Guide to World Maps

map scale
1:18,000,000
1:16,000,000
1:15,000,000

1:12,000,000

1:9,000,000
1:8,000,000

1:6,000,000
1:4,500,000

1:3,500,000
and larger

124 page reference

114
108
62
124
110
128
126
JAPAN
KAZAKHSTAN
MONGOLIA
116
NORTH KOREA
SOUTH KOREA
118
UZBEKISTAN
KYRG.
TURKMENISTAN
TAJIK.
CHINA
TURKEY
GEO. ARM. AZER.
IRAN
AFGHANISTAN
TAIWAN
SYRIA
IRAQ
120
ISRAEL
JORDAN
KUWAIT
PAKISTAN
NEPAL
BHU.
132
HONG KONG 131a
130
134
EGYPT
SAUDI ARABIA
QATAR
U.A.E.
OMAN
INDIA
BNGL.
MYANMAR (BURMA)
LAOS
THAILAND
CAMBODIA
VIETNAM
PHILIPPINES
SUDAN
YEMEN
ERITREA
DJIBOUTI
ETHIOPIA
122
SRI LANKA
BRUNEI
MALAYSIA
SINGAPORE
134a
SOMALIA
204
UGANDA
KENYA
RWANDA
BURUNDI
TANZANIA
202
MAHE
207c
INDONESIA
135b
JAVA
PAPUA NEW GUINEA
140
142
ZAMBIA
207d
COMOROS
MADAGASCAR
ZIMBABWE
INDIAN OCEAN
58
FIJI 147c
MOZAMBIQUE
SWANA
SWAZILAND
MAURITIUS
207e
REUNION
205a
AUSTRALIA
144
LESOTHO
TH NCA
138
TASMANIA
145a
146 NEW ZEALAND

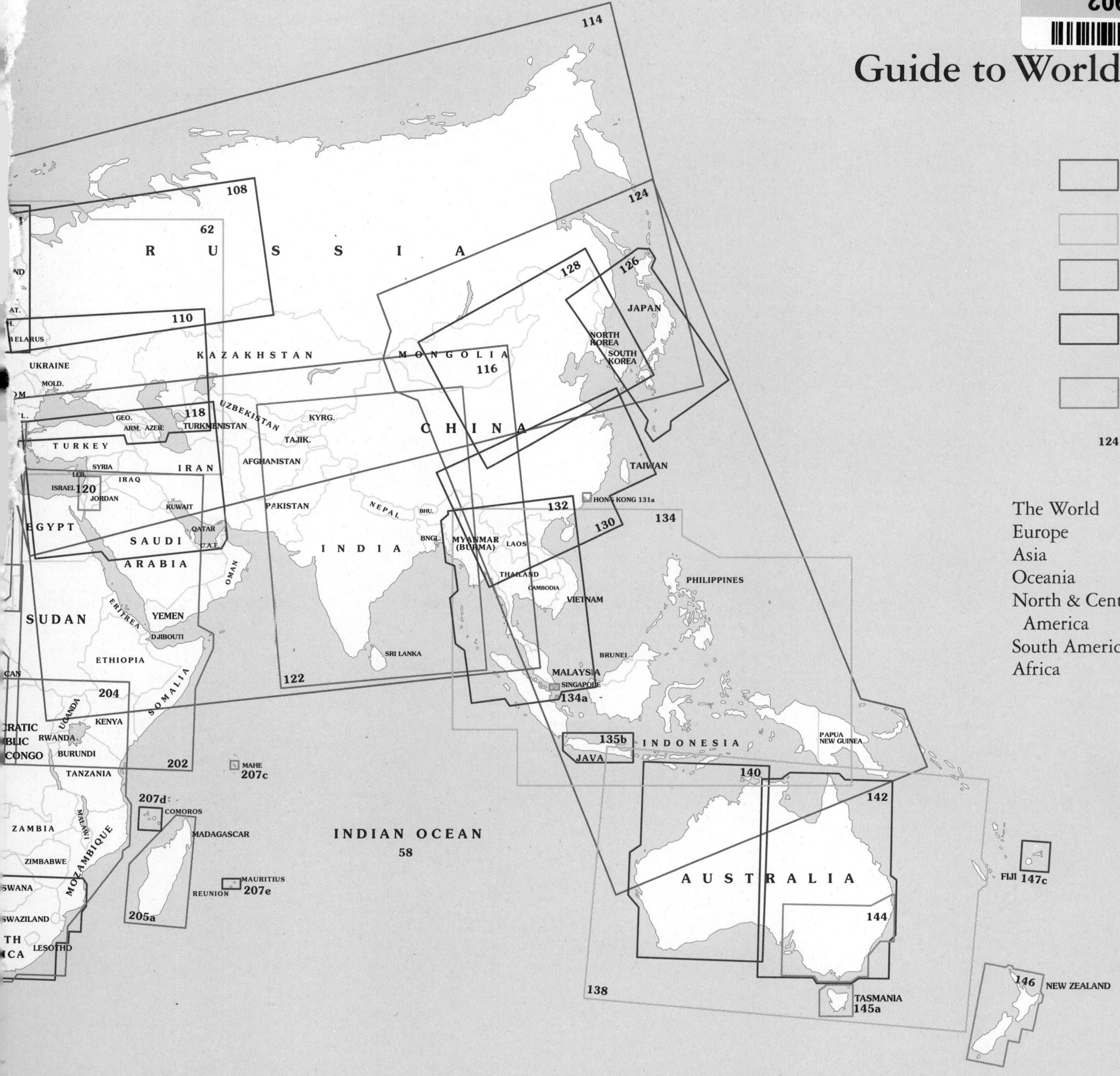

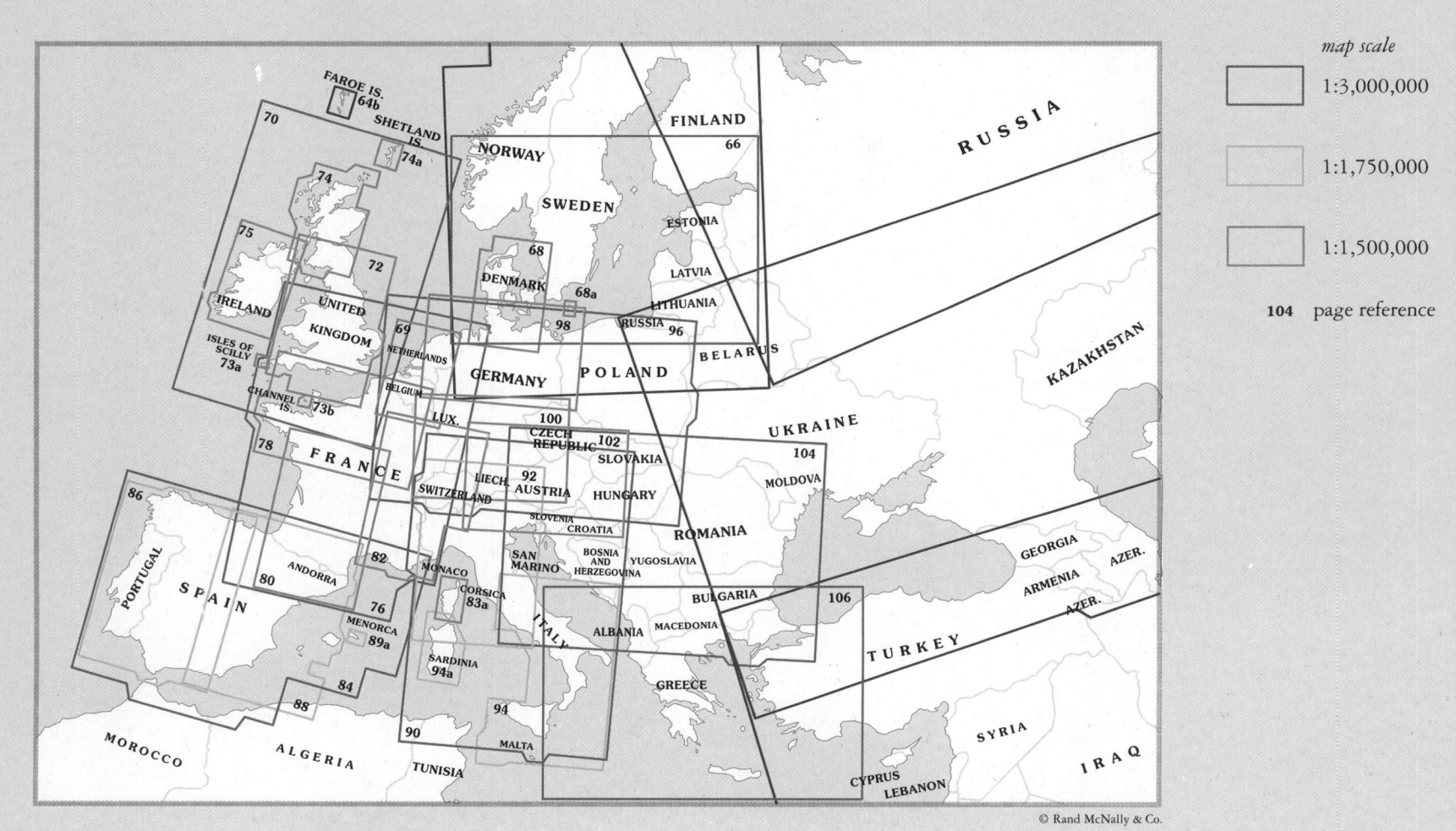

map scale
1:3,000,000

1:1,750,000

1:1,500,000

104 page reference

FAROE IS.
64b
70
SHETLAND IS.
74a
NORWAY
FINLAND
66
SWEDEN
RUSSIA
74
75
72
68
ESTONIA
68a
DENMARK
LATVIA
IRELAND
UNITED KINGDOM
69
LITHUANIA
RUSSIA 96
98
ISLES OF SCILLY
73a
NETHERLANDS
BELGIUM
GERMANY
POLAND
BELARUS
CHANNEL IS. 73b
LUX.
100
UKRAINE
78
CZECH REPUBLIC
102
SLOVAKIA
104
MOLDOVA
KAZAKHSTAN
FRANCE
92
AUSTRIA
HUNGARY
SWITZERLAND
LIECH.
86
SLOVENIA
CROATIA
ROMANIA
82
MONACO
SAN MARINO
BOSNIA AND HERZEGOVINA
YUGOSLAVIA
GEORGIA
AZER.
PORTUGAL
SPAIN
80
ANDORRA
CORSICA
83a
BULGARIA
106
ARMENIA
AZER.
76
MENORCA
89a
ITALY
ALBANIA
MACEDONIA
TURKEY
88
84
SARDINIA
94a
94
GREECE
SYRIA
MOROCCO
ALGERIA
90
TUNISIA
MALTA
CYPRUS
LEBANON
IRAQ

READER'S DIGEST
ILLUSTRATED
ATLAS
OF THE
WORLD

Published by The Reader's Digest Association Limited
London • New York • Sydney • Montreal

EDITOR Robin Hosie
ASSOCIATE EDITOR Michael Davison
ART EDITOR Bob Hook
CARTOGRAPHIC EDITOR Alison Ewington
ASSISTANT CARTOGRAPHIC EDITOR David Irvine

Maps of the World
The maps on pages 56 to 208 and the map index were
specially created for this atlas by Rand McNally & Company.
1997 © Rand McNally & Company.
Map captions by David MacFadyen

The Story of the Earth and Nations of the World
Edited and designed for Reader's Digest by
Duncan Baird Publishers Limited and
Siena Artworks Limited, London
MANAGING EDITOR Catherine Bradley
ART DIRECTOR Tony Cobb
ART EDITOR Iona McGlashan
EDITORS Slaney Begley, Maggie Ramsay,
Tom Ruppel, Louisa Somerville
Nations of the World: design John Grain;
cartography Eugene Fleury

CONTRIBUTORS
The Story of the Earth: Laura Ivill, Chris Madsen,
Rebecca Renner, Dr Brian Turner
Nations of the World, country profiles (text): Michael
Chisholm, Emeritus Professor of Geography at the
University of Cambridge, England

CONSULTANTS
Michael Allaby, Nei Curtis, David Gould,
Gareth Wyn Jones, Robert MacDonald, Sally Morgan,
Dr Douglas Palmer, Giles Sparrow, Martin Walters

Statistical information from *The Europa World
Year Book* supplied courtesy of Europa
Publications Limited, London

Colour reproduction by Colourscan, Singapore

Reader's Digest General Books
EDITORIAL DIRECTOR Cortina Butler
ART DIRECTOR Nick Clark
EXECUTIVE EDITOR Julian Browne
PUBLISHING PROJECTS MANAGER Alastair Holmes
DEVELOPMENT EDITOR Ruth Binney

First edition Copyright © 1997
The Reader's Digest Association Limited,
11 Westferry Circus, Canary Wharf, London E14 4HE

Reprinted with amendments 1999

South African edition published by Heritage Publishers (Pty)
Limited, representing Reader's Digest in Southern Africa.

INTRODUCTION

As we stand at the threshold of a new century, never has the need for an understanding of the complexity of our planet been greater. The Reader's Digest *Illustrated Atlas of the World* will take you on a voyage of discovery from the outer reaches of the Universe through the immensity of the Solar

The core of the atlas is a comprehensive set of world maps that have been specially designed and arranged to lead the reader from a view of the world as a whole to more detailed maps of all its continents, and finally to revealing close-ups of their most densely populated areas. The maps have been

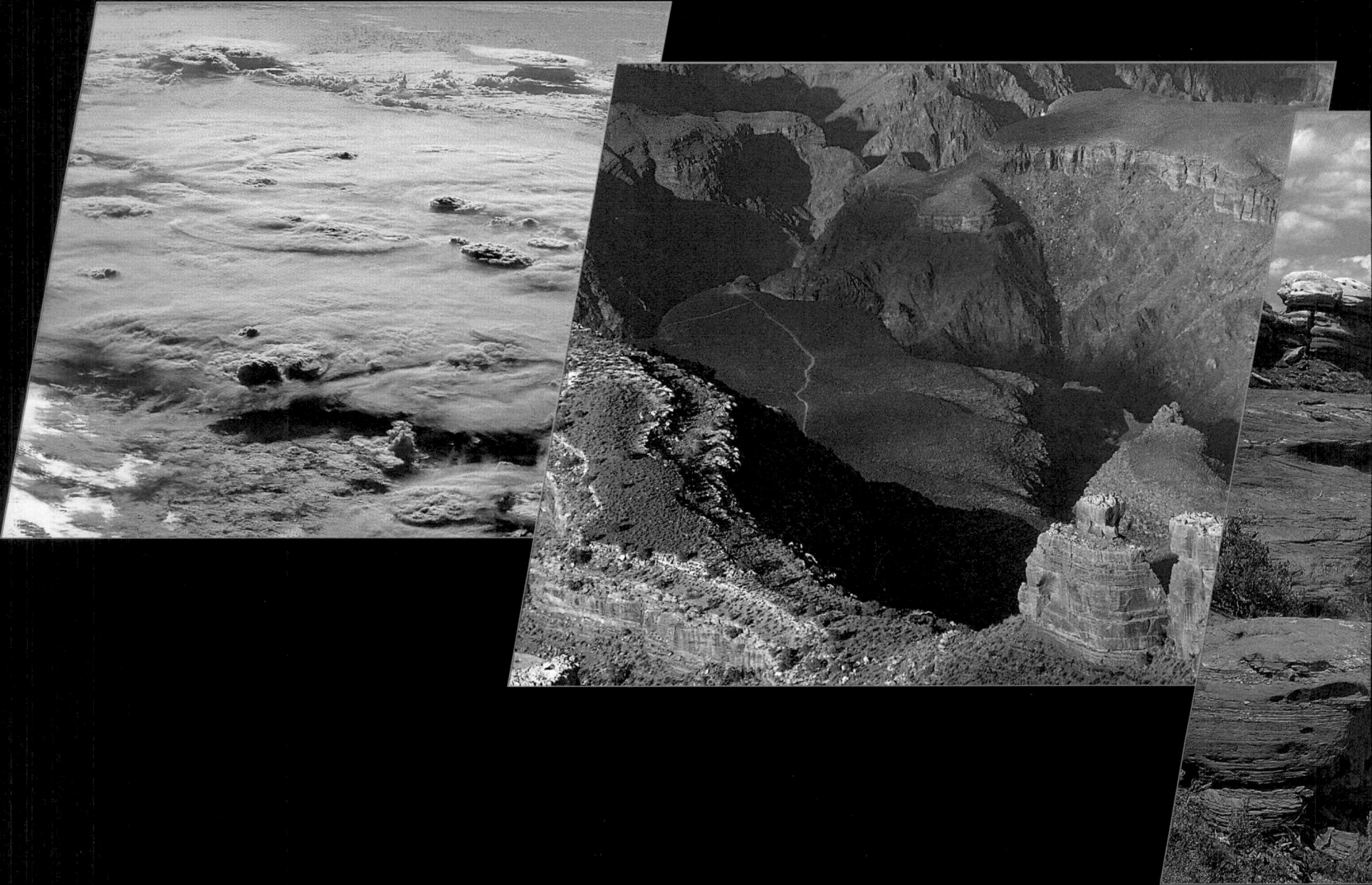

Front and rear endpapers: Guide to World Maps

OUR PLACE IN THE UNIVERSE

The Big Bang: an artist's impression

The Universe is thought to have been created in a vast explosion, the 'Big Bang', between 15 and 10 billion years ago. All the matter that exists formed in a fraction of a second, in an infinitesimally small space, simultaneously hurtling outwards at incredibly high speed. As the Universe expanded, the matter flung out began to cool from the immeasurably high temperatures initially generated. As it cooled, tiny, fundamental particles combined to form protons and neutrons, which themselves formed atoms of the gases hydrogen and helium. These gases make up most of the Universe today. Astronomers have discovered that the Universe is still expanding outwards from the original explosion, although one day it may slow to a halt, before contracting again in a final 'Big Crunch'.

Giant in space
The Andromeda galaxy (main picture) is the closest large group of stars to our own Milky Way galaxy, yet light from it still takes 2.2 million years to reach Earth. Andromeda is spiral-shaped, like our own galaxy – but it contains almost twice as many stars.

The scale of the Universe
Looking out from our small planet, we can see that the Universe is made up of successively larger structures. Earth is just one of nine planets orbiting the Sun, and the Sun is one among 200 billion stars in the Milky Way galaxy. The Milky Way is a large member of a cluster known as the Local Group, which is itself a member of our Local Supercluster – one of around 50 such clusters which together make up the largest known structure in the Universe.

The Universe
The Big Bang's cosmic afterglow and remains of the structure that it formed are captured in this image from COBE, the Cosmic Background Explorer satellite.

Supercluster
Between the vast superclusters of galaxies, the Universe contains voids – areas where almost no matter is detectable. The Local Supercluster to which our Local Group belongs is so big that it takes light 100 million years to cross it.

Local Group
Our home galaxy, the Milky Way, is one of a cluster of galaxies in nearby space called the Local Group. This cluster is roughly 2.5 million light years across, and contains the Andromeda galaxy (main picture) as well as about 30 smaller, elliptical galaxies.

Milky Way
The Sun is just one of 200 billion stars within the spiral disc of our Milky Way galaxy. Our Solar System lies in one of the Milky Way's spiral 'arms', which is why most stars as seen from Earth – looking along the disc – appear in a white band across the sky.

Solar System
Nine known planets, together with smaller objects such as comets and asteroids, form the Solar System in orbit around our Sun. The outer curve of Pluto's orbit stretches as far as 6 billion km (4 billion miles) from the Sun. Planets orbit other stars than the Sun: bodies as large as Jupiter orbit several nearby stars.

The life and death of a star

A star like our Sun is a ball of hydrogen gas, pulled together by gravitational forces so powerful that, at its core, atoms of hydrogen fuse together. This fusion creates helium gas and causes energy to be released. The hydrogen is used up over billions of years, until the star becomes unstable, swells into a 'red giant', then dwindles into a tiny burnt-out star – a 'white dwarf'. Larger stars than the Sun can destroy themselves in vast explosions, called supernovae.

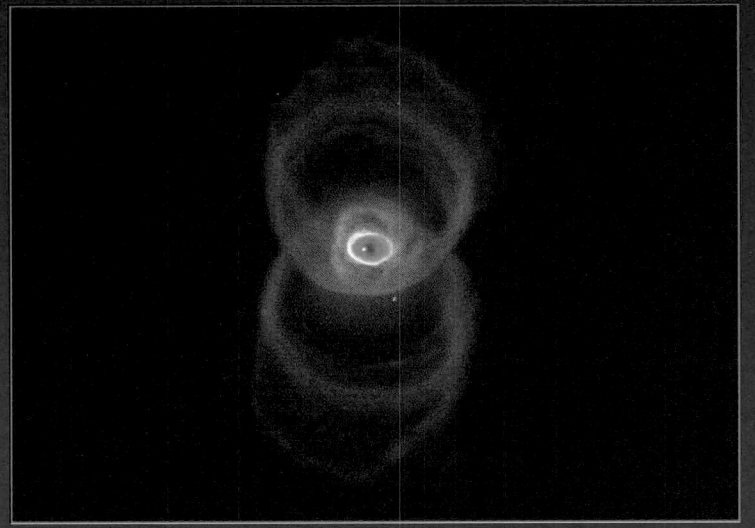

Deathly glow

When a star of a similar size to the Sun has almost run out of fuel for its internal nuclear reactions, it undergoes a series of violent convulsions. These throw off the star's outer gas layers, which become a glowing nebula such as MyCn18 (left). Often the nebula is seen as circles of bright gas around the dull dot of the dying star. The hourglass shape of MyCn18 may be caused by a ring of matter which circles the star's equator, absorbing some of the ejected material and forcing the gas to expand in two huge lobes above and below the star. Cooler, outer gas layers are dark red while younger layers, closer to the central star, glow white hot.

Nurseries of the stars

A star is born when a pressure wave passes through a huge interstellar gas cloud. The galaxy generates these waves as it rotates, or they can result from distant supernova explosions of huge stars. The wave compresses gas in the cloud, so that molecules begin to come together under gravity, pulling in more matter from around themselves to form spinning balls of gas. At the core of these balls, atoms are packed so closely together that their tiny nuclei collide, triggering a chain of nuclear reactions. The energy released by these becomes the first light emitted by the new star.

Trifid Nebula

The Trifid Nebula (left) is a cloud of dust and gas. It has no light of its own, and shines only by reflection. The region glowing red is made up of hydrogen gas, lit by the young stars forming within it. Above is an area of dust reflecting blue light from an older star within the nebula.

Black holes

The centres of many galaxies may contain black holes: collapsed stars with gravity so powerful that even light is sucked in. In active galaxies (above) gas is trapped in a black hole's magnetic field, and ejected at the poles, forming gas jets (shown above as pale blue and green areas).

THE SOLAR SYSTEM

Five billion years ago, the solar system existed only as a cloud of dust and gas floating in space. A supernova explosion in our Milky Way galaxy is thought to have created an immense pressure wave, which swept through this cloud. A small part of it was compressed to the point at which it collapsed under its own gravity, pulling in gas from all around, and heating up until nuclear reactions began in its core. Around this new-born star – the Sun – orbited a huge disc of gas and dust. The rocky inner planets Mercury, Venus, Earth and Mars were formed close to the Sun in a belt swept free of gas; the giant planets Jupiter, Saturn, Uranus and Neptune were created in a part that was still rich in gas. The disc's outer regions were the birthplace of the planet Pluto and a stream of asteroids and comets.

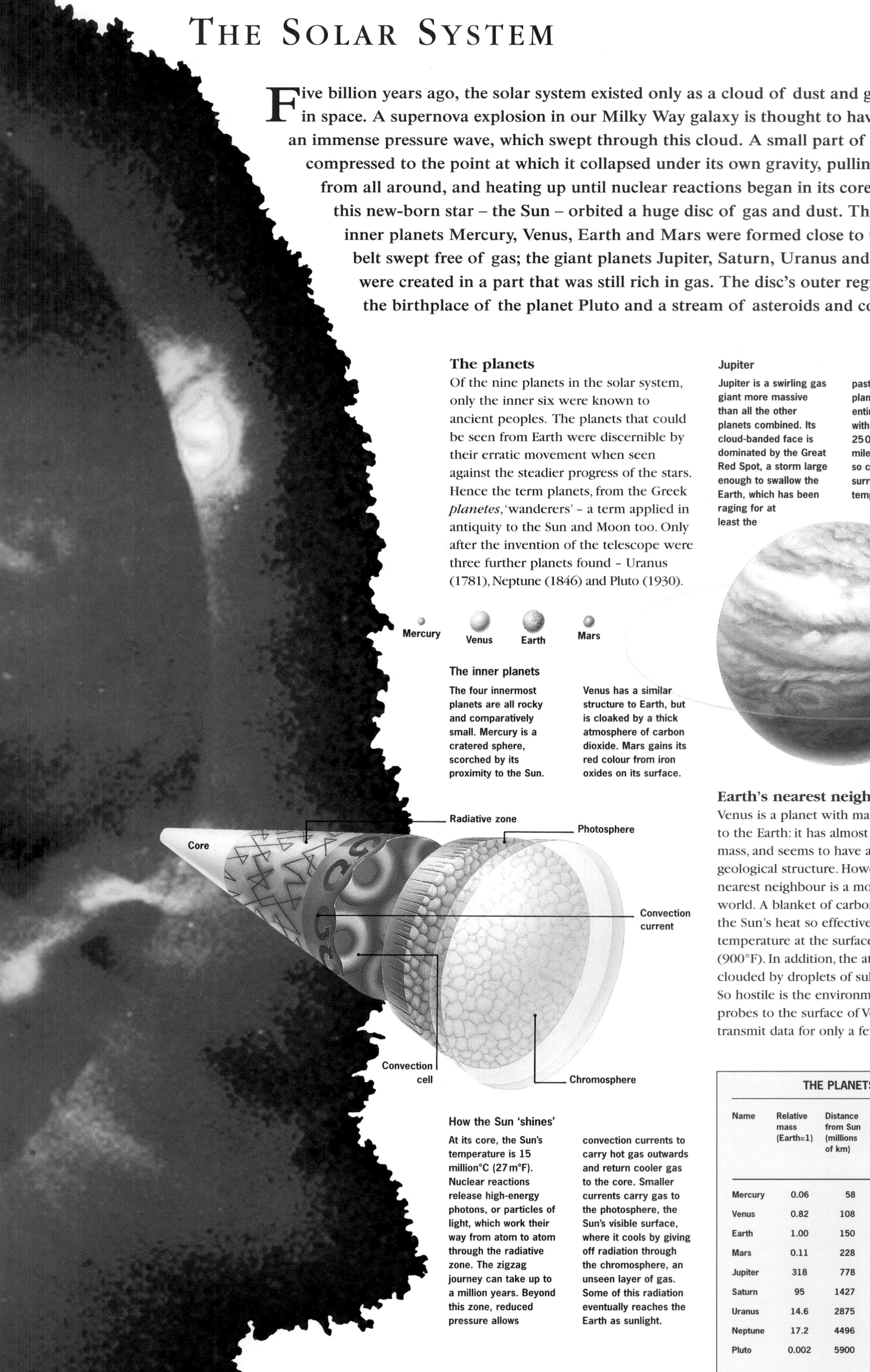

The planets

Of the nine planets in the solar system, only the inner six were known to ancient peoples. The planets that could be seen from Earth were discernible by their erratic movement when seen against the steadier progress of the stars. Hence the term planets, from the Greek *planetes*, 'wanderers' – a term applied in antiquity to the Sun and Moon too. Only after the invention of the telescope were three further planets found – Uranus (1781), Neptune (1846) and Pluto (1930).

Mercury **Venus** **Earth** **Mars**

The inner planets

The four innermost planets are all rocky and comparatively small. Mercury is a cratered sphere, scorched by its proximity to the Sun.

Venus has a similar structure to Earth, but is cloaked by a thick atmosphere of carbon dioxide. Mars gains its red colour from iron oxides on its surface.

Jupiter

Jupiter is a swirling gas giant more massive than all the other planets combined. Its cloud-banded face is dominated by the Great Red Spot, a storm large enough to swallow the Earth, which has been raging for at least the past 300 years. The planet consists almost entirely of atmosphere, with a rocky core only 25 000 km (15 540 miles) wide. The core is so compressed by the surrounding gas that its temperature reaches 30 000°C (54 000°F).

Jupiter

Core

Radiative zone

Photosphere

Convection current

Convection cell

Chromosphere

Earth's nearest neighbour

Venus is a planet with many similarities to the Earth: it has almost the same mass, and seems to have a similar geological structure. However, our nearest neighbour is a most inhospitable world. A blanket of carbon dioxide traps the Sun's heat so effectively that the temperature at the surface is 480°C (900°F). In addition, the atmosphere is clouded by droplets of sulphuric acid. So hostile is the environment that probes to the surface of Venus can transmit data for only a few minutes.

How the Sun 'shines'

At its core, the Sun's temperature is 15 million°C (27 m°F). Nuclear reactions release high-energy photons, or particles of light, which work their way from atom to atom through the radiative zone. The zigzag journey can take up to a million years. Beyond this zone, reduced pressure allows convection currents to carry hot gas outwards and return cooler gas to the core. Smaller currents carry gas to the photosphere, the Sun's visible surface, where it cools by giving off radiation through the chromosphere, an unseen layer of gas. Some of this radiation eventually reaches the Earth as sunlight.

THE PLANETS				
Name	Relative mass (Earth=1)	Distance from Sun (millions of km)	Number of satellites	Period of one orbit in Earth years
Mercury	0.06	58	0	0.24
Venus	0.82	108	0	0.61
Earth	1.00	150	1	1.00
Mars	0.11	228	2	1.88
Jupiter	318	778	16+	11.86
Saturn	95	1427	21+	29.50
Uranus	14.6	2875	15+	84.00
Neptune	17.2	4496	8+	164.80
Pluto	0.002	5900	1	248.40

How planets move

The planets move in elliptical orbits. All except Pluto orbit very nearly on the same plane. Pluto's path is a more pronounced ellipse, inclined so that the planet sometimes approaches closer to the Sun than Neptune. The planets are not the only bodies orbiting the Sun. Between Jupiter and Mars is the asteroid belt, made up of rocky debris from the solar system's formation. On the system's outskirts are comets. The best known, Halley's comet, reappears every 76 years.

Planetary paths

The farther away a planet is from Earth, the more slowly it appears to move in relation to the stars. Lying between Earth and the Sun, Mercury and Venus are the 'inferior planets'; the other six are 'superior'. Owing to differences in relative speeds, planets can sometimes seem to move backwards when viewed from Earth.

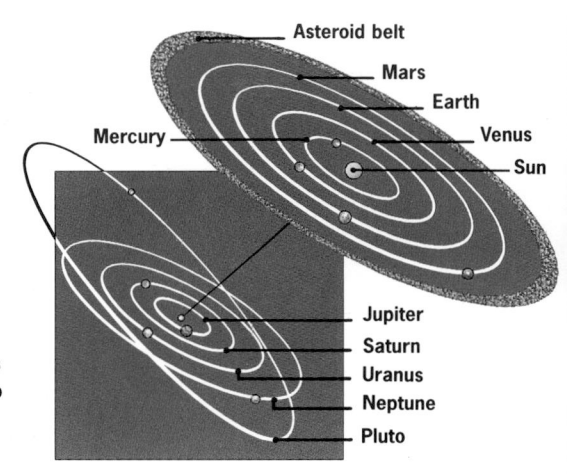

Asteroid belt
Mars
Earth
Venus
Sun
Mercury

Jupiter
Saturn
Uranus
Neptune
Pluto

Path of comet

Celestial streamers

Most comets voyage unseen at the outer limits of the solar system. The ones that we do see follow paths that take them close to the Sun. As a comet nears the inner planets (above), its forward surface is vaporised by solar radiation. Two tails form, pointing away from the Sun (not always away from the direction of the comet's motion): one tail is glowing gas, the other slower-moving dust.

Saturn

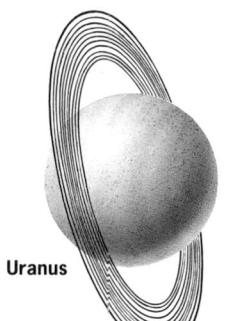

Uranus

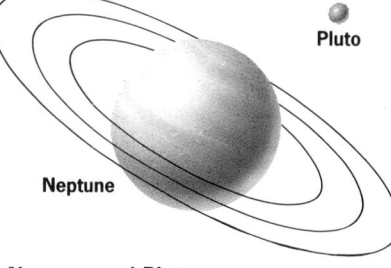

Pluto

Neptune

Uranus

This planet's green-blue hue derives from methane clouds in its atmosphere. Uranus is encircled by at least nine rings. Its largest moon is named Titania.

Neptune and Pluto

Neptune, the 'blue planet', has faint rings of methane ice crystals. Pluto is a tiny, icy body, with a moon, Charon, about half its own size.

Saturn

The second largest planet is a faintly banded globe encircled by a series of rings. The bands are caused by traces of water and ammonia compounds in the atmosphere of the planet. The rings are made up of dust and ice particles. Saturn's composition is thought to be very similar to that of Jupiter – mostly consisting of the gases hydrogen and helium.

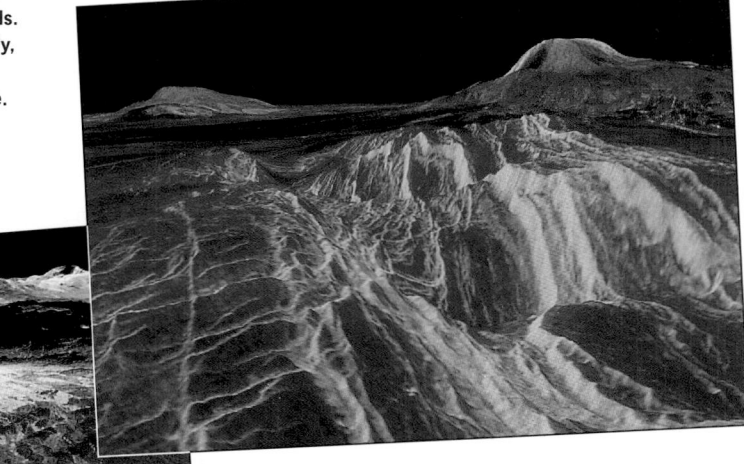

Venusian vista

The extinct volcano of Sapas Mons (left) on Venus is surrounded by bright solidified lava flows. Similar areas lie around Gula Mons (above). In all these Magellan images, the vertical scale has been exaggerated.

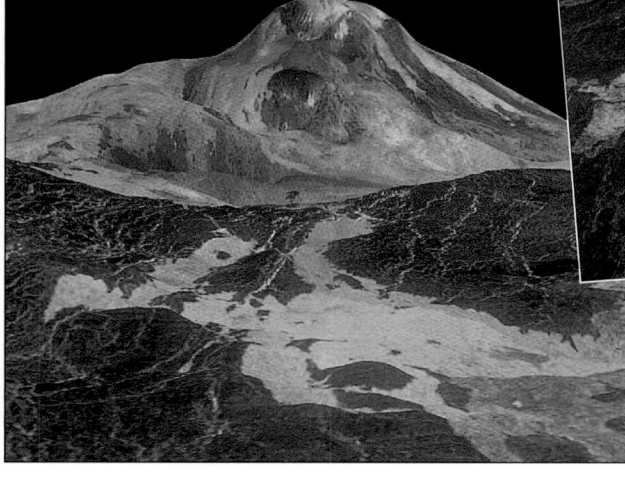

Volcano on Venus

In 1993 the Magellan probe used radar to penetrate Venus's thick clouds. Maat Mons (left) was one of the extinct volcanoes revealed.

Stormy weather

The banded appearance of Jupiter is caused by its own particular 'weather' – low-pressure belts where dark-coloured chemicals collect in the upper atmosphere, and high-pressure zones that reveal paler material below. At the boundaries between these areas huge turbulent storms rage, the most powerful of which is visible from Earth as the Great Red Spot. The Galileo probe, which entered Jupiter's atmosphere in 1995, found violent winds below the visible surface of the Spot with speeds up to 640 km/h (400 mph).

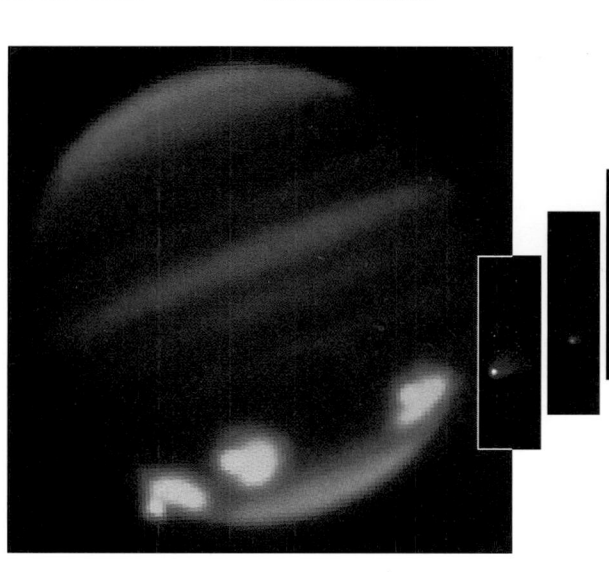

Cosmic collision

In July 1994, Comet Shoemaker-Levy was drawn by Jupiter's gravity into a collision with the planet (left). The immense forces exerted on the comet at first broke it up into smaller fragments, each with its own tail (above). The fragments entered the far side of the planet's atmosphere and became visible from Earth only as the planet turned to reveal its 'scars'. Three of them are clearly visible on this infrared image.

9

THE EVERCHANGING WORLD

The apparent solidity of the Earth conceals an inner turmoil that dates back to its origin approximately 4.5 billion years ago. The planet is thought to have formed from swirling clouds of dust, which gravity fused together into a sphere. The pressure and heat became more and more intense until a partial melting of the sphere's interior took place, forming an ocean of molten magma 200-400km (125-250 miles) below the surface. Gradually this swirling mass separated into distinct layers, with the least dense rock forming a crust on the outside and the most dense materials, iron and nickel, trapped in the central core. Signs of the tremendous energy contained within the Earth's structure can still be seen today in the violent, dynamic processes of volcanoes and earthquakes. Both phenomena are related to plate tectonics, the division of the Earth's crust into constantly moving slabs that carry both continents and oceans with them.

200 million years ago

135 million years ago

65 million years ago

Collision zone
Mid-ocean ridge
Transform fault

North American Plate
Eurasian Plate
African Plate
Pacific Plate
South American Plate
Indo-Australian Plate

Present day

The watery planet
The face of the Earth (right) when seen from space is dominated by the blue of the oceans and crossed by white streaks of cloud. There are an estimated 1.4 billion km³ (330 million cubic miles) of water on our planet. More than 97 per cent of this liquid vital to life is stored in the oceans, with less than 1 per cent in rivers and lakes. The rest is either ground water or vapour in the air.

A world in motion
The Earth's land-masses are plates of continental crust, separated by plates of ocean-floor crust. All are in continual, very slow motion. Some 200 million years ago all landmasses formed a single supercontinent called Pangaea (top left). Tectonic forces split this at first into two, then into today's smaller continents.
Plate boundaries are of three types: mid-ocean ridges, where tectonic forces pull the plates apart; collision zones, where one plate may dive under another in a process known as subduction; and transform faults, where two plates slide in opposite directions.

Magnetic patterns
Continental crust
Oceanic crust
Mid-ocean ridge
Himalayas
India
Trench

Continental drift
The idea of drifting continents, unsuspected until the early 1900s, is confirmed by evidence in the rocks of continents and ocean floors. The continental shelves around the coasts of Brazil and West Africa interlock like pieces of a jigsaw puzzle; and on both continents similar fossils of a land-living dinosaur have been found. In other parts of the globe there are signs left by sliding ice sheets on land that is now nearer the Equator than to the poles.

Such evidence supports the theory that 200 million years ago all the continents were joined together in one supercontinent. The forces of plate tectonics have split this landmass into the shapes familiar today.

Mantle
Ridge

Spreading out
New crust forms at a mid-ocean ridge (above), as molten rock wells up from the mantle between plates on the sea floor. As the new crust cools and is pushed away from the ridge, iron within the Earth's crust aligns with its magnetic field. The field changes its direction every few thousand years, so the rock's magnetic traces record crustal spread.

Plates colliding
At a collision or subduction zone (left), old crust is consumed as one plate dives beneath another. A deep ocean trench is formed and molten rock is pushed up into volcanoes. The Himalayas (above) were formed when the Indian and Eurasian plates collided 45 million years ago. The sea floor lying between the two continents folded to form the range. Everest's limestone summit was once below the sea.

Melting sediment
Volcanic mountains

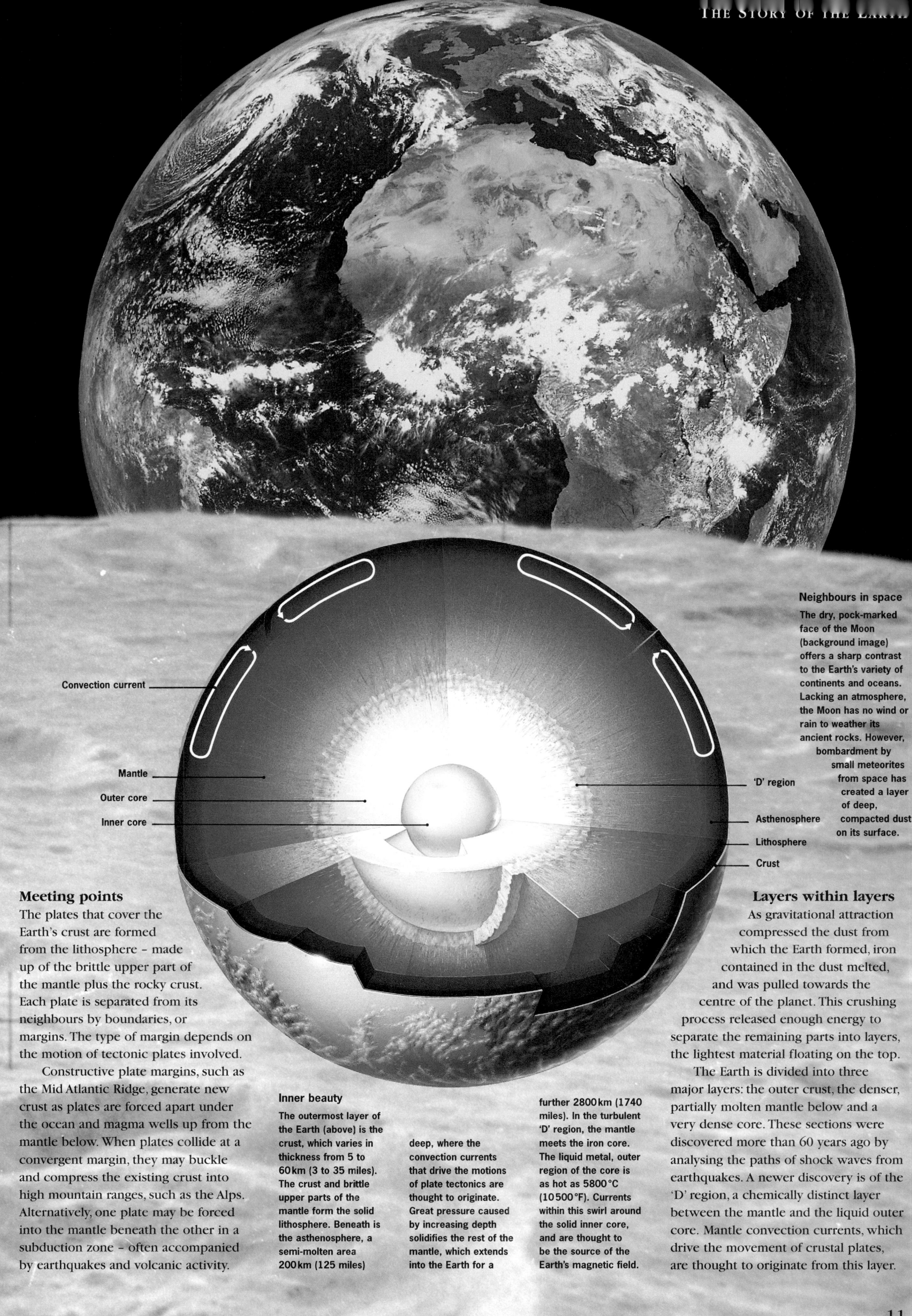

Convection current

Mantle

Outer core

Inner core

'D' region

Asthenosphere

Lithosphere

Crust

Neighbours in space
The dry, pock-marked face of the Moon (background image) offers a sharp contrast to the Earth's variety of continents and oceans. Lacking an atmosphere, the Moon has no wind or rain to weather its ancient rocks. However, bombardment by small meteorites from space has created a layer of deep, compacted dust on its surface.

Meeting points

The plates that cover the Earth's crust are formed from the lithosphere – made up of the brittle upper part of the mantle plus the rocky crust. Each plate is separated from its neighbours by boundaries, or margins. The type of margin depends on the motion of tectonic plates involved.

Constructive plate margins, such as the Mid Atlantic Ridge, generate new crust as plates are forced apart under the ocean and magma wells up from the mantle below. When plates collide at a convergent margin, they may buckle and compress the existing crust into high mountain ranges, such as the Alps. Alternatively, one plate may be forced into the mantle beneath the other in a subduction zone – often accompanied by earthquakes and volcanic activity.

Inner beauty
The outermost layer of the Earth (above) is the crust, which varies in thickness from 5 to 60 km (3 to 35 miles). The crust and brittle upper parts of the mantle form the solid lithosphere. Beneath is the asthenosphere, a semi-molten area 200 km (125 miles) deep, where the convection currents that drive the motions of plate tectonics are thought to originate. Great pressure caused by increasing depth solidifies the rest of the mantle, which extends into the Earth for a further 2800 km (1740 miles). In the turbulent 'D' region, the mantle meets the iron core. The liquid metal, outer region of the core is as hot as 5800 °C (10 500 °F). Currents within this swirl around the solid inner core, and are thought to be the source of the Earth's magnetic field.

Layers within layers

As gravitational attraction compressed the dust from which the Earth formed, iron contained in the dust melted, and was pulled towards the centre of the planet. This crushing process released enough energy to separate the remaining parts into layers, the lightest material floating on the top.

The Earth is divided into three major layers: the outer crust, the denser, partially molten mantle below and a very dense core. These sections were discovered more than 60 years ago by analysing the paths of shock waves from earthquakes. A newer discovery is of the 'D' region, a chemically distinct layer between the mantle and the liquid outer core. Mantle convection currents, which drive the movement of crustal plates, are thought to originate from this layer.

THE SCULPTING OF THE EARTH

Earth's amazing variety of rocks, and their formations, are the product of 4.5 billion years of change. Upwellings of the planet's slowly churning mantle alter the visible face of the outer crust, while at the same time old lands are worn down by weathering and erosion. First, the rocks are disintegrated by forces such as frost action, heating and cooling, abrasion, chemical reaction, and the impact of animals and plants. Then the debris is eroded and carried away by water, wind or ice, to be deposited elsewhere. The Grand Canyon in Arizona, USA, is a dramatic reminder of the erosive power of running water, for the Colorado River has maintained its level as the walls of the chasm have risen on either bank, creating a 1900 m (6250 ft) deep scar in the Earth's crust. The moving ice of glaciers also causes tremendous erosion. In the distant past, during the long, cold glacials, or ice ages, the effect of ice upon the landscape was profound, leaving a lasting topographical legacy.

Ice in retreat

During the last cold phase of the ice age 20 000 years ago, ice caps covered 28.5 million km² (11 million sq miles) of land that is free of ice today.

20 000 years ago

Present day

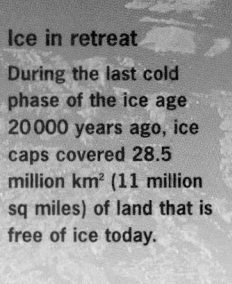

Cycles of ice

The term 'ice age' refers to any period of glaciation, but specifically the last one, in the Pleistocene epoch, at the close of prehistoric times. Over the last 2.5 million years, the Earth has passed through about 20 ice ages (glacials), separated by warmer 'interglacials'. A major factor in the cause of glacials is thought to be the periodic variation of the Earth's solar orbit. During each glacial, falling temperatures have promoted the growth of polar ice caps, and of mountain glaciers on the highest peaks around the world. Glacials could last tens of thousands of years but often ended fairly abruptly, with the glaciers and ice caps melting and shrinking back to approximately their present size. Major glacial advances 'locked up' such quantities of water that the sea level dropped significantly, exposing large areas of continental shelf.

An icy end

When a glacier is in retreat, meltwater is channelled through tunnels below the ice and runs out from the glacier's snout (below). Sub-glacier tunnels can be huge (inset).

Eventually tunnels become choked with glacial rock debris. The glacier finally melts, leaving behind ribbons of sediment (eskers) marking the old meltwater channels.

Rivers of ice

Glaciers such as this in Alaska (above) form on high mountain tops. When snow layers build up in hollows, the lower layers are compressed into ice. Where the ice touches rock, pressure melts its base, reducing friction so that a river of ice – a glacier – begins to slide down the mountainside. As it moves, it incorporates broken rock in its base layer, grinding away the underlying rock. Frost-shattered debris from the valley walls falls onto the glacier's edge and is carried along as a lateral moraine. Where two glaciers meet, their lateral moraines form a medial moraine, as in this second example from Alaska (above right). As the glacier descends, the ice begins to melt and streams bearing sediment issue from its snout. If the glacier stays still for a number of years, a terminal moraine may build up in front of it.

Formed by ice

Glaciated landscapes are characterised by erosion in mountains and by deposition on surrounding lowlands. U-shaped valleys, such as Glen Coe in Scotland's Grampian Highlands (above), were formed when an original V-shaped river valley was deeply excavated by an ice age glacier. Striated rocks, indicative of ice-scarring, are here as high as 1000 m (3280 ft). They show that the ice flow may have overtopped the mountains on its way towards the Atlantic.

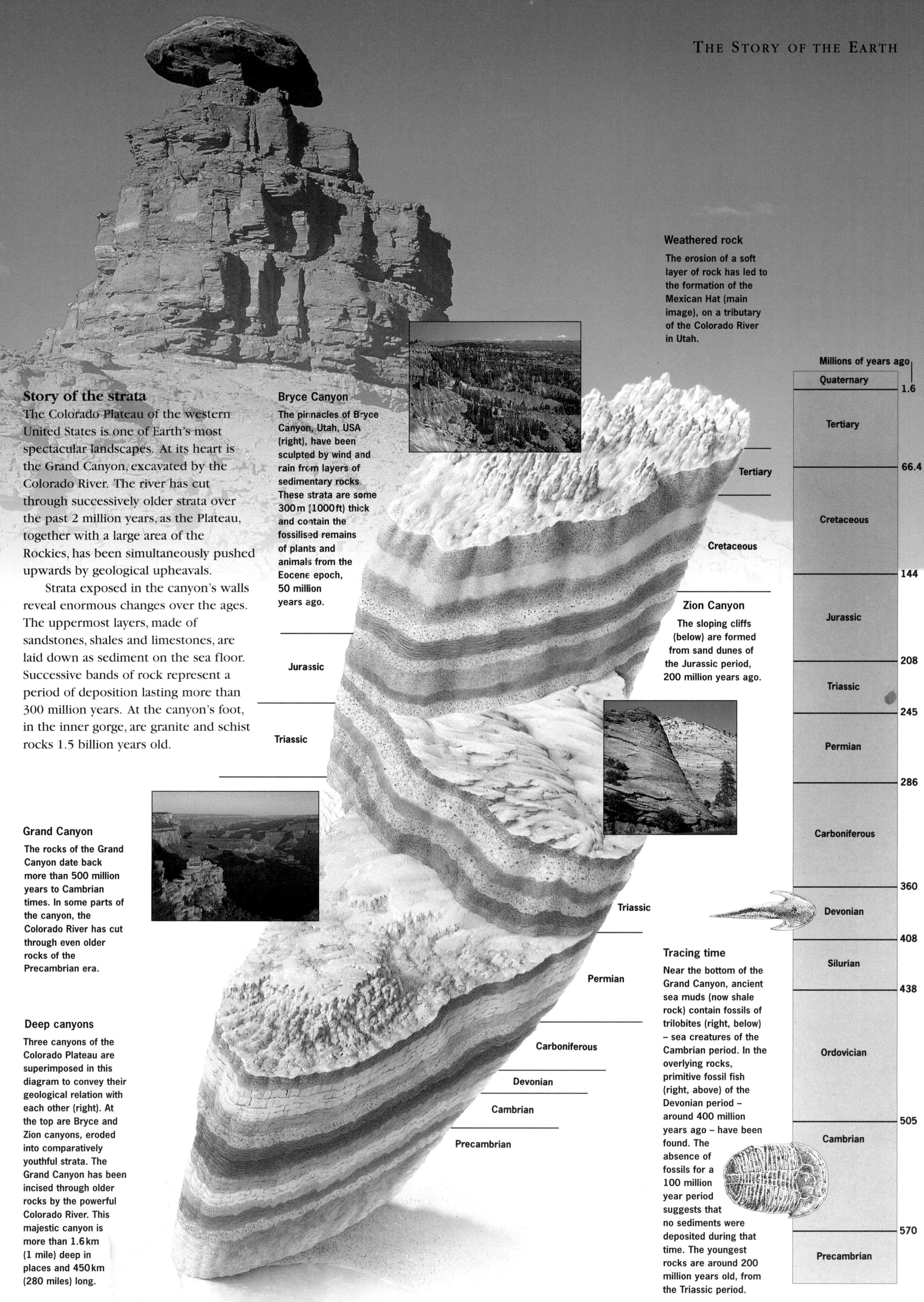

Weathered rock

The erosion of a soft layer of rock has led to the formation of the Mexican Hat (main image), on a tributary of the Colorado River in Utah.

Story of the strata

The Colorado Plateau of the western United States is one of Earth's most spectacular landscapes. At its heart is the Grand Canyon, excavated by the Colorado River. The river has cut through successively older strata over the past 2 million years, as the Plateau, together with a large area of the Rockies, has been simultaneously pushed upwards by geological upheavals.

Strata exposed in the canyon's walls reveal enormous changes over the ages. The uppermost layers, made of sandstones, shales and limestones, are laid down as sediment on the sea floor. Successive bands of rock represent a period of deposition lasting more than 300 million years. At the canyon's foot, in the inner gorge, are granite and schist rocks 1.5 billion years old.

Bryce Canyon

The pinnacles of Bryce Canyon, Utah, USA (right), have been sculpted by wind and rain from layers of sedimentary rocks. These strata are some 300m (1000ft) thick and contain the fossilised remains of plants and animals from the Eocene epoch, 50 million years ago.

Zion Canyon

The sloping cliffs (below) are formed from sand dunes of the Jurassic period, 200 million years ago.

Grand Canyon

The rocks of the Grand Canyon date back more than 500 million years to Cambrian times. In some parts of the canyon, the Colorado River has cut through even older rocks of the Precambrian era.

Deep canyons

Three canyons of the Colorado Plateau are superimposed in this diagram to convey their geological relation with each other (right). At the top are Bryce and Zion canyons, eroded into comparatively youthful strata. The Grand Canyon has been incised through older rocks by the powerful Colorado River. This majestic canyon is more than 1.6km (1 mile) deep in places and 450km (280 miles) long.

Tracing time

Near the bottom of the Grand Canyon, ancient sea muds (now shale rock) contain fossils of trilobites (right, below) – sea creatures of the Cambrian period. In the overlying rocks, primitive fossil fish (right, above) of the Devonian period – around 400 million years ago – have been found. The absence of fossils for a 100 million year period suggests that no sediments were deposited during that time. The youngest rocks are around 200 million years old, from the Triassic period.

Labels on diagram: Tertiary, Cretaceous, Jurassic, Triassic, Permian, Carboniferous, Devonian, Cambrian, Precambrian

Geological time scale (Millions of years ago):

Period	Millions of years ago
Quaternary	1.6
Tertiary	66.4
Cretaceous	144
Jurassic	208
Triassic	245
Permian	286
Carboniferous	360
Devonian	408
Silurian	438
Ordovician	505
Cambrian	570
Precambrian	

THE FURY WITHIN

Volcanoes and earthquakes are the most obvious and frightening evidence of the mighty forces of plate tectonics. Both are capable of enormous destruction. The first historically documented major volcanic event took place on August 24, AD 79 with the eruption of Mount Vesuvius and the destruction of the Roman towns of Pompeii and Herculaneum by clouds of ash and toxic gas. In recent times, the 1993 earthquake in the Maharashtra state of India levelled 50 towns in a few seconds and killed tens of thousands of people. The effects of such disasters may be felt worldwide. In 1991 the largest eruption this century blasted more than 8 km³ (2 cubic miles) of ash and 20 million tonnes of sulphur dioxide from Mount Pinatubo in the Philippines 20-25 km (12-15 miles) into the stratosphere. This created a haze that girdled the planet, reflecting sunlight back into space and so lowering average temperatures worldwide by 0.5°C (0.9°F).

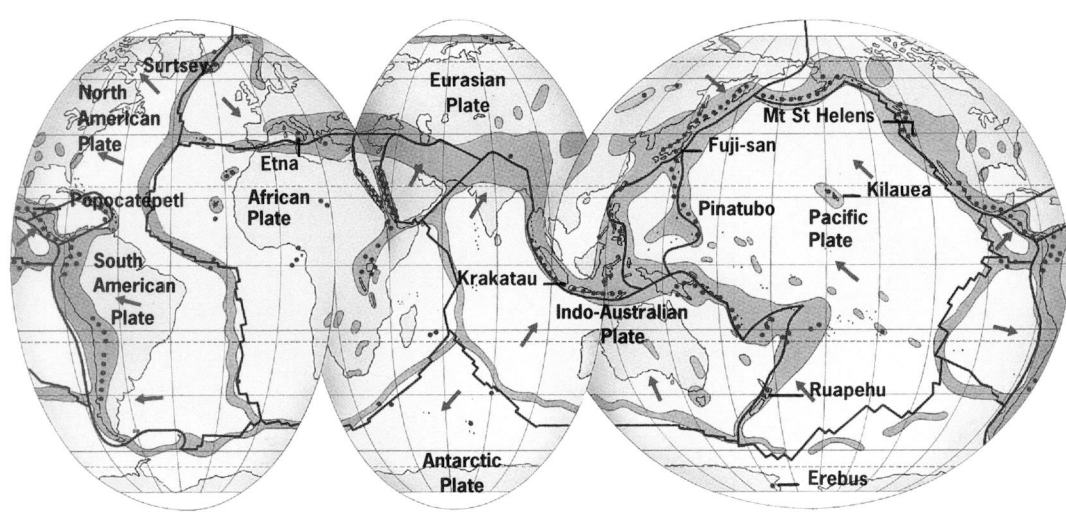

■ Earthquake zones   ·ᐟ· Volcanoes   ⌐ Plate margins

Interactive plates

The motion of one crustal plate against another fractures rocks, produces earthquakes and allows magma (molten rock) from the Earth's core to reach the surface and form volcanoes. Of the 600 or so active land volcanoes, the majority form where two plates collide. One such 'subduction' zone surrounds the Pacific Ocean, producing major faults in New Zealand and Japan and the 'ring of fire' comprising volcanoes from Mount Erebus in Antarctica around the Pacific rim to the Andes. Other earthquakes and volcanoes occur where plates pull apart to form new rocks on the ocean floor.

Plates under stress

Earthquakes can be terrifying natural phenomena. They are concentrated along fracture zones in the Earth's crust, where two plates move against one another. The huge pressures that build up are eventually released by faulting, and by violent earthquake motion.

Danger zones are monitored by satellite, but signs of impending disaster can also come from less scientific observations. In 1975 a tremor at Haicheng in China was heralded by animals becoming agitated, and wells bubbling. However, 18 months later no such signs were seen before another Chinese earthquake, which killed more than a quarter of a million people.

Structural damage

Earthquakes produce immense forces that oscillate several times per second, pulling apart the strongest structures, such as this highway, destroyed in the 1994 earthquake in Los Angeles.

Dividing line

This fracture (left) is part of the San Andreas Fault in California, USA. It occurs where the Pacific Plate and the North American Plate grind past each other at a rate of 2.5 cm (1 in) per year.

Earthquake zone

The San Andreas Fault runs out into the Pacific Ocean just south of San Francisco. It is shown as a red line on this satellite image (left). The arrows show the relative movements of the North American Plate and the Pacific Plate. Millions of years in the future, south-western California will become detached from the mainland and be carried north until it is an island off the coast of present-day Canada.

Fiery outpouring

Kilauea is not only the youngest of the Hawaiian volcanoes but also the most active volcano on Earth. During the 20th century it has been erupting molten rock at a rate of 5 m³ (177 cuft) per second to build up the vast, gently sloping flanks typical of a shield volcano. Lava has been pouring effusively from one of the craters on the eastern flank of Kilauea since 1983 (top right).

Rivers of rock

At more than 1130 °C (2066 °F), basalt lava flows readily, even on gentle slopes (middle row). As the upper surface cools, it forms a hard crust, beneath which molten lava continues to run (top left).

Solidifying rock

Hawaiian basalt lava has two main forms, both of which have local names: rubbly surfaced 'aa' and smooth 'pahoehoe'. Aa forms from fast flows. Pahoehoe (bottom left and bottom right) flows more slowly than aa, at the rate of 1 m (3 ft) per minute. Its surface can cool to form a thin shell that later cracks and bursts to release further weird-shaped bulges and coils of rope-like lava. In some places the pahoehoe flows directly into the sea where it solidifies fast in clouds of steam (bottom centre).

Types of volcano

The shape of a volcano is determined mostly by the nature of the lava that it produces, and in particular by the viscosity – resistance to flow – of the molten rock. This in turn depends on its chemical composition. The least viscous and fastest-flowing lavas are basalt lavas ejected by oceanic volcanoes, such as Kilauea and its sister volcano Mauna Loa in Hawaii. These have vast 'shield' slopes with a gentle gradient.

By contrast, classic, high cone-shaped volcanoes, such as those of the Pacific 'ring of fire', are more dangerous and highly unpredictable. Their molten rock, or magma, is much more viscous, so that it does not flow easily.

The build-up of gas pressure ejects magma in a fountain of incandescent fragments. The heaviest pieces of magma solidify in flight and fall back to Earth and, together with ash, form a steep-sided cinder cone.

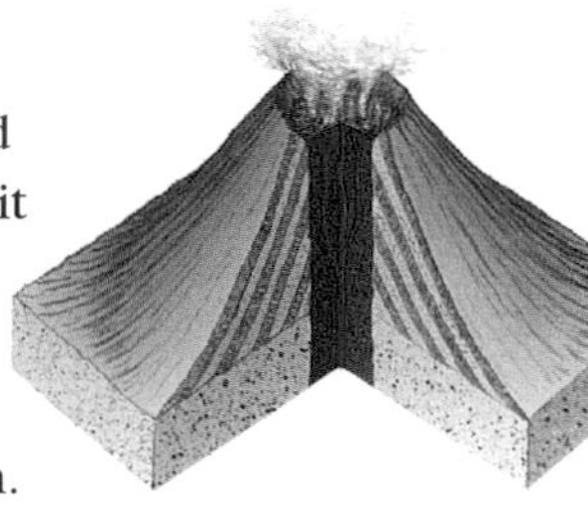

Cinder cone

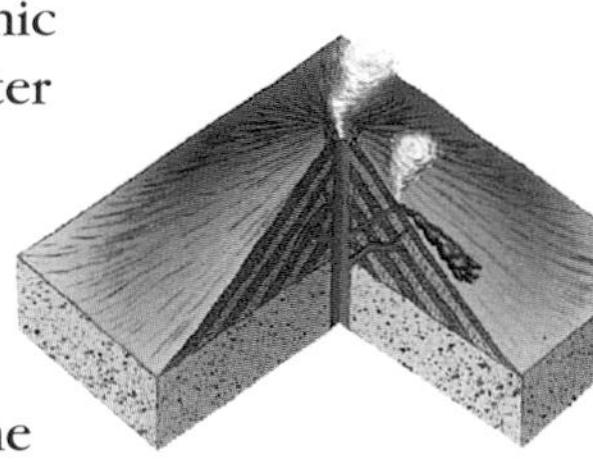

Composite cone

Volcanic variety

Cinder cones (top) formed from ash and rock fragments are steeper-sided than the composite cones formed from alternating layers of lava and cinder (above).

Power of destruction

Volcanic eruptions can release incredibly powerful blasts of ash, gas and steam. The force of the eruption in 1980 of Mount St Helens in Washington State, USA, was unexpected. On May 18, following two earthquakes, one side of the volcano collapsed, unleashing pent-up gas which vapourised the upper 410 m (1350 ft) of the mountain and sent 8 billion tonnes of rock avalanching down the mountainside at 250 km/h (155 mph).

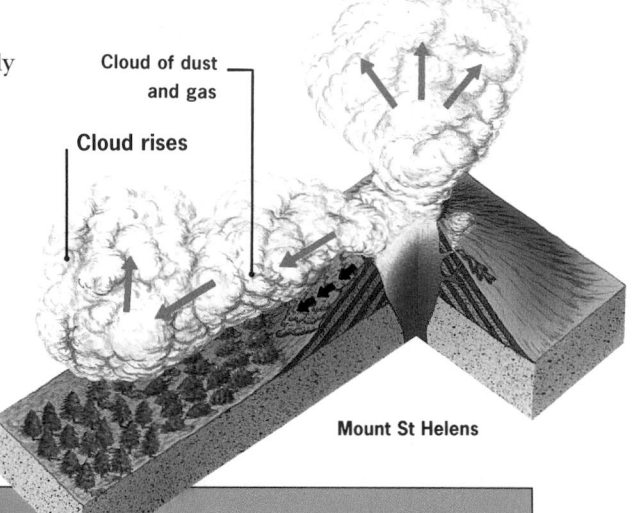

Cloud of dust and gas

Cloud rises

Mount St Helens

Lift off

After the collapse of the volcanic flank of Mount St Helens (right and above right), a cloud of gas and ash composed of pulverised rock and magma spread over an area of 400 km² (155 sq miles), flattening whole forests and rising 25 km (15 miles) into the atmosphere.

THE RECORD OF THE ROCKS

Solid and changeless though it appears, the rock of the Earth's crust has been constantly in motion and recycling itself over 4.6 billion years. In the course of its cycle, rock can pass through many different forms. Igneous rocks, formed from cooling magma, are ground down over the ages by wind or water. Rivers carry the particles to the oceans and deposit them on the sea bed. As yet more particles accumulate, pressure compacts them into sedimentary rock, which can be lifted into high mountain ranges by movements of the Earth's tectonic plates. Heat from deep within the Earth can transform sedimentary into metamorphic rock, creating smooth marble from chalky limestone. A more intense metamorphic process converts the soft carbon of graphite into the hardness of diamond. Further change can occur – tectonic movement may carry rocks into the Earth's depths, where they are remelted into magma and become the raw material of new rock.

Earth's building blocks

All the types of rock found on Earth, from the sky-grazing ramparts of the Himalayas to the hard, black pavements of Icelandic basalt or the sandstone towers of Monument Valley in Utah, USA, belong to one of three groups. The first group is igneous rock, which has crystallised from magma - molten lava formed deep in the Earth and often ejected in a volcanic eruption. Cooling takes place quickly and the rock thus formed has a fine-grained structure. Some masses of magma do not rise to the Earth's surface: instead they cool slowly underground to become much coarser-grained rocks.

Sedimentary rock, the second group, is formed by accumulations of sand, silt, mud and other detritus which become compacted and cemented by pressure. Erosion by wind, water, ice or heat can sculpt these rocks into dramatic forms, such as the Grand Canyon in Arizona.

Metamorphic rock, the third group, consists of existing rock transformed by pressure and heat. Italy's Carrara marble was once sedimentary limestone. It was compressed in the tectonic movement that formed the Alps.

Riches below ground

The Earth's crust is the source of all our mineral wealth. The most commonly used metals, such as iron and aluminium, are almost always found as ores – minerals in which the metal is in chemical compound with other elements. Rarer and more valuable are metals such as gold, which do not react with other elements. They are usually found in a native, uncombined state in veins deep underground.

Gemstones are much prized for their rarity and beauty. The most valuable have their origins deep in the Earth's crust. Here they were formed under extreme pressure and heat, which squeezed them into a compact crystal structure. This makes them extremely hard – diamond is the hardest known natural substance. Small, imperfect diamonds, unsuitable for shaping into gems, are used in industry for cutting or grinding.

Igneous outcrop
A granite outcrop (right) on the English coast is more resistant than surrounding rocks, but is still affected by weathering. Its crystal structure is revealed in polarised light (below).

Rock of fire
Igneous rock forms when molten rock solidifies. This can happen in one of two ways (right). In a volcano, magma forces its way to the surface from the mantle below. As it emerges, it can assume many forms, from glassy obsidian to sponge-like pumice. Alternatively, molten rock trapped deep in the Earth cools slowly into a large mass or pluton, with large mineral crystals. The commonest plutonic rock is granite.

Rising magma

Pluton (molten rock)

Volcanoes

Glittering prizes
Diamonds are crystals of pure carbon, formed under intense pressure and heat. Valued for their hardness, the colourless ones are particularly prized as gemstones. Ruby and sapphire are both forms of corundum, an oxide of aluminium. Their hues derive from traces of different metals trapped in the crystal structure. Emeralds are a form of the mineral beryl, coloured green by chromium. Silicon, with other chemicals, forms the basis of both opals and jadeite. Precious metals such as gold, silver and platinum are all found in a pure state in the Earth's crust.

Diamond (cut)   Sapphire   Gold

Ruby   Emerald   Silver

Opal   Jadeite   Platinum

The composition of the Earth

About 90 per cent of the mass of the Earth is made up of four elements: oxygen, silicon, aluminium and iron. In the planet as a whole, iron is the most abundant element – it is thought that it constitutes about 90 per cent of the Earth's core. However, it is only the fourth most common element in the crust, where oxygen is the most abundant. Silicon, the second most plentiful element, is found in virtually all rocks, as well as in sand, clays and soils.

Crust laid bare

A mere nine elements account for almost 99 per cent of the material of the Earth's crust (right). Of these, two elements – silicon and oxygen – make up about 72 per cent of the mass. In chemical combination, these are the basis of many different forms of mineral, from clear crystals of quartz to darker hornblende.

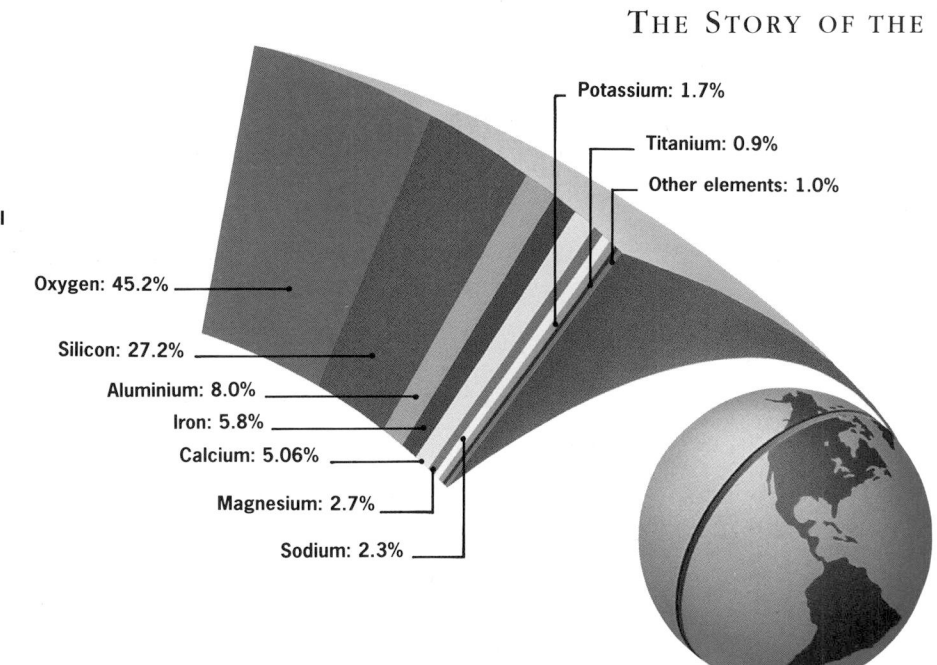

Potassium: 1.7%
Titanium: 0.9%
Other elements: 1.0%
Oxygen: 45.2%
Silicon: 27.2%
Aluminium: 8.0%
Iron: 5.8%
Calcium: 5.06%
Magnesium: 2.7%
Sodium: 2.3%

Rocks from the sea

The Badlands of South Dakota (above) are composed of soft sedimentary rocks, originally deposited on an ancient sea floor.

Colour within

A quartz geode (above) is a mineral formation within a rock cavity. Colourful layers of the mineral grow inwards from the cavity walls.

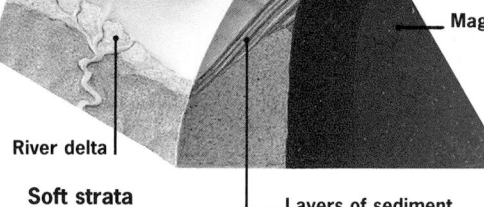

River delta

Soft strata

As layers of sediment are deposited on the sea floor (above), the cumulative pressure binds the particles together to form rock.

Magma

Layers of sediment

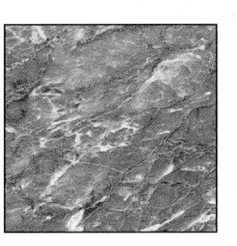

Streaked beauty

Marble forms when limestone is put under great heat or pressure. Impurities within the marble create the streaks of colour.

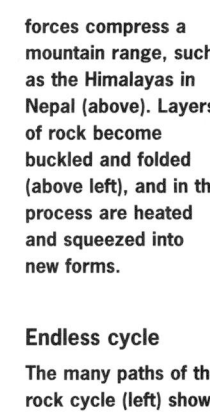

Folded layers

Mountain peaks

Changing states

Metamorphism occurs when extreme heat and pressure act on rock. This can happen when powerful tectonic forces compress a mountain range, such as the Himalayas in Nepal (above). Layers of rock become buckled and folded (above left), and in the process are heated and squeezed into new forms.

Endless cycle

The many paths of the rock cycle (left) show how rocks are transformed from one type to another, and recycled through the Earth's crust.

The cycle of the rocks

Rocks are converted from one form to another through the rock cycle. In this process a rock fragment can be carried far across the face of the Earth, as well as up or down within the crust. Rocks on the surface are eroded by weathering, then carried away as sediment and compacted into new sedimentary rock. This can then be pressed and heated into metamorphic rock, which in turn may be melted into magma and thrown to the surface by volcanic activity. When the magma solidifies into igneous rock and is exposed to the atmosphere, the whole cycle starts over again.

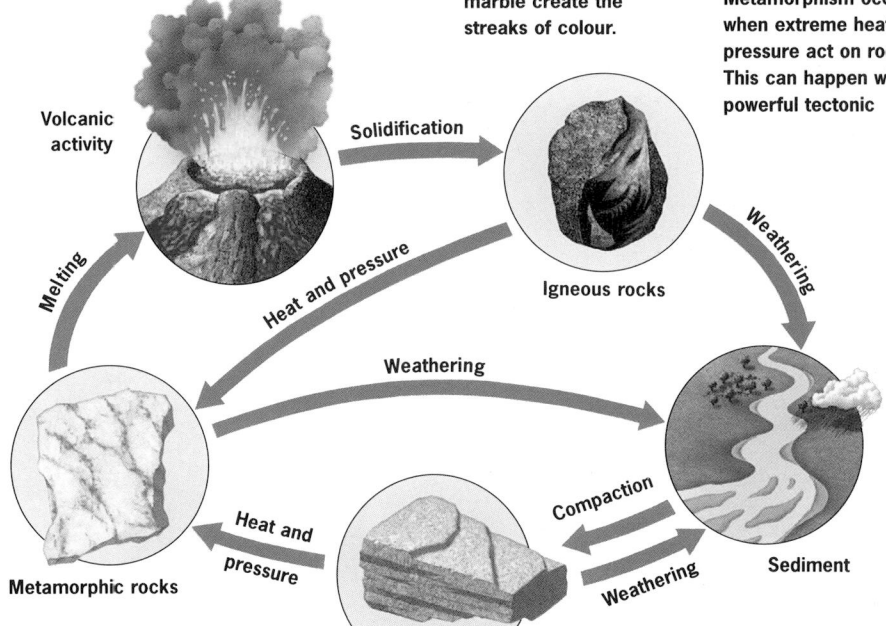

Volcanic activity
Solidification
Melting
Heat and pressure
Igneous rocks
Weathering
Weathering
Metamorphic rocks
Heat and pressure
Compaction
Weathering
Sediment
Sedimentary rocks

THE WEATHER MACHINE

The Earth's atmosphere is a turbulent mix of many gases, swirling in currents driven by the heat of the Sun. If the Earth did not spin on its axis, air would circulate in simple looping currents, or 'cells', as it heats up and cools. The currents would rise over the Equator, sink down over the poles and return low over the Earth's surface to the Equator. However, the rotation of the Earth complicates these patterns, as any air currents moving across the Earth will also start to spin. The uneven distribution of land and sea over the globe confuses the patterns further, making weather systems impossible to predict with complete precision. As currents of air circulate around the globe, they tend to form vortexes – the depressions and anticyclones familiar from weather forecasts. In a few places these vortexes can intensify, growing into mighty tropical storms. On a more local scale, in the right conditions, thunderclouds produce tornadoes, which create havoc along their narrow paths.

Tropical tempest

An astronaut on board a Space Shuttle took this photograph of Hurricane Elena as it approached the Caribbean Sea in 1985 (below). The distinctive spiral structure of a tropical storm can be clearly seen.

Swirling destruction

Severe tropical storms have a variety of names depending on where they occur. They are known as hurricanes over the Atlantic Ocean, typhoons over the Pacific and cyclones over the Indian Ocean. All these storms form and behave in the same way. In summer, the tropical sea surface warms. When it reaches 27°C (80°F), humid air evaporates from the surface and rises. The air cools as it lifts and its water vapour condenses, forming huge thunderclouds. High-altitude winds deflect the air above the thunderclouds, and more air is drawn up to take its place. The Earth's rotation sets the whole system of air currents and thunderclouds turning, producing huge spiral bands of cloud. The storm's most violent winds – which exceed 120 km/h (75 mph) – are concentrated around the centre of the spiral. Most damage occurs when this section of the storm crosses over land.

The 'eye' of a tropical storm is a region of very low air pressure. This forces the sea to bulge upwards, magnifying tides in a sea churning with stormy waves.

Twister

A tornado, or 'twister', forms inside a big thundercloud, where swirling air currents are rising and descending. As the spiral descends, the tornado narrows into a funnel shape, which intensifies the speed of the rotating air. Wind speed within a tornado may be as high as 480 km/h (300 mph).

Stormy structure

A hurricane forms when water evaporates from the warm tropical seas, creating updraughts of hot, moist air (right). As the air cools, water vapour condenses into thick clouds, which are shaped into wide spirals by air sucked in from the sea's surface. Above the storm most winds flow outwards, except for a small amount of air flowing downward in the calmer, cloud-free 'eye'.

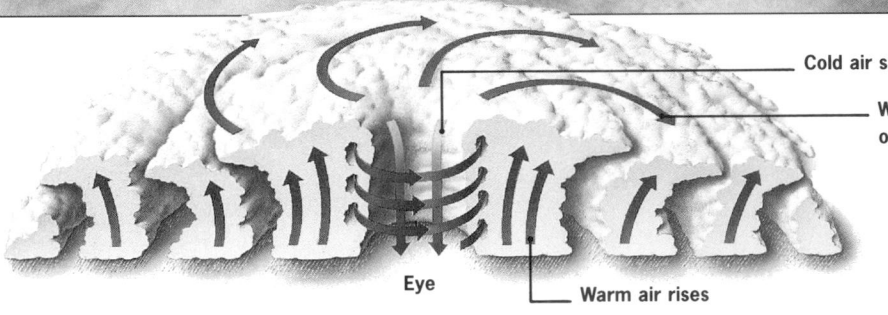

Cold air sinks

Winds flow outwards

Eye

Warm air rises

Weather zones

The continents of the Earth are divided into different climatic zones, each with a characteristic annual pattern of temperature and rainfall. Many factors govern the particular climate found at any one place. Latitude determines the amount of heat that a region receives from the Sun and is therefore a major influence on average temperatures. Distance from the ocean distinguishes dry continental interiors from moister coastal regions and islands. Ocean currents, which warm the air crossing over them, are also important. The mild climate of north-west Europe is partly caused by the passage of air over the warm waters of the Gulf Stream.

Physical features can also be significant – the 'rainshadow' effect of a mountain range can create regions as diverse as desert and tropical rain forest on its opposite slopes.

The winds of the world

The systems of vertically circulating air around the world are known as 'cells'. In 'Hadley cells', the looping air currents in the North and South Hemispheres, warm air rises at the Equator and then cools and sinks again at a latitude of 30°N and 30°S. Most of the cooler air is sucked back towards the low-pressure area of the Equator, but some of the sinking air moves towards the poles, forming the so-called 'Ferrel cells'. These circulate in the opposite direction to the Hadley cells. Each loop of air is skewed by the Earth's spin to form the lateral trade winds.

Atmospheric moves

A simplified diagram of the Earth's atmospheric patterns (above) shows the Hadley and Ferrel cells in both hemispheres. The vertical circulation of these cells is partly responsible for the world's climates. The Earth's rotation deflects these currents into belts of prevailing winds which blow horizontally over its surface. In the Tropics easterlies are known as 'trade winds'.

Legend:
- Tundra
- Boreal forest
- Temperate
- Mediterranean
- Desert
- Tropical rain forest
- Savanna
- Others

Polar

Eismitte in Greenland has a polar climate (below), with freezing temperatures all year. Cold air cannot carry much moisture, so the area has the low rainfall of a desert.

Continental

Krasnoyarsk in Russia has a typical continental climate (left), with bitterly cold winters and warm summers. Its distance from the sea gives the city a very low rainfall.

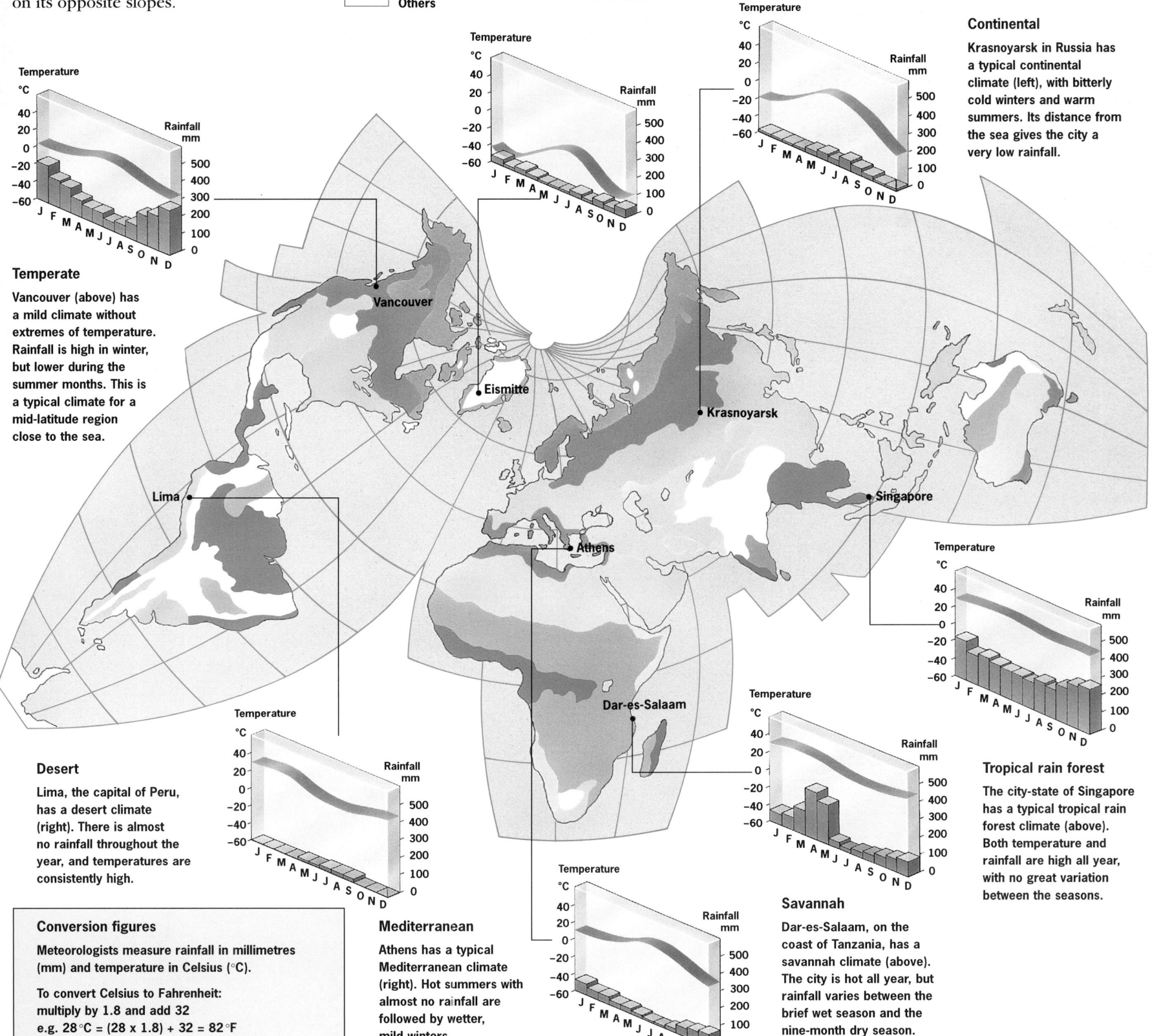

Temperate

Vancouver (above) has a mild climate without extremes of temperature. Rainfall is high in winter, but lower during the summer months. This is a typical climate for a mid-latitude region close to the sea.

Desert

Lima, the capital of Peru, has a desert climate (right). There is almost no rainfall throughout the year, and temperatures are consistently high.

Mediterranean

Athens has a typical Mediterranean climate (right). Hot summers with almost no rainfall are followed by wetter, mild winters.

Savannah

Dar-es-Salaam, on the coast of Tanzania, has a savannah climate (above). The city is hot all year, but rainfall varies between the brief wet season and the nine-month dry season.

Tropical rain forest

The city-state of Singapore has a typical tropical rain forest climate (above). Both temperature and rainfall are high all year, with no great variation between the seasons.

Conversion figures

Meteorologists measure rainfall in millimetres (mm) and temperature in Celsius (°C).

To convert Celsius to Fahrenheit: multiply by 1.8 and add 32
e.g. 28°C = (28 x 1.8) + 32 = 82°F

To convert millimetres to inches: multiply by 0.0394

THE BLUE PLANET

Where currents flow
A band of westward-flowing water at the Equator is diverted north and south when it strikes the barrier formed by the continental shelves of landmasses. Surface currents form great loops, which are known as gyres. Beneath them flow the cold currents that transport icy water from the Poles.

More than 70 per cent of the Earth's surface is covered by sea water. It extends to an average depth of 3.6 km (2¼ miles), and most of it is still largely unexplored. The great oceans interconnect to form a single global body of water in which the continents, for all their vastness, are only islands. The waters are in constant motion. Tidal 'bulges' are created by the gravitational pull of the Moon and Sun. At the same time, currents carry the oceans' waters about the planet in a complex, three-dimensional system driven by variations in water temperature and density, by the wind and by the Earth's rotation. Deep in the oceans, cold water flows away from the Poles; on the surface, winds push warm water, heated by the Sun, from one part of the world to the other in vast, meandering flows. The transfer of heat between ocean and atmosphere exerts an enormous influence on climate everywhere in the world, and on the distribution of life in the oceans.

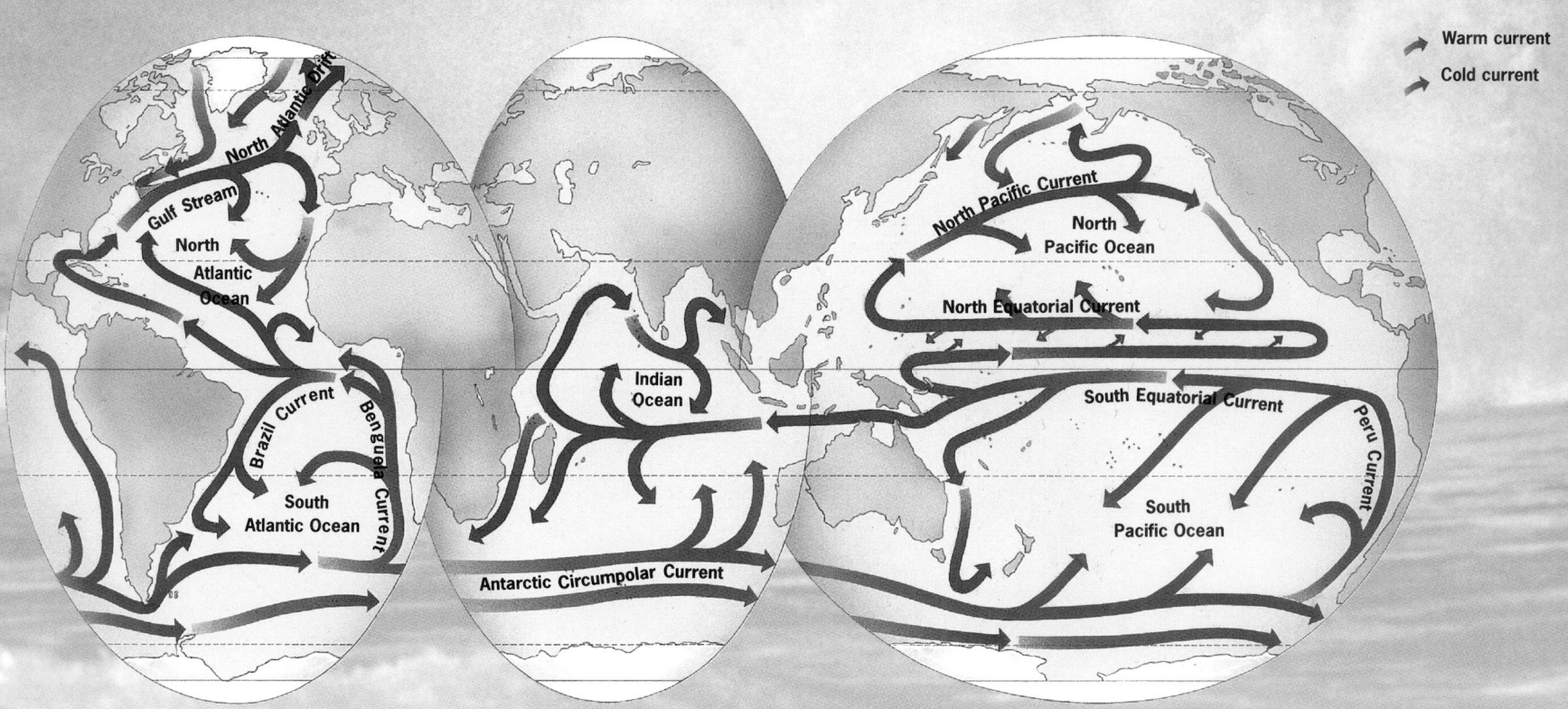

Warm current
Cold current

North Atlantic Drift
Gulf Stream
North Atlantic Ocean
Brazil Current
Benguela Current
South Atlantic Ocean
Indian Ocean
Antarctic Circumpolar Current
North Pacific Current
North Pacific Ocean
North Equatorial Current
South Equatorial Current
Peru Current
South Pacific Ocean

The global conveyor belt

There are 'rivers' in the sea – powerful currents that move water in such prodigious volumes as to make the flow of even the mighty Amazon seem puny. The largest deep current, carrying cold water from the Arctic into the North Atlantic, moves 5 million m³ (10 billion gallons) – 25 times the volume of the Amazon – every second.

Many of these currents are linked to a cycle that has been termed 'the global conveyor belt'. Warm surface water flows towards the North Atlantic Ocean. Between Florida and The Bahamas, the shape of the coast directs the water towards Europe. This current – the Gulf Stream – is driven by warm, moist, westerly winds that produce a warm wet climate in north-west Europe. The water cools as it approaches the North Pole. At these latitudes, ice forms on the surface of the sea. Because only fresh water freezes, the salinity of the remaining water is concentrated, which increases its density. It is this more saline, denser, colder water that feeds into the deep ocean currents, flowing more than 1 400 km (900 miles) into the South Atlantic and the Pacific.

Scourge of 'The Child'

Every ten years or so, a phenomenon known as El Niño occurs in the Pacific Ocean. During El Niño ('The Child' in Spanish, so called because it occurs around Christmas), the usual direction of the winds and ocean currents reverses – with disastrous effect. In 1982–83, the surface temperature of the Pacific Ocean at the Equator rose to almost 7°C (13°F) above normal. Peru's anchovy industry collapsed as fish fled to cooler waters. Indonesia and Australia were gripped by drought, while Ecuador and Peru were inundated by rainfall 300 times greater than normal. The causes of El Niño may be linked to higher sunspot activity occurring at similar intervals.

Good year
In a normal year (top, right), easterly winds across the Pacific drive warm surface water to Oceania. Here storm clouds form, bringing heavy summer rains. Off South America, cold, nutrient-rich water flows upwards, creating rich fishing grounds.

Bad year
When El Niño occurs (bottom, right), winds and ocean currents reverse. Warm currents and rain move eastwards across the Pacific, creating drought in Oceania. The cold upwelling off South America is suppressed. Fish stocks diminish.

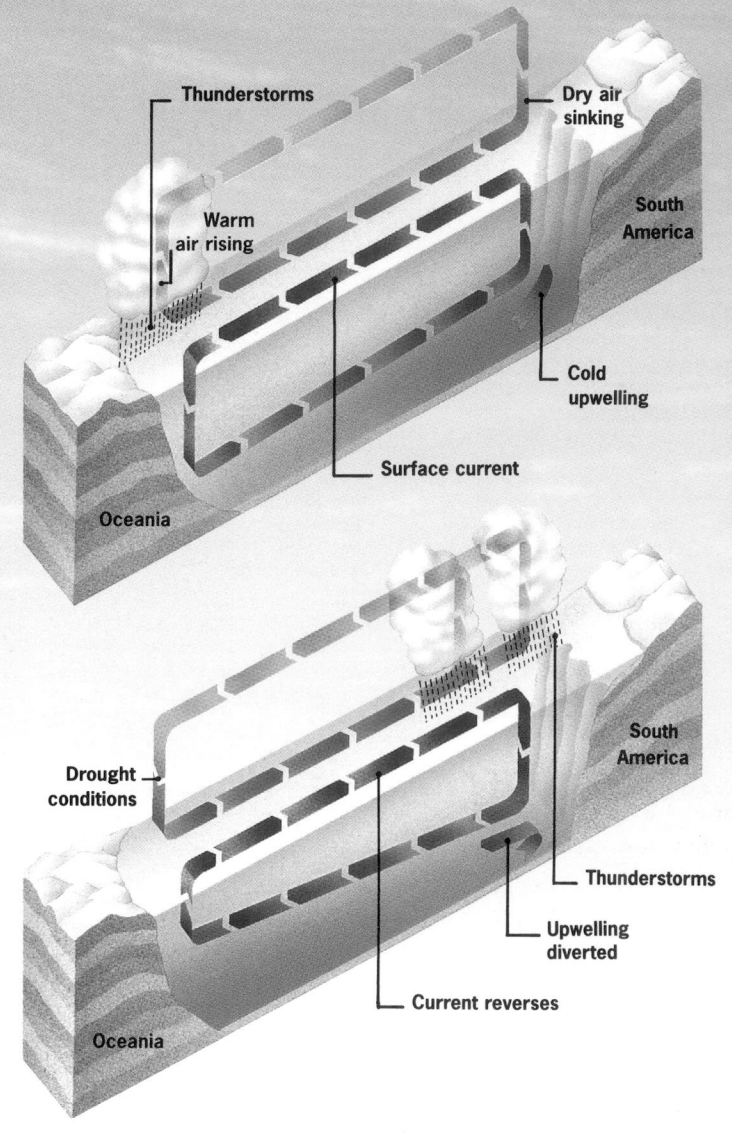

Thunderstorms
Warm air rising
Dry air sinking
South America
Cold upwelling
Surface current
Oceania

Drought conditions
South America
Thunderstorms
Upwelling diverted
Current reverses
Oceania

Warmer in the north

If the Earth were symmetrical, the surface of the oceans would be warmest at the Equator. However, surveys show that the highest temperatures occur a few degrees north of the Equator. One explanation for this is that most of the world's sea water lies in the Southern Hemisphere – only 19 per cent of which is land. As land heats faster than water, continents of the Northern Hemisphere make their surrounding seas warmer than those of the Southern Hemisphere.

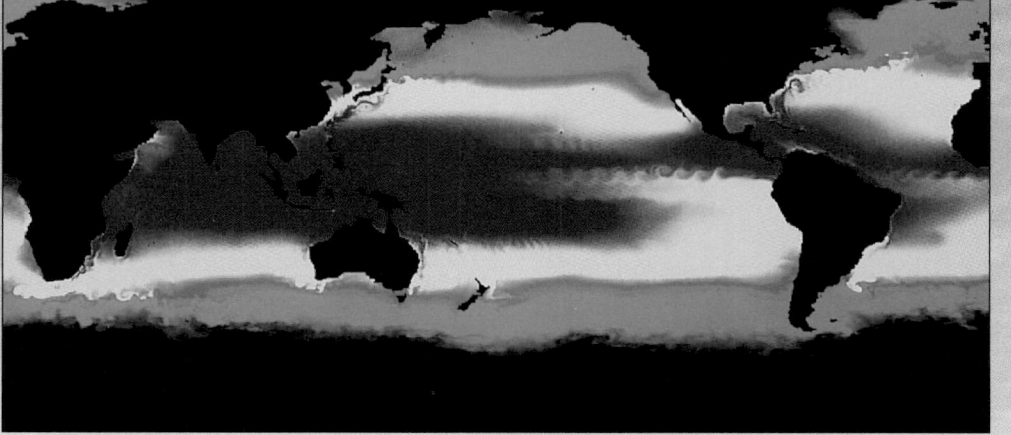

Global turbulence

A computer simulation (left) of sea surface temperatures clearly shows the warm band of water (coloured red) that stretches across equatorial seas. In the Pacific it can be seen breaking up into eddies. The model has been used to predict shifts in major currents, such as the Gulf Stream off North America.

How tides occur

Both the Moon and Sun exert a gravitational pull on the Earth, but the Sun, more distant, exerts a lesser pull. The pull of each body causes the oceans to bulge, producing tides.

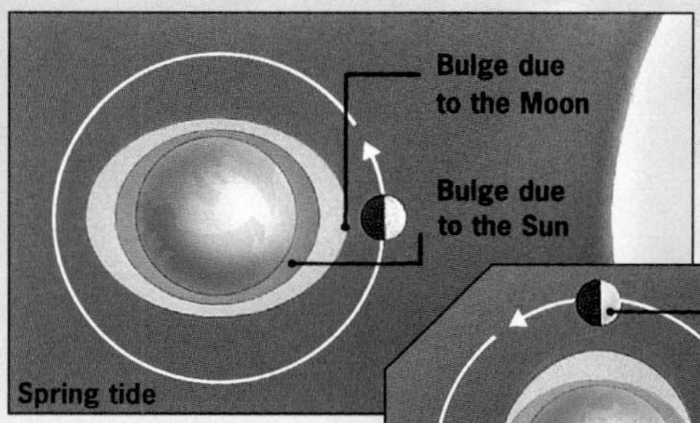

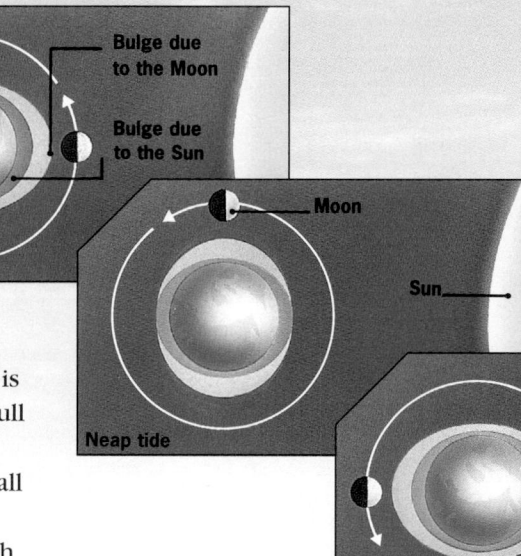

Bulge due to the Moon

Bulge due to the Sun

Spring tide

Moon

Sun

Neap tide

Spring tide

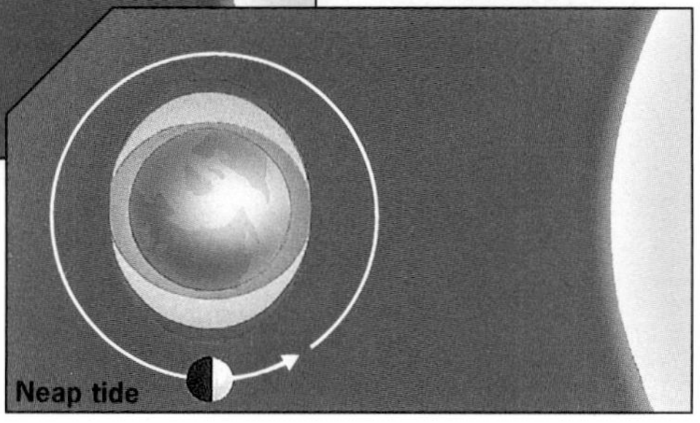

Neap tide

Ebb and flow

The constant slow rhythm of the tides is caused primarily by the gravitational pull of the Moon as it orbits the Earth. However, the effect is not the same in all parts of the globe. The precise tidal range at any place is influenced by such factors as the shape of a coastline, depth of water and the length of an inlet. The Mediterranean Sea is almost without tides, with a range of only 10–15 cm (4–6 in), yet the sea level in the Bay of Fundy on the east coast of Canada rises and falls by as much as 13.6 m (45 ft).

Spring tides

When the Sun, Moon and Earth are ranged along the same straight line (which occurs at either a new or a full moon), their tidal bulges coincide. This effect creates higher tides around the world, known as spring tides.

Opposite bulges

A tidal bulge forms on the side of the Earth nearest to the Moon (left). A second bulge – really a tail or 'wake' – occurs on the opposite side as the Moon's pull on the Earth is greater than its pull on the ocean on that side.

OCEANS AND SEAS OF THE WORLD	
Name	Area in km² (sq miles)
Pacific Ocean	165 384 000 (63 838 000)
Atlantic Ocean	82 217 000 (31 736 000)
Indian Ocean	73 481 000 (28 364 000)
Arctic Ocean	14 056 000 (5 426 000)
Mediterranean Sea	2 505 000 (967 000)
South China Sea	2 318 000 (895 000)
Bering Sea	2 269 000 (876 000)
Caribbean Sea	1 943 000 (750 000)

Neap tides

Twice a month, the Moon and Sun are at right angles relative to the Earth. The gravitational pulls of the Sun and Moon to some extent cancel each other out, making the lowest, or 'neap' tides.

LIFE IN THE SEAS AND OCEANS

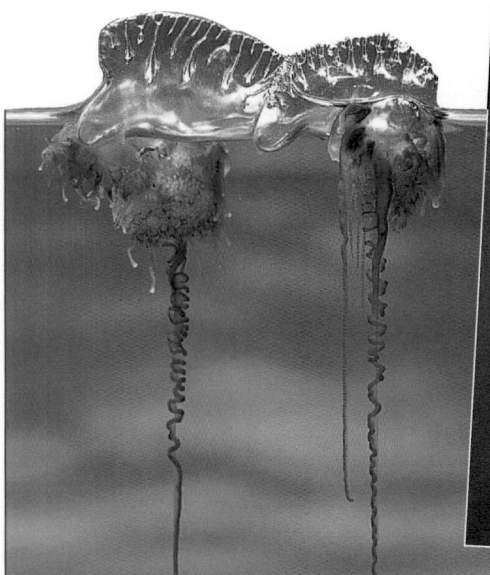

Ocean wanderer
Blue-footed boobies sleep on the surface of the sea and rarely visit land, except to breed. They catch fish by diving steeply from the sky.

Blue-footed booby

It was in the primeval oceans that life began 3.5 billion years ago. Today, the oceans cover two-thirds of the Earth's surface and support as rich and varied a community of animal life as any that can be found on land. This community depends ultimately upon the plant life of the sea, which consists overwhelmingly of minute algae, known as phytoplankton. Like all other plants, these rely on light to produce energy. Below a depth of around 100m (330ft), light intensity is not sufficient to support this energy production, so most phytoplankton are confined to the upper layers, as are the shoals of fish that feed on them and on each other. Life does exist at depths of 4km (2½ miles) or more. However, food here is scarce, consisting mainly of dead plants and animals, and other detritus that sinks from above. In shallow waters and coral reefs, on the other hand, the sea floor supports some of the most varied and colourful animal species on Earth.

Giant of the oceans
The main diet of the humpback whale (left) is krill, a shrimp-like animal abundant in cold, polar waters. These whales travel to warmer waters only to breed.

Rulers of the oceans

The undoubted rulers of the seas are the fish. There are two main groups: the first, which includes the sharks and rays, have skeletons made of cartilage, while the second, which includes most other fish, have skeletons made of bone. Only bony fish have developed the air-filled buoyancy sac known as the swim-bladder, which enables them to hover in the water: cartilaginous fish must swim continuously, or else they would sink.

Just as on land, there are herbivores and carnivores. Efficient killers, such as shark, tuna and barracuda, feed voraciously on the vast shoals of anchovy, sardine and herring that graze the abundant plankton.

Killer colony
A Portuguese man-of-war (above left) is not a single jellyfish, but a colony of individual polyps. Some polyps sting, some reproduce, some feed, while others form the sail-like float.

Sargassum fish

Swimming serpent
The sea-snake (left) secures its prey by injecting a fast-acting venom. This kills the victim before it has time to swim away.

Sea snake

Hiding out
The sargassum fish lives in the calm tropical waters of the Sargasso Sea. It is well camouflaged for lurking among the brown fronds of sargassum weed that form vast rafts in this sea.

Safety in numbers
Although shoals of anchovies (above) must attract the attention of predators because of their sheer size, massing together may intimidate the predator and certainly allows individual fish a better chance of survival.

Fishing with light
The deep-sea angler fish (below) uses a luminous lure to attract prey within reach of its mouth. These fish can live at depths of 4km (2½ miles).

Viper fish
The viper fish (right) has side lights to attract prey in the Pacific deeps. At 30cm (12in) long, it has a huge gaping mouth and sharp teeth.

Deep headlights
One way to signal in the dark is to shine a light. Many deep-sea creatures, including squid (below) and seapens (right), have evolved ways to convert chemical energy into light energy. Only part of the body is illuminated, in order to trap prey without attracting predators.

Fossil fan
The seapen (right) represents an early phase of evolution – fossils have been found in rocks more than 500 million years old. It filters food through fan-shaped polyps.

Luminous squid

Plankton soup

The ocean's food chain starts with uncountable billions of phytoplankton – microscopic plants – and equally vast numbers of zooplankton, the minute animals that feed on them. They multiply in the surface water, which is in effect a green 'soup'. Many marine species depend directly on this soup, from tiny fish and larvae to the largest living animal, the blue whale, which filters plankton through horny plates (baleen) suspended from the roof of its mouth.

Eight open arms

Octopuses are highly evolved relatives of slugs and snails. They have tentacles with suckers to seize prey.

Wide-eyed hunter

Hammerhead sharks (below) have a wide field of view and a keen sense of smell to guide them to food. They also use well-developed sensors on their heads to detect the electric field around their prey.

Coral community

Butterfly fish and parrot fish feed on coral, as does the voracious crown-of-thorns starfish. One starfish can devastate an area of 5 m² (55 sq ft) of coral in a year. Moray eels lurk in holes to catch unwary prey. Anemone fish, such as clown fish, live protected among the stinging tentacles of sea anemones, which are fatal to other fish.

Floating plants

Diatoms (left) are one of the main groups of single-celled plants that make up phytoplankton (from Greek words meaning 'wandering plants'). Magnification shows their elaborate and beautiful shells made of silica or lime. All phytoplankton use the energy of sunlight to convert water and carbon dioxide into sugars and oxygen.

Cleaner wrasse

Pacific cod

Moray eel

Brain coral

Crown-of-thorns starfish

Clown anemonefish

Parrot fish

Butterfly fish

Flashing blade

The exact function of the swordfish's blade-like nose has yet to be determined. One possibility is that it is used to slash at prey.

Hungry mouth

Deep-ocean fish must grab what they can get, whatever the size, but may suffocate on a big mouthful. However, a fangtooth (below) can swallow and breathe at the same time.

Colonies of colour

Coral reefs are home to a wider variety of sea creatures than any other marine habitat. All are attracted by the shelter and food sources that the reef creates. Coral itself is made up of huge communities of polyps – tiny creatures that filter out plankton from the sea. Each polyp builds its own hard limestone skeleton, and as each generation of polyps dies it adds its skeletons to the foundations of the reef.

Coral will grow only where the water is clear, shallow and warm, so reefs are found exclusively in tropical waters. The water temperature is most important – an average temperature lower than 20°C (68°F) would prevent the coral from flourishing.

Many reef residents are closely interdependent. Some small species of wrasse, for example, feed on the parasites attached to larger fish such as grouper and cod.

Long-term residents

Many of the ocean's inhabitants have changed little over hundreds of millions of years. Among them are the sea cucumbers, sea urchins and brittle stars, the jellyfish and sea anemones, and the marine 'worms'. Crustaceans, including sea spiders, shrimps, lobsters and crabs, are a primitive group as numerous in the world's seas as insects are on land. All these creatures have a constant food supply in the sediments of the sea bed and the nutrient-rich water.

Sea cucumber

Sea spider

Brittle star

At the Edges of the Oceans

Where the restless waters of the oceans meet the land, their sculpting power creates a wide variety of coastal formations. Surging waves carve arches and pillars out of cliff faces, or grind rocks down into shifting patterns of fine sand. Such diverse features bring a range of challenges and opportunities for living things. There are several different habitats, from the 'splash zone' – beyond the highest tides, but frequently soaked with salt spray – to the strip of beach closest to the sea and uncovered only at the lowest spring tides. The intertidal zone, submerged and then exposed twice daily by advancing and retreating tides, contains highly specialised communities of plants and animals. Sand and mud have a low oxygen content which, combined with pounding waves and grinding shingle, make this a demanding environment for shore life. However, rock pools provide safe havens for many species to await the returning tide.

The crumbling coast

The scouring power of water sweeping along a rocky coastline can create a natural gallery of dramatic features. Cliffs may contain areas of relatively soft rock, which waves erode, producing caves or cutting through a headland to form an arch. In time, the roof of the arch may collapse, leaving a lonely stack separated from the shore.

Sand is driven along shorelines by currents, accumulating in places where the current is weaker. It may pile up into spits, which lengthen over time to create bars, as well as lines of barrier islands.

The power of water

As ocean currents beat against a coastline (right), rock is ground into sand while the waves cut an arch and stack from the solid rock of a headland.

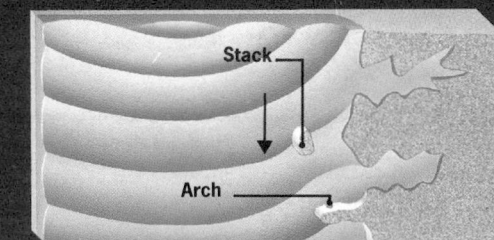

Further wear

Sand piles up into spits, and into tombolos linking rocks to the shore (left). The arch is eroded further until its roof collapses, leaving a second stack.

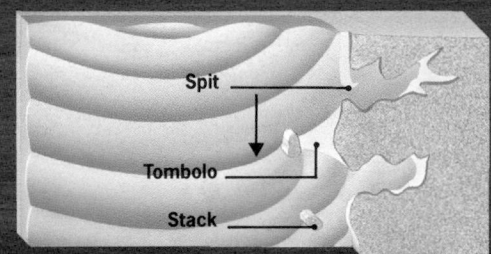

Reshaping the shore

As yet more sand accumulates (right), a spit gradually extends into a 'baymouth bar'. The stacks and other rock features are now completely worn away.

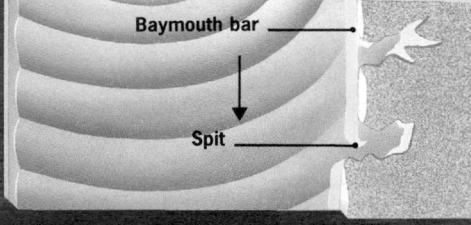

Shelter between the tides

For sea creatures, a rock pool provides a safe 'island' of water, surrounded at low tide by a 'sea' of rock and sand. Yet it is still an exacting environment for aquatic life, with temperature fluctuations and periodic dilution by rainwater. It may be home to crabs and other crustaceans that can survive saltiness, rainfall acidity and changes in temperature. Deeper pools may contain small fish, sea slugs and even jellyfish from farther offshore. Around the pool's edge barnacles and mussels endure the low tides, their shells clamped tightly shut.

Refuge from the tide

A temperate rock pool (right) is home to many hundreds of species. The predators include hermit crabs, starfish, sea anemones and the blenny, which lurks near the bottom of the pool. Mussels anchor themselves firmly to the rock, filtering their food from the water. When high tides cover the pool, limpets roam the rock surface, grazing on algae. They return at low water to niches ground into the rock.

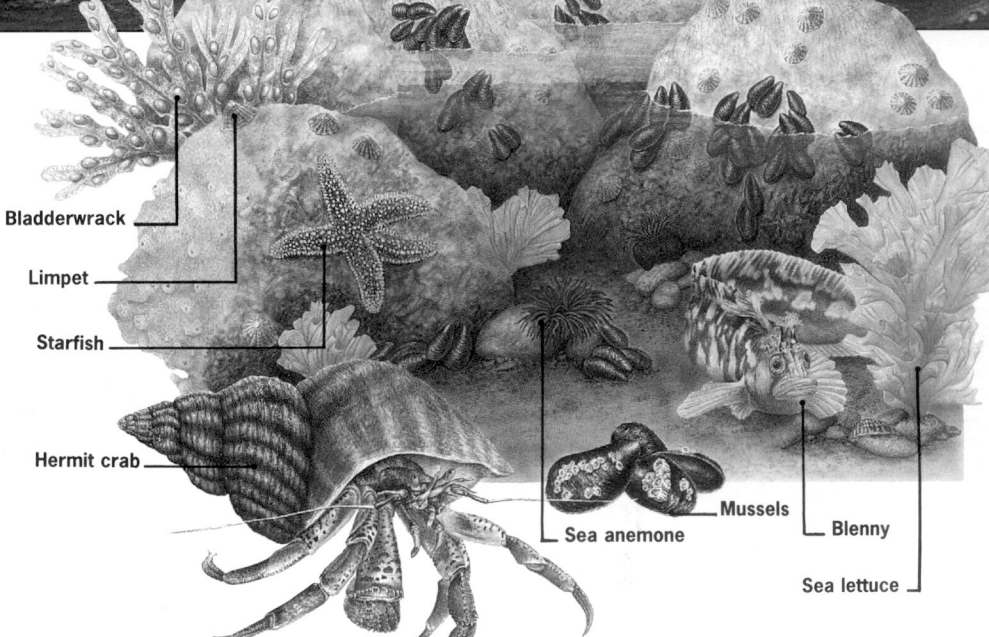

Bladderwrack
Limpet
Starfish
Hermit crab
Sea anemone
Mussels
Blenny
Sea lettuce

Life on the rocks

On a rocky shore, thousands of sea birds nest high on cliffs, while lichens encrust the 'splash zone' above high water. Kelp and seaweed forests growing under water provide a habitat for shellfish, and for fish and their predators, such as seals and sea otters. In the intertidal zone, rocks may carry limpets, barnacles and periwinkles, and also form pools for other creatures.

Cliff-nesting birds

Every spring, sea cliffs around the world become a temporary home for immense flocks of sea birds. Fulmars (left) breed on precarious cliff faces in the polar regions and along the coasts of northern Europe. Each pair lays a single white egg in a shallow dip on a ledge and incubates it for 50 days. The adult birds protect their only offspring ferociously, attacking any would-be predators with a volley of foul-smelling, half-digested food.

Sea-carved cliffs

The southern coast of Victoria in Australia (below) bears witness to the vast power of the sea which has sculpted an assortment of limestone stacks, arches and sand bars.

Ocean forest

Kelp is the 'tree' of the ocean floor. Pacific kelp (below) grows to a length of 60 m (200 ft). It is anchored to the rocky seabed by a grasping 'holdfast'.

The many hundreds of life-forms which hide within the cover of the kelp forest include sea urchins and abalones. The latter are feasted upon by sea otters.

Sandy shores

Sand is not the easiest of materials in which to make a home. At first, only marram grass takes root in the dry, salty dunes at the top of a beach, binding and compacting the sand for other plants, such as sea kale. Sand lower on the beach is equally inhospitable, being low in nutrients and regularly exposed to alternate wet and dry conditions. Rainfall may disturb its salt balance. Food supplies depend on the tides, which bring plankton to the burrowing shellfish and worms, whose presence is revealed by their casts left at low tide.

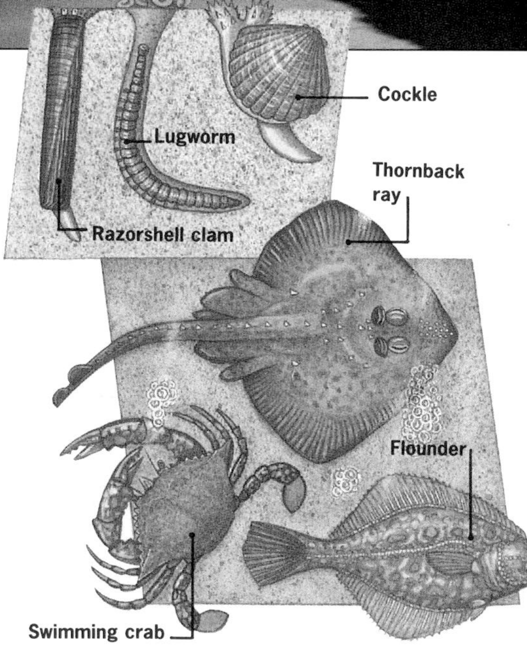

Cockle

Lugworm

Razorshell clam

Thornback ray

Flounder

Swimming crab

Filtering the sea

At high tide, razorshell clams, lugworms and cockles (left, top) extend their filters or siphons into the water to feed on its harvest of microscopic plankton.

Beyond the tides

In the sandy shallows offshore are found the swimming crabs, whose flattened legs propel them along. On the seabed lurk 'camouflaged' fish such as flounder and rays (left).

THE RIVER FROM SOURCE TO SEA

Rivers most often start at a mountain spring or lake, whose cold, fast-flowing headstreams tumble down to gentler slopes where they scour into the earth to cut narrow valleys. Where streams join together, the river proper begins, its pace slowing as the landscape becomes more gentle. In its lower reaches, a river may wind back and forth across its floodplain in a series of lazy meanders. On meeting the sea, it may fan out into a delta. As it passes through each of these different phases, a watercourse can play host to many forms of life – from mayfly and caddis fly larvae in the oxygen-rich mountain rills to the water snakes, caymans, crocodiles and hippopotamuses that thrive in the muddy waters of a tropical meander.

North American dipper

Primrose

Mountain bloom

High in the Pyrenees between France and Spain, a rushing stream provides moisture for colourful plants (top). Among the plants growing at these heights is the bird's-eye primrose (above).

High cascade

As it plunges into a pool, this waterfall in Mount Rainier National Park, Washington State, USA, provides a constant spray that encourages the growth of ferns, liverworts and spongy mosses.

Riverbank vegetation

As well as watering the soil, rivers add moisture to the air through spray and evaporation. Even in dry mountain air, crevices beside a stream may contain rich greenery. Delicate ferns benefit from the constant mist of a waterfall, which is also an ideal habitat for plants such as liverworts and mosses.

In a dense forest, a river provides a gap through which sunlight can reach the ground. River banks in such regions are therefore colonised by a wide range of light-seeking shrubs.

White water

Rapids, like those on a river in Nepal (above), develop when a river flows down a steep valley. Boulders protruding from the river bed force the water into a series of turbulent eddies.

Natural border

The River Zambezi (right), Africa's fourth longest river, forms a natural border between Zambia and Zimbabwe. It winds through scattered scrub on its wide floodplain and ends in a marshy delta.

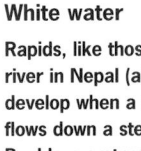

Long-eared bat

Red lechwe

Underground sculpture

As raindrops fall through the air, they absorb carbon dioxide to become a very weak acid. If this rainwater falls on an area of limestone, it gradually dissolves the rock. Over millions of years this process of erosion enlarges cracks and creates caves and underground streams and rivers. Where water drips from the roof of a cave, it gives up its dissolved load of limestone. The solution is deposited speck by speck to form either a hanging stalactite or an upward-pointing stalagmite.

Safe shelter

Stalactites (left) hang in a cave carved by an underground river. The stable humidity and low, even temperature of such caves make them ideal hibernation sites for the long-eared bat. Caves also support their own specialised species of fungi, which feed on other cave-dwellers' waste as well as on detritus deposited by the river.

Leaping lechwe

The red lechwe is a grazing antelope of the River Zambezi and its tributaries. It is threatened by dam construction, and the consequent loss of seasonally flooded grassland.

Along the watercourse

Rivers are fed by rain falling on high terrain. The volume of water given to the river system depends partly on the underlying geology – porous rocks may absorb as much as 85 per cent. Many rivers are dry for part of the year.

The fast water of a mountain stream scours away at the rock it passes over, carving out a steep-sided, V-shaped valley. Where the stream crosses an impervious layer of rock, its sculpting action is slowed. At a weak point in the rock the river can cut through the hard layer, rapidly eating away softer rocks below to form a waterfall. In other places, patches of harder rock protrude into the riverbed, creating violent rapids.

The lowland, mature river winds through its own floodplain of alluvial soil. This soil is easily eroded. Slight bends in the river's course are exaggerated as the faster water on the outside of each bend cuts more quickly into the bank, while the slower water on the inside deposits sediment. In this way a loop in the river may eventually become cut off from the main stream, forming an oxbow lake.

As it approaches the ocean, a large river widens and its current slows down. Sediment is deposited to form sandbanks. These divide the river into the myriad channels of a delta or estuary, which provides a rich habitat for aquatic and bird life.

Travelling geese

The migration paths of Brent geese (below) are both long and complex. From summer breeding grounds inside the Arctic Circle, the geese fly to feeding grounds in the temperate river estuaries of Europe and North America.

Brent goose

■ Winter
■ Summer
↔ Migration paths

Dipper's dive

A North American dipper (left) is never far from water. It swims underwater in search of insect larvae and other invertebrates, and can even walk along the riverbed. In places, these small birds have been seen to nest safely behind the constant protective curtain of a waterfall. The dipper is highly sensitive to acid rain. Its presence is a sure sign of pure water; while its disappearance may be interpreted as an early warning of environmental threat.

Drawing breath

Slow, warm waters, such as those of the muddy, meandering Norman River in Queensland, Australia (bottom), contain little oxygen. The Australian lungfish (below) has coped with this problem by evolving a primitive lung as well as a set of gills. When the water at the bottom is too foul and stagnant to sustain life, the lungfish makes its way to the surface and draws in a gulp of air before diving again.

Australian lungfish

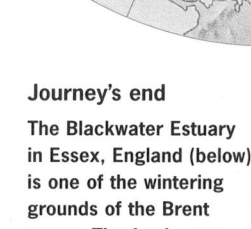

Journey's end

The Blackwater Estuary in Essex, England (below), is one of the wintering grounds of the Brent goose. The fresh water of the river mixes with seawater in shifting channels that cut through the sediment deposited by the river as it slows.

Vanishing waters

The Okavango River ends its journey in a landlocked basin in Botswana (above). The waters of the river are consumed by evaporation, forming a marshy 'delta' – home for the Nile crocodile, Africa's largest reptile (right).

Nile crocodile

LAKES AND WETLANDS

The lakes and wetlands of the world are among the most valuable, yet threatened, of our natural habitats. Lakes are formed either when hollows fill up with water, or when natural drainage is obstructed. Some are the result of movements in the Earth's crust; others are caused by glaciation, or are the craters of extinct volcanoes. Wetlands also take a variety of forms, from stagnant inland bogs to saltwater coastal mangrove swamps. Bodies of water may disappear altogether or acquire new features over time. Rivers can bring in silt and mud, which gradually build up into layers of sediment, reducing the depth of the water. In some wetlands, the level of nutrients increases slowly over thousands of years, accompanied by changes in the water's community of plants and animals. Sometimes the water will gradually silt up to become scrub, and then woodland. Abrupt changes in the ecology are experienced when a lake becomes polluted by industry, acid rain or intensive farming.

Under threat

Native sawgrass (below) and rush were once a dominant feature of the Florida Everglades. Development and drainage are causing this natural vegetation to be replaced by invasive species such as cat-tails.

Snail kite

Pink wader

The roseate spoonbill probes with its beak to find fish and shellfish in the muddy water of the Southern Everglades. An endangered species, it is being conserved at breeding sanctuaries on the island of Trinidad.

Roseate spoonbill

American alligator

Manatee

Garpike

Choosy eater

The main diet of the snail kite is the apple snail. Swamp drainage has reduced the snail population, so that now there are only 1000 or so snail kites in the USA.

Rapacious reptile

Both crocodiles and alligators are found in the Everglades National Park. The two can be differentiated by their teeth: alligators have a distinct overbite.

Vanishing wilderness

The Florida Everglades was once an immense freshwater marsh, home of the Florida panther and American crocodile. Now both are threatened by human activities, in particular by drainage and water pollution. Only a handful of panthers and a few hundred crocodiles remain. The Everglades is sustained by freshwater filtering down to the sea from Lake Okeechobee, which collects water from the Florida peninsula via the Kissimmee River. This river originally meandered, but was straightened to create dry land for building and agricultural use. It must now be returned to its natural state if sufficient water is to reach the Everglades National Park, the last remnant of this unique habitat.

Lurking carnivore

The wetlands, lakes and rivers of North America are home to the garpike. This carnivorous fish has large eyes and long jaws full of needle-like teeth for securing prey.

Hungry herbivore

The manatee is a herbivore that needs to eat 30 kg (66 lb) of food a day to maintain its weight. Sadly, many of these rare creatures are maimed by whirring speedboat propellers.

Mangrove swamps

Red mangroves cope with the unstable, stagnant mud of a shallow river estuary on the Everglades' margins (left) by growing a tangle of arching prop roots. The roots form rafts that support the plants in the unstable mud. Pores in the roots allow the plants to 'breathe' when the waters recede.

Dangerous interference

Lakes tend to develop specialised plant and animal communities that live together in a delicate balance. Disruption from direct pollution, acid rain or an introduced species can be disastrous.

The introduction of perch into Lake Victoria in Africa in 1958 has caused the extinction of many of the lake's 170 species of cichlid – nearly all of which were unique to the lake. This has wrecked the ecology of the lake and the livelihood of people on its shoreline.

The jewel of Siberia

Lake Baikal in Russia contains one-fifth of the world's fresh water. It is the world's deepest lake and occupies a rift valley that is seven times as deep as the Grand Canyon, and filled with 25 million years' accumulated sediment. The lake is fed by 300 rivers but drained by only one. A complete change of water takes at least 400 years, so the lake is vulnerable to pollution: the rivers carry industrial effluent, which is added to by pulp mills along the shoreline.

Lake Baikal

Lake Baikal (below) is literally a hotbed of life – its depths are stirred and heated by volcanic forces, creating swirling currents as warm water rises and cold water sinks. These currents prevent the stagnation usual in most deep lakes. At least half of the lake's 2600 animal and plant species are unique, and all are under threat.

Meagre catch

Before the Nile perch was brought to Lake Victoria (above), tilapia fish and cichlids fed the local people and sustained their economy.

Unwanted bloom

Water hyacinth is a weed found on Lake Victoria (right). It grows rapidly, forming dense rafts that cover the surface of the water.

THE WORLD'S LARGEST LAKES		
	Area	Max. depth
	km² (sq miles)	m (ft)
Caspian Sea	371 000 (143 250)	995 (3264)
Superior	82 400 (31 800)	406 (1332)
Victoria	69 500 (26 800)	85 (279)
Huron	59 600 (23 010)	228 (748)
Michigan	57 454 (22 180)	281 (922)
Aral Sea	37 000 (14 280)	68 (223)
Tanganyika	32 900 (12 700)	1480 (4855)
Great Bear	31 328 (12 100)	413 (1355)
Baikal	31 500 (12 160)	1620 (5315)
Malawi	23 300 (9000)	678 (2224)
LARGEST LAKES OF THE BRITISH ISLES		
Lough Neagh	382 (147)	31 (102)
Loch Lomond	70 (27)	189 (620)
Windermere	15 (6)	66 (216)

Bobbing about

The Baikal teal is a duck that breeds in and around Lake Baikal as well as other Siberian forest regions.

Siberian seal

The Baikal seal lives in Lake Baikal – 4000 km (2500 miles) from its nearest marine cousins. It is one of the very few freshwater seals in the world, and is the only mammal among the lake's 1400 animal species. The greatest numbers of Baikal seals live in the lake's less-polluted northern part.

Local delicacy

The omul is a species of salmon unique to Lake Baikal. Large numbers of the fish are farmed on the lake.

Baikal teal

Baikal sculpin

Baikal seal

Omul

Upwardly mobile

The Baikal sculpin amazes biologists by its daily migrations from the depths to the shallows of the lake in search of food.

Sponges

Baikal is unique among deep lakes in having freshwater sponges that thrive on the lake floor, thanks to deep currents that carry both oxygen and nutrients to them.

Baikal sponge

THE FROZEN WASTES

At the North Pole and South Pole, the Sun's rays make only glancing contact with the Earth's surface – making these regions the coldest places on the planet. Physically, the Arctic and Antarctic are quite dissimilar. The North Pole lies in the middle of the frozen expanse of the Arctic Ocean, while the South Pole sits on the frozen continent of Antarctica, which has mountain peaks of more than 4000 m (13 200 ft) emerging above the ice. Both regions are hugely inhospitable to life. Surprisingly, a lack of water – in its liquid form – is as much of a challenge as the intense cold. Few green plants can grow, as there are no soils to provide anchorage and nutrients. The animals that do live near the Poles are all endothermic (warm blooded) – there are no reptiles or amphibians on the ice caps – and most take their food from the sea. This means that the fauna of Polar regions is concentrated in a narrow strip beside unfrozen stretches of the oceans.

Life in Antarctica

The animal life of Antarctica includes many birds species, particularly penguins, and millions of ticks and lice. Two of the seal species are named after Antarctic seas: the Weddell seal, an expert deep diver that can stay below water for as long as 70 minutes, and the Ross seal which lives on the pack ice and can swim fast to catch squid and octopus. The most abundant Antarctic seal is the crab-eater, which has specialised teeth to filter krill from the water. The notorious leopard seal feeds on penguins, other sea birds, and even seals. The massive elephant seal takes its name from the male's flexible snout.

Both seals and penguins spend most of their life in the sea, coming ashore to produce offspring. Paddle-like limbs and heads merging smoothly into their bodies make them fast swimmers.

Emperors of the ice

Emperor penguins are the only species to breed on the ice during the harsh Antarctic winter. The female lays a single egg onto the ice. This is incubated by the male, who holds it on top of his feet, covered by a feathered fold of skin to keep it warm. Thousands of incubating males huddle together for warmth until the end of the winter when the eggs hatch, whereupon both parents feed the chicks.

Polar hunter

Killer whales are the largest species of the dolphin family. Males can grow to more than 9 m (30 ft). Living in shoals of about 50 individuals, they feed on a wide range of prey, including seals and penguins, as well as fish and other dolphins.

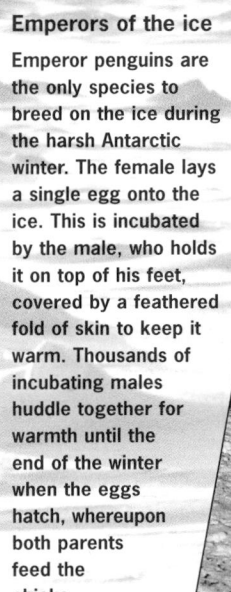

Sun at midnight

As the Earth orbits the Sun, its tilt remains constant. Across most of the world this is apparent from the seasons, with longer days in summer and shorter days in winter. But at the Poles the effect is much more extreme. During a polar midwinter, when the Pole is pointing away from the Sun, each day is a 24-hour 'night'. At midsummer, when the Pole is tilted towards the Sun, continuous daylight occurs (right). At evening, the Sun sinks lower as if about to set; but at midnight, still above the horizon, it starts to rise again. The Arctic and Antarctic circles mark the southern and northern limits of the regions where, for at least one day in the year, the Sun will neither rise nor set.

The ozone layer

Ultraviolet (UV) radiation from the Sun can split molecules of oxygen into their constituent atoms, which recombine to form ozone, a colourless gas. The ozone layer in the Earth's atmosphere is vital to life, as it absorbs damaging UV radiation. In the early 1980s a 'hole' – a region of depleted ozone – was found above the South Pole. Research showed that this was due to reactions involving synthetic chemicals called CFCs. These are now being phased out, but it may take up to a century for the ozone to replenish itself.

Broken shield

The ozone layer, 11-50 km (5-30 miles) above the Earth screens out harmful UV radiation (right). CFCs, used in coolants and aerosols, are broken down by UV radiation into chlorine, which attacks the ozone shield. Winter wind patterns over Antarctica create a region of almost still air, where ozone-depleting chlorine builds up, before being unleashed in spring.

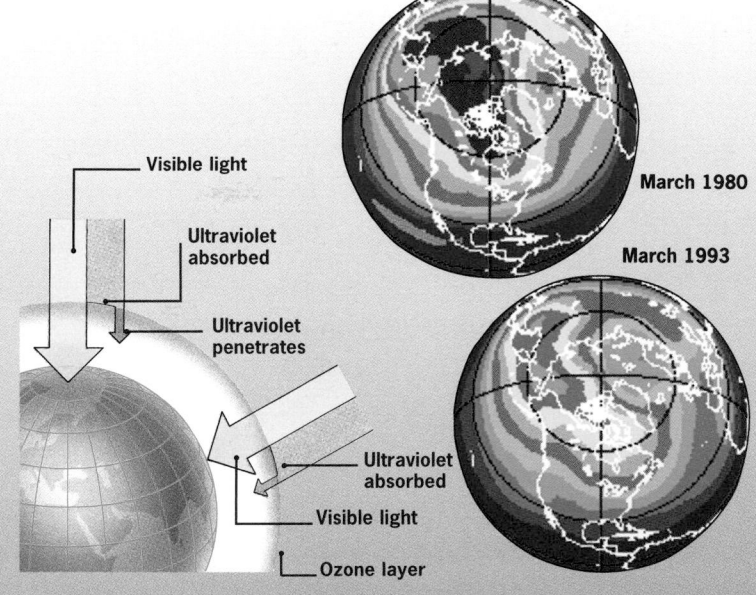

Visible light
Ultraviolet absorbed
Ultraviolet penetrates
Ultraviolet absorbed
Visible light
Ozone layer

March 1980
March 1993

Hole in the north

The ozone hole over the Arctic is smaller than that over the Antarctic, but still significant. The globe comparison (left) shows the enlargement of the ozone hole above the North Pole during a 13-year period. Areas of high ozone concentration are shown in red.

Life in the Arctic

The Arctic and Antarctic regions each contain a different set of mammals and birds, although seals as a group are common to both. In the Antarctic there is no counterpart of the northern polar bear, and the Arctic has no penguins.

The ringed seal is a small species common on the Arctic pack ice. Also native to the region are the harp seal, bearded seal and hooded seal.

As well as the polar bear, the land mammals of the Arctic include the arctic hare, the stoat or ermine, and the arctic fox, which all retreat south to the tundra during the coldest months.

The edges of the Arctic ice cap provide a rich feeding ground for birds such as guillemots, razorbills and puffins. Most of the breeding birds migrate to warmer climes at summer's end.

Seals and bears

Harp seals spend most of their time at sea, but climb onto the sea-ice to mate and have pups, as well as to moult. They breed in large colonies in the Arctic. The pups are white at first, moulting into a blotchy juvenile coat (bottom), before acquiring the adult pattern of light grey with a black head and harp-shaped flank patches (below). They are hunted by polar bears and the Inuit, who make use of their skin, flesh and fat.

Tusked titans

Like seals, walruses have to come onto land or solid ice to give birth. Both sexes have tusks (the males' slightly longer than the females'), used mainly in display to establish dominance. The moustache of stiff, sensitive bristles helps the walrus in the search for food, even in total darkness.

Lonely hunter

The polar bear hunts throughout the year on the Arctic pack ice. It is an accomplished swimmer, and fast and agile on land. Its hairy feet give a good grip on the slippery ice. Polar bears feed mostly on seals as they come up to breathe through holes in the ice. But they will eat anything available, including fish, young whales or walruses, or carrion.

31

BETWEEN FORESTS AND FROZEN WASTES

For a few brief weeks each summer, the land in Alaska, Canada, Greenland, Scandinavia and Siberia between the frozen Arctic Ocean and the northern fringes of the great forests bursts into life with fresh plant growth. This is the tundra, a region so cold that the ground a short way below the surface remains permanently frozen. Winter lasts eight to nine months, with temperatures falling to –30°C (–22°F). Only tough, low-growing plant species can survive on the acidic, waterlogged soils. Many of the animals are migrants, such as caribou or reindeer, drawn northwards in herds from the forests towards the rich summer foraging. In their wake follow their predators, the wolves. Perhaps the tundra's most populous summer inhabitants are mosquitoes. They emerge in such numbers that reindeer may take refuge on the lingering snowfields, where cold air deters these blood-seeking insects. Only a few animal species stay the long winter, burrowing into deep snow for shelter.

Changing coats

In winter the tundra merges into the polar regions, hidden below a thick covering of snow. But in summer the snows melt to leave a landscape of greens, browns and greys. A dark animal stands out against snow, while a white-coated animal is equally obvious against plants and rocks, so many residents of the tundra have evolved to change the colour of their fur or feathers with the seasons. Among the birds that show such changes are the ptarmigan and the snow goose; among the mammals are the Arctic hare and Arctic fox.

Land carved by cold

Just below the surface of the tundra, at a depth of about 50 cm (20 in), is a frozen layer called permafrost, which never thaws out. The soil above thaws in summer, but the water cannot drain away. It collects on the surface and forms marshy pools. The tundra is dotted with features that have been shaped by ice, such as domed polygons and ice hills. Of the Earth's total land surface, 26 per cent is permafrost. Global warming threatens the tundra: even a slight rise in temperature could melt some of the permafrost and cause flooding over huge areas.

Clear of frost

The Trans-Alaska pipeline, 122 cm (48 in) wide, carries oil from the state's northern shore to ice-free Valdez in the south. The pipe is raised on stilts to minimise freeze-thaw damage, to allow access for maintenance, and to limit damage to the sensitive permafrost beneath. The exploitation of oil and minerals continues to threaten the tundra.

Gyrfalcon

Grey hunter

The gyrfalcon is a tundra predator. Specimens from the north have white feathers; farther south, feathers are grey.

Polygons

Domed polygons (below) form when cracks in the ground fill with water. This water expands as it freezes, pushing the land upwards. Cold passes through rock more easily than through soil, so the ice forms first beneath the stones. As they are pushed to the surface, they roll into the ditches surrounding the polygons.

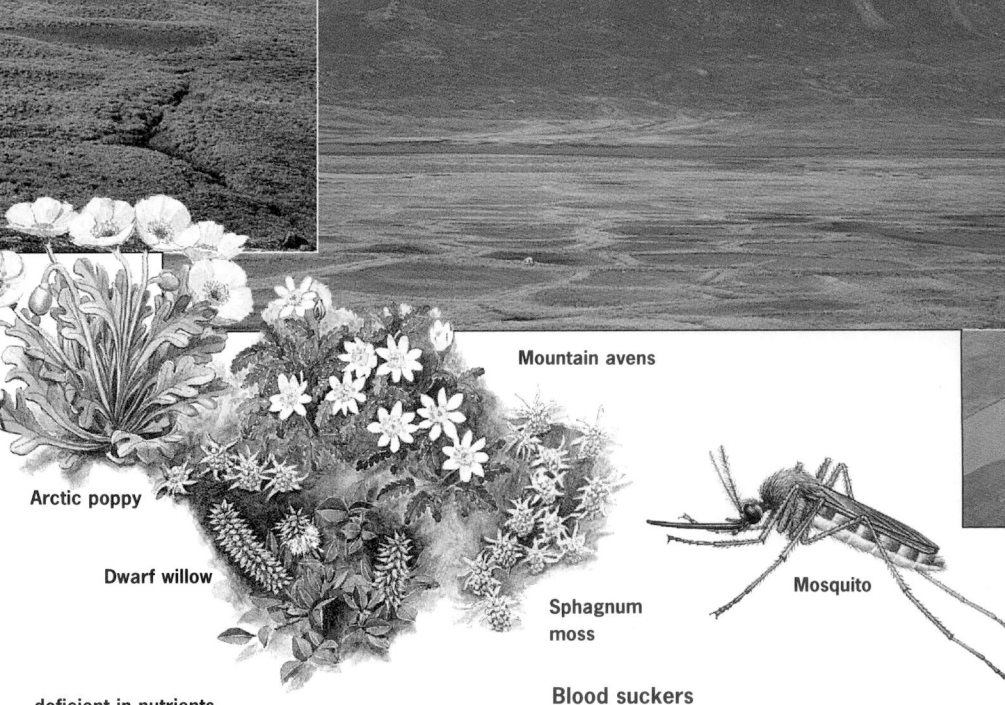

Tundra plants

The tundra is a windswept, treeless plain. Plants are mostly ground-hugging, such as moss, lichens and dwarf willow, or else hummock-forming, such as grasses, sedges and heathers. Other plants, such as the Arctic poppy, have thick, hairy stems that will not succumb to the fierce, icy winds. Plants survive the low winter temperatures beneath an insulating layer of snow. The soil is acidic, waterlogged and often deficient in nutrients. To overcome this, some plants, such as butterworts, are carnivorous, feeding on the insects that swarm during the tundra summer.

Mountain avens

Arctic poppy

Dwarf willow

Sphagnum moss

Mosquito

Blood suckers

In the spring, mosquito larvae hatch from eggs in pools of melting snow. By the summer, adults throng the air, the females thirsty for blood to fuel egg production. The vast numbers of mosquitoes attract migrant birds.

CANADA

Winter feeding grounds

Summer feeding grounds

The incredible journey

As the cold, dark days of winter approach, most large mammals leave the tundra for the protection of forests to the south. One exception is the musk ox, which builds up reserves of fat during summer. Other mammals, such as lemmings and stoats, are too small to make the journey. These remain through the winter, tunnelling under the snow to find food. Most tundra birds are migrants, which fly south when their insect food supply runs out in autumn.

The long trek

Caribou live in North American tundra regions. They are the same species as the Scandinavian reindeer, but have not been domesticated. Adults of both sexes have well-developed antlers, but those of the males are larger. Great herds of up to 100000 caribou migrate 1000 km (620 miles) from the forests of Canada northwards each summer to feed on the tundra (above). Along the way they often have to cross icy, fast-flowing rivers (right).

Ice hill

Ice mounds, or pingos, are common sights near tundra rivers or lakes (below). At the heart of each hill is a core of ice, gradually pushed upwards by pressure from the surrounding land.

These strange hills can be as high as 70 m (230 ft). When cracks on the mound become deep enough to expose the ice core, it melts, collapsing the mound and leaving a circular rampart.

Hare of the north

The Arctic hare (brown in summer, white in winter) is unlike other hares in that it digs a burrow, rather than sleeping in a shallow depression.

Arctic hare

Defensive formation

Shaggy-coated musk oxen (below) bunch together for protection from the cold of the tundra winter. Facing outwards, their horns defend them against hungry predators.

Arctic fox

Plumage

Ptarmigan (right) acquire white plumage during winter, and so remain hidden from predators such as the gyrfalcon. They feed on buds, shoots, berries, insects and worms.

Ptarmigan

Hidden hunter

Arctic foxes (right) feed on small mammals and birds, changing colour through the year to remain camouflaged. In winter they sometimes feed from frozen stores of earlier kills.

WHERE RAIN SELDOM FALLS

With less than 250 mm (10 in) of rain per year, the defining feature of a desert is aridity, not heat. The Sahara, by day, is one of the hottest places on Earth, with temperatures often exceeding 50 °C (122 °F), though heat loss under cloudless skies brings the thermometer down dramatically at night. Other deserts, such as the Gobi, are hot in summer but in winter can be as cold as –20 °C (–4 °F). Typically, warm deserts receive less than 120 mm (5 in) of rain annually, and most of that evaporates. With such a scarcity of water, it might be expected that this environment would be completely lifeless. In fact, most animal groups have species that are adapted to these conditions. And tough grasses, cacti and other spiny shrubs succeed, despite the scant soil, in pushing their roots down to reach any moisture lying beneath the surface of the sand. Other plants survive by having seeds that germinate and flower rapidly after seasonal rains, completing their life cycles within a few months.

Dry New World

A saguaro cactus dominates a stretch of the Sonoran Desert in south-western North America (right). These tree-like plants are the largest of all cacti, reaching heights up to 17 m (57 ft). They are topped with clusters of large, showy flowers that attract swarms of pollinating insects.

Saguaro cactus

Spiny sponge

Cacti are well adapted to desert conditions. They have thick, fleshy stems where moisture is stored, and in place of leaves they have sharp spines that deter grazers. The barrel cactus's rotund stem is adapted for storing water. The pads of the prickly pear face east-west, so that at midday only the edges catch the heat of the sun.

Prickly pear

Rattlesnake

Barrel cactus

Gila monster

Spadefoot toad

Kangaroo rat

North American deserts

The deserts of North America include the Great Basin Desert of Nevada, Utah and Oregon, and the Mojave, Sonoran and Chihuahuan Deserts of the south-west. These landscapes contain not golden dunes, but stony soils with rock outcrops. There are two rainy periods, one in winter and one in summer. Most cacti and annual flowers bloom after the winter rains. The deciduous creosote bush, whose oldest specimens are some 11 500 years old, puts out leaves at this season, but is able to flower at any time.

Audible warning

The rattlesnake belongs to a group of snakes called pit vipers. Heat-sensitive organs between the eye and nostril act like infrared 'eyes', so that the snake can find its prey in total darkness by tracking its body heat. Horny inter-locking segments at the end of the tail vibrate to make a rattling sound to warn off predators.

Lethal lizard

The gila monster (above) is a venomous reptile that feeds on small mammals and birds. Venom is produced by glands in its lower jaw, and flows through grooves in its teeth. The motion of chewing increases the flow of poison.

Going underground

The spadefoot toad, like all amphibians, needs water for the tadpole stage of its life cycle. The toad survives in the Sonoran Desert in the USA and in Mexico by remaining in a deep burrow for periods of up to nine months, emerging only when it rains. The kangaroo rat shelters from the sun in its burrow, where moisture loss is minimised. As it breathes, water vapour is absorbed by its store of seeds. The rat then regains the moisture by consuming the seeds. When it emerges to feed at night, it becomes vulnerable to many predators, such as owls and snakes.

Desert regions

Deserts and arid zones cover more than a quarter of the Earth's land surface – mainly in the interiors of continents where atmospheric pressure is high and rainfall low, or where distance from any ocean limits rainfall. Deserts also form in areas where off-shore winds predominate, such as the Atacama Desert in South America. Here the air is nearly always cool and dry, the winds having lost most of their moisture as they passed over adjacent land masses.

Desert markers

A pair of date palm trees marks a point in the dunes of the Sahara Desert (below) where the ground water is at or near the surface. Date palms thrive in the hot desert climate, but they must have frequent water during their fruiting season.

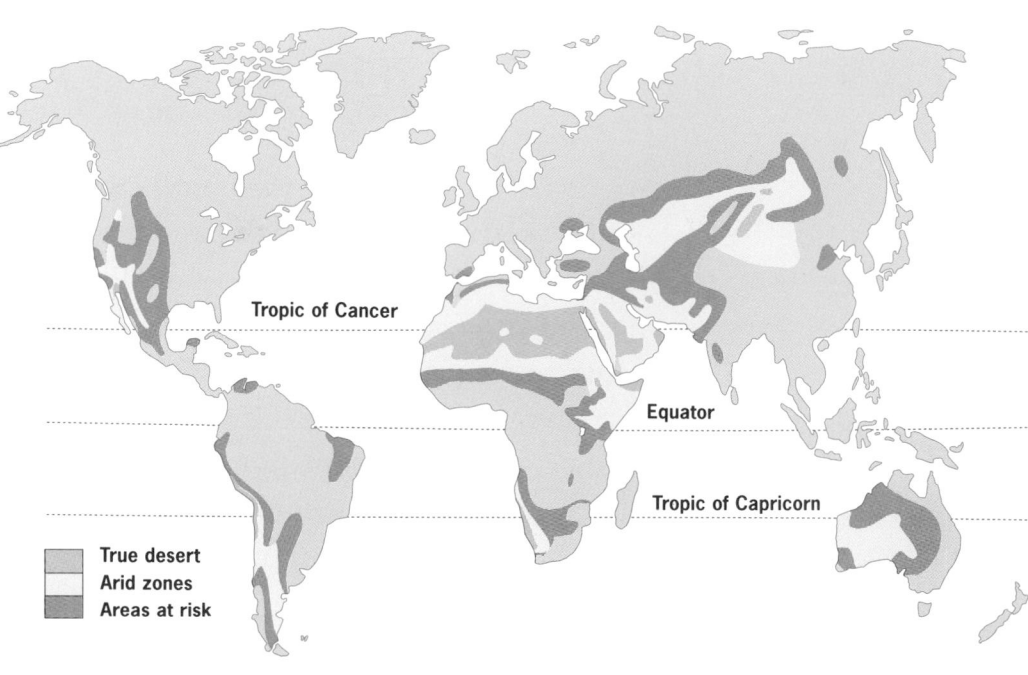

Tropic of Cancer

Equator

Tropic of Capricorn

True desert
Arid zones
Areas at risk

Spreading sands

Desertification – the spreading of deserts – is a problem in many areas (map above). It can be caused by climatic changes, tree-felling, or the overgrazing of desert edges by animals.

Barchan dunes

When a wind blows constantly in one direction across an area of sand, it produces tapering barchan dunes (below). As wind passes over a hump, it divides into several eddies, some of which swirl sideways to pile sand into scimitar-shaped arms. Another eddy tucks backwards, blowing sand upwards to form the steep lee slope of the dune.

Barchan dune

Prevailing wind direction

Eddies

Scimitar-shaped arms

Dromedary

Scimitar oryx

Fennec fox

Meerkat

Living stone

Living stone

Scorpion

Darkling beetle

African deserts

Africa has two distinct desert regions. The Sahara, the largest of the world's deserts, stretches across the north of the continent – a 9 million km² (3.5 million sq mile) landscape of dry hills, rocks and shifting sands. The sparse vegetation in this harsh environment supports few animals. Africa's other great arid area, in the south-west, is split in two. The Namib is a coastal strip that receives moisture from sea mists, while the Kalahari, farther inland, is an expanse of rolling sand dunes.

Living stones

Lithops, or living stones, are plants of the Kalahari Desert that closely resemble the rocks among which they grow. This camouflage protects them from being eaten by animals.

Lethal sting

Androctonus australis (above) is a scorpion of the Sahara region. Its sting is used in defence and to subdue struggling prey. Unlike most scorpions, it has venom powerful enough to kill humans.

Early drinker

The darkling beetle (above) of the Namib Desert comes out at dawn, holding its abdomen high off the sand. Droplets of fog condense on the beetle's body and run down into its mouth.

Saharan mammals

The fennec fox (left) is the smallest member of the fox family. It lives in the North African and Arabian deserts and is mainly nocturnal. It uses its large ears both to help to locate insects and other small prey, and also as radiators to prevent overheating.

Meerkats live in close-knit family groups. While some stand upright, alert for danger, others forage for insects, small rodents and lizards.

The dromedary, or Arabian camel, was domesticated centuries ago, and is now found mainly in eastern Africa and India. It has also been successfully introduced into Australia's central desert. A dromedary's spreading feet allow it to walk steadily even on soft sand.

The scimitar oryx lives along the southern edge of the Sahara Desert. Like all oryxes, it can survive for long periods without water, relying solely on moisture in the grasses and other plants in its diet.

'Seas' of Grass

Grasslands are found on all the continents (except Antarctica) as extensive plains, sometimes dotted with trees. There are two main kinds: the temperate grasslands, which include the prairies of North America, the steppes of Asia and the pampas of South America; and the drier tropical and subtropical grasslands or savannah, found in East Africa, Australia, Venezuela and Colombia. On the classic savannah landscape of East Africa herds of grazing animals roam, following the seasonal rains to take advantage of fresh grass. Predators such as cheetahs stalk the herds looking for a kill, usually an old or weak member which can be separated from the other animals. The fertility of the plains has not escaped human attention. Vast areas of temperate grasslands have been cleared of their wildlife and given over to the farming of wheat or corn – themselves both types of grass – or to the ranching of cattle or sheep.

Treetop browser
The giraffe's long neck allows it to reach into the trees for a year-round supply of green foliage not available to lower-level grazers. Its long legs make it a fast and graceful runner.

Powerful giants
The African elephant is the largest of all land mammals, weighing up to 6.5 tonnes. Its main diet is grass, plus the bark and foliage of trees and shrubs.

Elephants may appear destructive in stripping bark and pushing over trees. However, this natural thinning of trees allows the grassland to develop.

Cheetah

Struggle for survival

The greatest variety of grassland wildlife is found on the East African plains, where there is a constant battle between hunters and prey. There are few hiding places, so grazing animals such as wildebeest and gazelles have evolved other strategies to avoid predators. Safety lies in numbers – it is more difficult for a hunter to select a victim from a closely gathered herd. Lions, cheetahs and hyenas all choose their kill when an individual animal strays from its companions. Speed also provides protection: some grass-eaters can run at 52 km/h (32 mph), and a hunter will not waste energy pursuing a lost cause.

Grassland records

Some of the world's biggest, most powerful animals inhabit the African grassland. Lions are the largest predators. A pride of lions hunts as a team, but usually only the females take part. The adult male (above right) does little killing, despite its great strength and weight of up to 230 kg (500 lb).

The ostrich (centre right) is the world's largest bird, up to 2.75 m (9 ft) tall. It also lays the largest eggs, as long as 20 cm (8 in).

Race for life

A cheetah can sprint at 95 km/h (60 mph), but only for a short time. At 52 km/h (32 mph), the Thomson's gazelle is a slower runner, but may escape because of its greater stamina.

Rising from the flames

Fire has helped to create the open landscapes of the grasslands. It is vital for maintaining the ecological balance between the grasses, the trees and the animals that graze and browse on them. Some fires are caused by lightning, but most are started by deliberate human activity. Grassland soils are not naturally fertile: burning adds nutrient-rich ash and encourages new growth of grasses, which can easily regenerate from their roots. Saplings are usually destroyed, but some savannah trees have mechanisms for surviving a fire. In south-western Australia, for example, the mallee eucalyptus survives by thrusting out new stems from its fire-resistant roots. Some birds also take advantage of a fire. African secretary birds and storks lurk at the edge of a blaze, waiting for rodents and other small animals to be driven out of hiding by the flames.

Following the rains

Wildebeest roam the African plains in huge herds (below). In the Serengeti National Park in Tanzania, their migration follows the clockwise path of the seasonal rains. All the pregnant females of a herd give birth within a few days of each other, so predators are able to take only a few of the vulnerable young.

Bush fire

A bush fire in Meru National Park, Kenya (above), rages out of control – but new grass will grow on soil enriched by the ash.

King of the prairies

Around 60 million bison roamed the American prairies before 1800. After being hunted almost to extinction their numbers have now recovered to about 25 000.

Wild horse

Przewalski's horses once roamed the Asian steppe, but the species is now endangered. Genetic tests have shown them to be the closest ancestors of the modern horse.

Thomson's gazelle

American bison

Przewalski's horse

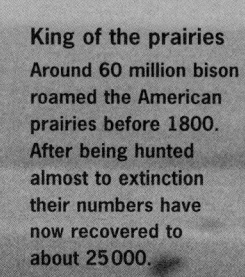

Prairies

Asian steppe

Outback

© Bartholomew

Guanaco

Pampas

African savannah

Red kangaroo

Zebra

◼ Savannah
◼ Semi-arid grasslands

Inhabitants of the grasslands

In similar environments around the world, animals and plants possess related characteristics that have evolved independently. The savannahs of South America, Africa and Australia, for example, all contain large, plant-eating flightless birds – the rhea, ostrich and emu respectively. Plant-eaters are the dominant animals in all grassland areas, and are preyed upon by only a few carnivores, such as the lion in Africa. In Australia the lion's role was once filled by the thylacine, a marsupial 'lion', and in the Americas by the sabre-toothed cat. Both animals are now extinct.

Pampas native

The guanaco grazes on the tough grasses of the South American pampas. It is a type of llama, related to the camel: both can survive on little water.

Counterparts

Each of the world's grasslands is grazed by large grass-eating animals. The guanaco of South America has its counterparts in the African zebra and the Australian kangaroo.

Safety stripes

The striped markings of zebras vary between individuals. The patterns of stripes on the moving zebras may confuse predators.

Hopping herbivore

The red kangaroo is a pouched mammal, or marsupial. Its heavy tail acts as a counter-balance to its body when it hops.

TROPICAL RAIN FORESTS

The tropical rain forests of South America, central Africa and South-east Asia are among the Earth's most vital resources. They contain by far the greatest diversity of plants and animals of any habitat, with as many as 200 species of trees and more than 60 000 species of insects and spiders in a single hectare (2½ acres). Some trees are invaluable, such as the Amazonian liana tree, the source of a drug used to treat multiple sclerosis and Parkinson's disease. As producers of oxygen and absorbers of carbon dioxide, the forests make a huge contribution to the planet's ability to sustain life, yet they are being stripped at an alarming rate, for short-term logging and ranching purposes. The cleared land takes centuries to recover. However, vast areas of the Amazon, the Congo and the East Indies are still virgin forest, and concerted efforts are being made in Brazil and Costa Rica to develop sustainable agroforestry that preserves the precious environment.

Rain-forest life

A permanently warm, damp climate ensures that plants grow larger and more luxuriantly in the rain forest than elsewhere. There is scarcely a tree that is not entwined with lianas and creepers. Bromeliads root themselves into trees, absorbing rainwater through their scales and trapping it amid their fleshy leaves in standing pools, inhabited by lizards, snakes and even crabs and frogs.

The crowns of trees rise to more than 40 m (130 ft) to form the green canopy, while in places single trees, known as 'emergents', grow half as tall again. In these upper heights dwell insect-eating birds such as the massive-billed toucan, as well as huge birds of prey that swoop onto monkeys in the canopy below. Snakes and big cats lie in wait for their prey among the lower branches. Leaves near the forest floor provide foraging for tapirs, gorillas and other large mammals.

Treetop life

The leafy canopy (right) teems with animals, all adapted to life above the ground. Red tree frogs are found in Amazonia, while the birdwing butterfly is a brightly coloured resident of the South-east Asian forest.

On the floor

Many rain-forest trees (right) spread strong stabilising buttresses up to 10 m (33 ft) from the bases of their trunks.

Okapi

Hunters and hunted

In each of the world's rain forests, the emergent layer that towers above the canopy (right) is home to a species of large eagle. In central Africa, eagles prey on several species of red colobus monkey, eaters of leaves, flowers and fruit. The harpy eagle of South America swoops through the treetops at 80 km/h (50 mph) in pursuit of small monkeys such as the capuchin and the squirrel monkey.

Tree frog

Red colobus monkey

Harpy eagle

Asian birdwing butterfly

Scarlet macaw

The middle layer

The blotched markings of the jaguar – South America's only big cat – provide good camouflage in the dense foliage of the middle layer of the forest. This layer is also home to many bird species, including the colourful scarlet macaw. Many rain-forest plants, such as bromeliads, are epiphytes – plants that grow on the trunks and branches of forest trees, but do not draw nutrients from their hosts as parasites do.

Jaguar

Plant-eaters

The abundant rain-forest vegetation supports a wealth of species. In South American forests, large quantities of leaves are taken by leaf-cutter ants, which cultivate them to grow fungi in huge underground nests. Some Equatorial African forests are host to gorillas, which eat mainly leaves and the stems of shrubs and climbing plants. The okapi of central Africa is a shy, solitary, often nocturnal animal which browses on the leaves of tree saplings. Its finely tuned senses of smell and hearing enable it to detect and evade predators.

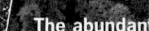
Leaf-cutter ant

Gorilla

Disappearing Eden

The luxuriance of the rain forest depends not on rich soils – the nutrient level is actually very low – but on the recycling of great quantities of leaf litter on the forest floor. Once trees have been removed and the ground cleared of vegetation, there is nothing to prevent heavy rains from washing away the soil – leaving in their wake a denuded landscape that can take several centuries to regenerate to mature forest.

An estimated 18 million hectares (44.5 million acres) of forest are cleared around the world each year, not only for timber and farmland but also for mining and settlement. To slow down the destruction, it is increasingly recognised that rain-forest countries must be helped by the world community to develop effective forest management policies and alternative sources of income.

Lone survivor

A single tree is left standing in an area of Amazonian forest (right). After clearance, the plot will be farmed for a only few years before the soil nutrients are exhausted. Only about 85 per cent of the Amazonian rain forest remains. Preserving this natural heritage has become a major focus of international concern.

Spreading scar

A huge clearing in the forest of northern Brazil (left) was made to allow oil prospecting. It is being enlarged by erosion as rainwater carries away fertile soil and cuts deep gulleys into exposed slopes.

Conditions of growth

Rain forests are restricted to a belt around the Equator, between the tropics of Cancer and Capricorn. Here are constant temperatures of at least 24 °C (75 °F) and rainfall of 2300 mm (90 in) or more per year – in some places the annual rainfall is as high as 7600 mm (300 in). This creates humid conditions where plants grow rapidly. Because there are no seasons in the Equatorial belt, the vegetation grows in abundance all year round. The climate need not be constantly wet, however: some of the world's rain-forest regions show monsoon characteristics.

Lost heritage

A map of tropical rain-forest regions (below) shows the huge loss of habitat over the past 50 years. Almost half the original rain-forest extent has already been destroyed.

Remaining tropical rain forest

Forest cleared since 1945

© Bartholomew

Raggiana bird of paradise

Fer-de-lance snake

Fine forest dwellers

The rain forests are legendary for their profusion of exotic species. The fer-de-lance is a beautiful, but feared, snake of South America. It normally feeds on rodents, but can give a fatal bite to humans if disturbed. The forests of New Guinea are home to spectacular birds of paradise, such as the Raggiana, whose feathers are used to adorn traditional costumes for festivals.

39

THE GREAT FORESTS

Hunter of the north
The great grey owl grows to a length of 70 cm (27 in). It is a native of the dense boreal forest, but hard winter weather sometimes drives it farther south into the United States and Germany.

Great grey owl

Cold-climate trees

Most coniferous forest is in the Northern Hemisphere. Farther south, mountain ranges such as the Andes in Chile (right) provide similar conditions.

Cone cruncher

Crossbills are a group of finches with beaks adapted for prising apart the scales of pine cones and extracting the seeds.

Crossbill

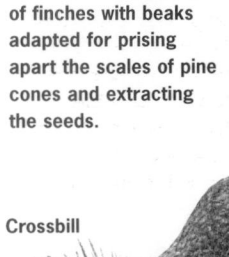

Broadleaf trees thrive wherever rainfall is spread evenly through the year and the summers are warm and not too short. Most of the world's temperate regions fall into this category but, because these areas are heavily populated, much of their ancient woodland has been cleared for agriculture. The fertility of the land derives from the trees that used to grow there, dropping their leaves onto the ground year after year for thousands of years. If farming ceased, the trees would slowly recolonise their natural territory. In regions where summers are short and the risk of frost is always present, evergreen trees predominate. Coniferous forests stretch across the north of America, Scandinavia and Russia in a broad swathe known as the boreal (northern) forest. The term 'taiga', sometimes used interchangeably with boreal forest, describes the marshy conifer forests of Siberia. The frontier between coniferous and broadleaf zones is determined by both climate and altitude.

Native browser

Moose (known as elk in Europe) are the largest of all deer. They live in the boreal forest and adjacent open country and swamps, eating bark, twigs, grasses and water-plants.

Tree feller

A North American beaver (above) fells trees by gnawing with its strong incisor teeth. The trees are used to build both dams and the lodge where the beaver lives. This is a complex construction, with underwater entrances, in the centre of the dammed pond.

Forest feline

The densely furred feet and short tail of the lynx (above) help it to stay warm in the forests of northern Europe. The lynx hunts at night, using its keen eyesight and sense of smell.

Coniferous forests

Evergreen forests grow in regions with long, hard winters. The boreal forest has no equivalent in the Southern Hemisphere because there is no land mass at the corresponding latitude.

The shape of many evergreen trees allows snow to slide off their branches, rather than building up and breaking them. Roots cannot extract water from frozen ground: evergreen leaves are therefore designed to conserve water. Leaves are reduced in size and are often needle-like, with a waxy coating to reduce evaporation. An evergreen tree can start to manufacture food as soon as the spring warmth comes because its leaves are in place already. It also conserves energy because it does not have to generate new leaves each year.

Acid rain

One of the major threats to woodlands comes from acid rain. Sulphur dioxide from the burning of fossil fuels and nitrogen oxides from motor vehicle exhausts combine with moisture in the air to form sulphuric and nitric acids. Clouds may travel 1000 km (620 miles) or more before raining down their acid far from the original source.

The effect of acid rain is worst where the soil is already acidic in content – notably in the evergreen belt. Acids can release toxic metals in the soil and destroy soil bacteria on which trees depend. By the time the effects are seen, the soil may be damaged beyond redemption. The trees start to shed their needles and become less resistant to drought, frost and disease.

Death from above

These dying conifers (above) bear witness to the effects of acid rain, which can be 1000 times more acidic than 'natural' rain. Acid rain drains into rivers and lakes, carrying with it aluminium from the soil which is poisonous to fish. The increased acidity of the water damages the whole community that depends on it, from the tiniest plankton to waterbirds and mammals at the top of the food chain.

The broadleaf forests

Deciduous trees are active in summer and dormant in winter. During the summer their broad leaves make full use of the abundant light. In winter, when roots are less able to replace water from the soil, evaporation through the leaves would be too great, so they are shed as the days shorten.

The fallen leaves are broken down by fungi and bacteria and their nutrients are released back into the soil. Leaf-fall allows light to penetrate to the forest floor during winter and spring, so that bulbs and other early plants can sprout before the trees grow new foliage. The floor of a deciduous wood is therefore richer in herbs and shrubs than either tropical or evergreen forest.

The dominant tree species in a forest depends on soil, rainfall and climate. Beeches grow on alkaline, well-drained soils. Oaks thrive on heavy clay: common oaks favour neutral soils but sessile oaks can tolerate acid conditions.

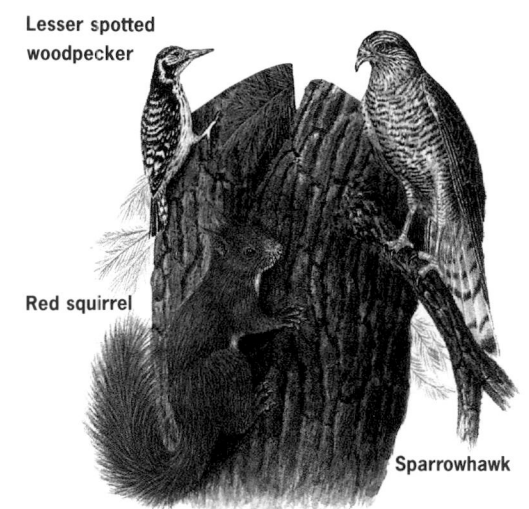

Lesser spotted woodpecker

Red squirrel

Sparrowhawk

Forest fellows

Deciduous woods support many small birds and mammals (left). Woodpeckers probe tree bark for grubs. Both red and grey squirrels feed on seeds, berries and nuts; grey squirrels occasionally take birds' eggs. The swift flight of a sparrowhawk allows it to chase its songbird prey through the forest. In spring, sunlight reaching the forest floor when the trees are still leafless encourages flowers such as primroses, daffodils and bluebells to bloom (left).

Eurasian jay

Careful cleaner

Jays clean themselves by 'anting'. They allow ants to run over their feathers, squirting formic acid which acts as a natural pesticide, killing lice and mites.

Wild boar

Red fox

Longhorn beetle

Tree beetle

The longhorn beetle larva burrows into a tree to feed. It surfaces just before pupating, so that the weak-jawed adult (left) can emerge.

Woodland deer

The North American wapiti (above) is closely related to the red deer of western Europe and central Asia. Second in size only to the moose, these deer inhabit coniferous forests. The smaller, dappled fallow deer is found in deciduous woodland throughout Eurasia.

Wild boar

The wild boar (above) is the ancestor of the domestic pig. It eats nuts, roots, fungi, worms and snails.

Adaptable animal

The red fox, naturally an animal of deciduous forests, is becoming a common sight in the cities of Europe and North America.

Leaf litter animals

The ground beneath the trees acts like an extensive compost heap. Fallen leaves support a complex community of life on the forest floor. The amount of warmth and moisture determines the level of activity: decomposition is normally faster in deciduous woodland than in evergreen forest. Most of the organisms are tiny, but are present in enormous numbers. A handful of litter might contain hundreds of springtails. These tiny wingless insects, together with worms, snails and woodlice, are preyed on by beetles, centipedes and spiders. Fungi play an important part in decomposition, and are eaten by small invertebrates, which themselves may be food for a mole. Mites are parasites of moles and other mammals.

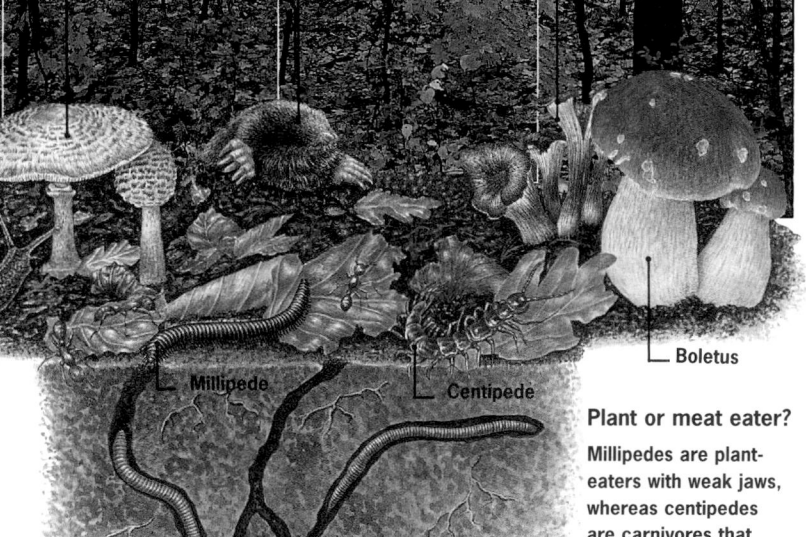

Tricholoma

Shaggy parasol

Mole

Horn of plenty

Wood blewit

Chanterelle

Snail

Millipede

Centipede

Boletus

Life on the floor

Many fungi thrive in the shady warmth of the woodland floor. A network of fungal filaments spreads through the leaf litter, from which the fungi absorb nutrients.

Springtail

Earthworm

Mite

Plant or meat eater?

Millipedes are plant-eaters with weak jaws, whereas centipedes are carnivores that can give a painful bite.

41

THE ROOF OF THE WORLD

The great mountain ranges of the world – the Alps, Himalayas, Rockies and Andes – reach heights of more than 4 km (2½ miles) above sea level. Because the temperature drops by approximately 2°C (3.5°F) for every 300 m (1000 ft) of altitude gained, high mountains near the Equator, such as Mt Kilimanjaro, have permanent snow and ice on their summits while their lower slopes are bathed in tropical warmth. The ranges have been created by collision of the Earth's crustal plates – the interlocking pieces that form the planet's outermost layer. Forces within the Earth push one plate against another until the crumpled rocks in the crust are forced upwards to form mountains. At the same time, some of the rocks are pushed down as far as 90 km (40 miles) into the Earth's hot interior. At this depth the rocks melt and become hot, molten magma, which in due course may well up and rise above the Earth's surface, as volcanic mountains.

Southern fiords

The Southern Alps of New Zealand's South Island lie in an active fault zone. Milford Sound (below) is in the Fiordland region at the island's western tip. Mitre Peak (left), 1691 m (5500 ft) high, is the only habitat of the kakapo, a flightless nocturnal parrot facing extinction. The Southern Alps' highest peak, at 3764 m (12 349 ft), is Mount Cook (also known as Aoraki) whose eastern slope carries the Tasman glacier. To the south of the chain, parallel mountain ridges form a complex, dissected terrain.

Life on the peaks

The ascent of any mountain climbs through a sequence of vegetation zones. In the Tropics this may resemble a journey from the Equator to the Poles, from rain forest in the foothills to tundra nearer the summit.

Plant and animal species vary not only according to vegetation zone, but also from sunny side to shady side. In spring, alpine meadows can be a blaze of colour, with flowers such as gentian and campions. On the summits, few mammals can survive. Those that do have thick coats to combat the cold, and agility and sure-footedness to reach sparse grazing on ledges. Giant birds of prey, such as eagles and falcons, glide and soar on mountain winds.

Unbroken barrier

The 7500 km (4600 miles) of the Andes (right) form the longest continuous mountain range, with 40 peaks over 6100 m (20 000 ft).

Forested flanks

The Rockies (below) extend 4800 km (3000 miles) from Alaska to New Mexico. The tree-line, above which no trees can grow, is clearly defined.

Porcupine

Spiny climber

The North American porcupine is a spiny-quilled rodent which lives in the extensive conifer forests on the slopes of the Rocky Mountains. Despite their poor eyesight and slow movement, porcupines climb high trees in search of nuts, bark, leaves and twigs.

Giant of the hills

The grizzly bear, a species of brown bear, used to roam the length of the Rockies but now survives only in a few national parks in Alaska and Canada.

Grizzly bear

Kea

Threatened bird

The kea is a large, powerful parrot of New Zealand's Southern Alps. It uses its sharp, hooked beak to feed on fruit, insects and plant buds. Its reputation for attacking sheep has led to its near eradication by farmers.

The magnificent Andes

The high plateaus and soaring peaks of the Andes stretch from South America's Caribbean coast, in the north, to the southern tip of the continent. They comprise a succession of mountain chains, or cordilleras, standing above a 'subduction zone', where the Pacific Plate is wedged under the South American Plate (right).

This belt of tectonic plate movement is the site of both earthquakes and active volcanoes. Aconcagua, in Argentina, is at 6960 m (22 835 ft) the highest peak in the Americas.

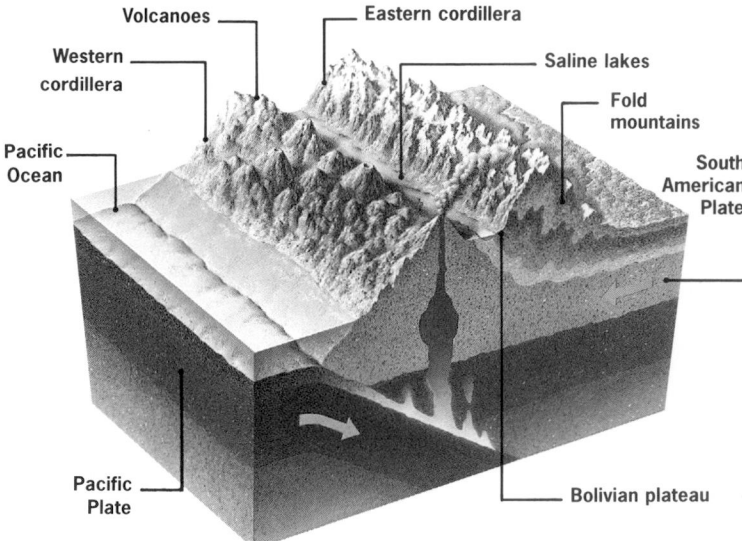

Volcanoes • Eastern cordillera
Western cordillera • Saline lakes
Pacific Ocean • Fold mountains
South American Plate
Pacific Plate • Bolivian plateau

Mountain building

A cross-section of the central Andes (left) shows the differing nature of the two main cordilleras. The western cordillera is volcanic. The eastern one, with its folds and faults, was pushed upwards as the western margin of the South American plate crumpled under the pressure of the Pacific plate. Between them lies the high Bolivian plateau with its string of saline lakes, including Lake Titicaca.

Patrolling the peaks

The Andean condor (below) is the world's heaviest bird of prey. It has a wingspan of 3 m (10 ft) and can soar to heights of up to 7000 m (23 000 ft). These giant scavengers are exceptionally long-lived: one survived in captivity at Moscow Zoo for 72 years. They have been known to raid the nests of seabirds, taking young chicks and eggs.

Andean condor

Mountain cat

The snow leopard (right) is an extremely rare wild cat, found only in the Himalayan region. Despite official protection, it is still hunted for its fur.

On top of the world

The Himalayan peaks (left) are the highest in the world. Few creatures can survive for long in the oxygen-starved, icy wastes.

Snow leopard

Warm coats

Chinchillas, which shelter in burrows or rock crevices in the high Andes, have been extensively hunted for their fur, and only a few communities remain in the wild.

Chinchilla

Parched plains

Much of the Andes has a very dry climate with permanent snow only above 6500 m (21 300 ft). Grassland plateaus in these mountains are suitable for grazers, such as the guanaco (above).

High water

Set 3800 m (12 500 ft) above sea-level, on the borders of Peru and Bolivia, Lake Titicaca (right) is the world's highest navigable lake. It offers sanctuary to many water-birds, amphibians and fish.

Bills for sifting

Andean flamingos sift food from the salt waters of Lake Titicaca with their specially adapted beaks.

Andean flamingo

Ranges of North America

The Appalachians extend for 2500 km (1550 miles) down the east coast of the United States. In a pattern that started more than 600 million years ago, successive phases of folding constructed the mountains while continuing erosion reduced their height. Now no peak is higher than 2037 m (6684 ft).

West of the Great Plains are the Rocky Mountains and, farther west, the Pacific Range. The latter contains, in eastern California, the Sierra Nevada, created only 15 million years ago, when a massive granite range was thrust upwards. The tallest peak, Mt Whitney, is 4418 m (14 494 ft) high.

To the north, in Washington State, are the Cascades, which are volcanic. They contain Mount St Helens, which last erupted in May 1980.

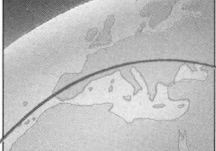

Scaling the peaks

A trajectory across Europe from the Canaries to the Caucasus (left) cuts through many different types of mountain (below). Teide, on Tenerife, is a volcano. The Pyrenees, Alps and Carpathians are young mountains created by the collision between tectonic plates. The Massif Central is an older highland, and El'brus is another volcano. High in the Alps stands the glacial pyramid of the Matterhorn (right).

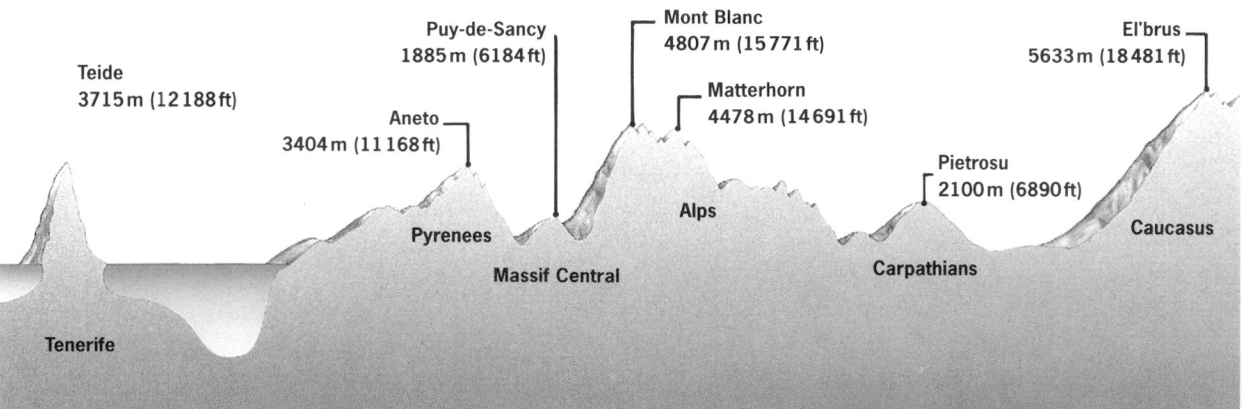

Teide 3715 m (12 188 ft)

Puy-de-Sancy 1885 m (6184 ft)

Mont Blanc 4807 m (15 771 ft)

Matterhorn 4478 m (14 691 ft)

El'brus 5633 m (18 481 ft)

Aneto 3404 m (11 168 ft)

Pietrosu 2100 m (6890 ft)

Tenerife

Pyrenees

Massif Central

Alps

Carpathians

Caucasus

PEOPLING THE PLANET

One of the earliest surviving traces of the ancestors of our human species is a trail of footprints made by human-like creatures walking upright some 3.7 million years ago, found at Laetoli, in present-day Tanzania. Most of the globe was populated by early humans walking from one place to another, perhaps as hunters following migratory herds or in search of new food supplies. The fossil record shows a complex story of evolution, with several species fanning out across the planet, probably from a common ancestry in Africa. Our own sub-species, *Homo sapiens sapiens*, appeared in Africa more than 100 000 years ago and seems to have spread northwards, reaching most parts of the world by 10 000 years ago. At that time the world's estimated population was between 5 and 10 million; today it is more than 5400 million. People continue to migrate from place to place – today in search of political freedom, religious tolerance or better economic prospects.

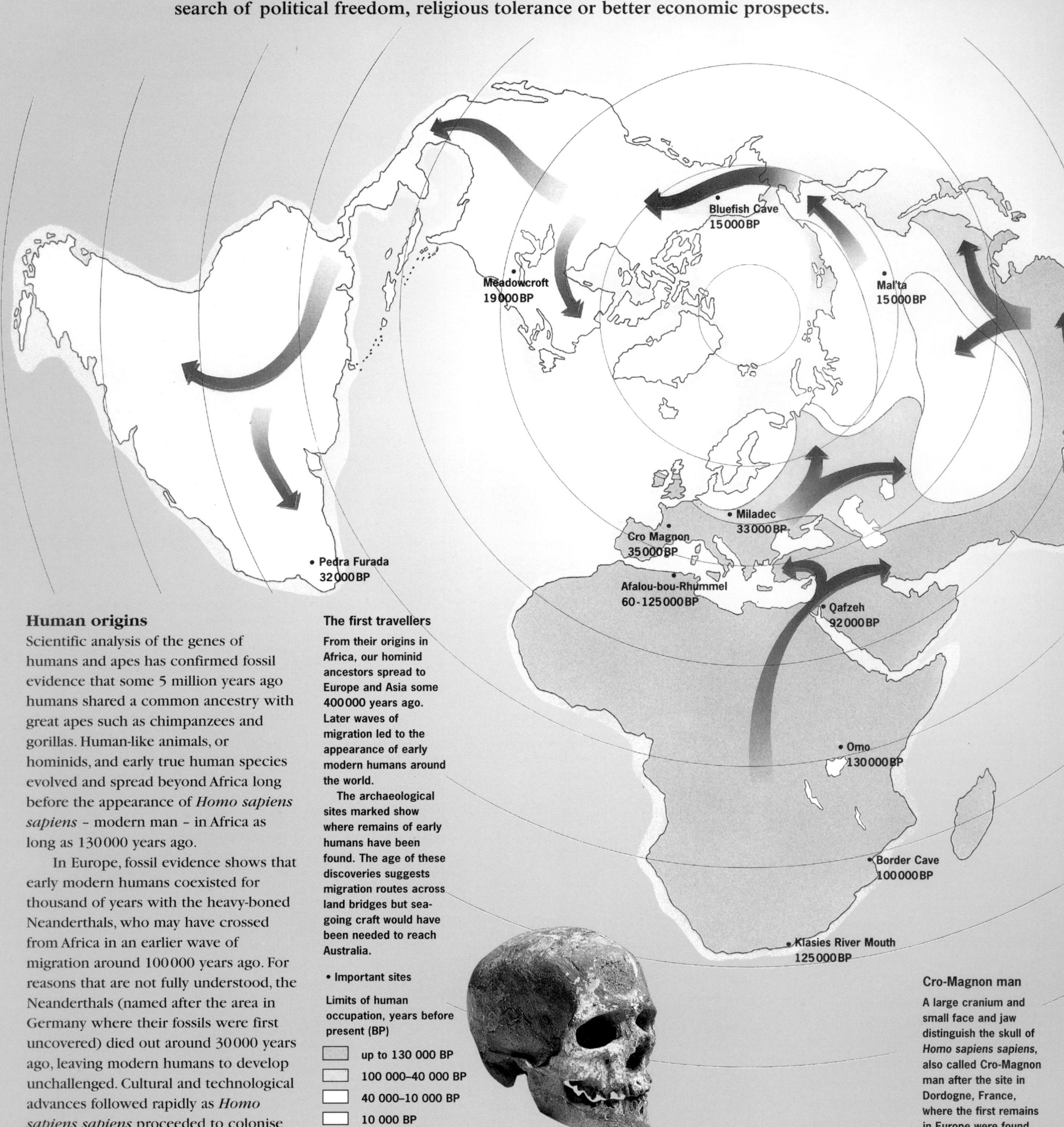

Bluefish Cave
15 000 BP

Meadowcroft
19 000 BP

Mal'ta
15 000 BP

Miladec
33 000 BP

Cro Magnon
35 000 BP

Afalou-bou-Rhummel
60 - 125 000 BP

Qafzeh
92 000 BP

Pedra Furada
32 000 BP

Omo
130 000 BP

Border Cave
100 000 BP

Klasies River Mouth
125 000 BP

Human origins

Scientific analysis of the genes of humans and apes has confirmed fossil evidence that some 5 million years ago humans shared a common ancestry with great apes such as chimpanzees and gorillas. Human-like animals, or hominids, and early true human species evolved and spread beyond Africa long before the appearance of *Homo sapiens sapiens* – modern man – in Africa as long as 130 000 years ago.

In Europe, fossil evidence shows that early modern humans coexisted for thousand of years with the heavy-boned Neanderthals, who may have crossed from Africa in an earlier wave of migration around 100 000 years ago. For reasons that are not fully understood, the Neanderthals (named after the area in Germany where their fossils were first uncovered) died out around 30 000 years ago, leaving modern humans to develop unchallenged. Cultural and technological advances followed rapidly as *Homo sapiens sapiens* proceeded to colonise the habitable world.

The first travellers

From their origins in Africa, our hominid ancestors spread to Europe and Asia some 400 000 years ago. Later waves of migration led to the appearance of early modern humans around the world.

The archaeological sites marked show where remains of early humans have been found. The age of these discoveries suggests migration routes across land bridges but sea-going craft would have been needed to reach Australia.

- Important sites

Limits of human occupation, years before present (BP)

- up to 130 000 BP
- 100 000–40 000 BP
- 40 000–10 000 BP
- 10 000 BP
- ice age land masses

Cro-Magnon man

A large cranium and small face and jaw distinguish the skull of *Homo sapiens sapiens*, also called Cro-Magnon man after the site in Dordogne, France, where the first remains in Europe were found.

Lake Mungo
38 000 BP

Tabon Cave
30 000 BP

Devil's Lair
38 000 BP

Luijiang
67 000 BP

Historic movements

Throughout history peoples have moved overland from one place to another – aided by the horse and the camel, both domesticated between 6000 and 5000 years ago. The Aryans, thought to be the ancestors of most of the peoples of Europe, the Middle East and the Indian subcontinent, probably came from the steppes of central Asia some 3000 years ago. These areas are still linked by a group of related languages, from Celtic to Hindi, that are spoken by their inhabitants. More recent major migrations have included the 'barbarians' of the 4th and 5th century sweeping from the steppes into the disintegrating Roman Empire, and the 13th-century Mongols leaving their Asian heartland to conquer large swathes of the Middle East and Eastern Europe. Other peoples were great seafarers – and the greatest of these were the Polynesians, who had spread their culture across the islands of the vast Pacific Ocean by AD 1000.

America the goal

The USA has long been a magnet to people seeking a new life (below). In the 19th century most of the migrants came from Europe, spurred on by political unrest, economic hardship or religious persecution in their homelands. Many workers from China and Japan were brought in through the ports of the west coast to work on the railways.

Going west

Many of the great migrations of history originated in Asia (below). The Huns came from central Asia in the 4th century, the Mongols 900 years later. In the 8th century the Arabs brought Islamic rule to Spain before being turned back. In the 9th and 10th centuries the Vikings travelled as far as Newfoundland.

⇒ Vikings
⇒ Huns
→ Arabs
→ Mongols

The peopling of America

No fossils of early *Homo sapiens* have been found in the Americas. The most ancient remains date from around 32 000 years ago. The ancestors of today's Native Americans are thought to have walked from north-eastern Asia across the Bering Strait, when a glacial period caused sea levels to fall and dry land to appear across the strait.

The first Europeans to set eyes on North America were Norsemen from Greenland and Iceland: Viking legends of a colony across the Atlantic are backed up by archaeological evidence of a Norse settlement in Newfoundland around AD 1020. However, following Columbus's voyage to the New World in 1492, many European countries established colonies in the Americas. During the 19th century the USA became the target for the greatest migration in human history, as millions of Europeans arrived to build new lives in a new land. Not all migration was voluntary, however – the slave trade brought more than 6 million people from Africa against their will.

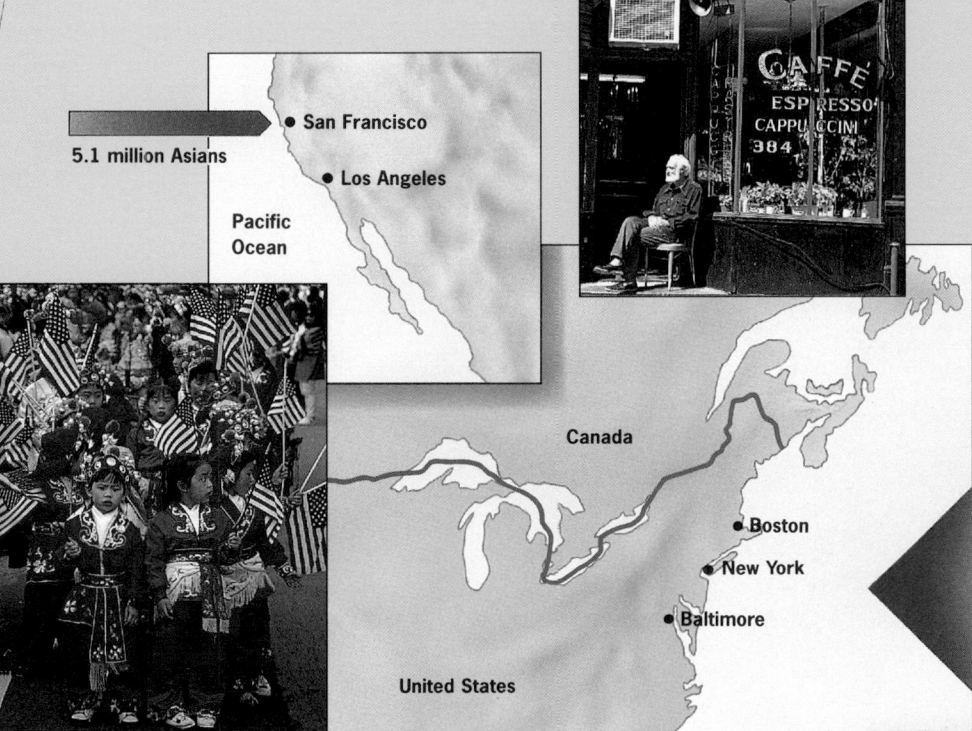

5.1 million Asians

● San Francisco

● Los Angeles

Pacific Ocean

Canada

● Boston
● New York
● Baltimore

United States

Atlantic Ocean

Mexico

Home from home

New settlers often chose to live and work in one particular area, such as Little Italy in New York (left).

1820–1990

| 8.1 million Eastern Europeans |
| 7.0 million Germans |
| 5.3 million Italians |
| 5.1 million British |
| 4.7 million Irish |
| 2.5 million Scandinavians |

Ethnic pride

Chinese-American children in Los Angeles (above) show pride in both their ethnic origin and American citizenship.

Land of freedom

One of the attractions of the USA to groups such as the Amish (above right) was the Constitutional freedom to practise any religion.

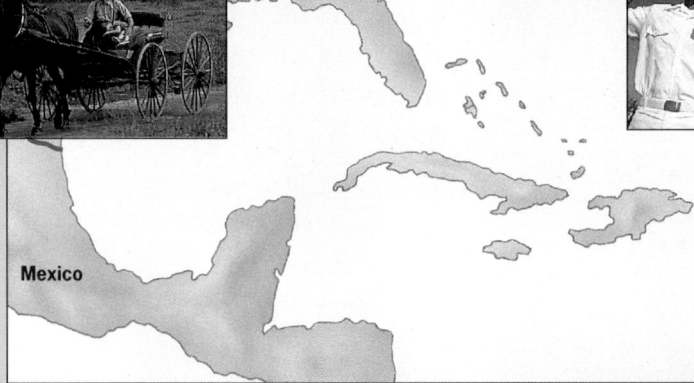

All American

Three US Navy sailors salute the flag (above) in a striking illustration of modern America's ethnic diversity.

PUTTING THE EARTH TO WORK

Our ability to harvest the natural resources of land and sea is a cornerstone of our success as a species, motivating enterprises from small farms and fishing boats to the vast silver mines of Mexico and cattle ranges of Australia. Two-fifths of our planet's land surface has been 'domesticated', primarily for crops and livestock. The yield is massive: every year, the Earth provides over 500 million tonnes of rice, 100 million tonnes of fish and 22 billion barrels of oil. Such exploitation is often damaging: the excavation of ore, coal and stone leaves huge scars on the landscape; industry pollutes air, rivers, seas and land; chemical fertilisers and pesticides eventually impoverish the soil; and the clearing of forests for farms may have long-term climatic effects. The fossil fuels upon which the modern world depends are finite resources which will one day be exhausted. Their husbanding, and eventual replacement, is one of the great challenges of the future.

Back to nature

Modern farming techniques enable the developed world to produce far more food than it needs, though at considerable cost to the environment and, potentially, to health. Organic farming is being reintroduced as an alternative to intensive methods of producing food. Farm waste is better for soil structure and long-term fertility than chemicals, while regular rotation of crops – for example, alternately sowing cereals, roots and legumes in the same field – makes sure that all levels of the soil are used and protects it from becoming exhausted. At the same time, pests find it harder to become established, reducing pesticide use.

The bread basket
In many cereal-growing areas such as Michigan, USA (right), farmers have created vast fields to allow tractors and combine harvesters to operate without obstacle. The eradication of trees and hedges can bring soil erosion and nutrient loss – controlled by the use of chemicals.

The ocean's harvest

Fishing provides about a quarter of the world's protein, and a livelihood for millions. The use of modern factory ships has quadrupled the total catch since 1950; it now stands at some 100 million tonnes a year. In order to halt the alarming depletion of many species, including tuna and cod, governments have closed some fishing grounds and imposed quotas limiting the catches that fleets can land. To help stocks to recover, nets must have holes large enough for young fish to swim through.

The rice bowl
In warm, wet areas of Asia such as India (left), the staple food is rice, planted and harvested using traditional – and often labour-intensive – methods.

How land is used
Many factors affect patterns of land use (below). Topography, soil, climate, social organisation and levels of investment in farming all play a part.

- Nomadic herding
- Hunting and gathering
- Subsistence farming
- Mixed farming
- Ranching
- Forestry
- Barren land

© Bartholomew

Floating factory

A typical modern fishing vessel (below) is a complete processing plant. Within its 115 m (377 ft) length, fish can be caught, filleted, frozen and packed. Such a boat might tow a net 800 m (2600 ft) long, which opens wide enough to engulf whole shoals of fish. Shoals are located using sonar, and possibly even a spotter plane. Such efficient factory ships have decimated fish stocks around the world. In 30 years, the proportion of different species caught off the Gulf of Maine, USA, has swung dramatically from the traditional cod and flounder to the less popular dogfish and skate (table below).

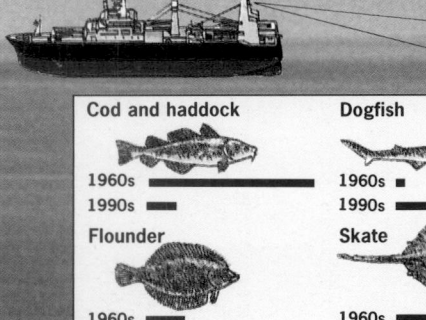

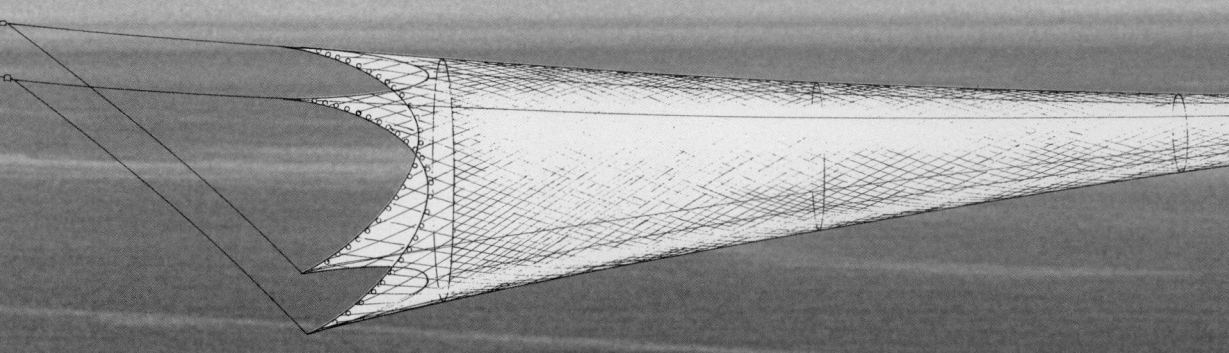

Cod and haddock	Dogfish
1960s	1960s
1990s	1990s
Flounder	Skate
1960s	1960s
1990s	1990s
0 10 20 30 40 50	0 10 20 30 40 50

Fish catch (1000s of tonnes)

Black gold

Oil is the most important of the Earth's fossil fuels, supplying some 40 per cent of the world's energy needs. Together with natural gas, it is a by-product of the decomposition of microscopic plants and organisms deposited in ancient sedimentary rock. Despite the expense and technical difficulty of extracting oil from under the sea, reserves have been successfully tapped beneath the North Sea, the Gulf of Mexico and the Arctic Ocean.

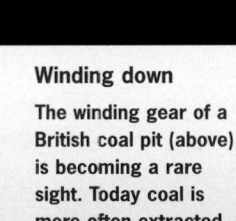

Winding down

The winding gear of a British coal pit (above) is becoming a rare sight. Today coal is more often extracted by open-cast methods.

The fuel formed from forests

Just as oil originates from ancient marine organisms, coal is the fossilised remains of extinct plants. Most of the 350 billion tonnes of coal reserves in Europe and the Americas were formed 290–325 million years ago during the Upper Carboniferous or Pennsylvanian era, when large areas of the Earth were covered by vast swampy forests.

Dead plant matter was attacked by microbes to form peat-like bogs. As layers of sediment accumulated above it, the peaty material was compressed: first into soft, brown lignite, and then into harder, cleaner-burning bituminous coal. The most widely used type – brown coal – can be turned into industrial coke.

The increased cost of deep mining has led to the development of large-scale open-cast strip mines in the Americas, Australia and China, which produce cheaper coal than the old-fashioned shaft-and-tunnel mines.

Plumbing the depths

A combination of bacteria, chemical catalysts, heat from the Earth's core and pressure from crustal movements turns organic deposits within sedimentary rock into oil and gas. These move upwards through porous rock (such as sandstone) until they are trapped under an impermeable layer of, for instance, clay. This often takes place in a dome-shaped formation known as an anticline, from which they can be extracted.

- Sediment
- Borehole
- Fault
- Impermeable rock
- Gas
- Oil-bearing rock
- Porous rock

Open-cast mining

The world's largest copper mine, Bingham Canyon, near Salt Lake City in Utah, USA, is the largest man-made hole in the world. It is 7.2 km² (2¾ sq miles) in area and 800 m (2600 ft) deep. Over a billion tonnes of ore have been extracted – around a third of the total available. Open-cast mines efficiently extract bauxite (aluminium ore), iron ore and other minerals, but have a greater environmental impact than deep-shaft mines.

THE POPULATION EXPLOSION

I n the past 500 years the population of the Earth has risen from around 300 million people to approximately 6 billion, a twentyfold increase. According to UN projections continuing growth, though slower than expected a few years ago, will increase the world's population to 9.4 billion people by 2050. Such an increase is the result of many factors – in particular, improved sanitation and medical treatment, which allow more babies to survive their dangerous first year and go on to live longer lives. Until now, advances in technology have enabled us to produce sufficient food to feed the burgeoning population, but it is uncertain for how long agriculture will be able to meet the demand. One of the consequences of increasing populations in developing countries is a steady drift of people from the country to the city to find work. Such urbanisation results in shanty towns appearing on the outskirts of cities, without proper services and amenities, thus posing grave risks to health.

City of contrasts
Rio de Janeiro has a population of more than 10 million, swollen by migrants from the countryside. Lack of both money and space forces people to live in favelas, shanty towns that cling to the hills surrounding the city.

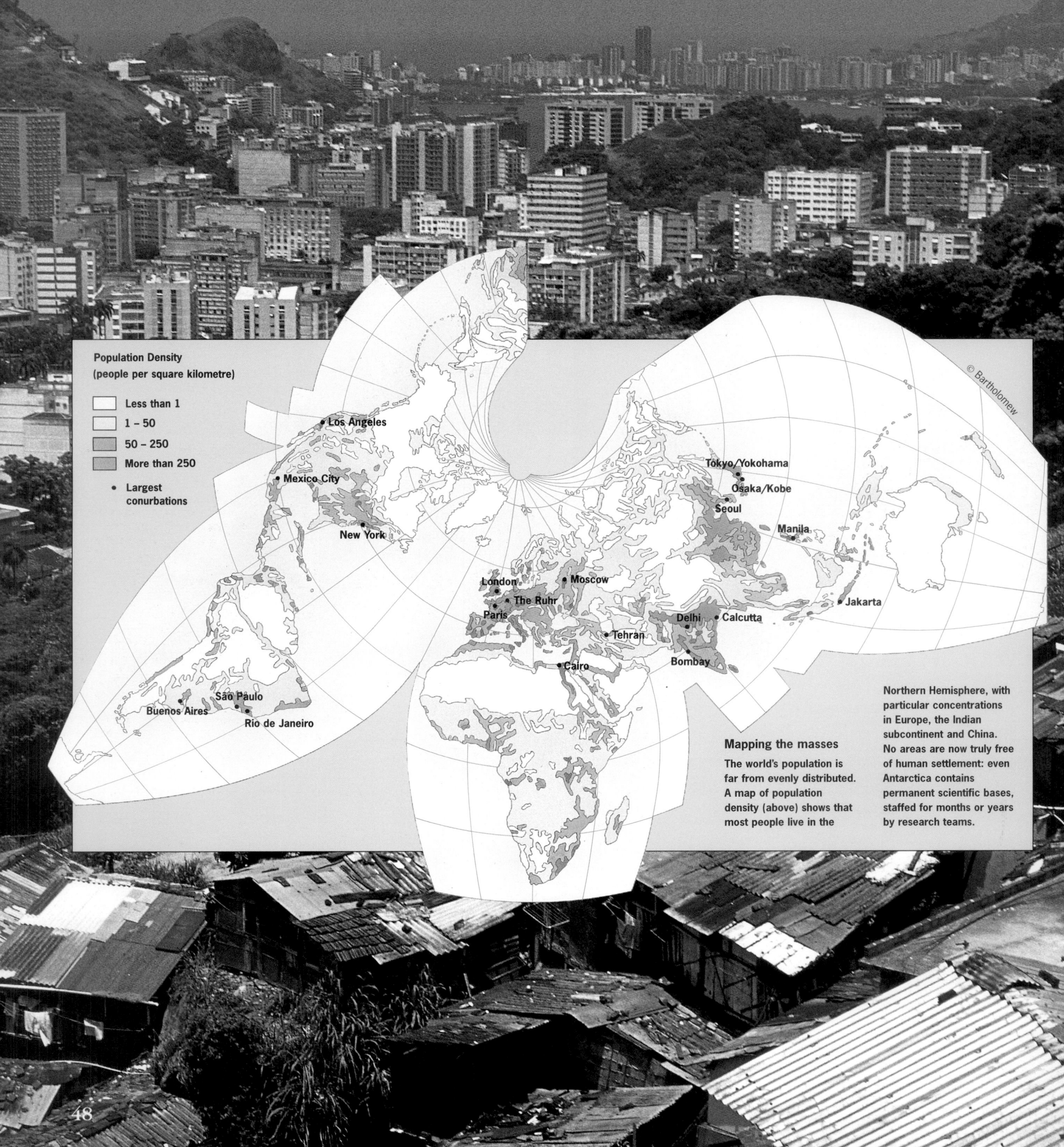

© Bartholomew

Population Density
(people per square kilometre)

- Less than 1
- 1 – 50
- 50 – 250
- More than 250

• Largest conurbations

Los Angeles
Mexico City
New York
Tokyo/Yokohama
Osaka/Kobe
Seoul
Manila
London
Moscow
The Ruhr
Paris
Jakarta
Delhi • Calcutta
Tehran
Cairo
Bombay
São Paulo
Buenos Aires
Rio de Janeiro

Mapping the masses

The world's population is far from evenly distributed. A map of population density (above) shows that most people live in the Northern Hemisphere, with particular concentrations in Europe, the Indian subcontinent and China. No areas are now truly free of human settlement: even Antarctica contains permanent scientific bases, staffed for months or years by research teams.

Predicting the peak

The term 'population explosion' describes the huge increase in the number of people on Earth over the past 200 years. The explosion occurred at different times in different parts of the world; it is now most marked in developing countries. In West and Central Africa, for example, population is growing by more than 3 per cent a year. By contrast, Europe's population, which increased most rapidly in the late 19th century, is now rising at only 0.4 per cent, and may soon decline.

Many governments encourage birth control. The growth rate of China's population has been checked by restricting state benefits to a family's first child.

Too many people?

The chart (left) shows the historic pattern of world population increase. Fastest growth now occurs in the developing regions of Africa and Asia. The global population has increased by more than ten times since 1750, and may double again before a stable level is reached.

- Asia
- Americas
- Russia
- Africa
- Oceania
- Europe

Global population (billions)

3
2
1

1950
1900
1850
1800
1750

2000
1950
1900
1850
1800
1750

Feeding the world

The most feared consequence of a rising global population is worldwide famine. Such a catastrophe was originally forecast by the English economist Thomas Malthus in 1798, when the population of the planet was around 600 million. Now it is 6 billion, yet the predicted shortages have not arisen. Localised famines do occur, but are almost always the consequence of human conflict. In recent times world food production, aided by new strains of rice and wheat, has increased at a greater rate than the population. Between 1980 and 1992 food production rose by 28 per cent while the increase in population was only 24 per cent.

Rice produced (thousands of tonnes)

190 180 170 160 150 140 130 120 110 100 90 80 70 60 50 40 30 20 10

China
India
Indonesia

Rice consumed (thousands of tonnes)

10 20 30 40 50 60 70 80 90 100 110 120 130 140 150

Bangladesh
Vietnam
Thailand
Myanmar (Burma)
Brazil
Philippines
Japan

Rice production

The staple food of eastern Asia is rice, one of the most productive of crops, though highly labour-intensive. Several of the world's most populous nations are in Asia, yet as a chart of rice production and consumption (above) shows, all but one of these countries produce more rice than they consume annually. The exception is Japan, which being the richest nation in the region can afford to import rice.

A picture of population

The scientific study of population is called demography. One of its most commonly used tools is a 'population pyramid', a graph that shows the numbers of men and women in each age group, the youngest at the bottom.

A great deal can be learned from a country's population pyramid. A truly pyramidal shape, with a wide base tapering towards the top, indicates a high birthrate and low life expectancy – characteristics of many countries in the developing world. Countries with a lower rate of population growth and longer life expectancies have a differently shaped pyramid, with a narrower base and much less tapering towards the top. In many developed countries, a wide waist to the pyramid reflects the large numbers born during the 'baby-boom' years after the Second World War. For every country, the lopsided shape of the pyramid reflects the fact that women, on average, live longer than men.

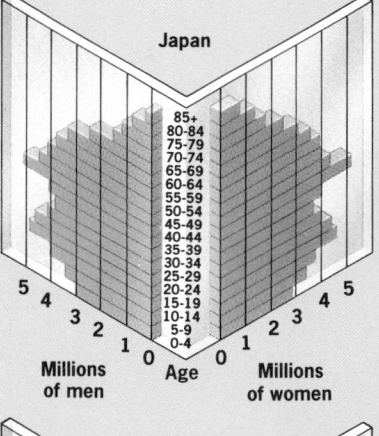

Japan

85+
80-84
75-79
70-74
65-69
60-64
55-59
50-54
45-49
40-44
35-39
30-34
25-29
20-24
15-19
10-14
5-9
0-4

5 4 3 2 1 0   0 1 2 3 4 5

Millions of men   Age   Millions of women

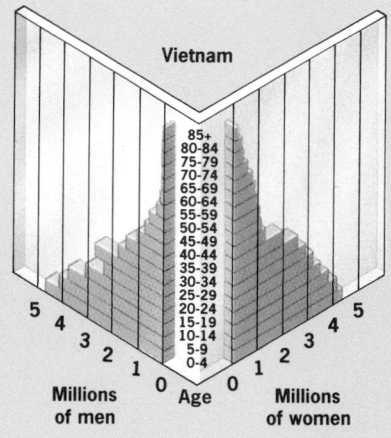

Vietnam

85+
80-84
75-79
70-74
65-69
60-64
55-59
50-54
45-49
40-44
35-39
30-34
25-29
20-24
15-19
10-14
5-9
0-4

5 4 3 2 1 0   0 1 2 3 4 5

Millions of men   Age   Millions of women

Pyramids of people

The population pyramids (right) of two countries in the Far East correspond closely to their different economic and social circumstances. Vietnam is experiencing rapid growth after the strife-torn middle years of the 20th century. This growth is reflected in the wide base of its population pyramid. The diagram dwindles to a narrow peak, reflecting both the casualties of war and the low life expectancy in a country that has seen its health care facilities ravaged by conflict. Japan, by contrast, shows a population pyramid typical of a mature, industrialised economy. Many more people survive into old age, and a low birthrate is reflected in the relatively small number of children.

THE ENERGY AUDIT

Much of the world's population aspires to an energy-hungry, affluent 'Western' lifestyle – owning a car, living and working in heated or air-conditioned premises, and using labour-saving devices that depend on electricity. Countries of the developed world consume vastly more energy – mostly derived from irreplaceable fossil fuels – than countries of the developing world. Even the intensive agriculture of the developed world uses far more energy to produce each kilogram of food than the subsistence farming of developing lands. The use of fossil fuels pumps pollutants into the air and boosts the proportion of carbon dioxide in the atmosphere, so trapping long-wave radiation and overheats the Earth's surface. As concern about this 'greenhouse effect' mounts, and as oil, coal and other non-renewable resources become scarcer and more expensive, the search for alternative sources of energy that harness sunlight, wind and water has become more urgent.

Farming the wind

This forest of metal pylons topped by whirring blades (main image) is one of the USA's many wind farms, turning the wind's energy into electricity. Hundreds of wind turbines are needed to replace a small power station.

Alternative sources

People in the developed world consume fossil fuels at an alarming rate. In 1995 the average North American used the equivalent of 6 tonnes of oil – more than six times the world average for the same year. Even without increasing consumption, the known oil reserves of the world would run out in 2039, and natural gas would last only until 2061.

Alternative sources of energy bring their own disadvantages: reservoirs and tidal barrages created to harness hydroelectric power can engulf sensitive habitats; start-up costs for extracting worthwhile amounts of solar power are high; and wind farms are noisy and dominate the landscape. Controlled nuclear fusion – which holds out the promise of releasing unlimited energy from sea water, leaving no harmful waste – is still in the experimental stage.

Energy-hungry Earth

Throughout the world, most of the energy used derives from the three principal fossil fuels: oil, coal and gas. A graph of consumption in the main land areas (left) shows that in most places oil or gas is the predominant fuel. The graph also reveals the huge difference between developed and developing worlds in the total amount of energy consumed. However, the gap is decreasing, and in most parts of the world consumption is rising. An exception is the group of countries that used to form the Soviet Union, where the political upheavals of the early 1990s resulted in reduced consumption.

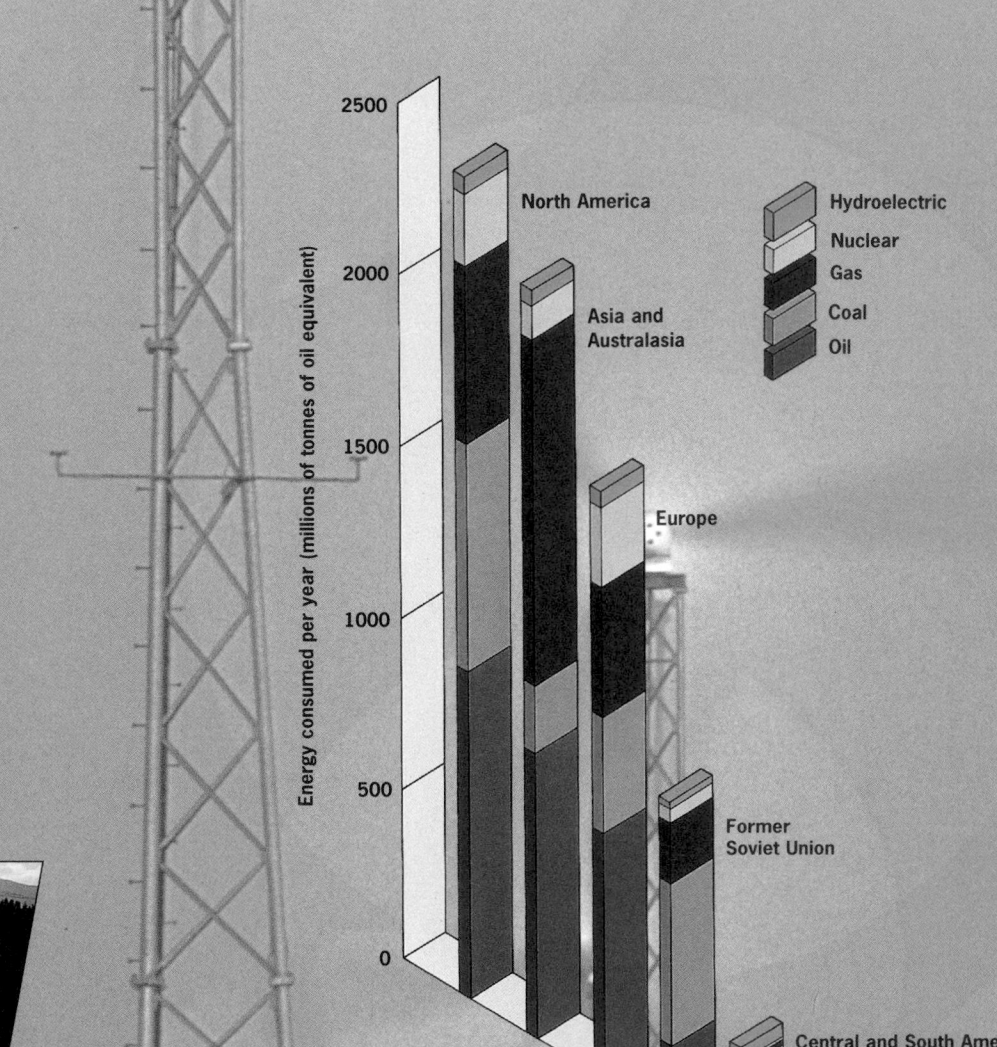

Energy consumed per year (millions of tonnes of oil equivalent)

- 2500
- 2000
- 1500
- 1000
- 500
- 0

North America

Asia and Australasia

Europe

Former Soviet Union

Central and South America

Middle East

Africa

Hydroelectric
Nuclear
Gas
Coal
Oil

Water power

The dam at Loch Laggan in the Scottish Highlands (above) creates enough water pressure to drive a set of powerful turbines and generators. Hydroelectricity is the most widely used form of renewable energy.

Sun power

Solar cells (above) are made from layers of silicon which convert sunlight directly into electricity. Commonly used to power pocket calculators, they are too expensive for large-scale power generation.

Steam power

More than half the homes in Iceland use water heated by hot volcanic rocks to keep warm. Natural steam from deep underground is also piped to the surface to drive power stations (right).

Nuclear power

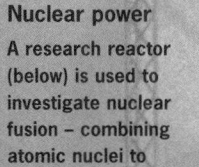

A research reactor (below) is used to investigate nuclear fusion – combining atomic nuclei to release 'clean' energy.

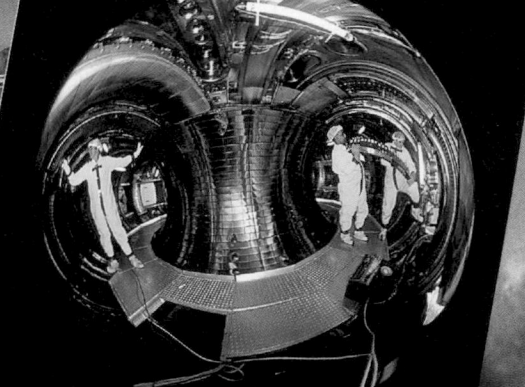

Choking the roads

There are more than 600 million motor vehicles on the world's roads. Vehicle registrations rose by 3.3 per cent between 1982 and 1992 – along with a consequent steady increase in the amount of pollution pumped out by their engines. Some countries have passed legislation to limit exhaust emissions. The US state of California has set manufacturers the task of ensuring that by the year 2003, cars with 'zero emissions' will account for 10 per cent of all sales. This might make electric vehicles more common, but at present they have neither the performance nor the range of their internal combustion engine-powered rivals.

Polluting industry

Beijing (left) has comparatively few motor vehicles and a large number of bicycles. However, the city's air quality is poor, because of uncontrolled industrial pollution.

Smog city

Car-loving Los Angeles (above, left) is hemmed in on three sides by mountains. With onshore breezes, they form a trap for a low-lying layer of hot air that contains pollutants, especially smog (the result of sunlight on exhaust fumes).

Hands on the wheel

An examination of levels of car ownership around the world shows the stark divide between the developed and developing worlds. The USA, for instance, has 147 million cars on the road – statistically one vehicle for less than two people. In contrast, Bangladesh has a population of almost 120 million, but only 43 000 cars.

Number of cars per 1000 people

600
500
400
300
200
100

USA
Germany
Australia
UK
Japan
Ireland
Oman
Brazil
Zimbabwe
Indonesia
India
China
Bangladesh

Power to the people

The energy sources used in developing countries vary enormously, depending on natural resources. Africa has few fossil fuels and limited ability to buy them, so wood and dried manure supply more than 80 per cent of energy needs. Chinese homes and factories alike burn a lot of coal, of which China is the world's second largest producer.

Although they consume less fuel per head than their Western counterparts, developing countries face their own energy problems. The felling of trees for firewood can quickly strip an area of its trees, leading to soil erosion. Gathering and burning cattle dung deprives fields of valuable nutrients.

Alternative sources of energy are available, but are harnessed on a smaller scale than in the developed world. Solar electricity needs expensive equipment – but a simple reflecting dish can focus sunlight on to a pot to boil water. Building dams for hydroelectric power is also costly, and can damage sensitive ecosystems – but a 'micro-hydro' scheme can use rivers to drive a small turbine, providing local electricity with minimal disruption to the environment.

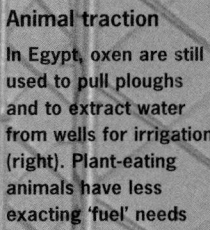

Animal traction

In Egypt, oxen are still used to pull ploughs and to extract water from wells for irrigation (right). Plant-eating animals have less exacting 'fuel' needs than a petrol engine.

Daily harvest

In Vietnam and other developing countries, collecting wood for fuel is one of the day's most important tasks (left). However, the scale of felling is damaging many forests.

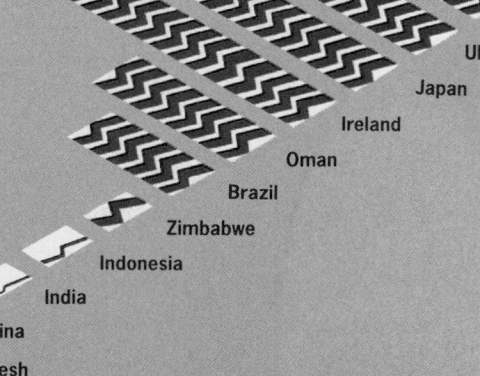

Sun baked

A wide dish made from recycled metal sheets focuses the Sun's rays onto a solar oven (right). In bright sunshine, the energy concentrated on the oven can raise the temperature high enough to bake bread.

Remodelling our Planet

Seen from outer space, the face of the Earth appears to be entirely the work of nature, sculpted by forces such as tectonics and erosion. Closer examination, however, reveals how radically the land has been altered by human activity. Many major rivers have been diverted or dammed to prevent flooding, to irrigate crops, regulate water supply or to generate electricity; vast areas of natural woodland have been cleared for agriculture, and new forests have been planted for timber and papermaking. Features of the landscape, such as ridges and hills, have been modified to create defensive structures, immune from attack. Population pressure and land shortages have motivated the reclamation of marshland by drainage and the use of vertical space through terraces in steep hillsides, or skyscrapers in confined city centres. The skills of the engineer have created canals and tunnels to cut through natural barriers, and bridges to span rivers and harbours.

Ancient barrier
The Great Wall of China (main image) marked the ancient northern border of China. Its principal section, 3460km (2150 miles) long, was completed by 210 BC.

Built for defence
From the days of the first cave dwellers, natural features have been exploited to provide protection against the elements, animals and other humans. A mountain ridge, topped by a wall, becomes an impenetrable barrier; a hill is an easily defended stronghold. The acropolis, at the highest point of ancient Greek cities, was both citadel and sanctuary.

Fortified temple
The Incas flattened a mountain ridge to create the fortress city of Machu Picchu. Its impregnable position is 600m (2000ft) above the Urubamba river in the Andes.

Winning more space
Humans have always shown ingenuity in putting seemingly inhospitable terrain to good use. If level land is at a premium, hillside terraces allow the cultivation of grapes in Europe and rice in Asia. The Aztecs in the 15th century used a system of dykes and ditches to convert the swampy Lake Chalco into productive farmland. Reclamation of land from the sea has increased the area of the Netherlands by almost 3000 km^2 (1160 sq miles) since 1900.

Land from the sea
Polders, or areas of reclaimed land, are seen as a green patchwork in a satellite image of the Netherlands (below).

Reach for the sky
The skyline of the financial district of New York shows how architects have built upwards to provide much-needed office space above the streets of crowded Manhattan Island.

Across the divide

Natural features that once formed barriers between peoples and nations are crossed every day in the course of modern trade and travel. Advances in steel technology since the 1850s have revolutionised the building of bridges, making it possible to span increasingly wide spaces. The bridge across the Akashi Strait in Japan, completed in 1998, has a main span nearly 2 km (1¼ miles) long. Tunnels are now dug by huge machines, which chew their way through rock like giant mechanical earthworms. Such machines excavated the 50 km (31 mile) tunnel under the English Channel, linking England to France in 1990. Major canals provide short cuts for trade around peninsulas, and sometimes whole continents. The Suez Canal, opened in 1869, linked the Mediterranean with the Red Sea, allowing ships from Europe to avoid the trip around the Cape of Good Hope on their way to India and Australia.

Narrow passage

The Corinth Canal (left) cuts through the 6.3 km (4 mile) isthmus that joins the Peloponnese peninsula to mainland Greece, shortening the voyage from Piraeus to the Ionian Sea by over 320 km (200 miles).

Desert track

The city of Perth is separated from the rest of Australia by vast deserts. The Nullarbor Plain is crossed by a railway (below) with the longest straight section in the world, stretching for 478 km (297 miles).

Mountain fields

Man-made terraces, such as these rice paddies in the Philippines, allow steep hillsides to be used for growing food.

Graceful span

The Humber Bridge in England (left) has a central section of 1410 m (4625 ft). When completed in 1981, it included the world's longest single span. It cuts out a lengthy detour inland.

BUILDING IT BIG

Longest multispan bridge	
Lake Pontchartrain Causeway, Louisiana, USA	38.4 km (24 miles)
Longest navigable tunnel	
Seikan rail tunnel, Japan	53.9 km (33½ miles)
Highest structure	
CN Tower, Toronto, Canada	553 m (1814 ft)
Longest canal for ocean-going vessels	
Suez Canal, Egypt	168 km (105 miles)
Highest dam	
Nurek, on the Vakhsh River, Tajikistan	300 m (984 ft)
Largest man-made lake	
Lake Volta, Ghana	8482 km² (3274 sq miles)

CONTENTS

KEY TO MAPS

CITIES AND TOWNS

	MAP SCALES	MAP SCALES
	1:300,000-1:9,000,000	1:12,000,000-1:18,000,000
Major city	**Chicago**	**Chicago**
Large city	**Iquitos**	Iquitos
Towns	Tacna	Tacna
Other settlements	Old Crow	Old Crow
●	Urban areas	

CAPITALS OF POLITICAL UNITS

PARIS ORANJESTAD	Independent country and dependent territory
Winnipeg Pierre	State, province, etc
Waukegan	County, oblast, etc

POLITICAL BOUNDARIES

	International
	International disputed de jure
	International disputed de facto
	Demarcation line
	Indefinite, undefined, over open water
	Main administrative state, province, etc
	Other administrative county, oblast, etc
AUSTRALIA MALAYSIA	Independent country
GREENLAND PUERTO RICO	Dependent territory
PARÁ COOK	Administrative area
NORMANDIE ALENTEJO	Cultural, historic region

TRANSPORTATION

	Motorway, special highway
	Main road
	Other road
	Track
	Main railway
	Other railway
	Tunnel, road
	Tunnel, rail

Bridge, road or rail

Car and rail ferries

International airport

Other airport

TOPOGRAPHIC FEATURES

Matterhorn 4478 m — Elevation above sea level

76 m — Elevation below sea level

Mount Fuji 3776 m — Volcano

Mountain pass

Rock

Lava

Sand desert, dunes

ANDES La Gran Sabana — Mountain range, plateau, plain etc

NEW GUINEA Hispaniola — Island

Cape York Pen. Lizard Point — Peninsula, cape, point, etc

PATAGONIA Barkly Tableland — Physical region, desert, forest, etc

Elevation & depth tints

HEIGHT

3000m (9842ft)

2000m (6562ft)

1000m (3281ft)

500m (1640ft)

200m (656ft)

Sea level

200m (656ft)

2000m (6562ft)

DEPTH

HYDROGRAPHIC FEATURES

River, stream

Intermittent river

Salto Ángel — Falls

764m ▽ — Depth of water

Navigable canal

Irrigation or drainage canal

Los Angeles Aqueduct — Aqueduct

Intracoastal waterway

Reef

Kumdah ○ — Oasis, spring, geyser

Cree Lake — Lake, reservoir

(395m) — Height of lake above sea level

Dam

Intermittent lake, reservoir

Salt lake

Dry lake bed, salt pan

Swamp, marsh

Glacier, ice cap

PACIFIC SEA OF JAPAN — Ocean, sea

Amazon Orinoco — River, canal

CULTURAL FEATURES

YELLOWSTONE — National park, reserve, reservation, historic site

Andrews A.F.B. — Military installations

Ruin

Ancient wall

Windsor Castle — Site of special interest

28 — Page continuation arrow

MAPS HAVE UNDERGONE many changes in recent decades. First there came the major East and West alignments, then the demands of colonies for independence which, once gained, led to further adjustments of boundaries. With the end of the Eastern Bloc there reappeared on maps names unseen since 1914. Nationhood remains a potent force, by no means submerged in initials such as EU, UN, OAS or CIS.

57

ABBREVIATED COUNTRY NAMES USED ON THIS MAP

ALB.	Albania
ARM.	Armenia
AZER.	Azerbaijan
BANGL.	Bangladesh
BEL.	Belgium
BOS. & HERZ.	Bosnia and Herzegovina
CZECH REP.	Czech Republic
LUX.	Luxembourg
MAC.	Macedonia, Former Yugoslav Republic of
NETH.	Netherlands
RUS.	Russia
SLOV.	Slovakia
SLVN.	Slovenia
SWITZ.	Switzerland
U.K.	United Kingdom
U.S.	United States of America
W. & F.	Wallis and Futuna
YUGO.	Yugoslavia (Serbia and Montenegro)

0   500 1000   2000   3000   4000   5000   6000   7000   8000 Kilometres

0   500   1000   2000   3000   4000   5000 Miles

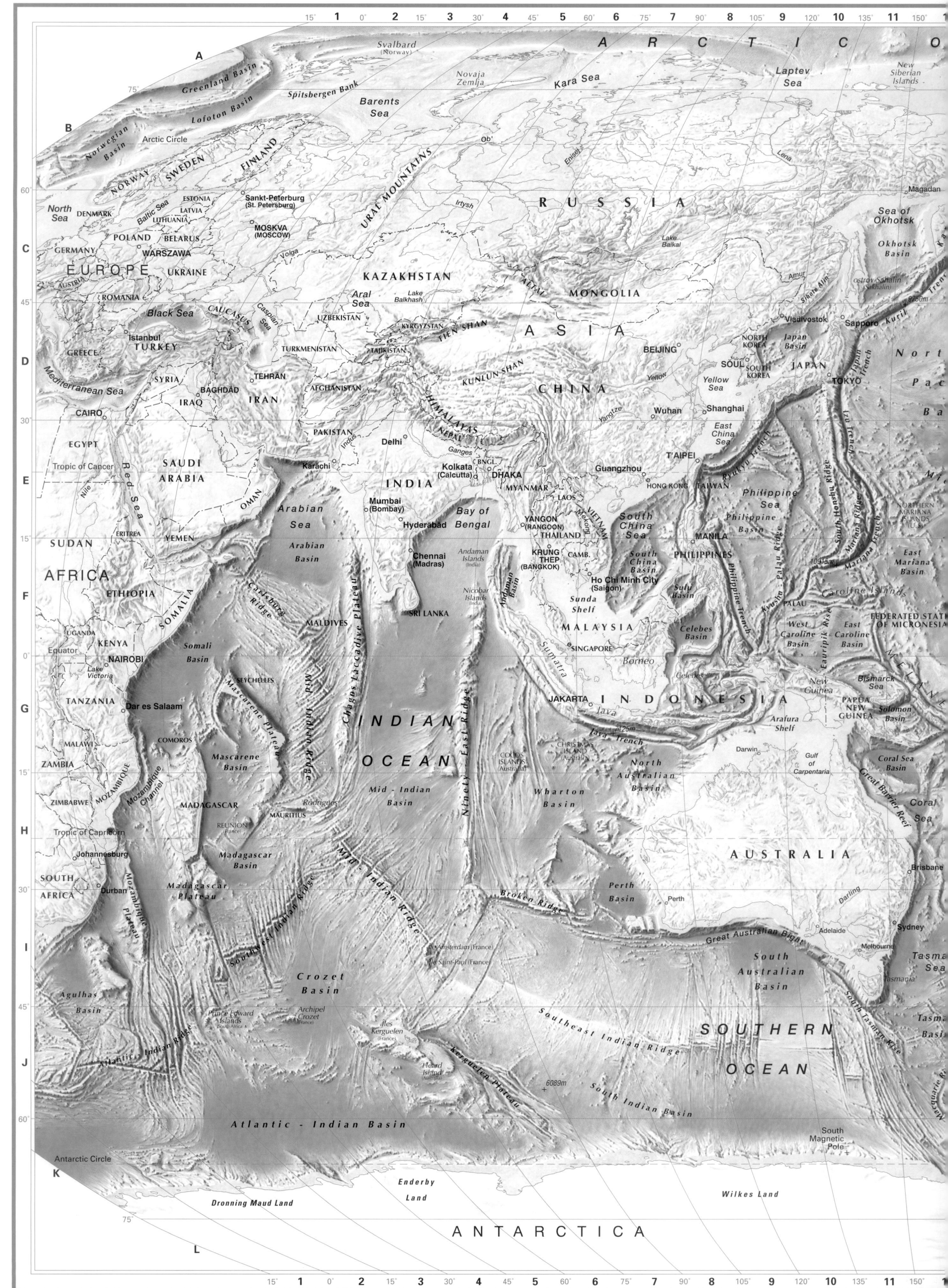

Robinson Projection

Scale 1:60,000,000

One centimetre represents 600 kilometres.

One inch represents approximately 950 miles.

OCEAN OF SUPERLATIVES, the Pacific, with its attendant seas and channels, covers about a third of the Earth's surface. Its floor is a succession of mountain ranges and valleys made by the thrust of the planet's crustal plates. An average depth of 4200 m (13 780 ft) plunges, in the Mariana Trench, into an abyss of 10 915 m (35 810 ft). The Indian Ocean has its greatest depth of 7125 m (23 376 ft) in the Java Trench.

59

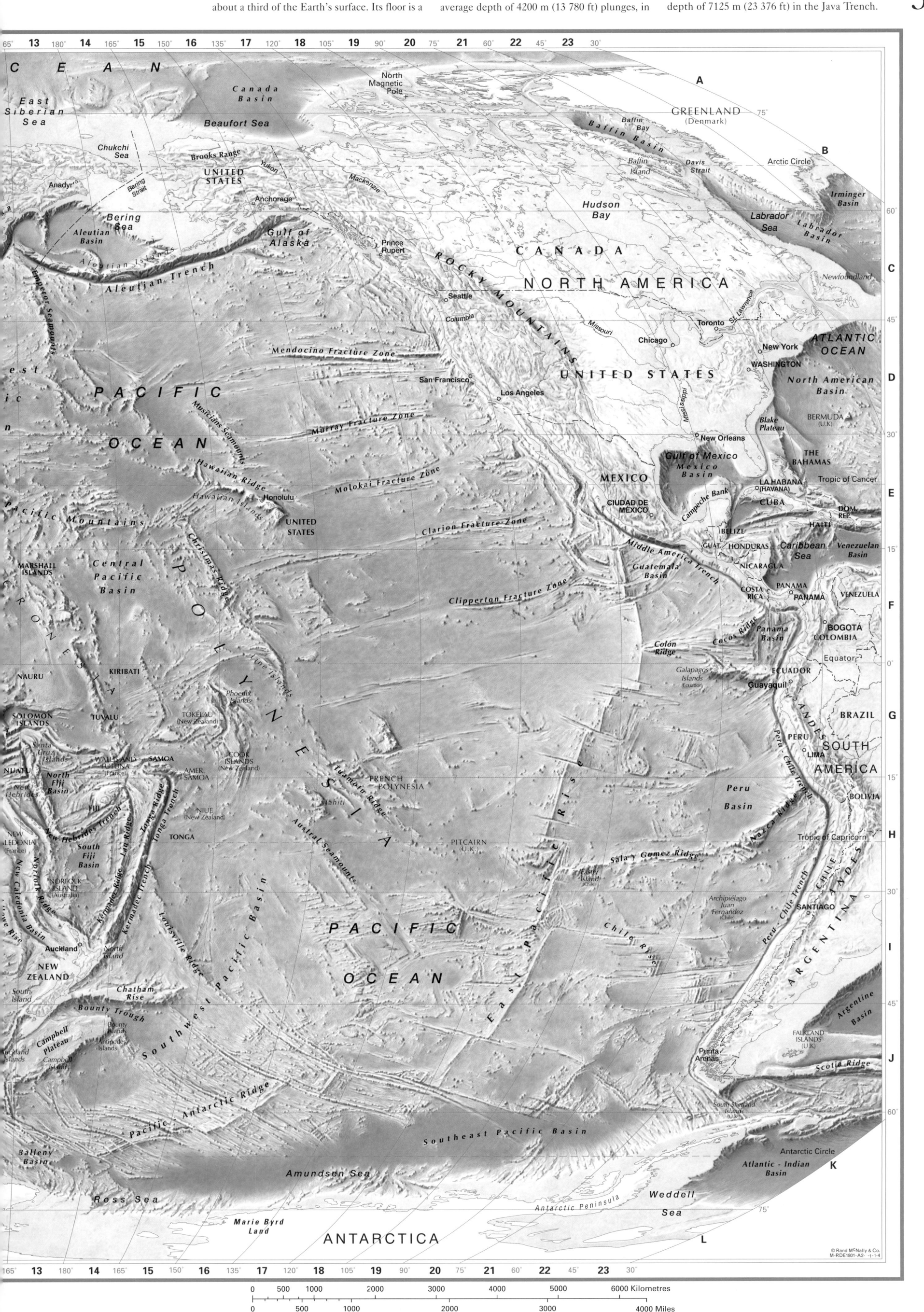

0   500   1000   2000   3000   4000   5000   6000 Kilometres

0   500   1000   2000   3000   4000 Miles

THE MID-ATLANTIC Ridge rises from the ocean floor, and molten rock continually seeps from it, pushing the ocean's edges wider apart.

The ridge is flanked by vast abyssal plains, buried hundreds of metres deep in sediments laid down by rivers like the Amazon and Congo.

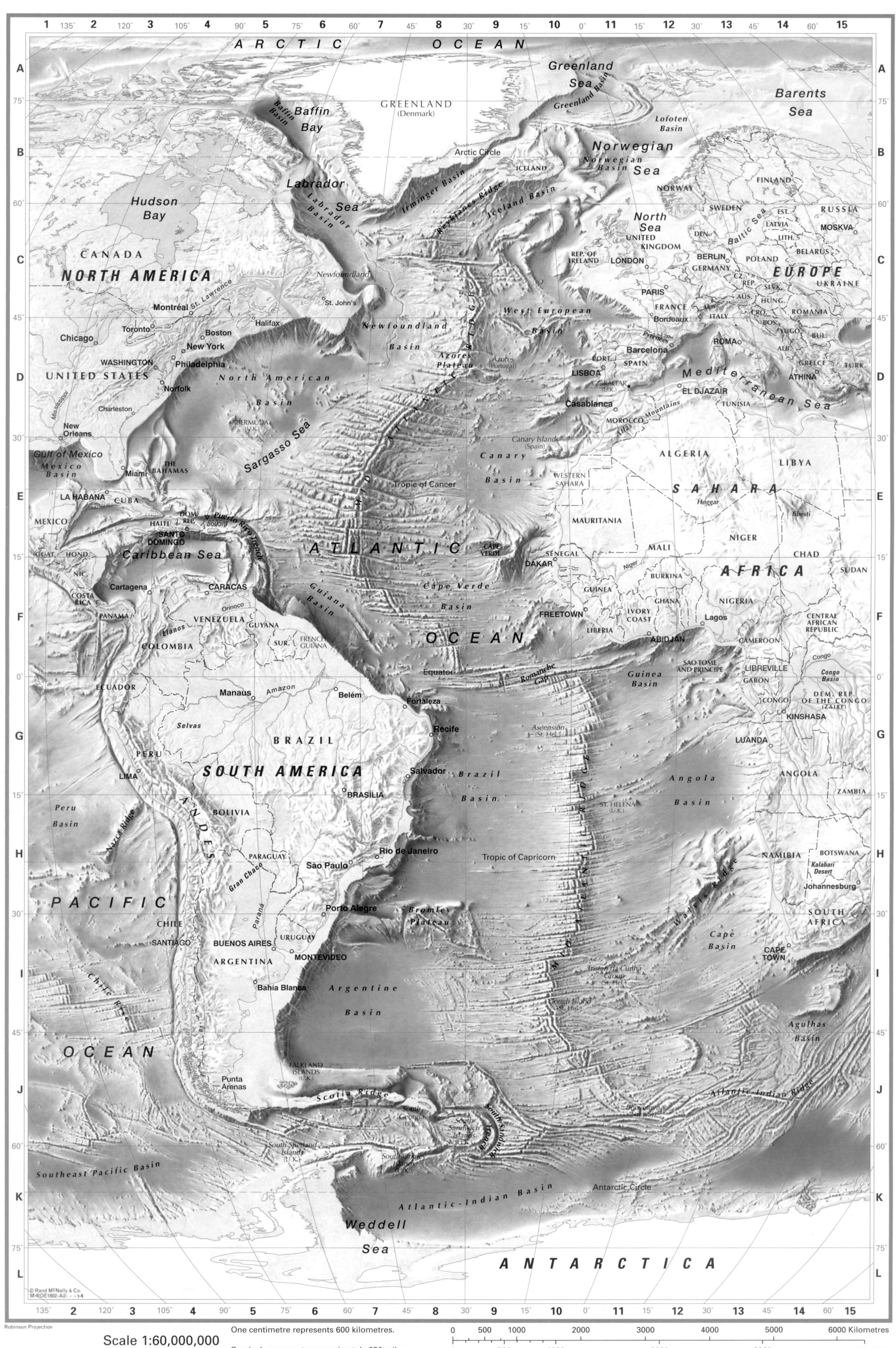

Robinson Projection

Scale 1:60,000,000

One centimetre represents 600 kilometres.

One inch represents approximately 950 miles.

| 0 | 500 | 1000 | 2000 | 3000 | 4000 | 5000 | 6000 Kilometres |

| 0 | 500 | 1000 | 2000 | 3000 | 4000 Miles |

© Rand McNally & Co.
M-RDE1802-A2- - -14

THREE CONTINENTS RING the smallest of the world's oceans, near whose frozen centre is the North Pole. Pack ice up to 3m (10ft) thick covers much of the ocean throughout the year, and the East Greenland and Labrador currents carry icebergs far into the Atlantic.

PACIFIC OCEAN

Aleutian Trench

Gulf of Alaska Seamount Province

Gulf of Alaska

Aleutian Basin

Bering Sea

Okhotsk Basin

ostrov Sahalin (Sakhalin)

Sea of Okhotsk

Kuril Trench

Petropavlovsk-Kamcatskij

St. Lawrence Island

Anadyr

Magadan

Arctic Circle

Nome

Anchorage

Juneau

UNITED STATES

Yukon

Bering Strait

Chukchi Sea

ostrov Vrangelja (Wrangel I.)

East Siberian Sea

Ambarcik

Kolyma

Cerskij hrebet

Jakutsk

Mackenzie Mountains

Brooks Range

Barrow

NEW SIBERIAN ISLANDS

NORTH AMERICA

Mackenzie

Inuvik

Beaufort Sea

Canada Basin

ARCTIC OCEAN

Mendeleyev Ridge

Makarov Basin

Laptev Sea

ASIA

Sachs Harbour

Banks Island

Alpha Cordillera

Lomonosov Ridge

Fram Basin

Nansen Cordillera

Nansen Basin

NORTH LAND

RUSSIA

Nordvik

Victoria Island

Ikaluktutiak

QUEEN ELIZABETH ISLANDS

North Magnetic Pole

North Pole

Noril'sk

Enisej

CANADA

Parry Channel

Dikson

Ellesmere Island

Etah

Alert

Lincoln Sea

FRANZ JOSEF LAND

Thule

Baffin Island

Baffin Basin

Baffin Bay

NOVAJA ZEMLJA

Kara Sea

Salehard

Ob'

URAL MOUNTAINS

Iqaluit

Godhavn

Davis Strait

Baffin Strait

SVALBARD (Norway)

Spitsbergen Bank

Barents Sea

Labrador Sea

Greenland Sea

Greenland Basin

Murmansk

Arhangel'sk (Archangel)

GREENLAND (Denmark)

GODTHÅB

Arctic Circle

Mohns Ridge

Hammerfest

Tromso

Kandalaksa

White Sea

Labrador Basin

Jan Mayen Ridge

Jan Mayen (Norway)

Lofoten Basin

EUROPE

Angmagssalik

Julianehåb

Denmark Strait

Norwegian Sea

Trondheim

FINLAND

Sankt-Peterburg (St. Petersburg)

Irminger Basin

Norwegian Basin

SWEDEN

HELSINKI

MOSKVA (MOSCOW)

Reykjanes Ridge

REYKJAVIK

ICELAND

FAROE ISLANDS (Denmark)

NORWAY

OSLO

STOCKHOLM

ESTONIA

LATVIA

Iceland Basin

Rockall Rise

North Sea

DENMARK

KØBENHAVN (COPENHAGEN)

Baltic Sea

LITHUANIA

BELARUS

ATLANTIC OCEAN

UNITED KINGDOM

GERMANY

POLAND

UKRAINE

© Rand McNally & Co.
M-RDE2000-A2

Lambert Azimuthal Equal Area Projection

Scale 1:25,000,000

One centimetre represents 250 kilometres.

One inch represents approximately 390 miles.

0 250 500 1000 1500 2000 2500 Kilometres

0 250 500 1000 1500 Miles

EUROPE

Scale 1:12,000,000

One centimetre represents 120 kilometres.

One inch represents approximately 190 miles.

Conic Equidistant Projection

WITH ITS SEPARATION from Asia defined by an arbitrary line along the crests of the Ural and Caucasus Mountains to the Black Sea and the Bosporus, Europe's inner frontiers form a kaleidoscopic pattern that has been constantly stirred and resettled down the centuries. Yet this small and stormy continent, with its diversity of language and culture, has provided some of the greatest inspirations in human history.

63

RUSSIA

FINLAND

APPLAND

KARELIJA

ESTONIA

LATVIA

LITHUANIA

BELARUS

UKRAINE

MOLDOVA

ROMANIA

BULGARIA

TURKEY

ASIA MINOR

SYRIA

CYPRUS

LEBANON

IRAQ

MESOPOTAMIA

IRAN

GEORGIA

ARMENIA

AZERBAIJAN

TURKMENISTAN

UZBEKISTAN

KAZAKHSTAN

KOMI

UDMURTIJA

TATARIJA

MARIJ EL

CUVASIJA

MORDOVIJA

BAŠKIRIJA

KALMYKIJA

DAGESTAN

ADYGEJA

Barents Sea

White Sea

Black Sea

Caspian Sea (-28m)

Aral Sea (41m)

Sea of Azov

Aegean Sea

Sea of Crete

Sea of Marmara

West Siberian Plain

URAL MOUNTAINS

CAUCASUS

CASPIAN DEPRESSION

USTIURT PLATEAU

Kara Kum (Garagum)

Arctic Circle

MOSKVA (MOSCOW)

Sankt-Peterburg (St. Petersburg) (Leningrad)

HELSINKI

TALLINN

RIGA

MINSK

KYYIV (KIEV)

CHIŞINĂU

BUCUREŞTI (BUCHAREST)

ISTANBUL

ANKARA

TBILISI

YEREVAN

BAKI (BAKU)

BAGHDAD

TEHRĀN

NICOSIA

Murmansk

Arhangel'sk (Arhangel)

Severodvinsk

Vorkuta

Nižnij Novgorod (Gorky)

Kazan'

Perm'

Ekaterinburg

Celjabinsk

Ufa

Samara

Orenburg

Volgograd (Stalingrad)

Rostov-na-Donu

Krasnodar

Omsk

Magnitogorsk

Astrahan (Astrakhan)

ISTANBUL

1200 Kilometres

800 Miles

Scandinavia

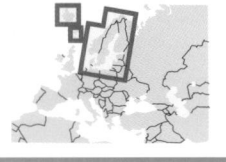

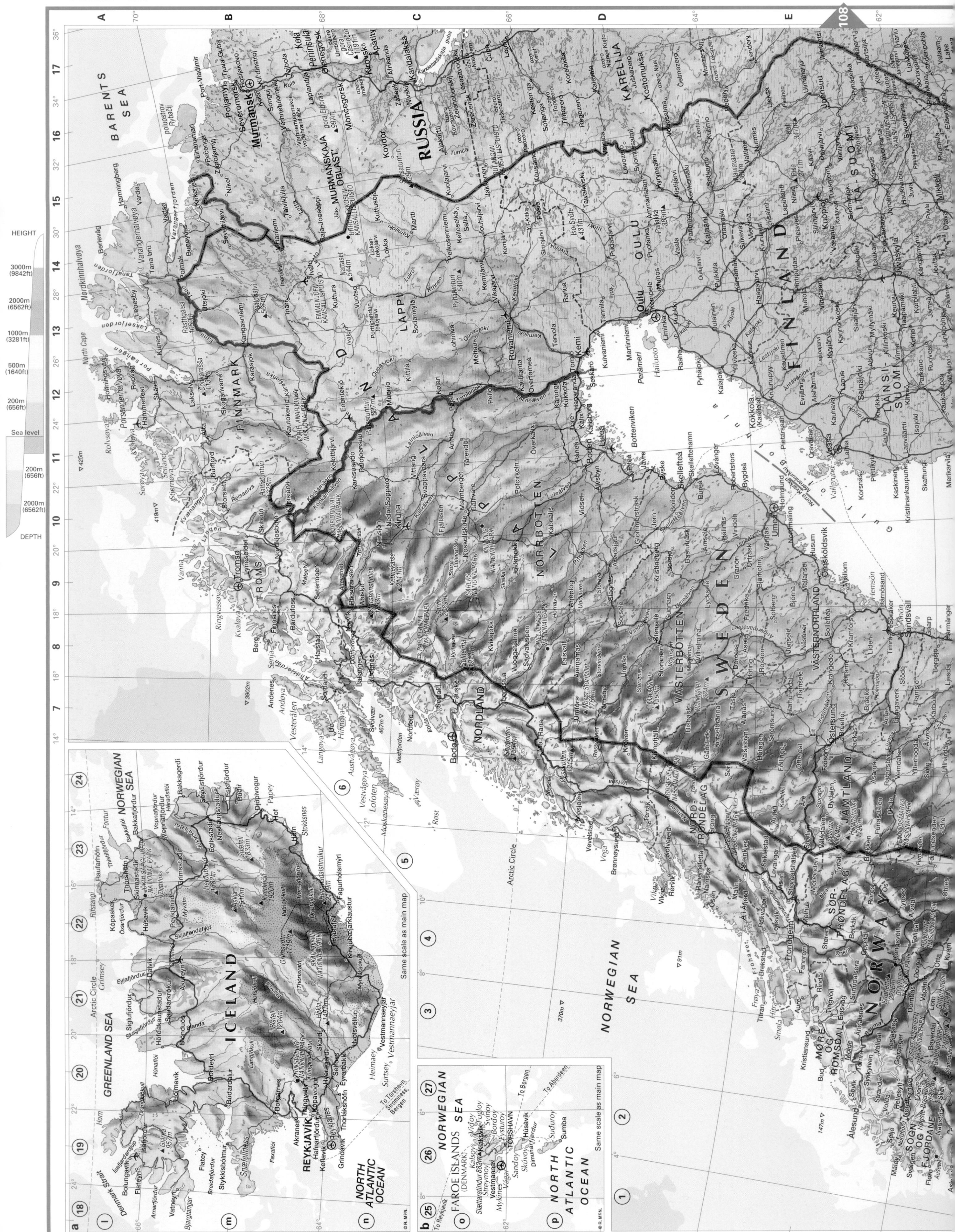

Conic Equidistant Projection

Scale 1:4,500,000

One centimetre represents 45 kilometres.

One inch represents approximately 71 miles.

THE SEA HAS been the sustaining factor in these northern lands. It impelled the outward thrust of the Vikings, it provides the livelihoods of Iceland and the Faroes, and makes every Scandinavian capital a seaport. Iceland was once a Norwegian colony. In the 16th century, Denmark and Sweden divided Scandinavia between them and fought a 134 year war, and for a century Finland was a Russian province.

65

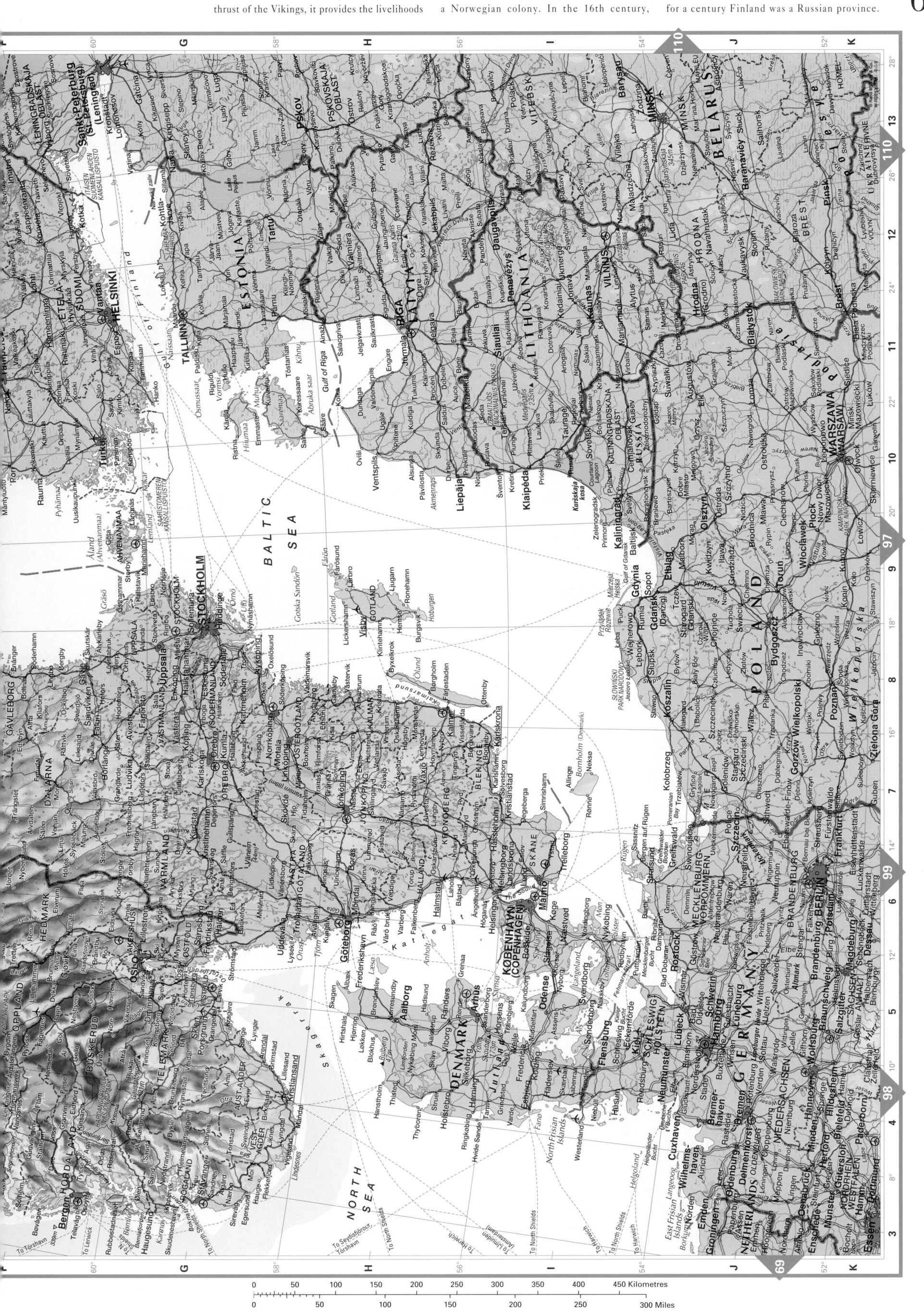

0   50   100   150   200   250   300   350   400   450 Kilometres

0   50   100   150   200   250   300 Miles

HEIGHT

3000m
(9842ft)

2000m
(6562ft)

1000m
(3281ft)

500m
(1640ft)

200m
(656ft)

Sea level

200m
(656ft)

2000m
(6562ft)

DEPTH

Conic Equidistant Projection

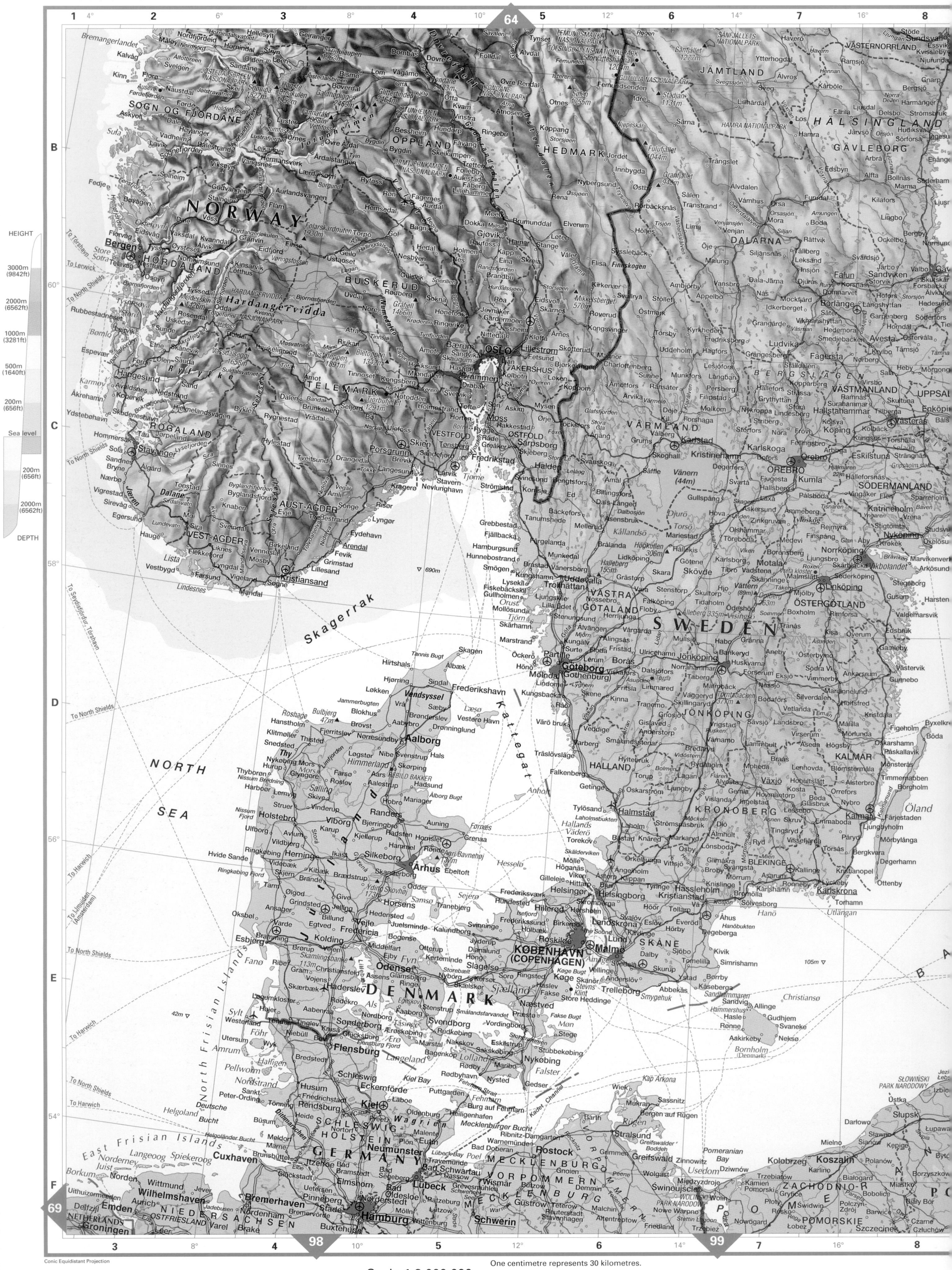

Scale 1:3,000,000

One centimetre represents 30 kilometres.

One inch represents approximately 47 miles.

TO THE TRADITIONAL harvests of forest and sea, modern, oil-rich Norway has added petroleum products and high-tech industry, while Sweden has turned to cars, aircraft and fine craftsmanship. Finland offers shipbuilding, engineering and superb modern architecture. The neighbouring Baltic states of Lithuania, Latvia and Estonia are struggling to re-create themselves after centuries of foreign control.

67

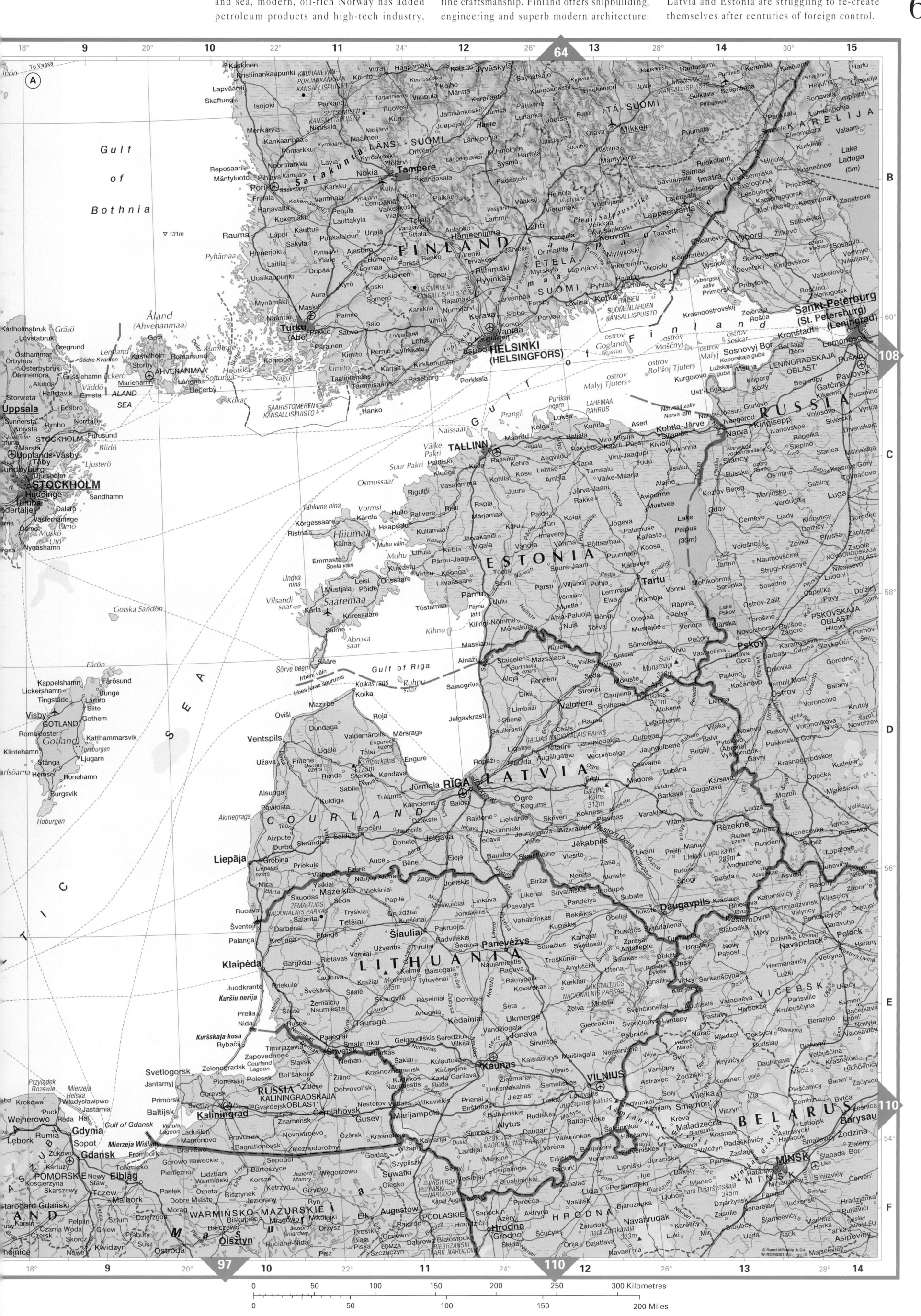

A PENINSULA AND 400 islands make up Denmark, which stands nowhere higher than 173m (568ft). The densely populated Belgium and the Netherlands share a low coastal plain, while the forested Ardennes plateau extends from eastern Belgium into tiny Luxembourg.

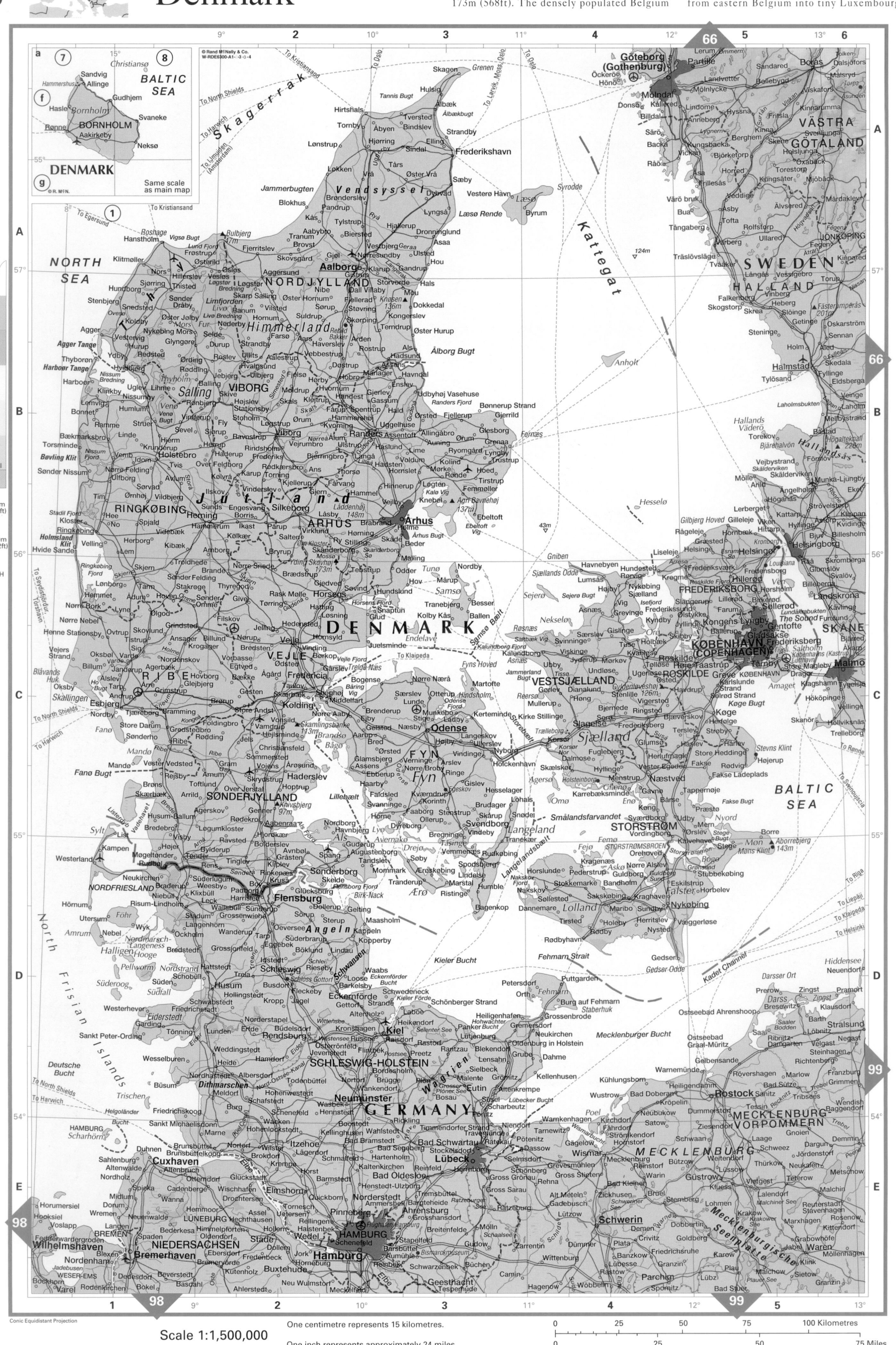

© Rand McNally & Co.
W-RDE6300-A1--3-3-4

Conic Equidistant Projection

Scale 1:1,500,000

One centimetre represents 15 kilometres.

One inch represents approximately 24 miles.

0	25	50	75	100 Kilometres

0	25	50	75 Miles

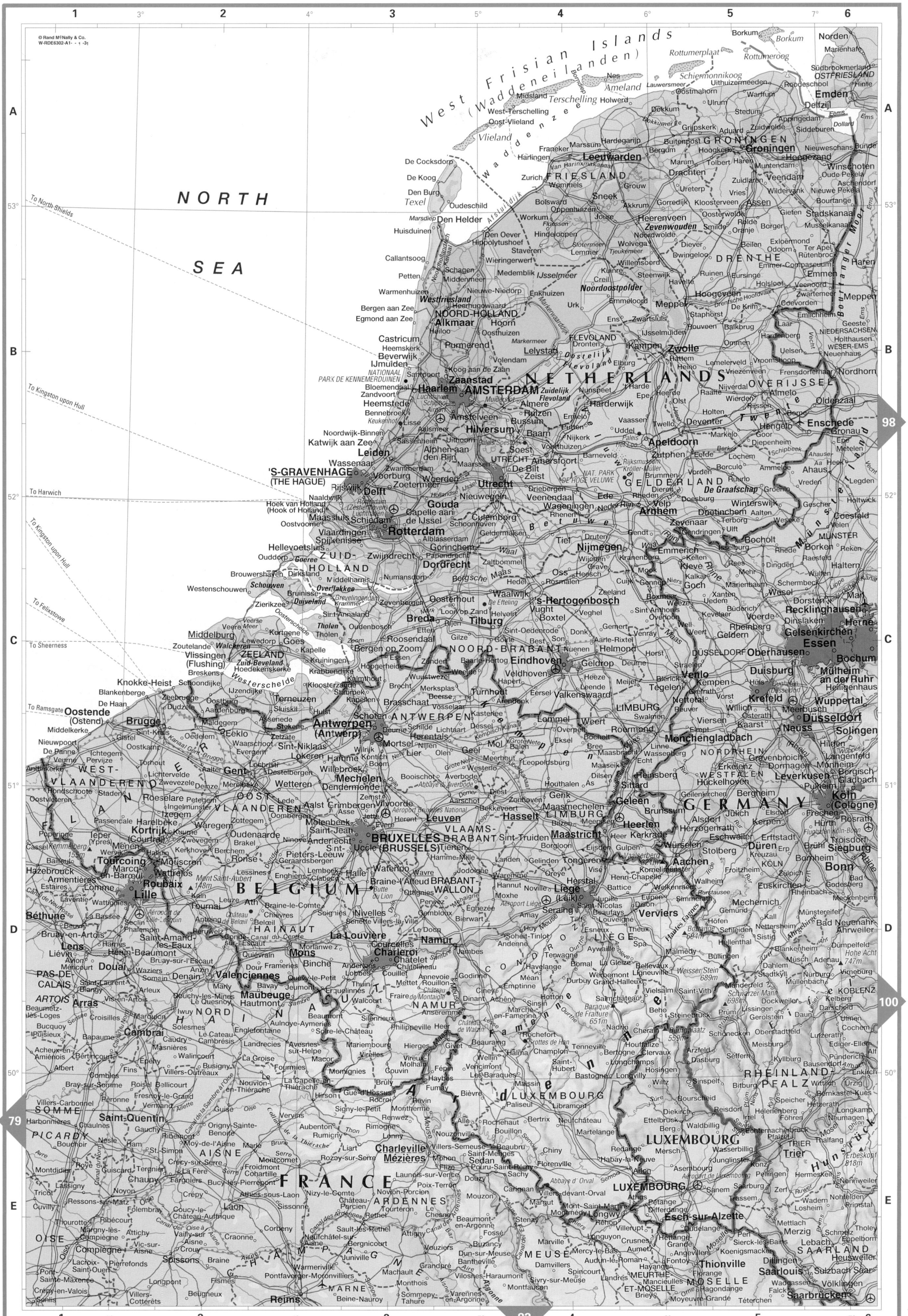

Scale 1:1,500,000

Conic Equidistant Projection

One centimetre represents 15 kilometres.

One inch represents approximately 24 miles.

| 0 | 25 | 50 | 75 | 100 Kilometres |

| 0 | 25 | 50 | 75 Miles |

HEIGHT

3000m
(9842ft)

2000m
(6562ft)

1000m
(3281ft)

500m
(1640ft)

200m
(656ft)

Sea level

200m
(656ft)

2000m
(6562ft)

DEPTH

NORWAY

To Bergen

NORTH SEA

NORTH ATLANTIC OCEAN

Shetland Islands

Orkney Islands

SCOTLAND

Aberdeen

Glasgow

Edinburgh

Newcastle upon Tyne

Sunderland

Middlesbrough

Outer Hebrides

Isle of Lewis

Island of Skye

Sea of the Hebrides

NORTHERN

Belfast

Londonderry

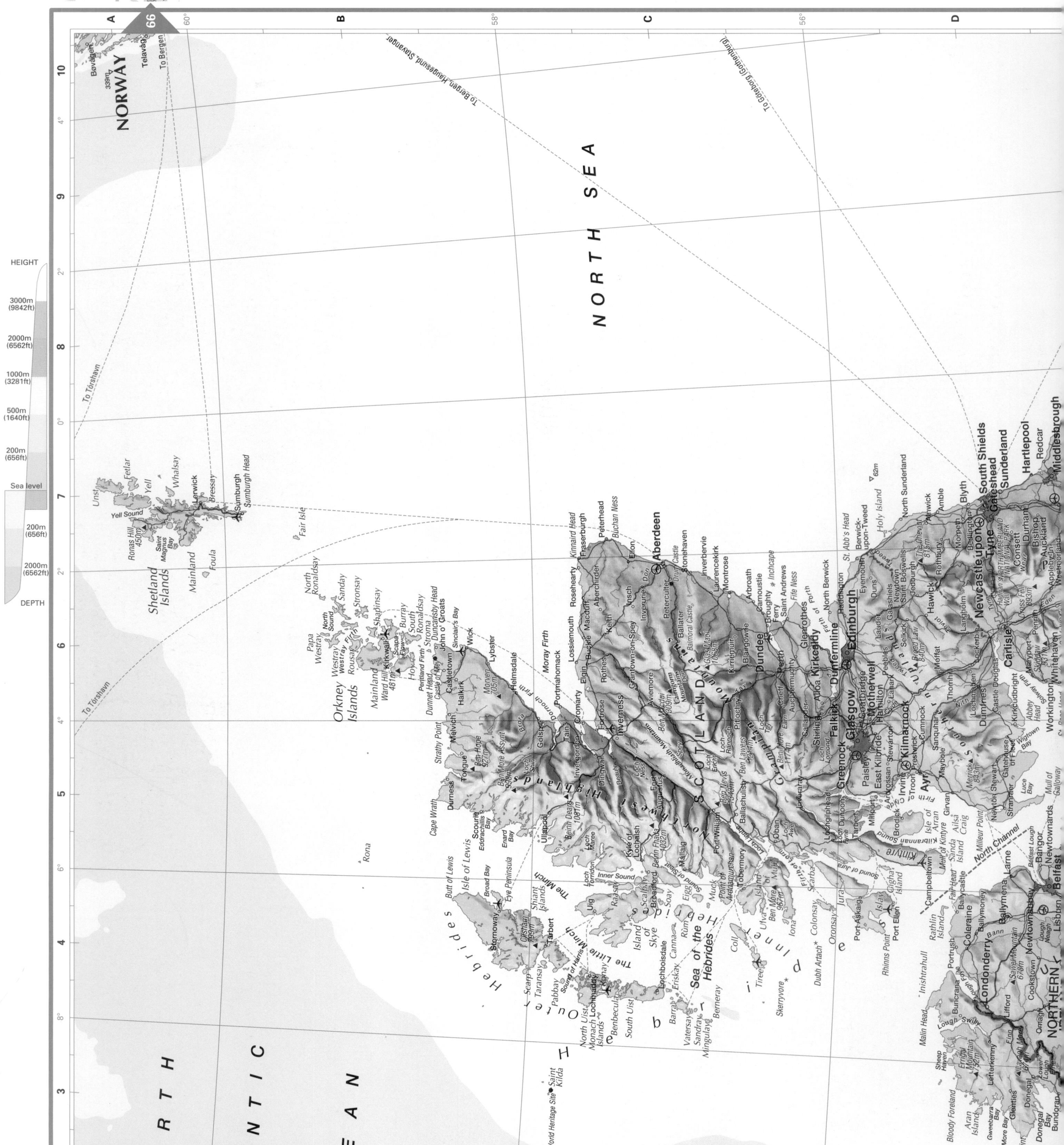

Conic Equidistant Projection

Scale 1:3,000,000

One centimetre represents 30 kilometres.

One inch represents approximately 47 miles.

FROM THE SANDY heaths of Norfolk to the
750 m (2462 ft) cliffs of the Dingle Peninsula in
Ireland, and from the deep red loams of Devon
to the world's oldest known rocks about Loch
Torridon, this small group of western European
islands offers, within a few hours travelling, an
immense variety of landscape. The surrounding
waters have not deterred waves of immigrants,
and a tunnel now links Britain to the Continent.

71

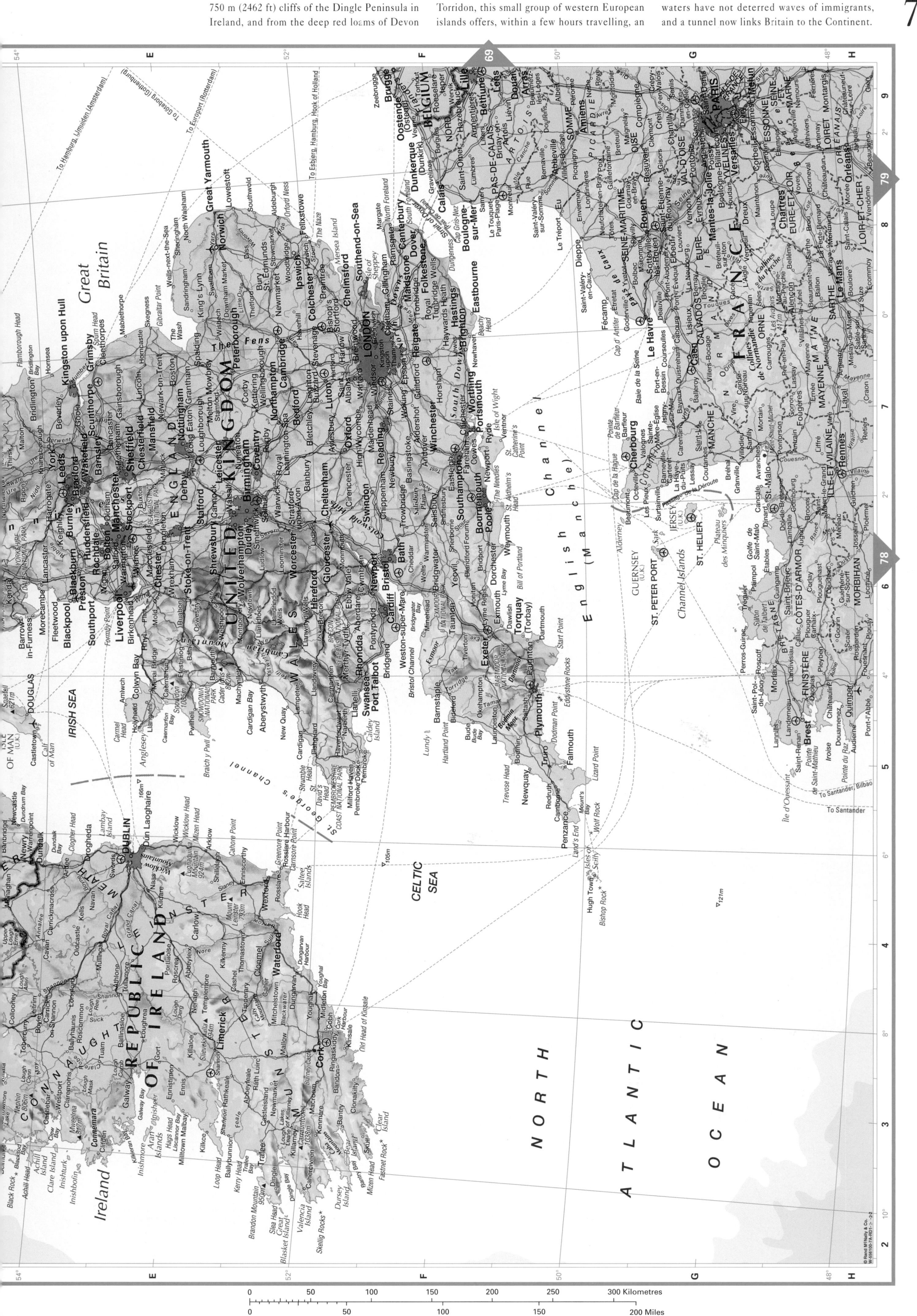

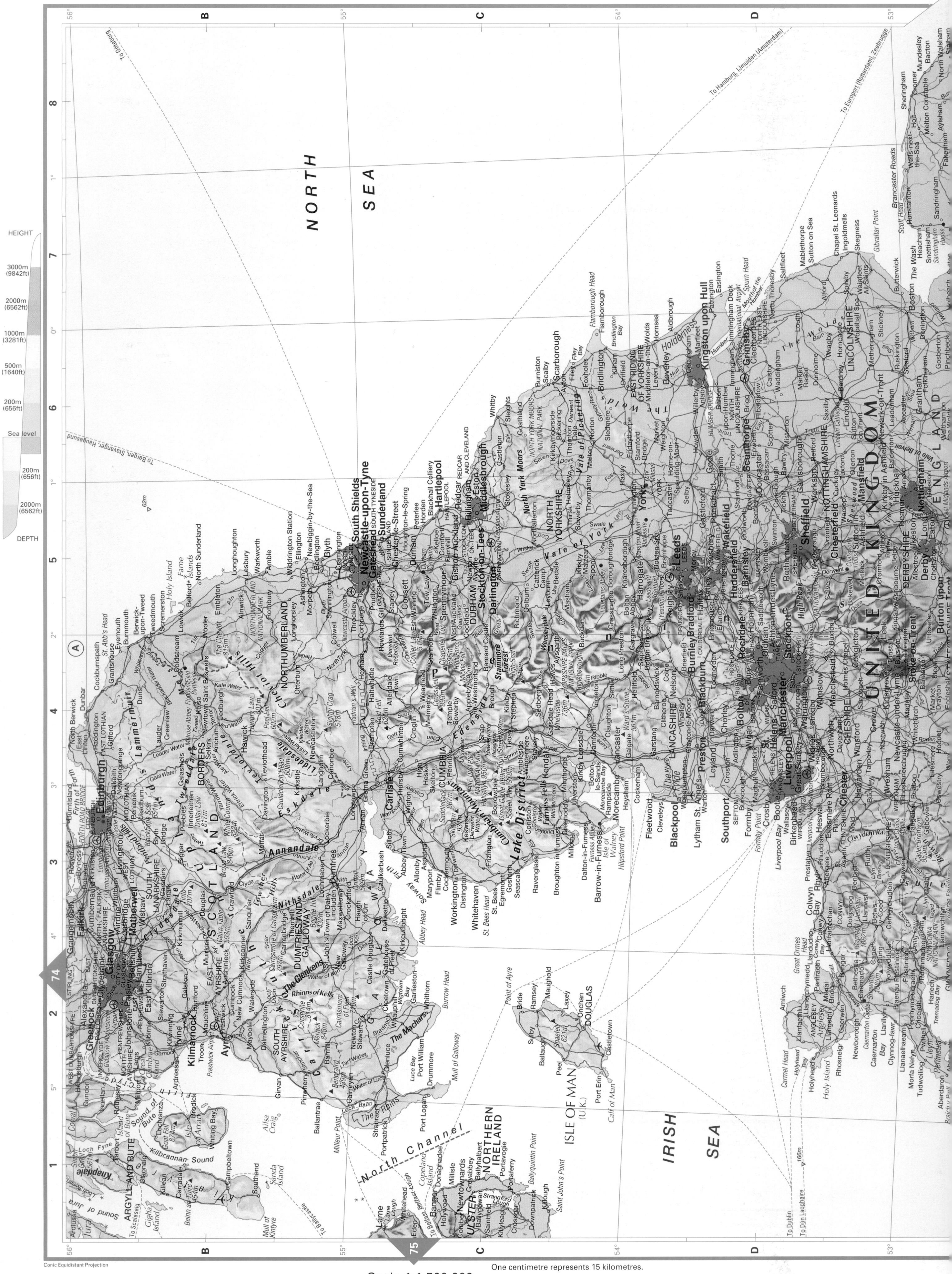

Conic Equidistant Projection

Scale 1:1,500,000

One centimetre represents 15 kilometres.

One inch represents approximately 24 miles.

MUCH OF ENGLAND and Wales – including downs, fens and Norfolk Broads, hedged fields and cathedral cities – has been shaped by human toil. But here and there the older bones of the land show through, as in the granite cap of Dartmoor and the splendours of Snowdonia. The west has the highest points in the two countries, Snowdon itself and Scafell Pike. Parts of East Anglia are actually lower than sea level.

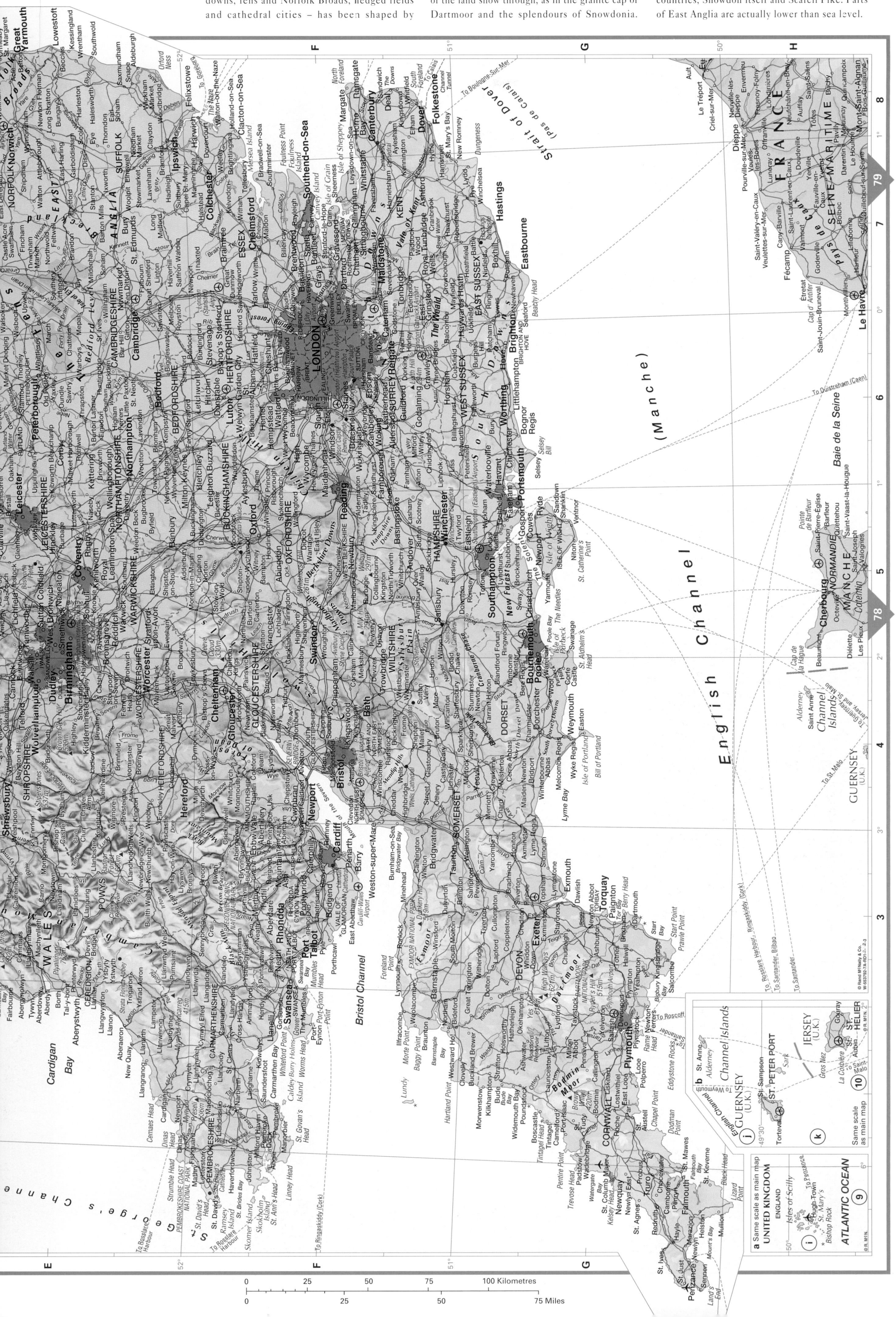

0   25   50   75   100 Kilometres

0   25   50   75 Miles

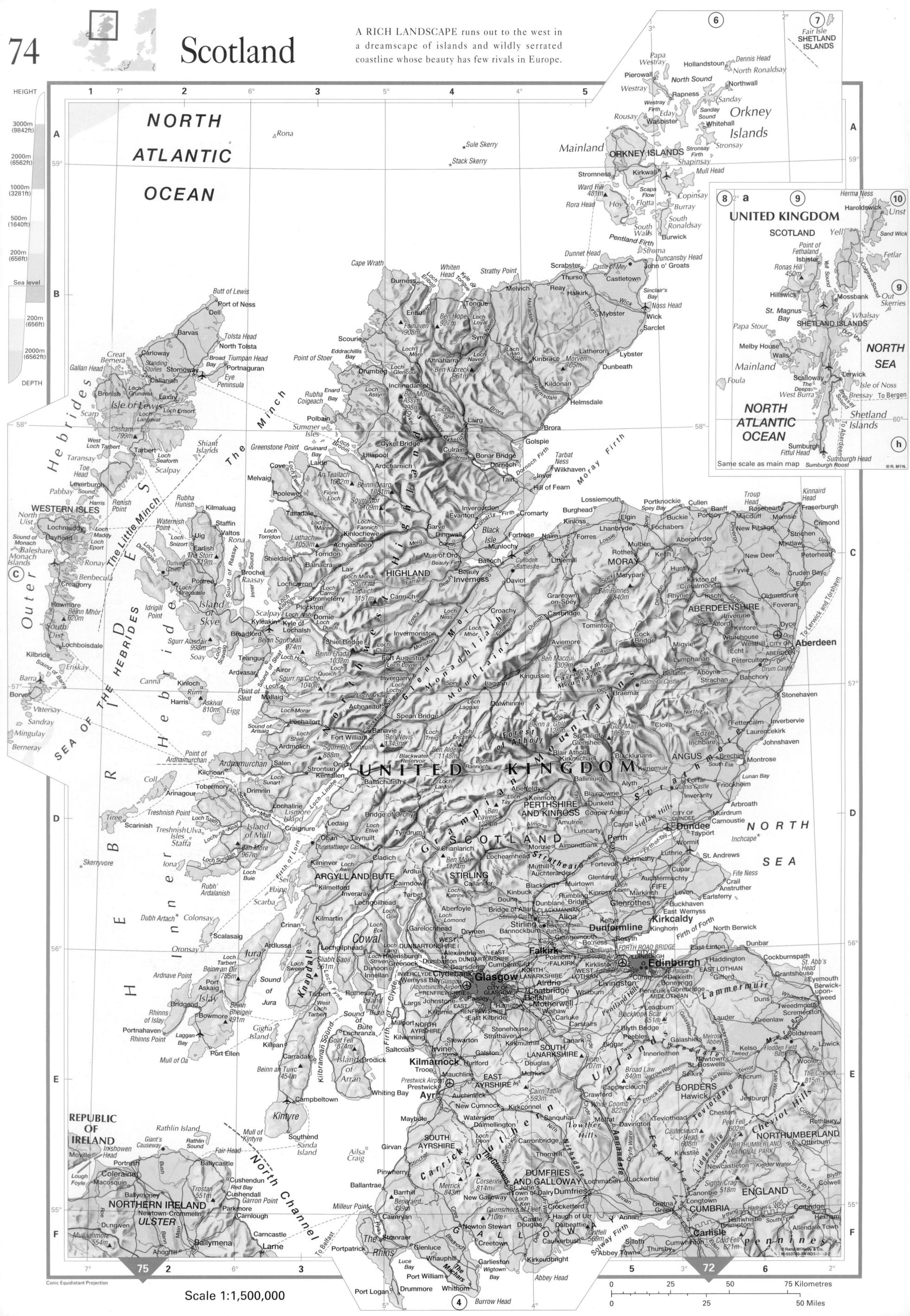

Scotland

A RICH LANDSCAPE runs out to the west in
a dreamscape of islands and wildly serrated
coastline whose beauty has few rivals in Europe.

HEIGHT

3000m
(9842ft)

2000m
(6562ft)

1000m
(3281ft)

500m
(1640ft)

200m
(656ft)

Sea level

200m
(656ft)

2000m
(6562ft)

DEPTH

NORTH

ATLANTIC

OCEAN

Orkney
Islands

ORKNEY ISLANDS

Mainland

UNITED KINGDOM

SCOTLAND

SHETLAND ISLANDS

NORTH
SEA

NORTH
ATLANTIC
OCEAN

Shetland
Islands

Same scale as main map

© R. McN.

The Minch

Hebrides

Isle of Lewis

WESTERN ISLES

Outer Hebrides

The Little Minch

SEA OF THE HEBRIDES

Island of Skye

HIGHLAND

Inverness

MORAY

ABERDEENSHIRE

Aberdeen

Inner Hebrides

Island of Mull

UNITED KINGDOM

Grampian Mountains

ANGUS

NORTH

SEA

ARGYLL AND BUTE

STIRLING

PERTHSHIRE
AND KINROSS

SCOTLAND

Dundee

FIFE

Glasgow

Edinburgh

BORDERS

Islay

ENGLAND

REPUBLIC
OF
IRELAND

NORTHERN IRELAND

ULSTER

North Channel

DUMFRIES
AND GALLOWAY

CUMBRIA

Carlisle

Pennines

Conic Equidistant Projection

Scale 1:1,500,000

0   25   50   75 Kilometres

0   25   50 Miles

NEAT AND COMPACT, Ireland consists of limestone plains and moorland generously endowed with lakes and rivers and surrounded by low hills. Much of the countryside is as bright a green as legend would have it, but its peaceful natural face is at odds with its turbulent history.

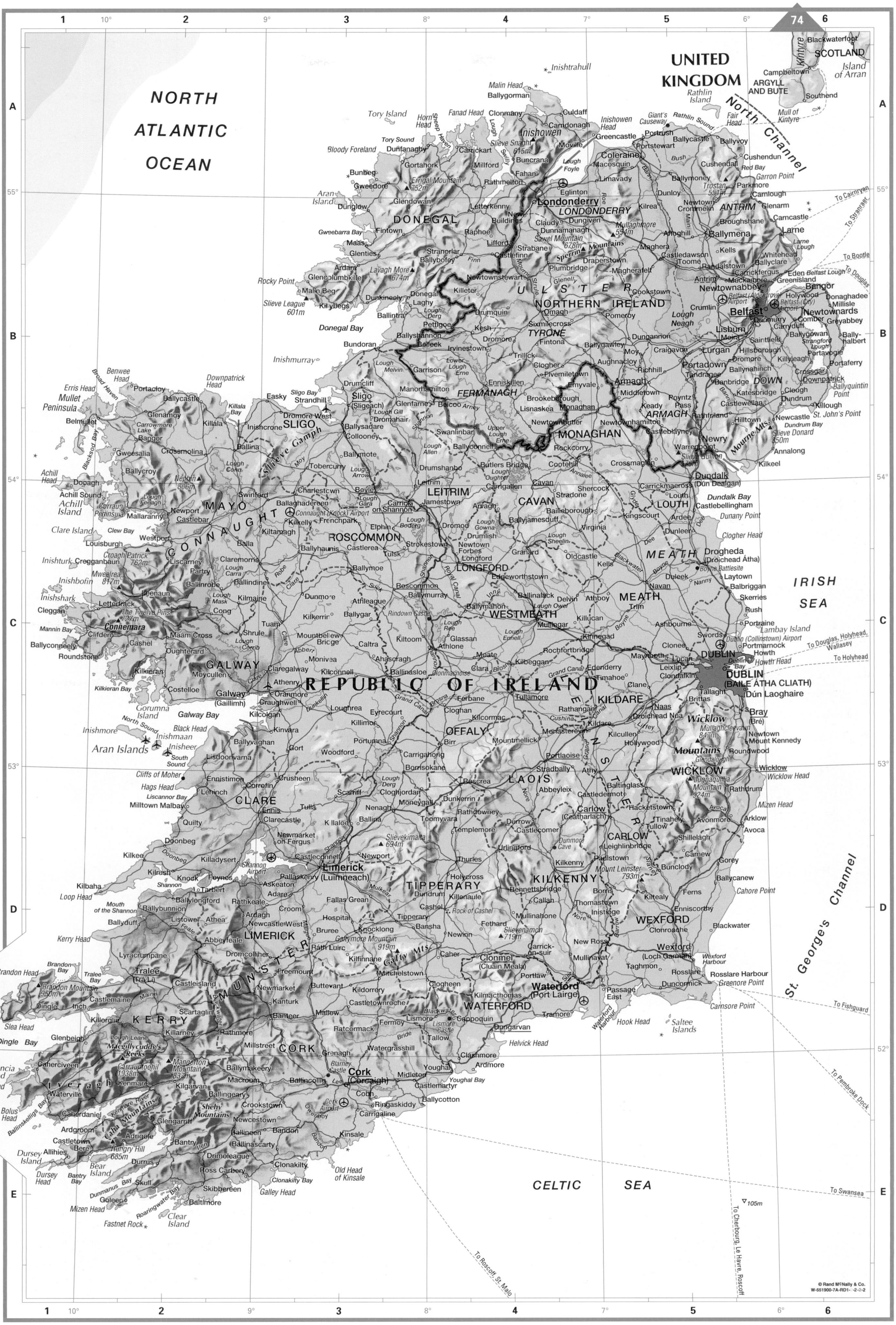

Scale 1:1,500,000

One centimetre represents 15 kilometres.

One inch represents approximately 24 miles.

Conic Equidistant Projection

© Rand McNally & Co.
W-551900-7A-RD1-.-2-2-2

Scale 1:3,000,000

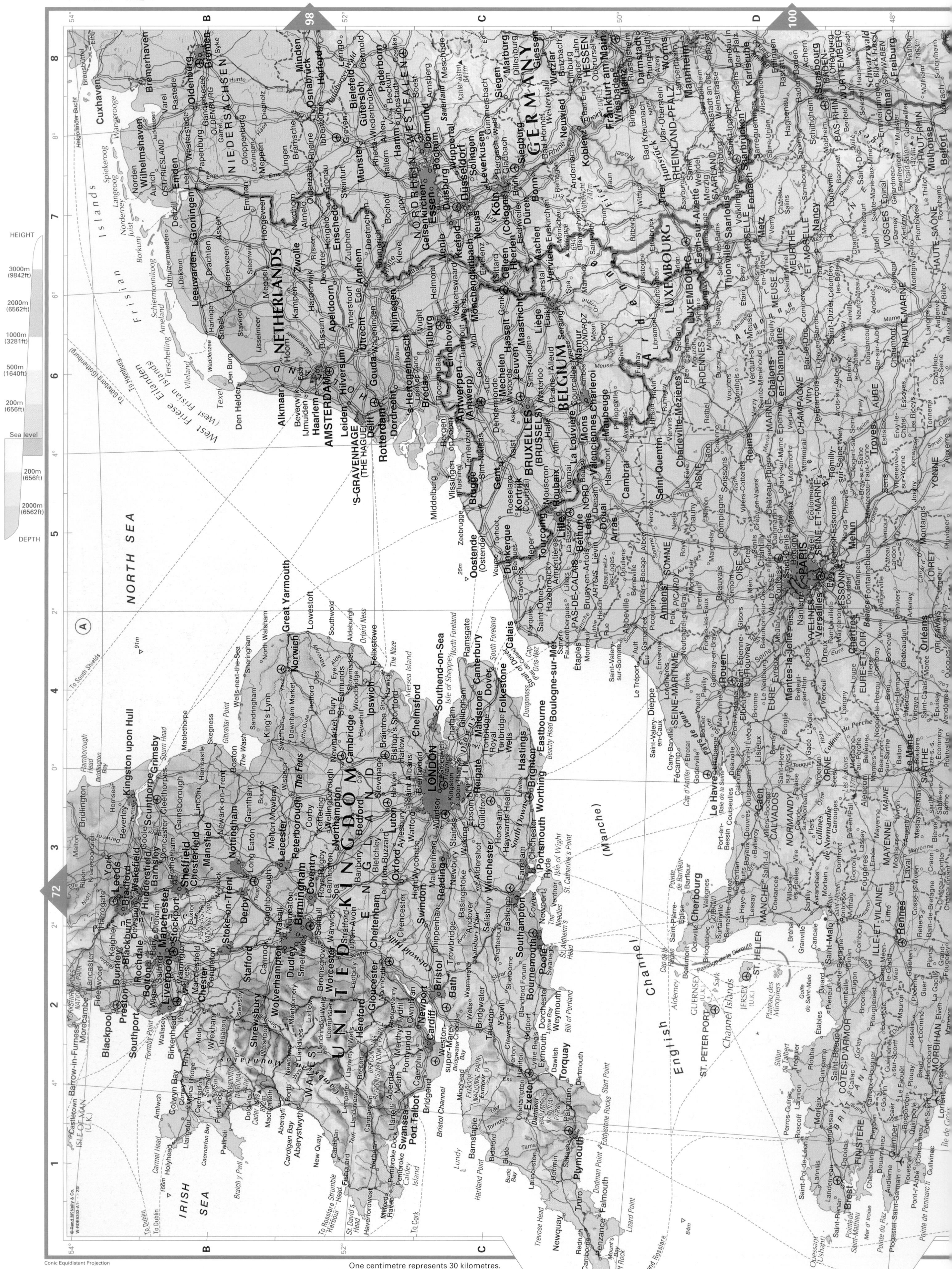

One centimetre represents 30 kilometres.

One inch represents approximately 47 miles.

Conic Equidistant Projection

HEIGHT

3000m (9842ft)
2000m (6562ft)
1000m (3281ft)
500m (1640ft)
200m (656ft)
Sea level
200m (656ft)
2000m (6562ft)

DEPTH

FRANCE IS OF both the south and the north, encompassing the coal mines and grey skies of Arras and the sunflowers and crystal light of Provence. Three seas wash its long coastline, and its landward frontiers are emphasised by the bastions of the Alps, the Pyrenees and the Vosges. Among its people are Basques and Bretons, Corsicans and Alsatians. Out of such variety emerges the harmony that is France.

77

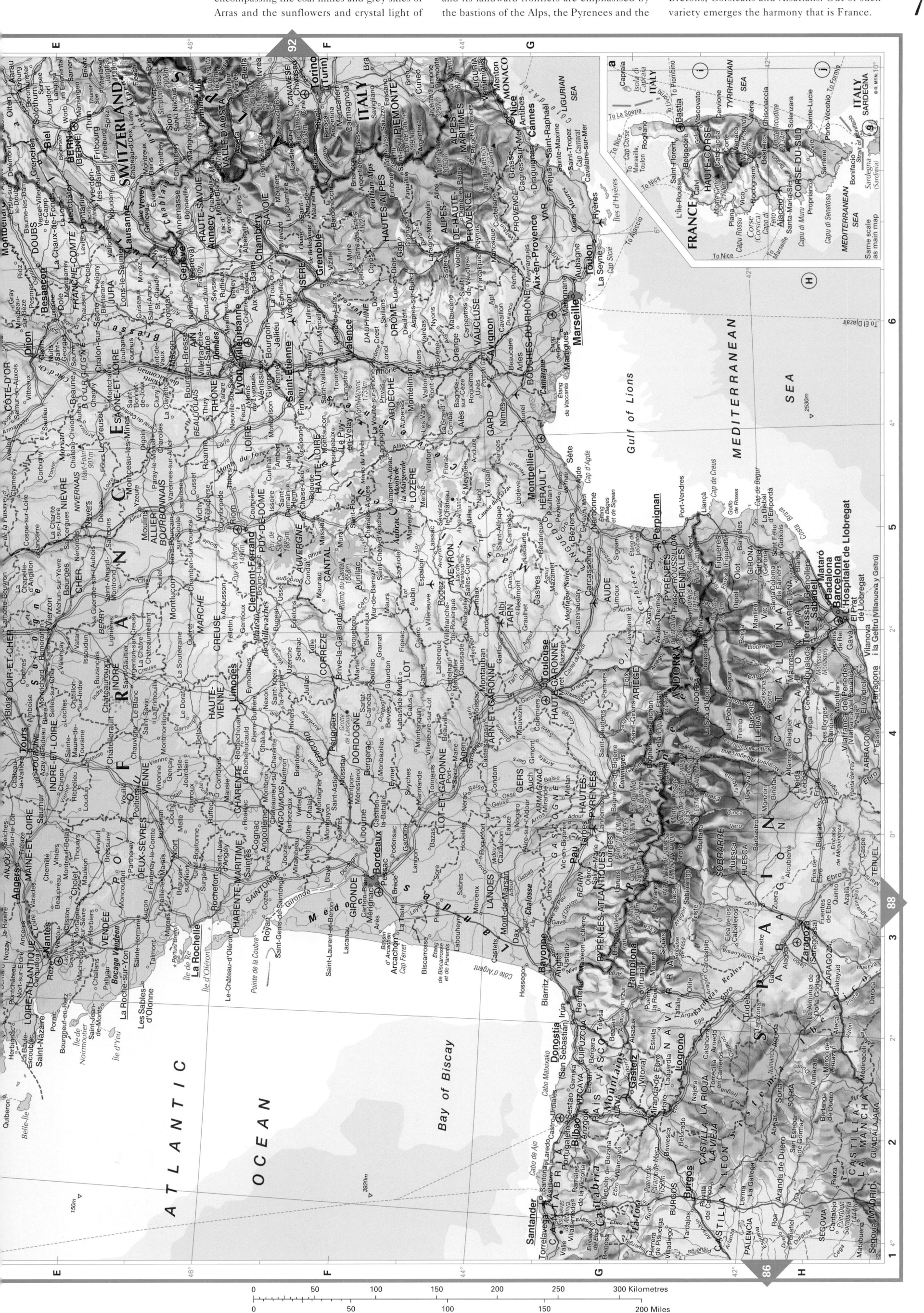

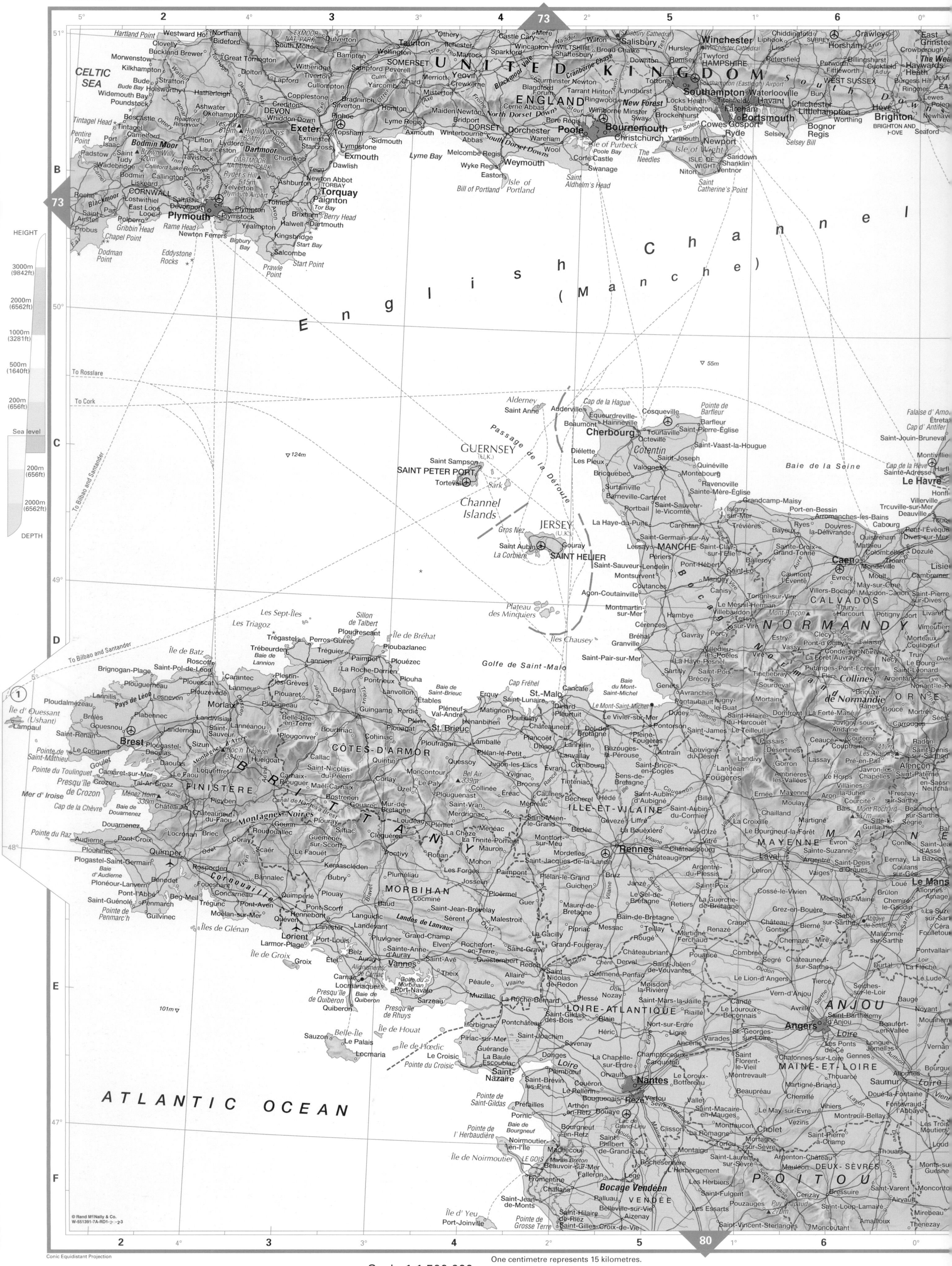

Scale 1:1,500,000

One centimetre represents 15 kilometres.

One inch represents approximately 24 miles.

Conic Equidistant Projection

© Rand McNally & Co.
W-551391-7A-RD1-?-?-?3

THE FRETTED COAST and many islands of Brittany make up a third of the entire French seaboard, and the moors and forests inland are strewn with the megalithic monuments of an ancient past. Normandy, whose Norse founders conquered England and Sicily, is a land of orchards and handsome old ports like Honfleur, from which the Seine can be followed upstream to that most celebrated of capitals, Paris.

79

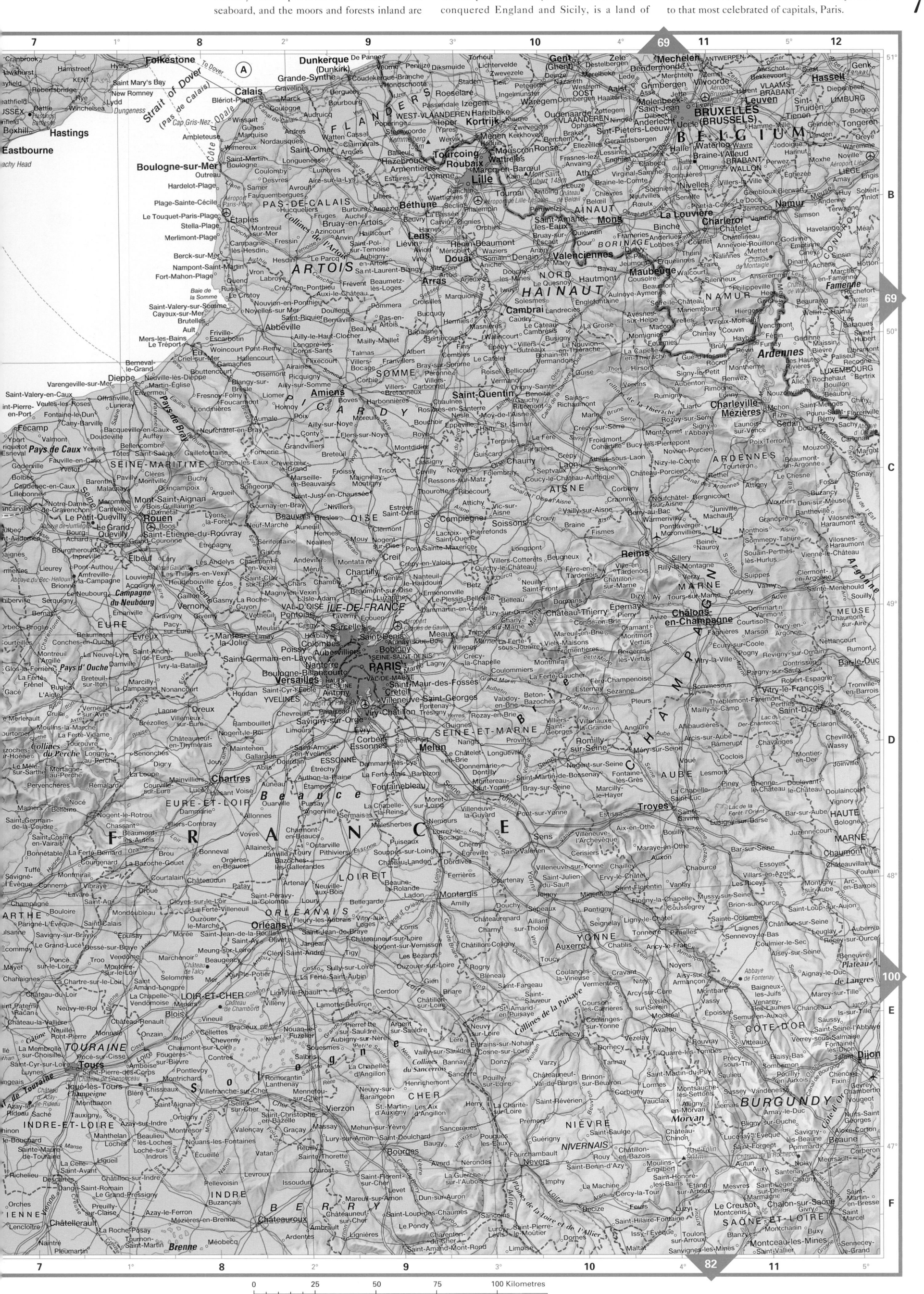

South-west France

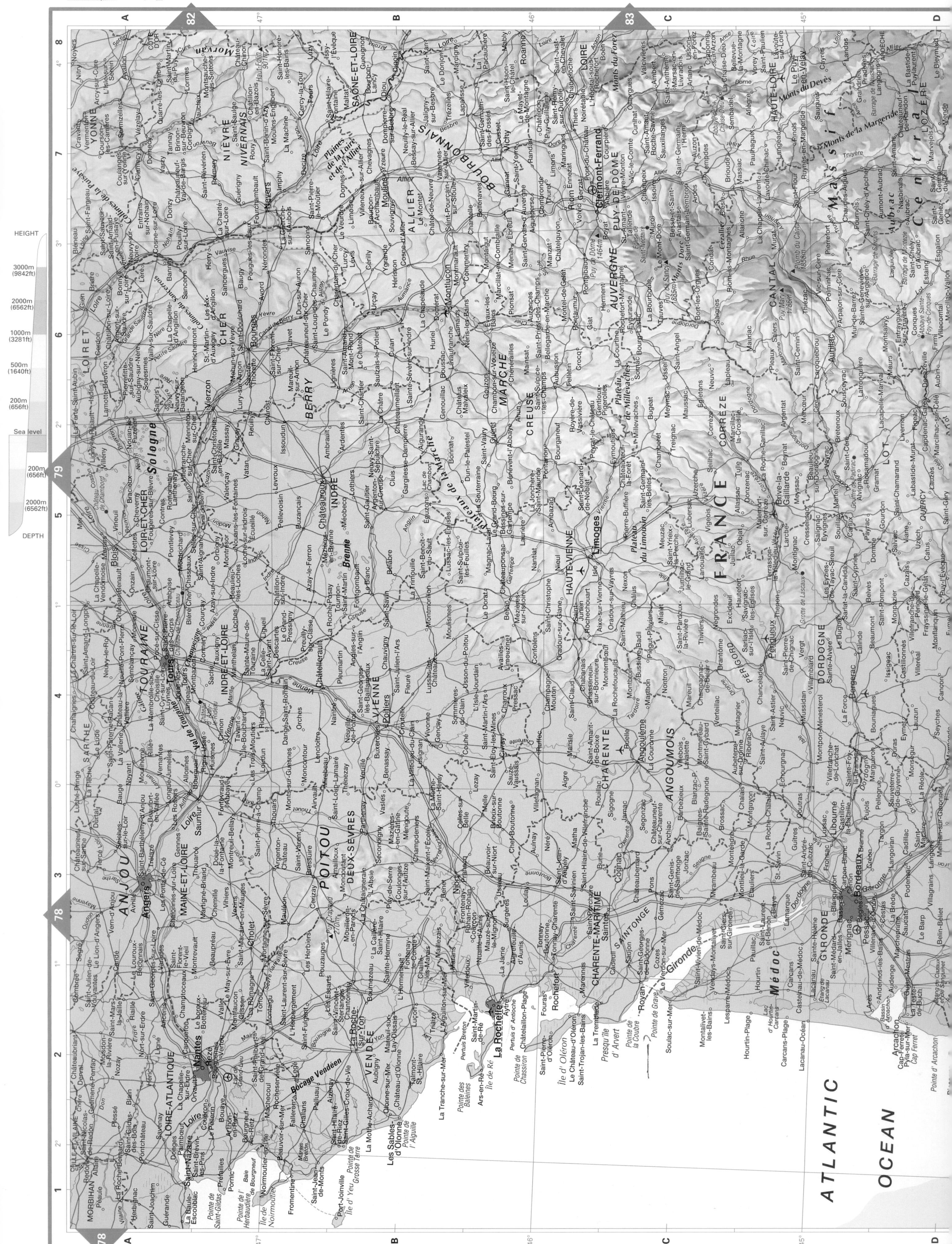

HEIGHT

3000m (9842ft)
2000m (6562ft)
1000m (3281ft)
500m (1640ft)
200m (656ft)
Sea level
200m (656ft)
2000m (6562ft)

DEPTH

ATLANTIC OCEAN

Conic Equidistant Projection

Scale 1:1,500,000

One centimetre represents 15 kilometres.

One inch represents approximately 24 miles.

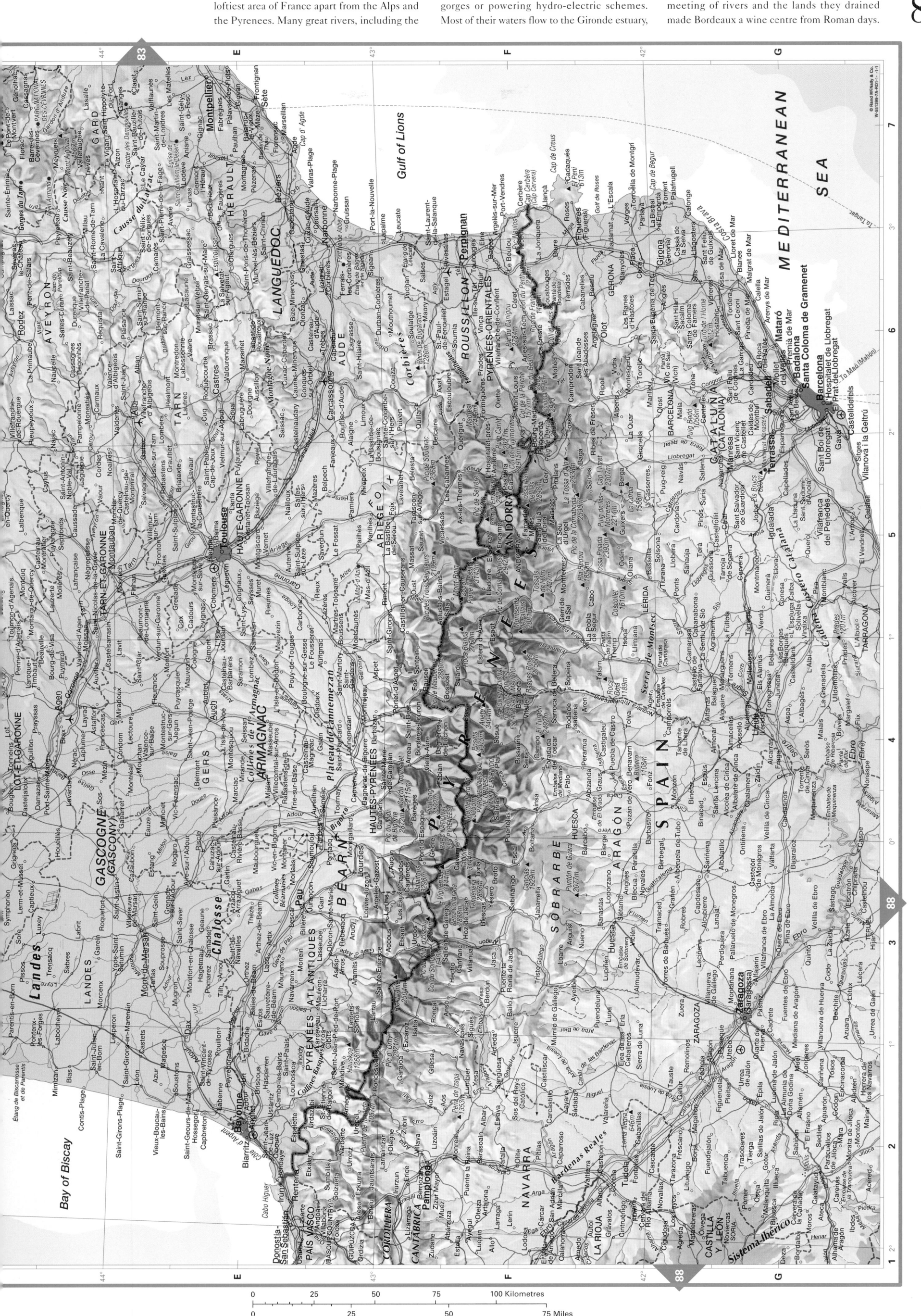

THE VAST GRANITE Massif Central is the loftiest area of France apart from the Alps and the Pyrenees. Many great rivers, including the Dordogne, are born there, thundering through gorges or powering hydro-electric schemes. Most of their waters flow to the Gironde estuary, joined by the Garonne that rises in Spain. This meeting of rivers and the lands they drained made Bordeaux a wine centre from Roman days.

81

South-east France

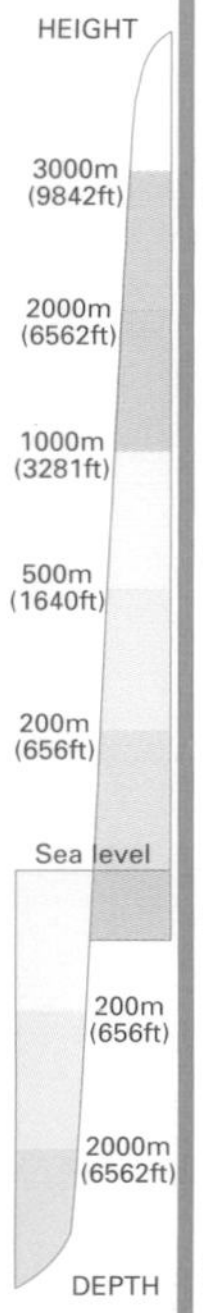

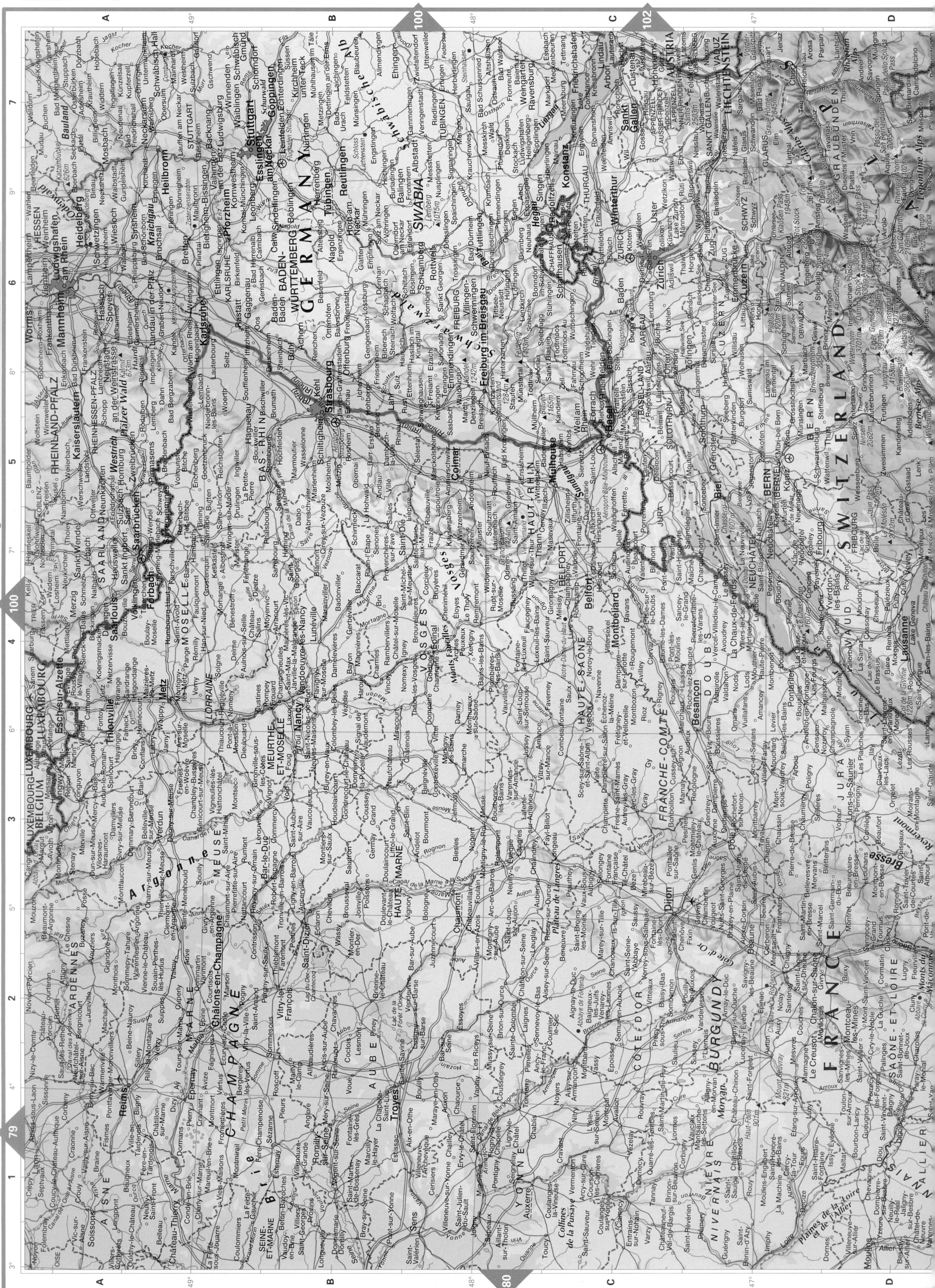

Scale 1:1,500,000

One centimetre represents 15 kilometres.

One inch represents approximately 24 miles.

Conic Equidistant Projection

TO THE EAST, France shares something of the flavour of five neighbours. The industries, cuisine, wines and beers of Lorraine and Alsace are reflected across the Rhine. Franche-Comté, along the slopes of the Jura, was an invaders' route, while beyond it the French Alps rise to meet those of Switzerland and Italy. Provence is the 'Province' of the Romans; even they were latecomers to Marseille, founded by the Greeks.

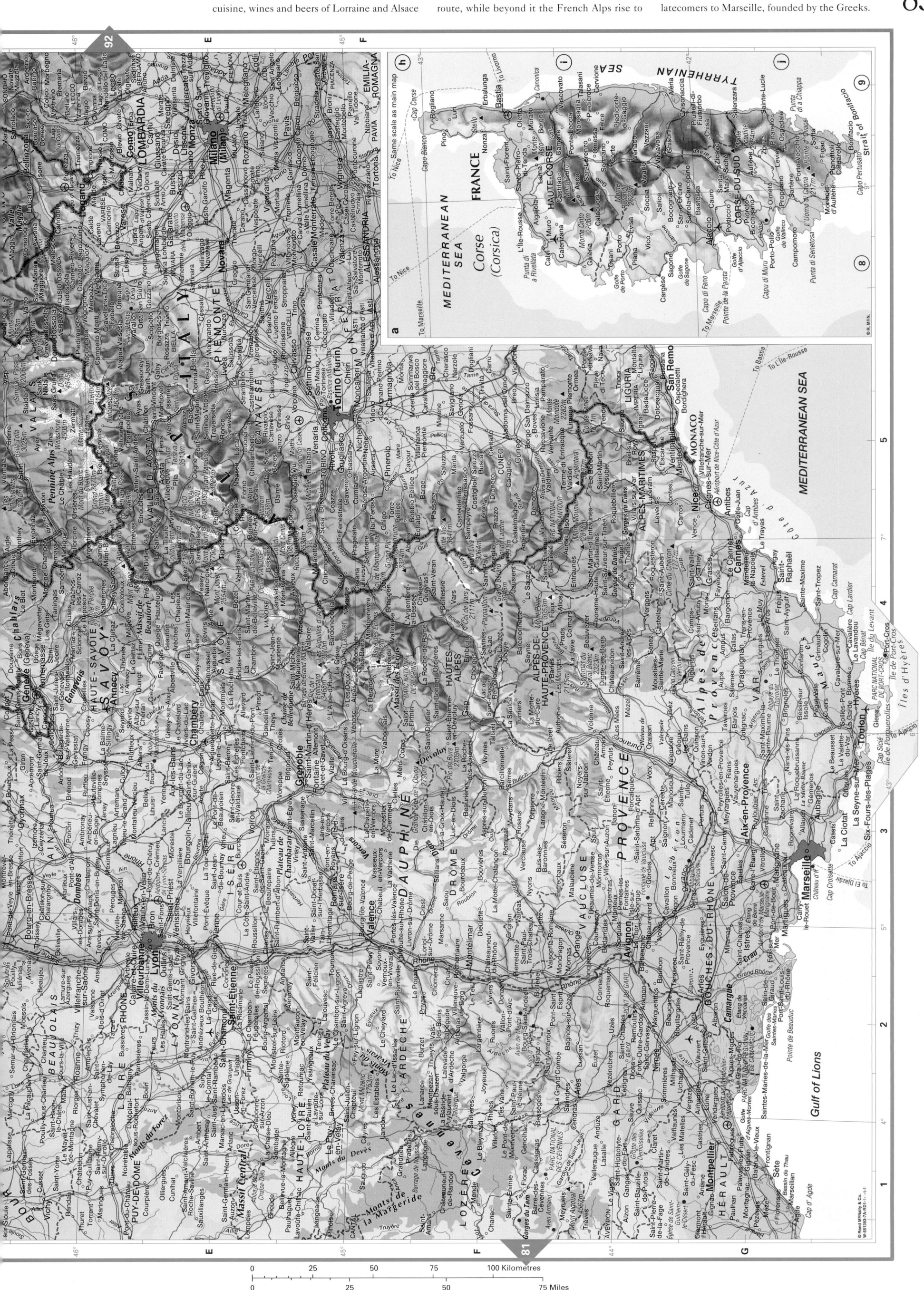

MEDITERRANEAN SEA

Corse (Corsica)

FRANCE

HAUTE-CORSE

CORSE-DU-SUD

TYRRHENIAN SEA

Gulf of Lions

MEDITERRANEAN SEA

0	25	50	75	100 Kilometres

0	25	50	75 Miles

THE IBERIAN PENINSULA, embracing Spain, Portugal and tiny Andorra, is cobbled roughly onto the remainder of Europe by the Pyrenees. Spain, the largest portion, is divided by mountain ranges, and its provinces, over the centuries, have each evolved their own strong and particular flavours. Stretches of the north coast are rugged, damp and green, while the south can be as hot and dry as Morocco.

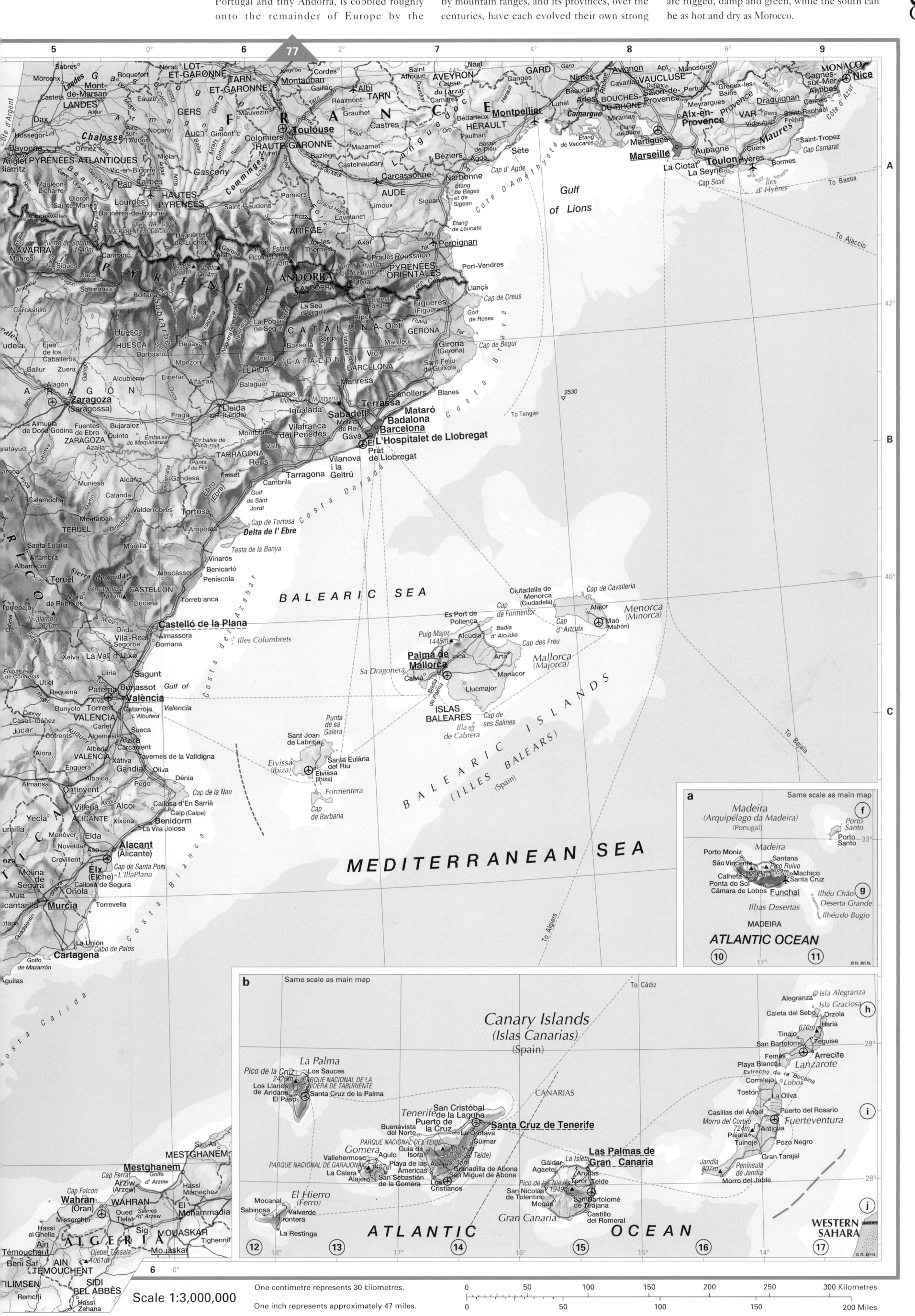

Scale 1:3,000,000

One centimetre represents 30 kilometres.

One inch represents approximately 47 miles.

Western Spain and Portugal

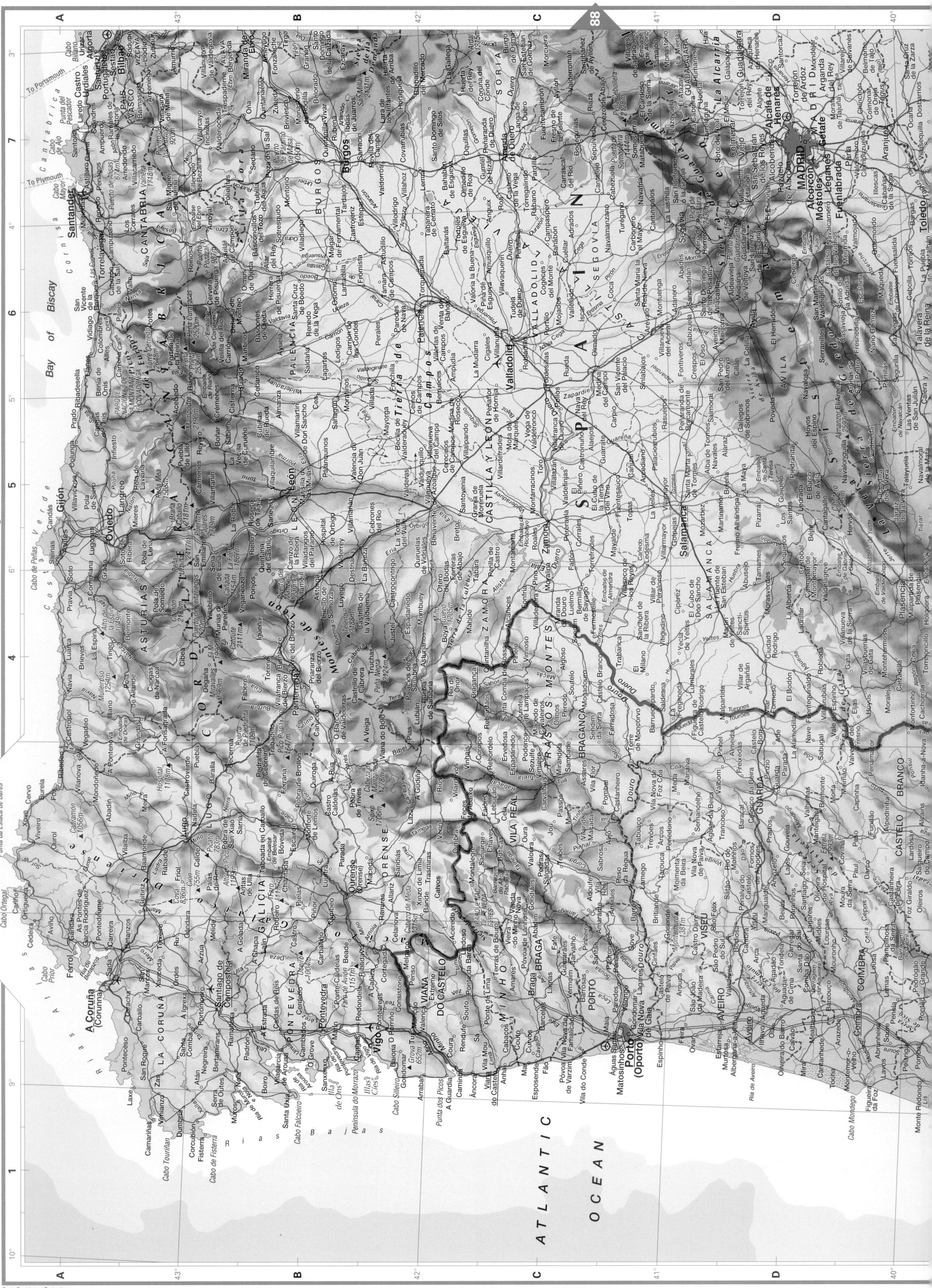

HEIGHT

3000m
(9842ft)

2000m
(6562ft)

1000m
(3281ft)

500m
(1640ft)

200m
(656ft)

Sea level

200m
(656ft)

2000m
(6562ft)

DEPTH

Conic Equidistant Projection

Scale 1:1,750,000

One centimetre represents 17.5 kilometres.

One inch represents approximately 28 miles.

ALL PORTUGAL'S COAST faces the Atlantic, but south of the River Tagus the 'feel' of the country, with its orange groves, cork plantations and beaches, is Mediterranean. North of the Tagus lie tiny fields of maize and root crops. Far upstream on the river's 1010 km (628 mile) course through Spain is the Meseta, a treeless plateau, torrid in summer and freezing in winter, on which is set Madrid, the Spanish capital.

87

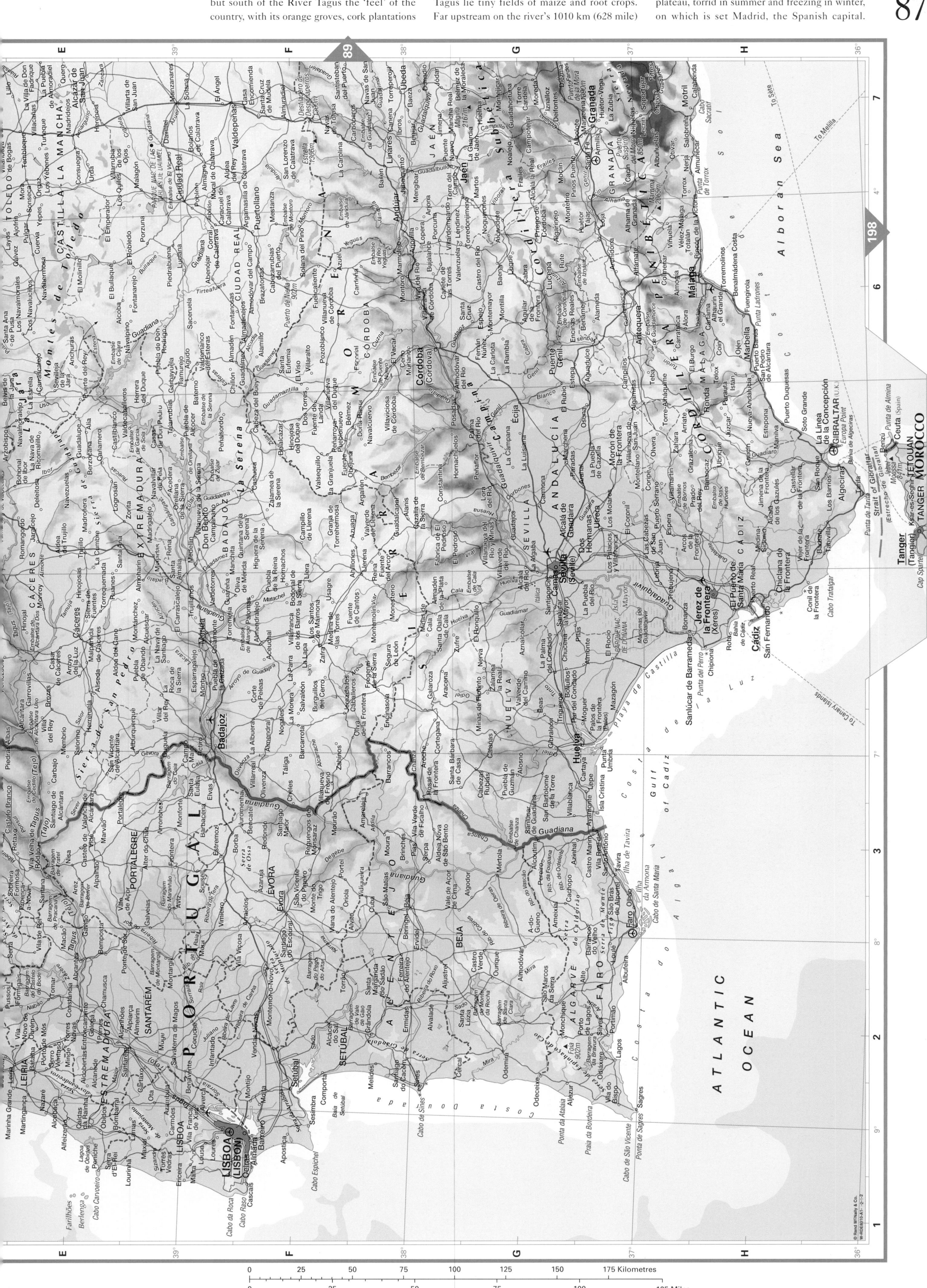

Eastern Spain

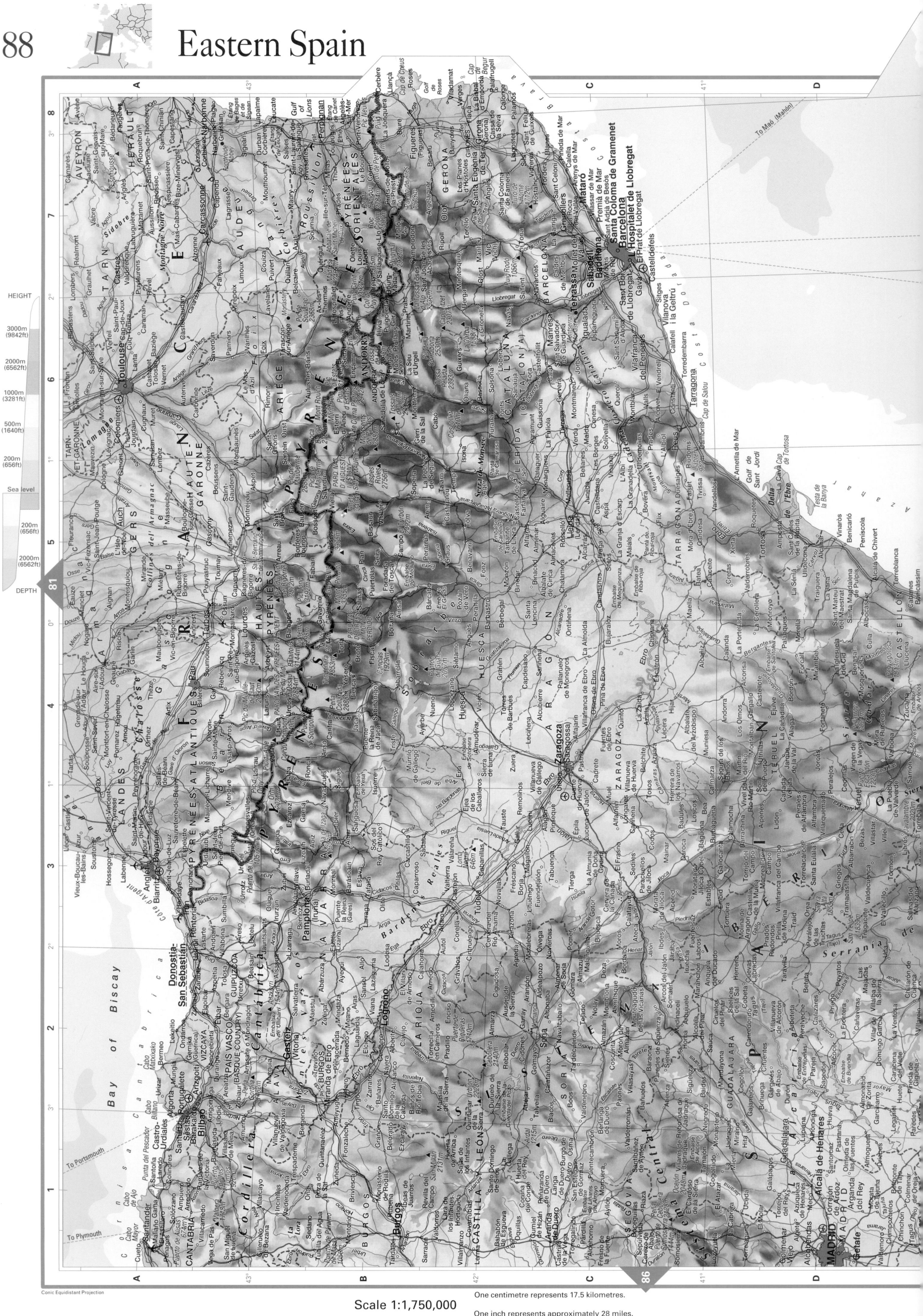

Scale 1:1,750,000

One centimetre represents 17.5 kilometres.

One inch represents approximately 28 miles.

FROM THE PYRENEES, ten legend-haunted passes through the mountains lead southwards to the huge distances of Castile and to bustling Barcelona and the bays and inlets of the Costa Brava. Here, and offshore in the Spanish-owned Balearic Islands, begins the Spain familiar to the holidaymaker. Farther south, sunny Andalucia also embraces the ice-capped Sierra Nevada and, at Almeria, Europe's only true desert.

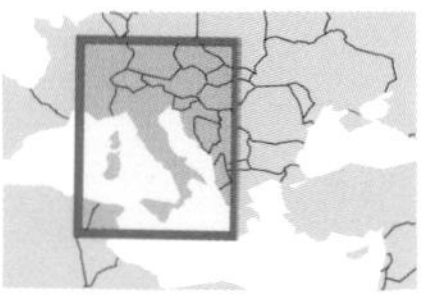

HEIGHT

3000m (9842ft)
2000m (6562ft)
1000m (3281ft)
500m (1640ft)
200m (656ft)
Sea level
200m (656ft)
2000m (6562ft)

DEPTH

Countries and regions (selected labels): CZECH REPUBLIC, SLOVAKIA, GERMANY, BAYERN, BADEN-WÜRTTEMBERG, FRANCE, SWITZERLAND, LIECHTENSTEIN, VORARLBERG, ÖSTERREICH (NIEDERÖSTERREICH, OBERÖSTERREICH, STEIERMARK, KÄRNTEN, TIROL, BURGENLAND), HUNGARY, SLOVENIA, CROATIA, BOSNIA AND HERZEGOVINA, CRNA GORA, ITALY (PIEMONTE, LOMBARDIA, VENETO, TRENTINO-ALTO ADIGE, FRIULI-VENEZIA GIULIA, EMILIA-ROMAGNA, LIGURIA, TOSCANA, UMBRIA, MARCHE), MONACO

Major cities (selected): BRATISLAVA, WIEN (VIENNA), BUDAPEST, GRAZ, ZAGREB, LJUBLJANA, SARAJEVO, München (Munich), Stuttgart, Augsburg, Regensburg, Salzburg, Innsbruck, Bolzano, Trento, Verona, Venézia (Venice), Padova, Vicenza, Treviso, Trieste, Udine, Rijeka, Split, Milano (Milan), Torino (Turin), Genova (Genoa), Bologna, Firenze (Florence), Ancona, Rimini, Ravenna, Ferrara, Modena, Parma, Piacenza, Brescia, Bergamo, Bern (Berne), Zürich, Lausanne, Genève (Geneva), Nice, Menton, San Marino

Seas: ADRIATIC, LIGURIAN SEA, Gulf of Genoa, Gulf of Venice

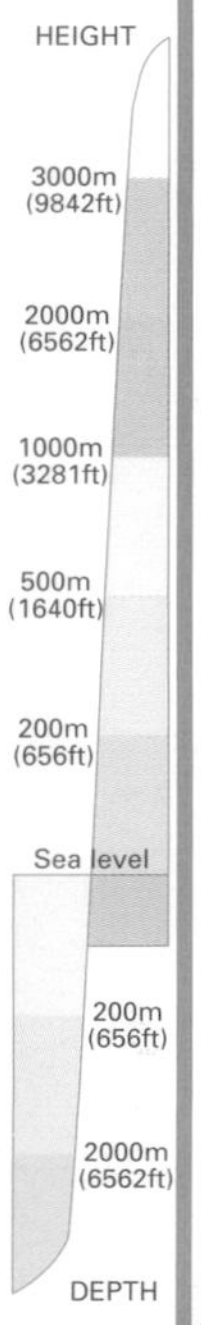

Conic Equidistant Projection

CURVED AROUND ITALY'S frontier is an arc of mountains and lakes which yields abruptly to the great northern plain. This contains the industrial triangle of Milan, Turin and Genoa as well as the nation's most productive farmlands. Close by Genoa rise the Apennines, the volcanic mountain chain that runs down the centre of the peninsula. A mountain chain across Sicily has a spectacular culmination in Mount Etna.

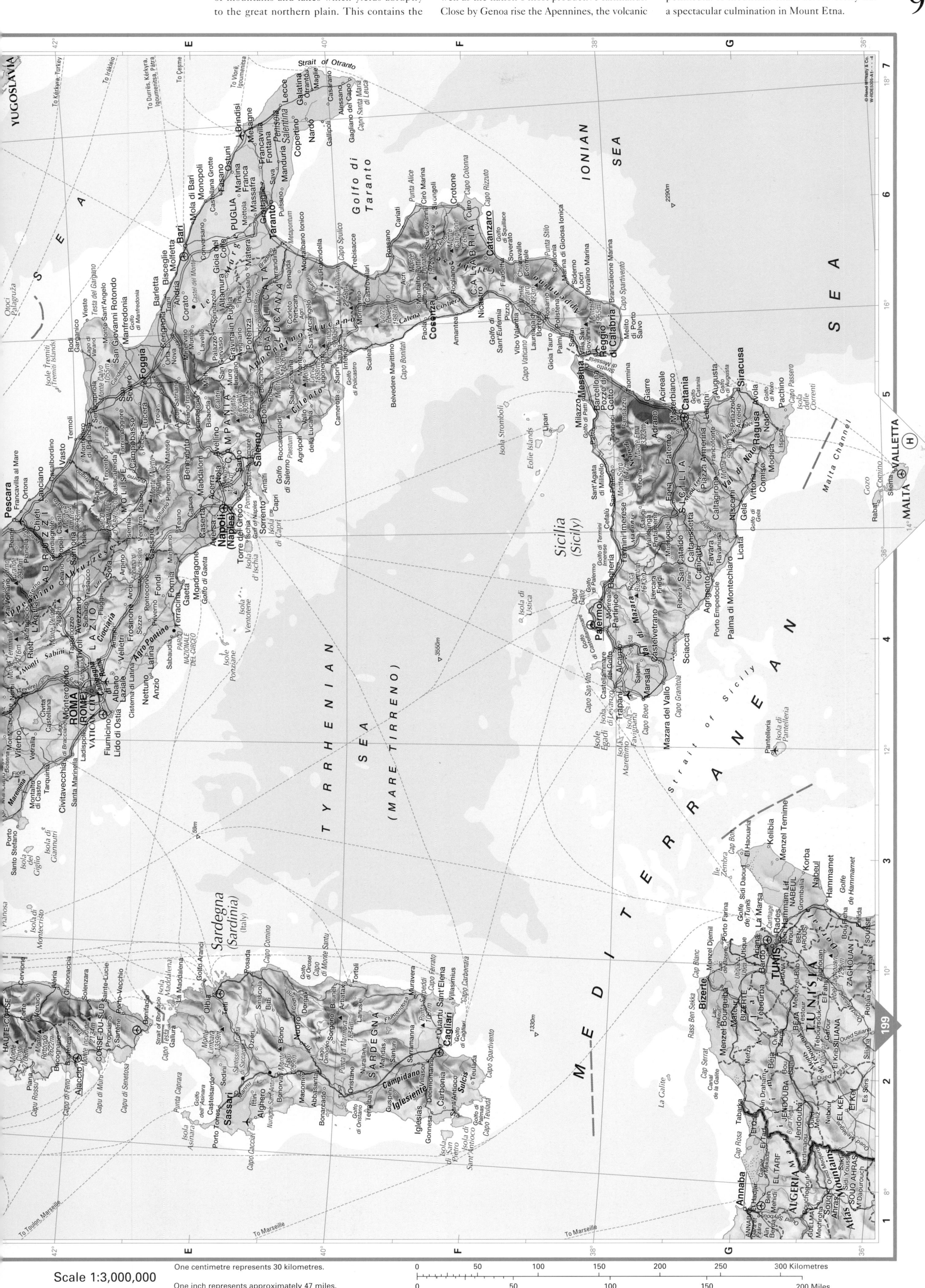

Scale 1:3,000,000

One centimetre represents 30 kilometres.

One inch represents approximately 47 miles.

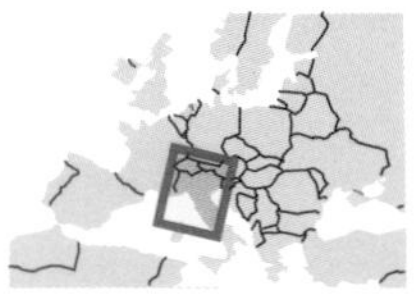

Northern Italy and Switzerland

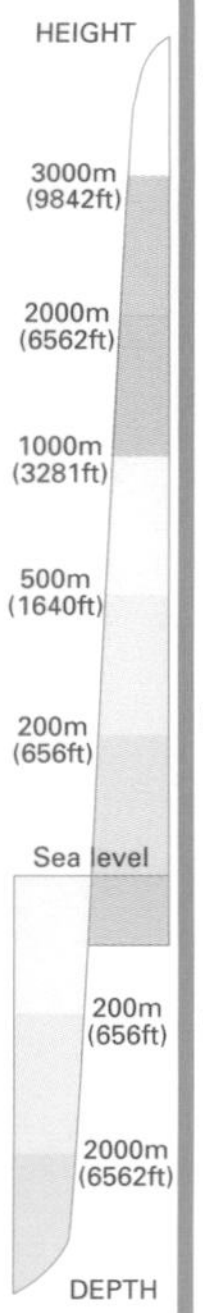

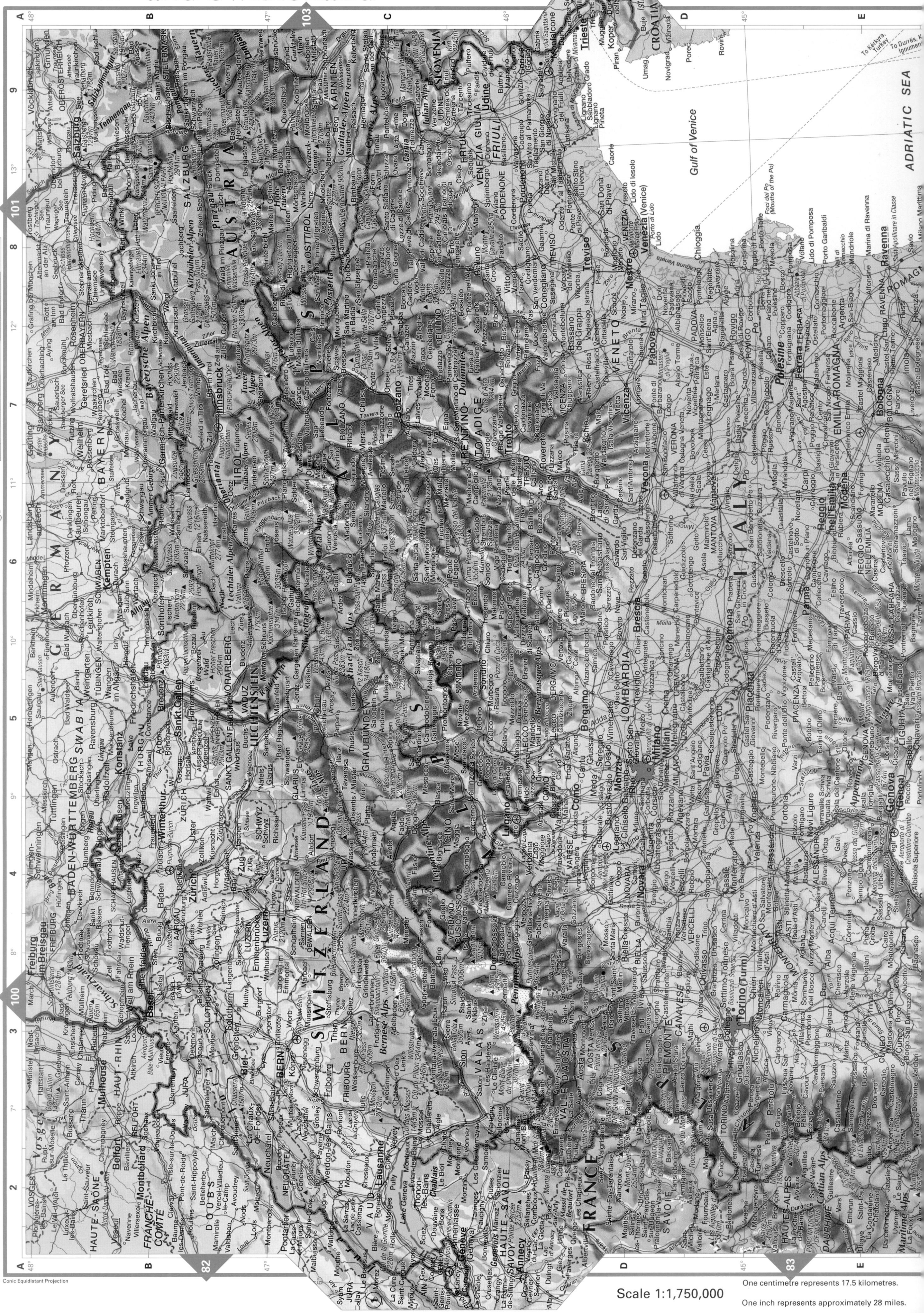

Scale 1:1,750,000

One centimetre represents 17.5 kilometres.

One inch represents approximately 28 miles.

Conic Equidistant Projection

HEIGHT

3000m (9842ft)
2000m (6562ft)
1000m (3281ft)
500m (1640ft)
200m (656ft)
Sea level
200m (656ft)
2000m (6562ft)

DEPTH

THE PYRAMID OF the Matterhorn towers over the border regions of Italy and Switzerland, whose inhabitants' native speech might be French, German, Italian, Slovene or Romansch. Southward lie the great cities of Rome, Venice and Florence and the lovely towns of Tuscany and Umbria, cradle of the Renaissance, whose great stirring lives on in the verve and style of the products of Italy's modern industries.

93

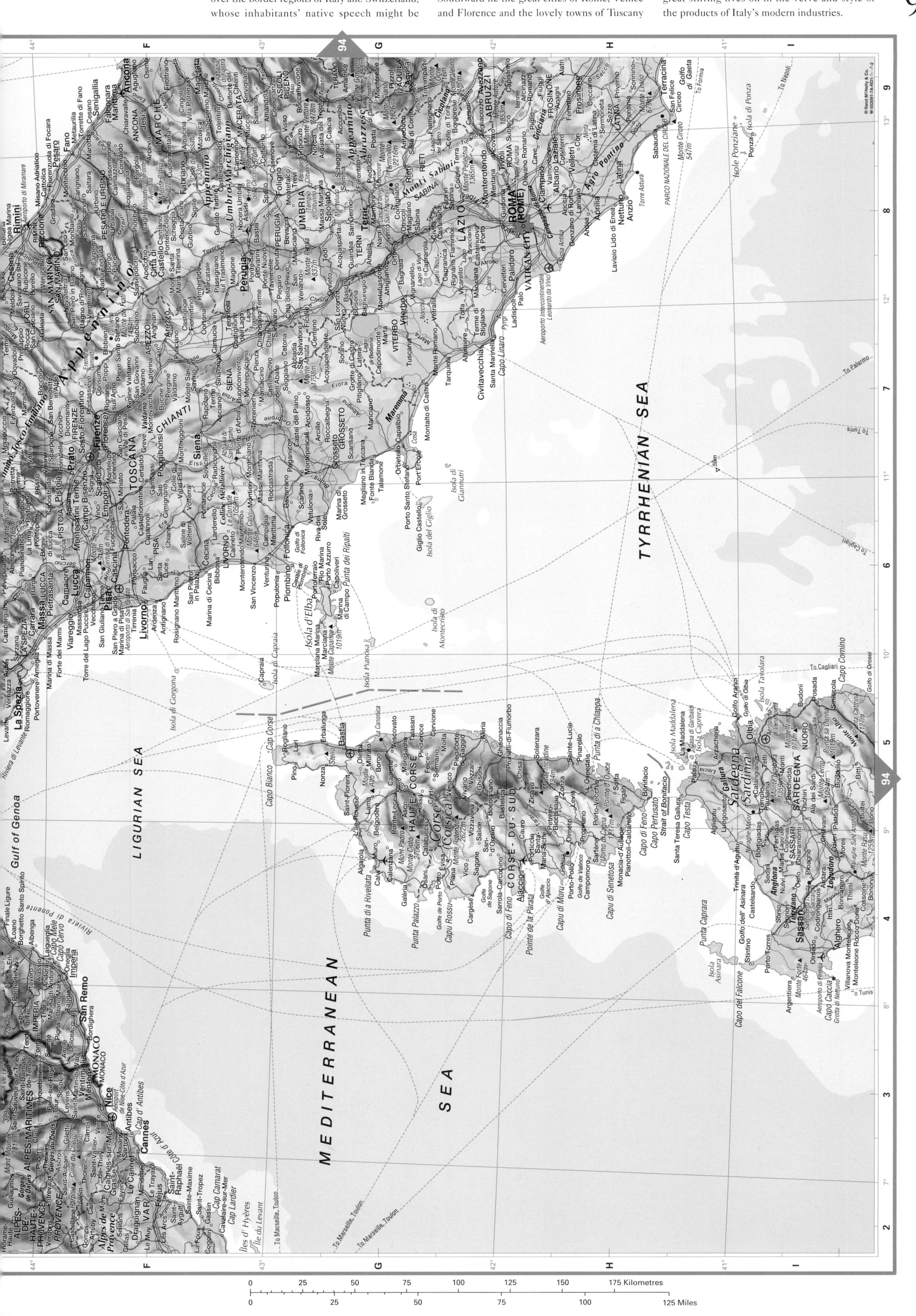

0   25   50   75   100   125   150   175 Kilometres

0   25   50   75   100   125 Miles

Southern Italy

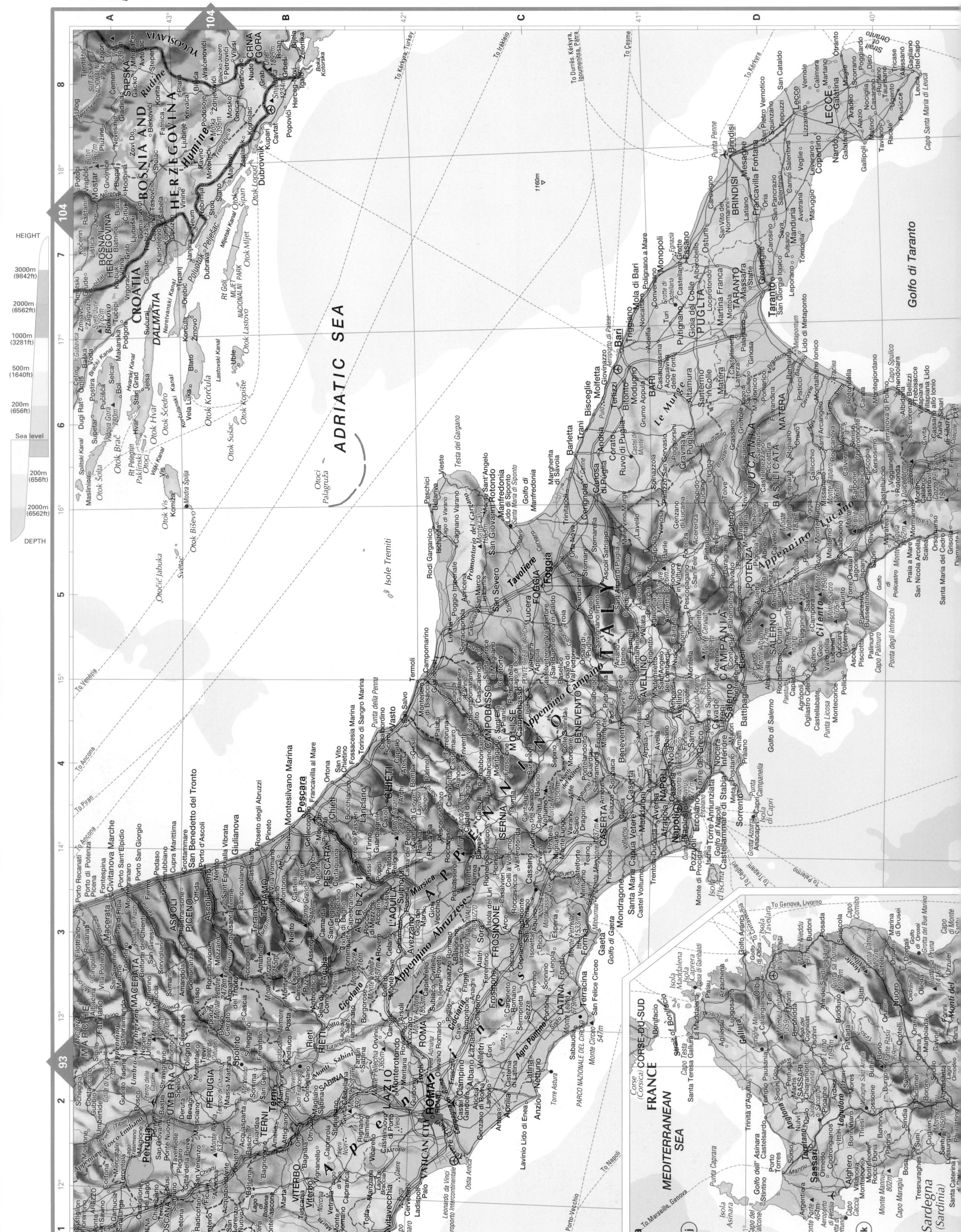

HEIGHT

3000m
(9842ft)

2000m
(6562ft)

1000m
(3281ft)

500m
(1640ft)

200m
(656ft)

Sea level

200m
(656ft)

2000m
(6562ft)

DEPTH

Conic Equidistant Projection

Scale 1:1,750,000

One centimetre represents 17.5 kilometres.

One inch represents approximately 28 miles.

SOUTH OF ROME, ancestral city to half of Europe, lies an Italy that is hotter, craggier, poorer than the north. In Campania, there are ancient Pompeii and teeming, exciting Naples; Basilicata and Calabria, at the bottom of Italy's 'boot', are remote, mountainous and harsh. The south has beckoned visitors since Roman emperors first went to Capri, and captivates them still with the beauty of the Amalfi coast.

95

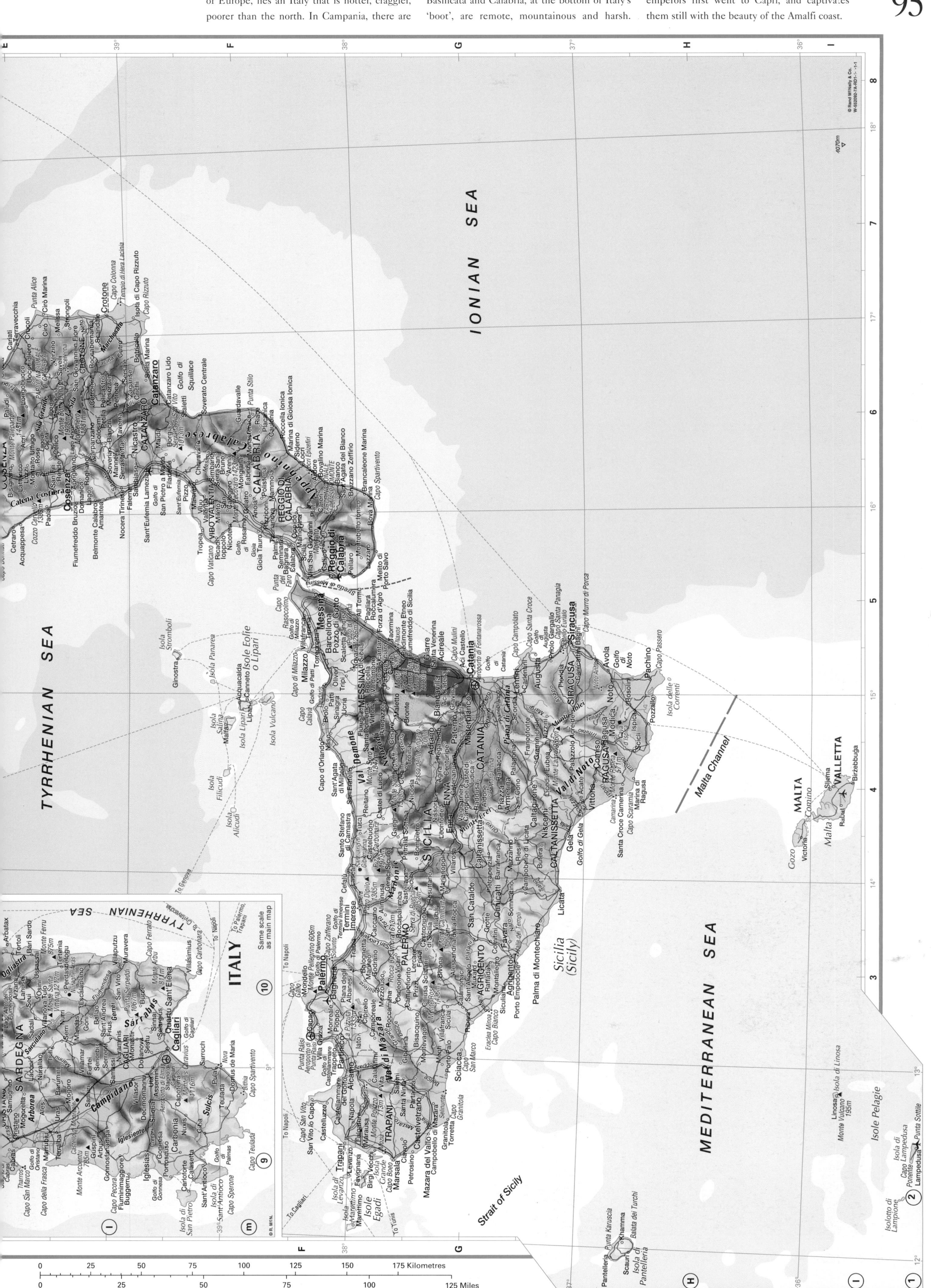

0   25   50   75   100   125   150   175 Kilometres

0   25   50   75   100   125 Miles

THE BROAD SWEEP of the North European
Plain rolls across Germany and Poland. All its
major rivers flow into the Baltic Sea or the
North Sea. To the south the land rises through
the Bavarian Alps and the Carpathian
Mountains, which form a natural border
between Poland and Slovakia. The mighty
Danube, a major transport artery, flows through
ten countries on its course to the Black Sea.

97

Scale 1:1,500,000

One centimetre represents 15 kilometres.

One inch represents approximately 24 miles.

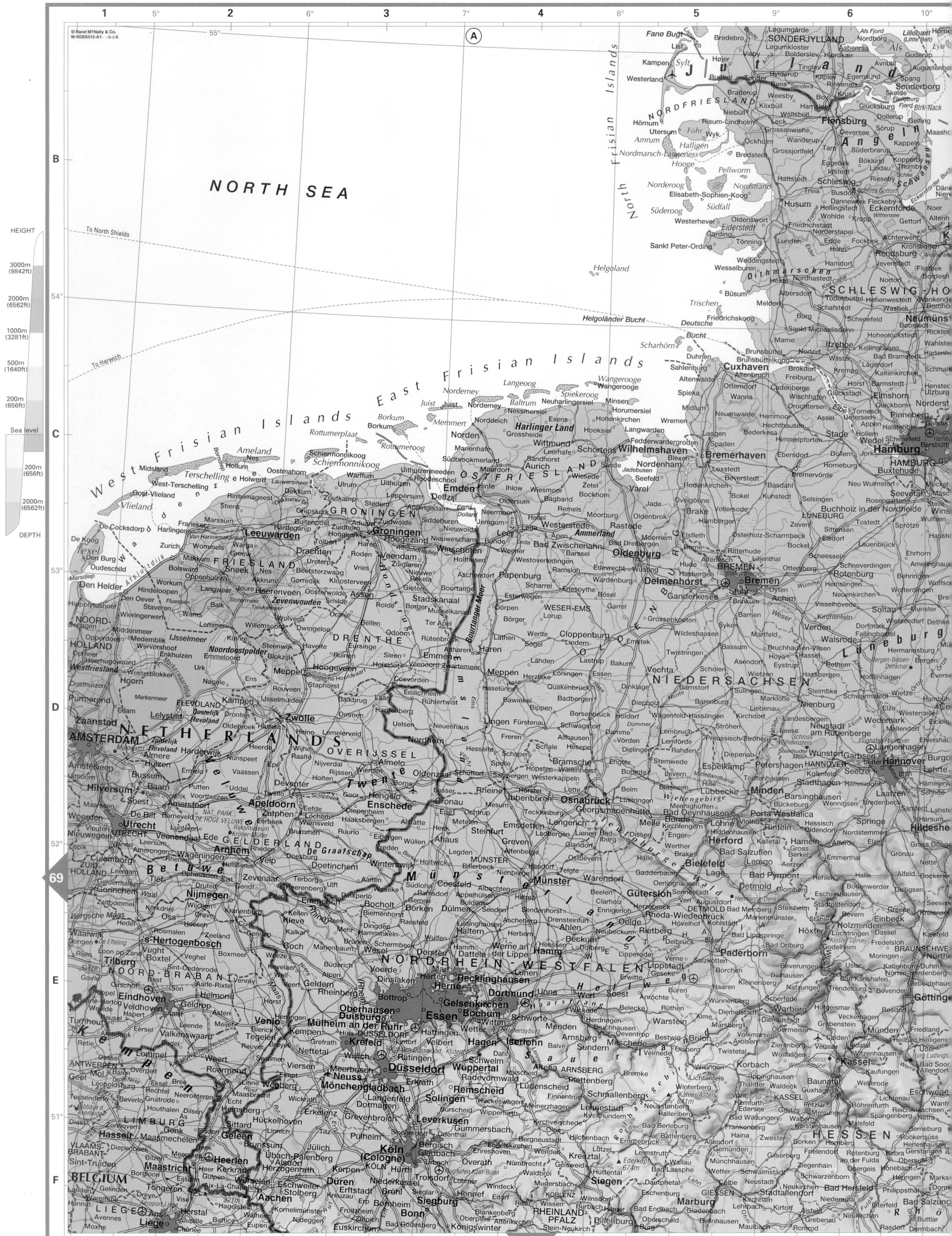

Conic Equidistant Projection

THE BERLIN WALL crumbled in 1989, and within a year reunited Germany was again the heart of Europe. Berlin looks towards the vast expanse of Eastern Europe, but Cologne, on the Rhine, is of the West. Hamburg is a gateway to the world. The lower Ruhr valley is one of the world's largest industrial areas, but with the closure of many coal mines its towns are today developing lighter, computer-based industries.

99

0   25   50   75   100 Kilometres

0   25   50   75 Miles

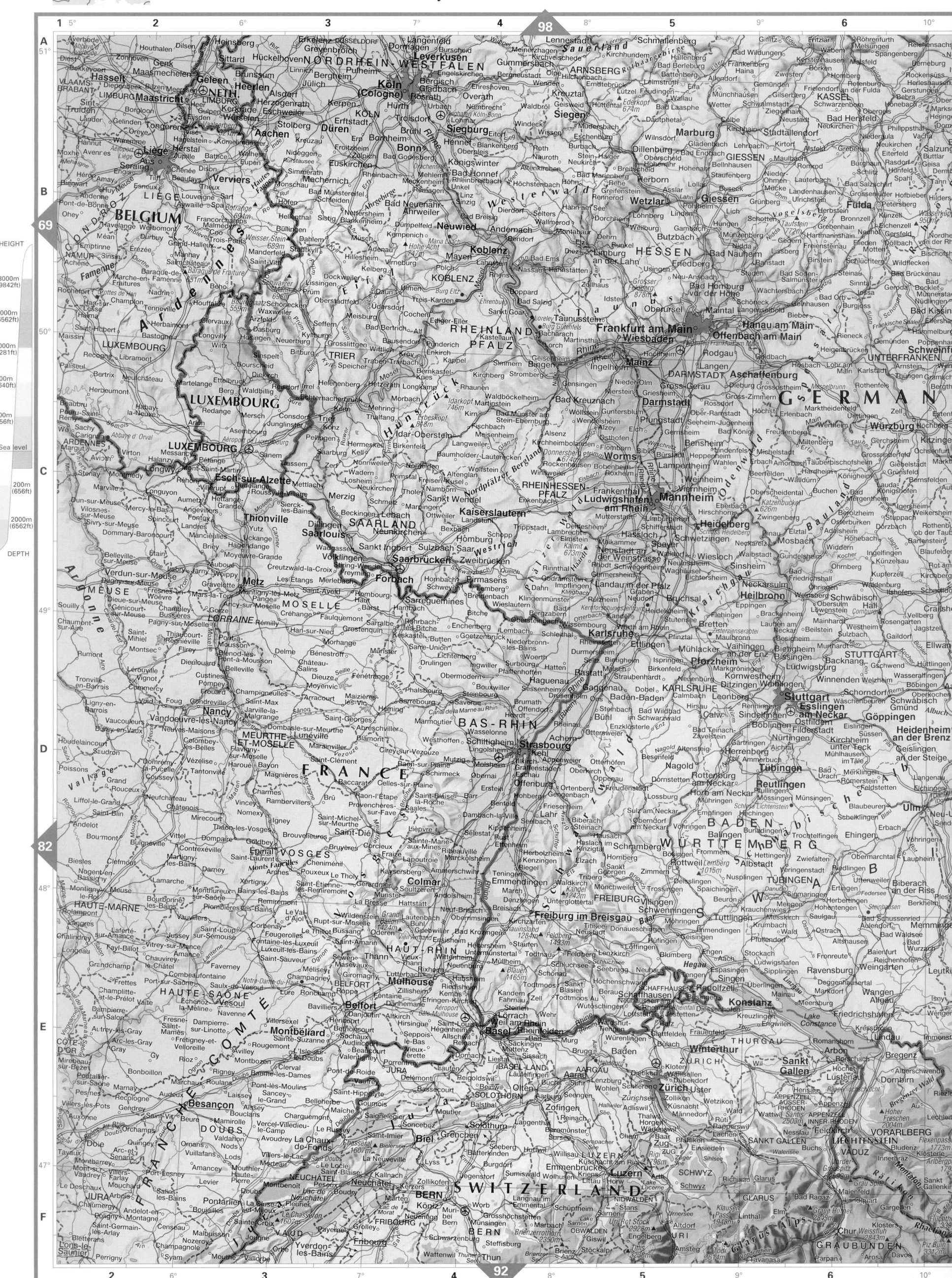

Scale 1:1,500,000

One centimetre represents 15 kilometres.

One inch represents approximately 24 miles.

BADEN-WÜRTTEMBERG AND Bavaria, the states of southern Germany, are large and prosperous. They embrace Stuttgart, maker of world-famous cars, and Munich, third largest of German cities, yet proudly provincial. They contain ancient universities such as Freiburg and Heidelberg, ethereal castles, and the Black Forest's pine-clad wilderness. Lake Constance is shared with Switzerland and Austria.

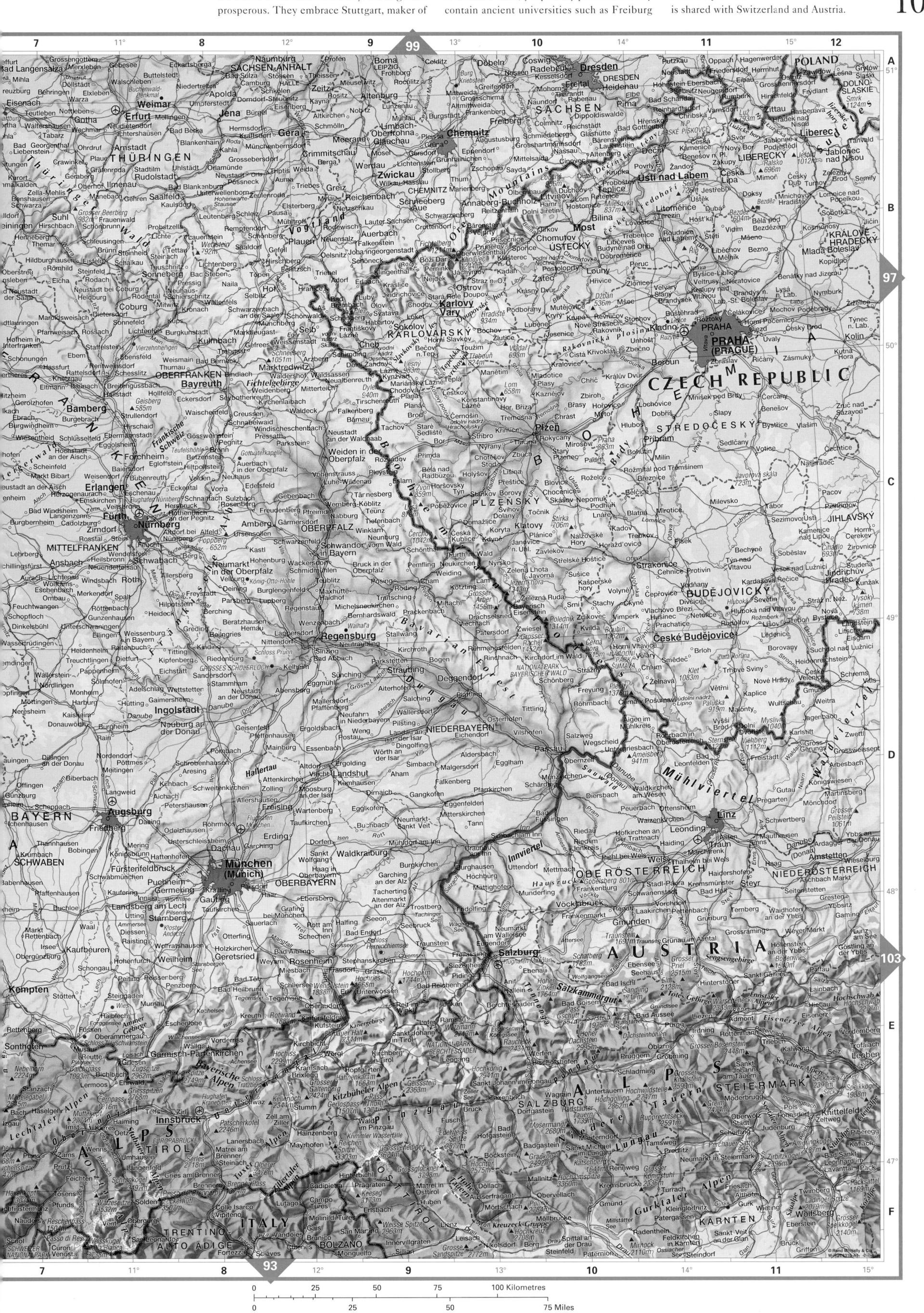

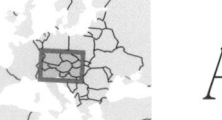

Scale 1:1,500,000

One centimetre represents 15 kilometres.

One inch represents approximately 24 miles.

Conic Equidistant Projection

MANY NORTH EUROPEANS see Austria as an intermediary between their own stern surroundings and the imagined joys of life in the south. It is an image that Austria has done much to foster in the gaiety of its music, in the elegance of its capital city, Vienna, and the exuberant baroque of its architecture. Nowhere is far from the mountains, with their sparkling air, tumbling rivers and numerous ski resorts.

103

South Central Europe

Conic Equidistant Projection

Scale 1:3,000,000

One centimetre represents 30 kilometres.

One inch represents approximately 47 miles.

| 0 | 50 | 100 | 150 | 200 | 250 | 300 Kilometres |

| 0 | 50 | 100 | 150 | 200 Miles |

HEIGHT

3000m (9842ft)

2000m (6562ft)

1000m (3281ft)

500m (1640ft)

200m (656ft)

Sea level

200m (656ft)

2000m (6562ft)

DEPTH

THE FORMER YUGOSLAVIA has fallen apart, but other states along the eastern Danube preserve their nationhood and seek to exploit their natural assets. Landlocked Hungary is dominated by a fertile plain where agriculture thrives; Bulgaria's long Black Sea coast attracts tourists; Romania drops from the forested Carpathian Mountains through rich farmlands to the wildlife paradise of the Danube delta.

105

Greece and Western Turkey

Conic Equidistant Projection

Scale 1:3,000,000

One centimetre represents 30 kilometres.

One inch represents approximately 47 miles.

THERE IS HARDLY a name on the map of Greece that does not evoke some memory in the rest of the world, or perhaps a touch of awe that such places as Marathon, Delphi and Mount Olympus are real. The islands of the Aegean are as full of beauty as the ancient poets proclaimed. Turkey, too, preserves settlements that date back 3000 years, and Istanbul remains the gateway between Europe and Asia.

107

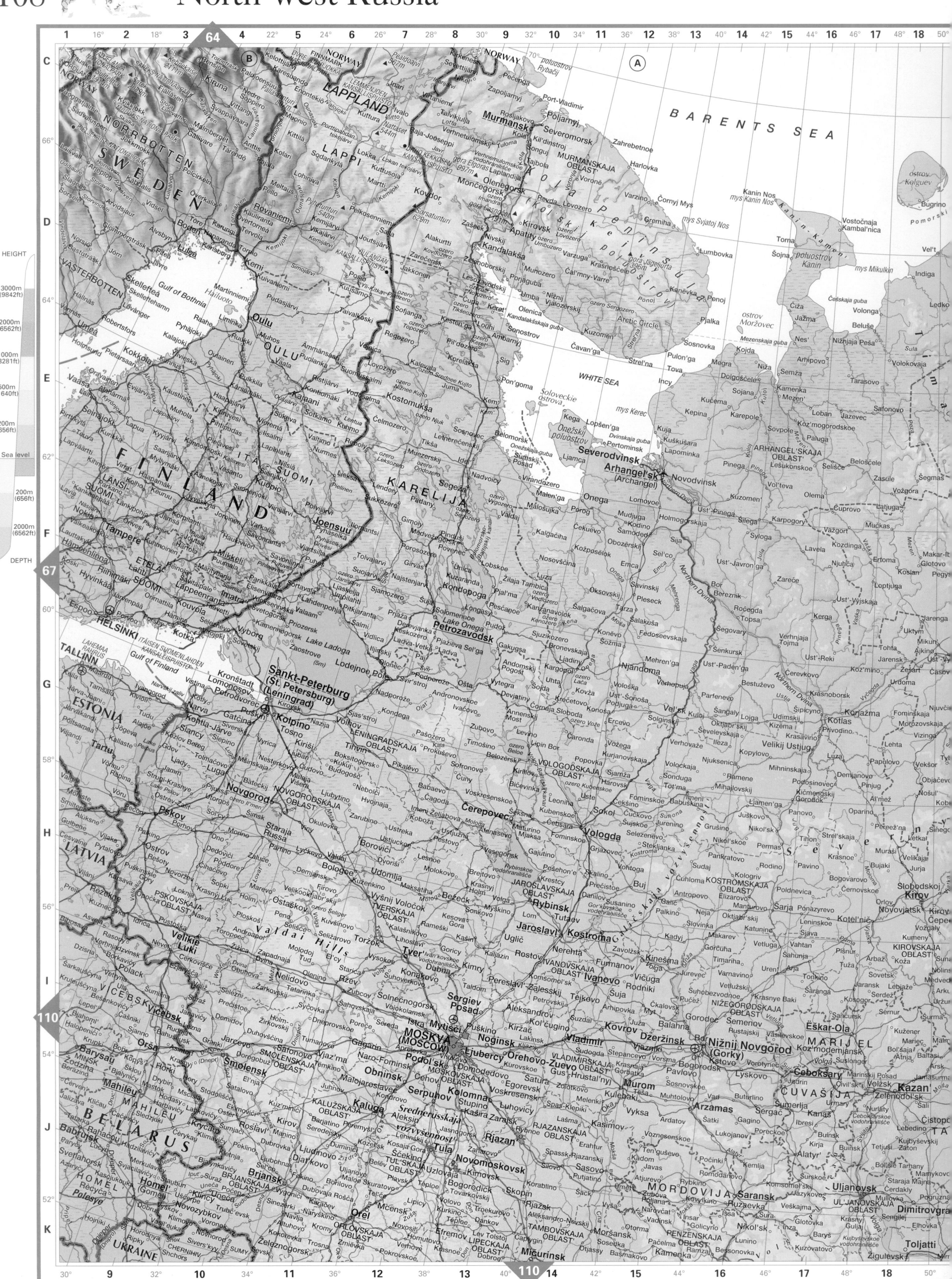

EUROPEAN RUSSIA IS the centre of the world's largest country, containing its two most important cities, Moscow and St Petersburg, and three-quarters of its population. The terrain is rolling steppe with forests and lakes in the north, where oil and gold reserves have made Archangel a boom city. The Volga, flowing south east for 3688 km (2292 miles), is Europe's longest river and an ancient trade link with Asia.

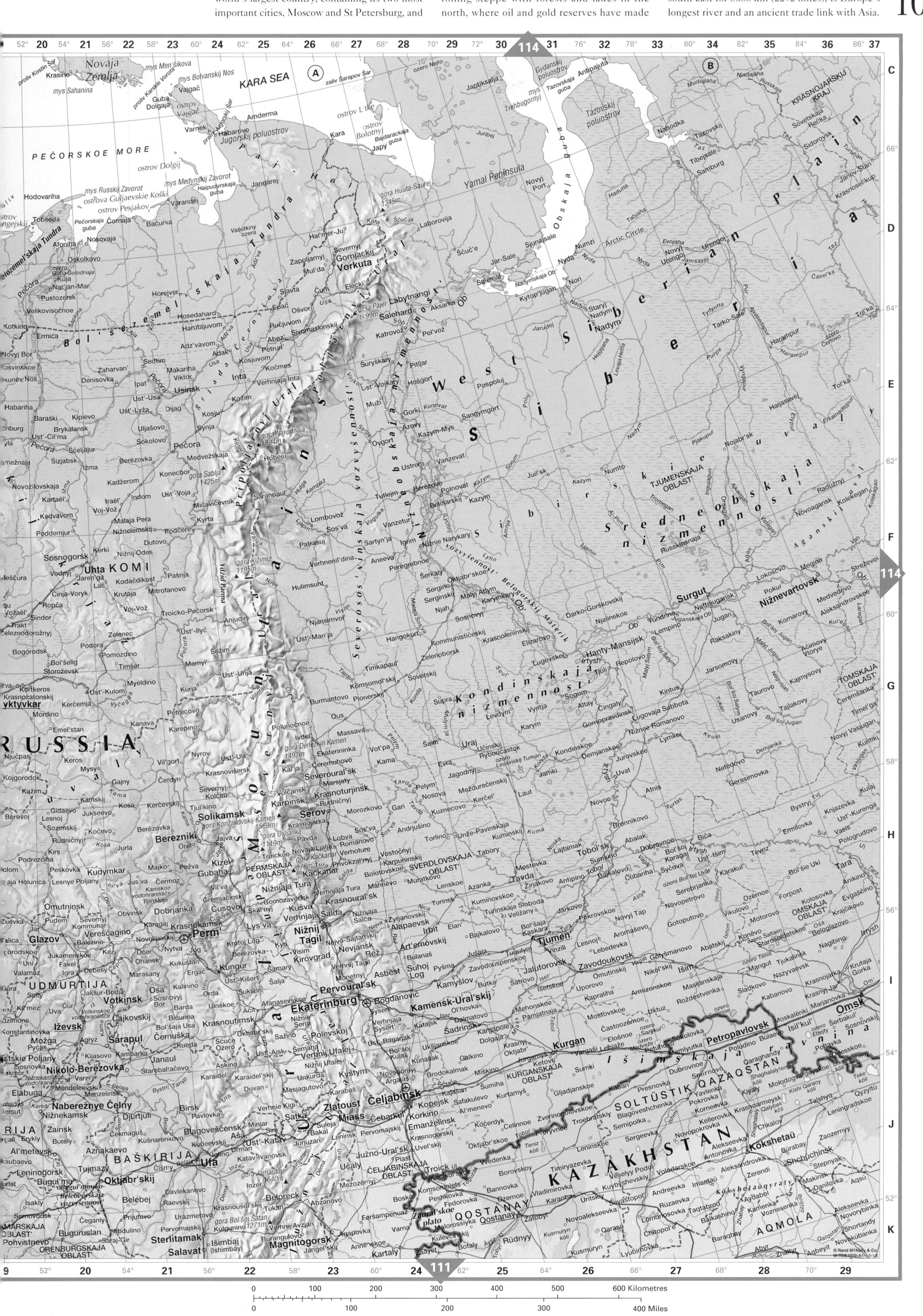

South-west Russia, Belarus and Ukraine

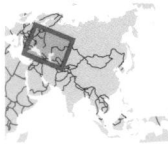

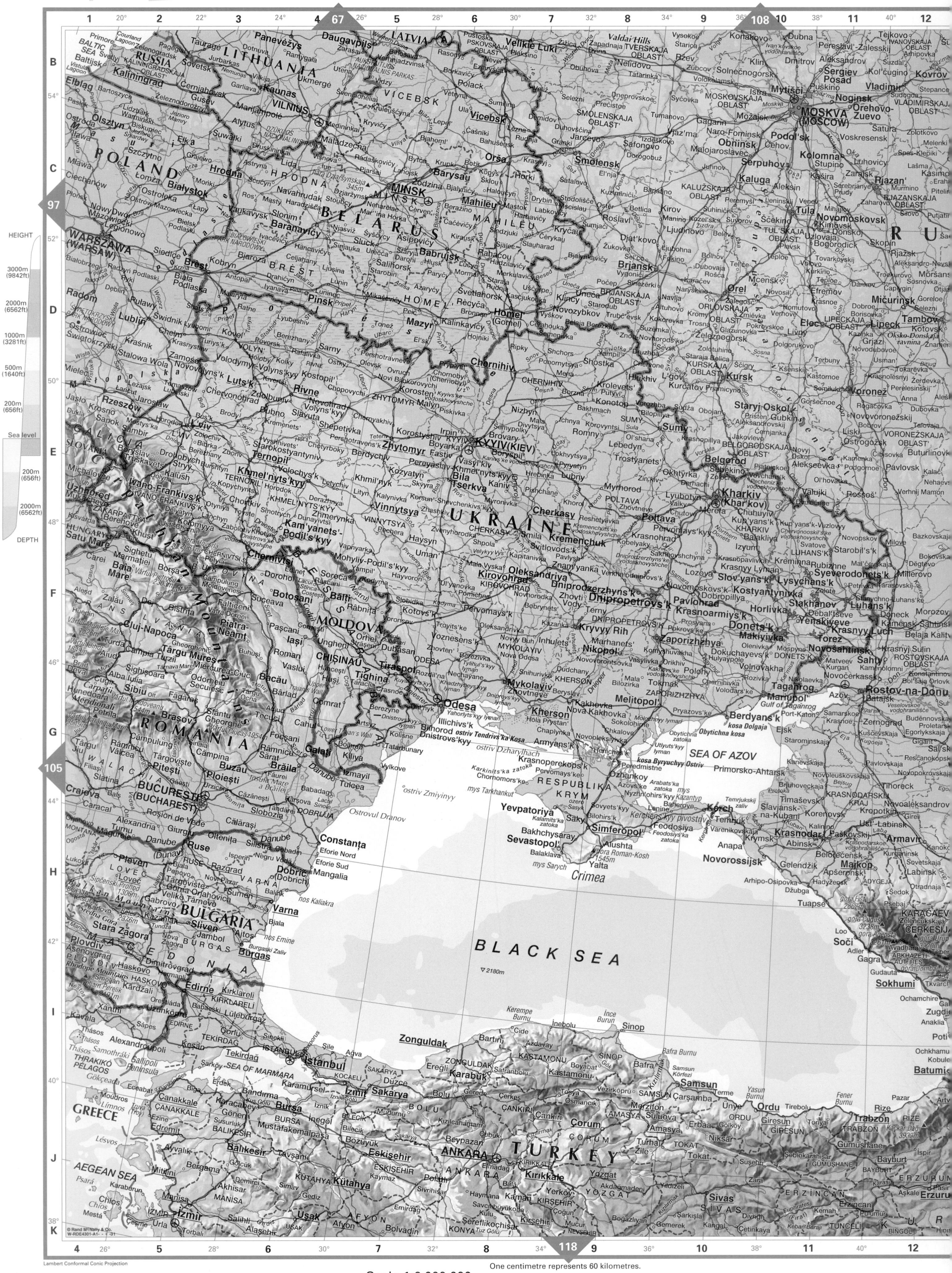

Lambert Conformal Conic Projection

Scale 1:6,000,000

One centimetre represents 60 kilometres.

One inch represents approximately 95 miles.

BELARUS, UKRAINE AND Russia, the key republics of the USSR, were also the three that dissolved it in the Minsk Declaration of 1991. Now, within the looser federation of the Commonwealth of Independent States, each on its own strives for political stability and economic progress. Russia still plays a dominant role, but the Ukraine has vast potential in its fertile soil, industries and Black Sea coastline.

ASIA

A THIRD OF THE world's landmass, Asia is where 60 per cent of its people live. It embraces permafrost, jungle, desert and Earth's highest and lowest surface points in Everest and the Dead Sea. In this continent civilisation was born, and from it the great religions emerged.

Lambert Azimuthal Equal Area Projection

Scale 1:28,000,000

One centimetre represents 280 kilometres.

One inch represents approximately 440 miles.

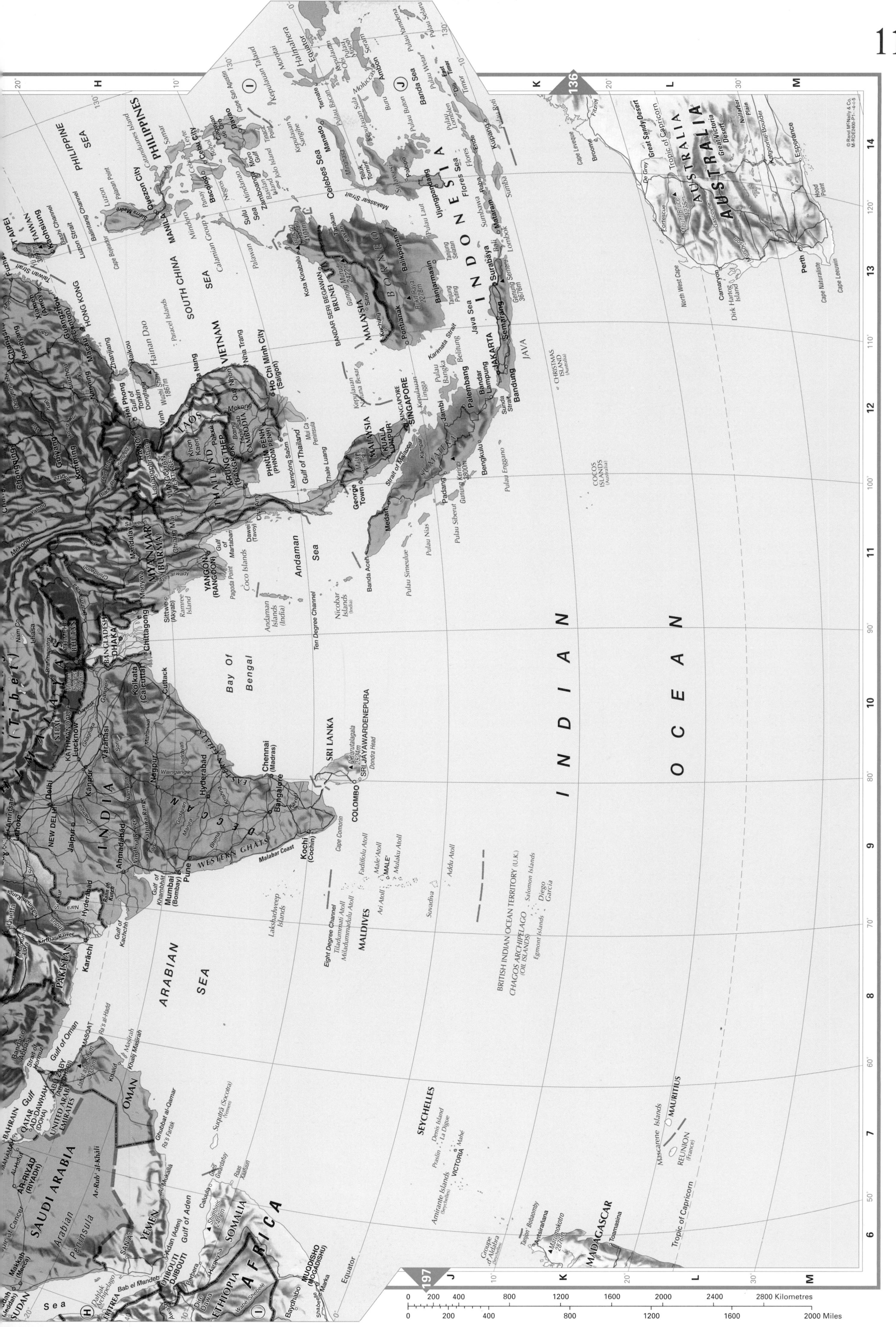

AUSTRALIA

Great Sandy Desert

Great Victoria Desert

Tropic of Capricorn

Perth

Cape Leeuwin

Cape Naturaliste

Esperance

PHILIPPINE
SEA

TAIPEI

Kaohsiung

TAIWAN

HONG KONG

Macau

SOUTH CHINA
SEA

PHILIPPINES

Luzon

MANILA

Quezon City

Cebu City

Bacolod

Davao

Mindanao

Palawan

Celebes Sea

INDONESIA

BORNEO

MALAYSIA

BANDAR SERI BEGAWAN

BRUNEI

Kota Kinabalu

Banjarmasin

Balikpapan

Pontianak

Kuching

Banda Sea

Halmahera

Equator

Molucca Sea

Manado

Flores Sea

Java Sea

Makassar Strait

Timor
Sea

JAVA

JAKARTA

Bandung

Semarang

Surabaya

Ujungpandang

Bali

Lombok

Sumbawa

Flores

Kupang

VIETNAM

Da Nang

Nha Trang

Ho Chi Minh City
(Saigon)

LAOS

THAILAND

KRUNG THEP
(BANGKOK)

CAMBODIA

PHNOM PENH

Gulf of Thailand

MYANMAR
(BURMA)

Mandalay

YANGON
(RANGOON)

Andaman
Sea

Gulf of
Martaban

Bay Of
Bengal

SRI LANKA

COLOMBO

Chennai
(Madras)

Bangalore

Hyderabad

INDIA

Mumbai
(Bombay)

Pune

WESTERN GHATS

Kochi
(Cochin)

Malabar Coast

Cape Comorin

MALDIVES

MALE'

DECCAN

Nagpur

Ahmadabad

Jaipur

NEW DELHI

Delhi

Kanpur

Lucknow

KATHMANDU

NEPAL

BHUTAN

BANGLADESH

DHAKA

Chittagong

Kolkata
(Calcutta)

Cuttack

HIMALAYA

(Tibet)

Lhasa

ARABIAN
SEA

PAKISTAN

Karachi

Hyderabad

Gulf of
Kachchh

Gulf of
Khambhat

BRITISH INDIAN OCEAN TERRITORY (U.K.)

CHAGOS ARCHIPELAGO
(OIL ISLANDS)

Diego
Garcia

Salomon Islands

Egmont Islands

INDIAN

OCEAN

COCOS
ISLANDS
(Australia)

CHRISTMAS
ISLAND
(Australia)

SEYCHELLES

VICTORIA

MAURITIUS

REUNION
(France)

Mascarene Islands

MADAGASCAR

Tropic of Capricorn

OMAN

MASQAT

Gulf of Oman

UNITED ARAB
EMIRATES

ABU ZABY
(ABU DHABI)

QATAR

AD-DAWHAH
(DOHA)

BAHRAIN

Gulf

Strait of
Hormuz

SAUDI ARABIA

AR-RIYAD
(RIYADH)

Arabian
Peninsula

YEMEN

SANA

Gulf of Aden

DJIBOUTI

DJIBOUTI

ERITREA

ETHIOPIA

SOMALIA

MUQDISHO
(MOGADISHU)

AFRICA

Equator

Red
Sea

SUDAN

Bab el Mandeb

© Rand McNally & Co.
M-RDE800-P1-4-4-5

| 0 | 200 | 400 | 800 | 1200 | 1600 | 2000 | 2400 | 2800 Kilometres |

| 0 | 200 | 400 | 800 | 1200 | 1600 | 2000 Miles |

Northern Asia

BESTRIDING NORTHERN ASIA is the tremendous bulk of Siberia and eastern Russia. The region's turbulent history is matched by the volcanic drama of the Kamchatka Peninsula, while the waters of Lake Baikal offer a peaceful contrast. A panorama of immense birch forests

Lambert Azimuthal Equal Area

Scale 1:18,000,000

One centimetre represents 180 kilometres.

One inch represents approximately 284 miles.

punctuated by brightly painted villages unrolls
along the Trans-Siberian Railway on the 6½ day
journey between Moscow and Vladivostok.

115

HINGED BY THE towering Hindu Kush, Afghanistan is the swing door of Asia. On one side, via the Kyber Pass, is the sub-continent of India, while on the other lie the former Soviet republics of Tajikistan, Uzbekistan, Kyrgyzstan, Turkmenistan and Kazakhstan. Today the Kyber Pass, the route of traders and invaders, leads into Pakistan, a nation divided between hill and plains dwellers though bound by Islam.

117

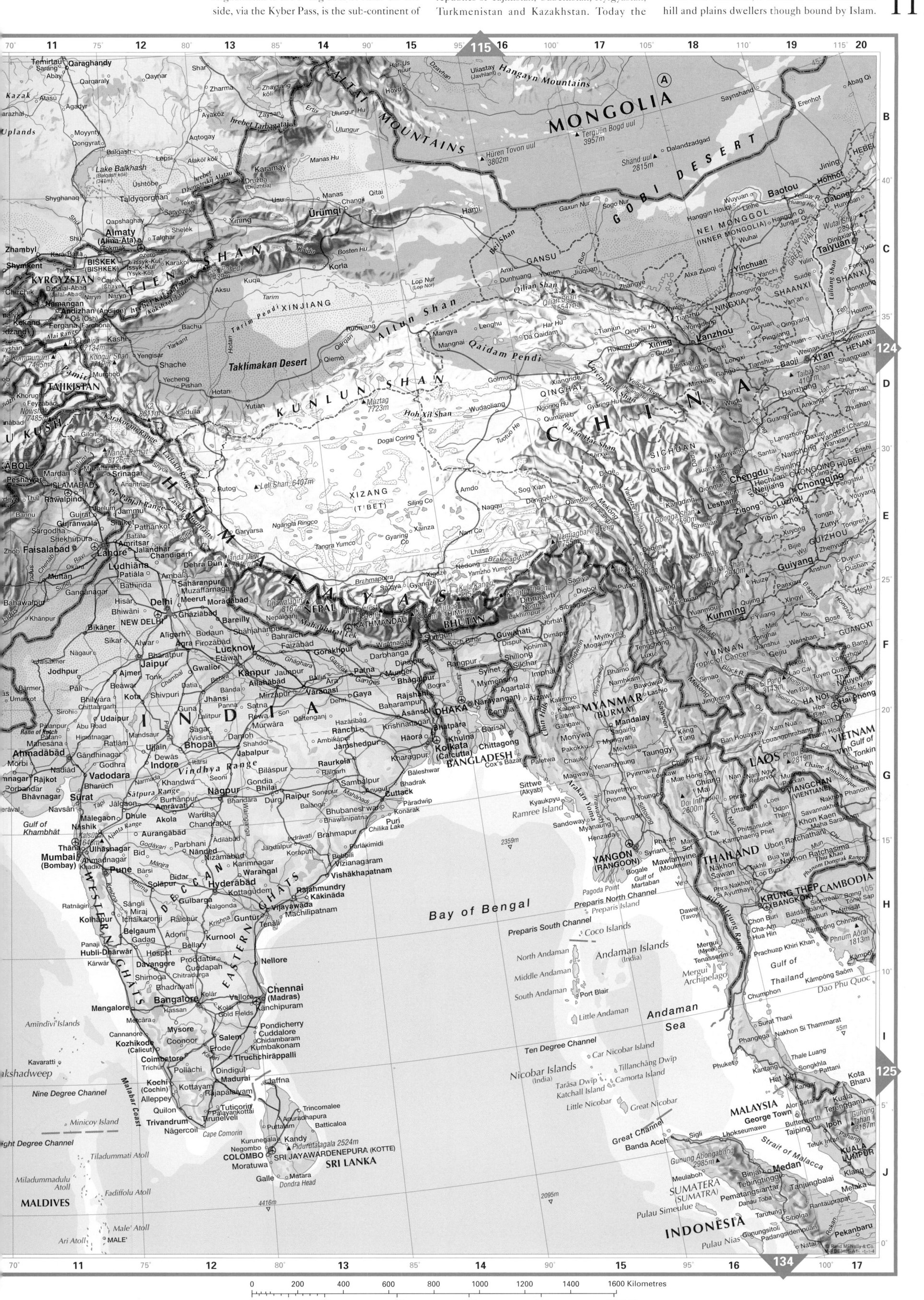

0   200   400   600   800   1000   1200   1400   1600 Kilometres

0   200   400   600   800   1000 Miles

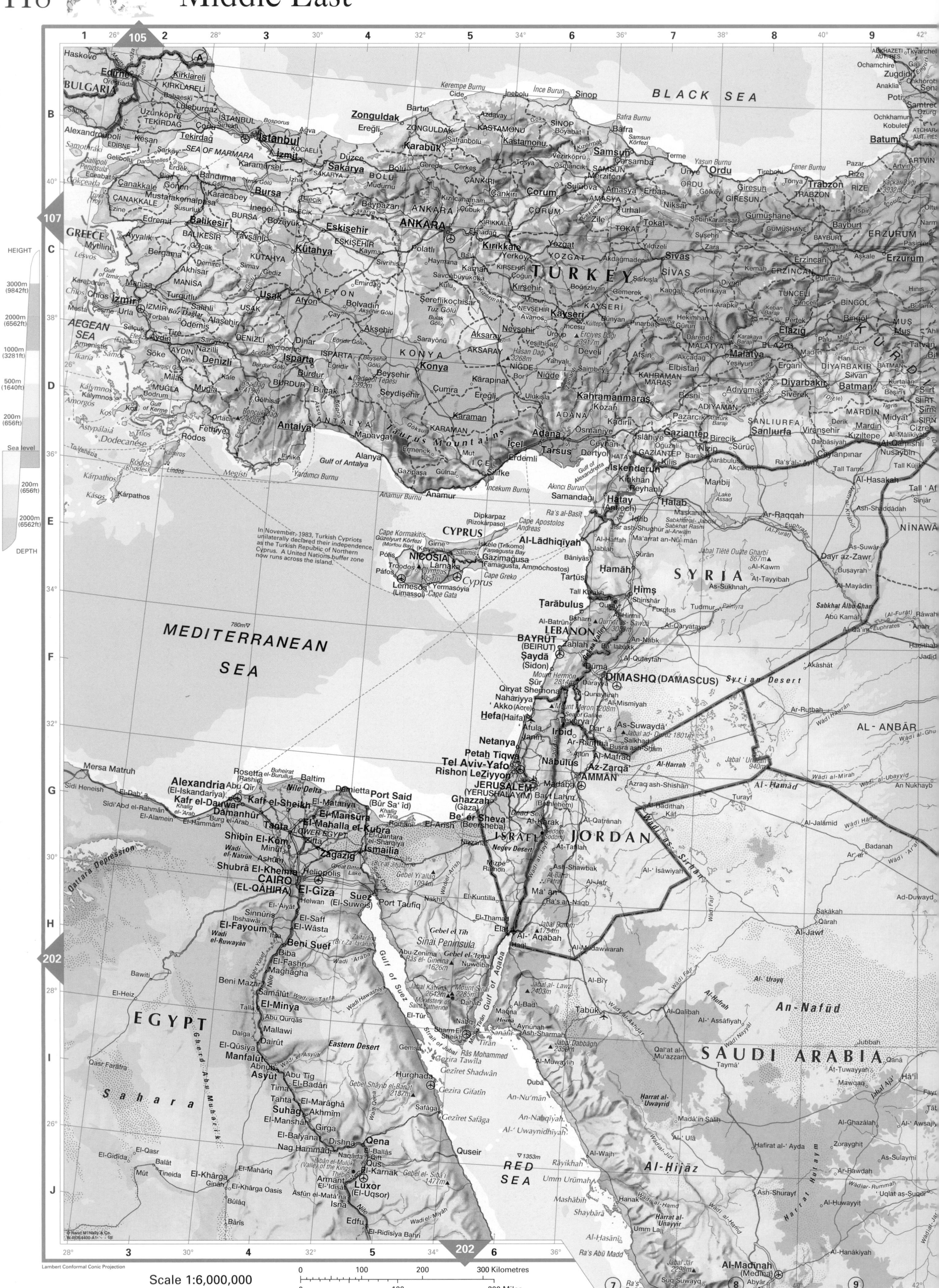

Scale 1:6,000,000

0   100   200   300 Kilometres
0   100   200 Miles

CIVILISATIONS ROSE AND fell in the lands at the head of the Persian Gulf. Where Iraq is now, Babylon and Assyria once flourished, and there too was Mesopotamia, the land between Tigris and Euphrates whose annual flooding facilitated early agriculture. Damascus may be the world's oldest city, and Iran is ancient Persia. Each of these desert nations has been made rich by oil, but it has brought them little joy.

119

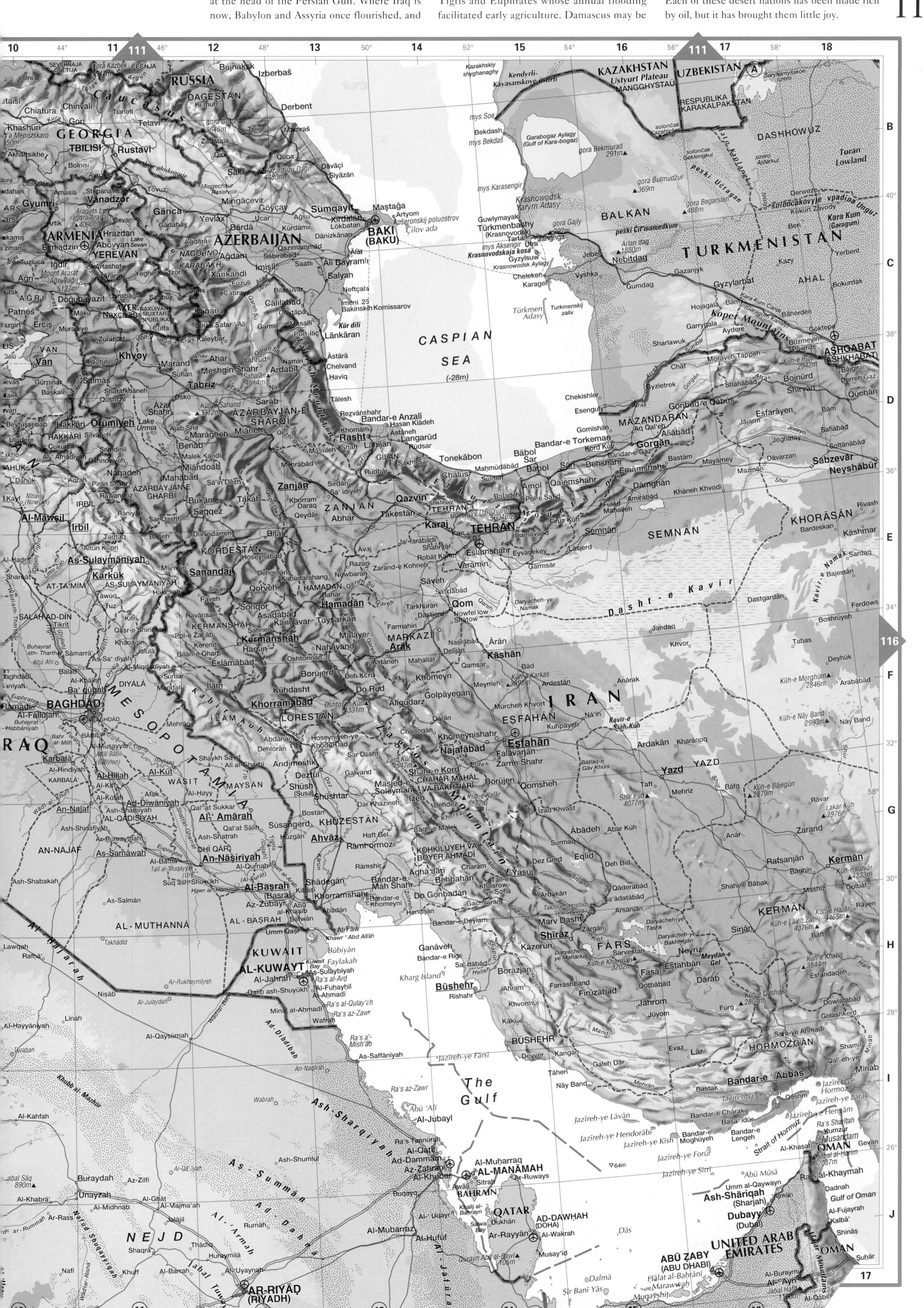

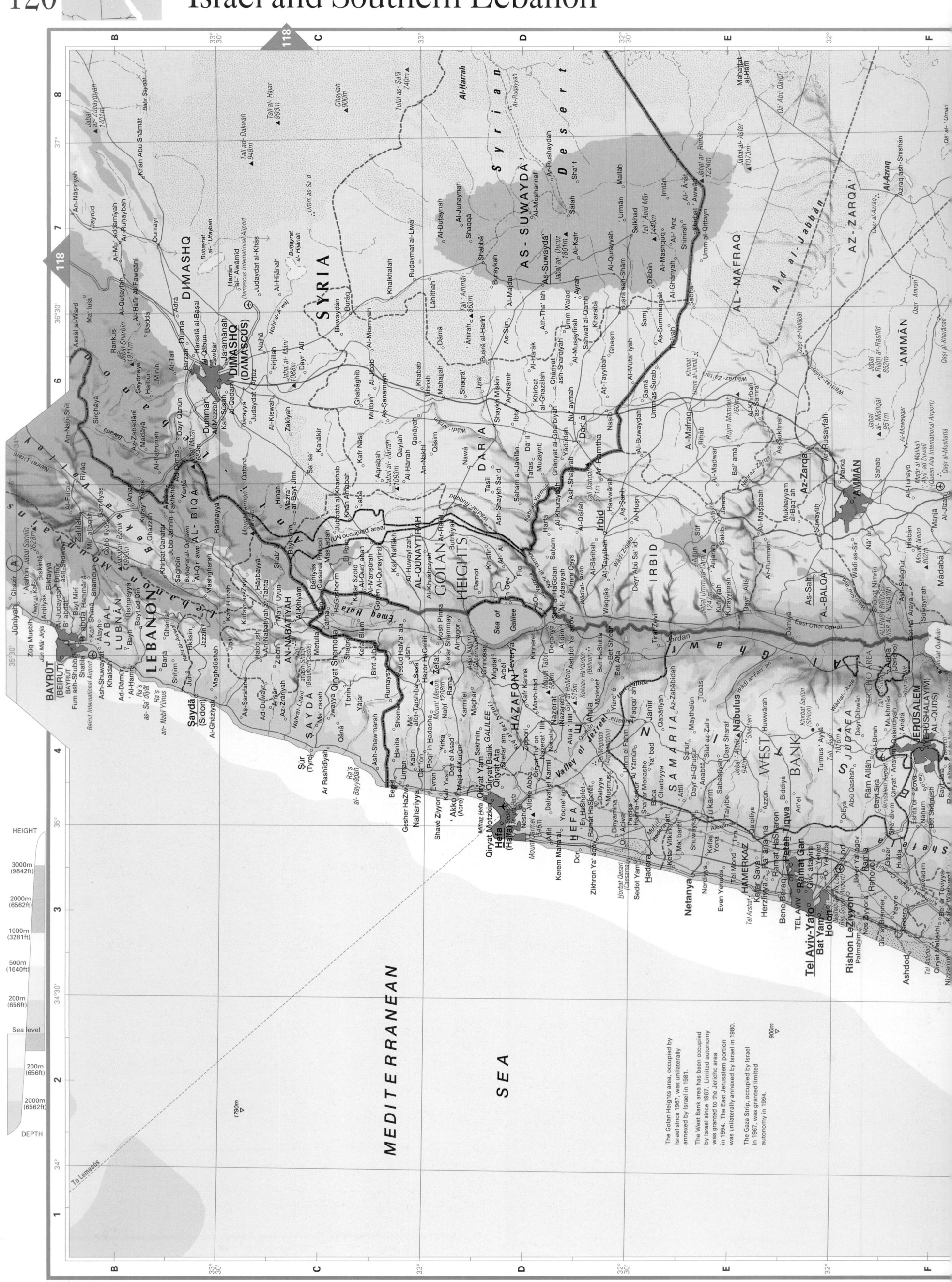

HEIGHT

3000m
(9842ft)

2000m
(6562ft)

1000m
(3281ft)

500m
(1640ft)

200m
(656ft)

Sea level

200m
(656ft)

2000m
(6562ft)

DEPTH

The Golan Heights area, occupied by
Israel since 1967, was unilaterally
annexed by Israel in 1981.

The West Bank area has been occupied
by Israel since 1967. Limited autonomy
was granted to the Jericho area
in 1994. The East Jerusalem portion
was unilaterally annexed by Israel in 1980.

The Gaza Strip, occupied by Israel
in 1967, was granted limited
autonomy in 1994.

Lambert Conformal Conic Projection

Scale 1:1,000,000

One centimetre represents 10 kilometres.

One inch represents approximately 16 miles.

AMONG THE SHRINES of Islam, Judaism and Christianity, modern Israel in a short half-century created a Jewish homeland and made the desert productive, but not without bitter conflicts with its neighbours. Despite the loss of the West Bank, Jordan still tries to keep a balance in the area. Lebanon, once a jewel of the Mediterranean, is gradually recovering from the ravages of a 16 year civil war.

121

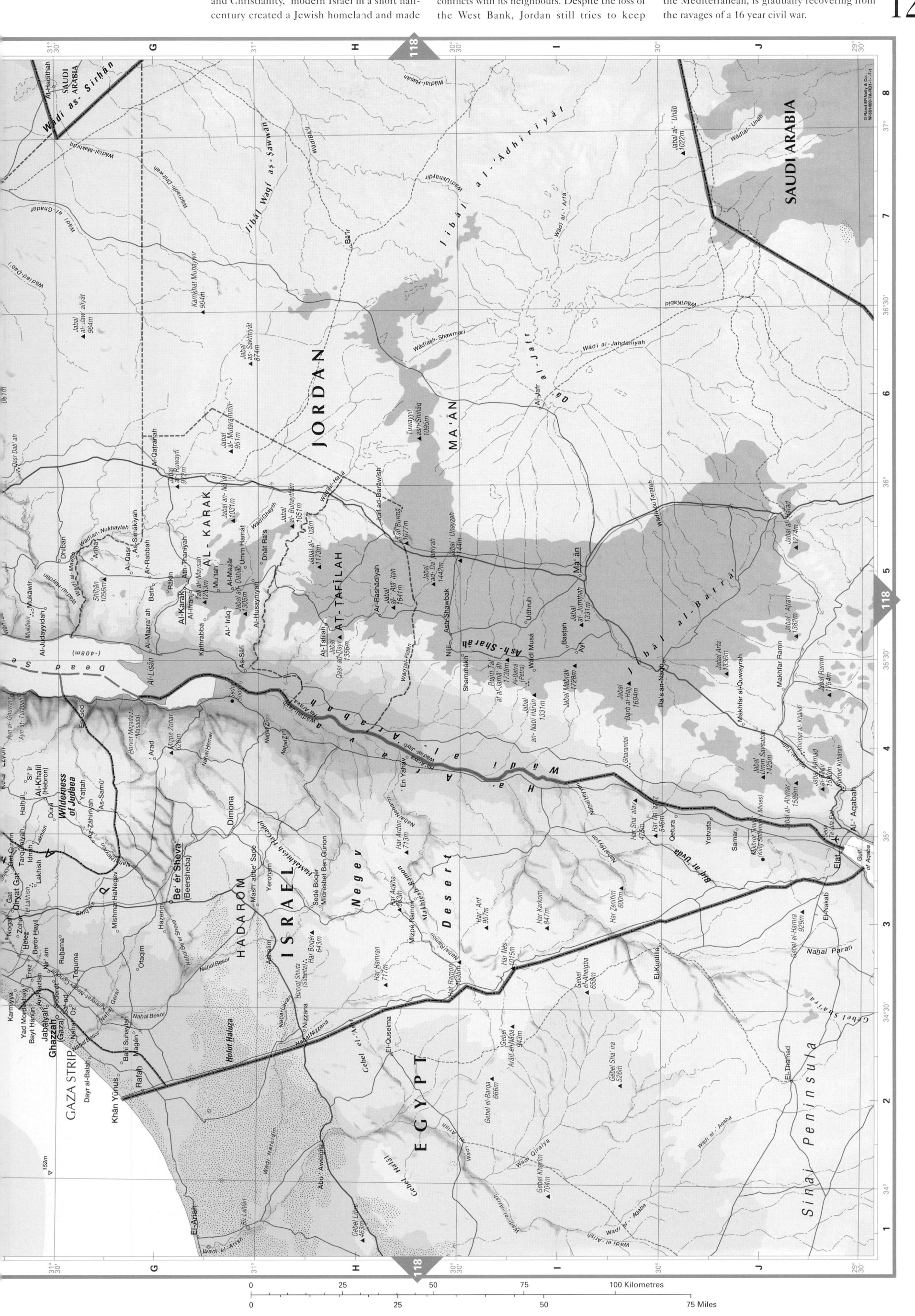

HEIGHT

3000m
(9842ft)

2000m
(6562ft)

1000m
(3281ft)

500m
(1640ft)

200m
(656ft)

Sea level

200m
(656ft)

2000m
(6562ft)

DEPTH

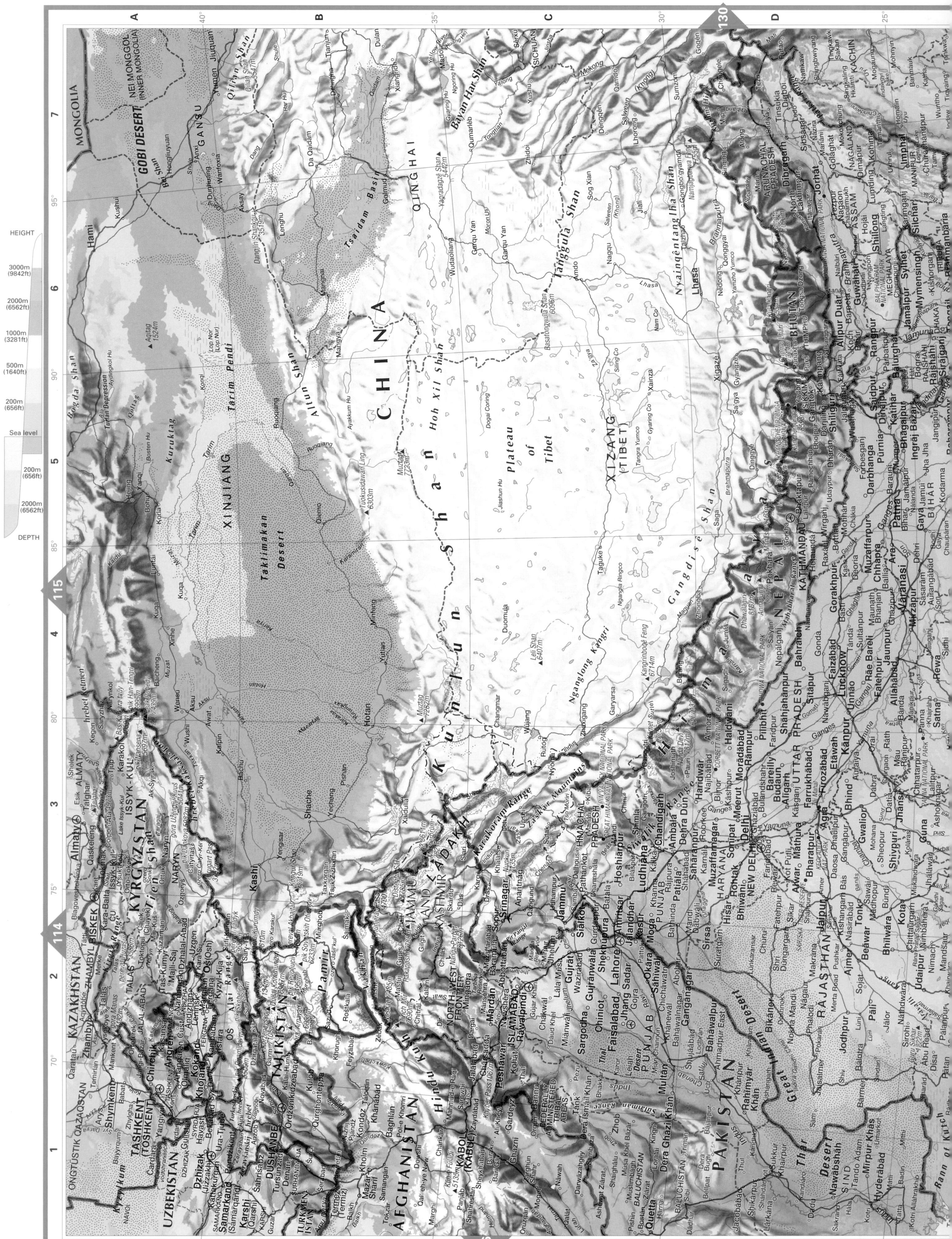

Lambert Conformal Conic Projection

Scale 1:9,000,000

One centimetre represents 90 kilometres.

One inch represents approximately 142 miles.

INDIA IS MORE a continent than a country, with a continent's variety in landscapes, from northern snows to southern jungles, in peoples, languages and customs. Its cap is the awesome beauty of the Himalayas and Kashmir. Below are Uttar Pradesh and the flat Ganges plain, in contrast to the romantic palaces of Rajasthan. There are teeming cities like Kolkata - and the ancient, silent temples of Mararashtra.

123

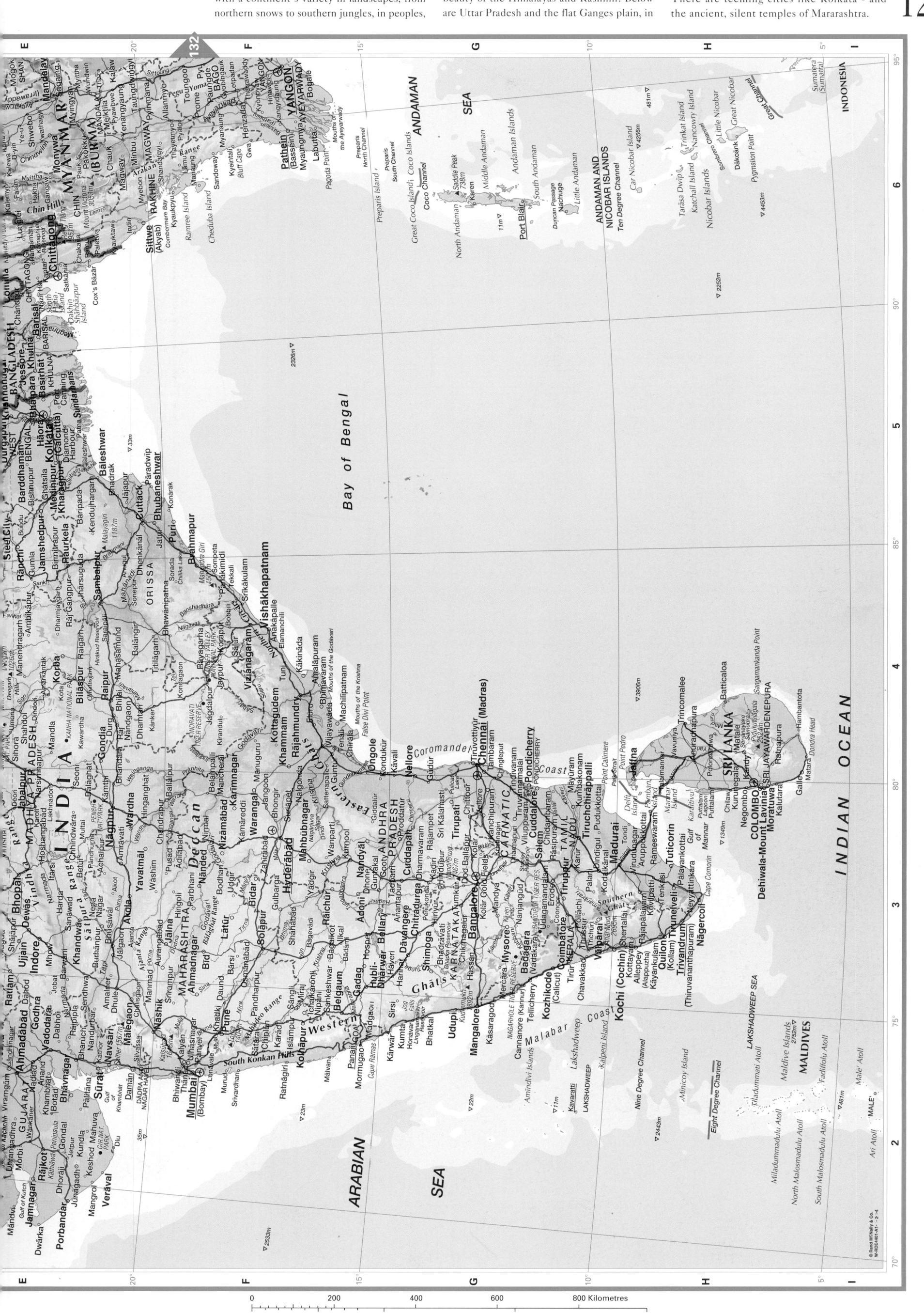

0   200   400   600   800 Kilometres

0   200   400   600 Miles

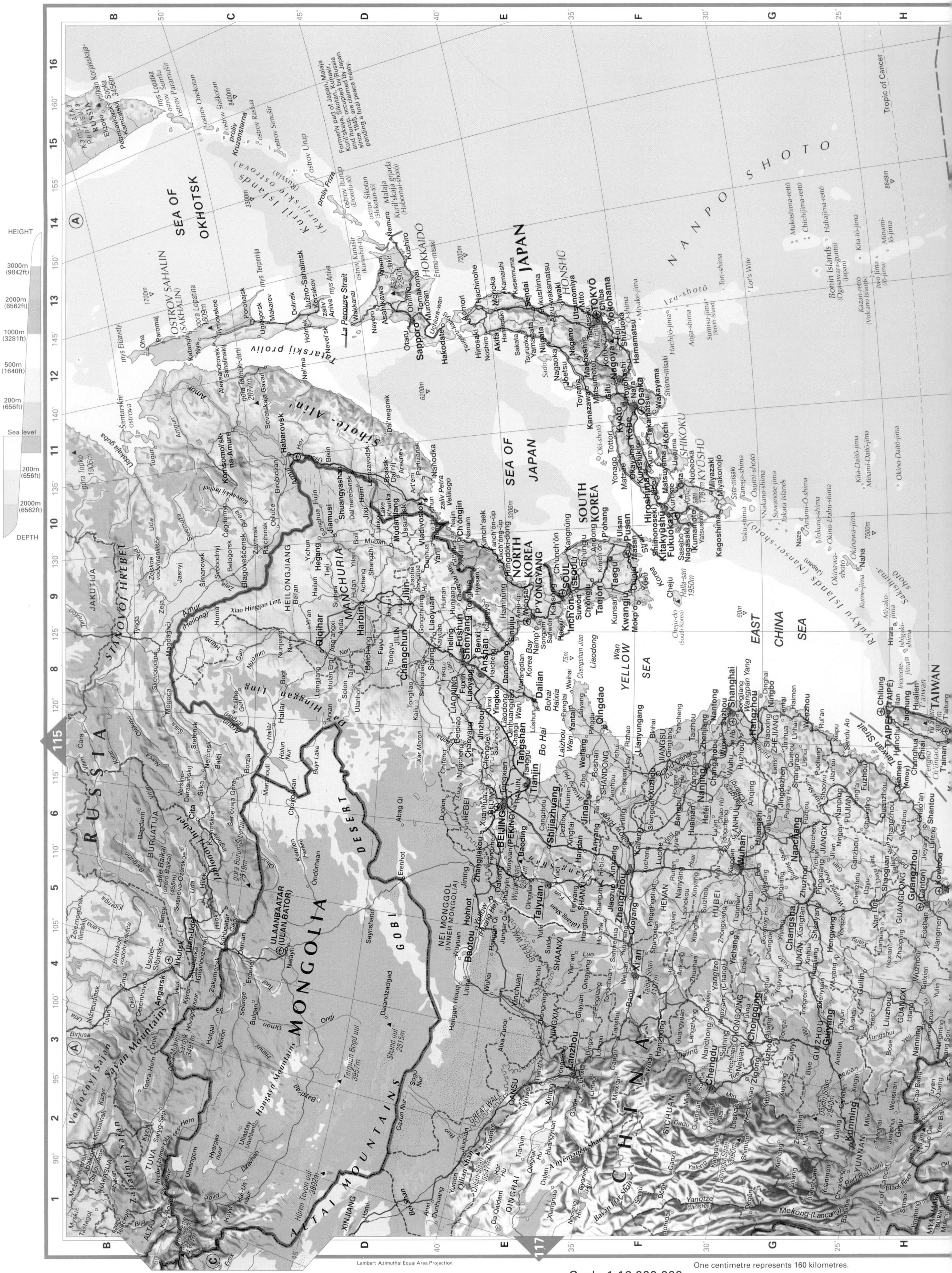

THE CHINA SEA is divided into East and South by the Taiwan Strait. About its shores are ancient empires and kingdoms, many peoples and ideologies. Once pirate-haunted, the China Sea is now a trading area served by ports like Hong Kong, Shanghai, Manila and Singapore.

125

PACIFIC OCEAN

PHILIPPINE SEA

NORTHERN MARIANA ISLANDS (U.S.)

GUAM (U.S.)
HAGÅTÑA

Challenger Deep ▼10915m

FEDERATED STATES OF MICRONESIA

Caroline Islands

PALAU
KOROR

BISMARCK SEA
Bismarck Archipelago
New Ireland
New Britain

SOLOMON SEA

D'Entrecasteaux Islands

PAPUA NEW GUINEA
PORT MORESBY
Gulf of Papua

Owen Stanley Range

CORAL SEA

Torres Strait
Cape York
Cape York Peninsula

AUSTRALIA
NORTHERN TERRITORY
Darwin

ARAFURA SEA

TIMOR SEA

BANDA SEA (LAUT BANDA)

MOLUCCAS (MALUKU)

Molucca Sea (Laut Maluku)

Halmahera

Ceram Sea

IRIAN JAYA

Jayapura

PHILIPPINES
MANILA
Quezon City
Luzon
Sierra Madre
Mindoro
Panay
Negros
Cebu City
Bacolod
Samar
Leyte
Mindanao
Davao
General Santos

SULU SEA

CELEBES SEA

SULAWESI (CELEBES)

Ujungpandang
Makassar Strait (Selat Makasar)

BORNEO

KALIMANTAN

MALAYSIA
BRUNEI
BANDAR SERI BEGAWAN
Kota Kinabalu

SOUTH CHINA SEA

Spratly Islands
(claimed by Brunei, China, Malaysia, the Philippines, Taiwan and Vietnam)

Paracel Islands
(claimed by China, Taiwan and Vietnam)

Hainan Dao
HAIKOU

VIETNAM
Da Nang
HO CHI MINH CITY (SAIGON)

CAMBODIA
PHNOM PENH

THAILAND
KRUNG THEP (BANGKOK)

Gulf of Thailand

Mekong

MALAYSIA
KUALA LUMPUR

SINGAPORE
SINGAPORE

SUMATERA (SUMATRA)

Palembang

INDONESIA

JAVA SEA (LAUT JAWA)

JAKARTA
Bandung
Semarang
Surabaya
JAVA (JAWA)
Yogyakarta

BALI SEA
Bali
Denpasar

FLORES SEA (LAUT FLORES)
Flores

SAVU SEA
Timor
Kupang

LESSER SUNDA ISLANDS

GREATER SUNDA ISLANDS

CHRISTMAS ISLAND (Australia)

INDIAN OCEAN

© Rand McNally & Co.

0 200 400 600 800 1000 1200 1400 1600 Kilometres
0 200 400 600 800 1000 Miles

Japan

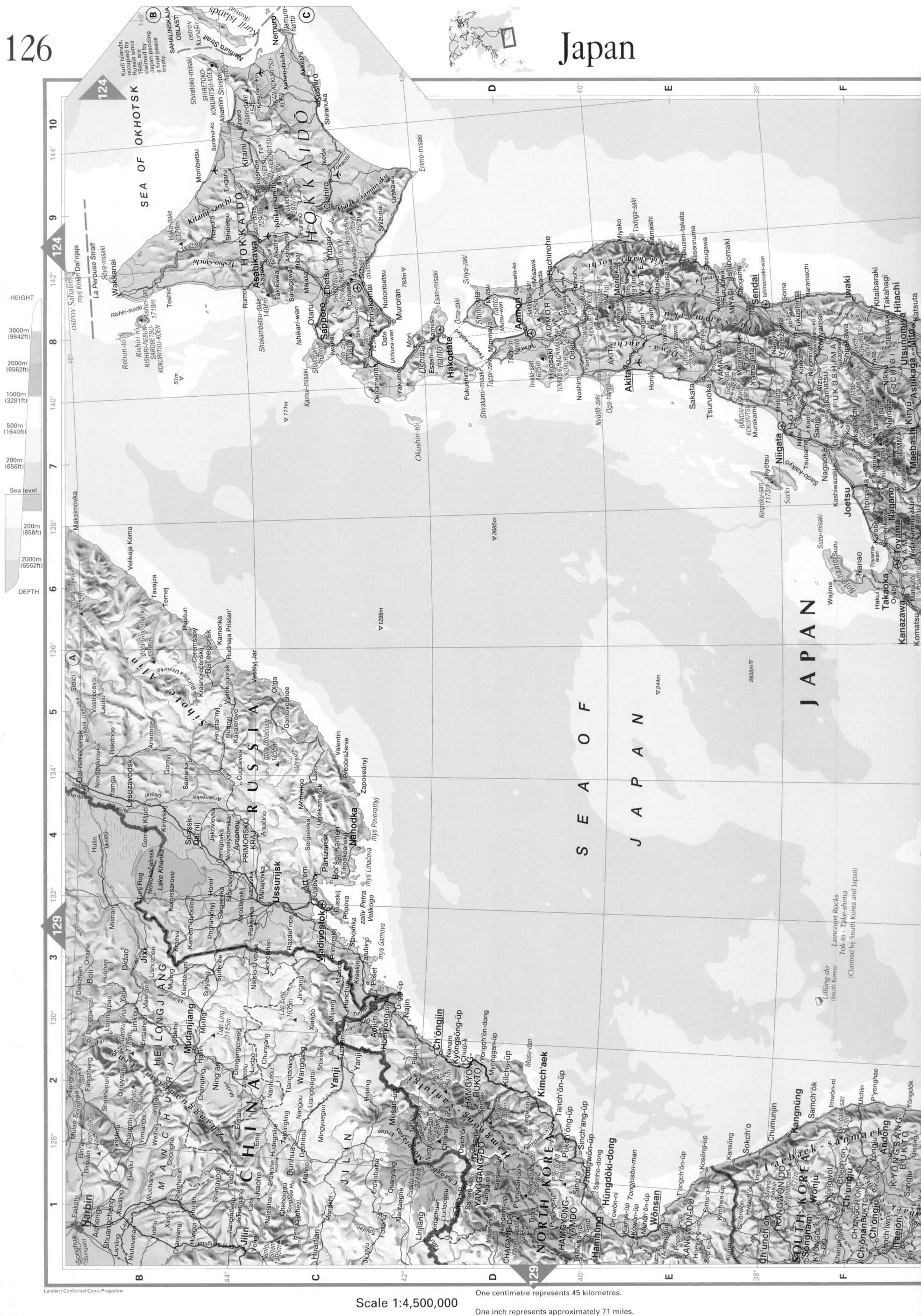

Lambert Conformal Conic Projection

Scale 1:4,500,000

One centimetre represents 45 kilometres.

One inch represents approximately 71 miles.

A NATION OFF whose coasts lie both tropical reefs and ice floes, Japan extends through some 4000 islands, of which four – Honshu, Kyushu, Shikoku and Hokkaido – are the largest. About 80 per cent of the country is mountainous, the small remainder being coastal plains into which industry, tiny farms, cities and suburbs crowd together. Earthquakes are a constant menace in a nation that straddles the Pacific 'ring of fire'.

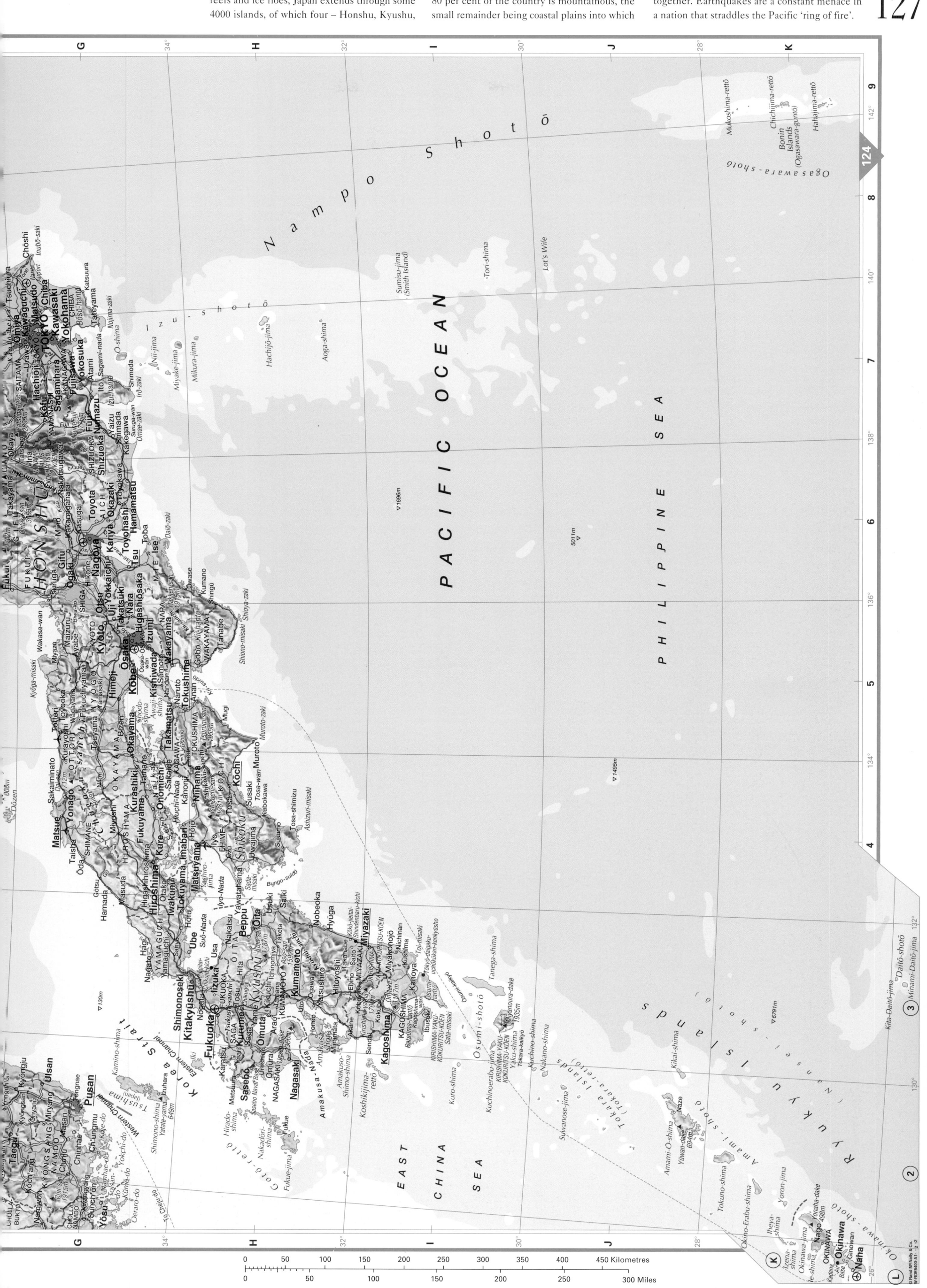

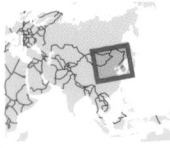

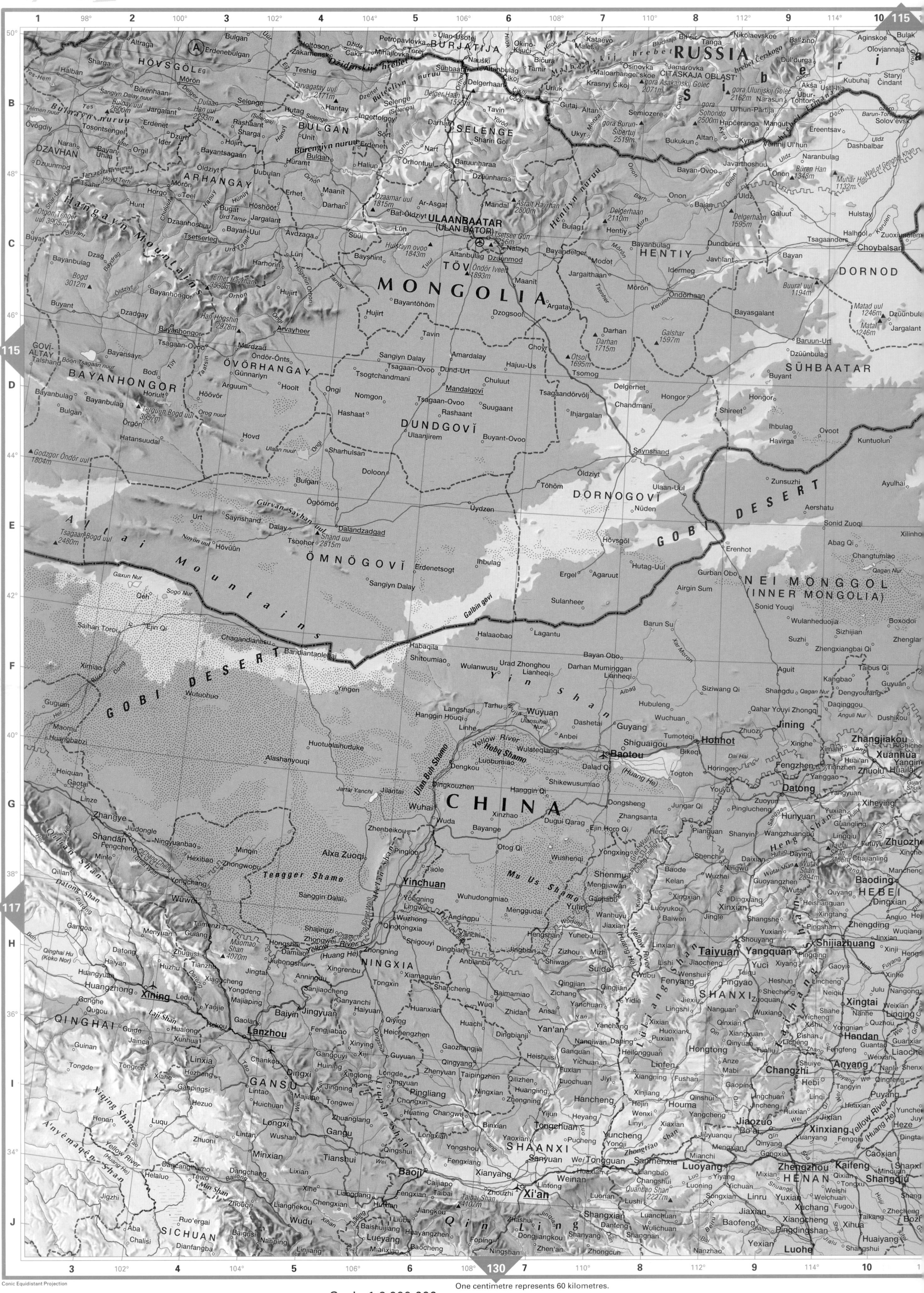

HEIGHT

3000m
(9842ft)

2000m
(6562ft)

1000m
(3281ft)

500m
(1640ft)

200m
(656ft)

Sea level

200m
(656ft)

2000m
(6562ft)

DEPTH

Conic Equidistant Projection

Scale 1:6,000,000

One centimetre represents 60 kilometres.

One inch represents approximately 95 miles.

FOR 2500 YEARS the Chinese called their land the Middle Kingdom – that is, the centre of the Universe. This sense of superior isolation was buttressed in 206 BC by the building of a Great Wall. Beijing, part monument to old Imperial China and part industrial conurbation, has a population of 11 million. Neighbouring North Korea, isolated under the world's only Marxist dynasty, is at permanent odds with South Korea.

129

0   100   200   300   400   500   600 Kilometres

0   100   200   300   400 Miles

Scale 1:6,000,000

Conic Equidistant Projection

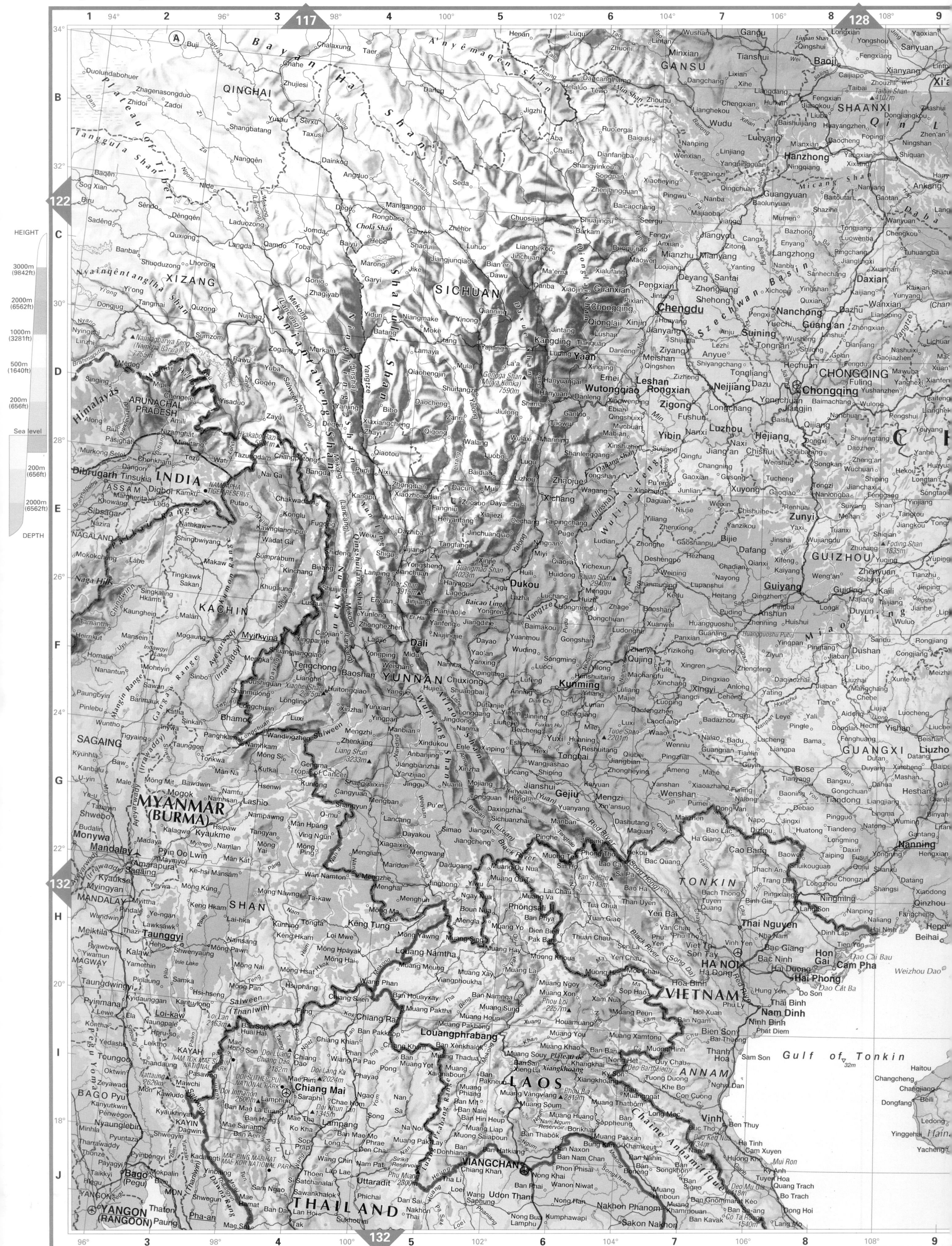

One centimetre represents 60 kilometres.

One inch represents approximately 95 miles.

PADDY FIELDS AND terraced hillsides in the green and well-watered south create the most familiar image of China to Western eyes. But today Shanghai, overflowing with foreign investment, sprouts factories and skyscrapers. In Guanghzhou (Canton), the country's gateway for 1000 years, trade is booming, and even the island province of Hainan is offering tropical beach holidays to people from Hong Kong.

131

South-east Asia

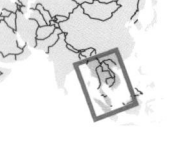

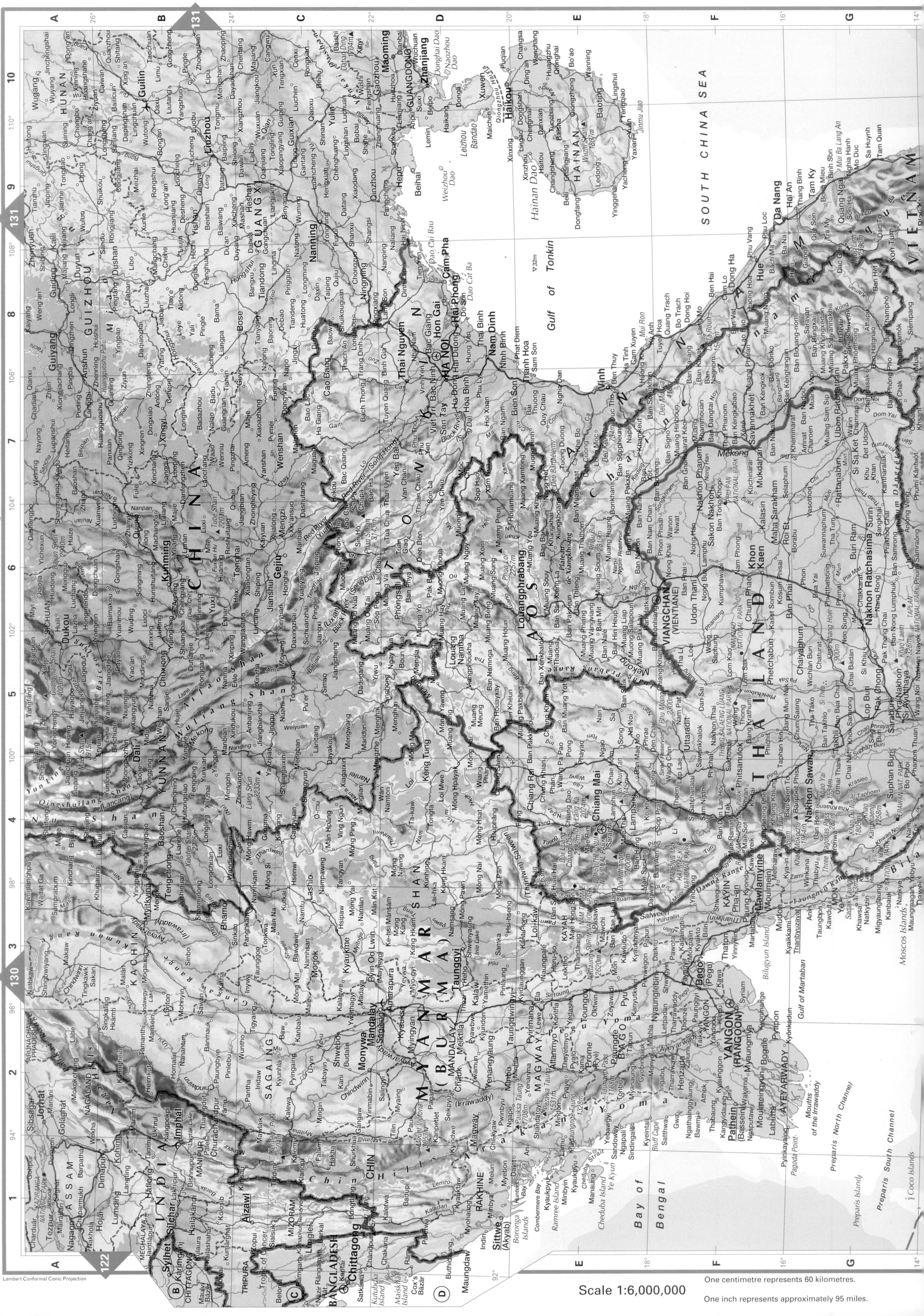

HEIGHT
3000m (9842ft)
2000m (6562ft)
1000m (3281ft)
500m (1640ft)
200m (656ft)
Sea level
200m (656ft)
2000m (6562ft)
DEPTH

Lambert Conformal Conic Projection

Scale 1:6,000,000

One centimetre represents 60 kilometres.

One inch represents approximately 95 miles.

IN THIS SADLY troubled corner of the globe, Myanmar (Burma) once defined by the golden serenity of Buddhist temples, has long been a playground of private armies. The great empire of Cambodia was devastated by Khmer Rouge, and Vietnam shows the cost of fighting the French and then the USA. Only uncolonised Thailand still wears an unscarred mantle of forests, rice fields, crystal rivers and silver sands.

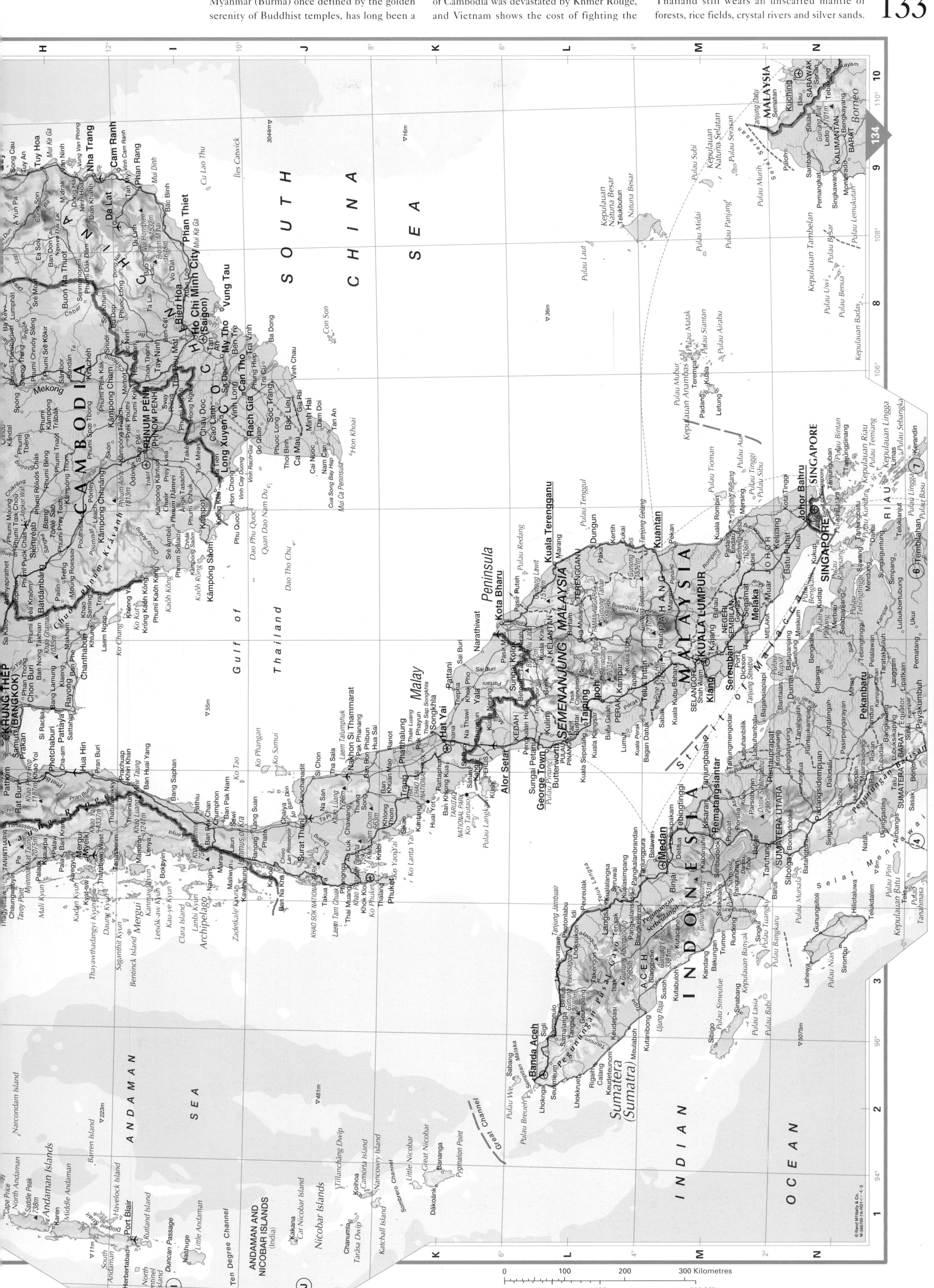

HEIGHT

3000m
(9842ft)

2000m
(6562ft)

1000m
(3281ft)

500m
(1640ft)

200m
(656ft)

Sea level

200m
(656ft)

2000m
(6562ft)

DEPTH

Lambert Conformal Conic Projection

Scale 1:12,000,000

One centimetre represents 120 kilometres.

One inch represents approximately 190 miles.

Scale 1:608,000

© Rand McNally & Co.
M-RDE3403-A1- 4-4-4

THE 13 777 TROPICAL islands that comprise Indonesia – the fabled East Indies – range from a myriad uninhabited islets to Sumatra, the size of California. The Philippines, a mere 7000 islands, is the only Catholic nation in South-east Asia and has English as its second language. The East Malaysian states of Sabah and Sarawak are divided from Peninsular Malaysia by 640 km (400 miles) of the South China Sea.

135

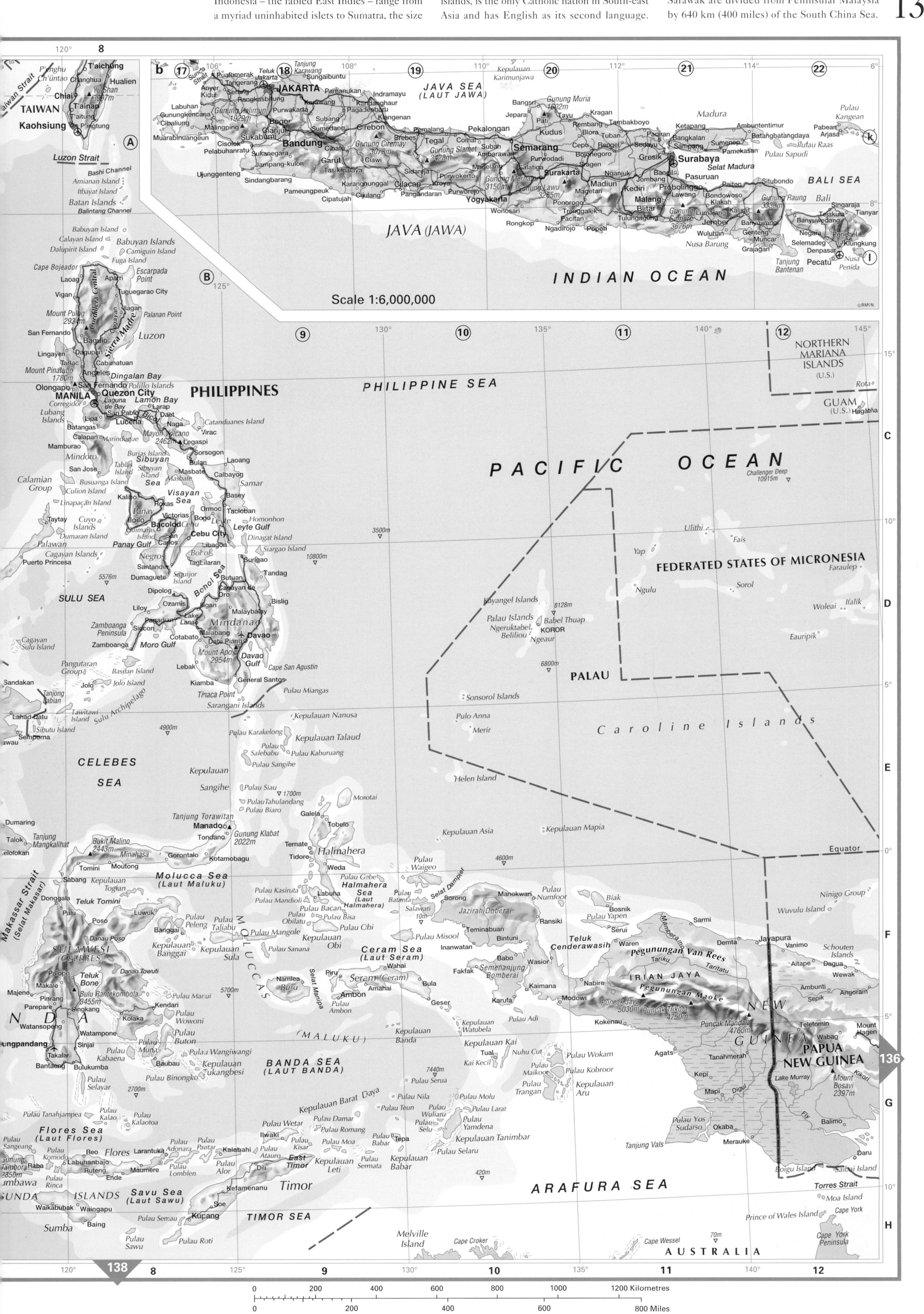

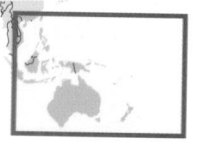

OCEANIA

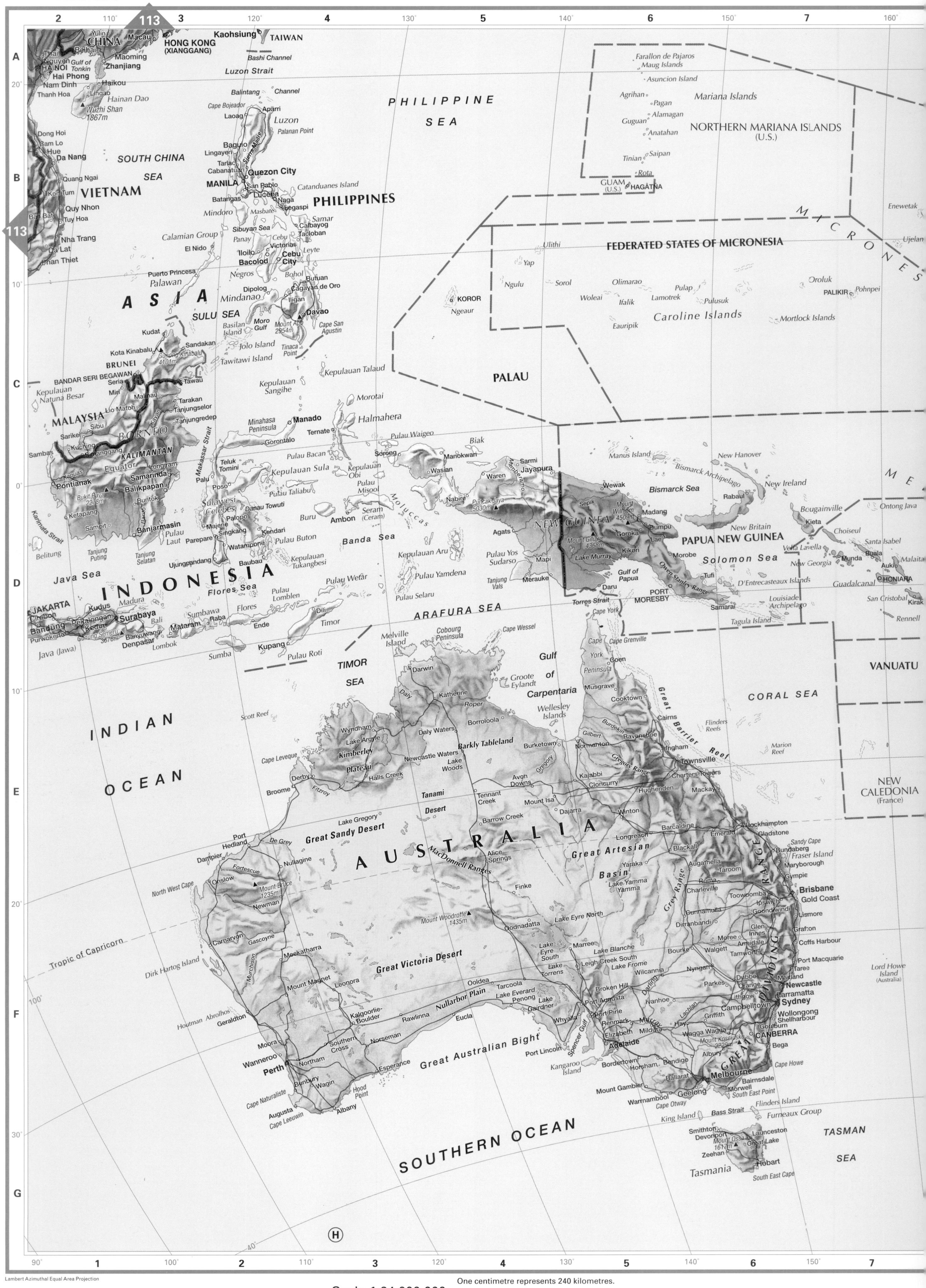

Lambert Azimuthal Equal Area Projection

Scale 1:24,000,000

One centimetre represents 240 kilometres.

One inch represents approximately 380 miles.

A FRAGMENTED 'CONTINENT' scattered across vast expanses of the Pacific comprises Australia, New Zealand and tens of thousands of islands. Only 3000 have names, though many are grouped into Micronesia, Melanesia and Polynesia – 'Little', 'Black' and 'Many' islands. Indigenous cultures have fallen under the influence of Christian missionaries, European and American colonists and Australian traders.

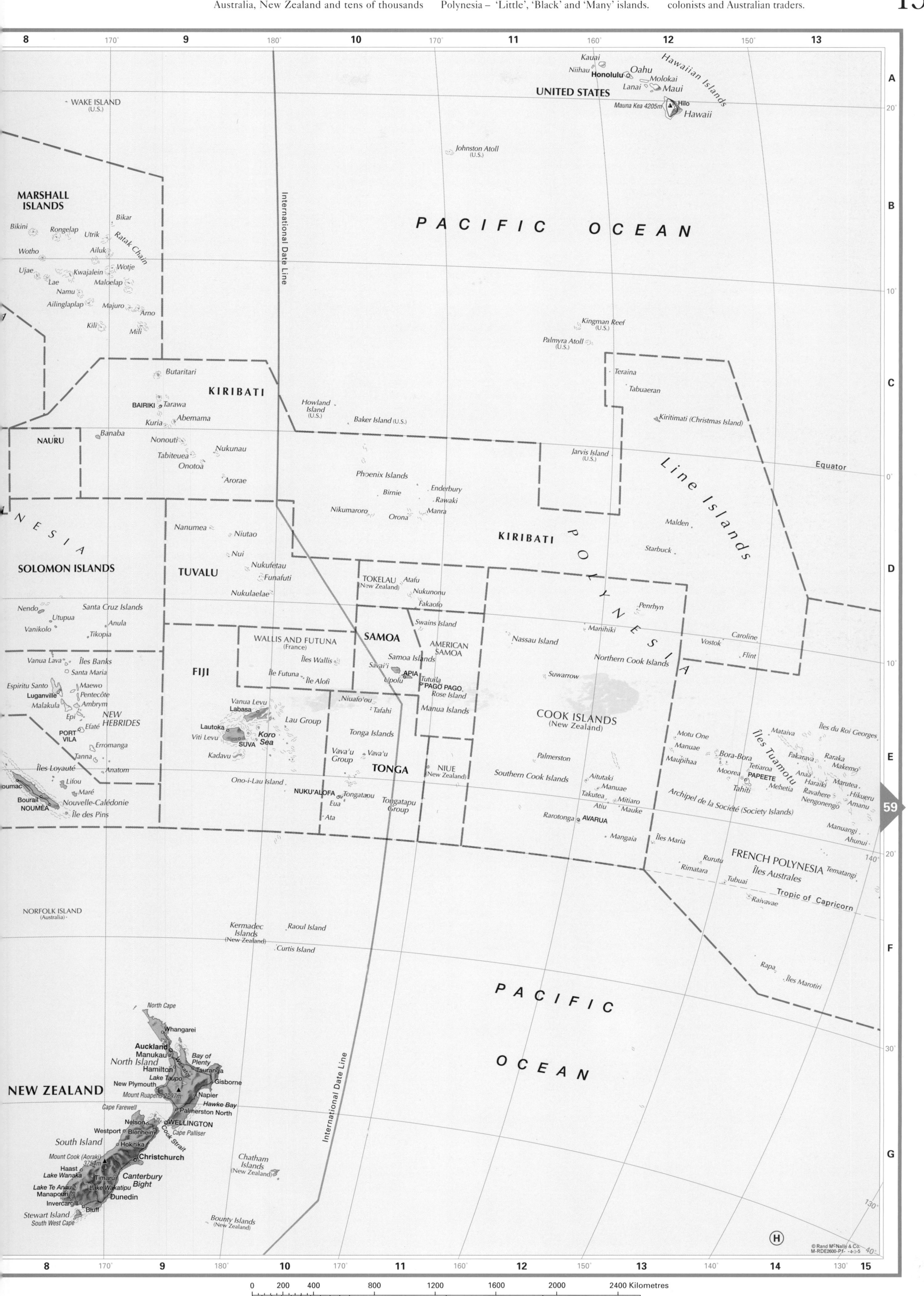

HEIGHT

3000m
(9842ft)

2000m
(6562ft)

1000m
(3281ft)

500m
(1640ft)

200m
(656ft)

Sea level

200m
(656ft)

2000m
(6562ft)

DEPTH

INDONESIA

Madura
Bangkalan Pamekasan
Kepulauan Kangen
Bali Sea
Surabaya
Bondowoso
Blitar Malang
Jember
Banyuwangi
Denpasar
Bali
Singaraja
Mataram
Praya
Lombok
JAVA (JAWA)
Waikabubak
Sumbawa Besar
Sumbawa
Sumba
Baing
Flores Sea
Guigung Tambora
2850m
Raba
Reo
Labuhanbajo
Ende
Lesser Sunda Islands
Waingapu
Flores
Larantuka
Maumere
Kepulauan Solor
Soe
Savu Sea
Pulau
Sawu
Pulau Roti
Kupang
Dili
Timor
Ketamenanu
Larantuka

INDIAN

OCEAN

Ashmore Islands
Cartier Islands

Scott Reef

Rowley Shoals

TIMOR

SEA

Cape Londonderry

Admiralty
Gulf

York Sound

Collier
Bay

Cape Leveque

King
Sound

Derby

Broome

Eighty Mile Beach

Lagrange

ARAFURA SEA

Cobourg
Peninsula Cape Croker
Melville Island
Bathurst Island
Van Diemen
Gulf
Beagle
Gulf
Darwin
Point Blaze
Rum Jungle
Pine Creek
Katherine
Daly
Roper
Cape Wessel
Wessel
Islands
Cape
Arnhem
ARNHEM LAND
Maria Island
Sir Edward
Pellew Gro
Groote
Eyland

Joseph
Bonaparte
Gulf
Wyndham
Kununurra
Lake
Argyle
Victoria
River Downs
Ord
Halls Creek
Fitzroy Crossing
Drysdale
Victoria
Kimberley Plateau
Mount Ord
947m
Fitzroy

Birdum
Daly Waters
Newcastle Waters
Wave Hill
Lake
Woods
Barkly Tableland
Borroloola

NORTHERN
TERRITORY
TANAMI
DESERT
Lake Gregory
Tennant Creek
Barrow Creek
Lake White
Lake Mackay
Lake
Macdonald
Lake Neale

Shay Gap
De Grey
Marble Bar
Nullagine
Lake Dora
Lake Auld
GREAT SANDY DESERT
Port Hedland
Dampier Roebourne
Marble Bar

Barrow Island
North West Cape
Onslow Pannawonica
Hamersley Range
Mount Brockman
1132m
Fortescue
Mount Bruce
1235m
Tom Price
Mount Meharry
1253m
Newman
Paraburdoo
Exmouth

Lake
Disappointment

Lake
Essendon
910m

WESTERN
AUSTRALIA
GIBSON DESERT
Mount Augustus
1105m
Lake Macleod
Mount Essendon

Mount Liebig
1274m
Mount Zeil
1531m
Mount Leisler
897m
MacDonnell Ranges
Alice Springs
SIMPSON
DESERT
Avon
Dow

Mount Olga
(Kata Tjuta)
1066m
Ayers Rock (Uluru)
863m
Lake Amadeus
Mount Cockburn
1134m
Finke
K Ilgera

Mount Aloysius
932m
Mount Woodroffe
1435m

Oodnadatta

AUSTRAL

Bernier Island
Carnarvon
Gascoyne
Dorre Island
Shark
Bay
Denham
Dirk Hartog Islands
Steep Point
Wooramel
Murchison
Peak Hill
Wiluna
Lake Gillen
Lake Carnegie
Lake Wells
Yeo Lake

GREAT VICTORIA DESERT

Meekatharra
Nannine
Cue
Lake Austin
Sandstone
Agnew
Mount Magnet
Mount Redcliffe
562m
Laverton
Lake Carey
Leonora
Lake
Ballard
Menzies
Lake Minigwal
Lake Maurice
Maralinga

SOUTH
AUSTRALIA
Lake Eyre North
-16m
Lake Eyre South
Lake Torrens
Woomera

Kalbarri
Northampton
Yalgoo
Mullewa
Houtman Abrolhos
Geraldton
Dongara
Three
Springs
Morgers Lake
Lake Barlee
Lake Moore
Ooldea
Tarcoola
Lake Everard
Penong Ceduna
Lake
Gairdner
Gawler Ranges
Iron Knob
Kimba
Elliston
Whyall
Eyre
Peninsula
Spencer
Gulf

Moora
Dalwallinu
Bonnie Rock
Bencubbin
Bullfinch
Southern Cross
Coolgardie
Kalgoorlie-Boulder
Zanthus
Rawlinna
Forrest
Deakin
NULLARBOR PLAIN
Eucla
Cape Adieu
Investigator
Group
Mount Hope
Port Lincoln

Wanneroo
Perth
Fremantle
Pinjarra
Northam
York
Beverley
Merredin
Kellerberrin
Hyden
Lake
Johnston
Lake Cowan
Norseman
Lake Dundas
Darling Range
Narrogin
Wagin
Newdegate
Ravensthorpe
Esperance
Point Culver
Cape Arid
Great Australian Bight
Cape Radstock
Port Lincoln
West Point
Cape Spencer

Bunbury
Collie
Nyabing
Katanning
Gnowangerup
Hopetoun
Archipelago
of the Recherche
Cape Naturaliste
Busselton
Bridgetown
Manjimup
Bluff Knoll
1096m
Hood Point
Augusta
Cape Leeuwin
Pemberton
Denmark
Mount Barker
Albany
West
Cape
Howe
Point D' Entrecasteaux

Kangaroo
Island

5670m

SOUTHERN   OCEAN

Tropic of Capricorn

Scale 1:12,000,000

Lambert Conformal Conic Projection

One centimetre represents 120 kilometres.

One inch represents approximately 190 miles.

SOME TWO-THIRDS of the world's smallest continent is taken up by the vast, arid Western Plateau, while the entire eastern seaboard is dominated by the heights of the Great Dividing Range. Separating these regions are the Central Lowlands, mostly grazing country whose rivers drain into Lake Eyre. Some 85 per cent of all Australians live in cities, leaving most of the continent to empty, sunburned distances.

Western Australia

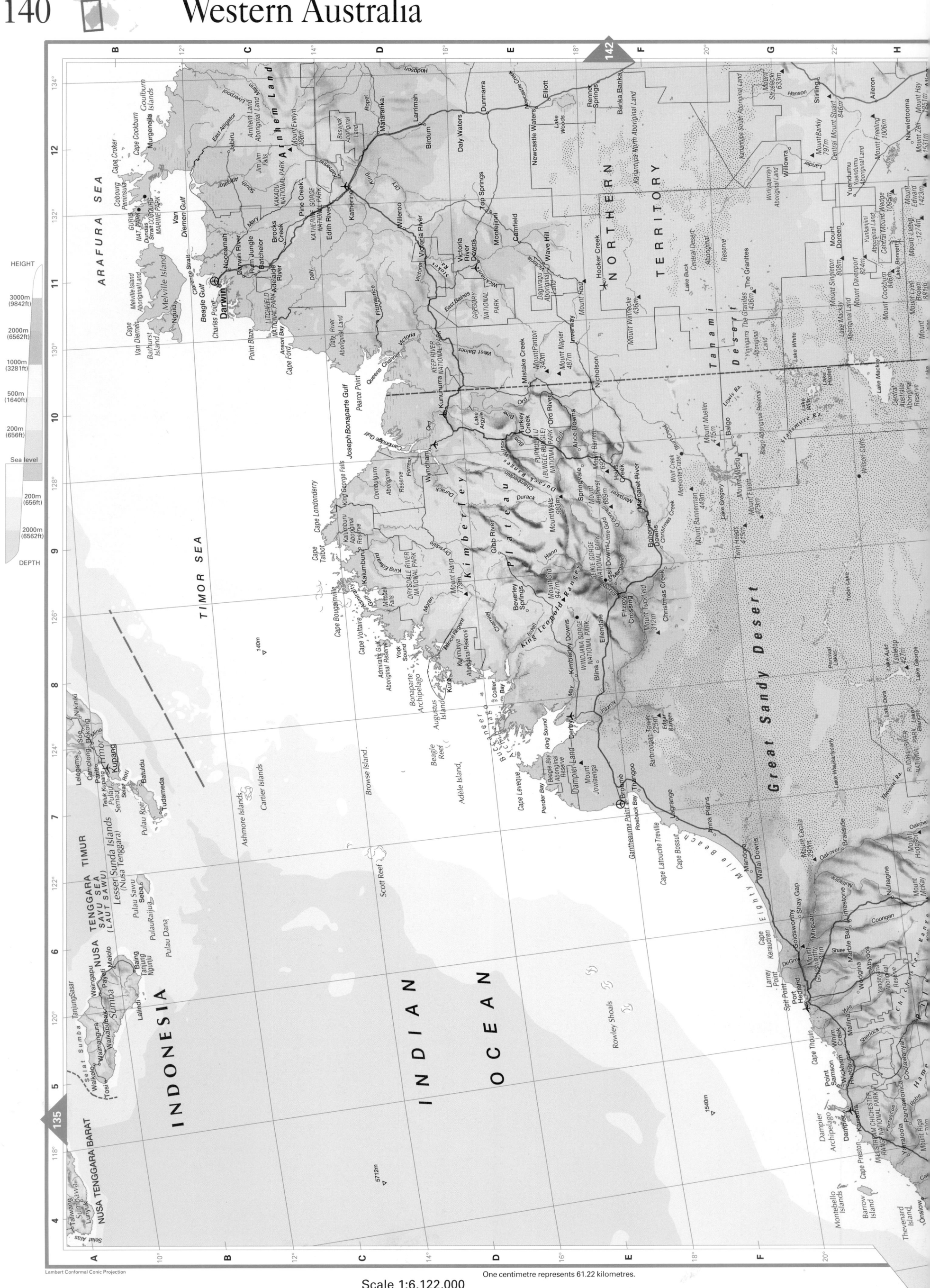

HEIGHT

3000m
(9842ft)

2000m
(6562ft)

1000m
(3281ft)

500m
(1640ft)

200m
(656ft)

Sea level

200m
(656ft)

2000m
(6562ft)

DEPTH

Lambert Conformal Conic Projection

Scale 1:6,122,000

One centimetre represents 61.22 kilometres.

One inch represents approximately 97 miles.

COASTAL FARMLANDS SOON give way to the flat, arid spaces, largely empty of people, that are characteristic of Western Australia. Deserts reach out towards the Indian Ocean, but there are virgin forests too and strange geological forms, such as the sandstone beehives of the Bungle Bungles and the huge, petrified Wave Rock. In Northern Territory is Ayers Rock, the sacred Uluru of the Aborigines.

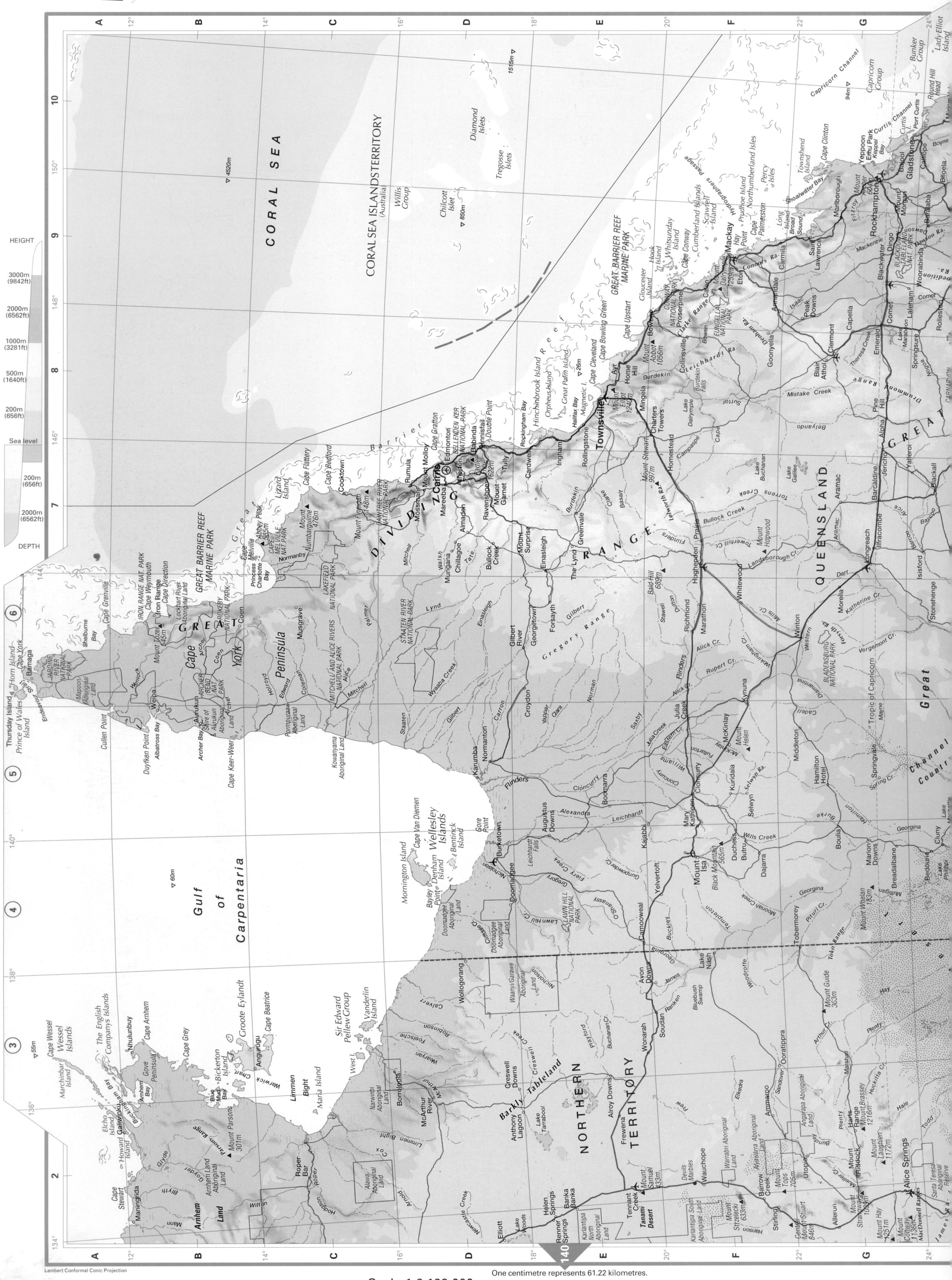

Lambert Conformal Conic Projection

Scale 1:6,122,000

One centimetre represents 61.22 kilometres.

One inch represents approximately 97 miles.

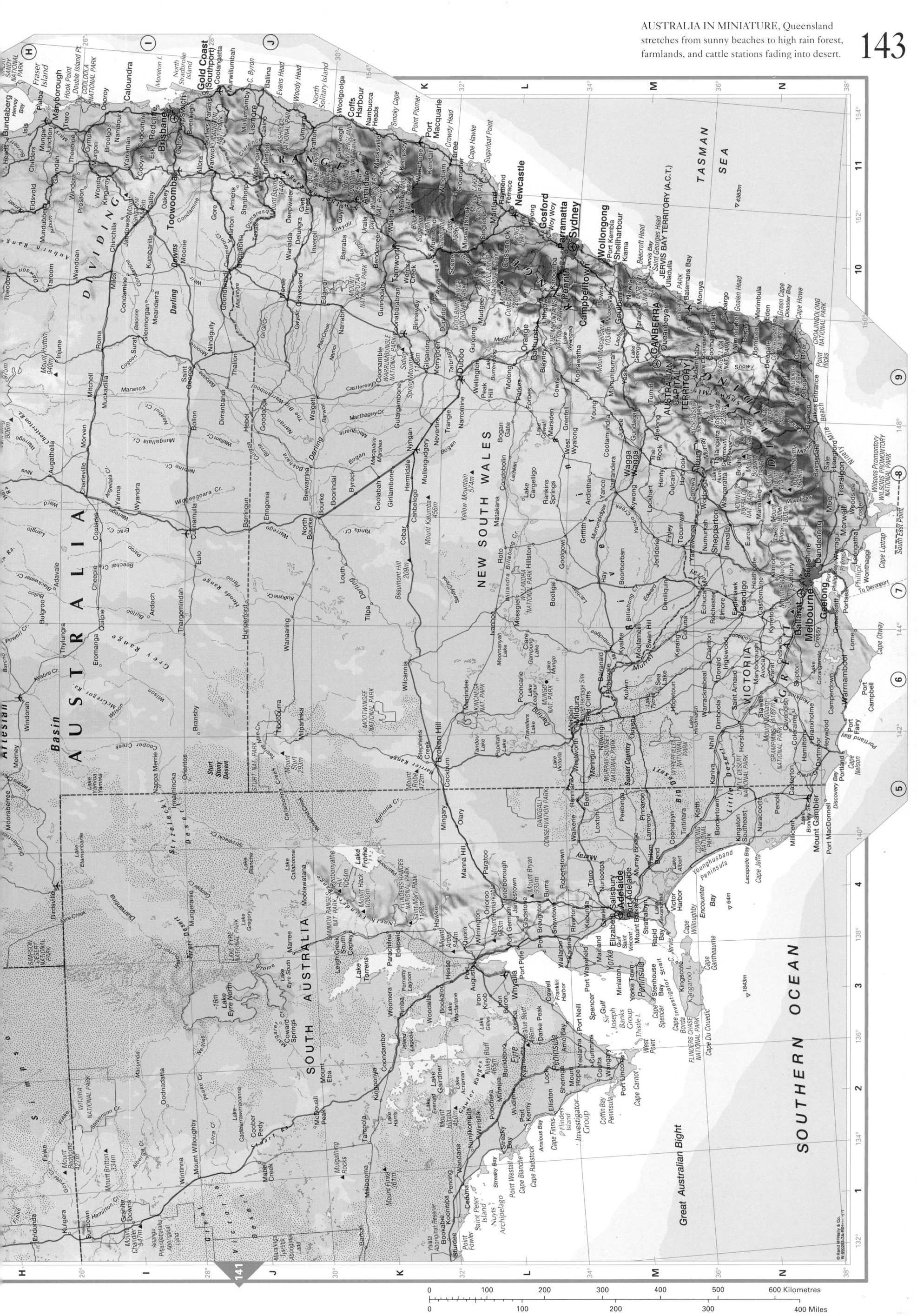

AUSTRALIA IN MINIATURE, Queensland stretches from sunny beaches to high rain forest, farmlands, and cattle stations fading into desert.

143

HEIGHT

3000m
(9842ft)

2000m
(6562ft)

1000m
(3281ft)

500m
(1640ft)

200m
(656ft)

Sea level

200m
(656ft)

2000m
(6562ft)

DEPTH

143

Lake Eyre North · LAKE EYRE NATIONAL PARK · Tirari Desert · Lake Koolkootinnie · Lake Mulapula · Lake Puntawolona · Cooper Creek · Lake Hope · **Strzelecki Desert** · Cooper Creek

Sturt Stony Desert · STURT NATIONAL PARK

Grey Range · Bulloo · Bulloo Downs · Warri Warri Creek · Bulloo Lake · Titheroo Creek · Lake Wyara · Mooning · Hoods Range

Lake Eyre South · Madigan Gulf · -16m · Etadunna · Lake Gregory · Lake Palankarinna · Strzelecki Creek · Callabonna Creek · Mount Sturt 293m · Tibooburra · Twelve Mile Creek · Currawinya · Paroo · Hungerford · Barringun

Marree · Frome · Lake Blanche · Moolawatana · Lake Callabonna · Mount Shannon 332m · Milparinka · Colane · Wanaaring · Wangamana · North Bourke · Bourke

GAMMON RANGES NATIONAL PARK · Leigh Creek South · Copley · Benbonyathe Hill 1064m · Border Downs · Packsaddle Creek · Louth · Darling · Mount Gunderbooka 495m

Andamooka Island · Lake Torrens · Mount Hack 1086m · Teatree · Lake Frome · Big John Creek · White Cliffs · Peery Lake · Momba · Tilpa

Lake Windabout · Pernatty Lagoon · Woocalla · Andamooka Ranges · Parachilna · Edeowie · FLINDERS RANGES NATIONAL PARK · Saint Mary Peak 1188m · Euriowie Creek · Corona 435m · MOOTWINGEE NATIONAL PARK · Gnalta Peak 433m · Wilcannia · Beaumont Hill 209m · Cobar

Hesso · Mount Arden 844m · Mount Plantagenet 952m · **SOUTH AUSTRALIA** · Mount Robe 472m · Barrier Range · Stephens Creek · Culpaulin · Barnato

Quorn · Carrieton · Binberrie Hill 500m · Bimbowrie · Mingary · **Broken Hill** · Stephens Creek · Scope 354m · Sandy Creek · Gilgunnia 524m

Port Augusta · Mount Brown 969m · Wilmington · Yunta · Olary · Cockburn · Pine Point · Menindee · Bambilla · Yallock

CORUNNA NORTH · Mount Remarkable 960m · MOUNT REMARKABLE NATIONAL PARK · Ororoo · Booleroo Centre · Paratoo · Quinna Hill 704m · Mannahill · KINCHEGA NATIONAL PARK · Tandou Lake · Darnick · Moornanyah Lake · Ivanhoe · Conoble Lake · Waranary Hill 309m · Mount Hope · Matakana · Roto · **NEW**

Iron Knob · Iron Baron · Port Germein · Peterborough · Manunda Creek · Oakbank · Coombah Roadhouse · Lake Mindona · Karoola · Popiltah Lake · Pooncarie · Clare · Mossgiel · WILLANDRA NATIONAL PARK · Willandra Billabong Creek

Whyalla · Germein Bay · Port Pirie · Jamestown · Mount Bryan 935m · DANGGALI CONSERVATION PARK · Popil Lake · Travellers Lake · Garnpung Lake · Manfred · Moolbong Creek · Lachlan · Hillston · Lake Ballyrogan

Eyre · Spencer Gulf · Gladstone · Burra · Lake Leaghur · Top Hut · Lake Mungo · Hatfield · Booligal

Cowell · Port Broughton · Brinkworth · MUNGO NATIONAL PARK · Goolgowi

Franklin Harbor · Illawarra Hill 434m · Snowtown · Manoora · Robertstown · Waikerie · Murray · Renmark · Wentworth · Murray · MALLEE CLIFFS NATIONAL PARK · Box · Lachlan · Griffith

Wallaroo · Kadina · Lochiel · South Hummocks 331m · Peters Hill 522m · Riverton · Mount Rufus 547m · Berri · Loxton · Merbein · **Mildura** · Red Cliffs · Pitarpunga Lake · Maude · Carrathool · Hanwood

Moonta · Port Wakefield · Kulpara · Balaklava · Kapunda · Truro · Nuriootpa · Meningur · Nowingi · Robinvale · Balranald · Murrumbidgee

Mount Arthurton 235m · Wild Horse Plains · Windsor · Roseworthy · Gawler · Lyndoch · Paruna · MURRAY-SUNSET NATIONAL PARK · Sunset Country · Ouyen · Kulwin · Manangatang · Booroorban · Coleambally Creek · **Riverina**

Yorke · Maitland · Urania · Gulf Saint Vincent · Elizabeth · Tea Tree Gully · Mount Pleasant · Murray · Peebinga · Kooloonong · Kyalite · Wanganella · Yanco Creek

Wardang Island · Minlaton · Port Vincent · **Salisbury** · Marne · Karoonda · Piangil · Lake Tyrrell · Swan Hill · Moulamein · Billabong Creek · Jerilderie

Corny Point · Hardwicke Bay · **Adelaide** · Marion · Mount Lofty 727m · Mount Barker · Murray Bridge · Pinnaroo · Patchewollock · Sea Lake · Kerang · Edward · Deniliquin · Finley

INNES NATIONAL PARK · Yorketown · Edithburgh · Noarlunga · Strathalbyn · Bremer · Tailem Bend · Lameroo · WYPERFELD NATIONAL PARK · Hopetoun · Culgoa · Cohuna · Mathoura · Tocumwal

Stenhouse Bay · Investigator Strait · Troubridge Point · Aldinga · Myponga Hill 441m · Lake Alexandrina · **Big Desert** · Birchip · Leitchville · Echuca

Cape Spencer · Point Rapid Bay · Fleurieu Peninsula · Victor Harbor · Encounter Bay · Coonalpyn · Tintinara · Lake Hindmarsh · Warracknabeal · Lake Buloke · Charlton · Rochester · Shepparton

Mount McDonnell 271m · Marsden · Cape Jervis · Kingscote · Black Bullock Hill 353m · Younghusband · Lake Albert · Mount Boothby 129m · Keith · Nhill · Dimboola · Donald · Elmore · Waranga Basin · Benalla

Kangaroo Island · Cygnet River · Cape Willoughby · Macdonnel Peninsula · **Peninsula** · Bordertown · Kaniva · **Little Desert** · LITTLE DESERT NAT. PARK · Natimuk · Murtoa · Saint Arnaud · Avoca · Inglewood · Eaglehawk · Wangaratta Hill · Euroa

FLINDERS CHASE NATIONAL PARK · Cape Du Couedic · Cape Gantheaume · COORONG NATIONAL PARK · Lacepede Bay · Kingston Southeast · Naracoorte · Horsham · Mount Bealiba 500m · Bendigo · **VICTORIA** · Heathcote · Mount Alexander 601m · Castlemaine · Seymour · Mansfield

64m · Cape Jaffa · Lake Eliza · Penola · Mount Difficult 810m · Stawell · GRAMPIANS NAT. PARK · Maryborough · Newstead · Malmsbury · Kyneton · Broadford · Goulburn · Yea · Mount Hickey 805m

1843m · Cape Lannes · Robe · Nangwarry · Mount William 1167m · Ararat · Maroona · Beaufort · Creswick · Mount Blackwood 1011m · The Camels Hump · KINGLAKE NAT. PARK

Great Australian Bight · Millicent · Mount Burr 240m · Casterton · Coleraine · Dunkeld · Mount Misery · Glenthompson · Skipton · Ballan · Bacchus Marsh · Sunbury · **Keilor** · **Broadmeadows** · Nunawading · Knox

CANUNDA NATIONAL PARK · Bonney SE · Mount Gambier · Nangwarry · Hamilton · Mortlake · Buninyong · **Ballarat** · Sebastopol · Meredith · Sunshine · **Melbourne** · Waverley · Springvale · Dandenong

SOUTHERN OCEAN · Port MacDonnell · LOWER GLENELG NATIONAL PARK · Mount Richmond 229m · Heywood · Milltown · Darlington · Camperdown · Colac · Winchelsea · **Geelong** · Mordialloc · Frankston

Discovery Bay · Cape Bridgewater · Cape Nelson · Portland · Portland Bay · Port Fairy · Warrnambool · Port Campbell · OTWAY NATIONAL PARK · Lorne · Mount Cowley 689m · Cape Otway · **Bass Strait** · Barwon Heads · Mornington Peninsula · Flinders · Phillip Island · Cowes · Cape Paterson

© Rand McNally & Co. · W-990294-7A-RD1-1- 4 -1

Lambert Conformal Conic Projection

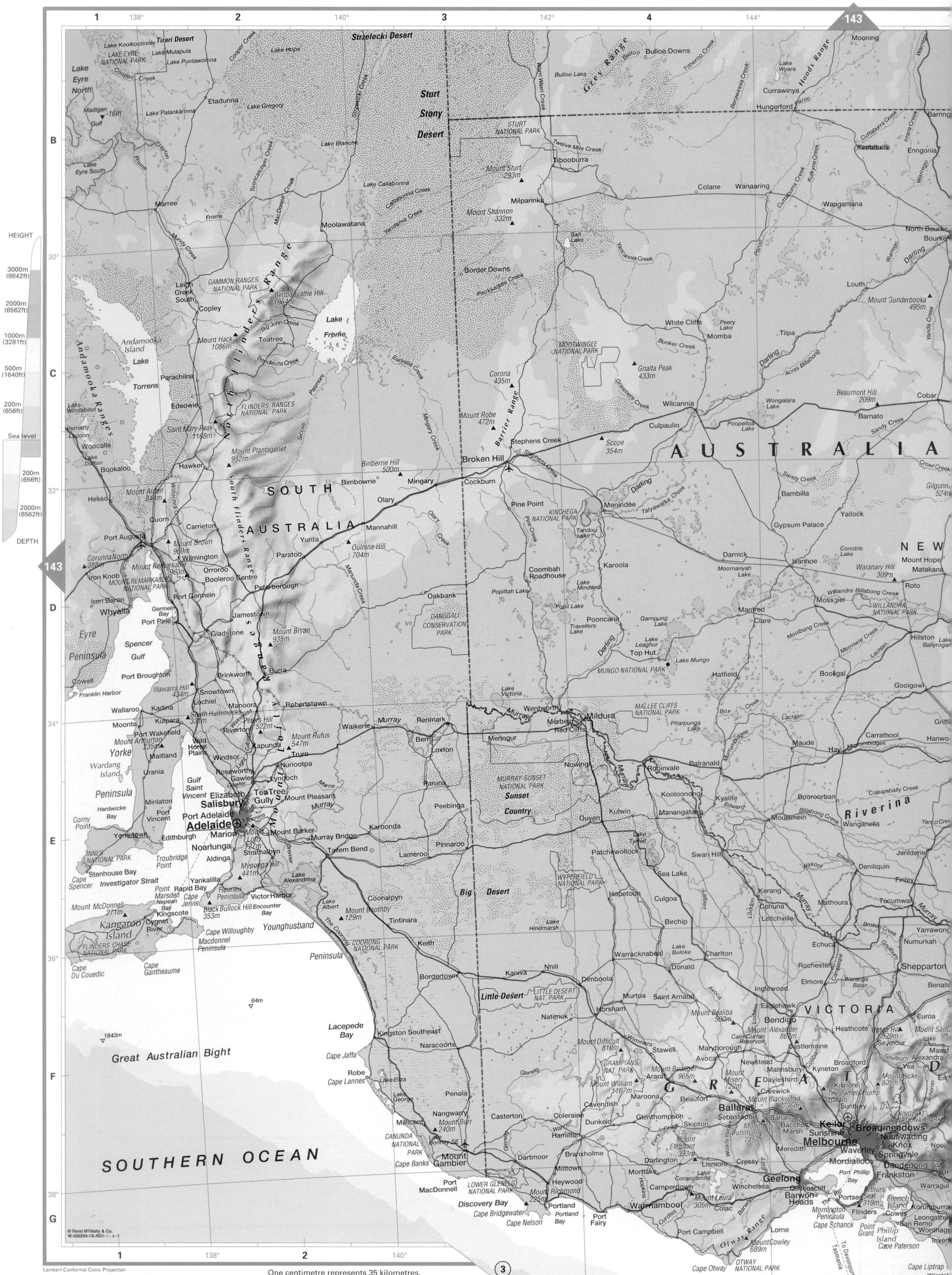

Scale 1:3,500,000

One centimetre represents 35 kilometres.

One inch represents approximately 55 miles.

NEW SOUTH WALES was where European Australia began. It is still the most populous state, with the nation's oldest and largest city, Sydney. To the south-west lies Melbourne, capital of Victoria. Between these two cities sits Canberra, in its Australian Capital Territory.

QUEENSLAND

NEW SOUTH WALES

SOUTH PACIFIC OCEAN

TASMAN SEA

CANBERRA
AUSTRALIAN
CAPITAL
TERRITORY

Sydney
Parramatta
Blacktown
Bankstown
Fairfield
Campbelltown
Wollongong

Newcastle

Gosford

Brisbane
Gold Coast
(Southport)
Surfers Paradise
Coolangatta

a Same scale as main map

Bass Strait

TASMANIA

Launceston

Hobart

TASMAN SEA

SOUTHERN OCEAN

Furneaux Group

| 0 | 50 | 100 | 150 | 200 | 250 | 300 | 350 Kilometres |

| 0 | 50 | 100 | 150 | 200 | 250 Miles |

© R. McN.

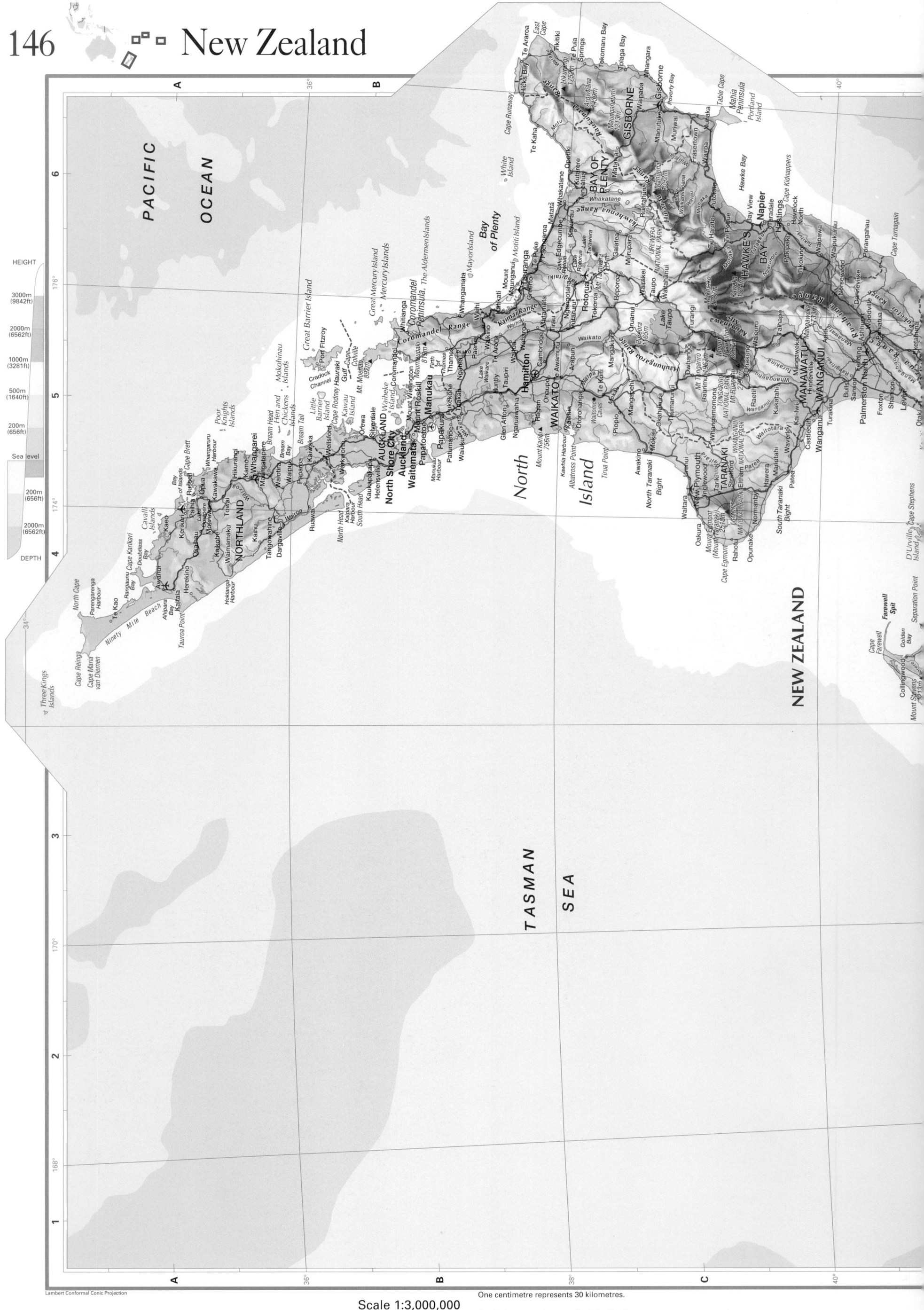

PACIFIC

OCEAN

HEIGHT

3000m
(9842ft)

2000m
(6562ft)

1000m
(3281ft)

500m
(1640ft)

200m
(656ft)

Sea level

200m
(656ft)

2000m
(6562ft)

DEPTH

Three Kings
Islands

North Cape
Cape Reinga
Cape Maria van Diemen
Te Kao
Parengarenga Harbour
Rangaunu
Cape Karikari
Doubtless Bay
Cavalli Islands
Kaitaia
Ahipara Bay
Awanui
Kaeo
Kerikeri
Ohaua
Bay of Islands
Paihia
Russell
Cape Brett
Ninety Mile Beach
Herekino
Kaikohe
Okaihau
Kaikino
Taurea Point
Hokianga Harbour
Whangaruru Harbour
Whangarei
Mangakahia
Hikurangi
Kamo
Whangaroa
Waimamaku
Kaihu
Dargaville
NORTHLAND
Tangowahine
Waipoua
Waipu
Bream Head
Bream Bay
Bream Tail
Poor Knights Islands
Hen and Chickens Islands
Little Barrier Island
Kawau Island
Great Barrier Island
Port Fitzroy
Cradock Channel
Cape Colville
Mt. Moehau 892m
Coromandel
Firth of Thames
Thames
Paeroa
Waihi
Mt. Te Aroha
Cape Rodney
Warkworth
Wellsford
Silverdale
Orewa
Helensville
Waimauku
Kaukapakapa
North Head
South Head
Kaipara Harbour
Ruawai
North Head
Papakura
AUCKLAND
North Shore City
Waitemata
Auckland
Manukau
Papatoetoe
Mount Wellington
Mount Roskill
Papakura
Waiheke Island
Hauraki Gulf
Manukau Harbour
Waiuku
Pukekohe
Huntly
Ngaruawahia
Cambridge
Hamilton
WAIKATO
Glen Afton
Te Kuiti
Raglan
Kawhia
Kawhia Harbour
Albatross Point
Tirua Point
Te Awamutu
Otorohanga
Waitomo Caves
Piopio
Mokau
North Taranaki Bight
Awakino
Waitara
New Plymouth
Inglewood
Oakura
Mount Egmont (Mount Taranaki) 2518m
Opunake
Rahotu
Cape Egmont
TARANAKI
Stratford
Eltham
Normanby
Hawera
Patea
South Taranaki Bight
Waverley

NEW ZEALAND

TASMAN

SEA

Te Araroa
East Cape
Hicks Bay
Te Puia Springs
Hikurangi 1752m
Tokomaru Bay
Tolaga Bay
Cape Runaway
Whangara
GISBORNE
Gisborne
Poverty Bay
Cape Kidnappers
Table Cape
Mahia Peninsula
Portland Island
Bay of Plenty
White Island
Mayor Island
Motiti Island
Whakatane
Kawerau
Opotiki
Matata
Whakatane
Tauranga
Te Puke
Katikati
Mount Maunganui
Waihi
Whangamata
UREWERA NATIONAL PARK
Wairoa
Hawke Bay
Bay View
Napier
Hastings
Havelock North
HAWKE'S BAY
Waipawa
Waipukurau
Takapau
Dannevirke
Woodville
Pahiatua
Pongaroa
Cape Turnagain
Rotorua
Lake Rotorua
Reporoa
Murupara
Lake Taupo
Taupo
Turangi
Mangakino
Tokoroa
Putaruru
Matamata
Kaimai Range
Kawhia
Te Kuiti
Mangaweka
Taihape
Mt. Ruapehu 2797m
Mt. Ngauruhoe 2291m
Mt. Tongariro 1967m
TONGARIRO NATIONAL PARK
Ohakune
Raetihi
Waiouru
WHANGANUI NATIONAL PARK
Wanganui
Marton
Bulls
Feilding
Palmerston North
MANAWATU
Foxton
Levin
Shannon
Himatangi
Waikanae

Bay of Plenty

North

Island

NEW ZEALAND

Cape Farewell
Farewell Spit
Collingwood
Golden Bay
Separation Point
D'Urville Island
Mount Stephens
Cape Stephens

Scale 1:3,000,000

One centimetre represents 30 kilometres.

One inch represents approximately 47 miles.

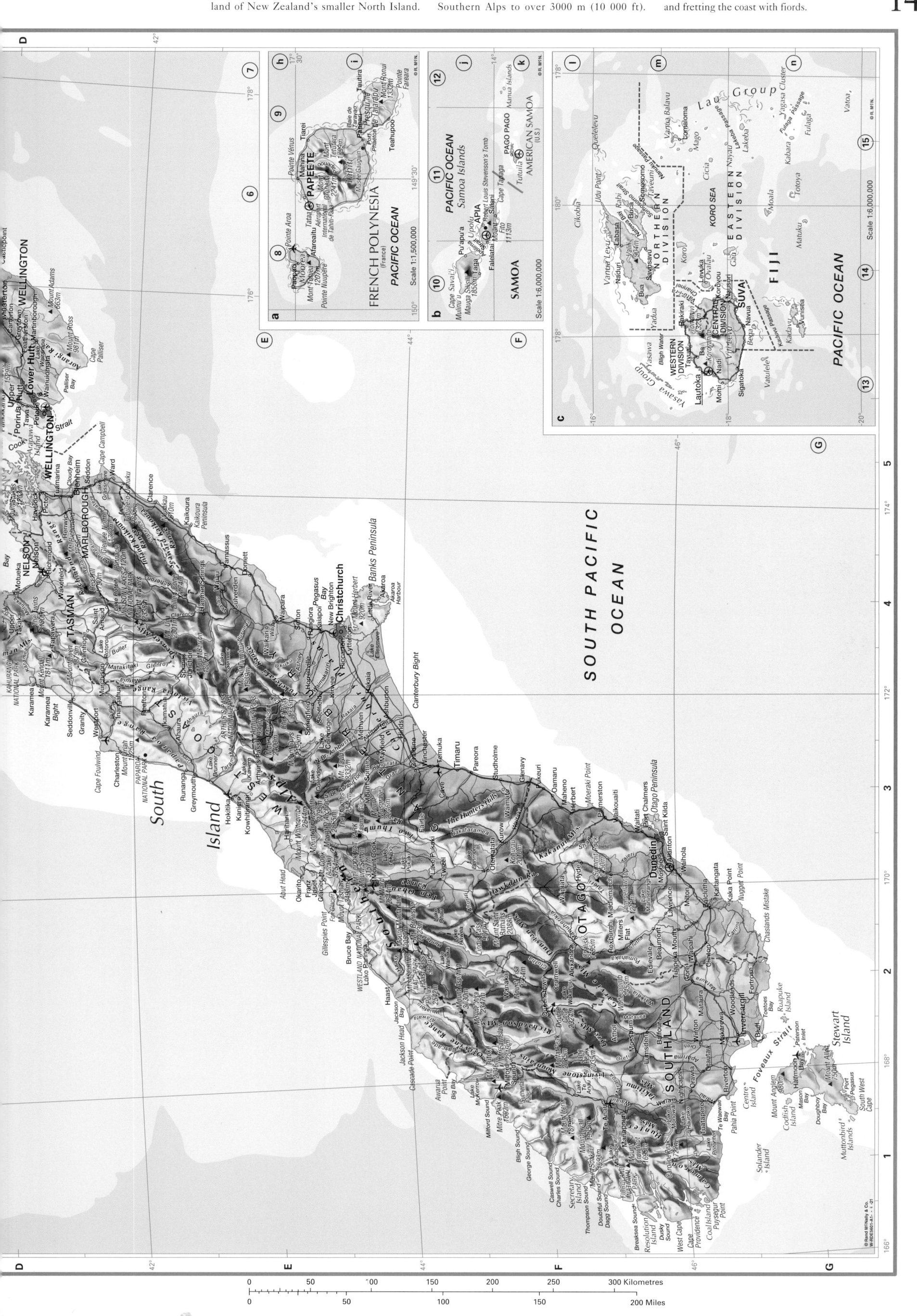

ACTIVE VOLCANOES, GEYSERS and hot bubbling springs flank the fertile sheep grazing land of New Zealand's smaller North Island.

In the larger but less populated South Island, below-ground activity has raised the peaks of the Southern Alps to over 3000 m (10 000 ft).

Their glaciers have created a diverse landscape by scooping out lakes, bringing forth tumbling rivers and fretting the coast with fiords.

147

EUROPE

Jaroslavl'
Nizhnii Novgorod
Vologda
MOSKVA
(MOSCOW)
Sankt-Peterburg
(St. Petersburg)
Lake Onega
Lake Ladoga
HELSINKI
TALLINN
EST.
LAT.
LITH.
OSLO
STOCKHOLM
SWEDEN
NORWAY
FINLAND
Gulf of Finland
Gulf of Bothnia
Gotland
Kiruna
Trondheim
Bergen
Lofoten
Narvik
Murmansk
Arhangel'sk
Kola Peninsula
White Sea
Mezen'
Pechora
Onega
North Cape (Nordkapp)
Svalbard
Spitsbergen
Edgeøya
Nordaustlandet
Jan Mayen (Norway)
Shetland Islands (U.K.)
FAROE ISLANDS (Denmark)
ICELAND
REYKJAVIK
Denmark Strait
Kap Brewster
Scoresbysund
Ammassalik

Norwegian Sea
Greenland Sea
Barents Sea
Kara Sea
White Sea

FRANZ JOSEF LAND
NORTH LAND
NOVAYA ZEMLYA

URAL MTS
SIBERIA
RUSSIA
ASIA
CHINA

Vorkuta
Usta
Pechora
Ukhta
ostrov Kolguyev
ostrov Belyi
Yamal Peninsula
Ob'
Dudinka
Noril'sk
Dikson
Taymyr Peninsula
ostrov Oktjabr'skoy Revolyutsii
Komsomolets
ostrov Taymyr
Khatanga
Essei
Tura
Anabar
ostrov Bol'soy Begičev
Lena
Olenek
Vilyuy
NEW SIBERIAN ISLANDS
ostrov Novaja Sibir'
ostrov Kotel'nyj
Laptev Sea
Yana
Indigirka
ostrov Ajon
Kolyma
Alazeja
ostrov Vrangelja (Wrangel Island)
East Siberian Sea
Chukchi Sea
Ambarcik
Anadyr'
Makovo
Uel'kal
Provideniya
Anadyr'
mys Dežnëva
Kamchatka Peninsula
gora Ledjanaja 2561m
Kaväčen
mys Oljutorskij
Palana
Shelekhov Gulf
Magadan
Jamsk
Ohotsk
Sea of Okhotsk
Ola
Ostrov Sahalin (Sakhalin)
Aldan
Jakutsk

GREENLAND
(KALAALLIT NUNAAT)
(Denmark)
GODTHÅB
Gunnbjørn Field 3700m
Peary Land
Kap Morris Jesup
Nordost-rundingen
Cape Columbia
Barbeau Peak 2616m
Ellesmere Island
Thule
Kap York
Nares Strait
Alert
Lincoln Sea

ARCTIC OCEAN
North Pole

Arctic Circle

Davis Strait
Baffin Bay
Labrador Sea
Godhavn
Upernavik
Disko
Holsteinsborg
Egedesminde

Baffin Island
Lancaster Sound
Devon Island
Cumberland Sound
Foxe Basin
Prince Charles Island
Southampton Island
Coats Island
Mansel Island
Belcher Islands
Smallwood Reservoir
George
Ungava Bay
Peninsula d'Ungava
Ivujivik
Hudson Strait

Hudson Bay
CANADA
Churchill
York Factory
Lynn Lake
Reindeer Lake
Southern Indian Lake
Nejanilini Lake

QUEEN ELIZABETH ISLANDS
Axel Heiberg Island
Meighen Island
Amund Ringnes Island
Ellef Ringnes Island
Melville Island
Bathurst Island
Cornwallis Island
Somerset Island
Prince of Wales Island
Boothia
Peninsula
Gulf of Boothia
Parry Channel
M'Clintock Channel
Banks Island
Victoria Island
Prince Albert Peninsula
Amundsen Gulf
Sachs Harbour
Cambridge Bay
Kugluktuk
Queen Maud Gulf
Great Bear Lake
Great Slave Lake
Yellowknife
Slave
Lake Athabasca
Fort McMurray
Lake Claire
Peace
Fort Nelson
Mackenzie
Mackenzie Mountains
Norman Wells
Keele Peak 2972m

Beaufort Sea
Point Barrow
Barrow
Cape Bathurst
Prudhoe Bay
Brooks Range
Colville
Yukon
UNITED STATES
ALASKA
Fairbanks
Tanana
Anchorage
Mount McKinley 6194m
Wrangell Mountains
Kuskokwim
Bethel
Yukon
Seward Peninsula
Nome
Norton Sound
Point Hope
Bering Strait
Saint Lawrence Island
Nunivak Island
Bristol Bay
Kodiak Island
Alaska Peninsula
Unimak Island
Unalaska
Pribilof Islands
Saint Matthew Island
mys Navarin
mys Čukotskij

Bering Sea
Gulf of Alaska
Queen Charlotte Islands
Cape Commeroy
Ketchikan
Juneau
ROCKY MOUNTAINS
Yukon
Whitehorse
Pelly Mountains
Cassiar Mountains
Stikine
Coast Mountains

ALEUTIAN ISLANDS
Attu Island

THE VAST TERRAIN that runs from within 800 km (500 miles) of the North Pole to Panama is dominated by Canada and the United States.

Central America, the land of the ancient Maya empire, includes Mexico and the smaller states that stretch south to the Colombian border.

188

Grid references: F, G, H, I, J (top and bottom); 7, 8, 9, 10, 11, 12, 13 (right side)

Oceans and seas: PACIFIC OCEAN, ATLANTIC OCEAN, Gulf of Mexico, CARIBBEAN SEA, Gulf of California

Countries/regions: NORTH AMERICA, UNITED STATES, MEXICO, CANADA, SOUTH AMERICA, BRAZIL, VENEZUELA, COLOMBIA, GUATEMALA, BELIZE, HONDURAS, NICARAGUA, COSTA RICA, PANAMA, EL SALVADOR, CUBA, JAMAICA, HAITI, DOMINICAN REPUBLIC, THE BAHAMAS

Cities: Montreal, OTTAWA, Toronto, Quebec, Boston, Providence, New York, Philadelphia, Baltimore, WASHINGTON, Richmond, Norfolk, Buffalo, Rochester, Pittsburgh, Cleveland, Detroit, Columbus, Cincinnati, Lexington, Charlotte, Raleigh, Columbia, Charleston, Savannah, Jacksonville, Daytona Beach, Orlando, Tampa, Miami, Atlanta, Birmingham, Montgomery, Tallahassee, Nashville, Knoxville, Louisville, Indianapolis, Chicago, Milwaukee, Madison, Minneapolis, St. Paul, Des Moines, St. Louis, Memphis, Jackson, New Orleans, Baton Rouge, Shreveport, Little Rock, Springfield, Kansas City, Tulsa, Oklahoma City, Wichita, Omaha, Dallas, Fort Worth, Austin, San Antonio, Houston, Corpus Christi, Brownsville, Denver, Cheyenne, Santa Fe, Albuquerque, El Paso, Amarillo, Phoenix, Las Vegas, Salt Lake City, Boise, Spokane, Seattle, Portland, Sacramento, San Francisco, Oakland, Los Angeles, San Diego, Reno, Winnipeg, Edmonton, Calgary, Vancouver, Victoria, Duluth, Fargo, Bismarck, Pierre

Mexico cities: CIUDAD DE MEXICO (MEXICO CITY), Guadalajara, Monterrey, Puebla, Veracruz, Acapulco, Tijuana, Mexicali, Ciudad Juárez, Chihuahua, Hermosillo, Culiacán, Mazatlán, Torreón, Durango, Aguascalientes, San Luis Potosí, Querétaro, Tampico, Mérida, Villahermosa, Oaxaca, Matamoros, Nuevo Laredo, La Paz, Ciudad Obregón, Ciudad Victoria, Gómez Palacio

Central America/Caribbean: GUATEMALA, Belize City, BELMOPAN, TEGUCIGALPA, San Pedro Sula, SAN SALVADOR, MANAGUA, SAN JOSÉ, PANAMÁ, Colón, LA HABANA (HAVANA), Santiago de Cuba, Camagüey, Holguín, Matanzas, Cienfuegos, NASSAU, KINGSTON, PORT-AU-PRINCE, SANTO DOMINGO, SAN JUAN, CARACAS, Maracaibo, BOGOTÁ, Medellín, Cali, Barranquilla, Cartagena

Physical features: Sierra Madre Oriental, Sierra Madre Occidental, Sierra Madre del Sur, Great Basin, Rocky Mountains, Sierra Nevada, Coast Ranges, Mississippi, Missouri, Rio Grande, Colorado, Appalachian, Lake Superior, Lake Michigan, Lake Huron, Lake Erie, Lake Ontario, Lake Winnipeg, Tropic of Cancer, Equator, Baja California, Yucatán Peninsula

Islands: BERMUDA (U.K.), PUERTO RICO (U.S.), VIRGIN ISLANDS, CAYMAN ISLANDS (U.K.), TURKS AND CAICOS ISLANDS (U.K.), LESSER ANTILLES, GREATER ANTILLES, Leeward Islands, Windward Islands, Isla de Coco (Costa Rica), Île Clipperton (France)

Scale bars:
0 200 400 600 800 1200 1600 2000 2400 Kilometres
0 200 400 600 800 1200 1600 Miles

© Rand McNally & Co.

Lambert Conformal Conic Projection

Scale 1:12,000,000

One centimetre represents 120 kilometres.

One inch represents approximately 190 miles.

THE WORLD'S SECOND largest country after Russia, Canada has 30 million people, most of whom reside close to the long border with the United States. Only a few make their living in the northern immensity of forest and tundra. Confederation of the original colonies into a predominantly English union was completed in 1949; however, French-speaking Canadians still aspire to influence the ultimate national pattern.

151

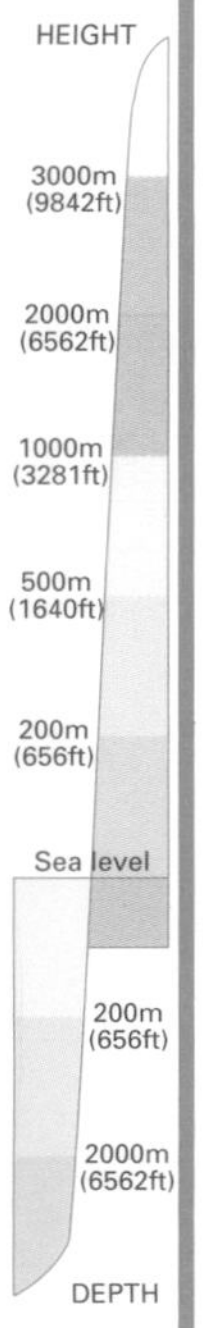

United States and Mexico

THE UNITED STATES is so broad that dawn comes to people living in California 3 hours later than to those in Maine. Yet they and all the millions of Americans in between belong to a single nation whose promise of opportunity was amply fulfilled in the richest economy on Earth. Mexico has never enjoyed the same economic prosperity as its neighbour to the north, and its population is today outstripping its resources.

153

Scale 1:12,000,000

One centimetre represents 120 kilometres.

One inch represents approximately 190 miles.

© Rand McNally & Co.

M-RDE3101-A1- -1-1-2

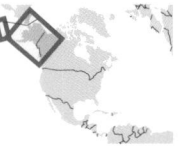
HEIGHT

3000m (9842ft)
2000m (6562ft)
1000m (3281ft)
500m (1640ft)
200m (656ft)
Sea level
200m (656ft)
2000m (6562ft)

DEPTH

CHUKCHI SEA

RUSSIA

Siberia (Sibir')

ČUKOTSKIJ AVTONOMNYJ OKRUG

Čukotskij poluostrov

Anadyrskij zaliv

Arctic Circle

Bering Strait

BERING SEA

Aleutian Islands

Islands of Four Mountains

Saint Paul Island
Pribilof Islands
Saint George Island

Hall Island
Saint Matthew Island
Pinnacle Island

Gambell
Savoonga
Saint Lawrence Island
Southwest Cape
Northeast Cape
Southeast Cape

BROOKS RANGE
Endicott Mountains
De Long Mountains
Baird Mountains
Schwatka Mountains
GATES OF THE ARCTIC NATIONAL PARK

Barrow
Point Barrow
Plover Islands
Point Franklin Peard Bay
Wainwright
Icy Cape
Ledyard Bay
Cape Lisburne
Lisburne Peninsula
Point Hope

Seward Peninsula
CAPE KRUSENSTERN NATIONAL MONUMENT
Kotzebue
Kotzebue Sound
Nome
Norton Sound
Norton Bay

UNITED STATES

ALASKA

Yukon

Bethel

Kuskokwim Bay

Bristol Bay

Kodiak Island
Kodiak

ALASKA Peninsula
KATMAI NATIONAL PARK
ANIAKCHAK NATIONAL MONUMENT

Shumagin Islands

DENALI NATIONAL PARK
Mount McKinley 6194m
Mount Foraker 5304m

ALASKA RANGE

LAKE CLARK NATIONAL PARK

Cook Inlet
Kenai Peninsula

PACIFIC OCEAN

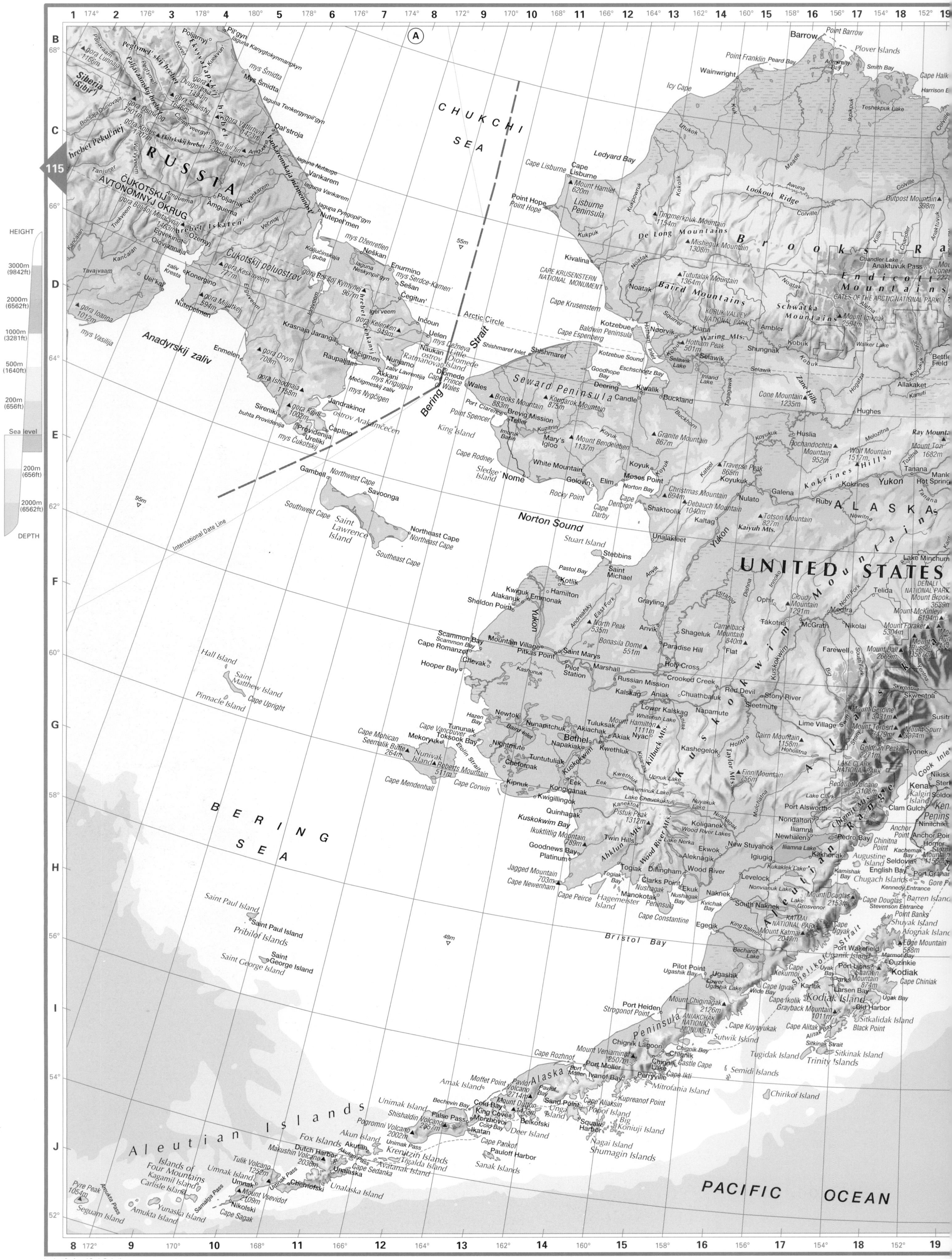

Lambert Conformal Conic Projection

Scale 1:6,000,000

One centimetre represents 60 kilometres.

One inch represents approximately 95 miles.

BOUGHT FROM RUSSIA by US Secretary of State William H. Seward in 1867, Alaska was contemptuously labelled 'Seward's Icebox'. However, gold, fisheries, timber and iron soon proved the shrewdness of the bargain, and oil later reconfirmed it. Today, Alaskans boast the highest per capita income in the Union. Canada's Yukon region, too, is rich in gold and minerals, but oil wealth has so far eluded it.

155

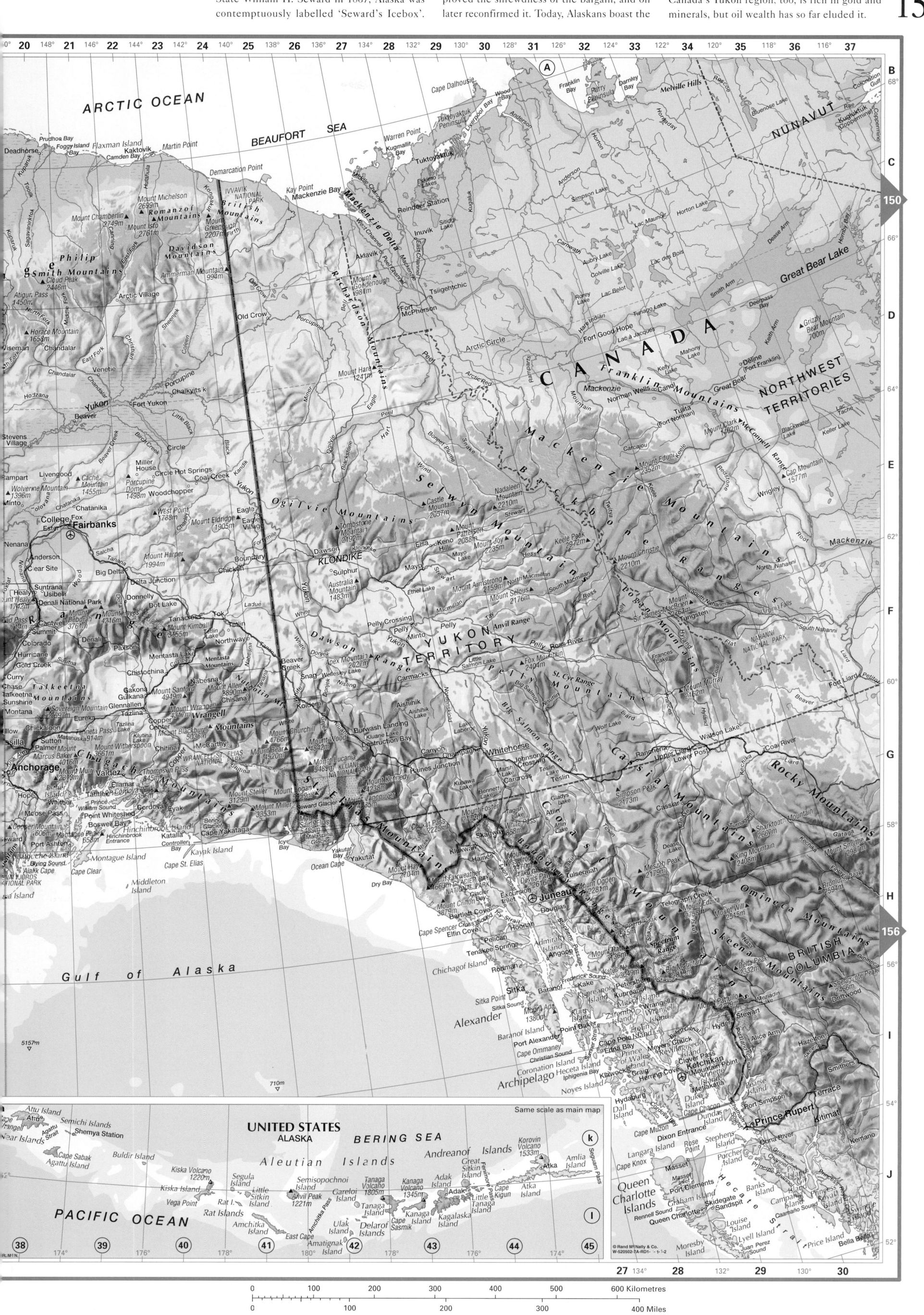

HEIGHT

3000m
(9842ft)

2000m
(6562ft)

1000m
(3281ft)

500m
(1640ft)

200m
(656ft)

Sea level

200m
(656ft)

2000m
(6562ft)

DEPTH

© Rand McNally & Co.
W-520294-7A-RQ1 -1-1-1

Lambert Conformal Conic Projection

Scale 1:4,500,000

One centimetre represents 45 kilometres.

One inch represents approximately 71 miles.

CROWNED GLORIOUSLY BY the Rockies, Alberta and British Columbia beckon tourists. Other attractions they offer are the Calgary Stampede in July, the Englishness of Victoria and the variety of British Columbia's scenery, flora and fauna. Alberta grew rich on farming, forestry and coal, then upon oil and gas strikes. On the Pacific coast, Vancouver Island is the largest of North America's west coast islands.

157

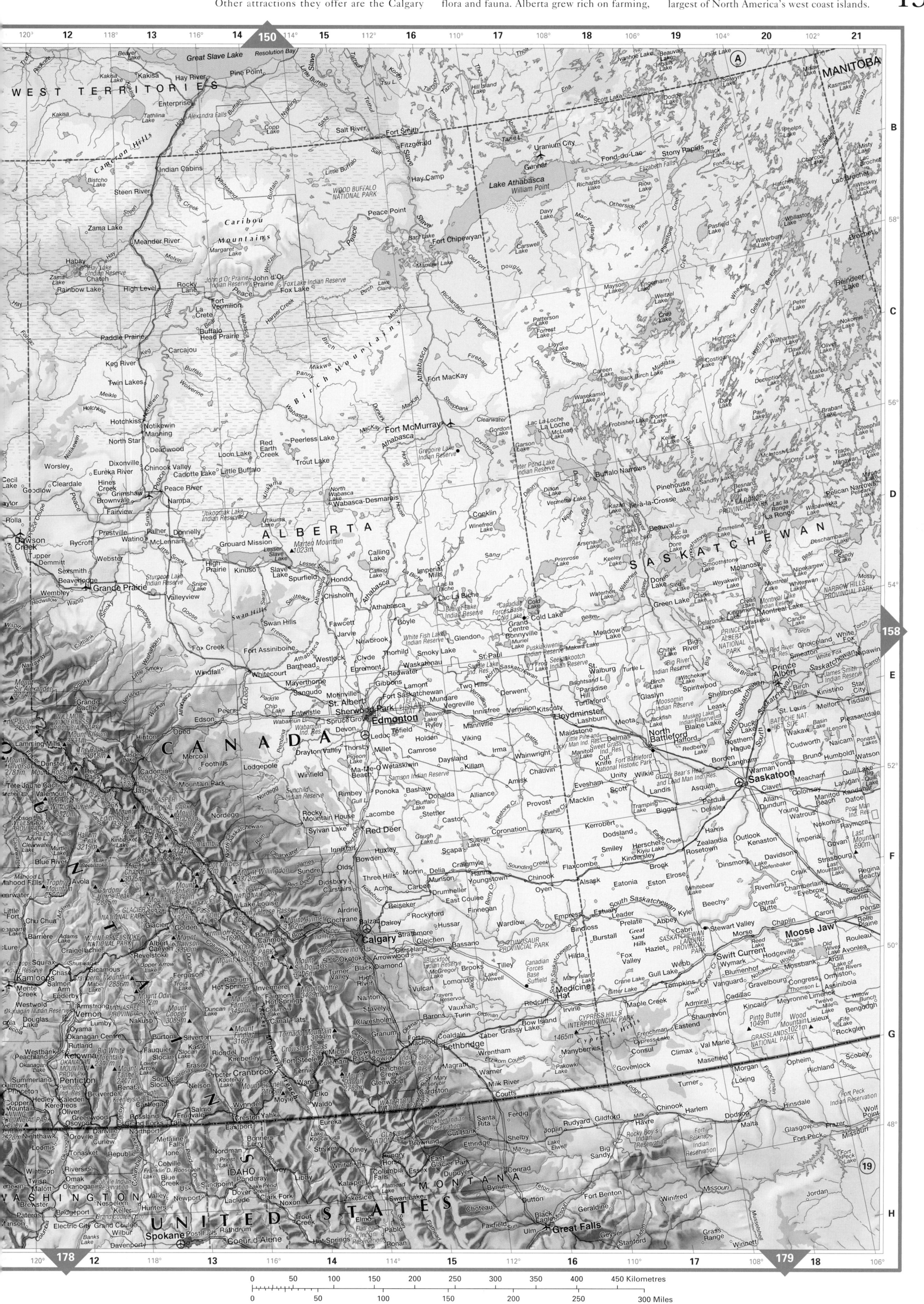

0   50   100   150   200   250   300   350   400   450 Kilometres

0   50   100   150   200   250   300 Miles

South Central Canada

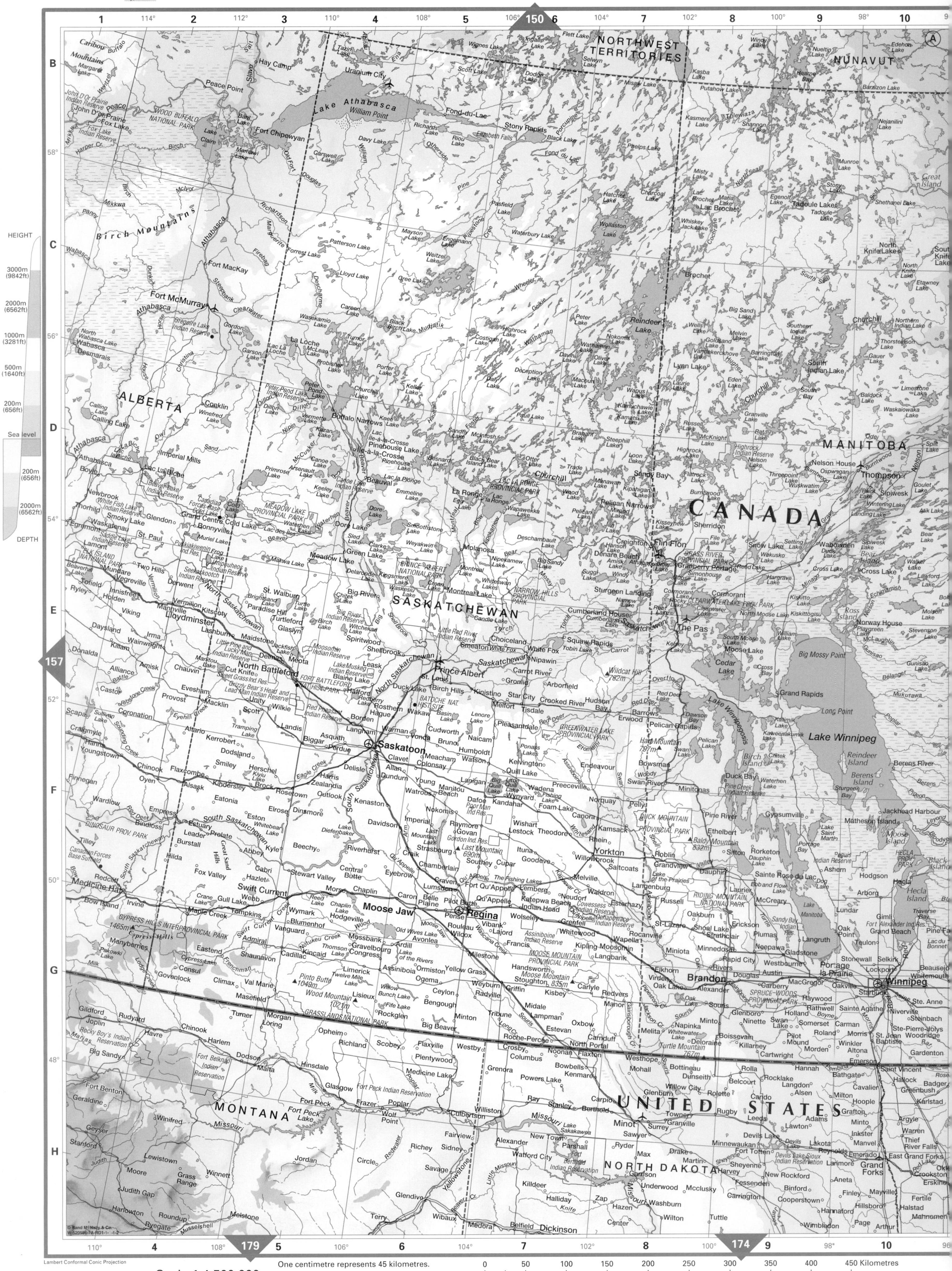

Scale 1:4,500,000

One centimetre represents 45 kilometres.

One inch represents approximately 71 miles.

Lambert Conformal Conic Projection

© Rand McNally & Co.

| 0 | 50 | 100 | 150 | 200 | 250 | 300 | 350 | 400 | 450 Kilometres |

| 0 | 50 | 100 | 150 | 200 | 250 | 300 Miles |

WIDE SEAS OF grass and wheat occupy the southern parts of Saskatchewan and Manitoba. Winnipeg, south of the huge lake of the same name, has one of the world's biggest wheat markets. Northwards the prairies give way to forest, lakes and rivers and finally to the arctic tundra on the shores of Hudson Bay. Lakes also dot the rocky northern part of Ontario, which is rich in nickel, copper, gold, silver and platinum.

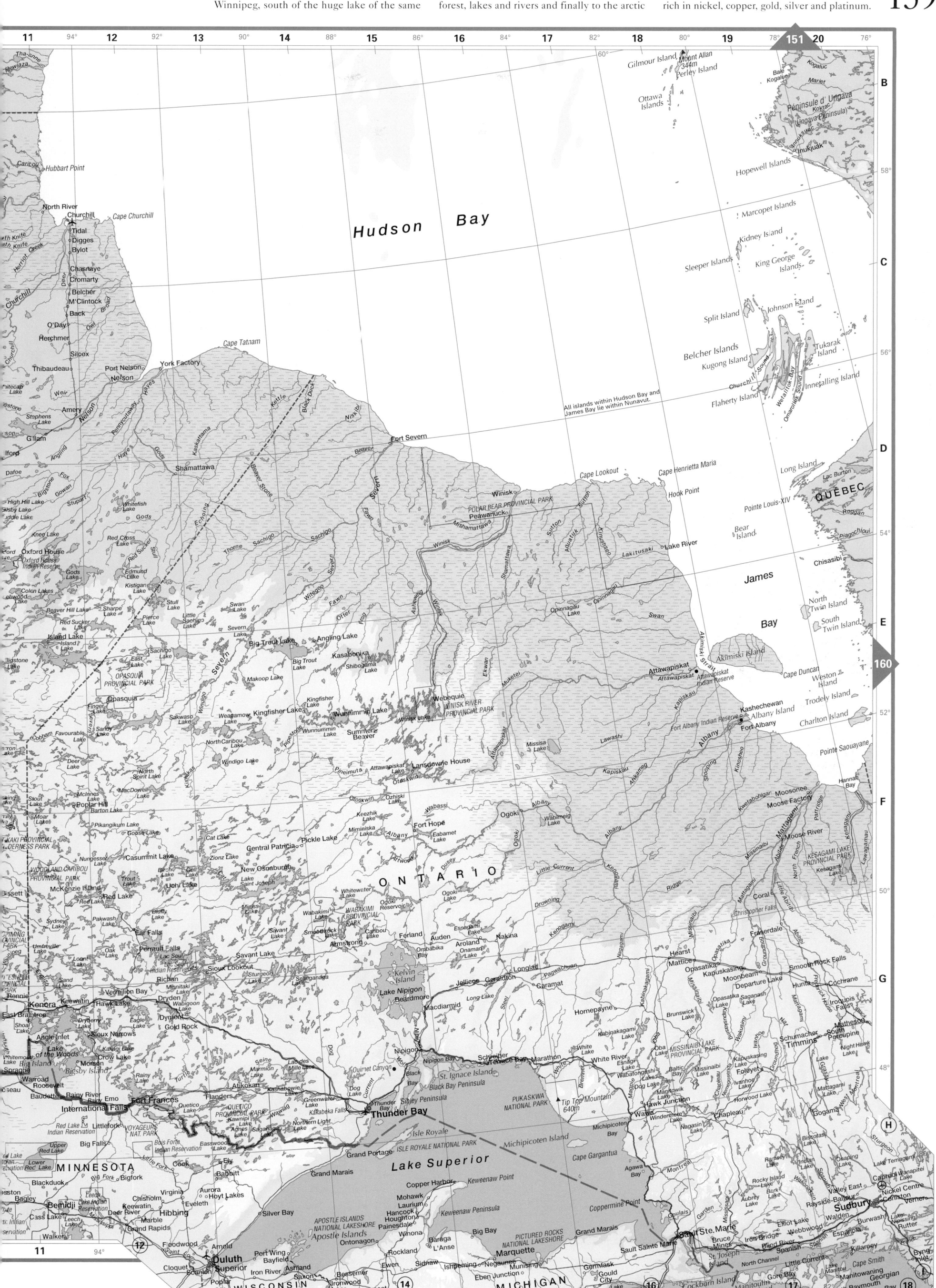

HEIGHT

3000m
(9842ft)

2000m
(6562ft)

1000m
(3281ft)

500m
(1640ft)

200m
(656ft)

Sea level

200m
(656ft)

2000m
(6562ft)

DEPTH

159

162

163

Lambert Conformal Conic Projection

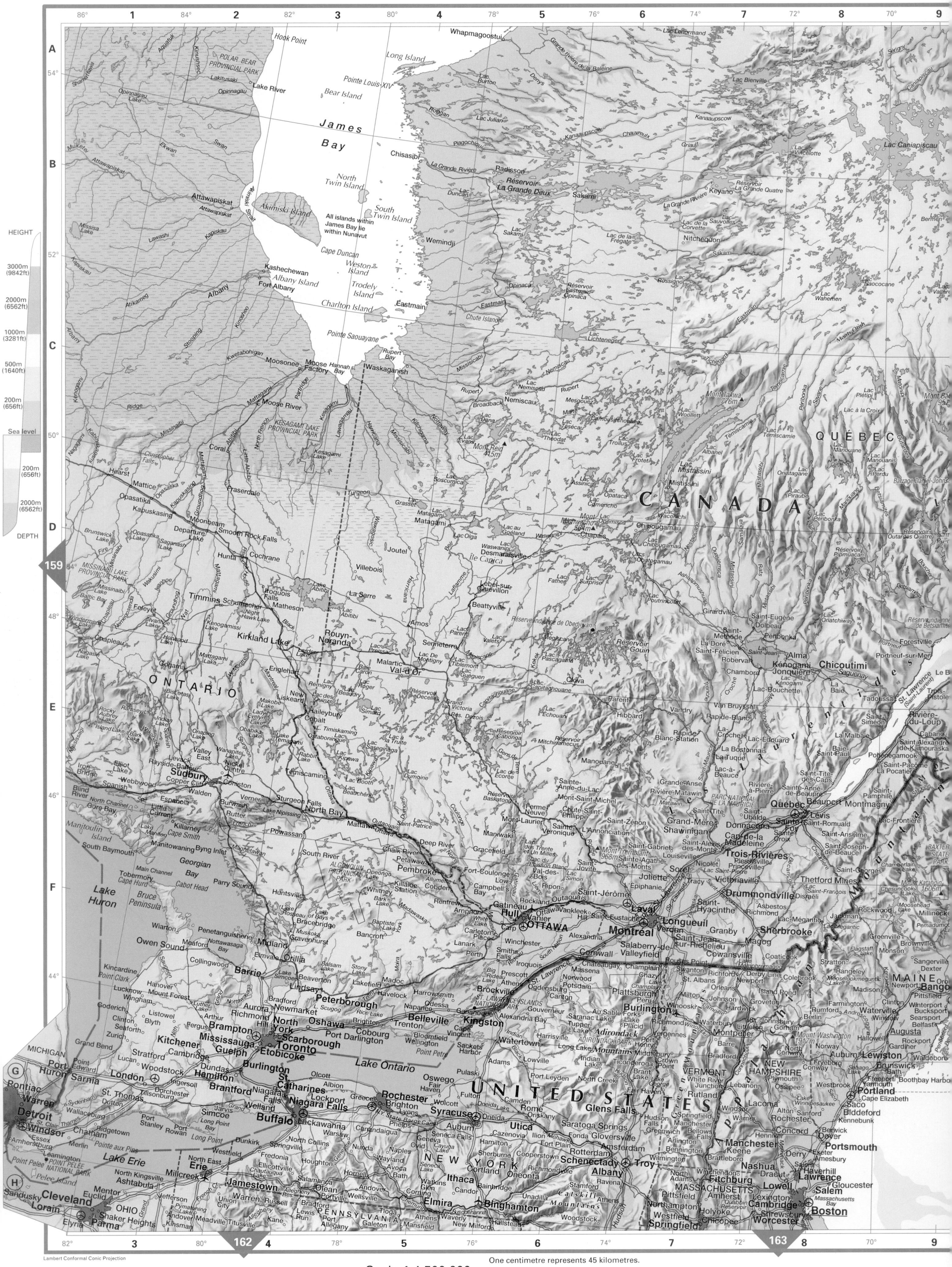

Scale 1:4,500,000

One centimetre represents 45 kilometres.

One inch represents approximately 71 miles.

HERE LIVE MOST of Canada's people, a rich blend of national flavours. Toronto, the hub of English-speaking Canada, has large Hindu, Italian and Chinese communities, while Quebec City is almost as French as Paris. Most exhilarating is Montreal, also French-speaking with an atmosphere that is part old Europe and part Manhattan. Many people from the Maritime Provinces also boast European roots.

161

ATLANTIC OCEAN

LABRADOR SEA

ATLANTIC OCEAN

Gulf of St. Lawrence

Gulf of Maine

0   50   100   150   200   250   300   350   400   450 Kilometres
0   50   100   150   200   250   300 Miles

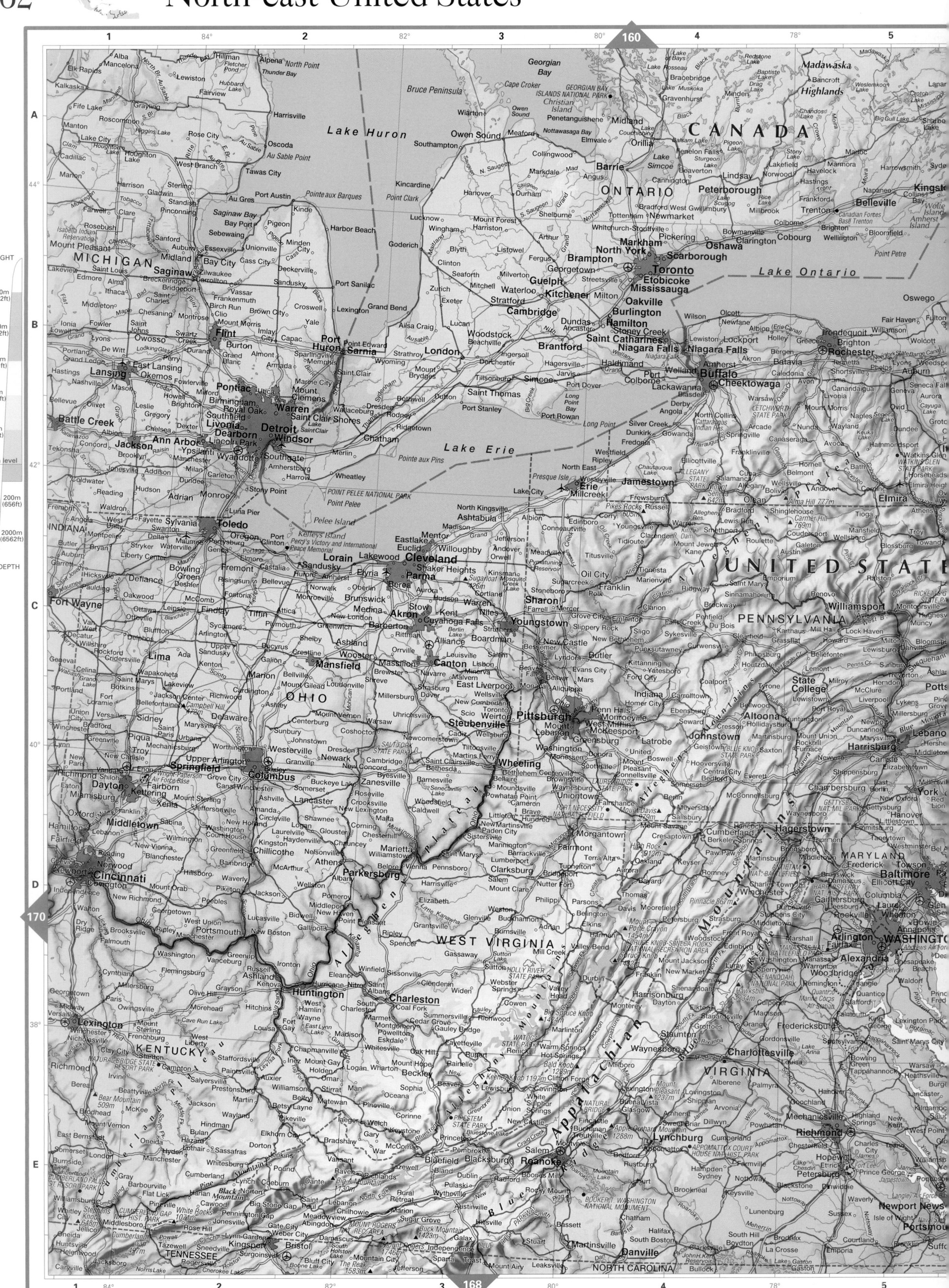

Albers Conic Equal Area Projection

Scale 1:3,000,000

One centimetre represents 30 kilometres.

One inch represents approximately 47 miles.

THE WEALTH OF USA's north-east stemmed from heavy industry. Unsullied nature survives in the grandeur of the Appalachian Mountains.

163

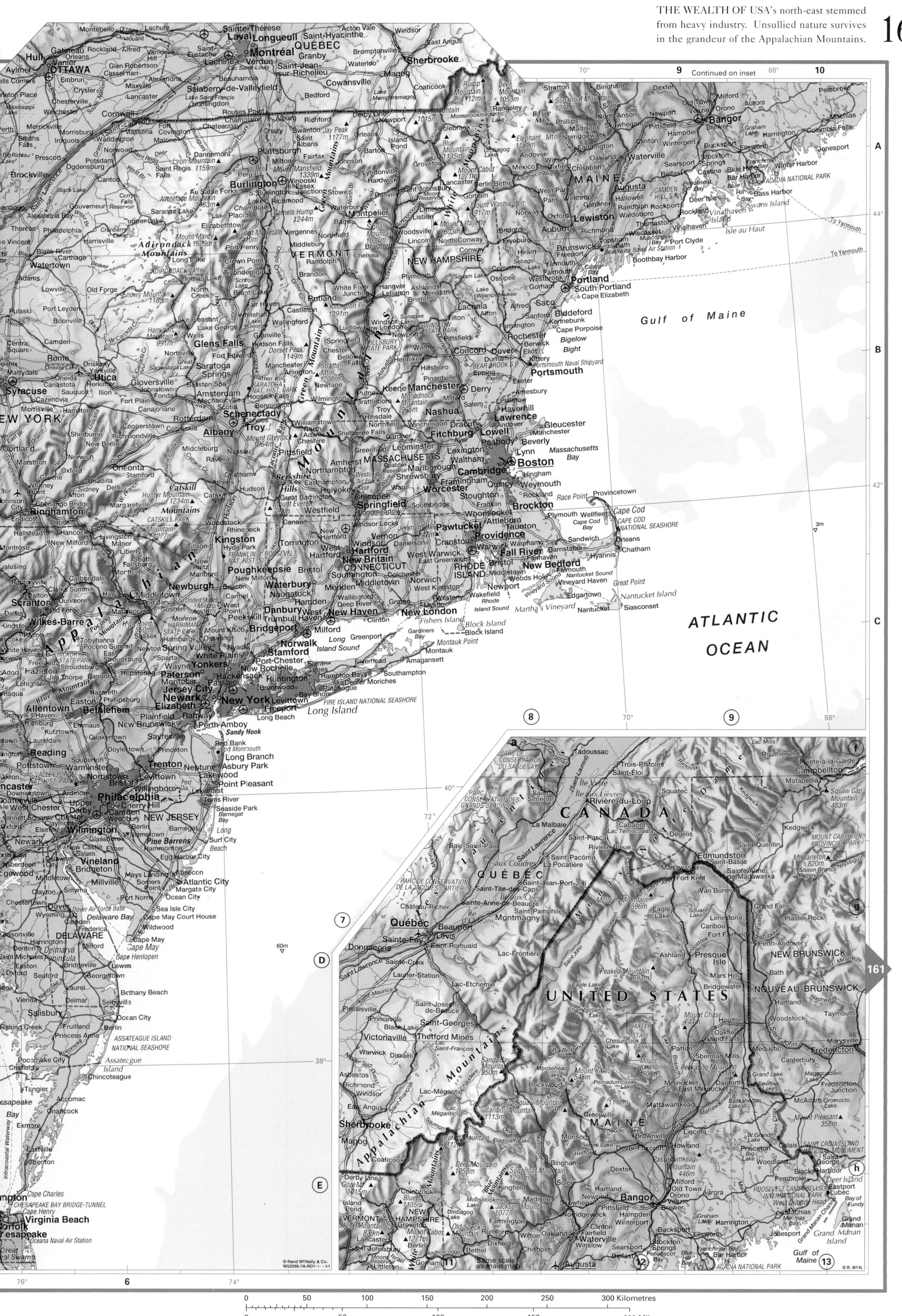

ATLANTIC OCEAN

Gulf of Maine

CANADA

QUÉBEC

UNITED STATES

NEW BRUNSWICK
NOUVEAU-BRUNSWICK

MAINE

NEW HAMPSHIRE

VERMONT

MASSACHUSETTS

CONNECTICUT

RHODE ISLAND

NEW YORK

NEW JERSEY

DELAWARE

163
162
160

HEIGHT

3000m
(9842ft)

2000m
(6562ft)

1000m
(3281ft)

500m
(1640ft)

200m
(656ft)

Sea level

200m
(656ft)

2000m
(6562ft)

DEPTH

CANADA

QUÉBEC

MAINE

NEW HAMPSHIRE

VERMONT

NEW YORK

MASSACHUSETTS

ONTARIO

Lake Ontario

Montréal

Ottawa

Boston

Portsmouth

Cape Ann

Kingston

Syracuse

Rochester

Albany

Burlington

Lake Champlain

Saint Lawrence

Hudson

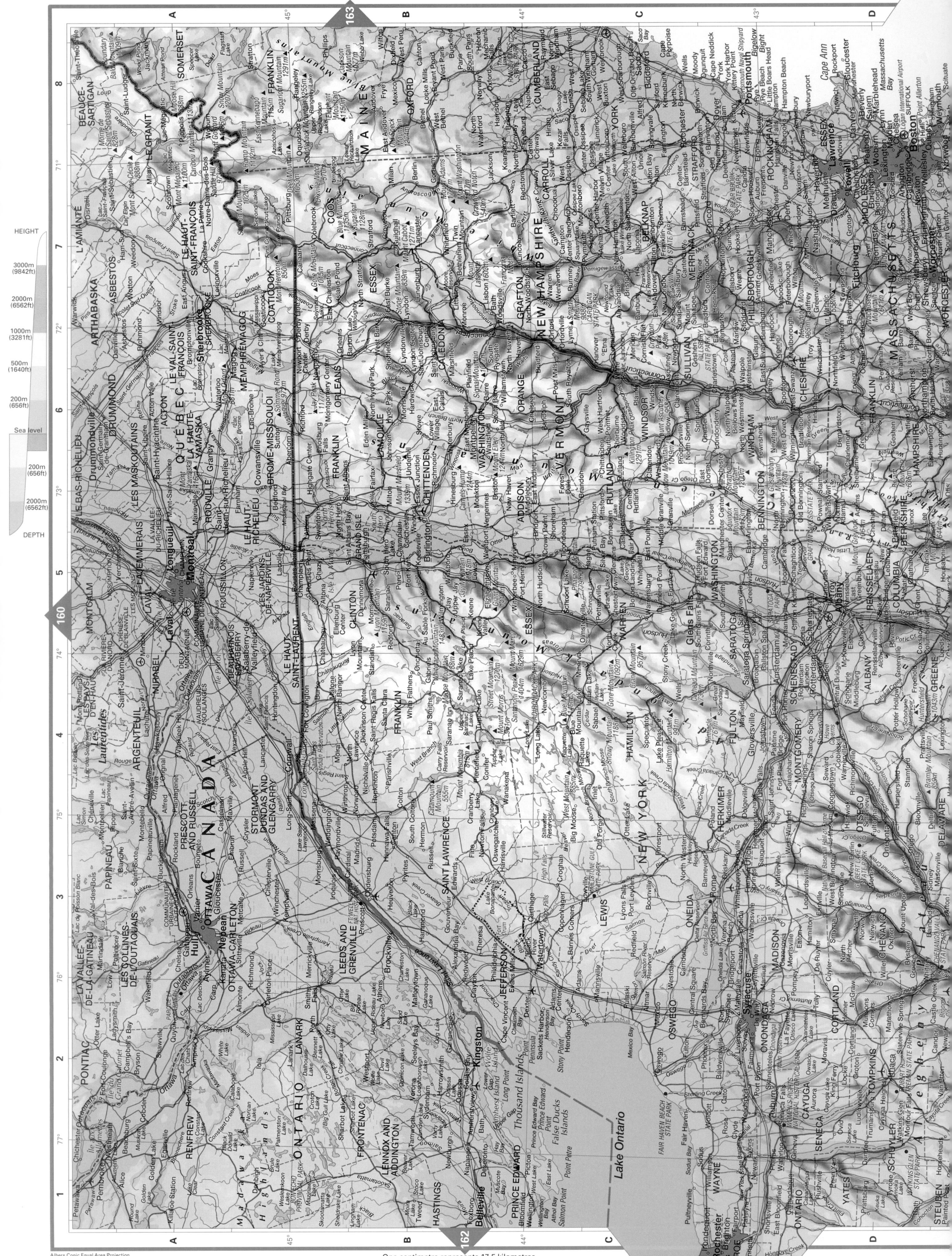

Albers Conic Equal Area Projection

Scale 1:1,750,000

One centimetre represents 17.5 kilometres.

One inch represents approximately 28 miles.

EARLY SETTLEMENTS ON the Atlantic coast, from Boston to north Virginia, nourished the flame of American independence. In more recent times they have gradually coalesced to form a 800 km (500 mile) long conurbation that its inhabitants have dubbed 'Megalopolis'.

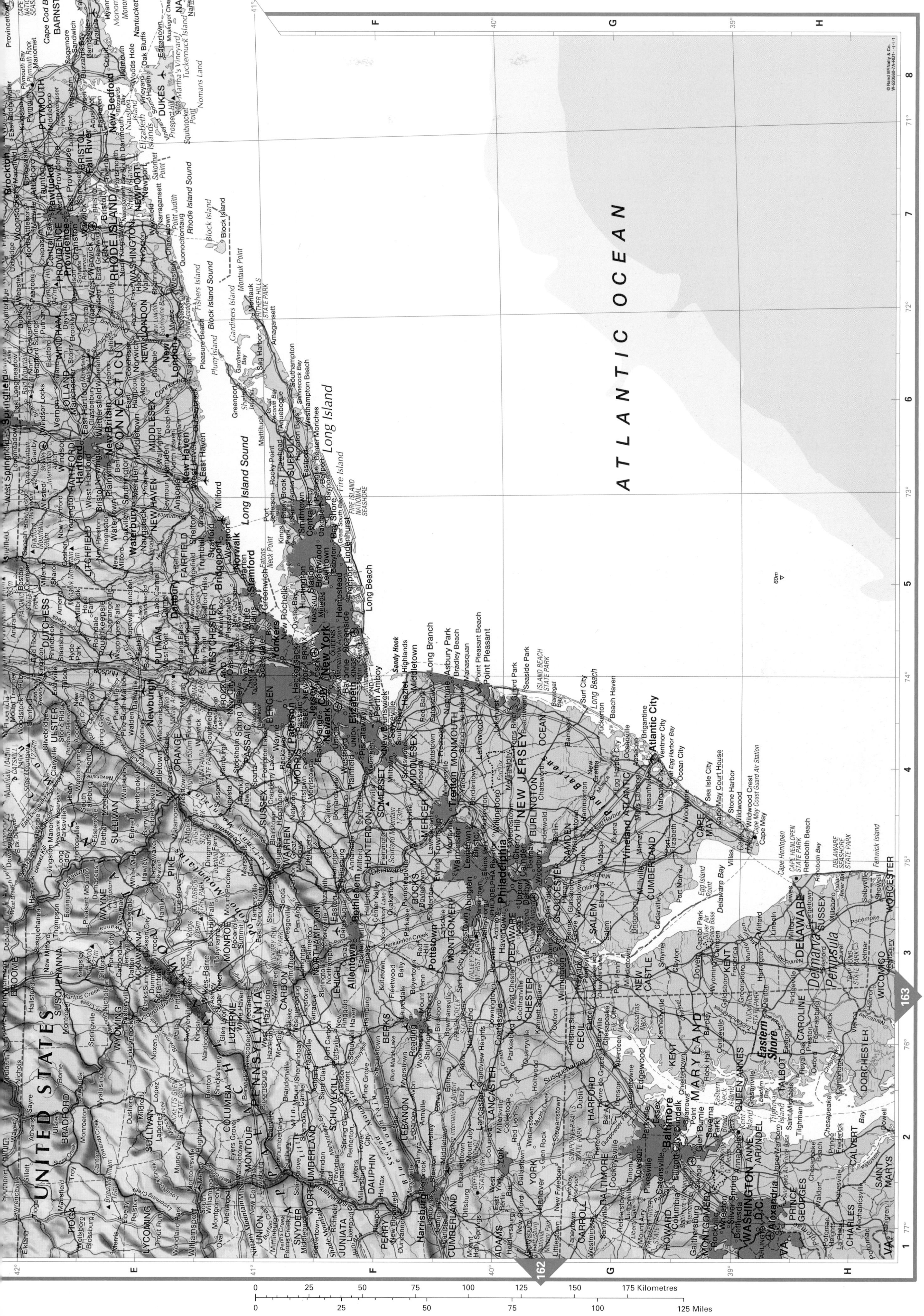

ATLANTIC OCEAN

UNITED STATES

PENNSYLVANIA

NEW JERSEY

MARYLAND

CONNECTICUT

RHODE ISLAND

Long Island

Long Island Sound

Cape Cod

Nantucket

Martha's Vineyard

New Bedford

Fall River

Providence

Newport

New London

New Haven

Hartford

Waterbury

Bridgeport

Stamford

Norwalk

New York

Yonkers

New Rochelle

Newark

Jersey City

Elizabeth

Paterson

Trenton

New Brunswick

Sandy Hook

Long Branch

Asbury Park

Point Pleasant

Atlantic City

Cape May

Philadelphia

Camden

Wilmington

DELAWARE

Dover

Baltimore

Annapolis

WASHINGTON, D.C.

Alexandria

Allentown

Bethlehem

Easton

Reading

Harrisburg

Lancaster

York

Chesapeake Bay

Delaware Bay

Delmarva Peninsula

Eastern Shore

| 0 | 25 | 50 | 75 | 100 | 125 | 150 | 175 Kilometres |

| 0 | 25 | 50 | 75 | 100 | 125 Miles |

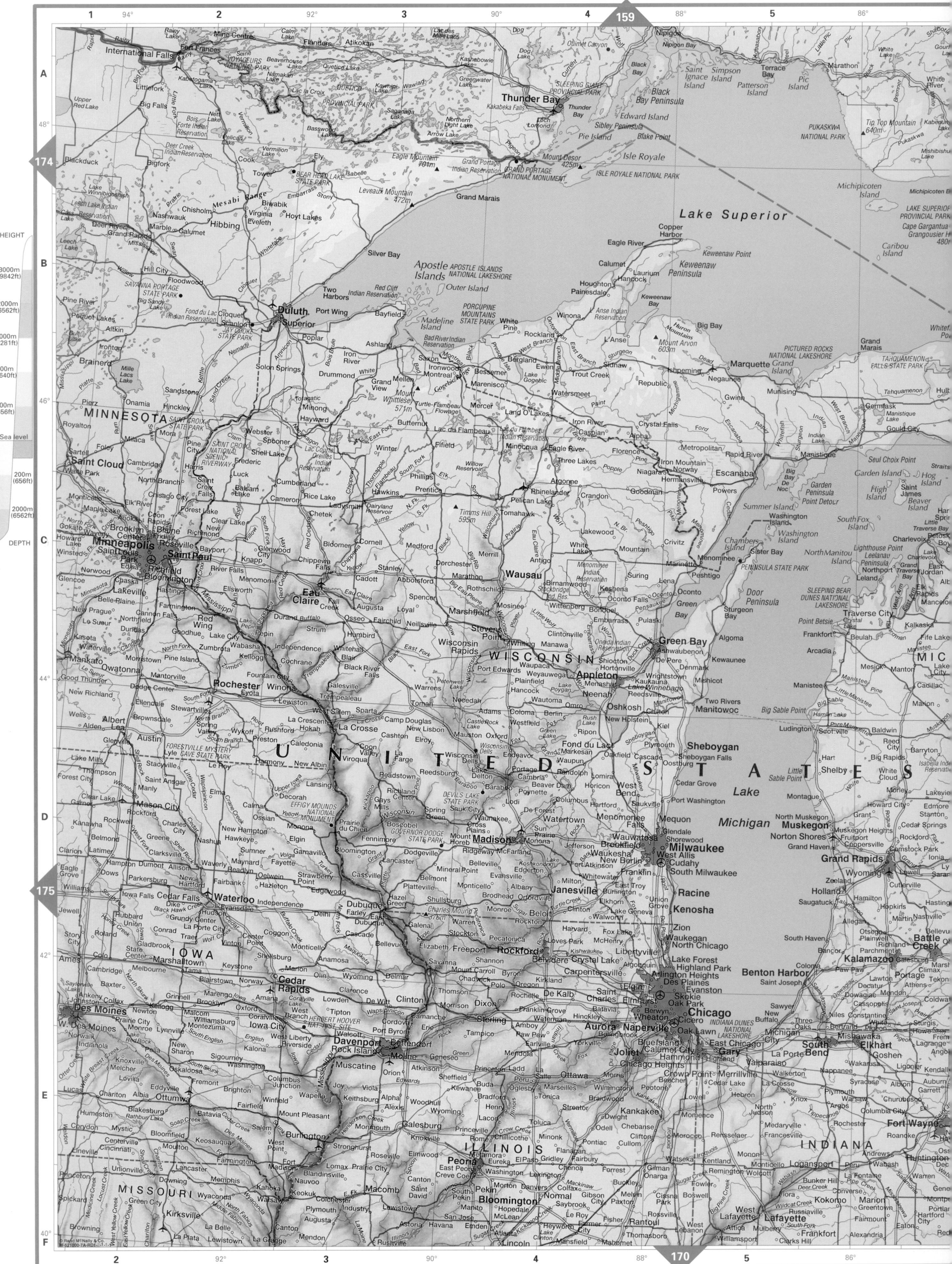

Scale 1:3,000,000

One centimetre represents 30 kilometres.

One inch represents approximately 47 miles.

THE GREAT LAKES, straddling the Canada-US border, together form the world's largest surface expanse of fresh water. Along their shores, a scenic backdrop of forest, bluffs and wide beaches gives way in places to the gritty decay of towns whose industries failed in the struggle to modernise. Bustling lakeside cities like Chicago and Toronto, however, hold the promise of an even more vigorous future.

167

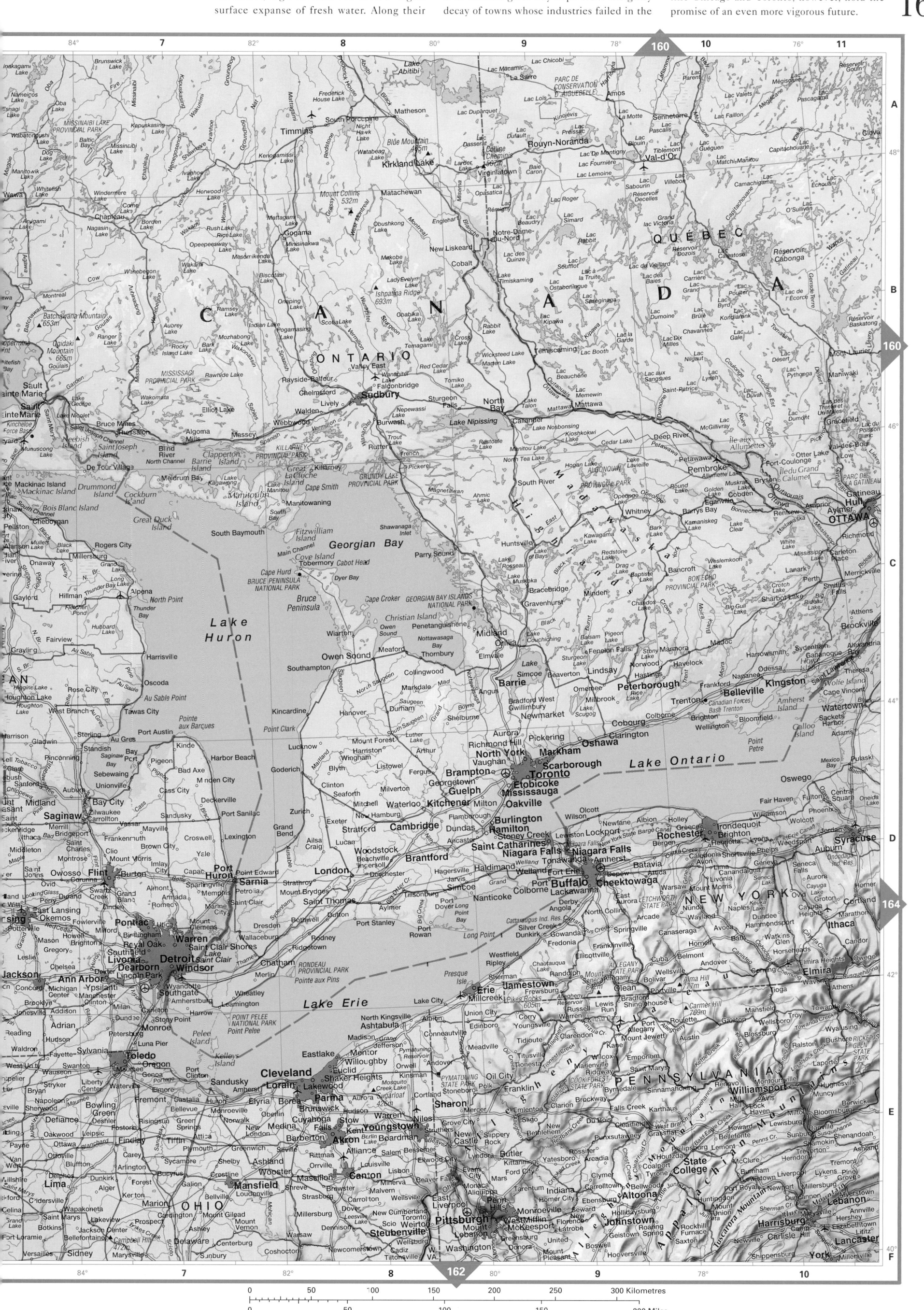

HEIGHT

3000m
(9842ft)

2000m
(6562ft)

1000m
(3281ft)

500m
(1640ft)

200m
(656ft)

Sea level

200m
(656ft)

2000m
(6562ft)

DEPTH

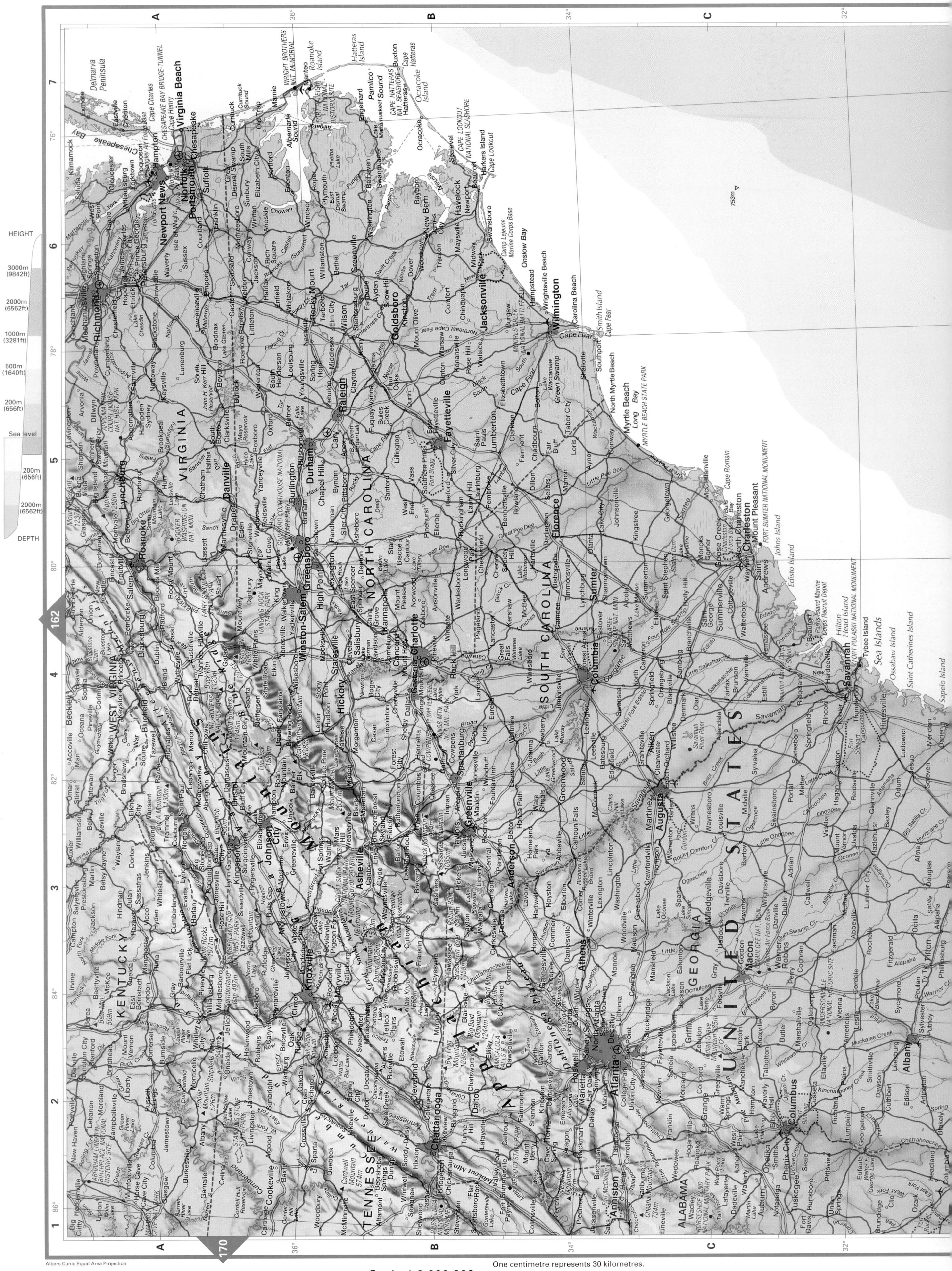

Albers Conic Equal Area Projection

Scale 1:3,000,000

One centimetre represents 30 kilometres.

One inch represents approximately 47 miles.

LEFT IN RUINS by the Civil War, the states of the south-east awoke slowly from an agrarian past. Florida, the southernmost state and known mostly for its beef, pork and oranges, led the way. After a railway reached Florida's tip in the early 1900s, a land boom followed, smart resorts sprang up, and people flocked to the 'Sunshine State', among whose attractions is delightful St Augustine, the oldest town in the USA.

169

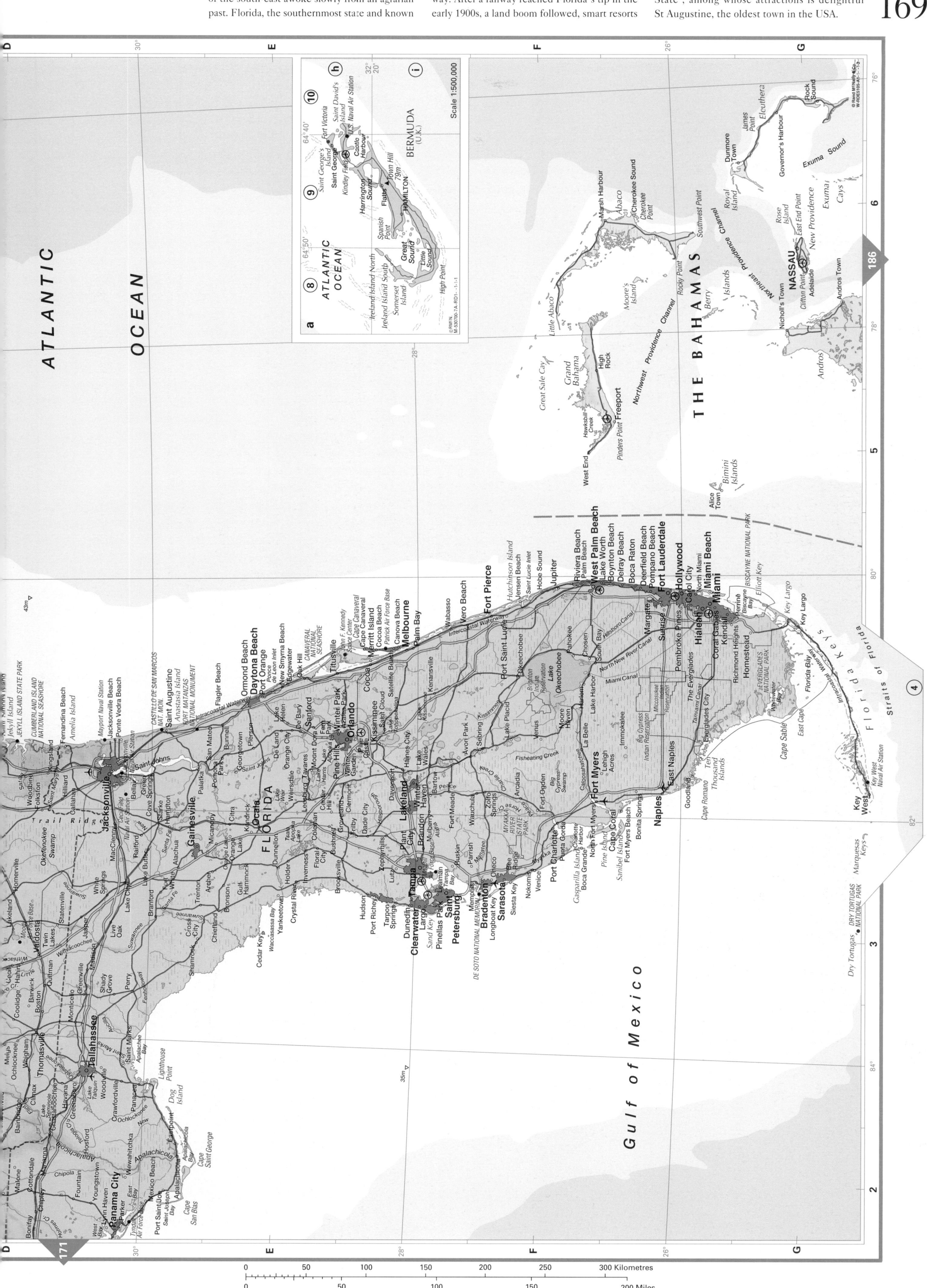

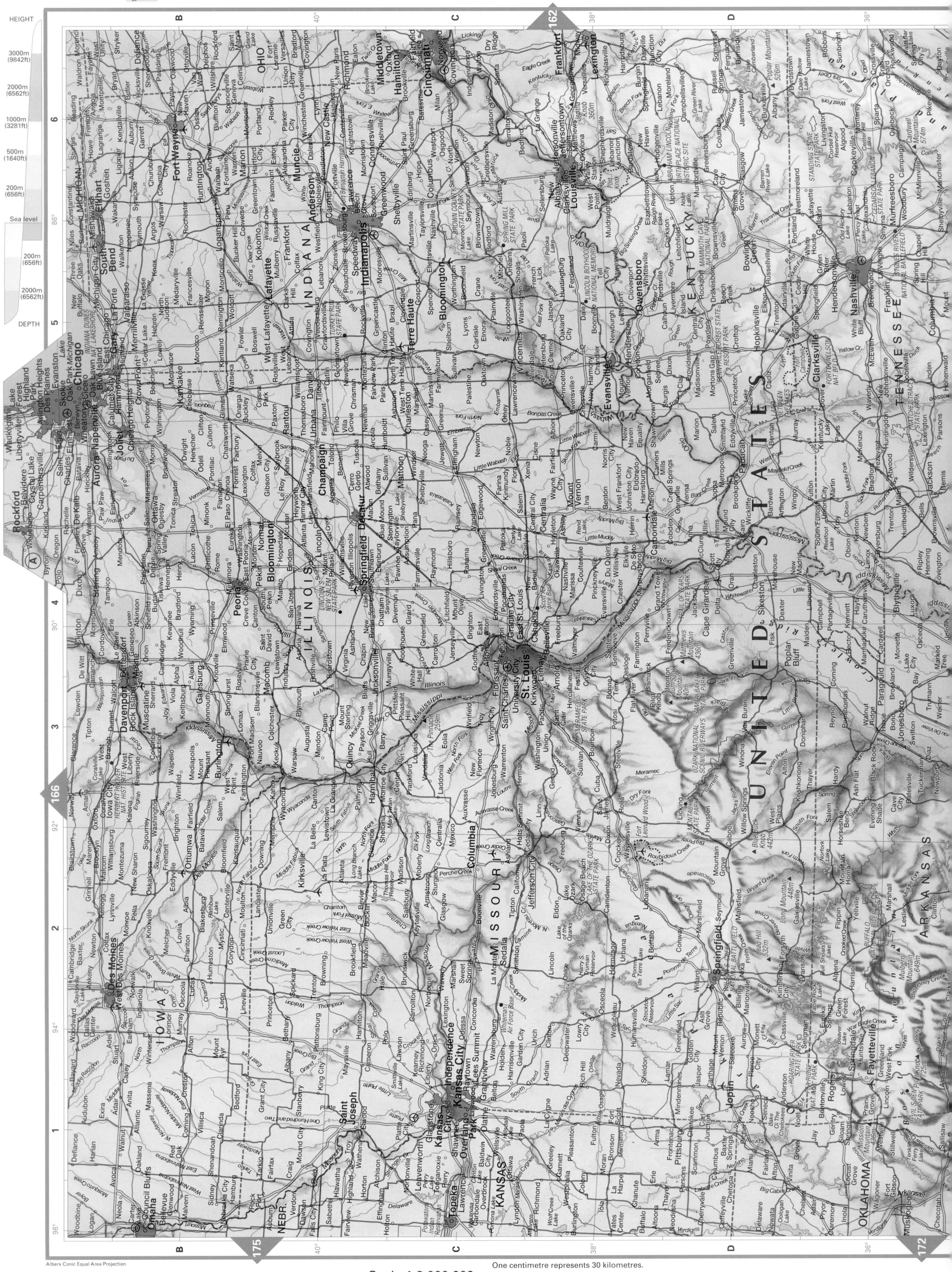

HEIGHT

3000m (9842ft)
2000m (6562ft)
1000m (3281ft)
500m (1640ft)
200m (656ft)
Sea level

200m (656ft)
2000m (6562ft)

DEPTH

OHIO

MICHIGAN

INDIANA

ILLINOIS

IOWA

MISSOURI

KENTUCKY

TENNESSEE

ARKANSAS

OKLAHOMA

KANSAS

NEBR.

UNITED STATES

Fort Wayne

Muncie

Anderson

Indianapolis

Cincinnati

Hamilton

Middletown

Frankfort

Lexington

Louisville

Clarksville

Nashville

Evansville

Owensboro

Terre Haute

Bloomington

Champaign

Decatur

Springfield

Bloomington

Normal

Peoria

Chicago

Rockford

Aurora

Naperville

Joliet

Gary

Hammond

South Bend

Elkhart

Des Moines

West Des Moines

Davenport

Rock Island

Iowa City

Burlington

Quincy

Columbia

Jefferson City

Springfield

Joplin

St. Louis

East St. Louis

Kansas City

Independence

Overland Park

Topeka

Lawrence

Leavenworth

Saint Joseph

Omaha

Council Bluffs

Fayetteville

Paducah

Mississippi

Missouri

Illinois

Ohio

Lake Michigan

Albers Conic Equal Area Projection

Scale 1:3,000,000

One centimetre represents 30 kilometres.

One inch represents approximately 47 miles.

GATEWAY TO THE west since its founding by the French, St Louis also looks to north and south along the Mississippi – 'Old Man River', dotted with towns whose names punctuate the Blues. Farthest south is the wide flood plain of the lower Mississippi, which once supported vast cotton plantations. Prominent features are the levees – huge embankments built to protect farms from inundation by 'Big Muddy'.

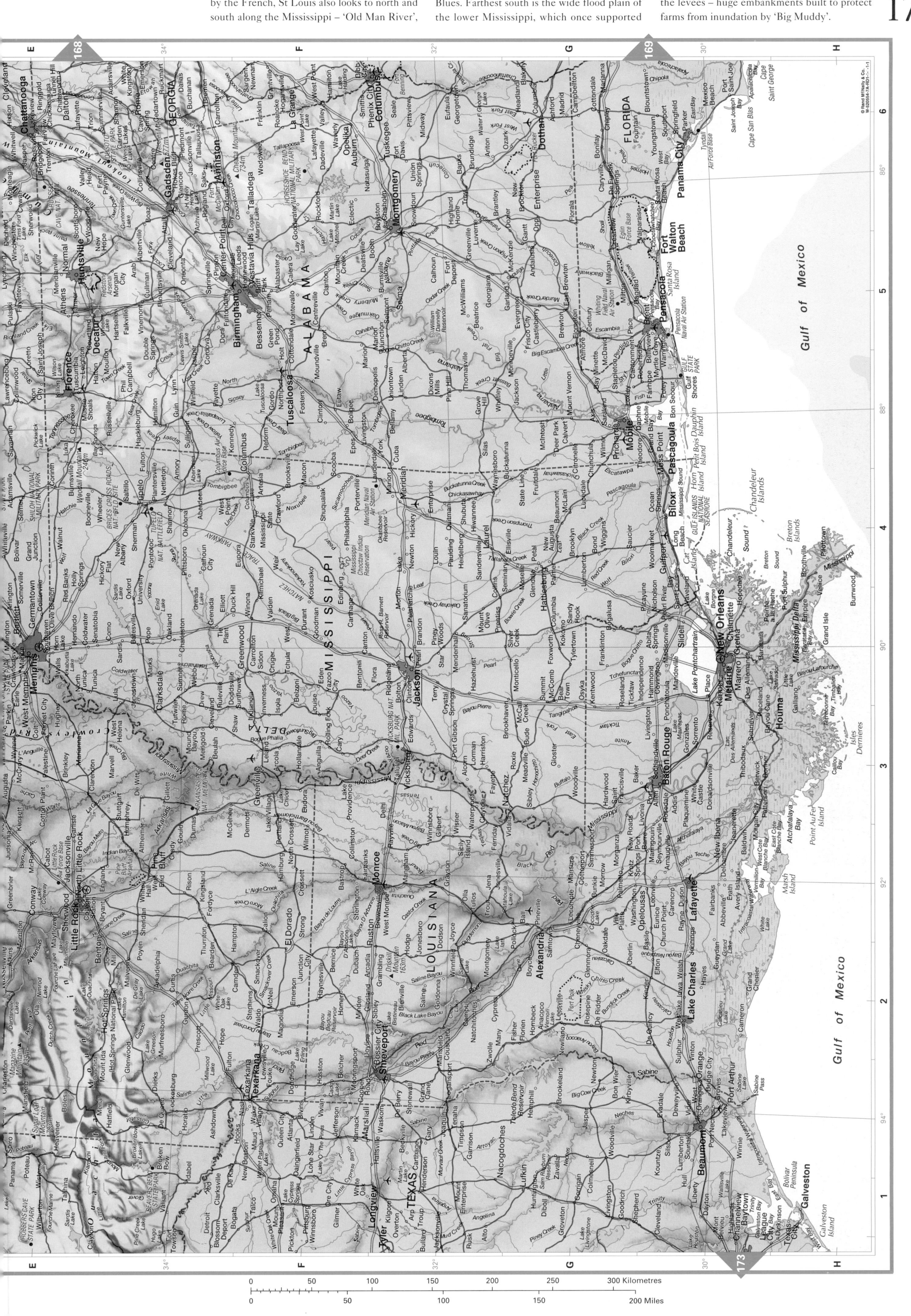

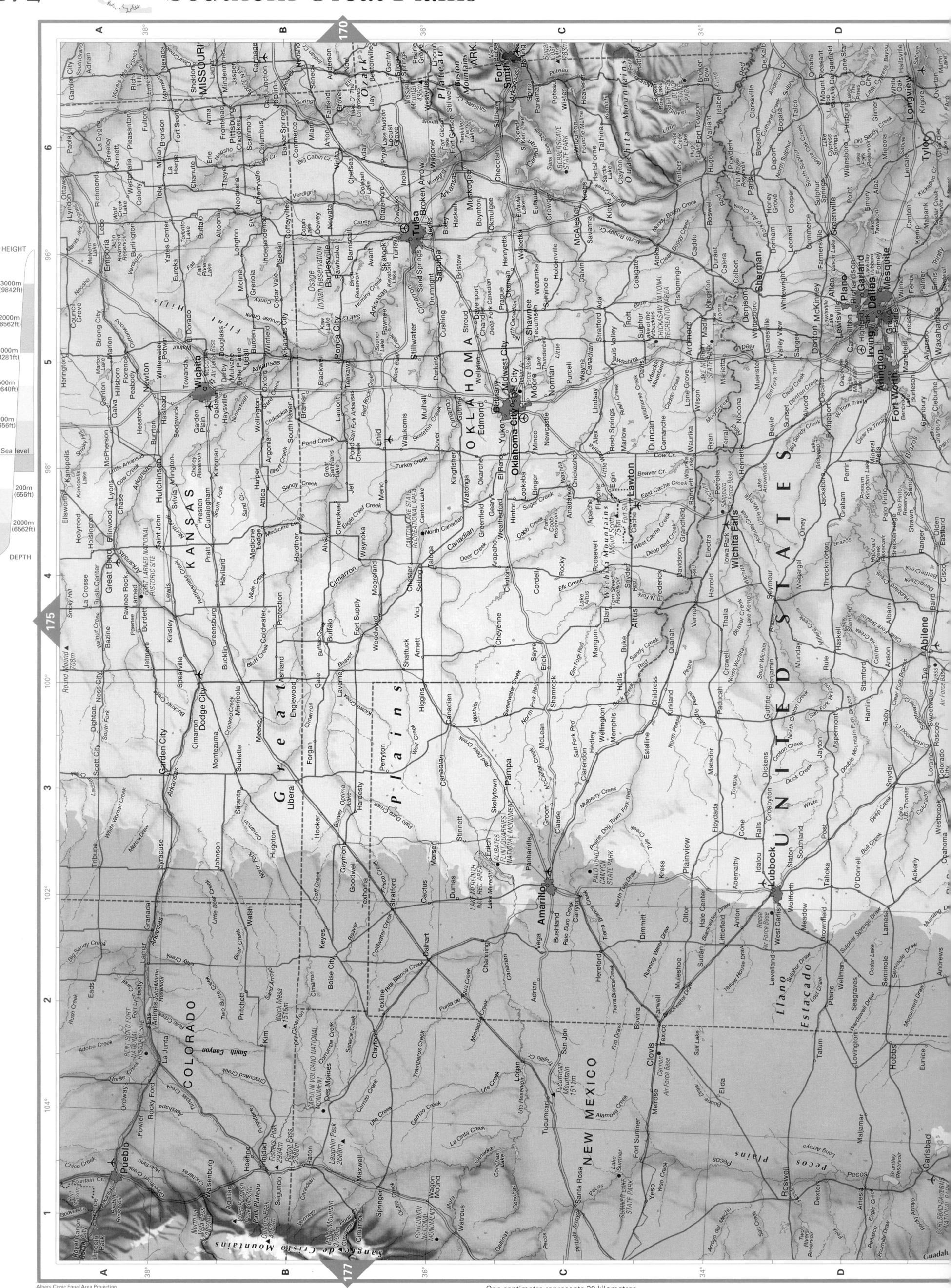

HEIGHT

3000m (9842ft)

2000m (6562ft)

1000m (3281ft)

500m (1640ft)

200m (656ft)

Sea level

200m (656ft)

2000m (6562ft)

DEPTH

EVEN LARGER THAN its legend, second state in size behind Alaska, Texas encompasses deserts and swamps, skyscraper cities and old Hispanic towns, oilfields and a tropical coast beset by hurricanes. Tornadoes plague the region, and in the 1930s unrelenting winds blew away tonnes of topsoil left dry as dust by years of drought. The fear of another such Dust Bowl hangs heavy over Oklahoma and its neighbours.

173

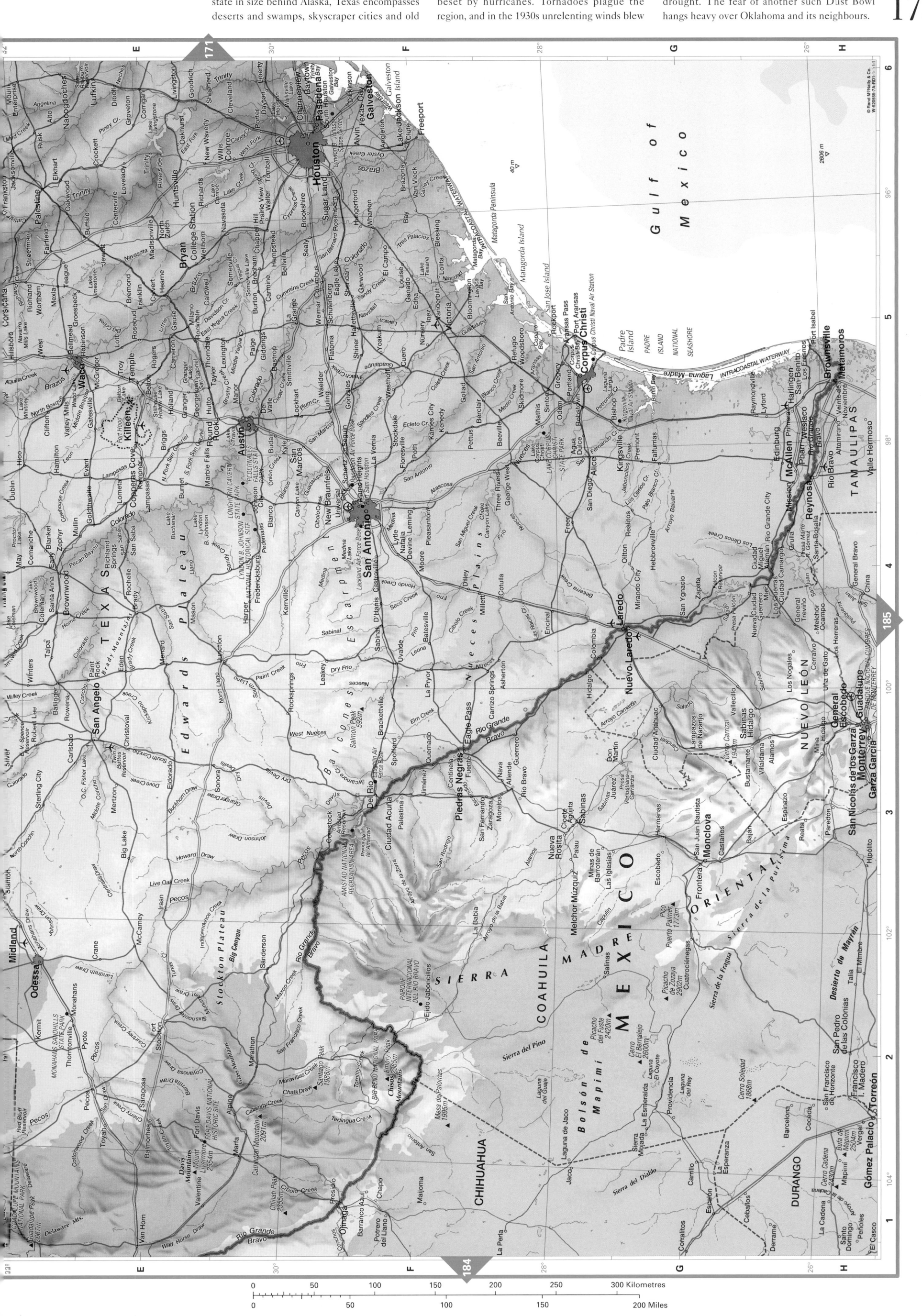

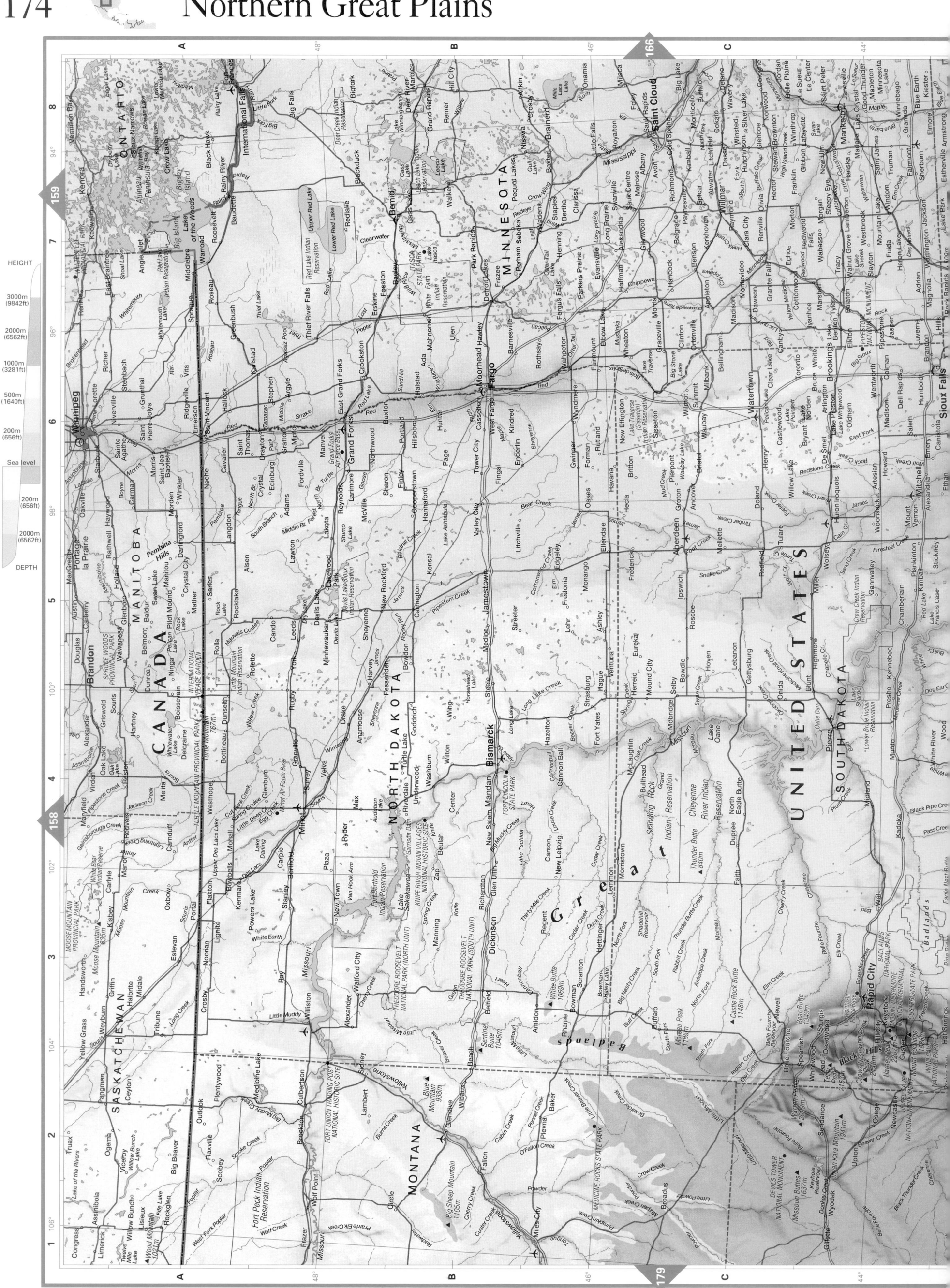

THE GREAT AMERICAN Desert, as old maps called the Great Plains, was transformed into the nation's breadbasket by the invention of the hardened steel plough, ending the glory days of the Plains Indians and the gunsmoke-filled saloons of cow towns such as Dodge City. Today the plains are sprinkled with the kind of towns that many city-dwelling Americans will forever associate with childhood and home.

175

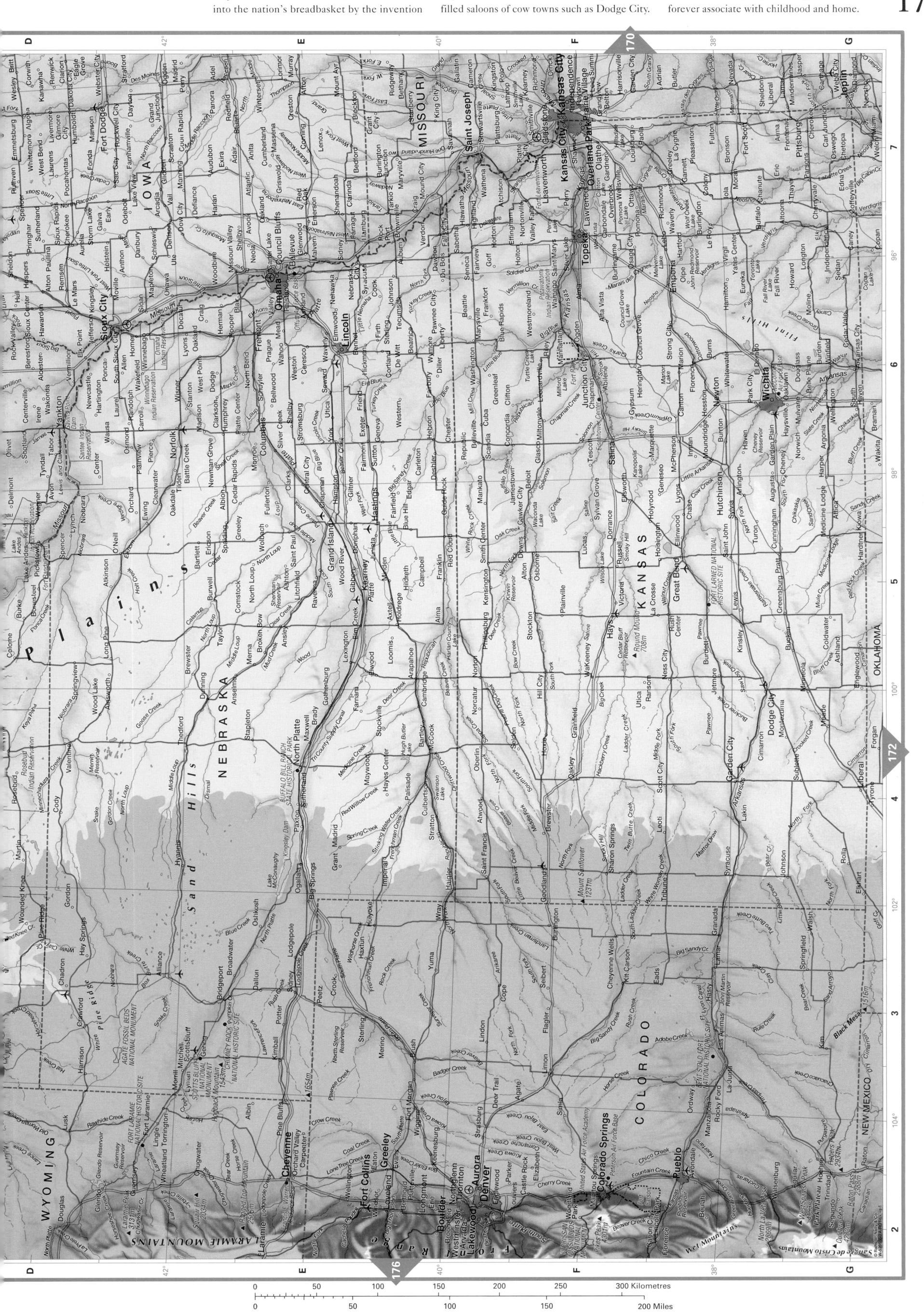

HEIGHT

3000m
(9842ft)

2000m
(6562ft)

1000m
(3281ft)

500m
(1640ft)

200m
(656ft)

Sea level

200m
(656ft)

2000m
(6562ft)

DEPTH

Albers Conic Equal Area Projection

Scale 1:3,000,000

One centimetre represents 30 kilometres.

One inch represents approximately 47 miles.

FROM THE SNOWY peaks of the Rocky Mountains to the dizzying depths of the Grand Canyon, this is one of the world's showplaces. It is embellished by the geysers at Yellowstone and the glowing red towers of Monument Valley; but most hauntingly beautiful perhaps is Canyon de Chelly, with its cliff houses built by the Anasazi people who lived and vanished 200 years before Europeans came to America.

177

0   50   100   150   200   250   300 Kilometres

0   50   100   150   200 Miles

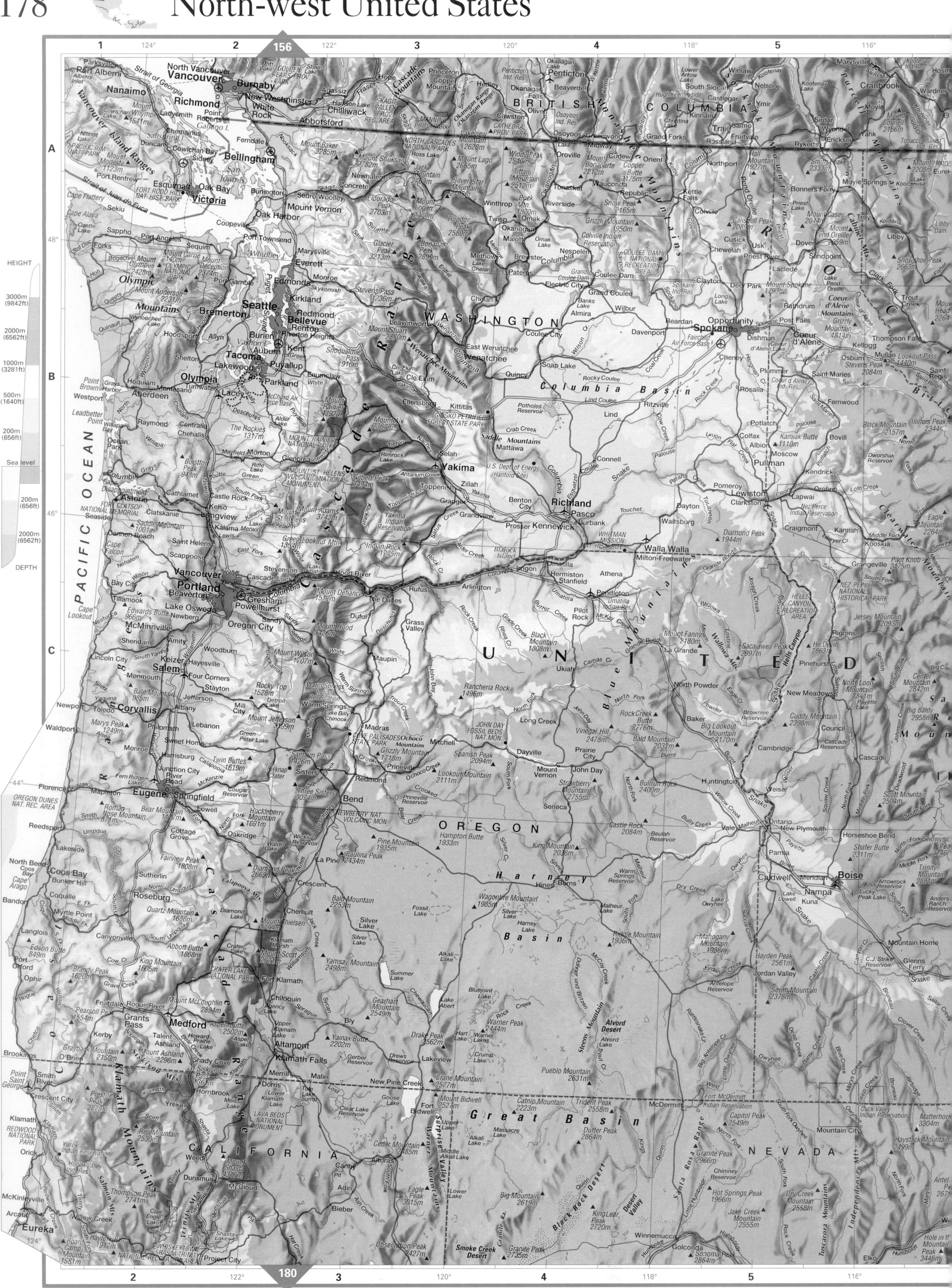

One centimetre represents 30 kilometres.

Scale 1:3,000,000

One inch represents approximately 47 miles.

Albers Conic Equal Area Projection

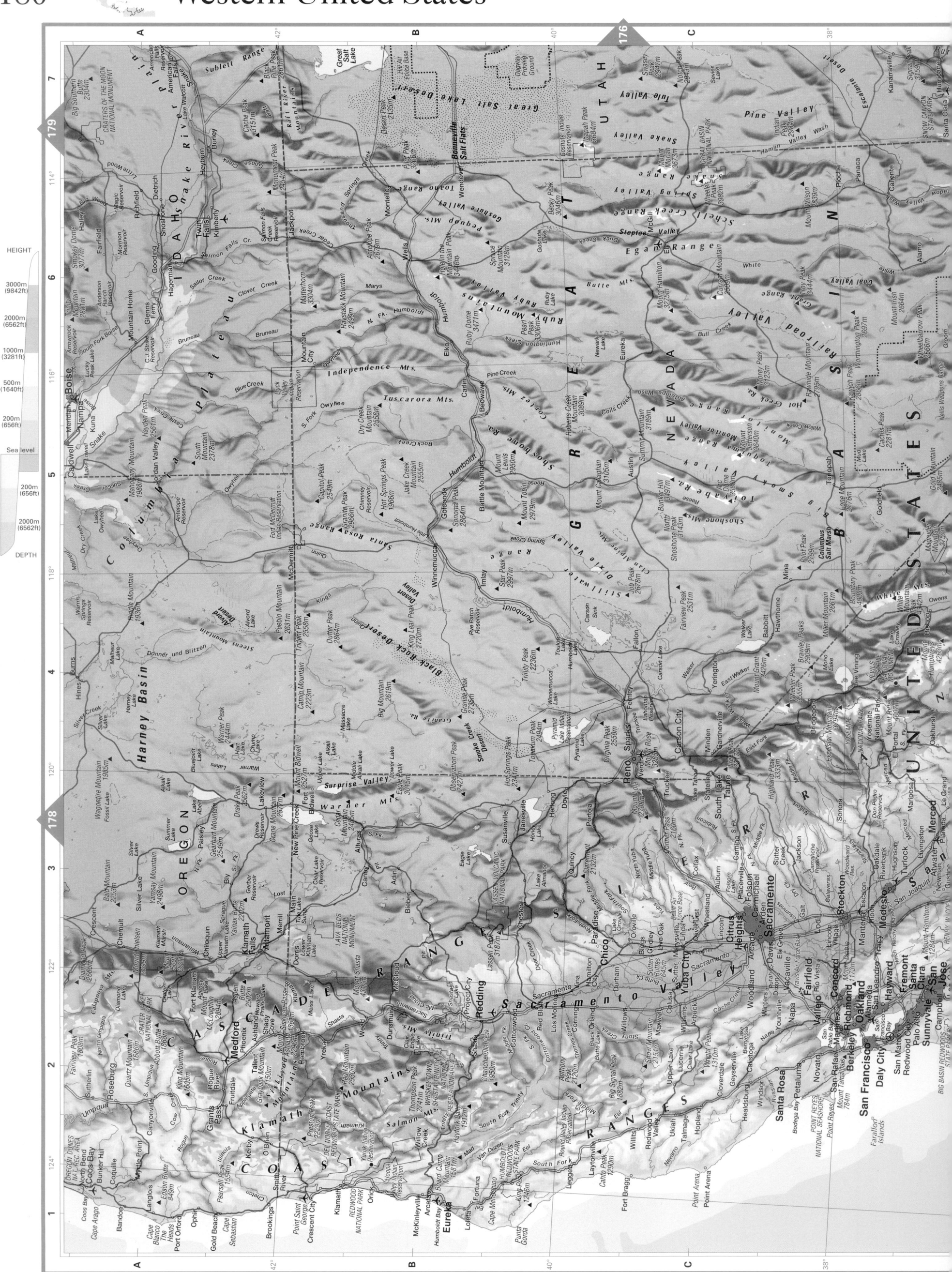

HEIGHT

3000m
(9842ft)

2000m
(6562ft)

1000m
(3281ft)

500m
(1640ft)

200m
(656ft)

Sea level

200m
(656ft)

2000m
(6562ft)

DEPTH

Albers Conic Equal Area Projection

Scale 1:3,000,000

One centimetre represents 30 kilometres.

One inch represents approximately 47 miles.

THE WORLD'S IMAGE of the USA, absorbed from a thousand films and books, is centred in the West. Here is the empty sagebrush plain of Nevada, lit in one corner by the neon oasis of Las Vegas. Here too are the unique splendours of California – its redwood forests, alpine Lake Tahoe, wind-burnished Death Valley and the glacial sculptures of Yosemite Park. Far out are the coral and volcanic islands of Hawaii.

181

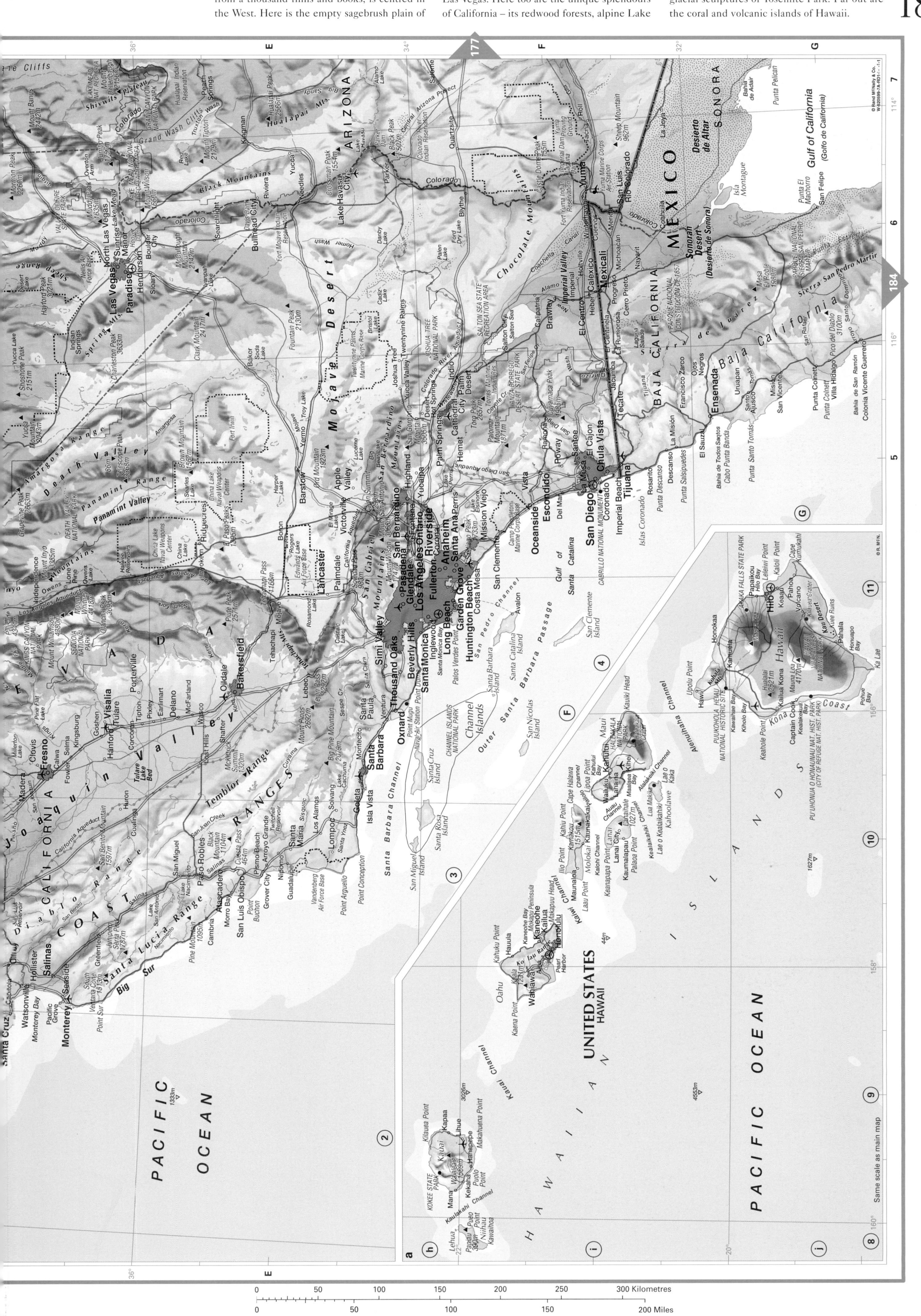

0   50   100   150   200   250   300 Kilometres

0   50   100   150   200 Miles

HEIGHT

3000m
(9842ft)

2000m
(6562ft)

1000m
(3281ft)

500m
(1640ft)

200m
(656ft)

Sea level

200m
(656ft)

2000m
(6562ft)

DEPTH

Albers Conic Equal Area Projection

Scale 1:1,750,000

One centimetre represents 17.5 kilometres.

One inch represents approximately 28 miles.

THERE ARE MANY California. To the south, Los Angeles is a brash, exuberant sprawl that has swallowed up a dozen or more towns, Hollywood for one, so that each suburb has a character all its own. The endless sunshine of Palm Springs attracts the rich and famous. Northerly San Francisco, however, can be chilly even in summer, but it is compact and relaxed, and its diverse architecture has a worldly air.

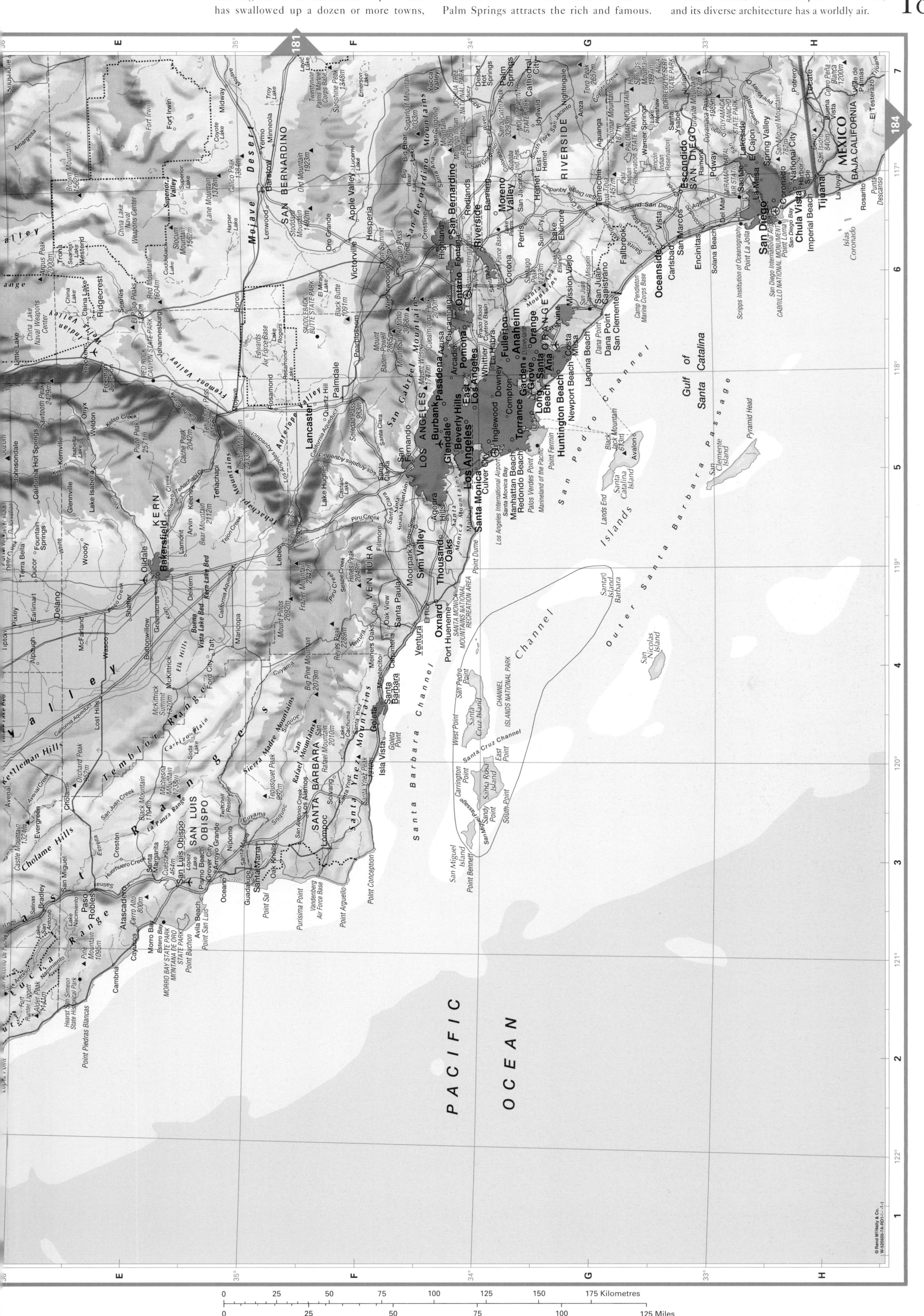

0   25   50   75   100   125   150   175 Kilometres

0   25   50   75   100   125 Miles

© Rand McNally & Co.
W-532000-7A-RD1-1--1-1

Lambert Conformal Conic Projection

Scale 1:6,000,000

One centimetre represents 60 kilometres.

One inch represents approximately 95 miles.

STYLISH YET POOR, full of ancient treasures and prone to earthquakes, Mexico City is Mexico in microcosm. Twenty million people somehow live in the city, and as their numbers grow many feel that emigration to the USA, legal or not, is their best hope. Human traffic of another kind flows the opposite way, as crowds of American tourists cross the border to marvel at the ruins and relics of Mexican civilisations.

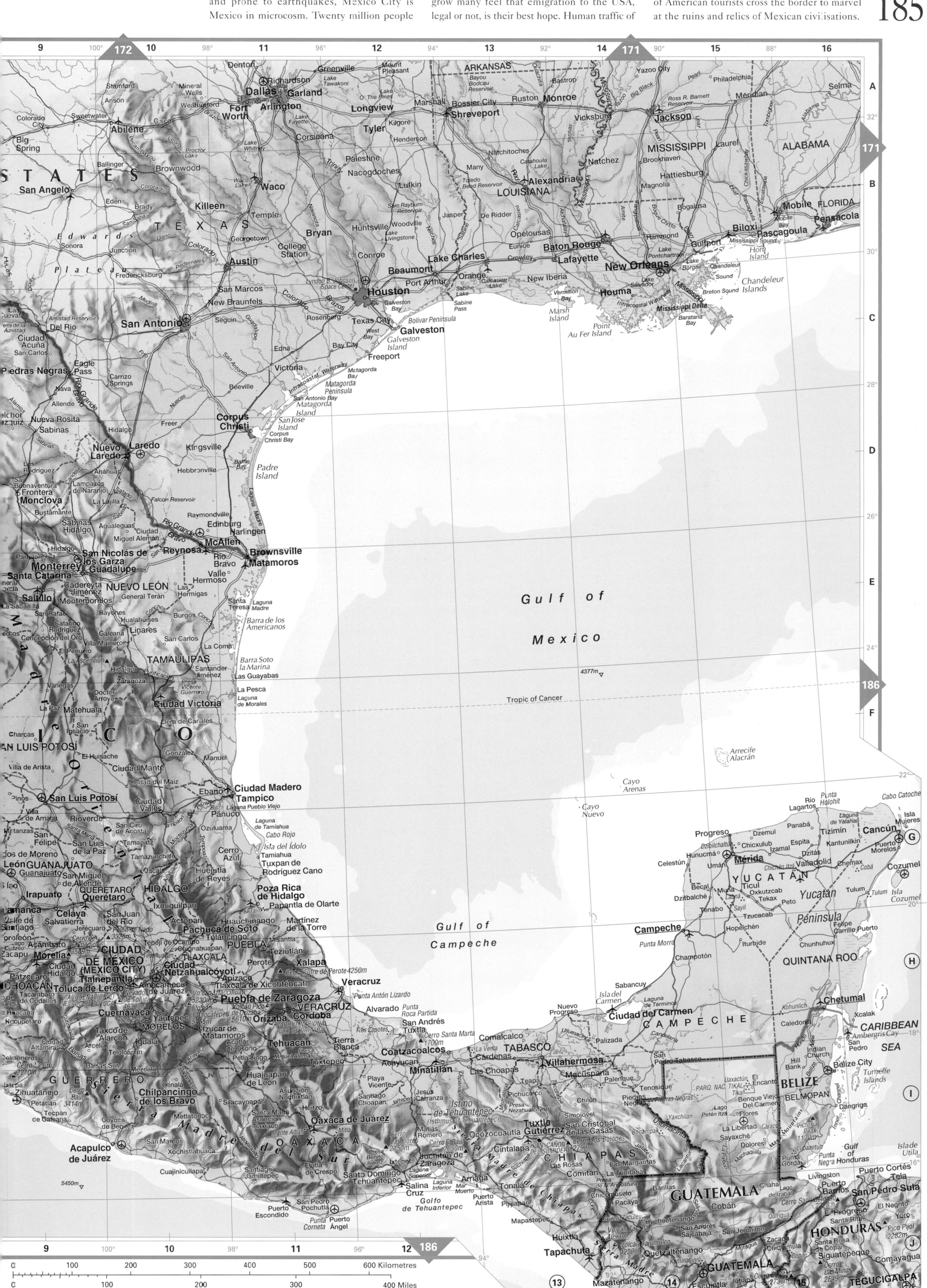

Scale 1:8,000,000

One centimetre represents 80 kilometres.

One inch represents approximately 126 miles.

Lambert Conformal Conic Projection

© Rand McNally & Co.
W-RDE4102-A1

VOLCANIC IN POLITICS as in geology, the nations of Central America and the larger islands of the Caribbean share histories of repression, revolution and counterrevolution. Fluctuating economies depend largely on coffee, bananas, tobacco, sugar and hardwoods. Tiny island countries like Antigua and Barbuda, and St Kitts and Nevis in the Leeward Islands, tempt their visitors with perfect beaches and warm seas.

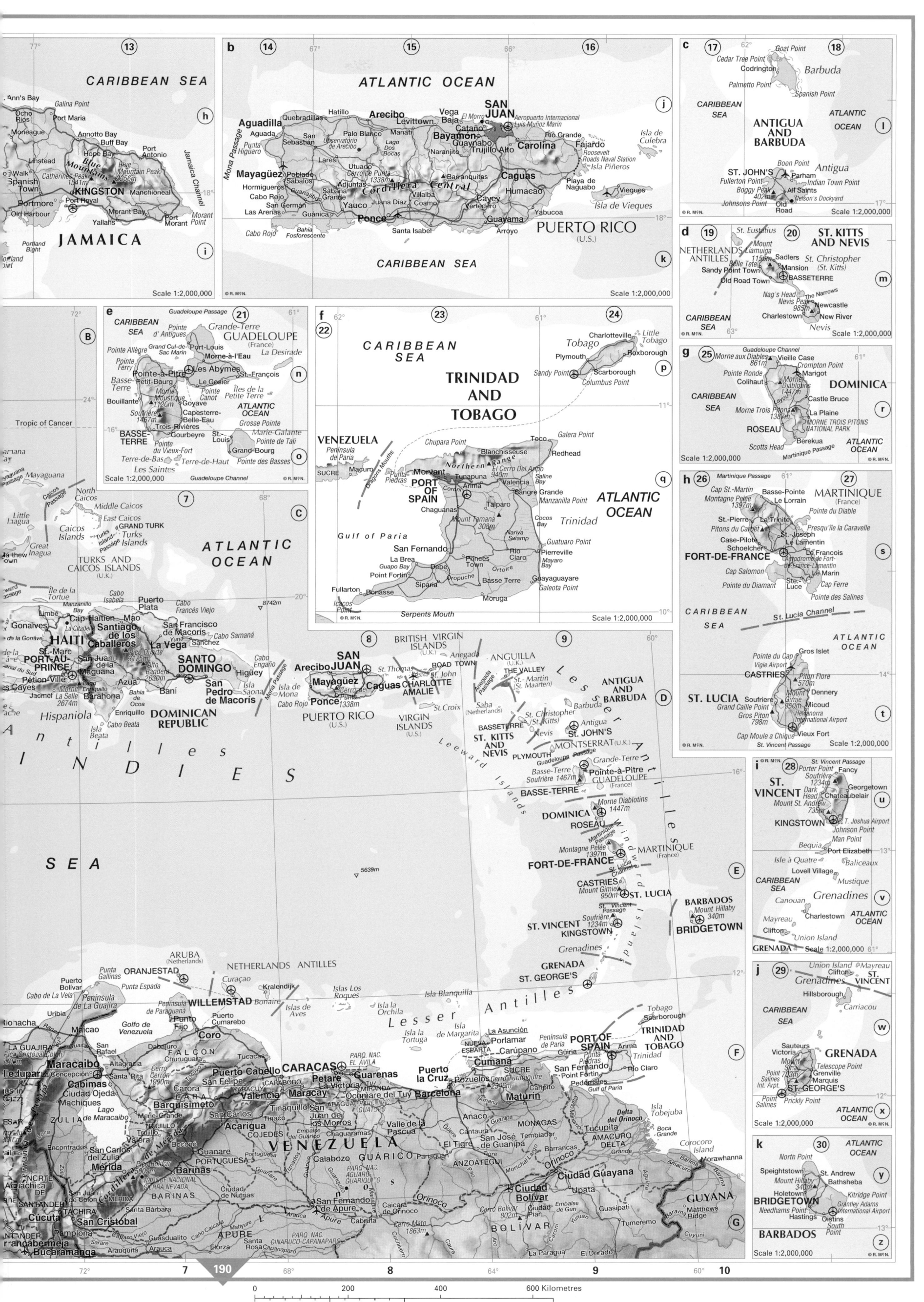

Lambert Azimuthal Equal Area Projection

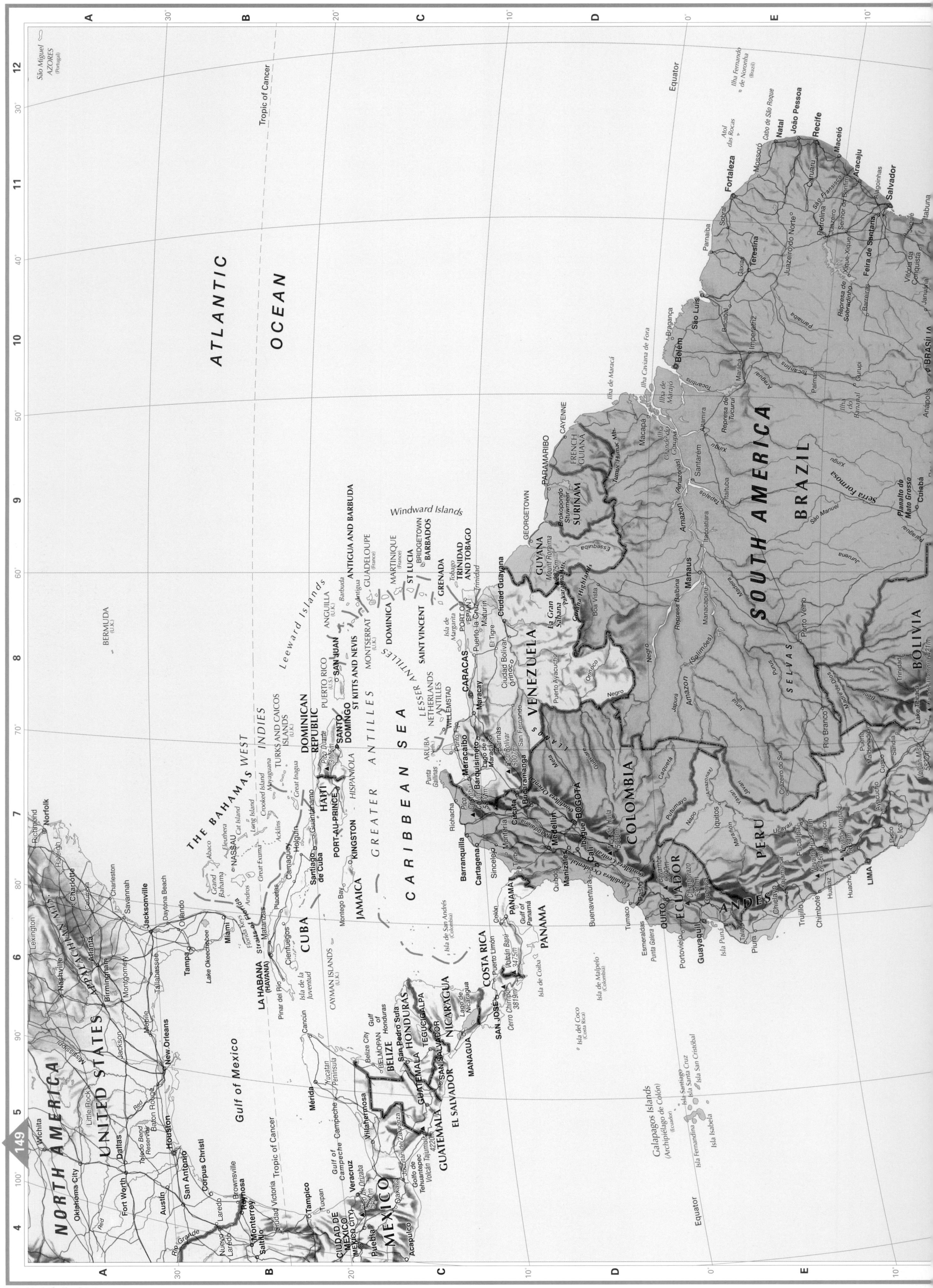

Scale 1:24,000,000

One centimetre represents 240 kilometres.

One inch represents approximately 380 miles.

SOUTH AMERICANS ARE mostly Roman Catholic and speak Spanish or Portuguese, yet their nations have very different histories.

Colombia and Peru were once great empires. Brutal wars cost Paraguay three-quarters of its people, and Bolivia more than half its territory.

Immigrants have brought a European flavour to Argentina, while recent industrialisation has hardly begun to tap Brazil's staggering potential.

189

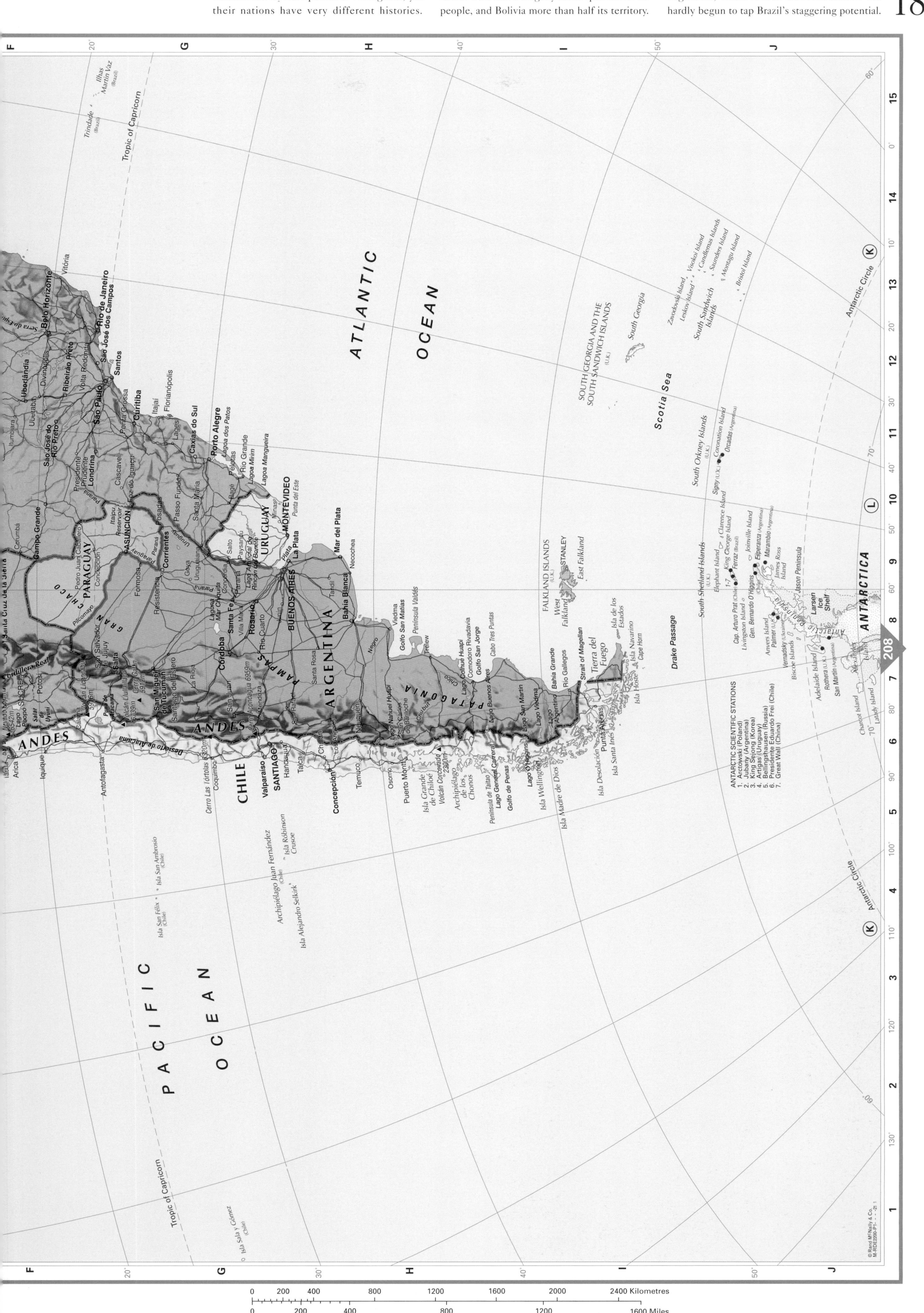

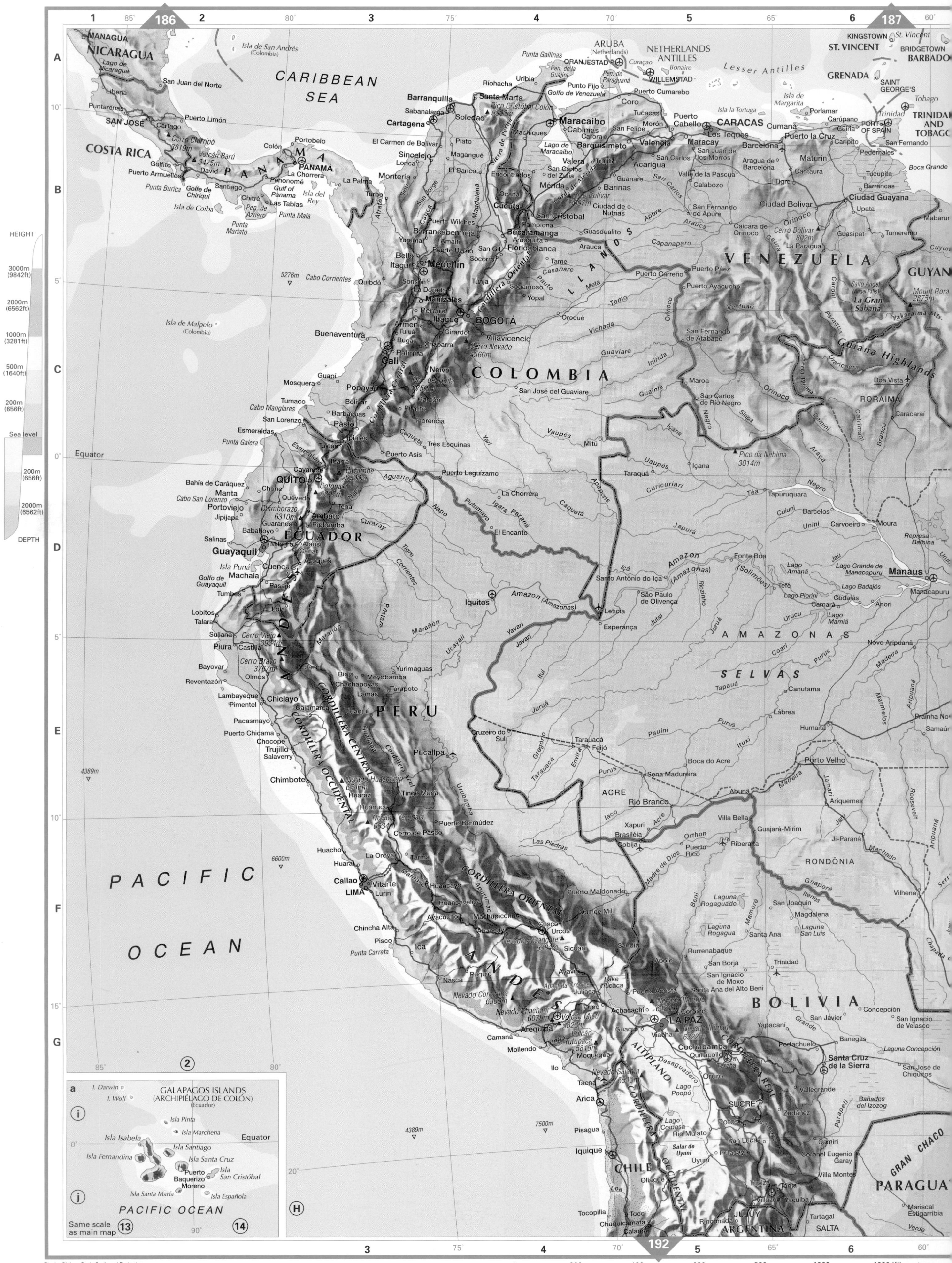

HEIGHT

3000m (9842ft)
2000m (6562ft)
1000m (3281ft)
500m (1640ft)
200m (656ft)
Sea level
200m (656ft)
2000m (6562ft)

DEPTH

GALAPAGOS ISLANDS (ARCHIPIÉLAGO DE COLÓN) (Ecuador)

Same scale as main map

Bipolar Oblique Conic Conformal Projection

Scale 1:12,000,000

One centimetre represents 120 kilometres.

One inch represents approximately 190 miles.

0 200 400 600 800 1000 1200 Kilometres

0 200 400 600 800 Miles

CAPPED WITH SNOW, the great bastion of the Andes runs for 7500 km (4600 miles) from Venezuela to Tierra del Fuego, stretching out in Bolivia to a width of 600 km (373 miles). Among the many rivers it gives birth to is the Amazon which, with its tributaries, drains a vast forest basin the size of Australia. In the Guiana Highlands, immense plateaus of sandstone rise abruptly out of grassland and jungle.

191

Southern South America

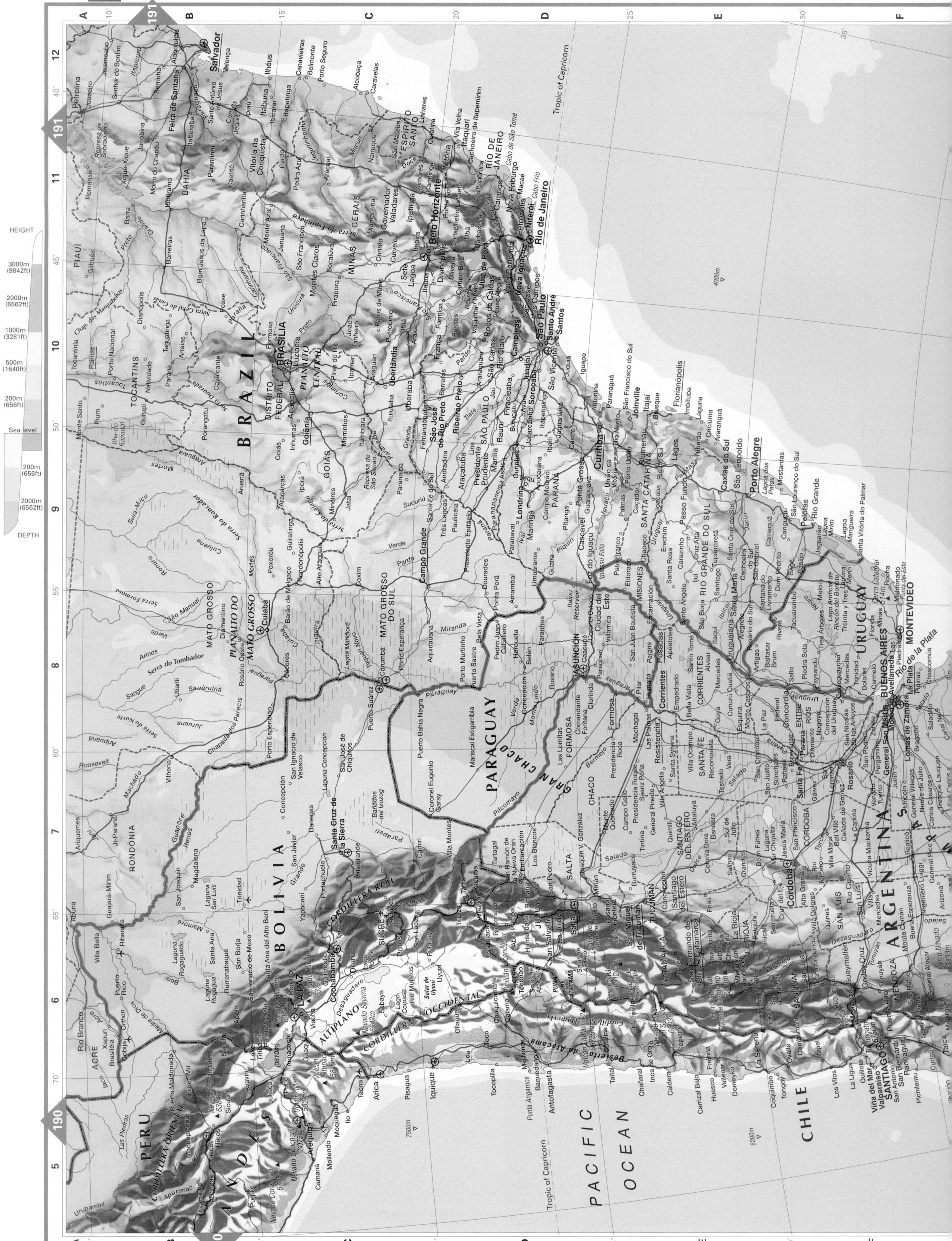

HEIGHT

3000m
(9842ft)

2000m
(6562ft)

1000m
(3281ft)

500m
(1640ft)

200m
(656ft)

Sea level

200m
(656ft)

2000m
(6562ft)

DEPTH

Lambert Conformal Conic Projection

Scale 1:12,000,000

One centimetre represents 120 kilometres.

One inch represents approximately 190 miles.

A LONG, THIN CURVE defined by the Andes, Chile is the backbone of South America, only 180 km (112 miles) wide but as long as the distance between New York and Los Angeles. It encompasses alps, lakes, volcanoes and desert, and at its tip is the old-time seamen's hell of Cape Horn. Aconcagua, at 6959 m (22 831 ft) the loftiest peak in the Western Hemisphere, straddles the Chile-Argentina border.

193

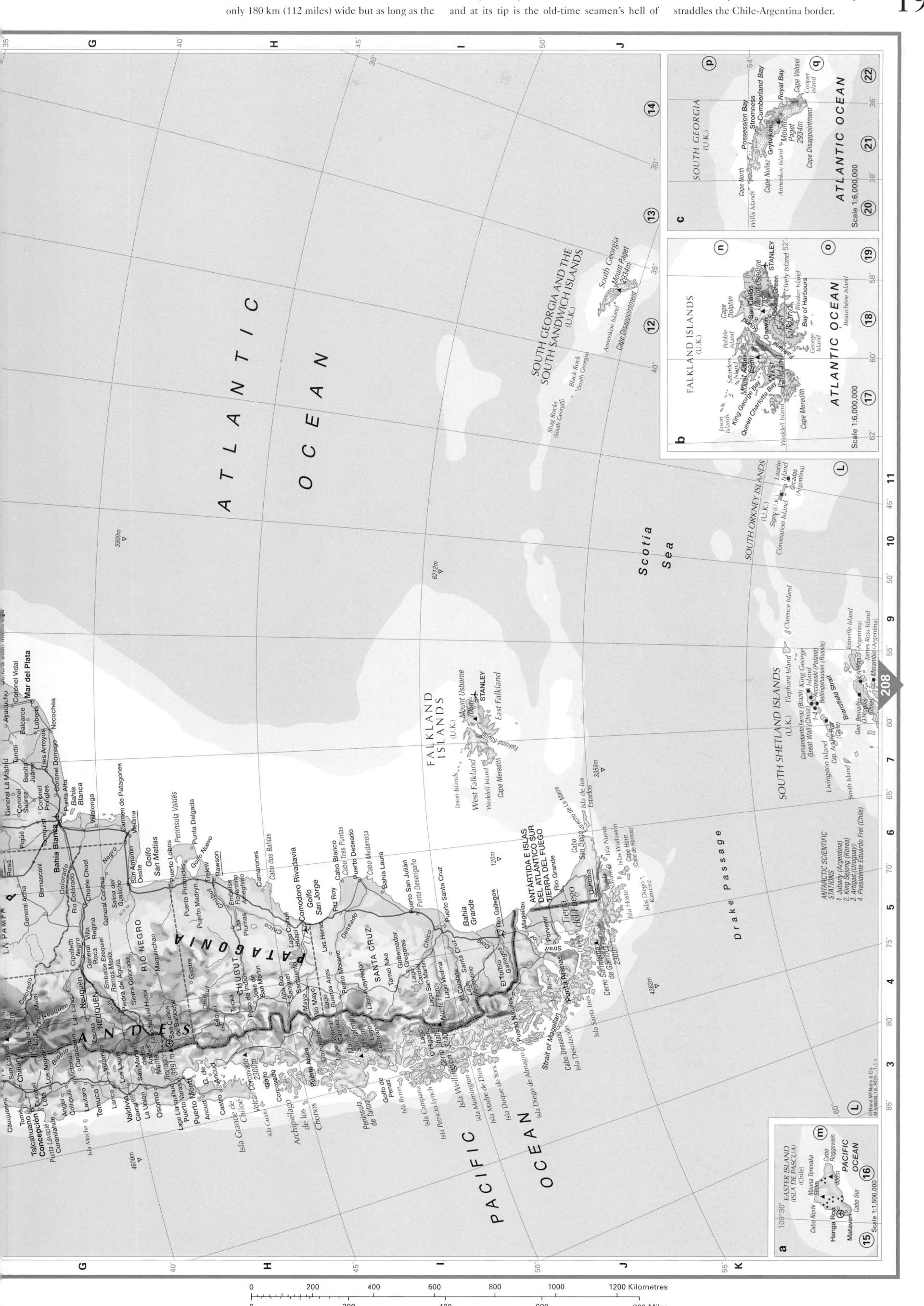

ATLANTIC OCEAN

PACIFIC OCEAN

ANDES

PATAGONIA

RÍO NEGRO

CHUBUT

SANTA CRUZ

NEUQUÉN

LA PAMPA

FALKLAND ISLANDS (U.K.)
West Falkland
East Falkland
STANLEY
Falkland Sound

SOUTH GEORGIA AND THE SOUTH SANDWICH ISLANDS (U.K.)

Scotia Sea

Drake Passage

Strait of Magellan

TIERRA DEL FUEGO

ANTÁRTIDA E ISLAS DEL ATLÁNTICO SUR

SOUTH ORKNEY ISLANDS

SOUTH SHETLAND ISLANDS (U.K.)

FALKLAND ISLANDS (U.K.)
Cape Dolphin
Jason Islands
Pebble Island
Saunders Island
Mount Adam 705m
Queen Charlotte Bay
Weddell Island
George Island
Beauchene Island
Bay of Harbours
Cape Meredith
Scale 1:6,000,000

SOUTH GEORGIA (U.K.)
Cape North
Possession Bay
Stromness
Grytviken
Royal Bay
Cumberland Bay
Cape Nuñez
Annenkov Island
Mount Paget 2934m
Cape Vahsel
Cooper Island
Cape Disappointment
Willis Islands
ATLANTIC OCEAN
Scale 1:6,000,000

EASTER ISLAND (ISLA DE PASCUA) (Chile)
Hanga Roa
Mataveri
Mauna Terevaka
Cabo Norte
Cabo Roggewein
Cabo Sur
PACIFIC OCEAN
Scale 1:1,500,000

ANTARCTIC SCIENTIFIC STATIONS
1. Jubany (Argentina)
2. King Sejong (Korea)
3. Artigas (Uruguay)
4. Presidente Eduardo Frei (Chile)

0   200   400   600   800   1000   1200 Kilometres
0   200   400   600   800 Miles

South-east Brazil

BUSY CITIES GREW up in south-east Brazil,
Uruguay and central Argentina on the wealth of
an area of intensive farming and cattle rearing.

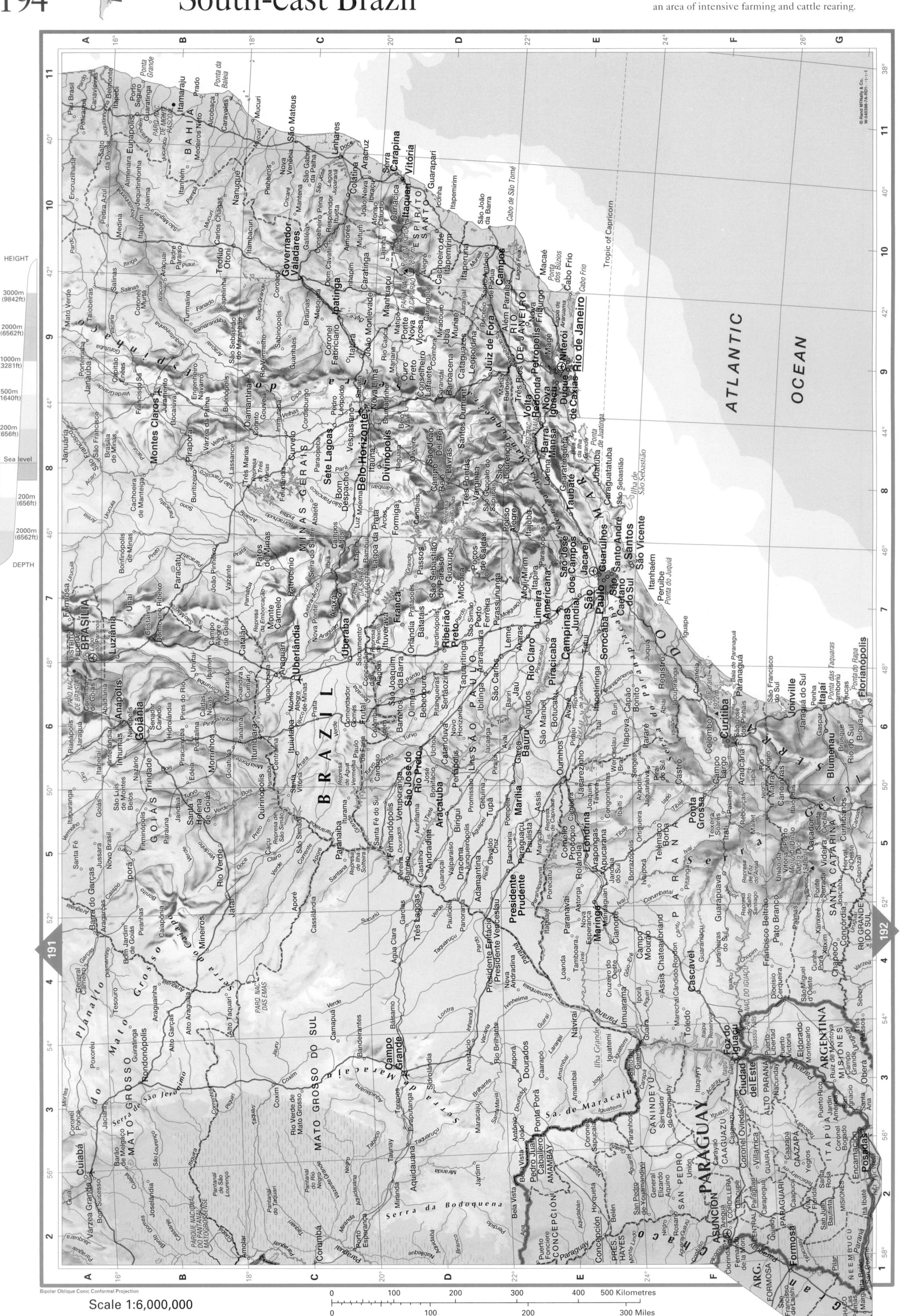

HEIGHT

3000m
(9842ft)

2000m
(6562ft)

1000m
(3281ft)

500m
(1640ft)

200m
(656ft)

Sea level

200m
(656ft)

2000m
(6562ft)

DEPTH

Bipolar Oblique Conic Conformal Projection

Scale 1:6,000,000

| 0 | 100 | 200 | 300 | 400 | 500 Kilometres |

| 0 | 100 | 200 | 300 Miles |

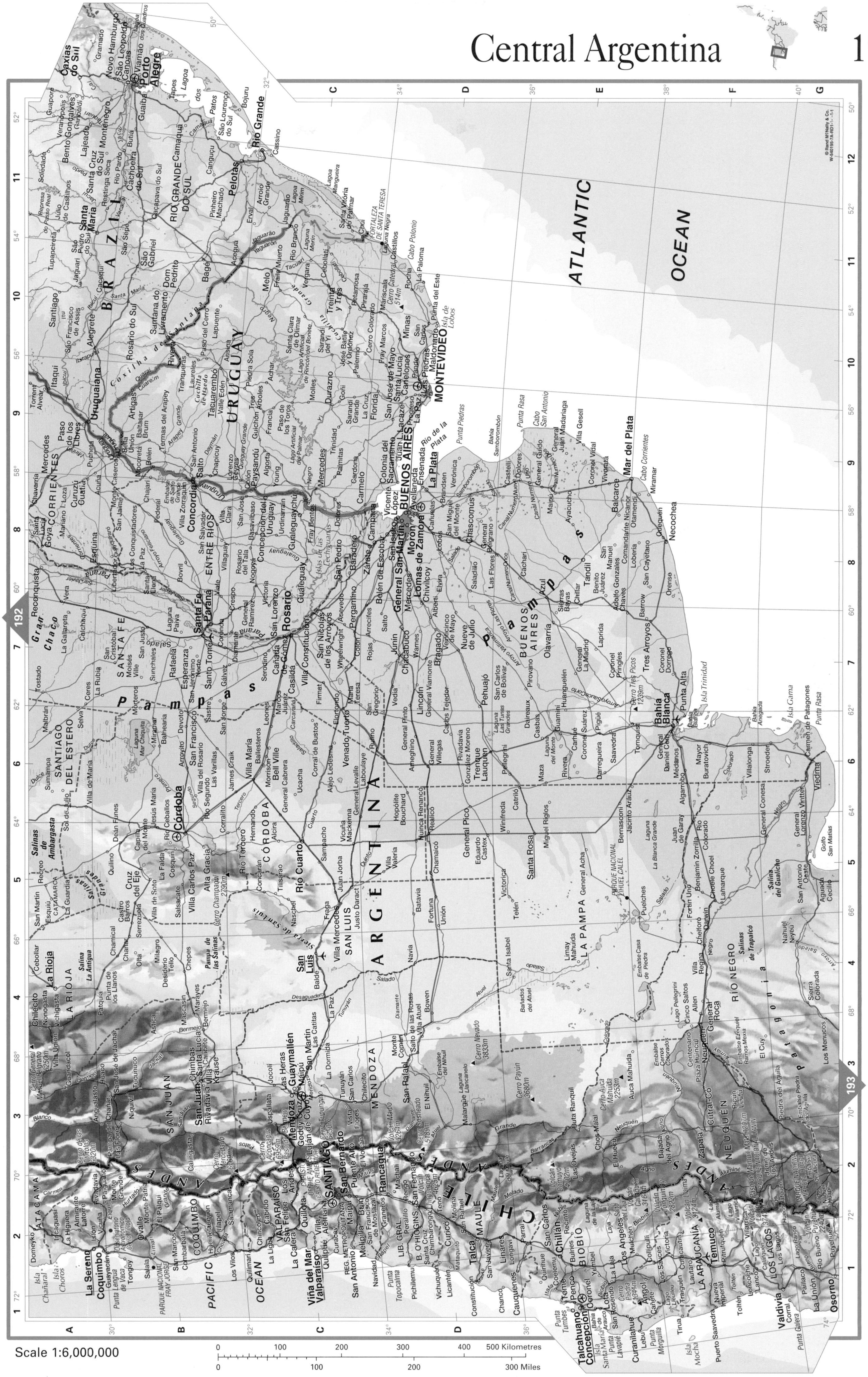

ATLANTIC OCEAN
PACIFIC OCEAN
ARGENTINA
URUGUAY
BRAZIL
CHILE
BUENOS AIRES
MONTEVIDEO
SANTIAGO
Córdoba
Rosario
Mendoza
La Plata
Mar del Plata
Bahía Blanca
Porto Alegre
Pampas
ANDES
Scale 1:6,000,000
500 Kilometres
300 Miles

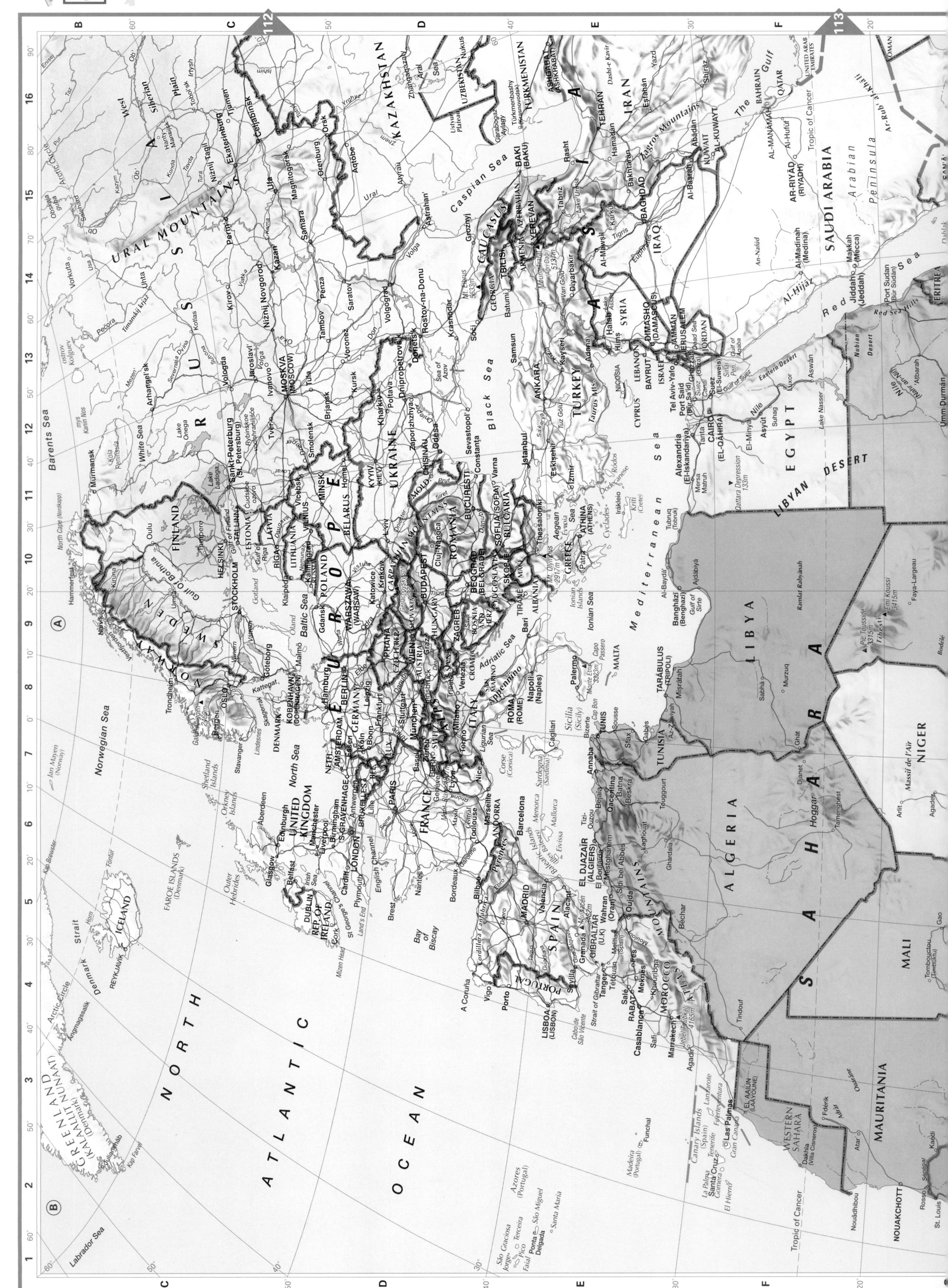

Scale 1:24,000,000

One centimetre represents 240 kilometres.

One inch represents approximately 380 miles.

FROM THE EQUATOR, Africa's awesome bulk extends north and south from rain forests, through tropical grasslands and deserts to the sunny extremities. Some of its countries have old roots but many, despite their present names, have their origins in European colonies gained in the 19th-century scramble for Africa. Their borders are the arbitrary lines of imperial map makers, having scant regard to natural features.

197

0   200   400   800   1200   1600   2000   2400 Kilometres

0   200   400   800   1200   1600 Miles

ATLANTIC OCEAN

Azores (Açores) (Portugal)

Corvo
Santa Cruz das Flores
Flores
Graciosa
Faial Velas São Jorge
Horta Pico
São Mateus Terceira
Angra do Heroismo
Santa Cruz da Graciosa
∇ 3090m
São Miguel
Ponta Delgada Povoação
Santa Maria
Vila do Porto

Same scale as main map

HEIGHT
3000m (9842ft)
2000m (6562ft)
1000m (3281ft)
500m (1640ft)
200m (656ft)
Sea level
200m (656ft)
2000m (6562ft)
DEPTH

ATLANTIC OCEAN

PORTUGAL

SPAIN

MADRID
LISBOA (LISBON)
Sevilla
Córdoba
Granada
Málaga
Cádiz
GIBRALTAR (U.K.)
Ceuta
Tanger (Tangier)
Tetouan

MOROCCO

RABAT
Casablanca
Mohammedia
El-Jadida
Safi
Marrakech
Essaouira
Agadir
Meknes
Fès
Taza
Oujda
Khouribga
Beni-Mellal
Er-Rachidia

ATLAS MOUNTAINS

Jbel Toubkal 4165m

ALGERIA

Béchar

Canary Islands (Spain)

La Palma
Santa Cruz de la Palma
La Gomera
El Hierro
Tenerife
Santa Cruz de Tenerife
Pico del Teide 3718m
Las Palmas de Gran Canaria
Gran Canaria
Lanzarote
Arrecife
Fuerteventura
Puerto del Rosario

Madeira (Portugal)
Funchal
Porto Santo
Ilhas Desertas

Ilhas Selvagens (Portugal)

EL AAIÚN (LAÂYOUNE)

WESTERN SAHARA

Semara

Dakhla (Villa Cisneros)

Cap Barbas

Nouâdhibou
Cap Blanc

MAURITANIA

TIRIS ZEMMOUR

Zouérat

ADRAR

INCHIRI

Atâr
Chinguetti

NOUAKCHOTT

TRARZA

BRAKNA

ASSABA

TAGANT

HODH ECH CHARGUI

HODH EL GHARBI

MALI

TOMBOUCTOU

Tombouctou (Timbuktu)

KIDAL

Adrar des Ifoghas

GAO

Gao

Tropic of Cancer

Sahara

Sahel (Sudan)

St. Louis

SENEGAL

GORGOL

KAYES

MOPTI

BURKINA

DAKAR

Lambert Azimuthal Equal Area Projection

Scale 1:9,000,000

One centimetre represents 90 kilometres.

One inch represents approximately 142 miles.

SOME 10,000 YEARS ago, the Sahara began to dry out, sealing off North Africa from the rest of the continent; but only the Mediterranean divided it from southern Europe. Phoenicians, Greeks and Romans all made their marks on North Africa, which the Moors repaid during their occupation of the Iberian Peninsula. More recent European colonies have given way to independent nations of varying fortunes.

199

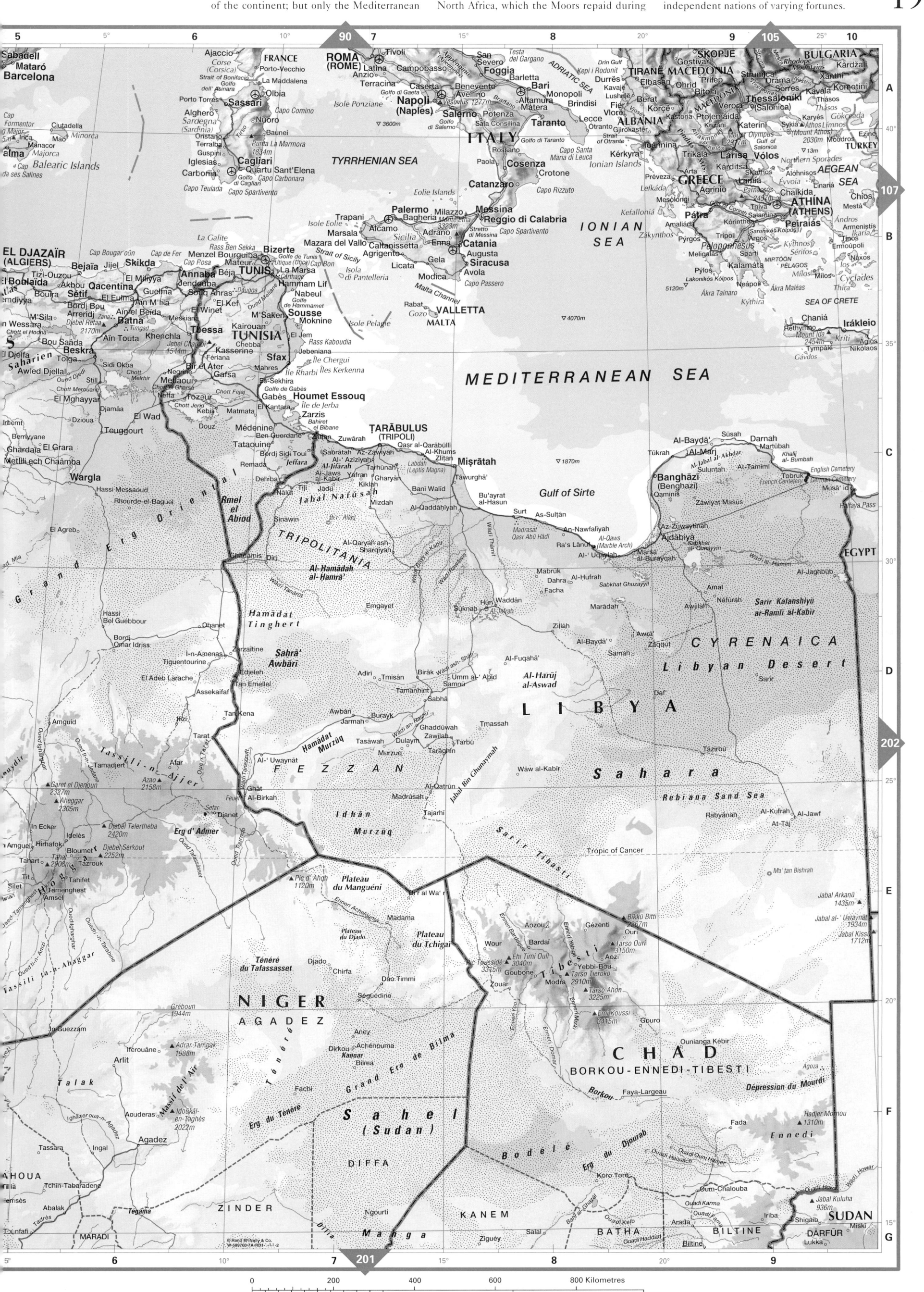

Western Africa

IN AN AREA akin to that of the USA, the West African mosaic shows a greater range of cultural differences than any comparable area on Earth.

A

B

C

D

E

HEIGHT

3000m (9842ft)

2000m (6562ft)

1000m (3281ft)

500m (1640ft)

200m (656ft)

Sea level

200m (656ft)

2000m (6562ft)

DEPTH

Lambert Azimuthal Equal Area Projection

Scale 1:9,000,000

One centimetre represents 90 kilometres.

One inch represents approximately 142 miles.

© Rand McNally & Co.
W-RDE4501-A1- - -14

ALGERIA

MAURITANIA

MALI

SENEGAL

THE GAMBIA

GUINEA-BISSAU

GUINEA

SIERRA LEONE

LIBERIA

IVORY COAST

BURKINA

GHANA

TOGO

BENIN

NIGER

NIGERIA

ATLANTIC OCEAN

Gulf of

Bight of Benin

Equator

a Same scale as main map

ATLANTIC OCEAN

CAPE VERDE
Arquipélago de Cabo Verde

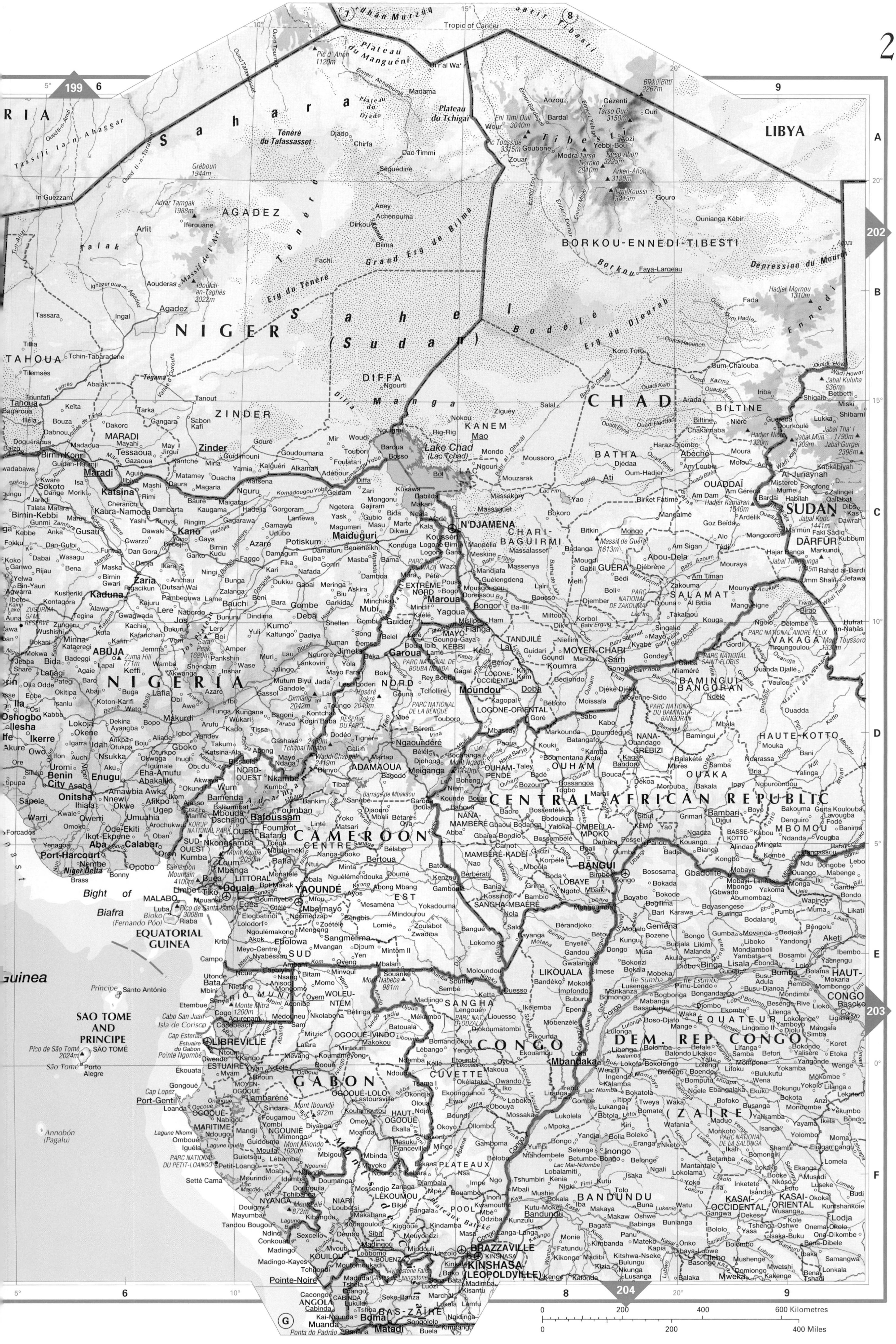

LIBYA

NIGER

Sahara

Ténéré du Tafassasset

AGADEZ

Sahel

(Sudan)

BORKOU-ENNEDI-TIBESTI

Dépression du Mourd

CHAD

BILTINE

SUDAN

DÂRFUR

ZINDER

DIFFA

KANEM

BATHA

OUADDAÏ

Lake Chad

N'DJAMENA

CHARI-BAGUIRMI

GUERA

SALAMAT

MARADI

Zinder

Maiduguri

Maroua

EXTRÊME-NORD

TANDJILÉ

MOYEN-CHARI

VAKAGA

Kano

Katsina

Kaduna

NIGERIA

ABUJA

Garoua

NORD

Moundou

LOGONE-OCCIDENTAL

LOGONE-ORIENTAL

Sarh

Koumra

BAMINGUI-BANGORAN

HAUTE-KOTTO

OUAKA

Ngaoundéré

ADAMAOUA

OUHAM

CENTRAL AFRICAN REPUBLIC

MBOMOU

Enugu

Benin City

Onitsha

CAMEROON

CENTRE

Bamenda

NORD-OUEST

OUEST

Bafoussam

Foumban

OUHAM-PENDE

NANA-MAMBÉRÉ

MAMBÉRÉ-KADÉÏ

BASSE-KOTTO

Bambari

Bangui

LOBAYE

Aba

Calabar

Douala

YAOUNDÉ

LITTORAL

SUD-OUEST

EST

SANGHA-MBAÉRÉ

MALABO

EQUATORIAL GUINEA

Bight of Biafra (Fernando Póo)

Bata

RIO MUNI

SUD

WOLEU-NTEM

LIKOUALA

SANGHA

HAUT-

CONGO

SAO TOME AND PRINCIPE

SÃO TOMÉ

LIBREVILLE

ESTUAIRE

OGOOUE-IVINDO

CONGO

CUVETTE

ÉQUATEUR

DEM. REP. CONGO

(ZAIRE)

GABON

OGOOUE-LOLO

MOYEN-OGOOUE

Lambaréné

Port-Gentil

OGOOUE-MARITIME

NGOUNIE

PLATEAUX

Mbandaka

BANDUNDU

NYANGA

NIARI

LEKOUMOU

POOL

KASAI-OCCIDENTAL

KASAI-ORIENTAL

KOUILOU

Pointe-Noire

BRAZZAVILLE

KINSHASA (LEOPOLDVILLE)

BAS-ZAÏRE

ANGOLA

CABINDA

Boma

Matadi

Annobón (Pagalu)

0   200   400   600 Kilometres

0   200   400 Miles

North-east Africa

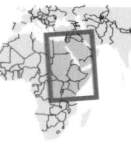

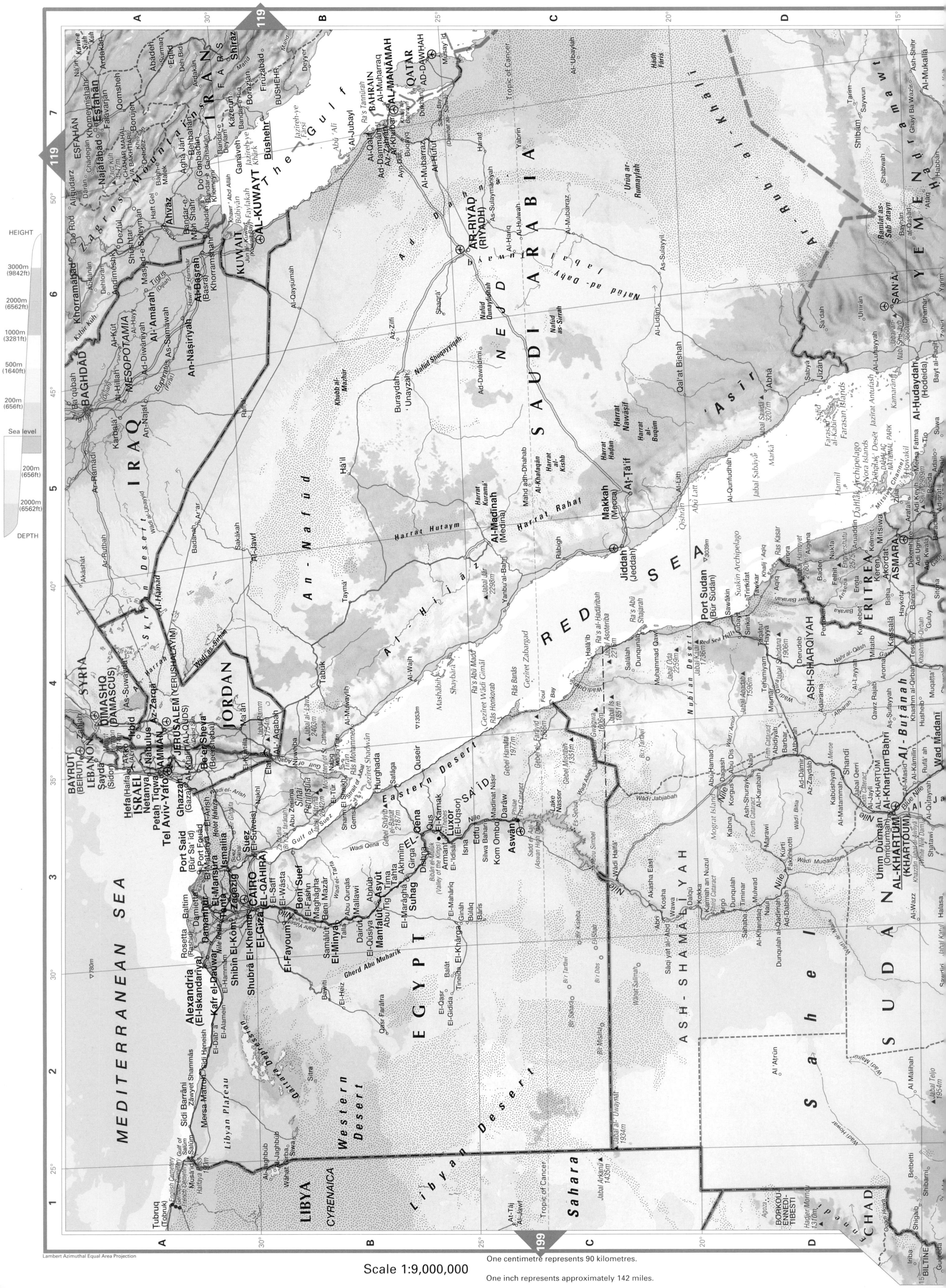

Lambert Azimuthal Equal Area Projection

Scale 1:9,000,000

One centimetre represents 90 kilometres.

One inch represents approximately 142 miles.

FOR 6000 YEARS the provider of life in Egypt has been the Nile, especially in the long, narrow oasis of its valley between the Sudan border and Cairo. Even today, 96 per cent of Egyptians live by the river, in one of the highest population densities to be found anywhere in the world.

| 0 | 200 | 400 | 600 | 800 Kilometres |

| 0 | 200 | 400 | 600 Miles |

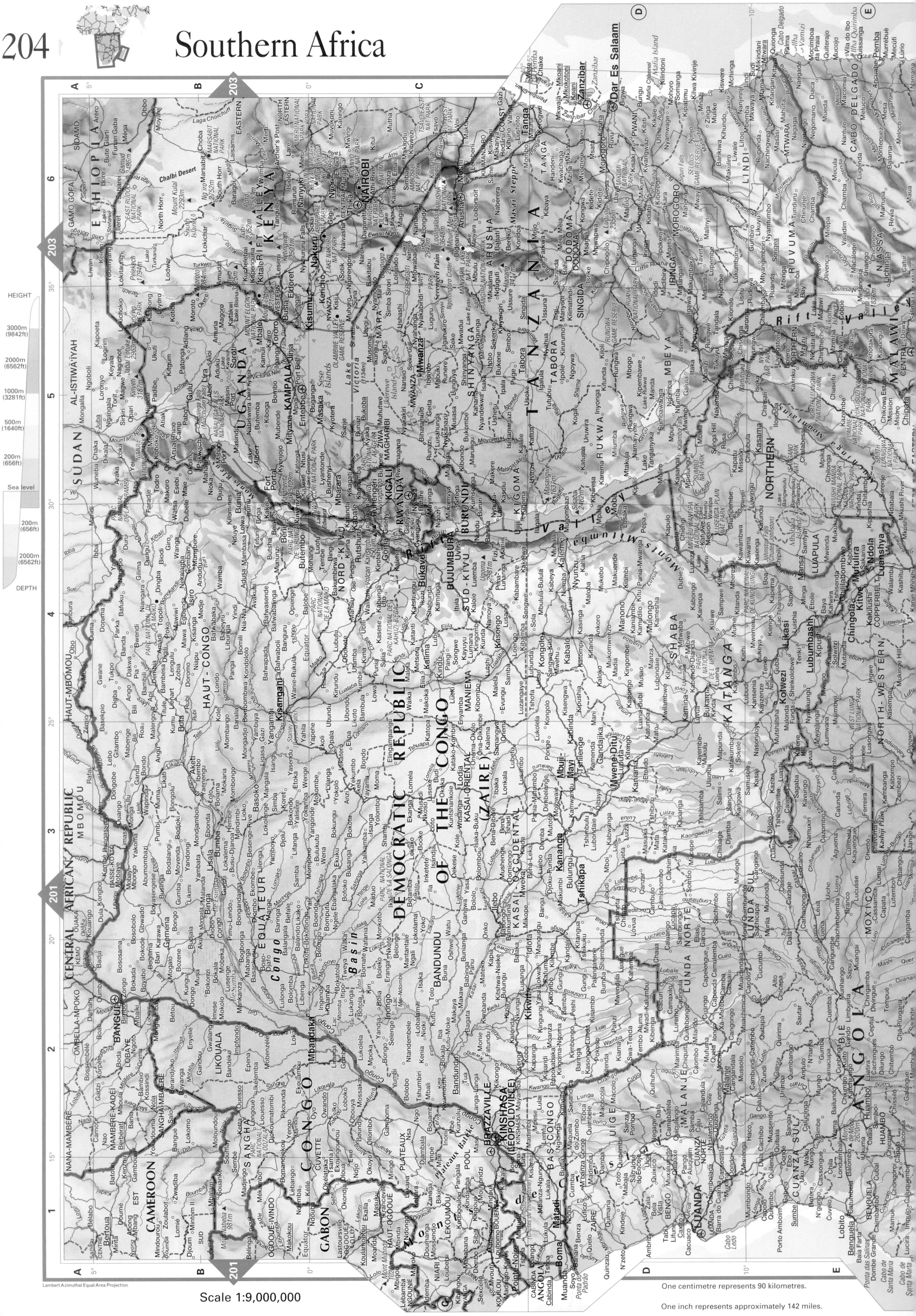

HEIGHT

3000m (9842ft)
2000m (6562ft)
1000m (3281ft)
500m (1640ft)
200m (656ft)
Sea level
200m (656ft)
2000m (6562ft)

DEPTH

ETHIOPIA

SUDAN

KENYA

UGANDA

TANZANIA

RWANDA

BURUNDI

DEMOCRATIC REPUBLIC OF THE CONGO (ZAIRE)

CENTRAL AFRICAN REPUBLIC

CAMEROON

GABON

CONGO

ANGOLA

MALAWI

NAIROBI

KAMPALA

KIGALI

BUJUMBURA

DODOMA

Dar Es Salaam

Zanzibar

BRAZZAVILLE

KINSHASA (LEOPOLDVILLE)

BANGUI

Lake Victoria (114m)

Lake Tanganyika

Rift Valley

Congo Basin

Equator

Lambert Azimuthal Equal Area Projection

Scale 1:9,000,000

One centimetre represents 90 kilometres.

One inch represents approximately 142 miles.

MOZAMBIQUE

MADAGASCAR

ANTANANARIVO

INDIAN OCEAN

Tropic of Capricorn

Mozambique Channel

ZAMBIA

ZIMBABWE

HARARE (SALISBURY)

Bulawayo

BOTSWANA

GABORONE

NAMIBIA

WINDHOEK

SOUTH AFRICA

Johannesburg

PRETORIA

SWAZILAND

MBABANE

LESOTHO

MASERU

Bloemfontein

MAPUTO

Durban

East London (Oos-Londen)

Port Elizabeth

CAPE TOWN (KAAPSTAD)

Cape of Good Hope

ATLANTIC OCEAN

INDIAN OCEAN

Kalahari Desert

Namib Desert

Okavango Delta

ANGOLA

Skeleton Coast

Wild Coast

© Rand McNally & Co.

0   200   400   600   800 Kilometres

0   200   400   600 Miles

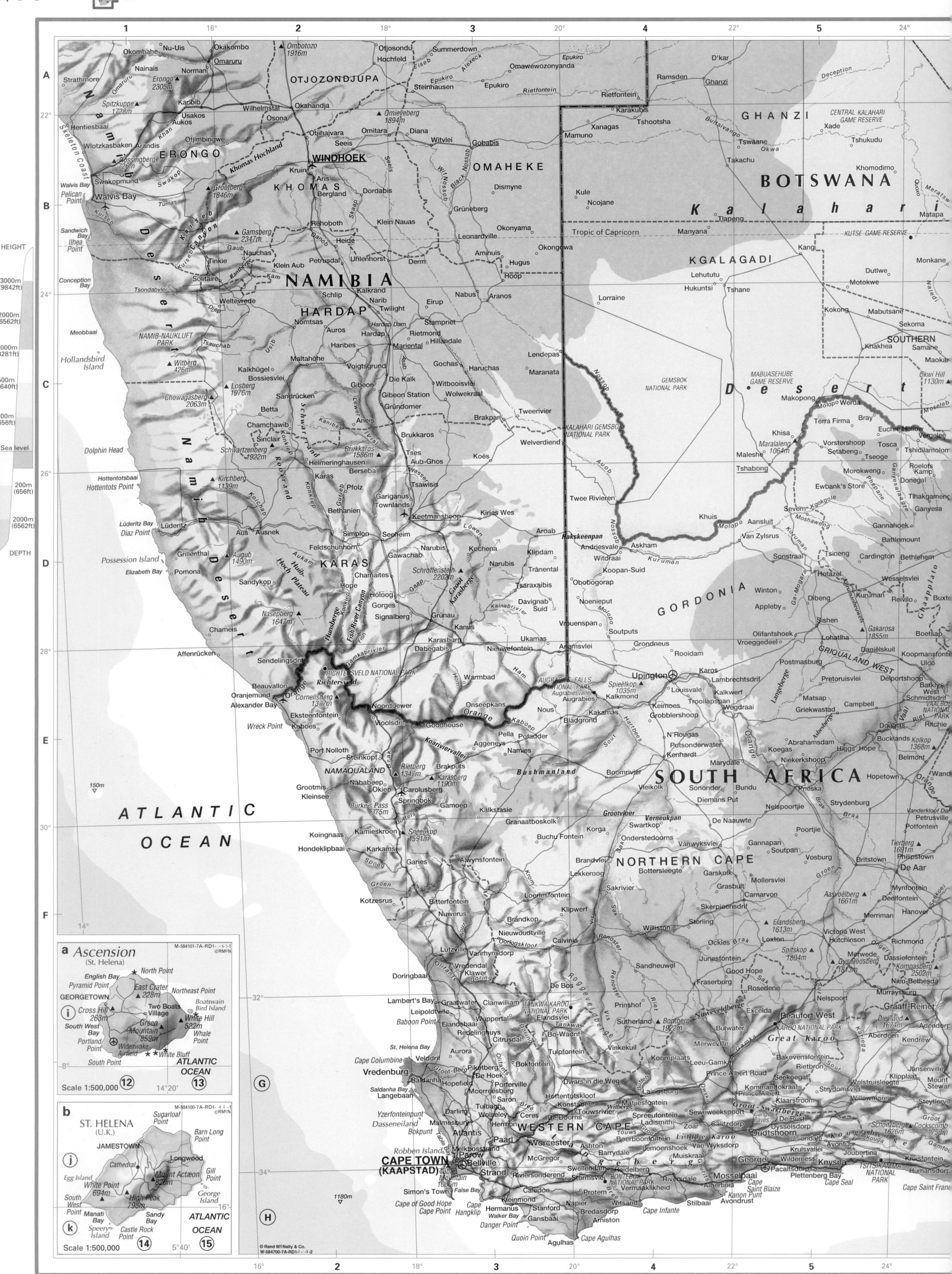

Scale 1:4,500,000

One centimetre represents 45 kilometres.

One inch represents approximately 71 miles.

Lambert Azimuthal Equal Area Projection

SHEER DIVERSITY ENCHANTS the visitor to South Africa, whether in the autumnal gold of the high veldt grasslands or among the towering bastions and airy waterfalls of the mountains. There is desert, rain forest, and the bushveldt, drenched in heat and full of game; there are white, empty beaches on which the rollers of two oceans break, and there are spring carpets of flower species that occur nowhere else.

207

Antarctica

AN ICE CAP thousands of metres thick covers isolated Antarctica. If it melted, the freed waters would drown all the world's coastal cities.

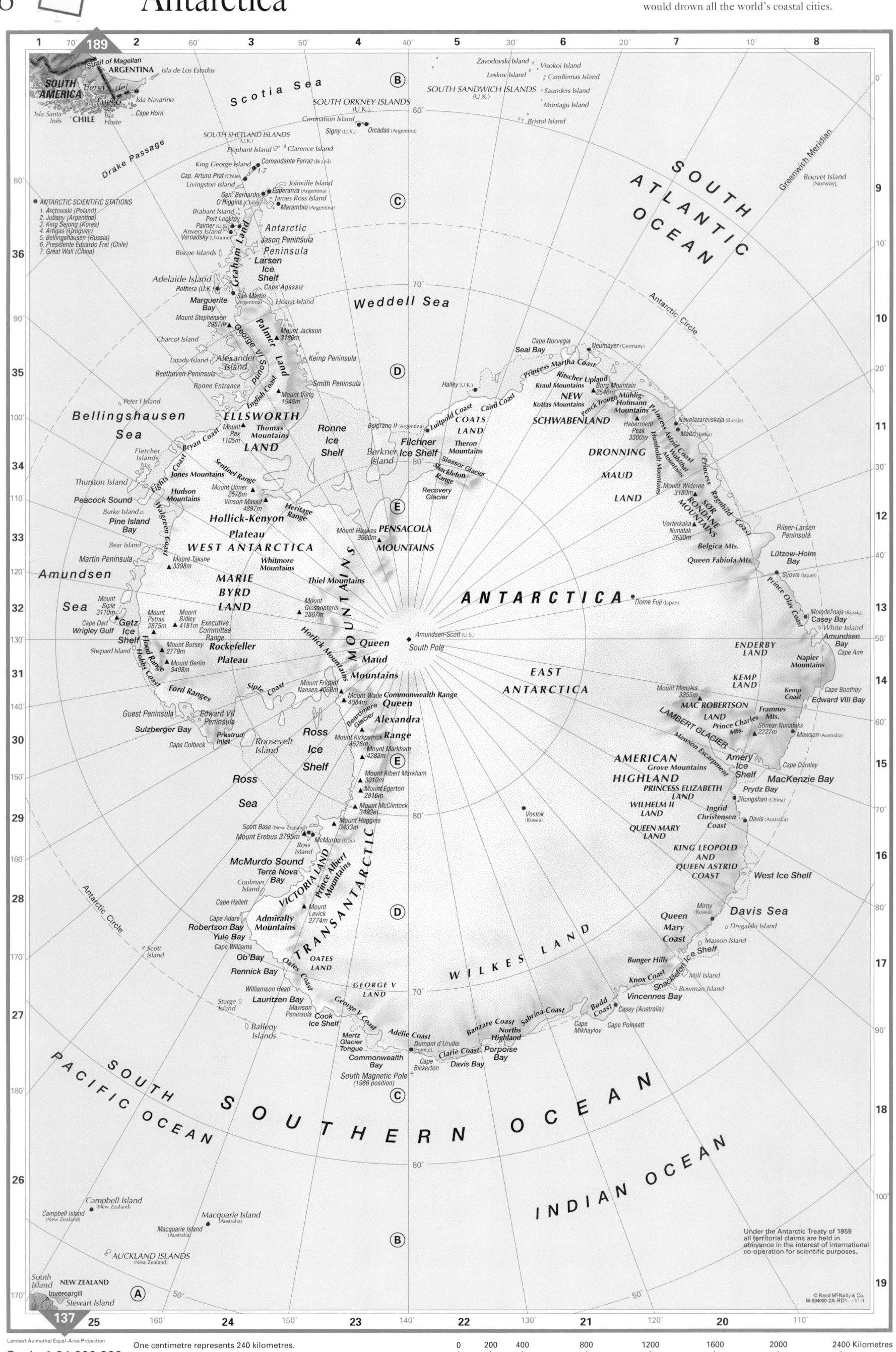

SOUTH ATLANTIC OCEAN

Scotia Sea

SOUTH ORKNEY ISLANDS (U.K.)

SOUTH SANDWICH ISLANDS (U.K.)

Zavodovski Island
Leskov Island
Visokoi Island
Candlemas Island
Saunders Island
Montagu Island
Bristol Island

Bouvet Island (Norway)

Greenwich Meridian

ARGENTINA
Strait of Magellan
Isla de los Estados
SOUTH AMERICA
Tierra del Fuego
CHILE
Isla Navarino
Cape Horn
Isla Santa Inés
Isla Hoste

Drake Passage

Coronation Island
Signy (U.K.)
Orcadas (Argentina)

SOUTH SHETLAND ISLANDS (U.K.)
Elephant Island
Clarence Island
King George Island
Comandante Ferraz (Brazil)
Cap. Arturo Prat (Chile)
Livingston Island
Joinville Island
Gen. Bernardo O'Higgins (Chile)
Esperanza (Argentina)
James Ross Island
Marambio (Argentina)

ANTARCTIC SCIENTIFIC STATIONS
1. Arctowski (Poland)
2. Jubany (Argentina)
3. King Sejong (Korea)
4. Artigas (Uruguay)
5. Bellingshausen (Russia)
6. Presidente Eduardo Frei (Chile)
7. Great Wall (China)

Brabant Island
Port Lockroy
Palmer (U.S.)
Anvers Island
Vernadsky (Ukraine)
Biscoe Islands

Antarctic Peninsula
Jason Peninsula
Larsen Ice Shelf
Cape Agassiz

Adelaide Island
Rothera (U.K.)
San Martín (Argentina)
Marguerite Bay
Hearst Island
Mount Stephenson 2987m
Mount Jackson 3189m

Weddell Sea

Cape Norvegia
Seal Bay
Neumayer (Germany)

Princess Martha Coast
Ritscher Upland
Kraul Mountains
Borg Mountain
Mühlig-Hofmann Mountains
Habermehl Peak 3300m

NEW SCHWABENLAND
Kottas Mountains
Penck Trough

Novolazarevskaja (Russia)
Maud (Yuke)

Charcot Island
Kemp Peninsula

Alexander Island
Latady Island
Beethoven Peninsula
Ronne Entrance
Smith Peninsula
English Coast
Mount Vang 1548m

Peter I Island

Bellingshausen Sea

ELLSWORTH LAND
Mount Rex 1105m
Thomas Mountains
Bryan Coast

Belgrano II (Argentina)
Luitpold Coast
Caird Coast
COATS LAND

Ronne Ice Shelf

Filchner Ice Shelf
Berkner Island
Theron Mountains
Slessor Glacier
Shackleton Range
Recovery Glacier

DRONNING MAUD LAND
Princess Astrid Coast
Mühlig-Hofmann
Humboldt Mountains
Mount Wideröe 3180m
SÖR RONDANE MOUNTAINS
Rasmussen Coast
Princess Ragnhild Coast

Fletcher Islands

Thurston Island
Jones Mountains
Sentinel Range
Mount Ulmer 2576m
Vinson Massif 4897m
Heritage Range

Peacock Sound
Hudson Mountains

Varterkaka Nunatak 3630m
Belgica Mts.
Queen Fiabola Mts.

Riiser-Larsen Peninsula
Lützow-Holm Bay
Syowa (Japan)
Prince Olav Coast

Burke Island
Pine Island Bay
Hollick-Kenyon Plateau
WEST ANTARCTICA

Mount Hawkes 3660m
PENSACOLA MOUNTAINS

Bear Island

Martin Peninsula

Amundsen Sea
Mount Takahe 3398m
Whitmore Mountains

MARIE BYRD LAND
Mount Glossopteris 2867m
Thiel Mountains

ANTARCTICA
Dome Fuji (Japan)

Moloděžnaja (Russia)
Casey Bay
White Island
Amundsen Bay
Cape Ann

Mount Siple 3110m
Cape Dart
Getz Ice Shelf
Wrigley Gulf
Mount Petras 2875m
Mount Sidley 4181m
Executive Committee Range

EAST ANTARCTICA

ENDERBY LAND

Napier Mountains

Shepard Island
Mount Bursey 2779m
Rockefeller Plateau
Mount Berlin 3498m

Horlick Mountains

Queen Maud Mountains

Mount Menzies 3355m

KEMP LAND
Kemp Coast
Cape Boothby
Edward VIII Bay

Flood Range
Habbs Coast

Siple Coast

MAC ROBERTSON LAND
LAMBERT GLACIER
Prince Charles Mts.
Mawson Escarpment
Framnes Mts.
Stinear Nunataks 2227m
Mawson (Australia)

Ford Ranges
Mount Fridtjof Nansen 4068m
Commonwealth Range
Mount Wade 4084m

Queen Alexandra Range
Mount Kirkpatrick 4528m

TRANSANTARCTIC MOUNTAINS

Guest Peninsula
Edward VII Peninsula
Sulzberger Bay
Cape Colbeck

Prestrud Inlet
Roosevelt Island

Ross Ice Shelf

Mount Markham 4282m
Mount Albert Markham 3010m
Mount Egerton 2816m
Mount McClintock 3492m

Grove Mountains
AMERICAN HIGHLAND
PRINCESS ELIZABETH LAND
WILHELM II LAND

Amery Ice Shelf
MacKenzie Bay
Prydz Bay
Zhongshan (China)

Ross Sea

Mount Huggins 3433m
Scott Base (New Zealand)
Mount Erebus 3795m
McMurdo (U.S.)
Ross Island

QUEEN MARY LAND

Vostok (Russia)

Ingrid Christensen Coast
Davis (Australia)

McMurdo Sound
Terra Nova Bay
Coulman Island

VICTORIA LAND
Prince Albert Mountains

KING LEOPOLD AND QUEEN ASTRID COAST

West Ice Shelf

Cape Hallett

Cape Adare
Robertson Bay
Yule Bay
Cape Williams
Ob' Bay

Admiralty Mountains
Mount Levick 2774m

Mirny (Russia)

Queen Mary Coast

Davis Sea
Drygalski Island

Rennick Bay
Williamson Head
Sturge Island

OATES LAND
George V Land

WILKES LAND

Bunger Hills
Knox Coast
Shackleton Ice Shelf
Mill Island
Vincennes Bay
Bowman Island

Balleny Islands

Lauritzen Bay
Mawson Peninsula
Cook Ice Shelf

George V Coast

Adélie Coast
Mertz Glacier Tongue
Commonwealth Bay
Dumont d'Urville (France)
Cape Bickerton
Davis Bay
Clarie Coast
Porpoise Bay

Banzare Coast
Norths Highland
Sabrina Coast
Budd Coast
Cape Mikhaylov
Casey (Australia)
Cape Poinsett

South Magnetic Pole (1986 position)

PACIFIC OCEAN

SOUTH SOUTHERN OCEAN

INDIAN OCEAN

Antarctic Circle

Campbell Island (New Zealand)
Macquarie Island (Australia)
AUCKLAND ISLANDS (New Zealand)
NEW ZEALAND
South Island
Invercargill
Stewart Island

Under the Antarctic Treaty of 1959 all territorial claims are held in abeyance in the interest of international co-operation for scientific purposes.

© Rand McNally & Co.
M-594000-2A-RD1- -1-1-1

Lambert Azimuthal Equal-Area Projection

Scale 1:24,000,000

One centimetre represents 240 kilometres.
One inch represents approximately 380 miles.

0 200 400 800 1200 1600 2000 2400 Kilometres
0 200 400 800 1200 1600 Miles

NATIONS OF THE WORLD

This section offers a brief guide to all the world's 192 independent countries. It gives a concise profile of each nation's physical geography, economy, politics and history, as well as statistical information, national flags and a regional map. Neighbouring countries are grouped together, as shown below, enabling the reader to compare the different nations in a particular region.

Statistics for each individual country are based on the following principles:

Capital city or town: The commonly accepted English version of the name is used, where available.

International organisations: The organisations to which each country is listed as belonging are those which are most influential in that particular region. The lists exclude some organisations to which the majority of countries belong, such as the United Nations, the International Monetary Fund and the World Trade Organisation. All the relevant abbreviations are explained in the left-hand column on each double-page spread.

Population: The figures cited are estimates published by the UN in 1999. Population growth rates

represent an average over recent years, and may be subject to external influences such as war or the influx or exodus of refugees.

Life expectancy: The figures are differentiated between males (m) and females (f) where this information is available.

Languages: Major or official languages for a country are shown in roman type. Other languages used within the country are in italic type.

Adult literacy rates: Many developed countries do not supply this data. UNESCO estimates of 'over 95%' have been used for such countries.

Currency: The dollar exchange rates specified are expressed as the average of those in operation by the International Monetary Fund on July 9, 1999.

Exchange rates fluctuate from day to day, so the figures quoted provide an approximate measure of the local currency rather than its precise current rate.

GDP: The Gross Domestic Product represents the total value of all goods and services produced within a country in a given period (usually a year) and the base upon which approximate economic comparisons are made.

GDP per head: This figure provides an estimate of relative income among each country's population. It is the standard measure of individual prosperity between different nations.

Principal sources: The United Nations publications, The Economist, the Economist Intelligence Unit and the Financial Times.

NORTH AND CENTRAL AMERICA
pages 228–29

BELIZE
CANADA
COSTA RICA
EL SALVADOR
GUATEMALA
HONDURAS
MEXICO
NICARAGUA
PANAMA
UNITED STATES

THE CARIBBEAN
pages 230–31

ANTIGUA & BARBUDA
THE BAHAMAS
BARBADOS
CUBA
DOMINICA
DOMINICAN REPUBLIC
GRENADA
HAITI
JAMAICA
ST KITTS & NEVIS
ST LUCIA
ST VINCENT & THE GRENADINES
TRINIDAD & TOBAGO

NORTHERN EUROPE
pages 210–11

AUSTRIA
BELGIUM
DENMARK
FINLAND
GERMANY
ICELAND
IRELAND
LUXEMBOURG
NETHERLANDS
NORWAY
SWEDEN
UNITED KINGDOM

SOUTHERN EUROPE
pages 212–13

ANDORRA
FRANCE
ITALY
LIECHTENSTEIN
MALTA
MONACO
PORTUGAL
SAN MARINO
SPAIN
SWITZERLAND
VATICAN CITY

CENTRAL AND SOUTH-EASTERN EUROPE
pages 214–15

ALBANIA
BOSNIA & HERZEGOVINA
CROATIA
CYPRUS
CZECH REPUBLIC
GREECE
HUNGARY
MACEDONIA
POLAND
SLOVAKIA
SLOVENIA
YUGOSLAVIA

RUSSIA AND WESTERN NEIGHBOURS
pages 216–17

BELARUS
BULGARIA
ESTONIA
LATVIA
LITHUANIA
MOLDOVA
ROMANIA
RUSSIA
UKRAINE

CENTRAL AND EASTERN ASIA
pages 222–23

CHINA
JAPAN
KAZAKHSTAN
NORTH KOREA
SOUTH KOREA
KYRGYZSTAN
MONGOLIA
TAIWAN
TAJIKISTAN
TURKMENISTAN
UZBEKISTAN

SOUTH-EAST ASIA
pages 224–25

BRUNEI
CAMBODIA
INDONESIA
LAOS
MALAYSIA
MYANMAR (BURMA)
PHILIPPINES
SINGAPORE
THAILAND
VIETNAM

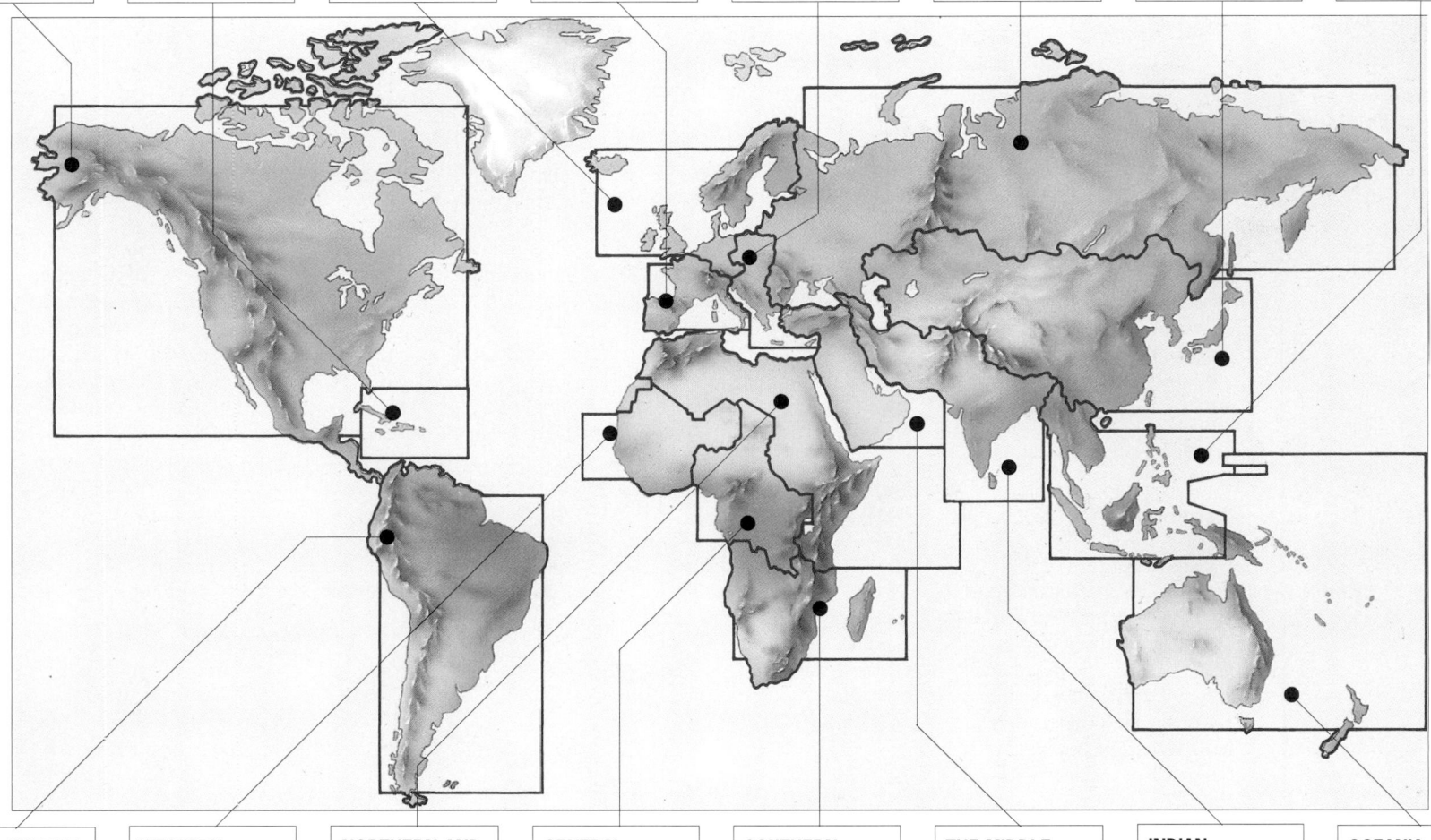

SOUTH AMERICA
pages 232–33

ARGENTINA
BOLIVIA
BRAZIL
CHILE
COLOMBIA
ECUADOR
GUYANA
PARAGUAY
PERU
SURINAM
URUGUAY
VENEZUELA

WESTERN AFRICA
pages 236–37

BENIN
BURKINA
CAPE VERDE
THE GAMBIA
GHANA
GUINEA
GUINEA-BISSAU
IVORY COAST
LIBERIA
MALI
MAURITANIA
NIGER
SENEGAL
SIERRA LEONE
TOGO

NORTHERN AND EASTERN AFRICA
pages 234–35

ALGERIA
DJIBOUTI
EGYPT
ERITREA
ETHIOPIA
KENYA
LIBYA
MOROCCO
SEYCHELLES
SOMALIA
SUDAN
TANZANIA
TUNISIA

CENTRAL AFRICA
pages 238–39

BURUNDI
CAMEROON
CENTRAL AFRICAN REPUBLIC
CHAD
CONGO
DEMOCRATIC REPUBLIC OF THE CONGO
EQUATORIAL GUINEA
GABON
NIGERIA
RWANDA
SÃO TOMÉ & PRÍNCIPE
UGANDA

SOUTHERN AFRICA
pages 240–41

ANGOLA
BOTSWANA
COMOROS
LESOTHO
MADAGASCAR
MALAWI
MAURITIUS
MOZAMBIQUE
NAMIBIA
SOUTH AFRICA
SWAZILAND
ZAMBIA
ZIMBABWE

THE MIDDLE EAST AND THE GULF
pages 218–19

BAHRAIN
IRAQ
ISRAEL
JORDAN
KUWAIT
LEBANON
OMAN
QATAR
SAUDI ARABIA
SYRIA
TURKEY
UNITED ARAB EMIRATES
YEMEN

INDIAN SUBCONTINENT AND NEIGHBOURS
pages 220–21

AFGHANISTAN
ARMENIA
AZERBAIJAN
BANGLADESH
BHUTAN
GEORGIA
INDIA
IRAN
MALDIVES
NEPAL
PAKISTAN
SRI LANKA

OCEANIA
pages 226–27

AUSTRALIA
FIJI
KIRIBATI
MARSHALL ISLANDS
MICRONESIA
NAURU
NEW ZEALAND
PALAU
PAPUA NEW GUINEA
SAMOA
SOLOMON ISLANDS
TONGA
TUVALU
VANUATU

NORTHERN EUROPE

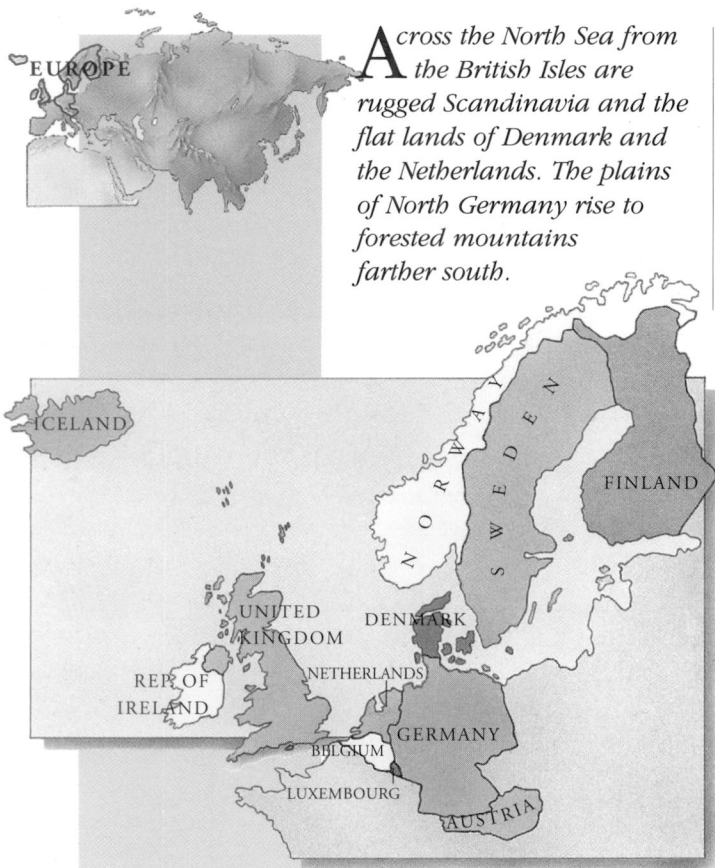

Across the North Sea from the British Isles are rugged Scandinavia and the flat lands of Denmark and the Netherlands. The plains of North Germany rise to forested mountains farther south.

Associated Territories

FAEROE ISLANDS
Parent country
DENMARK
Map page 64

GUERNSEY
Parent country
UK
Map page 73

ISLE OF MAN
Parent country
UK
Map page 72

JAN MAYEN
Parent country
NORWAY
Map page 56

JERSEY
Parent country
UK
Map page 73

SVALBARD
Parent country
NORWAY
Map page 57

Abbreviations
CE *Council of Europe*
COMM *Commonwealth*
EBRD *European Bank for Reconstruction and Development*
EFTA *European Free Trade Association*
EU *European Union*
G8 *Group of Eight Industrialised Countries*
NATO *North Atlantic Treaty Organisation*
OECD *Organisation for Economic Co-operation and Development*

GDP *Gross Domestic Product*

AUSTRIA

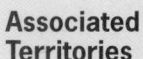

The Republic of Austria

Map pages 102–3

Area	83 858 km²
	(32 378 sq miles)
Capital	Vienna
Member of	CE, EBRD, EU, OECD

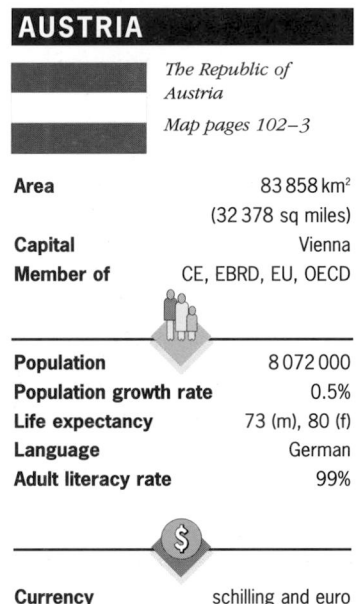

Population	8 072 000
Population growth rate	0.5%
Life expectancy	73 (m), 80 (f)
Language	German
Adult literacy rate	99%

Currency	schilling and euro
	(US $1 = 13.50 schilling
	1 euro = 13.76 schilling)
GDP (US million $)	215 000
GDP per head (US $)	26 641

Austria was the hub of the empire which the Habsburg dynasty built from 1246 and which endured until the First World War. The empire spanned Hungary, Czechoslovakia and parts of several other countries; Vienna was its glittering capital. Modern Austria was established in 1919, but was occupied by Germany during the Second World War. After that conflict, Austria was allowed to be independent provided it stayed neutral, although there has been a recent move towards NATO membership.

Both Salzburg and Vienna are famous musical cities (Mozart was born in Salzburg in 1756) and the opera house in Vienna is renowned. Outside the cities, Austria is a land of mountains, lakes, forests and picturesque villages, which cater for winter sports and summer holidays. Its sound economy has improved even more since joining the EU.

BELGIUM

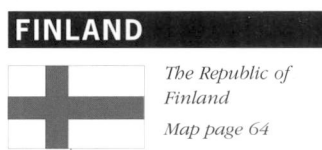

The Kingdom of Belgium

Map page 69

Area	30 528 km²
	(11 787 sq miles)
Capital	Brussels
Member of	CE, EBRD, EU, NATO, OECD

Population	10 188 000
Population growth rate	0.2%
Life expectancy	72 (m), 79 (f)
Languages	Flemish, French, German
Adult literacy rate	99%

Currency	Belgian franc and euro
	(US $1 = 39.58 Belgian francs,
	1 euro = 40.33 Belgian francs)
GDP (US million $)	245 000
GDP per head (US $)	24 019

Northern Belgium is inhabited by Flemings, whose language is related to Dutch, whereas French prevails in the south. Uneasy alliance between the Flemings and French-speaking Walloons gave birth to the modern nation in 1830.

Brussels, the wealthy capital, houses the main headquarters of the European Union. Cities such as Bruges and Antwerp gained prosperity from textiles and trade from the 15th century onwards. In the 19th century, iron and steel dominated the Meuse Valley, which remains a major industrial centre.

DENMARK

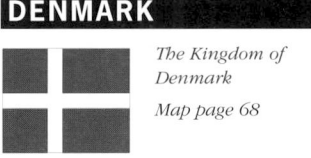

The Kingdom of Denmark

Map page 68

Area	43 094 km²
	(16 639 sq miles)
Capital	Copenhagen
Member of	CE, EBRD, EU, NATO, OECD

Population	5 294 860
Population growth rate	0.1%
Life expectancy	72 (m), 77 (f)
Language	Danish
Adult literacy rate	99%

Currency	Danish krone
	(US $1 = 7.2 kroner)
GDP (US million $)	173 000
GDP per head (US $)	32 641

Few natural resources exist in Denmark, which consists of massive sand dunes along the west coast, and glacial soils and bogs – now mostly drained – over the rest of the country. Yet historically it has been an important power through its control of the entrance to the Baltic Sea, the Øresund, and the taxes it could raise from the rich passing trade. Though its influence waned, Denmark remained part of the European cultural mainstream, and cities such as Ålborg and Copenhagen display this inheritance.

In the 19th century, the Danes successfully modernised their agriculture; butter and pork products, such as bacon, are notable exports. Considerable prosperity is created by Danish design and invention, as seen in industries as diverse as bridge building, pharmaceuticals and porcelain. A road and rail link with Sweden will open in 2000.

FINLAND

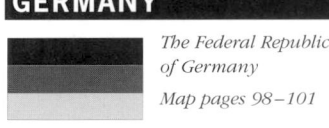

The Republic of Finland

Map page 64

Area	338 144 km²
	(130 558 sq miles)
Capital	Helsinki
Member of	CE, EBRD, EU, OECD

Population	5 140 000
Population growth rate	0.4%
Life expectancy	72 (m), 80 (f)
Languages	Finnish, Swedish, *Lapp*
Adult literacy rate	99%

Currency	markka and euro
	(US $1 = 5.8 markkaa,
	1 euro = 5.94 markkaa)
GDP (US million $)	121 400
GDP per head (US $)	23 804

The long-settled lands of Finland comprise Arctic tundra in the north (used for reindeer grazing), vast, well-managed forests and limited farming in the south. The major cities lie along the milder south coast. Controlled by Sweden and then Russia, Finland finally gained independence in 1917. Since the Second World War, the economy has been transformed with quality engineering and specialised manufactures such as icebreakers. At this latitude, day length and climate vary greatly between summer and winter.

GERMANY

The Federal Republic of Germany

Map pages 98–101

Area	356 974 km²
	(137 828 sq miles)
Capital	Berlin
Member of	CE, EBRD, EU, G8, NATO, OECD

Population	82 071 000
Population growth rate	0.7%
Life expectancy	72 (m), 79 (f)
Language	German
Adult literacy rate	99%

Currency	Deutschmark and euro
	(US $1 = 1.9 DM, 1 euro = 1.95 DM)
GDP (US million $)	2 140 000
GDP per head (US $)	26 097

The most populous country in modern Europe, Germany's history is dominated by the nation's alternate unification and fragmentation into small statelets. Historically, no single city managed to achieve supremacy; local rulers fostered their own political interests, helping to develop a rich seam of influence on European thought. Martin Luther, for example, published his doctrinal theses in Wittenberg in 1517, a decisive moment in the emergence of the Protestant faith. Germany has also made considerable contributions in philosophy, as for example in the works of Hegel and Kant, and in the arts and sciences.

The modern political state dates from the foundation of the Second German Reich in 1871 under Chancellor Otto von Bismarck, but has altered in the aftermath of military defeat in 1918 and again in 1945.

During the Second World War, there was enormous destruction of the industrial and transport systems. This was followed by the division of Germany into a Communist East and a capitalist West. These two parts were reunited in 1990, and Berlin has once again resumed its role as the nation's capital.

Germany has rich agricultural resources and widely varied landscapes, extending from the edge of the Alps to the north European plain. The country has been an important industrial power since the 19th century, with the development of coal, steel, engineering and textiles in the Ruhr, focused upon Essen. Since the Second World War, other modern industries have grown more rapidly in the south of the country around Stuttgart and Munich. Germany is noted for quality products, ranging from optics to motor vehicles, and Frankfurt has become an important financial centre.

West Germany was a founder member of the European Union. The united country is today among the world's economic and political leaders, despite the stresses caused by the integration of eastern provinces where living standards are much lower.

ICELAND

The Republic of Iceland

Map page 64

Area	103 000 km²
	(39 769 sq miles)
Capital	Reykjavik
Member of	CE, EBRD, EFTA, NATO, OECD

Population	271 000
Population growth rate	1.1%
Life expectancy	76 (m), 80 (f)
Language	Icelandic
Adult literacy rate	99%

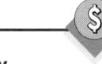

Currency Icelandic krona (US $1 = 72.1 kronur)
GDP (US million $) 7 400
GDP per head (US $) 27 407

The fishing industry, tourism and aluminium production are most important. This volcanic, icy land has few resources other than the geothermal energy of its many hot springs. Iceland has been independent since 1944.

IRELAND

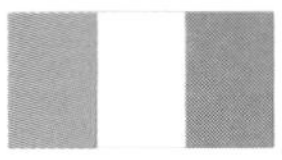

The Republic of Ireland
Map page 75

Area 70 285 km² (27 137 sq miles)
Capital Dublin
Member of CE, EBRD, EU, OECD

Population 3 661 000
Population growth rate 0%
Life expectancy 72 (m), 78 (f)
Languages Irish, English
Adult literacy rate 99%

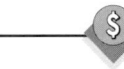

Currency Irish pound (punt) and euro (US $1 = IR£0.77, 1 euro = IR£0.78)
GDP (US million $) 75 400
GDP per head (US $) 20 944

Ireland emerged as a centre of monasticism as early as the 5th century AD. By the 8th century the wealth of the country was attracting destructive Viking raids. Norman invaders arrived in Ireland in 1168. Direct English rule of the entire island began in Tudor times and continued until 1921. The Irish bitterly resented British rule, with its curbs on Irish involvement in politics, business and commerce. In 1922, Ireland became an independent state in the British Commonwealth, and in 1949 it became fully independent as a republic. Six counties of Northern Ireland remained within the UK.

The potato famine in the mid 19th century ravaged Ireland; death and emigration brought a dramatic decline in population.

Ireland's distinguished literary tradition, elegant cities and beautiful countryside attract tourists. The mild, humid climate is ideally suited to the rearing of cattle. Since 1945, the Republic has developed a wide range of hi-tech industries and its economic growth outstrips all other European countries, earning it the title of 'Celtic tiger'.

LUXEMBOURG

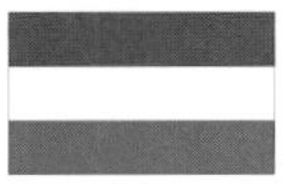

The Grand Duchy of Luxembourg
Map page 69

Area 2587 km² (999 sq miles)
Capital Luxembourg
Member of CE, EBRD, EU, NATO, OECD

Population 421 000
Population growth rate 1.0%
Life expectancy 70 (m), 77 (f)
Languages Letzeburgish (German-Moselle-Frankish dialect), French, German
Adult literacy rate 99%

Currency Luxembourg franc anc euro (US $1 = 39.58 Luxembourg francs, 1 euro= 40.33 Luxembourg francs)
GDP (US million $) 16 900
GDP per head (US $) 40 238

Luxembourg was created a Duchy by Emperor Charles IV in1354. The steel industry in the south brought prosperity in the 19th century, but the country is now primarily a banking centre. It is the home of many international bodies, such as the European Court of Justice. Of the 15 EU members, it has the highest standard of living and is now rated as one of the world's most prosperous nations.

NETHERLANDS

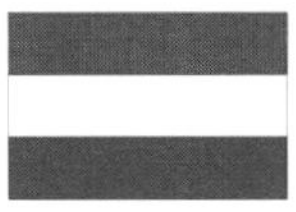

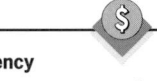

The Kingdom of the Netherlands
Map page 69

Area 33 939 km² (13 104 sq miles)
Capital Amsterdam
Member of CE, EBRD, EU, NATO, OECD

Population 15 604 000
Population growth rate 0.7%
Life expectancy 74 (m), 80 (f)
Language Dutch
Adult literacy rate 99%

Currency guilder and euro (US $1 = 2.16 guilders, 1 euro = 2.2 guilders)
GDP (US million $) 375 400
GDP per head (US $) 24 064

Commerce has been the lifeblood of the Netherlands since the 15th century, and its impact is visible in splendid cities such as Amsterdam and Delft. The Netherlands controls the mouth of the Rhine, a major gateway to Europe, and Rotterdam is one of the busiest ports in the world.

However, much of the delta is below sea level and there is a continuous battle to keep the rivers and the sea at bay. The sea defences in the south-west, built following a disastrous storm in 1953, are a monument to Dutch engineering skill.

The Netherlands gained full independence from Spain in 1648, subsequently lost Belgium and Luxembourg, and endured great privation in the Second World War. Today, manufacturing cities jostle with intensive farms and horticultural fields in the west, in contrast to the forests and heaths of the higher east.

NORWAY

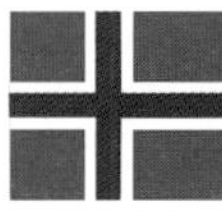

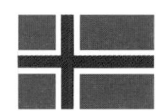

The Kingdom of Norway
Map page 64

Area 323 877 km² (125 050 sq miles)
Capital Oslo
Member of CE, EBRD, EFTA, NATO, OECD

Population 4 406 000
Population growth rate 0.4%
Life expectancy 74 (m), 80 (f)
Languages Norwegian (Bokmål and Nynorsk or neo-Norwegian), *Lapp*
Adult literacy rate 99%

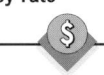

Currency Norwegian krone (US $1 = 7.96 kroner)
GDP (US million $) 149 000
GDP per head (US $) 33 863

Norway is a land of mountains, fiords and glaciers. Norwegians have been great seafarers since the Vikings of the 9th century. Both Bergen and Oslo are ancient ports. Dominated by Denmark and then by Sweden, Norway gained independence in 1905. Although fishing, forestry, tourism and hydroelectric power are still important, they are not as valuable as North Sea oil, which has created an economic independence that allows Norway to resist joining the EU while oil prices are high.

SWEDEN

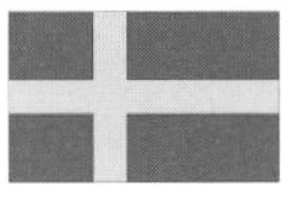

The Kingdom of Sweden
Map page 64

Area 449 964 km² (173 732 sq miles)
Capital Stockholm
Member of CE, EBRD, EU, OECD

Population 8 846 000
Population growth rate 0.5%
Life expectancy 76 (m), 81 (f)
Languages Swedish, *Finnish, Lapp*
Adult literacy rate 99%

Currency Swedish krona (US $1 = 8.55 kronor)
GDP (US million $) 225 000
GDP per head (US $) 25 568

Although Sweden has plentiful forests, hydroelectric resources and iron ore, the present-day wealth of the country depends on high-quality manufactures that are exported worldwide, such as defence equipment, aircraft, cars and glassware. Most development is in the south, where the climate is milder than the north. Once the dominant Baltic power, Sweden has been neutral since 1814. Even so, it maintains sizable and well-equipped armed forces.

UNITED KINGDOM

United Kingdom of Great Britain and Northern Ireland
Map pages 70–75

Area 241 752 km² (93 341 sq miles)
Capital London
Member of CE, COMM, EBRD, EU, G8, NATO, OECD

Population 59 009 000
Population growth rate 0.3%
Life expectancy 74 (m), 79 (f)
Languages English, *Welsh*
Adult literacy rate 99%

Currency pound sterling (US $1 = £0.64)
GDP (US million $) 1 413 300
GDP per head (US $) 23 954

The nation known as the United Kingdom was born of conquest. Norman invaders consolidated their control of England from 1066. Wales was united with England in 1536, and both were joined with Scotland in 1707. In 1800 the United Kingdom of Great Britain and Ireland was formed. Ireland continued to be restive, and by 1922 only six northern counties remained in the UK. The 1998 Good Friday Agreement raised hopes that the Northern Ireland problem could be solved.

The mild maritime climate and extensive lowlands give the United Kingdom an excellent agricultural base. The country was richly endowed with minerals, but most of these have been exhausted except for coal (much of which is now regarded as uneconomic) and North Sea oil and gas.

It was 16th-century maritime power that put Britain on the world map as a trading and colonial power; cities such as London, Bristol, Liverpool, Glasgow and Belfast quickly grew in importance. This wealth, and that derived from agricultural improvements in the 17th and 18th centuries, paved the way for the Industrial Revolution that took place in the late 18th and 19th centuries. Iron and steel, engineering goods, textiles, ceramics and much else made the country the 'workshop of the world'.

The final decades of the 20th century saw the passing of the British Empire as constituent nations gained independence, and closer economic and monetary relations with Europe. Traditional industries have declined, to be replaced by new businesses, often with foreign investment, and service industries have expanded.

Constitutional reform included the formation of new directly elected assemblies in Wales and Northern Ireland. In 1999 the new Scottish parliament took responsibility for its own affairs.

20TH-CENTURY LANDMARKS

1901 Finnish army disbanded; soldiers forced to join Russian army.

1910

1914–18 First World War sparked by assassination of Archduke Ferdinand. Belgium occupied by Germany.

1916 Easter Rising in Dublin. Battle of Jutland.

1917–19 Finland gains independence but endures civil war before republic is declared.

1920

1926 General Strike in Britain.

1929 Markets crash, causing Depression.

1930

1933 Hitler becomes German Chancellor.

1936 Germany and Italy sign Axis Pact.

1938 Austria annexed by Nazi Germany.

1939 Second World War begins.

1940

1940 German rule in Luxembourg, Norway, Belgium, Denmark and the Netherlands. Battle of Britain. London Blitz.

1941 Germany invades Soviet Union.

1944 D-Day landings. Belgium, Denmark and Luxembourg freed.

1945 German surrender. Nuremberg trials.

1949 Germany divided into East and West.

1950

1957 Treaty of Rome; Belgium, France, Italy, Luxembourg, the Netherlands and West Germany found EEC.

1960

1961 Berlin Wall built.

1970

1972 UK imposes direct rule on Northern Ireland.

1972–6 Iceland and UK engage in Cod War.

1973 Britain, Ireland and Denmark join EEC.

1980

1989 Berlin Wall razed.

1990

1990 Unification of East and West Germany.

1992 Single market between EU members.

1994 Northern Ireland peace process quickens.

1995 Austria, Finland and Sweden become members of EU.

1998 The EU prepares for European Monetary Union. Northern Ireland 'Good Friday' peace agreement.

1999 Euro currency is introduced by 11 of the 15 EU nations.

SOUTHERN EUROPE

*T*hese countries, with the exception of north and west France, are hilly or mountainous. They are watered by major rivers such as the Rhône, Tagus, Ebro and Po; the coastline is extensive.

Associated Territories

GIBRALTAR
Parent country
UK
Map page 87

Abbreviations
CE Council of Europe
EBRD European Bank for Reconstruction and Development
EFTA European Free Trade Association
EU European Union
G8 Group of Eight Industrialised Countries
NATO North Atlantic Treaty Organisation
OECD Organisation for Economic Co-operation and Development

GDP Gross Domestic Product

ANDORRA

The Principality of Andorra
Map page 88

Area	468 km²
	(181 sq miles)
Capital	Andorra la Vella
Member of	CE
Population	74 000
Population growth rate	5.3%
Life expectancy	79 (av. m/f)
Languages	Catalan, *French, Spanish*
Adult literacy rate	99%
Currency	French franc;
	Spanish peseta
GDP (US million $)	960
GDP per head (US $)	14 111

Andorra is self-governing, but nominal sovereignty is jointly held by France and Spain. Tourism and tax-free shopping are mainstays of the economy.

FRANCE

The French Republic

Map pages 78–83

Area	543 965 km²
	(210 026 sq miles)
Capital	Paris
Member of	CE, EBRD, EU, G8,
	NATO, OECD
Population	58 607 000
Population growth rate	0.5%
Life expectancy	73 (m), 81 (f)
Languages	French, *Breton, Basque*
Adult literacy rate	over 95%
Currency	French franc and euro
	(US $1 = FF6.4, 1 euro = FF6.5)
GDP (US million $)	1 413 900
GDP per head (US $)	24 128

A country that extends from the Mediterranean to the English Channel, from the Atlantic to the Alps, France encompasses great variations in climate and landscape: rolling plains in the Paris basin; a high and lightly inhabited plateau in the Massif Central; the Riviera popular with sun-worshippers. There are rich agricultural resources and, despite the population being relatively sparse, old towns and villages each possess their distinctive character. Some of these towns, such as Bordeaux, have prospered with overland and overseas trade.

Until after the Second World War, France outside the capital remained predominantly rural, with fine traditions of quality products, such as wines and cheeses. Most 19th-century industrialisation occurred in the north, around Lille and Metz for example, and in Paris. Since then, there has been widespread and rapid development of modern industries and commerce, creating cities such as Lyon and Marseille.

Within Europe, France was the pioneer of high-speed rail travel with the TGV, on specially built tracks. About three-quarters of the electricity used by the country is generated by nuclear power. French scientists and engineers also cooperate internationally in advanced aircraft design and construction, and in space research. Modern, computer-based industries have become a feature of the south. The French coasts and older cities, especially Paris, are major tourist destinations.

For many centuries, France has been a leading power with a worldwide influence on cultural and political issues. Following the French Revolution of 1789, when the monarchy was overthrown, France became the first modern republic, providing a model for other nations. In the 20th century, the country was a founder member and principal architect of the European Union. On the world scene, France is one of five permanent members of the United Nations Security Council.

The post-war loss of France's overseas possessions culminated in the independence of Algeria in 1962, resulting in the move of many people, particularly from North Africa, to France. This introduced important new cultural influences into French society, but has not lessened its fierce pride in French language, history and culture.

Despite its long and cohesive national history, the diversity of the country is reflected in active separatist movements – notably those of the Corsicans, Bretons and Basques. Since 1982, attempts have been made to meet some of the demands of these groups by decentralising the government of the country, including the establishment of a regional assembly for Corsica.

ITALY

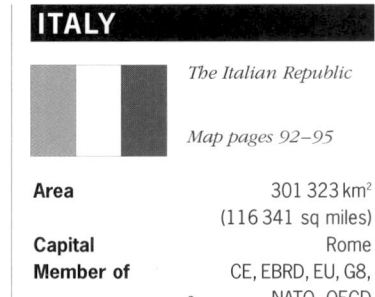

The Italian Republic

Map pages 92–95

Area	301 323 km²
	(116 341 sq miles)
Capital	Rome
Member of	CE, EBRD, EU, G8,
	NATO, OECD
Population	57 523 000
Population growth rate	0.1%
Life expectancy	74 (m), 80 (f)
Languages	Italian, *German, French*
	and other languages
Adult literacy rate	97.1%
Currency	lira and euro
	(US $1 = 1 900.2 lire,
	1 euro = 1936.2 lire)
GDP (US million $)	1 388 000
GDP per head (US $)	24 139

Between the Alps in the north and the Apennines forming Italy's mountainous spine, lies the Po valley, the country's one large area of flat and fertile land. Here irrigation supports intensive farming. Farther south in the peninsula and on the islands of Sicily and Sardinia the soil is generally poorer, the climate drier and agriculture is practised in a smaller way.

Though the peninsula had been united under the Romans, with the collapse of their empire the country became a mosaic of kingdoms and city-states. Trade with the rest of Europe in goods brought from the Far East (including gems, spices and silks) provided the medieval city-states of northern Italy such as Genoa and Venice with their great wealth.

Although the Portuguese discovery of the sea route to the Orient led to a decline in Italy's commercial fortunes, the Renaissance, which started around Florence in the 14th century, put Italy at the heart of Europe's cultural development. It marked a great flowering of art, science and architecture, the influence of which endured and spread across Europe. Cultural vitality was maintained through the 19th century and into the 20th century, as for example, in music and opera.

The country's reunification was finally achieved in 1870. But the disparity in wealth between northern Italy on the one hand and southern Italy, Sicily and Sardinia, on the other, provoked large-scale emigration from the southern regions to the United States of America. This trend only served to accentuate the contrast and the economic fortunes of the south have, over the years, been further damaged by the insidious activities of secret societies such as the Mafia. This economic disparity survives to the present, although successive governments have tried to minimise it. Nevertheless, the main commercial and industrial developments have occurred in the north around the major cities of Milan and Turin. In addition to its major industries such as car manufacturing, Italy is famous for its highly innovative small firms.

Italy's extensive coastline and rich artistic heritage in cities such as Venice, Rome, Florence and Pisa attract impressive numbers of tourists. The danger to both Venice (from flooding) and Pisa (from subsidence) lend a piquancy to Italy's tourism.

LIECHTENSTEIN

The Principality of Liechtenstein

Map page 102

Area	160 km²
	(61.8 sq miles)
Capital	Vaduz
Member of	CE, EBRD, EFTA
Population	32 000
Population growth rate	1.4%
Life expectancy	66 (m) 73 (f)
Language	German
	(Alemannic dialect)
Adult literacy rate	over 95%
Currency	Swiss franc
	(US $1 = 1.57 Swiss francs)
GDP (US million $)	1315
GDP per head (US $)	42 416

Wedged between Austria and Switzerland, this independent principality is economically linked to Switzerland. Excellent communications and lenient tax laws make Liechtenstein a favoured place for companies to base their headquarters. The economy, supported by tourism, is well diversified, with half the workforce in industry.

MALTA

The Republic of Malta

Map page 95

Area	316 km²
	(122 sq miles)
Capital	Valletta
Member of	CE, EBRD
Population	375 000
Population growth rate	0.3%
Life expectancy	75 (m), 79 (f)
Languages	Maltese, English, *Italian*
Adult literacy rate	87.9%
Currency	Maltese lira
	(US $1 = LM 0.4)
GDP (US million $)	3433
GDP per head (US $)	11 443

Small in size but strategically located, Malta has had a long history of foreign control. In 1964 the group of islands achieved independence from Britain, who abandoned its naval installations, bringing some hardship to the nation. Since then Malta has sought to diversify with emphasis on tourism, shipping and textiles.

MONACO

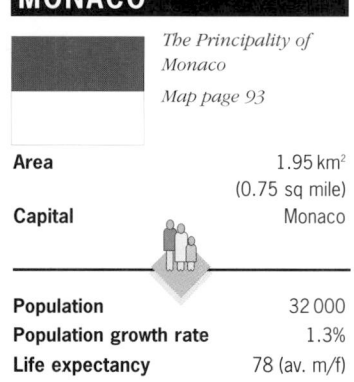

The Principality of Monaco
Map page 93

Area	1.95 km²
	(0.75 sq mile)
Capital	Monaco

Population	32 000
Population growth rate	1.3%
Life expectancy	78 (av. m/f)
Languages	French, *Monégasque*, *Italian, English*
Adult literacy rate	99%

Currency	French franc (US $1 = FF6.4)
GDP (US million $)	847
GDP per head (US $)	26 470

Ruled by a Genoese family since the 13th century, Monaco has a customs union with France. A haunt of the rich, it prospers from its casinos, the Monte Carlo Rally, the Monaco Grand Prix and other leisure activities that exploit the sea and sun.

PORTUGAL

The Portuguese Republic
Map pages 86–87

Area	92 270 km²
	(35 626 sq miles)
Capital	Lisbon
Member of	CE, EBRD, EU, NATO, OECD

Population	9 802 000
Population growth rate	−0.1%
Life expectancy	71 (m), 78 (f)
Language	Portuguese
Adult literacy rate	85%

Currency	escudo and euro
	(US $1 = 196.75 escudos,
	1 euro = 200.48 escudos)
GDP (US million $)	108 100
GDP per head (US $)	11 030

A nation-state since the 11th century, much of Portugal is dominated by low granite mountains that create a varied and fragmented landscape with diverse agricultural resources. The Atlantic gives Portugal a cooler and more moist climate than neighbouring Spain.

Seafaring Portugal pioneered Europe's period of exploration in the early 15th century, and gained enormous wealth in the process. Surpassed in the 17th century by Spain, England and the Netherlands, Portugal's stagnation only ended after the loss of overseas possessions and the death, in 1970, of Prime Minister António de Oliveira Salazar, who headed a right-wing dictatorship.

Modern Portugal's industries include a number based on local products, such as port wine. With low wage costs, the country makes an attractive manufacturing base for an increasing range of industries, including textiles and shoes. Agriculture remains important, but is being modernised. Tourism, especially along the Algarve coast, is of increasing value to the economy.

SAN MARINO

The Republic of San Marino
Map page 93

Area	61 km²
	(24 sq miles)
Capital	San Marino
Member of	CE

Population	26 000
Population growth rate	1.5%
Life expectancy	73 (m), 79 (f)
Language	Italian
Adult literacy rate	98.4%

Currency	Italian lira
	(US $1 = 1900.2 lire)
GDP (US million $)	478
GDP per head (US $)	19 121

Perched on the Apennines, San Marino derives its main income from tourists, attracted by its three picturesque 13th-century fortresses. Additional income is provided by agriculture, light industry and the issue of postage stamps. The country has close economic links with Italy.

SPAIN

The Kingdom of Spain
Map pages 86–89

Area	504 782 km²
	(194 897 sq miles)
Capital	Madrid
Member of	CE, EBRD, EU, NATO, OECD

Population	39 323 000
Population growth rate	0.3%
Life expectancy	73 (m), 80 (f)
Languages	Castilian Spanish, *others*
Adult literacy rate	95.8%

Currency	peseta and euro
	(US $1 = 163 pesetas,
	1 euro = 166 pesetas)
GDP (US million $)	550 000
GDP per head (US $)	13 995

Most of Spain's interior is a high plateau crowned by several mountain ranges; it is dry and suffers hot summers and cold winters. The most fertile land is found in the better-watered, mountainous north and in areas where irrigation is possible. These lie along the Mediterranean coast, around Valencia for example, and in the major river valleys, such as that of the Guadalquivir.

After the expulsion of the Moors, completed in 1492, and Columbus's voyage to America in the same year, Spain gained great wealth and power and an overseas empire in the 16th century. However, with the rise of England and the Netherlands, the influence of Spain declined, and its occupation by the French from 1808 to 1814 gave its colonies the opportunity to seize their independence. Spain entered the 20th century as a relatively poor nation with limited industrialisation and racked by internal dissension from groups such as the Basque separatist movement. These divisions culminated in the Spanish Civil War of the 1930s and the rise of the authoritarian General Francisco Franco. After his death and the restitution of the monarchy and democratic government, Spain is once more a major force in modern Europe.

The single most striking area of growth, which began in the early post-war period, has been the tourist industry, principally along the Mediterranean coast. Over 50 million visitors a year contribute about 10 per cent of the nation's gross domestic product (GDP), but competition from other countries is now forcing the industry to upgrade facilities. Efforts are also being made to exploit the potential of Spain's fine urban heritage in towns such as Granada. Major investment in the infrastructure, combined with relatively low wages, makes Spain an excellent manufacturing base. This has attracted inward investment, including car manufacture, and has spurred the development of Barcelona, Bilbao/Santander and Madrid in particular. Progress has been rapid in closing the economic gap with other European countries, although Spain was particularly affected by recession in the early 1990s. Lack of water poses a serious long-term problem in much of the country, and plans are being considered for major transfers from the wetter north-west.

Separatist pressures, especially from the Basque population, have resulted in a high degree of autonomy in the regions. The issue of Gibraltar's sovereignty comes to the fore periodically, but the Spanish government, while maintaining its claim to the territory, seems content to leave the matter on one side.

SWITZERLAND

The Swiss Confederation
Map page 92

Area	41 284 km²
	(15 940 sq miles)
Capital	Bern
Member of	CE, EBRD, EFTA, OECD

Population	7 089 000
Population growth rate	1%
Life expectancy	75 (m), 82 (f)
Languages	German, French, Italian, *and other languages*
Adult literacy rate	99%

Currency	Swiss franc
	(US $1 = 1.57 francs)
GDP (US million $)	262 200
GDP per head (US $)	37 428

This conservative country in the heartland of the Alps has prospered for centuries from transit trade with its neighbours, from dairy farming, precision industries such as clock-making and, above all, from tourism.

The environmental effect of road traffic traversing the country in increasing numbers is such that all transit lorries must pass through the country by rail.

The Swiss are also famous for their international banking and financial services industries.

The traditional neutrality of the nation has made it an ideal base for a number of worldwide organisations such as the International Red Cross and a number of agencies run by the United Nations.

VATICAN CITY

The State of the Vatican City
Map page 94

Area	0.44 km²
	(0.17 sq mile)
Capital	Vatican City

Population	1000
Languages	Italian, Latin
Adult literacy rate	100%

Currency	Italian lira
	(US $1 = 1900.2 lire)
GDP (US million $)	19
GDP per head (US $)	19 121

This tiny enclave within Rome is the smallest independent state in the world. It is the headquarters of the Roman Catholic Church (the Holy See) and seat of the Pope. Its treasures include St Peter's Basilica and the Sistine Chapel.

1904 France and UK sign Entente Cordiale.

— 1910 —

1910 Portugal declared a republic.

1914 First World War begins. Germany invades French territory.

1916 Battles of Somme and Verdun (France).

1918 First World War ends.

1919 Versailles Treaty.

— 1920 —

1922 Mussolini heads Italian government.

1923 Military overthrow monarchy in Spain.

1926 Military coup in Portugal is followed by right-wing dictatorship.

— 1930 —

1931 Second Republic declared in Spain.

1936–9 Spanish Civil War; Nationalist General Franco defeats Republican army.

1936 Italy and Germany sign Axis Pact.

1939 Second World War begins.

— 1940 —

1940 France occupied by Germany.

1943 Mussolini overthrown; Italy surrenders.

1944 D-Day landings in northern France.

1945 Second World War ends.

1946 Italy becomes a republic.

1946–58 Fourth Republic in France.

— 1950 —

1957 Treaty of Rome: France and Italy among six EEC founders.

1958 Fifth Republic declared in France.

— 1960 —

1962 France grants Algeria independence.

1968 Student unrest in France.

— 1970 —

1974 Dictatorship ends in Portugal.

1975 Death of General Franco; Juan Carlos becomes King of Spain.

1977 Democratic elections in Spain.

— 1980 —

1986 Portugal and Spain join EEC.

— 1990 —

1992 Single market between EU members.

1999 Euro currency is introduced in 11 of the 15 EU nations. Portugal returns Macau to China.

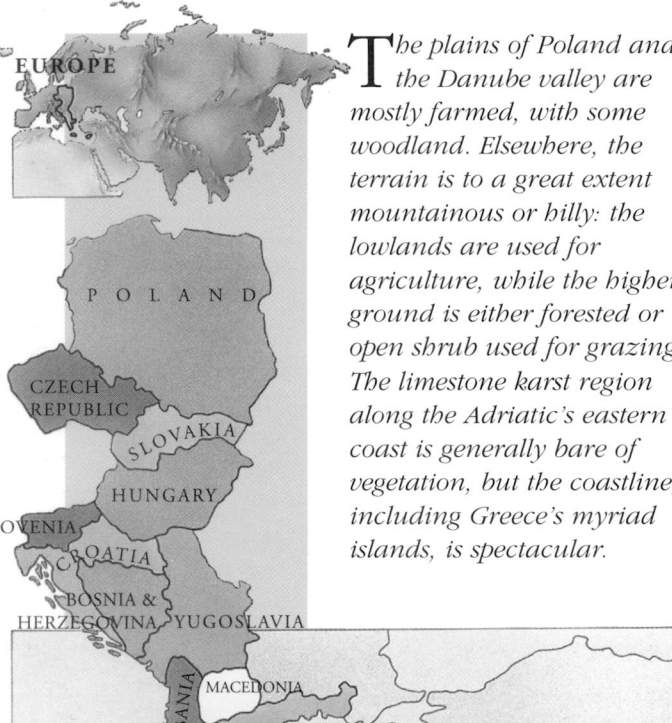

The plains of Poland and the Danube valley are mostly farmed, with some woodland. Elsewhere, the terrain is to a great extent mountainous or hilly: the lowlands are used for agriculture, while the higher ground is either forested or open shrub used for grazing. The limestone karst region along the Adriatic's eastern coast is generally bare of vegetation, but the coastline, including Greece's myriad islands, is spectacular.

ALBANIA

The Republic of Albania

Map page 106

Area	28 748 km²
	(11 100 sq miles)
Capital	Tirana
Member of	CE, EBRD

Population	3 731 000
Population growth rate	1.6%
Life expectancy	69 (m), 75 (f)
Language	Albanian (dialects: Gheg in the north, Tosk in the south)
Adult literacy rate	95%

Currency	lek (US $1 = 134.2 lekë)
GDP (US million $)	2937
GDP per head (US $)	793

This small, mountainous country is still dominated by agriculture, for which the natural resources are good: a Mediterranean climate and reasonably plentiful water supply nurture a wide range of crops.

Albania gained independence from the Turks in 1912; it was then invaded by the Italians during both world wars, and by the Germans in 1943. The partisan leader Enver Hoxha liberated the country in 1944. He imposed a strict Communist regime, aiming for maximum self-sufficiency and limited contact with the outside world.

Since the death of Hoxha in 1985, there has been considerable liberalisation, but Albania remains one of Europe's poorest countries. Its meagre resources were further strained by numerous ethnic Albanian refugees crossing its borders with Kosovo during 1999.

Abbreviations
CE *Council of Europe*
CEFTA *Central European Free Trade Association*
COMM *Commonwealth*
EBRD *European Bank for Reconstruction and Development*
EU *European Union*
NATO *North Atlantic Treaty Organisation*
OECD *Organisation for Economic Co-operation and Development*

GDP *Gross Domestic Product*

BOSNIA & HERZEGOVINA

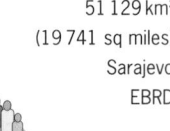

Bosnia and Herzegovina

Map page 104

Area	51 129 km²
	(19 741 sq miles)
Capital	Sarajevo
Member of	EBRD

Population	3 784 000
Population growth rate	–5.0%
Life expectancy	69 (m), 75 (f)
Language	Serbo-Croat (Muslims and Croats use Roman script, Serbs use Cyrillic)
Adult literacy rate	93%

Currency	marka (US $1 = 1.86 marka)
GDP (US million $)	968
GDP per head (US $)	271

Conquered by the Ottomans in 1463, Bosnia-Herzegovina gained its independence from Yugoslavia in 1992. It was then plunged into a dreadful conflict between the Muslim, Serb and Croat peoples, which involved neighbouring Croatia and the remaining provinces of the Federal Republic of Yugoslavia. A fragile peace was established in 1995 under the Dayton peace agreement and is sustained by a NATO presence. Sarajevo has been badly damaged in the civil war, and may never again be the multi-ethnic city it once was.

CROATIA

The Republic of Croatia

Map page 104

Area	56 610 km²
	(21 857 sq miles)
Capital	Zagreb
Member of	CE, EBRD

Population	4 572 000
Population growth rate	0.7%
Life expectancy	68 (m), 76 (f)
Language	Serbo-Croat
Adult literacy rate	93%

Currency	kuna (US $1 = 7.46 kuna)
GDP (US million $)	20 600
GDP per head (US $)	4577

The Croats fleetingly enjoyed independence during the Second World War before being reincorporated into Yugoslavia, from which they separated in 1992. The bare limestone Dinaric Alps dominate the west; the east is mainly fertile river lowlands. Croatia was one of the more prosperous parts of Yugoslavia, because of widespread industrialisation and the dramatic Adriatic coast, which attracted large numbers of tourists. The economy has suffered in the turmoil that followed the break-up of Yugoslavia, especially because of the conflicts in Bosnia and, more recently, Kosovo.

CYPRUS

The Republic of Cyprus

Map page 118

Area	9251 km²
	(3572 sq miles)
Capital	Nicosia
Member of	COMM, EBRD

Population	740 000
Population growth rate	1.1%
Life expectancy	75 (m), 79 (f)
Languages	Greek, *Turkish*
Adult literacy rate	94%

Currency	Cyprus pound (US $1 = 0.5 Cyprus pound)
GDP (US million $)	8800
GDP per head (US $)	11 891

Its Mediterranean position has given mountainous Cyprus a rich heritage of historic sites. After centuries of occupation, Cyprus became independent in 1960, although Britain maintains military Sovereign Base Areas, because of the island's strategic position. For years civil strife between the majority Greek and minority Turkish populations has afflicted Cyprus. In 1974 this culminated in a Turkish invasion and the establishment of a separate administration in the north. Attempts at reconciliation have failed.

CZECH REPUBLIC

The Czech Republic

Map page 97

Area	78 864 km²
	(30 450 sq miles)
Capital	Prague
Member of	CE, CEFTA, EBRD, NATO, OECD

Population	10 304 000
Population growth rate	0.1%
Life expectancy	70 (m), 77 (f)
Languages	Czech, *German and others*
Adult literacy rate	99%

Currency	Czech koruna (US $1 = 35.64 koruny)
GDP (US million $)	57 400
GDP per head (US $)	5572

Throughout their long history, the Czechs have managed to maintain close links with Western Europe; the wealth of Prague dates back to the 14th century, when it was the seat of the German Holy Roman Emperor and Charles University was founded.

The country has good soils which, with the continental climate, permit a wide range of crops to be grown; it also has important mineral deposits, including coal and uranium.

There is a long tradition of skilled workmanship, which provides the basis for numerous manufactures. However, the German occupation during the Second World War, followed by four decades of Communist rule, held back development. There is also a serious problem of industrial pollution, mainly in the north of the country.

The Republic was born after the peaceful dissolution of Czechoslovakia in 1993. Many Czechs opposed the separation of Slovakia from the former united republic, but the split was accomplished peacefully. The Czechs have managed the transition from Communism with considerable skill. They have successfully opened up their economy, with tourism being one of the largest growth areas; the potential for further expansion is considerable, particularly in Prague.

The Czech Republic joined NATO in 1999, and formal discussions are taking place regarding its membership of the European Union.

GREECE

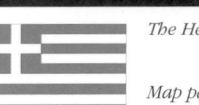

The Hellenic Republic

Map pages 106–7

Area	131 957 km²
	(50 949 sq miles)
Capital	Athens
Member of	CE, EBRD, EU, NATO, OECD

Population	10 522 000
Population growth rate	0.5%
Life expectancy	75 (m), 80 (f)
Language	Greek
Adult literacy rate	95.2%

Currency	drachma (US $1 = 318.9 drachmæ)
GDP (US million $)	120 100
GDP per head (US $)	11 438

Five hundred years before the birth of Christ, Greece was the centre of the Western world. The impact of the Hellenic legacy on language, culture, architecture, science and politics is immeasurable. The civilisation itself diminished with the rise of Rome and other powers. However, its language and culture were maintained in the Byzantine Empire, the eastern half of the Roman Empire and the heart of the Orthodox Church. Greece re-emerged as an independent nation in 1830 after war and centuries of occupation by the Ottoman Empire.

After German occupation in World War II, lengthy civil war and military rule, democracy was not restored until 1974. Greece was one of the most politically volatile and poor

nations in the European Union. Greater political and economic stability have now been achieved and Greece is expected to adopt the euro currency in 2001.

Greece is dominated by limestone mountains lacking soil and vegetation. Water is scarce and mineral resources are modest, but there are marble quarries. The scenic coastline and many islands attract tourists who are vital to the modern economy. Crops, such as olives and oranges, and large shipping interests are also important.

HUNGARY

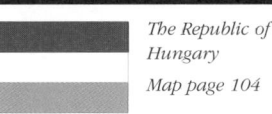

The Republic of Hungary

Map page 104

Area	93 030 km²
	(35 919 sq miles)
Capital	Budapest
Member of	CE, CEFTA, EBRD, EU (assoc.),
	NATO, OECD

Population	10 153 000
Population growth rate	−0.4%
Life expectancy	65 (m), 74 (f)
Language	Hungarian
Adult literacy rate	99%

Currency	forint (US $1 = 244.4 forint)
GDP (US million $)	46 600
GDP per head (US $)	4571

The landscape of Hungary is dominated by fertile plains suitable for a wide range of agriculture. Much is exported, especially livestock products. Rolling country west of the Danube, which links Hungary to the Black Sea, is dotted with spas, old towns, orchards and vineyards; Lake Balaton is an international holiday centre. In addition, coal, bauxite and other resources provide the basis for industrial development.

Magyar horsemen conquered the south-west of Hungary in the 9th century, bringing with them a language unique in Europe though related to Finnish. Thereafter, the country had a turbulent history, with a period of Turkish rule and then union with Austria. Only after the First World War did Hungary emerge, much reduced, as a separate state.

Communist rule after the Second World War was more liberal than in other Eastern European countries. A relatively progressive economic policy eased the transition to a post-Communist market; EU membership talks began in 1998 and it joined NATO in 1999. Budapest, the capital, is home to one-fifth of Hungary's population; it is an elegant city and a major cultural and industrial centre. Bartók, Kodály and Liszt are composers who testify to the nation's distinct musical tradition.

MACEDONIA

The Former Yugoslav Republic of Macedonia

Map page 106

Area	25 713 km²
	(9928 sq miles)
Capital	Skopje
Member of	CE, EBRD

Population	2 190 000
Population growth rate	−1.5%
Life expectancy	69 (m), 73 (f)
Languages	Macedonian, Albanian,
	Serbo-Croat
Adult literacy rate	93%

Currency	Macedonian denar
	(US $1 = 59.5 denars)
GDP (US million $)	3200
GDP per head (US $)	1454

Macedonia became independent in 1992. It shares its name with a neighbouring province of Greece, which was initially a matter of considerable political sensitivity. Macedonia also contains a sizable Albanian minority and has experienced ethnic tensions, which have been exacerbated by the conflict in neighbouring Kosovo and the temporary influx from there of ethnic Albanians.

POLAND

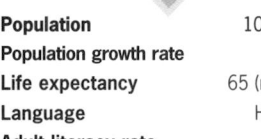

Republic of Poland

Map page 97

Area	312 685 km²
	(120 728 sq miles)
Capital	Warsaw
Member of	CE, CEFTA, EBRD,
	NATO, OECD

Population	38 650 000
Population growth rate	0.3%
Life expectancy	67 (m), 76 (f)
Languages	Polish, German
Adult literacy rate	99%

Currency	zloty
	(US $1 = 3.90 zlotys)
GDP (US million $)	148 800
GDP per head (US $)	3849

The Slavs who settled Poland formed their first kingdom in the 10th century and, between the 14th and 17th centuries, it became one of the great powers of Europe. Lacking natural frontiers on the north European plain, the country has suffered subjugation by neighbours, especially during the Second World War, in which 6 million Poles died, including 3 million Jews. A major adjustment of the border was imposed at that time, which was associated with huge population transfers. As a result, there are virtually no ethnic minorities.

Poland's agricultural lands are extensive, capable of producing a variety of vegetables and grains. Despite the restraints of Communist rule, the country managed to rebuild its shattered economy after 1945, exploiting in particular the acquisition of a Baltic coastline and southern Silesian coalfields to develop a wide range of industries, such as shipyards at Gdansk. It was here in 1980 that Solidarity was born, the first independent trade union in Eastern Europe since the war. It initiated a weakening of Communist control that led to free elections in 1989.

The medieval core of Kraków survived – the city is home to the country's oldest university, founded in 1364. Warsaw has been meticulously rebuilt, and similar restoration has taken place elsewhere, as for example at Torun, a Hanseatic town. On the other hand, the extensive use of low-grade coal and poor industrial equipment has left a serious legacy of pollution in the industrial south, which is of particular concern to its south-western neighbour, the Czech Republic. Poland joined NATO in 1999 and has begun formal negotiations for EU membership.

SLOVAKIA

The Slovak Republic

Map page 97

Area	49 036 km²
	(18 933 sq miles)
Capital	Bratislava
Member of	CE, CEFTA, EBRD

Population	5 383 000
Population growth rate	0.4%
Life expectancy	68 (m), 76 (f)
Languages	Slovak, Hungarian, Czech,
	and others
Adult literacy rate	93%

Currency	Slovak koruna
	(US $1 = 44.39 koruny)
GDP (US million $)	21 300
GDP per head (US $)	3959

Despite rule by foreign powers, mountainous terrain enabled the Slovaks to maintain their identity and ultimately to gain independence in 1993 from the former Czechoslovak federation. This move followed increasing resentment at the political and economic dominance of the wealthier Czechs. Bratislava, the Slovak capital, and the Danube plains form the economic core; forestry and ski resorts provide employment, while nature parks cover much of the highest land. A hydroelectric scheme on the Danube is being developed.

Slovakia has ambitions for closer links with the West through membership of NATO and, eventually, the EU.

SLOVENIA

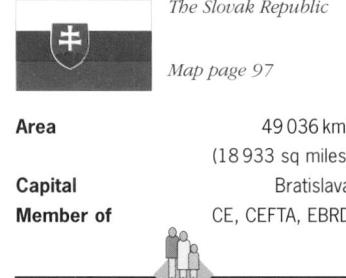

The Republic of Slovenia

Map page 103

Area	20 253 km²
	(7820 sq miles)
Capital	Ljubljana
Member of	CE, CEFTA, EBRD

Population	1 987 000
Population growth rate	0.7%
Life expectancy	70 (m), 77 (f)
Languages	Slovene, Hungarian, Italian
Adult literacy rate	99%

Currency	tolar (US $1 = 192.87 tolar)
GDP (US million $)	19 400
GDP per head (US $)	9763

It took 1000 years and a brief skirmish with the Yugoslav Federal Army in 1991 before Slovenia gained recognition as a separate nation in 1992. It was then spared the long and savage conflict which engulfed Croatia and Bosnia. Fine scenery – the Julian Alps rise to 2864 m (9396 ft) – attract increasing numbers of tourists, and a range of manufactures provide the basis for prosperity. Ljubljana, the capital, has many fine baroque buildings.

YUGOSLAVIA

The Federal Republic of Yugoslavia

Map page 104

Area	102 173 km²
	(39 449 sq miles)
Capital	Belgrade

Population	10 597 000
Population growth rate	0.9%
Life expectancy	68 (m), 74 (f)
Language	Serbo-Croat (Cyrillic script)
Adult literacy rate	89%

Currency	Yugoslav new dinar
	(US $1 = 11.49 new dinars)
GDP (US million $)	15 243
GDP per head (US $)	1487

A federation of Serbia and Montenegro is all that remains of the former Yugoslavia. The country suffered sanctions because of its support for Serbs in the Bosnian civil war. Then President Slobodan Milosevic annulled the autonomous status of Kosovo where the majority population was Albanian. This was followed by repression of the Albanians by the Serbs. Western ultimatums were rejected, leading to a NATO bombing campaign that lasted three months, inflicted severe damage and provoked yet more brutality – and even genocide – against the Albanian Kosovans. Eventually Serbia submitted to NATO's demands.

1908 Bosnia and Herzegovina annexed by Austria-Hungary.

— 1910 —

1912–13 Balkan Wars.

1914–18 Assassination of Archduke Ferdinand by Serb nationalist sparks First World War.

1918 Czechoslovakia, Hungary, Kingdom of Serbs, Croats and Slovenes (Yugoslavia) and Poland become republics.

— 1920 —

1928 King Zog, the former prime minister, is crowned in Albania.

— 1930 —

1939 Germany invades Poland; Second World War begins.

— 1940 —

1940 Hungary and Slovakia support the German-Italian Axis.

1941 Germany invades Yugoslavia and Greece.

1944 Soviet forces occupy Czechoslovakia, Hungary and Poland.

1945 Marshal Tito declares Communist rule in Yugoslavia.

1947 Czechoslovakia, Hungary and Poland become Communist.

— 1950 —

1956 Hungarian uprising suppressed by Soviet troops.

— 1960 —

1967 Greek colonels depose monarch.

1968 'Prague Spring' in Czechoslovakia crushed by Soviet troops.

— 1970 —

1973 Greece declared a republic.

1974 Northern Cyprus invaded by Turkey; the island is partitioned.

— 1980 —

1980 Solidarity trade union formed in Poland; martial law imposed (1981) after civil unrest.

1989 Czechoslovakia, Hungary and Poland overthrow Communism.

— 1990 —

1991 Independence of Croatia, Macedonia and Slovenia declared.

1992 Civil war starts in former Yugoslavia.

1993 Czechoslovakia divides into the Czech Republic and Slovakia.

1995 Fragile peace made in Croatia and in Bosnia and Herzegovina.

1998 Civil war in Kosovo sparked by Kosovans' desire for independence.

1999 NATO bombs Serbia to stop repression of Albanian Kosovans.

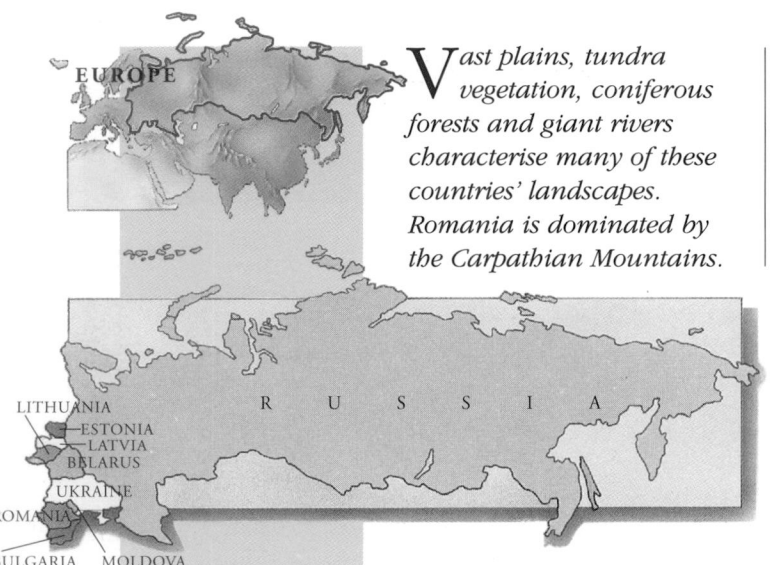

Vast plains, tundra vegetation, coniferous forests and giant rivers characterise many of these countries' landscapes. Romania is dominated by the Carpathian Mountains.

BELARUS

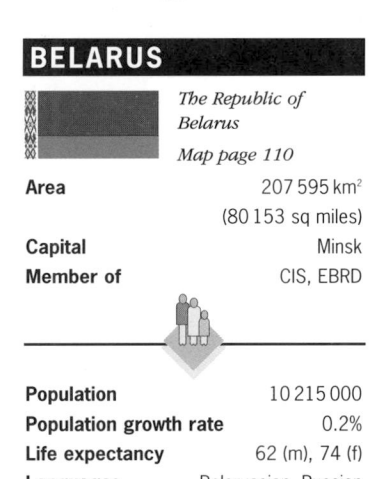

The Republic of Belarus

Map page 110

Area	207 595 km²
	(80 153 sq miles)
Capital	Minsk
Member of	CIS, EBRD

Population	10 215 000
Population growth rate	0.2%
Life expectancy	62 (m), 74 (f)
Languages	Belarussian, Russian
Adult literacy rate	97.9%

Currency	Belarussian rouble (interim currency)
	(US $1 = 315 000 roubles)
GDP (US million $)	14 800
GDP per head (US $)	1448

With the collapse of the Soviet Union, Belarus emerged as an independent state in 1991. The country, formerly known as Belorussia or 'White Russia', has a turbulent history, having been subject to competing territorial claims by Russia, Lithuania and Poland. Belarus was occupied by Germany in the Second World War, when the large Jewish population was exterminated. The country has no significant natural frontiers, and although the Belarussians are ethnically homogenous and proud of their culture, they generally speak Russian. They retain strong links with Russia, and there is even a move towards political and economic integration once more with Russia.

Summer rain and winter snow feed myriad lakes in the north of the country and the Pripet Marshes (Europe's largest swamp) in the south. The water is also used to nurture Belarus's thriving agriculture. About 70 per cent of the work force are involved in a wide range of basic manufacturing industries, many of which date back to the 19th century and the development of the railway network. Belarus industry and transport suffer because almost all fuel has to be imported, mainly from Russia, at prices the nation can barely afford.

BULGARIA

The Republic of Bulgaria

Map page 105

Area	110 994 km²
	(42 855 sq miles)
Capital	Sofia
Member of	BSEC, CE, CEFTA, EBRD

Population	8 306 000
Population growth rate	-0.2%
Life expectancy	67 (m), 74 (f)
Languages	Bulgarian, *Turkish and others*
Adult literacy rate	92%

Currency	lev (US $1 = 1.9130 leva)
GDP (US million $)	11 700
GDP per head (US $)	1409

As an identifiable people, the Bulgars may be traced back to about AD 500, but Bulgaria only emerged as a separate nation with the ending of 500 years of Turkish rule in 1878. Rich agricultural resources and the country's strategic position between Europe and Asia Minor has ensured a long history of prosperity, although Bulgaria's modernisation was restricted under Turkish rule. After the imposition of Communist rule in 1946, substantial industrial development took place, albeit with heavy reliance on the Soviet Union for manufacturing equipment. Initially, this made adaptation to the post-Soviet era more difficult, but Bulgaria has increasingly oriented its policy towards the West; indeed its currency has been pegged to the euro, bringing about greater confidence to the banking system. It cooperated with NATO during the 1999 Kosovo war.

Bulgaria has a developing tourist industry based on the Black Sea coast and skiing resorts in the mountains. It also exports wines to the West, attracting sufficient investment to modernise its operation.

ESTONIA

The Republic of Estonia

Map page 67

Area	45 227 km²
	(17 462 sq miles)
Capital	Tallinn
Member of	CE, EBRD

Population	1 458 000
Population growth rate	0.1%
Life expectancy	62 (m), 73 (f)
Languages	Estonian, *Russian*
Adult literacy rate	99.7%

Currency	kroon (US $1 = 15.35 kroons)
GDP (US million $)	5400
GDP per head (US $)	3703

The Estonians have lived along the Baltic shores for nearly 5000 years. Despite being ruled by more powerful neighbours for most of the modern period, they have maintained their cultural identity. Estonia has twice become independent of Russia – from 1918 to 1940 and again since 1991. As part of the Soviet Union, Estonia had to accept a large number of Russian immigrants, which left the newly independent state with an uncomfortable political and social legacy. Now a thriving state with close ties to Finland, Estonia began formal talks in 1998 about joining the EU.

Estonia is a land of islands and lakes, forests and marshes. Important industries include agriculture and forestry, as well as a wide range of consumer manufactures. Tallinn, the capital, is an attractive old port, now host to many visitors.

LATVIA

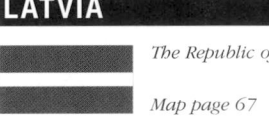

The Republic of Latvia

Map page 67

Area	64 589 km²
	(24 938 sq miles)
Capital	Rīga
Member of	CE, EBRD

Population	2 474 000
Population growth rate	-0.1%
Life expectancy	60 (m), 73 (f)
Languages	Latvian, *Russian*
Adult literacy rate	98%

Currency	100 santimi = 1 lats
	(US $1 = 60.7 santimi)
GDP (US million $)	5906
GDP per head (US $)	2387

After a short interlude as an independent state between 1918 and 1940, Latvia regained independence from Russia in 1991. Rīga, the capital, where one-third of the population lives, is a medieval port that, with Liepāja, has traditionally been a gateway to the Russian interior. Almost two-fifths of the land is forested, but this resource has been little developed and cattle are the mainstay of the rural economy.

The natural beauty of a landscape in which high hills alternate with loamy, fertile plains is enhanced by many rivers and over 3000 lakes.

There have been difficulties adjusting to independence because of the large number of Russians, immigrants during the Soviet era, who live in Latvia; only just more than 50 per cent of the population is actually Latvian.

The Latvian economy is now successfully adapting to trade with Western and Central Europe after years of looking East to the Russian hinterland.

LITHUANIA

The Republic of Lithuania

Map page 67

Area	65 300 km²
	(25 212 sq miles)
Capital	Vilnius
Member of	CE, EBRD

Population	3 706 700
Population growth rate	0.7%
Life expectancy	63 (m), 75 (f)
Languages	Lithuanian, *Russian, Polish, Yiddish*
Adult literacy rate	98.4%

Currency	litas (US $1 = 4.0 litai)
GDP (US million $)	10 491
GDP per head (US $)	2831

Largest of the Baltic states by population, Lithuania is also at present the least developed. Its low-lying, sandy coast has prevented the establishment of a major international port, with associated trade facilities.

On the other hand, Vilnius has the proud history of having been the capital of the Grand Duchy of Lithuania, which at one time extended through Russia and the Ukraine to the Black Sea. At the end of the 18th century, that independence was lost, but a much reduced Lithuania became independent again from 1918 to 1940 and then again from 1991. The port territory of Kaliningrad, south-west of Lithuania, is part of the Russian Federation.

With limited resources and the absence of a deep-water port, little industrialisation took place during the Soviet era, and there was therefore only a small inflow of Russian workers. As a result, Lithuania experiences little ethnic tension. Agriculture is still the mainstay of the economy, with cattle and dairy foods, vegetables and sugar beet being the principal products.

MOLDOVA

The Republic of Moldova

Map page 105

Area	33 700 km²
	(13 010 sq miles)
Capital	Chişinău
Member of	BSEC, CE, CIS, EBRD

Population	4 312 000
Population growth rate	0.5%
Life expectancy	62 (m), 69 (f)
Languages	Moldovan (Romanian), *Russian*
Adult literacy rate	96.4%

Currency	Moldovan leu
	(US $1 = 11.11 lei)
GDP (US million $)	1551
GDP per head (US $)	359

Moldova was part of Romania until 1940, when it was annexed by the Soviet Union. On gaining independence in 1991, it was thought that Moldovans would choose to re-unite with their kinsfolk; instead, in a plebiscite in 1994, they chose to remain independent. However, a high degree of autonomy has been granted to the easterly Dniester region, inhabited mainly by Russians, and to the southerly Gagauz area, dominated by people of Turkish extraction.

Moldova's economy is mainly agricultural, producing a wide range of crops, including grains, sugar beet, tobacco and wines, although farming methods are primitive and the people poor. In Europe, only Albania is poorer. Chişinău, the capital, has been largely rebuilt after its destruction in 1944. Frontage on the Danube gives the country access to international waters.

ROMANIA

Romania

Map page 105

Area	238 391 km²
	(92 043 sq miles)
Capital	Bucharest
Member of	BSEC, CE, CEFTA,
	EBRD
Population	22 565 000
Population growth rate	0.2%
Life expectancy	65 (m), 73 (f)
Languages	Romanian, Hungarian,
	German and others
Adult literacy rate	96.7%
Currency	Romanian leu
	(US $1 = 15 835 lei)
GDP (US million $)	41 400
GDP per head (US $)	1834

The Romanians are of Latin extraction but surrounded by Slav, Turkish and other peoples. Despite fighting tenaciously against occupation over many centuries, Romania only became independent in 1878. To the historical Romanian territories of Moldavia and Wallachia was added after the First World War Transylvania, whose triangular plateau is enclosed by the almost circular ring of the Carpathian Mountains, rising to 2663 m (8737 ft).

Although winters are usually very cold, the hot summers and rich, varied landscape provide the country with excellent agricultural conditions. Romania also has a wide range of other resources, including the massive hydroelectric facility in the Iron Gates of the Danube, built as a joint project with the former Yugoslavia. However, under post-1945 Communist rule, and especially under the regime of President Nicolae Ceausescu, a single-minded emphasis on

industrial development – mainly heavy industries such as iron, steel and chemical production – outstripped the available resources. It has left a serious environmental and economic legacy, since many of these plants had outdated equipment. At the same time, many of the traditional rural villages were razed and rebuilt in a 'modern' manner. Bucharest, the capital and by far the country's largest city, is known as 'the Paris of Eastern Europe', but while the older part of the city retains some of its former elegance, much was replaced during a postwar rebuilding programme.

Romania has much to interest the visitor, including the wildlife of the Danube delta and the beautiful Carpathian Mountains.

RUSSIA

The Russian Federation

Map pages 108–111, 114–15

Area	17 075 400 km²
	(6 592 850 sq miles)
Capital	Moscow
Member of	BSEC, CE, CIS, EBRD, G8
Population	147 105 000
Population growth rate	0.5%
Life expectancy	58 (m), 71 (f)
Languages	Russian, Tatar, Yakut,
	Chuvash, Bashkir and others
Adult literacy rate	99%
Currency	Russian rouble
	(US $1 = 24.42 roubles)
GDP (US million $)	307 500
GDP per head (US $)	2090

The vastness of Russia is hard to comprehend. Embracing about one-ninth of the world's total land area, it extends for about 10 000 km (6200 miles) from east to west, roughly equivalent to the distance from London to Los Angeles. Although there are mountains in the far east and south-east, the dominant feature of Russia is the vast extent of almost featureless plain. Being part of the Eurasian land mass, fronting onto the Arctic Ocean, which is itself largely covered in ice, Russia experiences bitterly cold winters – temperatures of -50°C (-58°F) are common. The summers can be intensely hot. These extremes are moderated in the more southerly latitudes around the Black Sea, and in the west where Atlantic maritime influences can penetrate.

Although summer warmth causes surface melting, the north of Russia is characterised by permanently frozen ground and stunted, low-growing vegetation. Farther south is a vast belt of coniferous forest, and to the south again lies the steppe – grasslands which, especially to the west of the Urals, have been converted for

agricultural use. The two most fertile areas are centred on Moscow, the capital, and the area between the Black Sea and the Caucasus Mountains.

The economic core of Russia lies in Moscow and its environs. This landlocked area has been subject to repeated invasion, beginning with the Vikings in the 9th century. Some of the bitterest fighting of the Second World War occurred in Russia, with up to 20 million soldiers and civilians being killed resisting the German forces. Over many centuries, the Russians have consistently sought to expand, in order to achieve secure natural frontiers and to gain access to the sea. They consequently incorporated numerous non-Russian peoples, especially with the formation of the Soviet Union. With the latter's dissolution, Russians comprise about 80 per cent of the country's population, although many Russians now live outside Russia itself.

Russia is one of the world's great powers, having inherited most of the nuclear capability of the Soviet Union and much of its capacity in space research and satellite technology. Its conventional army, air force and navy give it the ability greatly to influence events globally as well as around its borders, though in recent years Russia has been much less active internationally than the former Soviet Union was. A major reason has been that, for all the immense effort to build a powerful industrial base under Marxist-Leninist rule from 1917 (ideas which had a big influence outside Russia as well), the Russian economy now needs much modernisation, the likes of which can only be accomplished against a strong and stable background. The Russian Government under the capricious leadership of Boris Yeltsin has been anything but steadfast. The centre of economic power still lies west of the Urals in the old Russian core: east of that mountain range, and in the north of the country, important towns and cities are limited in number and separated by huge distances. Much of Russia's vast wealth of minerals and fossil fuels lies in Siberia, east of the Urals, but exploitation is hindered by accessibility and transport difficulties. Most of the fine monasteries and beautiful cities, such as St Petersburg, once the capital, are in the west.

The over-use of the rivers, notably the Volga, for irrigation and industrial purposes is a legacy from Communist days. Also, some of the non-Russian peoples have become restive, to the extent that, in the extreme case of Chechnya, they have fought to press their claim for full independence from Russia.

UKRAINE

The Republic of Ukraine

Map page 110

Area	603 700 km²
	(233 090 sq miles)
Capital	Kiev
Member of	BSEC, CE, CIS,
	EBRD
Population	50 698 000
Population growth rate	0.1%
Life expectancy	62 (m), 73 (f)
Languages	Ukrainian (Cyrillic script),
	Russian, Romanian, Hungarian, Polish
Adult literacy rate	96%
Currency	hryvnya
	(US $1 = 3.96 hryvnyas)
GDP (US million $)	40 700
GDP per head (US $)	802

The name 'Ukraina' means 'frontier land' – in this case between Russia, Poland and the former Ottoman Empire. A country of rich soils, plentiful coal and other industrial resources, and with access to the Black Sea, the Ukraine has been fought over for centuries, during which time it has been independent for limited periods. The Ukraine was incorporated into Russia in 1653 and only achieved independence in 1991.

The Ukraine was not only the breadbasket of Russia, but it also developed a large and diverse industrial sector, particularly in the coalfield area of the Donets Basin in the east. The Black Sea coast, and especially the Crimea, attracts visitors for the summer sun and water sports: the Black Sea moderates the extremes of winter cold and summer heat that are characteristic of the continental interior.

Ukraine inevitably maintains close links with Russia, although two-thirds of the population speak Ukrainian and are proud of their distinct nationality and recently found nationhood. This leads to a split approach to Ukrainian politics: at times they lean towards reassimilation with Russia, even though the years of separation have been characterised by bickering with their neighbour on matters such as the disposal of nuclear weapons and the division of the Black Sea fleet – matters which were however resolved in a 1997 Treaty of Friendship. At other times, the Ukrainian government has looked to the West and, for example, it welcomed NATO expansion as a force for European stability.

Some 90 km (55 miles) north of Kiev lies Chernobyl, scene in 1986 of the world's worst recorded civil nuclear accident. The fallout contaminated much of the country, leaving a serious health and economic legacy.

1904 Trans-Siberian railway completed.

— 1910 —

1914–18 First World War: Russia fights on Allies' side until 1917.

1917 Revolution in Russia: tsar abdicates. Lenin becomes leader.

1918–20 Civil war in Russia.

— 1920 —

1922 USSR formed.

1924 Lenin dies. Stalin becomes leader.

1928 Collectivisation of agriculture in USSR.

— 1930 —

1932–3 Millions die in Ukraine from famine started by Stalin to crush resistance.

1936–8 Millions killed or sent to labour camps in USSR's Great Purge.

1939 Stalin signs pact with Hitler. Second World War begins.

— 1940 —

1941 Germany invades USSR. Battle of Kerch and Siege of Leningrad.

1941–4 Belorussia (Belarus), Latvia and Lithuania occupied by Germany.

1942–3 Battle of Stalingrad.

1945 USSR controls Eastern Europe at end of Second World War.

1947 Cold War begins.

— 1950 —

1950 Chervenkov made Bulgarian Prime Minister and instigates purges.

1953 Stalin dies.

1955 Warsaw Pact.

— 1960 —

1962 Cuban missile crisis with USA.

1965 Ceausescu gains power in Romania.

— 1970 —

1972 Dissidents and intellectuals arrested in Ukraine by USSR.

— 1980 —

1985 Mikhail Gorbachev made leader of USSR; perestroika introduced.

1986 Chernobyl nuclear disaster in Ukraine.

1989 East European Communist regimes fall.

— 1990 —

1990 Bulgaria becomes democratic republic.

1991 USSR breaks up into separate states. CIS established. Boris Yeltsin President of Russian Federation. Warsaw Pact dissolved.

1993 Yeltsin overcomes attempted coup in Russian parliament.

1998 Russia joins G7.

THE MIDDLE EAST AND THE GULF

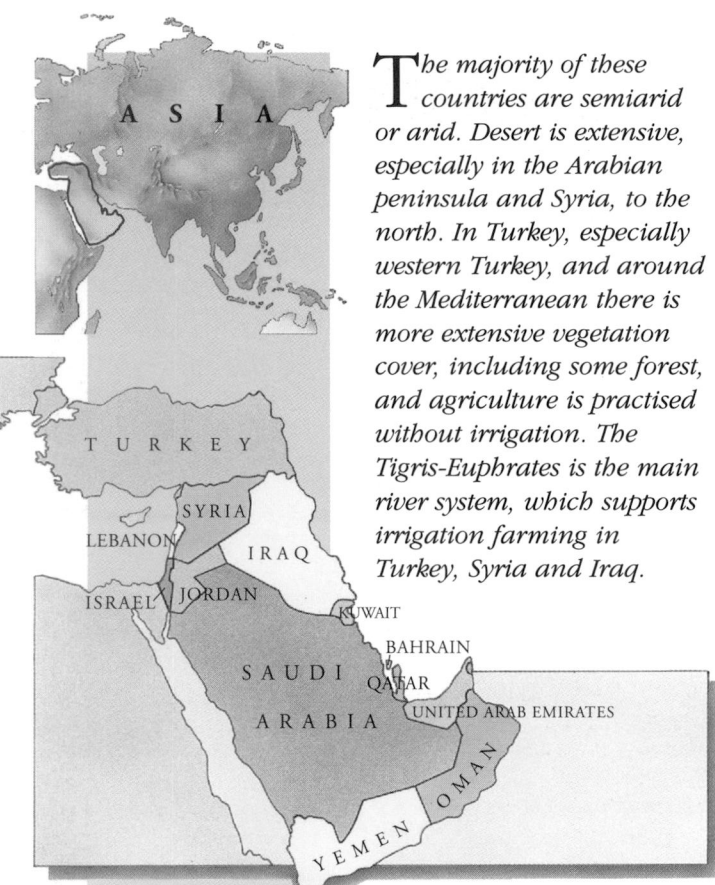

The majority of these countries are semiarid or arid. Desert is extensive, especially in the Arabian peninsula and Syria, to the north. In Turkey, especially western Turkey, and around the Mediterranean there is more extensive vegetation cover, including some forest, and agriculture is practised without irrigation. The Tigris-Euphrates is the main river system, which supports irrigation farming in Turkey, Syria and Iraq.

BAHRAIN

The State of Bahrain

Map page 119

Area	695.26 km²
	(268.44 sq miles)
Capital	Manama
Member of	CCASG, IDB, LAS, OAPEC, OIC
Population	620 000
Population growth rate	3.1%
Life expectancy	66 (m), 69 (f)
Languages	Arabic, *English*
Adult literacy rate	85.2%

Currency	1000 fils = 1 Bahrain dinar
	(US $1 = 377 fils)
GDP (US million $)	6000
GDP per head (US $)	9677

Bahrain became independent in 1971. Since the 1930s oil and gas-based industries have created much of its wealth and now about 50 per cent of its income. The island has also become a business and financial services centre for the Gulf area.

Much of its water comes from desalination plants. A causeway links Bahrain to Saudi Arabia.

IRAQ

The Republic of Iraq

Map page 119

Area	438 317 km²
	(169 235 sq miles)
Capital	Baghdad
Member of	CAEU, IDB, LAS, OAPEC, OIC, OPEC
Population	21 177 000
Population growth rate	2.9%
Life expectancy	77 (m), 78 (f)
Languages	Arabic, Kurdish, Turkoman
Adult literacy rate	58%

Currency	Iraqi dinar (US $1 = .3109 ID)
GDP (US million $)	227 229
GDP per head (US $)	11 308

The land between the Tigris and Euphrates rivers was the cradle of early civilisations. Cultivation of crops began by 5000 BC, and Nineveh and Babylon are world-renowned archaeological sites.

Independence was gained by modern Iraq in 1932. Although it is a desert country, the two rivers allow crops such as rice, wheat and vegetables to be intensively produced. Iraq's major oil reserves have been exploited for some 70 years.

In the 1960s and 1970s, Iraq prospered, but President Saddam Hussein's attack on Iran in 1980 started a crippling war.

In 1990, Iraq's invasion of Kuwait led to defeat. International efforts to eliminate Iraq's weapons of mass destruction provoke periodic resistance from Hussein and an increase in tension. Economic sanctions continue to bring hardship to a population afraid to show dissent.

ISRAEL

The State of Israel

Map pages 120–1

Area	21 946 km²
	(8473 sq miles)
Capital	Jerusalem
Member of	EBRD
Population	5 836 000
Population growth rate	2.7%
Life expectancy	75 (m), 79 (f)
Languages	Hebrew, *Arabic, many European languages*
Adult literacy rate	95.6%

Currency	100 agorot = 1 shekel
	(US $1 = 4.0 shekels)
GDP (US million $)	93 500
GDP per head (US $)	16 021

Israel's political and religious significance extends far beyond its size and resources. Jews, Christians and Muslims all claim Jerusalem as a religious centre, and the Israeli Government has designated it as the capital. However, this is not recognised by the UN, and most foreign embassies are in Tel Aviv. The creation in 1948 of a Jewish state within the former Palestine is deeply resented by Palestinian inhabitants. Israel has had several armed conflicts with its Arab neighbours, and terrorism continues. Most difficulties arise from the status of territories on the Jordan's West Bank, captured in 1967, where Israeli settlers resent any Palestinian autonomy.

Although the north receives enough rain for agriculture, the south is desert, and water is generally scarce. The Israelis

have developed their resources to the full, and agricultural exports (for example, oranges) are important. However, Israel is primarily an urban society, living by manufacturing and by commercial services. It also draws many tourists.

JORDAN

The Hashemite Kingdom of Jordan

Map page 118

Area	97 740 km²
	(37 738 sq miles)
Capital	Amman
Member of	CAEU, IDB, LAS, OIC
Population	5 774 000
Population growth rate	5.2%
Life expectancy	66 (m), 69 (f)
Language	Arabic
Adult literacy rate	86.6%

Currency	1000 fils = 1 Jordanian dinar
	(US $1 = 711 fils)
GDP (US million $)	7400
GDP per head (US $)	1281

Following independence in 1946, Jordan was embroiled in the Arab-Israeli conflict of 1948-9. Since 1967, its West Bank region has been administered by Israel, but in 1994 certain towns were granted limited autonomy under Palestinian administration.

Most of Jordan is desert or semidesert. Farm land is limited and water is scarce. Phosphates, financial services and transit trade are important sources of income, but Jordan's support of Iraq in the Gulf War has badly affected the economy. Tourists are attracted by Biblical sites, castles dating from the Crusades and the ancient city of Petra, founded about 1000 BC. More than a third of the country's population lives in the capital.

KUWAIT

The State of Kuwait

Map page 119

Area	17 818 km²
	(6880 sq miles)
Capital	Kuwait City
Member of	CAEU, CCASG, IDB, LAS, OAPEC, OIC, OPEC
Population	1 809 000
Population growth rate	−0.5%
Life expectancy	71 (m), 73 (f)
Languages	Arabic, *English*
Adult literacy rate	78.6%

Currency	1000 fils = 1 Kuwaiti dinar
	(US $1 = 307.5 fils)
GDP (US million $)	31 400
GDP per head (US $)	17 357

Kuwait is a desert country with pockets of arable and grazing land. The country has immense oil wealth and depends on large numbers of migrant workers to service its urban economy. Oil

wealth, combined with Kuwait's strategic location on The Gulf, prompted Iraq to invade in 1990. A UN-backed coalition of nations liberated the state, but not before its oil industry and its fragile desert ecology had been badly damaged. The economy has since largely recovered and the autocratic political system shows signs of liberalisation.

LEBANON

The Lebanese Republic

Map page 118

Area	10 452 km²
	(4036 sq miles)
Capital	Beirut
Member of	IDB, LAS, OIC
Population	3 144 000
Population growth rate	3.3% (est.)
Life expectancy	66 (m), 70 (f)
Languages	Arabic, *French, Kurdish, Armenian*
Adult literacy rate	92.4%

Currency	Lebanese pound
	(US $1 = £L1508)
GDP (US million $)	16 638
GDP per head (US $)	5292

With mountains rising to 3087 m (10 128 ft), Lebanon is a well-watered and fertile country astride ancient trade routes from the Mediterranean to the East. Home to the Phoenicians from the 14th to 9th centuries BC, Lebanon has been fought over ever since, not emerging as an independent state until the 1940s. It was then the most developed state in the Middle East, famous for its financial services and tourism. During the late 20th century it fell prey to partial occupation by Israel and Syria and savage civil wars among its numerous Christian and Muslim factions, although recent years have seen a return to peace and more stable rule.

OMAN

The Sultanate of Oman

Map page 116

Area	309 500 km²
	(119 500 sq miles)
Capital	Muscat
Member of	CCASG, IDB, LAS, OIC
Population	2 256 000
Population growth rate	4.4%
Life expectancy	67 (m), 71 (f)
Languages	Arabic, *English*
Adult literacy rate	41%

Currency	Omani rial
	(US $1 = 0.38 Omani rials)
GDP (US million $)	15 300
GDP per head (US $)	6782

Oman is a sparsely populated, mainly desert nation, although the northern mountains cause sufficient rain to support some small-scale agriculture. The capital, Muscat, was an important port long before its capture by the Portuguese in 1507. 1971 saw independence. It relies heavily on oil for revenue. Oman has close ties with Western nations because of its strategic position at the entrance to the Gulf.

QATAR

The State of Qatar
Map page 119

Area	11 437 km²
	(4416 sq miles)
Capital	Doha
Member of	CCASG, IDB, LAS, OAPEC,
	OIC, OPEC

Population	520 500
Population growth rate	4.5%
Life expectancy	68 (m), 74 (f)
Languages	Arabic, *English*
Adult literacy rate	79%

Currency	100 dirhams = 1 Qatar riyal
	(US $1 = 3.6 riyals)
GDP (US million $)	9800
GDP per head (US $)	18 846

Independent since 1971, Qatar used to rely on pearl diving, fishing and camel breeding for its revenue. The country's oil resources began to be exploited in 1949, and since then revenues from oil and gas have made Qatar a wealthy nation. Qatar's North Field is reputedly the world's largest single gas field, the development of which is expected to provide revenue long after the country's oil reserves have been exhausted.

SAUDI ARABIA

The Kingdom of Saudi Arabia
Map page 116

Area	2 240 000 km²
	(864 869 sq miles)
Capital	Riyadh
Member of	CCASG, IDB, LAS, OAPEC,
	OIC, OPEC

Population	19 494 000
Population growth rate	3.6%
Life expectancy	68 (m), 71 (f)
Language	Arabic
Adult literacy rate	63%

Currency	Saudi riyal
	(US $1 = 3.7 riyals)
GDP (US million $)	144 300
GDP per head (US $)	7402

The Arabian peninsula is a tilted plateau, rising above 3000 m (9800 ft) in the south-west and falling to sea level in the north-

east. The high land has enough rain to support vegetation and to supply underground aquifers. The interior and north-east of the country are desert, with some oases fed by ground water.

Tribal wars between 1902 and 1924 led to the establishment of modern Saudi Arabia. It was then a poor kingdom whose main income was derived from pilgrims visiting Mecca, where Muhammad, the founder of Islam, was born, and Medina, the second holy city of Islam.

Although oil was discovered in the 1930s, the extent of Saudi Arabia's oil reserves was only realised after the Second World War; the country is now the world's largest producer. The reserves lie in the north-east, around Ad-Dammàm, a region which is now thoroughly urbanised. Riyadh, the royal capital, and Jeddah the administrative capital and Red Sea port, have expanded greatly. During the second half of the 20th century, the economy has been transformed, and the population enjoys high living standards. Politically, the country remains in the control of the al-Saud dynasty with little sign of change.

SYRIA

The Syrian Arab Republic
Map page 118

Area	185 180 km²
	(71 498 sq miles)
Capital	Damascus
Member of	CAEU, IDB, LAS,
	OAPEC, OIC

Population	14 951 000
Population growth rate	3.5%
Life expectancy	64 (m), 68 (f)
Languages	Arabic, *Kurdish*
Adult literacy rate	79.4%

Currency	100 piastres = 1 Syrian pound
	(US $1 = £S45)
GDP (US million $)	50 749
GDP per head (US $)	3573

The Mediterranean climate of western Syria plus the waters of the Euphrates make this a reasonably fertile land, its situation enhanced by the historic associations of the ancient trade routes between Europe and Asia. Aleppo and Damascus are among the oldest continuously inhabited cities in the world, spanning 4500 years. Successive civilisations have left their marks, such as the impressive ruins of Palmyra on the edge of the Syrian desert.

Wheat, fruit, cotton and other crops are produced in large quantities, and there has been some industrialisation; oil is another significant resource.

Independent since 1946, Syria's development has been hindered by conflict with Israel, tense relations with neighbours and by international sanctions intended to end the terrorism it was said to encourage.

TURKEY

The Republic of Turkey
Map pages 107 & 118

Area	779 452 km²
	(300 948 sq miles)
Capital	Ankara
Member of	CE, EBRD, ECO, IDB,
	NATO, OECD, OIC

Population	63 705 000
Population growth rate	2.1%
Life expectancy	63 (m), 66 (f)
Languages	Turkish, *Kurdish*
Adult literacy rate	82.3%

Currency	Turkish lira
	(US $1 = 428 920 liras)
GDP (US million $)	197 900
GDP per head (US $)	3104

This long-settled land became the centre of the Byzantine Empire in AD 330, when the eastern Roman capital was moved to Constantinople (now Istanbul). Constantinople was captured by the Ottomans in 1453, and by the 16th century their empire extended from the Persian Gulf to the Danube.

The rich farms that flourish in the Mediterranean climate of the west and south merge into the drier and harsher Anatolian plateau, which forms the main granary of the country. The eastern mountains, which rise to over 5000 m (16 000 ft), are the source of the Euphrates and Tigris, rivers that supply hydro-electricity and irrigation waters.

Cotton and tobacco are important crops, and there are substantial mineral and other resources, providing the basis for much industrial development, mainly around Ankara, Istanbul, Izmit and Adana. A rich legacy of monuments and splendid coastline attracted many tourists, before the devastating earthquake of August 1999.

Turkey owes much to the dynamic leadership, after World War I, of Kemal Ataturk. He transformed the nation into a modern state, although that modernisation has caused tension throughout the 20th century among Muslim fundamentalist elements.

Turkey disputes with Greece the sovereignty of some Aegean islands and Cyprus, and its use of water from the Tigris and Euphrates affects Syria's economy, causing anger. Turkey also incurs international criticism by taking a hard line against its own Kurdish people.

UNITED ARAB EMIRATES

The United Arab Emirates
Map page 116

Area	77 700 km²
	(30 000 sq miles)
Capital	Abu Dhabi
Member of	CAEU, CCASG, IDB, LAS,
	OAPEC, OIC, OPEC

Population	2 580 000
Population growth rate	3.3%
Life expectancy	72 (m), 75 (f)
Languages	Arabic, *English*
Adult literacy rate	79.2%

Currency	100 fils = 1 UAE dirham
	(US $1 = 3.6 dirhams)
GDP (US million $)	42 000
GDP per head (US $)	16 279

The nation emerged as an independent state in 1971 through the merger of seven emirates (Dubai, Abu Dhabi, Sharjah, Ajman, Ras al Khaimah, Qaiwan and Fujairah). In earlier years these emirates depended on pearl-diving, fishing and trade in spices. The discovery and exploitation of oil since the 1960s transformed the economy and the citizens enjoy one of the world's highest living standards. Recent diversification affords protection against oil price fluctuations.

YEMEN

The Republic of Yemen
Map page 116

Area	536 869 km²
	(207 286 sq miles)
Capital	San'a
Member of	CAEU, IDB,
	LAS, OIC

Population	16 484 000
Population growth rate	4.1%
Life expectancy	55 (m), 56 (f)
Language	Arabic
Adult literacy rate	38%

Currency	Yemeni rial
	(US $1 = 148.15 Yemeni rials)
GDP (US million $)	5700
GDP per head (US $)	345

Yemen's mountains, which rise to 3760 m (12 336 ft), create well-watered lands in a region that is predominantly desert. This fact, combined with its strategically important location at the mouth of the Red Sea, has attracted civilisations since the 7th century BC; the port of Aden was occupied by the British from 1839 until 1967. The present Yemen dates from the union of two countries (North and South Yemen) in 1990. Despite oil and other resources, development is still limited.

1901–2 Abd al-Aziz, a member of the deposed Sa'udi family, regains his kingdom (Saudi Arabia).

— 1910 —

1914–18 Ottoman Empire (Turkey) sides with Germany during First World War.

1917 British support for a Jewish national home in Palestine outlined in the Balfour Declaration.

— 1920 —

1920 Iraq and Jordan mandated to Britain by League of Nations.

1923 Turkey becomes a republic; President Ataturk initiates reforms.

— 1930 —

1939–45 Genocide of Jews during Second World War increases international support for a Jewish homeland.

— 1940 —

1948–9 State of Israel proclaimed. After war with Arab neighbours, Israel emerges with 75% of western Palestine.

— 1950 —

1958 Iraqi monarchy overthrown by military. Syria merges with Egypt to form United Arab Republic (until 1961).

— 1960 —

1960 OPEC founded.

1964 PLO founded.

1967 Israel and Arab states fight Six-Day War.

— 1970 —

1970 Hafiz al-Assad seizes power in Syria.

1973 Egypt and Syria attack Israel, beginning Yom Kippur War.

1974 Turkish troops occupy northern Cyprus.

1975–89 Civil war in Lebanon.

1979 Saddam Hussein gains power in Iraq.

— 1980 —

1980–88 Iran-Iraq war ends in stalemate.

1982 Israel invades Lebanon.

1984 Separatist Kurds start guerrilla war in south-east Turkey.

1988 King Hussein of Jordan cedes claim to West Bank to PLO.

— 1990 —

1990–1 Gulf War: Iraq invades and annexes Kuwait; Kuwait liberated by multinational force.

1993 Israel recognises PLO, as stage in peace negotiations.

1998 Iraq's recalcitrance over UN weapons inspections brings threat of war once more.

1999 King Hussein of Jordan dies and is succeeded by his son Abdullah.

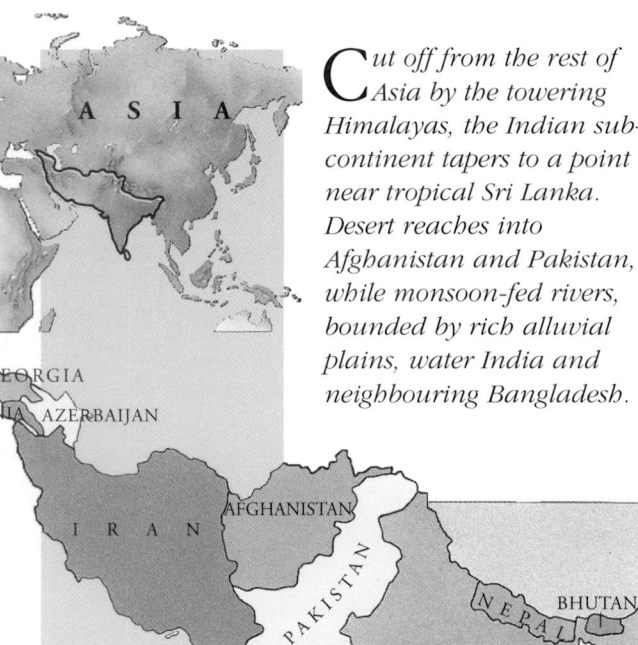

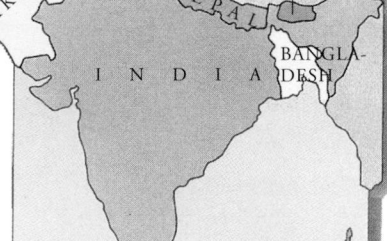

*C*ut off from the rest of Asia by the towering Himalayas, the Indian subcontinent tapers to a point near tropical Sri Lanka. Desert reaches into Afghanistan and Pakistan, while monsoon-fed rivers, bounded by rich alluvial plains, water India and neighbouring Bangladesh.

AFGHANISTAN

The Islamic State of Afghanistan

Map page 116

Area	652 225 km²
	(251 773 sq miles)
Capital	Kabul
Member of	ECO, IDB, OIC

Population	22 132 000
Population growth rate	−1%
Life expectancy	43 (m), 44 (f)
Languages	Pashto, Dari (dialect of Farsi or Iranian), many local languages
Adult literacy rate	31.5%

Currency	afghani (US $1 = Af4702)
GDP (US million $)	55 995
GDP per head (US $)	2848

Spectacular snow-covered mountains, rising to well over 6000 m (19 700 ft) dominate Afghanistan. The south-west is desert and semidesert, as is the north, where the Amu Darya provides water for irrigation. Herat, in the west, lies on the old trade route from Persia to India via the Khyber Pass.

Afghanistan has seldom known peace, partly because of its strategic position between Russia and India, and partly because its indigenous tribes have traditionally competed for power. The nation was thrown into turmoil by the Soviet occupation in 1979-80. Since then, civil war has ravaged the country, giving rise to Islamic extremist groups. One of these, the Taliban, holds sway over much of the country, which is now one of the world's poorest.

Abbreviations
CE Council of Europe
CIS Commonwealth of Independent States
COMM Commonwealth
EBRD European Bank for Reconstruction and Development
ECO Economic Co-operation Organization
IDB Islamic Development Bank
OIC Organisation of the Islamic Conference
OPEC Organisation of Petroleum Exporting Countries
SAARC South Asian Association for Regional Cooperation
GDP Gross Domestic Product

ARMENIA

The Republic of Armenia

Map page 111

Area	29 800 km²
	(11 500 sq miles)
Capital	Yerevan
Member of	CIS, EBRD

Population	3 642 000
Population growth rate	1.5%
Life expectancy	67 (m), 74 (f)
Languages	Armenian, Kurdish
Adult literacy rate	98.8%

Currency	dram (US $1 = 536.26 drams)
GDP (US million $)	1824
GDP per head (US $)	500

The Armenian people have inhabited the plateau between the Black Sea and the Caspian since the 7th century BC, and the Armenian Christian Church dates from the 2nd century AD. After centuries of suppression by neighbours, the country gained independence in 1991, since when it has been engaged in conflict with Azerbaijan over the territory of Nagorno-Karabakh, populated and controlled by Armenians since their 1993 invasion, but lying within Azerbaijan.

AZERBAIJAN

The Azerbaijan Republic

Map page 111

Area	86 600 km²
	(33 400 sq miles)
Capital	Baku
Member of	CIS, EBRD, ECO, IDB, OIC

Population	7 625 000
Population growth rate	1.3%
Life expectancy	65 (m), 74 (f)
Language	Azerbaijani (Azeri)
Adult literacy rate	97.3%

Currency	Azerbaijani manat (US $1 = 3950 manats)
GDP (US million $)	4 300
GDP per head (US $)	564

Formerly part of the Soviet Union, Azerbaijan became independent in 1991 but was soon embroiled with Armenia over Nagorno-Karabakh.

Rivers flowing to the Caspian give extensive irrigation to lands below sea level, for the growth of cotton in particular. Rich natural resources give the country excellent long-term prospects. The oil reserves of the Caspian Sea and Baku have long been important and are now being developed by Western oil companies; oil pollution along the Caspian must be tackled after years of neglect. Iron and copper ores, found in the Lesser Caucasus mountains, are also exploited.

BANGLADESH

The People's Republic of Bangladesh

Map pages 122–3

Area	147 570 km²
	(56 977 sq miles)
Capital	Dhaka
Member of	COMM, IDB, OIC, SAARC

Population	122 013 000
Population growth rate	2%
Life expectancy	57 (m), 56 (f)
Language	Bengali
Adult literacy rate	38%

Currency	taka (US $1 = 48.5 taka)
GDP (US million $)	33 900
GDP per head (US $)	277

Almost all of Bangladesh is formed by the huge delta of three great silt-bearing rivers. The heavy monsoon rains mean that much of the country is inundated every summer, providing ideal conditions for rice cultivation and inland fisheries. Dry-season irrigation enables two or three crops to be taken. Jute is an important cash crop. Villages are perched on the higher ground, often artificially raised, and houses are commonly built on stilts, raising them above the floods.

However, the floods remain unpredictable and periodically devastating; despite continuing control measures, it is unlikely that the rivers will ever be fully tamed. The country also suffers ferocious cyclones from the Bay of Bengal.

Bangladesh was ruled by the British until 1947, as part of Bengal. With the independence of India and Pakistan, the Muslim part of Bengal became the eastern wing of Pakistan. In 1971, the Bangladeshi people rebelled against domination by west Pakistan, and after serious conflict they achieved independence.

Urban development has been limited outside Dhaka. With rapid population growth, raising the nation's living standards is proving difficult.

BHUTAN

The Kingdom of Bhutan

Map page 122

Area	46 500 km²
	(17 954 sq miles)
Capital	Thimphu
Member of	SAARC

Population	1 862 000
Population growth rate	2.2%
Life expectancy	49 (m), 52 (f)
Language	Dzongkha
Adult literacy rate	42.2%

Currency	ngultrum (US $1 = Nu43.31)
GDP (US million $)	294
GDP per head (US $)	166

The mountainous kingdom of Bhutan, rising to over 7500 m (24 600 ft), has adopted an isolationist policy. Contact with the outside world is avoided and tourists are discouraged. Not until 1999 did it start a television service. The fortified monasteries are a distinctive feature, and the people work hard to make a poor living.

GEORGIA

Georgia

Map page 111

Area	69 700 km²
	(26 911 sq miles)
Capital	Tbilisi
Member of	CE, CIS, EBRD

Population	5 434 000
Population growth rate	0.4%
Life expectancy	68 (m), 76 (f)
Language	Georgian
Adult literacy rate	99%

Currency	lari (US $1 = 2.05 lari)
GDP (US million $)	5100
GDP per head (US $)	938

The Georgian people have occupied the Caucasus for more than 2000 years, but only gained independence in 1991. The country then suffered from civil war because minority groups wanted autonomy. The capital, Tbilisi, lies on a long-established trade route between Europe and Asia. It nestles between mountain ranges in the great trench that forms the heart of the country and where rich sub-tropical agriculture and a variety of mineral resources could allow Georgia to prosper.

INDIA

The Republic of India

Map page 122–3

Area	3 287 263 km²
	(1 269 219 sq miles)
Capital	New Delhi
Member of	COMM, SAARC

Population	955 220 000
Population growth rate	2%
Life expectancy	57 (m), 58 (f)
Languages	Hindi, English, many local languages
Adult literacy rate	52%

Currency	rupee (US $1 = 43.31 rupees)
GDP (US million $)	377 900
GDP per head (US $)	395

The world's second most populous country after China, India has a civilisation of great antiquity, on which successive invaders have left deep marks. Modern India emerged as an independent state in 1947, when the end of British rule saw the subcontinent divided between Muslim Pakistan and Hindu India. The division was accompanied by bitter strife, bringing floods of refugees and much loss of life. India retains a substantial non-Hindu minority, mainly in the north-west.

Relations with Pakistan have remained tense, because of Indian control of Kashmir (contested by Pakistan and by dissenting Kashmiris) and Indian assistance in establishing Bangladesh in 1971. Tension has been increased by the recent development and testing of nuclear weapons by both nations.

The great majority of Indians are poor farmers. Many are crammed into the fertile plains of the Ganges and Brahmaputra, which receive heavy summer monsoon rains and where dry-season irrigation is possible. The interior of the Deccan plateau is more arid and relatively sparsely peopled, except in the extreme south, which benefits from a second monsoon in the winter.

India has a long urban history and today several cities exceed 9 million inhabitants – though many live in squalid slums. The country has a large industrial sector, which includes several advanced industries such as nuclear engineering for electricity generation, and aircraft and space research. Bangalore, for example, is the centre of rapidly expanding electronics and computer manufacturing. With the recent opening of the country to outside investment, modernisation and development have gathered pace. India has a wide range of natural resources, including oil, coal and iron ore, making it largely self-sufficient.

Despite the legal abolition of caste, the caste system is still a dominating factor in Indian life, determining marriage partners, friends and employment. This and rapid population growth are two enduring problems. India's outstanding achievement has been the continued maintenance of parliamentary democracy since gaining independence.

Of the many monuments and buildings to attract visitors, the most famous is the Taj Mahal.

IRAN

The Islamic Republic of Iran

Map pages 119

Area	1 648 000 km²
	(636 296 sq miles)
Capital	Tehran (Teheran)
Member of	ECO, IDB, OIC, OPEC

Population	60 694 000
Population growth rate	3.3%
Life expectancy	58 (m), 59 (f)
Languages	Farsi (Iranian), Turkic, other local languages
Adult literacy rate	72.3%

Currency	Iranian rial (US $1 = 3000 rials)
GDP (US million $)	61 800
GDP per head (US $)	1018

Iran, formerly Persia, is heir to 2500 years' history. The Persian Empire, stretching from the Mediterranean to India, was founded in the 6th century BC. Though the empire waned, its heartland became modern Iran.

In the years after World War II, under the rule of the Shah, attempts were made to modernise the country on Western lines, and capitalise on Iran's oil wealth. Eventually opposition from Muslim fundamentalists prevailed; the Shah was overthrown and Ayatolla Khomeini was installed as leader. Since then, relations with Western nations have been frosty because Iran is suspected of fostering international terrorism. The 1980 invasion of Iran by Iraq led to almost a decade of debilitating war.

Tehran, the capital and principal city, is the focus of manufacturing industry. Much of the land is arid and suitable only for nomadic grazing, but intensive and varied agriculture is practised on the well-watered Elburz mountains and in the Caspian lowlands.

MALDIVES

The Republic of Maldives

Map page 58

Area	298 km²
	(115 sq miles)
Capital	Malé
Member of	COMM, IDB, OIC, SAARC

Population	273 000
Population growth rate	3.2%
Life expectancy	67 (m), 67 (f)
Language	Divehi (Maldivian, related to Sinhala)
Adult literacy rate	93.2%

Currency	rufiyaa (US $1 = 11.57 rufiyaa)
GDP (US million $)	274
GDP per head (US $)	1079

The low atolls which comprise the Maldives have few resources other than scenic beauty, which is beginning to attract tourists. Independent since 1968, the Maldives rely mainly on fishing, especially for tuna, for their livelihood and exports.

NEPAL

The Kingdom of Nepal

Map page 122

Area	147 181 km²
	(56 827 sq miles)
Capital	Kathmandau
Member of	ADB, SAARC

Population	22 591 000
Population growth rate	2.6%
Life expectancy	50 (m), 48 (f)
Languages	Nepali, Maithir, Bhojpuri
Adult literacy rate	27.5%

Currency	Nepalese rupee (NR) (US $1 = NRs 68.23)
GDP (US million $)	4800
GDP per head ($)	212

Nepal rises from the hot, humid Ganges plain to the peak of Everest, the highest mountain in the world at 8848 m (29 028 ft). Spectacular scenery attracts many visitors, but the country remains poor, having limited agricultural land and few mineral resources. Terrace farming is widely practised. Forestry, one of the major industries in Nepal, has led to a serious depletion of the country's forests.

In 1769 modern Nepal was established as a monarchy by Gurkha conquest. The king ruled absolutely until 1990 when multi-party democracy was established. The first years of democracy were characterised by political turbulence but more recently a degree of stability appears to have been achieved.

PAKISTAN

The Islamic Republic of Pakistan

Map pages 116–17

Area	796 095 km²
	(307 374 sq miles)
Capital	Islamabad
Member of	COMM, ECO, IDB, OIC, SAARC

Population	130 579 571
Population growth rate	2.8%
Life expectancy	59 (m), 59 (f)
Languages	Urdu, Punjabi, Pushto, Sindhi, Saraiki, English
Adult literacy rate	37.8%

Currency	Pakistani rupee (US $1 = 51.57 rupees)
GDP (US million $)	67 300
GDP per head (US $)	515

Pakistan emerged as a nation in 1947 when British rule in the Indian sub-continent ended. Muslim Pakistan initially included East and West territories, but East Pakistan rebelled and in 1971 became independent as Bangladesh. Throughout its history, since the early settlement of the Indus Valley around 3000 BC, the land has known instability, has often been invaded and ruled by different imperial powers. Today its politics are turbulent and lively; it has swayed between military and civilian rule, and between autocratic and more democratic government. Relations with India are difficult because of on-going disputes over Kashmir.

Pakistan has three distinct regions: the high Himalayas, which are well-watered but unsuitable for agriculture; the plains of the Indus and its tributaries which, with the help of irrigation, allow intensive agriculture including the production of rice; and the sparsely populated, semi-desert of Baluchistan in the west.

Industrialisation has been the key aim of recent Pakistani governments. Cotton textiles and leather goods have led the way but now more sophisticated engineering and defence industries are being developed.

Controversially, Pakistan has developed a nuclear capacity, and a certain amount of brinkmanship has taken place with India – which has also tested nuclear weapons.

SRI LANKA

Democratic Socialist Republic of Sri Lanka

Map page 123

Area	65 610 km²
	(25 332 sq miles)
Capital	Colombo
Member of	COMM, SAARC

Population	18 552 000
Population growth rate	1.3%
Life expectancy	67 (m), 71 (f)
Languages	Sinhala, Tamil, English
Adult literacy rate	90.2%

Currency	Sri Lanka rupee (US $1 = 71.51 rupees)
GDP (US million $)	15 500
GDP per head (US $)	835

Sri Lanka's rich resources have attracted traders and settlers for 5000 years. Under British rule (1796-1948) the island, then Ceylon, prospered from exports of coffee, tea and other produce. Since independence, conflict between the Sinhalese majority and the Tamil minority has limited development and caused serious violence in the 1990s.

Agriculture remains the main livelihood, but commerce and industry have grown rapidly, the latter particularly in and around Colombo, the capital. The beauty of the island and its ancient monuments provide great potential for tourism.

1906 Muslim League is founded in India to demand independent Islamic state.

— 1910 —

1915–22 1.5 million Armenians killed or deported by Ottomans.

— 1920 —

1920–2 Armenia, Azerbaijan and Georgia become part of Soviet Republic. Mahatma Gandhi leads India's first non-violent campaign for independence.

— 1930 —

1930–3 Second non-violent campaign for independence in India.

1939–45 India is an important manufacturing and military base during Second World War.

— 1940 —

1947 India and Pakistan become independent.

1948 Mahatma Gandhi assassinated. India and Pakistan at war over ownership of Kashmir.

— 1950 —

1956 Pakistan is made an Islamic republic.

— 1960 —

1962 India and China fight over border.

1965 India and Pakistan enter second war over Kashmir.

— 1970 —

1971 East Pakistan secedes from Pakistan to form Bangladesh; India declares third war on Pakistan in support of Bangladesh.

1973 Afghanistan is made a republic. Start of Mujaheddin rebellion.

1979 USSR invades Afghanistan. Shah of Iran deposed; Ayatollah Khomeini leads Islamic fundamentalist regime.

— 1980 —

1980–8 Iran-Iraq war ends in stalemate.

1983 Civil war between Tamils and Sinhalese erupts in Sri Lanka.

1989 Soviet troops suppress riots in the Georgian city of Tbilisi. Further conflict in Afghanistan follows Soviet withdrawal.

— 1990 —

1991 Armenia, Azerbaijan and Georgia gain independence when USSR collapses.

1993 Armenia and Azerbaijan declare war over Nagorno-Karabakh.

1998 India and Pakistan test nuclear weapons.

1999 India and Pakistan fight again in Kashmir.

CENTRAL AND EASTERN ASIA

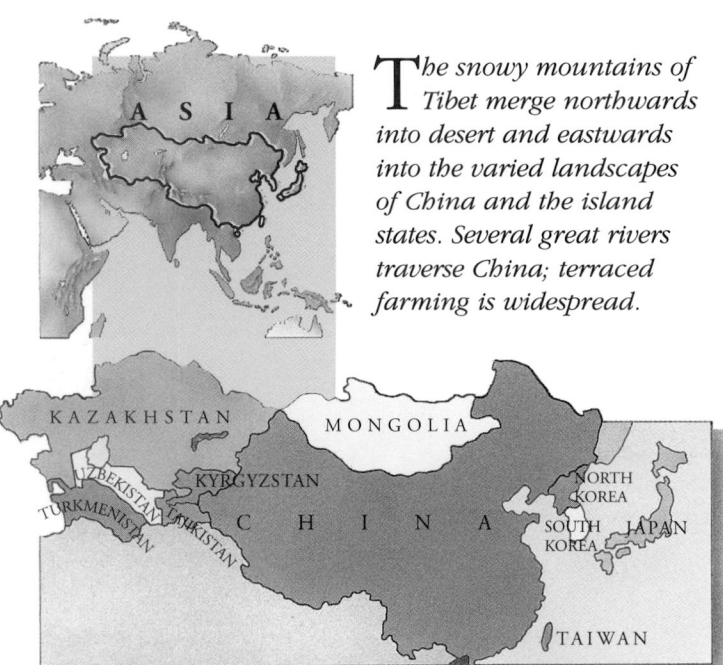

*T*he snowy mountains of Tibet merge northwards into desert and eastwards into the varied landscapes of China and the island states. Several great rivers traverse China; terraced farming is widespread.

CHINA

The People's Republic of China

Map pages 128–131

Area	9 571 300 km²
	(3 695 500 sq miles)
Capital	Beijing
Member of	APEC

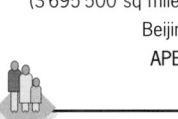

Population	1 250 659 000
Population growth rate	1.4%
Life expectancy	66 (m), 70 (f)
Languages	Northern Chinese (Mandarin) and others
Adult literacy rate	82.2%

Currency	yuan and Hong Kong dollar (US $1 = 8.27 yuan, US1$ = 7.7598 HK$)
GDP (US million $)	977 300
GDP per head (US $)	793

A continuous Chinese civilisation has existed since before 1700 BC, exerting considerable influence in the Asiatic realm but for many centuries unknown in Europe. In the 13th century AD, Marco Polo's account of China was widely disbelieved in Venice. Yet when the Industrial Revolution began in Europe, part of the purpose was to replace goods imported from China. Although the country could not entirely exclude foreign invaders in the 19th and early to mid 20th centuries, it has remained a distinct and powerful economic, cultural and political force.

Approximately 20–25 per cent of the world's population (about 1.2 billion people) inhabit the country, whose land area is third in size after Russia and Canada and extremely varied. The mountain basins and plateaus of the interior experience hot summers and cold winters and receive little rain. To the north, desert and semidesert conditions prevail. Most people live in the east, and especially on the plains of the Huang He (Yellow River) and Chang Jiang (Yangtze Kiang),

with their fertile alluvial soils. North of the Huang He, rainfall is limited and the dominant crops are wheat, millet and cotton. Farther south, higher rainfall and irrigation allow rice, the country's staple grain, to be grown in abundance, with tea, sugar cane and vegetables. Intense population pressure has led to the construction of flights of paddy terraces on the hillsides. Settlements are tightly clustered, to save valuable land.

China has plentiful coal supplies and a wide range of other fuels and industrial materials. Most of the industrial development is on or near the coast (for example, Guangzhou and Shanghai) or located where major sources of fuel and other resources are available, as at Harbin in the north-east. Recently, under more liberal government policies, Guangdong (Canton) province has enjoyed rapid growth of modern manufacturing industries, fuelled in part by investment from Hong Kong. After a turbulent 20th century, the Chinese colossus is now on the move, with the likelihood of momentous consequences for the whole world.

There are significant minorities within China, some of whom are restive under Chinese control, as in Tibet, for example, incorporated in 1965. The size and diversity of the area inhabited by the Han Chinese (over 90 per cent of the population) has created growing pressure for greater regional autonomy. Relations with the outside world have always posed problems, as exemplified by the Great Wall (built to repel northern invaders). Challenges that face the modern nation include establishing a rapprochement with the breakaway island of Taiwan and adapting to the 1997 absorption of Hong Kong after the termination of its 99-year lease to Britain.

JAPAN

Japan

Map pages 126–7

Area	377 750 km²
	(145 850 sq miles)
Capital	Tokyo
Member of	APEC, EBRD, G8, OECD

Population	125 638 000
Population growth rate	0.4%
Life expectancy	76 (m), 83 (f)
Language	Japanese
Adult literacy rate	99%

Currency	yen (US $1 = 122.36 yen)
GDP (US million $)	3 823 100
GDP per head (US $)	30 429

For two centuries until 1868, the ancient and distinct Japanese civilisation isolated itself from the rest of the world. Slowly Japan realised that this policy was not beneficial and became more militaristic. Since World War II, it has concentrated on developing a modernised and prosperous economy, with a gross domestic product second only to that of the United States.

Japan comprises more than 3000 islands, of which the chief are Hokkaido, Honshu, Shikoku and Kyushu. The archipelago lies in a geologically unstable area, and there are numerous active volcanoes and recurrent earthquakes. Mineral resources are limited, and the population is concentrated on the restricted areas of flat land on the four main islands, mostly along the south coast of Honshu. Protected by the mountain spine from the Manchurian winter winds and heavy snowfalls, these southerly lands have a climate suitable for paddy rice and intensive agriculture. Hokkaido in the north has a rather bleak climate and is sparsely inhabited.

Japan is largely self-sufficient in foodstuffs. Its traditional, small-scale farming is heavily subsidised, and any change in this policy could have major effects on the patchwork farming landscape. Pressure on available resources has caused the Japanese to exploit the seas with one of the world's biggest fishing fleets.

Late in the 19th century, Japan began to build an empire, inflicting defeats on China and Russia and annexing Korea and Taiwan. During the Second World War the country sought to dominate the western Pacific, but after defeat it withdrew into its island core. Since 1945 Japan has played only a limited role in international political and military affairs, but it has used the past 50 years impressively to create a strong economy founded upon a powerful manufacturing base. Japanese-produced items, such as motor cars, electronics, cameras and computer chips, compete with the best in the world, and its manufacturing and managerial methods have attracted worldwide interest and emulation. Japanese science and technology are at the leading edges of development, and the ethnically homogenous population has enjoyed a high standard of living. Recently the economy has faltered because of a fall in the value of the yen, sending shockwaves round the world and raising the spectre of unemployment in Japan.

Tokyo is arguably the world's largest city; about 40 million people live within 50 km (30 miles) of the capital's core. It is also one of the world's leading financial centres, and the home of many manufacturing giants.

KAZAKHSTAN

The Republic of Kazakhstan

Map page 114

Area	2 717 300 km²
	(1 049 150 sq miles)
Capital	Astana
Member of	CIS, EBRD, ECO

Population	16 832 000
Population growth rate	0.8%
Life expectancy	64 (m), 73 (f)
Languages	Kazakh, Russian
Adult literacy rate	97.5%

Currency	tenge (US $1 = 132.56 tenge)
GDP (US million $)	23 200
GDP per head (US $)	1378

This vast country is home to nearly as many Russians as Kazakhs, as well as numerous ethnic minorities. The influx of Russians dates from World War II when, as part of the Soviet Union, they settled to establish an industrial base and to exploit mineral resources well away from the war zone. Friction between the two main groups is the legacy.

Kazakhstan has an extreme continental climate; most of the country is open plain, with enough rain in the north for extensive wheat farming, but turning to grasslands and then desert farther south. There is large-scale irrigation farming, with cotton as the principal crop. However, this has had a disastrous ecological impact: much of the Aral Sea has dried up because of the damming and diversion for irrigation of the waters that feed it, and saline soil problems have become apparent. Serious radioactive pollution, a result of nuclear testing, has occurred around Semipalatinsk. With huge oil, iron, chromium, gold and other resources, Kazakhstan has the basis for prosperity and so far has managed its transition to independence, gained in 1991, with considerable success.

NORTH KOREA

Democratic People's Republic of Korea

Map page 129

Area	120 538 km²
	(46 540 sq miles)
Capital	Pyongyang

Population	22 837 000
Population growth rate	1.8%
Life expectancy	68 (m), 74 (f)
Language	Korean
Adult literacy rate	99%

Currency	won (US $1 = 2.2 won)
GDP (US million $)	5997
GDP per head (US $)	271

Until the end of the Second World War, North and South Korea shared a common history, consisting of about 1500 years of independent civilisation and political control, albeit with incursions from neighbouring China and Japan. From 1910 to 1945, as a Japanese colony, the peninsula was exploited primarily for its agricultural and mineral resources. At the end of the war, American and Soviet forces partitioned the country, leading to a devastating war from 1950 to 1953 and separation along the 38th parallel.

Under the late Kim Il Sung, and his son Kim Jong Il, North Korea has pursued repressive Stalinist policies. The leadership alarms the world as it seeks to develop a nuclear capability and tests missiles across the Pacific.

Their attempts to create a self-sufficient economy have failed utterly and the people live in desperate poverty.

SOUTH KOREA

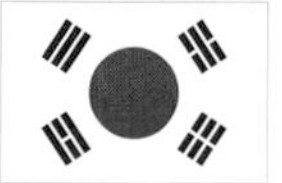

The Republic of Korea

Map page 129

Area	99 392 km² (38 375 sq miles)
Capital	Seoul
Member of	APEC, EBRD
Population	45 991 000
Population growth rate	1%
Life expectancy	67 (m), 75 (f)
Language	Korean
Adult literacy rate	98%
Currency	won (US $1 = 1185.5 won)
GDP (US million $)	304 300
GDP per head (US $)	6616

Since the damaging 1950–3 war (see North Korea), South Korea has built a formidable industrial base around steel, cars, ships and electronics, which has ensured its place as one of the dynamic emergent economies of Asia, despite recent financial instability. The deep roots of civilisation, outward-looking development policies and the need to achieve security from North Korea combined to create a common purpose. The result has been a radical transformation from an agricultural economy with rice as its staple ingredient to a significant industrial nation.

The main impact has been on the west and south. Seoul has more than 10 million inhabitants and is a major industrial centre, while Pusan, the second city and major port, has about 4 million people. In contrast, Kyongju, in the south-east, retains some 1000-year-old buildings from the former Korean kingdom. Relations with neighbours, especially North Korea, remain tense.

KYRGYZSTAN

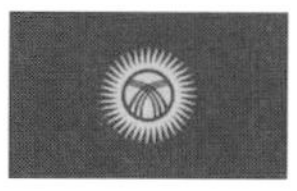

The Kyrgyz Republic

Map page 122

Area	198 500 km² (76 600 sq miles)
Capital	Bishkek
Member of	CIS, EBRD, ECO
Population	4 635 000
Population growth rate	1.7%
Life expectancy	61 (m), 70 (f)
Languages	Kyrgyz (Cyrillic script, Latin script to be reintroduced), *Russian*
Adult literacy rate	97%
Currency	som (US $1 = 37.448 soms)
GDP (US million $)	1800
GDP per head (US $)	388

Glaciers, alpine pastures and dry grassy basins dominate the landscape and sustain the nomadic livestock economy. There is some manufacturing and mining, especially for gold, but declining prices are a problem. The transition since independence in 1991 has been smooth, despite ethnic diversity.

MONGOLIA

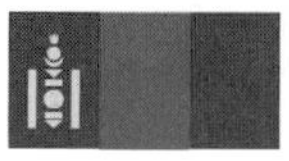

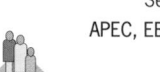

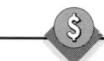

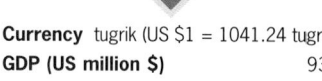

Mongolia

Map page 115

Area	1 566 500 km² (604 829 sq miles)
Capital	Ulan Bator
Member of	ADB
Population	2 313 000
Population growth rate	2.8%
Life expectancy	62 (m), 65 (f)
Languages	Khalkha Mongolian, *Kazakh*
Adult literacy rate	82.9%
Currency	tugrik (US $1 = 1041.24 tugrik)
GDP (US million $)	933
GDP per head (US $)	403

A land of mountains and high grasslands merging into deserts, experiencing a severe climate, Mongolia has long been home to hardy horse-riding nomads. The country was unified under Genghis Khan in the 13th century and later absorbed into China; it became independent, with Russian assistance, to become a Communist state in 1924, and has maintained close ties with Russia. Few nomads remain, but livestock on large cooperative ranches still provides an important source of income; the climate is too harsh for cultivation. Mining, the other main source of wealth, was developed with Russian aid. Despite recent economic and political liberalisation, Mongolia is a poor country, dependent on international aid and the goodwill of its powerful neighbours.

TAIWAN

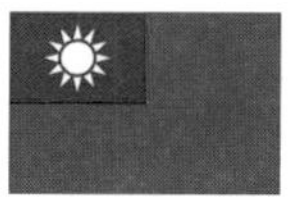

The Republic of China

Map page 131

Area	36 000 km² (13 900 sq miles)
Capital	Taipei
Member of	APEC
Population	21 740 000
Population growth rate	1.2%
Life expectancy	72 (m), 78 (f)
Languages	Northern Chinese (Mandarin), *Taiwanese*
Adult literacy rate	93.7%
Currency	NT$ (US $1 = NT$32.30)
GDP (US million $)	296 200
GDP per head (US $)	13 723

Taiwan is an anomaly. In 1949 Chinese Nationalists, defeated by the Communists, fled the mainland and seized control of Taiwan (formerly Formosa). Since then, Taiwan's *de facto* independence has not been accorded full international recognition. The country is now excluded from the UN, having held China's seat until 1971. China refuses to accept that Taiwan is a sovereign state.

The high mountain spine and tropical location provides Taiwan with plentiful rain and rich agricultural resources. Most people live in the western half of the island, where rice, sugar cane and tea are major crops. Since 1949 Taiwan's industrial progress has been spectacular. Its well-educated, hard-working population is a great asset.

TAJIKISTAN

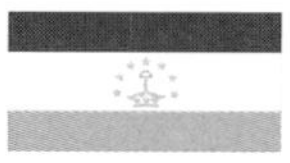

The Republic of Tajikistan

Map page 122

Area	143 100 km² (55 251 sq miles)
Capital	Dushanbe
Member of	CIS, EBRD, ECO
Population	6 046 000
Population growth rate	2.9%
Life expectancy	65 (m), 71 (f)
Languages	Tajik (Cyrillic script), *Russian*
Adult literacy rate	97.7%
Currency	Tajik rouble (interim currency) (US $1 = 1128 Tajik roubles)
GDP (US million $)	1000
GDP per head (US $)	165

Agriculture, confined to the deep valleys, together with some mining and manufacturing, provides a meagre living in this high land. There is great mineral and hydroelectric potential. Conflict broke out in ethnically diverse Tajikistan in 1991 after independence. An agreement in 1997 brought hope of peace, but fighting erupts sporadically.

TURKMENISTAN

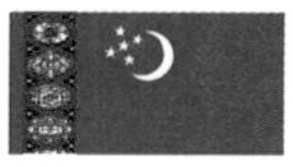

The Republic of Turkmenistan

Map page 116

Area	488 100 km² (188 456 sq miles)
Capital	Ashgabat
Member of	CIS, EBRD, ECO
Population	4 235 000
Population growth rate	2.5%
Life expectancy	62 (m), 68 (f)
Languages	Turkmen (Latin-based script), *Russian, Uzbek, Kazakh*
Adult literacy rate	98%
Currency	Turkmen manat (US $1 = 5350 manats)
GDP (US million $)	2200
GDP per head (US $)	519

Turkmenistan's desert economy relies on irrigated agriculture, the salt of the former Gulf of Kara-Bogaz, and rich reserves of fossil fuels. Diversion of the Amu Darya for irrigation is partly responsible for the reduced water level of the Aral Sea.

UZBEKISTAN

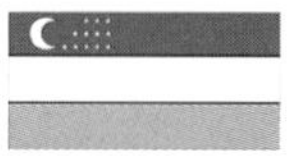

The Republic of Uzbekistan

Map page 116

Area	447 400 km² (172 740 sq miles)
Capital	Tashkent
Member of	CIS, EBRD, ECO
Population	23 667 000
Population growth rate	2.3%
Life expectancy	66 (m), 72 (f)
Languages	Uzbek (reverting to Latin script), *Russian, Kazakh*
Adult literacy rate	97%
Currency	som (US $1 = 625 som)
GDP (US million $)	11 500
GDP per head (US $)	486

Though much of Uzbekistan is flat desert and semidesert, the high mountains of the east are the source of major rivers which irrigate fertile farmland: cotton is the main crop, and silk worms are reared in the Fergana Valley. Poor mountain and desert pastures sustain livestock, notably the karakul sheep in the deserts. Oil, gold and other minerals provide additional income. Several ancient oasis cities were important stopping points on the famous Silk Road between China and Europe. They include Samarkand and Bukhara, renowned for its rugs and a major place of Muslim pilgrimage.

Uzbekistan gained its independence in 1991. Although civil strife between the diverse communities was avoided until 1999, when a bombing campaign shook Tashkent, the economy has not prospered.

20TH-CENTURY LANDMARKS

1900–1 Boxer Rebellion in China.

1904–5 Russo-Japanese war: Russia defeated; Japan gains control of Korea and Formosa (Taiwan).

1910

1911 China overthrows Manchu dynasty and becomes a republic under Sun Yat-sen.

1914 Japan declares war on Germany as First World War commences.

1920

1921 Communist Party is founded in China.

1923 Earthquake destroys the Japanese city of Yokohama.

1930

1931 Japan invades Manchuria.

1934–5 Chinese Communist Party flees 9500 km (5900 miles) on Long March; Mao Ze-dong is established as party leader.

1937 War between Japan and China begins.

1940

1941 Japan attacks US fleet at Pearl Harbor, bringing USA fully into Second World War.

1945 USA drops atomic bombs on Hiroshima and Nagasaki. Japan surrenders, losing all overseas possessions, including Korea and Taiwan.

1949 Chinese civil war ends in victory for Communists. Mao Ze-dong proclaims People's Republic of China.

1950

1950–1 China takes control of Tibet.

1950–3 Korean War.

1959 Dalai Lama flees Tibet.

1960

1962 China and India at war over border.

1966 Mao Ze-dong leads Cultural Revolution in China.

1970

1971 Taiwan is forced to relinquish UN seat in favour of China.

1980

1989 Chinese student protest is crushed in Tiananmen Square.

1990

1991 USSR is dissolved. Formation of the CIS.

1997 Hong Kong reverts to China.

1997-8 Economic difficulties beset Japan and South Korea.

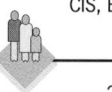

SOUTH-EAST ASIA

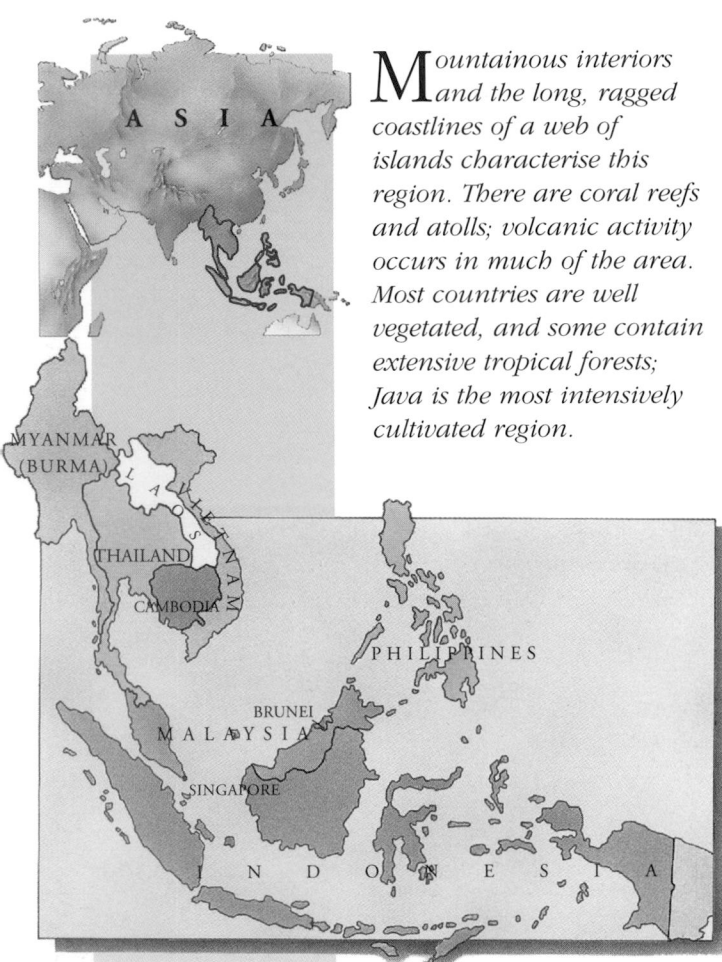

Mountainous interiors and the long, ragged coastlines of a web of islands characterise this region. There are coral reefs and atolls; volcanic activity occurs in much of the area. Most countries are well vegetated, and some contain extensive tropical forests; Java is the most intensively cultivated region.

Associated Territories

CHRISTMAS ISLAND
Parent country
AUSTRALIA
Map page 134

COCOS (KEELING) ISLANDS
Parent country
AUSTRALIA
Map page 134

PARACEL ISLANDS
Parent country
DISPUTED by China, Vietnam and Taiwan.
Map page 134

SPRATLY ISLANDS
Parent country
DISPUTED by China, Malaysia, Taiwan, Vietnam, Brunei and the Philippines.
Map page 134

Abbreviations
APEC *Asia-Pacific Economic Co-operation*
ASEAN *Association of South East Asian Nations*
COMM *Commonwealth*
IDB *Islamic Development Bank*
OPEC *Organisation of Petroleum Exporting Countries*

GDP *Gross Domestic Product*

BRUNEI

The Sultanate of Brunei
Map page 134

Area	5765 km²
	(2226 sq miles)
Capital	Bandar Seri Begawan
Member of	APEC, ASEAN, COMM, IDB
Population	307 000
Population growth rate	3.0%
Life expectancy	70 (m), 73 (f)
Languages	Malay, *Chinese, English*
Adult literacy rate	89%

Currency	Brunei dollar (US $1 = B $1.6)
GDP (US million $)	4888
GDP per head (US $)	16 683

Located on the north-west coast of Borneo, Brunei used to control much of that island, but its influence declined. In the 19th century, the Sultan signed a treaty with the United Kingdom for protection against pirates. Brunei became a protectorate in 1959 and then independent in 1984. The Sultanate still rules the country, which is bisected by a tongue of the Malaysian state of Sarawak. The interior is hilly, covered in rain forest and undeveloped, whereas the coastal plains, which merge into tidal swamps, are home to some of the richest people in the world. Rubber used to be the economic mainstay but has been neglected since oil and gas were discovered in the 1920s; they now constitute 90 per cent of exports. The revenue generated means no income tax for inhabitants and generous provision of public services.

CAMBODIA

The Kingdom of Cambodia
Map page 133

Area	181 035 km²
	(69 898 sq miles)
Capital	Phnom Penh
Member of	ASEAN
Population	11 426 223
Population growth rate	3.1%
Life expectancy	50 (m), 52 (f)
Language	Khmer
Adult literacy rate	35%

Currency	riel (US $1 = 3800 riels)
GDP (US million $)	2900
GDP per head (US $)	253

The temples of the ancient capital, Angkor Wat, testify to the power of the Khmer empire which prospered from the 6th to the mid-15th centuries. Since then, Cambodia has often fallen prey to neighbours. It had a period of stable prosperity as a French protectorate from 1863, becoming the 'rice bowl' of Asia. After independence in 1954, Cambodia was embroiled in the Vietnam war and then suffered terrible privations under the Pol Pot regime (1975–9); about 2 million people either died or fled the country. The ravages of civil war continued until the UN launched a peace plan in 1991. Since then a fragile stability has allowed reconstruction to start. Pol Pot died in 1998.

With high annual rainfall, the mountains that surround Cambodia are heavily forested, and timber and rubber are the two main export commodities. In the interior, the plains are dominated by the Mekong River and by Tonle Sab, both of which flood annually. This creates ideal conditions for rice cultivation and for large inland fisheries.

INDONESIA

The Republic of Indonesia
Map pages 134–5

Area	1 919 317 km²
	(741 053 sq miles)
Capital	Jakarta
Member of	APEC, ASEAN, IDB, OPEC
Population	199 867 000
Population growth rate	1.6%
Life expectancy	61 (m), 64 (f)
Languages	Bahasa Indonesia (a form of Malay), *many local languages*
Adult literacy rate	83.8%

Currency	rupiah (US $1 = 6625 Rp)
GDP (US million $)	93 200
GDP per head (US $)	466

Nearly 14 000 islands, stretching a greater distance from west to east than continental USA, together form Indonesia, home of the world's fourth largest population. It is a region of volcanoes and earthquakes; Krakatoa is the island remnant of what is seen as the world's largest natural explosion, which occurred in 1883. Easily eroded volcanic materials supply new soils, and the high mountains induce heavy rain which, with high temperatures, means that tropical forest is the natural vegetation cover.

The islands have attracted traders interested in the rich resources, including spices, for many centuries. The Portuguese, who arrived in 1509, were supplanted in 1619 by the Dutch. The latter ruled (with brief interruptions) until 1949, when the country became independent. Considerable development took place under the Dutch, especially in Java, where more than half the population lives.

Java has alkaline soils, which are considerably more fertile than the acidic ones of Sumatra. However, Java is overcrowded, and for decades there have been programmes to foster settlement in Sumatra, Kalimantan and, more recently, Irian Jaya.

Indonesia's varied agricultural resources include rice, coffee and tea. The country is also a major producer and exporter of rubber and palm oil. It still has large forest reserves and forestry provides important employment and exports; however, badly controlled felling is causing serious damage. Oil and gas have provided the country with a post-war bonanza which, in comparison with some other countries, has been wisely used to foster long-term development, including manufactures. These have expanded rapidly, with the help of inward investment, and Indonesia is now a significant industrial nation, with thriving electronics and aerospace industries. Hydroelectric power is an important energy source in Sumatra. Indonesia also has a wide range of minerals, as well as major tourist attractions, such as the island of Bali.

The Dutch influence is still visible, as in old Jakarta, though the capital has outgrown the colonial port to become a city of about 8 million people.

Stability in Indonesia has been achieved through authoritarian regimes. In 1998 popular power overthrew the long-time president Suharto. In 1999 democratic elections were held for the first time in 50 years. The new government faces separatist movements in Irian Jaya and North Sumatra; it failed to prevent horrific violence in East Timor after the majority voted for independence.

LAOS

The Lao People's Democratic Republic
Map page 132

Area	236 800 km²
	(91 400 sq miles)
Capital	Vientiane
Member of	ASEAN
Population	5 194 000
Population growth rate	3.1%
Life expectancy	49 (m), 52 (f)
Languages	Lao (Laotian), *French, many local languages*
Adult literacy rate	56.6%

Currency	new kip (US $1 = 7680 new kips)
GDP (US million $)	1700
GDP per head (US $)	327

Internal strife and external interference have characterised the history of Laos, one of the poorest countries in the world. Most of this hot monsoon land is mountainous, forested and inaccessible. About half the inhabitants are Lao, living along the Mekong; the remainder are various mountain peoples.

Development focuses on the Mekong, which forms the western boundary, provides fertile rice-growing plains and is the main communication artery. French colonial rule ended in 1954; since then, the effects of the Vietnam war and doctrinaire socialist policies have left the population, mostly subsistence farmers, impoverished and facing 100 per cent inflation with a greatly devalued currency.

MALAYSIA

Malaysia
Map page 134

Area	329 758 km²
	(127 320 sq miles)
Capital	Kuala Lumpur
Member of	APEC, ASEAN, COMM, IDB
Population	21 666 000
Population growth rate	2.5%
Life expectancy	68 (m), 73 (f)
Languages	Bahasa Malaysia, *English, Chinese, Tamil, Iban*
Adult literacy rate	83.5%

Currency	ringgit (US $1 = R3.8)
GDP (US million $)	72 100
GDP per head (US $)	3327

It was largely historical accident that after the Second World War mainland Malaya, and Sabah and Sarawak on Borneo, unified to form Malaysia in 1963. Despite the geographical separation and ethnic diversity, the country has enjoyed remarkable economic success although, for a while, financial instability in South East Asia generally hindered progress. The nation's politics

have been open to question; Prime Minister Mahathir governs autocratically and deals ruthlessly with his opponents.

The Strait of Malacca is the maritime route between China and India; Melaka, the former capital, bears the imprint of Portuguese, Dutch and British architecture, although it became much less important with the rise of Singapore.

In the 19th century, deposits of alluvial tin attracted major development along the west coast of the peninsula. Rubber plantations, exploiting the hot and humid climate, were also highly successful. Today, Malaysia is one of the world's leading exporters of timber, mostly from Sabah and Sarawak.

MYANMAR (BURMA)

The Union of Myanmar

Map page 132

Area	676 553 km² (261 218 sq miles)
Capital	Yangon (Rangoon)
Member of	ASEAN

Population	48 402 000
Population growth rate	2.1%
Life expectancy	57 (m), 63 (f)
Languages	Myanmar (Burmese) *and other local languages*
Adult literacy rate	83.1%

Currency	kyat (US $1 = 6.2 kyats)
GDP (US million $)	108 199
GDP per head (US $)	2399

Isolated from its neighbours by high and difficult mountains, Myanmar looks inwards to Mandalay, its traditional cultural centre, and southwards along its three great rivers towards Yangon (Rangoon), the premier port and capital.

In 1612, the British began to make inroads into this ancient kingdom, finally annexing the country in 1886. Myanmar, with its monsoon climate and huge river plains, was an important rice exporter; the extensive forests yielded valuable teak.

The Japanese invasion during the Second World War resulted in serious destruction. Following the grant of independence in 1948, a military dictatorship was declared. Repressive economic and political policies were subsequently imposed, which resulted in the nation's serious economic decline; rice exports, for example, fell to one-tenth their previous level. During the 1980s, Myanmar pursued more liberal policies – but not for long. In 1990 the military government quashed the result of a democratic election in which the party of Aung San Suu Kyi (who a year later was awarded the Nobel Peace Prize) won 80 per cent of the vote. Despite internal unrest and international pressure, the military leaders show no sign of giving way.

PHILIPPINES

The Republic of the Philippines

Map page 135

Area	300 000 km² (115 831 sq miles)
Capital	Manila
Member of	APEC, ASEAN

Population	73 527 000
Population growth rate	2.1%
Life expectancy	63 (m), 67 (f)
Languages	Filipino (based on Tagalog), *English, many other local languages*
Adult literacy rate	94.6%

Currency	Philippine peso (US $1 = 38.47 pesos)
GDP (US million $)	63 700
GDP per head (US $)	866

More than 100 distinct ethnic groups inhabit the Philippines, though most Filipinos are of Malay origin. Mountainous terrain and population pressure forced the early settlers to construct terraces and intricate water control systems for paddy rice, some of which are still in use after 3000 years.

The effects of Spanish rule from 1565 to 1898 are evident in all facets of life, though diluted from 1898 by American influence, which continued after independence in 1946. During the years of colonial rule considerable development took place, for example in the export of coconuts, paving the way for further exploitation of the substantial natural resources. These well-watered volcanic islands can grow tropical crops, such as pineapples and sugar cane, and yield large, but over-exploited, supplies of timber.

The Philippines suffered serious destruction during the Second World War, followed by problems of insurgency. From 1965 to 1986 the country was harshly and corruptly governed by President Marcos, and guerrilla war continued. More liberal rule has opened the country to rapid development, based on agriculture, forestry, mining and industry.

SINGAPORE

The Republic of Singapore

Map page 134

Area	646 km² (249.5 sq miles)
Capital	Singapore
Member of	ASEAN, COMM

Population	3 737 000
Population growth rate	1.1%
Life expectancy	74 (m), 78 (f)
Languages	Malay, *Chinese (Mandarin), Tamil, English*
Adult literacy rate	91.1%

Currency	Singapore dollar (US $1 = S$1.69)
GDP (US million $)	85 900
GDP per head (US $)	22 986

Until the 19th century Singapore was virtually uninhabited. Under British rule, however, its strategic commercial and naval position was rapidly exploited, triggering substantial Chinese immigration. Following Japanese rule during the Second World War, Singapore became self-governing in 1959. It briefly joined Malaysia, but in 1965 reverted to independence.

Following the closure of the naval base and sharply reduced trade with China after 1945, and lacking natural resources, the country had to find a new role. Under Lee Kuan Yew's austere premiership (1959–90), it became one of the world's richer countries, developing international finance and a wide range of modern manufactures, including computer equipment and telecommunications, which underpin the metropolitan economy. Tourism is also very important, aided by Singapore's position as a major airline hub.

THAILAND

The Kingdom of Thailand

Map page 132

Area	513 115 km² (198 115 sq miles)
Capital	Bangkok
Member of	APEC, ASEAN

Population	60 602 000
Population growth rate	1.6%
Life expectancy	64 (m), 69 (f)
Languages	Thai, *Chinese, Malay*
Adult literacy rate	93.8%

Currency	baht (US $1 = 37.1 baht)
GDP (US million $)	114 900
GDP per head (US $)	1895

Among the countries of South-east Asia, Thailand alone maintained its independence throughout the colonial period, though it was briefly occupied by the Japanese in the Second World War. Much of its culture has survived intact and the country abounds in temples and other monuments, many of which are very ancient.

The hot monsoon climate is ideal for rice in the river plains north of Bangkok, rubber in the peninsula, and teak and other timber in the north. The modern industries that evolved during the 1980s and 1990s, mainly around Bangkok, include textiles and electronics. The export of these and many other goods provided the basis for development, which was rapid until 1997 when the baht collapsed, signalling economic difficulty and triggering financial instability in the region. Recovery is underway now, however.

Rapid change has caused some serious problems. Among these are over-fishing of the coastal waters; excessive logging, leading to the official but only partially enforced ban on commercial felling; and the chaotic expansion of Bangkok.

VIETNAM

The Socialist Republic of Vietnam

Map page 132

Area	331 114 km² (127 844 sq miles)
Capital	Hanoi
Member of	ASEAN

Population	76 548 000
Population growth rate	2.1%
Life expectancy	63 (m), 67 (f)
Language	Vietnamese
Adult literacy rate	93.7%

Currency	dông (US $1 = 13 943 dông)
GDP (US million $)	25 500
GDP per head (US $)	333

At the end of the Second World War, France tried to re-establish control of Vietnam, but withdrew in 1954 after defeat in the battle for Dien Bien Phu. The nation was partitioned along latitude 17 degrees North, becoming Communist in the north and anti-Communist in the south. The ideological incompatibility between the two led to the devastating Vietnam war (1964–75), after which, despite massive American involvement, the country was forcibly united under northern rule in 1976. The war brought much destruction and loss of life, as well as an extensive refugee problem, and long-term environmental damage created by forest defoliation.

Initially, the Communist government adopted restrictive policies but has gradually introduced economic and social change. Inward investment has begun; the United States has lifted its trade embargo; exports are on the increase and the country is beginning to prosper.

20TH-CENTURY LANDMARKS

1901 Dutch policies in Indonesia spark nationalist movement.

1910

1917 Thailand joins Allies in First World War.

1920

1929 Oil extraction begins in Brunei.

1930

1930 Indo-China Communist Party founded in Vietnam.

1937 Burma (Myanmar) is separated from India.

1940

1941–5 All countries in the region are occupied by Japan during Second World War.

1945–54 Vietnam fights for independence from France.

1950

1954 Vietnam is divided into North Vietnam, supported by USSR, and South Vietnam, supported by USA.

1959 Brunei becomes Islamic state.

1960

1961–73 Vietnam War: US helps South Vietnam, but eventually pulls out; millions flee the country.

1962 Military coup in Myanmar sees start of isolationalist policy.

1965 Ferdinand Marcos elected president of the Philippines.

1970

1975 Indonesia invades East Timor. Laos becomes Communist. Khmer Rouge assumes power in Cambodia: hundreds of thousands die from hunger and disease under its rule.

1976 Pol Pot becomes prime minister of Kampuchea (Cambodia). Vietnam unites and becomes Communist.

1978 Vietnam invades Kampuchea and installs 'friendly' government; Khmer Rouge starts guerrilla war.

1979 Vietnam fights Nine-Day War with China.

1980

1986 Marcos exiled to USA from Philippines.

1988 Student riots in Myanmar. Vietnam withdraws from Cambodia.

1990

1991 Aung San Suu Kyi raises awareness of conditions in Myanmar.

1993 UN oversees elections in Cambodia.

1998 President Suharto of Indonesia is forced out of office. Financial instability besets South-East Asian countries.

1999 Democratic elections in Indonesia.

OCEANIA

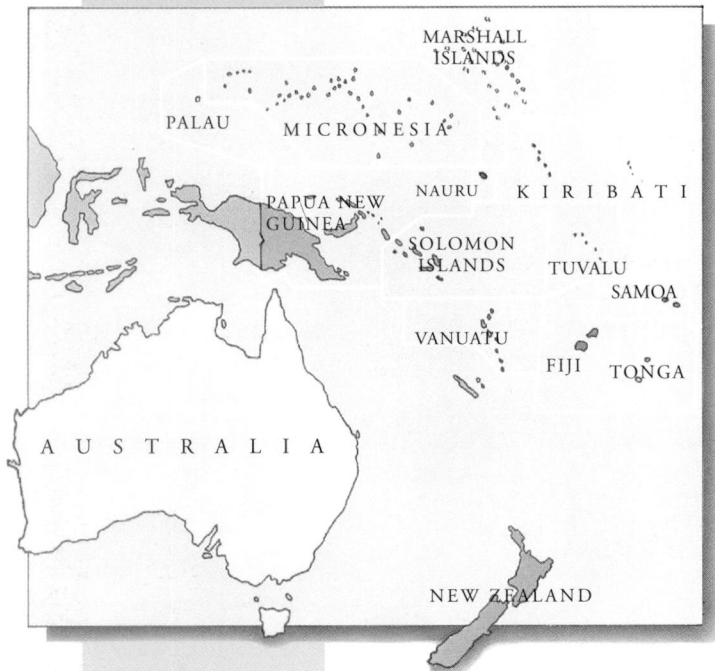

The thousands of islands scattered across the Pacific Ocean form three main groups: Melanesia, Micronesia and Polynesia. Most are ringed by coral reefs. Much of Australia's interior is flat desert, whereas New Zealand and Papua New Guinea are mountainous and green.

Associated Territories

AMERICAN SAMOA
Parent country USA
Map page 147

COOK ISLANDS
Parent country
NEW ZEALAND
Map page 137

FRENCH POLYNESIA
Parent country FRANCE
Map page 147

GUAM
Parent country USA
Map page 125

NEW CALEDONIA
Parent country FRANCE
Map page 139

NIUE
Parent country
NEW ZEALAND
Map page 137

NORTHERN MARIANA ISLANDS
Parent country USA
Map page 136

WALLIS AND FUTUNA ISLANDS
Parent country FRANCE
Map page 137

Abbreviations
ADB Asian Development
   Bank
APEC Asia-Pacific Economic
   Co-operation
COMM Commonwealth
ESCAP Economic and Social
   Commission for Asia and
   the Pacific
OECD Organisation for
   Economic Co-operation
   and Development
PC Pacific Community
SPF South Pacific Forum

GDP Gross Domestic Product

AUSTRALIA

The Commonwealth of Australia
Map pages 140–5

Area	7 682 300 km²
	(2 966 153 sq miles)
Capital	Canberra
Member of	APEC, COMM, OECD, PC, SPF

Population	18 532 000
Population growth rate	1.5%
Life expectancy	75 (m), 80 (f)
Languages	English, Aboriginal languages
Adult literacy rate	over 95%

Currency	Australian dollar
	(US $1 = $A 1.501)
GDP (US million $)	353 300
GDP per head (US $)	19 064

Most of Australia is arid land or desert. The extreme north of the country has a tropical climate, whereas the south-east and south-west have a more Mediterranean regime. The east coast and the Great Dividing Range are the main areas of plentiful rainfall. After the first settlement in 1788, European colonisation was confined to this area, where most Australians live today. However, by 1850 there were six self-governing states covering the whole country. In 1901, these were federated to create Australia.

In the 19th century, the economy grew with the export of farm produce, in particular wheat and wool. Important gold finds in 1851 began the exploitation of Australia's vast

mineral wealth, which include coal, iron ore, bauxite and copper, and contribute significantly to revenue.

Today Australia is a prosperous, primarily urban society. In the early days the population, apart from the indigenous Aboriginals, was almost exclusively of British descent. Then, after 1960, there was an influx from other European countries and Asia. Also, in former times, the focus of Australia's trade was with Europe; now it is directed more to the USA and to Asia which takes 60 per cent of Australian exports. This social and economic revolution has led many to favour turning the nation into a republic.

European settlement dispossessed the Aboriginal people and reduced their number. Many are now reasserting their land claims, which often brings them into conflict with mining interests. Australia also faces the problem of adapting European farming methods and livestock management to the soils and climate of the country, to avoid serious soil degradation.

The Great Barrier Reef along the north-east coast is one of the world's natural marvels; Ayers Rock, sacred Uluru to the Aboriginals, is another major attraction. The breathtaking architecture of Sydney Opera House is world famous.

FIJI ISLANDS

The Republic of Fiji Islands
Map page 147

Area	18 376 km²
	(7095 sq miles)
Capital	Suva, on Viti Levu
Member of	COMM, PC, SPF

Population	800 000
Population growth rate	1.4%
Life expectancy	70 (m), 74 (f)
Languages	Fijian, Hindi, *English*
Adult literacy rate	91.6%

Currency	Fiji dollar
	(US $1 = $F 1.968)
GDP (US million $)	2033
GDP per head (US $)	2593

The islands of Fiji export sugar, copra and other agricultural products, their coral reefs attract tourists, and there are good fish resources. Manufacturing is mostly confined to processing local produce, such as sugar.

Independence from Britain was gained in 1970. However, the country's considerable prosperity is marred by tension between the native Fijian population and those of Indian descent whose ancestors were brought by the British in the nineteenth century to work the sugar plantations.

KIRIBATI

The Republic of Kiribati
Map page 137

Area	810.5 km²
	(312.9 sq miles)
Capital	Bairiki, on Tarawa Atoll
Member of	COMM, PC, SPF

Population	81 000
Population growth rate	1.5%
Life expectancy	58 (av. m/f)
Languages	I-Kiribati (Gilbertese), English
Adult literacy rate	not available

Currency	Australian dollar
	(US $1 = $A 1.501)
GDP (US million $)	51
GDP per head (US $)	654

Kiribati, formerly known as the Gilbert Islands, is a nation of islands and atolls. It is seriously threatened by global warming and a rising sea level; indeed two islands were reportedly lost beneath the waves in 1999.

Once phosphate was mined on Banaba (Ocean Island) but the deposits have long been exhausted. Now fishing, coconuts and subsistence crops yield a modest living, and have to be supplemented by international aid.

MARSHALL ISLANDS

The Republic of the Marshall Islands
Map page 137

Area	180 km²
	(70 sq miles)
Capital	Dalap-Uliga-Darrit (Majuro Atoll)
Member of	PC, SPF

Population	61 000
Population growth rate	3%
Life expectancy	64 (m), 68 (f)
Languages	English, Marshallese, Japanese
Adult literacy rate	91%

Currency	US dollar
GDP (US million $)	91
GDP per head (US $)	1649

The Marshall Islands consist of more than 1000 coral atolls. US nuclear tests on the islands of Bikini and Enewetak between 1946 and 1958 resulted in serious contamination. Rent for an American military base – and US aid – underpin the nation's economy. The islands became independent in 1979.

MICRONESIA

The Federated States of Micronesia
Map page 136

Area	700 km²
	(270.3 sq miles)
Capital	Palikir
Member of	ESCAP, PC, SPF

Population	130 000
Population growth rate	1.8%
Life expectancy	71 (av. m/f)
Languages	English, *Trukese, Pohnpeian*
Adult literacy rate	not available

Currency	US dollar
GDP (US million $)	259
GDP per head (US $)	2104

As many as 600 widely scattered volcanic islands and coral atolls make up Micronesia, which depends on fishing, copra and – more recently – tourism for its living. Since independence from the USA in 1979, the country has received much economic aid.

NAURU

The Republic of Nauru
Map page 137

Area	21.3 km
	(8.2 sq miles)
Capital	No official capital
Member of	COMM, PC, SPF

Population	11 000
Population growth rate	2.3%
Life expectancy	not available
Languages	Nauruan, *English*
Adult literacy rate	99%

Currency	Australian dollar
	(US $1 = $A 1.501)
GDP (US million $)	368
GDP per head (US $)	33 476

Nauru's phosphate mines are now almost exhausted and other resources, including water, are limited. Property investment overseas is now the main source of revenue. Many Nauruans leave the island to seek work elsewhere. Nauru became independent in 1968.

NEW ZEALAND

New Zealand
Map pages 146–7

Area	270 534 km²
	(104 454 sq miles)
Capital	Wellington
Member of	APEC, COMM, OECD, PC, SPF

Population	3 761 000
Population growth rate	0.9%
Life expectancy	73 (m), 79 (f)
Languages	English, *Maori language*
Adult literacy rate	99%

Currency	NZ dollar (US $1 = $NZ 1.897)
GDP (US million $)	52 500
GDP per head (US $)	13 959

European settlement of New Zealand began in the early 19th

century and Britain took control of the country in 1840. It received full independence in 1947. The indigenous Maori population was much reduced after the arrival of Europeans, but the number of Maoris has increased in recent years. The question of land rights has not yet been fully resolved.

New Zealand has prospered from the export of butter, cheese, wool and meat – mainly to Europe and especially to Britain – since the late 19th century. After 1945 the focus of trade shifted towards Australia, South-east Asia and the United States. Simultaneously, there has been considerable industrial development, particularly around Auckland; industries include paper, textiles and steel manufacture.

Hydroelectricity provides about three-quarters of New Zealand's electricity and the potential for further development is huge, especially in the glaciated mountains of South Island, which rise to 3754 m (12 316 ft). Geothermal energy is also available around Rotorua, a volcanic area famous for geysers and hot springs. Most people live on North Island, which is warmer and less rugged than South Island. The latter's spectacular mountain scenery, including the fiords of the south-west, attracts tourists.

New Zealanders demonstrate a special concern for the environment. They protested loudly over French nuclear tests in the Pacific. The government has initiated far-sighted schemes for the protection and management of natural resources such as fish stocks and their unique and often vulnerable wildlife.

PALAU

The Republic of Palau
Map page 135

Area	508 km²
	(196 sq miles)
Capital	Koror, on Koror island
Member of	PC, SPF

Population	17 000
Population growth rate	2.1%
Life expectancy	60 (m), 63 (f)
Languages	Palauan, English
Adult literacy rate	not available

Currency	US dollar
GDP (US million $)	109
GDP per head (US $)	6417

Coral atolls and volcanic islands offer good opportunities for tourism in Palau, but natural resources other than copra and fishing are limited.

The nation declared its independence from the United States in 1994.

PAPUA NEW GUINEA

The Independent State of Papua New Guinea
Map page 136

Area	462 840 km²
	(178 704 sq miles)
Capital	Port Moresby
Member of	APEC, COMM, PC, SPF

Population	4 209 000
Population growth rate	2.2%
Life expectancy	55 (m), 57 (f)
Languages	Pidgin, English, Motu,
	many local languages
Adult literacy rate	72.2%

Currency	kina (US $1 = 2.584 kina)
GDP (US million $)	3800
GDP per head (US $)	902

The eastern half of the island of New Guinea forms the core of Papua New Guinea, with about 600 smaller islands. The coast and islands have long been in contact with the wider world: the original inhabitants, the Melanesians, established with Europeans a lucrative trade in copra and other products. However, until the discovery of gold, and missionary activity, in the 1930s, the interior was virtually unknown. Dense forests on the lower slopes of jagged mountains make communication difficult; the huge, swampy Sepik and Fly river basins are barely accessible. Under Australian rule, limited European settlement occurred in the basins between the mountains, with coffee as the main cash crop. Independence was achieved in 1975. Papua New Guinea is prone to natural disasters: in 1998 a tidal wave devastated the north-west Sepik coast, leaving thousands of people dead or missing.

Mainland Papua New Guinea is developing oil, gas, gold and other minerals. Bougainville island has one of the world's largest copper mines, but rebel activity has affected production. The 1998 ceasefire raises hopes that production will resume.

SAMOA

The Independent State of Samoa
Map page 147

Area	2831 km²
	(1093 sq miles)
Capital	Apia, on Upolu
Member of	COMM, PC, SPF

Population	168 000
Population growth rate	0.5%
Life expectancy	64 (m), 70 (f)
Languages	Samoan, English
Adult literacy rate	97%

Currency	tala (Samoan dollar)
	(US $1 = 3.0157 tala)
GDP (US million $)	173
GDP per head (US $)	1029

The two large and seven small islands of the then Western Samoa gained independence from New Zealand in 1962. The economy is diversifying from farming and fishing into tourism and light manufacturing. Minerals are lacking, but forest resources are being exploited.

SOLOMON ISLANDS

Solomon Islands
Map pages 136–7

Area	27 556 km²
	(10 639 sq miles)
Capital	Honiara, on Guadalcanal
Member of	COMM, PC, SPF

Population	404 000
Population growth rate	3.4%
Life expectancy	68 (m), 73 (f)
Languages	English, Melanesian,
	Pidgin, other local languages
Adult literacy rate	60%

Currency	SI dollar
	(US $1= SI $ 4.833)
GDP (US million $)	302
GDP per head (US $)	747

Melanesian settlement of the Solomon Islands dates from approximately 1000 BC. These coral-reefed volcanic islands have heavy rainfall, suitable for timber production, palm oil, cocoa and copra. The fishing industry is also important, and minerals include gold. Typhoons are a recurrent hazard.

The Solomons were a British protectorate from 1900 until independence in 1978. The island of Guadalcanal was the scene of fierce fighting during World War II.

TONGA

The Kingdom of Tonga
Map page 137

Area	748 km²
	(289 sq miles)
Capital	Nuku'alofa
Member of	COMM, PC, SPF

Population	99 000
Population growth rate	0.8%
Life expectancy	66 (m), 70 (f)
Languages	Tongan, English
Adult literacy rate	93%

Currency	pa'anga (Tongan dollar)
	(US $1 = $T 1.501)
GDP (US million $)	279
GDP per head (US $)	2818

A British protectorate from 1900, Tonga became independent in 1970. The islands are generally low coral atolls in the east and volcanic in the west. Much of the land is cultivated for subsistence crops and the production of copra. Mineral resources are lacking.

TUVALU

Tuvalu
Map page 137

Area	26 km²
	(10 sq miles)
Capital	Vaiaku, on Funafuti atoll
Member of	COMM, PC, SPF

Population	10 000
Population growth rate	0%
Life expectancy	not available
Languages	Tuvaluan, English
Adult literacy rate	95%

Currency	Australian dollar
GDP (US million $)	9
GDP per head (US $)	900

Coconuts and some food crops are grown on the coral atolls of Tuvalu, but the country's main resource is fish. The remittances of citizens working abroad and the issue of postage stamps help to support the economy.

Tuvalu, formerly the Ellice Islands, gained independence from Britain in 1978. It recently reinstated the flag of 1978.

VANUATU

The Republic of Vanuatu
Map page 136

Area	12 190 km²
	(4707 sq miles)
Capital	Port Vila
Member of	COMM, PC, SPF

Population	178 000
Population growth rate	2.5%
Life expectancy	63 (m), 67 (f)
Languages	Bislama, English, French,
	many local languages
Adult literacy rate	53%

Currency	vatu
	(US $1 = 129 vatu)
GDP (US million $)	254
GDP per head (US $)	1427

Volcanic Vanuatu has plentiful rain and abundant forest. Ruled jointly by Britain and France as the New Hebrides until 1980, the country has diversified its economy from copra, cocoa, fishing and timber to include beef farming, tourism and international finance. Tourism is helped by good air links with Australia and New Zealand.

1901 Commonwealth of Australia founded.

1906 Australia acquires Papua New Guinea.

— 1910 —

1914 First World War begins. Japan occupies Marshall Islands. New Zealand occupies Western Samoa. Nauru is held by Australia.

1915 Battle of Gallipoli.

1916 British colony established on Gilbert and Ellice islands (Kiribati and Tuvalu).

— 1920 —

1921 New Guinea mandated to Australia by League of Nations.

— 1930 —

1939 Second World War starts. Australia and New Zealand join Allies.

— 1940 —

1941 Pacific becomes major war zone.

1942 Battle of Midway.

1942–5 Kiribati, Papua New Guinea and Nauru occupied by Japanese.

1946–58 Nuclear tests conducted by USA in Marshall Islands.

— 1950 —

1957 Nuclear tests carried out by Britain near Christmas Island.

— 1960 —

1960 Nauru (not in UN) made 'special member' of Commonwealth.

— 1970 —

1975 Ellice Islands secede to form Tuvalu.

1975 Governor-general of Australia dismisses Labor government; calls for Australia to become a republic gain support.

— 1980 —

1985 Rainbow Warrior, Greenpeace flagship, sabotaged and sunk in Auckland Harbour.

1987 Military coup in Fiji establishes republic; Fiji suspended from Commonwealth.

— 1990 —

1990 Papua New Guinea blockades Bougainville island, where rebels seek independence.

1994 Papua New Guinea agrees ceasefire with Bougainville rebels.

1995 Large tracts of land in New Zealand returned to Maoris.

1995–6 French nuclear tests in Pacific cause widespread anger.

1998 Western Samoa drops 'Western' from its name – now Samoa.

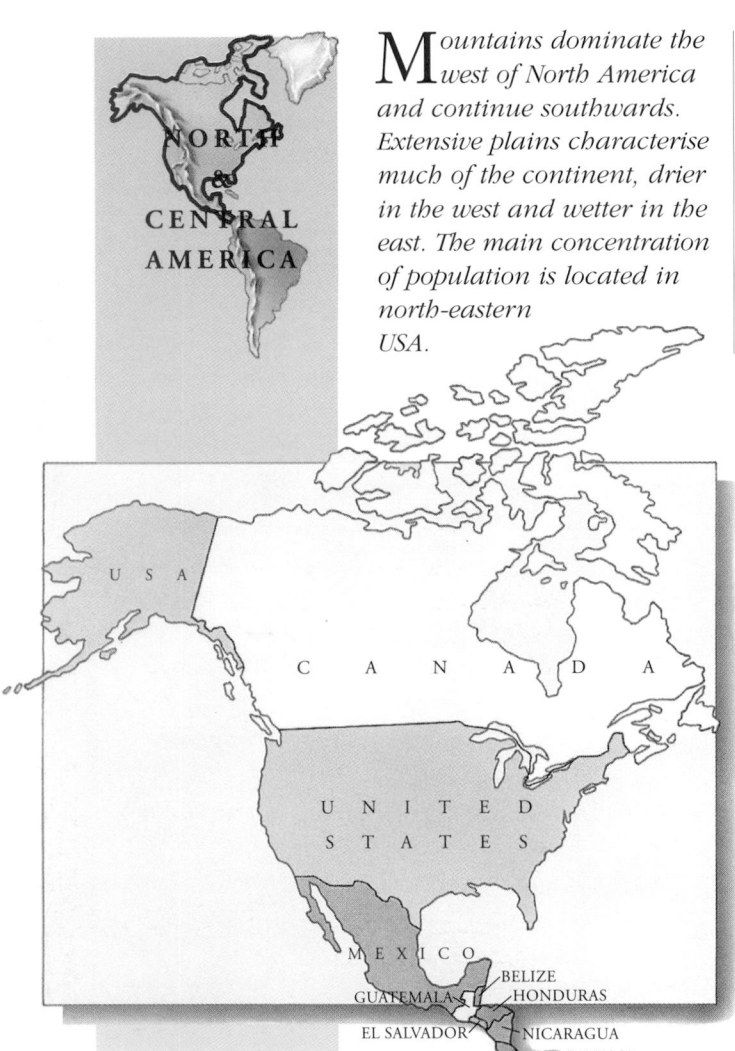

Mountains dominate the west of North America and continue southwards. Extensive plains characterise much of the continent, drier in the west and wetter in the east. The main concentration of population is located in north-eastern USA.

Associated Territories

BERMUDA
Parent country
UK
Map page 169

GREENLAND
Parent country
DENMARK
Map page 151

MIDWAY ISLANDS
Parent country
USA
Map page 56

ST PIERRE AND MIQUELON
Parent country
FRANCE
Map page 161

WAKE ISLAND
Parent country
USA
Map page 137

Abbreviations
ACS Association of Caribbean States
Andean Comm The Andean Community
CACM Central American Common Market
CARICOM Caribbean Community
COMM Commonwealth
EBRD European Bank for Reconstruction and Development
G8 Group of Eight Industrialised Countries
IADB Inter-American Development Bank
LAIA Latin American Integration Association
NAFTA North American Free Trade Agreement
NATO North Atlantic Treaty Organisation
OECD Organisation for Economic Co-operation and Development
GDP Gross Domestic Product

CANADA

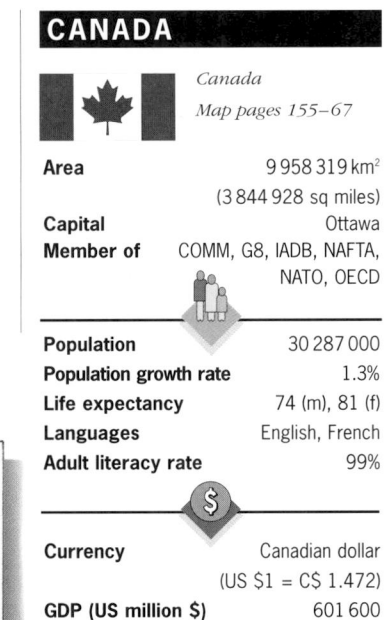

Canada
Map pages 155–67

Area	9 958 319 km²
	(3 844 928 sq miles)
Capital	Ottawa
Member of	COMM, G8, IADB, NAFTA, NATO, OECD
Population	30 287 000
Population growth rate	1.3%
Life expectancy	74 (m), 81 (f)
Languages	English, French
Adult literacy rate	99%
Currency	Canadian dollar
	(US $1 = C$ 1.472)
GDP (US million $)	601 600
GDP per head (US $)	19 863

Canada is a vast country which extends north of the Arctic Circle; its winters are bitterly cold but, in the south, summer temperatures can be high. Cultivation is possible only in the south, where the fertile plains of the Midwest enable Canada to be a major exporter of grain and producer of livestock. Ontario and Québec have more mixed agriculture, including fruit and vineyards in favourable locations. There is spectacular scenery, especially among the Rockies and at Niagara Falls.

Canada's great wealth lies in its minerals and forests. It produces large quantities of oil, gas, coal, nickel, gold and other minerals. Northern Canada was heavily glaciated, creating myriad lakes and waterways among the coniferous forests, which cover nearly 40 per cent of the land. The forests supply Canada with important export products of timber, wood pulp and paper. The country has enormous potential for generating hydroelectricity.

Most Canadians are urban, and manufacturing industries such as motor vehicles, aircraft, machinery and electronics employ many people. The St Lawrence Seaway enables ocean-going ships to reach the Great Lakes.

Modern Canada's history began with the fur trade and competition between French and British settlement from 1605. The French colonies were ceded to Britain in 1763, the borders with the United States were established in 1846, and an autonomous Dominion of Canada was formed in 1867 and gained independence in 1931. The transcontinental railway aided the nation's development.

Québec's French-speaking population has long held strong separatist aspirations. In the north of the country the Inuit people have achieved their wish for autonomy following the creation in 1999 of the self-governing territory of Nunavut.

BELIZE

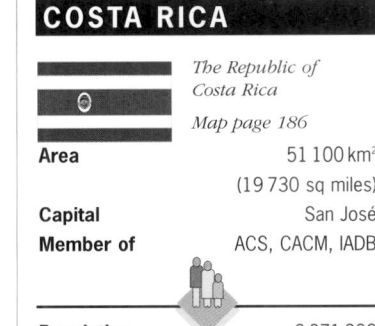

Belize
Map page 185

Area	22 965 km²
	(8867 sq miles)
Capital	Belmopan
Member of	ACS, CARICOM, COMM, IADB
Population	230 000
Population growth rate	2.6%
Life expectancy	70 (m), 74 (f)
Languages	English, Spanish, Creole, Garifuna, Maya, Ketchi, German dialect
Adult literacy rate	90%
Currency	Belizean dollar
	(US $1 = BZ $2.0)
GDP (US million $)	645
GDP per head (US $)	2804

The coastal plain of hot and humid Belize is low-lying and swampy; the southern interior is mountainous and forested. The ruined temples and cities of the ancient Maya civilisation, which peaked around AD 250–900, combined with fine off-shore coral reefs, offer scope for controlled tourist development. The country lacks minerals and depends upon the export of sugar, timber and citrus fruits. There is a developing clothes-manufacturing industry.

Belize was a British colony from 1862 until independence in 1981 and a few British troops remain in Belize, training the Belize Defence Force to protect themselves against possible aggression by Guatemala.

COSTA RICA

The Republic of Costa Rica
Map page 186

Area	51 100 km²
	(19 730 sq miles)
Capital	San José
Member of	ACS, CACM, IADB
Population	3 271 000
Population growth rate	2.5%
Life expectancy	73 (m), 78 (f)
Language	Spanish
Adult literacy rate	94.8%
Currency	Costa Rican colón
	(US $1 = 286.99 colónes)
GDP (US million $)	10 200
GDP per head (US $)	3118

Costa Rica's prosperity is based on the fertile valleys and benign climate of the uplands, rather than the coastal lowlands, which are swampy and inhospitable. Ruled by Spain from the 16th century, the country gained independence in 1821. Enlightened policies in the 19th century encouraged immigrants to establish smallholdings and grow coffee; the population is largely of European extraction.

The country has a reputation for stable government and a tradition of neutrality. Literacy rates are high and healthcare is good. The economy is expanding from coffee and banana exports to minerals and tourism.

EL SALVADOR

The Republic of El Salvador
Map page 186

Area	21 041 km²
	(8124 sq miles)
Capital	San Salvador
Member of	ACS, CACM, IADB
Population	5 928 000
Population growth rate	1.9%
Life expectancy	51 (m), 64 (f)
Language	Spanish
Adult literacy rate	71.5%
Currency	Salvadorean colón
	(US $1 = 8.647 colónes)
GDP (US million $)	12 100
GDP per head (US $)	2041

El Salvador was ruled by Spain until 1821 and achieved complete independence in the mid 19th century. It suffered internal strife and corrupt military dictatorships culminating, during the 1980s, in a disastrous civil war which came to an end only in 1992.

Although war has ceased, the country has continued to suffer. It is the most densely populated country in the western hemisphere, with subsistence farmers scraping a living in the cool uplands. Many have moved to the towns where conditions are poor and often squalid.

The country has been almost entirely deforested, the soil is eroded and the water polluted.

GUATEMALA

The Republic of Guatemala
Map page 186

Area	108 889 km²
	(42 042 sq miles)
Capital	Guatemala City
Member of	ACS, CACM, IADB
Population	10 517 000
Population growth rate	2.9%
Life expectancy	62 (m), 67 (f)
Languages	Spanish, many local languages
Adult literacy rate	55.6%
Currency	quetzal
	(US $1 = 7.349 quetzales)
GDP (US million $)	18 700
GDP per head (US $)	1778

Spain ruled Guatemala until 1821, and full independence followed in 1838. With little plantation development few African slaves were imported. People of European extraction dominate the nation's economy, while those of Amerindian descent have been forced onto the poorer land to eke out a living and to fight for their rights. Only in the latter years of the century has there been peace.

Exports are dominated by coffee, sugar and cotton. With a population of some 2 million, Guatemala City generates most of the country's manufacturing products; it also possesses a university founded in 1676.

Guatemala is a beautiful country with plentiful natural resources. It has a rich potential, given peace, though as yet the indigenous population is downtrodden, the army wields oppressive power, and discrimination against women is supported by the law.

HONDURAS

The Republic of Honduras
Map page 186

Area	112 088 km²
	(43 277 sq miles)
Capital	Tegucigalpa
Member of	ACS, CACM, IADB
Population	5 981 000
Population growth rate	3.0%
Life expectancy	65 (m), 70 (f)
Language	Spanish
Adult literacy rate	72.7%
Currency	lempira
	(US $1 = 14.30 lempiras)
GDP (US million $)	5400
GDP per head (US $)	902

From the 1920s to the 1950s, the United Fruit Company of America dominated Honduras's economy, with banana exports from the northern coast. The company also had considerable political influence. Most of the country's citizens remained poor, living in the mountainous and forested interior.

Today, coffee, cattle and sugar are important products, as well as tropical flowers and fruits. There is little manufacturing, but mineral deposits could be developed in the future.

The country suffered a massive setback in November 1998 when hurricane 'Mitch' caused widespread devastation.

MEXICO

	The United Mexican States
	Map pages 184–5
Area	1 958 201 km²
	(756 066 sq miles)
Capital	Mexico City
Member of	ACS, IADB, LAIA,
	NAFTA, OECD

Population	96 400 000
Population growth rate	2.2%
Life expectancy	68 (m), 74 (f)
Languages	Spanish, *many local*
	languages
Adult literacy rate	89.6%

Currency	Mexican peso
	(US $1 = 9.34 pesos)
GDP (US million $)	411 400
GDP per head (US $)	4267

An uneasy balance of tradition and modernity, Mexico's culture derives from the ancient Aztec and Maya civilisations and three centuries of Spanish colonial influence. At independence in the early 19th century, land and wealth were unequally divided, leading to a revolution in 1910. Extensive land reforms followed, but glaring inequalities in income and wealth remain a national problem.

Southern Mexico receives an adequate rainfall, supporting a wide range of crops. The north is largely desert. Mexico supplies most of its own food and has some surplus to export, such as coffee and sugar.

The nation's main wealth lies in minerals and manufactures. It is a major producer of oil (along the east coast). Mexico is one of the most industrialised of the developing countries, catering for both home and export markets. The main industrial centre, Mexico City, has serious problems of air pollution; it has a population of some 20 million, many of whom live in extensive slums.

Manufacturing has also rapidly expanded along the frontier with the United States.

From 1836 to 1848, Mexico lost more than half its territory, comprising the present states of Arizona, California, New Mexico, Texas and Utah, and parts of Colorado and Wyoming.

Despite the North American Free Trade Agreement being made operative in 1994, relations with the USA remain uneasy. This is exacerbated by the large numbers of Mexicans who try to enter the USA illegally in search of work.

NICARAGUA

	The Republic of Nicaragua
	Map page 186
Area	120 254 km²
	(46 430 sq miles)
Capital	Managua
Member of	ACS, CACM, IADB

Population	4 351 000
Population growth rate	3.1%
Life expectancy	63 (m), 69 (f)
Languages	Spanish, *English*
Adult literacy rate	65.6%

Currency	gold cordoba
	(US $1 = 11.87 gold cordobas)
GDP (US million $)	2000
GDP per head (US $)	459

With fertile volcanic soils and a humid climate, Nicaragua has the ideal conditions to produce many tropical crops. The capital, Managua, a commercial and industrial centre, contains about one in five of the population.

Following its independence in 1838, Nicaragua has a history of dictatorship and intervention by the USA. The Somoza family's regime was toppled in 1979 by a civil war that continued until the mid 1990s; its legacy is a devastated economy, an impoverished population, and difficult political relations with the United States.

PANAMA

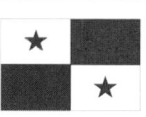

	The Republic of Panama
	Map page 186
Area	75 517 km²
	(29 157 sq miles)
Capital	Panama City
Member of	ACS, Andean Comm,
	CACM, IADB,

Population	2 719 000
Population growth rate	2.0%
Life expectancy	71 (m), 76 (f)
Language	Spanish
Adult literacy rate	90.8%

Currency	balboa (US $1 = 1.0 balboas)
GDP (US million $)	4657
GDP per head (US $)	1083

Located on the narrowest point of the isthmus joining north and south America, Panama spans a gap in the mountain chain. It has provided a favoured route between the Pacific and Atlantic for centuries, adapting to new technologies of transit; pack animals were first replaced by a railway and then, in 1914, by the Panama Canal. The United States, which considers Panama to be of strategic importance, leased the zone through which the canal was built; however, Panama gained full control of all its territory at the end of 1999.

The reasonably prosperous economy is heavily dependent on canal revenues. In addition, a large international fleet sails under the Panamanian 'flag of convenience', and there are major financial houses based in the country. Rice is the staple foodstuff of the population, and products such as bananas, sugar and coffee are exported.

In 1989, US troops invaded Panama and seized the dictator General Noriega, who was later convicted of drug trafficking. An elected government has been in power since then. Political stability has encouraged inward investment and enhanced the nation's prosperity.

UNITED STATES

	The United States of America
	Map pages 162–83
Area	9 809 155 km²
	(3 787 319 sq miles)
Capital	Washington D.C.
Member of	G8, IADB, NAFTA,
	NATO, OECD

Population	267 901 000
Population growth rate	1.0%
Life expectancy	72 (m), 79 (f)
Languages	English, *Spanish*
Adult literacy rate	over 95%

Currency	US dollar
GDP (US million $)	8 544 700
GDP per head (US $)	31 895

The USA is a huge country, with its immense plains, vast deserts, and the two long mountain chains of the Rocky Mountains and the Appalachians. The Grand Canyon in Arizona is perhaps the most famous natural feature. The climate east of the Rockies can be difficult; during winter, arctic winds bring bitterly cold weather, while east of the Mississippi River hot and humid summers are widespread. The western states enjoy a more pleasant climate, that of California being particularly attractive.

Native Americans lived and hunted on most of the land for thousands of years before the first permanent European settlement was established in Florida in 1565. Many thousands of European immigrants were attracted to the New World by the rich resources and prospect of religious freedom. In 1776, the original 13 colonies (along the eastern coast) issued their Declaration of Independence from Britain. The federation then began to extend westwards by voluntary accession, purchase and war, a process largely completed by 1868. During the 18th and early 19th centuries, large numbers of African slaves were brought to work on the southern plantations. The 20th century has seen an influx of Mexicans and Asiatics, especially to the west coast.

Railway construction in the 19th century was instrumental in the USA's physical and economic expansion. The rail network aided the export of grain and livestock from the Midwest, cotton and tobacco from the South, and timber from the northern regions. It also laid the foundations for massive industrial development, such as iron and steel at Pittsburgh and meat packing at Chicago.

Today the United States, with its incredibly varied society and diverse ethnic traditions, is the world's most powerful economy and military machine. It is also a major cultural influence and source of scientific innovation. The country is the industrial giant of the world, capable of making virtually anything. In the late 19th century, Henry Ford pioneered mass production techniques in car manufacture, for which Detroit is famous. Boeing, the aircraft giant, dominates Seattle, and Silicon Valley (south of San Francisco) spawned modern innovative firms in the information technology revolution based on the microchip. The USA has led the way in space research and satellite technology. New York is one of the world's leading financial centres, and Chicago the key place to trade in primary products. Pennsylvania has abundant seams of coal, and there are rich deposits of oil and gas in Texas.

However, economic success has had its price. The United States made the motor car its own, but despite massive road building, traffic clogs the cities and creates serious atmospheric pollution. The urban areas foster a violent society, notorious for its murder rate and widespread use of drugs. Despite the USA's ideals of freedom and equality of opportunity, many citizens remain poor, living in deprived neighbourhoods.

From 1945 to 1991, the USA confronted the Soviet Union in the Cold War, assuming the role of leader of the Western nations. Today, issues of international security have changed radically and isolationist pressures within the USA are evident, combining to force a reassessment of the country's role in the world.

1903 Panama Canal Zone ceded to USA.

— 1910 —

1910–11 Mexican Revolution, followed by civil war (1913).

1914 Panama Canal opens.

1914–18 First World War: Canada plays a major Allied role.

1917 USA enters First World War on Allied side.

— 1920 —

1929 Wall Street Crash precipitates worldwide economic depression.

— 1930 —

1933 US President Roosevelt introduces 'New Deal' for recovery and reform.

1935 Nationalisation and land redistribution programmes in Mexico.

1939–45 Second World War: Canada plays a major Allied role.

— 1940 —

1941 USA in Second World War after Japan attacks Pearl Harbor.

1942 Mexico joins Allies in Second World War.

1945 USA tests first A-bomb in New Mexico.

— 1950 —

1950 Sen. McCarthy begins anti-Communist hearings.

— 1960 —

1961–73 USA involved in Vietnam War.

1962 Cuban missile crisis with USSR.

1963 President John F. Kennedy assassinated.

1968 Martin Luther King assassinated.

— 1970 —

1974 President Nixon resigns over Watergate.

1979 Civil wars in El Salvador and Nicaragua.

— 1980 —

1982 Mexico defaults on international loans.

1989 Panama invaded by USA; General Noriega arrested.

— 1990 —

1990 Nicaragua holds democratic elections.

1992 Civil war ends in El Salvador. NAFTA agreed between USA, Canada and Mexico to promote trade.

1995 Québec votes narrowly to remain in Canadian Federation.

1999 Nunavut is established as an Inuit homeland in Northern Canada.

THE CARIBBEAN

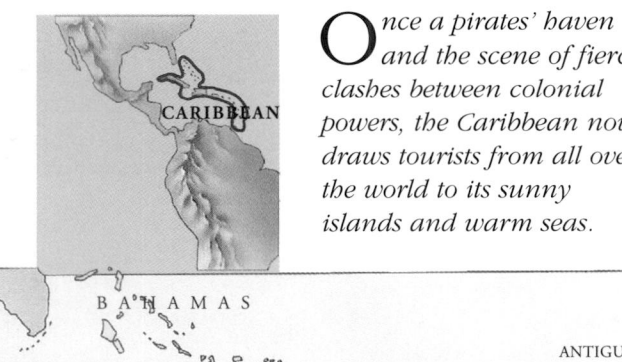

*O*nce a pirates' haven and the scene of fierce clashes between colonial powers, the Caribbean now draws tourists from all over the world to its sunny islands and warm seas.

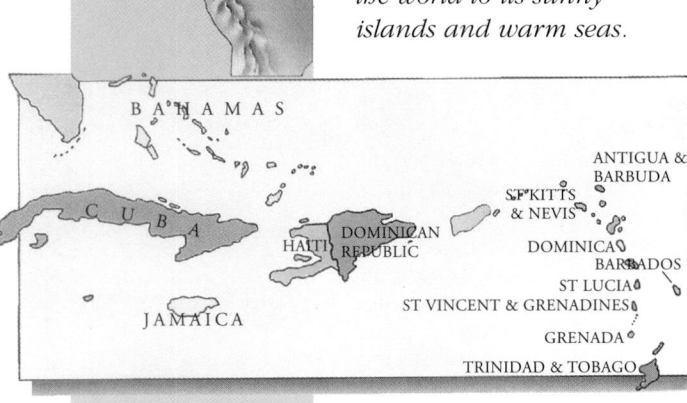

Associated Territories

ANGUILLA
Parent country UK
Map page 187

ARUBA
Parent country
NETHERLANDS
Map page 187

BRITISH VIRGIN ISLANDS
Parent country UK
Map page 187

CAYMAN ISLANDS
Parent country UK
Map page 186

GUADELOUPE
Parent country
FRANCE
Map page 187

MARTINIQUE
Parent country
FRANCE
Map page 187

MONTSERRAT
Parent country UK
Map page 187

NAVASSA ISLAND
Parent country USA
Map page 186

NETHERLANDS ANTILLES
Parent country
NETHERLANDS
Map page 187

PUERTO RICO
Parent country USA
Map page 187

TURKS AND CAICOS ISLANDS
Parent country UK
Map page 187

VIRGIN ISLANDS (US)
Parent country USA
Map page 187

Abbreviations
ACS Association of Caribbean States
CARICOM Caribbean Community
COMM Commonwealth
IADB Inter-American Development Bank
SELA Latin American Economic System

GDP Gross Domestic Product

ANTIGUA & BARBUDA

Antigua and Barbuda
Map page 187

Area	442 km²
	(170 sq miles)
Capital	St John's, on Antigua
Member of	ACS, CARICOM, COMM

Population	67 000
Population growth rate	0.5%
Life expectancy	74 (av. m/f)
Languages	English, *English patois*
Adult literacy rate	90%

Currency	East Caribbean dollar
	(US $1 = EC $2.7)
GDP (US million $)	603
GDP per head (US $)	9000

A British colony from 1632, the country gained independence in 1981. Most inhabitants live on Antigua, which is a historic naval base. The once-dominant sugar industry is now defunct, and the islands depend on tourism, sustained by their fine coral beaches. Farming and fishing are also important, as are the manufacture of petroleum products and textiles from imported materials, and the provision of financial services.

THE BAHAMAS

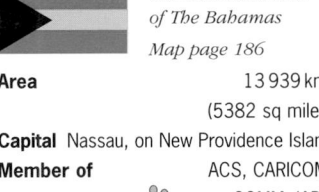

The Commonwealth of The Bahamas
Map page 186

Area	13 939 km²
	(5382 sq miles)
Capital	Nassau, on New Providence Island
Member of	ACS, CARICOM, COMM, IADB

Population	289 000
Population growth rate	1.7%
Life expectancy	68 (m), 75 (f)
Language	English
Adult literacy rate	98.2%

Currency	Bahamian dollar
	(US $1 = B$ 1.0)
GDP (US million $)	3875
GDP per head (US $)	13 408

Before the 1950s, the main industry on this group of 700 low coral islands was sponge fishing. The Bahamas lacks natural resources other than fine beaches, which are now the playground for several million visitors annually, the majority from the USA. The country also hosts many banks and financial institutions, taking advantage of the favourable tax regime, and a large merchant fleet operating under a flag of convenience. Nassau, the capital, has a fine harbour, which was once of great strategic importance. The Bahamas was controlled by Britain for almost 300 years until independence in 1973.

BARBADOS

Barbados
Map page 187

Area	430 km²
	(166 sq miles)
Capital	Bridgetown
Member of	ACS, CARICOM, COMM, IADB

Population	262 000
Population growth rate	0.3%
Life expectancy	72 (m), 77 (f)
Language	English
Adult literacy rate	97.4%

Currency	Barbados dollar
	(US $1 = Bds $2.0)
GDP (US million $)	2270
GDP per head (US $)	8664

Sugar plantations and rum used to be the basis of the economy of Barbados, but the industry has been hit by competition. Fringing coral reefs now attract large numbers of tourists, and the country has a diverse manufacturing industry, but many Barbadians leave to seek work abroad. The country has a tradition of good government and excellent education. The capital, Bridgetown, was founded in 1628 by the British; independence was gained in 1966. As the most easterly of the Caribbean Islands, Barbados has often been badly hit by seasonal hurricanes.

CUBA

The Republic of Cuba
Map page 186

Area	110 860 km²
	(42 803 sq miles)
Capital	Havana
Member of	ACS, SELA

Population	11 060 000
Population growth rate	0.9%
Life expectancy	74 (m), 77 (f)
Language	Spanish
Adult literacy rate	95.7%

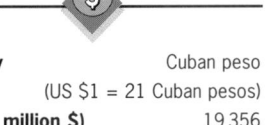

Currency	Cuban peso
	(US $1 = 21 Cuban pesos)
GDP (US million $)	19 356
GDP per head	1750

Cuba has the potential for considerable prosperity, but the economy still languishes. The country has extensive plains excellent for sugar cane, tobacco and many other crops, in addition to large deposits of iron ore, nickel, chromium and other minerals. The island also possesses wonderful beaches and a rich heritage of Spanish colonial architecture. Havana, the capital, has a fine natural harbour and a population of about 2 million; the city used to be the main cultural centre of the Caribbean.

Apart from a brief interlude, Spain controlled Cuba from the 16th century to the end of the 19th century, when Spain lost the Spanish-American war. Cuba became independent, but the USA was granted the right of intervention in the island's affairs and leased military bases, including Guantanamo, which it still maintains.

After independence, unstable political regimes and an unequal distribution of wealth fostered civil unrest. In 1959 this culminated in a Communist revolution led by Fidel Castro, who has remained in power ever since. As a Communist state on its threshold, Cuba attracted the hostility of the United States, most dangerously in 1962 when the Soviet Union unsuccessfully tried to establish missile bases on the island.

For some three decades after 1959, Cuba became heavily dependent on the Soviet Union for economic aid. That ended in 1990, although Russia remains Cuba's most important trading partner. Cuba no longer foments revolution elsewhere, which has improved relations with some nations but, so far, not the USA. The USA has maintained a trade embargo and other sanctions, which continue to damage the Cuban economy.

Sugar remains Cuba's largest export, followed by citrus fruits and nickel; the finest Havana cigars are now scarce. The country has to import large amounts of food and there are chronic shortages of oil, machinery and spare parts. There has been some relaxation of internal controls, but many Cubans still want to leave.

DOMINICA

The Commonwealth of Dominica
Map page 187

Area	750 km²
	(290 sq miles)
Capital	Roseau
Member of	ACS, CARICOM, COMM

Population	71 000
Population growth rate	– 0.2%
Life expectancy	72 (av. m/f)
Languages	English, *Creole*
Adult literacy rate	94.4%

Currency	East Caribbean dollar
	(US $1 = EC $2.7)
GDP (US million $)	244
GDP per head (US $)	3436

The volcanic mass of Dominica rises 1447 m (4747 ft) above the ocean, a rugged, well-watered island which is still heavily forested. Early European colonists were not attracted to it because its terrain would not support sugar cultivation, neither did it possess a good harbour. Ruled by Britain from 1805 until 1978, Dominica relies on the export of bananas, copra and citrus fruits and, increasingly, on tourists who are drawn to the forests' flora and fauna.

DOMINICAN REPUBLIC

The Dominican Republic
Map pages 186–7

Area	48 422 km²
	(18 696 sq miles)
Capital	Santo Domingo
Member of	ACS, IADB

Population	8 190 000
Population growth rate	2.1%
Life expectancy	68 (m), 72 (f)
Language	Spanish
Adult literacy rate	82.1%

Currency	Dominican Republic peso
	(US $1 = 15.94 pesos)
GDP (US million $)	15 300
GDP per head (US $)	1868

Santo Domingo, the capital, was founded in 1496 and is the oldest continuous European settlement in the Americas. During the colonial period, from 1492 until independence from Spain in 1865, the country had a troubled history. Successive revolutions and dictatorships followed until 1966, when the establishment of a democratic government created a degree of stability.

Occupying the eastern part of the island of Hispaniola, the Republic contains Pico Duarte, the highest Caribbean mountain (3175 m or 10 417 ft). It also possesses dramatic scenery, fertile lands and a wide range of export crops, such as tobacco, sugar and coffee. Gold and other metals are also exported.

The island's excellent beaches attract increasing numbers of tourists from Canada, Europe and the USA. However, the country's reputation is marred by accusations of a sizable illegal transit trade in drugs.

GRENADA

Grenada
Map page 187

Area	344 km²
	(133 sq miles)
Capital	St George's
Member of	ACS, CARICOM, COMM

Population	93 000
Population growth rate	0.2%
Life expectancy	71 (av. m/f)
Languages	English, *French patois*
Adult literacy rate	90%

Currency	East Caribbean dollar
	(US $1 = EC $2.7)
GDP (US million $)	333
GDP per head (US $)	3580

The volcanic and forested island of Grenada is well known for its spices, in particular nutmeg and mace. Other exports include cocoa and bananas. St George's has a modern deep-sea port. Grenada was under British rule from 1783 to 1974. In 1983 it was invaded by the USA, and a new non-Marxist administration was established. An international airport was opened in 1984, aiding tourism.

HAITI

The Republic of Haiti
Map page 186

Area	27 750 km²
	(10 714 sq miles)
Capital	Port-au-Prince
Member of	ACS, CARICOM, IADB

Population	7 492 000
Population growth rate	2%
Life expectancy	52 (m), 56 (f)
Languages	French, Creole
Adult literacy rate	45%

Currency	gourde
	(US $1 = 16.69 gourdes)
GDP (US million $)	3400
GDP per head (US $)	453

The modern country of Haiti was created by African slaves. Brought to work the estates of Spanish and French colonists, they revolted and declared independence in 1804. Since then Haiti has had a dictatorial government, punctuated by US intervention, most recently in 1994. The regimes of Duvalier, father and son (1957–86), were particularly brutal, causing many people to flee the country.

The country is mountainous and beautiful, but its potential for tourism is underdeveloped. Haiti lacks significant minerals, and agriculture provides a meagre living for most people and the outlook is still bleak. There has been no stable, let alone democratic, government for years and little prospect in the future. Serious crime is widespread; it is a centre for drugs exports, especially to the USA. Its people are the poorest in the western hemisphere.

JAMAICA

Jamaica
Map page 186

Area	10 991 km²
	(4244 sq miles)
Capital	Kingston
Member of	ACS, CARICOM, COMM, IADB

Population	2 554 000
Population growth rate	0.9%
Life expectancy	71 (m), 76 (f)
Languages	English, *local patois*
Adult literacy rate	85%

Currency	Jamaican dollar
	(US $1 = J $37.65)
GDP (US million $)	6900
GDP per head (US $)	2701

Jamaica is a beautiful and varied island, with land that rises above 2000 m (7000 ft). Kingston, the capital, is a busy, bustling city, the home of reggae music and 25 per cent of the population. It has a fine harbour but also poor districts where many live in considerable squalor.

Britain seized Jamaica from Spain in 1655 and granted the country independence in 1962. Sugar plantations used African slave labour, and the modern population is predominantly African in origin. Agriculture has diversified to include bananas, tobacco and high-quality Blue Mountain coffee; more recently, winter vegetables, flowers and honey have been produced. However, many rural people continue to farm at subsistence level.

Jamaica is the world's third largest producer of bauxite, the base ore of aluminium. This has underpinned the economy, but international prices are volatile. The country's manufacturing centres on the processing of primary products, such as sugar, molasses and rum, but cement and textiles also contribute to the economy. Tourism is now a major industry, especially along the north and west coasts. Foreign visitors, mainly from the USA and Canada, come to the large enclosed beach resorts, but do not venture into the villages of the mountainous interior. Despite the growing economy, large numbers of Jamaicans have emigrated since 1945.

Hurricanes periodically batter Jamaica, causing great damage. A more enduring problem is the illegal cultivation of narcotics, one of the more profitable of Jamaica's industries. Associated difficulties, such as gang warfare and lawlessness, have seriously impeded the island's general development.

ST KITTS & NEVIS

The Federation of Saint Kitts and Nevis
Map page 187

Area	261 km²
	(101 sq miles)
Capital	Basseterre, on St Kitts
Member of	ACS, CARICOM, COMM

Population	41 000
Population growth rate	– 0.5%
Life expectancy	67 (m), 70 (f)
Language	English
Adult literacy rate	97.3%

Currency	East Caribbean dollar
	(US $1 = EC $2.7)
GDP (US million $)	264
GDP per head (US $)	6439

These two islands, suitable for sugar cane cultivation, attracted both French and British colonial interest. Britain gained sole control in 1783; independence was granted in 1983. A vote to give Nevis independence from its larger neighbour was lost because the two-thirds majority required was not achieved.

The country is still dependent on the sugar industry, but encouragement is being given to market gardening, cotton and livestock rearing.

ST LUCIA

Saint Lucia
Map page 187

Area	616 km²
	(238 sq miles)
Capital	Castries
Member of	ACS, CARICOM, COMM

Population	146 000
Population growth rate	1.7%
Life expectancy	69 (m), 75 (f)
Languages	English, *French*
Adult literacy rate	81.5%

Currency	East Caribbean dollar
	(US $1 = EC $2.7)
GDP (US million $)	609
GDP per head (US $)	4171

Extinct volcanoes provide St Lucia with dramatic scenery, and its beautiful harbour of Castries is a regular port of call for cruise liners. Bananas, the country's traditional export, suffer from periodic drought and hurricanes, but tourism is expanding, as are some areas of manufacturing. St Lucia did not gain its independence from Britain until 1979.

ST VINCENT & THE GRENADINES

Saint Vincent and the Grenadines
Map page 187

Area	389 km²
	(150 sq miles)
Capital	Kingstown, on St Vincent
Member of	ACS, CARICOM, COMM

Population	112 000
Population growth rate	0.9%
Life expectancy	72 (av. m/f)
Language	English
Adult literacy rate	82%

Currency	East Caribbean dollar
	(US $1 = EC $2.7)
GDP (US million $)	300
GDP per head (US $)	2678

St Vincent, which gained independence from Britain in 1979, spans two distinct worlds. The main island, dominated by the sometimes destructive Soufriere volcano, is a land of farmers, the descendants of sugar plantation workers, who also grow bananas, arrowroot and increasingly, but illegally, marijuana. The smaller island to the south is a yachting paradise and a haven for wealthy tourists.

TRINIDAD & TOBAGO

The Republic of Trinidad and Tobago
Map page 187

Area	5128 km²
	(1980 sq miles)
Capital	Port of Spain, on Trinidad
Member of	ACS, CARICOM, COMM, IADB

Population	1 271 000
Population growth rate	1.2%
Life expectancy	72 (av. m/f)
Languages	English, *French, Spanish, Hindi, Chinese*
Adult literacy rate	97.9%

Currency	Trinidad and Tobago dollar
	(US $1 = TT$ 6.2)
GDP (US million $)	5800
GDP per head (US $)	4563

The first oil well in Trinidad was drilled in 1867 and has been in continuous production since. The island also contains the world's largest source of natural asphalt. The prosperity that these have brought has been considerable, but the economy remains vulnerable to price fluctuations.

Efforts are being made to develop new industries and to expand tourism, the main industry of Tobago. Traditional exports include sugar and cocoa. In 1962, the country gained independence from Britain.

1902 Cuba becomes independent republic.

1910

1914 Panama Canal opens, increasing trade potential of region.

1915–34 Haiti is occupied by US forces.

1916–24 Dominican Republic occupied by US military.

1920

1920–33 Bahamas is a bootlegging centre during US Prohibition.

1930

1933 Fulgencio Batista y Zaldivar comes to power in Cuba.

1937–8 Economic depression causes riots in Barbados.

1940

1940 Dominica joins Windward Islands group from Leeward Islands Federation.

1950

1959 Cuban revolution: Castro deposes Batista; US business interests seized; USA severs relations (1961).

1960

1962 Cuban missile crisis: USSR withdraws missile base.

1963 Military coup in Dominican Republic.

1965 Civil war and revolt in Dominican Republic; US troops suppress the violence.

1970

1972 Cuba establishes preferential trade links with USSR. Jamaica moves to left under premier Michael Manley.

1980

1983 Cabinet ministers and police commissioner implicated in Bahamas drug trade. Military coup in Grenada prompts US intervention.

1986 Haitian President 'Baby Doc' Duvalier is overthrown.

1988 Hurricane Gilbert devastates Jamaica.

1990

1991 President Aristide of Haiti overthrown by military coup.

1992 USA strengthens economic blockade on Cuba.

1994 USA occupies Haiti; President Aristide returns to power.

1995 Hurricane Luis causes severe damage to Antigua and Barbuda.

1997 Montserrat suffers severe damage from volcanic activity.

SOUTH AMERICA

SOUTH
AMERICA

VENEZUELA
GUYANA
COLOMBIA
SURINAM
ECUADOR
P E R U
B R A Z I L
BOLIVIA
PARAGUAY
A R G E N T I N A
CHILE
URUGUAY

The Andes Mountains run the length of the west coast, behind a narrow coastal plain. To the north the Guiana Highlands face the Atlantic. The forested Amazon basin covers a third of Brazil, whose southern plateau extends to the great plains, or pampas, of Uruguay and Argentina.

Associated Territories

FALKLAND ISLANDS
Parent country
UK
Map page 193

FRENCH GUIANA
Parent country
FRANCE
Map page 191

SOUTH GEORGIA AND SOUTH SANDWICH ISLANDS
Parent country
UK
Map page 193

Abbreviations
ACS Association of Caribbean States
Andean Comm Andean Community
CARICOM Caribbean Community
COMM Commonwealth
IADB Inter-American Development Bank
MERCOSUR Common Market of the South
OPEC Organisation of Petroleum Exporting Countries

GDP Gross Domestic Product

232

ARGENTINA

The Argentine Republic
Map pages 192–3

Area	2 766 889 km²
	(1 068 302 sq miles)
Capital	Buenos Aires
Member of	IADB
Population	35 672 000
Population growth rate	1.4%
Life expectancy	68 (m), 73 (f)
Language	Spanish
Adult literacy rate	96.2%
Currency	peso
	(US $1 = 0.9 peso)
GDP (US million $)	343 700
GDP per head (US $)	9635

As it lacked the precious metals found in other South American countries, Argentina was largely neglected by its 16th-century Spanish conquerors. It achieved independence from Spain in the mid 19th century after a lengthy civil war. The massive pampas were then settled by European immigrants who used the new technology of refrigeration and railways to supply meat, wool, hides and grain to the world market. By the early 20th century, Argentina had become one of the world's richest countries.

However, the two world wars caused serious disruptions to international trade. Since 1930, the government has alternated between military and civilian rule. The dominant political figure in the 20th century was Colonel Juan Perón, president from 1946 to 1955, when he was ejected in a military coup. Argentina's economic decline continued until 1983, when stable civilian government began to improve its prospects.

Argentina has extremely rich agricultural resources, including the vineyards of Mendoza and the sheep of Patagonia. The Andes have great hydroelectric and tourist potential, but limit access to the Pacific Ocean.

One-third of Argentinians live in Buenos Aires, the capital and main port. Argentina continues to claim sovereignty over the Falkland Islands, which it calls Islas Malvinas, despite the costly war fought with Britain in 1982. The deeply damaged relations that ensued are being mended.

BOLIVIA

The Republic of Bolivia
Map page 192

Area	1 098 581 km²
	(424 164 sq miles)
Capital	La Paz and Sucre
Member of	Andean Comm, IADB
Population	7 767 000
Population growth rate	2.2%
Life expectancy	59 (m), 63 (f)
Languages	Spanish, Quechua, Aymará
Adult literacy rate	83.1%
Currency	boliviano
	(US $1 = 5.76 bolivianos)
GDP (US million $)	8400
GDP per head (US $)	1081

In the 16th century Bolivia was conquered by Spain and was ruled until armed rebellion in 1825. The rich seams of silver attracted Spain, and minerals remain the basis of the Bolivian economy. Tin is important, but low world prices have reduced its value. The predominantly Amerindian population is poor, partly because of unstable government and partly because of widespread corruption. Many live by the illegal culture of coca, despite the international pressure which has forced the government to clamp down.

The rearing of livestock and some subsistence farming takes place on the high plateau. There has been some development on the Amazon lowlands in the east.

BRAZIL

The Federative Republic of Brazil
Map pages 191–2

Area	8 511 996 km²
	(3 286 500 sq miles)
Capital	Brasília
Member of	IADB, MERCOSUR
Population	159 636 000
Population growth rate	1.8%
Life expectancy	64 (m), 70 (f)
Language	Portuguese
Adult literacy rate	85.2%
Currency	100 centavos = 1 real
	(US $1 = 1.807 reais)
GDP (US million $)	768 800
GDP per head (US $)	4816

A land of astonishing contrasts, Brazil is the world's fifth largest country and contains its fourth greatest population. São Paulo has about 18 million people and is the heart of Brazil's large manufacturing industry, while in the Amazon basin Amerindians fight to maintain their ancient way of life.

Portugal established control over Brazil in the 16th century and brought large numbers of African slaves to work in the sugar plantations along the coast. Following independence, which occurred dramatically but peacefully in 1822, Brazil experienced rapid economic expansion, which still continues despite recurrent financial crises. Large mining enterprises combine with extensive coffee production and significant manufacturing; exports include cars, computers, aircraft and defence equipment. Because it possesses limited oil resources, Brazil has pioneered the use of methanol – derived from sugar cane – as a motor fuel, though the economics are doubtful. There are several schemes to generate hydroelectricity, such as the massive Itaipú project on the Paraná River. The Amazon basin is currently being opened up for mining, forestry and cattle rearing.

The Brazilian population is dominantly of European and African extraction. Marriages between the communities are common, and ethnic tension has been notably absent.

Rapid economic development has been bought at the cost of huge social inequalities in the country; the slums of the cities are notorious. Environmental destruction continues on a massive scale, especially in the rain forests of Amazonia.

CHILE

The Republic of Chile
Map pages 192–3

Area	756 626 km²
	(292 135 sq miles)
Capital	Santiago
Member of	IADB
Population	14 622 000
Population growth rate	1.7%
Life expectancy	72 (m), 77 (f)
Language	Spanish
Adult literacy rate	95.2%
Currency	Chilean peso
	(US $1 = 517.75 pesos)
GDP (US million $)	77 400
GDP per head (US $)	5293

The long narrow land of Chile stretches through three distinct climatic zones. To the north is the scorching Atacama desert, inhospitable and empty. In the south, the high winds, cool temperatures and heavy rainfall allow only sheep farming. The heart of the nation is found in the central zone, around the capital Santiago, with its benign, Mediterranean climate.

Agricultural exports, including fruit and wine, are important, but Chile's wealth comes largely from mining. Huge copper deposits in the desert and near Concepción, together with other minerals, have replaced the 19th-century export of nitrates. Manufacturing has also developed, processing local produce (such as fishmeal) and supplying the domestic market with textiles and cement.

Armed conflict ended Spanish rule in 1818. Between 1879 and 1893, Chile gained territory and minerals in the north in a war with Peru and Bolivia. The left-wing Allende government was overthrown in 1973 by a repressive military Junta led by General (later President) Pinochet. However, more stable, peaceful conditions have existed since 1990, allowing the economy to flourish.

COLOMBIA

The Republic of Colombia
Map page 190

Area	1 141 748 km²
	(440 831 sq miles)
Capital	Bogotá
Member of	ACS, Andean Comm, IADB
Population	36 162 000
Population growth rate	2.2%
Life expectancy	66 (m), 72 (f)
Language	Spanish
Adult literacy rate	91.3%
Currency	Colombian peso
	(US $1 = 1831.50 pesos)
GDP (US million $)	94 500
GDP per head (US $)	2613

A rich civilisation flourished in Colombia before the arrival of the Spanish, who found their El Dorado in the 16th century. Having pillaged the country of its gold, the colonists stayed until they were ejected in 1819, bequeathing an unequal division of land that has been a source of discord ever since. The rich cotton and sugar plantations of the fertile valleys are in strong contrast to the small, mainly Amerindian, farms of the mountains and lowland interior, which grow coffee for export and subsistence crops.

Colombia is an extremely diverse country with rich resources of emeralds, precious metals, coal and other mineral deposits. The capital, Bogotá, is a city of about 5 million people and the focus of manufacturing and commerce. To the east are extensive grassy plains and forests, which as yet have been little developed.

Efforts are being made to control and eliminate the huge illegal trade in marijuana and cocaine that supplies markets worldwide. Success depends upon finding alternative crops or work for the impoverished farmers, and by reaching an understanding with anti-government guerrilla groups who finance their activities through the drugs trade.

ECUADOR

The Republic of Ecuador

Map page 190

Area	272 045 km²
	(105 037 sq miles)
Capital	Quito
Member of	Andean Comm, IADB

Population	11 937 000
Population growth rate	2.3%
Life expectancy	67 (m), 72 (f)
Languages	Spanish, *Quechua*, other
	local languages
Adult literacy rate	90.1%

Currency	sucre
	(US $1 = 11 700 sucres)
GDP (US million $)	19 100
GDP per head (US $)	1600

The Incas of Peru seized control of Ecuador from its indigenous peoples in the 15th century. Within 100 years, however, they had been succeeded by the Spaniards, whose legacy of inequality survived Ecuador's independence in 1830.

The humid coast plain grows bananas, coffee and other crops for export, and at Guayaquil there is a major concentration of manufacturing. Oil was found in the Amazonian lowlands in the 1970s, but this sparsely inhabited area has not benefited from the resulting riches.

In recent times, Ecuador's economy has been badly affected by political wrangling and deadlock which frustrated effective decision-making.

GUYANA

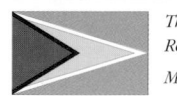

The Cooperative Republic of Guyana

Map page 190–1

Area	214 969 km²
	(83 000 sq miles)
Capital	Georgetown
Member of	ACS, CARICOM,
	COMM, IADB

Population	847 000
Population growth rate	0.5%
Life expectancy	62 (m), 68 (f)
Languages	English, *Hindi, Urdu,*
	Amerindian dialects
Adult literacy rate	98.1%

Currency	Guyana dollar
	(US $1 = SG 177.3)
GDP (US million $)	742
GDP per head (US $)	876

Formerly known as British Guiana, the country achieved independence in 1966. In the 17th century and later, African slaves and Asian workers were imported to work in the rice and sugar fields, resulting in an ethnically divided population. Most people live on the coastal lowlands, and much of Guyana's interior remains unexploited.

PARAGUAY

The Republic of Paraguay

Map page 192

Area	406 752 km²
	(157 048 sq miles)
Capital	Asunción
Member of	IADB, MERCOSUR

Population	5 085 000
Population growth rate	3%
Life expectancy	66 (m), 70 (f)
Languages	Spanish, *Guarani*
Adult literacy rate	92.1%

Currency	guarani
	(US $1 = 3320 guaranis)
GDP (US million $)	8700
GDP per head (US $)	1711

Asunción, the only sizable city in landlocked Paraguay, is the country's river port and gateway to international commerce. East of the Paraguay River, the fertile land allows for diverse farming, such as cotton, cereals, sugar cane and cattle; the western plains and swamps are lightly populated. Hydroelectric power provides virtually all the country's electricity.

Since independence from Spain in 1811, Paraguay's development has been hindered by wars with its neighbours, a succession of repressive governments and, now that infant democracy has replaced tyranny, political instability.

PERU

The Republic of Peru

Map page 190

Area	1 285 216 km²
	(496 225 sq miles)
Capital	Lima
Member of	APEC, IADB

Population	24 371 000
Population growth rate	2%
Life expectancy	66 (m), 70 (f)
Languages	Spanish, Quechua, Aymara
Adult literacy rate	88.7%

Currency	new sol
	(US $1 = 3.319 new sols)
GDP (US million $)	65 300
GDP per head (US $)	2679

Peru's coastal plain is desert, but crossed by several rivers that originate in the Andes. These enable many tropical crops to be grown on large estates. There are numerous cities lining the coast, including the capital, Lima, which has the continent's oldest university, dating from 1551. With a population of some 6 million people, however, Lima is better known for the size and squalor of its shanty towns. Most of the country's manufacturing is located along the coast; it

encompasses fish processing, textiles and metal refining.

Peru's high mountains are difficult to cultivate and yield a meagre income for the mainly Amerindian peasant population. The eastern lowlands have remained largely untouched, except by the recent exploitation of oil and natural gas.

Before the Spanish conquest in the 16th century, Peru was the heart of the Inca civilisation, which has left splendid remains, particularly at Cusco and Machu Picchu. Independence from Spain was gained in 1821. Until recently economic development was hindered by civil war and the cocaine trade, but firm leadership and the quelling of terrorist activity have improved prospects.

SURINAM

The Republic of Surinam

Map page 191

Area	163 265 km²
	(63 037 sq miles)
Capital	Paramaribo
Member of	ACS, CARICOM, IADB

Population	437 000
Population growth rate	1.1%
Life expectancy	64 (m), 71 (f)
Languages	Dutch, *Hindi, Javanese,*
	Sranang Tongo, Chinese, English
Adult literacy rate	93%

Currency	Surinam guilder
	(US $1 = 698.9 guilders)
GDP (US million $)	748
GDP per head (US $)	1711

Almost half the population of Surinam lives in Paramaribo; the interior of the country is largely forest and savannah. Bauxite and aluminium are the main exports; rice and sugar cane are important products. Surinam became independent from the Netherlands in 1975.

URUGUAY

The Eastern Republic of Uruguay

Map page 195

Area	176 215 km²
	(68 037 sq miles)
Capital	Montevideo
Member of	IADB, MERCOSUR

Population	3 221 000
Population growth rate	0.6%
Life expectancy	68 (m), 74 (f)
Language	Spanish
Adult literacy rate	96.8%

Currency	Uruguayan peso
	(US $1 = 11.43 pesos)
GDP (US million $)	20 200
GDP per head (US $)	6271

Uruguay gained independence from Spain in 1828 and then faced civil war and (along with Argentina and Brazil) conflict with Paraguay until the 1870s. Thereafter, immigration and expanding world markets for meat, wool and grain gave the country stability and prosperity until the mid 20th century. A period of recession, civil unrest and military government set the country's progress back, but civilian government since 1984 has seen major economic and social improvement. Financial services and tourism are helping to diversify Uruguay's economy.

VENEZUELA

The Republic of Venezuela

Map page 190

Area	912 050 km²
	(352 144 sq miles)
Capital	Caracas
Member of	ACS, Andean Comm,
	IADB, OPEC

Population	22 777 000
Population growth rate	2.5%
Life expectancy	69 (m), 75 (f)
Language	Spanish
Adult literacy rate	91.1%

Currency	bolivar
	(US $1 = 609.65 bolivars)
GDP (US million $)	107 500
GDP per head (US $)	4719

Emerging from a long period of Spanish rule in the early 19th century, Venezuela was a poor and backward country. A century later, the discovery of oil in Lake Maracaibo launched the country into a period of prosperity and rapid change. The huge reserves have been augmented by further finds in the Orinoco delta, but the country's excessive reliance on oil was compounded by a failure to develop its other resources adequately. During the 1980s, with the collapse of oil prices, Venezuela was afflicted by a serious recession.

Almost all the development is concentrated along the humid coast, notably at Caracas, which is the main manufacturing city. Caracas has grown explosively and now accommodates about 3.5 million people, many in slums. The interior consists of grassy plains, used for cattle ranching, and forested uplands, left largely to the Amerindians.

Venezuela has enormous reserves of oil, bauxite and iron ore. With its unspoilt beaches, tropical forests and in Angel Falls the world's highest waterfall, at 979 m (3212 ft), the country could also develop a thriving tourist industry. However, at present it has to import much of its food.

1903 Colombia loses Panama.

— 1910 —

1916 Hipólito Yrigoyen becomes first freely elected president of Argentina.

— 1920 —

1928–35 Chaco Wars between Bolivia and Paraguay.

— 1930 —

1930 Military coups in Argentina and Brazil.

1932 Civilian rule restored to Argentina.

1936 Fascist regime established in Paraguay.

— 1940 —

1942 Brazil enters Second World War on the side of the Allies.

1943 Military rule in Argentina.

1946–55 Juan Perón is President of Argentina.

1949–58 Some 200 000 die during 'La Violencia' in Colombia.

— 1950 —

1952 Eva (Evita) Perón, the popular wife of Juan Perón, dies.

1954 Military coup in Paraguay.

1955 Perón overthrown in military coup.

— 1960 —

1964 Bloodless right-wing coup in Brazil.

— 1970 —

1973 Military coup in Chile; junta, led by General Pinochet, aims to eradicate Marxism. Perón returned to power in Argentina.

1974 Perón dies.

1976 Military junta in Argentina; thousands of alleged left-wing activists 'disappear'.

— 1980 —

1982 Falklands War between Argentina and Britain.

1983 Free elections held in Argentina.

1985 Free elections held in Brazil and Uruguay.

1989 Free elections held in Chile.

— 1990 —

1991 Argentina, Brazil, Paraguay and Uruguay sign trade agreement.

1992 Peru gives Bolivia access to Pacific port of Ilo. Earth Summit held in Rio de Janeiro.

1993 Free elections held in Paraguay.

1996-7 Marxist revolutionaries hold hostages in Japanese Embassy in Peru.

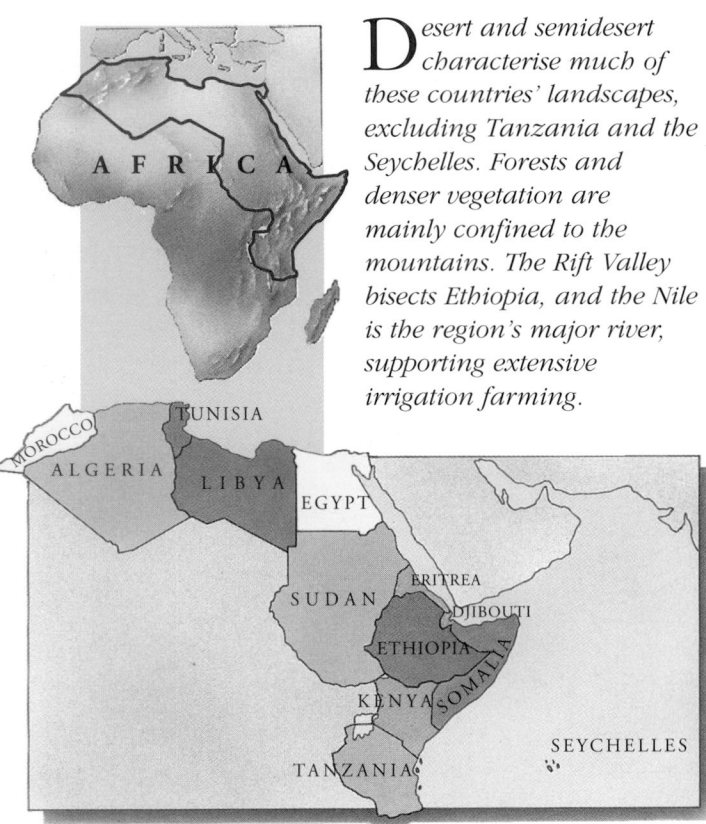

A F R I C A

TUNISIA

MOROCCO

ALGERIA   LIBYA

EGYPT

SUDAN

ERITREA

DJIBOUTI

ETHIOPIA

SOMALIA

KENYA

SEYCHELLES

TANZANIA

*D*esert and semidesert
characterise much of
these countries' landscapes,
excluding Tanzania and the
Seychelles. Forests and
denser vegetation are
mainly confined to the
mountains. The Rift Valley
bisects Ethiopia, and the Nile
is the region's major river,
supporting extensive
irrigation farming.

Associated Territories

**BRITISH INDIAN
OCEAN TERRITORY**
Parent country
UK
Map page 113

MAYOTTE
Parent country
FRANCE
Map page 197

WESTERN SAHARA
Parent country
DISPUTED Administered
by Morocco
Map page 198

Abbreviations

COMESA *Common Market
for Eastern and Southern
Africa*
COMM *Commonwealth*
IDB *Islamic Development
Bank*
LAS *League of Arab States*
NAM *Non-Aligned Movement*
OAPEC *Organisation of Arab
Petroleum Exporting
Countries*
OPEC *Organisation of
Petroleum Exporting
Countries*
SADC *Southern African
Development Community*

GDP *Gross Domestic Product*

ALGERIA

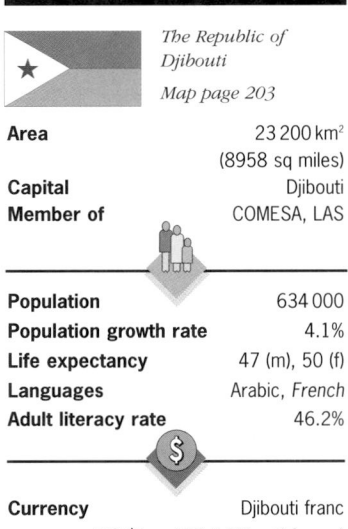

*The Democratic and
Popular Republic of
Algeria*
Map pages 198–9

Area	2 381 741 km²
	(919 595 sq miles)
Capital	Algiers
Member of	LAS, OPEC

Population	29 276 767
Population growth rate	2.5%
Life expectancy	65 (m), 66 (f)
Languages	Arabic, French, Berber
Adult literacy rate	61.6%

Currency	Algerian dinar
	(US $1 = 68.93 dinars)
GDP (US million $)	49 000
GDP per head (US $)	1673

Most Algerians live in the
northern coastal plain. South of
the Atlas Mountains is the Sahara
Desert.

Nomadic Berbers have lived in
Algeria since about 3000 BC. The
land has been ruled by a series
of invaders, who sought control
of the great camel trade routes
across the Sahara. France took
control of Algeria in 1830, and
encouraged French immigration.
Following protracted fighting,
there was a French withdrawal
in 1962, when about one million
settlers left Algeria.

The country has huge oil and
gas reserves which account for
96 per cent of Algeria's exports.
By the late 1990s, the economy
was severely affected by the
collapse in oil prices, an
unemployment rate of 20 per
cent and a civil war.

The army had been the key to
power since independence. In
1992 army chiefs cancelled the
country's first democratic
election to prevent an Islamist
government coming to power.
This provoked a civil war in
1997 and 1998.

DJIBOUTI

*The Republic of
Djibouti*
Map page 203

Area	23 200 km²
	(8958 sq miles)
Capital	Djibouti
Member of	COMESA, LAS

Population	634 000
Population growth rate	4.1%
Life expectancy	47 (m), 50 (f)
Languages	Arabic, French
Adult literacy rate	46.2%

Currency	Djibouti franc
	(US $1 = 177.7 Djibouti francs)
GDP (US million $)	444
GDP per head (US $)	893

Primarily a desert country,
Djibouti has few oases. The
majority of its people live in the
port of Djibouti, which gives
access to Ethiopia. Trade has
been disrupted by regional
conflicts, and this has led to
considerable poverty.

EGYPT

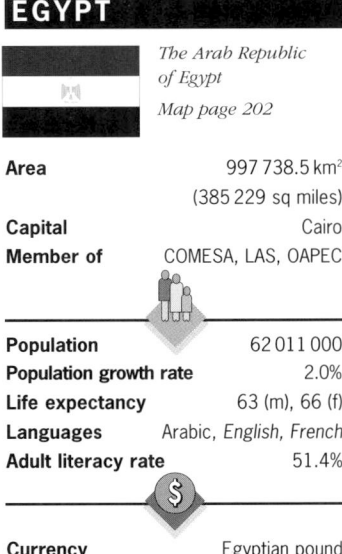

*The Arab Republic
of Egypt*
Map page 202

Area	997 738.5 km²
	(385 229 sq miles)
Capital	Cairo
Member of	COMESA, LAS, OAPEC

Population	62 011 000
Population growth rate	2.0%
Life expectancy	63 (m), 66 (f)
Languages	Arabic, English, French
Adult literacy rate	51.4%

Currency	Egyptian pound
	(US $1 = £E 3.4)
GDP (US million $)	82 100
GDP per head (US $)	1324

One of the world's earliest
civilisations flowered in Egypt
from about 3000 BC, leaving
magnificent monuments such as
the pyramids. However, Egypt
has been ruled by other empires
for most of the last 2500 years,
only gaining independence from
Britain in 1936.

Most of the country is desert,
traversed by a thin ribbon of
settlement and cultivation along
the Nile, which is Egypt's lifeblood. When the Suez Canal
opened in 1869, it significantly
reduced the length of sea
voyages between Europe and
the Far East; the canal revenues
continue to be an important
national asset to Egypt. The
Aswan Dam, completed in 1971,
regulates natural floods and
provides hydroelectricity and
water for irrigation. Now two
more vast irrigation schemes are
underway: the Al Salam canal in
the northeast and the Toshka
canal in the far south.

Modern Egypt has experienced
substantial commercial and
industrial development. Its
economy has been boosted by
11 years of oil production, which
accounts for half the total
exports. Abundant reserves of
natural gas in the Nile delta and
offshore in the Mediterranean
await exploitation.

The capital, Cairo, is a city of
some 16 million inhabitants.
Commercial sectors and
prosperous suburbs are in sharp
contrast to vast numbers of
small traders and sprawling
shanty towns. During the 1990s
terrorist acts by militant Islamic
fundamentalists affected Egypt's
important tourist industry.

ERITREA

The State of Eritrea
Map page 202

Area	121 144 km²
	(46 774 sq miles)
Capital	Asmara
Member of	COMESA

Population	3 409 000
Population growth rate	2.7%
Life expectancy	48 (m), 51 (f)
Languages	Arabic, Tigre, English
Adult literacy rate	20%

Currency	nakfa (US $1 = 7.30 nakfa)
GDP (US million $)	(1996) 714
GDP per head (US $)	209

Eritrea's 30 year long fight for
independence from Ethiopia,
achieved in 1993, devastated the
country. In 1997 trade relations
with Ethiopia deteriorated, and
Eritrea launched its own
currency. Territorial claims by
Ethiopia in 1998 led to border
clashes which finally developed
into full-scale war.

There is some mining, light
industry and fishing, but the
economy is largely dependent
on foreign aid.

ETHIOPIA

*The Federal Democratic
Republic of Ethiopia*
Map pages 203

Area	1 133 380 km²
	(437 600 sq miles)
Capital	Addis Ababa
Member of	COMESA

Population	60 148 000
Population growth rate	2.9%
Life expectancy	46 (m), 49 (f)
Languages	Amharic, English, many
	local languages
Adult literacy rate	35.5%

Currency	birr (US $1 = 7.51 birr)
GDP (US million $)	5663
GDP per head (US $)	94

Formerly known as Abyssinia,
Ethiopia has maintained its
independence for over 2000
years, with the exception of a
brief Italian occupation in the
1930s. Since AD 330 it has had its
own Christian Church.

Most of Ethiopia is plateau and
mountain, rising to over 4000 m
(13 100 ft). Rain is sufficient to
support grains, other crops and
livestock, though devastating
droughts occur periodically.
The surrounding lowlands are
desert and semidesert.

Ethiopia is a desperately poor
country. The majority of people
eke out a living from small
patches of land, and are virtually
self-sufficient. Roads, electricity
and other basic facilities are not
available for many people.

When Eritrea became
independent in 1993, Ethiopia
became landlocked, as its ports
were now in Eritrea. Conflicts of
interest led to a breakdown in
trading relationships.

Ethiopia is a multi-ethnic
state, dominated administratively
by Tigrayans from the northern
province of Tigray. In 1998 a
new Tigrayan map showed part
of Eritrea as Ethiopian. This
triggered border clashes which
developed into a vicious war.

KENYA

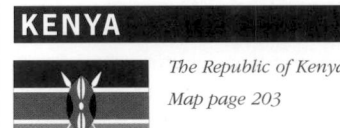

The Republic of Kenya
Map page 203

Area	580 367 km²
	(224 081 sq miles)
Capital	Nairobi
Member of	COMESA, COMM

Population	28 414 000
Population growth rate	2.9%
Life expectancy	57 (m), 61 (f)
Languages	Kiswahili, English,
	Kikuyu, Luo
Adult literacy rate	78.1%

Currency	Kenya shilling
	(US $1 = Ks 72.1)
GDP (US million $)	10 165
GDP per head (US $)	357

As a political entity, Kenya is
barely 100 years old. It includes
several major African tribes and
a number of European settlers,
the latter attracted by the climate
and fertility of the south-west
highlands and the potential for
cash crops, such as tea and
coffee. The rest of the country is
dry and sparsely inhabited.

For some 30 years after its
independence in 1963, Kenya
was regarded as a model of
economic success, producing tea
and a wide range of other crops
and developing significant
manufacturing. Tourism, based
on numerous game reserves and
national parks, provided the
chief source of foreign
exchange. However, in the late
1990s, Kenya's fortunes changed

because of tribal hostilities, political incompetence and corruption, along with debt and the withdrawal of foreign aid. Income from tourism has halved, roads and railways are in disrepair and the country has become politically and economically unstable.

LIBYA

The Great Socialist People's Libyan Arab Jamahiriya
Map page 199

Area	1 775 500 km²
	(685 524 sq miles)
Capital	Tripoli
Member of	IDB, LAS, OPEC

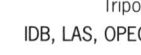

Population	5 784 000
Population growth rate	3.6%
Life expectancy	62 (m), 65 (f)
Languages	Arabic, English, Italian
Adult literacy rate	76.2%

Currency	1000 dirhams = 1 Libyan dinar
	(US $1 = 450 dirhams)
GDP (US million $)	29 727
GDP per head (US $)	5498

Primarily a desert country, Libya has been occupied and fought over for more than 2000 years. At independence in 1951, Libya was a poor country, but its economy has been transformed by oil reserves. Saharan ground water supplies huge irrigation schemes and the coastal cities, where major industrialisation has occurred. In the north of the country, winter rains allow grain and Mediterranean crops to grow.

Libyan leader Colonel Gaddafi's association with international terrorist organisations led to a UN ban on travel to Libya, and other sanctions, between 1992 and 1999. Some have been lifted.

MOROCCO

The Kingdom of Morocco
Map page 198

Area	710 850 km²
	(274 461 sq miles)
Capital	Rabat
Member of	IDB, LAS

Population	27 310 000
Population growth rate	2.2%
Life expectancy	62 (m), 66 (f)
Languages	Arabic, Berber, Spanish, French
Adult literacy rate	43.7%

Currency	Moroccan dirham
	(US $1 = 10.1 dirhams)
GDP (US million $)	37 300
GDP per head (US $)	1365

Morocco, with both Atlantic and Mediterranean coastlines, and with mountains rising to over 4000 m (13 100 ft), is a fertile

land: a wide range of vegetables, fruits and other crops provide major agricultural exports. The economy is also assisted by huge phosphate resources and substantial manufacturing growth, including fruit canning, textiles and car assembly plants.

After the Moorish invasion of Spain in the 8th century AD, Morocco became the centre of an empire which extended from the centre of Iberia to Senegal. Morocco's ancient cities, such as Fès and Marrakech, provide the basis of a flourishing tourist industry.

Independence, interrupted by French control from 1912, was regained peacefully in 1956.

Morocco has annexed the territory to the south known as Western Sahara, but a UN-organised referendum will settle the sovereignty of the area.

SEYCHELLES

The Republic of Seychelles
Map page 207

Area	454 km²
	(175.3 sq miles)
Capital	Victoria, on Mahé
Member of	COMESA, COMM, SADC

Population	75 000
Population growth rate	1.3%
Life expectancy	65 (m), 74 (f)
Languages	Creole, English, French
Adult literacy rate	85%

Currency	Seychelles rupee
	(US $1 = 5.41 rupees)
GDP (US million $)	535
GDP per head (US $)	7133

A chain of more than 100 coral and granite islands, the Seychelles lure tourists to a tropical paradise of white beaches and forested hills. First claimed by France and later by Britain, the Seychelles declared independence in 1976.

SOMALIA

The Somali Democratic Republic
Map pages 203

Area	637 657 km²
	(246 201 sq miles)
Capital	Mogadishu
Member of	LAS

Population	10 217 000
Population growth rate	1.6%
Life expectancy	45 (m), 49 (f)
Languages	Somali, Arabic, English, Italian
Adult literacy rate	24.1%

Currency	Somali shilling
	(US $1 = 2620 shillings)
GDP (US million $)	(1995) 1132
GDP per head (US $)	110

Only in Somalia's mountains is there enough rain to support agriculture and reasonable grazing. Rivers provide water for crops, including bananas for export, but the main exports are live animals, meat and hides.

In 1991, a 22 year long military dictatorship was overthrown. Since then the country has suffered such vicious tribal fighting that the UN, with the USA, intervened. The northern region has a government of sorts, but the rest is run by rival warlords. The country is very poor and suffers severe droughts.

SUDAN

The Republic of Sudan
Map pages 202–3

Area	2 505 813 km²
	(967 500 sq miles)
Capital	Khartoum
Member of	COMESA, LAS

Population	27 899 000
Population growth rate	2.9%
Life expectancy	49 (m), 52 (f)
Languages	Arabic, English and local languages
Adult literacy rate	46.1%

Currency	Sudanese dinar
	(US $1 = 254 Sudanese dinars);
	also Sudanese pound (1 dinar = £S 10)
GDP (US million $)	2400
GDP per head (US $)	86

Before national independence in 1956, the African peoples of southern Sudan rebelled against rule by the northern Arabs, and a civil war has continued ever since. About 1.3 million people have died in the conflict and more than 3 million have been displaced. Further suffering has been caused by famine following drought, which might have been alleviated if not for the fighting.

The north is desert but much of the rest of the country is savannah, suitable for growing tropical grains, groundnuts and livestock, which form the basis of its subsistence farming.

The Blue Nile and White Nile supply extensive irrigation to grow cotton, sugar cane and other tropical crops for export.

Because of internal repression and alleged support for inter-national terrorism, Sudan was isolated in the world community. Change came in 1999: the ban on multi-party politics was lifted and income was expected from the country's first oil exports.

TANZANIA

The United Republic of Tanzania
Map page 204

Area	945 087 km²
	(364 900 sq miles)
Capital	Dodoma
Member of	COMESA, COMM, SADC

Population	31 507 000
Population growth rate	3.1%
Life expectancy	52 (m), 55 (f)
Languages	Swahili, English, many local languages
Adult literacy rate	67.8%

Currency	Tanzanian shilling
	(US $1 = 737.5 Tanzanian shillings)
GDP (US million $)	8300
GDP per head (US $)	235

Much of the land is fairly high, rising to Mount Kilimanjaro, Africa's highest peak at 5895 m (19 341 ft). The interior is cooler than the lowland coastal strip, but rainfall is limited. The dramatic scenery and abundant wildlife provide excellent potential for tourism.

Tanzania came into existence with the union of Tanganyika and Zanzibar (with Pemba). Under the government of President Nyerere, 15 million people were moved from their scattered lands into villages. Farm production plummeted, and most people have drifted back to their own lands. This is a poor country with a crippling debt repayment burden, but a gold rush near Lake Victoria in the late 1990s could provide a significant boost to the economy.

TUNISIA

The Republic of Tunisia
Map page 199

Area	163 610 km²
	(63 170 sq miles)
Capital	Tunis
Member of	COMM, LAS, NAM

Population	9 215 000
Population growth rate	2.3%
Life expectancy	69 (m), 73 (f)
Languages	Arabic, Berber, French
Adult literacy rate	66.7%

Currency	1000 millimes = 1 Tunisian dinar
	(US $1 = 1235.4 millimes)
GDP (US million $)	19 900
GDP per head (US $)	2159

The eastern end of the Atlas Mountains gives northern Tunisia adequate rain for flourishing agriculture, such as olive and citrus groves. Oil, phosphates and other minerals are also important resources. Desert dominates the south, with large salt accumulations in the depressions.

There has been relatively stable rule since independence in 1956, allowing considerable development. A growing tourist industry is based on the Roman remains and the beaches.

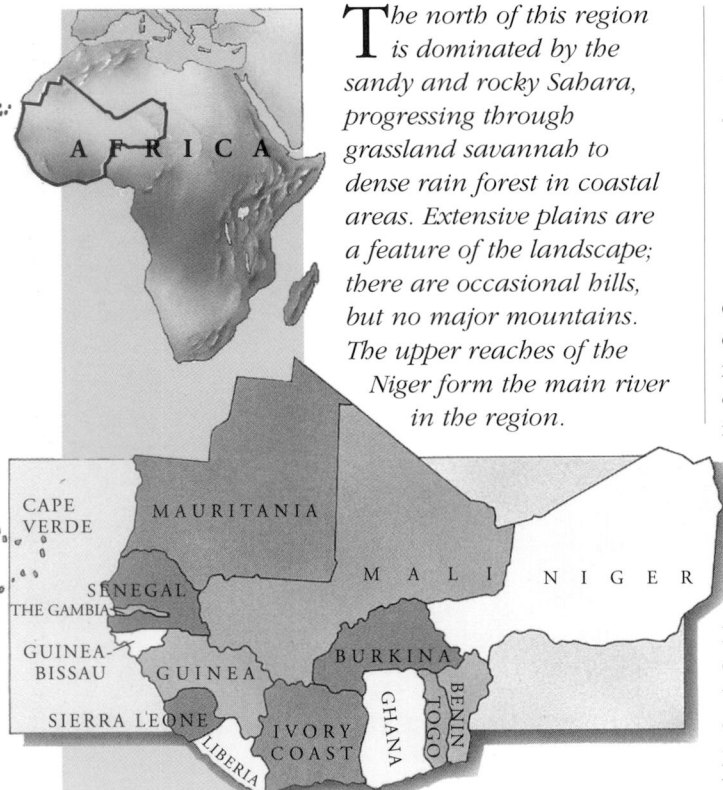

The north of this region is dominated by the sandy and rocky Sahara, progressing through grassland savannah to dense rain forest in coastal areas. Extensive plains are a feature of the landscape; there are occasional hills, but no major mountains. The upper reaches of the Niger form the main river in the region.

BENIN

The Republic of Benin

Map page 200

Area	112 622 km²
	(43 484 sq miles)
Capital	Porto-Novo
Member of	ECOWAS, FZ

Population	5 828 000
Population growth rate	3.0%
Life expectancy	51 (m), 56 (f)
Languages	French, Bariba, Fulani,
	Fon and Yoruba
Adult literacy rate	37.0%

Currency	CFA franc
	(US $1 = 643.7 CFA francs)
GDP (US million $)	2174
GDP per head (US $)	373

Benin became independent from France in 1960, and was known as Dahomey until 1975, when it was renamed after the Bight of Benin. It is an agricultural country with many subsistence farmers. Export crops such as oil palms and cocoa grow in the wetter, densely settled south. Cotonou is a thriving port and industrial centre. The north of the country is savannah grassland. Beautiful wildlife parks and a sandy coast offer potential for tourism.

BURKINA

The Republic of Burkina

Map page 200

Area	274 200 km²
	(105 870 sq miles)
Capital	Ouagadougou
Member of	ECOWAS, FZ

Population	11 087 000
Population growth rate	2.7%
Life expectancy	45 (m), 47 (f)

Languages	French, Mossi, many local
	languages
Adult literacy rate	19.2%

Currency	CFA franc
	(US $1 = 643.7 CFA francs)
GDP (US million $)	2395
GDP per head (US $)	216

Ouagadougou has been the capital of the Mossi people and their former empire since the 15th century, but they lost their independence to French rule from 1895 until 1960. Lying on the edge of the Sahara, Burkina's rainfall is low and variable and temperatures are high, allowing some crops and forage for livestock to grow. However, there have been severe droughts in recent decades, whilst unstable government and ethnic diversity have added to Burkina's problems. The Volta River, from which Burkina's former name of Upper Volta derives, provides potential for agricultural development.

CAPE VERDE

The Republic of Cape Verde

Map page 200

Area	4033 km²
	(1557 sq miles)
Capital	Praia
Member of	ECOWAS

Population	406 000
Population growth rate	2.3%
Life expectancy	64 (m), 71 (f)
Languages	Portuguese, Creole
Adult literacy rate	71.6%

Currency	Cape Verde escudo
	(US $1 = 94.71 escudos)
GDP (US million $)	425
GDP per head (US $)	1046

After 500 years of Portuguese rule, in 1975 Cape Verde gained independence. Despite highland rising to 2829 m (9281 ft), the islands suffer serious droughts. Fishing and farming are the main occupations; the beaches offer potential for tourism.

THE GAMBIA

The Republic of The Gambia

Map page 200

Area	11 295 km²
	(4361 sq miles)
Capital	Banjul
Member of	COMM, ECOWAS

Population	1 169 000
Population growth rate	4.1%
Life expectancy	43 (m), 47 (f)
Languages	English, Mandinka, Fula
	Wolof, other local languages
Adult literacy rate	38.6%

Currency	dalasi (US $1 = 11.72 dalasi)
GDP (US million $)	385
GDP per head (US $)	329

The country is dominated by the River Gambia, which is also a trade artery for Senegal. Fishing, groundnut cultivation, coastal tourism and subsistence farming are the main economic activities. British rule from 1664 to 1965 left a strong influence.

GHANA

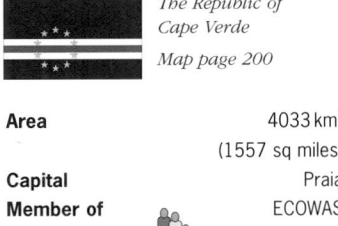

The Republic of Ghana

Map page 200

Area	238 537 km²
	(92 100 sq miles)
Capital	Accra
Member of	COMM, ECOWAS

Population	18 338 000
Population growth rate	3.1%
Life expectancy	54 (m), 58 (f)
Languages	English, many local
	languages
Adult literacy rate	64.5%

Currency	cedi
	(US $1 = 2569 cedis)
GDP (US million $)	7194
GDP per head (US $)	392

From the 15th to 19th centuries, Ghana – then known as the Gold Coast – was a source of gold and slaves for European traders. Kumasi, founded in the 17th century, was capital of the Ashanti empire until the British destroyed it and brought the area under British control. In 1957 the country became the first African state to achieve independence from Britain, and was named Ghana.

At independence, Ghana was relatively rich. Cocoa, oil palm and rubber, all grown in the south, were major exports, as was gold. Subsistence farming and livestock dominated the economies of the drier and less fertile centre and north.

Ghana has had a long period of political stability. The country, however, is poor. Economic mismanagement caused the decline of export crops in favour of subsistence farming, and debt repayments are high. More than a third of Ghana's income derives from exports from the Ashanti goldfields, but the continuing fall in the price of gold threatens growth.

GUINEA

The Republic of Guinea

Map page 200

Area	245 857 km²
	(94 926 sq miles)
Capital	Conakry
Member of	ECOWAS, IDB

Population	7 614 000
Population growth rate	2.9%
Life expectancy	44 (m), 45 (f)
Languages	French, Soussou, Manika,
	other local languages
Adult literacy rate	35.9%

Currency	franc guinéen
	(US $1 = 1340 francs guinéen)
GDP (US million $)	3566
GDP per head (US $)	468

In 1958, Guinea severed political connections with France. For the next 26 years, under the repressive rule of Sekou Toure, Guinea became one of the world's poorest countries. In the 1990s democracy was established and trading links with the West opened up. The country has become a haven for refugees from warring neighbouring countries. The land is well-watered and fertile, but the basis of the economy lies in rich deposits of minerals such as bauxite.

GUINEA-BISSAU

The Republic of Guinea-Bissau

Map page 200

Area	36 125 km²
	(13 948 sq miles)
Capital	Bissau
Member of	ECOWAS, FZ, IDB

Population	1 112 000
Population growth rate	2.1%
Life expectancy	41 (m), 44 (f)
Languages	Portuguese, Creole
Adult literacy rate	54.9%

Currency	CFA franc
	(US $1 = 643.7 CFA francs)
GDP (US million $)	141
GDP per head (US $)	131

A poor country when it gained independence from Portugal in 1974, Guinea-Bissau was then devastated by 11 years of civil war, which erupted once again in 1998 for a year. The main cash crop is groundnuts, but there are unexploited resources such as large areas of forest.

IVORY COAST

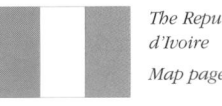

The Republic of Côte d'Ivoire

Map page 200

Area	322 462 km²
	(124 503 sq miles)
Capital	Yamoussoukro
Member of	ECOWAS

Population	14 300 000
Population growth rate	3.6%
Life expectancy	50 (m), 54 (f)
Languages	French, many local
	languages
Adult literacy rate	40.1%

Currency	CFA franc
	(US $1 = 643.7 CFA francs)
GDP (US million $)	11 270
GDP per head (US $)	736

Trade in ivory and slaves drew Europeans to the Ivory Coast from the 15th century to the 19th century. Towards the end of this period the country came under French control. Under the colonial regime, products such as rubber and cocoa made the south prosperous; the drier north remained little affected.

Since independence in 1960, relatively outward-looking policies have been pursued. Electrification has proceeded, there is a good road network and an efficient railway from Abidjan provides neighbouring Burkina with its only rail link to the sea. With approximately 3 million inhabitants, Abidjan is the centre for a major coastal tourist industry based on long, sandy beaches.

The Ivory Coast is the world's leading cocoa producer; most of the population is engaged in subsistence and cash crop farming. Droughts in the north in recent decades have caused considerable hardship. There are many African tribes and a significant number of European settlers in a country strongly influenced by the French language and customs.

LIBERIA

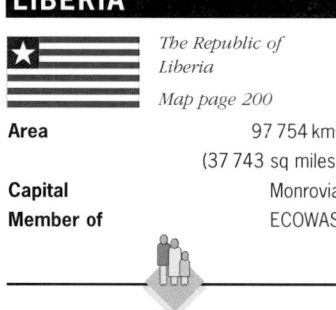

The Republic of Liberia

Map page 200

Area	97 754 km²
	(37 743 sq miles)
Capital	Monrovia
Member of	ECOWAS

Population	2 879 000
Population growth rate	3.2%
Life expectancy	54 (m), 57 (f)
Languages	English, many local
	languages and dialects
Adult literacy rate	38.3%

Currency	Liberian dollar (and US dollar)
	(US $1 = L $1)
GDP (US million $)	2385
GDP per head (US $)	1124

Early in the 19th century, Liberia was created by freed slaves returning from North America, and in 1847 it was recognised as an independent country. During the 20th century, large rubber plantations and a sizable fleet of ships trading under Liberia's flag of convenience have financed development. Despite substantial timber and mineral resources, the country remains poor, having been in the throes of a bloody civil war during the 1980s and much of the 1990s.

MALI

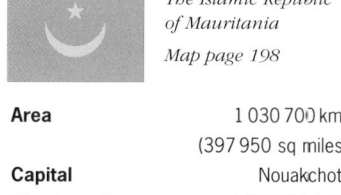

The Republic of Mali

Map pages 198 & 200

Area	1 240 192 km²
	(478 841 sq miles)
Capital	Bamako
Member of	ECOWAS

Population	11 480 000
Population growth rate	2.8%
Life expectancy	55 (m), 58 (f)
Languages	French and 12 other official
	languages
Adult literacy rate	31.0%

Currency	CFA franc
	(US $1 = 643.7 CFA francs)
GDP (US million $)	2672
GDP per head (US $)	232

Once the centre of a great empire, Mali is a landlocked arid waste which periodically suffers drought. Timbuktu on the Niger was founded in the 11th century and flourished with the trans-Sahara camel caravans. Independence in 1960 was followed by dictatorial rule, which ended in 1991. Most people depend on livestock and limited farming. Cotton growing and gold production are also important sources of revenue.

MAURITANIA

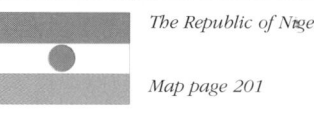

The Islamic Republic of Mauritania

Map page 198

Area	1 030 700 km²
	(397 950 sq miles)
Capital	Nouakchott
Member of	ECOWAS, LAS

Population	2 392 000
Population growth rate	2.5%
Life expectancy	50 (m), 53 (f)
Languages	Arabic, French, many local
	languages
Adult literacy rate	37.7%

Currency	ouguiya
	(US $1 = 208.1 ouguiyas)
GDP (US million $)	1098
GDP per head (US $)	459

Most of Mauritania is desert, but the country has major mineral resources and the south has enough rain for agriculture. Civil unrest has slowed development since independence in 1960.

NIGER

The Republic of Niger

Map page 201

Area	1 267 000 km²
	(489 191 sq miles)
Capital	Niamey
Member of	ECOWAS, IDB

Population	9 470 000
Population growth rate	3.2%
Life expectancy	45 (m), 48 (f)
Languages	French, many local
	languages
Adult literacy rate	13.6%

Currency	CFA franc
	(US $1 = 643.7 CFA francs)
GDP (US million $)	1857
GDP per head (US $)	196

There is enough rainfall for limited rain-fed agriculture in the south of this desert country, but the most fertile areas are those seasonally flooded by the Niger River, and around the shores of Lake Chad. Nomadic livestock herding is also important. The Sahel droughts that occurred from 1973 caused severe hardship, alleviated by international aid. Uranium mining in the Air Mountains gave a short-lived boost to the economy in the 1980s, and Niamey, the capital, is a modern and in places elegant city. However Niger, independent since 1960, continues to face a difficult future.

SENEGAL

The Republic of Senegal

Map page 200

Area	196 722 km²
	(75 955 sq miles)
Capital	Dakar
Member of	ECOWAS

Population	8 802 000
Population growth rate	2.7%
Life expectancy	48 (m), 50 (f)
Languages	French, many local
	languages
Adult literacy rate	33.1%

Currency	CFA franc
	(US $1 = 643.7 CFA francs)
GDP (US million $)	4824
GDP per head (US $)	548

Located on the western tip of Africa, Senegal has experienced serious but not devastating drought in recent decades. Most people live in the wetter west, where subsistence farming and groundnut production typify the country's agriculture.

Dakar, the capital, has a fine port and a railway link to Mali. A thriving modern city, it is both a tourist resort and a centre for manufacturing.

Despite a stable government since independence in 1960, a strong French influence and good education, the majority of Senegalese remain poor. Ethnic conflict is a recurrent problem. In the southern province of Casamance there has been 17 years of guerrilla warfare by rebels seeking independence.

SIERRA LEONE

The Republic of Sierra Leone

Map page 200

Area	71 740 km²
	(27 699 sq miles)
Capital	Freetown
Member of	COMM, ECOWAS

Population	4 428 000
Population growth rate	2.5%
Life expectancy	32 (m), 36 (f)
Languages	English, Krio (Creole), other
	local languages
Adult literacy rate	31.4%

Currency	leone (US $1 = 1726 leones)
GDP (US million $)	941
GDP per head (US $)	212

In 1787 Freetown, the capital, was founded as a refuge for freed African slaves. Sierra Leone came under British control in the 19th century; independence was granted in 1961. The nation has rich mineral resources, including diamonds, gold, iron ore and bauxite.

The country has endured an eight-year-long civil war between the government and a rebel movement seeking control of the areas rich in minerals. A Nigerian-led peace-keeping force intervened in 1998. Further fighting ensued but, by mid 1999, a peace settlement was drafted which resulted in the rebels having a share in government.

TOGO

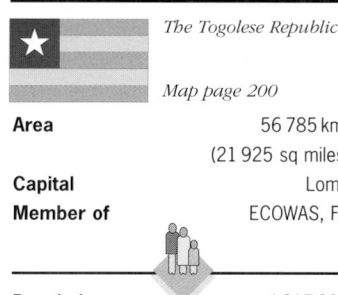

The Togolese Republic

Map page 200

Area	56 785 km²
	(21 925 sq miles)
Capital	Lomé
Member of	ECOWAS, FZ

Population	4 317 000
Population growth rate	3.1%
Life expectancy	49 (m), 52 (f)
Languages	French, Kabiye, Ewe,
	other local languages
Adult literacy rate	51.7%

Currency	CFA franc
	(US $1 = 643.7 CFA francs)
GDP (US million $)	1400
GDP per head (US $)	324

Subsistence farming is the dominant activity of Togo. Its main exports used to be cash crops, such as cocoa and groundnuts, but these have declined in recent years. There are phosphates, but their international prices are unreliable. The capital, Lomé, is the focus of modern economic development, which includes transit trade for inland states. Togo, which contains two main tribal groups, was granted independence in 1960.

20TH-CENTURY LANDMARKS

1901 Ashanti (Ghana) annexed by Britain.

1903–35 Railway built between Ivory Coast and Burkina.

— 1910 —

1914 Togo invaded by Britain and France.

1915 Guinea-Bissau interior subdued by Portuguese.

1919 Liberia cedes large inland areas to French control.

— 1920 —

1920 Mauritania made a French colony.

1926 Liberia grants 400 000 ha (1 000 000 acres) to Firestone Tire and Rubber Co.

— 1930 —

1931 Liberia examined by League of Nations after charges of forced labour and slavery.

— 1940 —

1940–2 Vichy government rules Ivory Coast.

1947 Upper Volta (Burkina) made part of the French Union.

— 1950 —

1959 Mali and Senegal form federation.

— 1960 —

1960 Senegal withdraws from federation with Mali.

1966 Military coups in Upper Volta and Ghana.

1968 Military coup in Mali; uranium mined in Niger.

— 1970 —

1970 Guinean exiles and Portuguese troops try to invade Guinea.

1973 Mali and Niger suffer droughts.

1974 Military coup in Niger.

— 1980 —

1980 Military coup in Liberia.

1982 The Gambia and Senegal form limited federation.

1984 Military coup in Guinea; drought in Niger.

1985 Mali and Burkina fight six-day war.

1987 Blaise Compaoré seizes power in Burkina.

— 1990 —

1990 Start of civil war in Liberia.

1992 Ghana and Mali hold multiparty elections.

1993 Niger holds democratic elections.

1997 General election in Liberia offers hope of peace. Military coup and civil war in Sierra Leone.

1998 Civil war in Guinea-Bissau.

1999 Civil war in Sierra Leone.

CENTRAL AFRICA

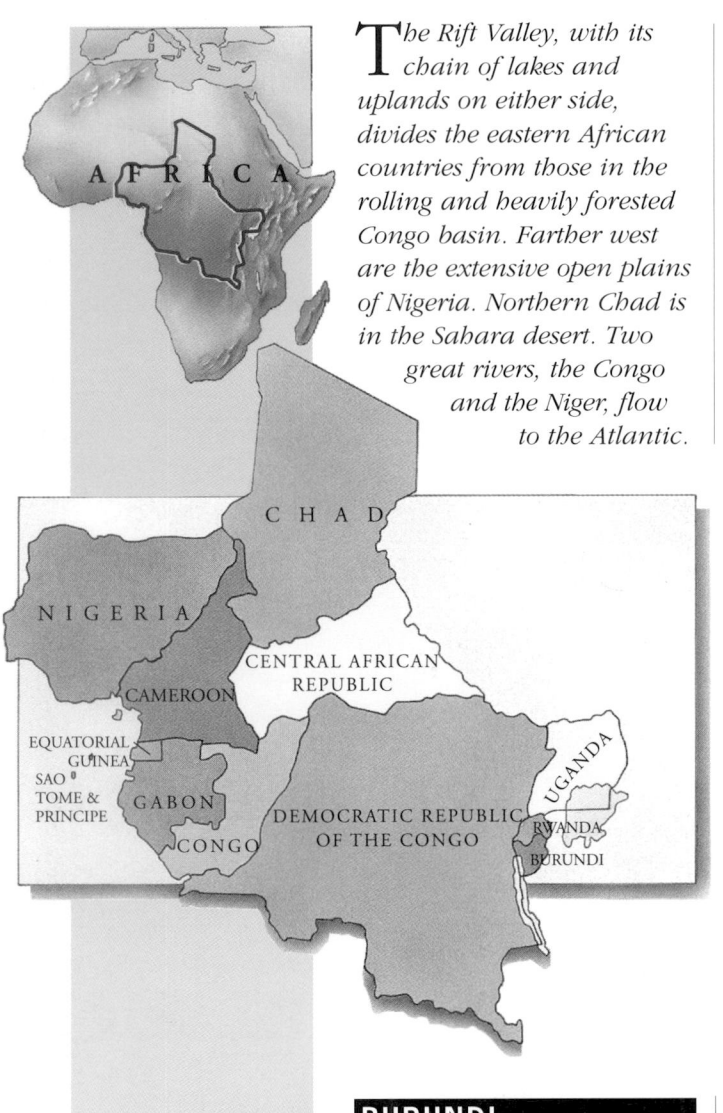

The Rift Valley, with its chain of lakes and uplands on either side, divides the eastern African countries from those in the rolling and heavily forested Congo basin. Farther west are the extensive open plains of Nigeria. Northern Chad is in the Sahara desert. Two great rivers, the Congo and the Niger, flow to the Atlantic.

BURUNDI

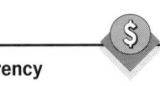

The Republic of Burundi

Map page 204

Area	27 834 km²
	(10 747 sq miles)
Capital	Bujumbura
Member of	COMESA

Population	6 194 000
Population growth rate	3%
Life expectancy	43 (m), 46 (f)
Languages	French, *Kirundi, Swahili*
Adult literacy rate	35.3%

Currency	Burundian franc
	(US $1 = 550.1 Burundian francs)
GDP (US million $)	1220
GDP per head (US $)	197

On the edge of the African Rift Valley, Burundi is a mountainous country. It is well watered and intensively farmed to feed its dense population. In addition to subsistence crops, some coffee is grown as a cash crop.

The Tutsi people gained control of Burundi in the 16th century and established feudal authority over the Hutu majority. Since its independence from Belgium in 1962, Burundi has been racked by ethnic strife. In 1993–4 some 1 million people fled to refugee camps in Zaire and Tanzania. Neighbouring countries imposed a trade embargo in 1996, but lifted it two years later when democracy was restored. The economy has deteriorated as a result of the sanctions and the continuing war between Tutsis and Hutus.

Abbreviations

CFA *Communauté Financière Africaine (African Financial Community)*

COMESA *Common Market for Eastern and Southern Africa*

COMM *Commonwealth*

ECOWAS *Economic Community of West African States*

FZ *The Franc Zone*

SADC *Southern African Development Community*

GDP *Gross Domestic Product*

CAMEROON

The Republic of Cameroon

Map page 201

Area	475 442 km²
	(183 569 sq miles)
Capital	Yaoundé
Member of	COMM

Population	13 937 000
Population growth rate	2.8%
Life expectancy	53 (m), 56 (f)
Languages	English, French, *many local languages*
Adult literacy rate	63.4%

Currency	CFA franc
	(US $1 = 643.7 CFA francs)
GDP (US million $)	8773
GDP per head (US $)	629

Mountains and high plateaus dominate central Cameroon. In the north, these uplands are covered with grass savannah, which merges into arid plains bordering Lake Chad. The southerly mountains and coastal lowlands are hot and steamy, covered with forest; eastwards, this is replaced by drier and more open country. The densest population occurs in the south-west of the country.

Aluminium, bauxite, cocoa, coffee, gas, oil and timber make up most of Cameroon's exports; Cameroon is the largest producer of logs in Africa. The country has enjoyed considerable development since independence in 1961. Yaoundé is a prosperous city; however, in the remote forests, pygmies still live in their traditional manner.

After the First World War, following the end of over 30 years of German control, most of Cameroon came under French administration and the remainder under British rule. At independence, the northern part of British Cameroon opted for union with Nigeria.

CENTRAL AFRICAN REPUBLIC

The Central African Republic

Map page 201

Area	622 984 km²
	(240 535 sq miles)
Capital	Bangui
Member of	FZ

Population	3 245 000
Population growth rate	2.5%
Life expectancy	47 (m) 52 (f)
Languages	French, *Sango*
Adult literacy rate	60%

Currency	CFA franc
	(US $1 = 643.7 CFA francs)
GDP (US million $)	1086
GDP per head (US $)	334

Most of the Republic consists of upland, which is dry savannah grassland in the east, but wet and forested in the south-west. External commerce passes through Bangui and along the River Oubangui, travelling onwards to the coast by river and rail. Rivers are also important for internal traffic.

In 1960 the Republic gained independence from France. From 1966 it was ruled for 13 years by President (later Emperor) Bokassa, who amassed a fortune from diamonds and ivory. As a result, the elephant population was reduced to a quarter of its earlier level, and the country came very close to bankruptcy. Diamonds and timber have remained significant exports, but most people continue to lead traditional self-sufficient lives, untouched by modern development. Game reserves in the east offer valuable potential for tourism.

CHAD

The Republic of Chad

Map page 201

Area	1 284 000 km²
	(495 800 sq miles)
Capital	N'Djamena
Member of	FZ

Population	6 702 000
Population growth rate	2.3%
Life expectancy	45 (m), 51 (f)
Languages	French, Arabic, *many local languages*
Adult literacy rate	48.1%

Currency	CFA franc
	(US $1 = 643.7 CFA francs)
GDP (US million $)	1244
GDP per head (US $)	185

Most of Chad's citizens live in the south, where there is enough rain to grow millet and similar crops. To the north, the country is empty desert, suitable only for nomadic grazing. In the south, Lake Chad and the rivers which feed it provide important fisheries. Chad has experienced serious droughts in recent years and has had to depend on international aid to survive the crises these caused.

The country has lacked major commercial mineral deposits, but recent oil discoveries may transform this situation. Chad suffers from long and difficult transport links, both internally and through neighbouring countries to the outside world.

Independence from France occurred in 1960; it was followed by civil war and a Libyan invasion in 1973. Only in 1994 did Libya recognise the international boundary and finally withdraw.

CONGO

The Republic of the Congo

Map page 201

Area	342 000 km²
	(132 047 sq miles)
Capital	Brazzaville
Member of	FZ

Population	2 745 000
Population growth rate	3%
Life expectancy	48 (m), 54 (f)
Languages	French, *Kikongo, Lingala, other local languages*
Adult literacy rate	74.9%

Currency	CFA franc
	(US $1 = 643.7 CFA francs)
GDP (US million $)	2287
GDP per head (US $)	833

Congo receives plentiful rain, and dense forest covers much of the south; the northern plains have extensive swamps and seasonal flooding. Oil is the main source of export revenue, but timber, sugar and coffee are also significant. Most of the population are subsistence farmers, who eke out a living on patches of land.

Brazzaville, founded in 1880, became in 1910 the capital of French Equatorial Africa, which extended beyond the present state of Congo. The city is located at the lowest navigable point on the Congo River. Independent since 1960, Congo has suffered from recurrent political instability, accompanied by civil war.

DEMOCRATIC REPUBLIC OF THE CONGO

Democratic Republic of the Congo (formerly Zaire)

Map page 204

Area	2 344 885 km²
	(905 365 sq miles)
Capital	Kinshasa
Member of	COMESA, SADC

Population	48 040 000
Population growth rate	3.3%
Life expectancy	50 (m), 54 (f)
Languages	French, *many Sudanese and Bantu dialects*
Adult literacy rate	77.3%

Currency	Congolese franc
	(US $1 = 4.5 FC)
GDP (US million $)	1030
GDP per head (US $)	21

The Democratic Republic of the Congo (formerly Zaire) is a huge land of rivers and forests, rising eastwards to open savannah and mountains along the Rift Valley. Some of the hydroelectric potential has been exploited, and the country has very rich mineral resources. Diamonds and copper are the major exports,

followed by coffee, cobalt and crude oil.

At the time of first European contact – with the Portuguese – in 1482, much of the area was ruled by the powerful Kongo kingdom, which subsequently sold slaves for the Americas. Direct European influence on the interior did not begin until the late 19th century, when the country came under Belgian control. Foreign investment in mining and plantations was encouraged, but little was done to prepare the country for independence in 1960. A bid by the copper-producing region of Katanga (now Shaba) to secede in 1960 was ended by United Nations troops in 1963.

For 32 years General Mobutu presided with authoritarian rule over a country consisting of hundreds of tribes and vast mineral wealth. Mismanagement and corruption drove the economy into steep decline. Mobutu was ousted in 1997 by Laurent Kabila, who changed the country's name back to Congo and soon became unpopular. The economy collapsed. Invasions by rebel groups from neighbours such as Rwanda soon developed into a scramble for control of the gold and diamond centres. Other neighbours intervened and also became involved in the crisis.

EQUATORIAL GUINEA

The Republic of Equatorial Guinea
Map page 201

Area	28 051 km²
	(10 830 sq miles)
Capital	Malabo
Member of	FZ

Population	420 000
Population growth rate	2.5%
Life expectancy	46 (m), 50 (f)
Languages	Spanish, Fang, many local languages
Adult literacy rate	78.5%

Currency	CFA franc
	(US $1 = 643.7 CFA francs)
GDP (US million $)	446
GDP per head (US $)	1061

This tiny country, independent from Spain since 1968, was until recently almost entirely dependent on foreign aid. Since 1996, oil production has soared and a new refinery will provide income and employment for local people.

GABON

The Gabonese Republic
Map page 201

Area	267 667 km²
	(103 347 sq miles)
Capital	Libreville
Member of	FZ

Population	1 138 000
Population growth rate	1.8%
Life expectancy	52 (m), 55 (f)
Languages	French, Fang, Bantu dialects
Adult literacy rate	63.2%

Currency	CFA franc
	(US $1 = 643.7 CFA francs)
GDP (US million $)	5528
GDP per head (US $)	5007

Libreville, founded in 1849 as a home for freed African slaves, houses a quarter of Gabon's population. Since independence from France in 1960, uranium, manganese and oil have generated considerable wealth.

NIGERIA

The Federal Republic of Nigeria
Map pages 200–1

Area	923 768 km²
	(356 669 sq miles)
Capital	Abuja
Member of	COMM, ECCWAS

Population	118 369 000
Population growth rate	2.9%
Life expectancy	49 (m), 52 (f)
Languages	English, Hausa, Yoruba, Ibo
Adult literacy rate	57.1%

Currency	naira (US $1 = 102 naira)
GDP (US million $)	43 800
GDP per head (US $)	370

Nigeria is the most populous country in Africa. There are four main groups: the Hausa, Fulani, Yoruba and Ibo. They were joined under a British administration in 1914, from which Nigeria became independent in 1960.

The Ibo declared their own independence, leading to the Biafran civil war (1967–70), which they lost. Since then there have been several disputed elections and military governments. In May 1999, the last 15 years of military rule ended with the inauguration of President Olesegun Obasanjo who immediately took steps to try to eliminate the endemic corruption for which Nigeria has become notorious.

The south of the country is covered in rain forest and is suitable for cocoa, rubber and oil palms as commercial crops. Subsistence crops are also grown. This is the most densely populated part. To the north, rainfall decreases and is less reliable. The middle belt of tree-covered savannah is rather infertile and sparsely populated. Fertile soils in the north make up for a low and erratic rainfall – conditions which allow dense settlement around Kano and other northern cities which

used to engage in caravan trade across the Sahara.

Until the 1970s, agricultural products dominated Nigeria's exports; Nigeria supplied 20 per cent of the world's cocoa. Following the discovery of huge oil reserves in the Niger delta, oil now accounts for more than 95 per cent of exports, but the industry is threatened by increasing ethnic violence in the Delta region. The development of the oil industry has been matched by a decline in export crops and indigenous food production; Nigeria now has enormous international debts, and the average standard of living has declined. Industrial development has been limited.

RWANDA

The Rwandan Republic
Map page 204

Area	26 338 km²
	(10 169 sq miles)
Capital	Kigali
Member of	COMESA

Population	5 883 000
Population growth rate	2.7%
Life expectancy	45 (m), 48 (f)
Languages	French, English, Kinyarwanda, Kiswahili
Adult literacy rate	60.5%

Currency	Rwandan franc
	(US $1 = 338.7 Rwandan francs)
GDP (US million $)	1843
GDP per head (US $)	313

Centuries-old enmity between the Tutsi minority and the Hutu majority has diminished the benefits of the independence gained from Belgium in 1962. In 1994 nearly a million Rwandans were slaughtered and more than a million refugees fled the country to Tanzania and what was then Zaire; many returned two years later.

With the exception of Lake Kivu, most of Rwanda is well-watered, intensively cultivated highland. The scarcity of land prompts the terracing of many hillsides. Most people are subsistence farmers, and cash crops, such as pyrethrum and coffee, are of lesser importance.

Civil strife and lack of non-agricultural resources have left the population impoverished, with very little development.

SAO TOME & PRINCIPE

The Democratic Republic of São Tomé e Príncipe
Map page 201

Area	1001 km²
	(386.5 sq miles)
Capital	São Tomé

Population	138 000
Population growth rate	2.1%
Life expectancy	67 (av. m/f)
Languages	Portuguese, many local dialects
Adult literacy rate	25%

Currency	dobra
	(US $1 = 2390 dobras)
GDP (US million $)	33
GDP per head (US $)	239

The two islands of São Tomé and Príncipe were ruled from 1740 by the Portuguese, who established cocoa plantations. After independence, production declined from mismanagement, but it has now been revived.

UGANDA

The Republic of Uganda
Map page 203

Area	241 139 km²
	(93 104 sq miles)
Capital	Kampala
Member of	COMESA, COMM

Population	20 438 000
Population growth rate	3.2%
Life expectancy	40 (m), 42 (f)
Languages	English, Luganda, other local languages
Adult literacy rate	61.8%

Currency	new shilling
	(US $1 = 1453 new shillings)
GDP (US million $)	6720
GDP per head (US $)	328

The ancient kingdoms of what is now Uganda were combined in 1895 as a British protectorate – not a colony – and remained so until independence in 1962. By then, Uganda's considerable prosperity was based on coffee and cotton exports, the growth of internal commerce and the provision of roads and schools.

After 1962, ethnic rivalries culminated in severe repression under President Amin (1971–9). The Asian community was expelled and its assets siezed. In the 1980s, faltering steps were taken to restore the economy and society, but no real progress was made until the 1990s. By the end of the decade, Uganda had political stability and a fast-growing economy, although the involvement in the Congo war and allegations of corruption threatened the country's image.

Much of Uganda, especially around Lake Victoria, is fertile and well watered. The country also possesses considerable copper, gold and cobalt. Tourist attractions include spectacular waterfalls and game reserves. Uganda has considerable potential, but the devastating AIDS pandemic casts a serious shadow over the country.

1900 Protectorate of Northern Nigeria established by Britain.

1908 Congo Free State (Zaire) becomes a Belgian colony.

— 1910 —

1914 Northern and Southern Nigeria (both British Protectorates) merge to form Nigeria.

1916 Urundi (Burundi) occupied by Belgium during First World War.

1919 Cameroon divided by French and British.

— 1920 —

1923 Ruanda-Urundi (Rwanda and Burundi) mandated to Belgium by League of Nations.

— 1930 —

1939–45 Second World War disrupts trade.

— 1940 —

1940 Free French troops take over Gabon from Vichy government.

1946 Ruanda-Urundi made UN trusteeship.

— 1950 —

1958 Central African Republic gains autonomy from France.

— 1960 —

1962 Ruanda-Urundi divides into Rwanda and Burundi.

1965 Military coups in Central African Republic (led by Bokassa) and Zaire (led by Mobutu).

1966 Burundi deposes monarch and becomes a republic. Military coup in Nigeria.

1967–70 Civil war in Nigeria.

1968 Macías Nguema begins 11-year reign in Equatorial Guinea.

— 1970 —

1971–9 Idi Amin heads military rule in Uganda.

1972 Some 100 000 Hutus massacred by Tutsis in Burundi.

1973 'Aozou strip' in Chad occupied by Libya.

1979–82 Civil war in Chad between Muslims and Christians.

— 1980 —

1988 Further mass slaughter of Tutsis and Hutus in Burundi.

— 1990 —

1990–7 Thousands killed in war between Hutus and Tutsis in Burundi, Rwanda and Zaire. Rebels oust General Mobutu and rename Zaire as Democratic Republic of the Congo.

1998–9 War in Democratic Republic of the Congo.

1999 Nigeria gets a civilian government.

SOUTHERN AFRICA

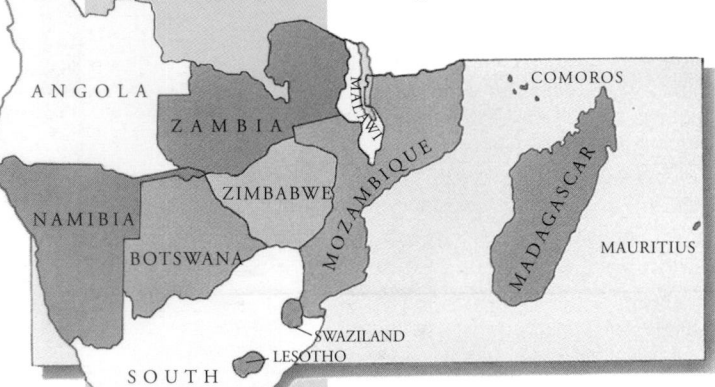

The southern countries of Africa have much dry or desert land and extensive plains, while the northern countries and Madagascar possess large forests. The Great Rift Valley extends into Malawi, with mountains to the east. The main rivers of the area are the Limpopo, the Orange and the Zambezi.

Associated Territories

BOUVET ISLAND
Parent country
NORWAY
Map page 208

REUNION
Parent country
FRANCE
Map page 207

ST HELENA AND DEPENDENCIES
Parent country
UK
Map page 206

Abbreviations
COMESA *Common Market for Eastern and Southern Africa*
COMM *Commonwealth*
FZ *The Franc Zone*
SADC *Southern African Development Community*

GDP *Gross Domestic Product*

240

ANGOLA

The Republic of Angola

Map page 204

Area	1 246 700 km²
	(481 354 sq miles)
Capital	Luanda
Member of	COMESA, SADC

Population	11 569 000
Population growth rate	3.2%
Life expectancy	45 (m), 48 (f)
Languages	Portuguese, *Umbundo,*
	Kimbundo, Chokwe, Ganguela
Adult literacy rate	41.7%

Currency	readjusted kwanza
	(US $1 = 2 326 945 readjusted kwanzas)
GDP (US million $)	4592
GDP per head (US $)	397

The population of Angola was severely depleted between the 16th and 19th centuries, as Portuguese colonists sold some 3 million into slavery in the New World. When that trade ceased, the development of Angola began with the establishment of roads, plantations and the Benguela railway to the copper mines of the Congo. After nearly 15 years' rebellion against colonial rule, independence was achieved in 1975. Guerrilla war continued into the 1990s. A peace accord was implemented in 1994, but to no avail; civil war had flared up again by the end of 1998.

Much of the country has been devastated by the conflict, although the coastal oil industry has prospered and diamond mining in the north-east has continued. Other rich mineral deposits await development.

Angola's climate and soils are suitable for a wide range of crops. The cold Benguela current keeps the coast cool and relatively dry; but inland the Planalto Plateau is well watered.

BOTSWANA

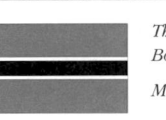

The Republic of Botswana

Map page 205

Area	581 730 km²
	(224 607 sq miles)
Capital	Gaborone
Member of	COMM, SADC

Population	1 533 000
Population growth rate	3.3%
Life expectancy	56 (m), 62 (f)
Languages	English, *Setswana*
Adult literacy rate	69.8%

Currency	pula (US $1 = 4.6 pula)
GDP (US million $)	4586
GDP per head (US $)	2991

Most Botswanans live in the south-east, which supports livestock and limited farming. Desert lies to the south-west, and the north is occupied by the Okavango Delta, a wildlife paradise. Stable government, meat exports, diamonds and other minerals give Botswana a measure of prosperity. Formerly the British protectorate of Bechuanaland, the country gained independence in 1966.

COMOROS

The Federal Islamic Republic of the Comoros

Map page 207

Area	1862 km²
	(719 sq miles)
Capital	Moroni
Member of	COMESA, FZ, LAS

Population	651000
Population growth rate	2.7%
Life expectancy	55 (m), 56 (f)
Languages	Comorian (Swahili and
	Arabic), French, Arabic
Adult literacy rate	57.3%

Currency	Comoros franc
	(US $1 = 491.9 Comoros francs)
GDP (US million $)	229
GDP per head (US $)	351

With few natural resources, the economy of these volcanic islands depends on subsistence farming and the production of vanilla and cloves. Comoros has been politically unstable since gaining independence in 1975.

LESOTHO

The Kingdom of Lesotho

Map page 207

Area	30 355 km²
	(11 720 sq miles)
Capital	Maseru
Member of	COMM, SADC

Population	2 131 000
Population growth rate	2.7%
Life expectancy	56 (m), 59 (f)
Languages	English, Sesotho
Adult literacy rate	71.3%

Currency	loti, plural maloti
	(US $1 = 6.09 maloti)
GDP (US million $)	942
GDP per head (US $)	442

Lesotho, completely surrounded by South Africa, gained its independence in 1966. Its people live by growing maize, rearing livestock and wages sent home by migrant workers in South Africa. A tourist industry, based on skiing, has developed. Violence afflicted the country in 1998 when the opposition and the army rebelled following a general election which they claimed had been rigged. The government asked the South African army to restore order.

MADAGASCAR

The Republic of Madagascar

Map page 205

Area	587 041 km²
	(226 658 sq miles)
Capital	Antananarivo
Member of	COMESA

Population	15 845 000
Population growth rate	3%
Life expectancy	55 (m), 58 (f)
Languages	Malagasy, French, *Hova,*
	other local languages
Adult literacy rate	45.7%

Currency	franc malgache (MG)
	(US $1 = 6604 francs MG)
GDP (US million $)	3552
GDP per head (US $)	224

Madagascar possesses a wealth of unique plants and animals, and is inhabited by non-African people from south-east Asia. The island resisted all attempts at colonisation until French rule was established in 1896. It regained independence in 1960.

The country's east coast is humid, the high grassy plateaus in the centre are cooler but also well watered, and the west is drier; droughts are a general problem. Most people are subsistence farmers, depending on rice or cassava, although coffee, vanilla, cloves and sugar are exported. There is potential for hydroelectricity, and minerals have been discovered, including oil and chromite. The main industrial centre is Antananarivo.

Although progress has been held back by political upheavals and a devastating cyclone in 1994, more stable government and the growth of tourism have improved the island's prospects.

MALAWI

The Republic of Malawi

Map page 204

Area	118 484 km²
	(45 747 sq miles)
Capital	Lilongwe
Member of	COMESA, COMM, SADC

Population	10 441 000
Population growth rate	4.5%
Life expectancy	43 (m), 46 (f)
Languages	English, *Chichewa, other*
	local languages
Adult literacy rate	56.4%

Currency	Malawian kwacha
	(US $1 = 42.9 kwacha)
GDP (US million $)	1794
GDP per head (US $)	171

Following independence from Britain in 1964, Malawi, formerly Nyasaland, was governed for 30 years by President Hastings Banda, who died in 1997. During this period, commercial plantation farming of crops such as tobacco was encouraged, but the majority of people continue to subsist on small plots of land with few modern facilities. Lake Malawi – rich in fish – and the highlands provide the country with considerable tourist appeal.

Industrial development has been limited, and there are few industrial resources other than hydroelectric power. Landlocked Malawi was seriously affected by civil war in Mozambique, but since 1992 greater stability and more liberal internal policies have offered an opportunity for significant development, but Malawians remain very poor.

MAURITIUS

The Republic of Mauritius

Map page 207

Area	2040 km²
	(788 sq miles)
Capital	Port Louis
Member of	COMESA, COMM,
	SADC

Population	1 148 000
Population growth rate	0.9%
Life expectancy	66 (m), 74 (f)
Languages	English, *Creole, other local*
	languages
Adult literacy rate	82.9%

Currency	Mauritian rupee
	(US $1 = 25.22 rupees)
GDP (US million $)	4178
GDP per head (US $)	3639

Mauritius is a fertile volcanic island surrounded by coral reefs. Its economy benefits from tourist revenues, and the export of sugar and clothing. It has been independent since 1968.

MOZAMBIQUE

The Republic of
Mozambique

Map pages 204–5

Area	799 380 km²
	(308 641 sq miles)
Capital	Maputo
Member of	COMM, SADC

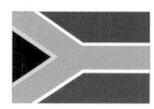

Population	16 543 000
Population growth rate	2%
Life expectancy	44 (m), 47 (f)
Languages	Portuguese, many local languages
Adult literacy rate	40.1%

Currency	metical
	(US $1 = 12 597 meticals)
GDP (US million $)	1925
GDP per head (US $)	116

Portuguese rule of Mozambique lasted from the 16th century until the country's independence in 1975. Virtually all the people of European descent had gone by 1977, leaving a largely illiterate population. The Mozambique National Resistance then engaged in a guerrilla war that made 4.5 million citizens homeless; a political accord was reached in 1992. In 1995 Mozambique was admitted to the Commonwealth as adjoining states are members.

Hot and humid plains crossed by numerous rivers dominate the south of the country; farther north greater altitude gives cooler conditions, suitable for rearing cattle. Most people are subsistence farmers on the coastal lowlands. The country has modest mineral resources, but has considerable fish stocks.

Top priority after the civil war is reconstruction, which involves the clearance of land mines and the resettlement of displaced people. Substantial international aid will be needed for some time, although increasing foreign investment and economic growth promise a better future.

NAMIBIA

The Republic of
Namibia

Map page 205

Area	824 292 km²
	(318 261 sq miles)
Capital	Windhoek
Member of	COMESA, COMM, SADC

Population	1 613 000
Population growth rate	2.7%
Life expectancy	54 (m), 57 (f)
Languages	English, Afrikaans, German, local languages
Adult literacy rate	62%

Currency	Namibian dollar
	(US $1 = N $6.093)
GDP (US million $)	2883
GDP per head (US $)	1787

A desert state, Namibia has enormous reserves of diamonds, uranium, copper and other minerals, as well as rich offshore fishing. Divisions in the country, between a wealthy elite and the poor majority largely untouched by modern development, are acute. Independence from South Africa was gained in 1990 after a long and highly damaging guerrilla war.

SOUTH AFRICA

The Republic of
South Africa

Map pages 206–7

Area	1 219 080 km²
	(470 689 sq miles)
Capital	Pretoria (administrative), Cape Town (legislative), Bloemfontein (judicial)
Member of	COMM, SADC

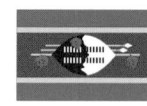

Population	43 336 000
Population growth rate	2.4%
Life expectancy	60 (m), 66 (f)
Languages	Afrikaans, English and nine African languages
Adult literacy rate	81.8%

Currency	rand
	(US $1 = 6.093 rand)
GDP (US million $)	117 000
GDP per head (US $)	2699

Territories controlled by Afrikaans-speaking and English-speaking descendants of settlers, who had been arriving in Cape Province since the late 17th century, were united in 1910 to form South Africa. The country gained independence from Britain in 1934.

In 1886, the world's largest gold find was made in the Witwatersrand, triggering substantial development and a further influx of settlers. Rich finds of diamonds and other minerals, the fertile lands and the moderate climate drew in yet more foreigners. Today, about three-quarters of the people are black, belonging to various linguistic groups, and about 14 per cent are white, speaking Afrikaans or English.

South Africa is the most industrialised and urbanised country in Africa, with a high standard of living for most of the whites, but grinding poverty for the majority of blacks. The government's enforcement of apartheid (separate development) from 1948 condemned most of the population to live either in huge and ill-provided urban settlements like Soweto, south-west of Johannesburg, or in overpopulated 'homelands', such as KwaZulu, in Natal.

After years of agitation by the African National Congress, white rule ended in 1994, following the first elections in which blacks could vote. Nelson Mandela, released after more than 27 years' imprisonment, succeeded F.W. de Klerk as president. A multi-ethnic democracy is taking root in the country, such that a second election passed off without incident in 1999, and Nelson Mandela retired, to be succeeded by Thabo Mbeki.

South Africa is a large and varied country, rising to the Drakensberg escarpment in the east and the Great Karroo mountains in the south. Fertile coastal lowlands give way to a drier interior, merging into desert in the west. The country is very beautiful and has fine wildlife reserves. Johannesburg, the largest city, with more than 5 million inhabitants, is an area with much manufacturing. Most of the other main cities are on the coast, including Cape Town picturesquely situated beneath Table Mountain.

SWAZILAND

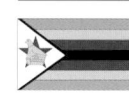

The Kingdom of
Swaziland

Map page 207

Area	17 363 km²
	(6704 sq miles)
Capital	Mbabane
Member of	COMESA, COMM, SADC

Population	906 000
Population growth rate	3.4%
Life expectancy	55 (m), 60 (f)
Languages	English, siSwati
Adult literacy rate	76.7%

Currency	lilangeni, plural emalangeni
	(US $1 = 6.093 emalangeni)
GDP (US million $)	1138
GDP per head (US $)	1256

A British protectorate until 1968, Swaziland possesses substantial agricultural and mineral resources, combined with a firm manufacturing base. Sugar forms one-third of its exports.

ZAMBIA

The Republic of
Zambia

Map pages 204–5

Area	752 614 km²
	(290 586 sq miles)
Capital	Lusaka
Member of	COMESA, COMM, SADC

Population	8 478 000
Population growth rate	3.3%
Life expectancy	50 (m), 53 (f)
Languages	English, Nyanja, Bemba, Tonga, Lozi, Lunda, Luvale
Adult literacy rate	78.2%

Currency	Zambian kwacha
	(US $1 = 2540 kwacha)
GDP (US million $)	1601
GDP per head (US $)	188

Although the country can support many crops, high transport costs create difficulties for exports other than tobacco. Most farming is for subsistence or for food crops to sell to the towns; recurrent drought is a serious problem. Zambia is one of the world's major producers of copper, which dominates the nation's economy, accounting for over 80 per cent of exports. The Copper Belt, centred on Ndola, is heavily urbanised.

Zambia gained independence in 1964, after nearly a century of British rule as Northern Rhodesia. It then suffered from the imposition of economic sanctions against Zimbabwe, conflicts in Angola and Mozambique and a substantial fall in copper prices. Recently the government has been accused of corruption and stifling opposition.

ZIMBABWE

The Republic of
Zimbabwe

Map page 205

Area	390 759 km²
	(150 873 sq miles)
Capital	Harare
Member of	COMESA, COMM, SADC

Population	12 294 000
Population growth rate	3%
Life expectancy	58 (m), 62 (f)
Languages	English, Chishona, Sindebele and other local languages
Adult literacy rate	85.1%

Currency	Zimbabwe dollar
	(US $1 = Z $37.95)
GDP (US million $)	5500
GDP per head (US $)	447

Britain took control of the area, which later became known as Southern Rhodesia, late in the 19th century, in pursuit of the country's gold and other minerals. The land was also attractive to European farmers, with tobacco as the main cash crop.

Denied self-government when its former Federal partners, Nyasaland and Northern Rhodesia, became self-governing, the all-white government of Southern Rhodesia unilaterally declared independence from Britain in 1965. International sanctions and civil war finally brought black majority rule in 1980. Threats to seize land from white farmers have caused stress, as have rising interest rates, inflation and unemployment, all at more than 50 per cent.

Most of Zimbabwe is over 300 m (1000 ft) above sea level, which moderates temperatures and attracts useful amounts of rain. Hydroelectricity is generated at the famous Kariba Dam on the Zambezi River.

20TH-CENTURY LANDMARKS

1899–1902 Boer War between Britain and South Africa.

1903 Swaziland made British protectorate.

— 1910 —

1910 Union of South Africa formed.

1912 ANC founded.

1914 South African forces enter German-occupied South West Africa (Namibia).

— 1920 —

1920 South West Africa (Namibia) becomes South African mandate.

1925 Black majority banned from skilled jobs in South Africa.

— 1930 —

1939–45 Second World War disrupts trade.

— 1940 —

1948 National Party gains power in South Africa and introduces apartheid.

— 1950 —

1950 South Africa refuses to hand South West Africa (Namibia) mandate to UN.

1953 Southern and Northern Rhodesia (Zimbabwe and Zambia) and Nyasaland (Malawi) are federated.

— 1960 —

1960 South Africa becomes a republic.

1964 Armed struggle for independence starts in Mozambique.

1965 Guerrilla war against white rule in Southern Rhodesia.

1966 South Africa's apartheid laws extended to South West Africa (Namibia); resistance movement begins.

— 1970 —

1975 Civil war breaks out in Angola.

1976 Mozambique closes border with Southern Rhodesia.

— 1980 —

1980 Black majority wins independence for Zimbabwe.

1985 International sanctions imposed on South Africa.

1989 Civil war in Mozambique.

— 1990 —

1992 Peace accord in Mozambique.

1994 ANC wins first democratic elections in South Africa. Nelson Mandela is South Africa's first black president.

1999 After 5 years of relative peace, civil war affects Angola again. Nelson Mandela retires.

World Gazetteer

This index includes in a single alphabetical list more than 42 000 names of features that appear on the maps. Each name is followed by a map reference and a page reference.

Names Local official names are used on the maps and in the index. The names are shown in full, including diacritical marks. Features that extend beyond the boundaries of one country and have no single official name are usually named in English. Many conventional English names and former names are cross-referenced to the official names.

Transliteration For names in languages not written in the Roman alphabet, the locally official transliteration system has been used where one exists. Thus, the transliteration for mainland Chinese names follows the Pinyin system, which has been officially adopted in mainland China. For languages with no one locally accepted system, transliteration closely follows a system adopted by the United States Board on Geographic Names.

Abbreviation and Capitalisation Abbreviations of names on the maps have been standardised as much as possible. Names that are abbreviated on the maps are generally spelt out in full in the index. Periods are used after all abbreviations regardless of local practice. The abbreviation 'St.' is used only for 'Saint'. The German 'Sankt' and other forms of this term are spelt out.

Most initial letters of names are capitalised, except for generic terms in Russia and a number of other countries in eastern Europe and central Asia, and a few Dutch names,

such as ''s-Gravenhage'. Capitalisation of noninitial words in a name generally follows local practice.

Alphabetisation Names are alphabetised in the order of the letters of the English alphabet. ñ, for example, is not treated as a distinct letter. Furthermore, diacritical marks are disregarded in alphabetisation–German or Scandinavian ä or ö are treated as a or o.

The names of physical features may appear inverted, since they are always alphabetised under the proper, not the generic, part of the name, thus: 'Gibraltar, Strait of ʯ'. Otherwise every entry, whether consisting of one word or more, is alphabetised as a single continuous entity. 'Lakeland', for example, appears after 'La Crosse' and before 'La Salle'. Names beginning with articles other than 'The' (Le Havre, Den Helder, Al-Qāhirah, As-Suways) are not inverted. Names beginning 'St.' and 'Sainte' are alphabetised as though spelt 'Saint'.

In the case of identical names, towns are listed first, then political divisions, then physical features. Entries that are completely identical (including symbols, explained below) are distinguished by abbreviations of their country names. The abbreviations used for places in the United States, Canada and United Kingdom indicate the state, province or political division in which the feature is located. (See List of Abbreviations below.)

Symbols The names of cities and towns are not followed by symbols. The names of all other features are followed

by symbols that graphically represent broad categories of features, for example, ʌ for mountain (Everest, Mount ʌ). Superior numbers indicate finer distinctions, for example, ʌ¹ for volcano (Fuji, Mount ʌ¹). A complete list of symbols, including those with superior numbers, follows the List of Abbreviations.

All cross-references are indicated by the word 'see'.

Map References and Page References The map references and page references are found in the last two columns of each entry.

Each map reference consists of a letter followed by a number. The letters to which they refer appear along the sides of the maps and numbers appear across the top and bottom of the maps.

Map references for point features, such as towns, cities and mountain peaks, indicate the locations of the symbols. For extensive features, such as countries, mountain ranges and rivers, locations are given for the position of the name.

The page number generally refers to the map that shows the feature at the most appropriate scale. Countries, mountain ranges and other extensive features are usually indexed to maps that not only show the features completely but also show them in their relationships to broader areas. Page references to two-page maps always refer to the left-hand page. If a page contains several maps or insets, a lower-case letter identifies the specific map or inset.

List of Abbreviations

Ab., Can.	Alberta, Can.	D.C., U.S.	District of Columbia, U.S.	Kaz.	Kazakhstan	N.H., U.S.	New Hampshire, U.S.	S. Mar.	San Marino
Afg.	Afghanistan	De., U.S.	Delaware, U.S.	Kir.	Kiribati	Nic.	Nicaragua	Sol. Is.	Solomon Islands
Afr.	Africa	Den.	Denmark	Ks., U.S.	Kansas, U.S.	Nig.	Nigeria	Som.	Somalia
Ak., U.S.	Alaska, U.S.	Dji.	Djibouti	Kuw.	Kuwait	N. Ire., U.K.	Northern Ireland, U.K.	Sp. N. Afr.	Spanish North Africa
Al., U.S.	Alabama, U.S.	Dom.	Dominica	Ky., U.S.	Kentucky, U.S.	N.J., U.S.	New Jersey, U.S.	Sri L.	Sri Lanka
Alb.	Albania	Dom. Rep.	Dominican Republic	Kyrg.	Kyrgyzstan	N. Kor.	North Korea	St. Hel.	St. Helena
Alg.	Algeria	D.R.C.	Democratic Republic of the	La., U.S.	Louisiana, U.S.	N.M., U.S.	New Mexico, U.S.	St. K./N.	St. Kitts and Nevis
Am. Sam.	American Samoa		Congo	Lat.	Latvia	N. Mar. Is.	Northern Mariana Islands	St. Luc.	St. Lucia
And.	Andorra	Ec.	Ecuador	Leb.	Lebanon	Nmb.	Namibia	S. Tom./P.	Sao Tome and Principe
Ang.	Angola	El Sal.	El Salvador	Leso.	Lesotho	Nor.	Norway	St. P./M.	St. Pierre and Miquelon
Ant.	Antarctica	Eng., U.K.	England, U.K.	Lib.	Liberia	Norf. I.	Norfolk Island	St. Vin.	St. Vincent and the
Antig.	Antigua and Barbuda	Eq. Gui.	Equatorial Guinea	Liech.	Liechtenstein	N.S., Can.	Nova Scotia, Can.		Grenadines
Ar., U.S.	Arkansas, U.S.	Erit.	Eritrea	Lith.	Lithuania	N.T., Can.	Northwest Territories, Can.	Sur.	Surinam
Arg.	Argentina	Est.	Estonia	Lux.	Luxembourg	Nu., Can.	Nunavut, Can.	Swaz.	Swaziland
Arm.	Armenia	Eth.	Ethiopia	Ma., U.S.	Massachusetts, U.S.	Nv., U.S.	Nevada, U.S.	Swe.	Sweden
Aus.	Austria	Eur.	Europe	Mac.	Macedonia, Former Yugoslav	N.Y., U.S.	New York, U.S.	Switz.	Switzerland
Austl.	Australia	Falk. Is.	Falkland Islands		Republic of	N.Z.	New Zealand	Tai.	Taiwan
Az., U.S.	Arizona, U.S.	Far. Is.	Faroe Islands	Madag.	Madagascar	Oc.	Oceania	Taj.	Tajikistan
Azer.	Azerbaijan	Fin.	Finland	Malay.	Malaysia	Oh., U.S.	Ohio, U.S.	Tan.	Tanzania
Bah.	Bahamas	Fl., U.S.	Florida, U.S.	Mald.	Maldives	Ok., U.S.	Oklahoma, U.S.	T./C. Is.	Turks and Caicos Islands
Bahr.	Bahrain	Fr.	France	Marsh. Is.	Marshall Islands	On., Can.	Ontario, Can.	Thai.	Thailand
Barb.	Barbados	Fr. Gu.	French Guiana	Mart.	Martinique	Or., U.S.	Oregon, U.S.	Tn., U.S.	Tennessee, U.S.
B.C., Can.	British Columbia, Can.	Fr. Poly.	French Polynesia	Maur.	Mauritania	Pa., U.S.	Pennsylvania, U.S.	Tok.	Tokelau
Bdi.	Burundi	Ga., U.S.	Georgia, U.S.	May.	Mayotte	Pak.	Pakistan	Trin.	Trinidad and Tobago
Bel.	Belgium	Gam.	Gambia, The	Mb., Can.	Manitoba, Can.	Pan.	Panama	Tun.	Tunisia
Bela.	Belarus	Gaza	Gaza Strip	Md., U.S.	Maryland, U.S.	Pap. N. Gui.	Papua New Guinea	Tur.	Turkey
Ber.	Bermuda	Geor.	Georgia	Me., U.S.	Maine, U.S.	Para.	Paraguay	Turk.	Turkmenistan
Bhu.	Bhutan	Ger.	Germany	Mex.	Mexico	P.E., Can.	Prince Edward Island, Can.	Tx., U.S.	Texas, U.S.
B.I.O.T.	British Indian Ocean Territory	Gib.	Gibraltar	Mi., U.S.	Michigan, U.S.	Phil.	Philippines	U.A.E.	United Arab Emirates
Bngl.	Bangladesh	Golan	Golan Heights	Micron.	Micronesia, Federated States	Pit.	Pitcairn	Ug.	Uganda
Bol.	Bolivia	Grc.	Greece		of	Pol.	Poland	U.K.	United Kingdom
Bos.	Bosnia and Herzegovina	Gren.	Grenada	Mid. Is.	Midway Islands	Port.	Portugal	Ukr.	Ukraine
Bots.	Botswana	Grnld.	Greenland	Mn., U.S.	Minnesota, U.S.	P.R.	Puerto Rico	Ur.	Uruguay
Braz.	Brazil	Guad.	Guadeloupe	Mo., U.S.	Missouri, U.S.	Qc., Can.	Quebec, Can.	U.S.	United States
Bru.	Brunei	Guat.	Guatemala	Mol.	Moldova	Reu.	Reunion	Ut., U.S.	Utah, U.S.
Br. Vir. Is.	British Virgin Islands	Gui.	Guinea	Mon.	Monaco	R.I., U.S.	Rhode Island, U.S.	Uzb.	Uzbekistan
Bul.	Bulgaria	Gui.-B.	Guinea-Bissau	Mong.	Mongolia	Rom.	Romania	Va., U.S.	Virginia, U.S.
Ca., U.S.	California, U.S.	Guy.	Guyana	Monts.	Montserrat	Rw.	Rwanda	Vat.	Vatican City
Cam.	Cameroon	Hi., U.S.	Hawaii, U.S.	Mor.	Morocco	S.A.	South America	Ven.	Venezuela
Camb.	Cambodia	Hond.	Honduras	Moz.	Mozambique	S. Afr.	South Africa	Viet.	Vietnam
Can.	Canada	Hung.	Hungary	Mrts.	Mauritius	Sau. Ar.	Saudi Arabia	V.I.U.S.	Virgin Islands of the U.S.
C.A.R.	Central African Republic	Ia., U.S.	Iowa, U.S.	Ms., U.S.	Mississippi, U.S.	S.C., U.S.	South Carolina, U.S.	Vt., U.S.	Vermont, U.S.
Cay. Is.	Cayman Islands	I.C.	Ivory Coast	Mt., U.S.	Montana, U.S.	Scot., U.K.	Scotland, U.K.	Wa., U.S.	Washington, U.S.
Christ. I.	Christmas Island	Ice.	Iceland	Mwi.	Malawi	S.D., U.S.	South Dakota, U.S.	Wake I.	Wake Island
Co., U.S.	Colorado, U.S.	Id., U.S.	Idaho, U.S.	Myan.	Myanmar	Sen.	Senegal	Wal./F.	Wallis and Futuna
Col.	Colombia	Il., U.S.	Illinois, U.S.	N.A.	North America	Sey.	Seychelles	W.B.	West Bank
Com.	Comoros	In., U.S.	Indiana, U.S.	N.B., Can.	New Brunswick, Can.	S. Geor.	South Georgia and the South	Wi., U.S.	Wisconsin, U.S.
Cook Is.	Cook Islands	Indon.	Indonesia	N.C., U.S.	North Carolina, U.S.		Sandwich Islands	W. Sah.	Western Sahara
C.R.	Costa Rica	I. of Man	Isle of Man	N. Cal.	New Caledonia	Sing.	Singapore	W.V., U.S.	West Virginia, U.S.
Cro.	Croatia	Ire.	Republic of Ireland	N.D., U.S.	North Dakota, U.S.	Sk., Can.	Saskatchewan, Can.	Wy., U.S.	Wyoming, U.S.
Ct., U.S.	Connecticut, U.S.	Isr.	Israel	Ne., U.S.	Nebraska, U.S.	S. Kor.	South Korea	Yk., Can.	Yukon Territory
C.V.	Cape Verde	Jam.	Jamaica	Neth.	Netherlands	S.L.	Sierra Leone	Yugo.	Yugoslavia
Cyp.	Cyprus	Jer.	Jericho Area	Neth. Ant.	Netherlands Antilles	Slvk.	Slovakia	Zam.	Zambia
Czech Rep.	Czech Republic	Jord.	Jordan	Nf., Can.	Newfoundland, Can.	Slvn.	Slovenia	Zimb.	Zimbabwe

Key to Symbols

ʌ	Mountain	⅀	Cape	⊥⁴	Cliff	c	Bay, Gulf	₸²	Sea	◻²	Dependency	●	Cultural Institution	●	Miscellaneous
ʌ¹	Volcano	⅀¹	Peninsula	⊥⁵	Cave, Caves	c¹	Estuary	₸³	Anchorage			●¹	Religious Institution		
ʌ²	Hill	⅀²	Spit, Sand Bar	⊥⁶	Crater	c²	Fjord	₸⁴	Oasis, Well, Spring	◻³	State, Canton,	●²	Educational Institution	●¹	Region
				⊥⁷	Depression	c³	Bight				Republic	●³	Scientific, Industrial	●²	Desert
				⊥⁸	Dunes								Facility		
⊀	Mountains	ı	Island	⊥⁹	Lava Flow	⌷	Lake, Lakes	✛	Submarine Features	◻⁴	Province, Region,			●³	Forest, Moor
⊀¹	Plateau	ı¹	Atoll			⌷¹	Reservoir	✛¹	Depression		Oblast	⊥	Historical Site	●⁴	Reserve, Reservation
⊀²	Hills	ı²	Rock	≈	River			✛²	Reef, Shoal					●⁵	Transportation
				≈¹	River Channel	⧎	Swamp	✛³	Mountain, Mountains	◻⁵	Department, District,	●	Recreational Site		
⨯	Pass	ıı	Islands					✛⁴	Slope, Shelf		Prefecture			●⁶	Dam
		ıı¹	Rocks	≋	Canal	⋈	Ice Features, Glacier			◻⁶	County	⊞	Airport	●⁷	Mine, Quarry
⌵	Valley, Canyon	⊥	Other Topographic	≋¹	Aqueduct					◻⁷	City, Municipality				
			Features			₸	Other Hydrographic					■	Military Installation	●⁸	Neighbourhood
≃	Plain	⊥¹	Continent	∟	Waterfall, Rapids		Features	◻	Political Unit	◻⁸	Miscellaneous				
≃¹	Basin	⊥²	Coast, Beach			₸¹	Ocean	◻¹	Independent Nation	◻⁹	Historical				
≃²	Delta	⊥³	Isthmus	ʯ	Strait										

Aabenraa — Al-Muwaqqar

Name	Map Ref.	Page
A		
Aabenraa	C 2	68
Aachen	F 3	98
Aakirkeby	f 7	68a
Aalborg	A 2	68
Aalen	D 7	100
Aalestrup	B 2	68
Aali, Sadd el- (Aswan High Dam) ◆[6]	C 3	202
Aalsmeer	B 3	69
Aalst	D 3	69
Aalten	C 5	69
Aalter	C 2	69
Aansluit	D 5	206
Aarau	C 5	82
Aarburg	C 5	82
Aare ≃	C 6	82
Aargau □[3]	C 6	82
Aarschot	D 3	69
Aasiaat see Egedesminde	C 22	150
Aba, China	B 6	130
Aba, Nig.	D 6	200
Abā al-Bawl, Qurayn ∧[2]	J 14	118
Abaco I	F 6	168
Ābādān	G 13	118
Ābādeh	G 15	118
Abadla	C 4	198
Abaeté	C 8	194
Abaetetuba	D 9	190
Abag Qi	E 10	128
Abaj see Abay	A 11	116
Abakaliki	D 6	200
Abakan	B 2	124
Abakan ≃	B 1	124
Abala	C 5	200
Abalak	G 28	108
Abancay	F 4	190
Abano Terme	D 7	92
Abarán	F 3	88
Abar Kūh	G 15	118
Abashiri	B 10	126
Abau	B 10	138
Abay	A 11	116
Ābaya Hāyk' ⊜	F 4	202
Abbadia San Salvatore	G 7	92
Abbasanta	E 2	90
Abbeville, Fr.	B 8	78
Abbeville, Ga., U.S.	C 3	168
Abbeville, La., U.S.	H 2	170
Abbey	F 17	156
Abbeyleix	D 4	75
Abbiategrasso	D 4	92
Abbotsford	G 10	156
Abbotspoort	B 7	206
Abbottābād	C 2	122
'Abd al-Kūrī I	E 7	202
'Abd Allāh, Khawr ʮ	H 13	118
Abdulino	J 20	108
Abéché	C 9	200
Abéjar	C 2	88
Abemama I[1]	C 9	136
Abengourou	D 4	200
Abensberg	D 8	100
Abeokuta	D 5	200
Aber	G 3	202
Abercarn	F 3	72
Aberchirder	C 6	74
Abercrombie ≃	D 7	144
Aberdare	F 3	72
Aberdeen, Austl.	D 8	144
Aberdeen, Scot., U.K.	C 6	74
Aberdeen, Md., U.S.	G 2	164
Aberdeen, S.D., U.S.	C 5	174
Aberdeen, Wa., U.S.	B 2	178
Aberdeen Lake ⊜	D 13	150
Aberdovey	E 2	72
Abergavenny	F 3	72
Abergele	D 3	72
Abertillery	F 3	72
Aberystwyth	E 2	72
Abetone	E 6	92
Abhā	D 5	202
Abhar	D 13	118
Ābhē Bid Hāyk' ⊜	E 5	202
Abidjan	D 4	200
Abiengama	G 2	202
Abilene, Ks., U.S.	F 6	174
Abilene, Tx., U.S.	D 4	172
Abingdon, Eng., U.K.	F 5	72
Abingdon, Va., U.S.	E 2	162
Abington	F 3	164
Abinsk	G 11	110
Abiod, Rmel el ◆[1]	C 6	198
Abisko	B 9	64
Abitau ≃	B 17	156
Abitibi ≃	C 3	160
Abitibi, Lac (Abitibi, Lake) ⊜	D 3	160
Abitibi, Lake (Abitibi, Lac) ⊜	D 3	160
Ābīy Ādī	E 4	202
Ābīyata Hāyk' ⊜	F 4	202
Abja-Paluoja	C 12	66
Abkhazeti Autonomis Respublika □[3]	H 12	110
Abnûb	I 4	118
Åbo see Turku	B 11	66
Abohar	C 2	122
Abomey	D 5	200
Abongabong, Gunung ∧	L 3	132
Abong Mbang	E 7	200
Abony	B 6	104
Aborigen, pik ∧	C 17	114
Abou	G 5	202
Abou-Deïa	C 8	200
Abou Simbel ⊥	C 3	202
Abovyan (Abovjan)	I 14	110
Abrantes	E 2	86
Abra Pampa	D 6	192
Abrene see Pytalovo	H 7	108
'Abrī	E 3	202
Absaroka Range ⋏	C 9	178
Absecon	G 4	164
Abū 'Alī I	I 13	118
Abū al-Khaṣīb	G 12	118
Abu Dhabi see Abū Ẓaby	J 16	118
Abū Dīs	D 3	202
Abuja	D 6	200
Abū Jubayhah	E 3	202
Abū Kamāl	E 9	118
Abū Kulaywāt	E 2	202
Abū Madd, Ra's ➤	J 7	118
Abunã	E 5	190
Abu Qîr ◆[8]	G 4	118
Abu Qurqâs	I 4	118
Ābu Road	E 2	122
Abū Shajarah, Ra's ➤	C 4	202
Abū Shanab	E 2	202
Abū Sunbul see Abou Simbel ⊥	C 3	202
Abu Tîg	I 4	118
Abū Zabad	E 2	202
Abū Ẓaby (Abu Dhabi)	J 16	118
Abwong	F 3	202
Aby, Lagune ⊜	D 4	200
Abyaḍ	E 2	202
Abyei	F 2	202
Abyr	K 28	108
Acajutla	E 2	186
Acámbaro	H 9	184
A Cañiza	B 2	86
Acaponeta	F 7	184
Acaponeta ≃	F 7	184
Acapulco de Juárez	I 9	184
Acarai Mountains ⋏	C 7	190
Acaraú	D 10	190
Acaraú ≃	D 10	190
Acaray ≃	F 3	194
Acari ≃	A 8	194
Acarigua	F 7	186
Acâș	B 7	104
Acatlán de Osorio	H 10	184
Acayucan	H 12	184
Accoville	A 4	168
Accra	D 4	200
Acerra	E 5	90
Aceuchal	F 4	86
Achacachi	G 5	190
Achalpur	E 3	122
Acharnés	C 5	106
Acheng	D 16	128
Achénouma	B 7	200
Achern	D 4	100
Achill Head ➤	B 1	75
Achill Island I	C 1	75
Achim	C 6	98
Achwa ≃	B 5	204
Aci Castello	G 5	94
Aci Catena	G 5	94
Acı Göl ⊜	D 8	106
Ačinsk	D 12	114
Acireale	G 5	94
Ackerly	D 3	172
Acklins I	C 6	186
Aconcagua, Cerro ∧	C 3	195
Aconibe	E 7	200
A Coruña (Corunna)	A 2	86
Acquapendente	G 7	92
Acquaviva delle Fonti	D 6	94
Acqui Terme	E 4	92
Acraman, Lake ⊜	L 2	142
Acre see 'Akko	D 4	120
Acre □[3]	E 5	190
Acre ≃	F 5	190
Acri	E 6	94
Acton Vale	A 6	164
Actopan	G 10	184
Ada, Ok., U.S.	C 5	172
Ada, Yugo.	C 6	104
Adâfer el Abiod ◆[1]	F 2	198
Adailo	E 5	202
Adair	D 1	170
Adair, Cape ➤	B 18	150
Adairville	D 5	170
Adak	I 43	155a
Adam, Mount ∧	n 18	193b
Adamantina	D 5	194
Adamawa ⋏	D 7	200
Adamello ⋏	C 6	92
Adamów	C 12	96
Adams, N.D., U.S.	A 5	174
Adams, N.Y., U.S.	C 2	164
Adams, Mount ∧[1]	B 3	178
Adams Lake ⊜	F 12	156
'Adan (Aden)	E 6	202
Adana	D 6	118
Adanero	D 6	86
Adare, Cape ➤	D 20	208
Adavale	H 7	142
Adda ≃	D 5	92
Ad-Dabbah	D 3	202
Ad-Dahnā' ◆[2]	B 6	202
Ad-Dāmir	D 3	202
Ad-Dammām	I 13	118
Ad-Dawḥah (Doha)	J 14	118
Ad-Dibdibah ◆[1]	H 12	118
Addis Ababa see Ādīs Ābeba	F 4	202
Addison	B 1	162
Ad-Dīwānīyah	F 11	118
Ad-Du'ayn	E 2	202
Ad-Duwaym	E 3	202
Adébour	C 7	200
Adel	B 1	170
Adelaide	E 2	144
Adelaide Island I	C 2	208
Adelaide River	C 11	140
Adèle Island I	D 7	140
Adelfia	C 6	94
Adelie Coast ⩡[2]	C 23	208
Adelong	E 6	144
Aden see 'Adan	E 6	202
Aden, Gulf of ⊂	E 6	202
Adendorp	G 6	206
Adi, Pulau I	F 10	134
Adige (Etsch) ≃	D 8	92
Ādīgrat	E 4	202
Adıgüzel Barajı ⊜[1]	C 8	106
Adi Keyih	E 4	202
Adi Kwala	E 4	202
Ādilābād	F 3	122
Adilang	G 3	202
Adīrī	D 7	198
Adirondack Mountains ⋏	C 4	164
Ādīs Ābeba (Addis Ababa)	F 4	202
Ādīs Zemen	E 4	202
Adi Ugri	E 4	202
Adıyaman	D 8	118
Adler	H 11	110
Adliswil	C 6	82
Admiral	G 17	156
Admiralty Bay ⊂	A 16	154
Admiralty Gulf ⊂	D 9	140
Admiralty Island I	H 27	154
Admiralty Islands II	M 13	124
Admiralty Mountains ⋏	D 25	208
Adolfo Gonzales Chaves	E 8	195
Adolfo López Mateos, Presa ⊜[1]	E 6	184
Adonara, Pulau I	G 8	134
Ādoni	F 3	122
Adorf	B 9	100
Adour ≃	E 2	80
Adra	H 1	88
Adrano	G 4	94
Adrar	D 4	198
Adrâr ◆[1]	E 2	198
Adré	C 9	200
Adria	D 8	92
Adrian, Mi., U.S.	C 1	162
Adrian, Mn., U.S.	D 7	174
Adrian, Mo., U.S.	C 1	170
Adrian, W.V., U.S.	D 3	162
Adrianople see Edirne	B 7	106
Adriatic Sea ⫧[2]	G 11	62
A Dun ≃	H 9	132
Ādwa	E 4	202
Adyča ≃	C 16	114
Adygeja □[3]	G 12	110
Adyk	G 14	110
Adzopé	D 4	200
Aegean Sea ⫧[2]	C 6	106
Aegina see Aígina	D 5	106
Aegviidu	C 12	66
Ærø I	D 3	68
Ærøskøbing	D 3	68
A Estrada	B 2	86
Afadé	C 7	200
Afar	D 6	198
Afféry	D 4	200
Afghanistan □[1]	F 8	112
Afgooye	G 6	202
Afikpo	D 6	200
Aflao	D 5	200
Aflou	C 5	198
Afognak Island I	G 18	154
Afoniha	B 20	108
A Fonsagrada	A 3	86
Afragola	D 4	94
Africa ⩡[1]	G 8	196
Afrikanda	C 16	64
Afşin	C 7	118
Afton, N.Y., U.S.	D 3	164
Afton, Ok., U.S.	D 1	170
'Afula	D 4	120
Afyon	C 9	106
Agadez	B 6	200
Agadez, Ighazer oua-n- ≃	B 6	200
Agadir	C 2	198
Agadyr	A 11	116
Agaie	D 6	200
Agan ≃	F 31	108
Agana see Hagåtña	C 12	134
Agano ≃	F 7	126
Agapovka	J 23	108
Āgaro	F 4	202
Agartala	E 6	122
Agassiz Pool ⊜	A 6	174
Agate	F 3	174
Agats	G 11	134
Agattu Strait ʮ	k 38	155a
Agboville	D 4	200
Ağdam	I 15	110
Agde	G 1	82
Agen	D 4	80
Aggeneys	E 3	206
Āghā Jārī	G 13	118
Aghzoumal, Sabkhat ⊜	E 2	198
Agía Paraskeví	C 7	106
Aginskoe	A 10	128
Ágio Óros □[3]	B 6	106
Ágios Kírykos	D 7	106
Ágios Nikólaos	E 6	106
Agíou Órous, Kólpos ⊂	B 5	106
Agira	G 4	94
Agliana	F 6	92
Agnibilékrou	D 4	200
Agnita	C 8	104
Agogo	D 4	200
Agou, Mont ∧	D 5	200
Agoura Hills	F 5	182
Āgra	D 3	122
Agreda	C 3	88
Ağrı	C 10	118
Ağrı Dağı see Ararat, Mount ∧	C 10	118
Agrigento	G 3	94
Agrigento □[6]	G 3	94
Agrihan I	I 13	124
Agrínio	C 4	106
Agrópoli	D 4	94
Agro Pontino ◆[1]	H 8	92
Agryz	H 20	108
Ağsu	I 16	110
Aguachica	F 6	186
Aguadilla	j 14	187b
Aguadulce, Pan.	F 4	186
Aguadulce, Spain	H 2	88
Agualeguas	D 10	184
Aguán ≃	E 3	186
Aguanaval ≃	E 8	184
Aguanish ≃	C 12	160
Agua Prieta	B 5	184
A Guardia	C 2	86
Aguarico ≃	D 3	190
Aguasabon ≃	A 5	166
Aguascalientes	G 8	184
Águas Santas	C 2	86
Água Vermelha, Represa de ⊜[1]	C 6	194
Agua Zarca	G 3	176
A Gudiña	B 3	86
Agudos	E 6	194
Aguié	C 6	200
Aguijan I	J 13	124
Aguilar	G 2	174
Aguilar de Campoo	B 6	86
Aguilar de la Frontera	G 6	86
Águilas	G 3	88
Aguit	F 9	128
Agujita	G 3	172
Agulhas	H 3	206
Agulhas, Cape (Agulhas, Kaap) ➤	H 4	206
Agulhas Basin ✦[1]	I 12	60
Agustín Codazzi	F 6	186
Agwarra	C 5	200
Ahaggar see Hoggar ⋏	E 6	198
Ahaggar, Tassili ta-n- ⋏[1]	E 6	198
Ahal □[3]	C 18	118
Ahangaran	A 1	122
Ahar	C 12	118
Ahaus	D 4	98
Ahipara Bay ⊂	A 4	146
Ahlat	C 10	118
Ahlbeck	C 11	98
Ahlen	E 4	98
Ahmadābād	E 2	122
Ahmadnagar	F 2	122
Ahmadpur East	D 2	122
Ahmar Mountains ⋏	F 5	202
Ahmetli	C 7	106
Ahon, Tarso ∧	A 8	200
Ahoskie	A 6	168
Ahrensbök	B 7	98
Ahrensburg	C 7	98
Ahtuba ≃	F 15	110
Ahtubinsk	E 15	110
Ahumada	B 6	184
Ahunui I[1]	E 13	136
Åhus	E 7	66
Ahvāz	G 13	118
Ahvenanmaa □[3]	B 10	66
Aichach	D 8	100
Aiea	i 9	181a
Aigen im Mühlkreis	B 5	102
Aigínio	B 5	106
Aígio	C 5	106
Aigle	D 4	82
Aigueperse	B 7	80
Aigüestortes i Estany Sant Maurici, Parque Nacional d' ♦	B 5	88
Aigurande	B 5	80
Aiken	C 4	168
Ailao Shan ⋏	F 5	130
Ailinglaplap I[1]	C 8	136
Ailuk I[1]	B 8	136
Aimorés	C 10	194
Aïn Defla	H 6	88
Aïn Deheb	C 5	198
Aïn Draham	G 2	90
Aïn el Beïda	B 6	198
Aïn M'lila	B 6	198
Aínos National Park ♦	C 4	106
Ainring	C 4	102
Aïn Sefra	C 4	198
Ainslie Lake ⊜	E 13	160
Ainsworth	D 4	174
Aïn Témouchent	B 4	198
Aïn Touta	B 6	198
Aïn Wessara	B 5	198
Aiora	E 3	88
Aïr, Massif de l' ⋏	B 6	200
Airdrie, Ab., Can.	F 14	156
Airdrie, Scot., U.K.	B 3	72
Aire-sur-l'Adour	E 3	80
Aire-sur-la-Lys	B 9	78
Air Force Island I	C 18	150
Airolo	D 6	82
Aishihik	F 26	154
Aishihik Lake ⊜	F 26	154
Aisne ≃	C 9	78
Aïssa, Djebel ∧	C 4	198
Aitape	M 12	124
Aitkin	B 2	166
Aït-Melloul	C 3	198
Aitutaki I[1]	E 12	136
Aiud	B 7	104
Aix-en-Provence	G 3	82
Aix-La-Chapelle	F 2	98
Aix-les-Bains	E 3	82
Āīzawl	E 6	122
Aizkraukle	D 12	66
Aizu-wakamatsu	F 7	126
Aj ≃	B 21	110
'Ajab Shīr	D 11	118
Ajaccio	j 8	83a
Ajana	J 3	140
Ajanta Range ⋏	E 3	122
Ajasse	D 5	200
Ajdābiyā	C 9	198
Ajdarkul', ozero ≣	I 20	110
Ajdovščina	E 5	102
Ajjer, Tassili-n- ⋏[1]	D 6	198
Ajka	C 9	102
'Ajlūn	E 5	120
'Ajmān	J 16	118
Ajmer	D 2	122
Ajni	B 1	122
Ajo	A 3	184
Ajon, ostrov I	C 19	114
Ajtos	D 9	104
Akaba	D 5	200
Akabira	C 9	126
Akagera see Kagera ≃	C 5	204
Akaroa	E 4	146
'Akāshāt	F 8	118
Akbou	B 5	198
Akbulak	D 19	110
Akçadağ	C 7	118
Akçakale	D 8	118
Akçakoca	B 9	106
Akchâr ◆[1]	F 2	198
Akdağmadeni	C 6	118
Aken	E 8	98
Aketi	B 3	204
Akhaltsikhe	I 13	110
Akhḍar, Wādī al- ≃	H 7	118
Akhisar	C 7	106
Akhmîm	I 4	118
Akiachak	F 14	154
Akimiski Island I	B 3	160
Akita	E 7	126
Akjoujt	F 2	198
Akka	D 3	198
Akkani	D 9	154
Akkeshi	C 10	126
'Akko (Acre)	D 4	120
Aklavik	B 27	154
Akmola see Astana	D 10	114
Akmolinsk see Astana	D 10	114
Aknīste	D 12	66
Ākobo (Akūbū) ≃	F 3	202
Akok	E 7	200
Akola	E 3	122
Akor	C 3	200
Akordat	D 4	202
Akot	E 3	122
Akoupé	D 4	200
Akpatok Island I	D 19	150
Akranes	m 19	64a
Åkrehamn	C 2	66
Akrítas, Ákra ➤	D 4	106
Akron, Oh., U.S.	C 3	162
Akron, Pa., U.S.	F 2	164
Akša	A 9	128
Aksaray	C 5	118
Akšatau see Aqshataū	E 19	110
Aksay	D 18	110
Akşehir	C 9	106
Akşehir Gölü ⊜	C 9	106
Aksu	A 4	122
Aksu ≃	D 9	106
Aksubaevo	I 19	108
Āksum	E 4	202
Aktanyš	B 19	110
Aktau see Aqtaū	H 17	110
Aktjubinsk see Aqtöbe	D 20	110
Aktyubinsk see Aqtöbe	D 20	110
Aku	D 6	200
Akūbū	F 3	202
Akūbū (Ākobo) ≃	F 3	202
Akune	H 3	126
Akure	D 5	200
Akureyri	m 21	64a
Akutan	I 11	154
Akutan Pass ʮ	I 11	154
Akwaya	D 6	200
Akyab see Sittwe	D 1	132
Akyazı	B 9	106
Ål	B 4	66
Ala ≃	A 5	122
Alabama □[3]	E 10	152
Alabama ≃	G 5	170
Alabaster	F 5	170
Alacant (Alicante)	F 4	88
Alachua	E 3	168
Aladža manastir ◗[1]	D 10	104
Alagoas □[3]	E 11	190
Alagoinhas	F 11	190
Alagón	C 3	88
Alagón ≃	E 4	86
Alaior	C 8	84
Alai Range ⋏	B 2	122
Alajõe	C 13	66
Alajuela	F 3	186
Alaköl köli ⊜	A 13	116
Alakurtti	C 9	108
Al-'Amādīyah	D 10	118
Alamagan I	I 13	124
Al-'Amārah	G 12	118
Ālamat'ā	E 4	202
Alameda	C 1	182
Alameda □[6]	C 2	182
Alamo	D 1	176
Alamo ≃	F 6	180
Alamogordo	F 6	176
Alamo Indian Reservation ◆[4]	E 5	176
Álamos ≃	C 9	184
Alamosa	D 5	176
Åland (Ahvenanmaa) II	B 9	66
Aland Sea ⫧[2]	B 9	66
Alanson	C 6	166
Alanya	D 4	118
Alaotra, Farihy ⊜	k 9	205a
Alapaevsk	H 24	108
Alapaha ≃	D 3	168
Alaplı	B 9	106
Al-'Aqabah	J 4	120
Alarcón	E 2	88
Alarcón, Embalse de ⊜[1]	E 3	88
Al-'Arīsh see El-Arish	G 1	120
Alas, Selat ʮ	A 4	140
Alaşehir	C 8	106
Alaska □[3]	D 18	154
Alaska, Gulf of ⊂	G 21	154
Alaska Peninsula ➤[1]	H 15	154
Alaska Range ⋏	E 20	154
Alassio	E 4	92
Alastaro	B 11	66
Älät	I 16	110
Alatna ≃	C 18	154
Alatri	H 9	92
Alatyr'	I 17	108
Alatyr' ≃	I 16	108
Alausí	D 3	190
Alava □[3]	B 2	88
Alava □[6]	B 2	88
Alava, Cape ➤	A 1	178
Alawa	C 6	200
Alawa Aboriginal Land ◆[4]	C 2	142
Al-'Ayn	J 16	118
Alazeja ≃	B 18	114
Al-'Azīzīyah	C 7	198
Al-Azraq ◆[1]	F 7	120
Alba, Italy	E 4	92
Alba, Tx., U.S.	D 6	172
Alba □[3]	B 7	104
Albacete	F 3	88
Albacete □[6]	F 3	88
Ålbæk	A 3	68
Albaida	F 4	88
Alba Iulia	B 7	104
Albal	E 4	88
Al-Balqā' □[3]	E 5	120
Albanel, Lac ⊜	C 7	160
Albania □[1]	G 11	62
Albano Laziale	H 8	92
Albany, Austl.	N 4	140
Albany, Ga., U.S.	D 2	168
Albany, Ky., U.S.	D 6	170
Albany, N.Y., U.S.	D 5	164
Albany, Oh., U.S.	D 2	162
Albany, Tx., U.S.	D 4	172
Albany □[6]	D 4	164
Albany ≃	F 16	150
Albarracín	D 3	88
Al-Barrah	J 11	118
Al-Baṣrah (Basra)	G 12	118
Al-Baṣrah □[3]	G 12	118
Albatera	F 4	88
Al-Bāṭinah ◆[1]	F 8	116
Al-Batrā' (Petra) ⊥	I 4	120
Albatross Bay ⊂	B 5	142
Al-Bayḍā', Libya	C 9	198
Al-Baydā', Libya	D 8	198
Albemarle Sound ʮ	A 6	168
Albenga	E 4	92
Alberene	E 4	162
Alberga Creek ≃	I 2	142
Alberic	E 4	88
Alberobello	D 7	94
Albert	B 9	78
Albert, Lake ⊜, Afr.	B 5	204
Albert, Lake ⊜, Austl.	E 2	144
Alberta	F 5	170
Alberta □[3]	F 10	150
Alberta, Mount ∧	E 13	156
Albertirsa	B 5	104
Albertkanaal ⩨	C 4	69
Albert Lea	D 2	166
Albert Markham, Mount ∧	E 24	208
Albert Nile ≃	G 3	202
Alberton	E 11	160
Albertville see Kalemie, D.R.C.	D 4	204
Albertville, Fr.	E 4	82
Albertville, Al., U.S.	E 5	170
Albi	E 6	80
Al Bidia	C 9	200
Albignasego	D 7	92
Albin	E 2	174
Albina	B 8	190
Albino	D 5	92
Albion, Mi., U.S.	B 1	162
Albion, Ne., U.S.	E 5	174
Albion, N.Y., U.S.	B 4	162
Albion, Pa., U.S.	C 3	162
Albion Park	E 8	144
Al-Biqā' □[3]	B 5	120
Al-Bīrah	F 4	120
Al-Birkah	E 7	198
Albisola Superiore	E 4	92
Alblasserdam	C 3	69
Albolote	G 7	86
Alboran Sea ⫧[2]	D 4	84
Alboraya	E 4	88
Ålborg see Aalborg	A 2	68
Albox	G 2	88
Albstadt	D 6	100
Ālbū Gharz, Sabkhat ⩦	E 9	118
Albuñol	H 1	88
Albuquerque	E 5	176
Alburquerque	E 4	86
Albury	F 6	144
Al-Buṭānah ◆[1]	D 3	202
Alcácer do Sal	F 2	86
Alcalá de Guadaira	G 5	86
Alcalá de Henares	D 7	86
Alcalá del Río	G 4	86
Alcalá la Real	G 7	86
Alcalde	D 5	176
Alcamo	G 2	94
Alcanar	D 5	88
Alcañiz	C 4	88
Alcántara	E 4	86
Alcantarilla	G 3	88
Alcaudete	G 6	86
Alcázar de San Juan	E 7	86
Alcester	D 6	174
Alcobaça, Braz.	B 11	194
Alcobaça, Port.	E 1	86
Alcobendas	D 7	86
Alcoi (Alcoy)	F 4	88
Alcolu	C 4	168
Alcora	D 4	88
Alcorcón	D 7	86
Alcorn	G 3	170
Alcoy see Alcoi	F 4	88
Alcubierre	C 4	88
Alcúdia	E 8	88
Alcúdia, Badia d' ⊂	E 8	88
Aldabra, Groupe d' II	I 12	196
Aldan	D 15	114
Aldan ≃	C 15	114
Aldan Plateau see Aldanskoe nagor'e ⋏[1]	D 15	114
Aldanskoe nagor'e ⋏[1]	D 15	114
Alderney I	j 10	73b
Aldershot	F 6	72
Alderson	A 4	168
Aleg	F 2	198
Alegre	D 10	194
Alegrete	A 10	195
Alejandro Selkirk, Isla I	H 6	188
Alejsk	D 11	114
Aleksandro-Nevskaja	H 14	110
Aleksandrov	H 13	108
Aleksandrov Gaj	D 15	110
Aleksandrovskij	D 10	110
Aleksandrovsk-Sahalinskij	B 12	124
Aleksandrów Kujawski	B 10	96
Alekseevka, Kaz.	J 29	108
Alekseevka, Kaz.	J 28	108
Alekseevka, Russia	D 11	110
Aleksin	I 12	108
Aleksinac	D 6	104
Além Paraíba	D 9	194
Alençon	D 6	78
Alenquer	D 8	190
Alentejo □[9]	F 2	86
Aleppo see Ḥalab	D 7	118
Aléria	i 9	83a
Alert	A 13	148
Alès	F 2	82
Aleški	D 12	110
Alessándria	E 4	92
Alessandria □[6]	E 4	92
Ålesund	E 2	64
Aleutian Basin ✦[1]	A 4	61
Aleutian Islands II	k 42	155a
Aleutian Trench ✦[1]	C 14	58
Alevina, mys ➤	D 18	114
Alexander	G 8	158
Alexander Archipelago II	H 26	154
Alexander Bay	E 2	206
Alexander Island I	C 1	208
Alexandra	F 2	146
Alexandra Falls ⌊	A 13	156
Alexandretta see İskenderun	D 7	118
Alexandretta, Gulf of ⊂	D 6	118
Alexandria, B.C., Can.	E 10	156
Alexandria, On., Can.	F 6	160
Alexandria (El-Iskandarîya), Egypt	G 3	118
Alexandria, Rom.	D 8	104
Alexandria, S. Afr.	C 9	206
Alexandria, Scot., U.K.	A 2	72
Alexandria, La., U.S.	G 2	170
Alexandria, Mn., U.S.	C 7	174
Alexandria, Va., U.S.	H 1	164
Alexandria Bay	B 3	164
Alexandrina, Lake ⊜	E 2	144
Alexandroúpoli	B 6	106
Alexis Creek	E 10	156
Al-Fallūjah	F 10	118
Alfaro	B 3	88
Alfarràs	C 5	88
Al-Fāshir	E 2	202
Alfatar	C 9	104
Al-Fayyūm see El-Fayoum	H 4	118
Alfeld	D 6	98
Alföld (Great Alfold) ⩦	B 7	90
Alfonsine	E 8	92
Alfred	C 8	164
Alfred National Park ♦	F 7	144
Alfreton	D 5	72
Alfta	B 8	66
Al-Fuḥayḥīl	H 13	118
Al-Fuqahā'	D 8	198
Algarve □[9]	G 2	86
Algarve, Costa do ⩡[2]	H 3	86
Algeciras	H 5	86
Algemesí	E 4	88
Alger	E 7	166
Algeria □[1]	F 8	196
Algete	D 7	86
Algha	E 20	110
Al-Ghawr ⩛	E 5	120
Alghero	I 4	92
Algiers see El Djazaïr	B 5	198
Alginet	E 4	88
Algoa Bay ⊂	G 6	206
Algoma	C 5	166
Algona	D 7	174
Algonquin	D 4	166
Algonquin Provincial Park ♦	F 4	160
Algorta, Spain	A 7	86
Algorta, Ur.	C 9	195
Alguazas	F 3	88
Al-Ḥajarah ◆[1]	H 10	118
Al-Ḥamād ⩦	G 8	118
Alhama de Murcia	G 3	88
Alhambra	F 1	88
Al-Ḥarīq	C 6	202
Al-Ḥarrah ⩡[9]	F 7	118
Al-Harūj al-Aswad ⋏[2]	D 8	198
Al-Ḥasakah	D 9	118
Alhaurín el Grande	H 6	86
Al-Ḥawrah	E 6	202
Al-Ḥijāz ◆[1]	B 4	202
Al-Ḥillah	F 11	118
Al-Hoceima	B 4	198
Al-Hoceima □[3]	E 3	84
Al-Huḍayb	E 3	202
Al-Ḥudaydah (Hodeida)	E 5	202
Al-Ḥufrah ◆[1]	H 8	118
Al-Hufūf	J 13	118
Alía	E 5	86
'Alīābād	D 16	118
Aliaga, Spain	D 4	88
Aliağa, Tur.	C 7	106
Aliákmonas ≃	B 5	106
Alibates Flint Quarries National Monument ♦	C 3	172
Äli Bayramlı	J 16	110
Alibey, ozero ⊜	C 10	104
Alicante see Alacant	F 4	88
Alicante □[6]	F 4	88
Alice	G 4	172
Alice Arm	D 7	156
Alice Springs	G 1	142
Alice Town	G 5	168
Alicurá, Embalse de ⊜[1]	G 2	195
Alīgarh	D 3	122
Alignements de Carnac ⊥	E 3	78
Alīgūdarz	F 13	118
Alikovo	B 15	110
Alima ≃	C 2	204
Alingsås	D 6	66
Ālīpur Duār	D 5	122
Aliquippa	C 3	162
Al-Istiwā'īyah □[3]	F 3	202
Alitak Bay ⊂	H 17	154
Alivéri	C 6	106
Al-Jabalayn	E 3	202
Al-Jaghbūb	D 9	198
Al-Jahrah	H 12	118
Al-Jalāmīd	G 8	118
Al-Jawf, Libya	E 9	198
Al-Jawf, Sau. Ar.	H 8	118
Al-Jawlān see Golan Heights □[2]	D 5	120
Al-Jaylī	D 3	202
Al-Jazīrah ◆[1]	E 3	202
Aljezur	G 2	86
Al-Jubayl	I 13	118
Al-Jufrah ⫧[4]	D 8	198
Al-Junaynah	E 1	202
Al-Kahfah	I 10	118
Alkamari	C 7	200
Al-Karabah	D 3	202
Al-Karak	G 5	120
Al-Karak □[3]	G 5	120
Al-Kawm	E 8	118
Al-Khābūrah	F 8	116
Al-Khafaqān ⩦	C 5	202
Al-Khalīl (Hebron)	F 4	120
Al-Kharṭūm (Khartoum)	D 3	202
Al-Kharṭūm □[3]	D 3	202
Al-Kharṭūm Baḥrī	D 3	202
Al-Khaṣab	I 16	118
Al-Khatam ◆[1]	K 16	118
Al-Khubar	I 13	118
Al-Khums	C 7	198
Alkmaar	B 3	69
Al-Kūfah	F 11	118
Al-Kufrah	E 9	198
Al-Kūt	F 11	118
Al-Kuwayt	H 12	118
Al-Lādhiqīyah	E 6	118
Al-Lagowa	E 2	202
Allahābād	D 4	122
Allan	F 18	156
Allanmyo	E 2	132
Allanridge	D 7	206
Allanton	F 3	146
'Allāq, Bi'r ⫧[4]	C 7	198
Allaqi, Wadi ≃	C 3	202
Allatoona Lake ⊜[1]	B 2	168
Allauch	G 3	82
Alldays	B 8	206
Allegany	B 4	162
Allegany State Park ♦	B 4	162
Allegheny ≃	C 4	162
Allegheny Mountains ⋏	D 4	162
Allegheny Plateau ⋏[1]	C 4	162
Allegheny Reservoir ⊜[1]	B 4	162
Allemands, Lac Des ⊜	H 3	170
Allen, Arg.	F 4	195
Allen, Ne., U.S.	D 6	174
Allen, Tx., U.S.	D 5	172
Allenby Bridge (Ḥusayn, Jisr al-) ◆[5]	F 5	120
Allendale	C 4	168
Allende	C 9	184
Allentown	F 3	164
Alleppey (Alappuzha)	H 3	122
Allevard	E 4	82
Allgäu ◆[1]	E 7	100
Alliance, Ne., U.S.	D 3	174
Alliance, Oh., U.S.	C 3	162
Al-Lidām	C 5	202
Allier □[3]	B 7	80
Allier ≃	B 7	80
Allinge	f 7	68a
Al-Lisān ➤[1]	G 4	120
Al-Līth	C 5	202
Alloa	D 5	74
Allonnes	E 7	78
Allora	B 8	144
Allschwil	C 5	82
Al-Luḥayyah	D 5	202
Allumette Lake ⊜	F 5	160
Allumettes, Île aux I	A 1	164
Allyn	B 2	178
Alma, Qc., Can.	D 8	160
Alma, Ks., U.S.	F 6	174
Alma-Ata see Almaty	A 3	122
Almacelles	C 5	88
Almada	F 1	86
Almaden, Austl.	D 7	142
Almadén, Spain	F 6	86
Al-Madīnah (Medina)	J 8	118
Al-Mafraq	E 6	120
Al-Mafraq □[3]	E 7	120
Almagro	F 7	86
Al-Manāmah	I 14	118
Al-Manāqil	E 3	202
Almansa	F 3	88
Almanza	B 5	86
Al-Marj	C 9	198
Almassora	E 4	88
Al-Matammah	D 3	202
Almaty	A 3	122
Almaty □[3]	A 3	122
Al-Mawṣil	D 10	118
Almeida	D 4	86
Almejas, Bahía ⊂	E 4	184
Almelo	B 5	69
Almenara	B 10	194
Almenar de Soria	C 2	88
Almendra, Embalse de ⊜[1]	C 4	86
Almendralejo	F 4	86
Al'menevo	I 25	108
Almería	H 2	88
Almería □[6]	G 2	88
Almeria, Costa de ⩡[2]	H 3	88
Almería, Golfo de ⊂	H 2	88
Al'metevsk	I 19	108
Al-Mijlad	E 2	202
Al-Miqdādīyah	E 11	118
Almira	B 4	178
Almirante Latorre	A 2	195
Almodôvar	G 2	86
Almodóvar del Campo	F 6	86
Almonte, On., Can.	A 2	164
Almonte, Spain	G 4	86
Almora	D 3	122
Al-Mubarraz	J 13	118
Al-Mudawwarah	H 7	118
Almudévar	B 4	88
Al-Muḥarraq	I 14	118
Al-Mukallā	E 6	202
Al-Mukhā	E 5	202
Almuñécar	H 7	86
Almussafes	E 4	88
Al-Muthanná □[3]	G 11	118
Al-Muwaqqar ⊥	F 6	120

Symbols in the index entries represent the broad categories identified in the key at the right. Symbols with superior numbers (⋌¹) identify subcategories (see complete key on page 242).

▲ Mountain   ⋌ Mountains   ⋊ Pass   ⋁ Valley   ≃ Plain   ⊁ Cape   I Island   II Islands   ⊥ Other Topographic Feature   ≃ River   ≈ Canal

Arnhem Land Aboriginal Land — Balears

Name	Map Ref.	Page
Arnhem Land Aboriginal Land ✦4	B 2	142
Árnissa	B 4	106
Arno I1	C 9	136
Arno ≃	F 6	92
Arno Bay	L 3	142
Arnold, Eng., U.K.	D 5	72
Arnold, Mn., U.S.	H 12	158
Arnold, Mo., U.S.	C 3	170
Arnprior	F 5	160
Arnsberg	E 4	98
Arnsberg □6	E 4	98
Arnsdorf	E 10	98
Arnstadt	F 7	98
Aroab	D 3	206
Aroland	F 15	158
Arolsen	E 5	98
Aromaševo	H 28	108
Arona	D 4	92
Aroostook ≃	g 12	163a
Arop Island I	M 13	124
Arorae I	D 9	136
Arp	F 1	170
Arqalyq	D 9	114
Arquata Scrivia	E 4	92
Arques	B 9	78
Arrah	D 4	200
Ar-Rahad	E 3	202
Arraias	F 9	190
Ar-Ramādī	F 10	118
Ar-Ramthā	D 6	120
Ar-Rank	E 3	202
Ar-Raqqah	D 8	118
Arras	B 9	78
Arras, Nuraghe ⊥	I 10	94a
Arrasate o Mondragón	A 2	88
Ar-Rawḍah	I 9	118
Ar-Rayyān	J 14	118
Arrecife	i 17	85b
Arrecifes	D 7	195
Arriaga	I 12	184
Arrigorriaga	A 2	88
Ar-Riyāḍ (Riyadh)	J 12	118
Arroio Grande	C 11	195
Arronches	E 3	86
Arros ≃	E 4	80
Arroyito	B 6	195
Arroyo	k 15	187b
Arroyo de la Luz	E 4	86
Arroyo Grande	E 3	182
Arroyo Hondo	D 6	176
Ar-Rub' al-Khālī (Empty Quarter) ✦2	G 6	116
Ar-Ruqayyah ⊥	D 8	120
Ar-Ruṣayfah	E 6	120
Ar-Ruṣayriṣ	E 3	202
Ar-Ruṭbah	F 8	118
Arsanjān	H 15	118
Arsenault Lake ⊜	D 17	156
Arsenev	B 4	126
Arsenevka ≃	B 4	126
Ars-en-Ré	B 2	80
Ārsī □3	F 4	202
Arsk	H 18	108
Ars-sur-Moselle	A 3	82
Árta, Grc.	C 4	106
Artà, Spain	E 8	88
Artashat	J 14	110
Arteaga	H 8	184
Art'em	C 4	126
Artemisa	C 4	186
Art'emovskij	H 24	108
Artern	E 8	98
Artesia	D 1	172
Artesian	C 6	174
Arthabaska □6	A 7	164
Arthur	H 10	158
Arthurs Lake ⊜1	i 12	145a
Arthur's Pass)(	E 3	146
Arthur's Pass National Park ♦	E 3	146
Arthur Stone	C 9	206
Arthur's Town	B 5	186
Artigas	B 9	195
Artigas ◗3	L 8	192
Artik	I 13	110
Artillery Lake ⊜	D 11	150
Artois □9	B 9	78
Artsyz	B 10	104
Artvin	B 9	118
Artvin □3	B 10	118
Artyom	I 17	110
Aru, Kepulauan II	G 10	134
A Rúa, Spain	B 3	86
Arua, Ug.	G 3	202
Aruanã	F 8	190
Aruba □2	H 13	148
Arucas	i 15	85b
Arufu	D 6	200
Arunāchal Pradesh □3	D 6	122
Arun Qi	B 14	128
Aruppukkottai	H 3	122
Arusha	C 6	204
Arusha □3	C 6	204
Arusha National Park ♦	C 6	204
Aruvi ≃	H 4	122
Aruwimi ≃	B 3	204
Arvada	F 2	174
Arviat (Eskimo Point)	D 14	150
Arvidsjaur	D 9	64
Arvika	C 6	66
Arvon, Mount ▲	B 4	166
Arvonia	E 4	162
Arxan	C 13	128
Arys	A 1	122
Arzamas	I 15	108
Arzew see Arziw	B 4	198
Arzgir	G 14	110
Arzignano	D 7	92
Arziw (Arzew)	B 4	198
Ås	C 5	66
Aša	I 22	108
Asaba	D 6	200
Asadābād	E 12	118
Asahan ≃	M 4	132
Asahi-dake ▲1	C 9	126
Asahikawa	C 8	126
Āsale ⊜	E 4	202
Asamankese	D 4	200
Asankranguaa	D 4	200
Asan-man c	H 16	128
Āsānsol	E 5	122
Åsarna	E 7	64
Asbest	H 24	108
Asbestos	F 8	160
Asbestos □6	A 7	164
Asbestos Range National Park ♦	i 12	145a
Asbury Park	F 5	164
Ascensión	B 6	184
Ascension I	I 6	196
Aschaffenburg	C 6	100
Ascheberg	E 4	98
Aschendorf	C 4	98
Aschersleben	E 8	98
Ascoli Piceno	B 3	94
Ascoli Piceno □6	B 3	94
Ascoli Satriano	C 5	94
Ascona	D 6	82
Aseb	E 5	202
Āsela	F 4	202
Åsele	D 8	64
Asenovgrad	D 8	104
Aseri	C 13	66
Asfûn el-Matâ'na	J 5	118
Ashbourne	D 5	72
Ashburton	E 3	146
Ashburton ≃	H 3	140
Ashburton Downs	H 4	140
Ashby-de-la-Zouch	E 5	72
Ashdod	F 3	120
Ashdod, Tel ⊥	F 3	120
Asheboro	B 5	168
Asherton	F 4	172
Asheville	B 3	168
Asheweig ≃	D 15	158
Ashford, Eng., U.K.	F 7	72
Ashford, Al., U.S.	G 6	170
Ash Fork	E 2	176
Ashgabat	J 21	110
Ashibetsu	C 9	126
Ashikaga	F 7	126
Ashington	B 5	72
Ashland, Ks., U.S.	G 5	174
Ashland, Ky., U.S.	D 2	162
Ashland, Me., U.S.	g 12	163a
Ashland, Mo., U.S.	C 2	170
Ashland, Mt., U.S.	C 10	178
Ashland, Oh., U.S.	C 2	162
Ashland, Or., U.S.	D 2	178
Ashland, Wi., U.S.	B 3	166
Ashley, Austl.	B 7	144
Ashley, N.D., U.S.	B 5	174
Ashoknagar	E 3	122
Ashqelon	F 3	120
Ash-Shamālīyah □3	C 2	202
Ash-Shāmīyah	G 11	118
Ash-Sharāh ✦1	I 5	120
Ash-Shāriqah (Sharjah)	J 16	118
Ash-Sharqāṭ	E 10	118
Ash-Sharqīyah □3	D 4	202
Ash-Sharqīyah ✦1	I 13	118
Ash-Shaṭrah	G 12	118
Ash-Shiḥr	E 6	202
Ash-Shināfīyah	G 11	118
Ashtabula	C 3	162
Ashtead	F 6	72
Ashton, S. Afr.	G 4	206
Ashton, Ia., U.S.	D 7	174
Ashton-under-Lyne	D 4	72
Ashuanipi Lake ⊜	B 11	160
Ashûm	G 4	118
Ashville	D 2	162
Ashwaubenon	C 4	166
'Āṣī ≃	E 7	118
Asia •1	C 18	56
Asia, Kepulauan II	E 10	134
Asia Minor □9	H 14	62
Asilah	B 3	198
Asinara, Golfo dell' c	I 4	92
Asino	D 11	114
Asipovičy	F 14	66
'Asīr ✦1	D 5	202
Aşkale	C 9	118
Askarovo	C 21	110
Askham	D 4	206
Askja ▲1	m 22	64a
Askvoll	B 2	66
Asmara	D 4	202
Asmera see Asmara	D 4	202
Ašmjany	E 12	66
Asnæs	C 4	68
Åsnen ⊜	D 7	66
Asola	D 6	92
Āsosa	E 3	202
Asouf, Oued ≃	D 5	198
Asp	F 4	88
Aspen	C 5	176
Aspendos ⊥	D 9	106
Aspiring, Mount ▲	F 2	146
As Pontes de García Rodríguez	A 2	86
Aspres-sur-Buëch	F 3	82
Aspromonte, Parco Nazionale dell' ♦	F 6	94
Assa	D 3	198
Assab see Aseb	E 5	202
Assaba □3	F 2	198
Assad, Lake ⊜1	D 8	118
As-Salṭ	E 5	120
Assam □3	D 6	122
As-Samāwah	G 11	118
Assateague Island I	D 6	162
Assateague Island National Seashore ♦	D 6	162
Asse	D 3	69
Assemini	I 9	94a
Assen	A 5	69
Assenede	C 2	69
Assens	C 2	68
Asseria ⊥	C 3	104
As-Sīb	F 8	116
Assíni ⊥	D 5	106
Assiniboine ≃	G 9	158
Assiniboine, Mount ▲	F 13	156
Assiniboine Indian Reserve ✦4	F 7	158
Assinica, Lac ⊜	C 6	160
Assis	E 5	194
Assis Chateaubriand	F 4	194
Assisi	F 8	92
Asslar	B 5	100
As-Sulaymānīyah, Iraq	E 11	118
As-Sulaymānīyah, Sau. Ar.	C 6	202
As-Sulaymānīyah □3	E 11	118
As-Sulayyil	C 6	202
Aş-Şummān ✦1	I 12	118
Assumption	C 4	170
As-Suwaydā'	D 7	120
As-Suwaydā' □3	D 7	120
Astakós	C 4	106
Astana (Aqmola)	D 10	114
Āstāneh	D 14	118
Āstārā	C 13	118
Asten	E 2	98
Asti	E 4	92
Asti □6	E 4	92
Astillero	A 7	86
Astorga, Braz.	E 5	194
Astorga, Spain	B 4	86
Astoria, Il., U.S.	B 3	170
Astoria, Or., U.S.	B 2	178
Åstorp	D 6	66
Astrachanskaja oblast' □6	F 15	110
Astrahan (Astrakhan)	F 16	110
Astravec	E 12	66
Astudillo	B 6	86
Astura, Torre ⊥	H 8	92
Asturias □3	A 4	86
Asunción	F 2	194
Asuncion Island I	I 13	124
Åsunden ⊜	D 7	66
Asveja	D 14	66
Aswân	C 3	202
Aswan High Dam see Aali, Sadd el- ✦6	C 3	202
Asyût	I 4	118
Aszód	B 5	104
Ata I	F 10	136
Atacama □3	A 2	195
Atacama, Desierto de ✦2	D 6	192
Atacama, Puna de ⋀1	D 6	192
Atacama, Salar de ≡	D 6	192
Atafu I1	D 10	136
Atakpamé	D 5	200
Atalánti	C 5	106
Atami	G 7	126
Aṭar	E 2	198
Atascadero	E 3	182
Atasū	A 11	116
Atatürk Barajı ⊜1	D 8	118
Atauro, Pulau I	G 9	134
Atbara see 'Aṭbarah ≃	D 3	202
'Aṭbarah	D 3	202
'Aṭbarah ≃	D 3	202
Atbasar	E 21	62
Atchafalaya ≃	G 3	170
Atchafalaya Bay c	H 3	170
Atchara Autonomis Respublika □3	I 13	110
Atchison	C 1	170
Atebubu	D 4	200
Aterno ≃	B 3	94
Ath	D 2	69
Athabasca	D 15	156
Athabasca ≃	C 16	156
Athabasca, Lake ⊜	B 17	156
Athapapuskow Lake ⊜	D 7	158
Athena	C 4	178
Athens see Athína, Grc.	D 5	106
Athens, Al., U.S.	E 5	170
Athens, Ga., U.S.	B 3	168
Athens, Mi., U.S.	D 6	166
Athens, N.Y., U.S.	B 7	162
Athens, Oh., U.S.	D 2	162
Athens, Tn., U.S.	B 2	168
Athens, Tx., U.S.	D 6	172
Atherton	D 7	142
Athi ≃	H 4	202
Athína (Athens)	D 5	106
Athi River	H 4	202
Athol	F 2	146
Áthos (Athos, Mount) ▲	B 6	106
Athos, Mount see Áthos ▲	B 6	106
Athus	E 4	69
Athy	C 4	75
Ati	C 8	200
Atienza	C 2	88
Atigun Pass)(	B 20	154
Atikaki Provincial Wilderness Park ♦	F 11	158
Atik Lake ⊜	D 10	158
Atikokan	G 13	158
Atikonak Lake ⊜	B 11	160
Atiu I	E 12	136
Atkarsk	D 14	110
Atkins	E 2	170
Atkinson	D 5	174
Atlanta, Ga., U.S.	C 2	168
Atlanta, Tx., U.S.	F 1	170
Atlantic	B 1	170
Atlantic □6	G 4	164
Atlantic City	G 4	164
Atlantic-Indian Basin ⊹1	K 4	58
Atlantic-Indian Ridge ⊹3	J 3	58
Atlántico □3	F 6	186
Atlantic Ocean ⫪1	E 8	60
Atlantis	G 3	206
Atlas, Rias •2	A 2	86
Atlas Mountains ⋀	C 4	198
Atlas Saharien ⋀	C 5	198
Atlas Tellien see Maritime Atlas ⋀	B 5	198
Atlin Lake ⊜	B 5	156
Atlin Provincial Park ♦	B 5	156
Atmore	G 5	170
Atnarko ≃	E 9	156
Atoka	C 5	172
Atoui, Khaṭṭ ≃	E 2	198
Atoyac ≃	H 10	184
Atrå	C 4	66
Atrak (Atrek) ≃	D 16	118
Ätran ≃	D 6	66
Atrato ≃	B 3	190
Atrek (Atrak) ≃	D 16	118
Atri	B 3	94
Atripalda	D 4	94
Aṭ-Ṭafīlah	H 5	120
Aṭ-Ṭafīlah □3	H 5	120
Aṭ-Ṭā'if	C 5	202
At-Ta'mīm □3	E 10	118
Attapu	G 8	132
Attawapiskat	B 2	160
Attawapiskat ≃	E 17	158
Attawapiskat Indian Reserve ✦4	E 17	158
Attawapiskat Lake ⊜	E 14	158
Attica, Ks., U.S.	G 5	174
Attica, N.Y., U.S.	D 9	166
Attica, Oh., U.S.	C 2	162
Attica □9	C 5	106
Attikí □3	C 5	106
Attleboro	E 7	164
Attnang	A 2	104
Attu Island I	k 38	155a
Aṭ-Ṭuwayyah	I 9	118
Atuel ≃	D 4	195
Atuel, Bañados del ≡	E 4	195
Åtvidaberg	G 8	64
Atwater	C 3	182
Atwood, Ks., U.S.	F 4	174
Atwood, Tn., U.S.	E 4	170
Atyraū	F 17	110
Atyraū □3	F 17	110
Aubagne	G 3	82
Aube □3	D 11	78
Aubenas	F 2	82
Aubervilliers	D 9	78
Aub-Ghos	C 3	206
Aubigny-sur-Nère	E 9	78
Aubinadong ≃	B 7	166
Aubry Lake ⊜	C 31	154
Auburn, Al., U.S.	F 6	170
Auburn, Ca., U.S.	B 2	182
Auburn, In., U.S.	B 6	170
Auburn, Ma., U.S.	D 7	164
Auburn, Me., U.S.	A 8	162
Auburn, Mi., U.S.	B 1	162
Auburn, N.Y., U.S.	B 5	162
Auburn, Wa., U.S.	B 2	178
Auburn ≃	H 10	142
Aubusson	C 6	80
Auch	E 4	80
Auchel	B 9	78
Auchterarder	D 5	74
Auckland	B 5	146
Auckland □3	B 5	146
Aude □3	E 6	80
Auden	F 15	158
Audierne	D 2	78
Audincourt	C 4	82
Audubon Lake ⊜1	B 4	174
Aue	B 9	100
Auerbach	B 9	100
Augathella	H 8	142
Auge, Pays d' ✦1	C 7	78
Augrabies	E 4	206
Augrabies Falls National Park ♦	E 4	206
Augsburg	D 7	100
Augusta, Austl.	N 3	140
Augusta, Italy	G 5	94
Augusta, Ga., U.S.	C 3	168
Augusta, Il., U.S.	B 3	170
Augusta, Me., U.S.	A 9	162
Augusta, Wi., U.S.	C 3	166
Augustdorf	E 5	98
Augustów	B 12	96
Augustus, Mount ▲	I 4	140
Augustus Downs	E 4	142
Auki	A 13	138
Aukstaitijos nacionalnis parkas ♦	E 12	66
Aulanko	B 12	66
Auld, Lake ⊜	H 7	140
Aulendorf	E 6	100
Aulla	E 5	92
Aulnay	B 3	80
Aulnay-sous-Bois	D 9	78
Aulnoye-Aymeries	B 10	78
Aumale	C 8	78
Aumance ≃	B 6	80
Aumühle	C 7	98
Auna	C 5	200
Auning	B 3	68
Auob ≃	D 4	206
Auraiya	D 3	122
Aurangābād, India	E 3	122
Aurangābād, India	E 4	122
Auray	E 3	78
Aurich	C 4	98
Auriflama	D 5	194
Aurillac	D 6	80
Aurlandsvangen	B 3	66
Aurora, On., Can.	F 4	160
Aurora, Co., U.S.	F 2	174
Aurora, Il., U.S.	B 4	170
Aurora, Me., U.S.	A 9	162
Aurora, N.Y., U.S.	D 2	164
Aurora, Oh., U.S.	C 3	162
Aurora, W.V., U.S.	D 4	162
Aurukun	B 5	142
Au Sable ≃	A 2	162
Au Sable Forks	B 5	164
Auschwitz see Oświęcim	C 10	96
Ausevik ⊥	B 2	66
Ausnek	D 2	206
Aust-Agder □3	C 4	66
Austerlitz see Slavkov u Brna	A 8	102
Austin, In., U.S.	C 6	170
Austin, Mn., U.S.	D 2	166
Austin, Pa., U.S.	C 4	162
Austin, Tx., U.S.	E 5	172
Austin, Lake ⊜	J 5	140
Austinville	E 3	162
Australes, Îles II	F 13	136
Australia □1	F 4	136
Australian Capital Territory □3	G 10	138
Austria □1	F 10	62
Autlán de Navarro	H 7	184
Autun	F 11	78
Auvergne □9	C 6	80
Auxerre	E 10	78
Auxier	E 2	162
Auxvasse	C 3	170
Auzangate, Nevado ▲	F 4	190
Avakubi	B 4	204
Avallon	E 10	78
Avalon Peninsula ≻1	E 17	160
Avanos	C 6	118
Avaré	E 6	194
Avarua	F 12	136
Avebury Stone Circle ⊥	F 5	72
Aveiro	D 2	86
Aveiro □3	D 2	86
Avella	D 4	94
Avellaneda	D 8	195
Avellino	D 4	94
Avellino □6	C 5	94
Avenal	D 3	182
Averbode, Abbaye d' ◗1	C 3	69
Aversa	D 4	94
Avesnes-sur-Helpe	B 10	78
Avesta	B 8	66
Aveyron □3	D 6	80
Avezzano	G 9	92
Aviano	C 8	92
Aviemore	C 5	74
Avigliana	D 3	92
Avignon	G 2	82
Ávila	D 6	86
Ávila □6	D 5	86
Avilés	A 5	86
Avinurme	C 13	66
Avion	B 9	78
Aviz	E 3	86
Avoca, Ia., U.S.	B 1	170
Avoca, N.Y., U.S.	B 5	162
Avola	H 5	94
Avon, Mn., U.S.	C 7	174
Avon, N.Y., U.S.	B 5	162
Avon ≃	E 5	72
Avondrust	H 4	206
Avon Park	F 4	168
Avontuur	G 5	206
Avranches	D 5	78
Awaji-shima I	G 5	126
Awakino	C 5	146
Āwasa	F 4	202
Āwash	F 4	202
Āwash ≃	E 5	202
Āwash Bihērawī Kilil ♦	F 4	202
Awbārī	D 7	198
Awbārī, Ṣaḥrā' ✦1	D 7	198
Awdal □3	E 5	202
Awled Djellal	C 5	198
Awlef	D 5	198
'Awrā'	D 8	198
Axel Heiberg Island I	B 10	148
Axim	E 4	200
Axiós (Vardar) ≃	E 7	104
Axis	G 4	170
Ax-les-Thermes	F 5	80
Axminster	G 3	72
Ayabe	G 5	126
Ayacucho, Arg.	E 8	195
Ayacucho, Peru	F 4	190
Ayakkum Hu ⊜	B 5	122
Ayaköz	A 13	116
Ayamé	D 4	200
Ayamonte	G 3	86
Ayapel	F 6	186
Ayaviri	F 4	190
Aydar ≃	E 11	110
Aydere	J 20	110
Aydın	D 7	106
Aydın □3	D 7	106
Āyelu Terara ▲1	E 5	202
Ayer	D 7	164
Ayer Chawan, Pulau I	j 14	134a
Ayer Merbau, Pulau I	j 14	134a
Ayers Rock (Uluru) ▲	I 11	140
Ayeyarwady □3	F 2	132
Ayeyarwady (Irrawaddy) ≃	F 2	132
Ayeyarwady, Mouths of the ≃1	F 6	122
Ayina ≃	B 1	204
Äyke köli ⊜	D 22	110
Aylesbury	F 6	72
Aylmer, On., Can.	D 8	166
Aylmer, Qc., Can.	A 3	164
Aylmer Lake ⊜	D 11	150
Ayod	F 3	202
Ayon Island see Ajon, ostrov I	C 19	114
Ayos	E 7	200
'Ayoûn el 'Atroûs	F 3	198
Ayr, Austl.	E 8	142
Ayr, Scot., U.K.	B 2	72
Ayre, Point of ≻	C 2	72
Ayrum	I 14	110
Ayvalık	C 7	106
Azahar, Costa del •2	D 5	88
Azalea Park	E 4	168
Azamatovo	C 18	110
Azanka	G 26	108
Azaouâd ✦1	B 4	200
Azaouagh ≃	B 5	200
Azärbaycan see Azerbaijan □1	E 6	112
Āzārbāyjān-e Gharbī □3	D 11	118
Āzārbāyjān-e Sharqī □3	D 13	118
Azare	C 7	200
Āzar Shahr	D 11	118
Azay-le-Rideau, Château d' ⊥	E 7	78
Azeffâl •8	E 2	198
Azemmour	C 3	198
Azerbaijan □1	E 6	112
Azëry	F 12	66
Azghyr	F 15	110
Azilal	C 3	198
Aznakaevo	I 20	108
Azogues	D 3	190
Azores II	h 12	198a
Azoum, Bahr ('Aẓūm, Wādī) ≃	C 9	200
Azov	F 11	110
Azov, Sea of ⫪2	F 10	110
Azovs'ke	G 9	110
Azpeitia	A 2	88
Azraq ash-Shīshān	F 7	120
Azrou	C 3	198
Azua	D 7	186
Azuaga	F 5	86
Azuero, Península de ≻1	G 4	186
Azuga	C 8	104
Azul	E 8	195
Azul, Cordillera ⋀	E 3	190
'Aẓūm, Wādī see Azoum, Bahr ≃	C 9	200
Azur, Côte d' •2	G 5	82
Azusa	F 6	182
Az-Zabadānī	B 6	120
Aẓ-Ẓahrān	I 13	118
Az-Zarqā'	E 6	120
Az-Zarqā' □3	F 7	120
Az-Zāwiyah	C 7	198
Az-Zaydāb	D 3	202
Azzel Matti, Sebkha ⊜	D 5	198
Az-Zubayr	G 12	118
Azzurra, Grotta •5	D 4	94
Az-Zuwaytīnah	C 9	198
B		
Ba	m 13	147c
Ba ≃, China	C 8	130
Ba ≃, China	C 12	130
Ba ≃, Viet.	H 9	132
Baar	C 6	82
Baar ✦1	E 5	100
Baardheere	G 5	202
Baarn	B 4	69
Baba Burnu ≻	C 6	106
Babadağ	D 8	106
Babaeski	B 7	106
Babaevo	G 11	108
Babahoyo	D 3	190
Babana	C 5	200
Babanka	A 11	104
Babanūsah	E 2	202
Babar, Kepulauan II	G 9	134
Babar, Pulau I	G 9	134
Babbitt	H 13	158
B'abdā	B 5	120
Bab el Mandeb see Mandeb, Bab el ʞ	E 5	202
Babel Thuap I	D 10	134
Babia, Arroyo de la ≃	F 3	172
Babian ≃	G 5	130
Bābil □3	F 11	118
Bābil, Aṭlāl (Babylon) ⊥	F 11	118
Babina Greda	C 5	104
Babine ≃	D 8	156
Babine Lake ⊜	D 9	156
Babinga	C 2	204
Babiogórski Park Narodowy ♦	D 10	96
Babo	F 10	134
Bābol	D 15	118
Bābol Sar	D 15	118
Babrujsk	C 6	110
Babuyan Island I	B 8	134
Babuyan Islands II	B 8	134
Babylon	F 5	164
Babylon see Bābil, Aṭlāl ⊥	F 11	118
Bacaadweyn	F 6	202
Bacabal	D 10	190
Bacan, Pulau I	F 9	134
Bacău	B 9	104
Bacău □3	B 9	104
Bac Binh	I 9	132
Baccarat	B 4	82
Bacchus Marsh	F 5	144
Bačėjkava	E 14	66
Bac Giang	D 8	132
Bachiniva	C 6	184
Bach Thong	C 7	132
Back ≃	C 13	150
Bačka ✦1	C 5	104
Bačka Palanka	C 5	104
Bačka Topola	C 5	104
Back Creek ≃	D 4	162
Bäckefors	C 5	66
Backnang	D 6	100
Bac Lieu	J 7	132
Bac Ninh	D 7	132
Bacolod	C 8	134
Bácsalmás	B 5	104
Bács-Kiskun □3	B 5	104
Bačurka	B 22	108
Bad ≃	B 1	162
Badagara (Vadakara)	G 3	122
Bad Aibling	E 8	100
Badajós, Lago ⊜	D 6	190
Badajoz	F 4	86
Badajoz □6	F 5	86
Badalona	C 7	88
Bādāmi	F 3	122
Badanah	G 9	118
Badanga	C 8	200
Bad Aussee	C 5	102
Bad Bergzabern	C 4	100
Bad Berleburg	E 5	98
Bad Bevensen	C 7	98
Bad Blankenburg	B 8	100
Bad Bramstedt	C 6	98
Baddeck	E 13	160
Bad Doberan	B 8	98
Bad Driburg	E 6	98
Bad Düben	E 9	98
Bad Dürkheim	A 6	82
Bad Dürrenberg	E 9	98
Bad Dürrheim	B 6	82
Bad Ems	B 4	100
Baden, Aus.	B 8	102
Baden, Switz.	C 6	82
Baden-Baden	D 5	100
Bad Endbach	F 5	98
Baden-Powell, Mount ▲	F 6	182
Badenweiler	C 5	82
Baden-Württemberg □3	D 5	100
Bad Frankenhausen	E 7	98
Bad Freienwalde	D 11	98
Bad Friedrichshall	C 6	100
Badgastein	C 5	102
Badger	D 15	160
Bad Hall	B 6	102
Bad Harzburg	E 7	98
Bad Hersfeld	F 6	98
Bad Homburg vor der Höhe	B 5	100
Bad Honnef	B 4	100
Badia Polesine	D 7	92
Badīar, Parc National du ♦	C 2	200
Bad Iburg	D 5	98
Bad Ischl	C 5	102
Bad Kissingen	B 7	100
Bad König	C 5	100
Bad Kreuznach	C 4	100
Bad Krozingen	E 4	100
Badlands ⋀2, S.D., U.S.	D 3	174
Badlands ⋀2	B 3	174
Badlands National Park ♦	D 3	174
Bad Langensalza	E 7	98
Bad Lausick	E 9	98
Bad Lauterberg im Harz	E 7	98
Bad Liebenstein	F 7	98
Bad Liebenwerda	E 10	98
Bad Lippspringe	E 5	98
Bad Mergentheim	C 6	100
Bad Münstereifel	B 3	100
Bad Muskau	E 11	98
Bad Nauheim	B 5	100
Bad Neuenahr-Ahrweiler	B 4	100
Bad Neustadt an der Saale	B 7	100
Bad Oeynhausen	D 5	98
Bad Oldesloe	C 7	98
Badong	C 10	130
Bad Orb	B 6	100
Badoumbé	C 2	200
Bad Pyrmont	D 6	98
Bad Ragaz	D 7	82
Bad Reichenhall	E 9	100
Bad River Indian Reservation ✦4	B 3	166
Bad Sachsa	E 7	98
Bad Säckingen	E 4	100
Bad Salzuflen	D 5	98
Bad Salzungen	F 7	98
Bad Sankt Leonhard im Lavanttal	C 6	102
Bad Schmiedeberg	E 9	98
Bad Schussenried	E 6	100
Bad Schwalbach	C 4	96
Bad Schwartau	C 7	98
Bad Segeberg	C 7	98
Bad Sooden-Allendorf	E 6	98
Bad Tölz	E 8	100
Bad Urach	D 6	100
Bad Vöslau	C 8	102
Bad Waldsee	E 6	100
Bad Wildbad im Schwarzwald	D 5	100
Bad Wildungen	E 5	98
Bad Windsheim	C 7	100
Bad Wörishofen	E 6	96
Bad Wurzach	E 6	100
Bad Zwischenahn	C 4	98
Baena	G 6	86
Bærum	C 5	66
Baeza	G 7	86
Bafang	D 7	200
Bafatá	C 2	200
Baffin Basin ⊹1	B 29	61
Baffin Bay c, N.A.	B 13	148
Baffin Bay c, Tx., U.S.	G 5	172
Baffin Island I	C 19	150
Bafia	E 7	200
Bafilo	D 5	200
Bafoulabé	C 2	200
Bafoussam	D 7	200
Bāfq	G 16	118
Bafra	B 6	118
Bāft	H 17	118
Bafwasende	B 4	204
Bagaces	F 3	186
Bāgalkot	F 3	122
Bagansiapiapi	M 5	132
Bagata	C 2	204
Bagawi	E 3	202
Bagdad see Baghdād	F 11	118
Bagdarin	B 6	124
Bagé	B 10	195
Bagenkop	D 3	68
Bāgevādi	F 3	122
Baghdād	F 11	118
Baghdād □3	F 11	118
Bāgh-e Malek	G 13	118
Bagheria	F 3	94
Baghlān	B 1	122
Bagnara Cálabra	F 5	94
Bagnères-de-Bigorre	E 4	80
Bagnères-de-Luchon	F 4	80
Bagni di Lucca	E 6	92
Bagnols-sur-Cèze	F 2	82
Bago (Pegu)	F 3	132
Bago □3	E 2	132
Bagoé ≃	C 3	200
Bagolino	D 6	92
Bagrationovsk	E 10	66
Baguio	B 8	134
Bahamas, The □1	G 12	148
Bahār	E 13	118
Baharampur	E 5	122
Bahau	M 6	132
Bahāwalnagar	C 2	122
Bahāwalpur	D 2	122
Bäherden	J 20	110
Baherove	G 9	110
Bahia □3	F 10	190
Bahía, Islas de la II	D 3	186
Bahía Blanca	F 6	195
Bahía de Caráquez	D 2	190
Bahía Kino	C 4	184
Bahía Laura	I 6	192
Bahir Dar	E 4	202
Bahraich	D 4	122
Bahrain □1	G 7	112
Baḥr al-Ghazāl □3	F 2	202
Baḥrayn, Khalīj al- c	J 14	118
Bahušėusk	B 7	110
Bai ≃	B 11	130
Baia de Aramă	C 7	104
Baia Mare	B 7	104
Baia Sprie	B 7	104
Baicheng, China	D 14	128
Baicheng, China	A 4	122
Baidoa see Baydhabo	G 5	202
Baie-Comeau	D 9	160
Baie-Johan-Beetz	C 12	160
Baiersbronn	B 6	82
Baie-Saint-Paul	E 8	160
Baie-Trinité	D 10	160
Baikal, Lake (Bajkal, ozero) ⊜	B 5	124
Băile Govora	C 8	104
Bailén	F 7	86
Băileşti	C 7	104
Bailieborough	C 4	75
Bailleul	B 9	78
Ba-Illi	C 8	200
Bailong ≃	B 7	130
Bainbridge, Ga., U.S.	D 2	168
Bainbridge, N.Y., U.S.	D 3	164
Baing	H 8	134
Bains-les-Bains	B 4	82
Baipu	B 15	130
Baiquan	C 16	128
Baird Inlet ⊜	F 12	154
Bairiki	C 9	136
Bairnsdale	F 6	144
Baisha, China	E 9	132
Baisha, China	D 8	130
Baishuijiang	B 8	130
Baixo Longa	F 2	204
Baiyin	H 5	128
Baiyü	C 4	130
Baïzo	C 5	200
Baja	D 10	102
Baja California □3	B 2	184
Baja California (Lower California) ≻1	C 2	184
Baja California Sur □3	D 3	184
Bajas, Rias •2	B 1	86
Bajdarackaja guba c	B 27	108
Bajina Bašta	C 5	104
Bajkalovo	H 27	108
Bajmak	C 21	110
Bajo Boquete	F 4	186
Bakacak	B 7	106
Bakal	I 23	108
Bakel	B 2	200
Baker, La., U.S.	G 3	170
Baker, Mt., U.S.	B 2	174
Baker, Mount ▲1	A 2	178
Baker Island I	C 10	136
Baker Lake ⊜	D 13	150
Baker Lake ⊜	J 9	140
Bakersfield	E 4	182
Bakersville	A 3	168
Bakhchysaray	G 8	110
Bakhmach	D 8	110
Bākhtarān see Kermānshāh	E 12	118
Bakhtegān, Daryācheh-ye ⊜	H 16	118
Bakı (Baku), Azer.	I 16	110
Baki, Som.	E 5	202
Bakitabu	H 4	202
Bakkaflói c	I 23	64a
Bakkagerði	m 24	64a
Bako	F 4	202
Bakony ⋀	D 9	102
Bakool □3	G 5	202
Bakouma	D 9	200
Bakovensfontein	G 5	206
Bakoy ≃	C 2	200
Baksan	H 13	110
Baksan ≃	H 13	110
Bakšty	F 13	66
Baku see Bakı	I 16	110
Bakwanga see Mbuji-Mayi	D 3	204
Balâ, Tur.	C 5	118
Bala, Wales, U.K.	E 3	72
Balabac Island I	D 7	134
Balabac Strait ʞ	D 7	134
Ba'labakk	F 7	118
Balad	F 10	118
Bālāghāt	E 3	122
Balaguer	C 5	88
Balahna	H 15	108
Balaklava	G 8	110
Balakliya	E 10	110
Balakovo	C 15	110
Balambangan, Pulau I	D 7	134
Balāngīr	E 4	122
Balaši	D 16	110
Balašov	D 13	110
Balassagyarmat	A 5	104
Balaton	C 7	174
Balaton ⊜	D 9	102
Balbieriškis	E 11	66
Balbina, Reprêsa ⊜1	D 7	190
Balcad	G 6	202
Balcarce	E 8	195
Balclutha	G 2	146
Bald Knob	E 3	170
Baldock	E 6	72
Baldock Lake ⊜	C 10	158
Baldone	D 12	66
Bald Rock National Park ♦	B 9	144
Baldwin	D 6	166
Baldwin City	C 1	170
Baldy Mountain ▲	F 8	158
Baldy Peak ▲	E 4	176
Bâle see Basel	C 5	82
Balē □3	F 5	202
Balearic Islands see Balears, Illes II	C 7	84
Balearic Sea ⫪2	E 6	88
Balears, Illes (Balearic Islands) II	C 7	84

Waterfall · ʞ Strait · c Bay, Gulf · ⊜ Lake · ≡ Swamp · Ice Feature · ⫪ Other Hydrographic Feature · ⊹ Submarine Feature · □ Political Unit · ◗ Cultural Institution · ⊥ Historical Site · ♦ Recreational Site · Airport · Military Installation · ✦ Miscellaneous

Name — Map Ref. — Page

Baleine ≃ E 19 150
Baleine, Grande rivière de la ≃ A 5 160
Balej B 7 124
Bale Mountain National Park ♦ F 4 202
Balen C 4 69
Bāleshwar E 5 122
Balestrand B 3 66
Balezino G 20 108
Balfour D 8 206
Balfour Downs H 6 140
Balgo G 9 140
Balgo Aboriginal Reserve ⬥[4] G 10 140
Balhaš see Balqash A 12 116
Bali I k 22 135b
Bali, Selat Ʉ G 6 134
Balige M 4 132
Balıkesir C 7 106
Balıkesir □[3] C 7 106
Balikpapan F 7 134
Balikumbat D 6 200
Balimo N 12 124
Balingen D 5 100
Balintang Channel Ʉ A 8 134
Bali Sea (Bali, Laut) ⊽[2] G 7 134
Balkan □[3] B 16 118
Balkan Mountains (Stara Planina) ⋏ D 8 104
Balkh B 1 122
Balkh ≃ B 1 122
Balkhash, Lake (Balqash köli) ◎ A 12 116
Ballachulish D 3 74
Ballālpur F 3 122
Ballan F 5 144
Ballangen B 8 64
Ballarat F 4 144
Ballard, Lake ◎ K 6 140
Ballater C 5 74
Ballenas, Bahía de c D 3 184
Ballengeich D 8 206
Balleny Islands II C 25 208
Ballerup C 5 68
Balleza ≃ D 6 184
Ballia D 4 122
Ballina, Austl. B 9 144
Ballina, Ire. B 2 75
Ballinasloe C 3 75
Ballincollig E 3 75
Ballinrobe C 2 75
Ballston Spa C 5 164
Ballycastle A 5 75
Ballymena B 5 75
Ballymoney A 5 75
Ballymote B 3 75
Ballyrogan, Lake ◎ D 5 144
Balma E 5 80
Balmaseda A 7 86
Balmoral Castle ⊥ C 5 74
Balmorhea E 2 172
Balonne ≃ B 7 144
Bālotra D 2 122
Balphakram National Park ♦ D 6 122
Balqash A 12 116
Balranald E 4 144
Balsam Lake C 2 166
Balsas A 9 190
Balsas ≃, Braz. E 9 190
Balsas ≃, Mex. H 9 184
Balsas Sur H 9 184
Bålsta C 8 66
Balsthal C 5 82
Balta B 10 104
Baltasar Brum B 9 195
Baltasi H 18 108
Bălți B 9 104
Baltic Sea ⊽[2] D 11 62
Baltijsk B 1 110
Baltijskaja kosa (Wiślany, Mierzeja) ›[2] A 10 96
Baltim G 4 118
Baltimore, S. Afr. B 8 206
Baltimore, Md., U.S. G 2 164
Baltimore □[6] G 2 164
Ba Lu ≃ G 9 132
Baluchistān □[3] D 1 122
Baluchistan □[9] C 1 122
Bālurghāt D 5 122
Balvi D 13 66
Balyn A 9 104
Balyqshy F 17 110
Bam E 8 116
Bama F 8 130
Bamaga A 6 142
Bamako C 3 200
Bambari D 9 200
Bamberg, Ger. C 7 100
Bamberg, S.C., U.S. C 4 168
Bambesa B 4 204
Bambio E 8 200
Bambouti F 2 202
Bambuí C 7 194
Bambuto ≃ G 3 176
Bamenda D 6 200
Bamfield G 9 156
Bamingui ≃ D 8 200
Bamingui-Bangoran □[3] D 9 200
Bamingui-Bangoran, Parc National du ♦ D 8 200
Bamokgoko C 8 206
Bampūr A 9 116
Bamy J 20 110
Bana E 5 204
Banaba I D 8 136
Banalia B 4 204
Banamba C 3 200
Bananal, Ilha do I F 8 190
Banaras see Vārānasi D 4 122
Banarlı B 7 106
Banās ≃ D 3 122
Banâs, Râs › C 4 202
Banat □[9] C 6 104
Banaz C 8 106
Banbridge B 5 75
Banbury E 5 72
Banc d'Arguin, Parc National du ♦ E 1 198
Banchory C 6 74
Bancroft see Chililabombwe E 4 204
Banda, D.R.C. B 4 204
Bānda, India D 4 122
Banda, Kepulauan II F 9 134
Banda Aceh L 2 132
Bandai-Asahi-kokuritsu-kōen ♦ E 7 126
Bandama ≃ D 4 200
Bandama Blanc ≃ D 3 200
Bandama Rouge ≃ D 3 200
Bandarbeyla F 7 202
Bandar-e 'Abbās I 16 118
Bandar-e Anzalī D 13 118
Bandar-e Deylam H 14 118
Bandar-e Gaz D 15 118
Bandar-e Khomeynī G 13 118
Bandar-e Lengeh I 16 118
Bandar-e Māh Shahr G 13 118
Bandar-e Shāhpūr see Bandar-e Khomeynī G 13 118
Bandar-e Torkeman D 15 118
Bandar Lampung G 5 134
Bandar Murcaayo E 6 202
Bandar Seri Begawan D 6 134
Banda Sea (Banda, Laut) ⊽[2] F 9 134
Bandeira, Pico da ∧ D 10 194
Bandeirantes C 3 194
Bandelier National Monument ♦ E 5 176
Bandera E 7 192
Banderas, Bahía de c G 7 184
Bandhavgarh National Park ♦ E 4 122
Bandiagara C 4 200
Bandiantaolehai F 5 128
Bandingilo National Park ♦ F 3 202
Bandipur Tiger Reserve ⬥[4] G 3 122
Bandırma B 8 106
Bandon E 3 75
Ban Don, Ao c J 4 132
Bandundu C 2 204
Bandundu □[3] C 2 204
Bandung, Indon. k 18 135b
Bandung, Indon. k 18 135b
Băneasa C 9 104
Banegas G 6 190
Bāneh E 11 118
Banes C 6 186
Banff, Ab., Can. F 14 156
Banff, Scot., U.K. C 6 74
Banff National Park ♦ F 13 156
Banfora C 4 200
Bangalore G 3 122
Bangassou E 9 200
Bangeta, Mount ∧ N 13 124
Banggai F 8 134
Banggai, Kepulauan II F 8 134
Banggi, Pulau I D 7 134
Banghāzī (Benghazi) C 9 198
Banghiang ≃ F 7 132
Bangil k 21 135b
Bangka, Pulau I F 5 134
Bangka, Selat Ʉ F 5 134
Bangkalan k 21 135b
Bangkinang N 5 132
Bangkok see Krung Thep H 5 132
Bangladesh □[1] G 10 112
Bang Mun Nak F 5 132
Bangolo D 3 200
Bangor, N. Ire., U.K. B 6 75
Bangor, Wales, U.K. D 2 72
Bangor, Me., U.S. A 9 162
Bangsri k 20 135b
Bangui E 8 200
Bangweulu, Lake ◎ E 5 204
Bangweulu Swamps ≋ E 5 204
Banhine, Parque Nacional de ♦ B 10 206
Bani, C.A.R. D 9 200
Baní, Dom. Rep. D 7 186
Bania E 8 200
Bani Bangou B 5 200
Banie B 8 96
Banifing ≃ C 3 200
Banima D 9 200
Banio, Lagune ◎ F 7 200
Bāniyās E 6 118
Banja Luka C 4 104
Banjarmasin F 6 134
Banjul (Bathurst) C 1 200
Bankass C 4 200
Bankilaré C 5 200
Bankja D 7 104
Banks, Îles II E 8 136
Banks Island I, B.C., Can. E 6 156
Banks Island I, N.T., Can. B 8 150
Banks Lake ◎[1] B 4 178
Banks Peninsula ›[1] E 4 146
Banks Strait Ʉ i 13 145a
Bankstown D 8 144
Bankumuna C 2 204
Bann ≃ A 5 75
Ban Nadou G 7 132
Ban Namnga D 5 132
Banner Elk A 4 168
Banning G 6 182
Banningville see Bandundu C 2 204
Bannockburn Battlesite ⊥ D 5 74
Bannu C 2 122
Bánokszentgyörgy D 8 102
Ban Pakneun E 5 132
Ban Phai F 6 132
Ban San Xieng La E 6 132
Banská Bystrica B 11 102
Banská Štiavnica B 10 102
Ban Songkhon E 7 132
Banstead F 6 72
Bantaeng G 7 134
Bantenan, Tanjung › I 22 135b
Ban Thabôk I 6 130
Banyo D 7 200
Banyoles B 7 88
Banyuwangi I 22 135b
Banyuwedang I 22 135b
Baode G 8 128
Baoding G 10 128
Baofeng B 11 130
Bao Ha C 7 132
Baoji A 8 130
Baojing D 9 130
Bao Lac I 8 132
Baoning G 8 130
Baoqing C 18 128
Baoshan F 4 130
Baoting I 9 130
Baotou F 8 128
Baoulé ≃ C 3 200
Baoying B 14 130
Bapaume B 9 78
Bāqa el Gharbiyya E 4 120
Ba'qūbah F 11 118
Baquedano D 5 192
Baraawe G 5 202
Baraboo D 4 166
Baracoa C 6 186
Baradero C 8 195
Baradine C 7 144
Baragoi G 4 202
Bārah E 3 202
Barahona D 7 186
Barāk ≃ E 6 122
Baraka (Barakah, Khawr) ≃ D 4 202
Barakah, Khawr (Baraka) ≃ D 4 202
Barakaldo A 1 88
Baraki C 1 122
Baram ≃ E 6 134
Barama ≃ G 9 186
Bārāmūla C 2 122
Baran' E 14 66
Baranavičy J 13 64
Baranoa F 6 186
Baranof Island I H 27 154
Baranya □[3] D 10 102
Baraolt B 8 104
Baraqbay J 27 108
Baraški D 20 108
Barataria H 3 170
Barat Daya, Kepulauan II G 9 134
Barauni D 5 122
Baravuha E 14 66
Barbacena D 9 194
Barbacoas C 3 190
Barbados □[1] H 14 148
Barbar D 3 202
Barbas, Cap › E 1 198
Barbastro B 5 88
Barbate H 5 86
Barbeau Peak ∧ A 12 148
Barberton, S. Afr. C 9 206
Barberton, Oh., U.S. C 3 162
Barbezieux C 3 80
Barbuda I I 18 187c
Barby E 8 98
Bârca C 7 104
Barcaldine G 7 142
Barcău (Berettyó) ≃ B 7 104
Barcellona Pozzo di Gotto F 5 94
Barcelona, Mex. D 8 184
Barcelona, Spain C 7 88
Barcelona, Ven. F 8 186
Barcelona □[6] C 6 88
Barcelos, Braz. D 6 190
Barcelos, Port. C 2 86
Barcoo ≃ H 6 142
Barcs E 9 102
Bärdä, Azer. I 15 110
Barda, Russia H 21 108
Bardai C 9 200
Barddhamān E 5 122
Bardejov D 11 96
Bardeskan E 17 118
Bardo G 3 90
Bardoc L 6 140
Bardstown D 6 170
Bardwell D 4 170
Bareilly D 3 122
Barentin C 7 78
Barentsøya I B 5 114
Barents Sea ⊽[2] B 6 114
Barentu D 4 202
Barga E 6 92
Barge F 5 82
Bargnop F 2 202
Bargoed F 3 72
Bargteheide C 7 98
Barguzin ≃ B 5 124
Bar Harbor A 9 162
Bari, D.R.C. B 2 204
Bari, Italy C 6 94
Bari □[3] E 7 202
Bari □[6] D 6 94
Barikiwa D 6 204
Baril Lake ◎ B 16 156
Barinas F 7 186
Barinas □[3] F 7 186
Bāripada E 5 122
Bariri E 6 194
Bârîs J 4 118
Barisāl E 6 122
Barisāl □[3] E 6 122
Barisan, Pegunungan ⋏, Indon. N 5 132
Barisan, Pegunungan ⋏, Indon. F 4 134
Barito ≃ F 6 134
Barjac F 2 82
Barjols G 4 82
Barkam C 6 130
Barkava D 13 66
Barkley, Lake ◎[1] D 5 170
Barkley Sound Ʉ G 9 156
Barkly East F 7 206
Barkly Tableland ⋏[1] E 2 142
Barla C 9 106
Bârlad B 9 104
Barleben D 8 98
Bar-le-Duc D 12 78
Barlee, Lake ◎ K 5 140
Barletta C 6 94
Barling E 1 170
Bārmer D 2 122
Barmstedt C 6 98
Barnard ≃ C 8 144
Barnard Castle C 4 72
Barnato C 5 144
Barnaul D 11 114
Barnesville B 6 174
Barnet □[6] F 6 72
Barneveld B 4 69
Barneville-Carteret C 5 78
Barnim ⬥[1] D 10 98
Barnoldswick D 4 72
Barnsley D 5 72
Barnsley □[6] D 5 72
Barnstable E 8 164
Barnstable □[6] E 8 164
Barnstaple F 2 72
Barnstaple Bay c F 2 72
Baro ≃ F 3 202
Baroua C 7 200
Barpeta D 6 122
Barques, Pointe aux › A 2 162
Barquisimeto F 7 186
Barra F 10 190
Barra, Ponta da › B 11 206
Barrackville D 3 162
Barra do Cuanza D 1 204
Barra do Garças A 4 194
Barra Falsa, Ponta da › B 11 206
Barrafranca G 4 94
Barra Mansa E 8 194
Barrancabermeja G 6 186
Barrancas F 9 186
Barranco do Velho G 2 86
Barranquilla F 6 186
Barrax E 2 88
Barre B 6 164
Barreiras F 10 190
Barreiro F 1 86
Barretos D 6 194
Barrhead D 14 156
Barrie F 4 160
Barrière F 11 156
Barrier Range ⋏ C 3 144
Barrington Lake ◎ C 8 158
Barrington Tops National Park ♦ D 8 144
Barringun B 5 144
Barrow, Arg. F 7 195
Barrow, Ak., U.S. A 16 154
Barrow ≃ D 5 75
Barrow, Point › A 16 154
Barrow-in-Furness C 3 72
Barrow Island I G 3 140
Barrows E 8 158
Barrow Strait Ʉ B 14 150
Barry F 3 72
Barrydale G 4 206
Barryton D 6 166
Barsbüttel C 7 98
Bārsi F 3 122
Barsinghausen D 6 98
Barssel C 4 98
Barstow F 6 182
Bar-sur-Seine D 11 78
Barth B 9 98
Bartholomew, Bayou ≃ F 3 170
Bartibougou C 5 200
Bartica B 7 190
Bartın B 5 118
Bartle Frere ∧ D 7 142
Bartlesville B 5 172
Bartlett, N.H., U.S. B 7 164
Bartlett, Tn., U.S. E 4 170
Bartley E 4 174
Barton-upon-Humber D 6 72
Bartoszyce A 11 96
Bartow, Fl., U.S. F 4 168
Bartow, Ga., U.S. C 3 168
Barú, Volcán ∧[1] F 4 186
Barumun ≃ M 5 132
Barung, Nusa I I 21 135b
Barun-Torej, ozero ◎ B 10 128
Barus N 4 132
Baruun-Urt C 9 128
Barwāni E 2 122
Barwice B 9 96
Barwon ≃ C 6 144
Barwon Heads G 5 144
Baryš J 17 108
Barysau E 14 66
Basankusu B 2 204
Basarabeasca B 10 104
Basatongwula Shan ∧ C 6 122
Basavilbaso C 8 195
Bas-Congo □[3] D 2 204
Basel (Bâle) C 5 82
Basel-Land □[3] C 5 82
Basey C 9 134
Bashaw E 15 156
Bashi Channel Ʉ H 15 130
Basilan Island I D 8 134
Basildon F 7 72
Basile G 2 170
Basiliano C 8 92
Basilicata □[3] D 6 94
Basílio F 9 192
Basingstoke F 5 72
Basīrhāt E 5 122
Başkale C 10 118
Baskatong, Réservoir ◎[1] E 6 160
Baškirija □[3] B 19 110
Baskomutan Milli Parkı ♦ C 9 106
Bašmakovo J 15 108
Bāsoda E 3 122
Basoko B 3 204
Basque Country see Vasco, País □[3] A 2 88
Basra see Al-Başrah G 12 118
Bas-Rhin □[3] B 5 82
Bassano del Grappa D 7 92
Bassar D 5 200
Bassein see Pathein F 2 132
Bassein (Pathein) ≃ F 6 122
Basse-Kotto □[3] D 9 200
Bassella B 6 88
Basse-Terre, Guad. o 21 187e
Basseterre, St. K./N. m 20 187d
Basse Terre, Trin. q 23 187e
Basse-Terre I n 21 187e
Bassikounou F 3 198
Bass River F 12 160
Bass Strait Ʉ G 5 144
Bassum D 5 98
Basswood Lake ◎ A 3 166
Bastak I 16 118
Bastelica j 8 83a
Basti D 4 122
Bastia, Fr. i 9 83a
Bastia, Italy F 8 92
Bastogne D 4 69
Bastrop F 2 170
Bata E 6 200
Batabanó, Golfo de c C 4 186
Batajsk F 11 110
Batala C 3 122
Batalha E 2 86
Batang C 4 130
Batangas C 8 134
Batangbatangdaya k 21 135b
Batan Island I H 8 124
Batan Islands II A 8 134
Batanta, Pulau I F 10 134
Batatais D 7 194
Batavia, Ia., U.S. B 2 170
Batavia, Il., U.S. B 4 170
Batavia, N.Y., U.S. B 4 162
Batchelor C 11 140
Bătdâmbâng H 6 132
Bateckij G 9 108
Batemans Bay E 8 144
Bate Pito ≃ G 4 176
Batesville, Ar., U.S. E 3 170
Batesville, In., U.S. C 6 170
Batesville, Tx., U.S. F 4 172
Bath, Eng., U.K. F 4 72
Bath, Me., U.S. B 9 162
Bath, N.Y., U.S. D 1 164
Batha □[3] C 8 200
Bath and North East Somerset □[6] F 4 72
Bathgate G 10 158
Bathinda C 2 122
Bathurst, Austl. D 7 144
Bathurst, N.B., Can. E 11 160
Bathurst see Banjul, Gam. C 1 200
Bathurst, S. Afr. G 7 206
Bathurst, Cape › B 7 150
Bathurst Inlet c C 11 150
Bathurst Island I, Austl. B 10 140
Bathurst Island I, Nu., Can. A 12 150
Batī E 5 202
Batié D 4 200
Bāṭin, Wādī al- ≃ H 12 118
Batley D 5 72
Batman D 9 118
Batman □[3] C 9 118
Batna B 6 198
Batoche National Historic Site ♦ E 19 156
Baton Rouge G 3 170
Batouala E 7 200
Batouri E 7 200
Battambang see Bătdâmbâng H 6 132
Batticaloa H 4 122
Battipaglia D 4 94
Battle ≃ E 16 156
Battle Creek, Mi., U.S. B 1 162
Battle Creek, Ne., U.S. E 6 174
Battlefields F 4 204
Battle Mountain B 5 180
Battonya B 6 104
Batu ∧ F 4 202
Batu, Kepulauan II F 3 134
Batu Gajah L 5 132
Batumi I 12 110
Batu Pahat N 6 132
Baturaja F 4 134
Baturité D 11 190
Bat Yam E 3 120
Batys Qazaqstan □[3] E 17 110
Baubau G 8 134
Bauchi C 6 200
Baud E 4 78
Bauland ⬥[1] C 6 100
Bauld, Cape › C 16 160
Baume-les-Dames C 4 82
Baunatal E 6 98
Baure C 6 200
Bauru E 6 194
Bauska D 12 66
Bautzen E 11 98
Bavaria see Bayern □[3] D 7 100
Bavarian Forest ⋏ C 9 100
Båven ◎ C 8 66
Bavispe ≃ B 5 184
Baw Baw National Park ♦ F 6 144
Bawean, Pulau I G 6 134
Bawiti H 3 118
Bawku C 4 200
Baxian G 11 128
Baxter, Mn., U.S. B 7 174
Baxter, Tn., U.S. A 2 168
Baxter State Park ♦ g 12 163a
Bay E 3 170
Bay □[3] G 5 202
Bay, Laguna de ◎ C 8 134
Bayamo C 5 186
Bayamón j 15 187b
Bayan C 16 128
Bayanga E 8 200
Bayan Har Shan ⋏ D 16 116
Bayanhongor C 3 128
Bayanhongor □[3] D 2 128
Bayano, Lago ◎[1] F 5 186
Bayan Obo E 7 128
Bayan-Ovoo B 8 128
Bayan-Uhaa B 2 128
Bayan-Uul C 3 128
Bayard B 1 170
Bayasgalant C 9 128
Bayboro B 6 168
Bayburt B 9 118
Bayburt □[3] B 9 118
Bay City, Mi., U.S. B 2 162
Bay City, Or., U.S. C 2 178
Bay City, Tx., U.S. F 5 172
Baydhabo G 5 202
Baydrag ≃ C 2 128
Bayerische Alpen ⋏ E 8 100
Bayerischer Wald, Nationalpark ♦ D 10 100
Bayern □[3] D 7 100
Bayeux C 6 78
Bayfield B 3 166
Bayhān al-Qaşāb E 6 202
Bayındır C 7 106
Bay Minette G 5 170
Bay of Plenty □[3] C 6 146
Bayonne, Fr. E 2 80
Bayonne, N.J., U.S. F 4 164
Bayou Bodcau Reservoir ◎[1] F 2 170
Bayou Cane H 3 170
Bayou D'Arbonne Lake ◎[1] F 2 170
Bayovar E 2 190
Bayport, Mn., U.S. C 2 166
Bayport, N.Y., U.S. F 5 164
Bayramiç C 7 106
Bayreuth C 8 100
Bay Roberts E 17 160
Bayrūt (Beirut) B 4 120
Bayrūt □[3] B 4 120
Bays, Lake of ◎ F 4 160
Bay Saint Louis G 4 170
Bay Shore F 5 164
Bay Springs Lake ◎[1] E 4 170
Bayt al-Faqīh E 5 202
Bayt Jālā F 4 120
Bayt Laḥm (Bethlehem) F 4 120
Baytown H 1 170
Bayy al-Kabīr, Wādī ≃ C 7 198
Bayyrqum A 1 122
Baza G 2 88
Bazardüzü Dağı ∧ I 15 110
Bazaruto, Ilha do I A 11 206
Bazas D 3 80
Bazhong C 8 130
Bazine A 4 172
Be, Nosy I j 9 205a
Beach B 2 174
Beachville B 3 162
Beacon E 5 164
Beaconsfield F 6 72
Beagle Bay Aboriginal Reserve ⬥[4] E 7 140
Beagle Gulf c C 11 140
Bealanana j 9 205a
Bear ≃ E 7 178
Bear Brook State Park ♦ C 7 164
Bearden F 2 170
Beardmore Glacier ⊓ E 26 208
Beardstown B 3 170
Bear Head Lake State Park ♦ B 2 166
Bear Island I D 33 208
Bear Lake C 8 156
Bear Lake ◎, Mb., Can. D 10 158
Bear Lake ◎ E 8 178
Béarn □[9] E 3 80
Bear River Range ⋏ E 8 178
Bearsden E 4 74
Beartooth Mountains ⋏ C 9 178
Beās ≃ C 3 122
Beasain A 2 88
Beata, Cabo › D 7 186
Beata, Isla I D 7 186
Beatrice E 6 174
Beatton ≃ C 11 156
Beatton River C 11 156
Beattyville E 2 162
Beaucaire G 2 82
Beauce ⬥[1] D 8 78
Beauce-Sartigan □[6] A 8 164
Beauchêne Island I o 18 193b
Beaudesert A 9 144
Beaufort, Austl. F 4 144
Beaufort, Malay. D 7 134
Beaufort, N.C., U.S. B 6 168
Beaufort Castle see Qal'at ash-Shaqīf ⊥ C 4 120
Beaufort Sea ⊽[2] B 6 148
Beaufort West G 5 206
Beaugency E 8 78
Beauharnois A 7 162
Beauharnois-Salaberry □[6] A 5 164
Beaujolais □[9] D 2 82
Beaumetz-lès-Loges B 9 78
Beaumont, Ms., U.S. G 4 170
Beaumont, Tx., U.S. G 1 170
Beaumont-sur-Oise C 9 78
Beaumont-sur-Sarthe D 6 78
Beaune E 11 78
Beauport E 8 160
Beaupréau E 6 78
Beausejour F 10 158
Beauvais C 8 78
Beauvais Lake ◎ A 19 156
Beauvallon E 2 206
Beauvoir-sur-Mer F 4 78
Beaver, Pa., U.S. C 3 162
Beaver, Ut., U.S. C 2 176
Beaver, W.V., U.S. E 3 162
Beaver ≃ A 9 156
Beaver ≃ D 18 156
Beaver ≃ B 4 172
Beaver Creek ≃, Ak., U.S. D 21 154
Beaver Creek ≃, Mt., U.S. A 9 178
Beaver Dam D 4 166
Beaverdell G 12 156
Beaver Falls C 3 162
Beaverhead ≃ C 7 178
Beaverhead Mountains ⋏ C 7 178
Beaver Hill Lake ◎ D 11 158
Beaver Island I C 6 166
Beaver Lake Indian Reserve ⬥[4] D 16 156
Beavers Bend State Park ♦ E 1 170
Beaverton C 2 178
Beāwar D 2 122
Bebedouro D 6 194
Béboto D 8 200
Bebra F 6 98
Bécancour ≃ E 8 160
Beccles E 8 72
Bečej C 5 104
Beceni C 9 104
Béchar C 4 198
Becharof Lake ◎ H 16 154
Bec-Hellouin, Abbaye du ◗[1] C 7 78
Bechet D 7 104
Bechevin Bay c I 12 154
Beckingen C 3 100
Beckley E 3 162
Beckum E 4 98
Beckville F 1 170
Bedale C 5 72
Bedford, Qc., Can. A 5 164
Bedford, Eng., U.K. E 6 72
Bedford, In., U.S. C 5 170
Bedford, Ma., U.S. D 7 164
Bedford, Pa., U.S. C 4 162
Bedford, Va., U.S. E 4 162
Bedfordshire □[6] E 6 72
Bédi C 8 200
Bedlington B 5 72
Bedok j 15 134a
Bedourie H 4 142
Beech Creek D 5 170
Beech Grove C 5 170
Beechy F 18 156
Beek F 2 98
Beelitz D 9 98
Beenleigh A 9 144
Beerse C 3 69
Be'ér Sheva' G 3 120
Beeskow D 11 98
Beeston E 5 72
Beethoven Peninsula ›[1] D 1 208
Beeville F 5 172
Befale B 3 204
Bega F 7 144
Begna ≃ B 5 66
Begoro D 4 200
Behbahān G 14 118
Behm Canal Ʉ I 29 154
Behshahr D 15 118
Bei ≃ G 11 130
Bei'an B 16 128
Beicheng F 6 130
Beihai H 9 130
Beijing (Peking) G 11 128
Beijing □[3] F 11 128
Beiliu G 10 130
Beipan ≃ F 7 130
Beipiao F 13 128
Beira F 5 204
Beira □[9] C 1 84
Beirut see Bayrūt B 4 120
Beiseker F 15 156
Bei Shan ⋏ A 7 122
Beitbridge B 9 206
Beizhen F 13 128
Beja, Port. F 3 86
Béja, Tun. B 6 198
Beja □[3], Port. G 2 86
Béja □[3], Tun. G 2 90
Bejaïa B 6 198
Béjar D 5 86
Béka D 7 200
Bekaa Valley V E 7 118
Bekabad A 1 122
Békés B 6 104
Békés □[3] B 6 104
Békéscsaba B 6 104
Bekily I 9 205a
Bekodoka k 8 205a
Bekwai D 4 200
Bekyem D 4 200
Bela E 10 116
Bélabo E 7 200
Bela Crkva C 6 104
Belaga E 6 134
Bel Air G 2 164
Belaja ≃ B 19 110
Belaja Berëzka C 8 110
Belaja Holunica G 19 108
Belaja Kalitva E 12 110
Belalcázar F 5 86
Belampalli F 3 122
Bela Palanka D 7 104
Belarus □[1] E 13 62
Bela Vista, Ang. D 1 204
Bela Vista, Braz. E 2 194
Belawan M 4 132
Belbubulo F 3 202
Bełchatów C 10 96
Belcher C 11 158
Belcher Islands II C 18 158
Belebej I 21 108
Belecke E 5 98
Beledweyne G 5 202
Belel D 7 200
Belém D 9 190
Belén, Arg. E 6 192
Belen, N.M., U.S. E 5 176
Belén de Escobar D 8 195
Belene D 8 104
Bélep, Îles II C 13 138
Beles ≃ E 4 202
Belet Uen see Beledweyne G 5 202
Belëv J 12 108
Belfast, N. Ire., U.K. B 5 75
Belfast, Me., U.S. A 9 162
Belfield B 3 174
Belfort C 4 82
Belfort □[3] C 4 82
Belgaum F 2 122
Belgium B 8 206
Belgium □[1] E 8 62
Belgorod D 10 110
Belgorodskaja oblast' □[6] D 10 110
Belgrade, Mn., U.S. C 7 174
Belgrade see Beograd, Yugo. C 6 104
Belgrano II ◗[3] D 5 208
Beliliou I D 10 134
Beli Manastir E 10 102
Belin-Beliet D 3 80
Belington D 4 162
Belitung I F 5 134
Belize □[1] H 11 148
Belize City I 15 184
Belknap □[6] C 7 164
Bell C 7 156
Bell ≃, Qc., Can. D 5 160
Bell ≃, Yk., Can. C 26 154
Bella Bella E 7 156
Bellac B 4 80
Bella Coola ≃ E 8 156
Bellair D 4 168
Bellaria E 8 92
Bellary F 3 122
Bella Unión B 9 195
Bella Vista E 8 192
Bellé C 2 200
Bellefontaine C 2 162
Bellefonte C 5 162
Belle Fourche ≃ C 3 174
Bellegarde-sur-Valserine D 3 82
Belle Glade B 4 186
Belle-Île I E 3 78
Belle Isle, Strait of Ʉ C 15 160
Bellenden Ker National Park ♦ D 7 142
Belle-Plaine, Sk., Can. F 19 156
Belle Plaine, Mn., U.S. C 2 166
Belleview G 5 170
Belleville, On., Can. F 5 160
Belleville, Il., U.S. C 3 170
Belleville, Ks., U.S. F 6 174
Bellevue, Ab., Can. A 6 178
Bellevue, Ne., U.S. B 1 170
Bellevue, Oh., U.S. C 2 162
Bellevue, Wa., U.S. B 2 178
Belley E 3 82
Bellingham, Mn., U.S. C 6 174
Bellingham, Wa., U.S. A 2 178
Bellingshausen ◗[3] L 8 192
Bellingshausen Sea ⊽[2] C 35 208
Bellinzago Novarese E 6 82
Bellinzona D 7 82
Bellmawr G 3 164
Bellmead E 5 172
Bello B 3 190
Bellpat D 1 122
Bells Corners A 5 162
Bellshill B 2 72
Belluno C 8 92
Belluno □[6] C 7 92
Bell Ville, Arg. C 6 195
Bellville, S. Afr. G 3 206
Bellville, Tx., U.S. F 5 172
Bellwood C 4 162
Belmond D 2 166
Belmont, N.Y., U.S. B 4 162
Belmont, Wi., U.S. D 3 166
Belmonte, Braz. A 11 194
Belmonte, Port. D 3 86
Belmonte, Spain E 2 88
Belmopan I 15 184
Beloe, ozero ◎ F 12 108
Belœil, Château de ◗ D 2 69
Belogorsk B 9 124
Beloha m 8 205a
Belo Horizonte C 8 194
Beloit D 4 166
Belojarskij E 27 108
Belomorsk D 11 108
Belomorsko-Baltijskij kanal ≊ E 11 108
Belorado B 7 86
Belorečensk G 11 110
Beloreck I 22 108
Beloščele D 17 108
Belo sur Mer I 8 205a
Belot, Lac ◎ C 31 154
Belo Vale D 8 194
Belovo D 11 114
Belozërsk F 12 108
Belper D 5 72
Belt B 8 178
Belton, Mo., U.S. C 1 170
Belton, Tx., U.S. E 5 172
Beluha, gora ∧ E 11 114
Belukha, Mount see Beluha, gora ∧ E 11 114
Belvedere Marittimo E 5 94
Belvidere, Il., U.S. A 4 170
Belvidere, N.J., U.S. F 3 164
Belvís de la Jara E 6 86
Belvoir see Kokhav HaYarden ⊥ D 4 120
Belyando ≃ G 8 142
Belyj, ostrov I B 10 114
Belyj Jar D 11 114
Belyy Island see Belyj, ostrov I B 10 114
Belz C 12 96
Belzig D 9 98
Belzoni F 3 170
Bembèrèkè C 5 200
Bembibre B 4 86
Bemidji B 7 174
Bemis E 4 170
Bena C 6 200
Benaadir □[3] G 6 202
Benāb D 12 118
Benahmed C 3 198
Benalla F 5 144
Benalmádena Costa H 6 86
Benares see Vārānasi D 4 122

Symbols in the index entries represent the broad categories identified in the key at the right. Symbols with superior numbers (⋏[1]) identify subcategories (see complete key on page 242).

∧ Mountain ⋏ Mountains)(Pass V Valley ≚ Plain › Cape I Island II Islands ⊥ Other Topographic Feature ≃ River ≊ Canal

Name	Map Ref.	Page
Ben Arous	G 3	90
Ben Arous □³	G 3	90
Benavarri	B 5	88
Benavente	C 5	86
Benbecula I	C 1	74
Ben Boyd National Park ♦	F 8	144
Bencubbin	L 4	140
Bend	C 3	178
Bendigo	F 5	144
Bendorf	B 4	100
Bēne	D 11	66
Bene Beraq	E 3	120
Benešov	C 11	100
Benetússer	E 4	88
Bénévent-l'Abbaye	B 5	80
Benevento	C 4	94
Benevento □⁶	C 4	94
Bengal, Bay of c	F 6	122
Bengbis	E 7	200
Bengbu	B 13	130
Benghazi see Banghāzī	C 9	198
Bengkalis	N 5	132
Bengkayang	N 9	132
Bengkulu	F 4	134
Bengo □³	D 1	204
Bengtsfors	C 5	66
Benguela	E 1	204
Benguela □³	E 1	204
Ben Guerdane	C 7	198
Beni	B 4	204
Beni ≃	F 5	190
Béni Abbès	C 4	198
Benicarló	D 5	88
Benicàssim see Benicàssim	D 5	88
Benicàssim (Benicasim)	D 5	88
Benicia	B 1	182
Benidorm	F 4	88
Benifaió	E 4	88
Benigànim	F 4	88
Beni Mazâr	H 4	118
Beni-Mellal	C 3	198
Benin □¹	G 8	196
Benin, Bight of c	E 5	200
Benin City	D 6	200
Beni Saf	E 5	84
Benissa	F 5	88
Beni Suef	H 4	118
Benito Juárez	E 8	195
Benito Juárez, Presa @¹	I 12	184
Benjamín Hill	B 4	184
Benkovac	C 3	104
Ben Lomond	C 1	182
Ben Lomond National Park ♦	i 12	145a
Ben Mehidi	G 1	90
Benmore, Lake @¹	F 3	146
Bennebroek	B 3	69
Bennett, Lake ≃	H 11	140
Bennett Lake	A 4	156
Bennettsville	B 5	168
Bennington	D 5	164
Bennington □⁶	C 5	164
Benoni	D 8	206
Bénoué (Benue) ≃	D 7	200
Bénoué, Parc National de la ♦	D 7	200
Bénoy	D 8	200
Ben Sekka, Rass ﹥	B 6	198
Bensheim	C 5	100
Benson	G 3	176
Bentiaba	E 1	204
Bentiaba □	E 1	204
Bentinck Island I	D 4	142
Bentley	D 5	72
Bento Gonçalves	A 11	195
Bentol	D 2	200
Benton, Ar., U.S.	E 2	170
Benton, Il., U.S.	C 4	170
Benton City	B 4	178
Benton Harbor	D 5	166
Bentonville	D 1	170
Ben Tre	I 8	132
Bent's Old Fort National Historic Site ♦	F 3	174
Benue (Bénoué) ≃	D 6	200
Benxi	F 14	128
Benza	D 1	204
Beograd (Belgrade)	C 6	104
Béoumi	D 3	200
Beppu	H 3	126
Běrandjoko	B 2	204
Berat	B 3	106
Berazino, Bela.	C 6	110
Berazino, Bela.	E 14	66
Berbegal	C 5	88
Berbera	E 6	202
Berbérati	E 8	200
Berchtesgaden	E 10	100
Berchtesgaden, Nationalpark ♦	E 9	100
Berdaale	G 5	202
Berdyans'k	F 10	110
Berdychiv	E 6	110
Berea, Ky., U.S.	E 1	162
Berea, Oh., U.S.	C 3	162
Berehove	A 7	104
Berekua	r 25	187g
Berekum	D 4	200
Berens ≃	E 10	158
Berens River	E 10	158
Beresford	D 6	174
Berettyó (Barcău) ≃	B 6	104
Berettyóújfalu	k 8	205a
Berevo-Ranobe	D 9	160
Berezhany	B 11	104
Berezivka	B 11	104
Berezniki	G 22	108
Berëzovka, Russia	D 21	108
Berëzovka, Russia	D 21	108
Berg	B 8	64
Berga	B 6	88
Bergama	C 7	106
Bergamo	D 5	92
Bergamo □⁶	D 5	92
Bergara	B 3	88
Bergen, Ger.	D 6	98
Bergen, Ger.	B 2	66
Bergen, Nor.	B 2	66
Bergen, N.Y., U.S.	B 4	162
Bergen □⁶	E 4	164
Bergen auf Rügen	B 10	98
Bergen-Belsen-Denkmal ♦	D 6	98
Bergen op Zoom	C 3	69
Bergerac	C 4	80
Bergheim	B 3	100
Bergisch Gladbach	F 4	98
Bergland	B 2	206
Bergische Maas ≃	C 4	69
Bergsjö	A 8	66
Bergslagen □⁹	C 7	66
Bergues	B 9	78
Berhala, Selat ﹗	F 4	134
Beri	J 21	110
Beringa, ostrov I	D 19	114
Bering Glacier ⌧	F 23	154
Bering Sea ⊂	D 2	148
Bering Strait ﹗	C 10	154
Berja	H 1	88
Berkane	C 4	198
Berkeley	C 1	182
Berkeley Springs	D 4	162
Berkhamsted	F 6	72
Berkner Island I	D 4	208
Berks □⁶	F 3	164
Berkshire □⁶, Eng., U.K.	F 5	72
Berkshire □⁶, Ma., U.S.	D 5	164
Berkshire Hills ↗²	D 5	164
Berland ≃	E 12	156
Berlevåg	A 14	64
Berlin, Ger.	D 10	98
Berlin, Md., U.S.	D 6	162
Berlin, N.H., U.S.	B 7	164
Berlin, Pa., U.S.	D 4	162
Berlin □³	D 10	98
Berlin, Mount ∧	D 31	208
Berlin-Ichthyosaur State Park ♦	B 6	182
Bermejillo	E 8	184
Bermejo ≃, Arg.	F 6	192
Bermejo ≃, S.A.	E 7	192
Bermejo, Paso del)(	C 3	195
Bermen, Lac @	B 9	160
Bermeo	A 2	88
Bermuda □²	F 13	148
Bern (Berne)	D 5	82
Bern □³	D 5	82
Bernalda	D 6	94
Bernau bei Berlin	D 10	98
Bernaville	C 7	78
Bernay	C 7	78
Bernburg	E 8	98
Berne, Ger.	C 5	98
Berne see Bern, Switz.	D 5	82
Berner Alpen (Bernese Alps) ↗	E 7	76
Bernese Alps see Berner Alpen ↗	E 7	76
Bernhardina	D 8	206
Bernier Island I	I 2	140
Bernina, Piz ∧	D 1	102
Bernkastel-Kues	C 4	100
Bernsdorf	E 11	98
Beroun	C 11	100
Berovo	E 7	104
Bertha	B 7	174
Berthoud	E 2	174
Berthoud Pass)(	C 5	176
Bertoua	E 7	200
Bertrand	B 5	170
Berwick, Me., U.S.	C 8	164
Berwick, Pa., U.S.	E 1	162
Berwick-upon-Tweed	B 5	170
Berwyn	F 8	110
Beryslav	F 8	110
Besançon	C 4	82
Bešankovičy	I 8	108
Besigheim	C 6	100
Beskids ↗	D 10	96
Beskra	C 6	198
Beslan	H 14	110
Besnard Lake @	D 18	156
Besozzo	E 6	82
Bessacarr	D 5	72
Bessarabia □⁹	B 10	104
Bessèges	F 2	82
Bessemer, Al., U.S.	F 5	170
Bessemer, Mi., U.S.	B 3	166
Bessheim	B 4	66
Bestuževo	F 15	108
Bestwig	E 5	98
Beswick Aboriginal Land ▵⁴	D 12	140
Betamba	C 3	204
Betanzos	A 2	86
Betbetti	D 1	202
Betera	E 4	88
Bétérou	D 5	200
Bethal	D 8	206
Bethanien	D 2	206
Bethany, Mo., U.S.	B 1	170
Bethany, Ok., U.S.	C 5	172
Bethel, Ak., U.S.	F 13	154
Bethel, Ct., U.S.	E 5	164
Bethel, N.C., U.S.	B 6	168
Bethesda	H 1	164
Bethlehem, S. Afr.	E 8	206
Bethlehem, S. Afr.	D 6	206
Bethlehem see Bayt Laḥm, W.B.	F 4	120
Bethulie	D 6	206
Béthune	B 9	78
Betong	L 5	132
Bétou	B 2	204
Bet Sh'ean	F 4	120
Bet Shemesh	F 4	120
Betsiamites	D 9	160
Betsiamites ≃	D 9	160
Betsiamites, Réserve indienne de ▵⁴	D 9	160
Betsiboka ≃	k 9	205a
Betta	C 2	206
Bettendorf	B 3	170
Bettiah	D 4	122
Bettül	E 3	122
Betuwe ↗¹	C 4	69
Beulah	B 4	174
B. Everett Jordan Lake @¹	B 5	168
Beverley	D 6	72
Beverley Springs	E 8	140
Beverly	D 8	164
Beverly Hills	F 5	182
Beverungen	E 6	98
Beverwijk	B 3	69
Bewdley	E 4	72
Bexbach	C 4	100
Bexhill	G 7	72
Bexley	D 2	162
Bexley □⁶	F 7	72
Beycuma	D 4	118
Beydaglan Olimpos Milli ♦	D 9	106
Beyla	D 3	200
Beyneu	G 19	110
Beypazarı	B 4	118
Beyra	F 6	202
Beyşehir	D 4	118
Beyşehir Gölü @	D 4	118
Bezaha	I 8	205a
Bezdēz ⊥	B 11	100
Bežeck	H 12	108
Béziers	E 7	80
Bhadrak	E 5	122
Bhadra Reservoir @¹	G 3	122
Bhadrāvati	G 3	122
Bhāgalpur	D 5	122
Bhakkar	C 2	122
Bhaktapur	D 5	122
Bhamo	B 3	132
Bhandāra	E 3	122
Bharatpur	D 3	122
Bharūch	E 2	122
Bhatkal	G 2	122
Bhātpāra	E 5	122
Bhāvnagar	E 2	122
Bhawānipatna	E 4	122
Bhilai	E 4	122
Bhilwāra	D 2	122
Bhīma ≃	F 3	122
Bhīmavaram	F 4	122
Bhind	D 3	122
Bhiwandi	F 2	122
Bhiwāni	D 3	122
Bhongīr	F 3	122
Bhopāl	E 3	122
Bhubaneshwar	E 5	122
Bhuj	E 1	122
Bhusāwal	E 3	122
Bhutan □¹	G 10	112
Bia, Phou ∧	E 6	132
Biafra, Bight of c	E 6	200
Biak I	F 11	134
Biała Piska	B 12	96
Biała Podlaska	B 12	96
Białogard	A 9	96
Białowieski Park Narodowy ♦	B 12	96
Białystok	B 12	96
Biancavilla	G 4	94
Biaro, Pulau I	E 9	134
Biarritz	E 2	80
Biasca	D 6	82
Biba	H 4	118
Bibai	C 8	126
Bibane, Bahiret el c	C 7	198
Bibân el-Mulūk (Valley of the Kings) ⊥	B 3	202
Bibbiena	F 7	92
Biberach an der Riss, Ger.	D 5	96
Biberach an der Riss, Ger.	D 6	100
Bibiani	D 4	200
Biblis	C 5	100
Biča	H 29	108
Bicaz	B 8	104
Bicester	F 5	72
Biche, Lac la @	D 15	156
Bichena	E 4	202
Bicheno	i 13	145a
Bicol ﹥¹	C 8	134
Bicuari, Parque Nacional do ♦	F 1	204
Bičura	A 6	128
Bid	F 3	122
Bida	D 6	200
Bidar	F 3	122
Biddeford	C 8	164
Bideford	F 2	72
Bidwell	D 2	162
Bié □³	E 2	204
Bieber	E 3	178
Biebrzański Park Narodowy ♦	B 12	96
Biel	C 5	82
Biel, Lake see Bielersee @	C 5	82
Bielawa	C 9	96
Bielefeld	D 5	98
Bielersee (Biel, Lake) @	C 5	82
Biella	D 4	92
Biella □⁶	D 4	92
Bielsk	B 10	96
Bielsko-Biała	D 10	96
Bielsk Podlaski	B 12	96
Bien Hoa	I 8	132
Bienne see Biel	C 5	82
Bien Son	D 7	132
Bienville, Lac @	A 7	160
Bierné	E 6	78
Biesiesvlei	D 6	206
Bieszczadzki Park Narodowy ♦	D 12	96
Bietigheim-Bissingen	D 6	100
Biga	B 7	106
Bigadiç	C 8	106
Big Bar Creek	F 10	156
Big Basin Redwoods State Park ♦	C 1	182
Big Bear Lake	F 7	182
Big Belt Mountains ↗	B 8	178
Big Bend	D 9	206
Big Bend National Park ♦	F 2	172
Big Bird Creek ≃	F 4	176
Big Clifty	A 1	168
Big Cypress Indian Reservation ▵⁴	F 4	168
Big Cypress Swamp ≃	F 4	168
Big Delta	D 21	154
Big Desert ﹦²	E 3	144
Bigfork	B 2	166
Biggar	E 17	156
Biggleswade	E 6	72
Bighorn ≃	C 10	178
Bighorn Canyon National Recreation Area ♦	C 9	178
Big Horn Lake @¹	C 10	178
Bighorn Mountains ↗	C 10	178
Big Island	A 5	168
Big Island I	D 18	150
Big Lake	D 1	172
Big Muddy Creek ≃	A 2	174
Bignona	C 1	200
Bigorre ↗⁹	E 4	80
Big Piney	D 8	178
Big Prairie Creek ≃	F 5	170
Big Quill Lake @	E 10	156
Big Rapids	D 5	166
Big Rideau Lake @	F 5	160
Big River Indian Reserve ▵⁴	E 18	156
Big Salmon ≃	F 28	154
Big Sand Lake @	C 8	158
Big Sandy	A 8	178
Big Sandy ≃	D 2	162
Big Sandy Creek ≃	F 3	174
Big Sandy Lake @	D 20	156
Big Sioux ≃	D 6	174
Big Spring	D 3	172
Bigstone ≃	D 11	158
Big Stone Gap	E 2	162
Bezaha	I 8	158
Big Sur ﹥¹	D 2	182
Big Thompson ≃	B 6	176
Big Trout Lake	E 14	158
Biguaçu	C 6	194
Bihać	C 3	104
Bihar	D 5	122
Bihār □³	E 5	122
Biharamulo	C 5	204
Bihor □³	B 6	104
Bihoro	C 10	126
Bija ≃	D 11	114
Bijagós, Arquipélago dos (Bissagos) II	C 1	200
Bijapur	E 12	118
Bijeljina	C 5	104
Bijelo Polje	D 5	104
Bikaner	D 2	122
Bikar I	B 9	136
Bikié	E 7	200
Bikin	C 20	128
Bikin ≃	C 20	128
Bikini I¹	B 8	136
Bikkū Bīttī ∧	E 8	198
Bilanga	E 4	200
Bilāspur, India	D 5	122
Bilāspur, India	E 4	122
Bilāsuvar	J 16	110
Bila Tserkva	E 7	110
Bilauktaung Range ↗	H 4	132
Bilbao	A 7	86
Bilbilis ⊥	C 11	96
Bilecik	B 8	106
Bilecik □³	B 8	106
Bilgoraj	C 12	96
Bilhorod-Dnistrovs'kyj	B 11	104
Biliran I	C 8	134
Bili	B 3	204
Bili ≃	B 2	204
Bilin	F 3	132
Bilin ≃	B 10	100
Bilina	B 10	100
Billabong Creek ≃	E 5	144
Billerbeck	D 4	98
Billère	E 3	80
Billericay	F 7	72
Billingham	C 7	72
Billings	E 9	178
Billingsfors	C 9	178
Bill Williams ≃	E 2	176
Biloela	H 10	142
Bilohirs'k	D 9	110
Bilopillya	D 9	110
Biloxi	G 4	170
Biltine ≃	C 9	200
Biltine □³	C 9	200
Biltmore Forest	B 3	168
Bilzen	D 4	69
Bimberi Peak ∧	E 7	144
Bimbila	E 4	200
Bimbo	D 2	144
Bimbowrie	D 2	144
Bimini Islands II	G 5	168
Bintimani ∧	C 2	200
Bint Jubayl	C 4	120
Bintulu	E 6	134
Bintuni	F 10	134
Binxian, China	H 11	128
Binxian, China	D 16	128
Binxian, China	I 7	128
Binyang	G 9	130
Bio Addo	F 6	202
Bioblo □³	E 1	195
Bioblo ≃	G 5	192
Biograd na moru	D 3	104
Biogradska Gora Nacionalni Park ♦	D 5	104
Bioko (Fernando Póo) I	E 6	200
Bira ≃	B 19	128
Birāk	D 7	198
Bi'r al Wa'r	E 7	198
Birao	C 9	200
Bircao see Buur Gaabo	H 5	202
Birch	B 5	156
Birch Creek ≃	C 22	154
Birch Island	A 7	162
Birch Mountains ↗²	C 15	156
Birch Run	B 2	162
Birchy Bay	D 8	144
Birdum	D 12	140
Bir el Ater	C 6	198
Bir Enzaran	D 4	198
Birigui	D 5	194
Biriljussy	D 8	116
Birjand	D 12	114
Birjusa ≃	D 9	114
Birkeland	G 4	66
Birkenfeld, Ger.	C 4	100
Birkenfeld, Ger.	C 4	100
Birkenwerder bei Berlin	D 10	98
Birkerød	G 3	72
Birkfeld	C 7	102
Birmingham, Eng., U.K.	E 4	72
Birmingham, Al., U.S.	F 5	170
Birmingham, Mi., U.S.	A 4	122
Birmitrapur	E 4	122
Birnin Gaouré	C 5	200
Birnin-Kebbi	C 6	200
Birnin Konni	C 6	200
Birnin Kudu	C 7	200
Birobidžan	B 19	128
Birsk	I 21	108
Birungu, Pac des ≃	C 4	204
Biržai	D 12	66
Bisa, Pulau I	E 9	134
Bisaccia	C 5	94
Biscarrosse	D 2	80
Biscay, Bay of c	D 2	76
Biscayne National Park ♦	G 4	168
Bisceglie	C 6	94
Bischofshofen	C 5	102
Bischwiller	B 5	82
Bisha	D 4	202
Bishnupur	E 5	122
Bisho	G 7	206
Bishop	G 5	172
Bishop Auckland	C 5	72
Bishop Indian Reservation ▵⁴	C 5	182
Bishop Rock II¹	i 9	73a
Bishop's Stortford	F 7	72
Bishrah, Ma'tan ﹖	E 9	198
Bisina, Lake @	G 3	202
Bišek	A 2	122
Biskupiec	B 11	96
Bislig	D 9	134
Bismarck	B 4	174
Bismarck Archipelago II	M 13	124
Bismarckmuseum ♦	C 7	98
Bismarck Range ↗	N 12	124
Bismarck Sea ⊤²	M 13	124
Bissau	C 1	200
Bissett	F 11	158
Bistcho Lake @	B 12	156
Bistineau, Lake @¹	F 2	170
Bistrica	D 8	102
Bistrița	B 8	104
Bistrița-Năsăud □³	B 7	104
Bitam	E 7	200
Bitburg	C 3	100
Bitche	A 5	82
Bitéa, Ouadi ≃	C 9	200
Bithia ⊥	m 9	94a
Bitkin	C 8	200
Bitlis	C 10	118
Bitlis □³	C 10	118
Bitola	E 6	104
Bitonto	C 6	94
Bitou	C 4	200
Bitterfeld	E 8	98
Bitterroot ≃	B 7	178
Bitterroot, West Fork ≃	C 6	178
Bitterroot Range ↗	B 6	178
Bitti	I 5	92
Biu	C 7	200
Biwabik	B 2	166
Biwa-ko @	G 5	126
Biyang	B 11	130
Bizana	F 8	206
Bizerte	B 6	198
Bizerte □³	G 2	90
Bizerte, Lac de @	G 2	90
Bjala Slatina	D 7	104
Bjalynyčy	B 6	110
Bjarëzina ≃	C 11	110
Bjargtangar ﹥	m 18	64a
Bjaroza	J 12	64
Bjarozaŭka	F 12	66
Bjärred	C 6	66
Bjelovar	E 8	102
Bjerringbro	B 2	68
Björna	E 9	64
Bjuv	D 6	66
Bla	C 3	200
Black ≃, Ak., U.S.	D 24	154
Black ≃, La., U.S.	B 3	170
Black ≃, N.Y., U.S.	E 3	164
Black Bear Island Lake @	D 6	158
Black Birch Lake @	C 18	156
Blackburn	D 4	72
Blackburn, Mount ∧	F 22	154
Black Canyon of the Gunnison National Monument ♦	C 5	176
Black Creek	G 9	156
Black Duck ≃	C 14	158
Black Eagle	B 8	178
Blackfeet Indian Reservation ▵⁴	A 7	178
Blackfoot	D 7	178
Blackfoot Indian Reserve ▵⁴	F 15	156
Black Forest see Schwarzwald ↗	D 5	100
Black Hills ↗	C 4	174
Black Lake @	B 19	156
Black Lake @	C 8	158
Black Mesa ∧	G 3	174
Blackmoor ﹥³	B 2	78
Black Mountain	E 2	162
Black Nossob ≃	B 3	206
Blackpool	D 4	72
Black River (Da, Song) (Lixian) ≃	D 7	132
Black River Falls	C 3	166
Black Rock Desert ﹦	A 7	178
Black Sea ⊤²	H 6	110
Blacks Fork ≃	B 6	178
Blacks Harbour	E 5	160
Blackstone	D 26	154
Black Tickle	B 16	160
Blacktown	D 8	144
Black Volta (Mouhoun) ≃	D 4	200
Blackwater	G 9	142
Blackwater Draw ≃	C 2	172
Blackwater Lake @	D 33	154
Blackwell	B 5	172
Blackwood ≃	M 4	140
Bladensburg National Park ♦	G 6	142
Bladgrond	E 3	206
Blaenau Gwent □⁶	F 3	72
Blagnac	E 5	80
Blagodarnyj	G 13	110
Blagodatovka	C 16	110
Blagoevgrad	E 7	104
Blagoveščensk, Russia	I 21	108
Blagoveščensk, Russia	A 16	128
Blaine	C 2	166
Blaine Lake	E 18	156
Blair	E 8	174
Blairstown	B 2	170
Blaj	B 7	104
Blakely	G 2	170
Blanc, Cap ﹥	A 4	198
Blanc, Mont ∧	A 1	82
Blanca, Bahía c, Arg.	G 4	192
Blanca, Costa ﹆²	F 6	88
Blanca Peak ∧	D 5	176
Blanca, Bahía c	H 7	140
Blanche, Lake @	D 3	144
Blanchisseuse ♦	q 23	187e
Blanco ≃	A 3	195
Blanco, Cabo ﹥	A 7	92
Blanco, Cape ﹥	A 1	180
Blanc-Sablon	C 15	160
Bland	E 3	162
Blandinsville	B 3	170
Blanes	C 7	88
Blankenberge	C 1	69
Blankenburg	E 7	98
Blankenfelde	D 10	98
Blankenheim	B 3	100
Blanquilla, Isla I	F 8	186
Blantyre	F 5	204
Blarney Castle ⊥	E 3	75
Blasdell	B 4	162
Blatná	C 10	100
Blaubeuren	D 6	100
Blaye	C 4	80
Bleaker Island I	o 18	193b
Bled, Lake @	B 2	102
Bleiburg	D 6	102
Bleicherode	E 7	98
Blekinge □³	D 7	66
Blenheim	D 4	146
Blenheim Palace ♦	F 5	72
Blerick	C 5	69
Blessing	F 5	172
Bletchley	F 6	72
Bleus, Monts ↗	B 5	204
Bligh Water ﹗	m 13	147c
Blina	E 8	140
Blind River	D 11	160
Blitar	j 21	135b
Block Island	E 7	164
Block Island I	E 7	164
Bloed ≃	D 9	206
Bloedel	F 9	156
Bloemendaal	B 3	69
Bloemfontein	E 6	206
Bloemhofdam @¹	D 6	206
Blois	E 8	78
Blokhus	A 2	68
Blomberg	D 6	98
Blönduós	m 20	64a
Bohemia see Čechy □⁹	D 8	96
Bohemian Forest ↗	C 10	100
Bohicon	D 5	200
Bohinjska Bistrica	D 5	102
Böhlen	E 9	98
Bohol	F 6	202
Bohol I	D 8	134
Bohol Sea ⊤²	D 8	134
Bohongou	C 5	200
Bohu	A 5	122
Boiano	C 4	94
Boiestown	E 10	160
Boiro	B 2	86
Bois ≃	C 5	194
Bois, Lac des @	C 32	154
Bois Blanc Island I	C 6	166
Bois de Sioux ≃	D 5	178
Boise	D 5	178
Boise, Middle Fork ≃	D 6	178
Boise, South Fork ≃	D 6	178
Bois Forte Indian Reservation ▵⁴	A 2	166
Bois-Guillaume	C 8	78
Boissevain	G 8	158
Boituva	C 7	98
Bojador, Cape ﹥	B 8	134
Bojnūrd	D 17	118
Bojonegoro	k 20	135b
Boju	D 6	200
Bokāro Steel City	E 5	122
Bokatola	C 2	204
Boki	C 2	200
Boknafjorden ﹗	C 2	66
Bokondo	B 3	204
Bokoro	C 8	200
Bokote	E 12	110
Boksitogorsk	G 10	108
Bokungu	C 3	204
Bokurdak	J 21	110
Bol	C 7	200
Bolama	B 8	204
Bolangir	E 5	122
Bolaños de Calatrava	F 7	86
Bolayır	B 7	106
Bolbec	C 7	78
Bolekhiv	A 7	104
Boles	E 1	170
Bolesławiec	C 8	96
Boleszkowice	B 8	96
Bolgatanga	C 4	200
Bolhov	C 9	110
Bolívar, Col.	C 3	190
Bolívar □³, Col.	F 6	186
Bolívar □³, Ven.	G 9	186
Bolívar, Cerro ∧	B 6	190
Bolívar, Pico ∧	F 8	188
Bolivia □¹	F 5	188
Bollnäs	B 8	66
Bollullos Par del Condado	H 5	86
Bolmen @	G 4	66
Bologna	E 7	92
Bologna □⁶	E 7	92
Bologoje	H 10	108
Bololo	C 3	204
Bolovens, Plateau des ↗¹	G 8	132
Bol'šaja Atnja	H 18	108
Bol'šaja Hobda see Ülken Qabda ≃	D 19	110
Bol'šaja Kaskara	C 14	66
Bol'šaja Osinovaja ≃	C 28	108
Bol'šaja Ussurka ≃	B 5	126
Bol'šelig	E 20	108
Bolsena, Lago di @	G 7	92
Bol'ševik, ostrov I	B 13	114
Bol'šije Uki	H 30	108
Bol'šoe Zagorse	C 19	114
Bolșoca	C 5	104
Bol'šoj Begičev, ostrov I	B 16	114
Bol'šoj Jugan ≃	F 31	108
Bol'šoj Kamen'	C 4	126
Bol'šoj Ljahovskij, ostrov I	B 17	114
Bol'šoj Uzen' ≃	D 16	110
Bolton, Eng., U.K.	D 4	72
Bolton, Ms., U.S.	C 2	170
Bolton □⁶	D 4	72
Bolu	B 9	106

ʟ Waterfall ﹗ Strait c Bay, Gulf @ Lake ≃ Swamp ⌧ Ice Feature ⊤ Other Hydrographic Feature ⌁ Submarine Feature □ Political Unit @ Cultural Institution ⊥ Historical Site ♦ Recreational Site ✈ Airport ▪ Military Installation ⊷ Miscellaneous

Name | Map Ref. | Page

Symbols in the index entries represent the broad categories identified in the key at the right.
Symbols with superior numbers (≃¹) identify subcategories (see complete key on page 242).

▲ Mountain ▱ Mountains)(Pass V Valley ≃ Plain ↠ Cape I Island II Islands ⊥ Other Topographic Feature ≃ River ≃ Canal

Burlington — Castellote

Name	Map Ref.	Page
Burlington, Wa., U.S.	A 2	178
Burlington □[6]	G 4	164
Burlit	C 20	128
Burma see Myanmar □[1]	G 11	112
Burnaby	G 10	156
Burnet	E 4	172
Burnett ≃	H 11	142
Burnham	E 10	166
Burnham-on-Sea	F 3	72
Burnie	i 11	145a
Burnley	D 4	72
Burns	D 4	178
Burnside ≃	C 11	150
Burnside, Lake ⊜	I 7	140
Burns Lake	D 8	156
Burnsville, Al., U.S.	F 5	170
Burnsville, W.V., U.S.	D 3	162
Burntisland	A 3	72
Burntwood	E 4	72
Burntwood ≃	D 10	158
Burntwood Lake ⊜	D 8	158
Burra	D 2	144
Burracoppin	L 5	140
Burragorang, Lake ⊜[1]	E 8	144
Burrel	B 3	106
Burrendong, Lake ⊜[1]	D 7	144
Burren Junction	C 7	144
Burrinjuck Reservoir ⊜[1]	E 7	144
Burrowa-Pine Mountain National Park ♦	F 6	144
Burruyacú	E 7	192
Burrwood	H 4	170
Bursa	B 8	106
Bursa □[3]	B 8	106
Burscheid	E 4	98
Burshtyn	E 4	110
Burslem	D 4	72
Bürstadt	C 5	100
Burt Lake ⊜	C 6	166
Burton, Mi., U.S.	B 2	162
Burton, Tx., U.S.	E 5	172
Burton upon Trent	E 5	72
Buru I	F 9	134
Buruc	E 6	202
Burullus, Buheirat el- ⊜	G 4	118
Burundi □[1]	I 11	196
Burun-Šibertuj, gora ∧	B 7	128
Burwell	E 5	174
Bury	D 4	72
Bury □[6]	D 4	72
Bury Saint Edmunds	E 7	72
Busanga	C 3	204
Busby	C 10	178
Buseck	B 5	100
Bushbush ≃	H 5	202
Būshehr	H 14	118
Būshehr □[3]	H 14	118
Bushenyi	H 3	202
Bushland	C 2	172
Bushmanland ◆[1]	E 3	206
Bushtyna	A 7	104
Busia	G 3	202
Businga	B 3	204
Busira ≃	C 2	204
Bus'k	D 4	110
Buskerud □[3]	B 4	66
Busko-Zdrój	C 11	96
Busovača	C 4	104
Busselton	M 3	140
Bussolengo	D 6	92
Bussoleno	D 3	92
Bussum	B 4	69
Bustamante	D 9	184
Busto Arsizio	D 4	92
Busto Garolfo	E 6	82
Busuanga Island I	C 8	134
Büsum	B 5	98
Buta	B 3	204
Butan	D 7	104
Butare	C 4	204
Butaritari I[1]	C 9	136
Bute Inlet c	F 9	156
Butemba	G 3	202
Butembo	B 4	204
Butha-Buthe	E 8	206
Buthidaung	D 1	132
Butiá	B 11	195
Butler, In., U.S.	B 6	170
Butler, Pa., U.S.	C 4	162
Buton, Pulau I	F 8	134
Butru	F 4	142
Butsha	B 4	204
Butte	B 7	178
Butte □[6]	A 2	182
Butte du Lion ⊥	D 3	69
Butterworth, Malay.	L 5	132
Butterworth, S. Afr.	G 8	206
Butuan	D 9	134
Buturlino	I 16	108
Buturlinovka	D 12	110
Butzbach	B 5	100
Bützow	C 8	98
Buulobarde	G 6	202
Buurgplaatz ∧	D 5	69
Buxtehude	C 6	98
Buxton, S. Afr.	D 6	206
Buxton, Eng., U.K.	D 5	72
Buxton, N.C., U.S.	B 7	168
Buyant ≃	C 2	128
Buyat	C 1	128
Buyo	D 3	200
Buyo, Barrage de ◆[6]	D 3	200
Buyr Lake ⊜	C 7	124
Buyr nuur see Buir Nur ⊜	C 11	128
Büyükçekmece	B 8	106
Büyükkale	C 7	106
Büyükmenderes ≃	D 7	106
Buzançais	F 8	78
Buzău	C 9	104
Buzău □[3]	C 9	104
Buzău ≃	C 9	104
Búzi ≃	F 5	204
Buziaș	C 6	104
Büzmeyin	C 17	118
Buzuluk	C 18	110
Byam Martin Island I	A 12	150
Bychawa	C 12	96
Bydalen	E 6	64
Bydgoszcz	B 10	96
Bygdeå	D 10	64
Bykovo	E 14	110
Bylnice	A 10	102
Bylot Island I	B 17	150
Byng Inlet	F 3	160
Bynum	B 5	168
Byrnedale	E 9	166
Byrock	C 6	144
Byron	A 4	170
Byron, Cape ≻	B 9	144
Byron, Isla I	I 4	192
Byrranga, gory ⋏	B 13	114
Byske	D 10	64
Bystřice pod Hostýnem	A 9	102
Bystrzyca Kłodzka	C 9	96
Bytča	E 14	66
Bytom	C 10	96
Bytów	A 9	96
Byxelkrok	D 8	66
Byzantium see İstanbul	B 8	106
C		
Ca ≃	I 7	130
Caacupé	F 2	194
Caaguazú □[3]	F 2	194
Caála	E 2	204
Caapucú	G 2	194
Caarapó	E 3	194
Caazapá	G 2	194
Caazapá □[3]	G 2	194
Cabaiguán	C 5	186
Caballo Reservoir ⊜[1]	F 5	176
Cabanatuan	B 8	134
Cabano	E 9	160
Cabeza del Buey	F 5	86
Cabimas	F 7	186
Cabinda	D 1	204
Cabinda □[3]	D 1	204
Cabo Blanco	I 6	192
Cabo Delgado □[3]	E 6	204
Cabo Frio	E 10	194
Cabonga, Réservoir ⊜[1]	E 5	160
Caboolture	I 11	142
Caborca	B 3	184
Cabo Rojo	j 14	187b
Cabot	E 3	170
Cabot Strait Ʉ	E 13	160
Cabourg	C 6	78
Cabo Verde, Arquipélago de II	h 11	200a
Cabra	G 6	86
Cabrayıl	J 15	110
Cabrera, Parc National de Archipiélago ♦	E 7	88
Cabriel ≃	E 3	88
Cabrillo National Monument ♦	H 6	182
Cabruta	G 8	186
Caçador	G 5	194
Čačak	D 6	104
Caçapava do Sul	B 11	195
Cacequi	A 10	195
Cáceres, Braz.	G 7	190
Cáceres, Spain	E 4	86
Cáceres □[6]	E 4	86
Čačèvičy	C 6	110
Cache	C 4	172
Cache Creek ≃	B 1	182
Cache la Poudre ≃	B 6	176
Cacheu	C 1	200
Cachimbo, Serra do ⋏	E 7	190
Cachingues	E 2	204
Cachoeira do Sul	B 11	195
Cachoeiro de Itapemirim	D 10	194
Cacín ≃	G 7	86
Căciulați	C 9	104
Cacolo	F 2	204
Cactus	B 2	172
Cactus Flat ≡	C 7	182
Cacuaco	D 1	204
Caculuvar ≃	F 1	204
Cacuri	D 2	204
Cadaqués	F 7	80
Čadca	A 10	102
Caddo Lake ⊜[1]	F 2	170
Cadereyta Jiménez	E 9	184
Cadibarrawirracanna, Lake ⊜	J 2	142
Cadillac, Fr.	D 3	80
Cadillac, Mi., U.S.	A 1	162
Cádiz	H 4	86
Cádiz □[6]	H 5	86
Cadiz, Gulf of (Cádiz, Golfo de) c	H 3	86
Cadiz Lake ⊜	E 6	180
Cadomin	E 13	156
Cadotte Lake	C 13	156
Caen	C 6	78
Caengo (Kwenge) ≃	D 2	204
Caere ⊥	G 8	92
Caernarfon	D 2	72
Caernarfon Bay c	D 2	72
Caernarfon Castle ⊥	D 2	72
Caernarvon see Caernarfon	D 2	72
Caerphilly	F 3	72
Caerphilly □[6]	F 3	72
Caesarea see Qesari, Ḥorbat ⊥	D 3	120
Caetité	F 10	190
Cafima	F 2	204
Cagayan ≃	B 8	134
Cagayan de Oro	D 8	134
Cagayan Islands II	D 8	134
Cagayan Sulu Island I	D 7	134
Cagli	F 8	92
Cagliari	F 2	90
Cagliari □[6]	I 10	94a
Cagliari, Golfo di c	F 2	90
Cagnano Varano	C 5	94
Cagnes-sur-Mer	G 5	82
Caguas	j 15	187b
Cahama	F 1	204
Caherciveen	E 1	75
Cahokia	C 3	170
Cahora Bassa, Albufeira ⊜[1]	F 5	204
Cahors	D 5	80
Cahul	C 10	104
Caianda	E 3	204
Caiapó, Serra do ⋏	G 8	190
Caibarién	C 5	186
Caicara de Orinoco	G 8	186
Caicó	E 11	190
Caicos Islands II	C 6	186
Caicos Passage Ʉ	C 6	186
Caiguna	M 8	140
Caijiapo	A 8	130
Caimanero, Laguna del ⊜	F 6	184
Caird Coast ≛[2]	D 7	208
Cairns	D 7	142
Cairo (El-Qâhira), Egypt	G 4	118
Cairo, Il., U.S.	D 4	170
Cairofa	E 1	204
Cairo Montenotte	E 4	92
Caiundo	F 2	204
Cajamarca	E 3	190
Cajarc	D 5	80
Čajek (Chayek)	A 2	122
Čajkovskij	H 21	108
Cajon Pass)(	F 6	182
Čakovec	D 8	102
Cala	F 7	206
Calabar	D 6	200
Calabozo	F 8	186
Calabria □[3]	F 6	94
Calabria, Parco Nazionale d' ♦	E 6	94
Calafat	C 7	104
Calafell	C 6	88
Calafquén, Lago ⊜	F 1	195
Calahorra	B 2	88
Calais	B 8	78
Calais, Pas de see Dover, Strait of Ʉ	F 8	70
Calama	D 6	192
Calamian Group II	C 8	134
Calamonte	F 4	86
Calañas	G 4	86
Calandula	D 2	204
Calangianus	I 5	92
Calapan	C 8	134
Călărași, Mol.	B 10	104
Călărași, Rom.	C 9	104
Călărași □[3]	C 9	104
Calasparra	F 3	88
Calatafimi	G 2	94
Calatayud	C 3	88
Calau	E 10	98
Calaveras □[6]	B 3	182
Calayan Island I	B 8	134
Calbayog	C 8	134
Calbe	E 8	98
Calcasieu Lake ⊜	H 2	170
Calcinato	E 2	102
Calcutta see Kolkata	E 5	122
Caldas da Rainha	E 1	86
Caldas de Reis	B 2	86
Caldas Novas	B 6	194
Caldera	E 5	192
Caldera de Taburiente, Parque Nacional de la ♦	i 13	85b
Calderdale □[6]	D 4	72
Caldes de Montbui	C 7	88
Caldicot	F 4	72
Caldwell, Id., U.S.	D 5	178
Caldwell, Oh., U.S.	D 3	162
Caledon	H 3	206
Caledon (Mohokare) ≃	E 7	206
Caledonia, Belize	H 15	184
Caledonia, Mn., U.S.	D 3	166
Caledonia □[6]	B 6	164
Caledonian Canal ≂	D 3	74
Calella	C 7	88
Calen	F 9	142
Calera	D 5	172
Calexico	F 6	180
Calgary	F 14	156
Calhoun, Al., U.S.	F 5	170
Calhoun, Ga., U.S.	B 2	168
Calhoun Falls	B 3	168
Cali	C 3	190
Calicut see Kozhikode	G 3	122
Calida, Costa ≛[2]	G 3	88
Caliente	D 1	176
California □[3]	D 4	152
California, Golfo de (California, Gulf of) c	C 3	184
California, Gulf of see California, Golfo de c	C 3	184
California Aqueduct ≂[1]	F 5	182
Călilabad	J 16	110
Călimănești	C 8	104
Calimere, Point ≻	G 3	122
Calion	F 2	170
Calitzdorp	G 4	206
Callabonna, Lake ⊜	B 3	144
Callahan	D 4	168
Callander	D 4	74
Callao	F 3	190
Callaquén, Volcán ∧[1]	E 2	195
Calling Lake	D 15	156
Callosa de Segura	F 4	88
Calmar	D 3	166
Calne	F 5	72
Calolziocorte	D 5	92
Calonga ≃	F 2	204
Calonge	C 8	88
Calore ≃	C 4	94
Caloundra	I 11	142
Calp (Calpe)	F 5	88
Caltagirone	G 4	94
Caltanissetta	G 4	94
Caltanissetta □[6]	G 4	94
Çaltılıbük	C 8	106
Calucinga	E 2	204
Caluire-et-Cuire	E 2	82
Calulo	E 2	204
Calumet	B 2	166
Calumet City	B 5	170
Calunda	E 3	204
Caluso	E 5	82
Caluula	E 7	202
Calvados □[3]	C 6	78
Calvert	G 4	170
Calvert □[6]	H 2	164
Calvert Island I	F 7	156
Calvi	i 8	83a
Calvià	E 7	88
Calvillo	G 8	184
Calvinia	F 3	206
Calw	D 5	100
Camagüey	C 5	186
Camaiore	F 6	92
Camaldoli, Eremo di ◗[1]	F 7	92
Camaná	G 4	190
Camanche	B 3	170
Camapuã	C 3	194
Camaquã	B 11	195
Camaquã ≃	B 12	195
Camará	D 6	190
Camarès	E 6	80
Camargue ◆[1]	G 2	82
Camargue, Parc Naturel Regional de ♦	G 2	82
Camarina ⊥	H 4	94
Camarones	H 6	192
Camas	G 4	86
Ca Mau	J 7	132
Ca Mau, Mui ≻	J 7	132
Camaxilo	D 2	204
Cambados	B 2	86
Cambará	E 5	194
Camberley	F 6	72
Cambodia □[1]	H 12	112
Cambooya	A 8	144
Camboriú	G 6	194
Camborne	G 1	72
Cambrai	B 10	78
Cambria	D 4	166
Cambrian Mountains ⋏	E 3	72
Cambridge, On., Can.	G 3	160
Cambridge, N.Z.	B 5	146
Cambridge, Eng., U.K.	E 6	72
Cambridge, Il., U.S.	B 3	170
Cambridge, Ma., U.S.	D 7	164
Cambridge, Md., U.S.	H 2	164
Cambridge, Mn., U.S.	C 2	166
Cambridge, N.Y., U.S.	C 5	164
Cambridge, Oh., U.S.	C 3	162
Cambridge Gulf c	D 10	140
Cambridgeshire □[6]	E 7	72
Cambrils	C 6	88
Cambundi-Catembo	E 2	204
Camden, Austl.	E 8	144
Camden, S. Afr.	D 8	206
Camden, Ar., U.S.	F 2	170
Camden, De., U.S.	G 3	164
Camden, N.J., U.S.	G 3	164
Camden □[6]	G 4	164
Camden Bay c	A 22	154
Camden Hills State Park ♦	A 9	162
Camenca	A 10	104
Cameri	D 4	92
Camerino	F 8	92
Cameron, La., U.S.	H 2	170
Cameron, Wi., U.S.	C 3	166
Cameron Hills ⋏[2]	A 13	156
Cameroon □[1]	H 9	196
Cameroon Mountain ∧[1]	E 6	200
Cametá	D 9	190
Camfield	E 11	140
Çamiçi Gölü ⊜	D 7	106
Camiguin Island I	B 8	134
Caminha	C 2	86
Camiri	H 6	190
Camissombo	D 3	204
Cam Lo	F 8	132
Camocim	D 10	190
Camooweal	E 4	142
Camousitchouane, Lac ⊜	C 6	160
Campagna	E 5	90
Campagna di Roma ◆[1]	H 8	92
Campana	D 8	195
Campana, Isla I	I 4	192
Campanario	F 5	86
Campania □[3]	D 5	94
Campania Island I	J 30	154
Campbell, Ca., U.S.	C 1	182
Campbell, Mo., U.S.	D 3	170
Campbell, Ne., U.S.	E 5	174
Campbell Hill ∧[2]	C 2	162
Campbell Island I	J 13	58
Campbell River	F 9	156
Campbellsville	D 6	170
Campbellton	D 10	160
Campbelltown	E 8	144
Campbeltown	B 1	72
Campeche	H 14	184
Campeche □[3]	H 14	184
Campeche, Gulf of c	H 12	184
Câmpeni	B 7	104
Camperdown	G 4	144
Cam Pha	D 8	132
Camp Hill	F 1	164
Câmpia Turzii	B 7	104
Campi Bisenzio	F 6	92
Campiglia Marittima	F 6	92
Campillos	G 6	86
Câmpina	C 8	104
Campina ◆[1]	G 5	86
Campina Grande	E 11	190
Campinas	E 7	194
Campi Salentina	D 7	94
Camplong	A 7	140
Campo	F 6	204
Campobasso	C 4	94
Campobasso □[6]	C 4	94
Campobello di Licata	G 3	94
Campobello di Mazara	G 2	94
Campo Belo	D 8	194
Campo de Criptana	E 1	88
Campo Gallo	E 7	192
Campo Grande, Arg.	G 3	194
Campo Grande, Braz.	D 3	194
Campo Largo	F 6	194
Campo Maior	D 10	190
Campo Mourão	F 4	194
Campos, Braz.	D 10	194
Campos, Spain	E 8	88
Campos Altos	C 7	194
Campotosto, Lago di ⊜[1]	G 9	92
Camp Point	B 3	170
Câmpulung	C 8	104
Câmpulung Moldovenesc	B 8	104
Campuzano	A 6	86
Cam Ranh	I 9	132
Cam Ranh, Vinh c	I 9	132
Camrose	E 15	156
Çan	B 7	106
Canaan	D 5	164
Canada □[1]	C 9	148
Canada Basin ✦[1]	C 36	61
Cañada de Gómez	C 7	195
Cañada Honda	F 6	192
Canadian ≃	C 6	172
Canajoharie	D 4	164
Çanakkale	B 7	106
Çanakkale □[3]	C 7	106
Canals	F 4	88
Canal Winchester	D 2	162
Canandaigua	D 1	164
Cananea	B 4	184
Cañar	D 3	190
Canarias □[3]	i 15	85b
Canarias, Islas (Canary Islands) II	h 15	85b
Canary Islands see Canarias, Islas II	h 15	85b
Cañas	F 3	186
Canastota	C 3	164
Canatlán	E 7	184
Canaveral, Cape ≻	E 4	168
Canaveral National Seashore ♦	E 4	168
Canavese □[9]	D 3	92
Canavieiras	A 11	194
Canbelego	C 6	144
Canberra	E 7	144
Canby	C 6	174
Cancon	D 4	80
Cancún	G 16	184
Candás	A 5	86
Candelaria ≃	H 14	184
Candle	D 13	154
Candle Lake ⊜	E 19	156
Candlemas Islands II	J 12	188
Cando	A 5	174
Candor	B 5	168
Canelli	E 4	92
Canelones	D 9	195
Cañete	E 1	195
Caney	G 7	174
Cangas	B 2	86
Cangas de Narcea	A 4	86
Canginge	E 3	204
Cangkuang, Tanjung ≻	G 5	134
Cangongo	D 2	204
Canguçu	B 11	195
Cangxi	C 7	130
Cangyuan	G 4	130
Cangzhou	G 11	128
Caniapiscau ≃	E 19	150
Caniapiscau, Lac ⊜[1]	A 8	160
Caniçado	C 10	206
Canicattì	G 3	94
Canim Lake ⊜	F 11	156
Canindeyú □[3]	F 3	194
Canjáyar	G 2	88
Çankırı	B 5	118
Çankırı □[3]	B 5	118
Canmore	F 14	156
Cannanore (Kannur)	G 2	122
Canne ⊥	C 6	94
Cannes	G 4	82
Canning ≃	B 22	154
Cannington	A 4	162
Cannock	E 4	72
Cannonball ≃	B 4	174
Cannon Beach	C 2	178
Canoas	A 12	195
Canoas ≃	G 5	194
Canoe Creek Indian Reserve ◆[4]	F 10	156
Canoe Lake ⊜	D 17	156
Canoe Lake Indian Reserve ◆[4]	D 18	156
Canoinhas	G 5	194
Canol	D 31	154
Canon City	F 2	174
Cañon del Sumidero, Parque Nacional ♦	I 13	184
Canonica, La ◗[1]	i 9	83a
Canosa di Púglia	C 6	94
Canova Beach	E 4	168
Canso	F 13	160
Cantabria □[3]	A 7	86
Cantábrica, Cordillera ⋏	A 3	84
Cantabrica, Cornisa ≛[2]	A 2	88
Cantal □[3]	C 6	80
Cantanhede	D 2	86
Cantaura	F 8	186
Canteleu	C 7	78
Canterbury	F 8	72
Canterbury □[3]	E 3	146
Canterbury Bight c	F 3	146
Canterbury Cathedral ◗[1]	F 7	72
Canterbury Plains ≡	E 3	146
Can Tho	I 7	132
Canton see Guangzhou, China	G 11	130
Canton, Ga., U.S.	B 2	168
Canton, Il., U.S.	B 3	170
Canton, Ks., U.S.	F 6	174
Canton, Ms., U.S.	F 3	170
Canton, N.C., U.S.	B 3	168
Canton, N.Y., U.S.	B 3	164
Canton, Oh., U.S.	C 3	162
Canton Lake ⊜[1]	B 4	172
Canton Lake State Recreational Area ♦	B 4	172
Cantù	D 5	92
Cantwell	E 20	154
Cañuelas	D 8	195
Canunda National Park ♦	F 3	144
Canutama	E 6	190
Čany, ozero ⊜	D 10	114
Cany-Barville	C 7	78
Canyon	C 2	172
Canyon de Chelly National Monument ♦	D 4	176
Canyon Lake ⊜[1]	F 4	172
Canyonlands National Park ♦	C 4	176
Canyonville	D 2	178
Cao Bang	C 7	132
Cao Lanh	I 7	132
Caombo	D 2	204
Caorle	D 8	92
Caoxian	I 10	128
Čapaevsk	C 16	110
Capala	E 1	204
Capanaparo ≃	B 5	190
Capannori	F 6	92
Capão Bonito	F 6	194
Caparaó, Parque Nacional do ♦	D 9	194
Capata	E 3	204
Cap-Chat	D 10	160
Cap-de-la-Madeleine	E 7	160
Cape ≃	F 8	142
Cape Arid National Park ♦	M 7	140
Cape Barren Island I	i 13	145a
Cape Basin ✦[1]	I 11	60
Cape Breton Highlands National Park ♦	E 13	160
Cape Breton Island I	E 13	160
Cape Canaveral	E 4	168
Cape Coast	D 4	200
Cape Cod Bay c	E 8	164
Cape Cod National Seashore ♦	E 8	164
Cape Coral	F 3	168
Cape Fear ≃	C 6	168
Cape Girardeau	D 4	170
Cape Hatteras National Seashore ♦	B 7	168
Cape Henlopen State Park ♦	H 3	164
Cape Krusenstern National Monument ♦	C 11	154
Capelinha	B 9	194
Cape Lisburne	B 11	154
Capella	G 9	142
Capelle aan de IJssel	C 3	69
Cape Lookout National Seashore ♦	B 6	168
Cape May	H 4	164
Cape May □[6]	G 4	164
Cape May Court House	G 4	164
Cape Melville National Park ♦	C 7	142
Cape Pole	H 28	154
Cape Range National Park ♦	H 2	140
Capernaum see Kefar Naḥum ⊥	D 5	120
Cape Romanzof	F 11	154
Capertee ≃	D 8	144
Capesterre-Belle-Eau	n 21	187e
Cape Town (Kaapstad)	G 2	206
Cape Verde □[1]	h 11	200a
Cape Verde Basin ✦[1]	F 8	60
Cape Vincent	B 2	164
Cape York Peninsula ≻[1]	B 6	142
Cap-Haïtien	D 6	186
Capim ≃	D 9	190
Capistrello	H 9	92
Capitán Arturo Prat ◗[3]	L 7	192
Capitão Enéas	B 9	194
Capitola	D 2	182
Capitol Reef National Park ♦	C 3	176
Capivara, Represa de ⊜[1]	E 5	194
Capiz see Roxas	C 8	134
Čapljina	D 4	104
Čaplygin	J 14	108
Capo d'Orlando	F 4	94
Capoterra	I 9	94a
Capraia	F 5	92
Caprarola	G 8	92
Capreol	H 18	158
Capri	D 4	94
Capri, Isola di I	D 4	94
Capricorn Channel Ʉ	G 11	142
Caprivi □[3]	F 3	204
Caprivi Strip □[9]	F 3	204
Cap Saint Jacques see Vung Tau	I 8	132
Captieux	D 3	80
Capua	C 4	94
Capulin Volcano National Monument ♦	B 2	172
Capuna	F 2	204
Caquetá (Japurá) ≃	D 4	190
Čara	A 7	124
Čara ≃	D 14	114
Carabobo □[3]	F 7	186
Caracal	C 8	104
Caracaraí	C 6	190
Caracas	F 8	186
Caracol ⊥	I 15	184
Caraguatatuba	E 8	194
Carajás, Serra dos ⋏[2]	E 8	190
Caramat	G 15	158
Carandaí	D 9	194
Carangola	D 9	194
Caransebeș	C 7	104
Carapina	D 10	194
Caraquet	E 11	160
Caraș-Severin □[3]	C 6	104
Caratasca, Laguna de c	E 3	186
Carate Brianza	E 7	82
Caratinga	C 9	194
Caravaca de la Cruz	F 3	88
Caravaggio	E 1	102
Carayaó	F 2	194
Carazinho	E 9	192
Carballiño	B 2	86
Carballo	A 2	86
Carbo	C 4	184
Carbon □[6]	F 3	164
Carbon-Blanc	D 3	80
Carbondale, Il., U.S.	D 4	170
Carbondale, Ks., U.S.	C 1	170
Carbondale, Pa., U.S.	E 3	164
Carbonear	E 17	160
Carbonia	F 2	90
Carcaixent	E 4	88
Carcajou	C 13	156
Carcajou ≃	D 31	154
Carcarañá ≃	C 6	195
Carcassonne	E 6	80
Carceri, Eremo delle ◗[1]	F 8	92
Carcross	A 4	156
Čardara	A 1	122
Čardarinskoe vodohranilišče ⊜[1]	A 1	122
Cardedeu	G 6	80
Cárdenas, Cuba	C 4	186
Cárdenas, Mex.	H 13	184
Cardiel, Lago ⊜	I 5	192
Cardiff	F 3	72
Cardiff □[6]	F 3	72
Cardigan	E 2	72
Cardigan Bay c	E 2	72
Cardigan State Park ♦	C 6	164
Cardington	D 5	206
Cardona, Spain	G 5	80
Cardona, Ur.	C 9	195
Cardston	G 15	156
Cardwell	E 7	142
Careen Lake ⊜	C 17	156
Carei	B 7	104
Carentan	C 5	78
Carey, Lake ⊜	K 7	140
Careysburg	D 2	200
Cariacica	D 10	194
Caribbean Sea ≂[2]	E 5	186
Cariboo ≃	E 11	156
Caribou, N.S., Can.	F 12	160
Caribou, Me., U.S.	g 12	163a
Caribou ≃	B 11	158
Caribou Mountains ⋏	B 14	156
Carignan	C 12	78
Carinhanha	F 10	190
Carinhanha ≃	F 10	190
Caripito	F 9	186
Carlentini	G 5	94
Carlet	E 4	88
Carleton	E 6	174
Carleton, Mount ∧	E 10	160
Carleton Place	F 5	160
Carletonville	D 7	206
Carlin	B 5	180
Carlisle, Eng., U.K.	C 3	72
Carlisle, In., U.S.	C 5	170
Carlisle, Pa., U.S.	F 1	164
Carl Junction	D 1	170
Carlos Casares	G 7	192
Carlos Chagas	B 10	194
Carlos Tejedor	D 6	195
Carlow (Ceatharlach)	D 4	75
Carlow □[3]	D 5	75
Carlsbad see Karlovy Vary, Czech Rep.	B 9	100
Carlsbad, Ca., U.S.	G 6	182
Carlsbad, N.M., U.S.	D 1	172
Carlsbad, Tx., U.S.	E 3	172
Carlsbad Caverns National Park ♦	D 1	172
Carluke	E 5	74
Carlyle Lake ⊜[1]	C 4	170
Carmagnola	E 3	92
Carman	G 10	158
Carmarthen	F 2	72
Carmarthenshire □[6]	F 2	72
Carmaux	D 6	80
Carmel, In., U.S.	C 5	170
Carmel, N.Y., U.S.	E 5	164
Carmel, Mount ∧	D 3	120
Carmel Head ≻	D 2	72
Carmelo	C 8	195
Carmel Valley	D 2	182
Carmen ≃	A 2	195
Carmen, Isla I	E 4	184
Carmen de Patagones	G 6	195
Carmichael	B 2	182
Carmila	F 9	142
Carmona	G 5	86
Carnarvon, Austl.	I 2	140
Carnarvon, S. Afr.	F 5	206
Carnarvon see Caernarfon, Wales, U.K.	D 2	72
Carnarvon National Park ♦	H 8	142
Carnatic □[9]	G 3	122
Carndonagh	A 4	75
Carnegie	I 7	140
Carnegie, Lake ⊜	J 7	140
Carnia ◆[1]	C 8	92
Carnoustie	D 6	74
Carnsore Point ≻	D 5	75
Carnwath ≃	C 30	154
Carol City	G 4	168
Carolina, Braz.	A 9	190
Carolina, P.R.	j 16	187b
Carolina Beach	B 6	168
Caroline □[6]	H 3	164
Caroline I[1]	D 12	136
Caroline Islands II	C 6	136
Caron	F 19	156
Caroní ≃	B 6	190
Carora	F 7	186
Carouge	D 4	82
Carovigno	D 7	94
Carp	F 5	160
Carpathian Mountains ⋏	F 12	62
Carpații Meridionali ⋏	F 12	62
Carpenedolo	D 6	92
Carpentaria, Gulf of c	B 4	142
Carpentersville	A 4	170
Carpentras	F 3	82
Carpi	E 6	92
Cărpineni	B 10	104
Carpineto Romano	C 3	94
Carpinteria	F 4	182
Carp Lake ⊜	D 10	156
Carquefou	E 5	78
Carrara	E 6	92
Carrauntoohil ∧	E 2	75
Carreta, Punta ≻	F 3	190
Carrick ◆[1]	B 2	72
Carrickfergus	B 6	75
Carrick on Shannon	C 3	75
Carrick-on-suir	D 4	75
Carrillo	D 8	184
Carrión de los Condes	B 6	86
Carrizal Bajo	E 5	192
Carrizo Creek ≃	B 2	172
Carrizo Springs	F 3	172
Carroll	C 8	144
Carroll □[6], Md., U.S.	G 1	164
Carroll □[6], N.H., U.S.	C 7	164
Carrollton, Ga., U.S.	F 6	170
Carrollton, Ky., U.S.	C 6	170
Carrollton, Mi., U.S.	B 2	162
Carrollton, Mo., U.S.	C 2	170
Carrollton, Tx., U.S.	D 5	172
Carrolltown	C 4	162
Carron ≃	D 5	142
Carrot ≃	E 7	158
Carrouges	D 6	78
Carry Falls Reservoir ⊜[1]	B 4	164
Çarşamba	B 7	118
Čarsk see Shar	A 13	116
Carsoli	G 9	92
Carson	B 4	174
Carson, East Fork ≃	B 4	182
Carson City	A 4	182
Carson City □[6]	A 4	182
Carson Range ⋏	A 4	182
Carson Sink ⊜	C 4	180
Cartagena, Col.	F 5	186
Cartagena, Spain	G 3	88
Cartago	F 4	186
Cartaxo	E 2	86
Cartaya	G 3	86
Cartersville	B 2	168
Carterton, N.Z.	D 5	146
Carterton, Eng., U.K.	F 5	72
Carthage, Mo., U.S.	D 1	170
Carthage, N.Y., U.S.	B 3	164
Carthage, Tx., U.S.	F 1	170
Carthage ⊥	B 7	198
Cartwright	B 15	160
Caruaru	E 11	190
Carúpano	F 9	186
Carutapera	D 9	190
Carvin	B 9	78
Carvoeiro	D 6	190
Cary	B 5	168
Caryville	G 6	170
Casablanca	C 3	198
Casacalenda	C 4	94
Casa de Piedra, Embalse ⊜[1]	F 4	195
Casa Grande	F 3	176
Casa Grande Ruins National Monument ♦	F 3	176
Casalecchio di Reno	E 7	92
Casale Monferrato	D 4	92
Casalpusterlengo	D 5	92
Casamance ≃	C 1	200
Casamassima	D 6	94
Casanare ≃	B 4	190
Casar	B 4	168
Casarano	D 8	94
Casas Adobes	F 3	176
Casas Grandes ≃	B 6	184
Casas-Ibáñez	E 3	88
Casavieja	D 6	86
Cascade, Ia., U.S.	D 3	166
Cascade, Wi., U.S.	D 4	166
Cascade Locks	C 2	178
Cascade Mountains (Cascade Range) ⋏	B 3	178
Cascade Range (Cascade Mountains) ⋏	A 3	178
Cascais	F 1	86
Cascavel	F 4	194
Cascina	F 6	92
Caserta	C 4	94
Caserta □[6]	C 4	94
Casey	B 1	170
Casey ◗[3]	C 19	208
Cashiers	B 3	168
Casilda	C 7	195
Casimcea	C 10	104
Casino	B 9	144
Čáslav	D 8	96
Čašniki	B 6	110
Casoria	D 4	94
Časovo	E 19	108
Caspe	C 4	88
Casper	D 10	178
Caspian Depression ≡	F 18	110
Caspian Sea ≂[2]	B 6	116
Cassà de la Selva	C 7	88
Cassai (Kasai) ≃	E 3	204
Cassamba	E 3	204
Cassanje ≃	B 2	194
Cassano allo Ionio	E 6	94
Cass City	B 2	162
Cassiar Mountains ⋏	G 30	154
Cassilândia	C 4	194
Cassinga	F 2	204
Cassino	C 3	94
Cass Lake ⊜	B 7	174
Cassoalala	D 1	204
Cassopolis	E 6	166
Cassville	D 2	170
Castalia	C 2	162
Castaños	G 3	172
Castelbuono	G 4	94
Castel del Piano	G 7	92
Castelfiorentino	F 6	92
Castelfranco Emilia	E 7	92
Castelfranco Veneto	D 7	92
Castellammare del Golfo	F 2	94
Castellammare di Stabia	D 4	94
Castellana Grotte	D 7	94
Castellane	G 4	82
Castellaneta	D 6	94
Castelldefels	C 6	88
Castelleone	D 5	92
Castelló de la Plana	D 5	88
Castellote	D 4	88

⌞ Waterfall Ʉ Strait c Bay, Gulf ⊜ Lake ≡ Swamp ⊓ Ice Feature ≂ Other Hydrographic Feature ✦ Submarine Feature □ Political Unit ◗ Cultural Institution ⊥ Historical Site ♦ Recreational Site ⊠ Airport ■ Military Installation ◆ Miscellaneous

Symbols in the index entries represent the broad categories identified in the key at the right. Symbols with superior numbers (☇¹) identify subcategories (see complete key on page 242).

∧ Mountain ☇ Mountains ⤳ Pass ∨ Valley ≃ Plain ⊁ Cape I Island II Islands ⸙ Other Topographic Feature ≃ River ≃ Canal

Choapa — Coswig

Name	Map Ref.	Page
Choapa ≃	B 2	195
Chobe □[3]	F 3	204
Chobe National Park ♠	F 3	204
Choch'iwŏn	F 1	126
Chociwel	B 8	96
Chocó □[3]	G 5	186
Chocope	E 3	190
Choctawhatchee ≃	D 2	168
Chodzież	B 9	96
Chofombo	E 5	204
Choichuff, Laga ≃	G 4	202
Choiseul I	D 7	136
Choix	D 5	184
Chojnice	B 9	96
Chojnów	C 8	96
Chōkai-san ∧[1]	E 8	126
Chókwe	C 10	206
Cholet	E 6	78
Chŏlla-bukto □[3]	I 16	128
Chŏlla-namdo □[3]	I 16	128
Choluteca	E 3	186
Choluteca ≃	E 3	186
Choma	F 4	204
Chomo Lhāri ∧	D 5	122
Chomutov	B 10	100
Ch'ŏnan	H 16	128
Chon Buri	H 5	132
Chone	D 3	190
Chong'an	E 14	130
Ch'ŏngjin	F 17	128
Ch'ŏngju	H 16	128
Chongming	C 15	130
Chongming Dao I	C 15	130
Chongoene	C 10	206
Chongqing, China	C 6	130
Chongqing, China	D 8	130
Chongqing □[3]	D 8	130
Chŏngŭp	I 16	128
Chongxin	I 6	128
Chongzuo	G 8	130
Chŏnju	I 16	128
Chonos, Archipiélago de los II	I 5	192
Chop	A 7	104
Chopim ≃	F 4	194
Chorges	F 4	82
Chorin ⊥	D 10	98
Chorley	D 4	72
Chornobyl' (Chernobyl)	D 6	110
Chornomors'ke	G 8	110
Choroszcz	B 12	96
Chortkiv	A 8	104
Ch'ŏrwŏn	G 16	128
Chosen	F 4	168
Chōshi	G 8	126
Chos Malal	E 2	195
Choszczno	B 8	96
Chotěboř	A 7	102
Choûm	E 2	198
Choybalsan	B 10	128
Chrissiesmeer	D 9	206
Christanshåb (Qasigiannguit)	C 22	150
Christchurch, N.Z.	E 4	146
Christchurch, Eng., U.K.	G 5	72
Christian, Cape ›	B 19	150
Christian Sound ʯ	H 27	154
Christie Bay ⊂	D 10	150
Christina ≃	C 16	156
Christmas Creek	F 8	140
Christmas Creek ≃	F 9	140
Christmas Island □[2]	K 12	112
Christmas Island see Kiritimati I[1]	C 12	136
Christmas Ridge ✢[3]	F 14	58
Christ of the Andes (Cristo Redentor) ⊥	C 2	195
Chrudim	D 8	96
Chrzanów	C 10	96
Chu (Xam) ≃	I 7	130
Chubbuck	D 7	178
Chūbu-Sangaku-kokuritsu-kōen ♠	F 6	126
Chubut □[3]	H 6	192
Chubut ≃	H 6	192
Chu Chua	F 11	156
Chūgoku-sanchi ⋏	G 4	126
Chuhuyiv	E 10	110
Chuí	C 11	195
Chukchi Sea ⊤[2]	B 4	61
Chula Vista	H 6	182
Chumbicha	E 6	192
Chum Phae	F 6	132
Chumphon	I 4	132
Chum Saeng	G 5	132
Chumunjin	F 2	126
Ch'unch'ŏn	H 16	128
Ch'ungch'ŏng-bukto □[3]	H 16	128
Ch'ungch'ŏng-namdo □[3]	H 16	128
Chung Hau	I 18	131a
Ch'ungju	H 16	128
Chungking see Chongqing	D 8	130
Ch'ungmu	I 17	128
Chunhuhux	H 15	184
Chuquicamata	D 6	192
Chur	D 7	82
Churāchāndpur	E 6	122
Churchill	B 11	158
Churchill □[6]	A 5	182
Churchill ≃, Nf., Can.	B 12	160
Churchill ≃	C 11	158
Churchill, Cape ›	B 12	158
Churchill, Mount ∧[1]	F 24	154
Churchill Falls ↳	B 12	160
Churchill Lake ◎	C 4	158
Church Point	G 2	170
Chūru	D 2	122
Churubusco	B 6	170
Chute-Saint-Philippe	E 6	160
Chutung	F 15	130
Chuŭl-li	D 2	126
Chuxian	B 13	130
Chuxiong	F 5	130
Chynadiyeve	A 7	104
Ciadâr Lunga	B 10	104
Ciampino	H 8	92
Cianjur	k 18	135b
Cianorte	E 4	194
Ciawi	k 19	135b
Cibaliung	k 17	135b
Cibatu	k 18	135b
Čibukli	H 21	110
Cicero	B 5	170
Cicolano ◆[1]	G 9	92
Ciechanów	B 11	96
Ciechanowiec	B 12	96
Ciego de Ávila	C 5	186
Ciempozuelos	D 7	86
Ciénaga	F 6	186
Cienfuegos	C 4	186
Cieszyn	D 10	96
Cieza	F 3	88
Çifteler	C 9	106
Cifuentes	D 2	88
Čiganak see Shyghanaq	A 11	116
Cigüela ≃	C 4	84
Cijara, Embalse de ◎[1]	E 6	86
Cijulang	k 19	135b
Čikoj	A 6	128
Čikoj (Cöch) ≃	B 6	128
Cilacap	k 19	135b
Çıldır Gölü ◎	B 10	118
Cilento ◆[1]	D 5	94
Cili	D 10	130
Cilleruelo de Bezana	B 7	86
Cil'ma ≃	D 19	108
Cimarron	B 1	172
Cimarron ≃	G 5	174
Čimbaj	H 21	110
Cimișlia	B 10	104
Cimljansk	F 13	110
Cimljanskoe vodohranilišče ◎[1]	E 13	110
Cina, Tanjung ›	G 4	134
Cinaruco-Capanaparo ♠	G 8	186
Cincinnati, Ia., U.S.	B 2	170
Cincinnati, Oh., U.S.	C 6	170
Cinco Saltos	F 4	195
Çine	D 8	106
Ciney	D 4	69
Cinfães	C 2	86
Cingoli	F 9	92
Cinisello Balsamo	D 4	92
Činja-Voryk	E 20	108
Cintalapa	I 13	184
Cinto, Monte ∧	i 8	83a
Cintruénigo	B 3	88
Ciociaria ◆[1]	H 9	92
Cipatujah	k 19	135b
Cipolletti	G 6	192
Circeo, Parco Nazionale del ♠	H 8	92
Circle	B 2	174
Circle Hot Springs	D 22	154
Circleville	D 2	162
Cirebon	k 19	135b
Ciremay, Gunung ∧	k 19	135b
Cirencester	F 5	72
Cirey-sur-Vezouze	B 4	82
Ciriè	D 3	92
Cirò Marina	E 7	94
Čirpan	D 8	104
Cislago	D 4	92
Čišmy	I 21	108
Cisnădie	C 8	104
Cisolok	k 18	135b
Cisséla	C 2	200
Cisterna di Latina	H 8	92
Cistierna	B 5	86
Čistopol'	I 19	108
Čita	B 6	124
Čitaskaja oblast' □[6]	A 8	128
Citlaltépetl, Volcán see Pico de Orizaba, Volcán ∧[1]	H 11	184
Citrus Heights	B 2	182
Cittadella	D 7	92
Città del Vaticano see Vatican City □[1]	E 4	90
Città di Castello	F 8	92
City of Refuge National Historical Park see Pu'uhonua o Honaunau National Historical Park ♠	j 10	181a
Ciuciuleni	B 10	104
Ciudad Acuña	C 9	184
Ciudad Altamirano	H 9	184
Ciudad Bolívar	F 9	186
Ciudad Camargo	D 7	184
Ciudad Constitución	E 3	184
Ciudad del Carmen	H 14	184
Ciudad del Este	F 3	194
Ciudad del Maíz	F 10	184
Ciudad de México (Mexico City)	H 10	184
Ciudad de Nutrias	F 7	186
Ciudadela	B 7	84
Ciudad Guayana	F 9	186
Ciudad Hidalgo	H 9	184
Ciudad Juárez	B 6	184
Ciudad Lerdo	E 8	184
Ciudad Madero	F 11	184
Ciudad Mante	F 10	184
Ciudad Miguel Alemán	D 10	184
Ciudad Netzahualcóyotl	H 10	184
Ciudad Obregón	D 5	184
Ciudad Ojeda	F 7	186
Ciudad Real	E 7	86
Ciudad Real □[6]	C 4	84
Ciudad Rodrigo	D 4	86
Ciudad Valles	F 10	184
Ciudad Victoria	F 10	184
Cividale del Friuli	C 9	92
Civil'sk	I 17	108
Civita Castellana	G 8	92
Civitanova Marche	A 3	94
Civitavecchia	G 7	92
Civray	B 4	80
Çivril	C 8	106
Cixi	C 15	130
Cizre	D 9	118
Čkalovsk	H 15	108
Clackmannan □[6]	D 5	74
Clacton-on-Sea	F 8	72
Claire, Lake ◎	B 15	156
Clair Engle Lake ◎[1]	E 2	178
Clam Gulch	F 18	154
Clanton	F 5	170
Claonaig	B 1	72
Clara City	C 7	174
Clare	B 1	162
Clare □[3]	D 3	75
Claremont	C 6	164
Claremore	D 1	170
Clarence, N.Z.	E 4	146
Clarence, Ia., U.S.	B 3	170
Clarence ≃	B 9	144
Clarence, Port ⊂	D 11	154
Clarence Island I	L 9	192
Clarence Strait ʯ, Austl.	C 11	140
Clarence Strait ʯ, Ak., U.S.	C 5	156
Clarendon	C 4	162
Clarens	E 8	206
Claresholm	F 15	156
Clarinda	B 1	170
Clarington	G 4	160
Clarion, Ia., U.S.	D 2	166
Clarion, Pa., U.S.	C 4	162
Clarión, Isla I	H 2	184
Clark, Lake ◎	F 17	154
Clarke ≃	E 7	142
Clarke Lake ◎	D 18	156
Clarkesville	B 3	168
Clark Fork ≃	A 6	178
Clarksburg	D 3	162
Clarksdale	E 3	170
Clarks Hill	B 5	170
Clarks Hill Lake ◎[1]	C 3	168
Clarkson	E 6	174
Clarks Summit	E 3	164
Clark's Town	h 12	186a
Clarksville, Ar., U.S.	E 2	170
Clarksville, Ia., U.S.	D 2	166
Clarksville, In., U.S.	C 6	170
Clarksville, Tn., U.S.	D 5	170
Clarkton	B 5	168
Claro ≃, Braz.	B 5	194
Claro ≃, Braz.	C 5	194
Claude	C 3	172
Clausthal-Zellerfeld	E 7	98
Claxton	C 4	168
Clay City	E 1	162
Claymont	G 3	164
Clayton, La., U.S.	G 3	170
Clayton, N.M., U.S.	B 2	172
Clayton, Wa., U.S.	A 5	178
Clear, Cape ›	G 21	154
Clearfield, Pa., U.S.	C 4	162
Clearfield, Ut., U.S.	E 7	178
Clearlake, Ca., U.S.	B 1	182
Clear Lake, Ia., U.S.	D 2	166
Clear Lake, Wi., U.S.	C 2	166
Clear Lake ◎	C 2	180
Clear Lake Reservoir ◎[1]	E 3	178
Clear Site	D 20	154
Clearwater, B.C., Can.	F 11	156
Clearwater, Fl., U.S.	F 3	168
Clearwater, Ne., U.S.	D 5	174
Clearwater ≃, Ab., Can.	E 14	156
Clearwater ≃, B.C., Can.	E 11	156
Clearwater ≃	C 16	156
Clearwater ≃, Id., U.S.	B 5	178
Clearwater ≃, Mt., U.S.	B 7	178
Clearwater, Middle Fork ≃	B 6	178
Clearwater Lake ◎	D 8	158
Clearwater Lake Provincial Park ♠	D 8	158
Clearwater Mountains ⋏	B 6	178
Cleburne	D 5	172
Cle Elum	B 3	178
Cle Elum ≃	B 3	178
Cleethorpes	D 6	72
Clelles	F 3	82
Clemson	B 3	168
Clermont, Austl.	G 8	142
Clermont, Fr.	C 9	78
Clermont, Fl., U.S.	E 4	168
Clermont-Ferrand	C 7	80
Cles	C 7	92
Clevedon	F 4	72
Cleveland, Al., U.S.	E 5	170
Cleveland, Ms., U.S.	F 3	170
Cleveland, Oh., U.S.	C 3	162
Cleveland, Tn., U.S.	E 6	170
Cleveland, Tx., U.S.	G 1	170
Cleveland, Mount ∧	A 6	178
Cleveleys	D 3	72
Clifton, Az., U.S.	A 5	184
Clifton, Ks., U.S.	F 6	174
Clifton, Tn., U.S.	E 4	170
Clifton Forge	E 4	162
Climax	D 6	166
Clinch ≃	A 3	168
Clingmans Dome ∧	B 3	168
Clinton, On., Can.	G 3	160
Clinton, N.Z.	G 2	146
Clinton, Ia., U.S.	B 3	170
Clinton, In., U.S.	C 5	170
Clinton, Me., U.S.	A 9	162
Clinton, Mi., U.S.	D 7	166
Clinton, Ms., U.S.	F 3	170
Clinton, N.C., U.S.	B 5	168
Clinton, Ok., U.S.	C 4	172
Clinton, Tn., U.S.	A 2	168
Clinton □[6]	B 5	164
Clintonville	C 4	166
Clio	B 2	162
Clitheroe	D 4	72
Clocolan	E 7	206
Clonakilty	E 3	75
Cloncurry	F 5	142
Cloncurry ≃	E 5	142
Clondalkin	C 5	75
Clonmacnoise ⊥	C 4	75
Clonmel (Cluain Meala)	D 4	75
Cloppenburg	D 4	98
Cloquet	B 2	166
Clorinda	F 2	194
Cloud Peak ∧	C 10	178
Clova	D 6	160
Cloverdale	C 2	180
Clovis, Ca., U.S.	D 4	182
Clovis, N.M., U.S.	C 2	172
Cluj □[3]	B 7	104
Cluj-Napoca	B 7	104
Cluny	H 4	142
Clusone	D 6	92
Clute	F 6	172
Clutha ≃	G 2	146
Clyde	C 2	164
Clyde ≃	B 2	72
Clyde, Firth of ⊂	B 2	72
Clydebank	B 2	72
Clydesdale	D 7	206
Cna ≃	I 15	108
Cnossus see Knosós ⊥	E 6	106
Côa ≃	D 3	86
Coacoyole	E 6	184
Coahuila	F 1	176
Coahuila □[3]	D 8	184
Coal ≃	F 31	154
Coaldale	G 15	156
Coal Fork	D 3	162
Coalinga	D 3	182
Coalport	C 4	162
Coal River	B 8	156
Coalville, S. Afr.	C 8	206
Coalville, Eng., U.K.	E 5	72
Coamo	j 15	187b
Coari ≃	E 6	190
Coast □[3]	H 4	202
Coast Mountains ⋏	D 7	156
Coast Ranges ⋏	C 3	152
Coatbridge	B 2	72
Coatesville	G 3	164
Coaticook	F 8	160
Coaticook □[6]	A 7	164
Coats Island I	D 16	150
Coats Land ◆[1]	D 6	208
Coatzacoalcos	H 12	184
Cobá ⊥	G 16	184
Cobalt	E 4	160
Cobán	J 14	184
Cobar	C 5	144
Cobargo	F 7	144
Cobden	F 5	160
Cobham ≃	E 11	158
Cobija	F 5	190
Cobourg	G 4	160
Cobourg Marine Park ♠	B 11	140
Cobre, Barranca del see Copper Canyon ♠	D 6	184
Coburg	B 7	100
Coburg Island I	A 17	150
Cocentaina	F 4	88
Cöch (Čikoj) ≃	B 6	128
Cochabamba	G 5	190
Cochem	B 4	100
Cochin see Kochi	H 3	122
Cochin China □[9]	I 8	132
Cochiti Indian Reservation ◆[4]	E 5	176
Cochrane, Ab., Can.	F 14	156
Cochrane, Wi., U.S.	C 3	166
Cochrane ≃	B 8	158
Cochrane, Lago (Pueyrredón, Lago) ◎	I 5	192
Cockburn	D 3	144
Cockburn, Mount ∧	I 10	140
Cockburn Island I	I 17	158
Cockermouth	C 3	72
Cockeysville	G 2	164
Cockpit Country ◆[1]	h 12	186a
Coco ≃	E 3	186
Coco, Cayo I	C 5	186
Coco, Isla del I	I 11	148
Cocoa	E 4	168
Cocoa Beach	E 4	168
Cocobeach	E 6	200
Coco Channel ʯ	G 6	122
Coco Islands II	G 1	132
Coconino Plateau ⋏[1]	E 2	176
Cocoparra National Park ♠	E 6	144
Cocos Islands □[2]	K 11	112
Cod, Cape ›[1]	D 8	164
Codăești	B 9	104
Codajás	D 6	190
Codigoro	E 8	92
Cod Island I	E 20	150
Codlea	C 8	104
Codó	D 10	190
Codogno	D 5	92
Codroipo	D 8	92
Cody	C 9	178
Coelemu	E 1	195
Coen	B 6	142
Coen ≃	B 6	142
Coesfeld	E 4	98
Coeur d'Alene	B 5	178
Coeur d'Alene Indian Reservation ◆[4]	B 5	178
Coevorden	B 5	69
Coffeyville	D 1	170
Coffs Harbour	C 9	144
Cognac	C 3	80
Cogo	E 6	200
Cogolludo	D 1	88
Cohocton ≃	B 5	162
Cohoes	D 5	164
Cohuna	E 5	144
Coiba, Isla de I	G 4	186
Coig ≃	J 6	192
Coihaique	I 5	192
Coimbatore	G 3	122
Coimbra	D 2	86
Coimbra □[3]	D 2	86
Coín	H 6	86
Coipasa, Lago ◎	G 5	190
Cojedes □[3]	F 7	186
Cokato	C 1	166
Colac	G 4	144
Colatina	C 10	194
Colbeck, Cape ›	D 29	208
Colbert	D 5	172
Colchester, Eng., U.K.	F 7	72
Colchester, Ct., U.S.	E 6	164
Cold Bay	I 13	154
Cold Bay ⊂	I 13	154
Colditz	E 9	98
Cold Lake ◎	D 16	156
Cold Spring	C 7	174
Coldstream	B 4	72
Coldwater	C 1	162
Coldwater ≃	E 3	170
Coldwater Indian Reserve ◆[4]	G 11	156
Coleen ≃	C 23	154
Coleford	F 4	72
Coleman, Ab., Can.	G 14	156
Coleman, Fl., U.S.	E 3	168
Coleman ≃	C 6	142
Coleraine, Austl.	F 3	144
Coleraine, N. Ire., U.K.	A 5	75
Colesberg	F 6	206
Colfax, Il., U.S.	B 4	170
Colfax, Wa., U.S.	B 5	178
Colhué Huapi, Lago ◎	I 6	192
Colico	C 5	92
Colima	H 8	184
Colima □[3]	H 7	184
Colima, Nevado de ∧[1]	H 7	184
Colinas	E 10	190
Coll I	D 2	74
Collarenebri	B 7	144
Colle di Val d'Elsa	F 6	92
Colleferro	H 8	92
College	D 20	154
Collegedale	B 2	168
College Park	C 2	168
College Station	E 5	172
Collegno	D 3	92
Collie	M 3	140
Collier Bay ⊂	E 8	140
Collier Range National Park ♠	I 5	140
Collierville	E 4	170
Colliford Lake Reservoir ◎[1]	B 2	78
Collingwood, On., Can.	F 3	160
Collingwood, N.Z.	D 4	146
Collins Bay	B 2	164
Collinsville	F 8	142
Collinwood	E 5	170
Collipulli	E 1	195
Colman	D 6	174
Colmar	B 5	82
Colmenar	H 6	86
Colmenar Viejo	D 7	86
Colne	D 4	72
Colo	D 2	166
Colo ≃	D 8	144
Cologna Veneta	D 7	92
Cologne see Köln	F 3	98
Coloma	D 5	166
Colomb-Béchar see Béchar	C 4	198
Colombes	D 9	78
Colombey-les-Belles	B 3	82
Colombia	G 4	172
Colombia □[1]	D 7	188
Colombo, Braz.	F 6	194
Colombo, Sri L.	H 3	122
Colomiers	E 5	80
Colón, Arg.	C 8	195
Colón, Arg.	C 7	195
Colón, Cuba	C 4	186
Colón, Pan.	F 5	186
Colona	L 12	140
Colonia del Sacramento	D 9	195
Colonia Dora	E 7	192
Colonia Vicente Guerrero	G 5	180
Colony	C 1	170
Colorado □[3]	D 6	152
Colorado ≃, Arg.	G 7	192
Colorado ≃, N.A.	E 5	152
Colorado ≃, Tx., U.S.	F 5	172
Colorado City	D 3	172
Colorado National Monument ♠	C 4	176
Colorado River Aqueduct ≋[1]	F 5	180
Colorado River Indian Reservation ◆[4]	F 1	176
Colorado Springs	F 2	174
Colorno	E 6	92
Colotlán	F 8	184
Čolpon-Ata	A 3	122
Colt	E 3	170
Columbia, Ky., U.S.	D 6	170
Columbia, Md., U.S.	G 2	164
Columbia, Mo., U.S.	C 2	170
Columbia, Ms., U.S.	G 4	170
Columbia, Pa., U.S.	F 2	164
Columbia, S.C., U.S.	C 4	168
Columbia, Tn., U.S.	E 5	170
Columbia □[6], N.Y., U.S.	D 5	164
Columbia □[6], Pa., U.S.	E 2	164
Columbia ≃	G 8	150
Columbia, Cape ›	A 12	148
Columbia, Mount ∧	E 13	156
Columbia Falls	A 10	162
Columbia Icefield ⊓	E 12	156
Columbia Mountains ⋏	F 12	156
Columbus, Ga., U.S.	F 6	170
Columbus, In., U.S.	C 6	170
Columbus, Ks., U.S.	D 1	170
Columbus, Ms., U.S.	F 4	170
Columbus, Mt., U.S.	C 9	178
Columbus, Ne., U.S.	E 6	174
Columbus, N.M., U.S.	G 5	176
Columbus, Oh., U.S.	D 2	162
Columbus, Tx., U.S.	F 5	172
Colusa	A 1	182
Colusa □[6]	A 1	182
Colville	A 5	178
Colville ≃	A 19	154
Colville, Cape ›	B 5	146
Colville Indian Reservation ◆[4]	A 4	178
Colville Lake ◎	C 31	154
Colwyn Bay	D 3	72
Comacchio	E 8	92
Comacchio, Valli di ◎	E 7	92
Comal	k 19	135b
Comalcalco	H 13	184
Comanche	C 5	172
Comandante Ferraz ◗[3]	L 8	192
Comandante Fontana	E 8	192
Comănești	B 9	104
Coma Pedrosa, Pic de ∧	B 6	88
Comayagua	E 3	186
Comber	B 6	75
Combermere Bay ⊂	E 1	132
Combomune	B 10	206
Combronde	C 7	80
Comburg ◗[1]	C 6	100
Comer	B 3	168
Comet ≃	H 9	142
Cometela	A 11	206
Comfort Bight	B 16	160
Comilla	E 6	122
Comino I	H 4	94
Comiso	H 4	94
Comitán	I 13	184
Commentry	B 6	80
Commerce	D 5	172
Commercy	B 3	82
Comminges ◆[1]	G 4	76
Committee Bay ⊂	C 15	150
Commondale	D 9	206
Communauté urbaine de l'Outaouais □[6]	A 3	164
Communauté urbaine de Montréal □[6]	A 5	164
Como	D 5	92
Como □[6]	D 5	92
Como, Lago di ◎	C 5	92
Comodoro Rivadavia	I 6	192
Comoé, Parc National de la ♠	D 4	200
Comores, Archipel des II	n 19	207d
Comorin, Cape ›	H 3	122
Comoros □[1]	J 12	196
Comox	G 9	156
Compiègne	C 9	78
Compostela	G 7	184
Comps-sur-Artuby	G 4	82
Compton	G 5	182
Comrat (Komrat)	B 10	104
Comstock	F 3	172
Conakry	D 2	200
Concarneau	E 3	78
Conceição das Alagoas	C 6	194
Conceição do Araguaia	A 9	190
Concepción, Arg.	E 6	192
Concepción, Bol.	G 6	190
Concepción, Chile	E 1	195
Concepción, Para.	E 2	194
Concepción □[3]	E 2	194
Concepción ≃	G 2	176
Concepción, Laguna ◎	G 6	190
Concepción, Volcán ∧[1]	F 3	186
Concepción del Oro	E 9	184
Concepción del Uruguay	C 8	195
Conception, Point ›	F 3	182
Conception Bay ⊂, Nf., Can.	E 17	160
Conception Bay ⊂, Nmb.	B 1	206
Concho	E 4	176
Conchos ≃, Mex.	E 10	184
Conchos ≃, Mex.	C 7	184
Concord, Ca., U.S.	C 1	182
Concord, Mi., U.S.	B 1	162
Concord, N.C., U.S.	B 4	168
Concord, N.H., U.S.	C 7	164
Concordia, Arg.	B 8	195
Concórdia, Braz.	G 4	194
Concordia, Mex.	F 6	184
Concordia Sagittaria ⊥	D 9	92
Concrete	A 3	178
Condamine ≃	I 10	142
Condat	C 6	80
Condé-sur-l'Escaut	D 2	69
Condé-sur-Noireau	D 6	78
Condobolin	D 6	144
Condroz □[9]	D 4	69
Cone	D 3	172
Conecuh ≃	G 5	170
Conegliano	D 8	92
Confuso ≃	F 2	194
Congaree Swamp National Monument ♠	C 4	168
Congaz	B 10	104
Conghua	G 11	130
Congjiang	F 9	130
Congleton	D 4	72
Congo □[1]	I 9	196
Congo ≃	C 2	204
Congo, Democratic Republic of the (Zaire) □[1]	I 10	196
Congress	G 18	156
Conil de la Frontera	H 4	86
Conimbla National Park ♠	D 7	144
Conisbrough	D 5	72
Conklin	D 16	156
Connaught □[9]	C 2	75
Conneautville	C 3	162
Connecticut □[3]	C 13	152
Connecticut ≃	E 6	164
Connellsville	C 4	162
Connemara ◆[1]	C 2	75
Connersville	C 6	170
Connors Range ⋏	F 9	142
Conrad	D 2	166
Conroe	E 6	172
Conroe, Lake ◎[1]	E 6	172
Conselheiro Lafaiete	D 9	194
Conselheiro Pena	C 10	194
Consett	C 5	72
Consolación del Sur	C 3	186
Con Son II	J 8	132
Constance, Lake (Bodensee) ◎	C 7	82
Constanța	C 10	104
Constanța □[3]	C 10	104
Constantí	C 6	88
Constantina	G 5	86
Constantine see Qacentina	B 6	198
Constantinople see İstanbul	B 8	106
Constitución	D 1	195
Constitución de 1857, Parque Nacional ♠	F 6	180
Consuegra	E 7	86
Consul	G 17	156
Contarina	D 8	92
Contas ≃	F 11	190
Contra Costa □[6]	C 2	182
Controller Bay ⊂	F 22	154
Contwoyto Lake ◎	C 10	150
Conty	C 9	78
Conversano	D 7	94
Conway, Ar., U.S.	E 2	170
Conway, Mo., U.S.	D 2	170
Conway, N.C., U.S.	A 6	168
Conway, S.C., U.S.	C 5	168
Conway National Park ♠	F 9	142
Conwy	D 3	72
Coober Pedy	J 2	142
Cook, Mn., U.S.	B 2	166
Cook, Ne., U.S.	E 6	174
Cook, Cape ›	F 7	156
Cook, Mount see Aoraki ∧	E 3	146
Cookeville	D 6	170
Cook Forest State Park ♠	E 9	166
Cookhouse	G 6	206
Cook Inlet ⊂	F 19	154
Cook Islands □[2]	E 11	136
Cook Strait ʯ	D 5	146
Cooktown	C 7	142
Coolabah	C 6	144
Coolah	C 7	144
Coolangatta	B 9	144
Coolgardie	L 6	140
Coolidge	F 3	176
Coolidge Dam ◆[6]	F 3	176
Cooloola National Park ♠	I 11	142
Cooma	F 7	144
Coombah Roadhouse	D 3	144
Coonabarabran	C 7	144
Coonalpyn	E 2	144
Coonamble	C 7	144
Coondambo	K 2	142
Coonoor	G 3	122
Coon Rapids, Ia., U.S.	E 7	174
Coon Rapids, Mn., U.S.	C 2	166
Cooper Creek ≃	B 1	144
Cooper Island I	q 22	193c
Cooper Road	F 2	170
Cooperstown	D 4	164
Coopracambra National Park ♠	F 7	144
Coorong National Park ♠	F 2	144
Coorow	K 4	140
Coos □[6]	B 7	164
Coosa ≃	F 5	170
Coos Bay	D 1	178
Cootamundra	E 7	144
Cootehill	B 4	75
Copan	G 7	174
Copán ⊥	J 15	184
Copenhagen see København, Den.	C 5	68
Copenhagen, N.Y., U.S.	C 3	164
Copertino	D 7	94
Copiapó	E 5	192
Coporolo ≃	E 1	204
Copparo	E 7	92
Copper ≃	F 22	154
Copperas Cove	E 4	172
Copperbelt □[3]	E 4	204
Copper Canyon ♠	D 6	184
Copper Center	F 22	154
Copper Harbor	B 4	166
Coppermine ≃	C 9	150
Copp Lake ◎	A 14	156
Coptos see Qift	I 5	118
Coquilhatville see Mbandaka	C 2	204
Coquille	D 1	178
Coquimbo	A 2	195
Coquimbo □[3]	B 2	195
Corabia	D 8	104
Coral Gables	G 4	168
Coral Sea ⊤[2]	C 9	142
Coral Sea Islands Territory □[2]	C 9	142
Coralville	B 3	170
Coram	A 6	178
Corangamite, Lake ◎	G 4	144
Corantijn (Corentyne) ≃	C 7	190
Corato	C 6	94
Corbeil-Essonnes	D 9	78
Corbetta	D 4	92
Corbett National Park ♠	D 3	122
Corbu	C 8	104
Corby	E 6	72
Corcoran	D 4	182
Corcovado, Golfo ⊂	H 5	192
Corcovado, Parque Nacional ♠	F 4	186
Corcovado, Volcán ∧[1]	H 5	192
Cordele	C 3	168
Cordell	C 4	172
Cordell Hull Reservoir ◎[1]	D 6	170
Cordenons	C 8	92
Cordillera □[3]	F 2	194
Córdoba, Arg.	B 5	195
Córdoba, Mex.	H 11	184
Córdoba (Cordova), Spain	G 6	86
Córdoba □[3], Arg.	F 7	192
Córdoba □[3], Col.	F 6	186
Córdoba □[6]	F 6	86
Cordova see Córdoba, Spain	G 6	86
Cordova, Al., U.S.	F 5	170
Cordova Bay ⊂	I 28	154
Corella	B 3	88
Corentyne (Corantijn) ≃	C 7	190
Corfu see Kérkyra I	C 3	106
Cori	H 8	92
Coria	E 4	86
Coria del Río	D 2	84
Corinne	E 3	162
Corinth	E 4	170
Corinth, Gulf of ⊂	C 5	106
Corinto	C 8	194
Corjeuți	A 9	104
Cork (Corcaigh)	E 3	75
Cork □[3]	D 3	75
Corleone	G 3	94
Çorlu	B 7	106
Cormons	D 9	92
Cormorant	D 8	158
Cormorant Lake ◎	D 8	158
Čornaja Sloboda	F 12	108
Cornelia	D 8	206
Cornélio Procópio	E 5	194
Cornell	C 3	166
Corner Brook	D 14	160
Cornești	B 9	104
Corneta, Punta ›	J 11	184
Corning, Ca., U.S.	C 2	180
Corning, Ia., U.S.	B 1	170
Corning, N.Y., U.S.	D 1	164
Corno Grande ∧	B 3	94
Cornouaille ◆[1]	E 3	78
Cornwall	F 6	160
Cornwall □[6]	G 2	72
Cornwallis Island I	A 14	150
Čornyj Mys	B 13	108
Coro	F 7	186
Coroaci	C 9	194
Coroico	G 5	190
Coromandel Coast ⊥[2]	G 4	122
Coromandel Peninsula ›[1]	B 5	146
Corona, Ca., U.S.	G 6	182
Corona, N.M., U.S.	E 6	176
Coronado	H 6	182
Coronado, Bahía de ⊂	F 3	186
Coronado National Memorial ♠	G 3	176
Coronation Gulf ⊂	C 10	150
Coronation Island I	L 10	192
Coronda	B 7	195
Coronel	E 1	195
Coronel Bogado	G 2	194
Coronel Dorrego	F 7	195
Coronel Fabriciano	C 9	194
Coronel Oviedo	F 2	194
Coronel Pringles	E 7	195
Coronel Suárez	E 6	195
Coropuna, Nevado ∧	G 4	190
Çorovodë	B 4	106
Corowa	E 6	144
Corozal, Belize	D 2	186
Corozal, Col.	F 6	186
Corpus Christi	G 5	172
Corpus Christi, Lake ◎[1]	F 4	172
Corpus Christi Bay ⊂	G 5	172
Corral de Almaguer	E 7	86
Corral de Bustos	C 6	195
Correggio	E 6	92
Corregidor I	C 8	134
Corrèze	C 5	80
Corrèze □[3]	C 5	80
Corrientes	E 8	192
Corrientes □[3]	E 8	192
Corrientes ≃, Arg.	A 8	195
Corrientes ≃, S.A.	D 3	190
Corrientes, Cabo ›, Col.	B 3	190
Corrientes, Cabo ›, Mex.	G 6	184
Corrigin	M 4	140
Corrumpa Creek ≃	B 2	172
Corry	C 4	162
Corse, Cap ›	h 9	83a
Corse-du-Sud □[3]	j 8	83a
Corsham	F 4	72
Corsica	D 5	174
Corsica (Corse) I, Fr.	i 8	83a
Corsica see Corse I, Fr.	i 8	83a
Corsicana	D 5	172
Corsico	D 5	92
Corte	i 9	83a
Cortemilia	E 4	92
Cortés, Mar de see California, Golfo de ⊂	C 3	184
Cortina d'Ampezzo	C 7	92
Cortland, N.Y., U.S.	D 2	164
Cortland, Oh., U.S.	C 3	162
Cortland □[6]	D 2	164
Cortona	F 7	92
Corubal (Koliba) ≃	C 2	200
Coruche	F 2	86
Çoruh ≃	B 9	118
Çorum, Tur.	B 6	118
Çorum, Tur.	C 8	106
Çorum □[3]	B 6	118
Corumbá	C 2	194
Corumbá ≃	G 9	190
Corund	B 8	104
Corunna see A Coruña	A 2	86
Coruripe	F 11	190
Corvallis	C 2	178
Corvette, Lac de la ◎	B 7	160
Corvey, Kloster ◗[1]	E 6	98
Corvo I	h 11	198a
Corwith	D 8	174
Corydon	B 2	170
Cosa ⊥	G 7	92
Cosenza	E 6	94
Cosenza □[6]	E 6	94
Coshocton	C 2	162
Cosmo Newberry Aboriginal Reserve ◆[4]	K 7	140
Cosne-sur-Loire	E 9	78
Coso Peak ∧[1]	D 6	182
Cosquín	B 5	195
Cossato	D 4	92
Cossé-le-Vivien	E 6	78
Costa Mesa	G 6	182
Costa Rica	E 6	184
Costa Rica □[1]	I 11	148
Costermansville see Bukavu	C 4	204
Costești	B 10	104
Cosumnes ≃	B 2	182
Coswig, Ger.	E 10	98

↳ Waterfall ʯ Strait ⊂ Bay, Gulf ◎ Lake ≋ Swamp ⊓ Ice Feature ⊤ Other Hydrographic Feature ✢ Submarine Feature □ Political Unit ◗ Cultural Institution ⊥ Historical Site ♠ Recreational Site ⊠ Airport ■ Military Installation ◆ Miscellaneous

Coswig — Dendermonde

Name	Map Ref.	Page
Coswig, Ger.	E 9	98
Cotabato	D 8	134
Cotati	B 1	182
Côte d'Ivoire see Ivory Coast □[1]	H 7	196
Côte-d'Or □[3]	C 2	82
Cotentin ›[1]	C 5	78
Côtes-d'Armor □[3]	D 4	78
Cotija de la Paz	H 8	184
Cotonou	D 5	200
Cotopaxi ∧[1]	D 3	190
Cotswold Hills ⋀[2]	F 4	72
Cottage Grove	D 2	178
Cottbus	E 11	98
Cottian Alps ⋀	F 4	82
Cottingham	D 6	72
Cottondale	G 6	170
Cotton Plant	E 3	170
Cotulla	F 4	172
Couchiching, Lake ⊜	A 4	162
Coudekerque-Branche	A 9	78
Coudersport	C 5	162
Couillet	D 3	69
Coulee City	B 4	178
Coulee Dam National Recreation Area ♠	A 4	178
Coulommiers	D 10	78
Coulonge ≃	E 5	160
Coulta	M 2	142
Coulterville	C 4	170
Council Bluffs	B 1	170
Council Grove	F 6	174
Coupeville	A 2	178
Courcelles	D 3	69
Courland □[9]	D 11	66
Courland Lagoon ⊂	E 10	66
Courpière	E 1	82
Courson-les-Carrières	E 10	78
Courtenay	G 9	156
Courtland	E 5	162
Courtrai see Kortrijk	D 2	69
Coushatta	G 2	170
Coutras	C 3	80
Covane	A 10	206
Covasna □[3]	C 9	104
Coventry	E 5	72
Cove Palisades State Park ♠	C 3	178
Covered Wells	F 2	176
Covilhã	D 3	86
Covington, Ga., U.S.	C 3	168
Covington, Ky., U.S.	C 6	170
Covington, La., U.S.	G 3	170
Covington, Tn., U.S.	E 4	170
Cowal, Lake ⊜	D 6	144
Cowan	E 5	170
Cowan, Lake ⊜	L 7	140
Cowansville	F 7	160
Cowell	D 1	144
Cowen	D 3	162
Cowes, Austl.	G 5	144
Cowes, Eng., U.K.	G 5	72
Cowessess Indian Reserve ◆[4]	F 7	158
Cowley	G 14	156
Cowlic	B 4	184
Cowlitz ≃	B 2	178
Cowpens	B 4	168
Cowpens National Battlefield ♠	B 4	168
Cowra	D 7	144
Coxim	C 3	194
Coxim ≃	C 3	194
Coxsackie	D 5	164
Cox's Bāzār	E 6	122
Coyah	D 2	200
Coyote Wash ≃	D 4	176
Cozes	C 3	80
Cozumel	G 16	184
Cozumel, Isla I	G 16	184
Cracow see Kraków	C 10	96
Cradle Mountain-Lake Saint Clair National Park ♠	i 11	145a
Cradock	G 6	206
Craig, Ak., U.S.	I 28	154
Craig, Co., U.S.	B 5	176
Craigavon	B 5	75
Craigellachie	F 12	156
Craigmyle	F 15	156
Craik	F 18	156
Crailsheim	C 7	100
Craiova	C 7	104
Cramlington	B 5	72
Cranbrook, Austl.	N 4	140
Cranbrook, B.C., Can.	G 13	156
Crandon	C 4	166
Crane	C 5	170
Cranston	E 7	164
Craon	E 5	78
Craponne-sur-Arzon see Craponne	E 1	82
Crasna	B 9	104
Crater Lake ⊜	D 2	178
Crater Lake National Park ♠	D 2	178
Craters of the Moon National Monument ♠	D 7	178
Crateús	E 10	190
Crato	E 11	190
Crau ◆[1]	G 2	82
Craven	F 19	156
Crawford	F 4	170
Crawfordsville	B 5	170
Crawfordville	D 2	168
Crawley	F 6	72
Creal Springs	D 4	170
Crean Lake ⊜	D 18	156
Cree ≃	B 19	156
Creel	D 6	184
Cree Lake ⊜	C 18	156
Creighton	F 8	206
Creil	C 9	78
Crema	D 5	92
Cremona	D 6	92
Cremona □[6]	D 5	92
Crépy-en-Valois	C 9	78
Cres	C 3	104
Cres, Otok I	C 3	104
Crescent	D 3	178
Crescent City	E 1	178
Crespo	C 7	195
Cresson	C 4	162
Crest	F 3	82
Crestline	F 6	182
Creston	G 13	156
Crestview	G 5	170
Creswell Downs	D 2	142
Crete see Kríti I	E 6	106
Crete, Sea of ⊤[2]	D 6	106
Créteil	D 9	78
Cretin, Cape ›	N 13	124
Creuse □[3]	B 6	80
Creussen	C 8	100
Creutzwald-la-Croix	C 3	100
Crevalcore	E 7	92
Crevillent	F 4	88
Crewe	D 4	72
Criciúma	E 10	192
Crieff	C 6	70
Crimea ›[1]	G 9	110
Crimmitschau	F 9	98
Crisfield	E 6	162
Cristalina	B 7	194
Cristóbal Colón, Pico ∧	A 4	190
Crișul Repede (Sebes Körös) ≃	B 7	104
Criuleni	B 10	104
Crivitz	C 8	98
Crna Gora (Montenegro) □[3]	D 5	104
Črnomelj	E 7	102
Croajingolong National Park ♠	F 7	144
Croatia □[1]	F 10	62
Crockett	E 6	172
Crocodile ≃, S. Afr.	C 7	206
Crocodile ≃, S. Afr.	C 9	206
Croghan	C 3	164
Croker, Cape ›	B 12	140
Cromarty	B 11	158
Cromwell	F 2	146
Crooked ≃	C 3	178
Crooked Creek	F 15	154
Crooked Island I	C 6	186
Crooked Island Passage ⋓	C 6	186
Crookston	B 6	174
Crosby, Eng., U.K.	D 3	72
Crosby, N.D., U.S.	A 3	174
Crosbyton	D 3	172
Cross ≃	D 6	200
Crossett	F 2	170
Cross Fell ∧	C 4	72
Cross Hands	F 2	72
Cross Lake	D 10	158
Cross Lake ⊜[1]	D 9	158
Cross Sound ⋓	G 26	154
Crothersville	C 6	170
Crotone	E 7	94
Crotone □[6]	E 6	94
Crottendorf	B 9	100
Crowborough	F 7	72
Crow Creek ≃	E 2	174
Crow Creek Indian Reservation ◆[4]	C 5	174
Crowdy Bay National Park ♠	C 9	144
Crowell	D 4	172
Crow Indian Reservation ◆[4]	C 10	178
Crow Lake	G 12	158
Crowley	B 13	184
Crown Point, In., U.S.	B 5	170
Crownpoint, N.M., U.S.	E 4	176
Crown Point, N.Y., U.S.	C 5	164
Crown Prince Frederik Island I	B 15	150
Crowsnest Pass	G 14	156
Crowsnest Pass)(	G 14	156
Croydon □[6]	F 6	72
Crozet Basin ◆[1]	I 5	58
Crozon	D 2	78
Cruger	F 3	170
Cruz, Cabo ›	D 5	186
Cruz Alta	A 9	192
Cruz del Eje	B 5	195
Cruzeiro do Oeste	E 4	194
Cruzeiro do Sul	E 4	190
Crysler	A 3	164
Crystal City	C 3	170
Crystal Falls	B 4	166
Crystal Lake	A 4	170
Crystal Springs	G 3	170
Csepel-sziget I	C 10	102
Csesznek ⊥	B 4	104
Csongrád	B 6	104
Csongrád □[3]	B 6	104
Csurgó	D 9	102
Ču □[3]	A 2	122
Ču see Shū ≃	B 11	116
Cuácua ≃	F 6	204
Cuamato	F 1	204
Cuando Cubango □[3]	F 2	204
Cuangar	F 2	204
Cuango	E 2	204
Cuango (Kwango) ≃	C 2	204
Cuanza ≃	D 2	204
Cuanza Norte □[3]	D 2	204
Cuanza Sul □[3]	E 1	204
Cuareim (Quaraí) ≃	B 9	195
Cuarto ≃	C 6	195
Cuatrociénegas	D 8	184
Cuauhtémoc	C 6	184
Cuba, Ks., U.S.	F 6	174
Cuba, N.Y., U.S.	B 4	162
Cuba □[1]	G 11	148
Cubal	E 1	204
Cubango see Okavango ≃	F 3	204
Čubariha	H 28	108
Çubuk	B 5	118
Cucamonga	F 6	182
Cuchi ≃	E 2	204
Cuchivero ≃	G 8	186
Cuckfield	F 6	72
Čučkovo	G 14	108
Cúcuta	G 6	186
Cudahy	D 5	166
Cuddalore	G 3	122
Cuddapah	G 3	122
Čudovo	G 9	108
Cudworth, Sk., Can.	E 19	156
Cudworth, Eng., U.K.	D 5	72
Cuéllar	C 6	86
Cuenca, Ec.	D 3	190
Cuenca, Spain	D 2	88
Cuenca □[6]	E 2	88
Cuencamé de Ceniceros	E 8	184
Cuernavaca	H 10	184
Cuero	F 5	172
Cuers	G 4	82
Cuervo, Laguna del ⊜	C 7	184
Cuesta Pass)(	E 3	182
Cuevas, Las ⊥	A 6	86
Cuevas del Almanzora	G 2	88
Cugir	C 7	104
Cugo ≃	D 2	204
Cuiabá	A 2	194
Cuiabá ≃	G 7	190
Cuilco (Grijalva) ≃	J 13	184
Cuilo (Kwilu) ≃	D 2	204
Cuimba	D 1	204
Cuíto ≃	F 2	204
Cuito Cuanavale	F 2	204
Cuitzeo, Lago de ⊜	H 9	184
Cuiuni ≃	D 6	190
Čuja	D 14	114
Cukai	L 6	132
Čukotskij, mys ›	C 21	114
Čukotskij avtonomnyj okrug □[6]	A 14	154
Čukotskij poluostrov ›[1]	C 21	114
Culbertson	A 2	174
Culcairn	E 6	144
Culemborg	C 4	69
Culgoa	E 4	144
Culgoa ≃	B 6	144
Culiacán	E 6	184
Culion Island I	C 7	134
Cullera	E 4	88
Cullman	E 5	170
Culloden Battlesite ⊥	C 4	74
Cullowhee	B 3	168
Culpeper	D 4	162
Culuene ≃	F 8	190
Culver City	G 5	182
Culverden	E 4	146
Čulym ≃	D 11	114
Cuma ⊥	D 4	94
Cumaná	F 8	186
Cumari	C 6	194
Cumberland, Ia., U.S.	E 7	174
Cumberland, Ky., U.S.	E 2	162
Cumberland, Md., U.S.	D 4	162
Cumberland □[6], Me., U.S.	C 8	164
Cumberland □[6], N.J., U.S.	G 3	164
Cumberland □[6], Pa., U.S.	F 1	164
Cumberland ≃	D 6	170
Cumberland, Lake ⊜[1]	A 2	168
Cumberland Bay ⊂	q 21	193c
Cumberland Falls State Resort Park ♠	E 1	162
Cumberland Gap)(	E 2	162
Cumberland Gap National Historical Park ♠	E 2	162
Cumberland House	E 7	158
Cumberland Island National Seashore ♠	D 4	168
Cumberland Lake ⊜	E 7	158
Cumberland Sound ⋓	C 19	150
Cumbernauld	B 3	72
Cumbres de Monterrey, Parque Nacional ♠	H 3	172
Cumbria □[6]	C 4	72
Cumnock	B 2	72
Çumra	D 5	118
Cumuripa	C 4	184
Čuna ≃	D 12	114
Cunani	C 8	190
Cundeelee Aboriginal Reserve ◆[4]	L 7	140
Cunene □[3]	F 2	204
Cunene see Kunene ≃	F 1	204
Cuneo	E 3	92
Cuneo □[6]	E 3	92
Cunhinga	E 2	204
Čunja ≃	C 12	114
Cunlhat	C 7	80
Cunnamulla	J 7	142
Čuny	G 12	108
Cuorgnè	D 3	92
Cupar	D 5	74
Čur	H 20	108
Curaçao I	E 7	186
Curacautín	F 1	195
Curanilahue	E 1	195
Curaray ≃	D 3	190
Curcani	C 9	104
Curcuriari ≃	D 5	190
Curecanti National Recreation Area ♠	C 5	176
Curepipe	q 21	207e
Curicó	D 2	195
Curitiba	F 6	194
Curitibanos	G 5	194
Curlewis	C 8	144
Curoca ≃	F 1	204
Currais Novos	E 11	190
Currawinya	B 5	144
Curry	E 20	154
Curtea de Argeș	C 8	104
Curtis	E 2	170
Curtis, Port ⊂	G 10	142
Curtis Channel ⋓	G 10	142
Curtis Island I, Austl.	G 10	142
Curtis Island I, N.Z.	G 10	136
Curuá ≃, Braz.	E 8	190
Curuá ≃, Braz.	C 7	190
Cururupu	D 10	190
Curuzú Cuatiá	A 8	195
Curvelo	C 8	194
Curwensville	C 4	162
Cusco	F 4	190
Cusick	A 5	178
Čusovaja ≃	G 22	108
Čusovoj	G 22	108
Cusseta	C 2	168
Čust	A 2	122
Custer, Mt., U.S.	B 10	178
Custer, S.D., U.S.	D 3	174
Custer State Park ♠	D 3	174
Cut, Nuhu I	G 10	134
Cutato ≃	E 2	204
Cut Bank Creek ≃	A 7	178
Cut Knife	E 17	156
Cutler	D 4	182
Cutlerville	D 6	166
Cutral-Có	F 3	195
Cutro	E 6	94
Cuttack	E 5	122
Cutzamalá ≃	H 9	184
Čuvašija □[3]	I 17	108
Cuvette □[3]	C 2	204
Cuvo ≃	E 2	204
Cuxhaven	C 5	98
Cuyahoga Falls	C 3	162
Cuyama ≃	F 3	182
Cuyamaca Peak ∧	G 7	182
Cuyamaca Rancho State Park ♠	H 7	182
Cuyo Islands II	C 8	134
Cuyuni ≃	B 7	190
Cwmbran	F 4	72
Cyangugu	C 4	204
Cybinka	B 8	96
Cyclades II	D 6	106
Cygnet River	E 1	144
Cypress	G 2	170
Cypress Hills ⋀[2]	G 17	156
Cypress Hills Interprovincial Park ♠, Ab., Can.	G 16	156
Cypress Hills Interprovincial Park ♠, Sk., Can.	G 4	158
Cypress Point ›	D 1	182
Cyprus □[1]	F 5	112
Cyprus I	E 5	118
Cyrenaica □[9]	D 9	198
Czarne	B 9	96
Czechowice-Dziedzice	D 10	96
Czech Republic □[1]	F 10	62
Czempiń	B 9	96
Czersk	B 9	96
Częstochowa	C 10	96
Człopa	B 9	96

D

Name	Map Ref.	Page
Da ≃	D 14	130
Da'an	D 15	128
Dabajuro	F 7	186
Dabat	E 4	202
Dabatou	C 2	200
Dabeiba	G 5	186
Dabhoi	E 2	122
Dabie Shan ⋀	C 12	130
Dabilda	C 7	200
Dabola	C 2	200
Daborow	F 6	202
Dabou	D 4	200
Dabra	D 3	122
Dąbrowa Białostocka	B 12	96
Dacca see Dhaka	E 5	122
Dac Glei	G 8	132
Dachau	D 8	100
Dačice	A 7	102
Dade City	E 3	168
Dādhar	D 1	122
Ḍadnah	J 17	118
Dādra and Nagar Haveli □[3]	E 2	122
Dādu	D 1	122
Dadu ≃	D 6	130
Daet	C 8	134
Daf'	D 9	198
Dafang	E 7	130
Dafeng	B 15	130
Dáfni	D 5	106
Dafoe	F 19	156
Dafoe ≃	D 11	158
Daga Post	F 3	202
Dağardı	C 8	106
Dagda	D 13	66
Dagestan □[3]	H 15	110
Dagoretti	H 4	202
Dagu	G 11	128
Daguan	E 7	130
Dagupan	B 8	134
Daguragu Aboriginal Land ◆[4]	E 11	140
Dagwin	E 3	132
Dahalac National Park ♠	D 5	202
Da Hinggan Ling ⋀	C 8	124
Dahl	E 4	98
Dahlak Archipelago II	D 5	202
Dahlak Kebir see Dehalak' Desēt I	D 5	202
Dahme	E 10	98
Dāhod	E 2	122
Dahra	D 8	198
Dahūk	D 10	118
Dahūk □[3]	D 10	118
Daḥy, Nafūd ad- ◆[2]	C 6	202
Daia	C 8	104
Dai Hai ⊜	F 9	128
Daik-u	F 3	132
Dailing	C 17	128
Daimiel	E 7	86
Dainkog	B 4	130
Daintree River National Park ♠	D 7	142
Daireaux	E 6	195
Dairen see Dalian	G 13	128
Dairût	I 4	118
Dai-sen ∧[1]	G 4	126
Daisetsu-zan-kokuritsu-kōen ♠	C 9	126
Daixian	G 9	128
Dajarra	F 4	142
Dajian Shan ∧	E 6	130
Dakar	C 1	200
Daketa ≃	F 5	202
Dakhin Shāhbāzpur Island I	E 6	122
Dakhla (Villa Cisneros)	E 1	198
Dakhlet Nouâdhibou □[3]	E 1	198
Dakoro	C 6	200
Đakovica	D 6	104
Đakovo	E 10	102
Dala	E 2	204
Dalaba	C 2	200
Dalad Qi	F 7	128
Dala-Järna	B 7	66
Dalälven ≃	B 8	66
Dalama	D 8	106
Dalaman	D 8	106
Dalandzadgad	E 5	128
Dalane ◆[1]	C 3	66
Dalarna □[3]	B 7	66
Da Lat	H 9	132
Dālbandin	E 9	116
Dalbeattie	C 3	72
Dalby	I 10	142
Dale, Nor.	B 2	66
Dale, Nor.	B 2	66
Dale Hollow Lake ⊜[1]	D 6	170
Daleszyce	C 11	96
Daleville	B 6	170
Dalga	I 4	118
Dalhart	B 2	172
Dalhousie, N.B., Can.	D 10	160
Dalhousie, India	C 3	122
Dalhousie, Cape ›	A 29	154
Dali	F 5	130
Dalian	G 13	128
Daliang Shan ⋀	D 6	130
Dalías	H 2	88
Dalin	E 14	128
Daling ≃	F 13	128
Dalkeith	B 3	72
Dallas, Ga., U.S.	F 6	170
Dallas, N.C., U.S.	B 4	168
Dallas, Tx., U.S.	D 5	172
Dall Island I	I 28	154
Dalmatia □[9]	D 6	90
Dalmatovo	H 25	108
Dalmine	E 7	82
Dal'negorsk	B 5	126
Dal'nerečensk	A 5	126
Daloa	D 3	200
Dalroy	F 15	156
Dalrymple, Lake ⊜[1]	F 8	142
Dāltenganj	E 4	122
Dalton, S. Afr.	E 9	206
Dalton, Ga., U.S.	E 6	170
Dalton, Pa., U.S.	E 3	164
Dalton-in-Furness	C 3	72
Dalupiri Island I	B 8	134
Dalwallinu	L 4	140
Daly ≃	C 11	140
Daly City	C 1	182
Daly Lake ⊜	C 19	156
Daly River Aboriginal Land ◆[4]	D 10	140
Daly Waters	E 12	140
Dam ≃	B 1	130
Damagum	C 7	200
Damān	E 2	122
Damanhûr	G 4	118
Damar, Pulau I	G 9	134
Damascus see Dimashq, Syria	C 6	120
Damascus, Ar., U.S.	E 2	170
Damascus, Md., U.S.	D 5	162
Damaturu	C 7	200
Damāvand	E 15	118
Damāvand, Qolleh-ye ∧[1]	D 14	118
Damboa	C 7	200
Dâmbovița □[3]	C 8	104
Dâmbovița ≃	C 8	104
Dam Gamad	E 2	202
Dāmghān	D 16	118
Dămienești	B 9	104
Damietta	G 4	118
Dammarie-lès-Lys	D 9	78
Damme	D 5	98
Damoh	E 3	122
Damongo	D 4	200
Damous	H 6	88
Dampier	G 4	140
Dampier, Selat ⋓	F 10	134
Dan ≃	B 9	130
Danai	N 6	132
Danakil ◆[1]	E 5	202
Danané	D 3	200
Da Nang	F 9	132
Dana Point	G 6	182
Danba	C 5	130
Danbury, Ct., U.S.	E 5	164
Danbury, N.C., U.S.	A 4	168
Danby Lake ⊜	E 1	176
Dandenong	G 5	144
Dandong	F 14	128
Dänew	C 9	116
Danfeng	B 10	130
Dang ≃	A 6	122
Dangchang	A 7	130
Danggali Conservation Park ♠	D 3	144
Dangila	E 4	202
Dângrêk, Chuŏr Phnum ⋀	G 6	132
Dangriga	I 15	184
Dangshan	A 13	130
Dangtu	C 14	130
Dangyang	C 10	130
Daniel-Johnson, Barrage ◆[6]	C 9	160
Daniëlskuil	E 5	206
Daniels Pass)(	B 3	176
Danielsville	B 3	168
Danilov	G 14	108
Dänizkänarı	I 16	110
Danja	C 6	200
Danjiangkou Shuiku ⊜[1]	B 10	130
Dankov	J 13	108
Danleng	C 6	130
Danlí	E 3	186
Dannemora	B 8	66
Dannenberg	C 7	98
Dannevirke	D 6	146
Dannhauser	E 9	206
Danshui	G 12	130
Dante	E 2	162
Danube (Donau) (Dunav) ≃	G 12	62
Danvers	D 8	164
Danville, Ca., U.S.	C 2	182
Danville, Ga., U.S.	C 3	168
Danville, Il., U.S.	B 5	170
Danville, Ky., U.S.	D 6	170
Danville, Pa., U.S.	F 2	164
Danville, Va., U.S.	E 4	162
Danville, Wa., U.S.	G 12	156
Danxian	I 9	130
Danyang	C 14	130
Danzig see Gdańsk	A 10	96
Daodi	G 12	128
Daosa	D 3	122
Daoukro	D 4	200
Daoura, Oued ≃	D 4	198
Daoxian	F 10	130
Daozhen	D 8	130
Dapaong	C 4	200
Da Peneda-Geres, Parque Nacional ♠	C 3	86
Daphne	G 4	170
Da Qaidam	B 7	122
Dar'ā	D 6	120
Dar'ā □[3]	D 6	120
Dārāb	H 16	118
Darabani	A 9	104
Daragodle	E 5	202
Dārān	F 14	118
Darâw	C 3	202
Dārayyā	C 6	120
Darbėnai	D 10	66
Darbhanga	D 5	122
Darby	B 6	178
D'Arcy	F 10	156
Dardanelle	B 4	182
Dardanelles ⋓	B 7	106
Darende	C 7	118
Dar es Salaam	D 6	204
Darfo	D 6	92
Dārfūr □[3]	E 1	202
Dargai	C 2	122
Darganata	B 9	116
Dargaville	A 4	146
Darhan	B 5	128
Darıca	B 8	106
Darien, Ct., U.S.	E 5	164
Darien, Ga., U.S.	D 4	168
Darien, Parque Nacional ♠	G 5	186
Darién, Serranía del ⋀	F 5	186
Dar'inskoe	D 17	110
Darjeeling see Dārjiling	D 5	122
Dārjiling	D 5	122
Darke Peak	L 3	142
Darling ≃	D 4	144
Darling Downs ◆[1]	I 9	142
Darlingford	A 5	174
Darling Range ⋀	M 4	140
Darlington, Austl.	F 4	144
Darlington, Eng., U.K.	C 5	72
Darlington □[8]	C 5	72
Darlington Dam ⊜[1]	G 6	206
Darlot, Lake ⊜	J 6	140
Darłowo	A 9	96
Darmstadt	C 5	100
Darmstadt □[6]	C 5	100
Darnah	C 9	198
Darnétal	C 8	78
Darney	B 4	82
Darnley, Cape ›	C 15	208
Darnley Bay ⊂	C 8	150
Daroca	C 3	88
Darou Mousti	B 1	200
Darra	A 9	144
Darreh Gaz	D 18	118
Darsser Ort ›	B 9	98
Dartford	F 7	72
Dartmoor	F 3	144
Dartmoor ◆[3]	G 3	72
Dartmoor National Park ♠	G 3	72
Dartmouth, N.S., Can.	F 12	160
Dartmouth, Eng., U.K.	G 3	72
Dartmouth Reservoir ⊜[1]	F 6	144
Daru	N 12	124
Darwāzahgêy	C 1	122
Darwen	D 4	72
Darwin, Austl.	C 11	140
Darwin, Falk. Is.	n 18	193b
Darwin, Isla I	i 13	190a
Darwin River	C 11	140
Dār Zubi	E 1	202
Dashhowuz	G 19	62
Dashhowuz □[3]	B 18	118
Dashitou	E 17	128
Dasht ≃	E 9	116
Dassiefontein	F 6	206
Date	C 8	126
Datia	D 3	122
Datian	F 13	130
Datong, China	H 3	128
Datong, China	F 9	128
Datong, China	C 15	128
Datong ≃	H 4	128
Datteln	E 4	98
Datu, Tanjung ›	M 9	132
Datu Piang	D 8	134
Daugai	E 12	66
Daugavpils	E 13	66
Daun	B 3	100
Daund	F 2	122
Daung Kyun I	H 3	132
Dauphin	F 8	158
Dauphin □[6]	F 2	164
Dauphiné □[9]	F 3	82
Dauphin Island I	G 4	170
Dauphin Lake ⊜	F 9	158
Dautphetal	F 5	98
Däväçi	I 16	110
Dāvangere	G 3	122
Davao	D 9	134
Davao Gulf ⊂	D 9	134
Davegoriale	F 5	202
Davenport, Ia., U.S.	B 3	170
Davenport, Ok., U.S.	C 5	172
Daventry	E 5	72
Davey, Port ⊂	j 11	145a
David	F 4	186
Davidson, Sk., Can.	F 18	156
Davidson, N.C., U.S.	B 4	168
Davin Lake ⊜	C 20	156
Davis, Ca., U.S.	B 2	182
Davis, Ok., U.S.	C 5	172
Davis ◗[3]	C 16	208
Davis, Mount ∧	D 4	162
Davisboro	C 3	168
Davis Dam ◆[6]	E 1	176
Davis Sea ⊤[2]	C 17	208
Davis Strait ⋓	C 21	150
Davlekanovo	I 21	108
Davos	C 5	92
Davutlar	D 7	106
Dawa ≃	G 5	202
Dawaki	C 6	200
Dawei (Tavoy)	G 3	132
Dawlish	G 3	72
Dawna Range ⋀	F 4	132
Dawrah	E 1	202
Dawson, Yk., Can.	D 25	154
Dawson, Ne., U.S.	B 1	170
Dawson ≃	G 9	142
Dawson, Isla I	J 5	192
Dawson Creek	D 11	156
Dawson Range ⋀	E 25	154
Dawsonville	B 2	168
Dax	E 2	80
Daxian	C 8	130
Daxing	G 11	128
Daxue Shan ⋀	C 5	130
Dayao	F 5	130
Daye	C 12	130
Daylesford	F 5	144
Daym Zubayr	F 2	202
Dayong	D 10	130
Dayr az-Zawr	E 9	118
Dayton, Ia., U.S.	D 7	174
Dayton, Oh., U.S.	D 1	162
Dayton, Tx., U.S.	G 1	170
Dayton, Wa., U.S.	B 5	178
Daytona Beach	E 4	168
Dayu	F 12	130
Dayu Ling ⋀	F 12	130
Da Yunhe see Grand Canal ≆	F 7	124
Dazhu	C 8	130
Dazu	D 7	130
Dcheïra	C 2	198
De Aar	F 6	206
Deadman's Cay	C 6	186
Dead Sea ⊜	G 4	120
Deadwood, Ab., Can.	C 13	156
Deadwood, S.D., U.S.	C 3	174
Deal	F 8	72
Deale	D 5	162
De'an	D 12	130
Dean ≃	E 9	156
Deán Funes	B 5	195
Dearborn	B 2	162
Dease ≃	B 7	156
Dease Arm ⊂	C 34	154
Dease Lake	B 7	156
Dease Lake ⊜	B 6	156
Dease Strait ⋓	C 11	150
Death Valley V	D 7	182
Deatsville	F 5	170
Deauville	C 6	78
Deba	C 7	200
Debal'tseve	E 11	110
Debar	E 6	104
De Bary	E 4	168
Debe	q 23	187e
De Berry	F 1	170
Dębica	C 11	96
De Bilt	B 4	69
Dęblin	C 11	96
Deborah West, Lake ⊜	L 5	140
Debra Sīna	F 4	202
Debre Birhan	F 4	202
Debrecen	B 6	104
Debre Mark'os	E 4	202
Debre Tabor	E 4	202
Debre Zeyit	F 4	202
Debrzno	B 9	96
Decatur, Al., U.S.	E 5	170
Decatur, Ga., U.S.	C 2	168
Decatur, Il., U.S.	C 4	170
Decatur, In., U.S.	C 1	162
Decatur, Tx., U.S.	D 5	172
Decazeville	D 6	80
Deccan ⋀[1]	F 3	122
Decelles, Réservoir ⊜[1]	E 5	160
Deception Lake ⊜	C 19	156
Děčín	B 11	100
Decize	F 10	78
Decorah	D 3	166
Decs	D 10	102
Deder	F 5	202
Dedham	D 7	164
De Doorns	G 3	206
Dédougou	C 4	200
Dedu	B 16	128
Dedza	E 5	204
Dee ≃, Scot., U.K.	C 6	74
Dee ≃	E 3	72
De Efteling ♠	C 4	69
Deelfontein	F 5	206
Deep River, On., Can.	E 5	160
Deep River, Ct., U.S.	E 6	164
Deepwater	C 2	170
Deer Creek Indian Reservation ◆[4]	B 2	166
Deerfield Beach	F 4	168
Deer Lake	D 15	160
Deer Lake ⊜	E 11	158
Deer Lodge	B 7	178
Deero Eri	F 6	202
Deer Park	A 5	178
Deerpass Bay ⊂	D 33	154
Deer Trail	F 2	174
Defiance	B 6	170
De Funiak Springs	G 5	170
Dêgê	C 4	130
Degeberga	E 7	66
Degerby	B 10	66
Degerfors	C 7	66
Deggendorf	D 9	100
De Graafschap ◆[1]	B 5	69
De Grey ≃	G 5	140
Dëgtevo	E 12	110
Dehalak' Desēt I	D 5	202
Deh Bīd	G 15	118
Dehiwala-Mount Lavinia	H 3	122
Deh Kord	F 13	118
Dehra Dūn	C 3	122
Dehri	D 4	122
Dehua	F 14	130
Dehui	D 15	128
Deinze	C 2	69
Dej	B 7	104
De Kalb, Il., U.S.	B 4	170
De Kalb, Tx., U.S.	F 1	170
Dekemhare	D 4	202
Dekese	C 3	204
Dékoa	D 8	200
De Land	E 4	168
Delano, Ca., U.S.	E 4	182
Delano, Mn., U.S.	C 8	174
Delaronde Lake ⊜	D 18	156
Delaware, Oh., U.S.	C 2	162
Delaware, Ok., U.S.	D 1	170
Delaware □[3]	D 12	152
Delaware □[6], N.Y., U.S.	D 4	164
Delaware □[6], Pa., U.S.	G 3	164
Delaware ≃	G 3	164
Delaware, East Branch ≃	D 4	164
Delaware Bay ⊂	G 3	164
Delaware Seashore State Park ♠	H 3	164
Delbrück	E 5	98
Delcambre	H 3	170
Del City	C 5	172
Délembé	D 9	200
Delémont	C 5	82
Delfoí (Delphi) ⊥	C 5	106
Delft	B 3	69
Delfzijl	A 5	69
Delgado, Cabo ›	E 7	204
Delger ≃	B 3	128
Delgerhaan	A 6	128
Delhi, India	D 3	122
Delhi, La., U.S.	F 3	170
Delhi, N.Y., U.S.	D 4	164
Delhi □[3]	D 3	122
Delicias	C 7	184
Delījān	E 14	118
Delingha	B 7	122
Delitzsch	E 9	98
Delle	C 5	82
Delmar	H 3	164
Delmarva Peninsula ›[1]	D 6	162
Delmas	E 17	156
Delmenhorst	C 5	98
Delnice	E 6	102
Del Norte	D 5	176
Del Norte Coast Redwood State Park ♠	B 2	180
Deloraine	G 8	158
Delos see Dílos ⊥	D 6	106
Delphi see Délfoi ⊥	C 5	106
Delray Beach	F 4	168
Del Rio	F 3	172
Delta, Mo., U.S.	D 4	170
Delta, Ut., U.S.	C 2	176
Delta □[9]	F 3	170
Delta ≃	E 21	154
Delta Amacuro □[3]	F 9	186
Delta du Saloum, Parc National du ♠	C 1	200
Delta Junction	D 22	154
Delta Peak ∧	C 7	156
Delyatyn	A 8	104
Dëma ≃	B 20	110
Demarcation Point ›	B 24	154
Demavend, Mount see Damāvand, Qolleh-ye ∧[1]	D 14	118
Demba	D 3	204
Dembia	B 4	204
Dembī Dolo	F 3	202
Demidov	I 9	108
Deming, N.M., U.S.	F 5	176
Deming, Wa., U.S.	G 10	156
Demini ≃	C 6	190
Demirci	C 8	106
Demirtaş	B 8	106
Demjanka ≃	D 10	114
Demjansk	H 10	108
Demjanskoe	G 28	108
Demmin	C 10	98
Demmitt	D 12	156
Democratic Republic of the Congo see Congo, Democratic Republic of the □[1]	I 10	196
Demone, Val ◆[1]	G 4	94
Demopolis	F 5	170
Dempo, Gunung ∧	F 4	134
Demta	F 12	134
Denain	B 10	78
Denakil see Danakil ◆[1]	E 5	202
Denali National Park	E 20	154
Denali National Park ♠	E 19	154
Denare Beach	D 7	158
Denau	B 1	122
Denbigh	D 3	72
Denbighshire □[6]	D 3	72
Den Chai	E 5	132
Dendermonde	C 3	69

Symbols in the index entries represent the broad categories identified in the key at the right. Symbols with superior numbers (⋀[1]) identify subcategories (see complete key on page 242).

∧ Mountain ⋀ Mountains)(Pass V Valley ≍ Plain › Cape I Island II Islands ⊥ Other Topographic Feature ≃ River ≆ Canal

Dengkou — Dysselsdorp

Name | Map Ref. | Page

Dengkou F 6 128
Dêngqên C 2 130
Dengxian B 11 130
Denham, Mount ∧ h 12 186a
Denham Range ⋏ F 8 142
Den Helder B 3 69
Dénia F 5 88
Dénié C 3 200
Deniliquin E 5 144
Denis Island I J 7 112
Denison D 5 172
Denisovka C 21 108
Denizli D 8 106
Denizli □[3] D 8 106
Denmark, Austl. N 4 140
Denmark, S.C., U.S. C 4 168
Denmark □[1] D 9 62
Denmark Strait ⋃ C 17 148
Dennery t 27 187h
Dennilton C 8 206
Dennison E 8 166
Denpasar I 22 135b
Denton, Md., U.S. H 3 164
Denton, Tx., U.S. D 5 172
D'Entrecasteaux Islands II N 14 124
D'Entrecasteaux National Park ♦ N 3 140
Denver, Co., U.S. C 6 176
Denver, Pa., U.S. F 2 164
Denzlingen D 4 100
Deori E 3 122
Deoria D 4 122
De Panne C 1 69
De Pere C 4 166
Depew D 9 166
Deport F 1 170
Depue B 4 170
Dêqên D 4 130
Deqing G 10 130
De Queen E 1 170
Dera, Lach ≃ G 5 202
Dera Ghāzi Khān C 1 122
Dera Ismāīl Khān C 2 122
Derazhnya E 5 110
Derbent H 16 110
Derby, Austl. E 7 140
Derby, Eng., U.K. E 5 72
Derby, Ks., U.S. B 5 172
Derby, N.Y., U.S. B 4 162
Derby Line A 6 164
Derbyshire □[6] D 5 72
Derecske B 6 104
Dergači D 16 110
Dergaon A 1 132
Derhachi D 9 110
De Ridder G 2 170
Derik D 9 118
Derjalyk H 21 110
Derre F 6 204
Derry
see Londonderry, N. Ire., U.K. B 4 75
Derry, N.H., U.S. D 7 164
Derudeb D 4 202
Derventa C 4 104
Derwent E 16 156
Derwent ≃ j 12 145a
Derwent Water ⊜ C 3 72
Derweze I 21 110
Derzhavinsk E 21 62
Desaguadero ≃, Arg. F 6 192
Desaguadero ≃, S.A. G 5 190
Des Allemands H 3 170
Descanso F 5 180
Deschambault Lake ⊜ D 19 156
Deschutes ≃ C 3 178
Desē E 4 202
Deseado ≃ I 6 192
Deseado, Cabo > J 5 192
Desengaño, Punta > I 6 192
Desenzano del Garda D 6 92
Deseronto B 1 164
Désert ≃ B 10 166
Desert Hot Springs G 7 182
Desert Lake ⊜ D 1 176
Deshler E 6 174
Deshnok D 2 122
Desio D 5 92
Desirade, La I n 21 187e
Deskáti C 4 106
Desloge D 3 170
Des Moines B 2 170
Des Moines ≃ C 9 152
Desna ≃ D 7 110
Desolación, Isla I J 5 192
De Soto National Memorial ♦ F 3 168
De Soto State Park ♦ E 6 170
Des Plaines A 5 170
Des Plaines ≃ D 5 166
Despotovac C 6 104
Dessau E 9 98
Dessau □[6] E 9 98
Dessel C 4 69
Destelbergen C 2 69
Desvres B 8 78
Detmold E 5 98
Detmold □[6] E 5 98
De Tour Village B 7 166
Detroit, Mi., U.S. B 2 162
Detroit, Tx., U.S. F 1 170
Detroit ≃ B 2 162
Det Udom G 7 132
Detva D 10 96
Deua National Park ♦ E 7 144
Deurne C 4 69
Deutsche Bucht c B 4 98
Deutschlandsberg D 7 102
Deux Balé, Forêt des ✦[4] C 4 200
Deux-Montagnes □[6] A 5 164
Deux-Sèvres □[3] B 3 80
Deva C 7 104
Dévaványa E 11 96
Devecser C 9 102
Develi C 6 118
Deventer B 5 69
Devils ≃ F 3 172
Devil's Den State Park ♦ E 1 170
Devils Lake Sioux Indian Reservation ✦[4] B 5 174
Devils Lake State Park ♦ D 4 166
Devils Marbles ♦ F 2 142
Devils Postpile National Monument ♦ C 4 182
Devils Tower National Monument ♦ C 2 174
Devizes F 4 72
Devjatiny F 12 108
Devoll ≃ B 4 106
Devon E 15 156
Devon □[6] G 3 72
Devon Island I A 15 150
Devonport, Austl. i 12 145a
Devonport, Eng., U.K. G 2 72
Devrek B 9 106
Dewās E 3 122
Dewetsdorp E 7 206
Deweyville G 2 170
De Witt, Ar., U.S. E 3 170
De Witt, Mi., U.S. B 1 162
De Witt, N.Y., U.S. C 2 164
Dewsbury D 5 72
Dexing D 13 130
Dexter, Me., U.S. A 9 162
Dexter, N.M., U.S. D 1 172
Deyang C 7 130
Dey-Dey, Lake ⊜ K 11 140
Deyhūk F 17 118
Deyyer I 14 118
Dez ≃ F 13 118
Dezfūl F 13 118
Dezhou H 11 128
Dežneva, mys > C 22 114
Dgâmcha, Sebkhet Te-n- ⊜ F 1 198
Dhaka E 5 122
Dhaka □[3] E 6 122
Dhamār E 5 202
Dhamtari E 4 122
Dharān D 5 122
Dharmapuri G 3 122
Dharmavaram G 3 122
Dharmjaygarh E 4 122
Dharmshāla C 3 122
Dhaulpur D 3 122
Dhawalāgiri ∧ D 4 122
Dhenkānāl E 5 122
Dhërmi ◗[1] B 3 106
Dhī Qār □[3] G 12 118
Dhone F 3 122
Dhoomadheere G 5 202
Dhorāji E 2 122
Dhrāngadhra E 2 122
Dhud ≃ E 7 202
Dhule E 2 122
Dhurbo E 7 202
Dhuusamarreeb F 6 202
Diablo, Mount ∧ C 2 182
Diablo, Pico del ∧ B 2 184
Diablo Range ⋏ C 2 182
Diablotins, Morne ∧[1] r 25 187g
Diabo D 3 200
Diafarabé C 3 200
Diaka ≃ B 4 200
Diamante C 7 195
Diamante ≃ D 4 195
Diamantina C 9 194
Diamantina ≃ I 4 142
Diamantino F 7 190
Diamond G 7 174
Diamond Harbour E 5 122
Dianbai H 10 130
Dian Chi ⊜ F 6 130
Dianjiang C 8 130
Dianópolis F 9 190
Diaoyu Islands (Senkaku-shotō) II F 16 130
Diawala C 3 200
Diaz E 3 170
Dibāng ≃ D 7 122
Dibete B 7 206
Dibo F 5 202
Dibrugarh D 6 122
Dibs E 1 202
Dickinson, N.D., U.S. B 3 174
Dickinson, Tx., U.S. H 1 170
Didao D 18 128
Didcot F 5 72
Dīdēsa ≃ F 4 202
Didimbo F 3 204
Didymóteicho B 7 106
Die F 3 82
Diébougou C 4 200
Dieburg C 5 100
Diefenbaker, Lake ⊜[1] F 18 156
Diego de Almagro, Isla I J 4 192
Diego Garcia I J 9 112
Diego Ramírez, Islas II K 6 192
Diégo-Suarez
see Antsirañana j 9 205a
Diemans Put E 4 206
Dien Bien D 6 132
Dien Bien Phu
see Dien Bien D 6 132
Diepenbeek B 2 100
Diepholz D 5 98
Dieppe, N.B., Can. E 11 160
Dieppe, Fr. C 8 78
Dieren B 5 69
Dierks E 1 170
Di'er Songhua ≃ E 16 128
Diessen E 8 100
Diest C 4 69
Dietikon C 6 82
Dietrich D 6 178
Dieuze B 4 82
Diez B 4 100
Diffa C 7 200
Diffa □[3] B 7 200
Differdange E 4 69
Digboi D 7 122
Digby F 11 160
Dighton A 3 172
Digne-les-Bains C 1 90
Digoin D 1 82
Digui D 9 200
Digul ≃ G 11 134
Diinsor G 5 202
Dijon E 12 78
Dik D 8 200
Dikala G 3 202
Dikebu C 7 206
Dikili C 7 106
Dikli D 12 66
Diksmuide A 9 78
Dikson B 11 114
Dikwa C 7 200
Dīla F 4 202
Dilbeek B 11 78
Dilek Yarımdası Milli Parkı ♦ D 7 106
Dili G 9 134
Diligent Strait ⋃ H 1 132
Dillenburg F 5 98
Dilley F 4 172
Dilling E 2 202
Dillingen C 3 100
Dillingen an der Donau D 7 100
Dillingham G 15 154
Dillon B 5 168
Dillwyn E 4 162
Dilolo E 3 204
Dilsen C 4 69
Dimāpur D 6 122
Dimashq (Damascus) C 6 120
Dimashq □[3] B 7 120
Dimbelenge D 3 204
Dimbokro D 3 200
Dimitrovgrad, Blg. D 8 104
Dimitrovgrad, Russia I 18 108
Dimlang
see Vogel Peak ∧ D 7 200
Dimona G 4 120
Dinagat Island I C 9 134
Dinājpur D 5 122
Dinan D 4 78
Dinant D 3 69
Dinar C 9 106
Dinara ∧ C 4 104
Dinard D 4 78
Dinaric Alps ⋏ D 6 90
Dindar, Nahr ad- (Dinder) ≃ E 3 202
Dinde E 1 204
Dinder (Dindar, Nahr ad-) ≃ E 4 202
Dinder National Park ♦ E 4 202
Dindigul G 3 122
Dindiza B 10 206
Dindori E 4 122
Dingalan Bay c B 8 134
Ding'an I 10 130
Dingbian H 6 128
Dingelstädt E 7 98
Dinggyê D 5 122
Dingnai C 15 130
Dinge D 1 75
Dinge Bay c D 1 75
Dingnan F 12 130
Dingolfing D 9 100
Dingshuzhen C 14 130
Dingtao I 10 128
Dinguira-Logo C 2 200
Dinguiraye C 2 200
Dingwall C 4 74
Dingxi I 5 128
Dingxian G 10 128
Dingxiang G 9 128
Dingyuan B 13 130
Dinh Lap D 8 132
Dinkelsbühl C 7 100
Dinklage D 5 98
Dinokana C 6 206
Dinosaur B 4 176
Dinosaur National Monument ♦ B 4 176
Dinosaur Provincial Park ♦ F 16 156
Dinslaken E 3 98
Dinuba D 4 182
Dinwiddie E 5 162
Diobo B 3 204
Diois ✦[1] F 3 82
Diomede D 10 154
Diouloulou C 1 200
Dioura C 3 200
Diourbel C 1 200
Dipolog D 8 134
Dippoldiswalde F 10 98
Dīr B 2 122
Diré B 4 200
Dirē Dawa F 5 202
Dirk Hartog I I 2 140
Dirranbandi B 7 144
Dīsa E 2 122
Disappointment, Cape >, S. Geor. q 21 193c
Disappointment, Cape >, Wa., U.S. B 1 178
Disappointment, Lake ⊜ H 6 140
Disaster Bay c F 8 144
Discovery Bay I 18 131a
Discovery Bay c I 19 131a
Discovery Bay c G 3 142
Disentis / Mustér D 6 82
Dishman B 5 178
Dishna I 5 118
Disko I C 22 150
Disneyland ♦ G 6 182
Dispur D 6 122
Disraëli F 8 160
Diss E 8 72
Distrito Federal □[3] G 9 190
Dithmarschen ✦[1] B 6 98
Ditzingen D 5 100
Diu E 2 122
Dīvāndarreh E 12 118
Divenskaja C 15 66
Divingue E 2 204
Divinópolis D 8 194
Divo D 3 200
Divriği C 8 118
Dixfield B 8 164
Dixon, Ca., U.S. B 2 182
Dixon, Il., U.S. B 4 170
Dixon, Ky., U.S. D 5 170
Dixon Entrance ⋃ D 5 156
Dixonville C 12 156
Diyālā □[3] F 11 118
Diyālā (Sīrvān) ≃ F 11 118
Diyarbakır D 8 118
Diyarbakır □[3] C 9 118
Dja ≃ E 8 200
Djado, Plateau du ⋏[1] A 7 200
Djamâa C 6 198
Djambala C 1 204
Djanet E 6 198
Djaret, Oued ≃ D 5 198
Djat'kovo J 11 108
Djébrène C 8 200
Djedi, Oued ≃ C 6 198
Djéké Djéké D 8 200
Djember C 8 200
Djenné C 4 200
Djérem ≃ D 7 200
Djibo C 4 200
Djibouti E 5 202
Djibouti □[1] G 12 196
Djoku-Punda D 3 204
Djoua ≃ B 1 204
Djougou D 5 200
Djouna C 8 200
Djugu B 5 204
Djurås B 7 66
Djursholm C 9 66
Djurtjuli I 21 108
D'kar A 4 206
Dmitrija Lapteva, proliv ⋃ B 17 114
Dmitrov A 10 110
Dneprovskoe I 10 108
Dnieper ≃ F 8 110
Dniester (Dnister) (Nistru) ≃ F 7 110
Dniprodzerzhyns'k E 8 110
Dniprodzerzhyns'ke vodoskhovyshche ⊜[1] E 9 110
Dnipropetrovs'k E 9 110
Dnipropetrovs'k □[6] E 9 110
Dno H 9 108
Doany j 9 205a
Doba D 8 200
Dobele D 11 66
Döbeln E 10 98
Doberai, Jazirah >[1] F 10 134
Doberlug-Kirchhain E 10 98
Dobiegniew B 8 96
Doboj C 5 104
Dobra B 8 96
Dobrič (Dobrich) D 9 104
Dobrich
see Dobrič D 9 104
Dobříš C 11 100
Dobrjanka G 21 108
Dobropillya E 10 110
Dobroteasa C 8 104
Dobruja □[9] C 10 104
Dobruš J 9 108
Dobruška C 9 96
Dobryanka A 11 104
Dobrzyń nad Wisłą B 10 96
Doce ≃ G 10 190
Döch ≃ B 10 128
Docker River I 10 140
Dod Ballāpur G 3 122
Doddridge F 2 170
Dodecanese II D 7 106
Dodéo D 7 200
Dodge City G 4 174
Dodola F 4 202
Dodoma D 6 204
Dodoma □[3] D 6 204
Dodsland F 17 156
Dodson A 9 178
Doesburg B 5 69
Doetinchem C 5 69
Dogai Coring ⊜ C 5 122
Doğanbey C 7 106
Dog Creek F 10 156
Dōgo I F 4 126
Do Gonbadān G 14 118
Dogondoutchi C 5 200
Doğubayazıt C 11 118
Doguéraoua C 6 200
Doha
see Ad-Dawḥah J 14 118
Doiran, Lake ⊜ E 7 104
Doi Suthep-Pui National Park ♦ E 4 132
Dokka B 5 66
Dokkum A 5 69
Dokuchayevs'k F 10 110
Dolbeau D 7 160
Dol-de-Bretagne D 5 78
Dole C 3 82
Dolgellau E 3 72
Dolgorukovo C 10 110
Dolgoščele C 15 108
Dolinsk C 12 124
Dolisie
see Loubomo C 1 204
Dolj □[3] C 7 104
Dolni Lom D 7 104
Dolnośląskie □[3] C 8 96
Dolo D 8 92
Dolomites ⋏ C 7 92
Doloon D 5 128
Dolores, Arg. E 9 195
Dolores, Guat. I 15 184
Dolores, Spain F 4 88
Dolores, Ur. C 8 195
Dolores ≃ C 4 176
Dolphin, Cape > n 18 193b
Dolphin and Union Strait ⋃ C 9 150
Dolyna A 8 104
Dolžicy C 14 66
Domasi F 6 204
Dombås A 4 66
Dombasle-sur-Meurthe D 3 100
Dombe Grande E 1 204
Dombes ✦[1] D 3 82
Dombóvár D 10 102
Dome Creek E 11 156
Dome Fuji ◗[3] D 13 208
Domeyko A 2 195
Domeyko, Cordillera ⋏ D 6 192
Domfront D 6 78
Dominica □[1] H 13 148
Dominica Channel
see Martinique Passage ⋃ E 9 186
Dominican Republic □[1] H 12 148
Dominica Passage
see Guadeloupe Channel ⋃ o 21 187e
Dominion, Cape > C 18 150
Domiongo C 3 204
Domnești C 8 104
Domodedovo I 12 108
Domodossola C 4 92
Domoni o 19 207d
Dom Pedrito B 10 195
Domuyo, Volcán ∧[1] G 5 192
Don ≃ D 12 110
Donada, Costa ⊥[2] C 6 88
Donaghadee B 6 75
Donalda E 15 156
Donalsonville D 2 168
Doñana, Parque Nacional de ♦ G 4 86
Donard, Slieve ∧ B 6 75
Donau
see Danube ≃ G 12 62
Donaueschingen E 5 100
Donauwörth D 7 100
Don Benito F 5 86
Doncaster D 5 72
Doncaster □[6] D 5 72
Dondo F 5 204
Dondra Head > H 4 122
Dondușeni A 9 104
Doneck E 12 110
Donegal B 3 75
Donegal □[3] B 4 75
Donegal Bay c B 3 75
Donetsk
see Doneck, Russia E 12 110
Donets'k, Ukr. E 10 110
Donets'k □[6] F 10 110
Dong ≃, China F 3 128
Dong ≃, China G 12 130
Donga ≃ D 7 200
Dong'an E 10 130
Dongara K 3 140
Dongchuan E 6 130
Dongen E 1 98
Dongfang I 9 130
Dongfeng E 15 128
Donggala F 7 134
Dongguan G 11 130
Dongguang H 11 128
Dong Ha F 8 132
Dong Hoi F 8 132
Dongjingcheng D 17 128
Dong Nai ≃ I 8 132
Dongo E 2 204
Dongping I 11 128
Dongsheng G 8 128
Dongtai B 15 130
Dongting Hu ⊜ D 11 130
Dongue F 1 204
Dongwe ≃ E 3 204
Dongxi D 8 130
Dongxiang D 13 130
Dongxing C 16 128
Dongzhi C 13 130
Doniphan D 3 170
Donjek ≃ E 25 154
Donji Vakuf C 4 104
Don Martín G 3 172
Donnacona E 7 160
Donnelly E 22 154
Donner Memorial State Park ♦ A 3 182
Donner Pass)(A 3 182
Donner und Blitzen ≃ D 4 178
Donnybrook, Austl. M 3 140
Donnybrook, S. Afr. E 8 206
Donostia
see Donostia-San Sebastián A 2 88
Donostia-San Sebastián A 2 88
Donskoj C 11 110
Doolow G 5 202
Doomadgee Aboriginal Land ♦ D 4 142
Doomadgee Aboriginal Land ✦[4] D 4 142
Doonerak, Mount ∧ B 19 154
Door Peninsula >[1] C 5 166
Dora, Lake ⊜ H 7 140
Dora Baltea ≃ D 3 92
Dorcheat, Bayou ≃ F 2 170
Dorchester, Eng., U.K. G 4 72
Dorchester, Wi., U.S. C 3 166
Dorchester □[6] H 2 164
Dordabis B 2 206
Dordogne □[3] D 4 80
Dordogne ≃ C 3 80
Dordrecht C 3 69
Doré Lake D 18 156
Dore Lake ⊜ D 18 156
Dorfen D 9 100
Dorgali E 2 90
Doring ≃ F 3 206
Dorking F 6 72
Dormagen E 3 98
Dormans C 10 78
Dornbirn C 1 102
Dornoch C 4 74
Dornod □[3] C 10 128
Dornogovĭ □[3] D 7 128
Dorog C 10 102
Dorogobuž I 10 108
Dorohoi A 9 104
Doromo B 4 204
Dorrance F 5 174
Dorre Island I I 2 140
Dorsale ⋏ G 3 90
Dorset □[6] G 4 72
Dorsten E 3 98
Dortmund E 4 98
Dorton E 2 162
Dörtyol D 6 118
Do Rūd F 13 118
Dos, Canal Numero ≋ E 9 195
Dos Bahías, Cabo > I 6 192
Dos Hermanas G 5 86
Do Son D 8 132
Dos Palos C 3 182
Dosso C 5 200
Dosso □[3] C 5 200
Dossor F 18 110
Dothan G 6 170
Doting Cove D 17 160
Dotnuva E 11 66
Douai B 9 78
Douala E 6 200
Douarnenez D 2 78
Double Springs E 5 170
Doubs □[3] C 4 82
Doubs ≃ D 3 82
Doubs, Saut du ʟ C 4 82
Doubtful Sound ⋃ F 1 146
Doubtless Bay c A 4 146
Douchy-les-Mines B 10 78
Douentza C 4 200
Dougga ⊥ B 6 198
Douglas, Mb., Can. G 9 158
Douglas, I. of Man C 2 72
Douglas, S. Afr. E 5 206
Douglas, Az., U.S. G 4 176
Douglas, Ga., U.S. D 3 168
Douglas □[6] A 4 182
Douglas, Cape > G 18 154
Douglas, Mount ∧[1] G 17 154
Douglas Channel ⋃ E 7 156
Douglas Lake ⊜[1] B 3 168
Douglass G 6 174
Doulaincourt D 12 78
Doullens B 9 78
Doumanaba C 3 200
Doumdégué D 8 200
Douna C 4 200
Dounguila F 7 200
Dour D 2 69
Dourada, Costa ⊥[2] G 2 86
Dourada, Serra ⋏[1] F 9 190
Dourados E 3 194
Dourkoulé C 9 200
Douro (Duero) ≃ B 2 84
Douz C 6 198
Dove Creek D 4 176
Dover, Austl. j 12 145a
Dover, Eng., U.K. F 8 72
Dover, De., U.S. G 3 164
Dover, Id., U.S. A 5 178
Dover, N.H., U.S. C 8 164
Dover, N.J., U.S. F 4 164
Dover, Oh., U.S. C 3 162
Dover, Strait of (Calais, Pas de) ⋃ F 8 70
Dover-Foxcroft h 12 163a
Dovre A 4 66
Dovrefjell Nasjonalpark ♦ E 4 64
Dowa E 5 204
Dowerin L 4 140
Dowlatābād H 17 118
Down □[8] B 6 75
Downey G 5 182
Downieville A 3 182
Downing B 2 170
Downingtown F 3 164
Downpatrick B 6 75
Doyle B 3 180
Doylestown F 3 164
Doyline F 2 170
Dra, Oued ≃ D 3 198
Dra'a, Hamada du ✦[2] D 3 198
Dracena D 5 194
Drachenfels ⊥ B 4 100
Drachten A 5 69
Dracut D 7 164
Dragalina C 9 104
Drăgănești-Vlașca C 8 104
Drăgășani C 8 104
Dragons Mouths ⋃ q 23 187e
Dragør C 5 68
Draguignan G 4 82
Drahičyn J 12 64
Drake B 9 144
Drakensberg ⋏ D 9 206
Drake Passage ⋃ J 8 188
Drakesboro D 5 170
Dráma B 6 106
Drammen C 5 66
Drangajökull ⊓ I 19 64a
Draper ✦[8] A 5 168
Drau (Dráva) (Drava) ≃ D 6 102
Drava (Drau) (Dráva) ≃, Eur. E 10 102
Dráva (Drau) (Drava) ≃, Eur. E 10 102
Drawieński Park Narodowy ♦ B 9 96
Drawno B 8 96
Drayton A 6 174
Drayton Valley E 14 156
Drenthe □[3] B 5 69
Drépano, Ákra > C 5 106
Dresden, On., Can. B 2 162
Dresden, Ger. E 10 98
Dresden □[6] E 11 98
Drètun' E 14 66
Dreux D 8 78
Drezdenko B 9 96
Driebergen B 4 69
Driffield C 6 72
Driftwood D 8 156
Drin ≃ A 3 106
Drina ≃ C 5 104
Drin Gulf
see Drinit, Gjiri i c E 5 104
Drinit, Gjiri i (Drin Gulf) c E 5 104
Driskill Mountain ∧[2] F 2 170
Drobeta-Turnu Severin C 7 104
Drochia A 9 104
Drochtersen C 6 98
Drogheda (Droichead Átha) C 5 75
Drohiczyn B 12 96
Drohobych E 3 110
Droichead Nua C 5 75
Droitwich E 4 72
Drôme □[3] F 3 82
Drömling ✦[1] D 7 98
Dronfield D 5 72
Dronninglund A 3 68
Dronning Maud Land ✦[1] D 9 208
Drouin G 5 144
Drum Castle ⊥, Scot., U.K. C 6 70
Drum Castle ⊥, Scot., U.K. C 6 74
Drumheller F 15 156
Drummond B 7 178
Drummond □[6] A 6 164
Drummond Island I C 7 166
Drummondville F 7 160
Druskininkai E 12 66
Družba (Druzhba) A 13 116
Druzhba
see Družba, Kaz. A 13 116
Druzhba, Ukr. C 9 110
Dry Bay c G 25 154
Dry Cimarron ≃ G 3 174
Dryden G 12 158
Dry Ridge C 6 170
Drysdale ≃ D 9 140
Drysdale River National Park ♦ D 9 140
Dry Tortugas II G 3 168
Dry Tortugas National Park ♦ G 3 168
Drzewica C 11 96
Drzewice B 8 96
Dschang D 6 200
Du ≃ B 10 130
Du'an F 8 130
Duarte, Pico ∧ D 7 186
Duayaw-Nkwanta D 4 200
Ḍubā I 6 118
Dubai
see Dubayy J 16 118
Dubăsari B 10 104
Dubăsari, Lacul ⊜[1] B 10 104
Dubawnt ≃ D 12 150
Dubawnt Lake ⊜ D 12 150
Dubayy (Dubai) J 16 118
Dubbo D 7 144
Dübendorf E 5 100
Dubí B 10 100
Dubie D 4 204
Dublin (Baile Átha Cliath), Ire. C 5 75
Dublin, Ga., U.S. C 3 168
Dublin, Va., U.S. E 3 162
Dublin □[3] C 5 75
Dubna H 12 108
Dubnica nad Váhom B 10 102
Dubno D 4 110
Du Bois, Pa., U.S. C 4 162
Dubois, Wy., U.S. D 9 178
Dubovka, Russia E 14 110
Dubovka, Russia D 12 110
Dubrovnik D 4 104
Dubrovnoe, Kaz. I 28 108
Dubrovnoe, Russia G 28 108
Dubrovytsya K 13 64
Dubuque D 3 166
Duchang D 12 130
Duchesne ≃ B 4 176
Duchess F 4 142
Duck ≃ E 5 170
Duck Hill F 4 170
Duck Lake ⊜ D 9 158
Duck Mountain Provincial Park ♦ F 8 158
Duck Valley Indian Reservation ✦[4] E 6 178
Duc Tho E 7 132
Dudchany F 8 110
Dudelange E 5 69
Duderstadt E 7 98
Dudinka C 11 114
Dudley E 4 72
Dudley □[6] E 4 72
Dudwa National Park ♦ D 4 122
Duékoué D 3 200
Duero (Douro) ≃ B 2 84
Dueville D 7 92
Dufourspitze ∧ E 5 82
Dufur C 3 178
Dugi Otok I D 3 104
Duisburg E 3 98
Duiveland ✦[1] C 3 69
Duiwelskloof B 9 206
Duke C 4 172
Dukes □[6] E 8 164
Duk Fadiat F 3 202
Dukhān J 14 118
Dukla D 11 96
Dukla Pass)(D 11 96
Dukou E 5 130
Dūkštas E 13 66
Dulan B 7 122
Dulce ≃ E 7 192
Dulgalah ≃ C 16 114
Dullstroom C 9 206
Dülmen E 4 98
Dulovo D 9 104
Duluth B 2 166
Duluthulu B 9 206
Dūmā B 6 120
Dumaguete D 8 134
Dumai N 5 132
Dumaran Island I C 7 134
Dumaring E 7 134
Dumas C 3 172
Dumbarton E 4 74
Dumbleyung M 4 140
Dumbrăveni B 8 104
Dumfries B 3 72
Dumfries and Galloway □[6] B 3 72
Duminiči J 11 108
Dummar B 6 120
Dümmer ⊜ D 5 98
Dumoine, Lac ⊜ E 5 160
Dumont D 2 166
Dumont d'Urville ◗[3] C 22 208
Dunaföldvár D 10 102
Dunaharaszti C 11 102
Dunajská Streda B 9 102
Dunakeszi C 11 102
Dunărea Veche, Brațul ≃ C 10 104
Dunaújváros D 10 102
Dunav
see Danube ≃ G 12 62
Dunav-Tisa-Dunav, Kanal ≋ C 5 104
Dunayivtsi A 9 104
Dunbar A 4 72
Dunblane D 5 74
Duncan, B.C., Can. G 10 156
Duncan, Ok., U.S. C 5 172
Duncan Lake ⊜[1] F 13 156
Duncannon F 1 164
Duncan Passage ⋃ G 6 122
Duncansby Head > B 5 74
Dundaga D 11 66
Dundalk (Dún Dealgan), Ire. B 5 75
Dundalk, Md., U.S. G 2 164
Dundalk Bay c C 5 75
Dundas G 3 160
Dundas, Lake ⊜ M 6 140
Dundas Strait ⋃ B 11 140
Dundee, S. Afr. E 9 206
Dundee, Scot., U.K. D 6 74
Dundee, Mi., U.S. C 2 162
Dundee, City of □[6] D 6 74
Dundgovĭ □[3] D 6 128
Dundurn F 18 156
Dunedin, N.Z. F 3 146
Dunedin, Fl., U.S. E 3 168
Dunfermline D 5 74
Dungannon B 5 75
Dūngarpur E 2 122
Dungarvan D 4 75
Dungau ✦[1] D 9 100
Dungeness > G 7 72
Dungog D 8 144
Dungu B 4 204
Dungu ≃ B 4 204
Dungun L 6 132
Dunhua E 16 128
Dunhuang A 6 122
Dunkerque (Dunkirk) A 9 78
Dunkirk
see Dunkerque, Fr. A 9 78
Dunkirk, N.Y., U.S. B 4 162
Dunkirk, Oh., U.S. E 7 166
Dunkwa D 4 200
Dún Laoghaire C 5 75
Dunlap E 6 170
Dunmore E 3 164
Dunmore Town G 6 168
Dunmurry B 6 75
Dunn B 5 168
Dunning E 4 174
Dunoon B 1 72
Dunqulah D 3 202
Duns B 4 72
Dunsmuir E 2 178
Dunstable F 6 72
Dunstaffnage Castle ⊥ D 3 74
Dun-sur-Auron F 9 78
Dunvegan Castle ⊥ C 2 74
Duobukur ≃ A 15 128
Duolun E 11 128
Duomula C 4 122
Duozhu G 12 130
Dupnica D 7 104
Dupree C 4 174
Duque de Caxias E 9 194
Duque de York, Isla I J 4 192
Du Quoin C 4 170
Durack ≃ D 9 140
Durack Ranges ⋏ E 9 140
Durand C 3 166
Durango, Mex. F 7 184
Durango, Spain A 2 88
Durango, Co., U.S. D 5 176
Durango □[3] E 7 184
Durant, Ms., U.S. F 4 170
Durant, Ok., U.S. D 5 172
Durazno C 9 195
Durban E 9 206
Durbe D 10 66
Đurđevac D 9 102
Düren F 3 98
Durg E 4 122
Durgāpur E 5 122
Durham, Eng., U.K. C 5 72
Durham, N.C., U.S. A 5 168
Durham, N.H., U.S. C 8 164
Durham □[6] C 5 72
Durham Cathedral ◗[1] C 5 72
Durham Heights ∧ B 8 150
Durlești B 10 104
Durmersheim D 5 100
Durmitor ∧ D 5 104
Durmitor Nacionalni Park ♦ D 5 104
Durness B 4 74
Durón D 2 88
Durrës B 3 106
Dursley F 4 72
Dursunbey C 8 106
Duru B 4 204
D'Urville Island I D 4 146
Dusetos E 12 66
Dushan F 8 130
Dushanbe B 1 122
Düsseldorf E 3 98
Düsseldorf □[6] E 3 98
Dutchess □[6] E 5 164
Dutch Harbor J 11 154
Dutovo E 22 108
Dutton G 3 160
Dutton, Lake ⊜ C 1 144
Dutton, Mount ∧[1] I 13 154
Duvan I 22 108
Duxun G 13 130
Duyun E 8 130
Düzce B 9 106
Dve Mogili D 8 104
Dvinskaja guba c D 13 108
Dwārka E 1 122
Dwars in die Weg G 4 206
Dwight B 4 170
Dworshak Reservoir ⊜[1] B 6 178
Dyce C 6 74
Dyer, Cape > C 20 150
Dyersburg D 4 170
Dyhtau, gora ∧ H 13 110
Dyje (Thaya) ≃ B 8 102
Dyment G 12 158
Dysselsdorp G 5 206

ʟ Waterfall ⋃ Strait c Bay, Gulf ⊜ Lake ≋ Swamp ⊓ Ice Feature ⊤ Other Hydrographic Feature ✧ Submarine Feature □ Political Unit ◗ Cultural Institution ⊥ Historical Site ♦ Recreational Site ⊠ Airport ■ Military Installation ✦ Miscellaneous

Symbols in the index entries represent the broad categories identified in the key at the right.   ∧ Mountain   ∧ Mountains   ↗ Pass   ∨ Valley   ≃ Plain   ↘ Cape   I Island   II Islands   ⊥ Other Topographic Feature   ≃ River   ≈ Canal
Symbols with superior numbers (↗1) identify subcategories (see complete key on page 242).

Ethridge — Franklin

Name	Map Ref.	Page
Ethridge	A 7	178
Eticoga	C 1	200
Etna	D 8	178
Etna, Monte (Mongibello) ∧[1]	G 5	94
Etobicoke	G 4	160
Etolin Strait ⊔	F 12	154
Eton, Austl.	F 9	142
Eton, Eng., U.K.	F 6	72
Etosha National Park ♦	F 2	204
Etosha Pan ≚	F 2	204
Etoumbi	E 8	200
Etowah ≃	B 2	168
Étretat	C 7	78
Etsch see Adige ≃	D 8	92
Ettelbruck	E 4	69
Ettlingen	D 5	100
Etzikom Coulee ≃	G 16	156
Eu	B 8	78
Eua I	F 10	136
Euabalong West	D 6	144
Euboea, Gulf of c	C 5	106
Eucla	L 10	140
Euclid	C 3	162
Eucumbene, Lake ◎[1]	F 7	144
Eudora	F 3	170
Eufaula	G 6	170
Eufaula Lake ◎[1]	C 6	172
Eugene	C 2	178
Eugenia, Punta ›	D 2	184
Eugowra	D 7	144
Eunápolis	B 11	194
Eungella National Park ♦	F 9	142
Eunice, La., U.S.	G 2	170
Eunice, N.M., U.S.	D 2	172
Eupen	D 4	69
Euphrates (Al-Furāt) (Fırat) ≃	C 8	118
Eure □[3]	C 7	78
Eure-et-Loir □[3]	D 8	78
Eureka, Ca., U.S.	E 1	178
Eureka, Ks., U.S.	G 6	174
Eureka, Nv., U.S.	C 6	180
Eureka, S.D., U.S.	C 5	174
Eureka □[6]	A 7	182
Eureka River	C 12	156
Eurialo, Castello ⊥	G 5	94
Euroa	F 5	144
Europa, Picos de ∧∧	A 6	86
Europabrücke ◆[5]	C 3	102
Europa Point ›	H 5	86
Europe ⊥[1]	C 13	56
Euskal Herriko see Vasco, País □[3]	A 2	88
Euskirchen	F 3	98
Eutaw	F 5	170
Eutin	B 7	98
Evans	E 2	174
Evans, Lac ◎	C 5	160
Evans, Mount ∧	C 6	176
Evans Head	B 9	144
Evans Strait ⊔	D 16	150
Evanston, Il., U.S.	A 5	170
Evanston, Wy., U.S.	E 8	178
Evansville, Il., U.S.	C 4	170
Evansville, In., U.S.	C 5	170
Evansville, Wy., U.S.	D 10	178
Evant	E 4	172
Eva Perón see La Plata	D 9	195
Evaz	I 16	118
Eveleth	B 2	166
Everard, Lake ◎	K 2	142
Evere	D 3	69
Everest, Mount ∧	D 5	122
Everett, Pa., U.S.	C 4	162
Everett, Wa., U.S.	A 2	178
Evergem	C 2	69
Everglades, The ≋	G 4	168
Everglades City	G 4	168
Everglades National Park ♦	G 4	168
Evergreen, Al., U.S.	G 5	170
Evergreen, Ca., U.S.	E 3	182
Evesham, Sk., Can.	E 17	156
Evesham, Eng., U.K.	E 5	72
Évian-les-Bains	D 4	82
Evje	C 3	66
Évora	F 3	86
Évora □[3]	F 3	86
Evra	F 26	108
Evrejskaja avtonomnaja oblast' □[6]	B 19	128
Évreux	D 8	78
Évros (Marica) (Meriç) ≃	E 9	104
Évry	D 9	78
Evungu	C 4	204
Évvoia I	C 5	106
Ewen	B 4	166
Ewenkiku Zizhiqi	B 12	128
Ewing Township	F 4	164
Ewo	C 1	204
Excelsior	E 7	206
Executive Committee Range ∧∧	D 32	208
Exeter, On., Can.	B 3	162
Exeter, Eng., U.K.	G 3	72
Exeter, Ca., U.S.	D 4	182
Exeter, N.H., U.S.	C 8	164
Exmoor National Park ♦	F 3	72
Exmore	E 6	162
Exmouth, Austl.	G 3	140
Exmouth, Eng., U.K.	G 3	72
Exmouth Gulf c	H 3	140
Exploits ≃	D 15	160
Extremadura □[3]	E 5	86
Extrême-Nord □[3]	C 7	200
Exuma Sound ⊔	B 5	186
Eyak	F 22	154
Eyasi, Lake ◎	C 5	204
Eye	E 8	72
Eyemouth	B 4	72
Eyjafjördur c	I 21	64a
Eyl (Deex Nugaaleed) ≃	F 6	202
Eymet	D 4	80
Eyota	C 2	166
Eyre	M 9	140
Eyre Creek ≃	I 4	142
Eyre North, Lake ◎	J 3	142
Eyre Peninsula ›[1]	L 2	142
Eyre South, Lake ◎	J 3	142
Ezequiel Ramos Mexía, Embalse ◎[1]	G 6	192
Ezine	C 7	106
Ezjaryšča	B 6	110
Ežva	F 19	108

F

Name	Map Ref.	Page
Faaborg	C 3	68
Fabala	D 3	200
Fåberg	B 5	66
Faber Lake ◎	D 9	150
Fabero	B 4	86
Fabriano	F 8	92
Fachi	B 7	200
Fada	B 9	200
Fada-Ngourma	C 5	200
Faddoi	F 3	202
Faenza	E 7	92
Fafa	B 5	200
Fafa ≃	D 8	200
Fafen ≃	F 5	202
Făgăraș	C 8	104
Fagernes	B 4	66
Fagersta	B 7	66
Faggo	C 7	200
Faguibine, Lac ◎	B 4	200
Fagwir	F 3	202
Faial I	E 5	196
Fairbanks, Ak., U.S.	D 21	154
Fairbanks, La., U.S.	F 2	170
Fairborn	D 1	162
Fairbury	E 6	174
Fairfax, Va., U.S.	D 5	162
Fairfax, Vt., U.S.	B 5	164
Fairfield, Austl.	D 8	144
Fairfield, Ca., U.S.	B 1	182
Fairfield, Id., U.S.	D 6	178
Fairfield, Il., U.S.	C 4	170
Fairfield, Ne., U.S.	E 5	174
Fairfield, Oh., U.S.	C 6	170
Fairfield, Tx., U.S.	E 5	172
Fairfield □[6]	E 5	164
Fairhaven, Ma., U.S.	E 8	164
Fair Haven, N.Y., U.S.	C 2	164
Fair Haven Beach State Park ♦	C 2	164
Fairhope	G 5	170
Fair Isle I	A 7	74
Fairlie	F 3	146
Fairmont, Mn., U.S.	D 7	174
Fairmont, N.C., U.S.	B 5	168
Fairmont, W.V., U.S.	D 3	162
Fairmont Hot Springs	F 14	156
Fairmount, In., U.S.	B 6	170
Fairmount, N.D., U.S.	B 6	174
Fairmount, N.Y., U.S.	C 2	164
Fair Oaks	C 2	168
Fairview, Mi., U.S.	A 1	162
Fairview, Mt., U.S.	H 6	158
Fairview, Ut., U.S.	C 3	176
Fairview Park	C 5	170
Fairweather, Mount ∧	B 3	156
Fairy Stone State Park ♦	A 4	168
Fais I	D 12	134
Faisalabad	C 2	122
Faistós ⊥	E 6	106
Faizābād	D 4	122
Fajardo	j 16	187b
Fajr, Wādī ≃	G 8	118
Fakaofo I[1]	D 10	136
Fakarava I[1]	E 13	136
Fakel	H 20	108
Fakfak	F 10	134
Fakse	C 5	68
Fakse Bugt c	C 5	68
Faku	E 14	128
Faladié	C 3	200
Falaise	D 6	78
Fālākāta	D 5	122
Falam	C 1	132
Falāvarjān	F 14	118
Fălciu	B 10	104
Falcón □[3]	F 7	186
Falcón, Presa see Falcon Reservoir ◎[1]	G 4	172
Falconara Marittima	F 9	92
Falcon Reservoir (Falcón, Presa) ◎[1]	G 4	172
Faléa	C 2	200
Falémé ≃	C 2	200
Falerii Novi ⊥	G 8	92
Fălești	B 9	104
Falfurrias	G 4	172
Falkenberg, Ger.	E 10	98
Falkenberg, Swe.	D 6	66
Falkensee	D 9	98
Falkenstein	B 9	100
Falkirk	A 3	72
Falkirk □[6]	B 3	72
Falkland Islands □[2]	J 8	188
Falkland Sound ⊔	n 18	193b
Falköping	C 6	66
Falkville	E 5	170
Fallbrook	G 6	182
Fallersleben	D 7	98
Fallingbostel	D 6	98
Fallon	A 5	182
Fall River, Ks., U.S.	G 6	174
Fall River, Ma., U.S.	E 7	164
Falls City	B 1	170
Falls Lake ◎[1]	A 5	168
Falmey	C 5	200
Falmouth, Jam.	h 12	186a
Falmouth, Eng., U.K.	G 1	72
Falmouth, Ma., U.S.	E 8	164
False Bay c	H 3	206
False Divi Point ›	F 4	122
False Pass	I 13	154
Falset	C 8	86
Falster I	D 4	68
Fălticeni	B 9	104
Falun	B 7	66
Famagusta see Ammochostos	E 5	118
Famagusta Bay c	E 5	118
Fameck	A 4	82
Famenne ◆[1]	D 4	69
Family Lake ◎	F 11	158
Fana	C 3	200
Fanchang	C 14	130
Fanchon, Pointe ›	D 6	186
Fandriana	I 9	205a
Fangak	F 3	202
Fangcheng	B 11	130
Fangxian	B 10	130
Fangzheng	D 17	128
Fanjiatun	E 15	128
Fannrem	E 4	64
Fano	F 9	92
Fan Si Pan ∧	G 6	130
Faradje	B 4	204
Faradofay see Tôlañaro	m 9	205a
Farafangana	I 9	205a
Farāh	D 9	116
Fara in Sabina	G 8	94
Farallon de Medinilla I	I 13	124
Farallon de Pajaros I	H 12	124
Faramana	C 3	200
Faranah	D 2	200
Farasān al-Kabīr I	D 5	202
Farasān, Jazā'ir II	D 5	202
Faraulep I[1]	D 12	134
Fareham	G 5	72
Farewell	E 17	154
Farewell, Cape ›	D 4	146
Fargo	B 6	174
Farīdābād	D 3	122
Farīdpur	D 3	122
Farié	C 5	200
Farina	C 4	170
Faringdon	F 5	72
Fāris, Ḥādh ⊥[8]	C 7	202
Farkwa	D 6	204
Farmersburg	C 5	170
Farmersville	C 4	170
Farmington, Me., U.S.	A 8	162
Farmington, Mo., U.S.	D 3	170
Farmington, N.H., U.S.	C 7	164
Farmington, N.M., U.S.	D 4	176
Farmington, Ut., U.S.	E 8	178
Farmville	E 4	162
Farnam	E 4	174
Farnborough	F 6	72
Farnham, Qc., Can.	A 5	164
Farnham, Eng., U.K.	F 6	72
Farnworth	D 4	72
Faro, Braz.	D 7	190
Faro, Port.	G 3	86
Faro □[3]	G 2	86
Faro ≃	D 7	200
Faro, Réserve du ◆[4]	D 7	200
Faroe Islands □[2]	C 6	62
Farrāshband	H 15	118
Farrell	C 3	162
Farrukhābād	D 3	122
Fārs □[3]	H 15	118
Fársala	C 5	106
Farsund	C 3	66
Fartak, Ra's ›	G 7	116
Farum	C 5	68
Farvel, Kap ›	E 24	150
Farwell	C 2	172
Fasā	H 15	118
Fasano	D 7	94
Fastiv	D 6	110
Fatehpur, India	D 4	122
Fatehpur, India	D 2	122
Father, Lac ◎	D 6	160
Fatick	C 1	200
Fatoto	C 2	200
Faulquemont	A 4	82
Fauquier	G 12	156
Fauresmith	E 6	206
Fåvang	B 4	66
Favara	G 3	94
Faversham	F 7	72
Favourable Lake ◎	E 11	158
Fawcett	D 14	156
Fawn ≃	D 14	158
Faxaflói c	m 19	64a
Faya-Largeau	B 8	200
Fayence	G 4	82
Fayette, Ia., U.S.	D 3	166
Fayette, Ms., U.S.	G 3	170
Fayetteville, Ar., U.S.	D 1	170
Fayetteville, N.C., U.S.	B 5	168
Fayetteville, W.V., U.S.	D 3	162
Fayl-Billot	C 3	82
Fazao Malfakassa, Reserve de Faune de ♦	D 5	200
Fdérik	E 2	198
Fear, Cape ›	C 6	168
Feather ≃	A 2	182
Feather, Middle Fork ≃	A 2	182
Fécamp	C 7	78
Fedala see Mohammedia	C 3	198
Federal	B 8	195
Federally Administered Tribal Areas □[3]	C 1	122
Federated States of Micronesia see Micronesia, Federated States of □[1]	C 6	136
Fedje	B 2	66
Fedorovka	C 23	110
Fedoseevskaja	E 14	108
Fehérgyarmat	A 7	104
Fehmarn I	B 8	98
Fehmarn Strait ⊔	B 8	98
Feia, Lagoa c	E 10	194
Fei Huang ≃	A 14	130
Feijó	E 4	190
Feilding	D 5	146
Feira de Santana	F 11	190
Feixi	C 13	130
Feixian	I 11	128
Fejaj, Chott ◎	C 6	198
Fejér □[3]	C 10	102
Felanitx	E 8	88
Feldbach	D 7	102
Feldkirch	C 1	102
Feldkirchen in Kärnten	D 6	102
Feldschuhhorn	D 2	206
Felhit	D 4	202
Felipe Carrillo Puerto	H 15	184
Felixlândia	C 8	194
Felixstowe	F 8	72
Felletin	C 6	80
Feltre	C 7	92
Femés	i 17	85b
Femunden ◎	E 5	64
Femundsmarka Nasjonalpark ♦	E 6	64
Fen ≃	G 9	128
Fenelon Falls	A 4	162
Fénérive see Fenoarivo Atsinanana	k 9	205a
Fengcheng, China	F 14	128
Fengcheng, China	D 12	130
Fengdu	D 8	130
Fengfeng	H 10	128
Fenggang	D 8	130
Fengjie	C 9	130
Fengle	D 15	128
Fengning	F 11	128
Fengqing	B 4	132
Fengqiu	I 10	128
Fengtai	G 11	128
Fengxian	B 8	130
Fengyüan	F 15	130
Fengzhen	F 9	128
Feni	E 6	122
Fenicia Moncata ⊥	G 4	94
Fenimore Pass ⊔	k 44	155a
Fenoarivo	I 9	205a
Fenoarivo Atsinanana	k 9	205a
Fenouillèdes ◆[1]	F 6	80
Fenyang	H 8	128
Fenyi	E 12	130
Feodosiya	G 9	110
Fer, Cap de ›	B 6	198
Ferdinand	C 5	170
Ferdows	E 18	118
Fère-en-Tardenois	C 10	78
Ferentino	H 9	92
Fergana	A 2	122
Fergana □[6]	A 2	122
Fergus	G 3	160
Fergus Falls	B 6	174
Ferguson	C 3	170
Fergusson Island I	N 14	124
Fériana	C 6	198
Ferkéssédougou	D 3	200
Ferland	F 14	158
Ferlo ◆[1]	B 2	200
Ferlo, Vallée du ≃	B 1	200
Fermanagh □[8]	B 4	75
Fermo	A 3	94
Fermont	B 10	160
Fermoy	D 3	75
Fernandina, Isla I	j 13	190a
Fernandina Beach	D 4	168
Fernando de la Mora	F 1	194
Fernando de Noronha, Ilha I	E 11	188
Fernandópolis	D 5	194
Fernando Póo see Bioko I	E 6	200
Fernán-Núñez	G 6	86
Fernie	G 14	156
Fernley	A 4	182
Ferrandina	D 6	94
Ferrara	E 7	92
Ferrara □[6]	E 7	92
Ferreira	E 7	206
Ferriday	G 3	170
Ferris	D 5	172
Ferro see El Hierro I	j 13	85b
Ferrol	A 2	86
Ferryhill	C 5	72
Feršampenuaz	J 23	108
Ferto-tavi Nemzeti Park ♦	C 8	102
Fès (Fez)	C 4	198
Feshi	D 2	204
Festus	C 3	170
Fetești	C 9	104
Fethiye	D 8	106
Feucht	C 8	100
Feuchtwangen	C 7	100
Feuilles ≃	E 18	150
Feurs	E 2	82
Feyẕābād	B 2	122
Fez see Fès	C 4	198
Fezzan □[9]	D 7	198
Ffestiniog	E 2	72
Fianarantsoa	I 9	205a
Fianarantsoa □[3]	I 9	205a
Fianga	D 8	200
Fiastra, Abbazia di ◗[1]	F 9	92
Fichē	F 4	202
Ficksburg	E 7	206
Fidenza	E 5	92
Fier	B 3	106
Fierzës, Liqeni i ◎[1]	A 4	106
Fiesch	D 6	82
Fife □[6]	D 5	74
Fife Ness ›	D 6	74
Fifield	C 3	166
Fifth Cataract ⌞	D 3	202
Figeholm	D 8	66
Figline Valdarno	F 7	92
Figueira da Foz	D 2	86
Figueras see Figueres	B 7	88
Figueres (Figueras)	B 7	88
Figuig	C 4	198
Fihaonana	k 9	205a
Fiji □[1]	E 9	136
Fika	C 7	200
Filabusi	G 4	204
Filatova Gora	D 13	66
Filchner Ice Shelf ⊓	D 5	208
Filderstadt	D 6	100
Filiași	C 7	104
Filingué	C 5	200
Fílippoi ⊥	B 6	106
Filipstad	C 6	66
Filitosa ⊥	j 8	83a
Fillmore, Ca., U.S.	F 5	182
Fillmore, Ut., U.S.	C 2	176
Filton	F 4	72
Fimi ≃	C 2	204
Finale Ligure	E 4	92
Fincastle	E 4	162
Findlay	C 2	162
Fingal	i 12	145a
Finger Lake ◎	E 12	158
Finike	D 9	106
Finistère □[3]	D 2	78
Finisterre, Cabo de see Fisterra, Cabo de ›	B 1	86
Finke ≃	H 2	142
Finke Gorge National Park ♦	I 12	140
Finland □[1]	C 13	62
Finland, Gulf of c	B 13	66
Finlay ≃	C 9	156
Finley, Austl.	E 5	144
Finley, N.D., U.S.	B 6	174
Finne ◆[1]	E 8	98
Finnegan	F 15	156
Finnentrop	E 4	98
Finnmark □[3]	B 12	64
Finskij zaliv see Finland, Gulf of c	B 13	66
Finspång	C 7	66
Finsterwalde	E 10	98
Fiordland National Park ♦	F 1	146
Fiorenzuola d'Arda	E 5	92
Fīq	D 5	120
Fire Island I	F 6	164
Fire Island National Seashore ♦	F 5	164
Firenze (Florence)	F 7	92
Firenze □[6]	F 7	92
Firenzuola	E 7	92
Firmat	C 7	195
Firminy	E 2	82
Firovo	H 10	108
Fīrozābād	D 3	122
First Cataract ⌞	C 3	202
Firth ≃	B 24	154
Fīrūzābād	H 15	118
Fish (Vis) ≃, Nmb.	D 2	206
Fish ≃, S. Afr.	F 4	206
Fisher	B 4	170
Fishguard	F 1	72
Fishing Lake ◎	E 11	158
Fish River Canyon ∨	D 2	206
Fisk	D 3	170
Fiskebäckskil	C 5	66
Fisterra, Cabo de ›	B 1	86
Fitchburg	D 7	164
Fito, Mount ∧[1]	k 11	147b
Fitri, Lac ◎	C 8	200
Fitzgerald	B 16	156
Fitzgerald River National Park ♦	N 5	140
Fitz Roy	I 6	192
Fitzroy ≃	G 10	142
Fitzroy, Monte (Cerro Chaltel) ∧	I 5	192
Fitzroy Crossing	F 8	140
Fiuggi	H 9	92
Fiume see Rijeka	E 6	102
Fiumicino ◆[8]	E 4	90
Fivizzano	E 6	92
Fiwila Mission	E 4	204
Fjällåsen	C 10	64
Fjerritslev	A 2	68
Flagler	F 3	174
Flagstaff, S. Afr.	F 8	206
Flagstaff, Az., U.S.	E 3	176
Flagstaff Lake ◎[1]	h 11	163a
Flamborough	D 8	166
Fläming ◆[1]	D 9	98
Flaming Gorge National Recreation Area ♦	E 9	178
Flaming Gorge Reservoir ◎[1]	E 9	178
Flanagan	B 4	170
Flanders □[9]	D 2	69
Flat ≃, N.T., Can.	F 31	154
Flat ≃, N.C., U.S.	A 5	168
Flatey	m 19	64a
Flathead ≃	B 6	178
Flathead, North Fork ≃	A 6	178
Flathead, South Fork ≃	B 7	178
Flathead Indian Reservation ◆[4]	B 6	178
Flathead Lake ◎	B 6	178
Flat Lick	E 2	162
Flatonia	F 5	172
Flat River	D 3	170
Flatrock Lake ◎	D 8	158
Flattery, Cape ›	A 1	178
Flaxton	A 3	174
Fleetwood, Eng., U.K.	D 3	72
Fleetwood, Pa., U.S.	F 3	164
Flemingsburg	D 2	162
Flemington	F 4	164
Flen	C 8	66
Flensburg	B 6	98
Fletcher	B 3	168
Fleur-de-Lys	C 15	160
Fleury-les-Aubrais	E 8	78
Flevoland □[3]	B 4	69
Flinders	G 5	144
Flinders ≃	E 5	142
Flinders Bay c	N 3	140
Flinders Chase National Park ♦	M 3	142
Flinders Island I	h 12	145a
Flinders Ranges National Park ♦	C 2	144
Flinders Reefs ✢[2]	E 6	136
Flin Flon	D 8	158
Flint, Wales, U.K.	D 3	72
Flint, Mi., U.S.	B 2	162
Flint I	E 12	136
Flint ≃	D 2	168
Flintshire □[6]	D 3	72
Flisa	B 6	66
Floby	C 6	66
Flodden Field Battlesite ⊥	B 4	72
Flöha	F 10	98
Flomaton	G 5	170
Flora	B 5	170
Floral City	E 3	168
Florange	A 4	82
Florence see Firenze, Italy	F 7	92
Florence, Al., U.S.	E 5	170
Florence, Az., U.S.	F 3	176
Florence, Or., U.S.	D 1	178
Florence, S.C., U.S.	B 5	168
Florence, Wi., U.S.	C 4	166
Florencia	C 3	190
Florentino Ameghino, Embalse ◎[1]	H 6	192
Flores	I 15	184
Flores I, Indon.	G 8	134
Flores I, Port.	h 11	198a
Flores Sea (Flores, Laut) ⊤[2]	G 8	134
Florești	B 10	104
Floresville	F 4	172
Floriano	E 10	190
Florianópolis	G 6	194
Florida, Cuba	C 5	186
Florida, Ur.	D 9	195
Florida □[3]	F 11	152
Florida, Straits of ⊔	B 4	186
Florida Bay c	G 4	168
Floridablanca	B 4	190
Florida Keys II	G 4	168
Floridia	G 5	94
Florido ≃	D 7	184
Flórina	B 4	106
Florisbad	E 6	206
Florissant	C 3	170
Florissant Fossil Beds National Monument ♦	F 2	174
Florvåg	B 2	66
Fluminimaggiore	I 9	94a
Flushing see Vlissingen	C 2	69
Fly ≃	N 12	124
Foča, Bos.	D 5	104
Foça, Tur.	C 7	106
Focșani	C 9	104
Fodé	D 9	200
Foeni	C 6	104
Fogang	G 11	130
Foggaret el Arab	D 5	198
Foggia	C 5	94
Foggia □[6]	C 5	94
Foggy Island Bay c	A 21	154
Fogo	D 16	160
Fogo I	h 11	200a
Fogo Island I	D 16	160
Fohnsdorf	C 6	102
Foix	F 5	80
Foix □[9]	E 5	80
Fokino	J 11	108
Fokku	C 5	200
Folda c	C 7	64
Foley	G 5	170
Foley Island I	C 17	150
Foligno	G 8	92
Folkestone	F 8	72
Folldal	A 5	66
Föllinge	E 7	64
Follonica	G 6	92
Folsom	B 2	182
Fominskaja	F 18	108
Fominskoe	G 13	108
Fonda, Ia., U.S.	D 7	174
Fonda, N.Y., U.S.	D 4	164
Fond du Lac	D 4	166
Fond du Lac ≃	B 19	156
Fond du Lac Indian Reservation ◆[4]	B 2	166
Fondi	C 3	94
Fonni	k 10	94a
Fonsagrada see A Fonsagrada	A 3	86
Fonseca, Golfo de c	E 2	186
Fontaine	E 3	82
Fontainebleau	D 9	78
Fontana	F 6	182
Fontana Lake ◎[1]	B 2	168
Fontas ≃	B 11	156
Fonte Avellana, Monastero di ◗[1]	F 8	92
Fonte Boa	D 5	190
Fontenay, Abbaye de ◗[1]	E 11	78
Fontenay-le-Comte	B 3	80
Fontfroide Abbey ◗[1]	E 6	80
Fontur ›	I 23	64a
Foothills	E 13	156
Foraker, Mount ∧	E 18	154
Forbach	A 4	82
Forbes	D 6	144
Forbesganj	D 5	122
Forcados	D 6	200
Forchheim	C 8	100
Ford City	C 4	162
Førde	B 2	66
Ford Ranges ∧∧	D 30	208
Fordsville	D 5	170
Fordyce	F 2	170
Forécariah	D 2	200
Foremost	A 8	178
Forest Acres	B 4	168
Forest City	D 2	166
Forestville	D 9	160
Forestville Mystery Cave State Park ♦	D 2	166
Forgan	G 4	174
Forillon, Parc national de ♦	D 11	160
Forked Deer ≃	D 4	170
Forks	A 1	178
Forlì	E 7	92
Forlì □[6]	E 8	92
Forlimpopoli	E 8	92
Formby	D 3	72
Formia	C 3	94
Formiga	D 8	194
Formigine	E 6	92
Formignana	E 7	92
Formosa, Arg.	G 1	194
Formosa, Braz.	A 7	194
Formosa □[3]	D 8	192
Formosa see T'aiwan I	G 15	130
Formosa, Serra ∧∧[1]	F 7	190
Fornæs ›	B 3	68
Forncelle	F 7	92
Forney	D 5	172
Forrest	B 4	170
Forrest City	E 3	170
Forsayth	E 6	142
Forsbacka	B 8	66
Forserum	D 7	66
Forssa	B 11	66
Forst	E 11	98
Forsyth	B 10	178
Fort Albany	B 3	160
Fort Albany Indian Reserve ◆[4]	E 17	158
Fort Alexander Indian Reserve ◆[4]	F 10	158
Fortaleza	D 11	190
Fort Apache Indian Reservation ◆[4]	E 3	176
Fort-Archambault see Sarh	D 8	200
Fort Atkinson	D 4	166
Fort Augustus	C 4	74
Fort Battleford National Historic Park ♦	E 17	156
Fort Belknap Agency	A 9	178
Fort Belknap Indian Reservation ◆[4]	A 9	178
Fort Berthold Indian Reservation ◆[4]	B 3	174
Fort Bidwell	E 3	178
Fort Clatsop National Memorial ♦	B 1	178
Fort Collins	E 2	174
Fort-Coulonge	F 5	160
Fort Covington	B 4	164
Fort-Dauphin see Tôlañaro	m 9	205a
Fort Davis, Al., U.S.	F 6	170
Fort Davis, Tx., U.S.	E 2	172
Fort Davis National Historic Site ♦	E 2	172
Fort-de-France	s 26	187h
Fort Deposit	G 5	170
Fort Dodge	D 7	174
Fort Donelson National Battlefield ♦	D 5	170
Forte dei Marmi	F 6	92
Fort Edward	C 5	164
Fort Erie	D 9	166
Fortescue ≃	G 4	140
Fort Frances	G 12	158
Fort Fraser	D 9	156
Fort Frederica National Monument ♦	D 4	168
Fort Gay	D 2	162
Fort Good Hope	C 30	154
Fort-Gouraud see Fdérik	E 2	198
Forth, Firth of c	D 6	74
Fort Hall Indian Reservation ◆[4]	D 7	178
Fort Hill see Chitipa	D 5	204
Fort Hope	F 15	158
Forth Road Bridge ◆[5]	A 3	72
Fortín Uno	F 5	195
Fort Johnston see Mangochi	E 6	204
Fort Klamath	D 3	178
Fort-Lamy see N'Djamena	C 8	200
Fort Laramie National Historic Site ♦	D 2	174
Fort Larned National Historic Site ♦	F 5	174
Fort Lauderdale	F 4	168
Fort Liard	A 10	156
Fort Lincoln State Park ♦	B 4	174
Fort MacKay	C 16	156
Fort Macleod	G 15	156
Fort Madison	B 3	170
Fort Matanzas National Monument ♦	E 4	168
Fort McDermitt Indian Reservation ◆[4]	D 5	178
Fort McMurray	C 15	156
Fort Meade	F 4	168
Fort Mojave Indian Reservation ◆[4]	E 1	176
Fort Myers	F 4	168
Fort Myers Beach	F 3	168
Fort Necessity National Battlefield ♦	D 4	162
Fort Nelson	B 10	156
Fort Ogden	F 4	168
Fort Payne	E 6	170
Fort Peck Dam ◆[6]	A 10	178
Fort Peck Indian Reservation ◆[4]	A 2	174
Fort Peck Lake ◎[1]	B 10	178
Fort Pierce	F 4	168
Fort Portal	G 3	202
Fort Providence	D 9	150
Fort Pulaski National Monument ♦	C 4	168
Fort Raleigh National Historic Site ♦	B 7	168
Fort Randall Dam ◆[6]	D 5	174
Fort Resolution	D 10	150
Fort Rodd Hill National Historic Park ♦	A 2	178
Fortrose	G 2	146
Fort Saint James	D 9	156
Fort Saint John	C 11	156
Fort Saskatchewan	E 15	156
Fort-Ševčenko see Fort-Shevchenko	G 16	110
Fort Severn	C 15	158
Fort-Shevchenko	G 16	110
Fort Smith, N.T., Can.	A 16	156
Fort Smith, Ar., U.S.	E 1	170
Fort Stockton	E 2	172
Fort Sumter National Monument ♦	C 5	168
Fort Supply	B 4	172
Fort Totten	H 9	158
Fortuna	B 1	180
Fortune Bay c	E 16	160
Fortune Harbour	D 16	160
Fort Union National Monument ♦	B 1	172
Fort Union Trading Post National Historic Site ♦	B 2	174
Fort Vermilion	B 13	156
Fort Walton Beach	G 5	170
Fort Washakie	D 9	178
Fort Wayne	B 6	170
Fort Wellington National Historic Park ♦	B 3	164
Fort William	D 3	74
Fort Worth	D 5	172
Fort Yates	B 4	174
Fortymile ≃	D 24	154
Forty Mile Flats	B 6	156
Fort Yuma Indian Reservation ◆[4]	F 1	176
Foshan	G 11	130
Foso	D 4	200
Fossano	E 3	92
Fossil Butte National Monument ♦	E 8	178
Fossil Lake ◎	D 3	178
Fossombrone	F 8	92
Foster ≃	D 19	156
Fosters	F 5	170
Fostoria	C 2	162
Fougamou	F 7	200
Fougères	D 5	78
Fouke	F 2	170
Foulatari	C 7	200
Foul Bay c	C 4	202
Foulness Island I	F 7	72
Foumban	D 7	200
Foumbot	D 7	200
Foum-Zguid	C 3	198
Foundiougne	C 1	200
Fountain	G 6	170
Fountain Inn	B 3	168
Fountains Abbey ◗[1]	C 5	72
Fourchu	F 13	160
Four Corners	C 2	178
Fourmies	B 11	78
Fournaise, Piton de la ∧[1]	q 20	207e
Fournier, Lac ◎	C 11	160
Fours	F 10	78
Fourth Cataract ⌞	D 3	202
Foux, Cap à ›	D 6	186
Foveaux Strait ⊔	G 2	146
Fowler, Ca., U.S.	D 4	182
Fowler, Mi., U.S.	B 1	162
Fox	D 21	154
Fox ≃, Mb., Can.	D 11	158
Fox ≃	E 4	166
Foxe Basin c	C 17	150
Foxe Channel ⊔	D 16	150
Foxen ◎	C 5	66
Foxe Peninsula ›[1]	D 17	150
Fox Glacier ⊓	E 2	146
Fox Lake	D 4	166
Fox Lake Indian Reserve ◆[4]	B 14	156
Foxton	D 5	146
Fox Valley	F 17	156
Foyle, Lough c	A 4	75
Foz do Areia, Represa de ◎[1]	F 5	194
Foz do Iguaçu	F 3	194
Foz Giraldo	E 3	86
Fqih-ben-Salah	C 3	198
Fraga	C 5	88
Fraile Muerto	C 10	195
Frameries	D 2	69
Framingham	D 7	164
Franca	D 7	194
Francavilla al Mare	B 4	94
Francavilla Fontana	D 7	94
France □[1]	F 8	62
Frances ≃	F 30	154
Frances Lake ◎	F 30	154
Francesville	B 5	170
Franceville see Masuku	F 7	200
Franche-Comté □[9]	C 3	82
Francis	F 7	158
Francis Case, Lake ◎[1]	D 5	174
Francisco Beltrão	F 4	194
Francisco I. Madero	E 7	184
Francisco Murguía	E 8	184
Francisco Zarco	F 5	180
Francistown	G 4	204
Francofonte	G 4	94
Francois Lake ◎	E 8	156
Franconia Notch)(	B 7	164
Francs Peak ∧	C 9	178
Franeker	A 4	69
Frangy	D 3	82
Franken □[9]	C 7	100
Frankenberg, Ger.	F 10	98
Frankenberg, Ger.	E 5	98
Frankenmuth	B 2	162
Frankenthal	C 5	100
Frankfield	h 12	186a
Frankford	A 5	162
Frankfort, In., U.S.	B 5	170
Frankfort, Ks., U.S.	F 6	174
Frankfort, Ky., U.S.	C 6	170
Frankfurt	D 11	98
Frankfurt am Main	B 5	100
Frank Hann National Park ♦	M 5	140
Fränkische Schweiz ◆[1]	C 8	100
Franklin, Az., U.S.	F 4	176
Franklin, Ma., U.S.	D 7	164
Franklin, Ne., U.S.	E 5	174
Franklin, N.H., U.S.	C 7	164
Franklin, N.J., U.S.	E 4	164
Franklin, Oh., U.S.	D 1	162
Franklin, Pa., U.S.	C 4	162
Franklin, Tn., U.S.	E 5	170
Franklin, Wi., U.S.	D 4	166
Franklin, W.V., U.S.	D 4	162
Franklin □[6], Ma., U.S.	D 6	164
Franklin □[6], Me., U.S.	A 8	164

⌞ Waterfall ⊔ Strait c Bay, Gulf ◎ Lake ≋ Swamp ⊓ Ice Feature ⊤ Other Hydrographic Feature ✢ Submarine Feature □ Political Unit ◗ Cultural Institution ⊥ Historical Site ♦ Recreational Site ⊠ Airport ▮ Military Installation ◆ Miscellaneous

---

Symbols in the index entries represent the broad categories identified in the key at the right. Symbols with superior numbers (⋀[1]) identify subcategories (see complete key on page 242).

⋀ Mountain   ⋒ Mountains   ⊀ Pass   V Valley   ≃ Plain   ⊁ Cape   I Island   II Islands   ⌐ Other Topographic Feature   ≃ River   ⌐ Canal

Name	Map Ref.	Page

Glacier F 13 156
Glacier Bay c G 26 154
Glacier Bay National Park ♦ G 26 154
Glacier National Park ♦, B.C., Can. F 12 156
Glacier National Park ♦, Mt., U.S. A 3 178
Glacier Peak ʌ¹ A 3 178
Gladenbach F 5 98
Gladsakse C 5 68
Gladstone, Austl. G 10 142
Gladstone, Mb., Can. F 9 158
Gladstone, Mo., U.S. A 1 170
Gladwin A 1 162
Gladys Lake B 5 156
Glafsfjorden ◻ C 6 66
Glåma ≈ D 6 122
Glamis Castle ⊥ D 6 74
Glamorgan, Vale of ◻⁶ F 3 72
Glamsbjerg C 3 68
Glan ≈ C 7 66
Glanum ⊥ G 2 82
Glaris see Glarus C 7 82
Glaris see Glarus ◻³ D 7 82
Glarus C 7 82
Glarus ◻³ D 7 82
Glasgow, Scot., U.K. B 2 72
Glasgow, Ky., U.S. D 6 170
Glasgow, Mo., U.S. C 2 170
Glasgow, Va., U.S. E 4 162
Glasgow, City of ◻⁶ B 2 72
Glassboro G 3 164
Glastonbury F 4 72
Glauchau F 9 98
Glazov G 20 108
Glazunovka C 10 110
Gleisdorf C 7 102
Gleiwitz see Gliwice C 10 96
Glenboro G 9 158
Glen Burnie G 2 164
Glen Canyon V F 4 176
Glen Canyon Dam ◄⁶ D 3 176
Glen Canyon National Recreation Area ♦ D 3 176
Glencoe, Al., U.S. F 6 170
Glencoe, Mn., U.S. C 1 166
Glendale, Az., U.S. F 2 176
Glendale, Ca., U.S. F 5 182
Glendale, Ms., U.S. G 4 170
Glendale, Wi., U.S. D 5 166
Glendalough ⊥ C 5 75
Glendo D 2 174
Glenelg ≈ F 3 144
Glenfield E 5 72
Glengyle H 4 142
Glen Innes B 8 144
Glen Lyon E 2 164
Glenmora G 2 170
Glenn ◻⁶ A 1 182
Glennallen E 21 154
Glennville D 3 168
Glenora C 6 156
Glen Rock G 2 164
Glenrothes D 5 74
Glens Falls C 5 164
Glenthompson F 4 144
Glen Ullin D 2 166
Glenville D 2 166
Glenwood, Nf., Can. D 16 160
Glenwood, Ia., U.S. B 1 170
Glenwood, Mn., U.S. C 7 174
Glenwood Springs D 10 176
Glienicke D 10 98
Glina E 8 102
Glinde C 7 98
Glittertinden ʌ B 4 66
Gliwice C 10 96
Gljadjanskoe I 26 108
Globe F 3 176
Glodeanu-Silistea C 9 104
Glodeni B 9 104
Glogau see Głogów C 8 96
Głogów C 8 96
Głogów Małopolski C 12 96
Glorieta E 4 176
Glotovka J 17 108
Gloucester, On., Can. A 3 164
Gloucester, Eng., U.K. F 4 72
Gloucester, Ma., U.S. D 8 164
Gloucester, Va., U.S. G 5 162
Gloucestershire ◻⁶ F 4 72
Glouster D 2 162
Gloversville C 4 164
Głowno C 10 96
Glubokoe see Hlybokae E 13 64
Głuchołazy C 9 96
Glücksburg B 6 98
Glückstadt C 6 98
Glyfa C 5 106
Glyngøre B 1 68
Gmünd, Aus. B 6 102
Gmünd, Aus. D 5 102
Gmunden C 5 102
Gnesen see Gniezno B 9 96
Gniew B 10 96
Gniezno B 9 96
Gnjilane D 6 104
Gnosjö D 5 66
Goa ◻³ F 2 122
Goa, Eth. F 4 202
Goba, Moz. D 10 206
Gobabis B 3 206
Gobernador Gregores I 5 192
Gobi Desert ◄² H 5 126
Gobō H 5 126
Goce Delčev E 7 104
Goch E 3 98
Godalming F 6 72
Godāvari ≈ C 4 122
Godāvari, Mouths of the ≈¹ F 4 122
God Colow G 5 202
Goderich G 3 160
Godfrey C 3 170
Godhavn (Qeqertarsuaq) C 22 150
Godhra E 2 122
Gödöllő B 5 104
Godoy Cruz C 3 195
Gods ≈ C 12 158
Gods Lake D 11 158
Godthåb (Nuuk) D 22 150
Godwin Austen, Mount see K2 ʌ B 3 122
Goéland, Lac au ◻ A 3 160
Goélands, Lac aux ◻ A 11 160
Goeree ✦¹ C 2 69
Goes C 2 69
Goff G 5 202
Goffstown C 7 164
Gogrial F 2 202

Goiânia B 6 194
Goiás A 5 194
Goiás ◻³ G 8 190
Goiatuba B 6 194
Goirle C 4 69
Gois, Le ◄⁵ F 4 78
Gojam ◻³ E 4 202
Gojeb ≈ F 4 202
Gojra C 2 122
Gökçeada I B 6 106
Gökçekaya Baraji ◻¹ B 9 106
Gökçen C 7 106
Gökova Körfezi (Kerme, Gulf of) c D 7 106
Göksu ≈ D 5 118
Göktepe J 20 110
Gokwe F 4 204
Golāghāt D 6 122
Gołańcz B 9 96
Goldbey B 4 82
Gold Bridge F 10 156
Gold Coast (Southport) A 9 144
Gold Coast ±² E 4 200
Golden F 13 156
Golden Bay c D 4 146
Golden City D 1 170
Golden Ears Provincial Park ♦ G 10 156
Golden Gate Highlands National Park ♦ E 8 206
Golden Spike National Historic Site ♦ E 7 178
Goldfield C 6 182
Gold River G 8 156
Goldsand Lake ◻ B 6 168
Goldsboro B 6 168
Goldsworthy G 5 140
Goldthwaite E 4 172
Goleniów B 8 96
Goleta A 4 182
Golfito F 4 186
Golfo Aranci H 5 92
Gölhisar D 8 106
Goliad F 5 172
Golina B 10 96
Gölköy B 7 118
Gollnow see Goleniów B 8 96
Gölmarmara C 7 106
Golodnaja Guba, ozero ◻ C 20 108
Golovin D 13 154
Golpāyegān F 14 118
Golyšmanovo H 28 108
Gomati ≈ D 4 122
Gombe C 7 200
Gombi C 7 200
Gomel (Homel') C 7 110
Gómez Palacio E 7 184
Gomišhān D 15 118
Gommern D 8 98
Gonābād D 8 118
Gonaïves D 6 186
Gonarezhou National Park ♦ G 5 206
Gonâve, Golfe de la c D 6 186
Gonâve, Île de la I D 6 186
Gonbad-e Qābūs D 16 118
Gonda D 4 122
Gondal E 2 122
Gonder E 4 202
Gonder ◻³ E 4 202
Gondia E 4 122
Gondomar C 2 86
Gönen B 7 106
Gonesse C 3 69
Gong'an C 10 130
Gongbo'gyamda D 6 122
Gongcheng F 10 130
Gongga Shan (Minya Konka) ʌ D 5 130
Gonghe H 3 128
Gongola ≈ C 7 200
Gongolon C 6 144
Gongxi E 12 130
Gongxian A 11 130
Gongzhuling E 15 128
Goñi C 9 195
Goniri C 7 200
Gonnesa F 2 90
Gonzales, Ca., U.S. D 2 182
Gonzales, La., U.S. G 3 170
Gonzales, Tx., U.S. F 5 172
González F 10 184
Goochland E 5 162
Goodeve F 7 158
Good Hope, Cape of ► G 2 206
Goodhope Bay c C 13 154
Good Hope Mountain ʌ F 9 156
Goodhouse E 3 206
Gooding D 6 178
Goodland F 4 174
Goodman C 5 102
Goodnews Bay G 13 154
Goodrich G 1 170
Goodwater F 5 170
Goole D 7 72
Googowi D 5 144
Goolgowi D 5 144
Goondiwindi B 8 144
Goongarrie L 6 140
Goongarrie National Park ♦ L 6 140
Goor B 5 69
Goose Creek C 4 168
Goose Green n 18 193b
Goose Lake ◻ E 3 178
Goose Lake ◻ D 8 158
Gooty F 3 122
Göppingen D 6 100
Goqên D 3 130
Góra C 9 96
Gorakhpur D 4 122
Gorczański Park Narodowy ♦ D 11 96
Gorda, Punta ►, Cuba C 4 186
Gorda, Punta ►, Ca., U.S. B 1 180
Gordon F 5 170
Gordon ≈ D 3 174
Gordon, Lake ◻¹ j 12 145a
Gordon Indian Reserve ◄⁴ F 6 158
Gore, Austl. B 8 144
Gore, N.Z. G 2 146
Gorebridge E 5 74
Goreloe C 12 110
Gore Range ʌ B 5 176
Goreville D 4 170
Gorgān D 16 118
Gorgān ≈ D 16 118
Gorges D 2 206
Gorgol ◻⁵ D 2 200

Gorgol el Abioḍ ≈ F 2 198
Gorgota C 8 104
Gorham C 8 164
Gori H 14 110
Gorica see Gorizia D 2 69
Goricy H 12 108
Gorinchem C 3 69
Goris J 15 110
Göritz see Górzyca D 11 98
Goriza (Gorica) D 9 92
Goriza ◻⁶ D 9 92
Gorj ◻³ C 7 104
Gorkhā D 4 122
Gor'kovskoe vodochranilišče ◻¹ G 14 108
Gorky see Nižnij Novgorod H 16 108
Gorlice D 11 96
Görlitz E 11 98
Gorna Orjahovica D 8 104
Gornjackij C 26 108
Gornja Radgona D 7 102
Gornji Milanovac C 6 104
Gorno-Altajsk D 11 114
Gornopravdinsk F 28 108
Gornozavodsk G 23 108
Gornye Ključi B 4 126
Gorodec, Russia H 15 108
Gorodec, Russia C 14 66
Gorodišče see Haradzišča J 12 64
Gorocino D 14 66
Goroka N 13 124
Gorontalo E 8 134
Górowo Iławeckie A 11 96
Gorseinon F 2 72
Gór Stołowych, Park Narodowy ♦ C 9 96
Gort C 3 75
Görz see Gorizia D 9 92
Gorzów Wielkopolski B 8 96
Gosford D 8 144
Gosforth C 3 72
Goshen, N.S., Can. F 13 160
Goshen, In., U.S. B 6 170
Goshen, N.Y., U.S. E 4 164
Goshute Indian Reservation ◄⁴ C 1 176
Goslar E 7 98
Gosnells M 4 140
Gosport, Eng., U.K. G 5 72
Gosport, In., U.S. C 5 170
Gossas C 1 200
Gossau C 7 82
Gossinga C 2 202
Gostivar E 6 104
Gostyń C 9 96
Gostynin B 10 96
Göta ≈ D 6 66
Göta kanal ◻ C 7 66
Göteborg (Gothenburg) D 6 66
Gotha F 7 98
Gothenburg see Göteborg, Swe. D 6 66
Gothenburg, Ne., U.S. E 4 174
Gotland ◻³ D 9 66
Gotland I D 8 66
Gotō-rettō II H 2 126
Gôtsu G 4 126
Göttingen E 6 98
Gottorf, Schloss ⊥ B 6 98
Gottvaldov see Zlín A 9 102
Götzis C 1 102
Goubangzi F 13 128
Goubcne A 8 200
Gouda C 3 69
Goudoumaria C 7 200
Gouéké D 3 200
Gough Island I I 10 60
Gouin, Réservoir ◻¹ D 6 160
Goulais ≈ H 16 158
Goulburn E 7 144
Goulburn ≈ F 5 144
Goulburn River National Park ♦ D 7 144
Gould City B 6 166
Gouldsboro State Park ♦ E 3 164
Goulmima C 4 198
Goumbati ʌ² C 2 200
Gouménissa B 5 106
Goundam B 4 200
Gound D 8 200
Gounou-Gaya D 7 200
Gourbassi C 2 200
Gourcy C 4 200
Gouré H 2 200
Gourits ≈ H 4 206
Gouro C 8 200
Gouverneur B 4 164
Govenlock G 17 156
Governador Valadares C 10 194
Governor Dodge State Park ♦ D 3 166
Govi-Altay ◻³ D 2 128
Govind Ballabh Pant Sāgar ◻¹ E 4 122
Gowanda B 4 162
Goya A 8 195
Göyçay I 15 110
Goz Beïda D 9 200
Gozo I H 4 94
Graaff-Reinet G 5 206
Graafwater G 3 206
Grabow C 6 98
Grabowiec C 12 96
Gračanica C 5 104
Gračanica, Manastir ◻ D 6 104
Graçay E 8 78
Graceville C 6 174
Gracias a Dios, Cabo ► E 5 196
Graciosa I E 5 196a
Gradačac C 5 104
Gradaús E 5 190
Grad Sofija ◻³ D 7 104
Grady B 5 172
Grafenau B 8 100
Gräfenhainichen E 9 98
Grafham Water ◻¹ E 9 72
Grafing bei München B 9 100
Grafton, Austl. B 9 144
Grafton ◻⁶ B 9 144
Grafton B 7 164
Grafton Lakes State Park ♦ D 5 164
Graham, N.C., U.S. C 5 168
Graham, Tx., U.S. A 1 172
Graham, Mount ʌ F 3 176
Graham Island I E 6 156
Graham Land ◄¹ C 2 208
Grahamstown G 5 206
Grajagan j 22 135b
Grajaú D 9 190
Grajaú ≈ D 9 190

Grajewo B 12 96
Gram C 2 68
Gramado A 12 195
Gramat D 5 80
Grammichele G 4 94
Grammont see Geraardsbergen D 2 69
Grampian Mountains ʌ D 5 74
Grampians National Park ♦ F 4 144
Gran see Esztergom C 10 102
Grana E 3 92
Granada, Nic. F 3 186
Granada, Spain G 7 86
Granada, Mn., U.S. D 7 174
Granada ◻⁶ D 4 84
Granadella see La Granadella C 5 88
Granby D 5 172
Granby, Qc., Can. F 7 160
Granby, Ct., U.S. E 6 164
Granby G 12 156
Gran Canaria I j 15 85b
Gran Chaco ◄¹ D 7 192
Grand ≈, On., Can. H 4 160
Grand ≈, Mi., U.S. D 6 166
Grand ≈, S.D., U.S. C 2 170
Grand ≈ C 2 170
Grand, East Fork ≈ C 1 170
Grand, North Fork ≈ C 3 174
Grandas A 4 86
Grand Bahama I F 5 168
Grand Ballon ʌ C 5 82
Grand Bank E 15 160
Grand-Bassam D 4 200
Grand Bay F 10 160
Grand Beach F 10 158
Grand Béréby E 3 200
Grand Bruit E 14 160
Grand Calumet, Île du I A 2 164
Grand Canal (Da Yunhe) ≈, China F 7 124
Grand Canal ≈, Ire. C 4 75
Grand Canyon D 2 176
Grand Canyon V D 2 176
Grand Canyon National Park ♦ D 2 176
Grand Cayman I D 4 186
Grand Centre D 16 156
Grand Chenier G 2 170
Grand Coulee Dam ◄⁶ A 4 178
Grand-Couronne C 6 78
Grande ≈, Bol. G 6 190
Grande ≈, Braz. F 10 190
Grande ≈, Braz. G 9 190
Grande ≈, Chile B 2 195
Grande ≈, Ven. F 9 186
Grande, Bahía c J 6 192
Grande, Boca ≈¹ C 6 196
Grande, Ilha I B 10 96
Grande, Rio (Bravo) ≈ F 7 152
Grande-Anse E 7 160
Grande Chartreuse, Couvent de la ⊥ E 3 82
Grande de Manacapuru, Lago ◻ D 6 190
Grande de Santiago ≈ G 7 184
Grande do Gurupá, Ilha I D 8 190
Grand Erg de Bilma ◄² B 7 200
Grand Erg Occidental ◄² C 5 198
Grand Erg Oriental ◄² C 5 198
Grande Prairie D 12 156
Grande Rivière, La ≈ B 4 160
Grande Ronde ≈ C 2 178
Grandes, Salinas ≈ E 7 192
Grand Falls (Grand Sault) E 10 160
Grand Falls-Windsor D 16 160
Grandfield C 4 172
Grand Forks, B.C., Can. G 12 156
Grand Forks, N.D., U.S. B 6 174
Grand-Fougeray E 5 78
Grand Haven D 5 166
Grandin, Lac ◻ D 9 150
Grand Island E 5 174
Grand Isle H 4 170
Grand Isle ◻⁶ B 5 164
Grand Junction, Co., U.S. C 4 176
Grand Junction, Tn., U.S. E 4 170
Grand Lake ◻, N.B., Can. F 11 160
Grand Lake ◻, N.A. h 13 163a
Grand Lake (Grand Lac) ◻, N.B., Can. F 11 160
Grand Lake ◻, La., U.S. H 3 170
Grand Ledge B 1 162
Grand Manan Island I B 3 166
Grand Marais B 3 166
Grand-Mère E 6 160
Grand Portage H 14 158
Grand Portage Indian Reservation ◄⁴ B 3 166
Grand Portage National Monument ♦ B 4 166
Grand Prairie C 5 172
Grand Rapids, Mb., Can. E 9 158
Grand Rapids, Mi., U.S. D 5 166
Grand Rhône ≈ G 2 82
Grands-Jardins, Parc de conservation des ♦ g 11 163a
Grand Teton ʌ D 8 178
Grand Teton National Park ♦ D 8 178
Grand Traverse Bay c C 6 166
Grand Turk C 7 186
Grandview, Mo., U.S. C 1 170
Grandview, Wa., U.S. B 3 178
Grand Wash Cliffs ±⁴ D 2 176
Graneros C 2 195
Grangemouth A 3 72
Granger, Wy., U.S. E 8 178
Granger Draw ≈ E 3 172
Granges see Grenchen C 5 82
Grängesberg B 7 66
Granite City C 7 170
Granite Downs I 1 142
Granite Peak ʌ¹ D 6 178
Granite Range ʌ E 4 178

Gran Paradiso ʌ D 3 92
Gran Paradiso, Parco Nazionale del ♦ D 3 92
Gran Rio ≈ C 7 190
Gransee C 10 98
Grant D 6 166
Grantham E 6 72
Grants E 5 176
Grants Pass D 2 178
Grantsville D 3 162
Granum G 15 156
Granville, Fr. D 5 78
Granville, Oh., U.S. C 2 162
Granville Lake C 8 158
Granvin B 3 66
Gras, Lac de ◻ D 10 150
Grasmere D 7 206
Grassano D 6 94
Grasse G 4 82
Grasset, Lac ◻ D 4 160
Grasslands National Park ♦ G 18 156
Grass Patch M 6 140
Grass River Provincial Park ♦ D 8 158
Grass Valley A 2 182
Grassy Lake G 16 156
Grästorp C 6 66
Graubünden ◻³ C 5 82
Graudenz see Grudziądz B 10 96
Graulhet E 5 80
Gravelines A 9 78
Gravenhage, 's- see 's-Gravenhage B 3 69
Gravenhurst B 4 160
Gravesend, Eng., U.K. F 7 72
Gravesend, Austl. B 8 144
Gravina G 4 94
Gravina in Puglia D 6 94
Gray, Fr. C 3 82
Gray, Ga., U.S. C 3 168
Grayling A 1 162
Grays F 7 72
Grays Harbor c B 1 178
Grayson G 5 172
Grays Peak ʌ C 6 176
Graz C 7 102
Grdelica D 7 104
Great Alföld see Alföld B 7 90
Great Artesian Basin ≈¹ H 5 142
Great Australian Bight c F 6 138
Great Barrier Island I B 5 146
Great Barrier Reef ◄² D 8 142
Great Barrier Reef Marine Park ♦ E 9 142
Great Barrington D 5 164
Great Basin ≈¹ D 4 152
Great Basin National Park ♦ C 1 176
Great Bear ≈ D 32 154
Great Bear Lake ◻ C 34 154
Great Bend F 5 174
Great Bitter Lake ◻ G 5 118
Great Britain I E 8 70
Great Dismal Swamp ≈ A 6 168
Great Divide Basin ≈¹ E 9 178
Great Dividing Range ʌ H 8 142
Great Exuma I C 5 186
Great Falls, Mt., U.S. B 8 178
Great Falls, S.C., U.S. B 4 168
Great Fish ≈ G 7 206
Great Grimsby see Grimsby D 6 72
Great Himalaya National Park ♦ C 3 122
Great Inagua I C 6 186
Great Indian Desert (Thar Desert) ◄² D 1 122
Great Karoo ≈¹ G 4 206
Great Kei ≈ G 7 206
Great La Cloche Island I G 7 160
Great Lake ◻¹ i 12 145a
Great Malvern E 4 72
Great Miami ≈ D 1 162
Great Nicobar I H 6 122
Great Ouse ≈ E 7 72
Great Pee Dee ≈ C 5 168
Great Plains ≈¹ B 3 172
Great Ruaha ≈ D 6 204
Great Sacandaga Lake ◻ C 4 164
Great Saint Bernard Pass ⤫ E 5 82
Great Salt Lake ◻ C 4 178
Great Salt Lake Desert ◄² B 2 176
Great Sand Dunes National Monument ♦ D 6 176
Great Sandy Desert ◄² C 4 140
Great Sandy National Park ♦ H 11 142
Great Sankey D 4 72
Great Scarcies (Kolenté) ≈ D 2 200
Great Slave Lake ◻ D 10 150
Great Smoky Mountains ʌ C 4 168
Great Smoky Mountains National Park ♦ A 3 168
Great Tenasserim ≈ H 4 132
Great Valley ≈¹ A 3 168
Great Victoria Desert ◄² E 5 140
Great Wall ◻¹ L 8 192
Great Wall see Chang Cheng ◄⁶ G 8 128
Great Yarmouth E 8 72
Great Zab ≈ C 11 118
Gréboun ʌ B 6 200
Greece ◻¹ H 12 62
Greeley, Co., U.S. E 2 174
Greeley, Ks., U.S. C 5 174
Greeley, Ne., U.S. E 7 174
Green ≈, N.D., U.S. C 1 174
Green ≈ C 1 174
Green Bay c C 4 166
Green Bay C 4 166
Green Brier c C 5 162
Greenbush A 6 170
Greencastle C 3 170
Green Cove Springs D 3 168
Greene D 4 166
Greeneville C 4 168

Greenfield, Oh., U.S. D 2 162
Greenisland B 6 75
Green Lake ◻ D 18 156
Greenland (Kalaallit Nunaat) ◻² B 15 148
Greenland Basin ◄¹ C 23 61
Greenland Sea ≈² C 23 61
Green Mountains ʌ C 6 164
Greenock B 2 72
Greenough K 3 140
Greenough ≈ K 3 140
Green River, Ut., U.S. C 3 176
Green River, Wy., U.S. E 9 178
Greensboro, Md., U.S. H 3 164
Greensboro, N.C., U.S. C 5 168
Greensburg, In., U.S. C 6 170
Greensburg, Ky., U.S. C 6 170
Greensburg, Pa., U.S. D 6 162
Greenvale E 7 142
Green Valley G 3 176
Greenville, Lib. E 3 200
Greenville, Al., U.S. G 5 170
Greenville, Il., U.S. C 4 170
Greenville, Me., U.S. h 12 163a
Greenville, Ms., U.S. F 3 170
Greenville, N.C., U.S. B 6 168
Greenville, Oh., U.S. B 6 170
Greenville, S.C., U.S. B 3 168
Greenville, Tx., U.S. D 5 172
Greenwater Lake Provincial Park ♦ E 7 158
Greenwich, Ct., U.S. E 5 164
Greenwich, N.Y., U.S. C 5 164
Greenwood, B.C., Can. G 12 156
Greenwood, Ms., U.S. F 3 170
Greenwood, S.C., U.S. B 3 168
Greenwood Lake ◻ E 4 164
Greers Ferry Lake ◻¹ E 3 98
Grefrath E 3 98
Gregbe D 3 200
Grégoire Lake Indian Reserve ◄⁴ C 16 156
Gregório ≈ E 4 190
Gregory G 5 172
Gregory ≈ C 6 144
Gregory, Lake ◻, Austl. B 2 144
Gregory, Lake ◻, Austl. I 5 140
Gregory, Lake ◻ F 9 140
Gregory National Park ♦ E 11 140
Gregory Range ʌ E 6 142
Greifenhagen see Gryfino B 8 96
Greifswald B 10 98
Greifswalder Bodden c B 10 98
Greiz E 9 100
Gremiha B 13 108
Gremjačinsk G 22 108
Grenada, Ms., U.S. F 4 170
Grenada ◻¹ H 13 148
Grenada Lake ◻¹ F 4 170
Grenadines II E 9 186
Grenchen C 5 82
Grenen ► B 2 68
Grenfell, Austl. D 7 144
Grenfell, Sk., Can. F 7 158
Grenoble E 3 82
Gréoux-les-Bains F 2 88
Gresham C 2 178
Gresik, Indon. k 21 135b
Gresik, Indon. k 21 135b
Gressåmoen Nasjonalpark ♦ D 5 64
Gresten C 7 102
Gretna H 3 170
Greve, Den. C 5 68
Greve, Italy F 7 92
Grevelingendam ◄⁵ C 3 69
Greven B 4 98
Grevená B 5 106
Grevenbroich E 3 98
Grevesmühlen C 8 98
Greve Strand C 5 68
Grey ≈ E 15 160
Greybull D 9 178
Greylock, Mount ʌ D 5 164
Greymouth E 3 146
Grey Range ʌ I 6 142
Greytown, N.Z. D 5 146
Greytown, S. Afr. D 5 206
Gribanovskij H 6 110
Gribbell Island I C 7 156
Gridley D 2 182
Griesheim C 5 100
Griffin, Sk., Can. G 7 158
Griffin, Ga., U.S. C 2 168
Griffith E 5 144
Grignan F 2 82
Grigny E 4 70
Grigoriopol B 10 104
Grijalva (Cuilco) ≈ J 13 184
Grillenthal D 1 206
Grim, Cape ► i 11 145a
Grimari C 2 202
Grimbergen D 3 69
Grimma D 10 98
Grimmen B 10 98
Grimnitzsee ◻ D 10 98
Grimsby D 6 72
Grimsel Pass ⤫ D 6 82
Grímsstaðir m 22 64a
Grimsvötn ʌ¹ n 19 64a
Grindavík n 19 64a
Grindsted B 2 68
Grinnell Peninsula ►¹ A 14 150
Gripsholm slott ⊥ C 2 66
Griqualand East ◻⁹ F 8 206
Griqualand West ◻⁹ E 5 206
Grischun see Graubünden ◻³ C 5 82
Gris-Nez, Cap ► B 8 78
Grisons see Graubünden ◻³ C 5 82
Griswold A 4 174
Grizzly Bear Mountain ʌ D 34 154
Grizzly Bear and Lead Man Indian Reserve ◄⁴ E 18 156
Grjazi C 11 110
Grjazovec G 14 108
Grobblershoop E 4 206
Groblersdal E 5 206
Gröditz E 10 98
Grodno see Hrodna F 11 66
Grodzisk Mazowiecki B 11 96
Groen ≈ F 3 206
Groenlo C 6 69
Grójec C 11 96
Grombalia H 5 94
Gronau, Ger. D 4 98
Gronau, Ger. D 4 98
Grong D 5 64

Groningen ◻³ A 5 69
Groom C 3 172
Groot ≈ G 6 206
Groot-Berg ≈ G 3 206
Grootdraaidem ◻¹ D 8 206
Groote Eylandt I B 3 142
Grootfontein F 2 204
Grootpan D 7 206
Groot-Swartberge ʌ G 5 206
Grootvloer ≈ E 4 206
Gropeni C 9 104
Gros Morne ʌ D 15 160
Gros Morne National Park ♦ D 14 160
Grossenhain E 10 98
Grossenkneten D 5 98
Grosser Arber ʌ C 10 100
Grosser Schulerloch ◻ D 8 100
Grosseto G 7 92
Grossglockner ʌ C 4 102
Grosshansdorf C 7 98
Grossostheim C 6 100
Grossräschen E 10 98
Grossvenediger ʌ C 4 102
Gross-Zimmern C 5 100
Grosvenor, Lake ◻ G 17 154
Groton C 5 174
Grottaglie D 7 94
Grottaminarda C 5 94
Grottammare B 3 94
Grouard Mission D 13 156
Groundhog ≈ D 2 160
Grove D 1 170
Grove City D 2 162
Grove Hill G 5 170
Grover City H 2 170
Groveton E 7 164
Growa Point ► B 3 200
Groznyj H 14 110
Grubišno Polje E 9 102
Grudziądz B 10 96
Grugliasco D 3 92
Gruia C 7 104
Grumo Appula C 6 94
Grums C 6 66
Grüna B 9 100
Grünberg B 5 100
Grundy Center D 2 166
Grundy Lake Provincial Park ♦ C 8 166
Grunthal A 6 174
Gruzdžiai D 11 66
Gryfice B 8 96
Gryfino B 8 96
Grythyttan C 6 66
Grytviken q 21 193c
Guacanayabo, Golfo de c C 5 186
Guadalajara, Mex. G 8 184
Guadalajara, Spain D 7 86
Guadalajara ◻⁶ C 6 86
Guadalcanal I A 13 138
Guadalimar ≈ F 7 86
Guadalmena ≈ F 2 88
Guadalmez ≈ C 4 86
Guadalquivir ≈ H 4 86
Guadalquivir, Marismas del ≈ H 4 86
Guadalupe, Mex. E 9 184
Guadalupe, Ca., U.S. E 3 182
Guadalupe ≈ F 5 172
Guadalupe Mountains National Park ♦ G 6 176
Guadalupe Peak ʌ E 1 172
Guadarrama ≈ D 8 86
Guadeloupe ◻² H 13 148
Guadeloupe Channel ◻ o 21 187e
Guadeloupe Passage ⥥ D 9 186
Guadiana ≈ H 4 86
Guadiana Menor ≈ G 1 88
Guadix G 1 88
Guafo, Isla I H 5 192
Guaíba C 12 195
Guaíra F 3 194
Guajará-Mirim F 5 190
Guaje, Laguna del ◻ E 8 184
Gualaco E 8 186
Gualdo Tadino F 7 92
Gualeguay F 8 195
Gualeguaychú G 8 195
Gualicho, Salina del ≈ H 6 192
Guam ◻² E 18 138
Guaminí E 5 195
Guamúchil E 5 184
Gua Musang L 5 132
Guanabacoa C 4 186
Guanajuato G 9 184
Guanajuato ◻³ G 9 184
Guanambi F 10 190
Guanare E 8 186
Guandacol A 3 195
Guane D 3 186
Guang'an E 12 130
Guangchang F 13 130
Guangde E 12 130
Guangdong ◻³ C 12 130
Guangfeng F 13 130
Guangji D 12 130
Guangnan B 7 130
Guangshui E 11 130
Guangyuan E 8 130
Guangze F 13 130
Guangzhou (Canton) C 11 130
Guanling B 7 130
Guánica j 15 187b
Guanta F 9 186
Guantánamo C 6 186
Guantao H 10 128
Guanting Shuiku ◻¹ G 10 128
Guanxian, China H 10 128
Guanxian, China H 10 128
Guanyun H 10 128
Guapí F 3 194
Guapiaçu E 6 194
Guaporé (Itenes) ≈ F 6 190
Guaqui G 6 190
Guaranda D 2 190
Guarapari E 8 194
Guarapuava B 11 195
Guaratinguetá A 12 195
Guarda F 3 86
Guardafui, Cape → see Gwardafuy, Raas ► F 9 204
Guárico ≈ F 8 186
Guarujá A 13 195
Guasave E 5 184
Guarenas F 8 186

Glacier — Guarenas

∟ Waterfall   ⌆ Strait   c Bay, Gulf   ◻ Lake   ≈ Swamp   ⧈ Ice Feature   ⊤ Other Hydrographic Feature   ✦ Submarine Feature   ◻ Political Unit   ◗ Cultural Institution   ⊥ Historical Site   ♦ Recreational Site   ⊕ Airport   ▣ Military Installation   ◄ Miscellaneous

Map
Name · Ref. · Page

Symbols in the index entries represent the broad categories identified in the key at the right. Symbols with superior numbers (✴¹) identify subcategories (see complete key on page 242).

∧ Mountain · ✴ Mountains · ✕ Pass · V Valley · ≈ Plain · ✶ Cape · I Island · ∐ Islands · ± Other Topographic Feature · ≈ River · ≈ Canal

Hennenman — Igara Paraná

Name | Map Ref. | Page

Hennenman E 7 206
Hennigsdorf D 10 98
Henniker C 7 164
Henning E 4 170
Henrietta D 4 172
Henrietta Maria, Cape ≻ D 17 158
Henry B 4 170
Henry, Cape ≻ E 6 162
Henry Cowell Redwoods State Park ♦ C 1 182
Henry Kater, Cape ≻ C 19 150
Henry W. Coe State Park ♦ C 2 182
Henstedt-Ulzburg C 6 98
Hentiy ▫[3] C 8 128
Henty E 6 144
Henzada F 2 132
Heppenheim C 5 100
Hepu H 9 130
Heqing A 5 132
Hequ G 8 128
Héraðsflói ⊂ m 23 64a
Hera Lacinia, Tempio di ⊥ E 7 94
Herāt D 9 116
Hérault ▫[3] G 5 76
Herbert F 3 146
Herbert Hoover National Historic Site ♦ B 3 170
Herbignac E 4 78
Herblay D 9 78
Herborn B 5 100
Herchmer C 11 158
Herculaneum see Ercolano ⊥ D 4 94
Hércules C 7 184
Herðubreið ∧[1] m 22 64a
Hereford, Eng., U.K. E 4 72
Hereford, Tx., U.S. C 2 172
Herefordshire ▫[6] E 4 72
Hereke B 8 106
Herencia E 7 86
Herent D 3 69
Herentals C 3 69
Herford D 5 98
Héricourt C 4 82
Herington F 6 174
Herisau C 7 82
Herkimer C 3 164
Herkimer ▫[6] C 4 164
Herlen see Kerulen ≃ C 6 124
Herlong B 3 180
Herman E 6 174
Hermanavičy E 13 66
Hermanns-Denkmal ⊥ E 5 98
Hermansverk B 3 66
Hermansville C 5 166
Hermidale C 6 144
Hermiston C 4 178
Hermitage E 15 160
Hermit Islands II M 13 124
Hermon, Mount ∧ C 5 120
Hermosillo C 4 184
Hermsdorf F 8 98
Hermus see Gediz ≃ C 7 106
Hernando, Arg. C 5 195
Hernando, Ms., U.S. E 4 170
Herne E 4 98
Herne Bay F 8 72
Herning B 1 68
Heron Lake D 7 174
Herrenberg D 5 100
Herrenchiemsee, Schloss ⊥ E 9 100
Herrin D 4 170
Herring Cove I 28 154
Herrljunga C 6 66
Herschel F 7 206
Herscher B 4 170
Hershey F 2 164
Herstal D 4 69
Herten E 4 98
Hertford F 6 72
Hertfordshire ▫[6] F 6 72
Hertsa A 9 104
Herval d'Oeste G 5 194
Hervey Bay ⊂ H 11 142
Herzberg E 10 98
Herzberg am Harz C 5 96
Herzebrock E 5 98
Herzliyya E 3 120
Herzogenaurach C 7 100
Herzogenrath F 3 98
Hesdin B 8 78
Heshan G 9 130
Heshun H 9 128
Hesperia F 6 182
Hess ≃ E 28 154
Hessen ▫[3] C 5 96
Hesso D 1 144
Heswall D 3 72
Heta ≃ B 12 114
Heṭauṇḍā D 4 122
Hetch Hetchy Aqueduct ≌[1] C 2 182
Hetch Hetchy Reservoir ⊜[1] C 4 182
Het Loo, Paleis ◗ B 4 69
Hettinger B 3 174
Hettstedt E 8 98
Heung (Huang) ≃ F 5 132
Heusweiler E 5 69
Heuvelton B 3 164
Heves B 6 104
Heves ▫[3] B 6 104
Hexham C 4 72
Hexian F 10 130
Hexigten Qi E 11 128
Heyang I 7 128
Heyrieux E 3 82
Heysham C 3 72
Heyuan G 12 130
Heze I 10 128
Hialeah G 4 168
Hian C 4 200
Hiawassee B 3 168
Hibbard E 6 160
Hibbing B 2 166
Hickory, Ms., U.S. F 4 170
Hickory, N.C., U.S. B 4 168
Hickory Run State Park ♦ F 3 164
Hicks, Point ≻ F 7 144
Hicks Bay B 7 146
Hico D 5 172
Hidalgo, Mex. D 9 184
Hidalgo, Mex. E 10 184
Hidalgo ▫[3] G 10 184
Hidalgo del Parral D 7 184
Hieflau C 6 102
Hierapolis see Pamukkale ⊥ D 8 106
Higashihiroshima G 4 126
Higashiōsaka G 5 126
Higgins B 3 172
Highland, Ca., U.S. F 6 182
Highland, In., U.S. B 5 170
Highland ▫[6] C 4 74
Highland Home G 5 170
Highland Park, Il., U.S. A 5 170
Highland Park, Tx., U.S. D 5 172
Highlands H 1 170
Highland Springs E 5 162
High Level B 13 156
High Peak ✜[1] D 5 72
High Point B 4 168
High Point ∧ E 4 164
High Point State Park ♦ E 4 164
High River F 14 156
High Rock F 5 168
Highrock Indian Reserve ✜[4] D 8 158
Highrock Lake ⊜, Mb., Can. D 8 158
Highrock Lake ⊜, Sk., Can. C 19 156
High Rock Lake ⊜[1] B 4 168
High Wycombe F 6 72
Higüero, Punta ≻ j 14 187b
Higüey D 7 186
Hiiraan ▫[3] G 6 202
Hiiumaa I C 11 66
Híjar C 4 88
Hikone G 6 126
Hikueru I[1] E 13 136
Hilda F 16 156
Hildburghausen B 7 100
Hilden C 5 69
Hildesheim D 6 98
Hill City, Mn., U.S. B 2 166
Hill City, S.D., U.S. D 3 174
Hillerød C 5 68
Hilliard D 4 168
Hillingdon ▫[6] F 6 72
Hill Island Lake ⊜ A 17 156
Hills D 6 174
Hillsboro, Ks., U.S. A 5 172
Hillsboro, N.H., U.S. C 7 164
Hillsboro, Oh., U.S. D 2 162
Hillsborough ▫[6] C 7 164
Hillston D 5 144
Hilo j 11 181a
Hilok B 6 124
Hilok ≃ B 5 124
Hílos (Delos) ⊥ D 6 106
Hilovo D 14 66
Hilton Head Island I C 4 168
Hiltrup E 4 98
Hilversum B 4 69
Hima A 3 168
Himāchal Pradesh ▫[3] C 3 122
Himalayas ⋏ D 4 122
Himatnagar E 2 122
Himeji G 5 126
Ḥimş E 7 118
Hinchinbrook Entrance ⩌ F 21 154
Hinchinbrook Island I E 8 142
Hinckley, Eng., U.K. E 5 72
Hinckley, Il., U.S. B 4 170
Hindman E 2 162
Hindmarsh, Lake ⊜ E 3 144
Hindu Kush ⋏ B 2 122
Hindupur G 3 122
Hinesville D 4 168
Hinganghāt E 3 122
Hingham D 8 164
Hingol ≃ E 10 116
Hingoli F 3 122
Hınıs C 9 118
Hinnøya I B 7 64
Hinojosa del Duque F 5 86
Hinsdale G 18 156
Hinterrhein ≃ D 7 82
Hinton, Ab., Can. E 13 156
Hinton, Ok., U.S. C 4 172
Hīrākud Reservoir ⊜[1] E 4 122
Hiram C 8 164
Hiraman ≃ H 4 202
Hirara H 8 124
Hiriyūr G 3 122
Hirnyk C 13 96
Hirosaki D 8 126
Hiroshima G 4 126
Hiroshima ▫[3] G 4 126
Hirschaid C 8 100
Hirson C 11 78
Hisār D 3 122
Hispaniola I D 6 186
Hita H 3 126
Hitachi F 8 126
Hitchin F 6 72
Hitchins D 2 162
Hither Hills State Park ♦ E 7 164
Hitoyoshi H 3 126
Hitra I E 4 64
Hiwannee G 4 170
Hiwassee ≃ B 2 168
Hixson E 6 170
Ḥiyyon, Naḥal ≃ I 4 120
Hjälmaren ⊜ C 7 66
Hjo C 7 66
Hjørring A 2 68
Hkakabo Razi ∧ D 3 130
Hkok (Kok) ≃ H 4 130
Hlathikulu D 9 206
Hlohovec B 9 102
Hlotse E 7 206
Hluboká ⊥ C 11 100
Hluboká nad Vltavou C 11 100
Hluhluwe E 10 206
Hluhluwe Game Reserve ✜[4] E 9 206
Hlukhiv D 8 110
Hluti D 9 206
Hlybokae E 13 66
Ho D 5 200
Hoa Binh D 7 132
Hoanib ≃ F 1 204
Hobart j 12 145a
Hobbs D 2 172
Hobbs Coast ⩟[2] D 31 208
Hobe Sound F 4 168
Hobro B 2 68
Hobyo F 6 202
Hocalar C 8 106
Höchberg C 6 100
Hochfeld A 2 206
Hochheim B 5 100
Ho Chi Minh City (Saigon) I 8 132
Hochkönig ∧ C 5 102
Höchst C 6 100
Höchstadt an der Aisch C 7 100
Hockenheim A 6 82
Ḥôḍ ✜[1] F 3 198
Hodeida see Al-Ḥudaydah E 5 202
Hodge F 2 170
Hodgeville F 18 156
Hodh ech Chargui ▫[3] F 3 198
Hodh el Gharbi ▫[3] F 2 198
Hódmezővásárhely B 6 104
Hodmo ≃ E 6 202
Hodna, Chott el ⊜ B 5 198
Hodonín B 9 102
Hodovariha B 20 108
Hoedspruit C 9 206
Hoek van Holland (Hook of Holland) C 2 69
Hoeryŏng-ŭp E 17 128
Hoeyang-ŭp G 16 128
Hof, Ger. B 8 100
Hof, Ice. m 23 64a
Hoffman C 7 174
Hofgeismar E 6 98
Hofmeyr F 6 206
Hofors B 8 66
Hofsjökull ⊓ m 21 64a
Hōfu H 3 126
Höganäs D 6 66
Hogansville F 6 170
Hoge Veluwe, Nationaal Park de ♦ B 4 69
Hoggar ⋏ E 6 198
Hohenau an der March B 8 102
Hohenems C 1 102
Hohenmölsen E 8 98
Hohensyburg ⊥ E 4 98
Hohenwald E 5 170
Hohenwarte-Stausee ⊜[1] B 8 100
Hohe Tauern ⋏ D 4 102
Hohhot F 8 128
Hohoe D 5 200
Hoh Xil Shan ⋏ B 5 122
Hoi An G 9 132
Hoi Xuan D 7 132
Hojāi D 6 122
Høje Taastrup C 5 68
Hojniki D 7 110
Hōjō H 4 126
Hokah D 3 166
Hokitika E 3 146
Hokkaidō ▫[3] C 9 126
Hokkaidō I C 9 126
Hokksund C 4 66
Hola Prystan' F 8 110
Holbæk C 4 68
Holbeach E 7 72
Holberg F 7 156
Holbrook E 3 176
Holden, Mo., U.S. C 1 170
Holden, W.V., U.S. E 2 162
Holder E 3 168
Holderness ≻[1] D 6 72
Holešov A 9 102
Holguín C 5 186
Holíč B 9 102
Hollabrunn B 8 102
Holladay E 8 178
Holland, Mi., U.S. D 5 166
Holland, Tx., U.S. E 5 172
Holland ▫[9] B 3 96
Hollandale F 3 170
Holland-on-Sea F 8 72
Hollandsbird Island I C 1 206
Hollick-Kenyon Plateau ⋏[1] D 35 208
Hollidaysburg C 4 162
Hollis C 4 172
Hollister D 2 182
Holly River State Park ♦ D 3 162
Holly Springs E 4 170
Hollywood F 4 168
Holm H 9 108
Holman B 9 150
Holmen B 5 66
Holmfirth D 5 72
Holmsjön ⊜ E 7 64
Holmsk C 12 124
Holm-Žirkovskij I 10 108
Holod B 6 104
Holon E 3 120
Holovanivs'k A 11 104
Holroyd ≃ C 6 142
Holstebro B 1 68
Holsteinborg ⊥ C 4 68
Holsteinsborg (Sisimiut) C 22 150
Holston ≃ A 3 168
Holston, North Fork ≃ E 3 162
Holsworthy G 2 72
Holton A 15 160
Holts Summit C 2 170
Holy Cross E 15 154
Holyhead D 2 72
Holyoke D 6 164
Holyrood F 5 174
Holyrood Palace ◗ B 3 72
Holzkirchen E 8 100
Holzminden E 6 98
Hom ≃ E 3 206
Homalin B 2 132
Homathko ≃ F 9 156
Homathko Icefield ⊓ F 9 156
Homberg E 6 98
Hombori Tondo ∧ B 4 200
Hombourg-Haut A 4 82
Hombre Muerto, Salar del ≌ E 6 192
Homburg C 4 100
Home Hill E 8 142
Homel' see Gomel C 7 110
Homel' ▫[3] C 6 110
Homeland Park B 3 168
Homer, Ak., U.S. G 19 154
Homer, La., U.S. F 2 170
Homer, Ne., U.S. D 6 174
Homerville D 3 168
Homestead G 4 168
Homewood F 5 170
Hommersåk C 2 66
Homonhon I C 9 134
Homutovo J 12 108
Honāvar G 2 122
Hondo H 3 126
Hondo ≃, N.A. I 15 184
Hondo ≃, N.M., U.S. F 6 176
Honduras ▫[1] H 11 148
Honduras, Gulf of ⊂ I 15 184
Honea Path B 3 168
Hønefoss B 5 66
Honesdale E 3 164
Honey Lake ⊜ B 3 180
Honeymoon Bay G 9 156
Honfleur C 7 78
Høng C 4 68
Hong, Song (Red River) (Yuan) ≃ C 7 132
Honga E 2 204
Hon Gai D 8 132
Honghe G 6 130
Hong Hu ⊜ D 11 130
Hongjiang E 9 130
Hong Kong see Victoria, China G 12 130
Hong Kong, China G 12 130
Hong Kong ▫[2] G 12 130
Hong Kong (Xianggang) ▫[3] I 19 131a
Hongshui ≃ F 8 130
Hongtong H 8 128
Honguedo, Détroit d' ⩌ D 11 160
Hongwŏn-ŭp D 2 126
Hongze B 14 130
Hongze Hu ⊜ B 14 130
Honiara A 12 138
Honiton G 3 72
Honjō E 7 126
Hönö D 5 66
Honolulu i 10 181a
Hon Quan I 8 132
Honshū I G 6 126
Hood, Mount ∧[1] C 3 178
Hood Canal ⊂ B 2 178
Hood River C 3 178
Hoogeveen B 5 69
Hoogezand A 5 69
Hooker B 3 172
Hook of Holland see Hoek van Holland C 2 69
Hooks F 1 170
Hoolt D 4 128
Hoop B 3 206
Hoopa Valley Indian Reservation ✜[4] E 2 178
Hoople G 10 158
Höör E 6 66
Hoorn B 4 69
Hoover Dam ✜[6] D 1 176
Hooversville C 4 162
Hopatcong F 4 164
Hope, B.C., Can. G 11 156
Hope, Ar., U.S. F 2 170
Hope, In., U.S. C 6 170
Hope, Point ≻ B 11 154
Hopedale B 4 170
Hopelchén H 15 184
Hopër ≃ D 13 110
Hopes Advance, Cap ≻ D 19 150
Hopetoun M 6 140
Hopetown E 5 206
Hope Valley E 7 164
Hopewell E 5 162
Hopi Indian Reservation ✜[4] E 3 176
Hopkins, Lake ⊜ I 10 140
Hopkinsville D 5 170
Hopland C 2 180
Hoquiam B 2 178
Hor C 20 128
Hor ≃ C 11 124
Horatio F 1 170
Horb am Neckar D 5 100
Hörby E 6 66
Hordaland ▫[3] B 3 66
Horden C 5 72
Horgen C 6 82
Hořice C 8 96
Horinger F 8 128
Horiult D 3 128
Horki B 7 110
Horley F 6 72
Horlick Mountains ⋏ E 31 208
Horlivka E 10 110
Hormigueros j 14 187b
Hormozgān ▫[3] I 16 118
Hormuz, Strait of ⩌ I 16 118
Horn B 7 102
Horn ≻ I 19 64a
Horn, Cape (Hornos, Cabo de) ≻ K 6 192
Hornaday ≃ B 33 154
Hornafjörður ⊂ m 22 64a
Hornavan ⊜ C 8 64
Hornby Bay ⊂ C 35 154
Horndal B 8 66
Hornell B 5 162
Hornindal B 3 66
Horní Počernice B 11 100
Horní Slavkov B 9 100
Horn Lake E 3 170
Horn Plateau ⋏[1] D 9 150
Hornsea D 6 72
Horodenka A 8 104
Horodkivka A 10 104
Horodnya K 9 108
Horodok, Ukr. E 3 110
Horodok, Ukr. E 5 110
Hořovice C 10 100
Horqin Youyi Zhongqi D 13 128
Horqin Zuoyi Houqi E 13 128
Horse Cave A 2 168
Horseheads D 2 164
Horsens C 2 68
Horseshoe Bend D 5 178
Horseshoe Bend National Military Park ♦ F 6 170
Horsham, Austl. F 4 144
Horsham, Eng., U.K. F 6 72
Hørsholm C 5 68
Hörstel D 4 98
Horta h 12 198a
Horten C 5 66
Hortobágy ✜[1] B 6 104
Hortobágyi Nemzeti Park ♦ B 6 104
Horton C 1 170
Horton ≃ B 32 154
Horton Lake ⊜ C 33 154
Horw C 6 82
Horwood Lake ⊜ D 2 160
Hory B 7 110
Hosa'ina F 4 202
Hösbach C 6 100
Hoséré Vokré ∧ D 7 200
Hošeutovo F 15 110
Hoshangābād E 3 122
Hoshiārpur C 3 122
Höshööt B 4 128
Hosmer A 6 178
Hospet F 3 122
Hospital de Órbigo B 5 86
Hosston F 2 170
Hoste, Isla I K 6 192
Hotan B 3 122
Hotan ≃ C 13 116
Hotarele C 9 104
Hotchkiss C 13 156
Hot Creek Range ⋏ B 7 182
Hotham Inlet ⊂ C 14 154
Hot Springs (Hot Springs National Park), Ar., U.S. E 2 170
Hot Springs, Mt., U.S. H 14 156
Hot Springs see Truth or Consequences, N.M., U.S. F 5 176
Hot Springs National Park see Hot Springs E 2 170
Hot Springs State Park ♦ D 9 178
Hottah Lake ⊜ C 9 150
Hottentotsbaai ⊂ D 1 206
Hottentotskloof G 3 206
Houdan D 8 78
Houghton G 4 160
Houghton Lake A 1 162
Houghton Lake ⊜ A 1 162
Houghton-le-Spring C 5 72
Houlton g 13 163a
Houma, China I 8 128
Houma, La., U.S. H 3 170
Houmet Essouq C 7 198
Housatonic D 5 164
Housatonic ≃ E 5 164
Houston, Mo., U.S. D 3 170
Houston, Tx., U.S. F 6 172
Houston, Lake ⊜[1] F 6 172
Hout ≃ B 8 206
Houthalen C 4 69
Hovd, Mong. C 2 124
Hovd, Mong. D 4 128
Hovd ≃ C 2 124
Hove G 6 72
Hövelhof E 5 98
Hoven C 5 174
Hovenweep National Monument ♦ D 4 176
Hoverla, hora ∧ A 8 104
Hövsgöl ▫[3] B 2 128
Hovsgol Lake see Hövsgöl nuur ⊜ B 4 124
Hövsgöl nuur ⊜ B 4 124
Hövüün E 4 128
Howa, Ouadi (Howar, Wādī) ≃ D 1 202
Howar, Wādī (Howa, Ouadi) ≃ D 2 202
Howard, Ks., U.S. G 6 174
Howard, S.D., U.S. D 6 174
Howard ▫[6] G 1 164
Howard Lake C 1 166
Howe, Cape ≻ F 7 144
Howeke E 3 200
Howick E 9 206
Howland Island I C 10 136
Howrah see Hāora E 5 122
Hoxie D 3 170
Höxter E 6 98
Høyanger B 3 66
Hoyerswerda E 11 98
Hoyos D 4 86
Hradec Králové C 8 96
Hrádek nad Nisou B 11 100
Hrandziči F 11 66
Hranice, Czech Rep. A 9 102
Hranice, Czech Rep. B 9 100
Hrazdan I 14 110
Hrebinka D 8 110
Hriňová D 10 96
Hrodna (Grodno) F 11 66
Hrodna ▫[3] J 12 64
Hron ≃ C 10 102
Hronov C 9 96
Hrubieszów C 12 96
Hsian see Xi'an A 9 130
Hsilo G 15 130
Hsinchu F 15 130
Hsintien F 15 130
Hsipaw C 3 132
Hua'an F 13 130
Huacho F 3 190
Huaco B 3 195
Huadian E 16 128
Hua Hin H 4 132
Huai ≃ B 13 130
Huai'an, China B 14 130
Huai'an, China F 10 128
Huaibin B 12 130
Huaidezhen E 15 128
Huaiji G 11 130
Huailai F 10 128
Huainan B 13 130
Huaining C 13 130
Huairou F 11 128
Huaiyang B 12 130
Huai Yot K 4 132
Huaiyuan B 13 130
Huajuapan de León I 11 184
Hualahuises E 10 184
Hualalai ∧[1] j 11 181a
Hualapai Indian Reservation ✜[4] E 2 176
Hualien F 15 130
Huallaga ≃ E 3 190
Huambo E 2 204
Huambo ▫[3] E 2 204
Huanan C 18 128
Huancavelica F 4 190
Huancayo F 3 190
Huang (Heung) ≃ F 5 132
Huangchuan B 12 130
Huanggai Hu ⊜ D 11 130
Huanggang C 12 130
Huang He see Yellow River ⊜ D 17 116
Huanghua G 11 128
Huangjinbu D 13 130
Huangling I 7 128
Huangnihe E 17 128
Huangpi C 12 130
Huangqi E 14 130
Huangshan D 14 130
Huangshi C 12 130
Huangtang Hu ⊜ C 11 130
Huangyan D 15 130
Huangyuan H 3 128
Huangzhong H 3 128
Huaning F 6 130
Huanjiang B 9 132
Huanren F 15 128
Huánuco E 3 190
Huanxian H 6 128
Huaral F 3 190
Huaraz E 3 190
Huascarán, Nevado ∧ E 3 190
Huasco E 5 192
Huatabampo D 5 184
Huatong F 13 128
Huauchinango G 10 184
Huaxian, China G 11 130
Huaxian, China I 10 128
Huaxian, China A 9 130
Huaynamota ≃ F 7 184
Huazamota F 7 184
Huazhou H 10 130
Hubbard Creek Reservoir ⊜[1] D 4 172
Hubbell Trading Post National Historic Site ♦ E 4 176
Hubei ▫[3] C 10 130
Hubli-Dhārwār F 3 122
Hückelhoven E 3 98
Hückeswagen E 4 98
Hucknall D 5 72
Huddersfield D 5 72
Huddinge C 9 66
Hude C 5 98
Huder B 13 128
Hudiksvall B 8 66
Hudson, Fl., U.S. E 3 168
Hudson, Ia., U.S. D 2 166
Hudson, Ma., U.S. D 7 164
Hudson, N.H., U.S. D 7 164
Hudson, N.Y., U.S. B 7 162
Hudson ▫[6] F 5 164
Hudson ≃ E 5 164
Hudson Bay E 7 158
Hudson Bay ⊂ D 15 150
Hudson Falls C 5 164
Hudson's Hope C 10 156
Hudson Strait ⩌ D 18 150
Hue F 8 132
Huechulafquen, Lago ⊜ F 2 195
Huehuetenango J 14 184
Huejutla de Reyes G 10 184
Huelgoat D 3 78
Huelva G 4 86
Huelva ▫[6] G 4 86
Huentelauquén B 2 195
Huércal-Overa G 3 88
Huesca B 4 88
Huesca ▫[6] B 4 88
Huéscar G 2 88
Huétor Tájar G 6 86
Ḥufrat an-Naḥās F 1 202
Huggins, Mount ∧ D 24 208
Hughenden F 7 142
Hughes C 17 154
Hughesville E 2 164
Hugh Keenleyside Dam ✜[6] G 12 156
Hugli ≃ E 5 122
Hugus B 3 206
Huichang F 12 130
Hŭich'ŏn F 16 128
Huichuan I 4 128
Huidong E 6 130
Huíla ▫[3] E 2 204
Huila, Nevado del ∧ C 3 190
Huilai G 13 130
Huili E 6 130
Huimin H 11 128
Huinan E 16 128
Huishui E 8 130
Huissen E 2 98
Huitong E 9 130
Huixian B 8 130
Huixtla J 13 184
Huize E 6 130
Huizen B 4 69
Huizhou G 12 130
Ḥukūmah E 4 202
Hulan C 16 128
Hulan ≃ C 16 128
Hulan Ergi C 14 128
Hulbert B 6 166
Hulga ≃ D 24 108
Hulin D 19 128
Hull, Qc., Can. F 6 160
Hull, Il., U.S. C 3 170
Hull, Ma., U.S. D 8 164
Hull, Tx., U.S. G 1 170
Hülscheid E 4 98
Hulst C 3 69
Hultsfred D 7 66
Hulun Nur ⊜ B 11 128
Hulyaypole F 10 110
Huma B 9 124
Huma ≃ B 8 124
Humacao j 16 187b
Humahuaca D 6 192
Humaitá, Braz. E 6 190
Humaitá, Para. E 8 192
Humansville D 2 170
Humber ≃ D 6 72
Humber Bridge ✜[5] D 6 72
Humbird C 3 166
Humboldt, Sk., Can. E 19 156
Humboldt, Il., U.S. C 4 170
Humboldt, Tn., U.S. E 4 170
Humboldt ≃ B 4 180
Humboldt, North Fork ≃ E 6 178
Humboldt Redwoods State Park ♦ B 2 180
Hume, Lake ⊜[1] F 6 144
Humenné D 11 96
Humine ✜[1] B 8 94
Humpata E 1 204
Humphrey E 3 170
Humphreys Peak ∧ E 3 176
Humppila B 11 66
Hun ≃, China F 15 128
Hun ≃, China F 14 128
Húnaflói ⊂ m 20 64a
Hunan ▫[3] E 10 130
Hunchun E 18 128
Hundested C 4 68
Hundred D 3 162
Hunedoara C 7 104
Hunedoara ▫[3] C 7 104
Hünfeld B 6 100
Hungary ▫[1] F 11 62
Hŭngdŏki-dong G 16 128
Hungen B 5 100
Hungerford B 5 144
Hungry Horse G 14 156
Hungry Horse Dam ✜[6] A 6 178
Hungry Horse Reservoir ⊜[1] A 7 178
Hunjiang E 16 128
Hunnebostrand C 5 66
Hunsberge ⋏ D 2 206
Hunstanton E 7 72
Hunter B 6 174
Hunter ≃ D 8 144
Hunterdon ▫[6] F 4 164
Hunter Island I, Austl. i 11 145a
Hunter Island I, B.C., Can. F 7 156
Hunters Bay ⊂ E 1 132
Hunterville C 5 146
Huntingdon, Eng., U.K. E 6 72
Huntingdon, Pa., U.S. C 5 162
Huntingdon, Tn., U.S. E 4 170
Huntington, Eng., U.K. D 5 72
Huntington, In., U.S. B 6 170
Huntington, N.Y., U.S. C 7 162
Huntington, Or., U.S. C 5 178
Huntington, Ut., U.S. C 3 176
Huntington, W.V., U.S. D 2 162
Huntington Beach G 5 182
Huntington Station F 5 164
Huntly B 5 146
Huntsville, On., Can. F 4 160
Huntsville, Al., U.S. E 5 170
Huntsville, Tx., U.S. E 6 172
Hunucmá G 14 184
Hunyuan G 9 128
Huong Hoa F 8 132
Huoqiu B 13 130
Huoshan C 13 130
Huoxian H 8 128
Hüramt B 4 128
Hurd, Cape ≻ F 3 160
Hüren Tovon uul ∧ D 3 124
Hure Qi E 13 128
Hurghada I 5 118
Huriel B 6 80
Hurlock H 3 164
Huron, Oh., U.S. C 2 162
Huron, S.D., U.S. C 5 174
Huron, Lake ⊜ A 2 162
Hurricane D 2 162
Hurtado ≃ B 2 195
Hürth F 3 98
Hurtsboro C 2 168
Húsavík I 22 64a
Huşi B 9 104
Huslia D 16 154
Husum B 6 98
Hutaym, Ḥarrat ⩟[9] J 9 118
Hutchinson, S. Afr. F 5 206
Hutchinson, Ks., U.S. F 5 174
Hutchinson, Mn., U.S. C 7 174
Hutuo ≃ G 9 128
Huwei G 15 130
Huy D 4 69
Hūzgān G 12 118
Huzhen D 15 130
Huzhou C 14 130
Huzhu H 4 128
Hvalynsk C 16 110
Hvannadalshnúkur ∧ m 22 64a
Hvar, Otok I D 4 104
Hveragerði m 20 64a
Hvolsvöllur n 20 64a
Hwali A 8 206
Hwange F 4 204
Hwange National Park ♦ F 4 204
Hwanghae-bukto ▫[3] G 16 128
Hwanghae-namdo ▫[3] G 15 128
Hyannis, Ma., U.S. E 8 164
Hyannis, Ne., U.S. D 4 174
Hyargas Lake see Hyargas nuur ⊜ C 2 124
Hyargas nuur ⊜ C 2 124
Hyde F 3 146
Hyden, Austl. M 5 140
Hyden, Ky., U.S. E 2 162
Hyde Park, N.Y., U.S. E 5 164
Hyde Park, Vt., U.S. B 6 164
Hyderābād, India F 3 122
Hyderābād, Pak. D 1 122
Hydrographers Passage ⩌ F 10 142
Hyères G 4 82
Hyères, Îles d' II H 4 82
Hyesan F 17 128
Hyland ≃ F 30 154
Hylestad C 3 66
Hyndman Peak ∧ D 6 178
Hyōgo ▫[3] G 5 126
Hyrynsalmi D 14 64
Hythe F 8 72
Hyūga H 3 126
Hyvinkää B 12 66

I

Iaco ≃ F 5 190
Iakora I 9 205a
Ialomiţa ▫[3] C 9 104
Ialomiţa ≃ C 9 104
Ianantsony I 8 205a
Iaşi B 9 104
Iaşi ▫[3] B 9 104
Ibadan D 5 200
Ibagué C 3 190
Ibaiti E 5 194
Ibaka C 3 204
Ibaraki ▫[3] F 8 126
Ibarra C 3 190
Ibb E 5 202
Ibba G 2 202
Ibbenbüren D 4 98
Ibérico, Sistema ⋏ C 3 88
Iberville, Mont d' (Caubvick, Mount) ∧ E 20 150
Ibeto C 5 200
Ibi F 4 88
Ibiá C 7 194
Ibiapaba, Serra da ⋏[2] D 10 190
Ibicaraí F 11 190
Ibicuí ≃ E 8 192
Ibiraçu C 10 194
Ibitinga D 6 194
Ibiza see Eivissa I F 5 88
Ibondo C 5 204
Ibotirama F 10 190
Ibrā F 8 116
Ibrah, Wādī ≃ E 2 202
İbriktepe B 7 106
Ibros F 7 86
Ibshawâi H 4 118
Ibusuki I 3 126
Ica F 3 190
Içá (Putumayo) ≃ D 5 190
Icacos Point ≻ q 22 187e
Içana C 5 190
Içana ≃ C 5 190
İçel D 6 118
İçel ▫[3] D 5 118
Iceland ▫[1] C 4 62
Ichaikaronji F 2 122
Ichkeul, Lac ⊜ G 2 90
Ichnya D 8 110
Ichtegem C 1 69
Ičinskaja Sopka, vulkan ∧[1] D 18 114
Icy Bay ⊂ G 24 154
Icy Cape ≻ A 13 154
Icy Strait ⩌ G 27 154
Ida, Mont ∧ E 6 106
Idah D 6 200
Idaho ▫[3] C 5 152
Idaho Falls D 7 178
Idaho National Engineering Laboratory ◗[3] D 7 178
Idanha-a-Nova E 3 86
Idar-Oberstein C 4 100
Idelès E 6 198
Ider ≃ B 2 128
Idi L 3 132
Idiofa D 2 204
Iditarod ≃ E 15 154
Idlib E 7 118
Idodi D 5 204
Ídolo, Isla del I G 11 184
Idoûkâl-en-Taghès ∧ B 6 200
Idrija E 5 102
Idstein B 5 100
Iecava D 12 66
Ieper D 1 69
Ierissós B 5 106
Ie-shima I K 1 126
Iesolo D 8 92
If, Château d' ⊥ G 3 82
Ifalik I[1] D 12 134
Ifanadiana I 9 205a
Ife D 5 200
Ifni ▫[9] D 2 198
Ifôghas, Adrar des ⋏ B 5 200
Ifon D 6 200
Ifrane C 3 198
Igalula D 5 204
Iganga G 3 202
Igara Paraná ≃ D 4 190

⌞ Waterfall ⩌ Strait ⊂ Bay, Gulf ⊜ Lake ≌ Swamp ⊓ Ice Feature ⊤ Other Hydrographic Feature ✢ Submarine Feature ▫ Political Unit ◗ Cultural Institution ⊥ Historical Site ♦ Recreational Site ⊠ Airport ▪ Military Installation ✜ Miscellaneous

Symbols in the index entries represent the broad categories identified in the key at the right. Symbols with superior numbers (←1) identify subcategories (see complete key on page 242).

∧ Mountain   ∦ Mountains   ⋈ Pass   V Valley   ≈ Plain   ≻ Cape   I Island   II Islands   ± Other Topographic Feature   ≈ River   ≖ Canal

260

Name	Map Ref.	Page

∟ Waterfall ⨆ Strait c Bay, Gulf @ Lake ≃ Swamp Ice Feature ⊁ Other Hydrographic Feature ✦ Submarine Feature □ Political Unit ♪ Cultural Institution ⊥ Historical Site ♦ Recreational Site ■ Airport ■ Military Installation ◄ Miscellaneous

261

Symbols in the index entries represent the broad categories identified in the key at the right.
Symbols with superior numbers (ʌ¹) identify subcategories (see complete key on page 242).

ʌ Mountain ⍫ Mountains ✕ Pass V Valley ≃ Plain ⍳ Cape I Island II Islands ⍑ Other Topographic Feature ≃ River ≈ Canal

Knik Arm — La Albuera

Name	Map Ref.	Page
Knik Arm c	F 20	154
Knin	C 4	104
Knislinge	D 7	66
Knittelfeld	C 6	102
Knjaževac	D 7	104
Knob Lake Junction	A 10	160
Knokke-Heist	C 2	69
Knosós (Cnossus) ⊥	E 6	106
Knowsley □[6]	D 4	72
Knox	F 5	144
Knox, Cape ›	D 5	156
Knox Coast ±[2]	C 19	208
Knoxville, Ga., U.S.	C 2	168
Knoxville, Il., U.S.	B 3	170
Knoxville, Tn., U.S.	A 3	168
Knysna	G 5	206
Koani	D 6	204
Kobayashi	H 3	126
Kōbe	G 5	126
Kobelyaky	E 9	110
København (Copenhagen)	C 5	68
København □[3]	C 5	68
Koblenz	B 4	100
Koblenz □[6]	B 4	100
K'obo	E 4	202
Kobroor, Pulau I	G 10	134
Kobryn	J 12	64
Kobuk	C 16	154
Kobuk ≃	C 14	154
Kobuk Valley National Park ♠	C 14	154
Kobuleti	I 12	110
Kocaali	B 9	106
Kocaavşar ≃	C 7	106
Kocaeli □[3]	B 8	106
Kočani	E 7	104
Koçarlı	D 7	106
Kočečum ≃	C 12	114
Kočerdyk	I 25	108
Kočevo	G 20	108
Kōch'ang	G 1	126
Koch Bihār	D 5	122
Kochi (Cochin), India	H 3	122
Kōchi, Japan	H 4	126
Kōchi □[3]	H 4	126
Koch Island I	C 17	150
Kock	C 12	96
Kočubej	G 15	110
Kodačdikost	E 21	108
Kodaikānal	G 3	122
Kodarma	E 5	122
Kodiak	H 18	154
Kodiak Island I	H 18	154
Kodok	E 3	202
Kodyma	A 10	104
Koës	C 3	206
Koffiefontein	E 6	206
Köflach	C 7	102
Koforidua	D 4	200
Kōfu	G 7	126
Koga	F 7	126
Kogaluc ≃	B 20	158
Kogaluc, Baie c	B 19	158
Kogaluk ≃	E 20	150
Køge	C 5	68
Kogin Baba	D 7	200
Kohāt	C 2	122
Kohila	C 12	66
Kohīma	D 6	122
Kohkīlūyeh va Boyer Aḥmadī □[3]	G 14	118
Kohtla-Järve	C 13	66
Kohunlich ⊥	H 15	184
Koide	F 7	126
Koidu-Sefagu	D 2	200
Koigi	C 12	66
Koimbani	n 18	207d
Koindu	D 2	200
Koiva see Gauja ≃	D 12	66
Kojda	C 15	108
Kojgorodok	F 19	108
Kojonup	M 4	140
Kok (Hkok) ≃	H 4	130
Kokee State Park ♠	h 9	181a
Kokemäenjoki ≃	B 11	66
Kokenau	F 11	134
Ko Kha	E 4	132
Kokhav HaYarden (Belvoir) ⊥	D 4	120
Kokka	D 3	202
Koko	C 5	200
Kokoda	A 10	138
Kokomo	B 5	170
Kokong	C 5	206
Koko Nor see Qinghai Hu ⊜	H 2	128
Kokrines	D 17	154
Koksan-ŭp	G 16	128
Kökshetaū	J 28	108
Koksoak ≃	E 19	150
Kokstad	F 8	206
Kokubu	I 3	126
Kola	B 10	108
Kolaka	F 8	134
Kola Peninsula (Kol'skij poluostrov) ›[1]	B 12	108
Kolār	G 3	122
Kolāras	D 3	122
Kolār Gold Fields	G 3	122
Kolárovo	C 9	102
Kolašin	D 5	104
Kolbotn	C 5	66
Kol'čugino	H 13	108
Kolda	C 1	200
Kolding	C 2	68
Kole	B 4	204
Kolea	H 7	88
Kolèntèn	C 2	200
Kolguev, ostrov I	B 18	108
Kolhāpur	F 2	122
Kolho	A 12	66
Koliba (Corubal) ≃	C 2	200
Koliganek	G 16	154
Kolín	B 12	100
Koljučinskaja guba c	C 7	154
Kolka	D 11	66
Kolkas rags ›	D 11	66
Kolkata (Calcutta)	E 5	122
Kölleda	E 8	98
Kollo	C 5	200
Köln (Cologne)	F 3	98
Köln □[6]	B 3	100
Koło	B 10	96
Kołobrzeg	A 8	96
Kologriv	G 16	108
Kolokani	C 3	200
Kolombangara I	A 12	138
Kolomna	I 13	108
Kolomyya	A 8	104
Kolondiéba	C 3	200
Kolosib	B 1	132
Kolosovka	H 30	108
Kolpa (Kupa) ≃	E 6	102
Kolpaševo	D 11	114
Kolpino	G 9	108
Kol'skij poluostrov see Kola Peninsula ›[1]	B 12	108
Koluszki	C 10	96
Kolva ≃	C 22	108
Kolwezi	E 4	204
Kolyma ≃	C 18	114
Kolyšlej	C 14	110
Kom see Qom	E 14	118
Kom ≃	E 7	200
Komadugu Yobe (Komadougou Yobé) ≃	C 7	200
Komandorskie ostrova II	D 19	114
Komandorski Islands see Komandorskie ostrova II	D 19	114
Komárno	C 10	102
Komarnyky	A 7	104
Komárom	C 10	102
Komárom-Esztergom □[3]	C 10	102
Komati (Incomati) ≃	C 10	206
Komatipoort	C 9	206
Komatsu	F 6	126
Kombissiri	C 4	200
Komering ≃	F 4	134
Komi □[3]	E 21	108
Komin-Yanga	C 5	200
Komló	D 10	102
Kommandokraal	G 5	206
Kommunističeskij	F 26	108
Kommunizm, Qullai ∧	B 2	122
Kommunizma, pik see Kommunizm, Qullai ∧	B 2	122
Komo ≃	E 7	200
Komodo, Pulau I	G 7	134
Komoé ≃	D 4	200
Kom Ombo	C 3	202
Komotiní	B 6	106
Kompasberg ∧	F 6	206
Komrat see Comrat	B 10	104
Komsomolec, ostrov I	A 12	114
Komsomolets	C 22	110
Komsomolets shyghanaghy c	G 17	110
Komsomol'sk	H 13	108
Komsomol'skij	I 16	108
Komsomol'sk-na-Amure	B 11	124
Komyshuvakha	F 9	110
Kona Coast ±[2]	j 11	181a
Konakovo	H 12	108
Konan	D 3	200
Konārak	F 5	122
Konda ≃	G 27	108
Kondagaon	F 4	122
Kondinin	M 5	140
Kondinskoe	G 27	108
Kondoa	C 6	204
Kondopoga	E 11	108
Kondoz	B 1	122
Kondrovo	I 11	108
Kondukūr	F 3	122
Koné	D 13	138
Konëvo	E 13	108
Konfara	C 3	200
Kong ≃	H 8	132
Kongakut ≃	B 24	154
Kongbo	E 9	200
Kongcheng	C 13	130
Kongens Lyngby	C 5	68
Kongolo, D.R.C.	D 4	204
Kongolo, D.R.C.	D 3	204
Kongoussi	C 4	200
Kongsvinger	B 6	66
Kongur Shan ∧	B 3	122
Kongwa	D 6	204
Konice	A 8	102
Königsberg see Kaliningrad	B 2	110
Königsbrück	E 10	98
Königsbrunn	D 7	100
Königsfelden ◗[1]	C 6	82
Königslutter	D 7	98
Königssee ⊜	E 9	100
Königswinter	F 4	98
Konin	B 10	96
Konispol	C 4	106
Kónitsa	B 4	106
Köniz	D 5	82
Konkiep ≃	D 2	206
Konkouré ≃	C 2	200
Konna	C 4	200
Konoša	F 13	108
Konotop	D 8	110
Konqi ≃	A 5	122
Konsankoro	D 3	200
Końskie	C 11	96
Konstantinovka	H 19	108
Konstantinovsk	F 12	110
Konstanz	E 6	100
Kontagora	C 6	200
Kontcha	D 7	200
Kontich	C 3	69
Kontiomäki	D 14	64
Kon Tum	G 8	132
Kontum, Plateau du ⋏[1]	H 8	132
Konya	D 5	118
Konya □[3]	C 5	118
Konz	C 3	100
Konžakovskij Kamen', gora ∧	D 8	114
Koocanusa, Lake ⊜[1]	A 6	178
Koog aan de Zaan	B 3	69
Koolau Range ⋏	i 10	181a
Koonga	C 12	66
Koopan-Suid	D 4	206
Koorawatha	E 7	144
Koosa	C 13	66
Kooskia	B 6	178
Kootenai (Kootenay) ≃	G 13	156
Kootenay (Kootenai) ≃	G 13	156
Kootenay Indian Reserve ◆[4]	A 6	178
Kootenay Lake ⊜	G 13	156
Kootenay National Park ♠	F 13	156
Kopanovka	F 15	110
Kópavogur	m 20	64a
Kopayhorod	A 9	104
Kopejsk	I 24	108
Koper	E 5	102
Kopervik	C 2	66
Kopetdag, hrebet ⋏	C 8	116
Köping	C 7	66
Koppang	B 5	66
Koppies	D 7	206
Koprivnica	D 8	102
Köprülü Kanyon Milli Parkı ♠	D 9	106
Köprüören	C 8	106
Kopylovo	F 16	108
Kor ≃	H 15	118
Korab (Korabit, Maja e) ∧	E 6	104
Korabit, Maja e (Korab) ∧	E 6	104
Korablino	I 14	108
Kora National Park ♠	H 4	202
Korāput	F 4	122
Korarou, Lac ⊜	F 4	198
Korba, India	E 4	122
Korba, Tun.	G 3	90
Korbach	E 5	98
Korbol	C 8	200
Korçë	B 4	106
Kordestān □[3]	E 12	118
Kord Kūy	D 15	118
Korea, North □[1]	E 14	112
Korea, South □[1]	F 14	112
Korea Bay c	G 14	128
Korea Strait ʊ	G 2	126
Korem	E 4	202
Koré Maïroua	C 5	200
Korenovsk	G 11	110
Korgus	D 3	202
Korhogo	D 3	200
Korinthiakós Kólpos see Corinth, Gulf of c	C 5	106
Kórinthos	D 5	106
Kōriyama	F 8	126
Korjakskaja Sopka, vulkan ∧	B 15	124
Korjakskoe nagor'e ⋏	C 20	114
Korjažma	F 17	108
Korkino	I 24	108
Korkuteli	D 9	106
Korla	A 5	122
Körmend	C 8	102
Kornati, Nacionalni Park ♠	D 3	104
Kornelimünster	F 3	98
Korneuburg	B 8	102
Kornsjø	C 5	66
Korntal-Münchingen	B 6	82
Kornwestheim	D 6	100
Koro	C 4	200
Koroleve	A 7	104
Koronowo	B 9	96
Koror	D 10	134
Koro Sea ⫪[2]	E 9	136
Korosten'	D 6	110
Korostyshiv	D 6	110
Koro Toro	B 8	200
Korovin Volcano ∧[1]	k 44	155a
Korovou	m 14	147c
Korpélé	E 8	200
Korppoo	B 10	66
Korsakov	C 12	124
Korselbränna	D 7	64
Korsnäs	B 7	66
Korso	B 12	66
Korsør	C 4	68
Korsun'-Shevchenkivs'kyy	E 7	110
Kortkeros	F 19	108
Kortrijk (Courtrai)	D 2	69
Korumburra	G 5	144
Korup National Park ♠	D 6	200
Kos	D 7	106
Kos I	D 7	106
Kosa	F 4	202
Kosa ≃	G 21	108
Koš-Agač	B 1	124
Kosaja Gora	I 12	108
Kościan	B 9	96
Kościerzyna	A 10	96
Kosciusko, Mount ∧	F 7	144
Kosciusko National Park ♠	F 7	144
Kose	C 12	66
Kōshoku	F 7	126
Kosi Bay c	D 10	206
Košice	D 11	96
Kosju	D 23	108
Koski	B 11	66
Koslan	E 18	108
Kosŏng-ŭp	G 17	128
Kosovo-Metohija □[6]	D 6	104
Kosovska Mitrovica	D 6	104
Kossindi	E 8	200
Kossou, Lac de ⊜[1]	D 3	200
Kostajnica	C 4	104
Koster	C 7	206
Kostomukša	D 9	108
Kostopil'	D 5	110
Kostroma	H 14	108
Kostroma ≃	G 14	108
Kostromskaja oblast' □[6]	G 16	108
Kostrzyn	B 8	96
Kostyantynivka	E 10	110
Koszalin	A 8	96
Kőszeg	C 8	102
Kota, India	E 4	122
Kota, India	D 3	122
Kota Belud	D 7	134
Kota Bharu	K 6	132
Kotabumi	F 4	134
Kotadabok	F 4	134
Kota Kinabalu	D 7	134
Kotamobagu	E 8	134
Kotari ◆[1]	C 3	104
Kota Tinggi	N 6	132
Kotcho Lake ⊜	B 11	156
Kotel'nič	G 17	108
Kotel'nikovo	F 13	110
Kotelny Island see Kotel'nyj, ostrov I	B 16	114
Kotel'nyj, ostrov I	B 16	114
Köthen	E 8	98
Kotido	G 3	202
Kotka	B 13	66
Kotlas	F 17	108
Kotlik	E 13	154
Koton-Karifi	D 6	200
Kotor Varoš	C 4	104
Kotouba	D 4	200
Kotovo	D 14	110
Kotovsk, Russia	C 12	110
Kotovs'k, Ukr.	B 10	104
Kot Pūtli	D 3	122
Kotri	D 1	122
Kottagūdem	F 4	122
Kottayam	H 3	122
Kotte see Sri Jayawardenepura	H 3	122
Kotto ≃	D 9	200
Kotuj ≃	B 13	114
Kotzebue Sound ʊ	C 13	154
Kötzting	C 9	100
Koubia	C 2	200
Kouchibouguac National Park ♠	E 11	160
Koudougou	C 4	200
Kouéré	C 4	200
Kougnohou	D 5	200
Kouilou □[3]	C 1	204
Kouilou ≃	C 1	204
Koulamoutou	F 7	200
Koulikoro	C 3	200
Koulikoro □[3]	C 3	200
Koumac	D 13	138
Koumameyong	E 7	200
Koumbia, Burkina	C 4	200
Koumbia, Gui.	C 2	200
Koumpentoum	C 1	200
Koumra	D 8	200
Koundâra	C 2	200
Koundian ⊥	C 2	200
Koundougou	C 3	200
Kountze	G 1	170
Koupéla	C 4	200
Kouri	C 3	200
Kourou	B 8	190
Kourouma	C 3	200
Kouroussa	C 3	200
Koussané	C 2	200
Kousséri	C 7	200
Koussi, Emi ∧	B 8	200
Koutia Ba	C 2	200
Koutiala	C 3	200
Kouvola	B 13	66
Kovada Milli Parkı ♠	D 9	106
Kovarskas	E 12	66
Kovdor	C 8	108
Kovdozero, ozero ⊜[1]	C 9	108
Kovel'	D 4	110
Kovilpatti	H 3	122
Kovrov	H 14	108
Kovylkino	I 15	108
Kovža	F 13	108
Kowalewo Pomorskie	B 10	96
Kowanyama Aboriginal Land ◆[4]	C 5	142
Kowie see Port Alfred	G 7	206
Kowkcheh ≃	B 2	122
Kowloon	G 12	130
Kowloon City	I 20	131a
Kowŏn-ŭp	G 16	128
Köyceğiz Gölü ⊜	D 8	106
Koyuk ≃	D 14	154
Koyukuk	D 15	154
Koyukuk ≃	D 16	154
Koyukuk, North Fork ≃	C 19	154
Koyukuk, South Fork ≃	C 20	154
Koža	H 18	108
Kozan	D 6	118
Kozáni	B 4	106
Kozara, Nacionalni Park ♠	C 4	104
Kozdinga	E 17	108
Kozel'sk	I 11	108
Kozhikode (Calicut)	G 3	122
Kozienice	C 11	96
Kožim	D 23	108
Kozlu	B 9	106
Koźmin	C 9	96
Koz'modemjansk	H 17	108
Kožposëlok	E 13	108
Kozyatyn	E 6	110
Kpalimé	D 5	200
Kra, Isthmus of ±[3]	I 4	132
Kraai ≃	F 7	206
Krabi	K 4	132
Krâchéh	H 8	132
Kragan	k 20	135b
Kragerø	C 4	66
Kragujevac	C 6	104
Kraichgau ◆[1]	C 5	100
Krajenka	B 9	96
Krakovets'	D 12	96
Kraków	C 10	96
Kraljevica	C 3	104
Kraljevo	D 6	104
Královéhradecký □[3]	C 8	96
Kralupy nad Vltavou	B 11	100
Kramfors	E 8	64
Kranenburg	E 2	98
Kranídi	D 5	106
Kranj	D 6	102
Kranji	i 14	134a
Kranji Reservoir ⊜[1]	i 14	134a
Krapina	D 7	102
Krasavino	F 16	108
Krasino	A 20	108
Krāslava	E 13	66
Kraslice	B 9	100
Krasnaja Gorbatka	I 14	108
Krasnaluki	E 14	66
Kraśnik	C 12	96
Kraśnik Fabryczny	C 11	96
Krasnoarmejskij	F 13	110
Krasnoarmejskoe	C 17	110
Krasnoarmeysk	J 28	108
Krasnoarmiys'k	E 10	110
Krasnobród	C 12	96
Krasnodar	G 11	110
Krasnodarskij kraj □[6]	G 11	110
Krasnoe	J 13	108
Krasnoe, ozero ⊜	C 20	114
Krasnogorskij	I 24	108
Krasnohrad	E 9	110
Krasnojarka	G 23	108
Krasnojarsk	D 12	114
Krasnojarskij	D 21	110
Krasnojarskij kraj □[6]	C 35	108
Krasnojarskoe vodohranilišče ⊜[1]	D 12	114
Krasnokamsk	G 21	108
Krasnolese	E 11	66
Krasnolesnyj	D 11	110
Krasnoostrovskij	B 14	66
Krasnoperekops'k	G 8	110
Krasnoščele	C 12	108
Krasnosielc	B 11	96
Krasnoslobodsk	E 14	110
Krasnoturjinsk	G 24	108
Krasnoufimsk	H 22	108
Krasnoural'sk	G 24	108
Krasnousol'skij	J 22	108
Krasnovišersk	F 22	108
Krasnovodsk see Türkmenbashy	B 15	118
Krasnowodsk Aylagy c	J 18	110
Krasnoznamensk	E 11	66
Krasnye Baki	H 16	108
Krasnye Gory	C 14	66
Krasnyj Čikoj	A 7	128
Krasnyj Guljaj	J 17	108
Krasnyj Holm	G 12	108
Krasnyj Jar	I 30	108
Krasnyj Kut	D 15	110
Krasnyj Oktjabr'	I 26	108
Krasnyj Sulin	F 12	110
Krasnystaw	C 12	96
Krasnyy Luch	E 11	110
Krasnyy Lyman	E 10	110
Kražiai	E 11	66
Krbava ◆[1]	C 3	104
Krečetovo	F 13	108
Krefeld	E 3	98
Kremastón, Technití Límni ⊜[1]	C 4	106
Kremenchuk	E 8	110
Kremenchuts'ke vodoskhovyshche ⊜[1]	E 8	110
Kremenets'	D 4	110
Kreminna	E 11	110
Krems an der Donau	B 7	102
Kress	C 3	172
Kressbronn	E 6	100
Kresta, zaliv c	D 5	154
Kretinga	E 10	66
Kreuzau	F 3	98
Kreuzlingen	C 7	82
Kreuztal	F 4	98
Krèva	E 13	66
Kribi	E 6	200
Kriebstein, Burg ⊥	E 10	98
Kriel	D 8	206
Kriens	C 6	82
Křimice	C 10	100
Krishna ≃	F 3	122
Krishna, Mouths of the ≃[1]	F 4	122
Krishnagiri	G 3	122
Krishnanagar	E 5	122
Kristiania see Oslo	C 5	66
Kristianopel	D 8	66
Kristiansand	C 4	66
Kristianstad	D 6	66
Kristianstad □[3]	D 6	66
Kristiansund	E 3	64
Kristiinankaupunki	A 10	66
Kristinehamn	C 6	66
Kríti □[3]	E 6	106
Kríti (Crete) I	E 6	106
Kriva Palanka	D 7	104
Krivoj Rog see Kryvyy Rih	F 8	110
Krivoy Rog see Kryvyy Rih	F 8	110
Križevci	D 8	102
Krk, Otok I	C 3	104
Krnov	C 9	96
Krokek	C 8	66
Krokowa	A 9	96
Krolevets'	D 8	110
Kröller-Müller, Rijksmuseum ◗	B 4	69
Kroměříž	A 9	102
Kromhoek	B 8	206
Kronach	B 8	100
Kronborg ⊥	B 5	68
Krŏng Kaôh Kŏng	I 6	132
Krŏng Kêb	I 7	132
Kronoberg □[3]	D 7	66
Kronockaja Sopka, vulkan ∧[1]	D 19	114
Kronshagen	B 6	98
Kronštadt	F 8	108
Kroonstad	D 7	206
Kropotkin	G 12	110
Krośniewice	B 10	96
Krosno	D 11	96
Krotoszyn	C 9	96
Krotz Springs	G 3	170
Kroya	k 19	135b
Kruger National Park ♠	C 9	206
Krugersdorp	D 7	206
Krui	G 4	134
Kruin	B 2	206
Kruisfontein	G 6	206
Krujë	B 3	106
Krumbach	D 7	100
Krung Thep (Bangkok)	H 5	132
Krupka	B 10	100
Krupki	B 6	110
Kruševac	D 6	104
Kruševo	E 6	104
Krutaja	E 21	108
Krutcy	D 14	66
Kruzensterna, proliv ʊ	C 14	124
Kryčaŭ	C 7	110
Krylbo	B 8	66
Krym, Respublika □[3]	G 9	110
Krymsk	G 10	110
Krynica	D 11	96
Kryve Ozero	B 11	104
Kryvyi Rih see Kryvyy Rih	F 8	110
Kryvyy Rih	F 8	110
Kryzhopil'	A 10	104
Krzepice	C 10	96
Krzyż	B 8	96
Ksar-el-Kebir (Alcazarquivir)	B 3	198
Kšenskij	D 10	110
Kstovo	H 16	108
Kū', Wādī al- ≃	E 2	202
Kuah	K 4	132
Kuala Kangsar	L 5	132
Kualakapuas	F 6	134
Kuala Krai	L 5	132
Kuala Kubu Baharu	M 5	132
Kuala Lipis	L 5	132
Kuala Lumpur	M 5	132
Kuala Nerang	K 5	132
Kuala Rompin	M 6	132
Kuala Sepetang	L 5	132
Kualasimpang	L 4	132
Kuala Terengganu	L 6	132
Kuandian	F 15	128
Kuantan	M 6	132
Kuban' ≃	G 10	110
Kubenskoe, ozero ⊜	G 13	108
Kuboes	E 2	206
Kubokawa	H 4	126
Kučema	D 14	108
Kuchelebai	G 4	202
Kuching	N 10	132
Kuçovë	B 3	106
Kudat	D 7	134
Kudirkos Naumiestis	E 11	66
Kudus	k 20	135b
Kudymkar	G 20	108
Kueda	H 21	108
Kuee Ruins ⊥	j 11	181a
Kufrinjah	E 5	120
Kufstein	C 4	102
Kugaluk ≃	B 29	154
Kugmallit Bay c	B 27	154
Kūhdasht	F 12	118
Kühlungsborn	B 8	98
Kuhmo	D 14	64
Kuiseb ≃	B 1	206
Kuitan	G 13	130
Kuito	E 2	204
Kuiu Island I	H 27	154
Kuivastu	C 11	66
Kuja	C 20	108
Kujang-ŭp	G 16	128
Kujawsko-Pomorskie □[3]	B 9	96
Kujawy ◆[1]	B 10	96
Kujbyševskij Zaton	I 18	108
Kujbyševskoe vodohranilišče ⊜[1]	C 16	110
Kujjuarapik see Whapmagoostui	A 4	160
Kujū-san ∧[1]	H 3	126
Kukaklek Lake ⊜	G 16	154
Kukawa	C 7	200
Kukkola	C 11	64
Kukmor	H 19	108
Kukup	N 6	132
Kula, Tur.	C 8	106
Kula, Yugo.	C 5	104
Kulai	N 6	132
Kula Kangri ∧	D 6	122
Kulautuva	E 11	66
Kuldīga	D 11	66
Kulebaki	I 15	108
Kulevčinskij	J 24	108
Kulgunino	J 22	108
Kulim	L 5	132
Kulju	B 11	66
Kulmbach	B 8	100
Kulob	B 1	122
Kuloj	F 15	108
Kuloj ≃	D 15	108
Kulpawn ≃	D 4	200
Kulsary	F 18	110
Kültepe ⊥	C 6	118
Kulu	C 5	118
Kulumadau	A 11	138
Kulundinskoe, ozero ⊜	D 11	114
Kum see Qom	E 14	118
Kuma ≃	G 14	110
Kumagaya	F 7	126
Kumamoto	H 3	126
Kumamoto □[3]	H 3	126
Kumano	H 6	126
Kumanovo	D 6	104
Kumārghāt	B 1	132
Kumarl	M 6	140
Kumasi	D 4	200
Kumba	E 6	200
Kumbakonam	G 3	122
Kumbarilla	I 10	142
Kumdanlı	C 9	106
Kŭm-gang ≃	H 16	128
Kŭmhwa	E 1	126
Kumi	G 3	202
Kuminovskoe	H 26	108
Kumla	C 7	66
Kumluca	D 9	106
Kumo	D 7	200
Kumskoj	G 15	110
Kumta	G 2	122
Kŭmya-ŭp	G 16	128
Kumzār	I 17	118
Kunašak	I 24	108
Kunashiri-tō see Kunašir, ostrov I	D 13	124
Kunašir, ostrov (Kunashiri-tō) I	D 13	124
Kunda	C 4	204
Kundelungu, Parc National de ♠	E 4	204
Kundla	E 2	122
Kunene □[3]	F 1	204
Kunene (Cunene) ≃	F 1	204
Kungana	D 7	200
Kungrad	H 21	110
Kungshamn	C 5	66
Kungsör	C 8	66
Kungur	H 22	108
Kungwane	B 6	206
Kunhegyes	B 6	104
Kunlong	C 4	132
Kunlun Shan ⋏	C 13	116
Kunming	F 6	130
Kunmunya Aboriginal Reserve ◆[4]	D 8	140
Kunsan	I 16	128
Kunszentmárton	B 5	104
Kununurra	D 10	140
Kunyo	F 5	202
Künzell	B 6	100
Künzelsau	C 6	100
Kuolajarvi	C 14	64
Kuopio	E 13	64
Kupa (Kolpa) ≃	E 7	102
Kupang	H 8	134
Kupang, Teluk c	B 7	140
Kupiškis	E 12	66
Kupreanof	H 28	154
Kupreanof Island I	H 28	154
Kup'yans'k	E 10	110
Kup'yans'k-Vuzlovyy	E 10	110
Kuqa, China	A 4	122
Kuqa, China	A 4	122
Kür (Kura) ≃, Asia	C 13	118
Kur ≃, Russia	B 20	128
Kura (Kür) ≃	A 10	118
Kuramā', Ḥarrat ±[9]	C 5	202
Kurashassayskiy	D 20	110
Kurashiki	G 4	126
Kurayoshi	G 4	126
Kurčatov	D 9	110
Kürdämir	I 16	110
Kurdistan □[9]	C 10	118
Kurdufān □[3]	E 3	202
Kure	G 4	126
Kurejka ≃	C 11	114
Kuressaare	C 11	66
Kurgan	I 26	108
Kurganinsk	G 12	110
Kurganskaja oblast' □[6]	I 26	108
Kuria I	C 9	136
Kuria Muria Islands (Halaaniyaat, Juzor al-) II	G 8	116
Kuridala	F 5	142
Kuril Islands (Kuril'skie ostrova) II	C 13	124
Kuril'skie ostrova see Kuril Islands II	C 13	124
Kuril Trench ✦[1]	D 12	58
Ku-Ring-Gai Chase National Park ♠	D 8	144
Kurjanovskaja	F 14	108
Kurkiëki	B 14	66
Kurkliai	E 12	66
Kurnool	F 3	122
Kurobe	F 6	126
Kurort Schmalkalden	F 7	98
Kurovskoe	I 13	108
Kurow	F 3	146
Kurri Kurri	D 8	144
Kuršėnai	D 11	66
Kuršiu nerija (Kuršskaja kosa) ›[2]	E 10	66
Kursk	D 10	110
Kurskaja	G 14	110
Kurskaja oblast' □[6]	D 9	110
Kuršskaja kosa (Kuršiu nerija) ›[2]	E 10	66
Kurtalan	C 9	118
Kurtamyš	I 26	108
Kūrtī	D 3	202
Kuruktag ⋏	A 5	122
Kuruman	D 5	206
Kuruman ≃	D 4	206
Kurume	H 3	126
Kurun ≃	F 3	202
Kurunegala	H 3	122
Kurunzulaj	A 11	128
Kusa	B 21	110
Kuşadası	D 7	106
Kusawa Lake ⊜	F 26	154
Kuş Cenneti Milli Parkı ♠	B 8	106
Kusel	C 4	100
Kuş Gölü ⊜	B 7	106
Kushima	I 3	126
Kushiro	C 10	126
Kushtia	E 5	122
Kushui	A 6	122
Kusiyāra ≃	E 6	122
Kuskokwim ≃	F 13	154
Kuskokwim, North Fork ≃	E 18	154
Kuskokwim, South Fork ≃	E 18	154
Kuskokwim Bay c	G 13	154
Kuskokwim Mountains ⋏	E 16	154
Kusmuryn	J 26	108
Kusmuryn köli ⊜	J 26	108
Küsnacht	C 6	82
Kušnarenkovo	I 21	108
Kussharo-ko ⊜	C 10	126
Küssnacht am Rigi	E 5	100
Kustanaj see Qostanay	C 23	110
Kūstī	E 3	202
Kušva	G 23	108
Kutabuloh	M 3	132
Kütahya	C 9	106
Kütahya □[3]	C 9	106
Kutaisi	H 13	110
Kutaradja see Banda Aceh	L 2	132
Kutch, Rann of ◆[1]	E 1	122
Kutina	E 8	102
Kutkai	C 3	132
Kutná Hora	C 12	100
Kutno	B 10	96
Kutse Game Reserve ◆[4]	B 5	206
Kuttusoja	C 14	64
Kutu	C 2	204
Kuty	A 8	104
Kuujjuaq	E 19	150
Kuurne	D 2	69
Kuusamo	C 14	64
Kuusankoski	B 13	66
Kuvandyk	D 20	110
Kuvšinovo	H 10	108
Kuwait □[1]	G 6	112
Kuwait Bay see Kuwayt, Jūn al- c	B 6	202
Kuwayt, Jūn al- (Kuwait Bay) c	B 6	202
Kuyal'nyts'kyy lyman ⊜	B 11	104
Kuye ≃	G 8	128
Kuyucak	D 8	106
Kuyukkol' köli ⊜	D 22	110
Kuzaranda	E 11	108
Kuženkino	H 11	108
Kuzneck	C 15	110
Kuzneckij Alatau ⋏	D 11	114
Kuznečnoe	B 14	66
Kuznecovo	G 25	108
Kuzomen'	C 12	108
Kvænangen c	A 10	64
Kvam	B 4	66
Kvarnerić c	C 3	104
Kverkfjöll ∧[1]	m 22	64a
Kvichak Bay c	G 16	154
Kvikkjokk	C 8	64
Kwa ≃	C 2	204
Kwai see Khwae Noi ≃	G 4	132
Kwajalein I[1]	C 8	136
Kwajok	F 2	202
Kwakoegron	B 7	190
Kwale	H 4	202
Kwa Mtoro	I 4	202
Kwando (Mashi) ≃	F 3	204
Kwangju	I 16	128
Kwango (Cuango) ≃	C 2	204
Kwangyang	G 1	126
Kwania, Lake ⊜	G 3	202
Kware	C 6	200
KwaZulu-Natal □[3]	E 9	206
Kwekwe	F 4	204
Kweneng □[3]	B 6	206
Kwenge (Caengo) ≃	D 2	204
Kwesimintim	D 4	200
Kwidzyn	B 10	96
Kwilu (Cuilo) ≃	C 2	204
Kwinana	M 3	140
Kyabé	D 8	200
Kyaikto	F 3	132
Kya-in	F 4	132
Kyaka	C 5	204
Kyancutta	L 2	142
Kyaukme	C 3	132
Kyaukpyu, Mya.	E 1	132
Kyaukpyu, Mya.	E 1	132
Kyaukse	D 2	132
Kyauktaw	D 1	132
Kyaunggon	F 2	132
Kyeintali	E 2	132
Kyiv see Kyyiv	D 7	110
Kyjov	A 9	102
Kyle	E 5	172
Kymijoki ≃	B 13	66
Kyn	H 23	108
Kyneton	F 5	144
Kyoga, Lake ⊜	G 3	202
Kyogle	B 9	144
Kyondo	F 4	132
Kyŏnggi-do □[3]	H 16	128
Kyŏnggi-man c	H 15	128
Kyŏngju	I 17	128
Kyŏngsan	G 2	126
Kyŏngsang-bukto □[3]	H 17	128
Kyŏngsang-namdo □[3]	I 17	128
Kyŏngsŏng-ŭp	F 17	128
Kyonpyaw	F 7	122
Kyōto	G 5	126
Kyōto □[3]	G 5	126
Kyparissiakós Kólpos c	D 4	106
Kyra	B 9	128
Kyra ≃	B 8	128
Kyren	B 4	124
Kyrgyzstan □[1]	E 9	112
Kyritz	D 9	98
Kyrönjoki ≃	E 11	64
Kyrösjärvi ⊜	B 11	66
Kyröskoski	B 11	66
Kyštym	I 24	108
Kýthira	D 5	106
Kýthira I	D 5	106
Kyūshū I	H 3	126
Kyūshū-sanchi ⋏	H 3	126
Kywong	E 6	144
Kyyiv (Kiev)	D 7	110
Kyyiv □[6]	D 7	110
Kyyivs'ke vodoskhovyshche ⊜[1]	D 6	110
Kyzyl	B 2	124
Kyzyl-Kija	A 2	122
Kyzyl Kum ◆[2]	B 9	116
Kyzyl-Suu ≃	B 2	122
Kzyl-Orda see Qyzylorda	B 10	116

L

Name	Map Ref.	Page
La'a	D 5	130
Laa an der Thaya	B 8	102
Laakirchen	C 5	102
La Albuera	F 4	86

⸤ Waterfall ʊ Strait c Bay, Gulf ⊜ Lake ≡ Swamp ⋌ Ice Feature ⫪ Other Hydrographic Feature ✦ Submarine Feature □ Political Unit ◗ Cultural Institution ⊥ Historical Site ♠ Recreational Site ⊠ Airport ■ Military Installation ◆ Miscellaneous

La Alcarria — Lentini

Name | Map Ref. | Page

La Alcarria ◆¹ D 2 88
La Algaba G 5 86
La Almunia de Doña Godina C 3 88
La Antigua, Salina ≚ A 4 195
La Araucanía □³ F 1 195
Laascaanood F 6 202
Laasqoray E 6 202
La Asunción F 9 186
Laatzen D 6 98
Laâyoune see El Aaiún D 2 198
La Baie D 8 160
La Bañeza B 5 86
La Barca G 8 184
Labasa m 14 147c
La Bassée B 9 78
La Baule-Escoublac E 4 78
Labdah (Leptis Magna) ⊥ C 7 198
Labé C 2 200
Labe (Elbe) ≃ F 11 98
La Belle B 2 170
Laberge, Lake ◎ F 27 154
Labian, Tanjong ❯ D 7 134
La Biche ≃ D 15 156
Labin C 3 104
Labinsk G 12 110
Labis M 6 132
La Bisbal d'Empordà C 8 88
Labkovičy C 7 110
La Blanca Grande, Laguna ◎ F 5 195
Labná ⊥ G 15 184
Laborovija C 27 108
Laboulaye D 6 195
Labrador ◆¹ B 13 160
Labrador Basin ◆¹ C 7 60
Labrador City B 10 160
Labrador Sea ⁼² E 21 150
Lábrea E 6 190
La Brède D 3 80
Labrit D 3 80
Labuan D 7 134
Labuan, Pulau I D 7 134
Labuha F 9 134
Labuhan k 17 135b
Labuhanbajo G 7 134
Labutta F 2 132
Labytnangi C 27 108
Lac □³ C 8 200
Lača, ozero ◎ F 13 108
Lac-à-Beauce E 7 160
La Calera, Chile C 2 195
La Calera, Spain i 13 85b
La Campana G 5 86
Lacanau D 2 80
Lacantum ≃ I 14 184
La Capelle-en-Thiérache C 10 78
La Carlota F 7 192
La Carolina F 7 86
Lacaune E 6 80
Lac-Bouchette D 7 160
Lac Brochet B 21 156
Laccadive, Minicoy and Amīndīvi Islands see Lakshadweep □³ G 2 122
Lac Courte Oreilles Indian Reservation ◆⁴ C 3 166
Lac du Flambeau Indian Reservation ◆⁴ C 4 166
Lacedonia C 5 94
La Ceiba E 3 186
Lacepede Bay ⊂ F 2 144
Lac-Etchemin g 11 163a
Lacey B 2 178
La Chaise-Dieu, Abbaye de ▶¹ E 1 82
La Chambre E 4 82
La Chapelle-Saint-Luc D 11 78
La Charité-sur-Loire E 10 78
La Châtaigneraie B 3 80
La Chaux-de-Fonds C 4 82
Lachine A 7 162
Lachkaltsap Indian Reserve ◆⁴ D 7 156
Lachlan ≃ E 5 144
La Chorrera, Col. D 4 190
La Chorrera, Pan. F 4 186
Lachute A 4 164
La Ciotat G 3 82
La Citadelle ⊥ D 6 186
La Ciudad F 6 184
Lackawanna B 4 162
Lackawanna □⁶ E 3 164
Lac La Biche D 16 156
Lac la Ronge Provincial Park ♦ D 18 156
Laclede A 5 178
Lac-Mégantic F 8 160
La Colorada C 4 184
Lacombe E 15 156
La Concepción, Pan. F 4 186
La Concepción, Ven. F 6 186
Laconia C 7 164
La Coruña see A Coruña A 2 86
La Coruña □⁶ A 2 86
La Courtine C 6 80
La Crete B 13 156
La Crosse, Ks., U.S. F 5 174
La Crosse, Wi., U.S. D 3 166
La Cruz C 9 195
Lac Seul Indian Reserve ◆⁴ F 12 158
Ladākh □⁹ B 3 122
Ladākh Range ∧ D 12 116
Ladd E 4 166
Ladder Creek ≃ F 4 174
Ládi B 7 106
La Digue I J 7 112
Ladispoli H 7 92
Ladoga, Lake ◎ F 9 108
La Dorada B 3 190
La Doré D 7 160
Ladra ≃ A 3 86
Ladva-Vetka F 10 108
Ladybrand F 7 206
Lady Frere F 7 206
Ladysmith, B.C., Can. A 2 178
Ladysmith, S. Afr. E 8 206
Ladyzhyn A 10 104
Lae N 13 124
Lae I¹ C 8 136
Lærdalsøyri B 3 66
La Esmeralda D 8 184
Læsø I A 4 68
La Esperanza E 2 186
La Falda B 5 195
Lafayette, Co., U.S. B 6 176
Lafayette, Ga., U.S. E 6 170
Lafayette, In., U.S. B 5 170
Lafayette, La., U.S. G 2 170
Lafayette, Tn., U.S. D 5 170
Lafayette, Mount ∧ B 7 164
La Ferté-Bernard D 7 78
La Ferté-Gaucher D 10 78
La Ferté-Saint-Aubin E 8 78
Lafia D 6 200
Lafiagi D 6 200
La Flèche E 6 78
La Fontaine B 6 170
La Fuente de San Esteban D 4 86
Lagan D 6 66
Lagan ≃ D 7 66
La Garde G 4 82
La Garriga C 7 88
Lage D 5 98
Lågen ≃, Nor. F 5 64
Lågen ≃, Nor. C 4 66
Lages A 9 192
Laghouat C 5 198
Lagkádia D 4 106
Lagny D 9 78
Lagoa da Prata D 7 194
La Gomera I i 13 85b
Lagos, Nig. D 5 200
Lagos, Port. G 2 86
Lagos de Moreno G 9 184
La Gouèra E 1 198
La Grand'Combe F 2 82
La Grande C 4 178
La Grande Deux, Réservoir ◎¹ B 5 160
La Grande Quatre, Réservoir ◎¹ B 7 160
La Grange, Ga., U.S. F 6 170
Lagrange, In., U.S. B 6 170
La Grange, Tx., U.S. F 5 172
La Gran Sabana ≚ B 6 190
La Grave E 4 82
La Guajira □³ F 6 186
La Guajira, Península de ❯¹ A 4 190
Laguépie D 5 80
La Guerche-de-Bretagne E 5 78
Laguiole D 6 80
Laguna E 10 192
Laguna Beach G 6 182
Laguna Dam ◆⁶ F 1 176
Laguna de Jaco G 2 172
Laguna Indian Reservation ◆⁴ E 5 176
Laguna Paiva B 7 195
Laha B 15 128
La Habana (Havana) C 4 186
La Habra G 6 182
Lahad Datu D 7 134
La Harpe D 1 170
Lahat F 4 134
La Haute-Yamaska □⁶ A 6 164
Lahdenpohja F 9 108
Lahemaa rahvus ♦ C 13 66
La Higuera A 2 195
Lahij E 5 202
Lāhījān D 13 118
Lahnstein B 4 100
Lahore C 2 122
Lahr D 4 100
Lahti B 12 66
Laï D 8 200
Lai Chau C 6 132
Laichingen B 1 102
Laifeng D 9 130
L'Aigle D 7 78
Laignes E 11 78
Laincourt Rocks II F 3 126
La Inmaculada C 4 184
Laīri C 8 200
Laīri, Batha de ≃ C 8 200
Lais F 4 134
Laissac D 6 80
Laitila B 10 66
Laives C 7 92
Laiwu H 11 128
Laixi H 13 128
Laiyang H 13 128
Laizhou Wan ⊂ H 12 128
Laja ≃ C 22 108
Laja, Laguna de la ◎ F 9 192
La Jara ◆¹ E 5 86
La Jarrie B 3 80
Lajeado A 11 195
Lajemmerais □⁶ A 5 164
Lajord F 6 158
Lajosmizse B 5 104
La Joya F 1 176
Lakamané C 3 200
Lake □⁶ A 1 182
Lake Andes D 5 174
Lakeba Passage ᛘ n 15 147c
Lake Butler D 3 168
Lake Cargelligo D 6 144
Lake Carmel E 5 164
Lake Charles G 2 170
Lake City, Ar., U.S. E 3 170
Lake City, Fl., U.S. D 3 168
Lake City, Pa., U.S. B 2 164
Lake Clark National Park ♦ F 17 154
Lake Coleridge E 3 146
Lake Corpus Christi State Park ♦ G 5 172
Lake Crystal C 7 174
Lake District ◆¹ C 3 72
Lake District National Park ♦ C 3 72
Lake Elsinore G 6 182
Lake Eyre National Park ♦ J 3 142
Lakefield National Park ♦ C 6 142
Lake Forest A 5 170
Lake Geneva D 4 166
Lake George C 5 164
Lake Harbor F 4 168
Lake Harbour D 19 150
Lake Havasu City E 1 176
Lakehurst F 4 164
Lake Jackson F 6 172
Lakeland F 4 168
Lake Louise F 13 156
Lake Mackay Aboriginal Land ◆⁴ H 10 140
Lake Malawi National Park ♦ E 5 204
Lake Manyara National Park ♦ C 6 204
Lake Mead National Recreation Area ♦ D 1 176
Lake Meredith National Recreation Area ♦ C 3 172
Lake Minchumina E 19 154
Lake Murray State Park ♦ C 5 172
Lake Nakuru National Park ♦ C 6 204
Lake Norden C 6 174
Lake of the Ozarks State Park ♦ C 2 170
Lake Oswego C 2 178
Lake Paringa E 2 146
Lake Placid B 4 164
Lake Pleasant C 4 164
Lake Preston C 6 174
Lake Pukaki F 3 146
Lakes Entrance F 7 144
Lakeside, Ca., U.S. H 7 182
Lakeside, Mt., U.S. A 6 178
Lake Superior Provincial Park ♦ B 6 166
Lake Tahoe-Nevada State Park ♦ A 4 182
Lake Traverse ◆⁴ C 6 174
Lakeview, Ga., U.S. E 6 170
Lake View, Ia., U.S. D 7 174
Lakeview, Mi., U.S. B 1 162
Lakeview, Or., U.S. D 3 178
Lakeville C 2 166
Lake Wales F 4 168
Lakewood, Co., U.S. F 2 174
Lakewood, N.J., U.S. F 4 164
Lakewood, Oh., U.S. C 3 162
Lakewood, Wa., U.S. B 2 178
Lake Worth F 4 168
Lakhnādon E 3 122
Lakin G 4 174
Lakinsk H 13 108
Lakonikós Kólpos ⊂ D 4 106
Laksefjorden ⊂ A 13 64
Lakselv A 12 64
Lakshadweep □³ G 2 122
Lakshadweep II G 2 122
Lakshadweep Sea ⁼² H 2 122
La Laja E 1 195
Lāla Mūsa C 2 122
Lalara E 7 200
L'Alcúdia E 4 88
Laleham G 9 142
L'Alfàs del Pi F 4 88
La Ligua C 2 195
Lalin ≃ D 16 128
Lalinde D 4 80
La Línea de la Concepción H 5 86
Lalitpur, India E 3 122
Lalitpur, Nepal D 5 122
La Loche C 17 156
La Loche, Lac ◎ C 17 156
La Louvière D 3 69
La Maddalena H 5 92
La Malbaie E 8 160
La Mancha ◆¹ E 2 88
Lamandau ≃ F 6 134
Lamar F 3 174
La Marmora, Punta ∧ F 2 90
La Marsa B 7 198
La Martre D 10 160
Lamas E 3 190
Lambaréné F 7 200
Lambayeque E 2 190
Lambert B 2 174
Lambert, Cape ❯ M 14 124
Lambert Glacier ◻ D 15 208
Lambertville F 4 164
Lambrechtsdrif E 4 206
Lamé D 7 200
Lamèque E 11 160
La Mesa, Ca., U.S. H 6 182
Lamesa, Tx., U.S. D 3 172
Lamía C 5 106
L'Amiante □⁶ A 7 164
Lamington National Park ♦ B 9 144
Lammermuir ◆¹ B 4 72
Lammeulo L 2 132
Lamming Mills E 11 156
Lamoille □⁶ B 6 164
Lamon Bay ⊂ C 8 134
Lamont, Ab., Can. E 15 156
Lamont, Ca., U.S. E 5 182
La Monte C 2 170
Lamotrek I¹ C 6 136
La Motte-Chalançon F 3 82
Lampang E 4 132
Lampasas E 4 172
Lampertheim C 5 100
Lampeter E 2 72
Lamphun E 4 132
Lāmu E 1 132
La Mure F 3 82
Lan' ≃ C 5 110
Lanai I i 10 181a
Lanai City i 10 181a
Lanark B 3 72
Lanark □⁶ B 2 164
Lancang G 5 130
Lancashire □⁶ D 4 72
Lancaster, Eng., U.K. C 4 72
Lancaster, Ca., U.S. F 5 182
Lancaster, Mo., U.S. B 7 174
Lancaster, N.H., U.S. B 7 164
Lancaster, Oh., U.S. D 2 162
Lancaster, Pa., U.S. F 2 164
Lancaster, Tx., U.S. D 5 172
Lancaster, Va., U.S. E 5 162
Lancaster, Wi., U.S. D 3 166
Lancaster □⁶ F 2 164
Lancaster Sound ᛘ B 16 150
Lanchyn A 8 104
Lanciano B 4 94
Lancun H 13 128
Łańcut C 12 96
Lancy D 4 82
Landau an der Isar D 9 100
Landau in der Pfalz C 5 100
Land Between the Lakes ◆¹ D 4 170
Landeck E 6 96
Lander D 9 178
Lander □⁶ A 6 182
Landerneau D 2 78
Landes □³ D 3 80
Landes ◆¹ E 3 80
Landing Lake ◎ D 10 158
Landis E 17 156
Lando B 4 168
Landquart D 7 82
Landsberg am Lech D 7 100
Landsberg an der Warthe see Gorzów Wielkopolski B 8 96
Land's End ❯ G 1 72
Landshut D 9 100
Landskrona E 6 66
Landstuhl C 4 100
Lanester E 3 78
Lanett C 2 168
Langa-Langa C 2 204
Langano, Lake ◎ F 4 202
Langarūd D 14 118
Langban C 7 66
Langdon A 5 174
Langeais E 7 78
Langeland I C 3 68
Langelsheim E 7 98
Langen, Ger. C 5 100
Langen, Ger. C 5 98
Langenau D 7 100
Langenburg F 8 158
Langenfeld E 3 98
Langenhagen D 6 98
Langenselbold B 6 100
Langenthal C 5 82
Langesund C 4 66
Langfang G 11 128
Langgapayung N 4 132
Langholm B 4 72
Langjökull ◻ m 20 64a
Langkawi, Pulau I K 4 132
Langley G 10 156
Langlo ≃ H 7 142
Langlois D 1 178
Langnau im Emmental D 5 82
Langogne F 1 82
Langoiran D 3 80
Langøya I B 7 64
Langreo A 5 86
Langres C 3 82
Langsa L 3 132
Langsa, Teluk ⊂ L 4 132
Langshan F 6 128
Lang Son D 8 132
Langudi Rassa National Park ♦ E 4 202
Languedoc □⁹ G 5 76
Langzhong E 8 130
Lanín, Parque Nacional ♦ F 2 195
Lanín, Volcán ∧¹ F 2 195
Länkäran J 16 110
Länkipohja B 12 66
Lannilis D 2 78
Lannion D 3 78
L'Annonciation E 6 160
Lanping E 4 130
Lansdale F 3 164
L'Anse-aux-Meadows National Historic Site ♦ C 16 160
L' Anse Indian Reservation ◆⁴ B 4 162
Lansing B 1 162
Länsi-Suomi □³ E 11 64
Lanslebourg-Mont-Cenis E 4 82
Lantau Island I G 11 130
Lantau Peak ∧ I 18 131a
La Nucia F 4 88
Lanusei F 2 90
Lanxi, China D 14 130
Lanxi, China C 16 128
Lanzarote I i 17 85b
Lanzhou H 6 128
Lanzo Torinese D 3 92
Laoag E 4 132
Laoang B 8 134
Laoang C 9 134
Lao Cai C 6 132
Laoha ≃ E 12 128
Laoheishan E 18 128
Laohekou B 10 130
Laois □³ D 4 75
Laon C 10 78
La Orchila, Isla I F 8 186
La Orotava i 14 85b
La Oroya F 3 190
Laos □¹ H 12 112
Lapa C 5 194
Lapalisse D 1 82
La Palma F 5 186
La Palma I i 13 85b
La Palma del Condado G 4 86
La Paloma D 10 195
La Pampa □³ G 6 192
La Paragua G 9 186
La Pasión ≃ I 14 184
La Paz, Arg. B 8 195
La Paz, Arg. C 4 195
La Paz, Bol. G 5 190
La Paz, Mex. E 4 184
La Paz, Ur. D 9 195
La Paz, Bahía de ⊂ D 4 184
La Perouse Strait ᛘ E 17 114
La Pesca F 11 184
La Piedad de Cabadas G 8 184
La Place G 3 170
Lap Lae F 4 132
Lapland see Lappland □⁹ C 9 64
Laplandija B 10 108
La Plata, Arg. D 9 195
La Plata, Md., U.S. H 1 164
La Plata, Mo., U.S. B 2 170
La Plata Peak ∧ C 5 176
La Pocatière E 8 160
Laporte, Co., U.S. B 6 176
La Porte, In., U.S. B 5 170
Laporte, Pa., U.S. E 2 164
La Porte City D 2 166
Lappajärvi ◎ E 11 64
Lappeenranta B 13 66
Lappersdorf C 8 100
Lappi □³ C 13 64
Lappland □⁹ C 9 64
La Pryor F 4 172
Laptev Sea (Laptevyh, more) ⁼² B 15 114
Laptevyh, more see Laptev Sea ⁼² B 15 114
Lapua E 11 64
La Puebla de Almoradiel E 7 86
La Puebla de Cazalla G 5 86
La Puebla del Río G 4 86
La Puebla de Montalbán E 6 86
Lapväärtti A 10 66
Łapy B 12 96
La Quiaca D 6 192
L'Aquila G 9 92
L'Aquila □⁶ B 3 94
Lār I 16 118
Lara □³ F 7 186
Laracha A 2 86
Larache B 3 198
La Rambla G 6 86
Laramie E 2 174
Laramie ≃ A 6 176
Laramie Mountains ∧ Wy., U.S. B 6 176
Laramie Mountains ∧ A 6 176
Laranjeiras do Sul B 6 192
Larantuka G 8 134
Larap C 8 134
Larat, Pulau I G 10 134
L'Arbresle E 2 82
Larchwood D 6 174
Lare G 4 202
Laredo, Spain A 7 86
Laredo, Tx., U.S. G 4 172
La Reforma E 5 184
L'Argentière-la-Bessée F 4 82
Largo F 3 168
Largs F 3 72
La Ricamarie E 2 82
Larimore B 6 174
La Rioja A 4 195
La Rioja □³, Arg. E 6 192
La Rioja □³, Spain B 2 88
Lárisa C 5 106
La Rivière-du-Nord □⁶ A 5 164
Lärkāna D 1 122
Lark Harbour D 14 160
Larnaka E 5 118
Larne B 6 75
Laro D 7 200
La Robla B 5 86
La Roca del Vallès C 7 88
La Roche-Bernard E 4 78
La Roche-Chalais C 3 80
La Rochefoucauld C 4 80
La Rochelle B 2 80
La Roche-sur-Yon B 2 80
La Roda E 2 88
Larrimah D 12 140
Larsen Ice Shelf ◻ C 2 208
La Rumorosa F 5 180
Laruns F 3 80
Larvik C 5 66
La Salle B 4 170
La Sarre D 4 160
Lasarte A 3 88
Las Ballenas, Canal de ᛘ C 3 184
Las Cabezas de San Juan H 5 86
Las Casitas ∧ F 5 184
Las Choapas I 12 184
Las Cruces, Mex. C 6 184
Las Cruces, N.M., U.S. F 5 176
La Selle, Morne ∧ D 6 186
La Serena A 2 195
La Serena ◆¹ F 5 86
La Seu d'Urgell B 6 88
La Seyne-sur-Mer G 3 82
Las Flores D 8 195
Las Flores, Arroyo ≃ E 7 195
Lashburn E 17 156
Las Heras, Arg. I 6 192
Las Heras, Arg. C 3 195
Lashio C 3 132
Las Hormigas E 10 184
Łasin B 10 96
Łask C 10 96
Laško D 7 102
Las Lajas G 5 192
Las Lomitas D 7 192
Lašma I 14 108
Las Margaritas I 14 184
Las Minas, Cerro ∧ E 2 186
Las Nieves D 7 184
La Solana F 7 86
Las Palmas de Gran Canaria i 15 85b
Las Pedroñeras E 2 88
La Spezia E 5 92
La Spezia □⁶ E 6 92
Las Piedras D 9 195
Las Piedras ≃ F 4 190
Las Plumas H 6 192
Las Rosas I 13 184
Lassay D 6 78
Lassen □⁶ A 3 182
Lassen Peak ∧¹ B 3 180
Lassen Volcanic National Park ♦ B 3 180
L'Assomption □⁶ A 5 164
Las Tablas G 4 186
Last Mountain Lake ◎ F 19 156
Las Tórtolas, Cerro ∧ E 6 192
Lastoursville F 7 200
Lastrup D 4 98
Las Tunas C 5 186
Las Tunas Grandes, Laguna ◎ E 6 195
La Suze-sur-Sarthe E 7 78
Las Varas G 7 184
Las Varillas B 6 195
Las Vegas, N.M., U.S. E 6 176
Las Vegas, Nv., U.S. D 1 176
Latady Island I D 1 208
Laterza D 6 94
La Teste-de-Buch D 2 80
Latiano D 7 94
Latimer D 2 166
Latina H 8 92
Latina □⁶ H 9 92
Latisana D 9 92
Latjuga D 18 108
La Tortuga, Isla I A 5 190
La Tour-du-Pin E 3 82
La Trimouille B 5 80
La Trinité s 26 187h
Latrobe, Austl. i 12 145a
Latrobe, Pa., U.S. C 4 162
La Trobe ≃ G 6 144
La Tuque E 7 160
Lātūr F 3 122
Latvia □¹ D 13 62
Lauchhammer E 10 98
Lauda-Königshofen C 6 100
Lauder B 4 72
Lauenburg C 7 98
Lauf an der Pegnitz D 6 96
Lauffen am Neckar C 6 100
Lau Group II E 10 136
Lauingen D 7 100
Laukaa E 12 64
Launceston, Austl. i 12 145a
Launceston, Eng., U.K. G 2 72
La Unión, Chile G 1 195
La Unión, Spain G 4 88
Laupheim D 6 100
Laureana di Borrello F 5 90
Laurel, Md., U.S. D 5 162
Laurel, Ms., U.S. G 4 170
Laurel, Mt., U.S. C 3 180
Laurel Hill B 5 168
Laurel Ridge State Park ♦ D 4 162
Laurencekirk D 4 72
Laurens B 3 168
Laurentides, Les (Les Laurentides) ∧¹ E 8 160
Laurie Island I L 11 192
Laurie Lake ◎ C 8 158
Laurier F 9 158
Laurière B 5 80
Laurinburg B 5 168
Laurium B 4 166
Lausanne D 4 82
Lausitzer Neisse (Nysa Łużycka) ≃ E 11 98
Laut, Pulau I F 7 134
Lauta C 7 96
Lautaro F 1 195
Lauterbach B 6 100
Lauterbrunnen D 5 82
Lauter Sachsen B 9 100
Laut Kecil, Kepulauan II F 7 134
Lautoka m 13 147c
Lauzerte D 5 80
Lava Beds National Monument ♦ E 3 178
Lava Hot Springs D 7 178
Laval, Qc., Can. F 7 160
Laval, Fr. D 6 78
Laval □⁶ A 5 164
La Valette-du-Var G 3 82
La Vall d'Uixó (Vall de Uxó) E 4 88
La Vallée-de-la-Gatineau □⁶ A 3 164
La Vallée-du-Richelieu □⁶ A 5 164
Lāvān, Jazīreh-ye I I 15 118
Lavapié, Punta ❯ G 5 192
Lavardac D 4 80
La Vega D 7 186
Lavela E 16 108
Lavello C 5 94
Laveno E 6 82
La Venta ⊥ H 13 184
La Vera ◆¹ D 5 86
La Vergne E 5 170
La Verna ▶¹ F 7 92
Laverne B 3 172
Laverton K 7 140
La Victoria F 8 186
Lavik B 2 66
La Vila Joiosa F 4 88
Lavonia B 3 168
Lavon Lake ◎¹ D 5 172
La Voulte-sur-Rhône F 2 82
Lavras D 8 194
Lavrentija, zaliv ⊂ D 9 154
Lávrio D 6 106
Lavushi Manda National Park ♦ E 4 204
Lawang k 21 135b
Lawas E 7 134
Lawes G 7 72
Lawford Lake ◎ D 10 158
Lawksawk H 3 130
Lawn D 4 172
Lawn Hill Creek ≃ E 4 142
Lawn Hill National Park ♦ B 4 162
Lawra C 4 200
Lawrence, In., U.S. C 6 170
Lawrence, Ks., U.S. C 1 170
Lawrence, Ma., U.S. D 7 164
Lawrenceburg E 5 170
Lawrenceville, Il., U.S. C 5 170
Lawrenceville, N.J., U.S. F 4 164
Lawton, N.D., U.S. A 5 174
Lawton, Ok., U.S. C 4 172
Lawu, Gunung ∧ k 20 135b
Lawz, Jabal al- ∧ I 8 116
Laxå C 7 66
Laxou B 4 82
Lay Lake ◎¹ F 5 170
Layton E 7 178
Laytonville C 2 180
Lázaro Cárdenas I 8 184
Lazdijai E 11 66
Lazio □³ E 4 90
La Zubia G 7 86
Leader F 17 156
Leadville C 5 176
Leaf ≃ G 4 170
Leaghur, Lake ◎ D 4 142
League City H 1 170
Leaksville E 3 162
Lealman F 3 168
Leamington, On., Can. G 2 160
Leamington see Royal Leamington Spa, Eng., U.K. E 5 72
Leamington Spa see Royal Leamington Spa E 5 72
Le'an E 12 130
Learmonth H 3 140
Leatherhead F 6 72
Leatherman Peak ∧ C 6 178
Leavenworth C 1 170
Leawood C 1 170
Lebach C 3 100
Lebak D 8 134
Lébamba F 7 200
Lebanon, In., U.S. B 5 170
Lebanon, Ky., U.S. D 6 170
Lebanon, N.H., U.S. C 6 164
Lebanon, Oh., U.S. D 1 162
Lebanon, Or., U.S. C 2 178
Lebanon, Pa., U.S. F 2 164
Lebanon, S.D., U.S. C 5 174
Lebanon, Tn., U.S. D 5 170
Lebanon □¹ F 5 112
Lebanon □⁶ F 2 164
Lebanon Junction D 6 170
Lebanon Mountains ∧ B 5 120
Le Bas-Richelieu □⁶ A 5 164
Lebedino I 18 108
Lebedyn D 9 110
Lebesby A 13 64
Le Bic D 9 160
Lebjaže I 27 108
Lebo F 7 174
Lebork A 9 96
Le Bourg-d'Oisans E 3 82
Lebrija H 4 86
Łebsko, Jezioro ◎ A 9 96
Lebu E 1 195
Le Cannet G 4 82
Le Cateau-Cambrésis B 10 78
Lecce D 8 94
Lecce □⁶ D 8 94
Lecco D 5 92
Lecco □⁶ D 5 92
Le Center C 8 174
Lech ≃ D 7 100
Le Chambon-Feugerolles E 2 82
Lechang F 11 130
Le Châtelet B 6 80
Le Cheylard F 2 82
Leck B 5 98
Lecompte G 2 170
Le Creusot F 11 78
Le Croisic E 4 78
Łęczyca B 10 96
Ledbury E 4 72
Lede D 2 69
Ledig C 7 206
Ledo F 7 122
Ledong I 9 130
Le Dorat B 4 80
Ledu H 4 128
Leduc E 15 156
Ledyard Bay ⊂ B 12 154
Lędyczek B 9 96
Leech Lake ◎ B 7 174
Leech Lake Indian Reservation ◆⁴ B 7 174
Leeds, Eng., U.K. D 5 72
Leeds, Al., U.S. F 5 170
Leeds ◻⁶ D 5 72
Leeds and Grenville □⁶ B 3 164
Leek D 4 72
Leer C 4 98
Leerdam E 2 98
Leesburg, Fl., U.S. E 4 168
Leesburg, Va., U.S. D 5 162
Lees Summit C 1 170
Leesville G 2 170
Leeudoringstad D 7 206
Leeuwarden A 4 69
Leeuwin, Cape ❯ N 3 140
Lee Vining C 4 182
Leeward Islands II D 9 186
Léfini ≃ C 2 204
Lefkáda C 4 106
Lefkáda I C 4 106
Léfka Óri ∧ E 6 106
Léfka Óri National Park ♦ E 5 106
Lefkímmi C 3 106
Lefroy, Lake ◎ L 6 140
Leganés D 7 86
Legaspi C 8 134
Leggett C 2 180
Legionowo B 11 96
Legnago D 7 92
Legnano D 4 92
Legnica C 9 96
Le Gosier n 21 187e
Le Grand-Quevilly C 7 78
Le Granit □⁶ A 8 164
Le Grau-du-Roi G 2 82
Legume B 9 144
Le Haut-Richelieu □⁶ A 5 164
Le Haut-Saint-François □⁶ A 7 164
Le Haut-Saint-Laurent □⁶ A 4 164
Le Havre C 7 78
Lehčevo D 7 104
Lehigh □⁶ F 3 164
Lehigh Acres F 4 168
Leho F 3 202
Lehrte D 7 98
Lehta F 18 108
Lehtse C 12 66
Lei ≃ E 11 130
Leiah C 2 122
Leibnitz D 7 102
Leicester E 5 72
Leicestershire □⁶ E 5 72
Leichhardt ≃ E 5 142
Leiden B 3 69
Leigh Creek South C 2 144
Leighton E 5 170
Leighton Buzzard F 6 72
Leinfelden-Echterdingen B 7 82
Leinster □⁹ C 4 75
Leipalingis E 11 66
Leipheim D 7 100
Leipsic C 2 162
Leipzig E 9 98
Leipzig □⁶ E 9 98
Leiria E 2 86
Leiria □³ E 2 86
Leisi C 11 66
Leisler, Mount ∧ H 10 140
Leisnig E 9 98
Leitchville E 5 144
Leitrim □³ C 4 75
Leivádia C 5 106
Leixlip C 5 75
Leiyang E 11 130
Leizhou Bandao ❯¹ H 9 130
Lekeitio A 2 88
Lekhureng B 8 206
Lékoni F 7 200
Lékoumou □³ C 1 204
Le Kreider C 4 198
Leksand B 7 66
Leksozero, ozero ◎ E 9 108
Le Lamentin s 26 187h
Leland C 6 166
Lelång ◎ C 5 66
Leli Shan ∧ C 4 122
Le Locle C 4 82
Le Lude E 7 78
Lelystad B 4 69
Le Maire, Estrecho de ᛘ J 7 192
Léman, Lac see Geneva, Lake ◎ D 4 82
Le Mans E 7 78
Lemay C 3 170
Lembeek D 3 69
Lemberg, Sk., Can. F 7 158
Lemberg see L'viv, Ukr. E 4 110
Lemdiyya B 5 198
Lemdiyya □³ H 7 88
Leme E 7 194
Lemesós (Limassol) D 5 118
Lemgo D 5 98
Lemhi ≃ C 7 178
Lemhi Pass ✕ C 7 178
Lemhi Range ∧ C 7 178
Lemmatsi C 13 66
Lemmenjoen kansallispuisto ♦ B 13 64
Lemmon, Mount ∧ F 3 176
Lemoenshoek G 4 206
Lemont C 5 162
Le Montet B 7 80
Lemoore D 4 182
Lempore E 2 186
Lemvig B 1 68
Lena ≃ B 15 114
Lenart D 7 102
Lengerich D 4 98
Lenggries E 9 102
Lenghu B 6 122
Lengshuitan E 10 130
Lengwe National Park ♦ F 5 204
Lenhovda D 7 66
Leninabad see Khujand A 1 122
Leninakan see Gyumri I 13 110
Leningrad see Sankt-Peterburg F 9 108
Leningradskaja oblast' □⁶ G 10 108
Leningradskoe J 29 108
Leninogorsk, Kaz. D 11 114
Leninogorsk, Russia I 19 108
Lenin Peak ∧ B 2 122
Leninsk, Russia I 23 108
Leninsk, Uzb. A 2 122
Leninskij I 12 108
Leninskoe, Kaz. I 26 108
Leninskoe, Russia B 19 128
Lennestadt E 5 98
Lennonville J 4 140
Lennox and Addington □⁶ B 1 164
Lennoxville A 7 164
Lenoir B 4 168
Lenore Lake ◎ E 19 156
Lenormand, Lac ◎ A 6 160
Lenox, Ga., U.S. D 3 168
Lenox, Tn., U.S. D 4 170
Lens B 9 78
Lensk C 14 114
Lenskoe G 25 108
Lentate D 8 94
Lentini G 5 94

Symbols in the index entries represent the broad categories identified in the key at the right. Symbols with superior numbers (∧¹) identify subcategories (see complete key on page 242).

∧ Mountain ∧ Mountains ✕ Pass ∨ Valley ≚ Plain ❯ Cape I Island II Islands ⊥ Other Topographic Feature ≃ River ≅ Canal

Lentsweletau — Louisville

Name — Map Ref. — Page

Lentsweletau C 6 206
Lentua ◎ D 14 64
Lentvaris E 12 66
Lenyenye B 9 206
Lenzburg C 6 82
Léo C 4 200
Leoben C 7 102
Leominster, Eng., U.K. E 4 72
Leominster, Ma., U.S. D 7 164
Léon, Fr. E 2 80
León, Mex. G 9 184
León, Nic. E 3 186
León, Spain B 5 86
León □6 B 5 86
Leon ≃ E 5 172
Léon, Pays de ◆1 D 2 78
Leonardville F 6 174
Leonberg D 5 100
Leonding B 6 102
Leonforte G 4 94
Leongatha G 5 144
Leonora K 6 140
Leonville G 2 170
Léopold II, Lac see Mai-Ndombe, Lac ◎ C 2 204
Leopoldina D 9 194
Leopoldsburg C 4 69
Léopoldville see Kinshasa C 2 204
Leova B 10 104
Le Palais E 3 78
Lepanto see Náfpaktos C 4 106
Lepe G 3 86
Le Péage-de-Roussillon E 2 82
Lepel' E 14 66
Le Petit-Quevilly C 7 78
Lephepe B 6 206
Leping D 13 130
L'Épiphanie F 7 160
Le Pont-de-Beauvoisin E 3 82
Le Port q 20 207e
Lepsi A 12 116
Le Puy E 1 82
Léraba ≃ D 4 200
Léré, Chad D 7 200
Lere, Nig. C 6 200
Lerici C 2 90
Lérida see Lleida C 5 88
Lérida (Lleida) □6 C 6 88
Lerma B 7 86
Le Roy F 7 174
Lerum D 6 66
Lerwick g 9 74a
Les Abymes n 21 187e
Les Andelys C 8 78
Les Borges Blanques C 5 88
Lésbos I C 7 106
L'Escala F 7 80
Lescar E 3 80
Les Cayes D 6 186
Les Collines-de-l'Outaouais □6 A 3 164
Lesdiboderi D 7 200
Les Échelles E 3 82
Leshan D 6 130
Les Herbiers F 5 78
Lesina C 5 94
Les Jardins-de-Napierville □6 A 5 164
Lesjaskog E 3 64
Lesko D 12 96
Leskovac D 6 104
Leskov Island I J 12 188
Les Laurentides see Laurentides, Les ⁂1 E 8 160
Leslie, S. Afr. D 8 206
Leslie, Mi., U.S. B 1 162
Les Maskoutains □6 A 6 164
Les Matelles E 7 80
Les Moulins □6 A 5 164
Lesneven D 2 78
Lesnoe G 11 108
Lesnoj H 27 108
Lesopil'noe C 19 128
Lesosibirsk D 12 114
Lesotho □1 K 10 196
Lesozavodsk B 4 126
Lesozavodskij C 10 108
Les Pays-d'en-Haut □6 A 4 164
Les Riceys D 11 78
Les Sables-d'Olonne B 2 80
Lessebo D 7 66
Lesser Antilles II D 9 186
Lesser Caucasus ⁂ B 12 118
Lesser Slave ≃ D 14 156
Lesser Slave Lake ◎ D 14 156
Lesser Sunda Islands II G 8 134
Lessines D 2 69
Lestijoki ≃ E 12 64
Le Sueur C 2 166
Leszno C 9 96
Letaba ≃ B 9 206
Letchworth F 6 72
Letchworth State Park ♦ B 4 162
Le Teil F 2 82
Lethbridge G 15 156
Leti, Kepulauan II G 9 134
Leticia D 5 190
Letka G 18 108
Letlhakane A 6 206
Letlhakeng C 7 206
Letpadan F 2 132
Le Trayas G 4 82
Le Tréport B 8 78
Letter D 6 98
Letterkenny B 4 75
Letychiv E 5 110
Leu C 8 104
Leuk D 5 82
Leuser, Gunung ∧ M 3 132
Leušinskij Tuman, ozero ◎ G 26 108
Leutkirch E 7 100
Leuven D 3 69
Leuze D 2 69
Levack E 3 160
Le Val-Saint-François □6 A 6 164
Levan C 3 176
Levante, Riviera di ⊥̲2 E 5 92
Levanto E 5 92
Levelland D 2 172
Levelock G 16 154
Leveque, Cape › E 7 140
Leverano D 7 94
Leverkusen E 4 98
Levice B 10 102
Levier D 4 82
Levin D 5 146
Lévis E 8 160
Levisa Fork ≃ E 2 162
Levittown, P.R. j 15 187b
Levittown, N.Y., U.S. F 5 164
Levittown, Pa., U.S. F 4 164
Levkosía see Nicosia E 5 118
Levroux F 8 78
Levuka m 14 147c
Lewe E 2 132
Lewes H 3 164
Lewis G 5 174
Lewis □6 C 3 164
Lewis, Butt of › B 2 74
Lewis, Isle of I B 2 74
Lewis and Clark Caverns State Park ♦ C 8 178
Lewis and Clark Lake ◎1 D 6 174
Lewis and Clark Range ⁂ B 7 178
Lewisburg, Pa., U.S. F 2 164
Lewisburg, Tn., U.S. E 5 170
Lewisporte D 16 160
Lewis Range ⁂ A 7 178
Lewiston, Id., U.S. B 5 178
Lewiston, Me., U.S. A 8 162
Lewiston, Mi., U.S. A 1 162
Lewistown, Il., U.S. B 3 170
Lewistown, Mt., U.S. B 9 178
Lewistown, Pa., U.S. C 5 162
Lewisville D 5 172
Lewisville Lake ◎1 D 5 172
Lexington, Ga., U.S. C 3 168
Lexington, Ky., U.S. C 6 170
Lexington, Ma., U.S. D 7 164
Lexington, Mo., U.S. C 2 170
Lexington, N.C., U.S. B 4 168
Lexington, S.C., U.S. B 4 168
Lexington, Tx., U.S. E 5 172
Lexington, Va., U.S. E 4 162
Lexington Park D 5 162
Leyden see Leiden B 3 69
Leye F 8 130
Leyland D 4 72
Leyte I C 8 134
Leyte Gulf ⊂ C 9 134
Lezhi C 7 130
Lëzna B 7 110
L'gov D 9 110
Lhasa D 6 122
Lhasa ≃ C 6 122
Lhoknga L 2 132
Lhokseumawe L 3 132
Lhorong C 3 130
L'Hospitalet de Llobregat C 7 88
Li F 4 132
Li ≃ D 9 130
Liamuiga, Mount ∧1 m 20 187d
Lian ≃ F 11 130
Liancheng F 13 130
Liangbao A 10 130
Liangdang B 7 130
Liangping C 8 130
Liangyuan B 13 130
Lianjiang H 10 130
Liannan F 11 130
Lianxian F 11 130
Lianyuan E 10 130
Lianyungang I 12 128
Liao ≃ F 14 128
Liaocheng H 10 128
Liaodong Bandao ›1 G 14 128
Liaodong Wan ⊂ F 13 128
Liaoning □3 F 14 128
Liaoyang F 14 128
Liaoyuan E 15 128
Liaozhong F 14 128
Liapádes C 3 106
Liard ≃ D 8 150
Libagon C 9 134
Libby A 6 178
Libby Dam ◆6 A 6 178
Liberal, Ks., U.S. G 4 174
Liberal, Mo., U.S. G 7 174
Liberec B 12 100
Liberecký □3 C 8 96
Liberia F 3 186
Liberia □1 H 6 196
Libertador General Bernardo O'Higgins □3 D 2 195
Liberty, Ky., U.S. A 2 168
Liberty, Mo., U.S. C 1 170
Liberty, S.C., U.S. B 3 168
Liberty, Tx., U.S. G 1 170
Libertyville A 4 170
Libibi E 2 204
Libo F 8 130
Liboi G 5 202
Libourne D 3 80
Libramont E 4 69
Libreville E 6 200
Libya □1 F 9 196
Libyan Desert ◆2 F 10 196
Licancábur, Volcán ∧1 D 6 192
Licantén D 1 195
Licata G 3 94
Lice C 9 118
Lich B 5 100
Licheng H 9 128
Lichfield E 5 72
Lichinga E 6 204
Lichtenau E 6 98
Lichtenburg D 7 206
Lichtenfels B 8 100
Lichtenstein F 9 98
Lichtenstein, Schloss ◗ D 6 100
Lichtervelde C 2 69
Lichuan, China E 13 130
Lichuan, China C 9 130
Lickershamn D 9 66
Licking ≃ D 1 162
Licungo ≃ F 6 204
Lida F 12 66
Liden E 8 64
Lidice ♦ B 11 100
Lidköping C 6 66
Lido di Ostia ◆8 E 4 90
Lidzbark B 10 96
Lidzbark Warmiński A 11 96
Liebertwolkwitz E 9 98
Liebig, Mount ∧ H 11 140
Liechtenstein □1 F 9 62
Liège (Luik) D 4 69
Liège □3 D 4 69
Lielvārde D 12 66
Lienen D 4 98
Lienz D 4 102
Liepāja D 10 66
Lier C 3 69
Liesjärven kansallispuisto ♦ B 11 66
Liestal C 5 82
Liévin B 9 78
Lièvre ≃ F 6 160
Liezen C 6 102
Lifanga B 3 204
Lifford B 4 75
Lifoku F 9 200
Lifou I D 14 138
Ligasa B 3 204
Lightning Ridge B 7 144
Lignières F 9 78
Ligny-en-Barrois B 3 82
Ligonha ≃ F 6 204
Ligonier B 6 170
Liguria □3 E 5 92
Ligurian Sea ⊤2 F 4 92
Lihoslavl' H 11 108
Lihue h 9 181a
Lihuel Calel, Parque Nacional ♦ E 5 195
Lihula C 11 66
Lijiang E 5 130
Likasi E 4 204
Likimi B 3 204
Likoma Island I E 5 204
Likouala □3 B 2 204
Likouala ≃ C 2 204
Lilanga C 3 204
L'Île-Rousse i 8 83a
Lilienthal C 5 98
Liling E 11 130
Lilla Edet C 6 66
Lille B 10 78
Lillebælt (Little Belt) ⊍ C 2 68
Lillebonne C 7 78
Lillehammer B 5 66
Lillerød C 5 68
Lillers B 9 78
Lillestrøm C 5 66
Lillhärdal B 7 66
Lillo E 7 86
Lillooet ≃ G 10 156
Lilongwe E 5 204
Liloy D 8 134
Lilydale i 12 145a
Lim ≃ D 5 104
Lima, Peru F 3 190
Lima, N.Y., U.S. D 1 164
Lima, Oh., U.S. C 1 162
Limarí ≃ B 2 195
Limassol see Lemesós E 5 118
Limavady A 5 75
Limay D 8 78
Limay ≃ G 6 192
Limbach-Oberfrohna F 9 98
Limbe, Cam. E 6 200
Limbe, Mwi. F 6 204
Limbueta E 2 204
Limburg □3, Bel. D 4 69
Limburg □3, Neth. C 4 69
Limburg an der Lahn B 5 100
Limburgerhof C 5 100
Lim Chu Kang i 14 134a
Limeira E 7 194
Limerick, Sk., Can. G 18 156
Limerick (Luimneach), Ire. D 3 75
Limerick □3 D 3 75
Limestone g 12 163a
Limestone ≃ C 11 158
Limestone, Lake ◎1 E 5 172
Limfjorden ◎ B 2 68
Limmared D 6 66
Limmen Bight ⊂ C 2 142
Límnos I C 6 106
Limoges C 5 80
Limon F 3 174
Limone Piemonte E 3 92
Limons C 7 80
Limoux E 6 80
Limpopo ≃ C 10 206
Linahamari B 15 64
Linapacan Island I C 7 134
Linares, Chile D 2 195
Linares, Mex. E 10 184
Linares, Spain F 7 86
Lincang G 6 130
Lincoln, Arg. D 7 195
Lincoln, Eng., U.K. D 6 72
Lincoln, Ar., U.S. E 1 170
Lincoln, Il., U.S. B 4 170
Lincoln, Ne., U.S. E 6 174
Lincoln Boyhood National Memorial ♦ C 5 170
Lincoln Cathedral ◗1 D 6 72
Lincoln City C 2 178
Lincoln Park, Ga., U.S. C 2 168
Lincoln Park, Mi., U.S. B 2 162
Lincoln Sea ⊤2 A 14 148
Lincolnshire □6 D 6 72
Lincoln's New Salem State Park ♦ B 4 170
Lincolnton C 3 168
Lind B 4 178
Linda A 2 182
Lindau E 6 100
Linden, Guy. B 7 190
Linden, Mi., U.S. D 7 166
Linden, Tn., U.S. E 5 170
Lindenhurst F 5 164
Lindenwold G 4 164
Lindesberg C 7 66
Lindesnes › D 3 66
Lindi D 6 204
Lindi □3 D 6 204
Lindi ≃ B 4 204
Lindian C 15 128
Lindome D 5 66
Líndos D 8 106
Líndos ⊥ D 7 106
Lindsay, On., Can. F 4 160
Lindsay, Ca., U.S. D 4 182
Line Islands II D 12 136
Lineville C 2 168
Linfen H 8 128
Linganamakki Reservoir ◎1 G 2 122
Lingao I 9 130
Lingayen B 8 134
Lingbi B 13 130
Lingbo B 8 66
Lingchuan I 9 128
Lingen D 4 98
Lingfengwei F 12 130
Lingga, Kepulauan II, Indon. N 7 132
Lingga, Kepulauan II, Indon. F 4 134
Lingolsheim D 4 100
Lingqiu G 10 128
Lingshan C 9 132
Lingshi H 8 128
Lingshui I 10 130
Linguère B 1 200
Lingwu G 6 128
Lingxian E 11 130
Lingyuan F 12 128
Linh, Ngoc ∧ G 8 132
Linhai D 15 130
Linhares C 10 194
Linhe F 6 128
Linjiang F 16 128
Linköping C 7 66
Linkou D 18 128
Linkuva D 12 66
Linnansaaren kansallispuisto ♦ E 14 64
Linqing H 10 128
Linqu H 12 128
Linquan B 12 130
Linru A 11 130
Lins D 6 194
Linstead h 12 186a
Lintan A 6 130
Lintao I 4 128
Linté D 7 200
Lintong A 9 130
Lintorf E 3 98
Linwu F 11 130
Linxi E 11 128
Linxia I 4 128
Linxian H 8 128
Linyi, China H 11 128
Linyi, China I 12 128
Linz, Aus. B 6 102
Linz, Ger. B 4 100
Linzgau ◆1 E 6 100
Linzolo F 7 200
Lio Matoh E 7 134
Lion, Golfe du (Lion, Gulf of) ⊂ A 8 84
Lion, Gulf of see Lion, Golfe du ⊂ A 8 84
Lionel Town i 12 186a
Liouesso B 2 204
Lipa C 8 134
Lipari F 4 94
Lipcani A 9 104
Lipeck C 11 110
Lipeckaja oblast' □6 C 11 110
Lipicy J 12 108
Liping E 9 130
Lipniški E 12 66
Lipno J 9 64
Lipno, údolní nádrž ◎1 D 10 100
Lipova B 6 104
Lippe ≃ E 5 98
Lippstadt E 5 98
Liptovský Mikuláš D 10 96
Lipu F 10 130
Lira G 3 202
Liranga C 2 204
Liri ≃ C 3 94
Lisakovsk C 23 110
Lisala B 3 204
Lisboa (Lisbon) F 1 86
Lisbon see Lisboa, Port. F 1 86
Lisbon, Oh., U.S. C 3 162
Lisbonne □3 F 1 86
Lisburn B 5 75
Lisburne, Cape › B 11 154
Lisburne Peninsula ›1 B 12 154
Lishe ≃ F 5 130
Lishi H 8 128
Lishu E 15 128
Lishui D 14 130
Lishuzhen D 18 128
Lisieux C 7 78
Lisitu D 5 204
Liski D 11 110
L'Isle-Adam C 9 78
L'Isle-sur-le-Doubs C 4 82
Lismore, Austl. B 9 144
Lismore, Austl. G 4 144
Lismore Castle ⊥ D 4 75
Lisse B 3 69
Lissone E 7 82
Listowel G 3 160
Lit E 7 64
Litang C 5 130
Litang ≃ D 5 130
Līṭānī, Nahr al- ≃ C 4 120
Litchfield, Mn., U.S. C 7 174
Litchfield, Ne., U.S. E 5 174
Litchfield □6 E 5 164
Litchfield National Park ♦ C 11 140
Lithgow D 8 144
Lithonia C 2 168
Lithuania □1 D 12 62
Lititz F 2 164
Litoměřice B 11 100
Litomyšl D 9 96
Litovko B 20 128
Littau C 6 82
Little ≃ E 5 172
Little Abaco I F 6 168
Little Andaman I G 6 122
Little Belt see Lillebælt ⊍ C 2 68
Little Bighorn ≃ C 10 178
Little Bighorn Battlefield National Monument ♦ C 10 178
Little Billabong E 6 144
Little Buffalo ≃ A 15 156
Little Cayman I D 4 186
Little Churchill ≃ C 11 158
Little Colorado ≃ E 3 176
Little Current E 3 160
Little Current ≃ F 16 158
Little Deschutes ≃ D 3 178
Little Desert ◆2 F 3 144
Little Desert National Park ♦ F 3 144
Little Diomede Island I D 10 154
Little Falls C 4 164
Littlefield D 2 172
Little Gold ≃ F 9 140
Littlehampton G 6 72
Little Inagua I C 6 186
Little Kanawha ≃ D 3 162
Little Karoo ⁂1 G 4 206
Little Lake ◎ H 3 170
Little London h 11 186a
Little Mecatina (Petit Mécatina) ≃ B 13 160
Little Minch, The see The Little Minch ⊍ C 2 74
Little Missouri ≃, Ar., U.S. F 2 170
Little Missouri ≃ B 3 174
Little Nicobar I H 6 122
Little Pine and Lucky Man Indian Reserve ◆4 E 17 156
Little Powder ≃ C 2 174
Little Rann of Kachchh ◆1 E 2 122
Little Red River Indian Reserve ◆4 E 19 156
Little Rock E 2 170
Little Sable Point › D 5 166
Little Sachigo Lake ◎ D 12 158
Little Salmon Lake ◎ E 27 154
Little Sandy Creek ≃ D 9 178
Little Scarcies ≃ D 2 200
Little Sioux ≃ E 7 174
Little Smoky ≃ D 13 156
Littlestown G 1 164
Littleton, Co., U.S. C 6 176
Littleton, W.V., U.S. D 3 162
Little Zab ≃ E 10 118
Littoral □3 E 7 200
Litvínov B 10 100
Liu ≃ F 9 130
Liuaniua see Ontong Java I1 D 7 136
Liucheng F 9 130
Liuhe E 15 128
Liuku B 4 132
Liuwa Plain National Park ♦ E 3 204
Liuyang D 11 130
Liuzhou F 9 130
Livada B 7 104
Līvāni D 13 66
Lively B 8 166
Lively Island I o 18 193b
Live Oak A 2 182
Livermore, Ca., U.S. C 2 182
Livermore, Ia., U.S. D 7 174
Liverpool, Eng., U.K. D 4 72
Liverpool, Pa., U.S. F 1 164
Liverpool, Cape › B 17 150
Liverpool Bay ⊂ B 29 154
Livigno C 6 92
Lívingston, Guat. J 15 184
Livingston, Scot., U.K. B 3 72
Livingston, Ca., U.S. C 3 182
Livingston, Tx., U.S. G 1 170
Livingstone, Nf., Can. B 10 160
Livingstone, Zam. F 4 204
Livingstone, Lake ◎1 E 6 172
Livingstone Falls ⌞ C 1 204
Livingston Island I L 7 192
Livno D 4 104
Livny C 10 110
Livonia, Mi., U.S. B 2 162
Livonia, N.Y., U.S. B 5 162
Livorno F 6 92
Livorno □6 F 6 92
Liwan G 4 202
Liwonde National Park ♦ F 5 204
Lixian, China D 10 130
Lixian, China A 7 130
Lixin B 13 130
Lixoúri C 4 106
Lixus ⊥ B 3 198
Liyang C 14 130
Lizard Point › H 1 72
Lizarra see Estella B 3 88
Ljadiny F 13 108
Ljamca D 12 108
Ljamin ≃ E 29 108
Ljan C 5 66
Ljuban' G 9 108
Ljubča F 13 66
Ljubercy I 12 108
Ljubimec E 9 104
Ljubinje D 5 104
Ljubljana D 6 102
Ljubohna J 10 108
Ljubuški D 4 104
Ljudinovo J 11 108
Ljungby D 6 66
Ljungbyholm D 8 66
Ljungskile C 5 66
Ljusina J 13 64
Ljusnan ≃ F 7 64
Ljutomer D 8 102
Llaima, Volcán ∧1 F 2 195
Llancanelo, Laguna ◎ D 3 195
Llandaff Cathedral ◗1 F 3 72
Llandrindod Wells E 3 72
Llandudno D 3 72
Llanelli F 2 72
Llanfyllin E 3 72
Llangollen E 3 72
Llano ≃ E 4 172
Llano Estacado see Estacado, Llano ≚ D 2 172
Llanos ≚ B 4 190
Llanquihue, Lago ◎ H 5 192
Llantrisant F 3 72
Llanwrtyd Wells E 3 72
Lleida (Lérida) C 5 88
Llerena F 5 86
Lleulleu, Lago ◎ F 1 195
Lleyn Peninsula ›1 E 2 72
Llíria E 4 88
Llivia B 6 88
Llodio A 7 86
Lloret de Mar G 6 80
Lloyd Lake ◎ C 17 156
Lloydminster E 17 156
Llucena D 4 88
Llucmajor E 7 88
Llullaillaco, Cerro ∧1 D 6 192
Lo ≃ H 7 130
Loa ≃ D 5 192
Loa, Mauna ∧1 j 11 181a
Loanda see Luanda, Ang. D 1 204
Loanda, Braz. E 4 194
Loange (Luangue) ≃ D 3 204
Loango D 1 204
Loano E 4 92
Lobamba D 9 206
Loban D 16 108
Lobatse C 6 206
Löbau E 11 98
Lobaye □3 E 8 200
Lobaye ≃ E 8 200
Lobería F 8 195
Łobez B 8 96
Lobito E 1 204
Lobitos D 2 190
Lobos D 8 195
Lobos, Isla de I D 10 195
Lobva G 24 108
Locarno D 6 82
Locate Triulzi E 7 82
Lochem B 5 69
Loch Garman see Wexford D 5 75
Lochgilphead D 3 74
Lochinvar National Park ♦ F 4 204
Lochmaben B 3 72
Lochristi C 2 69
Lochsa ≃ B 6 178
Lock L 2 142
Lockerbie B 3 72
Lockhart F 5 172
Lockhart River Aboriginal Land ◆4 B 6 142
Lock Haven C 5 162
Löcknitz C 11 98
Lockport B 4 162
Locks Heath G 5 72
Locminé E 4 78
Loc Ninh I 8 132
Locri Epizefiri ⊥ F 6 94
Locust Fork ≃ E 5 170
Locust Grove D 1 170
Lod F 3 120
Loddon ≃ E 4 144
Lodejnoe Pole F 10 108
Löderburg E 8 98
Lodge Creek ≃ G 17 156
Lodgepole E 14 156
Lodhrān D 2 122
Lodi, Italy D 5 92
Lodi, Ca., U.S. B 2 182
Lodi, Wi., U.S. D 4 166
Lodi □6 D 5 92
Lodja C 3 204
Lodwar G 4 202
Łódź C 10 96
Łódzkie □3 C 10 96
Loei F 5 132
Lofa ≃ D 2 200
Lofer C 4 102
Lofoten II B 6 64
Log E 13 110
Loga C 4 98
Logan, Austl. A 9 144
Logan, N.M., U.S. C 2 172
Logan, Ut., U.S. E 8 178
Logan, W.V., U.S. E 3 162
Logan, Mount ∧ F 24 154
Logan Martin Lake ◎1 F 5 170
Logan Mountains ⁂ F 30 154
Logan Pass)(A 7 178
Logansport B 5 170
Logirim G 3 202
Logone ≃ D 8 200
Logone Gana C 7 200
Logone-Occidental □3 D 8 200
Logone-Oriental □3 D 8 200
Logroño B 2 88
Logrosán E 5 86
Logtāk Lake ◎ E 6 122
Logudoro ◆1 I 4 92
Løgumkloster C 1 68
Lohiniva C 12 64
Lohit ≃ D 3 130
Lohmar F 4 98
Lohne, Ger. J 4 64
Löhne, Ger. D 5 98
Lohr am Main C 6 100
Loi (Nanlei) ≃ H 5 130
Loi-kaw E 3 132
Loimaa B 11 66
Loimijoki ≃ B 11 66
Loir ≃ D 8 78
Loire □3 E 2 82
Loire ≃ E 3 76
Loire-Atlantique □3 E 5 78
Loiret □3 D 9 78
Loir-et-Cher □3 E 8 78
Loitz C 10 98
Loja, Ec. D 3 190
Loja, Spain G 6 86
Loka B 2 204
Lokan tekojärvi ◎1 C 13 64
Lökbatan I 16 110
Løken C 5 66
Lokeren C 3 69
Lokhvytsya D 8 110
Lokichar G 4 202
Lokitaung G 4 202
Lokofa-Bokolongo B 2 204
Lokoja D 6 200
Lokoro ≃ C 3 204
Loks Land I D 20 150
Lol F 2 202
Lol ≃ F 2 202
Lolengi F 9 200
Loliondo C 6 204
Lolland I D 4 68
Lollar B 5 100
L'Olleria F 4 88
Lolo B 6 178
Lolodorf E 7 200
Lolo Pass)(B 6 178
Lom, Blg. D 7 104
Lom, Czech Rep. B 10 100
Lom, Nor. B 4 66
Lom ≃ D 7 200
Loma, Point › H 6 182
Lomagne ◆1 A 6 88
Lomami ≃ C 3 204
Lomas de Monreal G 3 176
Lomas de Zamora D 8 195
Lombardia □3 D 5 92
Lombe D 2 204
Lomblen, Pulau I G 8 134
Lombok I G 7 134
Lomé D 5 200
Lomela C 3 204
Lomela ≃ C 3 204
Lomié E 7 200
Lommatzsch E 10 98
Lomme B 9 78
Lommel C 4 69
Lomond, Loch ◎ D 4 74
Lomonosov G 8 108
Lomonosovka J 27 108
Lomovoe D 14 108
Lompoc F 3 182
Lom Sak F 5 132
Łomża B 12 96
Lonato D 6 92
Lonāvale F 2 122
Loncoche F 1 195
London, On., Can. G 3 160
London, Eng., U.K. F 6 72
London, Ky., U.S. E 1 162
Londonderry, N. Ire., U.K. B 4 75
Londonderry, N.H., U.S. D 7 164
Londonderry □8 B 4 75
Londonderry, Cape › C 9 140
Londrina E 5 194
Lone Grove C 5 172
Lone Star F 1 170
Long ≃ F 9 130
Longa ≃ E 1 204
Longarone C 8 92
Longaví D 2 195
Long Beach, Ca., U.S. G 5 182
Long Beach, Ms., U.S. G 4 170
Long Beach, N.Y., U.S. F 5 164
Long Branch F 5 164
Longchang D 7 130
Longchuan, China F 3 130
Longchuan, China F 12 130
Longchuan (Shweli) ≃ G 3 130
Long Creek C 4 178
Long Eaton E 5 72
Longford, Austl. G 6 144
Longford, Ire. C 4 75
Longford □3 C 4 75
Longhorn Cavern State Park ♦ E 4 172
Long Hu ◎ D 13 130
Longhua F 11 128
Longido C 6 204
Longiram F 7 134
Long Island I, Bah. C 6 186
Long Island I, N.Y., U.S. F 6 164
Long Island Sound ⊍ E 5 164
Longjiang C 14 128
Longleat ◗ F 4 72
Longli E 8 130
Longling F 4 130
Longmeadow D 6 164
Longmont E 2 174
Longnan F 12 130
Longnawan E 6 134
Longny-au-Perche D 7 78
Long Prairie C 7 174
Longquan D 14 130
Long Range Mountains ⁂ D 15 160
Longreach G 7 142
Long Reef ✦2 B 11 138
Longsheng F 9 130
Longs Peak ∧ B 6 176
Long Tom ≃ C 2 178
Longton G 6 174
Longuenesse B 9 78
Longueuil F 7 160
Longuyon A 3 82
Longview, Tx., U.S. F 1 170
Longview, Wa., U.S. B 2 178
Longwood Park B 5 168
Longwy A 3 82
Longxi I 5 128
Longxian A 8 130
Long Xuyen I 7 132
Longyan F 13 130
Longyou D 14 130
Longzhou G 8 130
Lonigo D 7 92
Löningen D 4 98
Lonquimay, Volcán ∧1 F 2 195
Lönsboda D 7 66
Lons-le-Saunier D 3 82
Lonton B 3 132
Loogootee C 5 170
Lookout, Cape › B 6 168
Lookout Mountain ⁂ E 6 170
Lookout Pass)(B 6 178
Loolmalassin ∧1 C 6 204
Loomis E 5 174
Loon Lake C 14 156
Loon Lake ◎ D 7 158
Lopatina, gora ∧ B 12 124
Lopatka, Cape see Lopatka, mys › B 15 124
Lopatka, mys › B 15 124
Lopatovo D 14 66
Lop Buri G 5 132
Lopez, Cap › F 6 200
Lop Nor see Lop Nur ◎ A 6 122
Lop Nur (Lop Nor) ◎ A 6 122
Lopori ≃ B 3 204
Lopšen'ga D 12 108
Lopuhovka D 14 110
Łopuszno C 11 96
Lora, Hāmūn-i- ◎ E 10 116
Lora Creek ≃ J 2 142
Lora del Río G 5 86
Lorain C 2 162
Loralai C 1 122
Lorca G 3 88
Lord Howe Island I G 7 136
Lordsburg F 4 176
Loreley ♦ B 4 100
Lorena E 8 194
Lorenzo Geyres C 9 195
Lorestān □3 F 13 118
Loreto A 9 190
Loretto E 5 170
Lorian Swamp ≡ G 4 202
Lorica F 5 186
Lorient E 3 78
Lőrinci B 5 104
Loriol-sur-Drôme F 2 82
Lorman G 3 170
Lorn, Firth of ⊂ D 3 74
Lorna Glen J 6 140
Lorne G 4 144
Loronyo G 3 202
Lorqui F 3 88
Lörrach E 4 100
Lorraine □9 A 4 82
Lorris E 9 78
Los Alamos, Ca., U.S. F 3 182
Los Alamos, N.M., U.S. E 5 176
Los Andes C 2 195
Los Angeles, Chile E 1 195
Los Angeles, Ca., U.S. F 5 182
Los Angeles □6 F 5 182
Los Angeles Aqueduct ⊤1 F 5 182
Los Banos C 3 182
Los Barrios H 5 86
Los Blancos D 7 192
Los Corrales A 6 86
Los Fresnos G 5 172
Los Gatos C 2 182
Losheim C 3 100
Los Herreras H 4 172
Loskopdam ◎1 C 8 206
Los Lagos F 1 195
Los Lagos □3 F 1 195
Los Llanos de Aridane i 12 85b
Los Mochis E 5 184
Los Navalmorales E 6 86
Lošnica E 14 66
Los Padillas E 5 176
Los Palacios y Villafranca G 4 86
Los Santos de Maimona F 4 86
Los Sauces F 1 195
Losser D 4 98
Los Teques A 5 190
Lost Hills E 4 182
Lost River Range ⁂ C 7 178
Lost Trail Pass)(C 7 178
Losuia N 14 124
Los Yébenes E 7 86
Lot □3 D 5 80
Lot ≃ D 4 80
Lota E 1 195
Lot-et-Garonne □3 D 4 80
Lothair D 9 206
Loto C 3 204
Lot's Wife I2 J 8 126
Lotta (Lutto) ≃ B 8 108
Lotung F 15 130
Louang Namtha D 5 132
Louangphrabang E 6 132
Loubetsi C 1 204
Loubomo C 1 204
Loudon B 2 168
Loudun E 7 78
Loue ≃ C 3 82
Louga B 1 200
Loughborough E 5 72
Loughrea C 3 75
Louin F 4 170
Louisa D 5 162
Louisbourg E 14 160
Louisbourg National Historic Site ♦ F 14 160
Louisburg A 5 168
Louise F 5 172
Louiseville E 7 160
Louisiade Archipelago II B 11 138
Louisiana C 3 170
Louisiana □3 E 9 152
Louisiana ◗ C 5 68
Louisville, Ga., U.S. C 3 168
Louisville, Ky., U.S. C 6 170

⌞ Waterfall ⊍ Strait ⊂ Bay, Gulf ◎ Lake ≡ Swamp ⍓ Ice Feature ⊤ Other Hydrographic Feature ✦ Submarine Feature □ Political Unit ◗ Cultural Institution ⊥ Historical Site ♦ Recreational Site ⊠ Airport ▮ Military Installation ◆ Miscellaneous

Symbols in the index entries represent the broad categories identified in the key at the right.
Symbols with superior numbers (∧¹) identify subcategories (see complete key on page 242).

∧ Mountain　∧ Mountains　⋊ Pass　V Valley　≃ Plain　‣ Cape　I Island　II Islands　⊥ Other Topographic Feature　≃ River　≈ Canal

Name	Map Ref.	Page

Manbij D 7 118
Mancha Real G 7 86
Manche □[3] C 5 78
Manche
  see English Channel
  ᴜ F 6 70
Mancheng G 10 128
Mancherāl F 3 122
Manchester, Eng., U.K. D 4 72
Manchester, Ct., U.S. E 6 164
Manchester, Ga., U.S. C 2 168
Manchester, Il., U.S. B 4 170
Manchester, Ky., U.S. E 2 162
Manchester, N.H., U.S. D 7 164
Manchester, Oh., U.S. D 2 162
Manchester, Vt., U.S. E 7 164
Manchioneal h 13 186a
Manchuria □[9] E 15 128
Manciano G 7 92
Mand ≏ H 15 118
Manda D 8 200
Mandabe I 9 205a
Mandaguari E 4 194
Mandala, Puncak ᴧ F 12 134
Mandalay C 2 132
Mandalay □[3] D 2 132
Mandalgovi D 6 128
Mandalī F 11 118
Mandan B 4 174
Mandara Mountains ᴧ C 7 200
Mandeb, Bab el ᴜ E 5 202
Mandelieu G 4 82
Mandello del Lario D 5 92
Mandera G 5 202
Mandeville, Jam. h 12 186a
Mandeville, La., U.S. G 3 170
Mandi C 3 122
Mandiana C 3 200
Mandi Dabwāli D 2 122
Mandimba E 6 204
Mandioli, Pulau I F 9 134
Mandiore, Lagoa ⊘ F 7 200
Mandji F 7 200
Mandla E 4 122
Mandora F 6 140
Mandrare I 9 205a
Mandronarivo I 9 205a
Mandsaur E 2 122
Mandurah M 3 140
Manduria D 7 94
Māndvi G 3 122
Mandya G 3 122
Manendragarh E 4 122
Manerbio D 5 92
Manfalūt I 4 118
Manfred D 4 144
Manfredonia C 6 94
Manfredonia, Golfo di C 6 94
Manga C 4 200
Manga ➝[1] B 7 200
Mangabeiras, Chapada
  das ᴧ[2] F 9 190
Mangaia I F 12 136
Mangakino C 5 146
Mangalia D 10 104
Mangalmé C 8 200
Mangalore G 2 122
Mangaweka C 5 146
Mange D 2 200
Mangghystaū □[3] H 18 110
Mangham D 7 170
Mangkalihat, Tanjung › E 7 134
Manglares, Cabo › C 3 190
Mangla Reservoir ⊘[1] C 5 122
Mangochi E 6 204
Mangoky ≏ I 8 205a
Mangole, Pulau I F 9 134
Mangoro ≏ k 9 205a
Mangotsfield F 4 72
Mangoupa F 1 202
Mangrol E 1 122
Mangueira, Lagoa C D 2 204
Mangungu D 2 204
Manhattan F 6 174
Manhattan Beach G 5 182
Manhiça C 10 206
Manhuaçu D 9 194
Mania ≏ k 9 205a
Maniago C 8 92
Manica F 5 204
Manica □[3] F 5 204
Manicaland □[3] F 5 204
Manic Deux, Réservoir
  ⊘[1] D 9 160
Manicouagan ≏ C 9 160
Manicouagan, Réservoir
  ⊘[1] C 9 160
Maniema □[3] C 4 204
Manihiki I[1] E 11 136
Maniitsoq
  see Sukkertoppen C 22 150
Mānikpur D 4 122
Manila C 8 134
Maningrida B 2 142
Manipa, Selat ᴜ F 9 134
Manipur □[3] E 6 122
Manipur ≏ B 1 132
Manisa C 7 106
Manisa □[3] C 7 106
Manistee C 5 166
Manistee ≏ C 5 166
Manito B 4 170
Manitoba □[4] F 13 150
Manitoba, Lake ⊘ F 9 158
Manitou ≏ A 8 174
Manitou, Lake ⊘ F 3 160
Manitou Beach F 19 156
Manitoulin Island I F 2 160
Manitou Springs F 2 174
Manitowaning F 3 160
Manitowoc C 5 166
Manizales B 3 190
Manja I 8 205a
Manjimup N 4 140
Mānjra ≏ C 3 122
Mankanza B 2 204
Mankato, Ks., U.S. F 5 174
Mankato, Mn., U.S. F 5 166
Mankono D 3 200
Manley Hot Springs B 7 88
Manlleu C 13 84
Manmād E 2 122
Manna F 4 134
Mannahili D 3 144
Mannar, Gulf of C H 3 122
Männedorf C 6 82
Mannheim C 5 100
Manning G 9 144
Manning Provincial Park
  ♦ G 11 156
Mannington D 3 162
Manokotak C 15 154
Manokwari F 10 134
Manono D 4 204
Manoora D 2 144
Manor E 5 172
Manosque G 3 82
Manouane, Lac ⊘[1] C 4 160

Manp'o F 16 128
Manra I[1] D 10 136
Manresa C 6 88
Mansa E 4 204
Mansabá C 1 200
Mānsehra C 2 122
Mansel Island I D 17 150
Mansfield, Austl. F 5 144
Mansfield, Eng., U.K. D 5 72
Mansfield, Ga., U.S. C 3 168
Mansfield, Il., U.S. B 4 170
Mansfield, Mo., U.S. D 2 170
Mansfield, Oh., U.S. C 2 162
Mansfield, Tx., U.S. D 5 172
Mansfield, Mount ᴧ B 6 164
Mansôa C 1 200
Manson H 11 156
Mansura G 2 170
Manta D 2 190
Manteca C 2 182
Mantena C 10 194
Manti C 3 176
Mantiqueira, Serra da ᴧ E 8 194
Mantorville C 2 166
Mántova D 6 92
Mantova □[3] D 6 92
Manturovo G 16 108
Mäntyharju B 13 66
Manua Islands II E 11 136
Manuae I[1] E 12 136
Manuangi I[1] E 13 136
Manuguru F 4 122
Manui, Pulau I F 8 134
Manukau B 5 146
Manukau Harbour C B 5 146
Manus Island I M 13 124
Manutahi C 5 146
Manvel A 6 174
Manville F 4 164
Manyame ≏ F 5 204
Manyana B 4 206
Manyč-Gudilo, ozero ⊘ F 13 110
Many Island Lake ⊘ F 16 156
Manyoni D 5 204
Manzanares E 7 86
Manzanillo, Cuba C 5 186
Manzanillo, Mex. H 7 184
Manzanillo, Punta › F 5 186
Manzanillo Bay C F 5 186
Manzanola F 2 174
Manzhouli B 11 128
Mao, Chad D 9 206
Mao, Dom. Rep. D 7 186
Maó (Mahón), Spain C 8 84
Maokeng D 7 206
Maoke, Pegunungan ᴧ F 11 134
Maoming H 10 130
Maowen C 6 130
Mapanza F 4 204
Mapastepec J 13 184
Mapi G 11 134
Mapia, Kepulauan II E 10 134
Mapimí, Bolsón de ᵈ[3] D 7 184
Maple Lake ⊘[2] C 2 166
Mapleton D 7 174
Mapoi F 2 202
Mapoon Aboriginal
  Land ᴫ[4] A 6 142
Mapuera ≏ D 7 190
Mapumulo E 9 206
Maputo □[3] C 10 206
Maputo (Lusutfu)
  (Usutu) ≏ D 9 206
Maqat F 18 110
Maquan ≏ C 4 122
Maquela do Zombo D 2 204
Maquinchao H 6 192
Mar, Serra do ᴧ F 7 194
Mara □[3] C 5 204
Mara ≏ C 5 204
Marabá A 9 190
Maraboon, Lake ⊘[1] D 8 142
Maracá, Ilha de I C 8 190
Maracaibo F 6 186
Maracaibo, Lago de ⊘ B 4 190
Maracaju D 3 194
Maracay F 8 186
Maradi C 6 200
Maradi □[3] C 6 200
Marägheh D 12 118
Marahoué, Parc
  National de la ♦ D 3 200
Marais des Cygnes ≏ F 7 174
Marajó, Baía de C D 9 190
Marajó, Ilha de I D 9 190
Maralaleng C 5 206
Maralaleng ᴧ C 5 206
Maralinga L 11 140
Maralinga Tjarutja
  Aboriginal Land ᴫ[4] K 11 140
Maramasike I A 13 138
Marambio ᴫ[3] L 8 192
Marampa D 2 200
Maramureş □[3] B 7 104
Maran M 6 132
Maranata C 3 206
Marand C 11 118
Marang, Malay. L 6 132
Marang, Mya. I 4 132
Maranhão □[3] A 9 190
Marano, Laguna di C D 9 92
Maranoa ≏ I 9 142
Marañón ≏ D 3 190
Marapong D 7 200
Marasany H 21 108
Marathon, On., Can. G 15 158
Marathon, N.Y., U.S. D 2 164
Marathon, Tx., U.S. E 2 172
Maráthonas C 5 106
Marawī D 3 202
Marbella H 6 86
Marble D 2 166
Marble Bar D 4 140
Marble Canyon V D 5 176
Marble Hall D 8 206
Marblehead D 8 164
Marburg F 5 98
Marca, Ponta da › F 1 204
March E 7 72
March (Morava) ≏ B 8 102
Marche □[3] D 4 90
Marche D 4 90
Marche □[3] B 6 90
Marchegg B 8 102
Marchena E 5 86
Marchena, Isla I i 13 190a
Marchesato □[3] E 6 94
Marcillac-Vallon E 9 82
Marcos Juárez G 6 195
Marcq-en-Barœul B 10 78
Marcus Baker, Mount ᴧ F 20 154

Marcy, Mount ᴧ B 5 164
Mardān C 2 122
Mardarivka B 10 104
Mar del Plata E 9 195
Mardin D 9 118
Mardin □[3] D 9 118
Maré I D 14 138
Marechal Cândido
  Rondon F 3 194
Mareeba D 7 142
Maremma ➝[1] G 7 92
Marengo B 2 170
Marengo ᴧ E 4 92
Marennes C 2 80
Marevo H 9 108
Marfa E 1 172
Margaree Harbour E 13 160
Margaret Lake B 14 156
Margaret River, Austl. M 3 140
Margaret River, Austl. F 9 140
Margarita, Isla de I A 6 190
Margate, Eng., U.K. F 8 72
Margate, Fl., U.S. F 4 168
Margate City G 4 164
Mārgherita E 2 130
Margherita di Savoia C 6 94
Margherita Peak ᴧ B 4 204
Marghita B 7 104
Margilan A 2 122
Margny-lès-Compiègne E 1 69
Marguerite Bay C C 1 208
Marha ≏ C 14 114
Marhanets' F 9 110
Maria, Îles II F 12 136
Maria Gail D 5 102
Mariager B 3 68
Maria Island National
  Park ♦ j 13 145a
Maria Laach ▶[1] B 4 100
Maria Lake B 8 158
María Madre, Isla I G 6 184
Mariana D 9 194
Mariana Islands II I 13 124
Mariana Trench ✦[1] F 11 58
Marian Guwaay G 5 202
Mariāni D 6 122
Marianna D 6 170
Mariannelund D 7 66
Mariánské Lázně C 9 100
Mariarano k 9 205a
Marias ≏ A 8 178
Marias Pass x A 7 178
Mariato, Punta › A 4 186
Maribo D 4 68
Maribor D 7 102
Marica (Évros) (Meriç)
  ≏ E 9 104
Marico ≏ C 7 206
Maricopa F 2 176
Maricopa Indian
  Reservation ᴫ[4] F 2 176
Maridī F 2 202
Marie Byrd Land ➝[1] C 33 208
Mariec H 18 108
Marie-Galante I o 21 187e
Mariehamn B 9 66
Marienbad
  see Mariánské Lázně C 9 100
Marienberg B 10 100
Marienburg
  see Malbork A 10 96
Marienfelde ➝[8] D 10 98
Mariental C 3 206
Marienville C 4 162
Marienwerder
  see Kwidzyn B 10 96
Mariestad C 6 66
Marietta, Ga., U.S. C 2 168
Marietta, Oh., U.S. D 3 162
Marieville A 5 164
Mariga C 6 200
Marignane G 3 82
Marigot r 25 187g
Mariinsk D 11 114
Marijampolė E 11 66
Marij El □[3] H 17 108
Marília E 5 194
Marimba D 2 204
Marín B 2 86
Marin □[6] B 1 182
Marina D 2 182
Marina di Ravenna E 8 92
Mar''ina Horka F 13 66
Marine-Ehrenmal ᴫ B 7 98
Marineland of the
  Pacific ▶[3] G 5 182
Marinette C 5 166
Maringá E 4 194
Maringa ≏ B 3 204
Maringouin G 3 170
Marinskij Posad H 17 108
Marion, Austl. E 2 144
Marion, Al., U.S. E 5 170
Marion, Ia., U.S. D 3 166
Marion, Il., U.S. B 6 170
Marion, In., U.S. B 6 170
Marion, Ks., U.S. C 5 174
Marion, Ky., U.S. C 5 170
Marion, Oh., U.S. C 2 162
Marion, S.D., U.S. D 6 174
Marion, Lake ⊘[1] A 4 168
Marion Bay j 12 145a
Marion Downs G 4 142
Marion Reef ✦[2] C 11 142
Marionville D 2 170
Mariposa C 4 182
Mariposa □[6] C 4 182
Mariscal Estigarribia D 7 192
Marissa C 4 170
Maritime Alps ᴧ C 1 90
Maritime Atlas (Atlas
  Tellien) ᴧ B 5 198
Mariupol' F 10 110
Marīvān E 11 118
Marjinsko C 14 66
Marka C 3 200
Markala A 3 200
Markaryd E 5 68
Markazī □[3] E 14 118
Markdorf E 6 100
Marked Tree E 3 170
Markermeer ⊘ B 6 90
Markerwaarddijk
  (Afsluitdijk) ➝[5] B 4 69
Market Drayton A 4 72
Market Harborough E 5 72
Market Weighton D 6 72
Markgröningen E 5 100
Markham D 6 160
Markham, Mount ᴧ E 24 208
Markleeville C 3 182
Markovo C 20 114
Markranstädt E 9 98
Marks D 15 110
Marktheidenfeld E 5 100
Marktoberdorf H 6 100
Marktredwitz E 8 100
Mark Twain Lake ⊘[1] C 3 170

Markundi E 1 202
Marl E 4 98
Marlborough, Austl. G 9 142
Marlborough, Eng.,
  U.K. F 5 72
Marlborough, Ma., U.S. D 7 164
Marlborough □[3] D 5 146
Marlborough Sounds ᴜ D 5 146
Marly B 10 78
Marma B 6 66
Marmande D 4 80
Marmara, Sea of ᴛ[2] B 8 106
Marmara Ereğlisi B 7 106
Marmaris D 8 106
Marmelos ≏ E 6 190
Marmolada ᴧ B 3 90
Marmolejo F 6 86
Marmora A 5 162
Marmot Bay C G 18 154
Marne C 6 98
Marne □[3] C 11 78
Marne ≏ D 5 76
Marne à la Saône,
  Canal de la B 3 82
Marne au Rhin, Canal
  de la ≍ B 5 82
Maroa C 5 190
Maroantsetra k 9 205a
Maroelaboom F 2 204
Marolambo I 9 205a
Maromme C 7 78
Maromokotro ᴧ j 9 205a
Marondera E 5 204
Maroni (Marowijne) ≏ C 8 190
Maros (Mureş) ≏ B 6 104
Marostica D 7 92
Marotandrano k 9 205a
Marotiri, Îles II J 1 136
Maroua D 7 200
Marovato k 9 205a
Marovoay k 9 205a
Marowijne (Maroni) ≏ C 8 190
Marpingen C 4 100
Marquard E 7 206
Marquette B 5 166
Marquise B 8 78
Marradi E 6 92
Marrah, Jabal ᴧ[2] E 1 202
Marrakech C 3 198
Marree B 2 144
Marrero H 3 170
Marrupa E 6 204
Marsabit G 4 202
Marsabit National Park
  ♦ G 4 202
Marsala G 2 94
Marsberg E 5 98
Marsciano C 7 200
Marseille G 3 82
Marseille-en-Beauvaisis C 8 78
Marshall, Il., U.S. C 5 170
Marshall, Mi., U.S. D 6 166
Marshall, Mn., U.S. C 7 174
Marshall, Tx., U.S. F 1 170
Marshall Islands □[2] B 8 136
Marshalltown B 2 166
Marshfield, Mo., U.S. D 2 170
Marshfield, Wi., U.S. C 5 166
Marsh Harbour F 6 168
Marsh Hill g 12 163a
Marsh Island I H 2 170
Marsh Lake A 4 156
Marsica ➝[1] C 3 94
Märsta C 8 66
Marstal D 3 68
Marston Moor
  Battlesite ᴫ D 5 72
Martaban C 6 200
Martaban, Gulf of C G 3 132
Martapura C 4 198
Marte C 7 200
Marte R. Gómez, Presa
  ⊘[1] G 4 172
Martha's Vineyard I E 8 164
Martí E 5 186
Martigny D 4 82
Martigues G 3 82
Martil E 3 84
Martin, Slvk. A 10 102
Martin, Tn., U.S. D 4 170
Martina Franca D 7 94
Martinengo E 1 102
Mărtineşti C 9 104
Martínez, Ca., U.S. B 1 182
Martínez, Ga., U.S. C 3 168
Martínez de la Torre G 11 184
Martinique □[2] H 13 148
Martinique Passage ᴜ E 9 186
Martin Lake ⊘[1] F 5 170
Martin Peninsula › D 33 208
Martinsberg C 9 104
Martinsburg D 9 184
Martin's Ferry D 3 162
Martinsville, In., U.S. C 5 170
Martinsville, Va., U.S. H 5 170
Martin Vaz, Ilhas II G 12 188
Martos G 7 86
Martre, Lac la ⊘ D 9 152
Martūbah C 9 198
Martuni C 5 204
Marungu E 5 204
Marutea I[1] E 13 136
Marv Dasht H 15 170
Marvell E 3 170
Mary (Merv) H 5 122
Maryborough, Austl. H 11 142
Maryborough, Austl. F 4 144
Marydale E 4 206
Mary Kathleen F 5 142
Maryland □[3] D 12 152
Marynivka B 11 104
Maryport C 3 72
Mary's Harbour B 16 160
Marysteown E 10 160
Marysville, N.B., Can. E 10 160
Marysville, Ks., U.S. F 6 174
Marysville, Oh., U.S. E 7 174
Marysville, Wa., U.S. E 7 174
Maryville, Mo., U.S. H 2 174
Maryville, Tn., U.S. B 3 168
Masada
  see Mezada, Horvot
  ᴫ G 4 120
Masai i 15 134a
Masai Mara Game
  Reserve ᴫ[4] H 3 202
Masai Steppe ᴫ[1] C 6 204
Masalembu Besar,
  Pulau I G 6 134
Masalli J 16 118
Mauganj G 4 172
Mauga Silisili ᴧ j 10 147b
Maui Islands II i 10 181a
Mauke I F 12 136

Masbate C 8 134
Masbate I C 8 134
Mascarene Islands II L 7 112
Maseru E 7 206
Mashan, China D 18 128
Mashan, China G 9 130
Mashar F 2 202
Masherbrum ᴧ B 3 122
Mashhad C 8 116
Mashi C 6 200
Mashi (Kwando) ≏ F 3 204
Mashonaland Central
  □[3] F 5 204
Mashonaland East □[3] F 5 204
Mashonaland West □[3] F 4 204
Masindi G 3 202
Maşīrah I F 8 116
Maşīrah, Khalīj C F 8 116
Masjed-e Soleymān F 13 118
Mask, Lough ⊘ G 2 75
Maska C 6 200
Masoala I B 11 66
Masoala, Saikanosy ›[1] k 9 205a
Mason, Tn., U.S. E 4 170
Mason, Tx., U.S. E 4 172
Mason City D 2 166
Masqaṭ (Muscat) F 8 116
Massa E 6 92
Massa-Carrara □[6] E 6 92
Massachusetts □[3] C 13 152
Massachusetts Bay C E 8 164
Massafra D 7 94
Massakory C 8 200
Massalassef C 8 200
Massamagrell E 4 88
Massa Marittima F 6 92
Massara F 5 204
Massarosa F 6 92
Massawa
  see Mitsiwa D 4 202
Massena, Ia., U.S. B 1 170
Massena, N.Y., U.S. B 4 164
Masset D 5 156
Masset Inlet C E 5 156
Massey B 7 166
Massiaru C 12 66
Massillon C 3 162
Massina ➝[1] C 4 200
Massinga B 11 206
Massingir F 9 206
Masson, Mount ᴧ C 5 176
Maştağa I 17 110
Masterton D 5 146
Mastok C 7 110
Mastung C 2 122
Masty J 12 64
Masu C 7 200
Masuda G 3 126
Masuku (Franceville) F 7 200
Masuria ➝[1] B 11 96
Masvingo F 5 204
Masvingo □[3] G 5 204
Matabeleland North □[3] F 4 204
Matachewan B 8 166
Matadi D 1 204
Matagalpa E 3 186
Matagami D 5 160
Matagorda Bay C F 5 172
Matagorda Island I F 5 172
Mataiva I[1] E 13 136
Matala E 1 204
Matale H 4 122
Matam B 5 146
Matamata B 5 146
Matamey C 6 200
Matamoros, Mex. E 11 184
Matamoros, Mex. E 8 184
Matandu ≏ D 6 204
Matane D 10 160
Matanuska ≏ F 21 154
Matanzas C 4 186
Matapa B 6 206
Matape ≏ C 4 184
Matapédia, Lac ⊘ D 10 160
Matara H 4 122
Mataram G 7 134
Mataró C 7 88
Matata B 6 146
Mataura G 2 146
Mataveri m 16 193a
Matawin ≏ C 9 160
Matehuala F 9 184
Matera D 6 94
Matera □[6] D 6 94
Matetsi F 4 204
Mateur B 6 198
Matha C 9 104
Matheson D 3 160
Mathis F 5 172
Mathura C 3 122
Matimekosh D 7 200
Matías Barbosa D 9 194
Matías Romero I 12 184
Matignon D 4 78
Matino D 8 94
Mātli E 1 122
Matlock D 5 72
Mato D 3 204
Mato, Cerro ᴧ D 8 186
Mato Grosso □[3] F 7 190
Mato Grosso, Planalto
  do ᴧ[1] F 8 190
Mato Grosso do Sul □[3] G 8 190
Matola C 10 206
Matosinhos C 2 86
Matrah F 8 116
Matsap E 5 206
Matsena C 7 200
Matsudo G 4 126
Matsue G 4 126
Matsumoto G 4 126
Matsu Tao I F 6 130
Matsutō F 6 126
Matsuura F 2 126
Matsuyama H 4 126
Mattamuskeet, Lake
  ⊘ C 3 160
Mattancheri H 3 122
Mattawa C 3 160
Mattawamkeag C 11 160
Mattawamkeag ≏ h 12 163a
Matterhorn (Cervino) ᴧ C 4 90
Mattersburg F 9 102
Matthews Ridge B 5 190
Mattighofen G 8 102
Mattoon C 10 206
Matuba C 10 206
Matumbo B 2 204
Maturín C 6 190
Matuskovo ... (unreadable)
Matveev Kurgan F 11 110
Maubeuge B 10 78
Maud F 1 170
Maués D 7 190
Maués ≏ D 7 190
Mauganj G 4 172

Mauldin B 3 168
Maule I D 2 195
Maule □[3] D 1 195
Maule, Laguna del ⊘ D 2 195
Mauléon F 6 78
Maumee C 2 162
Maumee ≏ E 7 166
Maumere G 8 134
McDonald, Lake ⊘ A 7 178
Mcensk J 12 108
McFarland E 4 182
McGill C 1 176
McGraw D 2 164
McGregor G 3 206
McGregor ≏ D 11 156
Maupin D 4 166
Mau Rānīpur C 3 178
McIntosh G 4 170
McIntosh Lake ⊘ D 19 156
McKeand D 19 156
McKeesport C 4 162
McKenzie G 5 170
McKenzie Island C 2 178
McKenzie F 6 88 ... (see note)
McKinlay F 5 142
McKinley, Mount ᴧ E 19 154
McKinleyville E 1 178
McKinney D 5 172
McKnight Lake ⊘ C 8 158
McLain G 4 170
McLean C 3 172
McLennan D 13 156
McLeod ≏ C 11 158
M'Clintock C 11 158
M'Clintock Channel ᴜ B 12 150
McLoughlin, Mount ᴧ D 2 178
McLure F 11 156
McMinnville, Or., U.S. E 2 178
McMinnville, Tn., U.S. E 6 170
McMurdo D 25 208
McMurdo Sound ᴜ D 26 208
McPherson F 6 174
McRae E 3 168
McVille B 5 174
Mdandu G 7 206
Mdantsana G 7 206
M'Daourouch G 1 90
Mead, Lake ⊘ D 1 176
Meadow D 2 172
Meadow Lake D 17 156
Meadow Lake
  Provincial Park ♦ D 4 158
Meadow Valley Wash
  ≏ D 1 176
Meadowview E 2 162
Meadville, Mo., U.S. C 2 170
Meadville, Pa., U.S. C 3 162
Meaford F 3 160
Méan D 4 69
Meander River B 13 156
Meath □[3] C 5 75
Meath □[9] C 5 75
Meaux D 9 78
Mecca
  see Makkah C 4 202
Mechanicsburg C 2 162
Mechanicsville E 5 162
Mechelen C 3 69
Mechernich B 3 100
Mechriyya C 4 198
Mečigmen B 28 154
Mečigmeskij zaliv C D 8 154
Meckenbeuren C 7 82
Meckenheim B 4 100
Mecklenburg □[9] C 8 98
Mecklenburg Bay
  see Mecklenburger
  Bucht C 8 98
Mecklenburger Bucht
  (Mecklenburg Bay) C B 8 98
Mecklenburgische
  Seenplatte ➝[1] C 9 98
Mecklenburg-
  Vorpommern □[3] C 9 98
Meconta E 6 204
Mecúfori E 6 204
Mecúbúri E 6 204
Mecula E 6 204
Meda D 5 92
Medan M 4 132
Medanosa, Punta › I 6 192
Mede D 7 104
Medeiros Neto B 10 194
Medellín B 3 190
Médéa C 6 198
Medenine C 6 198
Mederdra F 1 198
Medford, Or., U.S. D 2 178
Medford, Wi., U.S. C 10 104
Medgidia G 3 164
Media B 8 104
Mediaş E 7 92
Medicina C 5 176
Medicine Bow
  Mountains ᴧ S 5 176
Medicine Hat F 16 150
Medicine Rocks State
  Park ♦ C 2 174
Medina, Braz. B 10 194
Medina
  see Al-Madīnah, Sau.
  Ar. J 8 118
Medina, N.D., U.S. B 5 174
Medina, Oh., U.S. C 2 162
Medina del Campo C 5 86
Medina-Sidonia H 5 86
Medininkai E 12 66
Mediniņur F 2 122
Mediterranean Sea ᴛ[2] B 9 196
Medjerda, Oued ≏ G 2 90
Medjez el Bab B 6 198
Medkovec D 7 104
Mednogorsk D 20 110
Mednyj, ostrov D 19 114
Médoc ➝[1] D 4 69
Medora H 7 158
Meductic i 13 163a
Medvedica D 7 104
Medvedok H 19 108
Medvednica ᴧ D 1 202
Medveže, ozero I 27 108
Medvežegorsk F 4 108
Medway Towns F 7 72
Medzilaborce D 7 104
Meekatharra J 5 140
Meeker B 5 176
Meelpaeg Lake ⊘ D 15 160

McComas E 3 162
McComb G 3 170
McConnellsburg D 4 162
McCook C 4 174
McCormick C 3 168
McCrory E 3 170
McDermitt E 5 178

Masalli J 16 118
Mason, Tn., U.S. E 4 170

Meadow Lake D 2 172
Medeiros Neto B 10 194

Meda D 5 92
Medan M 4 132

Medina, Braz. B 10 194

(Column 7 entries)
Meda D 5 92
Medan M 4 132
Medanosa, Punta › I 6 192
Mede D 7 104
Medeiros Neto B 10 194
Medellín B 3 190
Médéa C 6 198
Medenine C 6 198
Mederdra F 1 198

Mauldin (see col 6)

Mega, Pulau I F 4 134
Mega, Mtn. ᴧ F 4 134
Megalópoli C 4 106
Mégara C 5 106

ᴸ Waterfall ᴜ Strait c Bay, Gulf ⊘ Lake ≋ Swamp ᴫ Ice Feature ᴛ Other Hydrographic Feature ✦ Submarine Feature □ Political Unit ▶ Cultural Institution ᴫ Historical Site ♦ Recreational Site ≍ Airport ■ Military Installation ➝ Miscellaneous

267

Meghālaya — Monessen

Name	Map Ref.	Page
Meghālaya □[3]	D 6	122
Meghna ≃	E 6	122
Mégiscane ≃	D 5	160
Megísti I	D 8	106
Mehadia	C 7	104
Meharry, Mount ∧	H 5	140
Mehedinți □[3]	C 7	104
Mehetia I	E 13	136
Mehonskoe	H 26	108
Mehrān ≃	I 15	118
Mehrīz	G 16	118
Mehun-sur-Yèvre	E 9	78
Mei ≃	F 13	130
Meia Meia	D 6	204
Meia Ponte ≃	C 6	194
Meichuan	C 12	130
Meiganga	D 7	200
Meihekou	E 15	128
Meiktila	D 2	132
Meinerzhagen	E 4	98
Meiningen	B 7	100
Meiringen	D 6	82
Meishan	D 7	130
Meissen	E 10	98
Meitan	E 8	130
Meizhou	F 13	130
Mejillones	D 5	192
Mek'elē	E 4	202
Mékhé	B 1	200
Meknès	C 3	198
Mekong (Khong) (Lancang) ≃	J 5	124
Mékrou ≃	C 5	200
Mel	C 8	92
Melaka	M 6	132
Melaka □[3]	M 6	132
Melanesia II	D 8	136
Melawi ≃	F 6	134
Melayu ≃	i 14	134a
Melbourne, Austl.	F 5	144
Melbourne, Fl., U.S.	E 4	168
Melby House	g 9	74a
Melchor Múzquiz	D 9	184
Melchor Ocampo	G 4	172
Meldola	E 8	92
Meldrum Bay	C 7	166
Melegnano	D 5	92
Melenki	I 14	108
Meleuz	C 19	110
Melfi, Chad	C 8	200
Melfi, Italy	C 5	94
Melfort	E 19	156
Melhus	E 5	64
Melide	B 2	86
Melilla	E 4	84
Melipilla	C 2	195
Melita	G 8	158
Melitopol'	F 9	110
Melk ◗[1]	B 7	102
Melksham	F 4	72
Mellansel	E 9	64
Melle	D 5	98
Mellègue, Oued ≃	G 2	90
Mellen	B 3	166
Mellette	C 5	174
Mělník	B 11	100
Mel'nikovo	B 14	66
Melo	C 10	195
Meloco	E 6	204
Melrhir, Chott ⊜	C 6	198
Melrose	C 7	174
Melrose Abbey ◗[1]	B 4	72
Melstone	B 10	178
Melsungen	E 6	98
Melton Mowbray	E 6	72
Meluco	E 6	204
Melúli ≃	F 6	204
Melun	D 9	78
Melunga	F 2	204
Melville	F 7	158
Melville, Cape ≻	C 7	142
Melville, Lake ⊜	B 14	160
Melville Bugt ⊂	B 13	148
Melville Island I, Austl.	B 11	140
Melville Island I	B 9	148
Melville Island Aboriginal Land ◆[4]	B 11	140
Melville Peninsula ≻[1]	C 16	150
Melvin	B 4	170
Melyana	H 7	88
Melzo	D 5	92
Memba	E 7	204
Memmingen	E 7	100
Mempawah	E 5	134
Memphis, Mi., U.S.	B 2	162
Memphis, Mo., U.S.	B 2	170
Memphis, Tn., U.S.	E 3	170
Memphrémagog □[6]	A 6	164
Memphremagog, Lake ⊜	A 6	164
Mena	D 8	110
Menai Bridge	D 2	72
Menai Strait ʯ	D 2	72
Ménaka	B 5	200
Menarandra ≃	I 9	205a
Menard	E 4	172
Menasha	C 4	166
Mendawai ≃	F 6	134
Mende	F 1	82
Mendeleevsk	I 20	108
Menden	E 4	98
Mendī	F 4	202
Mendocino, Cape ≻	B 1	180
Mendon	D 6	166
Mendota	B 4	170
Mendoza	C 3	195
Mendoza □[3]	F 6	192
Mendrisio	E 7	82
Ménéac	D 4	78
Mene Grande	F 7	186
Menemen	C 7	106
Menen	D 2	69
Menfi	G 2	94
Mengcheng	B 13	130
Mengen	D 6	100
Menghai	H 5	130
Mengíbar	G 7	86
Menglian	G 4	130
Mengxian	I 9	128
Mengyin	I 11	128
Mengzi	G 6	130
Menindee	D 4	144
Mennighüffen	D 5	98
Menominee	C 5	166
Menominee ≃	C 5	166
Menominee Indian Reservation ◆[4]	C 4	166
Menomonee Falls	D 4	166
Menomonie	C 2	166
Menongue	E 2	204
Menor, Mar ⊂	G 4	88
Menorca (Minorca) I	C 8	84
Mentana	G 8	92
Mentasta Lake	E 22	154
Mentawai, Kepulauan II	F 3	134
Mentawai, Selat ʯ, Indon.	N 4	132
Mentawai, Selat ʯ, Indon.	E 3	134
Menton	G 5	82
Mentor	C 3	162
Menzel Bourguiba	B 6	198
Menzelinsk	I 20	108
Menzel Temime	G 3	90
Menzies	K 6	140
Menzies, Mount ∧	D 15	208
Meobbaai ⊂	C 1	206
Meota	E 17	156
Meppel	B 5	69
Meppen	D 4	98
Meqerghane, Sebkha ⊜	D 5	198
Mequon	D 5	166
Meramec State Park ♠	C 3	170
Merano	C 7	92
Merate	C 2	90
Merauke	G 12	134
Merbabu, Gunung ∧	k 20	135b
Mercantour, Parc National du ♠	F 4	82
Mercāra	G 3	122
Mercato Saraceno	D 3	90
Merced	C 3	182
Merced □[6]	C 3	182
Merced ≃	C 3	182
Mercedes, Arg.	D 8	195
Mercedes, Arg.	A 9	195
Mercedes, Ur.	C 9	195
Mercer	C 3	162
Mercer □[6]	F 4	164
Mercerville	F 4	164
Merchtem	B 11	78
Mercoal	E 13	156
Mercy, Cape ≻	D 20	150
Meredith	F 5	144
Meredith, Cape ≻	o 17	193b
Meredith, Lake ⊜[1]	C 2	172
Merefa	E 10	110
Merelbeke	C 2	69
Mereni	B 10	104
Merenkurkku (Norra Kvarken) ʯ	E 10	64
Mergui (Myeik)	H 4	132
Mergui Archipelago II	I 3	132
Meriç	B 7	106
Meriç (Évros) (Marica) ≃	E 9	104
Méricourt	B 9	78
Mérida, Mex.	G 15	184
Mérida, Spain	F 4	86
Mérida, Ven.	F 7	186
Mérida □[3]	F 7	186
Mérida, Cordillera de ⩘	B 4	190
Meriden	E 6	164
Meridian, Id., U.S.	D 5	178
Meridian, Ms., U.S.	F 4	170
Meridianville	E 5	170
Mérignac	D 3	80
Merikarvia	B 10	66
Merimbula	F 7	144
Merín, Laguna (Mirim, Lagoa) ⊂	F 9	192
Mering	D 7	100
Meringur	E 3	144
Merir I	E 10	134
Merke	A 2	122
Merkendorf	C 7	100
Merlimau, Pulau I	j 14	134a
Merna	E 5	174
Meroe ⊥	D 3	202
Meron, Mount ∧	D 4	120
Merouane, Chott ⊜	C 5	198
Merredin	L 5	140
Merrickville	B 3	164
Merrill	D 3	178
Merrillville	B 5	170
Merrimack □[6]	C 7	164
Merrimack ≃	D 7	164
Merriman	F 5	206
Merritt	F 11	156
Merritt Island	E 4	168
Mersa Fatma	E 5	202
Mersa Matruh (Marsá Maṭrūḥ)	A 2	202
Merseburg	E 8	98
Mersey ≃	D 4	72
Mersing	M 6	132
Merthyr Tydfil	F 3	72
Merthyr Tydfil □[6]	F 3	72
Mértola	G 3	86
Méru, Fr.	C 9	78
Meru, Kenya	G 4	202
Meru, Mount ∧[1]	C 6	204
Meru National Park ♠	G 4	202
Merwede	F 5	206
Mëry	E 13	66
Merzifon	B 6	118
Merzig	C 3	100
Mesa, Moz.	E 6	204
Mesa, Az., U.S.	F 3	176
Mesabi Range ⩘[2]	B 2	166
Mesagne	D 7	94
Mesaména	E 7	200
Mesa Verde National Park ♠	D 4	176
Mescalero Apache Indian Reservation ◆[4]	F 6	176
Meschede	E 5	98
Meščura	E 19	108
Mesgouez, Lac ⊜	C 6	160
Meshgīn Shahr	C 12	118
Mesilinka ≃	C 9	156
Mesilla	F 5	176
Meskiana	B 6	198
Meskine	C 8	200
Mesocco	D 7	82
Mesola	E 8	92
Mesolóngi	C 4	106
Mesopotamia □[9]	F 11	118
Mespelbrunn ⊥	C 6	100
Mesquite	D 5	172
Messalo ≃	E 6	204
Messaoud, Oued ≃	D 4	198
Messina, Italy	F 5	94
Messina, S. Afr.	B 8	206
Messina □[6]	G 5	94
Messina, Stretto di ʯ	F 5	94
Messinge ≃	E 6	204
Messíni	D 4	106
Messíni ⊥	D 4	106
Messiniakós Kólpos ⊂	D 4	106
Mestá	C 6	106
Mesta (Néstos) ≃	E 7	104
Mestghanem	B 5	198
Mestghanem □[3]	D 6	84
Mestre	D 8	92
Mesum	D 4	98
Meszah Peak ∧[1]	B 6	156
Meta	D 4	94
Meta ≃	B 4	190
Metairie	H 3	170
Metaline Falls	G 13	156
Metán	E 7	192
Metangula	E 5	204
Metapán	E 2	186
Metapontum ⊥	D 6	94
Metéora ◗[1]	C 4	106
Meteor Crater ⊥[6]	E 3	176
Methóni	D 4	106
Methuen	D 7	164
Methven	E 3	146
Metković	D 4	104
Metlaoui	C 6	198
Metlatonoc	I 10	184
Metlili ech Chaâmba	C 5	198
Metropolis	D 4	170
Metsebotlhoko	C 6	206
Métsovo	C 4	106
Mettlach	C 3	100
Metu	F 4	202
Metuchen	F 4	164
Metz, Fr.	A 4	82
Metz, S. Afr.	C 9	206
Metzingen	B 7	82
Meu ≃	D 4	78
Meulaboh	L 2	132
Meurthe ≃	B 4	82
Meurthe-et-Moselle □[3]	B 3	82
Meuse □[3]	B 3	82
Meuse (Maas) ≃	C 6	76
Meuselwitz	E 9	98
Mevang	E 7	200
Mexiana, Ilha I	D 9	190
Mexicali	A 2	184
Mexico	C 2	170
Mexico □[1]	G 9	148
Mexico, Gulf of ⊂	F 9	152
Mexico Basin ✦[1]	E 19	58
Mexico Bay ⊂	C 2	164
Mexico Beach	H 6	170
Mexico City see Ciudad de México	H 10	184
Mey, Castle of ⊥	B 5	74
Meydān-e Gel ≚	H 16	118
Meyers Chuck	I 28	154
Meymac	C 6	80
Meymaneh	C 10	116
Meyo-Centre	E 7	200
Meyronne	G 18	156
Meẕada, Ḥorvot (Masada) ⊥	G 4	120
Mezcala	H 10	184
Mezcalapa ≃	I 13	184
Meždurečensk	B 1	124
Mèze	G 1	82
Mezen'	D 16	108
Mezen' ≃	D 16	108
Mezenskaja guba ⊂	C 15	108
Meziadin Lake ⊜	C 7	156
Mézières-en-Brenne	F 8	78
Mezőberény	B 6	104
Mezőcsát	B 6	104
Mezőföld ◆[1]	D 10	102
Mezőkövesd	B 6	104
Mezőtúr	B 6	104
Mezquital ≃	F 7	184
Mezzolombardo	B 3	90
Mgeta	D 6	204
M'Goun, Irhil ∧	C 3	198
Mhow	E 3	122
Mia, Oued ≃	C 5	198
Miajadas	E 5	86
Miaméré	D 8	200
Miami, Fl., U.S.	G 4	168
Miami, Ok., U.S.	D 1	170
Miami Beach	G 4	168
Miamisburg	D 1	162
Miān Channūn	C 2	122
Mianchi	A 10	130
Mīāndoāb	D 12	118
Mianduhe	B 13	128
Mīāneh	D 12	118
Miangas, Pulau I	D 9	134
Mianning	D 6	130
Miānwāli	C 2	122
Mianxian	B 8	130
Mianyang	C 7	130
Mianzhu	C 7	130
Miaoli	F 15	130
Miass	I 23	108
Miass ≃	I 26	108
Miasteczko Krajeńskie	B 9	96
Micaúne	F 6	204
Miccosukee Indian Reservation ◆[4]	F 4	168
Michalovce	D 11	96
Michel	G 14	156
Michelson, Mount ∧	B 22	154
Michelstadt	C 6	100
Michigan □[3]	C 11	152
Michigan ≃	B 5	176
Michigan, Lake ⊜	D 5	166
Michigan Center	D 6	166
Michigan City	B 5	170
Michipicoten Island I	H 15	158
Michoacán □[3]	H 9	184
Michów	C 12	96
Micoud	t 27	187h
Micronesia II	B 8	136
Micronesia, Federated States of □[1]	C 6	136
Mičurinsk	J 14	108
Mid-Atlantic Ridge ✦[3]	E 8	60
Middelburg, Neth.	C 2	69
Middelburg, S. Afr.	C 8	206
Middelburg, S. Afr.	F 6	206
Middelfart	C 2	68
Middelharnis	C 3	69
Middle ≃	D 9	156
Middle America Trench ✦[1]	F 19	58
Middle Andaman I	G 6	122
Middlebro	A 7	174
Middleburg	F 1	164
Middlebury	B 5	164
Middle Caicos I	C 7	186
Middle Channel ≃	B 27	154
Middle Loup ≃	E 5	174
Middlemarch	F 2	146
Middlesboro	E 2	162
Middlesbrough	C 5	72
Middlesex	B 5	168
Middlesex □[6], Ct., U.S.	E 6	164
Middlesex □[6], Ma., U.S.	D 7	164
Middlesex □[6], N.J., U.S.	F 4	164
Middle Stewiacke	F 12	160
Middleton, Austl.	G 5	142
Middleton, N.S., Can.	F 11	160
Middleton Island I	G 21	154
Middletown, Ct., U.S.	E 6	164
Middletown, De., U.S.	G 3	164
Middletown, Md., U.S.	D 5	162
Middletown, N.J., U.S.	F 4	164
Middletown, N.Y., U.S.	E 4	164
Middletown, Oh., U.S.	C 6	170
Middletown, Pa., U.S.	F 2	164
Midelt	C 4	198
Midi, Canal du ≅	E 5	80
Mid-Indian Basin ✦[1]	H 7	58
Mid-Indian Ridge ✦[3]	G 6	58
Midland, On., Can.	F 4	160
Midland, Mi., U.S.	B 1	162
Midland, S.D., U.S.	C 4	174
Midland, Tx., U.S.	D 2	172
Midlands □[3]	F 4	204
Midlothian □[6]	B 3	72
Mid-Pacific Mountains ✦[3]	E 13	58
Midville	C 3	168
Midway	F 6	170
Midway Islands □[2]	E 1	56
Midway Park	B 6	168
Midwest City	C 5	172
Midyat	D 9	118
Mie □[3]	G 6	126
Miechów	C 11	96
Międzychód	B 8	96
Międzyrzec Podlaski	B 12	96
Międzyrzecz	B 8	96
Mielec	C 11	96
Mielno	A 8	96
Miercurea-Ciuc	B 8	104
Mieres	A 5	86
Mieroszów	C 9	96
Miesbach	E 8	100
Mieszkowice	B 8	96
Mifflinburg	F 1	164
Migdol	D 6	206
Migennes	E 10	78
Miguel Alemán, Presa ⊜[1]	H 11	184
Miguel Auza	E 8	184
Miguel Hidalgo, Presa ⊜[1]	D 5	184
Mihai Viteazu	C 10	104
Mihajlov	B 11	110
Mihajlovka, Russia	D 13	110
Mihajlovka, Russia	C 4	126
Mihninskaja	F 16	108
Mikasa	C 8	126
Mikaševičy	J 13	64
Mikhrot Timna'(King Solomon's Mines) ⊥	J 3	120
Mikindani	E 7	204
Mikkeli	B 13	66
Mikkwa ≃	C 15	156
Mikrí Préspa National Park ♠	B 4	106
Mikulov	B 8	102
Mikumi National Park ♠	D 6	204
Mikun'	E 18	108
Milaca	C 2	166
Milagro	D 3	190
Milan see Milano, Italy	D 5	92
Milan, In., U.S.	C 6	170
Milan, N.M., U.S.	E 4	176
Milando	D 2	204
Milano (Milan), Italy	D 5	92
Milano, Tx., U.S.	E 5	172
Milano □[6]	D 5	92
Milâs	D 7	106
Milazzo	F 5	94
Mildenhall	E 7	72
Mildred	E 2	164
Mildura	E 4	144
Mile	F 6	130
Milepa	E 6	204
Miles City	B 2	174
Milestone	G 6	158
Milet (Miletus) ⊥	D 7	106
Milevsko	C 11	100
Milford, Ct., U.S.	E 5	164
Milford, Ma., U.S.	D 7	164
Milford, Me., U.S.	A 9	162
Milford, N.H., U.S.	D 7	164
Milford, Pa., U.S.	E 4	164
Milford, Ut., U.S.	C 2	176
Milford Haven	F 1	72
Milford Lake ⊜[1]	F 6	174
Milford Sound	F 1	146
Milford Sound ʯ	F 1	146
Milḥ, Baḥr al- ⊜[1]	F 10	118
Mili I[1]	C 9	136
Milk ≃	A 10	178
Milk River	G 15	156
Millau	D 7	80
Millboro	E 4	162
Millbrook	A 4	162
Millcreek, Pa., U.S.	B 3	162
Millcreek, Ut., U.S.	E 7	178
Mill Creek, W.V., U.S.	D 3	162
Milledgeville	C 3	168
Mille Îles ≃	A 5	164
Mille Lacs, Lac des ⊜	G 13	158
Mille Lacs Lake ⊜	B 2	166
Miller House	D 22	154
Millerovo	E 12	110
Millersburg, Ky., U.S.	D 1	162
Millersburg, Oh., U.S.	C 3	162
Millersville	G 2	164
Millet	E 15	156
Millicent	F 3	144
Milligan	G 5	170
Millington	E 4	170
Millinocket	h 12	163a
Millom	C 3	72
Millport	B 1	72
Millstatt	C 9	92
Millstream Chichester Range National Park ♠	G 4	140
Milltown	G 3	144
Milltown Malbay	D 2	75
Mill Valley	C 1	182
Millville	G 3	164
Millwood Lake ⊜[1]	F 2	170
Milo ≃	D 3	200
Mílos I	D 6	106
Milparinka	B 3	144
Milpitas	C 2	182
Milroy	C 5	162
Miltenberg	C 6	100
Milton, On., Can.	B 4	162
Milton, N.Z.	G 2	146
Milton, Fl., U.S.	G 5	170
Milton, N.D., U.S.	G 10	158
Milton, Vt., U.S.	B 5	164
Milton Keynes	E 6	72
Milton Keynes □[8]	E 6	72
Miltonvale	F 6	174
Milumba	D 5	204
Milwaukee	D 5	166
Mim	D 4	200
Miminiska Lake ⊜	F 14	158
Mimizan	D 2	80
Mimoň	B 11	100
Mimongo	F 7	200
Min ≃, China	F 14	130
Min ≃, China	D 7	130
Mina	G 3	172
Mīnā' al-Aḥmadī	H 12	118
Mīnāb	I 17	118
Minago ≃	D 9	158
Minahasa ≻[1]	E 8	134
Minamata	H 3	126
Minami-Alps-kokuritsu-kōen ♠	G 6	126
Minami-Daitō-jima I	L 3	126
Minami-Iō-jima I	H 12	124
Minas, Indon.	N 5	132
Minas, Ur.	D 10	195
Minas Basin ⊂	F 11	160
Minas de Ríotinto	G 4	86
Minas Gerais □[3]	G 10	190
Minatitlán	I 12	184
Minbu	D 2	132
Minbya	D 1	132
Minchika	C 7	200
Mincio ≃	D 6	92
Mindanao I	D 9	134
Mindelheim	B 2	102
Mindelo	h 11	200a
Minden, On., Can.	A 4	162
Minden, Ger.	D 5	98
Minden, La., U.S.	F 2	170
Minden, Nv., U.S.	B 4	182
Minden City	B 2	162
Mindon	E 2	132
Mindona, Lake ⊜	D 4	144
Mindoro I	C 8	134
Mindourou	E 7	200
Minehead	F 3	72
Mineiros	B 4	194
Mineola, N.Y., U.S.	F 5	164
Mineola, Tx., U.S.	D 6	172
Miner ≃	C 25	154
Mineral □[6]	B 5	182
Mineral'nye Vody	G 13	110
Mineral Wells	D 4	172
Minerva	C 3	162
Minervino Murge	C 5	94
Minfeng	B 4	122
Mingäçevir	I 15	110
Mingala	E 9	200
Mingan Archipelago National Park ♠	C 11	160
Mingāora	C 2	122
Mingary	D 3	144
Mingechaur Reservoir ⊜[1]	I 15	110
Mingela	E 8	142
Minglanilla	E 3	88
Mingorría	D 6	86
Mingshui	C 15	128
Mingyuegou	E 17	128
Minhang	C 15	130
Minh Hai	J 7	132
Minhla, Mya.	E 2	132
Minhla, Mya.	E 2	132
Minho □[9]	C 2	86
Minho (Miño) ≃	C 2	86
Minićevo	D 7	104
Minigwal, Lake ⊜	K 7	140
Minilya ≃	H 3	140
Miniota	F 8	158
Minjar	I 22	108
Min-Kuš	A 2	122
Minlaton	E 1	144
Minna	D 6	200
Minneapolis	C 2	166
Minnesota □[3]	B 9	152
Minnesota ≃	C 8	152
Minnesota Lake	D 8	174
Minnipa	L 2	142
Mino	G 6	126
Miño (Minho) ≃	C 2	86
Minong	B 3	166
Minorca see Menorca I	C 8	84
Minot	A 4	174
Minqing	E 14	130
Minquan	A 12	130
Minsk	F 13	66
Minsk □[3]	C 5	110
Mińsk Mazowiecki	B 11	96
Minto, Yk., Can.	E 26	154
Minto, Ak., U.S.	D 20	154
Minto Inlet ⊂	B 9	150
Mintom II	E 7	200
Mintoum	E 7	200
Minturnae ⊥	C 3	94
Minturno	C 3	94
Minûf	G 4	118
Minusinsk	B 2	124
Minute Man National Historical Park ♠	D 7	164
Minvoul	E 7	200
Minxian	A 7	130
Minya Konka see Gongga Shan ∧	D 5	130
Miquelon I	E 15	160
Mir	F 13	66
Mirabel	A 4	164
Mirabel □[6]	A 4	164
Mirador	E 10	190
Miraj	F 2	122
Miramar, Arg.	F 9	195
Miramar, Moz.	B 11	206
Miramare, Castello di ⊥	D 9	92
Mirambeau	C 3	80
Miramichi Bay ⊂	E 11	160
Mirampéllou, Kólpos ⊂	E 6	106
Miranda	D 2	194
Miranda □[3]	F 8	186
Miranda ≃	H 7	190
Miranda de Ebro	B 7	86
Mirando City	G 4	172
Mirandola	E 7	92
Mirano	D 8	92
Mira Táglio	D 8	92
Miravalles, Volcán ∧[1]	F 3	186
Mirbāṭ	G 7	116
Mirecourt	B 4	82
Miri	E 6	134
Miria	C 6	200
Miriam Vale	H 10	142
Mirim, Lagoa (Merín, Laguna) ⊂	F 9	192
Mirnyj, Russia	C 14	114
Mirnyj, Russia	J 19	108
Mirnyy ◗[3]	C 18	208
Mirogoma	B 9	206
Mirond Lake ⊜	D 7	158
Miroslav	B 8	102
Mirow	C 9	98
Mīrpur	C 2	122
Mīrpur Khās	D 1	122
Mirtóon Pélagos ▿[2]	D 5	106
Miryang	I 17	128
Mirzāpur	D 4	122
Misâha, Bîr ▿[4]	C 2	202
Misantla	H 11	184
Misawa	D 8	126
Mishan	D 18	128
Mishawaka	B 5	170
Mishicot	C 5	166
Mishmi Hills ⩘[2]	D 7	122
Misima Island I	B 11	138
Misiones □[3], Arg.	E 9	192
Misiones □[3], Para.	G 2	194
Miskī	G 9	198
Miskitos, Cayos II	E 4	186
Miskolc	A 6	104
Mislata	E 4	88
Mislippi	C 8	200
Misool, Pulau I	F 10	134
Miṣrātah	C 8	198
Missão Santa Cruz	F 3	204
Missinaibi ≃	C 2	160
Missinaibi Lake ⊜	D 2	160
Missinaibi Lake Provincial Park ♠	D 2	160
Mission, S.D., U.S.	D 4	174
Mission, Tx., U.S.	G 4	172
Mission Range ⩘	B 7	178
Mission Viejo	G 6	182
Mississagi ≃	H 17	158
Mississagi Provincial Park ♠	B 7	166
Mississauga	G 3	160
Mississinewa ≃	B 6	170
Mississippi □[3]	E 10	152
Mississippi ≃, On., Can.	F 5	160
Mississippi ≃	E 9	152
Mississippi Choctaw Indian Reservation ◆[4]	F 4	170
Mississippi Delta ≚[2]	H 4	170
Mississippi Sound ʯ	G 4	170
Mississippi State	F 4	170
Missoula	B 6	178
Missouri □[3]	D 9	152
Missouri ≃	D 9	152
Mistake Creek	E 10	140
Mistassibi ≃	D 8	160
Mistassini, Lac ⊜	C 7	160
Mistelbach an der Zaya	B 8	102
Misterbianco	G 4	94
Misti, Volcán ∧[1]	G 4	190
Mistissini	C 7	160
Misty Lake ⊜	B 21	156
Mita, Punta de ≻	G 7	184
Mitchell, Austl.	I 8	142
Mitchell, On., Can.	B 3	162
Mitchell, Or., U.S.	C 3	178
Mitchell, S.D., U.S.	D 6	174
Mitchell ≃, Austl.	F 6	144
Mitchell ≃, Austl.	C 6	142
Mitchell, Mount ∧	B 3	168
Mitchell and Alice Rivers National Park ♠	C 6	142
Mitchell River National Park ♠	F 6	144
Mitchelstown	D 3	75
Mitchinamecus, Réservoir ⊜[1]	E 6	160
Mitiaro I	E 12	136
Mitla ⊥	I 11	184
Mito	F 8	126
Mitsamiouli	n 18	207d
Mitsio, Nosy I	j 9	205a
Mitsiwa	D 4	202
Mitsiwa Channel ʯ	D 4	202
Mittagong	E 8	144
Mitta Mitta ≃	F 6	144
Mittelfranken □[6]	C 7	100
Mittellandkanal (Weser-Elbe-Kanal) ≅	D 8	98
Mittenwald	E 6	96
Mittersill	C 4	102
Mittimatalik (Pond Inlet)	B 17	150
Mittweida	E 9	98
Mitú	C 4	190
Mitumba, Monts ⩘	D 4	204
Mityana	G 3	202
Mitzic	E 7	200
Mixian	A 11	130
Miyagi □[3]	E 8	126
Miyake-jima I	G 7	126
Miyako	E 8	126
Miyako-jima I	G 9	124
Miyakonojō	I 3	126
Mīyaly	E 18	110
Miyazaki	I 3	126
Miyazaki □[3]	H 3	126
Miyazu	G 5	126
Miyoshi	G 4	126
Miyun	F 11	128
Mizen Head ≻	E 2	75
Mizhhir'ya	A 7	104
Mizhi	H 7	128
Mizil	C 9	104
Mizoram □[3]	E 6	122
Mizusawa	E 8	126
Mjadzel	E 13	66
Mjaksa	G 13	108
Mjanyana	F 7	206
Mjölby	C 7	66
Mjøsa ⊜	B 5	66
Mkalama	C 5	204
Mkoani	D 6	204
Mkokotoni	D 6	204
Mkomazi ≃	F 9	206
Mkushi	E 4	204
Mkuze	D 9	206
Mkuze ≃	D 10	206
Mkuzi Game Reserve ◆[4]	D 10	206
Mkwaya	E 6	204
Mladá Boleslav	B 12	100
Mlanje Peak see Sapitwa ∧	F 6	204
Mława	B 11	96
Mlembe (Emlembe) ∧	C 9	206
Mliba	D 9	206
Mlima Bénara ∧	o 19	207d
Mljet Nacionalni Park ♠	D 4	104
Mmabatho	C 6	206
Mmamabula	B 7	206
Mmashoro	B 7	206
Mníšek pod Brdy	C 11	100
Moa ≃	D 2	200
Moa, Pulau I	G 9	134
Moabi	F 7	200
Moanda	F 7	200
Moanza	D 2	204
Moar Lake ⊜	F 11	158
Moatize	F 5	204
Moba	D 4	204
Mobaye	E 9	200
Moberly	C 2	170
Mobile, Al., U.S.	G 4	170
Mobile, Az., U.S.	F 2	176
Mobile Bay ⊂	G 4	170
Moçâmedes see Namibe	F 1	204
Moccoidumis	G 5	202
Mocha, Isla I	G 5	192
Mochudi	C 7	206
Möckeln ⊜	D 6	66
Mockfjärd	B 7	66
Môco, Morro de ∧	E 2	204
Mococa	D 7	194
Mocodoene	B 11	206
Mocorito	E 6	184
Moctezuma ≃, Mex.	C 5	184
Moctezuma ≃, Mex.	G 10	184
Mocuba	F 6	204
Modder ≃	E 6	206
Módena	E 6	92
Modena □[6]	E 6	92
Modesto	C 2	182
Modica	H 4	94
Mödling	B 8	102
Modowi	F 10	134
Modra	A 8	200
Modugno	C 6	94
Moe	G 6	144
Moei (Thaungyin) ≃	F 3	132
Moerewa	A 4	146
Moga	C 2	122
Mogadishu see Muqdisho	G 6	202
Mogador see Essaouira	C 2	198
Mogadouro	C 4	86
Mogalakwena ≃	B 8	206
Mogami ≃	E 7	126
Mogapeng	C 9	206
Mogapinyana	B 7	206
Mogaung	B 3	132
Mogilno	B 9	96
Mogliano Veneto	D 8	92
Mogoča	B 7	124
Mogogh	F 3	202
Mogojwagojwe	C 6	206
Mogok	C 3	132
Mogollon Rim ⊥[4]	E 3	176
Mogorosi	B 7	206
Mogotón ∧	E 3	186
Moguer	G 4	86
Mohács	E 10	102
Mohammed, Râs ≻	I 6	118
Mohammedia	C 3	198
Mohawk	H 14	158
Mohawk ≃	D 4	164
Mohelnice	D 9	96
Mohns Ridge ✦[3]	C 23	61
Mohnyin	B 3	132
Mohyliv-Podil's'kyy	A 9	104
Moi	C 3	66
Moinești	B 9	104
Mo i Rana	C 7	64
Mõisaküla	C 12	66
Moisie ≃	C 10	160
Moïssala	D 8	200
Mojácar	G 3	88
Mojave ≃	E 5	180
Mojave Desert ◆[2]	E 5	180
Mojiang	G 5	130
Mojiguaçu ≃	E 7	194
Moji-Mirim	E 7	194
Mojo	F 4	202
Moju ≃	D 9	190
Mokaria	B 3	204
Mokau ≃	C 5	146
Moke	C 5	130
Moknine	B 7	198
Mokokchūng	D 6	122
Mokoro	B 7	206
Mokp'o	I 16	128
Mokša ≃	I 15	108
Mokwa	D 6	200
Mol	C 4	69
Mola di Bari	C 7	94
Molanosa	D 19	156
Molatedi	C 7	206
Mold	D 3	72
Moldau see Vltava ≃	B 11	100
Moldavia □[9]	B 9	104
Molde	E 3	64
Moldova □[1]	F 13	62
Moldoveanu, Vârful ∧	C 8	104
Mole Game Reserve ◆[4]	D 4	200
Molenbeek-Saint-Jean	D 3	69
Molepolole	C 6	206
Molėtai	E 12	66
Moletlane	C 8	206
Molfetta	C 6	94
Molina de Aragón	D 3	88
Molina de Segura	F 3	88
Moline	B 3	170
Molinella	E 7	92
Molins de Rei	C 7	88
Moliro	D 5	204
Molise □[3]	C 4	94
Mölkau	E 9	98
Mölle	D 6	66
Mollendo	G 4	190
Moller, Port ⊂	I 14	154
Mollerussa	C 5	88
Molles	C 9	195
Mollet del Vallès	C 7	88
Mölln	C 7	98
Mölndal	D 5	66
Molodežnaja ◗[3]	C 13	208
Mologa ≃	G 12	108
Molokai I	i 10	181a
Molokovo	G 12	108
Moloma ≃	G 18	108
Molopo ≃	D 4	206
Molou	C 9	200
Molson Lake ⊜	D 10	158
Molteno	F 7	206
Molu, Pulau I	G 10	134
Moluccas (Maluku) II	F 9	134
Molucca Sea (Maluku, Laut) ▿[2]	E 9	134
Moma	C 3	204
Momba	C 4	144
Mombasa	H 4	202
Mombetsu	B 9	126
Mombo	C 6	204
Momboyo ≃	C 2	204
Mombuey	B 4	86
Momi	m 13	147c
Mompós	F 6	186
Momskij hrebet ⩘	C 17	114
Mon □[3]	G 3	132
Møn I	D 5	68
Mona, Isla de I	D 8	186
Monaco □[1]	G 9	62
Monadhliath Mountains ⩘	C 4	74
Monadnock Mountain ∧	D 6	164
Monagas □[3]	F 9	186
Monaghan	B 4	75
Monaghan □[3]	B 4	75
Monahans	E 2	172
Monahans Sandhills State Park ♠	E 2	172
Monango	B 5	174
Mona Passage ʯ	D 8	186
Mona Quimbundo	E 3	204
Monarch Pass)(	C 5	176
Monashee Mountains ⩘	A 4	178
Monashee Provincial Park ♠	F 12	156
Monastery ⊥	B 6	88
Monastyrys'ka	A 8	104
Mona Vale	D 8	144
Monbazillac	F 4	76
Moncalieri	E 3	92
Mončegorsk	B 9	108
Mönchengladbach	E 3	98
Moncks Corner	C 5	168
Monclova	D 9	184
Moncoutant	F 6	78
Moncton	E 11	160
Mondego ≃	D 2	86
Mondello	F 3	94
Mondjamboli	B 3	204
Mondoro	C 4	200
Mondragone	C 3	94
Monemvasía	D 5	106
Monessen	C 3	162

Symbols in the index entries represent the broad categories identified in the key at the right. Symbols with superior numbers (⩘[1]) identify subcategories (see complete key on page 242).

∧ Mountain ⩘ Mountains)(Pass ∨ Valley ≚ Plain ≻ Cape I Island II Islands ⊥ Other Topographic Feature ≃ River ≅ Canal

Monesterio — Myall Lakes National Park

Name	Map Ref.	Page
Monesterio	F 4	86
Monetnyj	H 24	108
Monette	E 3	170
Monfalcone	D 9	92
Monferrato □[9]	E 4	92
Monforte	E 3	86
Monforte de Lemos	B 3	86
Mongadjo	B 3	204
Mongeri	D 2	200
Mongers Lake ◎	K 4	140
Möng Hawm	C 4	132
Möng Hsat	D 4	132
Mongibello see Etna, Monte ▲[1]	G 5	94
Möng Küng	D 3	132
Möng Mit	C 3	132
Mongo	C 8	200
Mongolia □[1]	E 11	112
Mongomo	E 7	200
Mongororo	C 9	200
Möng Pawn	D 3	132
Mong Tung Hang	I 19	131a
Mongu	F 3	204
Monheim, Ger.	C 5	69
Monheim, Ger.	D 7	100
Monida Pass)(	C 7	178
Monimpébougou	C 3	200
Monistrol-sur-Loire	E 2	82
Monitor Range ⋀	B 7	182
Mońki	B 12	96
Monmouth, Wales, U.K.	F 4	72
Monmouth, Or., U.S.	C 2	178
Monmouth □[6]	F 4	164
Monmouthshire □[6]	F 4	72
Mono □[6]	C 5	182
Mono ≃	D 5	200
Mono Lake ◎	B 5	182
Monona, Ia., U.S.	D 3	166
Monona, Wi., U.S.	D 4	166
Monongahela ≃	D 3	162
Monopoli	D 7	94
Monor	B 5	104
Monòver	F 4	88
Monreal del Campo	D 3	88
Monreale	F 3	94
Monreale, Castello di ⊥	I 9	94a
Monroe, La., U.S.	F 2	170
Monroe, Mi., U.S.	C 2	162
Monroe, Ne., U.S.	E 6	174
Monroe, Wa., U.S.	B 3	178
Monroe, Wi., U.S.	D 4	166
Monroe □[6], N.Y., U.S.	C 1	164
Monroe □[6], Pa., U.S.	E 3	164
Monroe Lake ◎[1]	C 5	170
Monroeville, Al., U.S.	G 5	170
Monroeville, Pa., U.S.	C 4	162
Monrovia	D 2	200
Mons	D 2	69
Monschau	B 3	100
Monsec, Serra de ⋀	F 4	80
Monselice	D 7	92
Mönsterås	D 8	66
Montabaur	B 4	100
Montagnana	D 7	92
Montagne d'Ambre, Parque National de la ♦	j 9	205a
Montagrier	C 4	80
Montague Island I	G 21	154
Montagu Island I	J 12	188
Montaigle, Château de ⊥	D 3	69
Montaigu	F 5	78
Montalbano Ionico	D 6	94
Montalegre	C 3	86
Montalto Uffugo	E 6	94
Montana	D 7	104
Montana □[3], Blg.	D 7	104
Montana □[3]	B 5	152
Montaña de Covadonga, Parque Nacional de la ♦	A 6	86
Montana de Oro State Park ♦	E 2	182
Montana-Vermala	D 5	82
Montargil	E 2	86
Montargis	D 9	78
Montataire	C 9	78
Montauban	D 5	80
Montauk State Park ♦	D 3	170
Montbard	E 11	78
Montbarrey	C 3	82
Montbéliard	C 4	82
Mont Belvieu	H 1	170
Montblanc	C 6	88
Montbrison	E 1	82
Montcalm □[6]	A 5	164
Montceau-les-Mines	F 11	78
Montchanin	F 11	78
Montclair	C 6	162
Mont-de-Marsan	E 3	80
Montdidier	C 9	78
Monte, Castel del ⊥	C 6	94
Monte, Laguna del ◎	E 6	195
Monteagle	E 6	170
Monte Albán ⊥	I 11	184
Monte Alegre	D 8	190
Monte Alegre de Minas	C 6	194
Monte Azul	G 10	190
Montebello Iónico	G 5	94
Montebelluna	D 7	92
Montecarlo	G 3	194
Monte Carmelo	C 7	194
Monte Caseros	B 8	195
Montecassino, Abbazia di ◗[1]	C 3	94
Montecatini Terme	F 6	92
Monte Comán	F 6	192
Montecuccolo ◗[1]	E 6	92
Monte di Procida	D 3	94
Montefalco	G 8	92
Montefiascone	G 8	92
Monteforte d'Alpone	D 7	92
Montego Bay	h 12	186a
Montegranaro	A 3	94
Montejicar	G 7	86
Montélimar	F 2	82
Monte Lindo ≃	D 8	192
Montella	D 5	94
Montellano	G 5	86
Montello	E 6	178
Monteluco ◗[1]	G 8	92
Montelupo Fiorentino	F 7	92
Montemorelos	E 9	184
Montemor-o-Velho	D 2	86
Montenegro	A 12	195
Montenegro see Crna Gora □[3]	D 5	104
Montenero di Bisaccia	C 4	94
Monte Pascoal, Parque Nacional de ♦	B 11	194
Monte Patria	B 2	195
Montepuez	E 6	204
Montepulciano	F 7	92
Monte Quemado	E 7	192
Monterādābād	G 9	92
Montereale	C 2	94
Montereau-Faut-Yonne	D 9	78
Monterey, Ca., U.S.	D 3	182
Monterey, Va., U.S.	D 4	162
Monterey □[6]	D 3	182
Monterey Bay c	D 1	182
Montería	F 6	186
Monterotondo	G 8	92
Monterrey	E 9	184
Montesano	B 2	178
Monte Sant'Angelo	C 5	94
Monte Santo, Braz.	E 9	190
Monte Santo, Braz.	E 9	190
Montesarchio	C 4	94
Montes Claros	B 8	194
Montesilvano Marina	B 4	94
Montevallo	F 5	170
Montevarchi	F 7	92
Montevideo	D 9	195
Montezic, Barrage de ✦[6]	D 6	80
Montezuma, In., U.S.	C 5	170
Montezuma, Ks., U.S.	G 4	174
Montezuma Castle National Monument ♦	E 3	176
Montgomery see Sāhīwāl, Pak.	C 2	122
Montgomery, Al., U.S.	F 5	170
Montgomery, La., U.S.	G 2	170
Montgomery □[6], Md., U.S.	G 1	164
Montgomery □[6], N.Y., U.S.	D 4	164
Montgomery □[6], Pa., U.S.	F 3	164
Montguyon	C 3	80
Monthey	D 4	82
Monthois	C 11	78
Monticello, In., U.S.	B 5	170
Monticello, Ky., U.S.	A 2	168
Monticello, Ms., U.S.	G 3	170
Monticello, N.Y., U.S.	E 4	164
Monticello, Wi., U.S.	D 4	166
Monticello ⊥	D 4	162
Montichiari	D 6	92
Montigny-le-Roi	B 3	82
Montigny-lès-Metz	A 4	82
Montijo, Port.	C 1	84
Montijo, Spain	F 4	86
Montilla	G 6	86
Montivilliers	C 7	78
Mont-Joli	D 9	160
Mont-Louis	F 6	80
Montluçon	B 6	80
Montmagny	E 8	160
Montmédy	C 12	78
Montmirail	D 10	78
Montmorillon	B 4	80
Montney	C 11	156
Monto	H 10	142
Montorio al Vomano	B 3	94
Montoro	F 6	86
Montour □[6]	E 2	164
Montoursville	E 2	164
Mont Peko, Parc National du ♦	D 3	200
Montpelier, In., U.S.	B 6	170
Montpelier, Vt., U.S.	B 6	162
Montpellier	G 1	82
Montréal, Qc., Can.	F 7	160
Montreal, Wi., U.S.	B 3	166
Montreal ≃, On., Can.	E 3	160
Montreal ≃, Sk., Can.	D 6	158
Montréal, Île de I	A 5	164
Montreal Lake ◎	D 19	156
Montreal Lake Indian Reserve ◆[4]	D 19	156
Montrésor	E 8	78
Montreuil-sur-Mer	B 8	78
Montreux	D 4	82
Montrichard	E 8	78
Montrose, Scot., U.K.	D 6	74
Montrose, Co., U.S.	C 4	176
Montrose, Pa., U.S.	E 3	164
Mont-Saint-Aignan	C 8	78
Mont-Saint-Hilaire	A 5	164
Mont-Saint-Martin	A 3	82
Mont-Saint-Michel, Baie du c	D 5	78
Mont-Saint-Michel, Le ◗[1]	D 5	78
Mont Sangbé, Parc National du ♦	D 3	200
Montserrat □[2]	H 13	148
Montserrat Monastery ◗[1]	C 6	88
Montuenga	C 6	86
Monument Valley V	D 3	176
Monyo	E 2	132
Monywa	C 2	132
Monza	D 5	92
Monze	F 4	204
Monzón	C 5	88
Mooi ≃	E 9	206
Mooihoek	C 8	206
Mookane	B 7	206
Moolman	C 9	206
Moonie	I 10	142
Moonie ≃	B 7	144
Moonta	E 1	144
Moora	L 3	140
Moorarie	I 4	140
Moore, Id., U.S.	D 7	178
Moore, Mt., U.S.	B 9	178
Moore, Ok., U.S.	C 5	172
Moore ≃	L 3	140
Moore, Lake ◎	L 4	140
Moorea I	E 13	136
Moores Creek National Battlefield ♦	B 5	168
Moorestown	G 4	164
Mooresville	C 5	170
Moorhead	B 6	174
Moornanyah Lake ◎	D 4	144
Moorpark	F 5	182
Moorreesburg	D 8	206
Moosburg an der Isar	D 8	100
Moose Factory	C 3	160
Moosehead Lake ◎	h 11	163a
Moose Jaw	F 18	156
Moose Lake	E 8	158
Mooselookmeguntic Lake ◎[1]	A 8	162
Moose Mountain Provincial Park ♦	G 7	158
Moose River	C 3	160
Moosomin Indian Reserve ◆[4]	E 17	156
Moosonee	C 3	160
Mootwingee National Park ♦	C 4	144
Mopipi	G 3	204
Mopti	C 4	200
Mopti □[3]	C 4	200
Moquegua	G 4	190
Mór	C 10	102
Mora, Cam.	C 7	200
Mora, Spain	E 7	86
Mora, Swe.	B 8	66
Morača, Manastir ◗[1]	D 5	104
Móra d'Ebre	C 5	88
Mora de Rubielos	D 4	88
Morąg	B 10	96
Moral de Calatrava	F 7	86
Morales, Laguna de c	F 11	184
Moramanga	k 9	205a
Moran	D 1	170
Morant Bay	i 13	186a
Morant Point ≻	i 13	186a
Moratalla	F 3	88
Moratuwa	H 3	122
Morava □[9]	D 9	96
Morava (March) ≃	B 8	102
Morāveh Tappeh	D 16	118
Moravské Budějovice	A 7	102
Morawa	K 4	140
Morawhanna	F 10	186
Moray □[6]	C 5	74
Moray Firth c	C 5	74
Morbach	C 4	100
Morbegno	C 5	92
Morbi	E 2	122
Morbihan □[3]	E 4	78
Morcenx	D 3	80
Morden	G 9	158
Mordialloc	F 5	144
Mordovija □[3]	I 15	108
Moreau ≃	C 4	174
Moreau, North Fork ≃	C 3	174
Morecambe	C 3	72
Morecambe Bay c	C 3	72
Moree, Austl.	B 7	144
Morée, Fr.	E 8	78
Morehouse	D 4	170
Moreland	C 2	168
Morelia	H 9	184
Morella	D 4	88
Morelos	F 3	172
Morelos □[3]	H 10	184
Morena, Sierra ⋀	C 3	84
Morenci	F 4	176
Moreni	C 8	104
Moreno Valley	G 6	182
Møre og Romsdal □[3]	E 3	64
Moresby Island I	E 5	156
Morestel	E 3	82
Moreton Island I	I 11	142
Morez	D 4	82
Morfou Bay see Güzelyurt Körfezi c	E 5	118
Morgan	A 10	178
Morgan City, Al., U.S.	E 5	170
Morgan City, La., U.S.	H 3	170
Morgan Hill	C 2	182
Morgantina ⊥	G 4	94
Morganton	B 4	168
Morgantown	D 4	162
Morganza	G 3	170
Morges	D 4	82
Morgongåva	C 8	66
Moriarty	E 5	176
Morice ≃	D 8	156
Morice Lake ◎	D 8	156
Morija	E 7	206
Moriki	C 6	200
Morin Dawa	B 15	128
Morino	H 9	108
Morinville	E 15	156
Morioka	E 8	126
Morīri, Tso ◎	C 3	122
Morkoka ≃	C 14	114
Morlaix	D 3	78
Morlanwelz	D 3	69
Morley	D 5	72
Mormal'	C 6	110
Mormugao	F 2	122
Morne-à-l'Eau	n 21	187e
Morne Trois Pitons National Park ♦	r 25	187g
Morney	H 5	142
Mornington, Isla I	I 4	192
Mornington Island I	D 4	142
Morobe	N 13	124
Morocco	B 5	170
Morocco □[1]	E 7	196
Morogoro	D 6	204
Morogoro □[3]	D 6	204
Moro Gulf c	D 8	134
Moroleón	G 9	184
Morombe	I 8	205a
Morón, Arg.	D 8	195
Morón, Cuba	C 5	186
Mörön, Mong.	B 3	128
Morón, Ven.	A 5	190
Mörön ≃	C 7	128
Morondava	I 8	205a
Morón de la Frontera	G 5	86
Morongo Indian Reservation ◆[4]	F 7	182
Moroni	n 18	207d
Moron Us ≃	C 6	122
Morotai I	E 9	134
Moroto	G 3	202
Morouba	D 8	200
Morozovsk	E 12	110
Morozovskaja	F 18	108
Morpeth	B 5	72
Morrilton	E 2	170
Morrinhos	B 6	194
Morris, Il., U.S.	B 4	170
Morris, Mn., U.S.	C 7	174
Morris □[6]	F 4	164
Morrisburg	B 3	164
Morris Jesup, Kap ≻	A 16	148
Morrison	B 4	170
Morristown, Mn., U.S.	C 2	166
Morristown, N.J., U.S.	F 4	164
Morristown, Tn., U.S.	A 3	168
Morrisville, N.Y., U.S.	D 3	164
Morrisville, Pa., U.S.	F 4	164
Morro Bay	E 3	182
Morro Bay State Park ♦	E 3	182
Morro do Chapéu	F 10	190
Morrosquillo, Golfo de c	F 5	186
Morrumbala	F 6	204
Mörrumsån ≃	D 7	66
Moršansk	J 14	108
Morse	F 18	156
Morson	G 11	158
Mortagne ≃	B 4	82
Mortagne-sur-Sèvre	E 6	78
Mortara	D 4	92
Morteau	C 4	82
Morteros	B 6	195
Mortes ≃	F 8	190
Mortesoro	E 3	202
Mortlock Islands II	C 7	136
Morton, Il., U.S.	B 4	170
Morton, Ms., U.S.	F 4	170
Morton, Wa., U.S.	B 2	178
Morton National Park ♦	E 8	144
Mortsel	C 3	69
Moruya	E 8	144
Morvant	q 23	187e
Morwa	C 7	206
Morwell	G 6	144
Moryń	B 8	96
Mosaneng	C 6	206
Mosbach	C 6	100
Mosborough	D 5	72
Moscow see Moskva, Russia	I 12	108
Moscow, Id., U.S.	B 5	178
Mosel (Moselle) ≃	B 4	100
Moselesenyane	A 6	206
Moselle □[3]	A 4	82
Moselle (Mosel) ≃	C 3	100
Moses Point	D 13	154
Mosgiel	F 3	146
Moshaweng ≃	D 5	206
Mosheim	A 3	168
Moshi	C 6	204
Moshi ≃	D 5	200
Mosinee	C 4	166
Moskalënki	I 29	108
Moskovskaja oblast' □[6]	I 12	108
Moskva (Moscow)	I 12	108
Moskva ≃	B 11	110
Mosonmagyaróvár	C 9	102
Mospyne	F 11	110
Mosquera	C 3	190
Mosquitos, Golfo de los c	F 4	186
Moss	C 5	66
Mossbank	F 18	156
Mosselbaai	H 5	206
Mossel Bay see Mosselbaai	H 5	206
Mossendjo	C 1	204
Mossgiel	D 5	144
Mössingen	D 6	100
Mossman	D 7	142
Mossoró	E 11	190
Moss Point	G 4	170
Moss Vale	E 8	144
Most	B 10	100
Mostar	D 4	104
Mostardas	F 9	192
Møsting, Kap ≻	D 24	150
Móstoles	D 7	86
Mostovka	G 26	108
Mosul see Al-Mawşil	D 10	118
Motaba ≃	B 2	204
Mota del Cuervo	E 2	88
Mota del Marqués	C 5	86
Motagua ≃	J 15	184
Motala	C 7	66
Motaze	C 10	206
Motherwell	B 3	72
Motihāri	D 4	122
Motloutse ≃	A 7	206
Motril	H 7	86
Motru	C 7	104
Mottola	D 7	94
Motueka	D 4	146
Motu One I[1]	E 12	136
Mouaskar	B 4	198
Mouaskar □[3]	E 6	84
Mouding	B 5	132
Moudjéria	D 8	156
Moúdros	C 6	106
Mougdi	C 8	200
Mouhoun see Black Volta ≃	D 4	200
Mouila	F 7	200
Mouit	F 2	198
Moulamein	E 5	144
Moulins	F 10	78
Moulins-la-Marche	D 7	78
Moulmein see Mawlamyine	F 3	132
Moulmeingyun	F 2	132
Moulouya, Oued ≃	C 4	198
Moulton	E 5	170
Moultrie	E 2	168
Moultrie, Lake ◎[1]	C 5	168
Mound City, Il., U.S.	D 4	170
Mound City, S.D., U.S.	C 4	174
Moundou	D 8	200
Mounds	D 4	170
Moundsville	D 3	162
Mountain	C 4	166
Mountain ≃	D 30	154
Mountainair	E 5	176
Mountain Ash	F 3	72
Mountain City	E 3	162
Mountain Grove	D 2	170
Mountain Home, Ar., U.S.	D 2	170
Mountain Home, Id., U.S.	D 6	178
Mountain Lake	D 7	174
Mountain Nile ≃	F 3	202
Mountain Point	I 29	154
Mountain View	C 1	182
Mountain Zebra National Park ♦	G 6	206
Mount Airy	E 3	162
Mount Aspiring National Park ♦	F 2	146
Mount Ayliff	E 9	206
Mount Barker	N 4	140
Mount Barney National Park ♦	B 9	144
Mount Beauty	F 6	144
Mount Brydges	B 3	162
Mount Buffalo National Park ♦	F 6	144
Mount Carleton Provincial Park ♦	g 13	163a
Mount Carmel	F 2	164
Mount Carroll	B 2	166
Mount Clemens	B 2	162
Mount Cook	E 3	146
Mount Cook National Park ♦	E 3	146
Mount Doreen	G 11	140
Mount Edgecumbe	C 4	156
Mount Edziza Provincial Park ♦	C 6	156
Mount Elgon National Park ♦	B 5	204
Mount Field National Park ♦	j 12	145a
Mount Fletcher	F 8	206
Mount Forest	F 3	160
Mount Gambier	F 3	144
Mount Garnet	D 7	142
Mount Gilead	C 2	162
Mount Holly	G 4	164
Mount Holly Springs	F 1	164
Mount Hope	M 2	142
Mount Isa	F 4	142
Mount Jacinto State Park ♦	G 7	182
Mount Jackson	D 4	162
Mount Kaputar National Park ♦	C 8	144
Mount Kenya National Park ♦	H 4	202
Mount Kisco	E 5	164
Mount Lebanon	C 3	162
Mount Magnet	K 4	140
Mount Maunganui	B 6	146
Mount McKinley National Park see Denali National Park ♦	E 19	154
Mountmellick	C 4	75
Mount Moorosi	F 7	206
Mount Morgan	G 10	142
Mount Morris	B 5	162
Mount Oeta National Park ♦	C 5	106
Mount Olive	G 4	170
Mount Olympus National Park ♦	B 5	106
Mount Orab	D 2	162
Mount Pleasant, Austl.	E 2	144
Mount Pleasant, Ia., U.S.	B 3	170
Mount Pleasant, Mi., U.S.	B 1	162
Mount Pleasant, S.C., U.S.	C 5	168
Mount Pleasant, Tn., U.S.	E 5	170
Mount Pleasant, Tx., U.S.	F 1	170
Mount Pleasant, Ut., U.S.	C 3	176
Mount Pulaski	B 4	170
Mount Rainier National Park ♦	B 3	178
Mount Remarkable National Park ♦	D 1	144
Mount Revelstoke National Park ♦	F 12	156
Mount Robson Provincial Park ♦	E 12	156
Mount Rogers National Recreation Area ♦	E 3	162
Mount Roskill	B 5	146
Mount Rushmore National Memorial ♦	D 3	174
Mount Saint Helens National Volcanic Monument ♦	B 3	178
Mount Savage	D 4	162
Mount's Bay c	G 1	72
Mount Somers	E 3	146
Mount Sterling	D 2	162
Mount Stewart	G 6	206
Mount Union	C 4	164
Mount Vernon, Al., U.S.	G 5	170
Mount Vernon, Il., U.S.	C 4	170
Mount Vernon, Mo., U.S.	D 1	170
Mount Vernon, Oh., U.S.	C 2	162
Mount Vernon, Wa., U.S.	A 2	178
Mount Wellington	B 5	146
Mount William National Park ♦	i 12	145a
Moura, Braz.	D 6	190
Moura, Port.	F 3	86
Mouraya	E 6	84
Mourdi, Dépression du ⊻[7]	B 9	200
Mourindi	F 7	200
Mourne Mountains ⋀	B 5	75
Mouscron	D 2	69
Moussa 'Ali ▲	E 5	202
Moussoro	C 8	200
Moutier	C 5	82
Moûtiers	E 4	82
Moutong	E 8	134
Mouzarak	C 8	200
Movenda	B 3	204
Moville	D 6	174
Moxico □[3]	E 3	204
Moya	o 19	207d
Moyahua	G 8	184
Moyale	B 6	204
Moyen Atlas ⋀	C 4	198
Moyen-Chari □[3]	D 8	200
Moyen-Ogooué □[3]	F 7	200
Moyeuvre-Grande	C 3	100
Moyie	G 14	156
Moyo	G 3	202
Moyo, Pulau I	G 7	134
Moyobamba	E 3	190
Moyynty	A 11	116
Možajsk	B 10	110
Mozambique □[1]	J 11	196
Mozambique Channel ʯ	J 12	196
Mozdok	H 14	110
Možga	H 20	108
Mozia ⊥	G 2	94
Mpaka	D 9	206
Mpama ≃	C 2	204
Mpé	C 1	204
Mphahlele	C 8	206
Mpigi	G 3	202
Mpika	E 5	204
Mpraeso	D 4	200
Mpumalanga □[3]	D 8	206
Mqanduli	F 8	206
Mragowo	B 11	96
M'Ramani	o 19	207d
Mrijo	D 6	204
Mrkopalj	C 3	104
Msagali	D 6	204
M'Saken	B 7	198
Mscislaŭ	B 7	110
Msciž	E 14	66
M'Sila	B 5	198
Msoro	E 5	204
Mtakataka	E 5	204
Mtama	E 6	204
Mtamvuna ≃	F 9	206
Mtubatuba	E 10	206
Mtwara	E 7	204
Mtwara □[3]	E 6	204
Mu ≃	C 2	132
Muacandala	D 2	204
Mualama	F 6	204
Muanda	D 1	204
Muang Hay	D 5	132
Muang Khammouan	F 7	132
Muang Không	G 7	132
Muang Khôngxédôn	G 7	132
Muang Pakxan	E 6	132
Muang Sing	D 5	132
Muang Vangviang	E 5	132
Muang Xaignabouri	I 5	130
Muar	M 6	132
Muar ≃	M 6	132
Muarabinuangeun	k 17	135b
Muarasiberut	F 3	134
Muaratewe	F 6	134
Mubende	G 3	202
Mubi	C 7	200
Muccan	G 5	140
Muchinga Mountains ⋀	E 5	204
Muchuan	D 6	130
Muckadilla	I 9	142
Mučkap	D 18	108
Mücke	B 6	100
Muconda	E 3	204
Mucope	F 1	204
Mucur	C 6	118
Mucuri ≃	G 10	190
Muda ≃	K 5	132
Mudan ≃	C 17	128
Mudanjiang	D 17	128
Mudanya	B 8	106
Mud Creek ≃	G 1	170
Muddus Nationalpark ♦	C 9	64
Muddy ≃	D 1	176
Mudgee	D 7	144
Mudjatik ≃	C 18	156
Mudon	F 3	132
Mudug □[3]	F 6	202
Mudurnu	B 9	106
Muenster	D 5	172
Muerto, Mar ◎	J 12	184
Muezerskij	D 10	108
Mufulira	E 4	204
Muggia	D 9	92
Mugi	H 5	126
Mu Gia, Deo)(	J 7	130
Muğla	D 8	106
Muğla □[3]	D 8	106
Mugron	E 3	80
Muhammad Qawl	C 4	202
Mühlacker	D 5	100
Mühldorf am Inn	D 9	100
Mühlhausen	E 7	98
Muhlig-Hofmann Mountains ⋀	D 9	208
Mühlviertel ◆[1]	B 6	102
Muhola	E 12	64
Muhutwe	C 5	204
Muiderslot ⊥	B 4	69
Muir Woods National Monument ♦	C 1	182
Muiskraal	G 4	206
Mui Wo	I 18	131a
Mujimbeji	E 3	204
Mujnak	H 21	110
Mukacheve	A 7	104
Mukah	E 6	134
Mukāwir ⊥	F 5	120
Mukdahan	F 7	132
Mukhayyam al-Baq'ah	E 5	120
Mukinbudin	L 5	140
Mukomwenzo	D 4	204
Mukoshima-rettō II	K 9	126
Mukry	C 10	116
Mukulushi ≃	E 3	204
Mukumbura	F 5	204
Mula	F 3	88
Mulan	D 16	128
Mulanje	F 6	204
Mulberry	F 3	168
Mulchatna ≃	F 16	154
Mulchén	E 1	195
Mul'da	C 25	108
Mulde ≃	E 9	98
Muldraugh	D 5	170
Muleshoe	C 2	172
Mulhacén ▲	H 7	62
Mulhall	B 5	172
Mülheim an der Ruhr	E 3	98
Mulhouse	C 5	82
Muli	E 5	130
Muling, China	D 18	128
Muling, China	D 18	128
Muling ≃	D 19	128
Mull, Island of I	D 3	74
Mullengudgery	C 6	144
Mullet Peninsula ≻[1]	B 1	75
Mullett Lake ◎	C 6	166
Mullewa	K 3	140
Müllheim	E 4	100
Mullingar	C 4	75
Mullumbimby	B 9	144
Mulongo	D 4	204
Multai	E 3	122
Multān	C 2	122
Mulvane	G 6	174
Muma	B 3	204
Mumbai see Bombay, India		122
Mumbai (Bombay), India	F 2	122
Mumbué	E 2	204
Mumcular	D 7	106
Mumra	G 15	110
Mun ≃	G 7	132
Muna	G 15	184
Muna ≃	C 15	114
Muna, Pulau I	F 8	134
Munayly	F 19	110
Muncar	I 22	135b
Münchberg	B 8	100
Müncheberg	D 11	98
München (Munich)	D 8	100
Münchenstein	C 5	82
Muncho Lake Provincial Park ♦	B 9	156
Munch'ŏn-ŭp	E 1	126
Muncie	B 6	170
Muncy	E 2	164
Munda	D 7	136
Mundaring	L 4	140
Münden	E 6	98
Mundrabilla	L 9	140
Munenga	D 1	204
Munfordville	D 6	170
Mungar Junction	H 11	142
Munger	D 5	122
Mungia	A 2	88
Mungindi	B 7	144
Mungo	E 2	204
Mungo National Park ♦	D 4	144
Munhango	E 2	204
Munhango ≃	E 2	204
Munich see München	D 8	100
Munising	B 5	166
Munkfors	C 6	66
Munku-Sardyk, gora ▲	B 4	124
Münsingen, Ger.	D 6	100
Münsingen, Switz.	D 5	82
Munson	B 10	170
Munster, Ger.	D 6	98
Münster, Ger.	D 7	98
Munster, Fr.	B 5	82
Münster □[6]	D 4	98
Munster □[9]	D 2	75
Münsterland ◆[1]	E 4	98
Muntok	F 5	134
Muonio	C 11	64
Mupfure ≃	F 4	204
Muping	H 13	128
Muqaddam, Wādī ≃	D 3	202
Muqatta'	E 5	120
Muqayshiţ I	J 15	118
Muqdisho (Mogadishu)	G 6	202
Mur (Mura) ≃	E 10	102
Mura (Mur) ≃	E 10	102
Muradiye	C 10	118
Murai Reservoir ◎[1]	i 14	134a
Murakami	E 7	126
Muramvya	D 5	204
Murat ≃	C 9	118
Muratlı	B 7	106
Murau	E 6	102
Murayama	C 8	126
Murça	C 3	86
Murchison	E 4	146
Murchison ≃	J 3	140
Murchison Falls see Kholombidzo Falls ⌊, Mwi.	F 5	204
Murchison Falls see Kabalega Falls ⌊, Ug.	G 3	202
Murchison Falls National Park ♦	G 3	202
Murcia	G 3	88
Murcia □[3]	G 3	88
Murdo	D 4	174
Mureş □[3]	B 8	104
Mureş (Maros) ≃	B 6	104
Muret	E 5	80
Murfreesboro, Ar., U.S.	E 2	170
Murfreesboro, Tn., U.S.	E 5	170
Murgab see Murghob	B 2	122
Murgab ≃	C 9	116
Murgeni	B 10	104
Murghob	B 2	122
Muri	D 7	200
Muria, Gunung ▲	k 20	135b
Muriaé	D 9	194
Muri-bei Bern	D 5	82
Muriedas	A 7	86
Muriege	D 3	204
Muriel Lake ◎	D 16	156
Müritz ◎	C 9	98
Muriwai	C 6	146
Murmansk	B 10	108
Murmanskaja oblast' □[6]	C 11	108
Murmino	B 12	110
Murnau	E 8	100
Muro de Alcoy	F 4	88
Muro Lucano	E 5	90
Murom	I 15	108
Muroran	C 8	126
Muroto	H 4	126
Murovani Kurylivtsi	A 9	104
Murphys	B 3	182
Murray, Ky., U.S.	D 4	170
Murray, Ut., U.S.	E 8	178
Murray ≃, Austl.	E 2	144
Murray ≃, B.C., Can.	D 11	156
Murray, Lake ◎	N 12	124
Murray Bridge	E 2	144
Murraysburg	G 6	206
Murray-Sunset National Park ♦	E 3	144
Murrēbuè	E 7	204
Murrhardt	D 6	100
Murrumbidgee ≃	E 4	144
Murrupula	F 6	204
Murska Sobota	D 8	102
Murtle Lake ◎	E 12	156
Murtosa	D 2	86
Murua Island I	A 11	138
Murud	F 2	122
Murud, Gunong ▲	E 7	134
Murupara	C 6	146
Murwāra	E 4	122
Murwillumbah	B 9	144
Murzuq	D 7	198
Murzūq, Idhān ◆[2]	E 7	198
Mürzzuschlag	C 7	102
Muş	C 9	118
Muş □[3]	C 9	118
Musa	B 2	204
Mūsa Khel Bāzār	C 1	122
Musala ▲	D 7	104
Musandam ≻[1]	I 17	118
Musan-ŭp	E 17	128
Musay'īd	J 14	118
Muscat see Masqaţ	F 8	116
Muscatine	B 3	170
Muscle Shoals	E 5	170
Mushenge	C 3	204
Mushie	F 8	200
Mushin	D 5	200
Mūsi ≃, India	F 3	122
Musi ≃, Indon.	F 4	134
Musicians Seamounts ◆[3]	D 14	58
Muskeg Lake Indian Reserve ◆[4]	E 18	156
Muskegon	D 5	166
Muskegon ≃	D 6	166
Muskegon Heights	D 5	166
Muskingum ≃	D 3	162
Muskogee	E 1	170
Muskwa ≃	B 10	156
Muslimbāgh	C 1	122
Musoma	C 5	204
Musquodoboit Harbour	F 16	160
Musselkanaal	B 6	69
Musselshell ≃	B 10	178
Mussidan	C 4	80
Mussomeli	G 4	90
Mustafakemalpaşa	B 8	106
Mustafa Kemal Paşa ≃	C 8	106
Mustang Draw ≃	D 3	172
Mustla	C 12	66
Mustvee	C 13	66
Muswellbrook	D 8	144
Mūt, Egypt	J 3	118
Mut, Tur.	D 2	118
Mutanda	G 5	204
Mutare	F 5	204
Mutsamudu	o 19	207d
Mutsu	D 8	126
Mutsu-wan c	D 8	126
Muttenz	C 5	82
Mutterstadt	C 5	100
Mutton Bay	C 14	160
Mutum Biyu	D 7	200
Muxaluando	D 1	204
Muyaga	C 5	204
Muzaffarābād	D 3	122
Muzaffarnagar	D 3	122
Muzaffarpur	D 5	122
Muzat ≃	A 4	122
Muži	D 26	108
Muzillac	E 4	78
Muzon, Cape ≻	I 28	154
Muztag ▲, China	B 4	122
Muztag ▲, China	C 4	122
Mvam	F 6	200
Mvela	E 6	204
Mvomero	D 6	204
Mvuma	F 5	204
Mwadui	C 5	204
Mwali I	J 12	196
Mwanza, Tan.	C 5	204
Mwanza, Zam.	E 5	204
Mwanza □[3]	C 5	204
Mwaya	E 6	204
Mweka	C 3	204
Mwemena	E 4	204
Mwene-Ditu	D 3	204
Mwenezi (Nuanetze) ≃	G 5	204
Mwenga	H 2	202
Mweni	H 4	202
Mweru, Lake ◎	D 4	204
Mweru Wantipa, Lake ◎	D 4	204
Mweru Wantipa National Park ♦	D 4	204
Mwingi	H 4	202
Myaing	D 2	132
Myakka River State Park ♦	F 3	168
Myall Lakes National Park ♦	D 9	144

⌊ Waterfall ʯ Strait c Bay, Gulf ◎ Lake ≋ Swamp ⊓ Ice Feature ≃ Other Hydrographic Feature ✦ Submarine Feature □ Political Unit ◗ Cultural Institution ⊥ Historical Site ♦ Recreational Site ⊠ Airport ■ Military Installation ◆ Miscellaneous

Name	Map Ref.	Page

Symbols in the index entries represent the broad categories identified in the key at the right. Symbols with superior numbers (∧¹) identify subcategories (see complete key on page 242).

∧ Mountain ∧ Mountains ✕ Pass ⋎ Valley ≃ Plain ⊁ Cape I Island II Islands ⊥ Other Topographic Feature ≃ River ≋ Canal

270

Ngqeleni — Odesa

Name | Map Ref. | Page

Ngqeleni F 8 206
Ngũ ≃ D 3 130
Nguigmi C 7 200
Nguiu B 11 140
Ngulu I1 D 11 134
Ngum ≃ E 6 132
Ngurore D 7 200
Nguru C 7 200
Ngwerere F 4 204
Nhabe ≃ G 3 204
Nhacoongo C 11 206
Nhamundá ≃ D 7 190
N'harea E 2 204
Nha Trang H 9 132
Nhill F 3 144
Nhlangano D 9 206
Nhoma F 3 204
Niagara Falls, On., Can. G 4 160
Niagara Falls, N.Y., U.S. B 4 162
Niagara Falls ∟ B 4 162
Niah E 6 134
Niakaramandougou D 3 200
Niamey C 5 200
Niamey □3 C 5 200
Niamtougou D 5 200
Nianfourando D 2 200
Niangara B 4 204
Niangay, Lac ◎ B 4 200
Niangoloko C 3 200
Nia-Nia B 4 204
Nianzishan C 14 128
Niari □3 C 1 204
Niari ≃ C 1 204
Nias, Pulau I N 3 132
Niassa □3 E 6 204
Nibe B 2 68
Nica ≃ H 25 108
Nicaragua □1 H 11 148
Nicaragua, Lago de ◎ F 3 186
Nicastro F 6 94
Nice G 5 82
Nichelino E 3 92
Nichinan I 3 126
Nicholas Channel ꓤ C 4 186
Nicholasville D 6 170
Nicholl's Town G 6 168
Nicholson E 3 164
Nicholson ≃ D 4 142
Nickel Centre E 3 160
Nicobar Islands II H 6 122
Nicola F 11 156
Nicolet E 7 160
Nicosia, Cyp. E 5 118
Nicosia, Italy G 4 94
Nicotera F 5 94
Nicoya, Golfo de ⊂ F 3 186
Nida E 10 66
Nidda B 5 100
Nidwalden □3 C 4 92
Nidzica B 11 96
Niebüll B 5 98
Niederbayern □6 D 9 100
Niederbronn-les-Bains D 4 100
Niedere Tauern ∧ C 6 102
Niederkassel F 3 98
Niederlausitz □9 E 11 98
Niederösterreich □3 B 7 102
Niedersachsen □3 D 5 98
Niederwiesa F 9 98
Niekerkshoop E 5 206
Niellim D 8 200
Niemba D 4 204
Nienburg, Ger. E 8 98
Nienburg, Ger. D 6 98
Niepołomice C 11 96
Niesky E 11 98
Nieuport see Nieuwpoort C 1 69
Nieuw Amsterdam B 8 190
Nieuwefontein E 3 206
Nieuwegein B 4 69
Nieuw Nickerie B 7 190
Nieuwpoort C 1 69
Nièvre □3 E 5 76
Niga C 3 200
Niğde D 6 118
Niğde □3 C 6 118
Nigel D 8 206
Niger □1 G 9 196
Niger ≃ G 8 196
Niger Delta ≃2 E 6 200
Nigeria □1 H 8 196
Nighthawk G 12 156
Nigrita B 5 106
Nihommatsu F 8 126
Nihuil, Embalse del ◎1 D 3 195
Niigata F 7 126
Niigata □5 F 7 126
Niihama H 4 126
Niihau I i 8 181a
Niitsu F 7 126
Nijar H 2 88
Nijkerk B 4 69
Nijlen C 3 69
Nijmegen C 4 69
Nijverdal B 5 69
Nikel' B 8 108
Nikiski F 19 154
Nikkō F 7 126
Nikkō-kokuritsu-kōen ♦ F 8 126
Nikolaevka, Russia F 15 110
Nikolaevka, Russia F 11 110
Nikolaevo C 14 66
Nikolaevsk E 14 110
Nikolai E 17 154
Nikolo-Berëzovka H 20 108
Nikol'sk, Russia J 16 108
Nikol'sk, Russia G 16 108
Nikolski J 10 154
Nikol'skoe G 16 108
Nikopol' F 8 110
Niksar B 7 118
Nikšić D 5 104
Nikumaroro I1 D 10 136
Nila, Pulau I G 9 134
Nile ≃ B 3 202
Nile Delta ≃2 G 4 118
Niles, Mi., U.S. B 5 170
Niles, Oh., U.S. C 3 162
Nilsiä E 13 64
Nīmach E 2 122
Nimba, Mount (Nimba, Mont) ∧ D 3 200
Nimbāhera F 3 120
Nîmes G 2 82
Nimule G 3 202
Nimule National Park ♦ G 3 202
Nīnawá □3 E 10 118
Nīnawá (Nineveh) ⊥ D 10 118
Nine Degree Channel ꓤ H 2 122
Ninette G 9 158
Ninetyeast Ridge ✢3 H 7 58
Ninety Mile Beach ⊥2 G 6 144
Nineveh see Nīnawá ⊥ D 10 118
Ninfa ⊥ H 8 92
Ning'an D 17 128
Ningari C 4 200
Ningbo D 15 130
Ningcheng F 12 128
Ningde E 14 130
Ningdu E 12 130
Ningguo C 14 130
Ninghai D 15 130
Ninghua E 13 130
Ningming G 8 130
Ningnan E 6 130
Ningqiang B 8 130
Ningshan B 9 130
Ningxia □3 H 5 128
Ningxiang D 11 130
Ningyuan F 10 130
Ninh Binh D 8 132
Ninigo Group II F 12 134
Ninohe D 8 126
Ninove D 2 69
Niny G 13 110
Niobrara ≃ D 5 174
Nioki C 2 204
Niokolo Koba, Parc National du ♦ C 2 200
Niono D 3 200
Nioro B 3 200
Nioro du Rip C 1 200
Niort B 3 80
Niou C 4 200
Nipāni F 2 122
Nipawin E 20 156
Nipigon G 14 158
Nipigon, Lake ◎1 G 14 158
Nipissing, Lake ◎ E 3 160
Nippers Harbour D 16 160
Niquero D 5 186
Nirmal F 3 122
Niš D 6 104
Niscemi G 4 94
Nisporeni B 10 104
Nisutlin ≃ F 28 154
Nītaure D 12 66
Niterói E 9 194
Nitra B 10 102
Nitro D 3 162
Niuafo'ou I E 10 136
Niue □2 E 11 136
Niulan ≃ E 6 130
Niut, Gunung ∧ N 9 132
Niutao I D 9 136
Niuzhuang F 14 128
Nivelles D 3 69
Nivernais □9 E 10 78
Niverville G 10 158
Nizāmābād F 3 122
Nižegorodskaja oblast' □6 H 16 108
Nizhyn D 7 110
Nizip D 7 118
Nízke Tatry, Narodny Park ♦ D 10 96
Nižnee Kujto, ozero ◎ D 9 108
Nižnee Romanovo G 28 108
Nižnekamsk I 20 108
Nižnekamskoe vodohranilišče ◎1 H 19 110
Nižnelemskij D 21 108
Nižneudinsk B 3 124
Nižnevartovsk F 31 108
Nižnie Sergi H 23 108
Nižnij Novgorod (Gorky) H 16 108
Nižnij Odes E 21 108
Nižnij Tagil H 23 108
Nižnij Ufalej I 23 108
Nižnjaja Salda G 24 108
Nižnjaja Tunguska ≃ C 11 114
Nižnjaja Tura G 23 108
Nizwá F 8 116
Nizza Monferrato E 4 92
Nizzana H 2 120
Njah E 26 108
Njalinskoe F 28 108
Njandoma F 14 108
Njansimvol' E 24 108
Njasviž J 13 64
Njazidja I J 12 196
Njombe D 5 204
Njombe ≃ D 5 204
Njučpas F 19 108
Njuk, ozero ◎ D 9 108
Njurba C 14 114
Njurunda A 8 66
Nkambe D 7 200
Nkandla E 9 206
Nkawkaw D 4 200
Nkhata Bay D 6 204
Nkhotakota E 5 204
Nkomi, Lagune ◎ F 6 200
Nkomo B 9 200
Nkongsamba D 6 200
Nkoto C 2 204
Nkwalini E 9 206
Nmai ≃ F 4 130
Nnewi D 6 200
Noarlunga E 2 144
Noatak ≃ C 13 154
Nobeoka H 3 126
Nobili C 4 200
Noblesville B 6 170
Noboribetsu C 8 126
Noce ≃ C 6 92
Nocera Inferiore D 4 94
Nocera Superiore D 4 94
Nocona D 5 172
Noel D 3 170
Nogales, Mex. B 4 184
Nogales, Az., U.S. G 3 176
Nogara D 7 92
Nōgata H 3 126
Nogent-le-Rotrou D 7 78
Nogent-sur-Oise C 9 78
Noginsk I 13 108
Nogoa ≃ H 8 142
Nogoyá C 8 195
Nógrád □3 C 4 104
Nohfelden C 4 100
Noia B 2 86
Noicattaro C 7 94
Noirmoutier, Île de I F 4 78
Nokha Mandi D 2 122
Nokia B 11 66
Nokomis F 19 156
Nokomis Lake ◎ C 20 156
Nokou C 7 200
Nola, C.A.R. E 3 202
Nola, Italy D 4 94
Nolinsk H 18 108
Nome D 12 154
Nomtsas C 2 206
Nonacho Lake ◎ D 11 150
Nonburg D 20 108
Nondweni E 9 206
Nong'an D 15 128
Nong Han F 7 132
Nong Khai F 6 132
Nongoma D 9 206
Nonoava D 6 184
Nonouti I1 D 9 136
Nonthaburi H 5 132
Nontron C 4 80
Nonvianuk Lake ◎ G 16 154
Noonamah C 11 140
Noondil, Lake ◎ K 5 140
Noord-Brabant □3 C 4 69
Noord-Holland □3 B 3 69
Noordoewer E 2 206
Noordoostpolder ◆1 B 4 69
Noordwijk-Binnen B 3 69
Noorvik C 14 154
Nootka Island I G 8 156
Nopiming Provincial Park ♦ F 11 158
Nora C 7 66
Nora ⊥ m 10 94a
Norberg B 7 66
Norchia ⊥ G 7 92
Norcia G 9 92
Nord □3, Cam. D 7 200
Nord □3, Fr. B 10 78
Nord, Canal du ≍ B 10 78
Nordaustlandet I B 5 114
Nordegg E 13 156
Norden C 4 98
Nordenham C 5 98
Norderney C 4 98
Norderstedt C 7 98
Nordfjord ⊂ B 2 66
Nordfold C 7 64
Nordfriesland □9 B 5 98
Nordhausen E 7 98
Nordhorn D 3 98
Nordjylland □3 A 2 68
Nordkapp see North Cape ≻ A 12 64
Nord-Kivu □3 C 4 204
Nordland □3 C 7 64
Nördlingen D 7 100
Nordmaling E 9 64
Nordostrundingen ≻ A 18 148
Nord-Ostsee-Kanal (Kiel Canal) ≍ A 5 96
Nord-Ouest □3 D 7 200
Nordrhein-Westfalen □3 C 4 96
Nordstemmen D 6 98
Nord-Trøndelag □3 D 6 64
Nordvik B 14 114
Nore B 4 66
Norfolk, Ne., U.S. D 6 174
Norfolk, Va., U.S. E 5 162
Norfolk □6, Eng., U.K. E 7 72
Norfolk □6, Ma., U.S. D 7 164
Norfolk Broads ◆1 E 8 72
Norfolk Island □2 F 8 136
Norfork Lake ◎1 D 2 170
Noril'sk C 11 114
Normal B 4 170
Normal ◆8 E 5 170
Norman C 5 172
Norman ≃ E 6 142
Norman Bay B 16 160
Normanby C 5 146
Normanby Island I N 14 124
Normand, Bocage ◆1 D 6 78
Normandie (Normandy) □9 G 7 70
Normandie, Collines de ∧2 D 6 78
Normandy see Normandie □9 G 7 70
Normanton D 5 142
Norrahammar D 6 66
Norra Kvarken (Merenkurkku) ꓤ E 10 64
Norrbotten □3 C 9 64
Nørresundby A 2 68
Norris Arm D 16 160
Norristown F 3 164
Norrköping C 7 66
Norrsundet B 8 66
Norrtälje C 9 66
Norseman M 6 140
Norsjö D 9 64
Norte, Cabo ≻ m 16 193a
Norte, Serra do ∧1 F 7 190
Norte de Santander □3 F 6 186
North C 4 168
North, Cape ≻, N.S., Can. E 13 160
North, Cape ≻, S. Geor. p 21 193c
North Adams D 5 164
Northallerton C 5 72
Northam, Austl. L 4 140
Northam, Eng., U.K. F 2 72
North America ⊥1 E 10 148
North American Basin ✢1 D 6 60
Northampton, Austl. K 3 140
Northampton, Eng., U.K. E 6 72
Northampton, Ma., U.S. D 6 164
Northampton, Pa., U.S. F 3 164
Northampton □6 F 3 164
Northamptonshire □6 E 6 72
North Andaman I G 6 122
North Anson A 9 162
North Atlanta C 2 168
North Attleboro E 7 164
North Ayrshire □6 B 2 72
North Battleford E 17 156
North Bay E 4 160
North Bend D 1 178
North Berwick A 4 72
North Branch C 2 166
North Caicos I C 6 186
North Canadian ≃ C 5 172
North Cape ≻, Nor. A 12 64
North Cape ≻, N.Z. A 4 146
North Caribou Lake ◎ E 13 158
North Carolina □3 D 12 152
North Cascades National Park ♦ A 3 178
North Channel ꓤ, On., Can. H 17 158
North Channel ꓤ D 5 70
North Charleston C 5 168
North Chicago D 5 166
North Collins B 4 162
North Creek C 5 164
North Dakota □3 B 7 152
North Downs ∧2 F 7 72
North Eagle Butte C 4 174
North East D 5 162
North-East □3 G 4 204
Northeast Cape E 10 154
North Eastern □3 G 4 202
North East Lincolnshire □6 D 6 72
Northeast Providence Channel ꓤ G 6 168
Northeim E 7 98
Northern □3, Mwi. E 5 204
Northern □3, S. Afr. C 8 206
Northern □3, Zam. E 5 204
Northern Cape □3 F 4 206
Northern Cheyenne Indian Reservation ◆4 C 10 178
Northern Cook Islands II E 11 136
Northern Division □3 m 14 147c
Northern Donets (Sivers'kyi Donets') ≃ E 10 110
Northern Dvina ≃ E 16 108
Northern Indian Lake ◎ C 10 158
Northern Ireland □3 B 5 75
Northern Mariana Islands □1 B 6 136
Northern Sporades II C 6 106
Northern Territory □3 D 7 138
Northfield, Mn., U.S. C 2 166
Northfield, Vt., U.S. B 6 164
North Flinders Range ∧ C 2 144
North Foreland ≻ F 8 72
North Fork ≃ D 2 170
North Fort Myers F 3 168
North Frisian Islands II D 1 68
Northglenn F 2 174
North Haven E 6 164
North Hero B 5 164
North Hero Island I B 5 164
North Highlands B 2 182
North Horr G 4 202
North Island I C 5 146
North Kingsville C 3 162
North Knife Lake ◎ B 10 158
North Lakhimpur D 6 122
North Lanarkshire □6 B 3 72
Northland □3 A 4 146
North Land II B 12 114
North Las Vegas D 1 176
North La Veta Pass)(G 2 174
North Lincolnshire □6 D 6 72
North Little Rock E 2 170
North Llano ≃ E 4 172
North Loup E 5 174
North Loup ≃ E 5 174
North Luangwa National Park ♦ E 5 204
North Macmillan ≃ E 28 154
North Magnetic Pole ◆ B 9 148
North Manitou Island I C 5 166
North Miami G 4 168
North Milk ≃ A 7 178
North Moose Lake ◎1 D 8 158
North Myrtle Beach C 5 168
North Nahanni ≃ E 32 154
North Platte E 4 174
North Platte ≃ C 7 152
North Pole ◆ D 13 61
Northport, Al., U.S. F 5 170
Northport, Wa., U.S. A 5 178
North Portal G 7 158
North Providence E 7 164
North Raccoon ≃ D 7 174
North Rim D 2 176
North River B 15 160
North Saskatchewan ≃ E 18 156
North Sea ⊤2 D 8 62
North Shore City B 5 146
North Siberian Lowland ⊻ C 13 114
North Spirit Lake ◎ E 12 158
North Stradbroke Island I A 9 144
North Sunderland B 5 72
North Sydney E 13 160
North Taranaki Bight ⊂ C 5 146
North Tunica E 3 170
North Tyneside □6 B 3 72
North Uist I C 1 74
Northumberland □6, Eng., U.K. B 4 72
Northumberland □6, Pa., U.S. F 2 164
Northumberland National Park ♦ B 4 72
Northumberland Strait ꓤ E 12 160
North Vancouver G 10 156
North Wabasca Lake ◎ C 15 156
North Walsham E 8 72
Northway E 23 154
North-West □3 D 6 206
North West Cape ≻ G 2 140
North-Western □3 E 4 204
North-West Frontier □3 B 2 122
Northwest Highlands ∧ C 4 74
Northwest Pacific Basin ✢1 D 12 58
Northwest Providence Channel ꓤ F 5 168
North West Somerset □6 F 4 72
Northwest Territories □3 D 9 150
Northwich D 4 72
North York G 4 160
North York Moors National Park ♦ C 6 72
North Yorkshire □6 C 5 72
North Zulch E 5 172
Norton, N.B., Can. F 11 160
Norton, Eng., U.K. C 6 72
Norton, Ks., U.S. F 5 174
Norton Bay ⊂ D 13 154
Norton Shores D 5 166
Norton Sound ꓤ E 12 154
Nortorf B 6 98
Norvegia, Cape ≻ D 7 208
Norwalk, Ct., U.S. E 5 164
Norwalk, Ia., U.S. B 2 170
Norwalk, Oh., U.S. C 2 162
Norway B 8 164
Norway □1 C 9 62
Norway Bay ⊂ B 12 150
Norway House D 10 158
Norwegian Basin ✢1 B 23 61
Norwegian Sea ⊤2 D 4 64
Norwich, Eng., U.K. E 8 72
Norwich, Ct., U.S. E 6 164
Norwich, N.Y., U.S. D 3 164
Norwood, On., Can. A 4 162
Norwood, Ma., U.S. D 7 164
Norwood, N.C., U.S. B 4 168
Norwood, Oh., U.S. C 6 170
Noshaq ∧ B 2 122
Noshiro D 7 126
Nosovo D 13 66
Nossebro C 6 66
Nossen E 10 98
Nossob ≃ D 4 206
Nosy-Varika I 9 205a
Noteć ≃ B 8 96
Notikewin C 13 156
Nótio Aigaío □3 D 7 106
Noto H 5 94
Noto, Golfo di ⊂ H 5 94
Noto, Val di ◆1 G 4 94
Noto Antica ⊥ H 5 94
Noto-hantō ≻1 F 6 126
Notozero, ozero ◎ C 10 108
Notre-Dame, Monts ∧ D 10 160
Notre Dame Bay ⊂ D 16 160
Notre-Dame-du-Haut ◗1 C 4 82
Notre-Dame-du-Nord B 9 166
Nottaway ≃ C 4 160
Nottingham E 5 72
Nottingham Island I D 17 150
Nottinghamshire □6 D 6 72
Notukeu Creek ≃ G 18 156
Notwane ≃ B 7 206
Nouâdhibou E 1 198
Nouakchott F 1 198
Nouméa D 14 138
Nouna C 4 200
Noupoort F 6 206
Nouveau-Québec, Cratère du ⊥6 D 18 150
Nouvelle D 10 160
Nouvelle-Calédonie (New Caledonia) I D 14 138
Nouzonville C 11 78
Nova Andradina E 4 194
Novabad B 1 122
Novacella ◗1 D 3 102
Nova Esperança E 4 194
Nova Freixo see Cuamba E 6 204
Nova Friburgo E 9 194
Nova Gradiška C 4 104
Nova Iguaçu E 9 194
Novaja Ljalja G 23 108
Novaja Sibir', ostrov I B 17 114
Novaja Zemlja II B 8 114
Nova Kakhovka F 8 110
Nova Lima D 9 194
Nova Lisboa see Huambo E 2 204
Nova Lusitânia F 5 204
Nova Odesa F 7 110
Nová Paka C 8 96
Novara D 4 92
Novara □6 D 4 92
Nova Scotia □3 H 20 150
Novato B 1 182
Nova Ushytsya A 9 104
Nova Varoš D 5 104
Nova Venécia C 10 194
Novaya Kazanka E 16 110
Novaya Sibir Island see Novaja Sibir', ostrov I B 17 114
Nova Zagora D 9 104
Nové Hrady D 11 100
Novelda F 4 88
Novellara E 6 92
Nové Město nad Váhom B 9 102
Nové Zámky B 10 102
Novgorod G 9 108
Novgorodskaja oblast' □6 G 10 108
Novhorod-Sivers'kyy J 10 108
Novi Bečej C 6 104
Novi Beograd C 6 104
Novi di Modena C 3 90
Novigrad C 2 104
Novi Ligure E 4 92
Novi Pazar, Blg. D 9 104
Novi Pazar, Yugo. D 6 104
Novi Sad C 5 104
Novo, Lago ◎ C 8 190
Novoaleksandrovsk G 12 110
Novoalekseevka J 26 108
Novoanninskij D 13 110
Novo Aripuanã E 6 190
Novočerkassk F 11 110
Novocimljanskaja E 13 110
Novodvinsk D 14 108
Novoe G 28 108
Novo Hamburgo A 12 195
Novo Horizonte D 6 194
Novohrad-Volyns'kyy D 5 110
Novoiljinskij G 21 108
Novokazalinsk see Zhangaqazaly A 9 116
Novokujbyševsk C 16 110
Novokurovka B 20 128
Novokuzneck D 11 114
Novolazarevskaja ◗3 C 10 208
Novo Mesto E 7 102
Novomoskovsk, Russia I 13 108
Novomoskovs'k, Ukr. E 9 110
Novonikolaevskij D 13 110
Novooleksiyivka F 9 110
Novoorsk D 21 110
Novopetrovo H 28 108
Novopskov E 11 110
Novorossijsk G 10 110
Novorybīnka K 29 108
Novošahtinsk F 11 110
Novosergievka C 18 110
Novosibirsk D 11 114
Novosibirskie ostrova see New Siberian Islands II B 17 114
Novosibirskoe vodohranilišče ◎1 D 11 114
Novosil's'ke C 10 104
Novostroevo E 10 66
Novotroick D 20 110
Novouzensk D 16 110
Novovjatsk G 18 108
Novovolyns'k D 4 110
Novovoronežskij D 11 110
Novozybkov J 9 108
Novska E 8 102
Nový Bohumín D 10 96
Nový Bor B 11 100
Novyj Bor C 19 108
Nový Jičín A 9 102
Novyj Oskol D 10 110
Novyj Port C 30 108
Novyy Buh F 8 110
Nowa Dęba C 11 96
Nowa Ruda C 9 96
Nowa Sól C 8 96
Nowbarān E 13 118
Nowe Miasto nad Pilicą C 11 96
Nowe Warpno B 8 96
Nowingi E 4 144
Nowitna ≃ D 18 154
Nowogród B 11 96
Nowra E 8 144
Nowshera C 2 122
Nowy Dwór Gdański A 10 96
Nowy Dwór Mazowiecki B 11 96
Nowy Sącz D 11 96
Nowy Targ D 10 96
Noxen E 2 164
Noyant E 7 78
Noyon C 9 78
Nqamakwe G 7 206
Nsa C 2 204
Nsanje F 6 204
Nsawam D 4 200
Nsoko D 9 206
Nsukka D 6 200
Ntem ≃ E 7 200
Ntomba, Lac ◎ C 2 204
N'Tsaoueni n 18 207d
Ntui E 7 200
Ntusi G 3 202
Ntwetwe Pan ⊻ G 4 204
Nubian Desert ◆2 C 4 202
Ñuble ≃ E 2 195
Nucet B 7 104
Nueces ≃ F 4 172
Nueltin Lake ◎ E 12 150
Nueva, Isla I K 6 192
Nueva-Andalucía H 5 86
Nueva Ciudad Guerrero G 4 172
Nueva Esparta □3 F 8 186
Nueva Gerona C 4 186
Nueva Imperial F 1 195
Nueva Italia de Ruiz H 8 184
Nueva Rosita C 9 184
Nueve, Canal Numero ≍ G 8 192
Nueve de Julio D 7 195
Nuevitas C 5 186
Nuevo, Golfo ⊂ H 7 192
Nuevo Casas Grandes B 6 184
Nuevo Laredo D 9 184
Nuevo León □3 E 10 184
Nuevo Progreso H 13 184
Nugaal □3 F 6 202
Nui I1 D 9 136
Nuia C 12 66
Nujiang C 3 130
Nuku'alofa F 10 136
Nukufetau I1 D 9 136
Nukulaelae I1 D 9 136
Nukunau I D 9 136
Nukunonu I D 10 136
Nukus H 21 110
Nules E 4 88
Nullagine G 6 140
Nullarbor National Park ♦ L 10 140
Nullarbor Plain ⊻ L 10 140
Numan D 7 200
Numancia ⊥ C 2 88
Numata F 7 126
Numazu G 7 126
Nümbrecht F 4 98
Numfoor, Pulau I F 10 134
Numurkah F 5 144
Nun ≃ E 6 200
Nunapitchuk F 13 154
Nunavut □3 C 14 150
Nunawading F 5 144
Nundah A 9 144
Nuneaton E 5 72
Nuñez, Cape ≻ q 21 193c
Nungarin L 5 140
Nungesser Lake ◎ F 11 158
Nunivak Island I F 11 154
Nunjiang B 15 128
Nunjikompita L 2 142
Nunspeet B 4 69
Nuomin ≃ B 14 128
Nuoro E 2 90
Nuoro □6 k 10 94a
Nuremberg see Nürnberg C 8 100
Nurlat I 19 108
Nurmes E 14 64
Nürnberg C 8 100
Nurri I 10 94a
Nürtingen D 6 100
Nusa Tenggara Barat □3 A 4 140
Nusa Tenggara Timur □3 A 6 140
Nusaybin D 9 118
Nushagak Bay ⊂ G 15 154
Nu Shan ∧ E 4 130
Nushki E 10 116
Nutauge, laguna ⊂ B 6 154
Nutrioso F 4 176
Nu-Uis A 1 206
Nuuk see Godthåb D 22 150
Nuwerus F 3 206
Nuweveldberge ∧ G 4 206
Nuyakuk Lake ◎ F 15 154
Nxai Pan National Park ♦ F 3 204
Nxaunxau F 3 204
Nyabing M 5 140
Nyack E 5 164
Nyahua D 5 204
Nyahururu Falls G 4 202
Nyainqêntanglha Shan ∧ C 6 122
Nyakakiri C 5 204
Nyala E 1 202
Nyamandhlovu F 4 204
Nyamtumbo E 6 204
Nyandekwa C 5 204
Nyanding, Khawr ≃ F 3 202
Nyang ≃ D 2 130
Nyanga □3 F 7 200
Nyanga ≃ F 7 200
Nyangana F 3 204
Nyanza C 4 204
Nyanza □3 H 3 202
Nyasa, Lake see Malawi, Lake ◎ E 5 204
Nyaunglebin F 3 132
Nyazura F 5 204
Nyborg C 3 68
Nybro D 7 66
Nyda C 30 108
Nye □6 B 7 182
Nyeri H 4 202
Nyika National Park ♦ E 5 204
Nyimba E 5 204
Nyingchi D 2 130
Nyiragongo, Volcan ∧1 C 4 204
Nyírbátor B 7 104
Nyíregyháza B 6 104
Nykøbing D 4 68
Nykøbing Sjælland C 4 68
Nyköping C 8 66
Nylstroom C 8 206
Nymboida ≃ B 9 144
Nymboida National Park ♦ B 9 144
Nymburk B 12 100
Nynäshamn C 8 66
Nyngan C 6 144
Nyon D 4 82
Nyong ≃ E 7 200
Nyons F 3 82
Nýrsko C 10 100
Nyš B 12 124
Nysa C 9 96
Nysa Łużycka (Lausitzer Neisse) ≃ E 11 98
Nytva H 21 108
Nyumba ya Mungu Dam ◆6 H 4 202
Nyungwe E 5 204
Nyunzu D 4 204
Nyzhankovychi D 12 96
Nyzhn'ohirs'kyy G 9 110
Nzébéla D 3 200
Nzérékoré D 3 200
Nzilo, Lac ◎1 E 4 204
Nzwani I J 12 196

O

Oahe, Lake ◎1 C 4 174
Oahe Dam ◆6 C 4 174
Oahu I i 9 181a
Oakbank D 3 144
Oak Bay G 10 156
Oakburn F 8 158
Oakdale, Ca., U.S. C 3 182
Oakdale, Ne., U.S. D 5 174
Oakengates E 4 72
Oakes B 5 174
Oakfield D 4 166
Oakham E 6 72
Oak Harbor A 2 178
Oak Hill E 3 162
Oakhurst E 6 172
Oak Lake ◎ G 8 158
Oakland, Ca., U.S. C 1 182
Oakland, Md., U.S. D 4 162
Oakland, Me., U.S. A 9 162
Oakland, Ne., U.S. E 6 174
Oak Lawn, Il., U.S. B 5 170
Oaklawn, Ks., U.S. G 6 174
Oakohay Creek ≃ F 4 170
Oakover ≃ G 6 140
Oak Park B 5 170
Oak Point F 10 158
Oakridge, Or., U.S. D 2 178
Oak Ridge, Tn., U.S. A 2 168
Oak Ridge National Laboratory ◗3 B 2 168
Oakura C 4 146
Oakville B 4 162
Oakwood B 6 170
Oamaru F 3 146
Oates Coast ⊥2 D 24 208
Oaxaca □3 I 11 184
Oaxaca de Juárez I 11 184
Ob' ≃ C 9 114
Obala E 7 200
Oban D 6 200
O Barco de Valdeorras B 4 86
Obed E 13 156
Obedjiwan, Réserve indienne ◆4 D 6 160
Obeliai E 12 66
Oberá G 3 194
Oberammergau E 7 100
Oberbayern □6 D 8 100
Oberfranken □6 B 8 100
Obergurgl D 3 102
Oberhausen E 3 98
Oberkirch D 5 100
Oberkochen D 7 100
Oberlausitz □9 E 11 98
Oberlin, Ks., U.S. F 4 174
Oberlin, Oh., U.S. C 2 162
Obernai B 5 82
Oberndorf am Neckar D 5 100
Oberösterreich □3 B 5 102
Oberpfalz □6 C 9 100
Oberpleis F 4 98
Ober-Ramstadt C 5 100
Oberstdorf C 2 102
Obersulm C 6 100
Oberueckersee ◎ C 10 98
Oberursel B 5 100
Obervellach D 5 102
Oberwart C 8 102
Obi D 6 200
Obi, Kepulauan II F 9 134
Obi, Pulau I F 9 134
Óbidos D 7 190
Obihiro C 9 126
Obilatu, Pulau I F 9 134
Obion D 4 170
Obion ≃ D 4 170
Obion, Middle Fork ≃ D 4 170
Oblivskaja E 13 110
Obluče B 18 128
Obninsk I 12 108
Obo A 4 204
Obock E 5 202
Obojan' D 9 110
Oborniki B 9 96
Obrenovac C 6 104
Obščij syrt ∧ D 17 110
Observatoire, Caye de l' I D 12 138
Obskaja guba ⊂ C 10 114
Obuasi D 4 200
Obudu D 6 200
Obuhova H 9 108
Obwalden □3 C 4 92
Ocala E 3 168
Ocaña, Col. F 6 186
Ocaña, Spain E 7 86
Occhito, Lago di ◎1 C 4 94
Occidental, Cordillera ∧ E 3 190
Ocean □6 G 4 164
Ocean City G 4 164
Oceano E 3 182
Ocean Park B 1 178
Oceanside, Ca., U.S. G 6 182
Oceanside, N.Y., U.S. F 5 164
Ocean Springs G 4 170
Očer H 21 108
Ochamchire H 12 110
Ochapowace Indian Reserve ◆4 F 7 158
Ochlocknee D 2 168
Ochlockonee ≃ D 2 168
Ochsenfurt C 7 100
Ochtrup D 4 98
Ocilla D 3 168
Öckerö D 5 66
Ocmulgee ≃ D 3 168
Ocmulgee National Monument ♦ C 3 168
Ocna Mureș B 7 104
Ocnița A 9 104
Ocoa, Bahía de ⊂ D 7 186
Oconee ≃ C 3 168
Oconee, Lake ◎1 C 3 168
Oconto Falls C 4 166
Ocosingo D 1 186
Ocotal E 3 186
Ocotlán G 8 184
Ocozocuautla I 13 184
Ocracoke Island I B 7 168
Ocumare del Tuy F 8 186
Oda, Ghana D 4 200
Ōda, Japan G 4 126
Oda, Jabal ∧ C 4 202
Odanakumadona G 3 204
Ōdate D 8 126
O'Day C 11 158
Odder C 3 68
Odebolt D 7 174
Ode-Ekiti D 6 200
Odei ≃ C 10 158
Odem G 5 172
Ödemiş C 7 106
Odendaalsrus D 7 206
Odense C 3 68
Odenthal E 4 98
Oder (Odra) ≃ C 11 98
Oderbruch ◆1 D 11 98
Oderzo D 8 92
Odesa (Odessa) B 11 104
Odesa □6 B 11 104

∟ Waterfall ꓤ Strait ⊂ Bay, Gulf ◎ Lake ≋ Swamp ⌇ Ice Feature ≍ Other Hydrographic Feature ✢ Submarine Feature □ Political Unit ◗ Cultural Institution ⊥ Historical Site ♦ Recreational Site ⊠ Airport ■ Military Installation ◆ Miscellaneous

Name / Map Ref. / Page

Symbols in the index entries represent the broad categories identified in the key at the right. Symbols with superior numbers (⋌¹) identify subcategories (see complete key on page 242).

▲ Mountain   ⋌ Mountains   ✕ Pass   V Valley   ≃ Plain   ➤ Cape   I Island   II Islands   ⊥ Other Topographic Feature   ≃ River   ≅ Canal

Pagon — Pic

Name	Map Ref.	Page
Pagon, Bukit ∧	E 7	134
Pago Pago	k 11	147b
Pagosa Springs	D 5	176
Pahama	B 7	206
Pahang □[3]	M 6	132
Pahang ≃	M 6	132
Pahoa	j 11	181a
Pahraničny	B 12	96
Pai ≃	I 3	130
Paide	C 12	66
Paignton	G 3	72
Paiguano	B 2	195
Päijänne ⊜	B 12	66
Paillaco	G 1	195
Paimio	B 11	66
Painesdale	B 4	166
Paint ≃	B 4	166
Painted Desert ◆[2]	E 3	176
Paint Lake ⊜	D 10	158
Paintsville	E 2	162
Paisley	B 2	72
Paiton	k 21	135b
Pajaro ≃	D 2	182
Paje	B 7	206
Pajer, gora ∧	C 26	108
Paj-Hoj ∧∧[2]	C 9	114
Pakaraima Mountains ∧∧	C 6	190
Pak Chong	G 5	132
Pakeng	F 3	202
Pakistan □[1]	G 8	112
Paklenica Nacionalni Park ♠	C 3	104
Pakokku	E 6	122
Pak Phanang	J 5	132
Pakrac	E 9	102
Pakruojis	E 11	66
Paks	D 10	102
Pak Thong Chai	G 5	132
Pakwash Lake ⊜	F 12	158
Pakxé	G 7	132
Pala	H 4	132
Palafrugell	C 8	88
Palagiano	D 6	94
Palagonia	G 4	94
Palagruža, Otoci II	D 4	104
Pala Indian Reservation ◆[4]	G 6	182
Palaiochóra	E 5	106
Palaiseau	D 9	78
Palamós	C 8	88
Palamu National Park ♠	E 4	122
Palamuse	C 13	66
Palana	D 18	114
Palanan Point ≻	B 8	134
Palanga	E 10	66
Palangkaraya	F 6	134
Palani	G 3	122
Palankarinna, Lake ⊜	B 2	144
Pālanpur	E 2	122
Palapye	B 7	206
Pālār ≃	G 3	122
Palas de Rei	B 3	86
Palatka, Russia	C 18	114
Palatka, Fl., U.S.	E 4	168
Palau	G 3	172
Palau □[1]	C 5	136
Palau Islands II	D 10	134
Palaw	H 4	132
Palawan I	D 7	134
Pālayankottai	H 3	122
Palazzolo Acreide	G 4	94
Palazzo San Gervasio	D 6	94
Palembang	F 4	134
Palencia	B 6	86
Palencia □[6]	B 6	86
Palenque	I 14	184
Palenque ⊥	I 13	184
Palermo, Italy	F 3	94
Palermo, Ur.	C 10	195
Palermo □[6]	G 3	94
Palestine, Ar., U.S.	E 3	170
Palestine, Tx., U.S.	E 6	172
Palestine □[9]	F 4	120
Pāli	D 2	122
Palidoro ◆[8]	H 8	92
Palikir	C 7	136
Palisade	C 4	176
Palisades	D 8	178
Palisades Reservoir ⊜[1]	D 8	178
Pālitāna	E 2	122
Palizada	H 13	184
Paljavaam ≃	B 2	154
Palkino	H 8	108
Palk Strait ꭒ	G 3	122
Pallasovka	D 15	110
Palling	D 8	156
Palliser, Cape ≻	D 5	146
Palma	E 7	204
Palma, Badia de ⊂	E 7	88
Palma del Río	G 5	86
Palma de Mallorca	E 7	88
Palma di Montechiaro	G 3	94
Palmar, Lago Artificial del ⊜[1]	C 9	195
Palmares	E 11	190
Palmas, Braz.	F 9	190
Palmas, Braz.	G 4	194
Palma Soriano	C 6	186
Palm Bay	E 4	168
Palm Beach	F 4	168
Palmdale	F 5	182
Palm Desert	F 5	180
Palmeira	F 5	194
Palmer, Ak., U.S.	F 20	154
Palmer, Ma., U.S.	D 6	164
Palmer, Tn., U.S.	E 6	170
Palmer ◗[3]	C 2	208
Palmer Land ◆[1]	D 2	208
Palmerston I[1]	E 11	136
Palmerston North	D 5	146
Palmerton	F 3	164
Palmi	F 5	94
Palmira	C 3	190
Palmitas	C 9	195
Palm Springs	G 7	182
Palmyra, N.Y., U.S.	C 1	164
Palmyra, Pa., U.S.	F 2	164
Palmyra ⊥	E 8	118
Palmyra Atoll I[1]	C 11	136
Palo Alto	C 1	182
Palo Duro Canyon State Park ♠	C 3	172
Palomar Mountain ∧	G 7	182
Palomar Mountain State Park ♠	G 7	182
Palopo	F 8	134
Palos see Palos de la Frontera	G 4	86
Palos de la Frontera (Palos)	G 4	86
Pålsboda	C 7	66
Palu, Indon.	F 7	134
Palu, Tur.	C 9	118
Paluke	D 3	200
Pama ≃	E 8	200
Pamanukan	k 18	135b
Pambeguwa	C 6	200
Pamekasan	k 21	135b
Pameungpeuk	k 18	135b
Pamiers	E 5	80
Pamir ∧∧	B 2	122
Pamlico Sound ꭒ	B 7	168
Pampa	C 3	172
Pampa del Chañar	B 3	195
Pampas ◆[1]	G 7	192
Pampeluna see Pamplona	B 3	88
Pamplona, Col.	G 6	186
Pamplona (Iruña), Spain	B 3	88
Pamukkale (Hierapolis) ⊥	D 8	106
Pamukova	B 9	106
Pana	C 4	170
Panaca	D 1	176
Panaitan, Pulau I	G 5	134
Panaji	F 2	122
Panamá, Braz.	C 6	194
Panamá, Pan.	F 5	186
Panama, Il., U.S.	C 4	170
Panama □[1]	I 11	148
Panamá, Bahía de ⊂	F 5	186
Panama, Gulf of ⊂	G 5	186
Panama, Isthmus of ⊥[3]	F 5	186
Panama Canal ≍	F 5	186
Panama City	G 6	170
Panamint Range ∧∧	D 6	182
Panamint Valley V	D 6	182
Panay I	C 8	134
Panay Gulf ⊂	C 8	134
Pančevo	C 6	104
Panciu	C 9	104
Pandan, Selat ꭒ	j 14	134a
Pandan Reservoir ⊜[1]	j 14	134a
Pandėlys	D 12	66
Pandharpur	F 2	122
Pāndhurna	E 3	122
Pando	D 10	195
Pandu	D 8	200
Panevėžys	E 12	66
Pāng ≃	C 4	132
Pangala	C 1	204
Pangandaran	k 19	135b
Pangani ≃	D 6	204
Pangi	C 4	204
Pangkalanbuun	F 6	134
Pangkalpinang	F 5	134
Pangutaran Group II	D 8	134
Panié, Mont ∧	D 13	138
Panj (Pyandzh) ≃	C 10	116
Panjgūr	E 9	116
Pankshin	D 6	200
Panlong see Lo ≃	H 7	130
P'anmunjŏm-ni	G 16	128
Panna	E 4	122
Panna National Park ♠	E 3	122
Pannirtuuq	C 19	150
Pannonhalma ◗[1]	C 9	102
Panora	E 7	174
Panorama	D 4	194
Panovo	G 17	108
Panshan	F 14	128
Pantanal Matogrossense, Parque Nacional do ♠	B 2	194
Pantar, Pulau I	G 8	134
Pantelleria, Isola di I	H 1	94
Panu	C 2	204
Pánuco	G 11	184
Pánuco ≃	F 10	184
Panvel	F 2	122
Panxian	F 7	130
Paola	E 5	94
Paoli	C 5	170
Pápa	C 9	102
Papagayo, Golfo de ⊂	F 3	186
Papago Indian Reservation ◆[4]	F 2	176
Papaikou	j 11	181a
Papakura	B 5	146
Papantla de Olarte	G 11	184
Paparoa National Park ♠	E 3	146
Papatoetoe	B 5	146
Papeete	i 8	147a
Papenburg	C 4	98
Papendrecht	C 3	69
Papigochic ≃	C 5	184
Papilė	D 11	66
Papineau □[6]	A 3	164
Papua, Gulf of ⊂	N 12	124
Papua New Guinea □[1]	D 6	136
Papun	E 3	132
Pará □[3]	E 8	190
Pará ≃	C 8	194
Paracatu	B 7	194
Paracatu ≃	B 8	194
Paracel Islands (Xisha Qundao) II	B 6	134
Parachilna	C 2	144
Paraćin	D 6	104
Paradas	G 5	86
Paradise, Ca., U.S.	A 2	182
Paradise, Nv., U.S.	D 1	176
Paradise Hill	E 15	154
Paradise River	B 15	160
Pāradwīp	E 5	122
Paragould	D 3	170
Paragua ≃	C 6	190
Paraguaçu ≃	F 11	190
Paraguaçu Paulista	E 5	194
Paraguai (Paraguay) ≃	C 8	192
Paraguaná, Península de ≻[1]	A 4	190
Paraguarí	F 2	194
Paraguarí □[3]	G 2	194
Paraguay □[1]	G 8	188
Paraguay (Paraguai) ≃	E 8	192
Paraíba □[3]	E 11	190
Paraíba do Sul ≃	H 10	190
Paraisópolis	E 7	194
Parakou	D 5	200
Paramaribo	B 7	190
Paramirim	F 10	190
Paramušir, ostrov I	B 15	124
Paraná, Arg.	B 7	195
Paranã, Braz.	F 9	190
Paraná □[3]	D 9	192
Paranã ≃, Braz.	F 9	190
Paraná ≃, S.A.	F 7	192
Paranaguá	F 6	194
Paranaguá, Baía de ⊂	F 6	194
Paranaíba	C 5	194
Paranaíba ≃	C 5	194
Paranam	B 8	190
Paranapanema ≃	H 8	190
Paranavaí	E 4	194
Paranoá, Lago do ⊜[1]	A 7	194
Paraopeba	C 8	194
Paraparaumu	D 5	146
Parapetí ≃	G 6	190
Paraúna	B 5	194
Paray-le-Monial	D 2	82
Pārbati ≃	E 3	122
Pārbatipur	D 5	122
Parbhani	F 3	122
Parchim	C 8	98
Parczew	C 12	96
Pardes Hanna-Karkur	E 4	120
Pardo ≃, Braz.	G 11	190
Pardo ≃, Braz.	H 9	190
Pardo ≃, Braz.	H 8	190
Pardubice	C 8	96
Pardubický □[3]	D 8	96
Parecis, Chapada dos ∧∧	F 7	190
Paredes de Nava	B 6	86
Parent	E 6	160
Pareora	F 3	146
Parepare	F 7	134
Parfenevo	F 15	108
Párga	C 4	106
Paria, Gulf of ⊂	F 9	186
Paricutín ∧[1]	H 8	184
Parika	B 7	190
Parikkala	B 14	66
Parima, Sierra ∧∧	C 6	190
Parintins	D 7	190
Paris, Fr.	D 9	78
Paris, Il., U.S.	C 5	170
Paris, Ky., U.S.	D 1	162
Paris, Tx., U.S.	D 6	172
Parita, Bahía de ⊂	F 4	186
Parit Buntar	L 5	132
Parkano	A 11	66
Parker, Co., U.S.	F 2	174
Parker, S.D., U.S.	D 6	174
Parker Dam ◆[6]	E 1	176
Parkersburg	D 3	162
Parkers Prairie	B 7	174
Parkes	D 7	144
Parkin	E 3	170
Parkland	B 2	178
Park Range ∧∧	B 5	176
Park Rynie	F 9	206
Parksville	A 1	178
Parkville	G 2	164
Parla	D 7	86
Parlākimidi	F 4	122
Parma, Italy	E 6	92
Parma, Id., U.S.	D 5	178
Parma, Oh., U.S.	C 3	162
Parma □[6]	E 6	92
Parnaíba	D 10	190
Parnaíba ≃	D 10	190
Parnassós ∧	C 5	106
Parnassós National Park ♠	C 5	106
Párnitha National Park ♠	C 5	106
Pärnu	C 12	66
Pärnu-Jaagupi	C 12	66
Paromaj	B 12	124
Paroo ≃	C 5	144
Páros	D 6	106
Parow	G 3	206
Parral	E 2	195
Parral ≃	D 7	184
Parramatta	D 8	144
Parras de la Fuente	E 8	184
Parrsboro	F 11	160
Parry Channel ꭒ	B 10	148
Parry Sound	F 3	160
Parshall	H 7	158
Parsnip ≃	D 10	156
Parsons, Ks., U.S.	D 1	170
Parsons, Tn., U.S.	E 4	170
Pärsti	C 12	66
Partanna	G 2	94
Parthenay	B 3	80
Partille	D 5	66
Partinico	F 3	94
Partizansk	C 4	126
Partizánske	B 10	102
Paru ≃	D 8	190
Paru de Oeste ≃	C 7	190
Părvomaj	D 8	104
Paryčy	C 6	110
Parys	D 7	206
Pasadena, Ca., U.S.	F 5	182
Pasadena, Tx., U.S.	F 6	172
Pasaje	D 3	190
Pa Sak ≃	F 5	132
Pascagoula	G 4	170
Pascagoula ≃	G 4	170
Paşcani	B 9	104
Pasco	B 4	178
Pascoag	E 7	164
Pas-de-Calais □[3]	B 9	78
Pasewalk	C 11	98
Pāsighāt	D 2	130
Pasinler	B 9	118
Pasir Gudang	i 15	134a
Pasir Mas	K 5	132
Pasir Panjang	j 14	134a
Pasirpengarayan	N 5	132
Pasir Puteh, Malay.	i 15	134a
Pasir Puteh, Malay.	L 6	132
Paškovskij	G 11	110
Pasłęk	A 10	96
Pasmore ≃	C 2	144
Pasni	E 9	116
Paso de Indios	H 6	192
Paso del Cerro	B 10	195
Paso de los Libres	A 9	195
Paso de los Toros	C 9	195
Paso Robles	E 3	182
Passadumkeag	F 9	160
Passaic	F 4	164
Passaic □[6]	E 4	164
Passau	D 10	100
Passero, Capo ≻	H 5	94
Passo Fundo	A 9	192
Passo Real, Represa do ⊜[1]	A 11	195
Passos	D 7	194
Pastavy	E 13	66
Pastaza ≃	D 3	190
Pasto	C 3	190
Pastol Bay ⊂	E 13	154
Pasuruan	k 21	135b
Pasvalys	D 12	66
Pásztó	B 5	104
Patagonia ◆[1]	H 6	192
Pātan	E 2	122
Patchewollock	E 4	144
Patchogue	F 5	164
Patea	C 5	146
Patensie	G 6	206
Paterna	E 4	88
Paternion	D 5	102
Paternò	G 4	94
Paterson, S. Afr.	G 6	206
Paterson, N.J., U.S.	F 4	164
Pathānkot	C 3	122
Pathein (Bassein)	F 2	132
Pathein see Bassein ≃	F 6	122
Pathfinder Reservoir ⊜[1]	D 10	178
Pati	k 20	135b
Patiāla	C 3	122
Pātkai Range ∧∧	D 7	122
Patna, India	D 5	122
Patna, India	E 5	122
Patnos	C 10	118
Pato Branco	G 4	194
Patonga	G 3	202
Patos	E 11	190
Patos ≃	C 3	195
Patos, Lagoa dos ⊂	F 9	192
Patos de Minas	C 7	194
Pátra	C 4	106
Patraikós Kólpos ⊂	C 4	106
Patricio Lynch, Isla I	I 4	192
Patrocínio	C 7	194
Pattada	I 5	92
Pattani	K 5	132
Pattaya	H 5	132
Patterson	C 2	182
Patterson, Mount ∧	D 27	154
Patti	F 4	94
Pattoki	C 2	122
Patuca ≃	E 3	186
Patumahoe	B 5	146
Patuxent ≃	D 5	162
Patuxent River State Park ♠	G 1	164
Pátzcuaro	H 9	184
Pau	E 3	80
Pauini ≃	E 5	190
Paulding	B 6	170
Paulhan	G 1	82
Paulicéia	D 4	194
Paulinzella ⊥	F 8	98
Paulistana	E 10	190
Paullo	E 7	82
Paulo Afonso	E 11	190
Pauls Valley	C 5	172
Paung	F 3	132
Paungde	E 2	132
Paunggyi	F 3	132
Pauri	C 3	122
Pauto ≃	B 4	190
Pāveh	E 12	118
Pavia	D 5	92
Pavia □[6]	D 5	92
Pavilion	F 11	156
Pāvilosta	D 10	66
Pavlikeni	D 8	104
Pavlodar	D 10	114
Pavlof Bay ⊂	I 14	154
Pavlof Volcano ∧[1]	I 13	154
Pavlohrad	E 9	110
Pavlovka	C 23	110
Pavlovo	I 15	108
Pavlovsk, Russia	D 12	110
Pavlovsk, Russia	C 15	66
Pavlysh	E 8	110
Pavullo nel Frignano	E 6	92
Pawan ≃	F 6	134
Pawn ≃	E 3	132
Pawnee	C 4	170
Pawnee City	E 6	174
Paw Paw, Il., U.S.	B 4	170
Paw Paw, W.V., U.S.	D 4	162
Pawtucket	E 7	164
Paxton	E 4	174
Payakumbuh	O 5	132
Paya Lebar	i 15	134a
Payerne	D 4	82
Payeti	A 6	140
Payette ≃	D 5	178
Payette, North Fork ≃	C 5	178
Paynes Find	K 4	140
Paysandú	C 8	195
Payson, Az., U.S.	E 3	176
Payson, Il., U.S.	C 3	170
Pazar	B 9	118
Pazarcık	D 7	118
Pazardžik	D 8	104
Pcič	C 6	110
Peabody, Ks., U.S.	A 5	172
Peabody, Ma., U.S.	D 7	164
Peace ≃	B 15	156
Peace River	C 13	156
Peachland	G 11	156
Peach Orchard	C 3	168
Peach Springs	E 2	176
Peak Charles National Park ♠	M 6	140
Peak District National Park ♠	D 5	72
Peake Creek ≃	J 2	142
Peak Hill, Austl.	I 5	140
Peak Hill, Austl.	D 7	144
Peard Bay ⊂	A 15	154
Pea Ridge National Military Park ♠	D 1	170
Pearl	F 3	170
Pearl ≃	G 3	170
Pearl Harbor ⊂	i 9	181a
Pearl Island I	k 18	131a
Pearl River	G 4	170
Pearse Island I	D 6	156
Pearston	G 6	206
Peary Land ◆[1]	A 16	148
Pebane	F 6	204
Pebble Island I	n 18	193b
Peć	D 6	104
Pecatu	I 22	135b
Pecica	B 6	104
Pečora	D 22	108
Pečora ≃	C 8	114
Pečorskaja guba ⊂	B 21	108
Pečorskoe more ⊤[2]	C 8	114
Pečory	H 7	108
Pecos	E 2	172
Pecos ≃	E 7	152
Pecos National Monument ♠	E 6	176
Pécs	D 10	102
Pedder, Lake ⊜[1]	j 11	145a
Peddie	G 7	206
Pedernales ≃	E 4	172
Pedernales Falls State Park ♠	E 4	172
Pedra Azul	A 10	194
Pedras Salgadas	C 3	86
Pedreiras	D 10	190
Pedro Afonso	A 9	190
Pedrógão Grande	E 2	86
Pedro Juan Caballero	E 3	194
Pedro Leopoldo	C 8	194
Pedro Muñoz	E 2	88
Peebles, Scot., U.K.	B 3	72
Peebles, Oh., U.S.	D 2	162
Pee Dee ≃	B 5	168
Peekskill	E 5	164
Peel ≃	C 27	154
Peel Channel ≃	B 27	154
Peel Sound ꭒ	B 13	150
Peene ≃	B 10	98
Peerless	A 11	178
Peers	E 13	156
Pegasus Bay ⊂	E 4	146
Pegau	E 9	98
Pegnitz	C 8	100
Pego	F 4	88
Pegtymel' ≃	B 3	154
Pegu see Bago	F 3	132
Pegu ≃	F 3	132
Peguis Indian Reserve ◆[4]	F 9	158
Pehčevo	E 7	104
Pehuajó	D 7	195
Pehula	B 11	66
Peigan Indian Reserve ◆[4]	G 15	156
Peikang	G 15	130
Peine	D 7	98
Peip'ing see Beijing	G 11	128
Peipus, Lake ⊜	C 13	66
Peiraiás (Piraeus)	D 5	106
Peissenberg	E 8	100
Peiting	E 7	100
Peixe ≃	D 5	194
Peixian	A 13	130
Peixoto, Represa de ⊜[1]	D 7	194
Pekalongan	k 20	135b
Pekan	M 6	132
Pekanbaru	N 5	132
Pekin	B 4	170
Peking see Beijing	G 11	128
Péla	D 3	200
Pelabuhanratu	k 18	135b
Pelagie, Isole II	I 2	94
Pelée, Montagne ∧[1]	s 26	187h
Pelee Island I	H 2	160
Peleng, Pulau I	F 8	134
Pelham	F 5	170
Pelhřimov	C 12	100
Pelican	H 27	154
Pelican Lake ⊜, Mb., Can.	E 8	158
Pelican Lake ⊜, Sk., Can.	D 7	158
Pelican Narrows	D 20	156
Pelister Nacionalni Park ♠	E 6	104
Pella	B 2	170
Pélla ⊥	B 5	106
Pell City	F 5	170
Pellegrini, Lago ⊜	F 4	195
Pellston	C 6	166
Pelly ≃	E 26	154
Pelly Crossing	E 26	154
Pelly Mountains ∧∧	F 28	154
Pelopónnisos □[3]	D 5	106
Pelopónnisos ≻[1]	D 5	106
Pelotas	B 11	195
Pelotas ≃	A 9	192
Pel'vož	C 27	108
Pelym	G 25	108
Pemadumcook Lake ⊜	h 12	163a
Pemalang	k 19	135b
Pematang	O 5	132
Pematangsiantar	M 4	132
Pemba	E 7	204
Pemba I	D 6	204
Pemba Channel ꭒ	D 6	204
Pemba North □[3]	H 5	202
Pemba South □[3]	I 5	202
Pemberton	N 4	140
Pembina ≃, Ab., Can.	E 14	156
Pembina ≃, N.A.	A 5	174
Pembroke, On., Can.	F 5	160
Pembroke, Wales, U.K.	F 2	72
Pembroke, Me., U.S.	A 10	162
Pembroke, Va., U.S.	E 3	162
Pembroke Pines	F 4	168
Pembrokeshire □[6]	F 1	72
Pembrokeshire Coast National Park ♠	E 1	72
Pembuang ≃	F 6	134
Pemigewasset ≃	C 7	164
Penafiel	C 2	86
Pena-Lunanga	C 4	204
Penápolis	D 5	194
Peñaranda de Bracamonte	D 5	86
Peñarroya-Pueblonuevo	F 5	86
Penarth	F 3	72
Penas, Golfo de ⊂	I 5	192
Pench National Park ♠	E 3	122
Penco	E 1	195
Pender Bay ⊂	E 7	140
Pendjari ≃	C 5	200
Pendjari, Parc National de la ♠	C 5	200
Pendleton, In., U.S.	B 6	170
Pendleton, Or., U.S.	C 4	178
Pend Oreille ≃	A 5	178
Pend Oreille, Lake ⊜	A 5	178
Pendžikent	B 1	122
Penebel	I 22	135b
Penedono	C 3	86
Penetanguishene	F 3	160
Penfield	C 4	162
Penganga ≃	F 3	122
Peng Chau	I 19	131a
Peng Chau I	I 19	131a
P'enghu Ch'üntao II	G 14	130
Penglai	H 13	128
Pengshui	D 9	130
Pengxi	C 7	130
Pengxian	C 6	130
Pengze	D 13	130
Penha	G 6	194
Penibética, Cordillera ∧∧	D 4	84
Peniche	E 1	86
Penicuik	B 3	72
Penida, Nusa I	I 22	135b
Peninsula State Park ♠	C 5	166
Penne	B 3	94
Penne-d'Agenais	D 4	80
Penneru ≃	G 3	122
Penn Hills	C 4	162
Pennines ∧∧	C 4	72
Penns Grove	G 3	164
Pennsville	G 3	164
Pennsylvania □[3]	C 12	152
Penn Yan	D 1	164
Pennyrile Forest State Resort Park ♠	D 5	170
Peno	H 10	108
Penobscot ≃	h 12	163a
Peñoles	H 1	172
Penong	K 1	142
Penonomé	F 4	186
Penrhyn I[1]	D 12	136
Penrith, Austl.	D 8	144
Penrith, Eng., U.K.	C 4	72
Pensacola	G 5	170
Pensacola Mountains ∧∧	E 4	208
Pentecost Island see Pentecôte I	E 8	136
Pentecôte I	E 8	136
Penticton	G 12	156
Penticton Indian Reserve ◆[4]	G 12	156
Pentland Firth ꭒ	B 5	74
Penukonda	G 3	122
Penza	C 14	110
Penzance	G 1	72
Penzberg	E 8	100
Penzenskaja oblast' □[6]	C 14	110
Penžinskij hrebet ∧∧	C 19	114
Peoria, Az., U.S.	F 2	176
Peoria, Il., U.S.	B 4	170
Peotone	B 5	170
Pepel	D 2	200
Peqin	B 3	106
Pequot Lakes	B 1	166
Perabumulih	F 4	134
Perak □[3]	L 5	132
Perak ≃	L 5	132
Perak, Kuala ⊂	L 5	132
Peralillo	D 2	195
Perämeri (Bottenviken) ⊂	D 11	64
Perchtoldsdorf	B 8	102
Percival Lakes ⊜	G 8	140
Perdido ≃	G 5	170
Perdido, Monte ∧	B 5	88
Perdue	E 18	156
Peregrebnoe	E 26	108
Perehins'ke	A 8	104
Perehonivka	A 11	104
Pereira	C 3	190
Pereira Barreto	D 5	194
Perelesinskij	D 12	110
Peremyšl'	I 11	108
Pereslavl'-Zalesskij	H 13	108
Pereyaslav-Khmel'nyts'kyy	E 7	110
Perg	B 6	102
Pergamino	C 7	195
Pergamum ⊥	C 7	106
Pergola	F 8	92
Péribonka ≃	D 8	160
Péribonka, Lac ⊜	C 8	160
Peridot	F 3	176
Périgord □[9]	C 4	80
Périgueux	C 4	80
Perijá, Sierra de ∧∧	A 4	190
Perim I	E 5	202
Periprava	C 10	104
Perito Moreno	I 5	192
Perkins	B 5	172
Perlas, Archipiélago de las II	F 5	186
Perlas, Laguna de ⊂	E 3	186
Perleberg	C 8	98
Perlis □[3]	K 5	132
Perm'	G 22	108
Permas	G 16	108
Përmet	B 4	106
Permskaja oblast' □[6]	G 23	108
Pernambuco □[3]	E 11	190
Pernatty Lagoon ⊜	C 1	144
Pernik	D 7	104
Péronne	C 9	78
Perosa Argentina	E 3	92
Perote	H 11	184
Perpignan	F 6	80
Perrin	D 4	172
Perrine	G 4	168
Perris	G 6	182
Perry, Ga., U.S.	C 3	168
Perry, Ia., U.S.	E 7	174
Perry, Mi., U.S.	B 1	162
Perry □[6]	F 1	164
Perry Lake ⊜[1]	C 1	170
Perrysburg	C 2	162
Perry's Victory and International Peace Memorial ⊥	C 2	162
Perryton	B 3	172
Perryville	D 3	170
Peršamajski	F 12	66
Persepolis see Takht-e Jamshīd ⊥	G 15	118
Pershotravens'k	D 5	110
Perstorp	H 6	64
Pertek	C 8	118
Perth, Austl.	L 3	140
Perth, On., Can.	F 5	160
Perth, Scot., U.K.	D 5	74
Perth Amboy	F 4	164
Perthshire and Kinross □[6]	D 5	74
Pertuis	G 3	82
Peru, Il., U.S.	B 4	170
Peru, In., U.S.	B 5	170
Peru □[1]	E 7	188
Perućačko jezero ⊜[1]	D 5	104
Peru-Chile Trench ✢[1]	I 21	58
Perugia	F 8	92
Perugia □[6]	G 8	92
Peruíbe	F 7	194
Perušić	C 3	104
Péruwelz	D 2	69
Pervomajsk	B 13	110
Pervomajskij, Russia	I 24	108
Pervomajskij, Russia	J 21	108
Pervomays'k	A 11	104
Pervomays'kyy	E 9	110
Pervoural'sk	H 23	108
Pesaro	F 8	92
Pesaro e Urbino □[6]	F 8	92
Pescadores see P'enghu Ch'üntao II	G 14	130
Pesčanoe	E 11	108
Pescantina	E 2	102
Pescara	B 4	94
Pescara □[6]	B 3	94
Pescara ≃	B 4	94
Pescia	F 6	92
Pescina	B 3	94
Pesek, Pulau I	j 14	134a
Peshāwar	C 2	122
Peshkopi	B 4	106
Peshtigo	C 5	166
Peso da Régua	C 3	86
Pesquería ≃	H 4	172
Pessac	D 3	80
Pest □[3]	B 5	104
Peštera	D 8	104
Pestovo	G 11	108
Pestravka	C 16	110
Petaḥ Tiqwa	E 3	120
Petaluma	B 1	182
Pétange	E 4	69
Petare	F 8	186
Petatlán	I 9	184
Petauke	E 5	204
Petawawa	F 5	160
Petegem	D 2	69
Petén Itzá, Lago ⊜	I 14	184
Petenwell Lake ⊜[1]	C 3	166
Peterborough, Austl.	D 2	144
Peterborough, On., Can.	F 4	160
Peterborough, Eng., U.K.	E 6	72
Peterborough, N.H., U.S.	D 7	164
Peterhead	C 7	74
Peter I Island I	C 36	208
Peterlee	C 5	72
Petermann Aboriginal Land ◆[4]	I 10	140
Peter Pond Lake ⊜	C 4	158
Peter Pond Lake Indian Reserve ◆[4]	C 16	156
Petersberg	B 6	100
Petersburg, Ak., U.S.	H 28	154
Petersburg, In., U.S.	C 5	170
Petersburg, Va., U.S.	E 5	162
Petersburg, W.V., U.S.	D 4	162
Petersfield	G 6	72
Petershagen, Ger.	D 5	98
Petershagen, Ger.	D 10	98
Petilia Policastro	E 6	94
Pétion-Ville	D 6	186
Petit-Bourg	n 21	187e
Petite Rivière Noire, Piton de la ∧	q 21	207e
Petit-Loango	F 6	200
Petit Mécatina (Little Mecatina) ≃	B 13	160
Petitot ≃	A 10	156
Petit Saint-Bernard, Col du)(	E 4	82
Petitsikapau Lake ⊜	A 10	160
Petlalcingo	H 11	184
Peto	G 15	184
Petone	D 5	146
Petoskey	C 6	166
Petra see Al-Batrā' ⊥	I 4	120
Petra Velikogo, zaliv ⊂	C 3	126
Petre, Point ≻	G 5	160
Petrer	F 4	88
Petrič	E 7	104
Petrified Forest National Park ♠	E 4	176
Petrila	C 7	104
Petrinja	E 8	102
Petrivka	B 11	104
Petrodvorec	G 8	108
Petrograd see Sankt-Peterburg	F 9	108
Petrolia	D 7	166
Petrolina	E 10	190
Petropavl see Petropavlovsk	I 28	108
Petropavlovka	A 5	128
Petropavlovsk	I 28	108
Petropavlovsk-Kamčatskij	B 15	124
Petrópolis	E 9	194
Petroşani	C 7	104
Petrovsk	C 14	110
Petrovskij	H 13	108
Petrov Val	D 14	110
Petrozavodsk	F 11	108
Petrusdal	B 2	206
Petrus Steyn	D 8	206
Pettus	F 5	172
Petuhovo	I 27	108
Peuerbach	B 5	102
Peuetsagoe, Gunung ∧[1]	L 3	132
Peykjahlid	m 22	64a
Peza ≃	D 18	108
Pézenas	G 1	82
Pezinok	B 9	102
Pfarrkirchen	D 9	100
Pfastatt	B 3	92
Pfinztal	C 5	100
Pflersch see Fleres	D 3	102
Pfolz	D 2	206
Pforzheim	D 5	100
Pfronten	E 6	96
Pfullendorf	E 6	100
Pfullingen	D 6	100
Pfungstadt	C 5	100
Pha-an	F 3	132
Phaephane	A 6	206
Phala	B 7	206
Phalaborwa	B 9	206
Phalodi	D 2	122
Phan	E 4	132
Phanom Dongrak Range ∧∧	C 4	134
Phanom Thuan	G 4	132
Phan Rang	I 9	132
Phan Si Pan ∧	C 6	132
Phan Thiet	I 9	132
Pharr	G 4	172
Phato	J 4	132
Phatthalung	K 5	132
Phayao	E 4	132
Phelps Lake ⊜	B 6	168
Phenix City	F 6	170
Phetchabun	F 5	132
Phetchabun Range ∧∧	F 5	132
Phetchaburi	H 4	132
Phichit	F 5	132
Philadelphia, Ms., U.S.	F 4	170
Philadelphia, Pa., U.S.	G 3	164
Philadelphia, Tn., U.S.	B 2	168
Philadelphia □[6]	F 3	164
Philae ⊥	C 3	202
Philippeville see Skikda, Alg.	B 6	198
Philippeville, Bel.	D 3	69
Philippi	D 3	162
Philippi, Lake ⊜	H 4	142
Philippine Basin ✢[1]	E 10	58
Philippines □[1]	H 14	112
Philippine Sea ⊤[2]	I 9	124
Philippine Trench ✢[1]	F 10	58
Philippopolis see Plovdiv	D 8	104
Philippsburg	A 6	82
Philipsburg	B 7	178
Philipstown	F 6	206
Phillip Island I	G 5	144
Phillips	B 8	164
Phillipsburg, Ks., U.S.	F 5	174
Phillipsburg, N.J., U.S.	F 3	164
Philo	C 4	170
Philpots Island I	B 17	150
Phimai	G 6	132
Phitsanulok	F 4	132
Phnom Penh see Phnum Pénh	I 7	132
Phnum Pénh (Phnom Penh)	I 7	132
Phoenix, Az., U.S.	F 2	176
Phoenix, N.Y., U.S.	C 2	164
Phoenix Islands II	D 10	136
Phon	G 6	132
Phôngsali	D 6	132
Phon Phisai	F 6	132
Phrae	E 5	132
Phra Nakhon Si Ayutthaya	G 5	132
Phuket	K 4	132
Phuket, Ko I	J 4	132
Phu Ly	D 7	132
Phum Duang ≃	J 4	132
Phumĭ Béng	H 7	132
Phumĭ Chhuk	I 7	132
Phumĭ Kâmpóng Trâbêk	H 7	132
Phuoc Long	I 8	132
Phu Pan National Park ♠	F 6	132
Phu Quoc, Dao I	J 6	132
Phu Tho	D 7	132
Piacenza	D 5	92
Piacenza □[6]	E 5	92
Pialba	H 11	142
Pianella	B 4	94
Piatra-Neamț	B 9	104
Piauí □[3]	E 10	190
Piave ≃	D 8	92
Piawaning	L 4	140
Piaxtla ≃	E 6	184
Piazza Armerina	G 4	94
Pic ≃	G 15	158

ᒪ Waterfall ꭒ Strait ⊂ Bay, Gulf ⊜ Lake ≋ Swamp ⍓ Ice Feature ⊤ Other Hydrographic Feature ✢ Submarine Feature □ Political Unit ◗ Cultural Institution ⊥ Historical Site ♠ Recreational Site ⊠ Airport ■ Military Installation ◆ Miscellaneous

Name	Map Ref.	Page

Symbols in the index entries represent the broad categories identified in the key at the right. Symbols with superior numbers (◄¹) identify subcategories (see complete key on page 242).

∧ Mountain ♦ Mountains ⌃ Pass V Valley ≃ Plain ► Cape I Island II Islands ⊥ Other Topographic Feature ≃ River ≃ Canal

Prince Edward — Redding

Name | Map Ref. | Page

Prince Edward □[6] B 1 164
Prince Edward Island □[3] G 20 150
Prince Frederick H 2 164
Prince George E 10 156
Prince Georges □[6] H 2 164
Prince of Wales, Cape ≻ D 10 154
Prince of Wales Island I, Austl. A 5 142
Prince of Wales Island I, Nu., Can. B 13 150
Prince of Wales Island I, Ak., U.S. I 28 154
Prince of Wales Strait ꭒ B 9 150
Prince Olav Coast ≛[2] C 13 208
Prince Patrick Island I B 8 148
Prince Regent ≃ D 8 140
Prince Regent Inlet ᑕ B 14 150
Prince Rupert D 6 156
Princess Anne D 6 162
Princess Astrid Coast ≛[2] D 10 208
Princess Charlotte Bay ᑕ C 6 142
Princess Martha Coast ≛[2] D 7 208
Princess Ragnhild Coast ≛[2] D 11 208
Princess Royal Island I E 7 156
Princes Town q 23 187e
Princeton, B.C., Can. G 11 156
Princeton, In., U.S. C 5 170
Princeton, Ky., U.S. D 5 170
Princeton, N.J., U.S. F 4 164
Princeville, Qc., Can. E 7 160
Princeville, Il., U.S. B 4 170
Prince William Sound ꭒ F 21 154
Príncipe I E 6 200
Prinshof G 4 206
Priolo Gargallo G 5 94
Priozersk F 9 108
Pripet ≃ D 6 110
Pristen' D 10 110
Priština D 6 104
Pritzwalk C 9 98
Privas F 2 82
Priverno H 9 92
Privodino F 17 108
Privolže C 16 110
Privolžskij, Russia F 15 110
Privolžskij, Russia D 15 110
Prizren D 6 104
Prizzi G 3 94
Prjaža F 10 108
Probolinggo k 21 135b
Probstzella B 8 100
Procter G 13 156
Proctor Lake ⊜[1] D 4 172
Proddatūr G 3 122
Progreso, Mex. G 15 184
Progreso, Mex. F 6 180
Progreso, Ur. D 9 195
Progress B 17 128
Prohladnyj H 14 110
Prokopevsk D 11 114
Prokuplje D 6 104
Prokuševo G 11 108
Proletarsk F 12 110
Prome (Pyè) E 2 132
Promissão D 5 194
Prophet ≃ C 10 156
Prophet River B 10 156
Prorva F 18 110
Proryvnoe I 26 108
Proserpine F 9 142
Prosotsáni B 5 106
Prosser B 4 178
Prostějov A 9 102
Protection B 4 172
Provadija D 9 104
Provence □[9] F 3 82
Provence, Alpes de ⋀ G 4 82
Providence, Ky., U.S. D 5 170
Providence, R.I., U.S. E 7 164
Providence □[6] E 7 164
Providencia, Isla de I E 4 186
Providenija D 8 154
Providenija, buhta ᑕ D 7 154
Provins D 10 78
Provo B 3 176
Provost E 16 156
Prrenjas B 4 106
Prudhoe C 5 72
Prudhoe Bay ᑕ A 20 154
Prudnik C 9 96
Prüm B 3 100
Prunn, Schloss ⊥ D 8 100
Pruszków B 11 96
Prut ≃ C 10 104
Pružany J 12 64
Pryazovs'ke F 9 110
Pryp'yat' D 6 110
Przasnysz B 11 96
Przedbórz C 10 96
Przemyśl D 12 96
Przysucha C 11 96
Psári D 4 106
Psebaj G 12 110
Psël ≃ E 8 110
Pskent A 1 122
Pskov H 8 108
Pskov, Lake ⊜ C 13 66
Pskovskaja oblast' □[6] H 8 108
Ptolemaḯda B 4 106
Ptuj D 7 102
Pualumerak k 18 135b
Pucallpa E 4 190
Pučež H 15 108
Pucheng, China I 7 128
Pucheng, China E 14 130
Pucheta A 9 195
Puchheim D 8 100
Pucioasa C 8 104
Puck A 10 96
Puçol E 4 88
Puding E 7 130
Pudož F 12 108
Pudu ≃ E 6 130
Pudukkottai G 3 122
Puebla □[3] H 11 184
Puebla de la Calzada F 4 86
Puebla de Sanabria B 4 86
Puebla de Zaragoza H 10 184
Pueblo F 2 174
Pueblo Viejo, Laguna ⊜ F 11 184
Puente Genil G 6 86
Puerco ≃ E 5 176
Puerto Acosta G 5 190
Puerto Aisén I 5 192
Puerto Ángel J 11 184
Puerto Armuelles F 4 186
Puerto Asís C 3 190
Puerto Ayacucho B 5 190
Puerto Bahía Negra D 8 192
Puerto Banús H 6 86
Puerto Baquerizo Moreno j 14 190a
Puerto Barrios J 15 184
Puerto Bermúdez F 4 190
Puerto Berrío B 4 190
Puerto Bolívar E 6 186
Puerto Cabello F 7 186
Puerto Cabezas E 4 186
Puerto Carreño B 5 190
Puerto Chicama E 3 190
Puerto Cortés E 3 186
Puerto Cumarebo F 7 186
Puerto de la Cruz i 14 85b
Puerto del Rosario i 17 85b
Puerto Deseado I 6 192
Puerto Duquesas H 5 86
Puerto Fonciere E 2 194
Puerto la Cruz F 8 186
Puerto Leguízamo D 4 190
Puerto Libertad F 3 194
Puerto Limón F 4 186
Puertollano F 6 86
Puerto Lobos H 6 192
Puerto Lumbreras G 3 88
Puerto Madryn H 6 192
Puerto Maldonado F 5 190
Puerto Montt H 5 192
Puerto Morelos G 16 184
Puerto Natales J 5 192
Puerto Padre C 5 186
Puerto Páez B 5 190
Puerto Peñasco B 3 184
Puerto Pirámides H 7 192
Puerto Plata D 7 186
Puerto Presidente Stroessner see Ciudad del Este F 3 194
Puerto Princesa D 7 134
Puerto Real H 4 86
Puerto Rico, Arg. G 3 194
Puerto Rico, Bol. F 5 190
Puerto Rico □[2] H 13 148
Puerto Rico Trench ✦[1] E 6 60
Puerto San José E 2 186
Puerto San Julián I 6 192
Puerto Santa Cruz J 6 192
Puerto Sastre D 8 192
Puerto Serrano H 5 86
Puerto Suárez G 7 190
Puerto Vallarta G 7 184
Puerto Varas H 5 192
Puerto Victoria G 3 194
Puerto Wilches G 6 186
Pueyrredón, Lago (Cochrane, Lago) ⊜ I 5 192
Pugačov C 16 110
Puge E 6 130
Puget Sound ꭒ B 2 178
Puget-Théniers G 4 82
Puglia □[3] D 7 94
Pugwash F 12 160
Puhja C 13 66
Puiești B 9 104
Puigcerdá B 6 88
Pui O I 18 131a
Pujiang D 14 130
Pukaki, Lake ⊜ F 3 146
Pukaskwa National Park ♦ G 15 158
Pukch'ŏng-ŭp F 17 128
Pukekohe B 5 146
Pukou, China E 14 130
Pukou, China B 14 130
Pula C 2 104
Pulacayo H 5 190
Pulaski E 5 170
Pulau Pinang □[3] L 5 132
Puławy C 11 96
Pulheim F 3 98
Puli G 15 130
Pulicat Lake ⊜ G 3 122
Pullman B 5 178
Pully D 4 82
Pul'mo C 12 96
Pulo ⊥ C 6 94
Pulo Anna I E 10 134
Pulog, Mount ∧ B 8 134
Pulon'ga C 14 108
Pulsano D 7 94
Pułtusk B 11 96
Pulusuk I C 6 136
Pumbi B 3 204
Puná, Isla I D 2 190
Punakha D 5 122
Punda Maria B 9 206
Pune F 2 122
Punggol i 15 134a
Punggol ≃ i 15 134a
P'ungsan-ŭp F 16 128
Pungué ≃ F 5 204
Punia C 4 204
Punjab □[3], India C 3 122
Punjab □[3], Pak. C 2 122
Punkalaidun B 11 66
Puno G 4 190
Punta, Cerro de ∧ j 15 187b
Punta Alta F 7 195
Punta Arenas J 5 192
Punta de Agua Creek (Tramperos Creek) ≃ B 2 172
Punta Delgada H 7 192
Punta Gorda, Belize I 15 184
Punta Gorda, Fl., U.S. F 3 168
Punta Gorda, Bahía de ᑕ F 4 186
Puntarenas F 3 186
Punta Umbría G 3 86
Puntawolona, Lake ⊜ B 2 144
Punto Fijo F 7 186
Punxsutawney C 4 162
Puqi, China D 11 130
Puqi, China D 15 130
Puquio F 4 190
Pur ≃ C 10 114
Purari ≃ N 12 124
Purcell C 5 172
Purcell Mountains ⋀ A 5 178
Purchena G 2 88
Purdy Islands II M 13 124
Pureora ∧[1] C 5 146
Purgatoire ≃ G 2 174
Puri F 5 122
Purificación ≃ E 10 184
Purmerend B 3 69
Pūrna ≃ E 3 122
Pūrnia D 5 122
Purnululu ♦ E 9 140
Purros F 1 204
Purus ≃ E 6 190
Puruvesi ⊜ F 14 64
Purwakarta k 18 135b
Purwodadi k 20 135b
Purwokerto k 19 135b
Purworejo k 20 135b
Pusad F 3 122
Pusan I 17 128
Pushkar D 2 122
Puskiakiwenin Indian Reserve ◆[4] E 16 156
Puškin G 9 108
Puškino H 12 108
Puškinskie Gory H 8 108
Pusŏng-ni D 1 126
Püspökladány B 6 104
Putaruru C 5 146
Putbus B 10 98
Putian F 14 130
Putignano D 6 94
Puting, Tanjung ≻ F 6 134
Putnam E 7 164
Putnam □[6] E 5 164
Putney D 6 164
Putorana, plato ⋀[1] C 12 114
Putsonderwater E 4 206
Puttalam H 3 122
Puttalam Lagoon ᑕ H 3 122
Putten B 4 69
Putumayo (Içá) ≃ D 6 190
Putuo C 16 130
Putyla A 8 104
Putyvl' D 8 110
Pu'uhonua o Honaunau National Historical Park ♦ j 10 181a
Puukohola Heiau National Historic Site ♦ i 10 181a
Puula ⊜ B 13 66
Puurmani C 13 66
Puyallup B 2 178
Puyang I 10 128
Puy-de-Dôme □[3] C 7 80
Puyehue, Volcán ∧[1] G 1 195
Puylaurens E 5 80
Puy-l'Évêque D 5 80
Puysegur Point ≻ G 1 146
Pwani □[3] D 6 204
Pweto D 4 204
Pyalo E 2 132
Pyandzh (Panj) ≃ C 10 116
Pyapon F 2 132
Pyawbwe D 2 132
Pyčas H 19 108
Pyè see Prome E 2 132
Pyhäjärvi ⊜ B 15 66
Pyhäjoki ≃ D 12 64
Pyhäselkä E 15 64
Pyhäselkä ⊜ E 14 64
Pyhtää B 13 66
Pyinmana E 2 132
Pyin Oo Lwin (Maymyo) C 3 132
Pyle F 3 72
Pymatuning Reservoir ⊜[1] C 3 162
Pymatuning State Park ♦ E 8 166
Pyngopil'gyn, laguna ᑕ C 7 154
Pyŏktong-ŭp F 15 128
P'yŏngan-bukto □[3] F 15 128
P'yŏngan-namdo □[3] G 16 128
P'yonghae F 2 126
P'yŏngt'aek H 16 128
P'yŏngyang G 15 128
Pyote E 2 172
Pyramid Lake ⊜ C 4 180
Pyramid Lake Indian Reservation ◆[4] B 4 180
Pyrenees ⋀ F 4 80
Pyrénées-Atlantiques □[3] E 3 80
Pyrénées Occident, Parc National des ♦ F 3 80
Pyrénées-Orientales □[3] F 6 80
Pyre Peak ∧[1] J 8 154
Pyrgi ⊥ H 7 92
Pýrgos D 4 106
Pyryatyn D 8 110
Pyšma H 25 108
Pyšma ≃ H 25 108
Pytalovo (Abrene) H 7 108
Pyu E 3 132

Q

Qacentina B 6 198
Qā'emshahr D 15 118
Qagan Nur ⊜ E 10 128
Qahar Youyi Zhongqi F 9 128
Qaidam ≃ B 7 122
Qala Ha Joele E 8 206
Qalāt C 1 122
Qal'at ash-Shaqīf (Beaufort Castle) ⊥ C 4 120
Qal'at Bīshah C 5 202
Qal'at Sukkar G 12 118
Qallābāt E 1 202
Qalqīlya E 3 120
Qalybek köli ⊜ J 29 108
Qamani'tuaq (Baker Lake) D 13 150
Qamar, Ghubbat al- (Qamar Bay) ᑕ G 7 116
Qamata F 7 206
Qamdo C 3 130
Qamşar F 14 118
Qamysty C 22 110
Qānā C 4 120
Qandala E 6 202
Qantur F 2 202
Qapshaghay B 12 116
Qaqortoq see Julianehåb D 23 150
Qarabutaq E 22 110
Qaraghandy, Kaz. A 11 116
Qaraghandy, Kaz. I 29 108
Qārah H 9 118
Qarataū A 1 122
Qarataū zhotasy ⋀ B 10 116
Qaraton F 18 110
Qarazhal A 11 116
Qareh Sū ≃ C 12 118
Qarqan ≃ B 5 122
Qarqaraly A 12 116
Qarshi see Karshi B 1 122
Qāsh, Nahr al- (Gash) ≃ D 4 202
Qasigiannguit see Christanshåb C 22 150
Qaskeleng A 3 122
Qaşr al-Azraq ⊥ F 7 120
Qaşr al-Hallābāt ⊥ E 6 120
Qaşr al-Kharānah ⊥ F 6 120
Qaşr al-Mushattá ⊥ F 6 120
Qaşr al-Qarābūllī C 7 198
Qaşr 'Amrah ⊥ F 7 120
Qaşr Ḍab'ah ⊥ F 6 120
Qasr el-Boukhari B 5 198
Qaṭanā C 6 120
Qatar □[1] G 7 112
Qattara Depression ≛[7] B 2 202
Qausuittuq (Resolute) B 14 150
Qawz Rajab D 4 202
Qax I 15 110
Qaynar A 12 116
Qazımämmäd I 16 110
Qazvīn D 14 118
Qeh E 3 128
Qena I 5 118
Qena, Wadi ≃ I 5 118
Qeqertarsuaq see Godhavn C 22 150
Qesari, Horbat (Caesarea) ⊥ D 3 120
Qeshm, Jazīreh-ye I I 16 118
Qeydār D 13 118
Qezel Owzan ≃ D 13 118
Qian ≃ G 9 130
Qian'an D 15 128
Qian Gorlos D 15 128
Qianning C 5 130
Qianshan C 13 130
Qianxi E 7 130
Qianyang E 9 130
Qiaojia E 6 130
Qidong E 11 130
Qiemo B 5 122
Qift I 5 118
Qijiang D 8 130
Qilian Shan ∧ E 3 124
Qilian Shan ⋀ C 16 116
Qimen D 13 130
Qin ≃ I 9 128
Qing ≃ C 10 130
Qing'an C 16 128
Qingdao H 13 128
Qingfeng I 10 128
Qinggang C 16 128
Qinghai □[3] B 6 122
Qinghai Hu (Koko Nor) ⊜ H 2 128
Qingjian H 7 128
Qingjiang, China D 12 130
Qingjiang, China B 14 130
Qinglong F 7 130
Qingshen D 6 130
Qingshui A 8 130
Qingshui ≃, China H 6 128
Qingshui ≃, China E 9 130
Qingtang F 11 130
Qingyang, China I 6 128
Qingyang, China C 13 130
Qingyuan, China G 11 130
Qingyuan, China E 15 128
Qingyuan, China E 14 130
Qingzhen E 8 130
Qinhuangdao G 12 128
Qin Ling ⋀ B 9 130
Qinshui I 8 128
Qinxian H 9 128
Qinyang I 9 128
Qinyuan H 9 128
Qinzhou G 9 130
Qionghai I 10 130
Qionglai C 6 130
Qiongzhou Haixia ꭒ H 10 130
Qiqihar C 15 128
Qiryat Ata D 4 120
Qiryat Bialik D 4 120
Qiryat Gat F 3 120
Qiryat Mal'akhi F 3 120
Qiryat Motzkin D 3 120
Qiryat Shemona C 4 120
Qiryat Tiv'on D 4 120
Qiryat Yam D 4 120
Qishn G 7 116
Qiṭā' Ghazzah see Gaza Strip □[2] G 2 120
Qitai B 14 116
Qitaihe D 18 128
Qiubei F 7 130
Qixia H 13 128
Qixian A 12 130
Qiyang E 10 130
Qizhou C 12 130
Qnadsa C 4 198
Qom E 14 118
Qomsheh G 15 118
Qondoz ≃ B 1 122
Qondūz see Kondoz B 1 122
Qongyrat A 11 116
Qorveh E 12 118
Qosshaghyl F 18 110
Qostanay C 23 110
Qostanay □[3] C 23 110
Qu ≃, China C 8 130
Qu ≃, China D 14 130
Quabbin Reservoir ⊜[1] D 6 164
Quadra Island I F 9 156
Quadros, Lagoa dos ⊜ B 12 195
Quakenbrück D 4 98
Quakertown F 3 164
Quanah C 4 172
Quang Ngai G 9 132
Quantico D 5 162
Quanzhou F 14 130
Qu'Appelle F 6 158
Qu'Appelle ≃ F 19 156
Quaraí (Cuareim) ≃ B 9 195
Quarryville G 2 164
Quartu Sant'Elena F 2 90
Quartzsite F 1 176
Quba I 16 110
Qūchān D 18 118
Qudhac Shiir G 6 202
Queanbeyan E 7 144
Queanbeyan ≃ E 7 144
Québec E 8 160
Quebec □[3] F 18 150
Quebeck E 6 170
Quedlinburg E 8 98
Queen Alexandra Range ⋀ E 24 208
Queen Annes □[6] H 2 164
Queen Charlotte E 5 156
Queen Charlotte Bay ᑕ n 17 193b
Queen Charlotte Islands II E 5 156
Queen Charlotte Sound ꭒ F 6 156
Queen Charlotte Strait ꭒ F 7 156
Queen Elizabeth Islands II B 10 148
Queen Mary Coast ≛[2] C 18 208
Queen Maud Gulf ᑕ C 12 150
Queen Maud Mountains ⋀ E 28 208
Queens □[6] F 5 164
Queens Channel ꭒ D 10 140
Queenscliff G 5 144
Queensland □[3] D 9 138
Queenstown, Austl. j 11 145a
Queenstown see Cobh, Ire. E 3 75
Queenstown, N.Z. F 2 146
Queenstown, S. Afr. F 7 206
Quela D 2 204
Quelimane F 6 204
Quemado F 3 172
Quemado, Punta de ≻ C 6 186
Quembo ≃ E 2 204
Quemoy I F 14 130
Quequén F 8 195
Quercy □[9] D 5 80
Querétaro G 9 184
Querétaro □[3] G 10 184
Querfurt E 8 98
Quesada G 1 88
Queshan B 11 130
Quesnel E 10 156
Quesnel ≃ E 11 156
Quesnel Lake ⊜ E 11 156
Questa D 6 176
Quetico Provincial Park ♦ G 13 158
Quetta C 1 122
Quettehou H 5 72
Quetzaltenango J 14 184
Quevedo D 3 190
Quezon City C 8 134
Qufu I 11 128
Quibala E 2 204
Quibdó B 3 190
Quiberon E 3 78
Quickborn C 6 98
Quiévrain D 2 69
Quihuhu D 2 204
Quila E 6 184
Quillacollo G 5 190
Quillan F 6 80
Quillota C 2 195
Quilon (Kollam) H 3 122
Quilpué C 2 195
Quimaria D 1 204
Quimbele D 2 204
Quimilí E 7 192
Quimper D 2 78
Quimperlé E 3 78
Quince Mil F 4 190
Quincy, Ca., U.S. C 3 180
Quincy, Il., U.S. C 3 170
Quincy, Ma., U.S. D 7 164
Quincy, Wa., U.S. B 4 178
Quines F 6 192
Quinhagak G 13 154
Quintanar de la Orden E 1 88
Quintanar del Rey E 3 88
Quintana Roo □[3] H 15 184
Quinto C 4 88
Quinto ≃ D 5 195
Quionga E 7 204
Quipungo E 1 204
Quiriguá ⊥ J 15 184
Quirima E 2 204
Quirindi C 8 144
Quirinópolis C 5 194
Quiroga B 3 86
Quissico C 11 206
Quiterajo E 7 204
Quitman F 4 170
Quito D 3 190
Quixadá D 11 190
Quixeré E 11 190
Qujing F 6 130
Qūlyköl köli ⊜ D 23 110
Qum see Qom E 14 118
Qumarlêb C 7 122
Qumbu F 8 206
Qumrān, Khirbat ⊥ F 4 120
Qunayfidhah, Nafūd ≛[8] C 6 202
Qunayyin, Sabkhat al- ⊜ C 9 198
Quoich ≃ D 14 150
Quorn D 1 144
Qŭrghonteppa B 1 122
Qus J 5 118
Quseir I 6 118
Quthing F 7 206
Quxian C 8 130
Quy Nhon H 9 132
Quyon A 2 164
Quzhou, China H 10 128
Quzhou, China D 14 130
Qyzylorda B 10 116
Qyzylorda □[3] G 22 110

R

Raab (Rába) ≃ D 8 102
Raalte B 5 69
Ra'ananna E 3 120
Raas, Pulau I k 22 135b
Raasiku C 12 66
Raba G 7 134
Rába (Raab) ≃ C 8 102
Rábade A 3 86
Rabak E 3 202
Rábaköz ◆[1] C 9 102
Rabat, Malta G 5 90
Rabat, Mor. C 3 198
Rabbit Ears Pass)(B 5 176
Rābigh C 4 202
Rabka D 10 96
Râbnița B 10 104
Rabyānah E 9 198
Raccoon ≃ B 2 170
Race, Cape ≻ E 17 160
Raceland H 3 170
Race Point ≻ D 8 164
Rach Gia J 7 132
Rach Gia, Vinh ᑕ J 7 132
Racibórz C 10 96
Racine D 5 166
Ráckeve C 10 102
Racula E 12 98
Rădăuți B 8 104
Råde C 5 66
Radeberg C 7 96
Radebeul E 10 98
Radenthein D 5 102
Rades G 3 90
Radevormwald E 4 98
Radford E 3 162
Rādhanpur E 2 122
Rădinești C 7 104
Raditshaba B 8 206
Radium Hot Springs F 13 156
Radolfzell E 5 100
Radom C 11 96
Radomir D 7 104
Radom National Park ♦ F 1 202
Radomsko C 10 96
Radoviš E 7 104
Radstadt C 5 102
Radstock F 4 72
Radviliškis E 11 66
Radville G 6 158
Radykovskoe F 13 110
Radykovskoje see Radykovskoe F 13 110
Radziejów B 10 96
Radzyń Podlaski C 12 96
Rae D 9 150
Rae ≃ B 37 154
Rāe Bareli D 4 122
Raeside, Lake ⊜ K 6 140
Rae Strait ꭒ C 14 150
Raetihi C 5 146
Raevskij I 21 108
Rafaela B 7 195
Rafaḥ G 2 120
Rafalivka D 5 110
Raffadali G 3 94
Rafḥā' H 10 118
Rafína C 6 106
Rafsanjān G 17 118
Raft ≃ D 7 178
Raft River Mountains ⋀ E 7 178
Ragged Island Range II C 6 186
Raglan B 5 146
Raguda, Qooriga ᑕ E 6 202
Ragusa H 4 94
Ragusa □[6] H 4 94
Raguva E 12 66
Rahačoŭ C 7 110
Rahad (Rahad, Nahr ar-) ≃ E 4 202
Rahad, Nahr ar- (Rahad) ≃ E 3 202
Rahaṭ, Ḥarrat ≛[9] C 5 202
Rahīmyār Khān D 2 122
Rahotu C 4 146
Rahway C 6 162
Rāichūr F 3 122
Raigarh E 4 122
Railton i 12 145a
Rainbow Bridge National Monument ♦ D 3 176
Rainier, Mount ∧[1] B 3 178
Rainy ≃ A 7 174
Rainy Lake ⊜ G 12 158
Raipur E 4 122
Raisin ≃ B 1 162
Raivavae I F 13 136
Rājahmundry F 4 122
Raja-Jooseppi B 14 64
Rajamäki B 12 66
Rājampet G 3 122
Rajang ≃ E 6 134
Rājapālaiyam H 3 122
Rājasthān □[3] D 2 122
Rajčihinsk B 17 128
Rāj Gangpur E 4 122
Rājgarh E 3 122
Rajka C 9 102
Rājkot E 2 122
Rāj Nāndgaon E 4 122
Rājpipla E 2 122
Rājpura C 3 122
Rājshāhi E 5 122
Rājshāhi □[3] E 5 122
Rakaia ≃ E 3 146
Rakamaz A 6 104
Rakaposhi ∧ B 2 122
Rakhine □[3] D 1 132
Rakhiv A 8 104
Rakiraki m 14 147c
Rakitnoe B 5 126
Rakkestad C 5 66
Rakovník B 10 100
Rakovski D 8 104
Råkvågen E 5 64
Rakvere C 13 66
Raleigh B 5 168
Ralls D 3 172
Ralston E 1 164
Ramacca G 4 94
Ramah Indian Reservation ◆[4] E 4 176
Rām Allāh F 4 120
Ramat Gan E 3 120
Ramat HaSharon E 3 120
Ramatlabama C 6 206
Rambervillers B 4 82
Rambouillet D 8 78
Rameški H 12 108
Rāmeswaram H 3 122
Rāmhormoz G 13 118
Ramingstein C 5 102
Ramla F 3 120
Ramlu ∧ E 5 202
Ramm, Jabal ∧ J 4 120
Râmnicu Sărat C 9 104
Râmnicu Vâlcea C 8 104
Ramona G 7 182
Ramos ≃ E 7 184
Ramotswa C 6 206
Rampart D 19 154
Ramparts ≃ C 29 154
Rāmpur D 3 122
Ramree Island I E 1 132
Ramsele E 8 64
Ramsey C 4 170
Ramsgate F 8 72
Rāmshīr G 13 118
Ramu G 5 202
Ramu ≃ M 12 124
Ramygala E 12 66
Ramzaj J 16 108
Rāna Pratāp Sāgar ⊜[1] E 2 122
Ranau D 7 134
Rancagua D 2 195
Rancharia E 5 194
Rancheria A 6 156
Rānchi E 4 122
Rancho Cordova B 2 182
Ranco, Lago ⊜ G 1 195
Randan D 1 82
Randazzo G 4 94
Randers B 2 68
Randlett C 4 172
Randolph, Ma., U.S. D 7 164
Randolph, Ne., U.S. D 6 174
Randolph, Vt., U.S. C 6 164
Randsfjorden ⊜ B 5 66
Råneå D 11 64
Ranérou B 2 200
Rāngāmāti E 6 122
Rangaunu Bay ᑕ A 4 146
Range Ponds State Park ♦ B 8 164
Ranger D 4 172
Rangiora E 4 146
Rangitaiki ≃ B 6 146
Rangkasbitung k 18 135b
Rangoon see Yangon F 2 132
Rangpur D 5 122
Rankamhaeng National Park ♦ F 4 132
Ranken ≃ F 3 142
Rankin's Pass C 7 206
Rankweil C 1 102
Rann of Kutch see Kutch, Rann of ◆[1] E 1 122
Ranomena I 9 205a
Ranong J 4 132
Ranongga I A 12 138
Ransäter C 6 66
Ransiki F 10 134
Rantasalmi A 14 66
Rantauprapat M 4 132
Rantekombola, Bulu ∧ F 8 134
Rantoul B 4 170
Ranua D 13 64
Råö D 5 66
Raohe C 19 128
Raon-l'Étape B 4 82
Raoping G 13 130
Raoul Island I F 10 136
Rapa I F 13 136
Rapallo E 5 92
Rapel ≃ D 2 195
Rapid Bay E 1 144
Rapid City C 3 174
Rapide-Blanc-Station E 7 160
Rapid River C 5 166
Rapla C 12 66
Rappahannock ≃ D 5 162
Rapperswil C 6 82
Raraka I[1] E 13 136
Rarotonga I F 12 136
Ra's al-Khaymah J 16 118
Râșcani A 9 104
Ras Dashen Terara ∧ E 4 202
Raseborg B 11 66
Raseiniai E 11 66
Ras el Ma C 4 198
Rashaant B 3 128
Rasht D 13 118
Rasimone C 7 206
Rāsipuram G 3 122
Ra's Lānūf C 8 198
Rasm al-Arwām, Sabkhat ⊜ E 7 118
Râșnov C 8 104
Rason Lake ⊜ K 8 140
Rasskazovo C 12 110
Rasšua. ostrov I C 14 124
Rassypnaja D 18 110
Ra's Tannūrah I 13 118
Rastatt D 5 100
Rastede C 5 98
Ratak Chain II C 9 136
Ratamka F 13 66
Rat Buri H 4 132
Ratekau C 7 98
Rāth D 3 122
Rathbun Lake ⊜[1] B 2 170
Rathdrum D 5 75
Rathenow D 9 98
Rathlin Island I A 5 75
Rathwell G 9 158
Ratingen E 3 98
Ratlām E 2 122
Ratmanova, ostrov I D 10 154
Ratnāgiri F 2 122
Ratnapura H 4 122
Raton G 2 174
Raton Pass)(G 2 174
Rattanaburi G 6 132
Rattling Brook D 15 160
Ratz, Mount ∧ C 5 156
Ratzeburg C 7 98
Rau N 4 132
Raub M 5 132
Raufoss B 5 66
Rauma B 10 66
Rauma ≃ E 3 64
Raung, Gunung ∧ I 22 135b
Raurkela E 4 122
Ravahere I[1] E 13 136
Ravanica, Manastir ◗[1] D 6 104
Ravanusa G 4 90
Rāvar G 17 118
Rava-Rus'ka C 12 96
Raven E 3 162
Ravenna, Italy E 8 92
Ravenna, Ne., U.S. E 5 174
Ravenna □[6] E 8 92
Ravensburg E 6 100
Ravensthorpe M 6 140
Rāvi ≃ C 2 122
Ravna Gora E 6 102
Rāwah E 9 118
Rawaki I[1] D 10 136
Rāwalpindi C 2 122
Rawicz C 9 96
Rawlinna L 8 140
Rawlins E 10 178
Rawson H 6 192
Raxāul D 4 122
Ray A 3 174
Ray, Cape ≻ E 14 160
Raya, Bukit ∧ F 6 134
Rāyagarha F 4 122
Raygorodok E 18 110
Ray Hubbard, Lake ⊜[1] D 5 172
Rayleigh F 7 72
Raymond B 2 178
Raymond Terrace D 8 144
Raymondville G 5 172
Rayne G 2 170
Rayong H 5 132
Rayside-Balfour E 3 160
Raytown C 1 170
Rayville F 3 170
Raz, Pointe du ≻ D 2 78
Ražanj D 6 104
Răzeni B 10 104
Razgrad D 9 104
Razlog E 7 104
Răzvani C 9 104
Ré, Île de I B 2 80
Reading, Eng., U.K. F 5 72
Reading, Oh., U.S. C 6 170
Reading, Pa., U.S. F 2 164
Readlyn D 2 166
Real, Cordillera ⋀ G 5 190
Realitos G 4 172
Reardan B 4 178
Reay B 5 74
Rebiana Sand Sea ◆[2] E 9 198
Rebild Bakker ♦ B 2 68
Recanati A 3 94
Recco E 5 92
Recherche, Archipelago of the II N 7 140
Recife E 12 190
Recklinghausen E 4 98
Reconquista A 7 195
Recreio D 9 194
Rector D 3 170
Rèčyča C 7 110
Red ≃, N.A. B 8 152
Red ≃ E 9 152
Red, North Fork ≃ C 4 172
Red, Prairie Dog Town Fork ≃ C 3 172
Reda A 10 96
Red Bank F 4 164
Red Banks E 4 170
Redberry Lake ⊜ E 18 156
Red Bluff B 2 180
Red Bluff Reservoir ⊜[1] E 2 172
Redbridge □[6] F 7 72
Redcar C 5 72
Redcar and Cleveland □[6] C 6 72
Redcliff F 4 204
Redcliffe I 11 142
Redcliffe, Mount ∧ K 6 140
Red Cliff Indian Reservation ◆[4] B 3 166
Red Cliffs E 4 144
Red Deer E 15 156
Red Deer ≃ F 16 156
Red Deer ≃ E 8 158
Red Deer Lake ⊜ E 8 158
Reddersburg E 7 206
Redding B 2 180

ᒪ Waterfall ꭒ Strait ᑕ Bay, Gulf ⊜ Lake ≋ Swamp ⩍ Ice Feature ⫪ Other Hydrographic Feature ✦ Submarine Feature □ Political Unit ◗ Cultural Institution ⊥ Historical Site ♦ Recreational Site ⌧ Airport ▪ Military Installation ◆ Miscellaneous

Redditch — Ruston

Name	Map Ref.	Page
Redditch	E 5	72
Red Earth Creek	C 14	156
Redfield	E 7	174
Redhead	q 24	187e
Red Indian Lake ⊜	D 15	160
Red Lake, On., Can.	F 12	158
Redlake, Mn., U.S.	B 7	174
Red Lake ⊜	F 12	158
Red Lake Indian Reservation ◆[4]	A 7	174
Redlands	F 6	182
Red Lodge	C 9	178
Redmond, Ut., U.S.	C 3	176
Redmond, Wa., U.S.	B 2	178
Redon	E 4	78
Redondela	B 2	86
Redondo Beach	G 5	182
Redoubt Volcano ∧[1]	F 18	154
Red Pass	E 12	156
Red Pheasant Indian Reserve ◆[4]	E 4	158
Red River (Hong, Song) (Yuan) ≃	C 7	132
Red Rock ≃	C 7	178
Red Rock Canyon State Park ♠	E 6	182
Redruth	G 1	72
Red Sea ⊤[2]	C 4	202
Red Sea Hills ⋏	D 4	202
Redstone	E 10	156
Redstone ≃	E 32	154
Red Sucker ≃	D 12	158
Red Sucker Lake ⊜	D 11	158
Red Volta (Nazinon) ≃	C 4	200
Redwater	E 15	156
Red Wing	C 2	166
Redwood City	C 1	182
Redwood Falls	C 7	174
Redwood National Park ♠	E 1	178
Redwood Valley	C 2	180
Ree, Lough ⊜	C 3	75
Reed Lake ⊜	D 9	158
Reedley	D 4	182
Reedsburg	D 3	166
Reefton	E 3	146
Reelfoot Lake ⊜	D 4	170
Rees	E 3	98
Reese ≃	B 5	180
Refuge Cove	F 9	156
Refugio	F 5	172
Regalbuto	G 4	94
Regen	B 5	102
Regen ≃	C 9	100
Regensburg	C 9	100
Regenstauf	C 9	100
Reggâne	D 4	198
Reggio di Calabria	F 5	94
Reggio di Calabria □[6]	F 6	94
Reggio nell'Emilia	E 6	92
Reggio nell'Emilia □[6]	E 6	92
Reghin	B 8	104
Regina	F 6	158
Región Metropolitana □[3]	C 2	195
Registro	F 6	194
Regozero	D 9	108
Rehau	C 6	96
Rehoboth	B 2	206
Reḥovot	F 3	120
Reichenbach	B 9	100
Reid	L 10	140
Reidsville	A 5	168
Reigate	F 6	72
Reims	C 10	78
Reinach	C 5	82
Reinbek	C 7	98
Reindeer Lake ⊜	C 7	158
Reindeer Station	B 27	154
Reinfeld	C 7	98
Reinga, Cape ≻	A 4	146
Reinosa	B 6	86
Reisterstown	G 2	164
Reivilo	D 6	206
Rejowiec Fabryczny	C 12	96
Reken	C 6	69
Reliance	D 11	150
Rellingen	E 2	68
Remagen	B 4	100
Remanso	E 10	190
Rembang	k 20	135b
Remchi	E 5	84
Remer	B 8	174
Remington	B 5	170
Remiremont	B 4	82
Remscheid	E 4	98
Remsen	D 7	174
Renata	G 12	156
Rencontre East	E 16	160
Rendova I	A 12	138
Rendsburg	B 6	98
Renens	D 4	82
Renews-Cappahayden	E 17	160
Renfrew	F 5	160
Renfrew □[6]	A 2	164
Renfrewshire □[6]	B 2	72
Rengat	F 4	134
Rengel	k 21	135b
Rengo	D 2	195
Reng Tlāng ∧	E 6	122
Renhua	F 11	130
Renhuai	E 8	130
Reni	C 10	104
Renick	D 3	162
Renko	B 12	66
Renmark	E 3	144
Renmin	C 15	128
Rennell I	B 13	138
Rennes	D 5	78
Rennie	G 11	158
Renningen	D 5	100
Reno	A 4	182
Reno ≃	E 7	92
Rensjön	B 9	64
Rensselaer, In., U.S.	B 5	170
Rensselaer, N.Y., U.S.	D 5	164
Rensselaer □[6]	D 5	164
Rentería	A 3	88
Renton	B 2	178
Renville	C 7	174
Renwick	D 8	174
Reo	G 8	134
Repolovo	F 28	108
Reposaari	B 10	66
Republic, Mo., U.S.	D 2	170
Republic, Wa., U.S.	A 4	178
Republican ≃	F 6	174
Republican, North Fork ≃	E 3	174
Republican, South Fork ≃	F 4	174
Requena	E 3	88
Réquista	D 6	80
Reserve	G 3	170
Resina see Ercolano	D 4	94
Resistencia	E 8	192
Reșița	C 6	104
Resolute see Qausuittuq	B 14	150
Resolution Island I	D 19	150
Restigouche ≃	E 10	160
Retamosa	C 10	195
Retezat, Parcul Național ♠	C 7	104
Retford	D 6	72
Rethel	C 11	78
Réthymno	E 6	106
Retie	E 2	98
Reunion □[2]	L 7	112
Reus	C 6	88
Reuterstadt Stavenhagen	C 9	98
Reutlingen	D 6	100
Revda	B 11	108
Revelstoke	F 12	156
Revelstoke, Lake ⊜[1]	E 12	156
Reventazón	E 2	190
Reviga	C 9	104
Revilla del Campo	B 7	86
Revillagigedo, Islas II	H 3	184
Revillagigedo Island I	I 29	154
Revin	C 11	78
Revubuè ≃	F 5	204
Rewa	E 4	122
Rewāri	D 3	122
Rexburg	D 8	178
Rey, Isla del I	F 5	186
Rey, Laguna del ⊜	D 8	184
Reyes, Point ≻	B 1	182
Reyhanlı	D 7	118
Reykjanes ≻[1]	n 19	64a
Reykjanes Ridge ✦[3]	C 8	60
Reykjavík	m 19	64a
Reyno	D 3	170
Reynosa	D 10	184
Rež	H 24	108
Reẕā'īyeh see Orūmīyeh	D 11	118
Rezé	E 5	78
Rēzekne	D 13	66
Rezina	B 10	104
Rezovo	D 10	104
Rezzato	D 6	92
Rhaetian Alps ⋏	C 5	92
Rhame	B 3	174
Rheda-Wiedenbrück	E 5	98
Rhede	C 5	69
Rheden	B 4	69
Rheinau	D 4	100
Rheinberg	E 3	98
Rheine	D 4	98
Rheinfelden	E 4	100
Rheinhessen-Pfalz □[6]	C 4	100
Rheinland-Pfalz □[3]	B 4	100
Rheinsberg	C 9	98
Rheinstetten	D 5	100
Rhenen	C 4	69
Rhine ≃	F 9	62
Rhinebeck	E 5	164
Rhinelander	C 4	166
Rhinns Point ≻	E 2	74
Rhino Camp	G 3	202
Rhir, Cap ≻	C 2	198
Rho	D 5	92
Rhode Island □[3]	C 13	152
Rhode Island I	E 7	164
Rhode Island Sound ɥ	E 7	164
Rhodes see Ródos I	E 8	106
Rhodes Matopos National Park ♠	G 4	204
Rhodes Nyanga National Park ♠	F 5	204
Rhodes' Tomb ⊥	G 4	204
Rhodope Mountains ⋏	E 8	104
Rhön ⋏	B 6	100
Rhondda	F 3	72
Rhondda Cynon Taff □[6]	F 3	72
Rhône □[3]	E 2	82
Rhône (Rotten) ≃	F 2	82
Rhône au Rhin, Canal du ≋	E 2	100
Rhourde-el-Baguel	C 6	198
Rhyl	D 3	72
Riachão	A 9	190
Rianápolis	A 6	194
Riaño	A 6	86
Riau □[3]	N 6	132
Riau, Kepulauan II	N 7	132
Ribadavia	B 2	86
Ribe	C 1	68
Ribe □[3]	C 1	68
Ribeira Grande	h 10	200a
Ribeirão Preto	D 7	194
Ribera	G 3	94
Riberalta	F 5	190
Ribnica	E 6	102
Ribnitz-Damgarten	B 9	98
Ricardo Flores Magón	B 6	184
Riccarton	E 4	146
Riccione	F 8	92
Rice	D 5	172
Riceville	B 2	168
Richards	E 6	172
Richards Bay	E 10	206
Richards Bay ⊂	E 9	206
Richards Lake ⊜	B 18	156
Richardson	D 5	172
Richardson ≃	B 16	156
Richardson Mountains ⋏	C 26	154
Richard Toll	B 1	200
Richelieu	E 7	78
Richey	H 6	158
Richfield, Mn., U.S.	C 2	166
Richfield, Pa., U.S.	F 1	164
Richfield Springs	D 4	164
Richland, Mt., U.S.	G 18	156
Richland, Tx., U.S.	E 5	172
Richland, Wa., U.S.	B 4	178
Richlands	E 3	162
Richmond, Austl.	F 6	142
Richmond, Austl.	j 12	145a
Richmond, Austl.	D 8	144
Richmond, B.C., Can.	G 10	156
Richmond, Qc., Can.	F 7	160
Richmond, N.Z.	D 4	146
Richmond, S. Afr.	F 5	206
Richmond, Eng., U.K.	C 5	72
Richmond, Ca., U.S.	C 1	182
Richmond, In., U.S.	C 6	170
Richmond, Ky., U.S.	E 1	162
Richmond, Me., U.S.	A 9	162
Richmond, Ut., U.S.	E 8	178
Richmond, Va., U.S.	E 5	162
Richmond, Vt., U.S.	B 6	164
Richmond □[6]	F 4	164
Richmond Hill	G 4	160
Richmondville	D 4	164
Rich Square	A 6	168
Richtersveld National Park ♠	E 2	206
Richwood	C 2	162
Ricketts Glen State Park ♠	E 2	164
Ricobayo, Embalse de ⊜[1]	C 4	86
Ridgecrest	E 6	182
Ridgeland, Ms., U.S.	F 3	170
Ridgeland, S.C., U.S.	C 4	168
Ridgetown	G 3	160
Ridgeway	E 7	174
Ridgway	C 4	162
Riding Mountain National Park ♠	F 8	158
Riebeek-Oos	G 7	206
Riedlingen	D 6	100
Riegersburg, Schloss ⊥	C 7	102
Riehen	C 5	82
Riesa	E 10	98
Riesco, Isla I	J 5	192
Riesi	G 4	94
Riet ≃	E 6	206
Rietavas	E 10	66
Rietberg	E 5	98
Rietbron	G 5	206
Rietfontein	C 7	206
Rieti	G 8	92
Rieti □[6]	G 8	92
Rif ⋏	C 4	198
Rift Valley □[3]	G 4	202
Rift Valley ∨	I 10	196
Rift Valley National Park ♠	F 4	202
Rīga	D 11	66
Riga, Gulf of ⊂	D 11	66
Riggins	C 5	178
Rigo	A 10	138
Rig-Rig	C 7	200
Riguldi	C 11	66
Riihimäki	B 12	66
Riiser-Larsen Peninsula ≻[1]	C 12	208
Rijeka	E 6	102
Rijen	C 3	69
Rijssen	B 5	69
Rijswijk	B 3	69
Riksgränsen	B 9	64
Rikuzen-takata	E 8	126
Rillieux	E 2	82
Rillito	F 3	176
Rilski manastir ◗[1]	D 7	104
Rima ≃	C 6	200
Rimatara I	F 12	136
Rimavská Sobota	D 10	96
Rimbo	C 9	66
Rimi	C 6	200
Rimini	E 8	92
Rimini □[6]	E 8	92
Rimouski	D 9	160
Rinca, Pulau I	G 7	134
Rincon	F 5	176
Rinconada	D 6	192
Rincón del Bonete, Lago Artificial de ⊜[1]	F 8	192
Rincón de Romos	F 8	184
Rincon Indian Reservation ◆[4]	G 7	182
Rindown Castle ⊥	C 3	75
Ringaskiddy	E 3	75
Ringe	C 3	68
Ringerike	B 5	66
Ringgold	E 6	170
Ringkøbing	B 1	68
Ringkøbing □[3]	B 1	68
Ringsted, Den.	C 4	68
Ringsted, Ia., U.S.	D 7	174
Ringvassøya I	B 9	64
Rinjani, Gunung ∧	G 7	134
Rinteln	D 6	98
Riobamba	D 3	190
Rio Branco	E 5	190
Río Bravo, Mex.	E 10	184
Río Bravo, Mex.	F 3	172
Río Bravo, Parque Internacional del ♠	F 2	172
Rio Brilhante	D 3	194
Río Bueno	G 1	195
Río Ceballos	B 5	195
Rio Claro, Braz.	E 7	194
Rio Claro, Trin.	q 23	187e
Río Colorado	F 5	195
Río Cuarto	C 5	195
Rio de Janeiro	E 9	194
Rio de Janeiro □[3]	H 10	190
Rio do Sul	G 6	194
Río Gallegos	J 6	192
Río Grande, Arg.	J 6	192
Rio Grande, Braz.	B 12	195
Río Grande, Mex.	F 8	184
Río Grande, P.R.	j 16	187b
Rio Grande do Norte □[3]	E 11	190
Rio Grande do Sul □[3]	E 9	192
Ríohacha	F 6	186
Rioja	E 3	190
Río Lagartos	G 15	184
Rio Largo	E 11	190
Riom	C 7	80
Río Mayo	I 5	192
Río Mulatos	G 5	190
Río Muni □[9]	E 7	200
Rio Negro	G 6	194
Río Negro □[3]	H 6	192
Rio Negro, Pantanal do ≣	C 2	194
Rionero in Vulture	D 5	94
Riópar	F 2	88
Rio Pardo	A 11	195
Rio Rancho	E 5	176
Río Segundo	B 6	195
Río Tercero	C 5	195
Rio Tinto	E 11	190
Rio Verde, Braz.	B 5	194
Ríoverde, Mex.	G 9	184
Rio Verde de Mato Grosso	C 3	194
Rio Vista	B 2	182
Riozinho ≃	D 5	190
Ripatransone	A 3	94
Ripley, Eng., U.K.	D 5	72
Ripley, Oh., U.S.	D 2	162
Ripley, Tn., U.S.	E 4	170
Ripoll	B 7	88
Ripon, Qc., Can.	F 6	160
Ripon, Eng., U.K.	C 5	72
Ripon, Ca., U.S.	C 2	182
Risca	F 3	72
Riscle	E 3	80
Rishā', Wādī ar- ≃	J 11	118
Rishiri-Rebun-Sarobetsu-kokuritsu-kōen ♠	B 8	126
Rishiri-suidō ɥ	B 8	126
Rishiri-tō I	B 8	126
Rishiri-zan ∧[1]	B 8	126
Rishon LeẔiyyon	F 3	120
Rising Star	D 4	172
Risingsun	C 2	162
Risør	C 4	66
Risti	C 12	66
Ritchie	E 6	206
Ritterhude	C 5	98
Ritzville	B 4	178
Rivadavia, Arg.	B 3	195
Rivadavia, Arg.	D 6	195
Rivadavia, Chile	A 2	195
Riva del Garda	D 6	92
Rivarolo Canavese	E 5	82
Rivas	F 3	186
Rive-de-Gier	E 2	82
Rivera, Arg.	E 6	195
Rivera, Ur.	B 10	195
River Cess	D 3	200
Riverdale	D 4	182
River Falls	C 2	166
Rivergaro	E 5	92
Riverhead	F 6	164
Riverina ◆[1]	E 5	144
River Road	C 2	178
Rivers	F 8	158
Riversdale	H 4	206
Riverside, Ca., U.S.	G 6	182
Riverside, Tx., U.S.	E 6	172
Riverside, Wa., U.S.	A 4	178
Riverside □[6]	G 7	182
Riverton, Austl.	E 2	144
Riverton, Wy., U.S.	D 9	178
Riverton Heights	B 2	178
Rivesaltes	F 6	80
Riviera ◆[8]	E 6	180
Riviera Beach	F 4	168
Rivière-à-Claude	D 11	160
Rivière-au-Tonnerre	C 11	160
Rivière-du-Loup	E 9	160
Rivière du Rempart	p 21	207e
Rivière-Pentecôte	D 10	160
Rivne	D 5	110
Rivne □[6]	K 13	64
Rivoli	D 3	92
Riyadh see Ar-Riyāḍ	J 12	118
Rize	B 9	118
Rize □[3]	B 9	118
Rizhao	I 12	128
Rjazan'	I 13	108
Rjazanskaja oblast' □[6]	I 14	108
Rjažsk	J 14	108
Rjukan	C 4	66
Rkîz, Lac ⊜	F 1	198
Roa	B 5	66
Roachdale	C 5	170
Roadford Reservoir ⊜[1]	G 2	72
Road Town	D 8	186
Roan Mountain	A 3	168
Roanne	D 2	82
Roanoke, In., U.S.	B 6	170
Roanoke, Va., U.S.	E 3	162
Roanoke (Staunton) ≃	A 6	168
Roanoke Rapids	A 6	168
Roaring River State Park ♠	D 2	170
Roatán, Isla de I	D 3	186
Robâa Oued Yahia	G 2	90
Robāṭ Karīm	E 14	118
Robben Island I	G 3	206
Robbers Cave State Park ♠	E 1	170
Robbinsville	B 3	168
Robe, Austl.	F 2	144
Robē, Eth.	F 4	202
Röbel	C 9	98
Robert H. Treman State Park ♠	D 2	164
Robert Louis Stevenson's Tomb ⊥	j 11	147b
Robert's Arm	D 16	160
Robertsdale	G 5	170
Robertsfors	D 10	64
Robert S. Kerr Lake ⊜[1]	E 1	170
Roberts Mountain ∧[1]	F 11	154
Robertson, Lac ⊜	C 14	160
Roberts Port	D 2	200
Roberval	D 7	160
Róbinson Crusoe, Isla I	H 7	188
Robinsons	D 14	160
Robinvale	E 4	144
Robledo	F 2	88
Robson, Mount ∧	E 12	156
Robstown	G 5	172
Roca, Cabo da ≻	F 1	86
Roca Partida, Isla I	H 3	184
Rocas, Atol das I[1]	D 12	190
Roccadaspide	D 5	94
Roccastrada	F 7	92
Rocha	D 10	195
Rochdale	D 4	72
Rochdale □[6]	D 4	72
Rochefort, Bel.	D 4	69
Rochefort, Fr.	C 2	80
Rochelle, Ga., U.S.	D 3	168
Rochelle, Il., U.S.	B 4	170
Roche-Percée	G 7	158
Rochepot, Château de la ⊥	F 11	78
Rochester, Austl.	F 5	144
Rochester, Eng., U.K.	F 7	72
Rochester, Mn., U.S.	C 2	166
Rochester, N.H., U.S.	C 8	164
Rochester, N.Y., U.S.	C 1	164
Rochlitz	E 9	98
Rock ≃	E 4	166
Rockall I	D 5	62
Rockefeller Plateau ⋏[1]	D 31	208
Rockenhausen	C 4	100
Rockford, Il., U.S.	A 4	170
Rockford, Mi., U.S.	D 6	166
Rockford, Oh., U.S.	B 6	170
Rockglen	G 19	156
Rockhampton	G 10	142
Rock Hill	B 4	168
Rockingham, Austl.	M 3	140
Rockingham, N.C., U.S.	B 5	168
Rockingham □[6]	D 7	164
Rockingham Bay ⊂	E 8	142
Rock Island	B 3	170
Rocklake	A 5	174
Rockland, On., Can.	F 6	160
Rockland, Ma., U.S.	D 8	164
Rockland, Me., U.S.	A 9	162
Rockland □[6]	E 4	164
Rocklin	B 2	182
Rock of Cashel ⊥	D 4	75
Rockport, Ma., U.S.	D 8	164
Rock Port, Mo., U.S.	B 1	170
Rockport, Tx., U.S.	G 5	172
Rock River	B 6	176
Rock Springs	E 9	178
Rockstone	B 7	190
Rockton	D 4	166
Rock Valley	D 6	174
Rockville, In., U.S.	C 5	170
Rockville, Md., U.S.	G 1	164
Rockwell	D 2	166
Rockwood	h 12	163a
Rocky	C 4	172
Rocky Boy's Indian Reservation ◆[4]	A 9	178
Rocky Cape National Park ♠	i 11	145a
Rockyford	F 15	156
Rocky Gully	N 4	140
Rocky Lake ⊜	D 8	158
Rocky Lane	B 13	156
Rocky Mount	B 6	168
Rocky Mountain House	E 14	156
Rocky Mountain National Park ♠	B 5	176
Rocky Mountains ⋏	E 8	148
Rocky Mountain Trench ∨	D 10	156
Rocky Point ≻	B 3	75
Rodalben	A 5	82
Rødby	D 4	68
Roddickton	C 15	160
Rödental	B 8	100
Rodeo	E 7	184
Roderick Island I	E 7	156
Rodewisch	B 9	100
Rodez	D 6	80
Rodgau	B 5	100
Rodi Garganico	C 5	94
Roding	C 9	100
Rodman	H 27	154
Rodniki	H 14	108
Ródos	D 8	106
Ródos (Rhodes) I	E 8	106
Rodrigues I	H 6	58
Roebourne	G 4	140
Roebuck Bay ⊂	F 6	140
Roermond	C 4	69
Roeselare	D 2	69
Roes Welcome Sound ɥ	D 15	150
Roff	C 5	172
Rogagua, Laguna ⊜	F 5	190
Rogaguado, Laguna ⊜	F 5	190
Rogaland □[3]	C 3	66
Rogaška Slatina	D 7	102
Rogers, Ar., U.S.	D 1	170
Rogers, Tx., U.S.	E 5	172
Rogers, Mount ∧	E 3	162
Rogers Lake ⊜	F 6	180
Rogers Pass)(	F 13	156
Rogersville	E 2	162
Roggewein, Cabo ≻	m 16	193a
Roggiano Gravina	E 6	94
Rogliano	E 6	94
Rogue ≃	D 1	178
Rogue River	D 2	178
Rohnert Park	B 1	182
Rohtak	D 3	122
Roi Et	F 6	132
Roi Georges, Îles du II	E 13	136
Roja	D 11	66
Rojas	D 7	195
Rojo, Cabo ≻	k 14	187b
Rokan ≃	N 5	132
Rokeby National Park ♠	B 6	142
Rokiškis	E 12	66
Rokycany	C 10	100
Roland	D 2	166
Rolândia	E 5	194
Røldal	C 3	66
Roll	F 2	176
Rolla, Ks., U.S.	G 4	174
Rolla, Mo., U.S.	D 3	170
Rolle	D 4	82
Rolleston	H 9	142
Rollingstone	E 8	142
Rolvsøya I	A 11	64
Roma, Austl.	I 9	142
Roma (Rome), Italy	H 8	92
Roma □[6]	H 8	92
Romagna □[9]	E 8	92
Romaine ≃	C 12	160
Roman	B 9	104
Romang, Pulau I	G 9	134
Romania □[1]	F 12	62
Roman-Kosh, hora ∧	G 9	110
Romano, Cape ≻	G 4	168
Romano, Cayo I	C 5	186
Romanovka	D 13	110
Romanovo	G 24	108
Romanshorn	C 7	82
Romans-sur-Isère	E 3	82
Rome see Roma, Italy	H 8	92
Rome, Ga., U.S.	E 6	170
Rome, Ms., U.S.	F 3	170
Rome, N.Y., U.S.	C 3	164
Romilly-sur-Seine	D 10	78
Romney	D 4	162
Romny	D 8	110
Romodanovo	I 16	108
Romorantin-Lanthenay	E 8	78
Romsey	G 5	72
Røn	B 4	66
Ron, Mui ≻	E 8	132
Rona I	A 3	74
Ronas Hill ∧[2]	g 9	74a
Roncador, Serra do ⋏[1]	F 8	190
Ronceverte	A 4	168
Ronchi dei Legionari	E 5	102
Ronchin	B 10	78
Ronda	H 5	86
Rondane Nasjonalpark ♠	B 5	66
Rønde	B 3	68
Rondeau Provincial Park ♠	D 8	166
Rondônia □[3]	F 6	190
Rondonópolis	B 3	194
Rong ≃	F 9	130
Rong'an	F 9	130
Rongcheng	H 14	128
Ronge, Lac la ⊜	D 19	156
Rongelap I[1]	B 8	136
Rongjiang	F 9	130
Rongkop	I 20	135b
Rongshui	B 9	132
Rongxian, China	G 10	130
Rongxian, China	D 7	130
Rønne	f 7	68a
Ronneby	D 7	66
Ronne Entrance ⊂	D 1	208
Ronne Ice Shelf ⌂	D 2	208
Ronse	D 2	69
Ronuro ≃	F 8	190
Roodhouse	C 3	170
Rooidam	E 4	206
Rooiwal	D 7	206
Roorkee	D 3	122
Roosendaal	C 3	69
Roosevelt, Az., U.S.	F 3	176
Roosevelt, Mn., U.S.	A 7	174
Roosevelt ≃	E 6	190
Roosevelt Campobello International Park ♠	h 13	163a
Roosevelt Island I	D 28	208
Root ≃	E 33	154
Ropaži	D 12	66
Roper	B 6	168
Roper ≃	C 2	142
Roquetas de Mar	H 2	88
Roquetes	D 5	88
Roraima □[3]	C 6	190
Roraima, Mount ∧	B 6	190
Rörbäcksnäs	B 6	66
Rorey Lake ⊜	C 30	154
Røros	E 5	64
Rorschach	C 7	82
Ros'	C 4	110
Rosales	C 7	184
Rosamond	F 5	182
Rosamond Lake ⊜	F 5	180
Rosans	F 3	82
Rosario, Arg.	C 7	195
Rosário, Braz.	D 10	190
Rosario, Mex.	F 7	184
Rosario, Para.	F 2	194
Rosario, Bahía del ⊂	C 1	184
Rosario de la Frontera	E 6	192
Rosario del Tala	C 8	195
Rosário do Sul	B 10	195
Rosário Oeste	F 7	190
Rosarito, Mex.	H 6	182
Rosarito, Mex.	C 3	184
Rosarno	F 5	94
Roščino	B 14	66
Roscoe	D 3	172
Roscommon, Ire.	C 3	75
Roscommon, Mi., U.S.	A 1	162
Roscommon □[3]	C 3	75
Rose, Mount ∧	A 4	182
Roseau, Dom.	r 25	187g
Roseau, Mn., U.S.	A 7	174
Rosebery	i 11	145a
Rosebud	D 4	174
Rosebud Indian Reservation ◆[4]	D 4	174
Roseburg	D 2	178
Rosebush	B 1	162
Rose City	A 1	162
Rosehearty	C 6	74
Rose-Hill, Mrts.	q 21	207e
Rose Hill, Va., U.S.	E 2	162
Rose Island I	E 11	136
Rosenberg	F 6	172
Rosendal	C 3	66
Rosenheim	E 9	100
Rosepine	G 2	170
Roses	B 8	88
Roseto degli Abruzzi	B 4	94
Rosetta (Rashid)	G 4	118
Roseville, Mn., U.S.	C 2	166
Roseville, Oh., U.S.	D 2	162
Rosewood	A 9	144
Rosice	A 8	102
Roșiori de Vede	C 8	104
Rositz	E 9	98
Roskilde	C 4	68
Roskilde □[3]	C 5	68
Roslavl'	J 10	108
Roslev	B 1	68
Rosljakovo	B 10	108
Rosmalen	C 4	69
Rosolini	H 4	94
Rosporden	E 3	78
Rösrath	B 4	100
Ross ≃	E 29	154
Rossano	E 6	94
Ross Béthio	B 1	200
Rossdorf	C 5	100
Ross Ice Shelf ⌂	E 27	208
Rossignol, Lac ⊜	B 6	160
Rossignol, Lake ⊜	F 11	160
Ross Island I	D 25	208
Rossiter	E 9	166
Rossland	G 12	156
Rosslau	E 9	98
Rosso	F 1	198
Rosso, Fiume ≃	C 7	132
Rossön	E 8	64
Ross-on-Wye	F 4	72
Rossoš'	D 11	110
Ross R. Barnett Reservoir ⊜[1]	F 4	170
Ross Sea ⊤[2]	D 27	208
Røssvatnet ⊜	D 7	64
Rossville	E 6	170
Rosthern	E 18	156
Rostock	B 9	98
Rostov	H 13	108
Rostov-na-Donu	F 11	110
Rostovskaja oblast' □[6]	F 12	110
Roswell, Ga., U.S.	B 2	168
Roswell, N.M., U.S.	D 1	172
Rota	H 4	86
Rota I	J 13	124
Rotanda	F 5	204
Rotenburg	C 6	98
Rotenburg an der Fulda	F 6	98
Roth	C 8	100
Röthenbach an der Pegnitz	C 8	100
Rothenburg ob der Tauber	C 6	100
Rothera ◗[3]	C 1	208
Rotherham	D 5	72
Rotherham □[6]	D 5	72
Rothesay	B 1	72
Rothschild	C 4	166
Roti, Pulau I	H 8	134
Roti, Selat ɥ	B 7	140
Rotondella	D 6	94
Rotorua	C 6	146
Rotorua, Lake ⊜	C 6	146
Rotten (Rhône) ≃	D 6	82
Rottenburg am Neckar	D 5	100
Rottenmann	C 6	102
Rotterdam, Neth.	C 3	69
Rotterdam, N.Y., U.S.	D 4	164
Rottweil	D 5	100
Roubaix	B 10	78
Roudnice nad Labem	B 11	100
Rouen	C 8	78
Rouge, Bassin (Sichuan, Bassin du) ≚[1]	C 7	130
Rougemont	C 4	82
Rough River Lake ⊜[1]	D 5	170
Rouleau	F 19	156
Round Mountain	B 6	182
Round Mountain ∧	C 9	144
Round Rock	E 5	172
Round Valley Indian Reservation ◆[4]	C 2	180
Rouses Point	B 5	164
Roussillon □[6]	A 5	164
Roussillon □[9]	F 6	80
Rouville □[6]	A 5	164
Rouxville	F 7	206
Rouyn-Noranda	D 4	160
Rovaniemi	C 12	64
Rovato	D 6	92
Rovereto	D 7	92
Rovigo	D 7	92
Rovigo □[6]	D 7	92
Rovinj	C 2	104
Rovnoe	D 15	110
Rovubo ≃	C 5	204
Rovuma see Ruvuma ≃	E 7	204
Rowan Lake ⊜	A 8	174
Rowena	B 7	144
Rowley Island I	C 17	150
Roxas	C 8	134
Roxboro	A 5	168
Roxburgh	F 2	146
Roxen ⊜	C 7	66
Roxie	G 3	170
Roy	E 7	178
Royal Bay ⊂	q 22	193c
Royal Canal ≋	C 4	75
Royale, Isle I	A 4	166
Royal Gorge ∨	A 1	172
Royal Leamington Spa	E 5	72
Royal Natal National Park ♠	E 8	206
Royal National Park ♠	E 8	144
Royal Oak	B 2	162
Royalton	C 1	166
Royal Tunbridge Wells	F 7	72
Royan	C 2	80
Royston, Eng., U.K.	E 6	72
Royston, Ga., U.S.	B 3	168
Rozdil'na	B 11	104
Rozivka	F 10	110
Rožňava	D 11	96
Rožnov pod Radhoštěm	A 10	102
Roztoczański Park Narodwy ♠	C 12	96
Roztoky	B 11	100
Rozzano	D 4	92
Rrëshen	B 3	106
Rtiščevo	C 13	110
Ru ≃	B 12	130
Ruacana	F 1	204
Ruacana Falls (Ruacaná, Quedas do) ⌞	F 1	204
Ruaha National Park ♠	D 5	204
Ruapehu, Mount ∧[1]	C 5	146
Ruatahuna	C 6	146
Rubbestadneset	C 2	66
Rubcovsk	D 11	114
Rubi	B 4	204
Rubi ≃	B 4	204
Rubicone ≃	E 8	92
Rubizhne	E 11	110
Rubondo Island National Park ♠	H 3	202
Rucava	D 10	66
Rucheng	F 11	130
Ručjuvom	C 24	108
Rudall River National Park ♠	H 7	140
Rūdbār	D 13	118
Rüdersdorf	D 10	98
Rūdiškės	E 12	66
Rudnaja Pristan'	B 5	126
Rudnik	C 12	96
Rudnja	I 9	108
Rudnytsya	A 10	104
Rūdnyy	C 23	110
Rudo	D 5	104
Rudolstadt	F 8	98
Rudong	B 15	130
Rudozem	E 8	104
Rūdsar	D 14	118
Rue	B 8	78
Rufā' ah	E 3	202
Ruffieux	E 3	82
Rufiji ≃	D 6	204
Rufino	D 6	195
Rufus	C 3	178
Rugao	B 15	130
Rugby, Eng., U.K.	E 5	72
Rugby, N.D., U.S.	A 4	174
Rugeley	E 4	72
Rügen I	B 10	98
Rugufu ≃	D 5	204
Ruhengeri	C 4	204
Ruhla	F 7	98
Ruhr ≃	E 5	98
Rui'an	E 15	130
Ruidoso ≃	F 6	176
Ruijin	F 12	130
Ruiz	F 7	184
Ruki ≃	C 2	204
Rukwa □[3]	D 5	204
Rukwa, Lake ⊜	D 5	204
Rule	D 4	172
Rulo	B 1	170
Rùm I	C 2	74
Rum ≃	C 2	166
Ruma	C 5	104
Rumaylah, 'Urūq ar- ⊥[8]	C 6	202
Rumbek	F 2	202
Rumburk	B 11	100
Rum Cay I	C 6	186
Rumia	A 10	96
Rumigny	C 11	78
Rummah, Wādī ar- ≃	J 10	118
Rumoi	C 8	126
Rumuruti	G 4	202
Runan	B 12	130
Runazi	C 5	204
Runde ≃	G 5	204
Rundēni	D 13	66
Rundu	F 2	204
Rungwa	D 5	204
Rungwa ≃	D 5	204
Rungwa Game Reserve ◆[4]	D 5	204
Rungwe	D 5	204
Runkel	B 5	100
Runn ⊜	B 7	66
Running Water Draw ≃	C 2	172
Runnymede ⊥	F 6	72
Ruo ≃	F 3	128
Ruo'ergai	B 6	130
Ruoxi	D 12	130
Rupert	E 3	162
Rupert ≃	C 5	160
Rural Retreat	E 3	162
Rurrenabaque	F 5	190
Rurutu I	F 12	136
Rusape	F 5	204
Ruṣayriṣ, Khazzān ar- ⊜[1]	E 3	202
Ruse	D 8	104
Ruse □[3]	D 9	104
Rushan	H 13	128
Rush Center	F 5	174
Rushford	D 3	166
Rushville	C 6	170
Ruskin	F 3	168
Rusnė	E 10	66
Russell, On., Can.	A 3	164
Russell, N.Z.	A 5	146
Russell, Ky., U.S.	D 2	162
Russell Cave National Monument ♠	E 6	170
Russell Island I	B 13	150
Russell Islands II	A 12	138
Russell Lake ⊜	C 8	158
Russellville, Al., U.S.	E 5	170
Russellville, Ar., U.S.	E 2	170
Rüsselsheim	D 5	96
Russi	E 7	92
Russia □[1]	C 9	112
Russian ≃	C 2	180
Russian Mission	F 14	154
Russka	C 14	66
Rustajskij	H 16	108
Rustavi	I 14	110
Rustenburg	C 7	206
Ruston	F 2	170

Symbols in the index entries represent the broad categories identified in the key at the right. Symbols with superior numbers (⋏[1]) identify subcategories (see complete key on page 242).

∧ Mountain ⋏ Mountains)(Pass ∨ Valley ≚ Plain ≻ Cape I Island II Islands ⊥ Other Topographic Feature ≃ River ≋ Canal

Rute — San Francisco de Macorís

Name / Map Ref. / Page

Rute G 6 86
Ruteng G 8 134
Rutenga G 5 204
Ruthin D 3 72
Rüti C 6 82
Rutland, B.C., Can. G 12 156
Rutland, Vt., U.S. C 6 164
Rutland □6 C 6 164
Rutland □8 E 6 72
Rutledge A 3 168
Rutshuru C 4 204
Rutter E 3 160
Ruvo di Puglia C 6 94
Ruvu D 6 204
Ruvuma □3 E 6 204
Ruvuma (Rovuma) ≃ E 7 204
Ruwenzori ⋀ B 4 204
Ruwenzori National Park ♦ H 2 202
Ruzaevka, Kaz. J 27 108
Ruzaevka, Russia I 16 108
Ružany J 12 64
Ruzizi ≃ C 4 204
Ružomberok A 11 102
Rwanda □1 I 10 196
Ryan C 5 172
Rybachye see Issyk-Kul' A 3 122
Rybačij E 10 66
Rybačij, poluostrov ›1 A 10 108
Rybinsk G 13 108
Rybinskoe vodohranilišče ⊜1 G 12 108
Rybnik C 10 96
Rybnoe I 13 108
Rychwał B 10 96
Ryd D 7 66
Ryde G 5 72
Ryder B 4 174
Rye F 5 164
Ryegate B 9 178
Ryfoss B 4 66
Ryfylke ✦1 C 3 66
Rygnestad C 3 66
Ryley E 15 156
Ryn A 11 96
Rypin B 10 96
Rysy ∧ A 5 104
Ryukyu Islands (Nansei-shotō) II G 9 124
Ryukyu Trench ✦1 E 10 58
Rzeszów C 12 96
Ržev H 11 108

S

Sa B 4 200
Saale ≃ E 8 98
Saalfeld B 8 100
Saalfelden C 4 102
Saar (Sarre) ≃ C 3 100
Saarbrücken C 4 100
Saarburg C 3 100
Saaremaa I C 11 66
Saarijärvi E 12 64
Saaristomeren kansallispuisto ♦ C 10 66
Saarland □3 C 3 100
Saarlouis C 3 100
Saatlı J 16 110
Saavedra E 6 195
Saba I D 9 186
Šabac C 5 104
Sabadell C 7 88
Sabah □3 D 7 134
Sabana Grande j 15 187b
Sabanalarga F 6 186
Sabancuy H 14 184
Sabang E 7 134
Sabará C 9 194
Sabarei G 4 202
Sābari ≃ F 4 122
Sābarmati ≃ E 2 122
Sab'atayn, Ramlat as- ✦8 D 6 202
Sabawanaag E 5 202
Şāberī, Hāmūn-e ⊜ D 9 116
Sabhā D 7 198
Sabie C 9 206
Sabile D 11 66
Sabina □9 G 8 92
Sabinal F 4 172
Sabiñánigo B 4 88
Sabinas D 9 184
Sabinas ≃, Mex. D 10 184
Sabinas ≃, Mex. D 9 184
Sabinas Hidalgo D 9 184
Sabine ≃ E 9 152
Sabine Lake ⊜ H 2 170
Sabine Pass ʮ H 2 170
Sabinov D 11 96
Sabirabad I 16 110
Sable ≃ A 9 160
Sable, Cape › G 11 160
Sable, Cape ›1 G 4 168
Sable, Île de I C 12 138
Sable Island I G 14 160
Sablé-sur-Sarthe E 6 78
Sablūkah, Ash-Shallāl as- ʟ D 3 202
Sabon Kafi C 6 200
Sabor ≃ C 3 86
Şabrātah C 7 198
Sabrina Coast ✦2 C 21 208
Sabugal D 3 86
Şabyā D 5 202
Sabzevār D 17 118
Sac City D 7 174
Sacedón D 2 88
Săcele C 8 104
Sachigo ≃ D 14 158
Sachigo Lake ⊜ E 12 158
Sachimbo D 3 204
Sachsen □3 C 7 96
Sachsen-Anhalt □3 E 8 98
Sachsenburg B 2 104
Sachs Harbour B 7 150
Sacile D 8 92
Šack I 14 108
Sackets Harbor C 2 164
Sackville F 11 160
Saco C 8 164
Saco ≃ C 8 164
Sacramento, Braz. C 7 194
Sacramento, Ca., U.S. B 2 182
Sacramento □6 B 2 182
Sacramento ≃ C 3 180
Sacramento Mountains ⋀ F 6 176
Sacramento Valley V C 2 180
Sacro Monte ◗1 E 6 82
Săcueni B 6 104
Şa'dah D 5 202
Sa Dao K 5 132
Saddleback Butte State Park ♦ F 6 182
Saddle Lake Indian Reserve ✦4 E 16 156
Saddleworth D 5 72
Sa Dec I 7 132
Sadiola C 2 200
Sado I F 7 126
Šadrinsk H 25 108
Sädvaluspen C 8 64
Şafā, Tulūl aş- ∧1 C 8 120
Safad see Zefat D 4 120
Safâga I 5 118
Safakulevo I 25 108
Säffle C 6 66
Safford F 4 176
Saffron Walden E 7 72
Safi C 3 198
Safonovo, Russia I 10 108
Safonovo, Russia D 17 108
Safranbolu B 5 118
Saga, China D 5 122
Saga, Japan H 3 126
Saga □3 H 3 126
Sagaba E 3 204
Sagaing D 2 132
Sagaing □3 E 6 122
Sagamihara G 7 126
Sagami-nada c G 7 126
Saganaga Lake ⊜ A 3 166
Sāgar E 3 122
Sagavanirktok ≃ B 20 154
Saghyz ≃ E 19 110
Saginaw B 1 162
Saginaw ≃ B 2 162
Saginaw Bay c B 2 162
Sagres H 2 86
Sagua de Tánamo C 6 186
Sagua la Grande C 4 186
Saguaro National Park ♦ F 3 176
Saguenay ≃ D 8 160
Saguenay, Parc de conservation du ♦ f 11 163a
Sagunt (Sagunto) E 4 88
Sagunto see Sagunt E 4 88
Sa'gya D 5 122
Sahaba D 3 202
Sahagún F 6 186
Sahalin, ostrov (Sakhalin) I B 12 124
Sahalinskaja oblast' □6 B 10 126
Sahara ✦2 F 7 196
Sahāranpur D 3 122
Sahasinaka I 9 205a
Sahel ✦1 G 9 196
Şahin B 7 106
Sāhīwāl C 2 122
Şahneh E 12 118
Šahovskaja H 11 108
Šahrisabz B 1 122
Šahty F 11 110
Sahuayo de José María Morelos G 8 184
Šahunja H 17 108
Šahy B 10 102
Saïda C 5 198
Saidpur D 5 122
Saigon see Ho Chi Minh City I 8 132
Saiki H 3 126
Saimaa ⊜ B 14 66
Saimaa Canal ≍ B 14 66
Saín Alto F 8 184
Sā'īn Dezh D 12 118
Sainte-Adresse C 6 78
Sainte Agathe G 10 158
Sainte-Agathe-des-Monts E 6 160
St.-Agrève E 2 82
St. Albans, Eng., U.K. F 6 72
St. Albans, Vt., U.S. B 5 164
St. Albans, W.V., U.S. D 3 162
St. Albert E 15 156
St.-Alexis-des-Monts E 7 160
St.-Amand-les-Eaux B 10 78
St.-Amand-Mont-Rond F 9 78
St.-Amant-Tallende C 7 80
St.-Amour D 3 82
St.-André, Cap see Vilanandro, Tanjona › k 8 205a
St.-André-Avellin A 3 164
St. Andrews, Scot., U.K. D 6 74
St. Andrews, S.C., U.S. C 4 168
Sainte-Anne-de-Beaupré g 11 163a
Sainte-Anne-du-Lac E 6 160
St. Ann's Bay h 12 186a
St.-Anselme E 8 160
St. Ansgar D 2 166
St. Anthony C 16 160
St.-Antonin-Noble-Val D 5 80
St. Arnaud F 4 144
St.-Auban G 4 82
St. Augustin ≃ C 14 160
St. Augustine E 4 168
St.-Aulaye C 4 80
St. Austell G 2 72
St.-Avold C 14 78
St. Barbe C 15 160
St.-Béat F 4 80
St. Bees Head › C 3 72
St.-Benoît-du-Sault B 5 80
St.-Bertrand-de-Comminges ◗1 A 5 88
St.-Brieuc D 4 78
St. Catharines G 4 160
St. Catherine, Monastery of ◗1 B 3 202
St. Catherines Island I D 4 168
St. Catherine's Point › G 5 72
St.-Céré D 5 80
St.-Chamond E 2 82
St. Charles, Il., U.S. B 4 170
St. Charles, Mi., U.S. B 1 162
St. Charles, Mo., U.S. C 3 170
St. Christopher (Saint Kitts) I m 20 187d
St.-Ciers-sur-Gironde C 3 80
St. Clair C 3 170
St. Clair ≃ B 2 162
St. Clair, Lake ⊜ B 2 162
St. Clair Shores B 2 162
St.-Claude D 3 82
St. Cloud, Fl., U.S. E 4 168
St. Cloud, Mn., U.S. C 1 166
Sainte-Croix D 4 82
St. Croix I D 8 186
St. Croix ≃, N.A. h 13 163a
St. Croix ≃ C 2 166
St. Croix Falls C 2 166
St. Croix Island National Monument ♦ h 13 163a
St. Croix National Scenic Riverway ♦ C 2 166
St. Croix State Park ♦ C 2 166
St.-Cyprien D 5 80
St.-Cyr-l'École D 8 78
St.-Cyr-sur-Loire E 7 78
St. David B 3 170
St. David's Cathedral ◗1 F 1 72
St. David's Head › F 1 72
St.-Denis, Fr. D 9 78
St.-Denis, Reu. q 20 207e
St.-Dié B 4 82
St.-Dizier D 11 78
St.-Donat-sur-l'Herbasse E 3 82
St.-Égrève E 3 82
St. Elias, Cape › G 22 154
St. Elias, Mount ∧ F 24 154
St. Elias Mountains ⋀ F 24 154
St.-Élie C 8 190
Sainte-Énimie F 1 82
St.-Étienne E 2 82
St.-Étienne-de-Saint-Geoirs E 3 82
St.-Étienne-du-Rouvray C 8 78
St.-Étienne-en-Dévoluy F 3 82
St.-Eugène D 7 160
St.-Eustache F 6 160
St. Faith's F 9 206
St.-Félicien D 7 160
St.-Florent-sur-Cher F 9 78
St.-Floris, Parc National ♦ D 9 200
St.-Flour C 7 80
St.-Fons E 2 82
Sainte-Foy E 8 160
Sainte-Foy-de-Conques, Abbaye ◗1 D 6 80
St. Francis ≃, N.A. g 12 163a
St. Francis ≃ D 3 170
St. Francis, Cape › H 6 206
St. Francis Bay c H 6 206
St. Francis Lake ⊜1 A 6 162
St. Francisville G 3 170
St.-François n 21 187e
St.-Gabriel D 9 160
St.-Gaudens E 4 80
St.-Gaultier B 5 80
St.-Genis-Laval E 2 82
St. George, Austl. I 9 142
St. George, N.B., Can. F 10 160
St. George, Ut., U.S. D 2 176
St. George, Cape › H 6 170
St.-Georges, Qc., Can. E 8 160
St.-Georges, Fr. Gu. C 8 190
St. George's, Gren. w 29 187j
St. George's Bay c, Nf., Can. D 14 160
St. Georges Bay c, N.S., Can. F 13 160
St. George's Channel ʮ E 5 70
St.-Georges-sur-Loire E 6 78
St.-Germain-en-Laye D 8 78
St.-Germain-l'Herm E 1 82
St.-Gervais-d'Auvergne B 6 80
St.-Gilles G 2 82
St.-Gilles-Croix-de-Vie F 5 78
St.-Guénolé E 2 78
St.-Guilhem-le-Désert, Église de ◗1 G 1 82
St. Helena □2 J 7 196
St. Helena Bay c G 2 206
St. Helens, Eng., U.K. D 4 72
St. Helens, Or., U.S. C 2 178
St. Helens □6 D 4 72
St. Helens, Mount ∧1 B 2 178
St. Helier k 10 73b
St.-Hippolyte C 4 82
St.-Hyacinthe F 7 160
St. Ignace C 6 166
St. Ignace Island I G 15 158
St.-Imier C 5 82
St. Ives G 1 72
St. James, Mi., U.S. C 6 166
St. James, Mo., U.S. C 3 170
St. James, N.Y., U.S. F 5 164
St. James, Cape › F 6 156
St.-Jean, Lac ⊜1 D 7 160
St.-Jean-d'Angély C 3 80
St.-Jean-de-Braye E 8 78
St.-Jean-de-Luz E 2 80
St.-Jean-de-Maurienne E 4 82
St.-Jean-de-Monts F 4 78
St.-Jean-Port-Joli g 11 163a
St.-Jean-sur-Richelieu F 7 160
St.-Jérôme F 6 160
St. Joe ≃ B 5 178
St. John F 10 160
St. John I D 8 186
St. John ≃ F 10 160
St. John, Cape › D 16 160
St. John's, Antig. I 18 187c
St. John's, Nf., Can. E 17 160
St. Johns, Mi., U.S. B 1 162
St. Johns ≃ D 4 168
St. Johnsbury B 6 164
St. Joseph, Mi., U.S. D 5 166
St. Joseph, Mo., U.S. C 1 170
St. Joseph ≃ E 5 166
St. Joseph, Lake ⊜ F 13 158
St.-Joseph-de-Beauce E 8 160
St. Joseph Island I H 17 158
St.-Jovite E 6 160
St.-Junien C 4 80
St.-Just-en-Chaussée C 9 78
St. Kilda F 3 146
St. Kilda I C 3 70
St. Kitts see Saint Christopher I m 20 187d
St. Kitts and Nevis □1 H 13 148
St.-Laurent (Saint Lawrence) ≃ D 9 160
St.-Laurent du Maroni B 8 190
St.-Laurent-et-Benon C 3 80
St. Lawrence E 16 160
St. Lawrence □6 B 3 164
St. Lawrence (Saint-Laurent) ≃ D 9 160
St. Lawrence, Gulf of c D 13 160
St. Lawrence Island I E 9 154
St. Lawrence Islands National Park ♦ F 6 160
St. Lazare F 8 158
St.-Lô C 5 78
St.-Louis, Fr. C 5 82
St.-Louis, Reu. q 20 207e
St.-Louis, Sen. B 1 200
St. Louis, Mi., U.S. B 1 162
St. Louis, Mo., U.S. C 3 170
St.-Louis de Kent E 11 160
St. Louis Park C 2 166
St. Lucia □1 H 13 148
St. Lucia, Lake ⊜ E 9 206
St. Lucia Channel ʮ s 27 187h
St. Lucia Game Reserve ✦4 E 10 206
Sainte-Lucie j 9 83a
St. Magnus Bay c g 9 74a
St.-Malo D 4 78
St.-Malo, Golfe de c D 4 78
St.-Marc D 6 186
St.-Marcellin E 3 82
Sainte-Marguerite ≃ C 10 160
Sainte-Marie, Cap see Vohimena, Tanjona › m 8 205a
Sainte Marie, Nosy I k 9 205a
Sainte-Marie-aux-Mines B 5 82
St. Maries B 5 178
St.-Martin (Sint Maarten) I D 9 186
St. Martin, Lake ⊜ F 9 158
St.-Martin-Boulogne B 8 78
St.-Martin-d'Hères E 3 82
St. Mary Lake ⊜ A 7 178
St. Mary Peak ∧ C 2 144
St. Marys, Austl. i 13 145a
St. Mary's, Nf., Can. E 17 160
St. Marys, Oh., U.S. B 6 170
St. Marys, W.V., U.S. D 3 162
St. Marys □6 H 2 164
St. Marys ≃ B 6 170
St. Marys ≃ D 4 168
St. Mary's, Cape › E 16 160
St. Mary's Bay c, Nf., Can. E 16 160
St. Marys Bay c, N.S., Can. F 10 160
St. Matthew Island I F 8 154
St. Matthews, Ky., U.S. C 6 170
St. Matthews, S.C., U.S. C 4 168
St.-Maur-des-Fossés D 9 78
St.-Maurice ≃ E 7 160
St.-Max B 4 82
Sainte-Maxime G 4 82
St.-Méen-le-Grand D 4 78
Sainte-Mère-Église C 5 78
St. Michaels H 2 164
St.-Michel-de-Cuxa, Abbatiale de ◗1 B 7 88
St.-Mihiel B 3 82
St.-Nazaire E 4 78
St.-Nectaire, Église de ◗1 C 6 80
St. Neots E 6 72
St.-Nicolas D 4 69
St.-Omer B 9 78
Saintonge □9 C 3 80
St.-Pacôme E 9 160
St.-Pascal g 12 163a
St. Paul, Ab., Can. D 16 156
St. Paul, In., U.S. C 6 170
St. Paul, Mn., U.S. C 2 166
St. Paul, Ne., U.S. E 5 174
St. Paul (Saint-Paul) ≃ C 15 160
St.-Paul, Île I I 7 58
St.-Paulien E 1 82
St. Pauls B 5 168
St.-Paul-Trois-Châteaux F 2 82
St. Peter C 8 174
St. Peter Island I L 1 142
St. Peter Port k 10 73b
St. Peters F 13 160
St. Petersburg see Sankt-Peterburg, Russia F 9 108
St. Petersburg, Fl., U.S. F 3 168
St.-Pierre, Mart. s 26 187h
St.-Pierre, Reu. q 20 207e
St.-Pierre I E 15 160
St.-Pierre, Lac ⊜ E 7 160
St. Pierre and Miquelon □2 E 14 148
St.-Pierre-des-Corps E 7 78
St.-Pierre-le-Moûtier F 10 78
St.-Pierreville F 2 82
St.-Pol-sur-Ternoise B 9 78
St.-Pons-de-Thomères E 6 80
St.-Priest E 2 82
St.-Quentin C 10 78
St.-Raphaël G 4 82
St. Regis Falls B 4 164
St. Regis Indian Reservation ✦4 B 4 164
St.-Romuald E 8 160
Sainte Rose du Lac F 9 158
Saintes C 3 80
St.-Savin B 4 80
Sainte-Savine D 11 78
St.-Sébastien, Cap see Anorontany, Tanjona › j 9 205a
St.-Sébastien, Morne de ∧ A 8 164
St.-Seine-l'Abbaye E 11 78
St. Simons Island D 4 168
St. Simons Island I D 4 168
Saintes-Maries-de-la-Mer G 2 82
St. Stephen C 4 168
St.-Sulpice-les-Feuilles B 5 80
Sainte-Thérèse A 7 162
St. Thomas, On., Can. G 3 160
St. Thomas, N.D., U.S. A 6 174
St. Thomas I D 8 186
St.-Tite E 7 160
St.-Tropez G 4 82
St.-Valery-en-Caux C 7 78
St.-Vallier, Fr. F 11 78
St.-Vallier, Fr. E 2 82
St.-Varent F 6 78
St. Vincent □1 H 13 148
St.-Vincent, Cap see Ankaboa, Tanjona › I 8 205a
St. Vincent, Gulf c E 2 144
St. Vincent and the Grenadines see Saint Vincent □1 H 13 148
St. Vincent Passage ʮ E 9 186
St.-Vith D 5 69
St.-Vivien-de-Médoc C 2 80
St. Walburg E 17 156
St.-Yvon D 11 160
Saipan I I 13 124
Saiqi E 14 130
Saitama □3 G 7 126
Saito H 3 126
Sai Yok National Park ♦ G 4 132
Sajama, Nevado ∧ G 5 190
Šajmak' B 2 122
Sajószentpéter A 6 104
Sak ≃ F 4 206
Sakaide G 4 126
Sakaiminato G 4 126
Sakākah G 9 118
Sakakawea, Lake ⊜1 B 3 174
Sakami B 5 160
Sakami ≃ B 7 160
Sakami, Lac ⊜ B 5 160
Sakaraha I 8 205a
Sakarya B 9 106
Sakarya □3 B 9 106
Sakarya ≃ B 4 118
Sakata E 7 126
Sakchu-ŭp F 15 128
Sakété D 5 200
Sakhalin see Sahalin, ostrov I B 12 124
Sakhnin D 4 120
Sakht Sar D 14 118
Şäki I 15 110
Šakiai E 11 66
Sakiet Sidi Youssef G 2 90
Sakishima-shotō II H 9 124
Sakon Nakhon F 6 132
Sakpiegu D 5 200
Sakrivier F 4 206
Sakskøbing D 4 68
Sakwaso Lake ⊜ E 12 158
Saky G 8 110
Säkylä B 11 66
Sal I h 11 200a
Sal ≃ F 12 110
Šal'a, Slvk. B 9 102
Sala, Swe. C 8 66
Salaberry-de-Valleyfield F 6 160
Salacgrīva D 12 66
Sala Consilina D 5 94
Salada, Laguna ⊜ A 1 184
Saladillo D 8 195
Saladillo ≃ C 6 195
Salado ≃, Arg. G 8 192
Salado ≃, Arg. G 6 192
Salado ≃, Arg. E 7 192
Salado ≃, Mex. D 10 184
Salado, Arroyo ≃ G 4 195
Salaga D 4 200
Şalāḥ ad-Dīn □3 E 10 118
Salahin G 6 202
Sălaj □3 B 7 104
Salajwe B 6 206
Salala D 3 200
Şalālah, Oman G 7 116
Şalālah, Sudan C 4 202
Salamanca, Mex. G 9 184
Salamanca, Spain D 5 86
Salamanca, N.Y., U.S. B 4 162
Salamanca □6 D 4 86
Salamat □3 C 9 200
Salamat, Bahr ≃ D 8 200
Salamína C 5 106
Salamis ⊥ E 5 118
Salani j 11 147b
Salantai D 10 66
Salatiga k 20 135b
Salavat J 21 108
Salaverry E 3 190
Salawati I F 10 134
Sala y Gómez, Isla I G 4 188
Salcia D 8 104
Šalčininkai E 12 66
Saldaña B 6 86
Saldanha Bay c G 2 206
Saldus D 11 66
Sale, Austl. G 6 144
Salé, Mor. C 3 198
Sale, Eng., U.K. D 4 72
Salebabu, Pulau I E 9 134
Sale Creek E 6 170
Salehard C 26 108
Salem, India G 3 122
Salem, Ia., U.S. E 3 166
Salem, Il., U.S. C 4 170
Salem, Ky., U.S. D 4 170
Salem, Ma., U.S. D 8 164
Salem, N.H., U.S. D 7 164
Salem, N.J., U.S. G 3 164
Salem, Oh., U.S. C 3 162
Salem, Or., U.S. C 2 178
Salem, S.D., U.S. D 6 174
Salem, Va., U.S. E 3 162
Salem □6 G 3 164
Salemi G 2 94
Sälen B 6 66
Salentina, Penisola ›1 E 6 90
Salerno D 4 94
Salerno □6 D 5 94
Salerno, Golfo di c D 4 94
Salford D 4 72
Šalgačova E 13 108
Salgótarján A 5 104
Salgueiro E 11 190
Sali D 4 198
Salihli C 8 106
Salihorsk J 13 64
Salim E 2 202
Salīmah, Wāḥat ⊤4 C 2 202
Salimani n 18 207d
Salina, Ks., U.S. F 6 174
Salina, Ut., U.S. C 3 176
Salina Cruz I 12 184
Salinas, Braz. B 9 194
Salinas, Ec. D 2 190
Salinas, Ca., U.S. D 2 182
Salinas ≃, N.A. I 14 184
Salinas ≃, Ca., U.S. D 2 182
Salinas, Pampa de las ≍ B 4 195
Salinas Pueblo Missions National Monument ♦ E 5 176
Saline F 2 170
Saline ≃ F 3 170
Salisbury, Austl. E 2 144
Salisbury, Eng., U.K. F 5 72
Salisbury, Md., U.S. H 3 164
Salisbury, Mo., U.S. C 2 170
Salisbury, N.C., U.S. B 4 168
Salisbury see Harare, Zimb. F 5 204
Salisbury Cathedral ◗1 F 5 72
Salisbury Island I D 17 150
Salisbury Plain ≍ F 5 72
Šalja H 23 108
Šalkar-Ega-Kara, ozero ⊜ D 22 110
Şalkhad E 7 120
Sallanches E 4 82
Sallent C 6 88
Salliq (Coral Harbour) D 16 150
Sallisaw E 1 170
Salluit D 17 150
Salmās C 11 118
Salmi F 9 108
Salmon C 6 178
Salmon ≃, N.B., Can. E 11 160
Salmon ≃, Id., U.S. C 5 178
Salmon, Middle Fork ≃ C 6 178
Salmon Arm F 12 156
Salmon Falls Creek ≃ D 6 178
Salmon River Mountains ⋀ C 6 178
Salmyš ≃ C 19 110
Salo, C.A.R. E 8 200
Salo, Fin. B 11 66
Salò, Italy C 3 90
Salobreña H 7 86
Salomon Islands II J 9 112
Salon-de-Provence G 3 82
Salonga, Parc National de la ♦ C 3 204
Salonica see Thessaloníki B 5 106
Salonica, Gulf of c B 9 198
Salonta B 6 104
Saloum ≃ C 1 200
Sal'sk F 12 110
Salt ≃ F 2 176
Salta D 6 192
Salta □3 D 7 192
Saltaim, ozero ⊜ H 29 108
Saltash G 2 72
Salt Basin ⊜ G 6 176
Saltcoats, Sk., Can. F 7 158
Saltcoats, Scot., U.K. E 4 74
Salt Fork State Park ♦ C 3 162
Saltillo E 9 184
Salt Lake City B 3 176
Salto, Arg. D 7 195
Salto, Ur. B 9 195
Salto, Lago del ⊜1 G 8 92
Salto da Divisa A 10 194
Salto del Guairá E 3 194
Salto Grande, Embalse de ⊜1 B 8 195
Salton Sea ⊜ F 6 180
Salton Sea State Recreation Area ♦ F 6 180
Salto Santiago, Represa de ⊜1 F 4 194
Salt River Indian Reservation ✦4 F 3 176
Saluda E 5 162
Saluda ≃ B 4 168
Salûm, Gulf of c A 2 202
Sālūr F 4 122
Saluzzo E 3 92
Salvador F 11 190
Salvador, Lake ⊜ H 3 170
Salvage D 17 160
Salvatierra G 9 184
Salviac D 5 80
Salwa Bay (Salwā, Dawḥat as-) c J 13 118
Salween ≃ F 16 116
Salyan J 16 110
Salyersville E 2 162
Salzburg C 5 102
Salzburg □3 C 5 102
Salzgitter D 7 98
Salzkammergut ✦1 C 5 102
Salzkotten E 5 98
Salzwedel D 8 98
Sam A. Baker State Park ♦ D 3 170
Samā'il F 8 116
Samalga Pass ʮ J 10 154
Samâlût H 4 118
Samandağı D 6 118
Samandıra B 8 106
Samane C 6 206
Samangān B 1 122
Samar I C 9 134
Samara C 17 110
Samara ≃, Russia C 18 110
Samara ≃, Ukr. E 9 110
Samarai O 14 124
Samaria □9 E 4 120
Samaria Gorge V E 5 106
Samarinda F 7 134
Samarka B 4 126
Samarkand (Samarqand) B 1 122
Samarkand □6 B 1 122
Sāmarrā' E 10 118
Samarskaja oblast' □6 C 17 110
Samarskoe F 11 110
Samaúna E 7 190
Samba Caju D 2 204
Sambalpur E 4 122
Sambas N 9 132
Sambava j 10 205a
Sāmbhar Lake ⊜ D 3 122
Sambiase F 6 94
Sambir E 3 110
Sambo E 2 204
Samborombón, Bahía c D 9 195
Sambungo D 3 204
Samch'ŏk H 17 128
Samer B 8 78
Samfya E 4 204
Samho-dong E 1 126
Sámi C 4 106
Şämkir I 15 110
Şamlı C 7 106
Samoa □1 E 10 136
Samoa Islands II E 10 136
Samobor E 7 102
Samofalovka E 13 110
Samokov D 7 104
Sámos I D 7 106
Samosir, Pulau I M 4 132
Samothrace see Samothráki I B 6 106
Samothráki B 6 106
Samothráki (Samothrace) I B 6 106
Sampang k 21 135b
Sampit F 6 134
Sampwe D 4 204
Sam Rayburn Reservoir ⊜1 G 1 170
Sam Son E 7 132
Samson Indian Reserve ✦4 E 15 156
Samsun B 6 118
Samsun □3 B 6 118
Samsun Körfezi c B 7 118
Samtredia H 13 110
Samui, Ko I J 5 132
Samut Prakan H 5 132
San C 3 200
San (Xan) ≃ H 8 132
Şan'ā' D 5 202
Sanaag □3 E 6 202
Sanaga ≃ E 7 200
San Agustin, Cape › D 9 134
San Ambrosio, Isla I G 7 188
Sanana, Pulau I F 9 134
Sanandaj E 12 118
San Andreas B 3 182
San Andrés E 4 186
San Andrés, Isla de I A 2 190
San Andrés Tuxtla H 12 184
San Andrés y Providencia □3 E 4 186
San Angelo E 3 172
San Antonio, Chile C 1 195
San Antonio, Ur. B 9 195
San Antonio, Tx., U.S. F 4 172
San Antonio, Cabo ›1 E 9 195
San Antonio, Cabo de › C 3 186
San Antonio, Mount ∧ F 6 182
San Antonio Abad see Sant Antoni de Portmany E 6 88
San Antonio Bay c F 5 172
San Antonio de Padua, Mission ◗1 D 2 182
San Antonio Mountain ∧ D 5 176
San Antonio Oeste G 5 195
Sanāwad E 3 122
San Bartolomeo in Galdo C 5 94
San Benedetto del Tronto B 3 94
San Benedetto Po D 6 92
San Benedicto, Isla I H 4 184
San Benito, Guat. D 2 186
San Benito, Tx., U.S. G 5 172
San Benito □6 D 2 182
San Benito ≃ D 2 182
San Bernardino F 6 182
San Bernardino □6 F 7 182
San Bernardino Mountains ⋀ F 7 182
San Bernardo C 2 195
San Blas D 5 184
San Blas, Cape › H 6 170
San Bonifacio D 7 92
San Borja F 5 190
San Buenaventura D 9 184
San Cándido C 8 92
San Carlos, Chile E 2 195
San Carlos, Falk. Is. n 18 193b
San Carlos, Mex. C 9 184
San Carlos, Mex. E 10 184
San Carlos, Phil. C 8 134
San Carlos, Ur. D 10 195
San Carlos, Ca., U.S. C 1 182
San Carlos, Ven. F 7 186
San Carlos ≃, C.R. F 3 186
San Carlos ≃, Ven. B 5 190
San Carlos de Bariloche H 5 192
San Carlos de Bolívar E 7 195
San Carlos del Zulia F 7 186
San Carlos de Río Negro C 5 190
San Carlos Indian Reservation ✦4 F 3 176
San Casciano in Val di Pesa F 7 92
San Cataldo G 3 94
Sancerre E 9 78
Sanchahe D 16 128
San Ciro de Acosta G 10 184
San Clemente, Spain E 2 88
San Clemente, Ca., U.S. G 6 182
San Clemente Island I H 5 182
Sancoins F 9 78
San Cristóbal, Arg. B 7 195
San Cristóbal, Ven. G 6 186
San Cristobal I B 13 138
San Cristóbal, Isla I j 14 190a
San Cristóbal, Volcán ∧1 E 3 186
San Cristóbal de la Laguna i 14 85b
San Cristóbal de las Casas I 13 184
Sancti Spíritus C 4 186
Sancy, Puy de ∧ C 6 80
Sand C 3 66
Sand ≃, S. Afr. B 9 206
Sand ≃, S. Afr. E 7 206
Sanda Island I B 1 72
Sandakan D 7 134
Sandane B 3 66
Sandaozhen C 15 128
Sandared A 5 68
Sandbach D 4 72
Sande C 5 98
Sandefjord C 5 66
Sandersdorf E 8 98
Sanderson E 2 172
Sandfly Lake ⊜ D 18 156
Sandhamn C 9 66
Sandia F 5 190
Sandia Indian Reservation ✦4 E 5 176
San Diego H 6 182
San Diego □6 G 7 182
San Diego, Cabo › J 6 192
San Diego Bay c H 6 182
Sandıklı C 9 106
Sand Lake ⊜ F 11 158
Sandnes C 2 66
Sandoa D 3 204
Sandomierz C 11 96
San Donà di Piave D 8 92
San Donato Milanese D 5 92
Sandoway E 2 132
Sandown G 5 72
Sandringham E 7 72
Sandringham House ⊥ E 7 72
Sandrücken C 2 206
Sand Springs, Ok., U.S. B 5 172
Sand Springs, Tx., U.S. D 3 172
Sandston A 6 168
Sandu Ao c E 14 130
Sandusky, Mi., U.S. B 2 162
Sandusky, Oh., U.S. C 2 162
Sandvika C 5 66
Sandviken B 8 66
Sandwell □6 E 4 72
Sandwich E 8 164
Sandwich Bay c, Nf., Can. B 14 160
Sandwich Bay c, Nmb. B 1 206
Sandy E 7 178
Sandy Bay Indian Reserve ✦4 F 9 158
Sandy Cape › H 11 142
Sandy Hook G 4 170
Sandy Hook ›2 F 5 164
Sandykop D 2 206
Sandy Lake ⊜ E 12 158
Sandy Springs C 2 168
Sandžak ✦1 D 5 104
San Felipe, Chile C 2 195
San Felipe, Mex. G 9 184
San Felipe, Mex. B 2 184
San Felipe, Ven. F 7 186
San Felipe Indian Reservation ✦4 E 5 176
San Félix, Isla I G 6 188
San Fernando, Chile D 2 195
San Fernando, Phil. B 8 134
San Fernando, Phil. B 8 134
San Fernando, Spain H 4 86
San Fernando, Trin. q 23 187e
San Fernando, Ca., U.S. F 5 182
San Fernando de Apure G 8 186
San Fernando de Atabapo C 5 190
San Fernando del Valle de Catamarca E 6 192
Sånfjällets Nationalpark ♦ A 6 66
Sanford, Fl., U.S. E 4 168
Sanford, Me., U.S. C 8 164
Sanford, N.C., U.S. B 5 168
Sanford ≃ J 4 140
Sanford, Mount ∧1 E 22 154
San Francesco, Convento ◗1 G 8 92
San Francisco, Arg. B 6 195
San Francisco, Ca., U.S. C 1 182
San Francisco □6 C 1 182
San Francisco ≃ F 4 176
San Francisco Bay c C 1 182
San Francisco de Horizonte H 2 172
San Francisco de Macorís D 7 186

ʟ Waterfall ʮ Strait c Bay, Gulf ⊜ Lake ≍ Swamp ⊓ Ice Feature ⊤ Other Hydrographic Feature ✦ Submarine Feature □ Political Unit ◗ Cultural Institution ⊥ Historical Site ♦ Recreational Site ✈ Airport ■ Military Installation ✦ Miscellaneous

Symbols in the index entries represent the broad categories identified in the key at the right. Symbols with superior numbers (↗¹) identify subcategories (see complete key on page 242).

∧ Mountain   ↗ Mountains   ✕ Pass   V Valley   ≖ Plain   ⊳ Cape   ⫽ Island   ⫽⫽ Islands   ≏ Other Topographic Feature   ≃ River   ⊘ Canal

⌐ Waterfall ∪ Strait c Bay, Gulf ∅ Lake ≈ Swamp ⊠ Ice Feature ∇ Other Hydrographic Feature ⊷ Submarine Feature □ Political Unit ⊳ Cultural Institution ⊥ Historical Site ⊠ Recreational Site ⊀ Airport ■ Military Installation ⊷ Miscellaneous

Symbols in the index entries represent the broad categories identified in the key at the right. Symbols with superior numbers (▲¹) identify subcategories (see complete key on page 242).

▲ Mountain ⌖ Mountains ⌣ Pass V Valley ≃ Plain ▸ Cape I Island II Islands ⊥ Other Topographic Feature ≃ River ⌇ Canal

Stavern — Tambakboyo

Name | Map Ref. | Page

Stavern C 5 66
Stavropol' G 13 110
Stavropol'skij kraj □[6] G 13 110
Stawell F 4 144
Stayton C 2 178
Steamboat Springs B 5 176
Stębark B 11 96
Stebbins E 13 154
Steele B 5 174
Steelville D 3 170
Steenwijk B 5 69
Steephill Lake ⊜ D 20 156
Stefanie, Lake ⊜ G 4 202
Stefansson Island I B 11 150
Ştefan Vodă C 9 104
Steffisburg D 5 82
Stegeborg C 8 66
Ştei B 7 104
Steiermark □[3] B 3 104
Steinach B 8 100
Steinamanger see Szombathely C 8 102
Steinau B 6 100
Steinbach G 10 158
Steinfurt D 4 98
Steinhausen A 3 206
Steinhausen ◗[1] D 6 100
Steinheim E 6 98
Steinhuder Meer ⊜ D 6 98
Steinkjer D 5 64
Stekene C 2 69
Stekljanka G 14 108
Stellarton F 12 160
Stelvio, Parco Nazionale dello ♦ C 6 92
Stenay C 12 78
Stendal D 8 98
Stenhouse Bay E 1 144
Stenstorp C 6 66
Stenungsund C 5 66
Stepanakert see Xankändi J 15 110
Stepanavan I 14 110
Stephanskirchen E 9 100
Stephen A 6 174
Stephens, Port ⊂ D 9 144
Stephens Lake ⊜[1] C 11 158
Stephenson, Mount ∧ C 1 208
Stephens Passage ʉ H 28 154
Stephenville, Nf., Can. D 14 160
Stephenville, Tx., U.S. D 4 172
Stepnoe G 14 110
Sterdyń B 12 96
Steréa Elláda □[3] C 5 106
Sterkstroom F 7 206
Sterling, Ak., U.S. F 19 154
Sterling, Co., U.S. E 3 174
Sterling, Il., U.S. B 4 170
Sterling, Mi., U.S. A 1 162
Sterling City E 3 172
Sterlitamak J 21 108
Šternberk D 9 96
Stęszew B 9 96
Stettin Lagoon ⊂ C 10 98
Stettler E 15 156
Steuben □[6] D 1 164
Steubenville C 3 162
Stevenage F 6 72
Stevenson B 2 168
Stevenson Creek ≃ I 2 142
Stevenson Entrance ʉ G 18 154
Stevenson Lake ⊜ E 10 158
Stevens Pass ✕ B 3 178
Stevens Point C 4 166
Stewart C 7 174
Stewart ≃ E 27 154
Stewart Island I G 2 146
Stewart Islands II A 13 138
Stewartstown G 2 164
Stewart Valley F 18 156
Stewartville D 2 166
Steynsrus D 7 206
Steyr B 6 102
Stickney, Eng., U.K. D 6 72
Stickney, S.D., U.S. D 5 174
Stigliano D 6 94
Stikine ≃ C 6 156
Stiklestad E 5 64
Stilfontein D 7 206
Stillwater, B.C., Can. G 9 156
Stillwater, Ok., U.S. B 5 172
Stinnett C 3 172
Štip E 7 104
Stiring-Wendel A 4 82
Stirling, Austl. L 3 140
Stirling, Austl. F 1 142
Stirling, Scot., U.K. D 4 74
Stirling □[6] A 2 72
Stirling Castle ⊥ D 4 74
Stirling Range National Park ♦ N 4 140
Stittsville A 3 164
Stockach E 6 100
Stockbridge C 2 168
Stockbridge Indian Reservation ◆[4] C 4 166
Stockelsdorf C 7 98
Stockerau B 8 102
Stockholm C 9 66
Stockholm □[3] C 9 66
Stockport D 4 72
Stockport □[6] D 4 72
Stockton, Ca., U.S. C 2 182
Stockton, Ks., U.S. F 5 174
Stockton-on-Tees C 5 72
Stockton-on-Tees □[6] C 5 72
Stockton Plateau ⋏[1] E 2 172
Stockton Springs A 9 162
Stoczek Łukowski C 12 96
Stodolišče I 10 108
Stœng Trêng H 7 132
Stoke-on-Trent E 4 72
Stolberg F 3 98
Stolin K 13 64
Stollberg B 9 100
Stöllet B 6 66
Stone E 4 72
Stoneboro C 3 162
Stone Harbor G 4 164
Stonehaven D 6 74
Stonehenge ⊥ F 5 72
Stone Indian Reserve ◆[4] F 10 156
Stone Mountain C 2 168
Stone Mountain Provincial Park ♦ B 9 156
Stones River National Battlefield ♦ E 5 170
Stoneville A 5 168
Stonewall F 10 158
Stoney Creek B 4 162
Stoney Indian Reserve ◆[4] F 14 156
Stony Brook F 5 164
Stony Creek Indian Reserve ◆[4] E 9 156
Stony Lake ⊜ B 9 158
Stony Point E 5 164
Stony Rapids B 19 156
Stopnica C 11 96
Stora Le ⊜ C 5 66
Stora Lulevatten ⊜ C 9 64
Storavan ⊜ D 9 64
Storby B 9 66
Storebælt ʉ C 3 68
Støren E 4 64
Storey □[6] A 4 182
Storlien E 6 64
Storm Bay ⊂ j 12 145a
Storm Lake D 7 174
Stormont, Dundas and Glengarry □[6] A 4 164
Stormsvlei H 4 206
Storoževsk E 20 108
Storozhynets' A 8 104
Storrs E 6 164
Storsjøen ⊜ B 5 66
Storsjön ⊜, Swe. B 8 66
Storsjön ⊜, Swe. E 6 64
Storstrøm □[3] C 4 68
Storstrømsbroen ◆[5] D 4 68
Storuman D 8 64
Storuman ⊜ D 7 64
Storvindeln ⊜ D 8 64
Storvreta B 8 66
Story City D 2 166
Stoŭbcy F 13 66
Stoughton, Sk., Can. G 7 158
Stoughton, Ma., U.S. D 7 164
Stourbridge E 4 72
Stourport-on-Severn E 4 72
Stout Lake ⊜ E 11 158
Stow C 3 162
Stowmarket E 7 72
Strabane B 4 75
Stradella D 5 92
Straelen C 5 69
Strafford □[6] C 7 164
Strahan j 11 145a
Strakonice C 10 100
Stralsund B 10 98
Strambino D 3 92
Strand H 3 206
Strangford Lough ⊂ B 6 75
Strängnäs C 8 66
Stranraer C 1 72
Strasbourg, Sk., Can. F 19 156
Strasbourg, Fr. B 5 82
Strasburg, Ger. C 10 98
Strasburg, N.D., U.S. B 4 174
Străşeni B 10 104
Strata Florida Abbey ◗[1] E 2 72
Stratford, Austl. F 6 144
Stratford, On., Can. G 3 160
Stratford, N.Z. C 5 146
Stratford, Ca., U.S. D 4 182
Stratford, Ct., U.S. E 5 164
Stratford, Tx., U.S. B 2 172
Stratford-upon-Avon E 5 72
Strathclair F 8 158
Strathcona Provincial Park ♦ G 8 156
Strathlorne E 13 160
Strathmore, Ab., Can. F 15 156
Strathmore, Ca., U.S. D 4 182
Strathroy B 3 162
Stratton E 4 174
Straubing D 9 100
Strausberg D 10 98
Strawberry ≃ B 3 176
Strawberry Reservoir ⊜[1] B 3 176
Strawn D 4 172
Strážske D 11 96
Streaky Bay L 2 142
Streaky Bay ⊂ L 1 142
Streator B 4 170
Středočeský □[3] D 8 96
Stredoslovenský □[3] D 10 96
Street F 4 72
Streetman E 5 172
Strehaia C 7 104
Strehla E 10 98
Strel'na ≃ C 13 108
Strel'skaja G 17 108
Stresa D 4 92
Striberg C 7 66
Stromboli, Isola I F 5 94
Stromness, S. Geor. q 21 193b
Stromness, Scot., U.K. B 5 74
Stromsburg E 6 174
Strömstad C 5 66
Strong F 2 170
Stronghurst B 3 170
Stropkov D 11 96
Stroud F 4 72
Stroudsburg F 3 164
Struer B 1 68
Strum C 3 166
Struma (Strimón) ≃ E 7 104
Strumica E 7 104
Struthers C 3 162
Strydomsvlei G 5 206
Stryker B 6 170
Stryków C 10 96
Strymónas ≃ E 7 104
Strymónas, Gulf of ⊂ B 6 106
Stryy E 3 110
Strzegowo-Osada B 11 96
Strzelce Opolskie C 10 96
Strzelecki Creek ≃ B 3 144
Strzelecki Desert ◆[2] I 5 142
Strzelecki National Park ♦ i 12 145a
Strzelin C 9 96
Strzelno B 9 96
Stuart, Fl., U.S. B 4 186
Stuart, Ia., U.S. B 1 170
Stuart ≃ D 9 156
Stuart Lake ⊜ D 9 156
Stubbington G 5 72
Studenica, Manastir ◗[1] D 6 104
Studholme F 3 146
Stuhr C 5 98
Stuie E 8 156
Stull ≃ D 12 158
Stull Lake ⊜ D 12 158
Stupino I 13 108
Sturge Island I C 25 208
Sturgeon C 2 170
Sturgeon Bay C 5 166
Sturgeon Falls E 4 160
Sturgeon Lake Indian Reserve ◆[4] D 13 156
Sturgis, Ky., U.S. D 5 170
Sturgis, Mi., U.S. B 6 170
Sturgis, S.D., U.S. C 3 174
Štúrovo C 10 102
Sturt National Park ♦ B 3 144
Sturt Stony Desert ◆[2] J 5 142
Stutensee C 5 100
Stutterheim G 7 206
Stuttgart, Ger. D 6 100
Stuttgart, Ar., U.S. E 3 170
Stuttgart □[6] D 6 100
Šu see Shū B 11 116
Suaçuí Grande ≃ C 9 194
Subačius E 12 66
Subah k 19 135b
Subang k 18 135b
Subansiri ≃ D 6 122
Subarnarekha ≃ E 5 122
Subate D 12 66
Subbética, Cordillera ⋏ G 1 88
Subeita see Shivta, Horvot ⊥ H 3 120
Subiaco H 9 92
Subotica B 5 104
Suceava B 9 104
Suceava □[3] B 8 104
Suchań C 12 98
Suchou see Suzhou C 15 130
Sucre G 5 190
Sucre □[3], Col. F 6 186
Sucre □[3], Ven. F 9 186
Sucuriú ≃ H 8 190
Sud □[3] E 7 200
Sud, Canal du ʉ D 6 186
Sudaj G 15 108
Sudan □[1] G 10 196
Sudbury, On., Can. E 3 160
Sudbury, Eng., U.K. E 7 72
Sudd ◆[1] F 3 202
Sudetes ⋏ C 8 96
Sudi E 6 204
Sud-Kivu □[3] C 4 204
Sudogda H 14 108
Sud-Ouest □[3] E 6 200
Sudža D 9 110
Sue ≃ F 2 202
Sueca E 4 88
Suez (El-Suweis) H 5 118
Suez, Gulf of ⊂ H 5 118
Suez Canal ≋ G 5 118
Suffolk E 5 162
Suffolk □[6], Eng., U.K. E 8 72
Suffolk □[6], Ma., U.S. D 8 164
Suffolk □[6], N.Y., U.S. F 6 164
Sugarcreek C 3 162
Sugar Land F 6 172
Suggi Lake ⊜ D 7 158
Sugoj ≃ C 18 114
Suhag I 4 118
Şuḥār J 17 118
Sühbaatar A 5 128
Sühbaatar □[3] C 9 128
Suhindol D 8 104
Suhiniči B 9 110
Suhl B 7 100
Suhobezvodnoe H 16 108
Suhoj Log H 25 108
Suhona ≃ G 15 108
Suhoverkovo H 11 108
Suhr E 5 100
Şuhut C 9 106
Šuiá-Miçu ≃ F 8 190
Suichuan E 12 130
Suide H 8 128
Suifenhe D 18 128
Suihua C 16 128
Suileng C 16 128
Suining, China C 7 130
Suining, China B 13 130
Suiping B 12 130
Suir ≃ D 4 75
Suisun City B 1 182
Suixi B 13 130
Suiyang, China E 8 130
Suiyang, China D 18 128
Suizhong F 13 128
Šuja H 14 108
Šuja ≃ E 10 108
Sujiatun F 14 128
Šujskoe G 14 108
Sukabumi k 18 135b
Sukagawa F 8 126
Sukanegara k 18 135b
Sukhothai F 4 132
Sukkertoppen (Maniitsoq) C 22 150
Sukkozero E 9 108
Sukkur D 1 122
Sukses G 2 204
Sukumo H 4 126
Sula ≃ C 18 108
Sula, Kepulauan II F 9 134
Sulaimaniya see As-Sulaymānīyah E 11 118
Sulaimān Range ⋏ C 2 122
Sulanheer E 7 128
Sulawesi (Celebes) I F 8 134
Sulaymān, Birak (Solomon's Pools) ⊥ F 4 120
Sulcis ◆[1] F 2 90
Sulechów B 8 96
Suleja I 23 108
Sulima D 2 200
Sulingen D 5 98
Sulitjelma ∧ C 8 64
Sulkava B 14 66
Sullana D 2 190
Sullivan, Il., U.S. C 4 170
Sullivan, In., U.S. C 5 170
Sullivan □[6], N.H., U.S. C 6 164
Sullivan □[6], N.Y., U.S. E 4 164
Sullivan □[6], Pa., U.S. E 2 164
Sulmona B 3 94
Sulphur, Yk., Can. E 25 154
Sulphur, La., U.S. G 2 170
Sulphur ≃ F 2 170
Sulphur Springs D 6 172
Sulphur Springs Draw ≃ D 2 172
Sultan Alanto, Lake ⊜ D 8 134
Sultandağı C 9 106
Sultanhisar D 8 106
Sultānpur D 4 122
Sulu Archipelago II D 8 134
Sulunṭah C 9 198
Suluova B 6 118
Sulu Sea ⫪[2] D 8 134
Sulz am Neckar D 5 100
Sulzbach-Rosenberg C 8 100
Sulzbach Saar C 4 100
Sulzberger Bay ⊂ D 29 208
Šumadija ◆[1] C 6 104
Sūmār F 11 118
Sumatera (Sumatra) I F 4 134
Sumatera Barat □[3] N 4 132
Sumatera Utara □[3] N 4 132
Sumatra see Sumatera I F 4 134
Sumba I H 7 134
Sumba, Selat ʉ A 5 140
Sumbar ≃ C 16 118
Sumbawa I G 7 134
Sumbawa Besar G 7 134
Sumbawanga D 5 204
Sumbe E 1 204
Sumbu National Park ♦ D 5 204
Sumburgh h 9 74a
Sumbuya D 2 200
Sumedang k 18 135b
Šumen D 9 104
Sumenep k 21 135b
Šumerlja I 17 108
Šumiha I 25 108
Sumiswald C 5 82
Šumjači J 10 108
Sumkino G 27 108
Summerdown A 3 206
Summerland G 11 156
Summerside E 11 160
Summerton C 4 168
Summerville C 4 168
Summit, Ak., U.S. E 20 154
Summit, S.D., U.S. C 6 174
Sumner D 2 166
Sumner Lake State Park ♦ C 1 172
Sumner Strait ʉ H 28 154
Sumoto G 5 126
Šumperk D 9 96
Sumqayıt I 16 110
Šumšu, ostrov I B 15 124
Sumter C 4 168
Sumy D 9 110
Sumy □[6] D 9 110
Sumzom D 3 130
Suna H 19 108
Sunagawa C 8 126
Sunburst A 7 178
Sunbury, Austl. F 5 144
Sunbury, N.C., U.S. A 6 168
Sunbury, Pa., U.S. F 2 164
Sunchales B 7 195
Sunchild Indian Reserve ◆[4] E 14 156
Sunch'ŏn G 1 126
Sunch'ŏn-ŭp G 15 128
Sun City, Az., U.S. F 2 176
Sun City, Ca., U.S. G 6 182
Sundance C 2 174
Sundarbans ◆[1] E 5 122
Sunda Shelf ✢[4] F 9 58
Sunda Strait ʉ G 5 134
Sundays ≃ I 3 204
Sundbyberg C 8 66
Sunderland C 5 72
Sunderland □[6] C 5 72
Sundern E 5 98
Sundgau ◆[1] C 5 82
Sundown I 1 142
Sundown National Park ♦ B 8 144
Sundsvall A 8 66
Sunflower F 3 170
Sunflower, Mount ∧ F 4 174
Sungaibuntu k 18 135b
Sungai Kolok L 5 132
Sungaipenuh F 4 134
Sungai Petani L 5 132
Sunjikāy E 2 202
Sunndalsøra E 4 64
Sunnersta C 8 66
Sunnyvale C 1 182
Sun Prairie D 4 166
Sunrise F 4 168
Sunrise Manor D 1 176
Sunset D 5 172
Sunset Country ◆[1] E 3 144
Sunset Crater National Monument ♦ E 3 176
Sunset Peak ∧ I 18 131a
Sunshine F 5 144
Sunshine Island I I 19 131a
Suntar-Hajata, hrebet ⋏ C 17 114
Suntrana E 20 154
Sun Valley D 6 178
Sunwu B 16 128
Sunyani D 4 200
Suojarvi E 9 108
Suomenlahti see Finland, Gulf of ⊂ B 13 66
Suō-nada ⫪[2] H 3 126
Suonenjoki E 13 64
Suontee ⊜ B 13 66
Superga, Basilica di ◗[1] D 3 92
Superior, Mt., U.S. B 6 178
Superior, Wi., U.S. B 2 166
Superior, Laguna ⊂ I 12 184
Superior, Lake ⊜ B 5 166
Suphan Buri G 4 132
Suphan Buri ≃ G 5 132
Supra F 26 108
Supung Reservoir ⊜[1] F 15 128
Sūq ash-Shuyūkh G 12 118
Şuq'at al-Jamal E 2 202
Suqian A 14 130
Suquṭrā (Socotra) I H 7 116
Şūr (Tyre), Leb. C 4 120
Şūr, Oman F 8 116
Sur, Cabo › m 16 193a
Sura J 16 108
Sura ≃ H 17 108
Surabaya k 21 135b
S'urachi, Nuraghe ⊥ k 9 94a
Surahammar C 7 66
Surakarta k 20 135b
Šurany B 10 102
Sūrat E 2 122
Sūratgarh D 2 122
Surat Thani J 4 132
Suraž, Bela. I 9 108
Suraž, Russia J 10 108
Šurči B 1 122
Surdulica D 7 104
Surfers Paradise B 9 144
Surgut F 30 108
Surhandarja □[6] B 1 122
Súria G 5 80
Suriāpet F 3 122
Surigao D 9 134
Surin G 6 132
Surinam □[1] D 9 188
Suring C 4 166
Sūrmaq G 15 118
Surovikino E 13 110
Surprise, Lac ⊜ D 6 160
Surrey A 4 174
Surrey □[6] F 6 72
Sursee C 6 82
Sursk C 14 110
Surt C 8 198
Surte D 6 66
Surtsey I n 20 64a
Sürüç D 8 118
Suruga-wan ⊂ G 7 126
Susa D 3 92
Sūsah C 9 198
Susaki H 4 126
Sūsangerd G 12 118
Susanino C 15 66
Susanville B 3 180
Suşehri B 7 118
Šušenskoe B 2 124
Susitna F 19 154
Susitna ≃ E 21 154
Suslonger H 17 108
Susong C 13 130
Suspiro del Moro, Puerto ✕ G 7 86
Susquehanna E 3 164
Susquehanna □[6] E 3 164
Susquehanna ≃ G 2 164
Susquehanna, West Branch ≃ C 5 162
Süssen D 6 100
Sussex, N.B., Can. F 11 160
Sussex, Va., U.S. E 5 162
Sussex □[6], De., U.S. H 3 164
Sussex □[6], N.J., U.S. E 4 164
Susuman C 17 114
Susurluk C 8 106
Susz B 10 96
Sutherland E 4 174
Sutherland Falls ⌞ F 1 146
Sutherlin D 2 178
Sutjeska Nacionalni Park ♦ D 5 104
Sutlej (Satluj) ≃ C 4 122
Sutter □[6] A 2 182
Sutter Buttes ∧ A 2 182
Sutter Creek B 3 182
Sutton E 6 174
Sutton □[6] F 6 72
Sutton Coldfield E 5 72
Sutton in Ashfield D 5 72
Suttor ≃ F 8 142
Süüj C 5 128
Suure-Jaani C 12 66
Suur Munamägi ∧[2] D 13 66
Suva n 14 147c
Suvorov B 10 110
Suvorove C 10 104
Suwałki A 12 96
Suwannee ≃ E 3 168
Suwanose-jima I J 2 126
Suwarrow I[1] E 11 136
Suwŏn H 16 128
Suzdal' H 14 108
Suzëmka C 9 110
Suzhi E 9 128
Suzhou, China B 13 130
Suzhou, China C 15 130
Suzu-misaki › F 6 126
Suzzara E 6 92
Svalbard II B 4 114
Svalyava A 7 104
Svaneke f 8 68a
Svanskog C 6 66
Svärdsjö B 7 66
Svartenhuk ›[1] B 21 150
Svatove E 11 110
Svay Riĕng I 7 132
Svėdasai E 12 66
Svegssjön ⊜ A 6 66
Sveindal C 3 66
Svelgen B 2 66
Švenčionėliai E 13 66
Švenčionys E 13 66
Svendborg C 3 68
Svenljunga A 5 68
Sverdlovskaja oblast' □[6] G 25 108
Švermov B 11 100
Sveti Arhandjel Mihajlo ◗[1] D 6 104
Svetlahorsk C 6 110
Svetlogorsk E 9 66
Svetlograd G 13 110
Svetlyj, Russia D 14 114
Svetlyj, Russia D 22 110
Svetlyj, Russia B 1 110
Svetogorsk F 8 108
Svidník D 11 96
Svilengrad E 9 104
Svinesund C 5 66
Svir E 13 66
Svir' ≃ F 11 108
Svislač B 12 96
Svištov D 8 104
Svitávka A 8 102
Svitavy D 9 96
Svitlovods'k E 8 110
Svjatoj Nos, mys › B 13 108
Svjatoslavka D 13 110
Svobodnyj B 9 124
Svolvær B 7 64
Swabia see Schwaben □[9] A 2 90
Swadlincote E 5 72
Swainsboro C 3 168
Swains Island I[1] E 10 136
Swakop ≃ B 1 206
Swakopmund B 1 206
Swanage G 5 72
Swanee see Suwannee ≃ E 3 168
Swan Hill E 4 144
Swan Islands II D 4 186
Swan Lake G 9 158
Swan Lake ⊜ E 8 158
Swanquarter B 6 168
Swan Range ⋏ B 7 178
Swan River E 8 158
Swansea, Austl. D 8 144
Swansea, Wales, U.K. F 2 72
Swansea, S.C., U.S. C 4 168
Swansea □[6] F 2 72
Swanton B 5 164
Swartberg F 8 206
Swart-Kei ≃ G 7 206
Swarzędz B 9 96
Swāt ≃ B 2 122
Swa-Tenda D 2 204
Swaziland □[1] K 11 196
Sweden □[1] C 10 62
Swedru D 4 200
Sweetgrass A 7 178
Sweet Grass Indian Reserve ◆[4] E 17 156
Sweet Home C 2 178
Sweetwater D 3 172
Swellendam H 4 206
Świdnica C 9 96
Świdnik C 12 96
Świdwin B 8 96
Świebodzice C 9 96
Świebodzin B 8 96
Świecie B 10 96
Świętokrzyskie □[3] C 11 96
Świętokrzyski Park Narodowy ♦ C 11 96
Swift Current F 18 156
Swifton E 3 170
Swindle Island I E 7 156
Swindon F 5 72
Swinford C 2 75
Świnoujście B 7 96
Swinton D 5 72
Switzerland □[1] F 9 62
Sycamore C 2 162
Syčova H 28 108
Syčovka I 10 108
Sydenham B 2 164
Sydney, Austl. D 8 144
Sydney, N.S., Can. E 13 160
Sydney Lake ⊜ F 11 158
Sydney Mines E 13 160
Syeverodonets'k E 11 110
Syke D 5 98
Sykiá B 5 106
Sykkylven E 3 64
Syktyvkar F 19 108
Sylhet D 6 122
Sylt I B 5 98
Sylvan Grove F 5 174
Sylvania C 2 162
Sylvan Lake E 14 156
Sylvester D 3 168
Šymkent see Shymkent A 1 122
Synevir A 7 104
Syowa ◗[3] C 13 208
Syracuse, In., U.S. B 6 170
Syracuse, Ne., U.S E 6 174
Syracuse, N.Y., U.S. C 2 164
Syrdarja A 1 122
Syrdarja □[6] A 1 122
Syr Darya ≃ B 10 116
Syria □[1] F 5 112
Syriam F 3 132
Syrian Desert ◆[2] F 8 118
Sysert' H 24 108
Sysmä B 12 66
Sysola ≃ F 19 108
Syzran' C 15 110
Szabolcs-Szatmár-Bereg □[3] B 7 104
Szamos (Someş) ≃ B 7 104
Szamotuły B 9 96
Szarvas B 6 104
Szczecin B 8 96
Szczecinek B 9 96
Szczekociny C 10 96
Szczytno B 11 96
Szeged B 5 104
Székesfehérvár C 10 102
Szekszárd D 10 102
Szentendre C 10 102
Szentes B 6 104
Szentgotthárd D 8 102
Szigetszentmiklós C 10 102
Szlichtyngowa C 8 96
Szolnok B 6 104
Szombathely (Steinamanger) C 8 102
Szprotawa C 8 96
Sztum B 10 96
Szydłowiec C 11 96

T

Taalintehdas B 11 66
Taatsïn ≃ D 3 128
Ţābah I 10 118
Tabarka G 2 90
Ţabas F 17 118
Tabasco □[3] H 13 184
Taber G 15 156
Taberg D 6 66
Tabiteuea I[1] D 9 136
Tabla C 5 200
Tablas de Daimiel, Parque Nacional de las ♦ E 7 86
Tablas Island I C 8 134
Table Bay ⊂ G 3 206
Table Mountain ∧ H 3 206
Table Rock Lake ⊜[1] D 2 170
Tabligbo D 5 200
Taboco ≃ C 3 194
Tábor C 11 100
Tabora C 5 204
Tabora □[3] D 5 204
Tabor City B 5 168
Tabou E 3 200
Tabrīz C 12 118
Tabuaço C 3 86
Tabuaeran I[1] C 12 136
Tabūk H 7 118
Täby C 9 66
Tacámbaro de Codallos H 9 184
Tacaná, Volcán ∧[1] J 13 184
Taché, Lac ⊜ D 34 154
Táchira □[3] G 6 186
Tachov C 9 100
Tacloban C 8 134
Tacna G 4 190
Tacoma B 2 178
Taconic Range ⋏ D 5 164
Taconic State Park ♦ D 5 164
Tacuarembó B 9 195
Tademaït, Plateau du ⋏[1] D 5 198
Tadjemout D 5 198
Tadjoura E 5 202
Tadjoura, Golfe de ⊂ E 5 202
Tadoule Lake ⊜ B 9 158
Tādpatri G 3 122
T'aean H 15 128
T'aebaek-sanmaek ⋏ H 17 128
Taech'ŏn H 16 128
Taedong-gang ≃ G 16 128
Taegu I 17 128
Taejŏn H 16 128
Taeng ≃ E 4 132
Taer A 4 130
Tafahi I E 10 136
Tafalla B 3 88
Tafassâsset, Oued ≃ E 6 198
Tafiré D 3 200
Taft, Iran G 16 118
Taft, Ca., U.S. E 4 182
Taganrog F 11 110
Taganrog, Gulf of ⊂ F 10 110
Tagant □[3] F 2 198
Tagânt ◆[1] F 2 198
Tagbilaran D 8 134
Taggia F 3 92
Taghit C 4 198
Tagish Lake ⊜ A 4 156
Tagliacozzo G 9 92
Taglio di Po E 8 92
Tagonos, poluostrov ›[1] C 19 114
Tagtabazar C 9 116
Taguatinga F 9 190
Taguke C 4 122
Tagula Island I B 11 138
Tagus (Tajo) (Tejo) ≃ C 1 84
Tah, Sebkha ⊜ D 2 198
Tahala C 4 198
Tahan, Gunong ∧ L 6 132
Tahanaout C 3 198
Tahat ∧ E 6 198
Tahiti I E 13 136
Tahoe, Lake ⊜ A 3 182
Tahoe City A 3 182
Tahoua C 5 200
Tahoua □[3] B 5 200
Tahquamenon Falls State Park ♦ B 6 166
Tahta I 4 118
Tahulandang, Pulau I E 9 134
Taï, Parc National de ♦ D 3 200
Tai'an H 11 128
Taibai Shan ∧ A 9 130
Taibus Qi F 10 128
T'aichung F 15 130
Taif see Aṭ-Ṭā'if C 5 202
Taigu H 9 128
Taihang Shan ⋏ H 9 128
Taihape C 5 146
Taihe, China E 12 130
Taihe, China B 12 130
Tai Ho I 18 131a
Taihu C 13 130
Tai Hu ⊜ C 15 130
Taikang A 12 130
Tailai C 14 128
Tai Lam Chung k 19 131a
Tailem Bend E 2 144
Tai Ling I 18 131a
T'ainan G 15 130
Taínaro, Ákra › D 5 106
Taining E 13 130
Taiobeiras A 9 194
T'aipei F 15 130
T'aipeihsien F 15 130
Taiping, China G 8 130
Taiping, Malay. L 5 132
Taisha G 4 126
Taishan G 11 130
Tai Shui Hang I 19 131a
Taishun E 14 130
Taitao, Península de ›[1] I 4 192
T'aitung G 15 130
Taivalkoski D 14 64
Taiwan □[1] G 14 112
T'aiwan (Formosa) I G 15 130
Taiwan Strait ʉ F 14 130
Taixing B 15 130
Taiyuan H 9 128
Taizhao D 6 122
Taizhou B 14 130
Taizi ≃ F 14 128
Ta'izz E 5 202
Tajbola B 10 108
Tajgonos, mys › C 18 114
Tajikistan □[1] F 9 112
Tāj Mahal ⊥ D 3 122
Tajmyr, ozero ⊜ B 13 114
Tajo see Tagus ≃ C 1 84
Tajšet D 12 114
Tajumulco, Volcán ∧[1] J 14 184
Tajuña ≃ D 1 88
Tak F 4 132
Takāb D 12 118
Takachu B 4 206
Takahagi F 8 126
Takahe, Mount ∧ D 34 208
Takakkaw Falls ⌞ F 13 156
Takalaou C 8 200
Takalar G 7 134
Takamatsu G 5 126
Takaoka F 6 126
Takasaki F 7 126
Takatsuki G 5 126
Takaungu H 4 202
Ta-kaw D 4 132
Takayama F 6 126
Takengon L 3 132
Tākestān D 13 118
Taketa H 3 126
Takêv I 7 132
Takhli G 5 132
Takht-e Jamshīd (Persepolis) ⊥ G 15 118
Takijuq Lake ⊜ C 10 150
Takikawa C 8 126
Takla Lake ⊜ D 9 156
Taklimakan Desert ◆[2] B 4 122
Takoradi E 4 200
Takotna E 16 154
Taku ≃ B 5 156
Taku Glacier ⊓ G 27 154
Takum D 6 200
Takutea I E 12 136
Talaimannar H 3 122
Talak ◆[1] B 6 200
Talant E 11 78
Talara D 2 190
Talas A 2 122
Talas □[3] A 2 122
Talas ≃ A 2 122
Talata Mafara C 6 200
Talaud, Kepulauan II E 9 134
Talavera de la Reina E 6 86
Talawdī E 3 202
Talbot □[6] H 2 164
Talca D 2 195
Talcahuano E 1 195
Talco F 1 170
Talcy, Château de ⊥ E 8 78
Taldom H 12 108
Taldyqorghan B 12 116
Talent D 2 178
Talghar A 3 122
Talia H 2 172
Taliabu, Pulau I F 8 134
Talien see Dalian G 13 128
Talihina E 1 170
Talish Mountains ⋏ D 13 118
Taliwang A 4 140
Talkheh ≃ C 12 118
Talla H 4 118
Talladega F 5 170
Tall 'Afar D 10 118
Tallaght C 5 75
Tallahassee D 2 168
Tallahatchie ≃ F 3 170
Tall al-Muqayyar (Ur) ⊥ G 11 118
Tallangatta F 6 144
Tallapoosa ≃ F 6 170
Tallard F 3 82
Tall as-Sulṭān ⊥ F 4 120
Tall-e Khosrow-ye Soflá G 14 118
Tallinn C 12 66
Tall Kalakh E 6 118
Tall Kūjik D 9 118
Tallulah F 3 170
Talmaz B 10 104
Talnah C 11 114
Talo ∧ E 4 202
Taloga B 4 172
Talok E 7 134
Tāloqān B 1 122
Talovaja D 12 110
Talsi D 11 66
Taltal E 5 192
Taltson ≃ D 10 150
Talu N 4 132
Talurqjuak (Spence Bay) C 14 150
Talwood B 7 144
Tama E 2 166
Tamale D 4 200
Tamalpais, Mount ∧ C 1 182
Tamana H 3 126
Tamanar C 3 198
Tamani C 3 200
Taman Negara ♦ L 6 132
Tamano G 4 126
Tamar ≃ i 12 145a
Tamarite de Litera C 5 88
Tamaulipas □[3] E 10 184
Tamazula E 6 184
Tamazunchale G 10 184
Tambacounda C 2 200
Tambakboyo k 20 135b

⌞ Waterfall ʉ Strait ⊂ Bay, Gulf ⊜ Lake ≡ Swamp ⊓ Ice Feature ⫪ Other Hydrographic Feature ✢ Submarine Feature □ Political Unit ◗ Cultural Institution ⊥ Historical Site ♦ Recreational Site ⊠ Airport ▪ Military Installation ◆ Miscellaneous

281

Name	Ref.	Page
Tāmbaram	G 4	122
Tambelan, Kepulauan II	N 8	132
Tambellup	N 4	140
Tambi-Kaboré, Parc National ◆	C 4	200
Tambo ⌒	G 4	190
Tambora, Gunung ∧	G 7	134
Tambov	C 12	110
Tambovka	F 15	110
Tambovskaja oblast' □⁶	C 13	110
Tambura	F 2	202
Tame	B 4	190
Tameapa ⌒	E 6	184
Tāmega ⌒	C 2	86
Tamel Aike	I 5	192
Tamenghest	E 6	198
Tamenghest, Oued ⌒	E 5	198
Tameside □⁶	D 4	72
Tamga	E 1	88
Tamiahua, Laguna de ⌒	G 11	184
Tamil Nādu □³	G 3	122
Tamiš (Timiş) ⌒	C 6	104
Tamis Ky	G 9	132
Tamms	A 3	170
Tampa	E 3	168
Tampa Bay c	F 3	168
Tampaon ⌒	G 10	184
Tampere	B 11	66
Tampico, Mex.	F 11	184
Tampico, Il., U.S.	B 4	170
Tampin	M 6	132
Tamri	C 2	198
Tamsalu	C 13	66
Tamu	B 2	132
Tamworth, Austl.	G 8	144
Tamworth, Eng., U.K.	E 5	72
Tana (Teno) ⌒, Eur.	B 13	64
Tana ⌒, Kenya	H 5	202
Tanabe	H 5	126
Tanafjorden ⌒	A 14	64
Tanaga Volcano ∧¹	k 42	155a
T'ana Hāyk' ⌒	H 1	202
Tanahbala, Pulau I	F 3	134
Tanahjampea, Pulau I	G 8	134
Tanahmerah, Indon.	G 12	134
Tanah Merah, Malay.	L 5	132
Tanami Desert ⌒²	G 10	140
Tan An, Viet.	I 8	132
Tan An, Viet.	J 7	132
Tanana	E 24	154
Tananarive see Antananarivo	k 9	205a
Tanbu	D 12	130
Tanch'ŏn-ŭp	F 17	128
Tanda, I.C.	D 4	200
Tānda, India	D 9	134
Tandag	D 5	204
Tandala	E 8	195
Tandil	D 8	200
Tandjilé □⁵	D 1	122
Tando Ādam	F 7	200
Tandou Bougou	D 4	144
Tandou Lake ⌒	C 6	146
Taneatua	A 5	122
Tanega-shima I	I 3	126
Tanezrouft ⌒²	E 4	198
Tanezzuft, Wādī ⌒	D 7	198
Tang	B 13	130
Tanga	C 6	204
Tanga □³	D 6	204
Tangail	E 5	122
Tanganyika, Lake ⌒	D 5	204
Tanger (Tangier)	B 3	198
Tanger □³	E 3	84
Tangerang	k 18	135b
Tangerhütte	D 8	98
Tangermünde	D 8	98
Tangfang	E 5	130
Tanggu	G 11	128
Tanggula Shan ⌒	C 6	122
Tanghe	B 11	130
Tangier see Tanger, Mor.	B 3	198
Tangier, Va., U.S.	E 6	162
Tangjiagou	C 13	130
Tangra Yumco ⌒	C 5	122
Tangshan	G 11	128
Tangulbei	G 4	202
Tangwang ⌒	C 17	128
Tangyan	I 10	128
Tangyuan	C 17	128
Tanimbar, Kepulauan II	G 10	134
Tanintharyi □³	H 4	132
Tanjungbalai	M 4	132
Tanjungbatu	N 6	132
Tanjungkarang-Telukbetung see Bandar Lampung	I 18	110
Tanjungpandan	F 5	134
Tanjungpinang	N 7	132
Tanjungredep	E 7	134
Tanjungselor	E 7	134
Tänk	C 2	122
Tan Kena	D 6	198
Tankwa Karoo National Park ◆	G 3	206
Tanna I	E 8	136
Tannenberg see Stębark	B 11	96
Tannu-Ola, hrebet ⌒	B 2	124
Tannūrah, Ra's ⌒	B 7	202
Tano ⌒	D 4	200
Tanout	B 6	200
Tanshui	F 15	130
Tanta	G 4	118
Tan-Tan	D 2	198
Tanumshede	C 5	66
Tanzania □¹	I 11	196
Tao ⌒	I 4	134
Tao'er ⌒	C 13	128
Taole	G 6	128
Taonan	D 14	128
Taormina	G 5	94
Taos	D 6	176
Taoudenni	C 3	198
Taounate	C 4	198
Taourirt	C 4	198
Taoussa	B 4	200
Taoyüan	F 15	130
Tapa	C 13	66
Tapachula	J 13	184
Tapah	L 5	132
Tapajós ⌒	D 7	190
Tapauá ⌒	E 5	190
Tapawera	B 12	195
Taphan Hin	F 5	132
Tāpi ⌒, India	E 3	122
Ta Pi ⌒, Thai.	I 5	132
Taplan National Park ◆	G 6	132
Tappahannock	E 5	162
Tapuruquara	D 6	190
Taquari ⌒	A 12	195
Taquari, Pantanal do ⌒	C 2	194
Taquari Novo ⌒	B 2	190
Taquaritinga	D 6	194
Tara	H 31	108

Name	Ref.	Page
Tara ⌒, Eur.	D 5	104
Tara ⌒, Russia	H 31	108
Taraba ⌒	D 7	200
Tarabine, Oued ti-n- ⌒	E 6	198
Tarābulus, Leb.	E 6	118
Tarābulus (Tripoli), Libya	C 7	198
Taraclia, Mol.	C 10	104
Taraclia, Mol.	B 10	104
Taradale	C 6	146
Tarago	E 7	144
Tarakan	E 7	134
Tarana	D 3	132
Tara Nacionalni Park ◆	D 5	104
Taranaki □³	C 5	146
Taranaki, Mount see Egmont, Mount ∧¹	C 4	146
Tarancón	E 1	88
Tarangire National Park ◆	C 5	204
Taranto	D 7	94
Taranto, Golfo di c	E 7	94
Tarapoto	E 3	190
Taraquá	E 2	82
Tarare	G 2	82
Tarascon	G 2	82
Tarasovo	C 17	108
Tarat	D 6	198
Tarata	G 5	190
Tarauacá	E 4	190
Tarauacá ⌒	E 4	190
Tarawa I¹	C 9	136
Tarawera, Mount ∧¹	C 6	146
Tarazona	C 3	88
Tarazona de la Mancha	E 3	88
Tarba	G 5	202
Tarbagataj, hrebet ⌒	A 13	116
Tarbela Reservoir ⌒¹	C 2	122
Tarbes	E 4	80
Tarboro	B 6	168
Tarcento	D 7	94
Tarcoola	K 2	142
Tardajos	B 7	86
Tardoki-Jani, gora ∧	C 11	124
Taree	C 9	144
Tarentum	E 9	166
Targhee Pass ⌒	C 8	178
Targon	D 3	80
Târgoviște, Blg.	D 9	104
Târgoviște, Rom.	C 8	104
Târgu Cărbunești	C 7	104
Târgu Jiu	C 7	104
Târgu Lăpuș	B 8	104
Târgu Mureș	B 9	104
Târgu-Neamț	B 9	104
Târgu Ocna	B 9	104
Târgușor	C 10	104
Tarhūnah	C 7	198
Tarifa	H 5	86
Tarija	H 9	190
Tariku ⌒	F 11	134
Tarim ⌒	A 5	122
Tarim Pendi ⌒¹	F 11	134
Tarītatu ⌒	F 11	134
Tarka	C 6	198
Tarkhankut, mys ⌒	G 7	110
Tarko-Sale	D 32	108
Tarkwa	D 4	200
Tarlac	B 8	134
Tarlo River National Park ◆	E 7	144
Tarm	C 1	68
Tarma	F 3	190
Tarn □³	B 4	80
Tarn ⌒	D 5	80
Tärnaby	D 7	64
Târnby	C 5	68
Tarn-et-Garonne □³	D 5	80
Tárnova	A 9	104
Tarnów	C 11	96
Tarnowskie Góry	C 10	96
Taro ⌒	H 9	142
Taroom	D 3	198
Taroudannt	E 3	168
Tarpon Springs	G 7	92
Tarquinia	E 2	142
Tarrabool, Lake ⌒	C 6	88
Tarragona	D 5	190
Tarragona □⁶	B 8	104
Tárrega	E 5	164
Tarrytown	D 6	118
Tarsus	I 18	110
Tarta	D 7	192
Tartagal	C 13	66
Tartu	B 7	106
Tartūs	B 10	104
Tarutao National Park ◆	K 4	132
Tarutung	M 4	132
Tarutyne	B 10	104
Tarvisio	C 9	92
Tašauz see Dashhowuz	D 19	62
Taseevo	D 12	114
Taşhk, Daryācheh-ye ⌒	H 15	118
Tashkent (Toshkent)	A 1	122
Tashkent □⁶	A 1	122
Tasikmalaya	k 18	135b
Tåsjö	D 7	64
Taškent see Tashkent □⁶	A 1	122
Taš-Kumyr	A 2	122
Tasman □³	B 11	195
Tasman Basin ⌒¹	J 12	58
Tasman Bay c	D 4	146
Tasman Glacier ⌒	E 3	146
Tasmania □³	j 12	145a
Tasmania I	H 8	142
Tasman Sea ⌒²	E 10	110
Tasoba	E 2	82
Tassin-la-Demi-Lune	G 11	114
Taštagol	D 11	114
Tata, Hung.	C 10	102
Tata, Mor.	D 3	198
Tatabánya	C 10	102
Tataouine	C 6	198
Tatarbunary	C 10	104
Tatarija □³	I 9	108
Tatarinka	H 10	108
Tatarlar	B 7	106
Tatarsk	D 10	114
Tatarskij proliv ⌒	G 12	124
Tateyama	G 7	126
Tathlina Lake ⌒	A 13	156
Tatiščevo	D 14	110
Tatitlek	F 21	154
Tatlatui Provincial Park ◆	E 7	144
Tatlayoko Lake ⌒	F 9	156
Tatnam, Cape ⌒	C 13	158
Tatranský Narodny Park ◆	D 10	96
Tatrzański Park Narodowy ◆	D 11	96
Tatsuno	G 7	126

Name	Ref.	Page
Tatta	E 1	184
Tätti	A 2	122
Tatui	E 7	194
Tatvan	C 10	118
Tau	C 2	66
Taubaté	E 8	194
Tauberbischofsheim	E 9	98
Taucha	D 8	100
Taufkirchen	D 17	114
Taujskaja guba c	E 7	144
Taum Sauk Mountain ∧	D 3	170
Taunay	D 2	132
Taungdwingyi	D 3	132
Taunggyi	F 3	72
Taunton, Eng., U.K.	B 7	164
Taunton, Ma., U.S.	B 5	100
Taunus ⌒¹	B 4	100
Taunusstein	C 6	146
Taupo	C 5	146
Taupo, Lake ⌒	E 11	66
Tauragė	B 6	146
Tauranga	F 5	94
Taurianova	E 8	94
Taurisano	A 4	146
Tauroa Point ⌒	D 5	118
Taurus Mountains ⌒	G 17	110
Taūshyq	C 3	88
Tauste	D 8	106
Tavares	D 26	108
Tavda	D 9	114
Tavda ⌒		
Taverne see Dawei	G 3	132
Tavşanlı	C 8	106
Tawa	C 5	146
Tawakoni, Lake ⌒¹	D 5	172
Tawas City	A 2	162
Tawau	E 7	134
Tawitawi Island I	D 8	134
Tawkar	D 4	202
Tāwūq	E 11	118
Taxco de Alarcón	H 10	184
Taxi	B 16	128
Tay ⌒, Yk., Can.	E 27	154
Tay ⌒, Scot., U.K.	D 5	74
Tay, Lake ⌒	M 6	140
Taylor, B.C., Can.	C 11	156
Taylor, Tx., U.S.	E 5	172
Taylor, Mount ∧	E 5	176
Taylors	B 3	168
Taylorsville	C 5	170
Taylorville	C 4	170
Taymouth	A 5	122
Taymyr, ozero ⌒ see Tajmyr, ozero ⌒	B 13	114
Taymyr Peninsula ⌒¹	B 13	114
Tay Ninh	I 8	132
Taytay	C 7	134
Tayu	k 20	135b
Taz ⌒	C 10	114
Taza	C 4	198
Taza □³	E 3	84
Tazewell	A 16	156
Tazin ⌒	C 12	156
Tazin Lake ⌒	B 17	156
Tāzirbū	D 9	198
Tazlina Lake ⌒	F 21	154
Tazovskaja guba c	B 31	108
Tazovski	C 33	108
Tazovski poluostrov ⌒¹	B 31	108
Tbessa	B 6	198
Tbilisi	I 14	110
Tchaourou	F 4	122
Tchentlo Lake ⌒	D 9	156
Tchetti	D 5	200
Tchibanga	F 7	200
Tchitondi	F 7	200
Tchula	F 3	170
Tczew	A 10	96
Téa ⌒	D 5	190
Teaca	B 8	104
Teague	E 5	172
Te Anau, Lake ⌒	F 1	146
Te Araroa	B 7	146
Te Aroha	B 5	146
Teatree	C 2	144
Tea Tree Gully	B 2	144
Te Awamutu	B 5	146
Tebakang	N 10	132
Tebicuary ⌒	G 2	194
Tebingtinggi	M 4	132
Tebingtinggi, Pulau I	N 6	132
Tebourba	G 2	90
Téboursouk	G 2	90
Tecalitlán	H 8	184
Tecate	H 7	182
Techiman	D 4	200
Techlé	E 1	198
Tecka	H 3	192
Tecomán	H 8	184
Tecpan de Galeana	I 9	184
Tecuci	C 9	104
Tecumseh	E 6	174
Teec Nos Pos	D 4	176
Tees ⌒	E 4	72
Tefé	B 3	128
Tefé ⌒	C 5	72
Tegal	k 19	135b
Tégama ⌒¹	B 6	200
Tegéa ⌒	D 5	106
Tegelen	E 8	69
Tegernsee	E 8	100
Tegina	D 3	198
Tegucigalpa	E 3	186
Tehachapi Mountains ⌒	H 5	182
Tehachapi Pass ⌒	E 5	182
Tehama	A 1	202
Tehamiyam	D 4	202
Teheran see Tehrān	E 14	118
Tehrān	E 14	118
Tehrān □³	D 14	118
Tehuantepec, Golfo de ⌒	H 11	184
Tehuantepec, Istmo de (Tehuantepec, Isthmus of) ⌒³	I 12	184
Teide, Mount (Teide, Pico de) ∧	i 14	85b
Teide, Parque Nacional del ◆	i 13	85b
Tejakula	k 22	135b
Tejen	C 9	116

Name	Ref.	Page
Tejkovo	H 14	108
Tejo see Tagus ⌒	C 1	84
Tejon Pass ⌒	F 5	182
Te Kaha	B 6	146
Tekapo, Lake ⌒	E 3	146
Tekax	G 15	184
Teke köli ⌒	J 30	108
Tekeli	B 12	116
Tekezē ⌒	E 4	202
Tekirdağ	B 7	106
Tekirdağ □³	B 7	106
Tekkali	F 4	122
Tekong, Pulau I	i 16	134a
Tekong Kechil, Pulau I	i 16	134a
Te Kuiti	C 5	146
Tel ⌒	F 4	122
Tela	J 16	184
Tel Arshaf ⌒	E 3	120
Tel Ashqelon ⌒	F 2	120
Telavåg	B 2	66
Telavi	H 14	110
Tel Aviv □³	E 3	120
Tel Aviv-Yafo	E 3	120
Telde	i 15	85b
Teleckoje, ozero ⌒	B 1	124
Telefomin	N 12	124
Telegraph Creek	C 6	156
Telêmaco Borba	F 5	194
Telemark □³	C 4	66
Telen ⌒	E 7	134
Teleneşti	B 10	104
Teleorman □³	C 8	104
Telertheba, Djebel ∧	E 6	198
Telescope Peak ∧	D 6	182
Telford	E 4	72
Telfs	C 3	102
Telgte	C 4	98
Telida	E 18	154
Télimélé	C 3	200
Tel Lakhish ⌒	F 3	120
Tell City	D 5	170
Tellicherry	G 3	122
Tellico Plains	B 2	168
Tel Megiddo (Armageddon) ⌒	D 4	120
Telmen nuur ⌒	A 4	128
Teloloapan	H 10	184
Telšiai	C 4	104
Telti	D 11	66
Teltow	D 10	98
Telukdalem	N 3	132
Teluk Intan	M 5	132
Tema	D 5	200
Temagami, Lake ⌒	E 3	160
Tematangi I¹	F 13	136
Temax	C 2	186
Tembesi ⌒	F 4	134
Tembilahan	O 6	132
Tembisa	C 8	206
Temblador	F 9	186
Temblor Range ⌒	E 4	182
Temecula	G 6	182
Temengor, Tasik ⌒¹	L 5	132
Temerin	C 5	104
Teminabuan	F 10	134
Temirlan	A 1	122
Temirtaū	A 11	116
Tetouan	B 3	198
Tetouan □³	E 3	84
Tetovo	B 3	104
Tettnang	C 1	102
Teulada	F 2	90
Teun, Pulau I	G 9	134
Teutoburger Wald ⌒²	D 5	98
Teuva	E 10	64
Tevere (Tiber) ⌒	D 4	120
Teverya	D 4	120
Te Waewae Bay c	G 1	146
Tewkesbury	E 4	72
Texada Island I	G 9	156
Texarkana, Ar., U.S.	F 1	170
Texarkana, Tx., U.S.	F 1	170
Texas □³	E 8	152
Texas City	A 1	170
Texel I	A 3	69
Texhoma	B 3	172
Texline	B 2	172
Texoma, Lake ⌒¹	A 6	172
Teyateyaneng	E 7	206
Teziutlán	H 11	184
Tezpur	B 2	122
Tezzeron Lake ⌒	D 5	156
Tha ⌒	B 5	132
Tha-anne ⌒	A 11	158
Thabana-Ntlenyana ∧	E 8	206
Thaba Nchu	D 8	206
Thai Binh	D 8	132
Thailand □¹	H 11	112
Thailand, Gulf of c	J 5	132
Thai Nguyen	C 2	132
Thal	C 2	122
Thale	D 9	98
Thalfang	C 3	100
Tha Li	B 5	132
Thallon	B 7	144
Thalwil	D 5	92
Thame	F 6	72
Thames	B 5	146
Thames ⌒	F 7	72
Thāna	E 2	122
Thanbyuzayat	G 3	132
Thanh Hoa	C 7	132
Thann	C 6	82
Thaon-les-Vosges	B 4	82
Tharād	G 2	122
Thar Desert (Great Indian Desert) ⌒²	D 1	122
Thargomindah	I 7	142
Thar Nhom	F 3	202
Tharrawaddy	F 2	132
Tharros ⌒¹	E 6	184
Tharthār, Buḩayrat ath- ⌒¹	E 10	118
Tharthār, Wādī ath- ⌒¹	E 10	118
Tharwa	E 7	144
Thássos I	C 7	106
Thássos I	C 7	106
Tha Tako	G 5	132
Thaton	G 3	132
Thau, Bassin de ⌒	F 7	82
Thaungyin (Moei) ⌒	G 3	132
Thaya (Dyje) ⌒	B 8	102
Thayer	A 7	104
Thayetmyo	F 2	132
Thazi	C 5	132
Thebes see Thíva	D 5	106
Thebes □¹	J 5	118
The Cheviot ∧	E 4	72
The Dalles	C 4	178
Thedford	E 10	190
Teresva ⌒	A 7	104
Terevaka, Mauna ∧	m 16	193a
Tergnier	C 10	78
Terlizzi	C 6	94
Termas del Arapey	B 9	195
Terme	B 7	118

Name	Ref.	Page
Termez (Termiz)	B 1	122
Termini Imerese	F 3	94
Términos, Laguna de c	H 14	184
Termiz see Termez	B 1	122
Termoli	B 4	94
Ternate	E 9	134
Ternej	B 6	126
Terneuzen	C 2	69
Terni	G 8	92
Terni □⁶	G 8	92
Ternitz	C 7	102
Ternivka	A 10	104
Ternopil'	E 4	110
Ternopil' □⁶	E 4	110
Terny	E 8	110
Terpenija, Cape see Terpenija, mys ⌒	C 12	124
Terpenije, mys ⌒	C 12	124
Terra Bella	E 4	182
Terrace	D 7	156
Terrace Bay	G 15	158
Terracina	H 9	92
Terral	D 5	172
Terra Nova Bay c	D 26	208
Terranova di Sicilia see Gela	G 4	94
Terra Nova National Park ◆	D 17	160
Terrassa	C 6	88
Terrebonne Bay c	H 3	170
Terre Haute	C 5	170
Terrenceville	E 16	160
Terry	H 6	158
Terschelling I	A 4	69
Teruel	D 3	88
Teruel □⁶	D 4	88
Tervakoski	B 12	66
Tervola	C 12	64
Teseney	E 4	202
Teshekpuk Lake ⌒	A 17	154
Tes-Hem ⌒	B 2	124
Teshig	A 4	128
Teslić	C 4	104
Teslin	G 28	154
Teslin Lake ⌒	B 5	156
Teton ⌒, Id., U.S.	D 8	178
Teton ⌒, Mt., U.S.	B 8	178
Teton Range ⌒	D 8	178
Tetouan	B 3	198
Tetovo	B 3	104
The Lakes National Park ◆	G 6	144
The Little Minch ⌒	C 2	74
Thelon ⌒	D 12	150
The Lynd	E 7	142
The Machars ⌒¹	C 2	72
The Minch ⌒	C 2	74
Théodat, Lac ⌒	C 5	160
Theodore Roosevelt ⌒	B 6	110
Theodore Roosevelt National Park ◆, N.D., U.S.	B 3	174
Theodore Roosevelt National Park ◆, N.D., U.S.	B 3	174
The Pas	E 8	158
Thepha	K 5	132
Thérèse-De Blainville □⁶	A 5	164
Thermopolis	B 8	178
Thermopylae see Thermopýles ⌒	C 5	106
Thermopýles (Thermopylae) ⌒	C 5	106
The Solent ⌒	G 5	72
Thessalía □⁹	C 5	106
Thessalon	B 7	166
Thessaloníki (Salonica)	B 5	106
Thessaly □⁹	C 5	106
The Steppes ⌒¹	E 19	110
Thetford	E 7	72
Thetford Mines	E 8	160
Theux	D 4	69
The Valley	D 9	186
The Wash c	E 7	72
The Weald ⌒¹	F 7	72
The Wrekin ⌒⁸	E 4	72
Thibaudeau	C 11	158
Thibodaux	H 3	170
Thielsen, Mount ∧	D 2	178
Thiene	D 7	92
Thiers	E 1	82
Thiès	C 1	200
Thiesi	I 4	92
Thika	H 4	202
Thimphu	D 5	122
Thingvallavatn ⌒	m 20	64a
Thingvellir	m 20	64a
Thingvellir National Park ◆	m 20	64a
Thio	D 14	138
Thionville	A 4	82
Third Cataract ⌒	D 3	202
Thíra (Santorini) I	D 6	106
Thistilfjörður c	I 23	64a
Thíva	C 5	106
Thiviers	C 4	80
Thjórsá ⌒	m 21	64a
Thlewiaza ⌒	A 11	158
Thohoyandou	B 9	206
Tholen □⁶	C 3	69
Tholen I	E 8	136
Thomasboro	B 4	170
Thomaston	C 5	164
Thomasville, Al., U.S.	G 5	170
Thomasville, Ga., U.S.	D 2	168
Thompson	D 10	158
Thompson ⌒, B.C., Can.	F 11	156
Thompson ⌒	C 2	170
Thomson	E 3	166
Thomson's Falls see Nyahururu Falls	G 4	202
Thonon-les-Bains	D 4	82
Thonze	F 2	132
Thorhild	D 15	156
Thórlákshöfn	n 20	64a
Thornbury	F 4	72
Thorndale	E 5	172
Thorne	D 6	72
Thornton, Ar., U.S.	F 1	170
Thornton, Co., U.S.	F 2	174
Thoronet, Abbaye du ◆¹	G 4	82
Thorsby	E 14	156
Thorsteinson Lake ⌒	C 10	158
Thouars	E 6	78
Thousand Islands II	B 2	164
Thousand Oaks	F 5	182
Thrakikó Pélagos ⌒²	B 6	106
Three Forks	C 8	178
Three Gorges Dam ◆	C 10	130
Three Kings Islands II	A 4	146
Three Lakes	C 4	162
Three Pagodas Pass ⌒	G 4	132
Three Points, Cape ⌒	E 4	200
Three Rivers	D 4	162
Three Sisters ∧	C 3	178
Three Springs	K 3	140
Thrissur (Trichūr)	G 3	122
Throckmorton	C 4	168
Throssel, Lake ⌒	J 8	140
Thu Dau Mot	I 8	132
Thueyts	F 2	82
Thule	B 13	148
Thun	D 3	92
Thunder Bay	G 14	158
Thunderbolt	C 4	168
Thunder See ◆	D 5	82
Thung Salaeng Luang National Park ◆	F 5	132
Thüringen □³	C 6	96
Thüringer Wald ⌒	B 7	100
Thurmont	B 7	162
Thurrock □⁶	F 7	72
Thurso	B 5	74
Thurston Island I	D 34	208
Thy ⌒¹	B 2	68
Thysville see Mbanza-Ngungu	D 1	204
Tianbao	F 3	130
Tianchang	B 14	130
Tianjin	H 14	128
Tianeti	H 14	110
Tiaret	B 5	198
Tiassalé	E 4	200

Name	Ref.	Page
Tibasti, Sarīr ⌒²	E 8	198
Tibati	D 7	200
Tiber see Tevere ⌒	G 8	92
Tiberias see Teverya	D 4	120
Tibesti ⌒	A 8	200
Tibet see Xizang □³	C 5	122
Tibet, Plateau of ⌒¹	C 5	122
Tibiri	C 5	200
Tibnīn	C 5	120
Tibro	C 7	66
Tiburón, Isla I	C 3	184
Ticino □³	D 6	82
Ticino ⌒	E 6	82
Tickfaw	G 3	170
Ticonderoga	C 5	164
Ticul	G 15	184
Tidaholm	C 6	66
Tidjikdja	F 2	198
Tidore	E 9	134
Tiébissou	D 3	200
Tiel	C 4	69
Tieli	C 17	128
Tieling	E 14	128
Tielt	A 10	78
Tienen	D 3	69
Tien Shan ⌒	B 12	116
Tie Plant	F 4	170
Tierra Blanca	H 11	184
Tierra Blanca Creek ⌒	C 2	172
Tierra de Campos ⌒¹	B 6	86
Tierra del Fuego I	J 6	192
Tietê ⌒	H 9	190
Tif	D 5	198
Tiffin	C 2	162
Tifton	D 3	168
Tighennif	B 10	104
Tighina	B 10	104
Tignère	D 7	200
Tigray □³	E 4	202
Tigre ⌒, Peru	C 3	190
Tigre ⌒, Ven.	F 9	186
Tigris (Dicle) (Dijlah) ⌒	G 12	118
Tiguentourine	D 6	198
Tih, Gebel el ∧¹	H 5	118
Tihert	B 5	198
Tihon	G 17	108
Tihookeanskij	C 4	126
Tihoreck	G 12	110
Tihvin	G 10	108
Tijesno	E 3	104
Tijuana	A 1	184
Tijucas	C 6	194
Tikal ⌒	I 15	184
Tikal, Parque Nacional ◆	I 15	184
Tikitiki	B 7	146
Tiko	E 6	200
Tikopia I	E 8	136
Tikrīt	E 10	118
Tiksa	D 10	108
Tikšeozero, ozero ⌒	C 9	108
Tiksi	B 15	114
Tilburg	C 4	69
Tile	D 4	200
Tilemsi, Vallée du ⌒	F 5	198
Tilff	D 4	69
Tilimsen	C 4	198
Tilimsen □³	E 5	84
Tilin	D 2	132
Tillabéri	C 5	200
Tillamook	C 2	178
Tilley	F 16	156
Tillson	E 4	164
Tillsonburg	C 5	198
Tilrhemt	C 7	164
Tima	I 4	118
Timah, Bukit ∧²	i 14	134a
Timanski krjaž ⌒²	C 8	114
Timaru	H 16	108
Timashevsk	G 11	110
Timbalier Bay c	H 3	170
Timbuktu see Tombouctou	B 4	200
Timgad ⌒¹	B 6	198
Timimoun	D 5	198
Timimoun, Sebkha de ⌒	D 5	198
Timinar	D 3	202
Timi Ouli, Ehi ∧¹	A 8	200
Timiris, Râs ⌒	F 1	198
Timirjazevo	E 10	66
Timiş □⁶	C 6	104
Timiş (Tamiš) ⌒	C 6	104
Timişoara	C 6	104
Timmendorfer Strand	C 7	98
Timmernabben	D 3	66
Timmins	G 15	158
Timms Hill ∧	C 9	162
Timor I	G 9	134
Timor Sea ⌒²	F 12	134
Timošino	F 12	108
Timpanogos Cave National Monument ◆	E 8	178
Timpson	D 15	114
Timptn	E 21	108
Timšer	F 9	114
Tin, Khalig el- c	G 5	118
Tinaca Point ⌒	D 5	132
Ti-n-Amzi ⌒	B 5	200
Tinaquillo	C 3	200
Tindila	C 3	200
Tindivanam	F 5	122
Tindouf	D 3	198
Tinerhir	C 3	198
Tinghert, Hamādat ⌒¹	D 7	198
Tingkawk Sakan	A 3	132
Tingo María	E 3	190
Tingsryd	D 6	66
Tinguiririca, Volcán ∧¹	C 2	194
Tinian I	J 13	124
Tinie I	B 5	186
Tinkisso ⌒	C 3	200
Tínos I	D 6	106
Tinsukia	A 3	132
Tintah	F 7	144
Tintina	G 7	192
Ti-n-Zaouâtene	A 5	200
Tioga	I 3	164
Tioga □⁵, N.Y., U.S.	D 2	164
Tioga □⁵, Pa., U.S.	B 7	164
Tioman, Pulau I	M 7	132
Tione di Trento	C 5	92
Tiou	C 4	200
Tipasa	H 7	88
Tipasa □³	E 4	84
Tipitapa	A 5	186
Tippecanoe ⌒	B 3	170
Tipperary	D 3	75
Tipperary □⁶	D 3	75
Tipton	D 4	164

Tipton — Tye

Name — Map Ref. — Page

Tipton, Mount ∧ E 1 176
Tip Top Mountain ∧ G 16 158
Tīra E 3 120
Tīrân, Madîq ʊ I 6 118
Tirana
 see Tiranë B 3 106
Tiranë (Tirana) B 3 106
Tirano C 6 92
Tiraspol B 10 104
Tirau B 5 146
Tire C 7 106
Tirebolu B 8 118
Tiree I D 2 74
Tires ✦[1] E 2 198
Tirich Mīr ∧ B 2 122
Tiris Zemmour □[3] E 3 198
Tírnavos C 5 106
Tirol □[3] C 3 102
Tirreno, Mare
 see Tyrrhenian Sea ⊤[2] E 3 90
Tirschenreuth C 9 100
Tirso ≃ F 2 90
Tirua F 1 195
Tiruchchirāppalli G 3 122
Tiruliai E 11 66
Tirunelveli H 3 122
Tirupati G 3 122
Tiruppur G 3 122
Tirūr G 3 122
Tiruvannāmalai G 3 122
Tirūvottiyūr G 4 122
Tisdale E 19 156
Tiskilwa B 4 170
Tissa D 7 200
Tīsta ≃ D 5 122
Tisza ≃ B 6 104
Tiszafüred B 6 104
Tiszaújváros B 6 104
Titaf D 4 198
Titel C 6 104
Titicaca, Lake ⊜ G 5 190
Titilāgarh E 4 122
Titisee-Neustadt E 5 100
Titovo Velenje D 7 102
Tittling D 10 100
Titu C 8 104
Titusville, Fl., U.S. E 4 168
Titusville, Pa., U.S. C 4 162
Tivaouane B 1 200
Tiverton G 3 72
Tivoli H 8 92
Tivoli ♦ C 5 68
Tizimín G 15 184
Tizi-Ouzou B 5 198
Tiznit D 3 198
Tjukalinsk I 29 108
Tjumen' H 26 108
Tjumenskaja oblast' □[6] E 30 108
Tjung ≃ C 14 114
Tjup A 3 122
Tjuva-Guba B 16 64
Tkvarcheli H 12 110
Tlalnepantla H 9 184
Tlaltenango de Sánchez
 Román G 8 184
Tlapeng B 4 206
Tlaquepaque G 8 184
Tlaxcala □[3] H 10 184
Tlaxcala de
 Xicohténcatl H 10 184
Tlhakgameng D 6 206
Tmīsān D 7 198
Tnâot ≃ I 7 132
Toahayana D 5 184
Toamasina k 9 205a
Toamasina □[3] k 9 205a
Toano E 6 92
Toano Range ⋀ B 1 176
Toast E 3 162
Toba, China C 3 130
Toba, Japan G 6 126
Toba, Danau ⊜ M 4 132
Tobacco Plains Indian
 Reserve ✦[4] A 6 178
Tobago I p 24 187e
Tobarra F 3 88
Tobelo E 9 134
Tobermorey G 4 142
Tobermory F 3 160
Tobin Lake ⊜ G 8 140
Tobin Lake ⊜[1] E 7 158
Tobique ≃ g 13 163a
Tobol'sk G 27 108
Tobor C 1 200
Tobruk
 see Ṭubruq A 1 202
Tobyhanna E 3 164
Tobyl ≃ D 9 114
Tobyš ≃ D 19 108
Tocantínia A 9 190
Tocantinópolis A 9 190
Tocantins □[3] F 9 190
Tocantins ≃ D 9 190
Tochigi □[3] F 7 126
Töcksfors C 5 66
Toco D 6 192
Toconao D 6 192
Tocopilla D 5 192
Tocumwal E 5 144
Tocuyo ≃ F 7 186
Todi G 8 92
Todmorden D 4 72
Todos Santos F 4 184
Todos Santos, Bahía
 de ⊂ B 1 184
Tofield E 15 156
Töfsingdalens
 Nationalpark ♦ A 5 66
Tofte C 5 66
Togano, Monte ∧ C 4 92
Togbo D 8 200
Togdheer □[3] F 6 202
Togiak Bay ⊂ G 14 154
Togian, Kepulauan II F 8 134
Togo □[1] H 8 196
Togtoh F 8 128
Togwotee Pass ⟩⟨ D 8 178
Tohopekaliga, Lake ⊜ E 4 168
Tohta E 18 108
Toijala B 11 66
Toiyabe Range ⋀ B 6 182
Tok E 23 154
Tokachi ≃ C 9 126
Tokachi-dake ∧[1] C 9 126
Tōkamachi F 7 126
Tokara-kaikyō ʊ I 2 126
Tokat B 7 118
Tokat □[3] B 7 118
Tokelau □[2] D 10 136
Toklat ≃ D 20 154
Tokmak, Kyrg. A 3 122
Tokmak, Ukr. F 9 110
Tokomaru Bay C 7 146
Tokoroa C 5 146
Toktogul A 2 122
Tokuno-shima I K 2 126
Tokushima G 5 126
Tokushima □[3] H 5 126
Tokuyama G 3 126
Tōkyō G 7 126
Tōkyō □[3] G 7 126
Tōkyō-daigaku-
 uchūkūkan-
 kenkyūsho ◗[3] I 3 126
Tôlañaro m 9 205a
Toledo, Braz. F 4 194
Toledo, Spain E 6 86
Toledo, Oh., U.S. C 2 162
Toledo, Or., U.S. C 2 178
Toledo □[6] C 3 84
Toledo, Montes de ⋀ E 6 86
Toledo Bend Reservoir
 ⊜[1] G 2 170
Tolentino F 9 92
Tolga C 5 198
Toliara I 8 205a
Toliara □[3] I 8 205a
Toljatti J 18 108
Tolland □[6] E 6 164
Tollarp E 6 66
Tolmačovo G 8 108
Tolmezzo C 9 92
Tolmin D 5 102
Tolna □[3] D 10 102
Tolosa A 2 88
Tolovana ≃ D 20 154
Tolstoj, mys › D 18 114
Toltén F 1 195
Toltén ≃ F 1 195
Toluca, Nevado de ∧[1] H 10 184
Toluca de Lerdo H 9 184
Tom' ≃ D 11 114
Tomah C 3 166
Tomakomai C 8 126
Tomanivi ∧ m 14 147c
Tomar E 2 86
Tomashpil' A 10 104
Tomasine ≃ B 10 166
Tomaszów Lubelski C 12 96
Tomaszów Mazowiecki C 10 96
Tombadonkéa C 1 200
Tombador, Serra do ⋀[1] F 7 190
Tombigbee ≃ F 5 170
Tombouctou (Timbuktu) B 4 200
Tombouctou □[3] E 4 198
Tombstone G 3 176
Tombstone Mountain ∧ D 25 154
Tomé, Chile E 1 195
Tome, Moz. B 11 206
Tomelloso E 1 88
Tomerong E 8 144
Tomichi Creek ≃ C 5 176
Tomini E 8 134
Tomini, Teluk ⊂ F 8 134
Tomislavgrad D 4 104
Tommot D 15 114
Tomo ≃ B 5 190
Tompkins F 17 156
Tompkins □[6] D 2 164
Tom Price, Mount ∧ H 4 140
Tomsk D 11 114
Tomskaja oblast' □[6] G 32 108
Toms River G 4 164
Tona C 7 88
Tonalá I 13 184
Tonasket A 4 178
Tonawanda D 9 166
Tonbridge F 7 72
Tondano E 8 134
Tønder D 1 68
Tondi H 3 122
Tondidji C 2 200
Tondi Kiwindi C 5 200
Tone ≃ G 8 126
Tonekābon D 14 118
Tonež D 5 110
Tonga F 3 202
Tonga □[1] E 10 136
Tongaat E 9 206
Tonga Islands II E 10 136
Tong'an F 13 130
Tongariro, Mount ∧[1] C 5 146
Tongariro National Park
 ♦ C 5 146
Tongatapu I F 10 136
Tongatapu Group II F 10 136
Tonga Trench ✢[1] H 14 58
Tongbai B 11 130
Tongbei C 16 128
Tongcheng C 13 130
T'ongch'ŏn-ŭp E 1 126
Tongchuan I 7 128
Tongde I 3 128
Tongeren D 4 69
Tong Fuk I 18 131a
Tongguan, China D 11 130
Tongguan, China A 10 130
Tonghai F 6 130
Tonghe C 17 128
Tonghua F 15 128
Tongjiang, China C 8 130
Tongjiang, China C 19 128
Tongjosŏn-man ⊂ G 16 128
Tongken ≃ C 16 128
Tongliang D 7 130
Tongliao E 13 128
Tongling C 13 130
Tonglu D 14 130
Tongnae G 2 126
Tongnan C 7 130
Tongobory I 8 205a
Tongoy B 2 195
Tongren E 9 130
Tongsa Dzong D 6 122
Tongtian ≃ C 7 122
Tongue B 4 74
Tongue ≃ B 2 174
Tongwei I 5 128
Tongxin H 5 128
Tongxu A 12 130
Tongyu D 14 128
Tongzi D 8 130
Tonica B 4 170
Tonk D 3 122
Tonkawa B 5 172
Tonkin □[9] D 7 132
Tonkin, Gulf of ⊂ I 8 130
Tonkwa C 3 132
Tônlé Sab, Bœng ⊜ H 6 132
Tonle Sap
 see Tônlé Sab,
 Bœng ⊜ H 6 132
Tonneins D 4 80
Tonnerre E 10 78
Tonopah B 6 182
Tonota A 7 206
Tønsberg C 5 66
Tonstad C 3 66
Tonto Creek ≃ E 3 176
Tonto National
 Monument ♦ F 3 176
Tonya B 8 118
Tooele E 7 178
Toora-Hem B 3 124
Toowoomba A 8 144
Tooxin E 7 202
Topeka C 1 170
Topia E 6 134
Topko, gora ∧ D 16 114
Topol'čany B 10 102
Topoli B 4 204
Topolog C 10 104
Topolovgrad D 9 104
Topozero, ozero ⊜ D 9 108
Top Springs E 11 140
Tor F 3 202
Torawitan, Tanjung › E 8 134
Torbalı C 7 106
Torbat-e Ḥeydarīyeh C 8 116
Torbat-e Jām C 9 116
Torbay
 see Torquay G 3 72
Torbay □[8] G 3 72
Torch ≃ E 7 158
Tordera C 7 88
Tordesillas C 6 86
Töreboda C 7 66
Torekov D 6 66
Torelló B 7 88
Torez E 11 110
Torfaen □[6] F 3 72
Torgau E 9 98
Torgelow C 11 98
Torghay ≃ A 9 116
Torghay üstirti ⋀[1] D 23 110
Torhamn D 7 66
Torhout C 2 69
Torino (Turin) D 3 92
Torino □[6] D 3 92
Tori-shima I I 8 126
Torit B 5 204
Tormes ≃ C 4 86
Tormosin E 13 110
Torneälven (Tornionjoki)
 ≃ C 11 64
Tornesch C 6 98
Torneträsk ⊜ B 9 64
Tornillo G 5 176
Tornionjoki (Torneälven)
 ≃ C 11 64
Toro C 5 86
Torodi C 5 200
Törökszentmiklós B 6 104
Toronto, On., Can. G 4 160
Toronto, S.D., U.S. C 6 174
Toropec H 9 108
Tororo G 3 202
Torpa ⊥ D 6 66
Torpo B 4 66
Torquay (Torbay) G 3 72
Torrance G 5 182
Torrão F 2 86
Torre Annunziata D 4 94
Torreblanca D 5 88
Torre del Campo G 7 86
Torre del Greco D 4 94
Torredonjimeno G 6 86
Torrejoncillo E 4 86
Torrejón de Ardoz D 7 86
Torrelavega A 6 86
Torremaggiore E 5 90
Torremolinos H 6 86
Torrens, Lake ⊜ C 1 144
Torrent, Arg. A 9 195
Torrent (Torrente),
 Spain E 4 88
Torrente
 see Torrent E 4 88
Torreón E 8 184
Torre Pellice F 5 82
Torreperojil F 7 86
Torres Martinez Indian
 Reservation ✦[4] F 5 180
Torres Strait ʊ A 9 138
Torres Vedras E 1 86
Torrevella G 4 88
Torrijos E 6 86
Torrington, Ct., U.S. E 5 164
Torrington, Wy., U.S. D 2 174
Torroella de Montgrí F 7 80
Torsås D 7 66
Torsburgen ⊥ D 9 66
Torshälla C 8 66
Tórshavn p 26 64b
Tortolì F 2 90
Tortona E 4 92
Tortosa D 5 88
Tortue, Île de la I C 6 186
Toruń B 10 96
Torup D 6 66
Toržok H 11 108
Torzym B 8 96
Tosa H 4 126
Tosa-shimizu H 4 126
Toscana □[3] F 7 92
Toscolano D 6 92
Toshkent
 see Tashkent A 1 122
Tosi A 5 140
Tosno G 9 108
Tosontsengel B 2 128
Tostado A 7 195
Tõstamaa C 11 66
Tosu H 3 126
Tosya B 6 118
Totana G 3 88
Tôtes C 7 78
Tot'ma F 15 108
Totnes G 3 72
Tottenham A 4 162
Totton G 5 72
Tottori G 5 126
Tottori □[3] G 4 126
Touba D 3 200
Toubkal, Jebel ∧ C 3 198
Toubori C 7 200
Touboro D 7 200
Touchwood Lake ⊜ D 11 158
Toudao ≃ E 16 128
Tougan C 4 200
Touggourt C 6 198
Tougouri C 4 200
Tougué C 2 200
Toul B 3 82
Toulépleu D 3 200
Touliu G 15 130
Toulnustouc ≃ C 10 160
Toulon G 3 82
Toulouse E 5 80
Toumodi D 3 200
Tounfafi B 6 200
Toungoo E 3 132
Touraine □[9] E 7 78
Tourane
 see Da Nang F 9 132
Tourcoing B 9 78
Tournai D 2 69
Tournon E 2 82
Tournus D 2 82
Tours E 7 78
Toussidé, Pic ∧[1] A 8 200
Toutle ≃ B 2 178
Touws ≃ G 4 206
Touwsrivier G 4 206
Töv □[3] C 6 128
Tovarkovskij J 13 108
Tovste A 8 104
Tovuz I 14 110
Towada D 8 126
Towada-Hachimantai-
 kokuritsu-kōen ♦ D 8 126
Towada-ko ⊜ D 8 126
Towanda, Ks., U.S. B 5 172
Towanda, Pa., U.S. E 2 164
Towcester E 6 72
Tower City B 6 174
Towerhill Creek ≃ F 7 142
Towner G 8 158
Townsend B 8 178
Townshend Island I G 10 142
Townsville E 8 142
Towson G 2 164
Towuti, Danau ⊜ F 8 134
Toxkan ≃ A 3 122
Toyah Creek ≃ E 2 172
Toyama F 6 126
Toyama □[3] F 6 126
Toyama-wan ⊂ F 6 126
Toyohashi G 6 126
Toyokawa G 6 126
Toyooka G 5 126
Toyota G 6 126
Tozeur C 6 198
Tpig I 15 110
Traben-Trarbach C 3 100
Trabzon B 8 118
Trabzon □[3] B 8 118
Tracy, Qc., Can. F 7 160
Tracy, Ca., U.S. C 2 182
Tracy, Mn., U.S. C 7 174
Tradate D 4 92
Trade Lake ⊜ D 20 156
Trælleborg ⊥ C 4 68
Trafalgar G 6 144
Trafalgar, Cabo › H 4 86
Trafford □[6] D 4 72
Traíd D 3 88
Traiguén F 1 195
Trail G 13 156
Trail of Tears State
 Park ♦ D 4 170
Traiskirchen C 8 102
Trakai E 12 66
Tralee (Trá Lí) D 2 75
Trá Lí
 see Tralee D 2 75
Trammel A 3 168
Tramperos Creek
 (Punta de Agua
 Creek) ≃ B 2 172
Tramping Lake ⊜ E 17 156
Trăn D 7 104
Tranås C 7 66
Trancoso D 3 86
Tranemo D 6 66
Trang K 4 132
Trangan, Pulau I G 10 134
Trani C 6 94
Tranqueras B 9 195
Transantarctic
 Mountains ⋀ D 25 208
Transylvania □[9] B 7 104
Trapalcó, Salinas de ⩡ F 4 195
Trapani F 2 94
Trapani □[6] G 2 94
Trap Pond State Park ♦ H 3 164
Traralgon G 6 144
Trarza □[3] F 1 198
Trârza ✦[1] F 1 198
Trasacco E 4 90
Trasimeno, Lago ⊜ F 7 92
Träslövsläge D 6 66
Trás-os-Montes □[9] C 3 86
Trasvase Tajo Segura,
 Canal de ≅ F 3 88
Trat H 6 132
Tratzberg, Schloss ⊥ C 3 102
Traun B 6 102
Traunreut B 8 92
Traunstein E 9 100
Travellers Lake ⊜ D 4 144
Traverse City C 6 166
Tra Vinh J 8 132
Travnik C 4 104
Trbovlje D 7 102
Třebechovice pod
 Orebem C 9 96
Trébevic, Nacionalni
 Park ♦ C 5 104
Třebíč A 7 102
Trebisacce E 6 94
Trebišov D 11 96
Třeboň C 11 100
Trebujena H 4 86
Trecate E 6 82
Tredici Archi, Ponte ✦[5] C 4 94
Treinta y Tres C 10 195
Trélazé A 3 80
Trelew H 6 192
Trelleborg E 6 66
Tremblant, Mont ∧ E 6 160
Tremont F 2 164
Tremp B 5 88
Trempealeau C 3 166
Trenčín B 10 102
Trenggalek I 20 135b
Trenque Lauquen D 6 195
Trent
 see Trento C 7 92
Trent ≃, On., Can. F 5 160
Trent ≃, Eng., U.K. D 6 72
Trente et Un Milles, Lac
 des ⊜ E 5 160
Trentino-Alto Adige □[3] C 7 92
Trento C 7 92
Trento □[6] D 7 92
Trentola-Ducenta D 3 94
Trenton, On., Can. F 5 160
Trenton, Ky., U.S. D 5 170
Trenton, N.C., U.S. B 6 168
Trenton, N.J., U.S. F 4 164
Trenton, Tn., U.S. E 4 170
Trepuzzi D 8 94
Tres Árboles C 9 195
Tres Arroyos F 7 195
Tres Esquinas C 3 190
Três Lagoas D 4 194
Três Marias C 8 194
Tres Marías, Islas II G 6 184
Três Marias, Represa
 de ⊜[1] C 8 194
Três Passos G 3 194
Tres Picos, Cerro ∧ F 7 195
Três Pontas D 8 194
Tres Puntas, Cabo › I 6 192
Três Rios E 9 194
Tres Zapotes ⊥ H 12 184
Tretten B 5 66
Treuchtlingen D 7 100
Treuenbrietzen D 9 98
Treviglio D 5 92
Treviso D 8 92
Treviso □[6] D 8 92
Trevorton C 5 162
Trezzo sull'Adda E 7 82
Trhové Sviny D 11 100
Triánta D 8 106
Triberg D 5 100
Tribune F 4 174
Tricarico E 5 90
Tricase E 8 94
Tricesimo C 9 92
Trichonída, Límni ⊜ C 4 106
Trieben C 6 102
Trier C 3 100
Trier □[6] C 3 100
Triest
 see Trieste D 9 92
Trieste D 9 92
Trieste □[6] D 9 92
Trieste, Gulf of ⊂ E 5 102
Triggiano C 6 94
Triglav ∧ D 5 102
Triglavski narodni park
 ♦ D 5 102
Trigueros G 4 86
Tríkala C 4 106
Trikora, Puncak ∧ F 11 134
Trim C 5 75
Trincheras B 4 184
Trincomalee H 4 122
Trindade B 6 194
Trindade I G 12 188
Trinidad, Bol. F 6 190
Trinidad, Ur. C 9 195
Trinidad, Co., U.S. G 2 174
Trinidad I q 24 187e
Trinidad and Tobago □[1] H 13 148
Trinitapoli C 5 94
Trinity E 6 172
Trinity ≃, Ca., U.S. E 2 178
Trinity ≃, Tx., U.S. E 6 172
Trinity, West Fork ≃ D 5 172
Trinity Bay ⊂, Nf., Can. D 17 160
Trinity Bay ⊂, Tx., U.S. H 1 170
Trinity Mountains ⋀ E 2 178
Trinity Site ⊥ F 5 176
Trino D 4 92
Trion E 6 170
Tripa ≃ L 3 132
Trípoli, Grc. D 5 106
Tripoli
 see Ṭarābulus, Libya C 7 198
Tripolis ⊥ D 8 106
Tripolitania □[9] C 7 198
Tripura □[3] E 6 122
Tristan da Cunha
 Group II I 10 60
Trivandrum
 (Thiruvananthapuram) H 3 122
Trivento C 4 94
Trnava B 9 102
Troia C 5 94
Troick I 24 108
Troickij D 13 110
Troickoe G 23 108
Troicko-Pečorsk E 22 108
Troïlus, Lac ⊜ C 6 160
Troina G 4 94
Troisdorf F 4 98
Trois Fourches, Cap
 des › B 4 198
Trois-Pistoles D 9 160
Trois-Rivières E 7 160
Trojan D 8 104
Trollhättan C 6 66
Troms □[3] B 9 64
Tromsø B 9 64
Trona E 6 182
Tronador, Monte ∧ H 5 192
Trondheim E 4 64
Trondheimsfjorden ⊂ E 5 64
Troodos E 5 118
Trooilapspan E 4 206
Troon B 2 72
Trophy Mountain ∧[1] F 12 156
Tropical, Costa ⩜[2] H 1 88
Troškūnai E 12 66
Trosna J 11 108
Trossingen D 5 100
Trostyanets', Ukr. D 9 110
Trostyanets', Ukr. A 10 104
Trout G 2 170
Trout ≃ A 12 156
Trout Creek B 6 178
Trout Lake A 11 156
Trout Lake ⊜, N.T.,
 Can. A 11 156
Trout Lake ⊜, On.,
 Can. F 12 158
Trouville-sur-Mer C 6 78
Trowbridge F 4 72
Troy, Al., U.S. G 5 170
Troy, Ks., U.S. C 1 170
Troy, Mt., U.S. A 5 178
Troy, N.H., U.S. D 6 164
Troy, N.Y., U.S. D 5 164
Troy, Oh., U.S. C 1 162
Troy, Pa., U.S. E 2 164
Troy
 see Truva ⊥ C 7 106
Troyes D 10 78
Troyits'ke B 11 104
Trstená D 10 96
Truax A 2 174
Trubč'evsk J 10 108
Truckee ≃ A 4 182
Trudfront G 15 110
Trujillo, Hond. E 3 186
Trujillo, Peru E 3 190
Trujillo, Spain E 5 86
Trujillo, Ven. B 4 190
Trujillo □[3] F 7 186
Trujillo Alto j 15 187b
Truman D 7 174
Trumansburg D 2 164
Trumbull E 5 164
Trumbull, Mount ∧ D 2 176
Truro, Austl. E 2 144
Truro, N.S., Can. F 12 160
Truro, Eng., U.K. G 1 72
Truskavets' E 3 110
Truth or Consequences F 5 176
Trutnov C 8 96
Truva (Troy) (Ilium) ⊥ C 7 106
Tryon B 3 168
Trysilelva (Klarälven) ≃ B 6 66
Trzcianka B 9 96
Trzciel B 8 96
Trzebież B 8 96
Trzebnica C 9 96
Tržič D 6 102
Tsagaandörvölj D 7 128
Tsaidam Basin ⩡[1] B 6 122
Tsangano F 5 204
Tsaratanana k 9 205a
Tsau G 3 204
Tsavo H 4 202
Tsavo East National
 Park ♦ H 4 202
Tsavo West National
 Park ♦ H 4 202
Tsawisis D 3 206
Tsekanyani F 4 204
Tselinograd
 see Astana D 10 114
Tseoge C 5 206
Tsesane B 6 206
Tsetserleg C 3 128
Tsévié D 5 200
Tshabong D 5 206
Tshane C 4 206
Tshangalele, Lac ⊜[1] E 4 204
Tshela C 1 204
Tshesebe A 7 206
Tshikapa D 3 204
Tshikapa
 see Chicapa ≃ D 3 204
Tshikuwi B 8 206
Tshilenge D 3 204
Tshimbulu D 3 204
Tshoa D 1 204
Tsholotsho F 4 204
Tshuapa ≃ C 3 204
Tshukudu B 5 206
Tshumbe (Chiumbe) ≃ E 3 204
Tsiafajavona ∧[1] k 9 205a
Tsianaloka k 8 205a
Tsimpsean Indian
 Reserve ✦[4] D 6 156
Tsingoni o 19 207d
Tsiombe m 9 205a
Tsiribihina ≃ k 8 205a
Tsitsihar
 see Qiqihar C 15 128
Tsitsikamma National
 Park ♦ H 5 206
Tsolo F 8 206
Tsu G 6 126
Tsubame F 7 126
Tsuchiura F 8 126
Tsugaru-kaikyō ʊ D 8 126
Tsu Lake ⊜ A 16 156
Tsumeb F 2 204
Tsumkwe F 3 204
Tsuruga G 6 126
Tsuruoka E 7 126
Tsushima II G 2 126
Tsuyama G 5 126
Tswatago C 8 206
Tuakau B 5 146
Tual G 10 134
Tuamarina D 4 146
Tuamotu, Îles II E 13 136
Tuapse G 11 110
Tuas j 13 134a
Tuatapere G 1 146
Tuban k 21 135b
Tubarão E 10 192
Ṭūbās E 4 120
Tübingen D 6 100
Tübingen □[6] D 6 100
Ṭubruq (Tobruk) A 1 202
Tubuai I F 13 136
Tuchów D 11 96
Tuckahoe State Park ♦ H 3 164
Tuckerman E 3 170
Tucson F 3 176
Tucumán □[3] E 6 192
Tucumcari C 2 172
Tucupita F 9 186
Tucuruí D 9 190
Tucuruí, Reprêsa de ⊜[1] D 9 190
Tuczna C 12 96
Tudela B 3 88
Tudela de Duero C 6 86
Tudmur E 8 118
Tugela E 9 206
Tugela ≃ E 9 206
Tugela Falls ∟ E 8 206
Tug Fork ≃ E 2 162
Tuggerah Lake ⊂ D 8 144
Tuguegarao City B 8 134
Tugulym H 26 108
Tugur B 11 124
Tui B 2 86
Tujmazy I 20 108
Tukangbesi, Kepulauan
 II G 8 134
Tūkrah C 9 198
Tukums D 11 66
Tukuyu D 5 204
Tula I 12 108
Tulaghi A 13 138
Tulancingo G 10 184
Tulangbawang ≃ F 5 134
Tulare D 4 182
Tulare □[6] D 5 182
Tulare Lake Bed ✦[1] D 4 182
Tularosa Valley ⩡[1] F 5 176
Tulcán C 3 190
Tulcea C 10 104
Tulcea □[3] C 10 104
Tul'chyn A 10 104
Tulemalu Lake ⊜ D 13 150
Tule River Indian
 Reservation ✦[4] D 5 182
Tuli A 8 206
Tulik Volcano ∧[1] J 10 154
Tulita (Fort Norman) D 32 154
Ṭūlkarm E 4 120
Tullahoma E 5 170
Tullamore C 4 75
Tulle C 5 80
Tullins E 3 82
Tulln B 8 102
Tullow D 5 75
Tully D 7 142
Tulsa B 6 172
Tulsequah B 4 156
Tul'skaja oblast' □[6] J 12 108
Tuluá C 3 190
Tulum G 16 184
Tulum ⊥ G 16 184
Tulun B 4 124
Tulungagung I 20 135b
Tuma ≃ E 3 186
Tumacacori National
 Monument ♦ G 3 176
Tumaco C 3 190
Tuman-gang (Tumen) ≃ C 3 126
Tumanovo I 11 108
Tumba C 8 66
Tumbes D 2 190
Tumblong E 7 144
Tumen E 17 128
Tumen (Tuman-gang) ≃ C 3 126
Tumenzi H 4 128
Tumeremo G 9 186
Tumkūr G 3 122
Tumoteqi F 8 128
Tumuc-Humac
 Mountains ⋀ C 8 190
Tumut E 7 144
Tumwater B 2 178
Tunago Lake ⊜ C 31 154
Tunapuna q 23 187e
Tunbridge Wells
 see Royal Tunbridge
 Wells F 7 72
Tunceli C 8 118
Tunceli □[3] C 8 118
Tunchang I 9 130
Tunduru E 6 204
Tundža ≃ D 8 104
Tunga ≃ G 3 122
Tungabhadra ≃ F 3 122
Tungaru E 3 202
Tung Chung I 18 131a
Tungshih F 15 130
Tuni F 4 122
Tunica E 3 170
Tunis B 6 198
Tunis, Golfe de ⊂ B 7 198
Tunisia □[1] E 8 196
Tunja B 4 190
Tunkhannock E 2 164
Tunliu H 9 128
Tunnelton D 4 162
Tunnsjøen ⊜ D 6 64
Tununak F 12 154
Tununirusiq (Arctic Bay) B 15 150
Tunuyán C 3 195
Tunuyán ≃ F 6 192
Tunxi D 14 130
Tuo ≃ D 7 130
Tuokusidawan Ling ∧ B 5 122
Tuolumne □[6] B 4 182
Tuolumne ≅ C 3 182
Tupã D 5 194
Tupaciguara C 6 194
Tupanciretã A 10 195
Tupelo E 4 170
Tupelo National
 Battlefield ♦ E 4 170
Tupiza H 5 190
Tupper D 11 156
Tupungato, Cerro ∧ F 6 192
Tuquan D 13 128
Tura ≃ D 9 114
Turakina D 5 146
Turbat E 9 116
Turbo F 5 186
Turda B 7 104
Turek B 10 96
Turfan Depression ⩜[7] A 5 122
Turgojak B 22 110
Turgutlu C 7 106
Turhal B 7 118
Türi, Est. C 12 66
Turi, Italy D 7 94
Túria ≃ E 4 88
Turin
 see Torino D 3 92
Turinsk G 25 108
Turinskaja Sloboda H 26 108
Turka A 7 104
Turkana, Lake ⊜ G 4 202
Turkey □[1] F 5 112
Turkey Run State Park
 ♦ C 5 170
Turki C 13 110
Türkmenbashy
 (Krasnovodsk) B 15 118
Turkmenistan □[1] F 7 112
Turkmenskij zaliv ⊂ J 18 110
Turks and Caicos
 Islands □[2] G 12 148
Turks Island Passage ʊ C 7 186
Turks Islands II C 7 186
Turku (Åbo) B 11 66
Turkwel ≃ G 4 202
Turlock C 3 182
Turnagain ≃ B 8 156
Turnagain Arm ⊂ F 20 154
Turneffe Islands II I 16 184
Turner G 17 156
Turnhout C 3 69
Türnitz C 7 102
Turnor Lake ⊜ C 4 158
Turnov B 12 100
Turnu Măgurele D 8 104
Turon G 5 174
Turquino, Pico ∧ D 5 186
Turritano ✦[1] I 4 92
Tursunzade B 1 122
Turtle Lake B 4 174
Turtle Lake ⊜ E 17 156
Turtle Mountain Indian
 Reservation ✦[4] A 4 174
Turtle Mountain
 Provincial Park ♦ A 4 174
Turuhan ≃ C 11 114
Turvo ≃ D 6 194
Turzovka A 10 102
Tuscaloosa F 5 170
Tuscania G 7 92
Tuskegee F 6 170
Tuszyn C 10 96
Tutaev H 13 108
Tuticorin H 3 122
Tutin D 6 104
Tutrakan C 9 104
Tuttle H 9 158
Tuttle Creek Lake ⊜[1] F 6 174
Tuttlingen E 5 100
Tutuila I E 10 136
Tutupaca, Volcán ∧[1] G 4 190
Tutzing C 3 102
Tuul ≃ C 5 128
Tuusniemi E 14 64
Tuva □[3] B 2 124
Tuvalu □[1] D 9 136
Ṭuwayq, Jabal ⋀ C 6 202
Tuxpan F 7 184
Tuxpan de Rodríguez
 Cano G 11 184
Tuxtepec H 11 184
Tuxtla Gutiérrez I 13 184
Tüy ≃, Mong. D 3 128
Tuy ≃, Ven. F 8 186
Tuyen Hoa F 8 132
Tuyen Quang D 7 132
Tuy Hoa H 9 132
Tūysarkān E 13 118
Tuz E 11 118
Tuz Gölü ⊜ C 5 118
Tuzigoot National
 Monument ♦ E 2 176
Tuzla C 5 104
Tuzluca B 10 118
Tvărdica D 8 104
Tvedestrand C 4 66
Tver' H 11 108
Tverskaja oblast' □[6] H 11 108
Twardogóra C 9 96
Tweed B 1 164
Tweed ≃ B 4 72
Tweedsmuir Provincial
 Park ♦ E 8 156
Tweerivier C 3 206
Twello B 5 69
Twente ✦[1] B 5 69
Twentynine Palms E 5 180
Tweya C 2 204
Twilight Cove ⊂ M 9 140
Twin Falls, Nf., Can. B 11 160
Twin Falls, Id., U.S. D 6 178
Twisp A 3 178
Twistringen D 5 98
Twitya ≃ E 30 154
Twizel F 3 146
Twofold Bay ⊂ F 7 144
Two Harbors B 3 166
Two Rivers C 5 166
Tyachiv A 7 104
Tybju F 19 108
Tychy C 10 96
Tye D 4 172

∟ Waterfall ʊ Strait ⊂ Bay, Gulf ⊜ Lake ≡ Swamp ⊓ Ice Feature ⊤ Other Hydrographic Feature ✢ Submarine Feature □ Political Unit ◗ Cultural Institution ⊥ Historical Site ♦ Recreational Site ⊠ Airport ▪ Military Installation ✦ Miscellaneous

Symbols in the index entries represent the broad categories identified in the key at the right. Symbols with superior numbers (⊀¹) identify subcategories (see complete key on page 242).

⋀ Mountain   ⊀ Mountains   ✗ Pass   V Valley   ≈ Plain   ⊩ Cape   I Island   II Islands   ⊥ Other Topographic Feature   ⇔ River   ≈ Canal

Vibank — Weatherford

Name / Map Ref. / Page

Vibank F 6 158
Viborg B 2 68
Viborg □[3] B 2 68
Vibo Valentia F 6 94
Vibo Valentia □[6] F 6 94
Vic (Vich) C 7 88
Vícam D 4 184
Vicebsk B 6 110
Vicebsk □[3] B 5 110
Vic-en-Bigorre E 3 80
Vicente Guerrero F 8 184
Vicente Guerrero, Presa ⊜[1] F 10 184
Vicente López D 8 195
Vicenza D 7 92
Vicenza □[6] D 7 92
Viceroy A 2 174
Vich see Vic C 7 88
Vichada ≃ C 4 190
Vichuquén D 1 195
Vichy D 1 82
Vicksburg F 3 170
Vicksburg National Military Park ♦ F 3 170
Viçosa D 9 194
Vicos-Aoos National Park ♦ C 4 106
Victor Harbor E 2 144
Victoria, Arg. C 7 195
Victoria, B.C., Can. G 10 156
Victoria, Chile F 1 195
Victoria see Hong Kong, China G 12 131a
Victoria, Malta H 4 94
Victoria, Sey. I 16 207c
Victoria, Ks., U.S. F 5 174
Victoria, Tx., U.S. F 5 172
Victoria □[3] G 9 138
Victoria ≃ D 10 140
Victoria, Lake ⊜, Afr. C 5 204
Victoria, Lake ⊜, Austl. F 6 144
Victoria, Lake ⊜, Austl. D 3 144
Victoria, Mount ∧, Mya. D 1 132
Victoria, Mount ∧, Pap. N. Gui. A 10 138
Victoria Falls F 4 204
Victoria Falls ⌞ F 4 204
Victoria Island I B 11 150
Victoria Land ⊸[1] D 25 208
Victoria Nile ≃ G 3 202
Victoria Peak ∧ I 15 184
Victoria River Downs E 11 140
Victorias C 8 134
Victoria Strait ⊔ C 12 150
Victoriaville E 7 160
Victorica E 5 195
Victorville F 6 182
Vičuga H 14 108
Vicuña Mackenna C 5 195
Vidalia, Ga., U.S. C 3 168
Vidalia, La., U.S. G 3 170
Videbæk D 4 66
Videira G 5 194
Vidigueira F 3 86
Vidin C 7 104
Vidisha E 3 122
Vidor G 1 170
Vidra C 9 104
Vidsel D 10 64
Viechtach C 9 100
Viedma G 6 195
Viedma, Lago ⊜ I 5 192
Vieil Armand ⊥ C 5 82
Viejo, Cerro ∧ D 3 190
Viekšniai D 11 66
Viella B 5 88
Vienenburg E 7 98
Vienna see Wien, Aus. B 8 102
Vienna, Il., U.S. D 4 170
Vienna, Mo., U.S. C 3 170
Vienna, W.V., U.S. D 3 162
Vienna Woods see Wienerwald ⋏ A 6 90
Vienne E 2 82
Vienne □[3] B 4 80
Vienne ≃ A 4 80
Vientiane see Viangchan F 6 132
Vieques, Isla de I j 16 187b
Viernheim C 5 100
Viersen E 3 98
Vierumäki B 12 66
Vierzehnheiligen ◗[1] B 8 100
Vierzon E 9 78
Viesīte D 12 66
Vieste C 6 94
Vietnam □[1] H 12 112
Viet Tri D 7 132
Vieux-Fort, Qc., Can. C 14 160
Vieux Fort, St. Luc. t 27 187h
Vievis E 12 66
Vigala C 12 66
Vigan B 8 134
Vigevano D 4 92
Vignanello G 8 92
Vignola E 7 92
Vigo B 2 86
Vigrestad C 2 66
Vihti B 12 66
Viinijärvi E 14 64
Viivikonna C 13 66
Vijayawāda F 4 122
Viken D 6 66
Viking E 16 156
Vikna D 5 64
Vikna I D 5 64
Viktor C 22 108
Vila de Rei E 2 86
Vila do Conde C 2 86
Vila Flor C 3 86
Vilafranca del Panadés see Vilafranca del Penedès C 6 88
Vilafranca del Penedès (Vilafranca del Panadés) C 6 88
Vila Franca de Xira F 1 86
Vila Gamito E 5 204
Vilagarcía de Arousa B 2 86
Vilaine ≃ E 4 78
Viļaka D 13 66
Vila Machado F 5 204
Vilanandro, Tanjona ≻ k 8 205a
Vilankulo B 11 206
Vila Nova de Foz Côa C 3 86
Vila Nova de Gaia C 2 86
Vilanova i la Geltrú (Villanueva y Geltrú) C 6 88
Vila Real, Port. C 3 86
Vila-Real (Villarreal), Spain F 1 88
Vila Real □[3] C 3 86
Vila Real de Santo António G 3 86
Vilassar de Mar C 7 88
Vila Velha H 10 190
Vila Velha de Ródão E 3 86
Vil'che D 12 96
Vildbjerg B 1 68
Vilejka E 13 66
Vilhena F 6 190
Vilija (Neris) ≃ E 12 66
Viljandi C 12 66
Viljoenskroon D 7 206
Viljuj ≃ C 15 114
Viljujskoe vodohranilišče ⊜[1] C 14 114
Vilkaviškis E 11 66
Vil'kickogo, proliv ⊔ B 13 114
Vilkija E 11 66
Villa Adriana ⊥ H 8 92
Villa Alemana C 2 195
Villa Ángela E 7 192
Villa Bella F 5 190
Villablino B 4 86
Villacañas E 7 86
Villa Carlos Paz B 5 195
Villacarrillo F 1 88
Villacastín D 6 86
Villach D 5 102
Villa Cisneros see Dakhla E 1 198
Villa Constitución C 7 195
Villa de Arriaga G 9 184
Villa del Río G 6 86
Villa del Rosario B 6 195
Villadiego B 6 86
Villa Dolores F 6 192
Villadossola C 4 92
Villafranca de los Barros F 4 86
Villafranca di Verona D 6 92
Villafranca Piemonte E 3 92
Villa Gesell E 9 195
Villaguay B 8 195
Villahermosa I 13 184
Villaines-la-Juhel D 6 78
Villa Insurgentes E 3 184
Villa Juárez D 4 184
Villa Krause B 3 195
Villalpando C 5 86
Villa María C 6 195
Villamartín H 5 86
Villa Mercedes C 4 195
Villa Montes H 6 190
Villanova Monteleone I 4 92
Villanueva de Córdoba F 6 86
Villanueva del Arzobispo F 1 88
Villanueva de la Serena F 5 86
Villanueva de la Sierra D 4 86
Villanueva de los Infantes F 2 88
Villanueva del Río y Minas G 5 86
Villanueva y Geltrú see Vilanova i la Geltrú C 6 88
Villa Ocampo E 8 192
Villarcayo B 7 86
Villardefrades C 5 86
Villa Regina F 4 195
Villarosa G 4 94
Villarreal see Vila-Real F 1 88
Villarrica, Chile F 1 195
Villarrica, Para. F 2 194
Villarrica, Lago ⊜ F 2 195
Villarrobledo E 2 88
Villarrubia de los Ojos E 7 86
Villa San Giovanni F 5 94
Villasanta E 7 82
Villasayas C 2 88
Villasor F 2 90
Villa Unión A 3 195
Villava B 3 88
Villaverde del Río G 5 86
Villavicencio C 4 190
Villaviciosa de Córdoba F 5 86
Villazón H 5 190
Villedieu-les-Poêles D 5 78
Villefranche-de-Rouergue D 6 80
Villefranche-sur-Mer G 5 82
Villefranche-sur-Saône D 2 82
Villena F 4 88
Villenauxe-la-Grande D 10 78
Villeneuve-de-Berg F 2 82
Villeneuve-Saint-Georges D 9 78
Villeneuve-sur-Lot D 4 80
Villers-Bocage C 6 78
Villers-Cotterêts C 10 78
Villersexel C 4 82
Villerupt C 2 100
Villeurbanne E 2 82
Villingen-Schwenningen D 5 100
Villisca B 1 170
Villorba D 8 92
Vilnius E 12 66
Vil'shanka A 11 104
Vilshofen D 10 100
Viluppuram G 3 122
Vil'va G 22 108
Vilvoorde D 3 69
Vimercate D 5 92
Vimianzo A 1 86
Vimoutiers D 7 78
Vimy B 9 78
Vina ≃ D 7 200
Viña del Mar C 1 195
Vinalhaven A 9 162
Vinaròs D 5 88
Vincennes C 5 170
Vinderup B 1 68
Vindhya Range ⋏ E 3 122
Vineland G 3 164
Vineuil E 8 78
Vineyard Haven E 8 164
Vingåker C 7 66
Vinh E 7 132
Vinhais C 3 86
Vinh Long I 7 132
Vinh Yen D 7 132
Vin'kivtsi A 9 104
Vinkovci E 10 102
Vinnytsya E 6 110
Vinnytsya □[6] A 10 104
Vinson Massif ∧ D 36 208
Vinstra B 4 66
Vinton D 2 166
Viny G 10 108
Vinzili H 26 108
Vioolsdrif E 2 206
Vipiteno C 7 92
Virac C 8 134
Viramgām E 2 122
Virandozero D 11 108
Viranşehir D 8 118
Virbalis E 11 66
Vire D 6 78
Virgil G 7 174
Virgin ≃ D 1 176
Virginia, S. Afr. E 7 206
Virginia, Mn., U.S. B 2 166
Virginia □[3] D 12 152
Virginia Beach E 6 162
Virginia City A 4 182
Virginia Falls ⌞ F 32 154
Virginia Peak ∧ A 4 182
Virginiatown A 9 166
Virgin Islands □[2] D 8 186
Virihaure ⊜ C 8 64
Virje D 9 102
Viroqua D 3 166
Virovitica E 9 102
Virrat A 11 66
Virserum D 7 66
Virton C 2 100
Virudunagar H 3 122
Viru-Jaagupi C 13 66
Virunga, Parc National de ♦ B 4 204
Virvytė ≃ E 11 66
Viry-Châtillon D 9 78
Visalia D 4 182
Visayan Sea ⍑[2] C 8 134
Visby D 9 66
Viscount Melville Sound ⊔ B 11 150
Visé D 4 69
Viseu D 3 86
Viseu □[3] D 3 86
Vișeu de Sus B 8 104
Vishākhapatnam F 4 122
Viskafors D 6 66
Višneva E 13 66
Viso, Monte ∧ E 3 92
Visoki Dečani, Manastir ◗[1] D 6 104
Visoko C 5 104
Visokoi Island I J 12 188
Visrivier F 6 206
Visselhövede C 6 98
Vista G 6 182
Vistina G 8 108
Vistula (Wisła) ≃ B 10 96
Vistula Lagoon ⊂ A 10 96
Vitanje D 7 102
Vitarte F 3 190
Viterbo G 8 92
Viterbo □[6] G 7 92
Viti Levu I E 9 136
Vitim ≃ D 14 114
Vítkov D 9 96
Vitória, Braz. D 10 194
Vitoria see Gasteiz, Spain B 2 88
Vitória da Conquista F 10 190
Vitoša Parki Narodowe ♦ D 7 104
Vitré D 5 78
Vitry-le-François D 11 78
Vitteaux E 11 78
Vittoria H 4 94
Vittorio Veneto C 8 92
Vittsjö D 6 66
Viveiro A 3 86
Vivian F 1 170
Vivonne B 4 80
Vizcaíno, Desierto de ⊸[2] D 3 184
Vizcaya □[6] A 2 88
Vize B 7 106
Vizianagaram F 4 122
Vizille E 3 82
Vižinada E 5 102
Vizzini G 4 94
Vjalikaja Berastavica B 12 96
Vjatka ≃ G 19 108
Vjatskie Poljany H 19 108
Vjazemskij C 20 128
Vjaz'ma I 11 108
Vjazniki H 15 108
Vjosës (Aóös) ≃ B 4 106
Vlaams-Brabant □[3] D 3 69
Vlaardingen C 3 69
Vlădeni B 9 104
Vladikavkaz H 14 110
Vladimir H 14 108
Vladimirskaja oblast' □[6] I 14 108
Vladivostok C 3 126
Vlašim C 11 100
Vleikolk E 4 206
Vlieland I A 4 69
Vlissingen (Flushing) C 2 69
Vlorë B 3 106
Vlotho D 5 98
Vltava (Moldau) ≃ B 11 100
Vnukovo I 12 108
Vočin E 9 102
Vöcklabruck B 5 102
Vodlozero, ozero ⊜ E 12 108
Vodnjan C 2 104
Vodosalma D 9 108
Voerde E 3 98
Vogel Peak ∧ D 7 200
Voghera D 4 92
Vogtland ⊸[1] B 9 100
Vohimena, Tanjona ≻ m 8 205a
Vohipeno I 9 205a
Vohitsara I 8 205a
Vöhringen D 6 100
Voi H 4 202
Voigtsgrund C 2 206
Voinești B 9 104
Voinjama D 3 200
Voiron E 3 82
Voitsberg C 7 102
Vojens C 2 68
Vojnica D 8 108
Vojvodina □[6] C 6 104
Voj-Vož E 21 108
Volcano Islands see Kazan-rettō II G 12 124
Volčansk F 23 108
Volda E 3 64
Volendam B 4 69
Volga ≃ F 17 62
Volga Plateau ⋏[1] C 15 110
Volgo-Baltijskij kanal ≡ G 13 108
Volgodonsk F 13 110
Volgograd (Stalingrad) E 13 110
Volgogradskoe vodohranilišče ⊜[1] E 14 110
Volhov F 10 108
Volhov ≃ G 9 108
Volintiri B 10 104
Volkach C 7 100
Völkermarkt D 6 102
Völklingen C 3 100
Volnovakha F 10 110
Volochys'k E 5 110
Volockaja F 15 108
Volodarskij F 16 110
Volodarskoe J 27 108
Volodymyr-Volyns'kyy D 4 110
Vologda G 14 108
Vologodskaja oblast' □[6] F 13 108
Volokolamsk H 11 108
Volonga C 17 108
Vólos C 5 106
Volos, Gulf of ⊂ C 5 106
Vološka F 14 108
Volosovo C 14 66
Volovo J 13 108
Volpago del Montello D 8 92
Volpiano D 3 92
Vol'sk D 15 110
Volta ≃ D 5 200
Volta Lake ⊜[1] D 5 200
Volta Redonda E 8 194
Volterra F 6 92
Voltri E 4 92
Volturno ≃ C 4 94
Vólvi, Límni ⊜ B 5 106
Volyn' □[6] C 13 96
Volžsk I 18 108
Volžskij E 14 110
Vom D 6 200
Vondrozo I 9 205a
Võnnu C 13 66
Voorburg B 3 69
Vopnafjörður ⊂ m 23 64a
Voranava E 12 66
Vorarlberg □[3] C 1 102
Vorderrhein ≃ D 7 82
Vordingborg C 4 68
Vóreio Aigaío □[3] C 6 106
Vorkuta C 26 108
Vorma ≃ B 5 66
Voroncov B 10 104
Voronež D 11 110
Voronež ≃ D 11 110
Voronežskaja oblast' □[6] D 12 110
Voronja ≃ B 11 108
Vorotynec H 16 108
Vorpommern □[9] C 10 98
Vorskla ≃ E 9 110
Vorsma H 15 108
Vorst C 5 69
Vorstershoop C 5 206
Vørterkaka Nunatak ∧ D 11 208
Võrtsjärv ⊜ C 12 66
Võru D 13 66
Vosges □[3] B 4 82
Vosges ⋏ B 4 82
Voskresensk I 13 108
Voskresenskoe C 20 110
Voss B 3 66
Vosselaar C 3 69
Vostočno-Sibirskoe more see East Siberian Sea ⍑[2] B 19 114
Vostočnyj G 24 108
Vostočnyj Sajan ⋏ D 12 114
Vostok I E 12 136
Vostok ◗[3] D 19 208
Votkinsk H 20 108
Votkinskoe vodohranilišče ⊜[1] H 20 108
Vot'pa F 25 108
Votuporanga D 5 194
Vougba D 9 200
Voulou D 9 200
Vovchans'k D 10 110
Voves D 8 78
Vovodo ≃ F 2 202
Voyageurs National Park ♦ A 2 166
Voynyliv A 8 104
Vožaël' E 19 108
Vože, ozero ⊜ F 13 108
Vožgora D 18 108
Voznesens'k F 7 110
Voznesenskoe I 15 108
Vozrozhdenīe araly I G 21 110
Vrå A 2 68
Vraca D 7 104
Vrådal C 4 66
Vrancea □[3] C 9 104
Vrangelja, ostrov (Wrangel Island) I B 20 114
Vranje D 6 104
Vrbas C 5 104
Vrbas ≃ C 4 104
Vrbovec E 8 102
Vrchlabí C 8 96
Vrede D 8 206
Vredefort Dome ⩡[6] D 7 206
Vreden D 3 98
Vredenburg G 2 206
Vredendal F 3 206
Vrena C 8 66
Vreta kloster ◗[1] C 7 66
Vries A 5 69
Vriezenveen B 5 69
Vrlika D 4 104
Vroeggedeel E 5 206
Vrouenspan D 4 206
Vršac C 6 104
Vryburg D 6 206
Vryheid D 9 206
Vsetín A 10 102
Vsevidof, Mount ∧[1] J 10 154
Vučitrn D 6 104
Vught C 4 69
Vukovar C 5 104
Vulcan C 7 104
Vulcănești C 10 104
Vulci ⊥ G 7 92
Vul'vyveem ≃ C 3 154
Vung Tau I 8 132
Vunisea n 14 147c
Vuohijärvi B 13 66
Vuoksa, ozero ⊜ B 14 66
Vuoksenniska B 14 66
Vuya F 2 202
Vyborg F 8 108
Vyčegda ≃ F 17 108
Východoslovenský □[3] D 11 96
Vygoniči J 11 108
Vygozero, ozero ⊜ E 11 108
Vyksa I 15 108
Vylkove C 10 104
Vynohradiv A 7 104
Vyntja F 27 108
Vyrica G 9 108
Vyšgorodok D 13 66
Vyshnivets' E 4 110
Vyškov A 9 102
Vyšnij Voloček H 11 108
Vysokae B 12 96
Vysokogorsk B 5 126
Vysokoye A 2 122
Vytegra F 12 108

W

Wa C 4 200
Waajid G 5 202
Waal ≃ C 4 69
Waalwijk C 4 69
Waanyi/Garawa Aboriginal Land ⊸[4] E 3 142
Waao F 7 130
Waarschoot C 2 69
Wabakimi Lake ⊜ F 13 158
Wabakimi Provincial Park ♦ F 14 158
Wabamun Indian Reserve ⊸[4] E 14 156
Wabamun Lake ⊜ E 14 156
Wabasca ≃ B 14 156
Wabasca-Desmarais D 15 156
Wabash B 6 170
Wabash ≃ C 4 170
Wabasha C 2 166
Wabē Gestro ≃ F 5 202
Wabē Shebelē ≃ H 12 196
Wąbrzeźno B 10 96
Wabush B 10 160
W.A.C. Bennett Dam ⊸[6] D 10 156
Wachau ⊸[1] B 7 102
Wächtersbach B 6 100
Waco E 5 172
Waco Lake ⊜[1] E 5 172
Waconda Lake ⊜[1] F 5 174
Waconichi, Lac ⊜ C 7 160
Wadayama G 5 126
Wad Bandah E 2 202
Wadbilliga National Park ♦ F 7 144
Waddenzee ⊔ A 3 69
Waddington B 3 164
Waddington, Mount ∧ F 9 156
Wade, Mount ∧ E 26 208
Wadena B 7 174
Wädenswil C 6 82
Wadern C 3 100
Wadgassen C 3 100
Wādī as-Sīr F 5 120
Wādī Ḥalfā' C 3 202
Wadley C 2 168
Wad Madanī E 3 202
Wadsworth A 4 182
Waelder F 5 172
Wafangdian G 13 128
Wafrah H 13 118
Wageningen C 4 69
Wager Bay ⊂ C 15 150
Wagga Wagga E 6 144
Waghäusel C 5 100
Wagin M 4 140
Waging am See C 4 102
Wagon Mound C 1 172
Wagrien ⊸[1] B 7 98
Wągrowiec B 9 96
Wahai F 9 134
Waharoa B 5 146
Wahiawa i 9 181a
Wahlstedt C 7 98
Wahpeton B 6 174
Wahran (Oran) B 4 198
Wahran □[3] E 5 84
Waiau E 4 146
Waiau ≃ G 1 146
Waiblingen D 6 100
Waidhofen an der Ybbs C 6 102
Waigeo, Pulau I F 10 134
Waiheke Island I B 5 146
Waihi B 5 146
Waika C 4 204
Waikabubak, Indon. A 5 140
Waikabubak, Indon. G 7 134
Waikato □[3] B 5 146
Waikato ≃ B 5 146
Waikelo A 5 140
Waikino B 5 146
Wailuku i 10 181a
Waimamaku A 4 146
Waimate F 3 146
Waimea see Kamuela j 11 181a
Wainganga ≃ E 3 122
Waingapu G 8 134
Wainuiomata D 5 146
Wainwright, Ab., Can. E 16 156
Wainwright, Ak., U.S. A 14 154
Waiouru C 5 146
Waipaoa C 6 146
Waipawa C 6 146
Waipu A 5 146
Waipukurau D 6 146
Wairarapa, Lake ⊜ D 5 146
Wairau ≃ D 4 146
Wairoa C 6 146
Waitahanui C 6 146
Waitaki ≃ F 3 146
Waitara C 5 146
Waitemata B 5 146
Waite Park C 1 166
Waitomo Caves ⩡[5] C 5 146
Waitsburg B 4 178
Wajima F 6 126
Wajir G 5 202
Waka, D.R.C. E 9 200
Waka, Eth. F 4 202
Wakasa-wan ⊂ G 5 126
Wakatipu, Lake ⊜ F 2 146
Wakaw E 19 156
Wakayama G 5 126
Wakayama □[3] H 5 126
WaKeeney F 5 174
Wakefield D 5 72
Wakefield □[6] D 5 72
Wake Island □[2] B 8 136
Wakema F 2 132
Wakhān see Vākhān □[9] B 2 122
Wakita G 6 174
Wakkanai B 8 126
Wakonda D 6 174
Walachia □[9] C 8 104
Walang D 5 130
Wal Athiang F 2 202
Wałbrzych C 9 96
Walcheren ⊸[1] C 2 69
Walcott D 8 156
Wałcz B 9 96
Wald E 5 100
Waldbröl F 4 98
Waldeck E 6 98
Walden E 4 164
Waldkirch D 4 100
Waldkirchen D 7 96
Waldkraiburg D 9 100
Waldo G 14 156
Waldorf H 2 164
Waldron B 6 170
Waldshut-Tiengen E 5 100
Waldviertel ⊸[1] B 7 102
Walenstadt C 7 82
Wales □[3] E 3 72
Wales Island I C 15 150
Walewale C 4 200
Walgett C 7 144
Walgreen Coast ⩡[2] D 34 208
Walhalla ⊥ C 9 100
Walheim F 3 98
Walikale C 4 204
Walker ≃ A 5 182
Walker, Lac ⊜ C 10 160
Walker Lake ⊜, Mb., Can. D 10 158
Walker Lake ⊜, Ak., U.S. C 17 154
Walker Lake ⊜ B 5 182
Walker River Indian Reservation ⊸[4] A 5 182
Walkerton B 5 170
Wall C 3 174
Wallaceburg G 2 160
Wallal Downs F 6 140
Wallaroo D 1 144
Wallasey D 3 72
Walla Walla B 4 178
Walldorf C 5 100
Walldürn C 6 100
Wallenhorst D 4 98
Wallerawang D 8 144
Wallingford, Eng., U.K. F 5 72
Wallingford, Ct., U.S. E 6 164
Wallis, Îles II E 10 136
Wallis and Futuna □[2] E 10 136
Wallisellen C 6 82
Wallisville Lake ⊜[1] H 1 170
Wallowa ≃ C 5 178
Walls E 3 170
Walls of Jericho National Park ♦ i 12 145a
Walmer ⊸[8] G 6 206
Walnut B 3 168
Walnut Canyon National Monument ♦ E 3 176
Walnut Cove A 4 168
Walnut Creek C 1 182
Walnut Grove C 7 174
Walnut Ridge D 3 170
Walpole N 4 140
Walsall E 4 72
Walsall □[6] E 5 72
Walsh G 3 174
Walsh ≃ D 7 142
Walsrode D 6 98
Walter F. George Lake ⊜[1] G 6 170
Waltershausen F 7 98
Waltham B 8 162
Walto D 2 200
Walton, Eng., U.K. F 6 72
Walton, N.Y., U.S. D 3 164
Walvis Bay B 1 206
Walvis Bay ⊂ B 1 206
Walvis Ridge ⊹[3] H 11 60
Walwa E 6 144
Walzin, Château de ⊥ D 3 69
Wama E 2 204
Wamba, D.R.C. B 4 204
Wamba, Kenya G 4 202
Wamba ≃ C 2 204
Wami ≃ D 6 204
Wampsville C 3 164
Wanaka F 2 146
Wanaka, Lake ⊜ F 2 146
Wan'an E 12 130
Wanda E 6 206
Wanderer F 5 204
Wandingzhen F 4 130
Wanfoxia A 7 122
Wangamana B 5 144
Wanganui C 5 146
Wanganui ≃ C 5 146
Wangaratta F 6 144
Wangary M 2 142
Wangcun H 11 128
Wangen im Allgäu E 6 100
Wangiwangi, Pulau I G 8 134
Wangkui C 16 128
Wangpan Yang ⊂ C 15 130
Wangqing E 17 128
Wanigela A 10 138
Wānkāner E 2 122
Wanlaweyn G 5 202
Wanneroo L 3 140
Wannian D 13 130
Wanning I 10 130
Wanparti F 3 122
Wanxian C 9 130
Wanyuan B 9 130
Wanzai D 12 130
Wanzleben D 8 98
Wapawekka Lake ⊜ D 19 156
Wapella F 8 158
Wapiti ≃ D 12 156
War E 3 162
Warakurna-Wingellina-Irrunytju Aboriginal Reserve ⊸[4] I 10 140
Waranga Basin ⊜[1] F 5 144
Warangal F 3 122
Waratah Bay ⊂ G 5 144
Warburg E 6 98
Warburton J 9 140
Warburton Aboriginal Reserve ⊸[4] I 8 140
Warburton Creek ≃ I 4 142
Warden D 8 206
Wardenburg C 5 98
Wardha E 3 122
Wardha ≃ F 3 122
Ward Hill ∧[2] B 5 74
Wardner G 14 156
Wardswell Draw ≃ D 2 172
Waregem D 2 69
Wareham G 4 72
Waremme D 4 69
Waren, Ger. C 9 98
Waren, Indon. F 11 134
Warendorf E 4 98
Ware Shoals B 3 168
Wargla C 6 198
Warialda B 8 144
Warin Chamrap G 7 132
Warkworth B 5 146
Warmbad, Nmb. E 3 206
Warmbad, S. Afr. C 8 206
Warm Baths see Warmbad C 8 206
Warmińsko-Mazurskie □[3] A 11 96
Warminster, Eng., U.K. F 4 72
Warminster, Pa., U.S. F 3 164
Warm Springs, Ga., U.S. C 2 168
Warm Springs, Mt., U.S. B 7 178
Warm Springs, Va., U.S. D 4 162
Warm Springs Indian Reservation ⊸[4] C 3 178
Warnemünde ⊸[8] B 8 98
Warner C 7 164
Warner Robins C 3 168
Waroona M 3 140
Warrabri Aboriginal Land ⊸[4] F 2 142
Warracknabeal F 4 144
Warragul G 5 144
Warrego ≃ C 5 144
Warren, Mi., U.S. B 2 162
Warren, Oh., U.S. C 3 162
Warren, Pa., U.S. C 4 162
Warren □[6], N.J., U.S. F 4 164
Warren □[6], N.Y., U.S. C 5 164
Warrenpoint B 5 75
Warrensburg, Mo., U.S. C 2 170
Warrensburg, N.Y., U.S. C 5 164
Warrenton, S. Afr. E 6 206
Warrenton, Ga., U.S. C 3 168
Warrenton, Va., U.S. D 5 162
Warri D 6 200
Warrington, Eng., U.K. D 4 72
Warrington, Fl., U.S. G 5 170
Warrnambool G 4 144
Warrumbungle National Park ♦ C 7 144
Warsaw see Warszawa, Pol. B 11 96
Warsaw, In., U.S. B 6 170
Warsaw, N.C., U.S. B 5 168
Warsaw, N.Y., U.S. B 4 162
Warsaw, Oh., U.S. C 3 162
Warshiikh G 6 202
Warsop D 5 72
Warstein E 5 98
Warszawa (Warsaw) B 11 96
Warta (Warthe) ≃ B 8 96
Wartburg A 2 168
Wartburg ⊥ F 7 98
Warthe see Warta ≃ B 8 96
Warwick, Austl. B 9 144
Warwick, Eng., U.K. E 5 72
Warwick, R.I., U.S. E 7 164
Warwick Channel ⊔ C 3 142
Warwickshire □[6] E 5 72
Wasagu C 6 200
Wasatch Range ⋏ B 3 176
Wasco E 4 182
Wasekamio Lake ⊜ C 17 156
Washburn B 4 174
Washburn Lake ⊜ B 11 150
Wāshīm E 3 122
Washington, D.C., U.S. H 1 164
Washington, Ia., U.S. B 3 170
Washington, Il., U.S. B 4 170
Washington, In., U.S. C 5 170
Washington, Mo., U.S. C 3 170
Washington, N.C., U.S. B 6 168
Washington, Pa., U.S. C 3 162
Washington, Ut., U.S. D 2 176
Washington, Va., U.S. D 4 162
Washington □[3] B 3 152
Washington □[6], N.Y., U.S. C 5 164
Washington □[6], R.I., U.S. E 7 164
Washington □[6], Vt., U.S. B 6 164
Washington, Mount ∧ B 7 164
Washington Court House D 2 162
Washington Island C 5 166
Washington Island I C 5 166
Washita ≃ C 5 172
Washoe □[6] A 4 182
Washpool National Park ♦ B 9 144
Wasilla F 20 154
Wasior F 10 134
Wāsiṭ □[3] F 11 118
Waskaiowaka Lake ⊜ C 10 158
Waskesiu Lake ⊜ E 18 156
Waskom F 1 170
Waspam E 4 186
Wassenaar B 3 69
Wasseralfingen D 6 100
Wassou C 2 200
Watampone F 8 134
Watamu Marine National Park ♦ H 4 202
Watansopeng F 7 134
Watarrka National Park ♦ I 11 140
Waterbury, Ct., U.S. E 5 164
Waterbury, Vt., U.S. B 6 164
Wateree Lake ⊜[1] B 4 168
Waterford (Port Lairge), Ire. D 4 75
Waterford, S. Afr. G 6 206
Waterford □[3] D 4 75
Waterhen ≃ D 17 156
Waterhen Lake ⊜, Mb., Can. E 9 158
Waterhen Lake ⊜, Sk., Can. D 17 156
Waterloo, Bel. D 3 69
Waterloo, On., Can. B 3 162
Waterloo, Qc., Can. A 6 164
Waterloo, S.L. D 2 200
Waterloo, Ia., U.S. D 2 166
Waterloo, N.Y., U.S. D 2 164
Waterlooville G 5 72
Waterman B 4 170
Watersmeet B 4 166
Waterton-Glacier International Peace Park ♦ A 7 178
Waterton Lakes National Park ♦ G 14 156
Watertown, Ct., U.S. E 5 164
Watertown, N.Y., U.S. C 3 164
Watertown, S.D., U.S. C 6 174
Watertown, Wi., U.S. D 4 166
Waterville, Me., U.S. A 9 162
Waterville, Mn., U.S. C 2 166
Watervliet D 5 164
Watford F 6 72
Watford City B 3 174
Wathaman ≃ C 19 156
Wathaman Lake ⊜ C 20 156
Watheroo National Park ♦ K 3 140
Watkins Glen D 2 164
Watkins Glen State Park ♦ D 2 164
Watoga State Park ♦ D 3 162
Watonga C 4 172
Watrous F 19 156
Watsa B 4 204
Watson E 19 156
Watson Lake A 7 156
Watsonville D 2 182
Wattignies B 9 78
Wattrelos B 10 78
Wattwil C 7 82
Watu C 3 204
Watubela, Kepulauan II F 10 134
Watzmann ∧ E 9 100
Wauchope F 2 142
Wauchula F 4 168
Waukarlycarly, Lake ⊜ G 7 140
Waukegan A 4 170
Waukesha D 4 166
Waukomis B 5 172
Waupaca C 4 166
Waurika C 5 172
Wausau C 4 166
Wauseon E 6 166
Wauwatosa D 4 166
Wave Hill E 11 140
Waverley, Austl. F 5 144
Waverley, S. Afr. F 7 206
Waverly, Al., U.S. F 6 170
Waverly, Ia., U.S. D 2 166
Waverly, Ks., U.S. F 7 174
Waverly, Mn., U.S. C 2 166
Waverly, Ne., U.S. E 6 174
Waverly, Tn., U.S. D 5 170
Wave Rock ♦ M 5 140
Wavre D 3 69
Wāw F 2 202
Wawa, Nig. D 5 200
Wawa, Sudan C 3 202
Wawayanda State Park ♦ E 4 164
Waxahachie D 5 172
Way, Lake ⊜ J 6 140
Waycross D 3 168
Wayi F 2 202
Wayland B 5 162
Wayne, N.J., U.S. F 4 164
Wayne, Ok., U.S. C 5 172
Wayne □[6], N.Y., U.S. C 1 164
Wayne □[6], Pa., U.S. E 3 164
Wayne City C 4 170
Waynesboro, Ms., U.S. G 4 170
Waynesboro, Pa., U.S. D 5 162
Waynesboro, Va., U.S. D 4 162
Waynesburg D 3 162
Waynesville D 2 170
Waynoka B 4 172
Waza, Parc National de ♦ C 7 200
Waziers B 10 78
Wazīrābād C 2 122
W du Benin, Parc National du ♦ C 5 200
W du Burkina Faso, Parc National du ♦ C 5 200
W du Niger, Parc National du ♦ C 5 200
Weagamow Lake ⊜ E 13 158
Weatherford, Ok., U.S. C 4 172

⌞ Waterfall ⊔ Strait ⊂ Bay, Gulf ⊜ Lake ≋ Swamp ⍓ Ice Feature ⍑ Other Hydrographic Feature ⊹ Submarine Feature □ Political Unit ◗ Cultural Institution ⊥ Historical Site ♦ Recreational Site ⌧ Airport ▮ Military Installation ⊸ Miscellaneous

Weatherford — Xigazê

Name | **Map Ref.** | **Page**

Weatherford, Tx., U.S. A 10 184
Weatherly F 3 164
Weaverville B 3 168
Webb F 3 170
Webbwood E 2 160
Weber City E 2 162
Webster D 7 164
Webster Springs D 3 162
Weda E 9 134
Weddell Island I n 17 193b
Weddell Sea ≂[2] D 4 208
Wedel C 6 98
Wedemark D 6 98
Wedowee F 6 170
Weebo J 6 140
Weedsport C 2 164
Weener C 4 98
Weert C 4 69
Weeze E 3 98
Wegberg E 3 98
Wegdraai E 4 206
Węgliniec C 8 96
Węgorzyno B 8 96
Wegscheid D 10 100
Wehr E 4 100
Wei ≃, China A 9 130
Wei ≃, China H 10 128
Weichang E 11 128
Weichuan A 12 130
Weida F 9 98
Weiden in der Oberpfalz C 9 100
Weifang H 12 128
Weihai H 14 128
Weil am Rhein E 4 100
Weilburg B 5 100
Weilheim E 8 100
Weimar, Ger. E 8 98
Weimar, Tx., U.S. F 5 172
Weinan A 9 130
Weiner E 3 170
Weinfelden C 7 82
Weingarten, Ger. E 6 100
Weingarten, Ger. A 6 82
Weinheim C 5 100
Weinsberg C 6 100
Weinviertel ◆[1] B 8 102
Weipa B 5 142
Weirsdale E 4 168
Weirton C 3 162
Weishan F 5 130
Weishan Hu ◎ I 11 128
Weishi A 11 130
Weismain B 8 100
Weissenburg in Bayern C 7 100
Weissenfels E 8 98
Weissenhorn B 2 102
Weisswasser E 11 98
Weitra B 6 102
Weitzel Lake ◎ C 18 156
Weixdorf E 10 98
Weixi E 4 130
Weixian, China H 10 128
Weixian, China H 10 128
Weiz C 7 102
Wejherowo A 9 96
Wekusko Lake ◎ D 9 158
Welch G 7 174
Weldiya E 4 202
Weleetka C 5 172
Welega □[3] F 4 202
Welk'ītē F 4 202
Welkom D 7 206
Welland G 4 160
Wellesley D 7 164
Wellesley Islands II D 4 142
Wellesley Lake ◎ E 25 154
Wellfleet E 8 164
Wellingborough E 6 72
Wellington, Austl. D 7 144
Wellington, N.Z. D 5 146
Wellington, Eng., U.K. G 3 72
Wellington, Eng., U.K. E 4 72
Wellington, Ks., U.S. G 6 174
Wellington, Ut., U.S. C 3 176
Wellington □[3] D 6 146
Wellington, Isla I I 5 192
Wellman D 2 172
Wells, Eng., U.K. F 4 72
Wells, Mn., U.S. D 2 166
Wells, N.Y., U.S. C 4 164
Wells, Lake ◎ J 7 140
Wellsboro E 1 164
Wellsburg C 3 162
Wells Cathedral ◗[1] F 4 72
Wells Gray Provincial Park ♦ E 11 156
Wells Lake ◎ C 8 158
Wellston D 2 162
Wellsville, Ks., U.S. C 1 170
Wellsville, Ut., U.S. E 8 178
Welmel ≃ F 5 202
Welo □[3] E 4 202
Wels B 5 102
Welsford F 10 160
Welshpool, Austl. G 6 144
Welshpool, Wales, U.K. E 3 72
Welverdiend C 3 206
Welwyn Garden City F 6 72
Welzheim D 6 100
Wembere ≃ C 5 204
Wenatchee B 3 178
Wenceslau Braz E 6 194
Wenchang I 10 130
Wenchi D 4 200
Wenchou see Wenzhou D 15 130
Wendelstein C 8 100
Wendeng H 13 128
Wendland ◆[1] D 8 98
Wendo F 4 202
Wendover B 1 176
Weng'an E 8 130
Wenjī F 4 202
Wenling D 15 130
Wenlock ≃ B 6 142
Wenlock Edge ±[4] E 4 72
Wennigsen D 6 98
Wenshan G 7 130
Wenshang I 11 128
Wenshui H 8 128
Wensu A 4 122
Wentworth, Austl. E 3 144
Wentworth, S.D., U.S. C 6 174
Wenxi I 8 128
Wenxian B 7 130
Wenzhou D 15 130
Werbellinsee ◎ D 10 98
Werda C 5 206
Werdau F 9 98
Werder D 9 98
Werl E 4 98
Werne an der Lippe E 4 98
Werneck C 7 100
Wernigerode E 7 98
Werra ≃ E 6 98
Werrikimbe National Park ♦ C 9 144
Wertheim C 6 100
Wervik D 1 69
Wesel E 3 98
Weser ≃ D 6 98
Weser-Elbe-Kanal see Mittellandkanal ≅ D 8 98
Weser-Ems □[6] D 4 98
Weslaco G 5 172
Wesley D 8 174
Wessel, Cape › A 3 142
Wessel Islands II A 3 142
Wesselsbron D 6 206
West E 5 172
West Acres C 9 206
West Allis D 5 166
West Antarctica ◆[1] D 34 208
West Bali National Park ♦ G 6 134
West Bank □[2] E 4 120
West Bay ᑕ F 6 172
West Bend, Ia., U.S. D 7 174
West Bend, Wi., U.S. D 4 166
West Bengal □[3] E 5 122
West Berkshire □[8] F 5 72
Westbourne F 9 158
West Branch, Ia., U.S. B 3 170
West Branch, Mi., U.S. A 1 162
West Bromwich E 5 72
Westbrook, Me., U.S. C 8 164
Westbrook, Tx., U.S. D 3 172
West Brother I I 18 131a
Westbury, Austl. i 12 145a
Westbury, Eng., U.K. F 4 72
West Cape › F 1 146
West Carlisle D 2 172
West Channel ≃ B 27 154
West Chester G 3 164
Westchester □[6] E 5 164
West Coast □[3] E 3 146
West Des Moines B 2 170
West Dolores ≃ D 4 176
West Dunbartonshire □[6] A 2 72
West End B 5 168
Westensee ◎ B 6 98
Westerkappeln D 4 98
Westerlo C 3 69
Westerly E 7 164
Western □[3], Kenya G 3 202
Western □[3], Zam. F 3 204
Western Australia □[3] D 5 138
Western Cape □[3] G 3 206
Western Channel ꭒ G 2 126
Western Desert ◆[2] B 2 202
Western Division □[3] m 13 147c
Western Dvina (Daugava) (Zaḫodnjaja Dzvina) ≃ H 12 64
Western Ghāts ⋀ F 2 122
Western Isles □[6] C 1 74
Western Sahara □[2] F 6 196
Western Samoa □[1] E 10 136
Western Sayans see Zapadnyj Sajan ⋀ D 12 114
Western Shore F 11 160
Westerschelde ᑕ[1] C 2 69
Westerstede C 4 98
Westerville C 2 162
West European Basin ◆[1] C 9 60
Westfalen see Westphalia □[9] E 5 98
West Falkland I n 17 193b
West Fargo B 6 174
Westfield, Ma., U.S. D 6 164
Westfield, N.J., U.S. F 4 164
Westfield, N.Y., U.S. B 4 162
West Frankfort D 4 170
Westfriesland ◆[1] B 3 69
West Frisian Islands II A 4 69
West Grand Lake ◎ h 13 163a
West Hamlin D 2 162
West Hartford E 6 164
West Haven E 6 164
West Helena E 3 170
Westhoff F 5 172
Westhuyzen D 6 206
West Ice Shelf ⊓ C 17 208
West Indies II D 6 186
West Jordan E 7 178
West Lafayette B 5 170
Westland National Park ♦ E 2 146
West Laramie B 6 176
West Liberty E 2 162
Westlock D 14 156
West Lothian □[6] B 3 72
West Lunga National Park ♦ E 3 204
West MacDonnell National Park ♦ H 11 140
Westmeath □[3] C 4 75
West Memphis E 3 170
West Mifflin C 4 162
Westminster, Co., U.S. F 2 174
Westminster, Md., U.S. G 1 164
West Monroe F 2 170
Westmoreland F 6 174
West Nicholson G 4 204
Weston D 3 162
Weston-super-Mare F 3 72
Westoverledingen C 4 98
West Palm Beach F 4 168
West Paris B 8 164
Westphalia C 1 170
Westphalia □[9] E 5 98
West Plains D 3 170
West Point, Ga., U.S. F 6 170
West Point, Ky., U.S. C 5 170
West Point, Ne., U.S. E 6 174
West Point, N.Y., U.S. E 5 164
West Point › M 2 142
Westport, N.S., Can. F 10 160
Westport, On., Can. B 2 164
Westport, Ire. C 2 75
Westport, Ct., U.S. E 5 164
West Quoddy Head › h 13 163a
Westrich ◆[1] C 4 100
West Road ≃ E 9 156
West Sacramento B 2 182
West Salem D 3 166
West Siberian Plain ≚ C 10 114
West Springfield D 6 164
West Sussex □[6] G 6 72
West Terre Haute C 5 170
West Union D 2 162
West Valley City E 7 178
West Vancouver G 10 156
Westville F 12 160
West Virginia □[3] D 11 152
West-Vlaanderen □[3] C 1 69
West Walker ≃ B 4 182
West Warwick E 7 164
Westwold F 11 156
West Wyalong D 6 144
West Yellowstone C 8 178
Wetar, Pulau I G 9 134
Wetaskiwin E 15 156
Wete C 6 204
Wethersfield E 6 164
Wet Mountains ⋀ F 2 174
Wetter, Ger. E 4 98
Wetter, Ger. F 5 98
Wetteren C 2 69
Wetumka C 5 172
Wetzikon C 6 82
Wetzlar B 5 100
Wewak M 12 124
Wexford (Loch Garman) D 5 75
Wexford □[3] D 5 75
Weyakwin Lake ◎ D 18 156
Weyauwega C 4 166
Weybridge F 6 72
Weyburn G 6 158
Weymouth, N.S., Can. F 11 160
Weymouth, Eng., U.K. G 4 72
Weymouth, Ma., U.S. D 8 164
Whakatane B 6 146
Whanganui National Park ♦ C 5 146
Whangara C 7 146
Whangarei A 5 146
Whapmagoostui A 4 160
Wharton F 5 172
Wharton Lake ◎ D 13 150
Whatley G 5 170
Wheatland D 2 174
Wheaton, Il., U.S. B 4 170
Wheaton, Md., U.S. G 1 164
Wheaton, Mn., U.S. C 6 174
Wheeler ≃ E 19 150
Wheeler Lake ◎[1] E 5 170
Wheeler Peak ∧, N.M., U.S. D 6 176
Wheeler Peak ∧, Nv., U.S. C 1 176
Wheeling C 3 162
Whetstone Gulf State Park ♦ C 3 164
Whidbey Island I A 2 178
Whim Creek G 4 140
Whiskeytown-Shasta-Trinity National Recreation Area ♦ B 2 180
Whitakers A 6 168
Whitburn B 3 72
Whitby C 6 72
Whitchurch E 4 72
Whitchurch-Stouffville B 4 162
White C 6 174
White ≃, N.A. E 25 154
White ≃, In., U.S. C 5 170
White ≃, Nv., U.S. D 1 176
White ≃, Tx., U.S. D 3 172
White ≃ E 3 170
White ≃ D 5 174
White, East Fork ≃ C 6 170
White, Lake ◎ G 10 140
White Bay ᑕ C 15 160
White Bear Indian Reserve ◆[4] A 3 174
White Butte ∧ B 3 174
White Cap Mountain ∧ h 12 163a
White Castle G 3 170
White Cliffs C 4 144
White Cloud D 6 166
Whitecourt D 14 156
White Earth Indian Reservation ◆[4] B 7 174
Whiteface Mountain ∧ B 5 164
Whitefish A 6 178
Whitefish Bay ᑕ B 6 166
Whitefish Lake ◎, Mb., Can. D 12 158
Whitefish Lake ◎, Ak., U.S. F 14 154
White Fish Lake Indian Reserve ◆[4] D 15 156
Whitefish Point › B 6 166
Whitefish Range ⋀ A 6 178
White Hall, Ar., U.S. E 2 170
Whitehall, Mt., U.S. C 7 178
Whitehaven, Eng., U.K. C 3 72
White Haven, Pa., U.S. E 3 164
Whitehorse F 27 154
White Island I, Nu., Can. C 16 150
White Island I, N.Z. B 6 146
White Lake C 4 166
White Lake ◎, On., Can. G 16 158
White Lake ◎, La., U.S. H 2 170
White Mountain Peak ∧ C 5 182
White Mountains ⋀, N.H., U.S. B 7 164
White Mountains ⋀ C 5 182
Whitemouth F 10 158
Whitemouth ≃ G 11 158
Whitemouth Lake ◎ G 10 158
White Nile ≃ E 3 202
White Nile Dam see Jabal al-Awliyā', Khazzān ◆[6] D 3 202
White Pass ⅹ B 4 156
White Pine A 3 168
White Plains, N.C., U.S. A 4 168
White Plains, N.Y., U.S. E 5 164
White River G 16 158
White Rock G 10 156
White Sands National Monument ♦ F 5 176
Whitesburg E 2 162
White Sea ≂[2] D 12 108
Whiteshell Provincial Park ♦ F 11 158
White Springs D 3 168
White Sulphur Springs E 3 162
Whiteville E 4 170
White Volta (Nakanbe) ≃ D 4 200
Whitewater D 4 166
Whitewater Lake ◎ G 8 158
Whitewood, Austl. F 6 142
Whitewood, Sk., Can. F 7 158
Whithorn h 11 186a
Whitianga B 5 146
Whitman D 8 164
Whitman Mission National Historic Site ♦ B 4 178
Whitney F 4 160
Whitney, Lake ◎[1] E 5 172
Whitney, Mount ∧ D 5 182
Whitstable F 7 72
Whittemore D 7 174
Whittier G 5 182
Whittle, Cap › C 13 160
Whittlesea G 7 206
Whittlesey E 6 72
Wholdaia Lake ◎ D 12 150
Whyalla D 1 144
Whycocomagh E 13 160
Wiasi C 4 200
Wiązów C 9 96
Wichita G 6 174
Wichita ≃ C 4 172
Wichita Falls D 4 172
Wichita Mountains ⋀ C 4 172
Wickede E 4 98
Wickenburg F 2 176
Wickham G 4 140
Wicklow D 5 75
Wicklow □[3] D 5 75
Wicklow Mountains ⋀ C 5 75
Wickrath E 3 98
Wicomico □[6] H 3 164
Wide Bay ᑕ H 16 154
Widen D 3 162
Wideroe, Mount ∧ D 11 208
Widnes D 4 72
Więcbork B 9 96
Wiederitzsch E 9 98
Wiehl C 7 76
Wieleń B 9 96
Wieliczka C 10 96
Wielkopolska ◆[1] C 9 96
Wielkopolskie □[3] B 9 96
Wielkopolski Park Narodowy ♦ B 9 96
Wieluń C 10 96
Wien (Vienna) B 8 102
Wien □[3] B 8 102
Wiener Neustadt C 8 102
Wienerwald (Vienna Woods) ⋀ A 6 90
Wieprz ≃ C 12 96
Wierden B 5 69
Wies ◗[1] E 7 100
Wiesbaden B 5 100
Wieselburg B 7 102
Wiesloch C 5 100
Wiesmoor C 4 98
Wigan D 4 72
Wigan □[6] D 4 72
Wiggins E 2 174
Wight, Isle of I G 5 72
Wigierski Park Narodowy ♦ A 12 96
Wigston E 5 72
Wigton C 3 72
Wijchen C 4 69
Wil C 7 82
Wilcannia C 4 144
Wilcox F 6 158
Wildau D 10 98
Wild Coast ±[2] G 8 206
Wilderness of Judaea ◆[2] G 4 120
Wildersville E 4 170
Wildervank A 5 69
Wildeshausen D 5 98
Wild Horse Plains E 2 144
Wildwood G 4 164
Wilge ≃ E 8 206
Wilhelm, Mount ∧ N 13 124
Wilhelmshaven C 5 98
Wilhelmshöhe, Schloss ⊥ E 6 98
Wilhelmstein, Schloss ⊥ D 6 98
Wilkau-Hasslau B 9 100
Wilkes-Barre E 3 164
Wilkesboro A 4 168
Wilkes Land ◆[1] D 21 208
Willamette ≃ C 2 178
Willamette, Middle Fork ≃ D 2 178
Willandra Billabong Creek ≃ D 5 144
Willandra National Park ♦ D 5 144
Willard, Mo., U.S. D 2 170
Willard, Ut., U.S. E 7 178
Willebroek C 3 69
Willemstad F 7 186
Willeroo D 11 140
William Bill Dannelly Reservoir ◎[1] F 5 170
William Lake ◎ E 9 158
Williams A 1 182
Williamsburg, Ia., U.S. B 2 170
Williamsburg, Va., U.S. E 5 162
Williams Lake E 10 156
Williams Lake Indian Reserve ◆[4] E 11 156
Williamson C 1 164
Williamson, Mount ∧ D 5 182
Williamsport, In., U.S. B 5 170
Williamsport, Pa., U.S. E 1 164
Williamstown, Ma., U.S. D 5 164
Williamstown, N.J., U.S. G 4 164
Williamstown, W.V., U.S. D 3 162
Willich E 3 98
Willimantic E 6 164
Willingboro F 4 164
Willis Islands II q 20 193c
Williston, Fl., U.S. A 4 186
Williston, N.D., U.S. A 3 174
Williston Lake ◎[1] C 9 156
Willisville D 4 170
Willmar C 7 174
Willmore Wilderness Provincial Park ♦ E 12 156
Willoughby C 3 162
Willow F 19 154
Willowbrook F 7 158
Willow City G 8 158
Willow Creek C 8 178
Willowra G 12 140
Willow River D 10 156
Willows A 1 182
Wills, Lake ◎ G 10 140
Wills Creek ≃ F 4 142
Willshire B 6 170
Wilmer D 5 172
Wilmington, De., U.S. G 3 164
Wilmington, N.C., U.S. B 6 168
Wilmington, Oh., U.S. D 2 162
Wilmington, Vt., U.S. D 6 164
Wilmot C 6 174
Wilmslow D 4 72
Wilson, N.C., U.S. B 6 168
Wilson, N.Y., U.S. B 4 162
Wilson ≃ I 6 142
Wilson, Cape › C 16 150
Wilson, Mount ∧ F 5 182
Wilson Lake ◎[1] E 5 170
Wilson's Creek National Battlefield ♦ D 2 170
Wilsons Promontory ›[1] G 6 144
Wilsons Promontory National Park ♦ G 6 144
Wilthen E 11 98
Wilton F 5 72
Wilton ≃ B 2 142
Wiltshire □[6] F 5 72
Wiluna J 6 140
Wimbledon H 9 158
Wimmera ≃ F 4 144
Winam ᑕ H 3 202
Winchelsea G 4 144
Winchendon D 6 164
Winchester, On., Can. F 6 160
Winchester, Eng., U.K. F 5 72
Winchester, Ky., U.S. E 1 162
Winchester, N.H., U.S. D 6 164
Winchester, Va., U.S. D 4 162
Winchester Cathedral ◗[1] F 5 72
Wind ≃, Yk., Can. D 27 154
Wind ≃, Wy., U.S. D 9 178
Windabout, Lake ◎ C 1 144
Windang E 8 144
Wind Cave National Park ♦ D 3 174
Windeck F 4 98
Windera H 10 142
Windermere C 4 72
Windermere Lake ◎ G 17 158
Windham □[6], Ct., U.S. E 6 164
Windham □[6], Vt., U.S. C 6 164
Windhoek B 2 206
Windigo ≃ E 13 158
Windigo Lake ◎ E 13 158
Windischgarsten C 6 102
Windjana Gorge National Park ♦ E 8 140
Windom D 7 174
Windorah H 6 142
Wind River Indian Reservation ◆[4] D 9 178
Wind River Peak ∧ D 9 178
Wind River Range ⋀ D 9 178
Windsor, Austl. E 2 144
Windsor, N.S., Can. F 11 160
Windsor, On., Can. G 2 160
Windsor, Qc., Can. A 7 164
Windsor, Eng., U.K. F 6 72
Windsor, Co., U.S. E 2 174
Windsor, Ct., U.S. E 6 164
Windsor, N.C., U.S. B 6 168
Windsor □[6] C 6 164
Windsor Castle ⊥ F 6 72
Windsor Locks E 6 164
Windward Islands II E 9 186
Windward Passage ꭒ C 6 186
Winfield, Ab., Can. E 14 156
Winfield, Ia., U.S. B 3 170
Winfield, Ks., U.S. G 6 174
Winfield, W.V., U.S. D 3 162
Wingham G 3 160
Wingo D 4 170
Winisk ≃ D 15 158
Winisk Lake ◎ E 14 158
Winisk River Provincial Park ♦ E 15 158
Winkana G 4 132
Winkler G 10 158
Winlaw A 5 178
Winneba D 4 200
Winnebago D 7 174
Winnebago ≃ D 2 166
Winnebago, Lake ◎ C 4 166
Winnebago Indian Reservation ◆[4] D 6 174
Winnemucca E 5 178
Winnemucca Lake ◎ B 4 180
Winnenden D 6 100
Winner D 5 174
Winnfield G 2 170
Winnibigoshish, Lake ◎ B 1 166
Winning H 3 140
Winnipeg G 10 158
Winnipeg ≃ F 11 158
Winnipeg, Lake ◎ E 9 158
Winnipegosis, Lake ◎ E 8 158
Winnsboro B 4 168
Winona, Mi., U.S. B 4 166
Winona, Mn., U.S. C 3 166
Winona, Mo., U.S. D 3 170
Winooski ≃ B 6 164
Winschoten A 6 69
Winsen C 7 98
Winsford D 4 72
Winslow, Az., U.S. E 3 176
Winslow, Me., U.S. h 12 163a
Winslow State Park ♦ C 7 164
Winsted C 1 166
Winston-Salem A 4 168
Winterberg E 5 98
Winter Garden E 4 168
Winter Harbor A 9 162
Winter Harbour F 7 156
Winter Haven E 4 168
Wintering Lake ◎ D 10 158
Winter Park E 4 168
Winterport A 9 162
Winters E 4 172
Winterswijk C 5 69
Winterthur C 6 82
Winterton E 8 206
Winterville C 3 168
Winthrop C 7 174
Wintinna I 2 142
Winton, Austl. G 6 142
Winton, N.Z. G 2 146
Winton, N.C., U.S. A 6 168
Wipperfürth E 4 98
Wirāṭnagar D 5 122
Wīrgañj D 4 122
Wirliyajarrayi Aboriginal Land ◆[4] G 11 140
Wirral □[6] D 3 72
Wirral ›[1] D 3 72
Wisbech E 7 72
Wiscasset A 9 162
Wisconsin □[3] C 10 152
Wisconsin ≃ D 3 166
Wisconsin Dells D 4 166
Wisconsin Dells ♦ D 4 166
Wisconsin Rapids C 3 166
Wishart F 7 158
Wishaw B 3 72
Wisła see Vistula ≃ B 10 96
Wiślany, Mierzeja (Baltijskaja kosa) ›[2] A 10 96
Wismar C 8 98
Wisner D 6 174
Wissen F 4 98
Wister E 1 170
Witbank C 8 206
Witbooisvlei C 3 206
Witham F 7 72
Witjira National Park ♦ I 2 142
Wit-Kei ≃ G 7 206
Witkowo B 9 96
Witney F 5 72
Witnica B 8 96
Wittelsheim C 5 82
Witten E 4 98
Wittenberge D 8 98
Wittenburg C 7 98
Wittenheim E 4 100
Wittenoom H 5 140
Wittensee ◎ B 6 98
Wittingen D 7 98
Wittlich B 3 100
Wittmund C 4 98
Wittstock C 9 98
Witu H 5 202
Witwatersrand ⋀ D 7 206
Witzenhausen E 6 98
Wiżajny A 12 96
Wleń C 8 96
Włocławek B 10 96
Włoszczowa C 11 96
Woburn D 7 164
Wodgina G 5 140
Wodonga F 6 144
Wodzisław Śląski C 10 96
Woerden B 3 69
Wohlen C 6 82
Woippy C 3 100
Wokam, Pulau I G 10 134
Wokha A 2 132
Woking F 6 72
Wokingham F 6 72
Woko National Park ♦ C 8 144
Wolbach E 5 174
Wolcott C 2 164
Woleai I[1] D 12 134
Woleu-Ntem □[3] E 7 200
Wolf ≃ C 4 166
Wolf, Isla I i 13 190a
Wolfach B 6 82
Wolf Creek B 7 178
Wolf Creek ≃ B 3 172
Wolf Creek Meteorite Crater ±[6] F 9 140
Wolf Creek Pass ⅹ D 5 176
Wolfen E 9 98
Wolfenbüttel D 7 98
Wolfhagen E 6 98
Wolf Lake ◎ A 6 156
Wolfratshausen E 8 100
Wolfsberg D 6 102
Wolfsburg D 7 98
Wolgast B 10 98
Woliński Park Narodowy ♦ B 8 96
Wollaston, Islas II K 6 192
Wollaston Lake ◎ E 12 150
Wollaston Peninsula ›[1] B 10 150
Wollemi National Park ♦ D 8 144
Wollogorang D 3 142
Wollondilly ≃ E 8 144
Wollongong E 8 144
Wolmirstedt D 8 98
Wołomin B 11 96
Wolseley F 7 158
Wolsey C 5 174
Wolvega B 4 69
Wolverhampton E 4 72
Wolverine C 6 166
Wolverton E 6 72
Wolwekraal C 3 206
Women's Rights National Historical Park ♦ D 2 164
Wongalara Lake ◎ C 5 144
Wŏnju H 17 128
Wonosari k 20 135b
Wonowon C 10 156
Wŏnsan G 16 128
Wonthaggi G 5 144
Wood D 4 174
Woodall Mountain ∧[2] E 4 170
Wood Bay ᑕ A 30 154
Woodbine, Ga., U.S. D 4 168
Woodbine, Ia., U.S. B 1 170
Woodbridge, Eng., U.K. E 8 72
Woodbridge, Va., U.S. D 5 162
Wood Buffalo National Park ♦ B 15 156
Woodburn C 2 178
Woodbury G 3 164
Woodchopper D 22 154
Woodhull B 3 170
Wood Lake ◎ D 7 158
Woodland, Ca., U.S. B 2 182
Woodland, Me., U.S. h 13 163a
Woodland Caribou Provincial Park ♦ F 11 158
Woodlands, N.Z. G 2 146
Woodlands, Sing. i 14 134a
Wood River G 15 154
Wood River Lakes ◎ G 15 154
Woodroffe, Mount ∧ J 11 140
Woodrow B 6 168
Woods, Lake ◎ E 12 140
Woods, Lake of the ◎ G 11 158
Woodsfield D 3 162
Woods Hole E 8 164
Woodstock, N.B., Can. E 10 160
Woodstock, On., Can. G 3 160
Woodstock, N.Y., U.S. D 4 164
Woodstock, Va., U.S. D 4 162
Woodstock, Vt., U.S. C 6 164
Woodsville B 6 164
Woodville, N.Z. D 5 146
Woodville, Al., U.S. E 5 170
Woodward, Ia., U.S. B 2 170
Woodward, Ok., U.S. B 4 172
Woolgangie L 6 140
Woollett, Lac ◎ C 7 160
Woolmarket G 4 170
Woomera K 3 142
Woonsocket D 7 164
Woorabinda H 9 142
Wooramel ≃ I 3 140
Wooster C 2 162
Woqooyi Gelbeed □[3] F 5 202
Worb D 5 82
Worcester, S. Afr. G 3 206
Worcester, Eng., U.K. E 4 72
Worcester, Ma., U.S. D 7 164
Worcester □[6], Ma., U.S. D 7 164
Worcester □[6], Md., U.S. H 3 164
Worcestershire □[6] E 4 72
Wörgl C 4 102
Workington C 3 72
Worksop D 5 72
Worland C 10 178
Worms C 5 100
Wortham E 5 172
Wörth am Rhein C 5 100
Worthing G 6 72
Worthington, Mn., U.S. D 7 174
Worthington, Oh., U.S. C 2 162
Wotho I[1] B 8 136
Wotje I[1] C 9 136
Woudi C 7 200
Wounded Knee D 3 174
Wounded Knee Creek ≃ D 3 174
Wour A 8 200
Wowoni, Pulau I F 8 134
Woy Woy D 8 144
Wrangel Island see Vrangelja, ostrov I B 1 114
Wrangell H 28 154
Wrangell, Cape › k 38 155a
Wrangell, Mount ∧[1] E 23 154
Wrangell Mountains ⋀ F 23 154
Wrangell-Saint Elias National Park ♦ F 23 154
Wrath, Cape › B 3 74
Wray E 3 174
Wrentham G 15 156
Wrexham D 4 72
Wrexham □[6] D 4 72
Wriezen D 11 98
Wright Brothers National Memorial ♦ A 7 168
Wright Patman Lake ◎[1] F 1 170
Wrightson, Mount ∧ G 3 176
Wrightstown C 4 166
Wrightsville Beach B 6 168
Wrigley E 32 154
Wrigley Gulf ᑕ D 32 208
Wrocław C 9 96
Września B 9 96
Wu ≃, China F 11 130
Wu ≃, China D 13 130
Wu ≃, China E 9 130
Wu ≃, China E 9 130
Wubu H 8 128
Wuchang D 16 128
Wuchuan, China H 10 130
Wuchuan, China F 8 128
Wuda G 6 128
Wudaoliang B 6 122
Wudi H 11 128
Wuding F 6 130
Wuding ≃ G 7 128
Wudu B 7 130
Wugang E 10 130
Wugong Shan ⋀ E 11 130
Wuhai G 6 128
Wuhan C 12 130
Wuhu C 14 130
Wuhua G 12 130
Wuhudongmiao G 6 128
Wukang C 14 130
Wulajia B 17 128
Wulateqianqi F 7 128
Wuliang Shan ⋀ F 5 130
Wuliaru, Pulau I G 10 134
Wulong D 8 130
Wuluhan I 21 135b
Wulumuch'i see Ürümqi B 14 116
Wum D 6 200
Wuming G 9 130
Wundwin H 2 130
Wuneba G 2 202
Wunnummin Lake ◎ E 14 158
Wun Rog F 2 202
Wunstorf D 6 98
Wuntho C 2 132
Wupatki National Monument ♦ E 3 176
Wuppertal E 4 98
Wuqi H 6 128
Wuqiang G 10 128
Würselen F 3 98
Würzburg C 6 100
Wurzen E 9 98
Wusanga C 3 204
Wushan A 7 130
Wusheng C 8 130
Wushenqi G 7 128
Wushi A 3 122
Wuskwatim Lake ◎ D 9 158
Wusuli (Ussuri) ≃ C 19 128
Wutai G 9 128
Wutai Shan ∧ G 9 128
Wuteve, Mount ∧ D 3 200
Wutong F 9 130
Wutongqiao D 6 130
Wuustwezel C 3 69
Wuvulu Island I M 12 124
Wuwei, China C 13 130
Wuwei, China H 4 128
Wuxi, China C 9 130
Wuxi, China C 15 130
Wuxuan G 9 130
Wuyi D 14 130
Wuyi Shan ⋀ E 13 130
Wuyuan, China D 13 130
Wuyuan, China F 7 128
Wuzhai G 8 128
Wuzhi Shan ∧ I 9 130
Wuzhong G 6 128
Wuzhou G 10 130
Wyaconda B 3 170
Wyalusing E 2 164
Wyandotte B 2 162
Wyangala, Lake ◎[1] D 7 144
Wye ≃ F 4 72
Wyk B 5 98
Wylie, Lake ◎[1] B 4 168
Wymark F 18 156
Wymondham E 8 72
Wyndham D 9 140
Wyndmere B 6 174
Wynne E 3 170
Wynyard, Austl. i 11 145a
Wynyard, Sk., Can. F 6 158
Wyola Lake ◎ K 11 140
Wyoming, Ia., U.S. D 3 166
Wyoming, Mi., U.S. D 6 166
Wyoming □[3] C 6 152
Wyoming □[6] E 2 164
Wyong D 8 144
Wyperfield National Park ♦ E 3 144
Wyreema A 8 144
Wysoka B 9 96
Wyszków B 11 96
Wyszogród B 11 96

X

Xaafuun, Raas › E 7 202
Xàbia F 5 88
Xaidulla B 3 122
Xai-Xai C 10 206
Xalapa H 11 184
Xalin F 6 202
Xam (Chu) ≃ H 7 130
Xam Nua D 7 132
Xá-Muteba D 2 204
Xan (San) ≃ H 8 132
Xangongo F 2 204
Xankändi J 15 110
Xanten C 5 69
Xánthi B 6 106
Xanxerê G 4 194
Xapuri F 5 190
Xar Moron ≃, China E 12 128
Xar Moron ≃, China E 8 128
Xàtiva E 4 88
Xau, Lake ≚ G 3 204
Xaxim G 4 194
Xcalak H 16 184
Xelva E 4 88
Xenia D 2 162
Xeres see Jerez de la Frontera H 4 86
Xi ≃, China F 3 128
Xi ≃, China G 11 130
Xiahe I 4 128
Xiajiezi E 5 130
Xiamen F 14 130
Xi'an A 9 130
Xianfeng D 9 130
Xiang ≃ D 11 130
Xiangcheng B 11 130
Xiangfan B 10 130
Xianggang see Hong Kong □[3] I 19 131a
Xiangkhoang E 6 132
Xiangride B 7 122
Xiangshan D 15 130
Xiangtan E 11 130
Xiangxiang E 11 130
Xiangyin D 11 130
Xiangyuan H 9 128
Xiangyun B 5 132
Xianju D 15 130
Xianshui ≃ B 4 130
Xiantao C 11 130
Xianyang, China A 9 130
Xianyang, China D 14 130
Xianyou F 14 130
Xiaodong G 9 130
Xiaogan C 11 130
Xiao Hinggan Ling ⋀ B 9 124
Xiaojin C 6 130
Xiaolongtan C 6 132
Xiaotanghe C 1 126
Xiaoxian A 13 130
Xiapu E 15 130
Xiaxian I 8 128
Xiaxiangcheng D 4 130
Xichang E 6 130
Xichong C 7 130
Xifeng E 8 130
Xigazê D 5 122

Symbols in the index entries represent the broad categories identified in the key at the right. Symbols with superior numbers (⋀[1]) identify subcategories (see complete key on page 242).

∧ Mountain ⋀ Mountains ⅹ Pass V Valley ≚ Plain › Cape I Island II Islands ± Other Topographic Feature ≃ River ≅ Canal

Xihan — Żywiec

Name / Map Ref. / Page

Xihan ≃ B 7 130
Xihe A 7 130
Xiheying G 10 128
Xihua B 12 130
Xiji H 5 128
Xiliao ≃ D 13 128
Ximakou C 11 130
Ximalin F 10 128
Xin ≃ D 13 130
Xin Barag Youqi B 11 128
Xin Barag Zuoqi B 11 128
Xincai B 12 130
Xinchang D 15 130
Xincheng G 10 128
Xinfeng F 12 130
Xing'an F 10 130
Xingcheng F 13 128
Xingguo E 12 130
Xinghe F 9 128
Xinghua B 14 130
Xinglong I 5 128
Xingren F 7 130
Xingtai H 10 128
Xingtang G 10 128
Xingu ≃ D 8 190
Xingxian G 8 128
Xingyi F 7 130
Xinhua E 10 130
Xining H 3 128
Xinji H 10 128
Xinjiang I 8 128
Xinjiang □3 A 5 122
Xinjin, China C 6 130
Xinjin, China G 13 128
Xinkai ≃ E 14 128
Xinli B 1 126
Xinlitun E 14 128
Xinmin E 14 128
Xinning A 10 132
Xinping F 5 130
Xintian F 11 130
Xinwen I 11 128
Xinxian, China C 12 130
Xinxian, China G 9 128
Xinxiang I 9 128
Xinyang B 12 130
Xinye B 11 130
Xinyi A 14 130
Xinyu E 12 130
Xinzha G 5 130
Xiongjiachang A 7 132
Xiongyuecheng F 13 128
Xiping, China D 14 130
Xiping, China B 12 130
Xique-Xique F 10 190
Xırdalan I 16 110
Xisha Qundao see Paracel Islands II B 6 134
Xishui C 12 130
Xiu ≃ D 12 130
Xi Ujimqin Qi D 11 128
Xiushui D 12 130
Xiuyan F 14 128
Xiva E 4 88
Xixian B 12 130
Xixiang B 8 130
Xiyang H 9 128
Xizang (Tibet) □3 C 5 122
Xizi F 12 128
Xochicalco ⊥ H 10 184
Xu ≃ E 13 130
Xuancheng C 14 130
Xuan'en D 9 130
Xuanhan C 8 130
Xuanhua F 10 128
Xuanwei E 7 130
Xuchang A 11 130
Xuddur G 5 202
Xun ≃, China G 10 130
Xun ≃, China B 16 128
Xunhua I 4 128
Xunle F 9 130
Xunwu F 12 130
Xupu E 10 130
Xúquer see Júcar ≃ E 4 88
Xuwen H 10 130
Xuyi B 14 130
Xuyong D 7 130
Xuzhou A 13 130
Xylókastro C 5 106

Y

Yaan D 6 130
Ya'bad E 4 120
Yabluniv A 8 104
Yabuli D 17 128
Yachi ≃ E 8 130
Yacuiba H 6 190
Yādgīr F 3 122
Yadkin ≃ B 4 168
Yadong D 5 122
Yafran C 7 198
Yageg G 5 202
Yagoua C 7 200
Yagradagzê Shan ▲ B 6 122
Yaguarón (Jaguarão) ≃ C 11 195
Yahyalı C 6 118
Yaita F 7 126
Yaizu G 7 126
Yajiang C 5 130
Yakeshi B 13 128
Yakima B 3 178
Yakima ≃ B 3 178
Yakima Indian Reservation ✦4 B 3 178
Yako C 4 200
Yakoma B 3 204
Yakumo C 8 126
Yaku-shima I I 3 126
Yakutat Bay c G 24 154
Yala, Ghana C 4 200
Yala, Thai. K 5 132
Yalahau, Laguna de c G 16 184
Yalata Aboriginal Land ✦4 L 11 140
Yale B 2 162
Yalgoo K 4 140
Yali F 8 130
Yalinga D 9 200
Yallingup Caves ♦ M 3 140
Yalobusha ≃ F 3 170
Yaloká D 8 200
Yalong ≃ E 5 130
Yalova B 8 106
Yalpuh, ozero ⊜ C 10 104
Yalta G 9 110
Yalu B 13 128
Yalu (Amnok-kang) ≃, Asia D 1 126
Yalu ≃, China C 14 128
Yalvaç C 9 106
Yamagata E 8 126
Yamagata □3 E 8 126
Yamaguchi G 3 126
Yamaguchi □3 G 3 126
Yamal Peninsula ≻1 B 10 114
Yamanashi □3 G 7 126
Yamasaki G 5 126
Yambéring C 2 200
Yambio G 2 202
Yamdena, Pulau I G 10 134
Yame H 3 126
Yamenying E 14 128
Yamethin D 3 132
Yamma Yamma, Lake ⊜ I 5 142
Yam O I 19 131a
Yamoussoukro D 3 200
Yampa ≃ B 4 176
Yampil', Ukr. A 10 104
Yampil', Ukr. D 8 110
Yamuna ≃ D 4 122
Yamzho Yumco ⊜ D 6 122
Yan ≃ H 7 128
Yan'an H 7 128
Yanbian A 5 132
Yanbu' al-Baḥr C 4 202
Yanceyville A 5 168
Yanchang H 8 128
Yancheng B 15 130
Yanchep National Park ♦ L 3 140
Yanchi H 6 128
Yanco E 6 144
Yandama Creek ≃ B 3 144
Yandeyarra Aboriginal Reserve ✦4 G 5 140
Yandoon F 2 132
Yangambi B 3 204
Yangcheng I 9 128
Yangchun G 10 130
Yanggang-do □3 F 16 128
Yanggao F 9 128
Yangiyul' A 1 122
Yangjiang H 10 130
Yangliuqing G 11 128
Yangon (Rangoon) F 2 132
Yangon □3 F 3 132
Yangonde C 3 204
Yangpingguan B 7 130
Yangquan H 9 128
Yangshan F 11 130
Yangshuo F 10 130
Yangtze (Chang) ≃ B 14 130
Yangxian B 8 130
Yangxin D 12 130
Yangyuan F 10 128
Yangzhou B 14 130
Yanhe D 9 130
Yanji, China E 17 128
Yanji, China E 17 128
Yankton D 6 174
Yankton Indian Reservation ✦4 D 5 174
Yanqi A 5 122
Yanqing F 10 128
Yanrey H 3 140
Yanshou D 17 128
Yantabulla B 5 144
Yantai H 13 128
Yanting C 7 130
Yanu A 10 138
Yanzhou I 11 128
Yao C 8 200
Yaojie H 4 128
Yaoundé E 7 200
Yaoxian A 9 130
Yap I D 11 134
Yapacaní G 6 190
Yapen, Pulau I F 11 134
Yaqui ≃ C 5 184
Yaracuy □3 F 7 186
Yarbasan C 8 106
Yardımcı Burnu ≻ D 9 106
Yardville F 4 164
Yarí ≃ C 4 190
Yarīm E 5 202
Yarkand see Shache B 3 122
Yarkant see Shache B 3 122
Yarkant ≃ A 4 122
Yarloop M 3 140
Yarlung see Brahmaputra ≃ E 6 122
Yarmouth, N.S., Can. G 10 160
Yarmouth see Great Yarmouth, Eng., U.K. E 8 72
Yarmouth, Me., U.S. B 8 162
Yarmūk, Nahr al- (HaYarmuk) ≃ D 5 120
Yarraman I 11 142
Yarrawonga F 5 144
Yarra Yarra Lakes ⊜ K 3 140
Yarumal B 3 190
Yasa-Lokwa D 2 204
Yashi C 6 200
Yasinya A 8 104
Yask C 7 200
Yasothon G 6 132
Yass E 7 144
Yāsūj G 14 118
Yatağan D 8 106
Yates □6 D 1 164
Yathkyed Lake ⊜ D 13 150
Yating F 8 130
Yatsushiro H 3 126
Yauco j 15 187b
Yautepec H 10 184
Yavarí (Javari) ≃ D 4 190
Yavatmāl E 3 122
Yavlenka I 28 108
Yavne F 3 120
Yavoriv D 12 96
Yaw ≃ E 6 122
Yawatahama H 4 126
Yaxchilan ⊥ I 14 184
Yazd G 16 118
Yazd □3 F 16 118
Yazoo ≃ F 3 170
Yazoo City F 3 170
Ybbs an der Donau B 6 102
Yding Skovhøj ▲2 C 2 68
Ye G 3 132
Yebawgyi E 2 132
Yebyu G 4 132
Yecheng B 3 122
Yech'ŏn F 2 126
Yecla F 3 88
Yedashe E 3 132
Yedi Göller Milli Parkı ♦ B 9 106
Yeghegnadzor J 14 110
Yegros G 2 194
Yehud E 3 120
Yei G 3 202
Yei ≃ F 3 202
Yeji, China C 12 130
Yeji, Ghana D 4 200
Yela Island I B 11 138
Yelarbon B 8 144
Yélimané B 2 200
Yellowdine L 5 140
Yellowhead Pass)(E 12 156
Yellowknife D 10 150
Yellow River (Huang He) ⊜ D 17 116
Yellow Sea ⊤2 E 8 124
Yellowstone ≃ B 7 152
Yellowstone Falls L C 8 178
Yellowstone Lake ⊜ C 8 178
Yellowstone National Park ♦ C 8 178
Yellowtail Dam ✦6 C 9 178
Yellville D 2 170
Yelwa C 5 200
Yemen □1 H 6 112
Yen E 7 200
Yenagoa D 6 200
Yenakiyeve E 11 110
Yenangyaung D 2 132
Yen Bai D 7 132
Yendi D 4 200
Yengisar B 3 122
Yengo National Park ♦ D 8 144
Yéni C 5 200
Yenişehir B 8 106
Yenshuichen G 15 130
Yentna ≃ E 19 154
Yeo Lake ⊜ J 8 140
Yeovil G 4 72
Yepes E 7 86
Yeppoon G 10 142
Yerbent J 21 110
Yerevan I 14 110
Yerington B 4 182
Yerköy C 6 118
Yermasóyia E 5 118
Yerupaja, Nevado ▲ F 3 190
Yerushalayim □3 F 3 120
Yeşilhisar C 6 118
Yeşilyurt C 8 118
Yeste F 2 88
Yetti ✦1 D 3 198
Ye-u C 2 132
Yeu, Île d' I F 4 78
Yevlax I 15 110
Yevpatoriya G 8 110
Yexian, China B 11 130
Yexian, China H 12 128
Yi ≃, China I 12 128
Yi ≃, China A 11 130
Yi ≃, Ur. C 9 195
Yi'an C 15 128
Yibin D 7 130
Yichang C 10 130
Yicheng C 10 130
Yichuan, China A 11 130
Yichuan, China H 7 128
Yichun, China E 12 130
Yichun, China C 17 128
Yidie H 8 128
Yidu, China C 10 130
Yidu, China H 12 128
Yifeng D 12 130
Yilan C 17 128
Yıldızeli C 7 118
Yiliang, China E 7 130
Yiliang, China F 6 130
Yimen F 5 130
Yimianpo D 17 128
Yinchuan G 6 128
Yindarlgooda, Lake ⊜ L 7 140
Yindi B 4 204
Ying ≃ B 12 130
Yingcheng C 11 130
Yingchengzi D 15 128
Yingde F 11 130
Yinggehai I 9 130
Yingkou, China F 14 128
Yingkou, China F 13 128
Yingshan C 8 130
Yingshang B 12 130
Yingshouyingzi F 11 128
Yingtan D 13 130
Yining B 13 116
Yiningarra Aboriginal Land ✦4 G 10 140
Yinjiang E 9 130
Yinnyein F 3 132
Yio Chu Kang i 15 134a
Yi'ong C 2 130
Yi'ong ≃ C 2 130
Yi Pak I 19 131a
Yirga 'Alem F 4 202
Yirwa F 2 202
Yishan F 9 130
Yishui I 12 128
Yishun i 15 134a
Yisuhe E 11 130
Yitong E 15 128
Yitulihe B 8 124
Yiwu D 14 130
Yixian F 13 128
Yiyang, China D 13 130
Yiyang, China D 11 130
Yiyang, China A 11 130
Yiyuan H 12 128
Yizhang F 11 130
Yizikong F 7 130
Yli-Kitka ⊜ C 13 64
Ylöjärvi B 11 66
Yoakum F 5 172
Yogyakarta k 20 135b
Yoho National Park ♦ F 13 156
Yokadouma E 7 200
Yokkaichi G 6 126
Yoko D 7 200
Yokohama G 7 126
Yokosuka G 7 126
Yokote E 8 126
Yola D 7 200
Yolo □6 B 2 182
Yolombo C 3 204
Yolöten C 9 116
Yom ≃ E 5 132
Yomou D 3 200
Yonago G 4 126
Yonezawa F 8 126
Yong'an E 13 130
Yongcheng B 12 130
Yŏngch'ŏn G 2 126
Yongch'ŏn-dong D 2 126
Yongchuan D 7 130
Yongdeng H 4 128
Yongding F 13 130
Yŏngdŏk H 17 128
Yongfeng E 12 130
Yŏngil-man c H 17 128
Yŏngju H 17 128
Yongkang D 14 130
Yongnian H 10 128
Yongning G 9 130
Yongping F 4 130
Yongshan D 6 130
Yongsheng E 5 130
Yongshou A 8 130
Yŏngwŏl F 2 126
Yongwŏn-ni D 2 126
Yongxing E 11 130
Yongxiu D 12 130
Yongzhou E 10 130
Yonkers F 5 164
Yonne □3 E 10 78
Yonne ≃ D 10 78
Yoontoy H 5 202
Yopal B 4 190
York, Eng., U.K. D 5 72
York, N.D., U.S. A 5 174
York, Ne., U.S. E 6 174
York, Pa., U.S. G 2 164
York □6, Eng., U.K. D 5 72
York □6, Me., U.S. C 8 164
York □6, Pa., U.S. G 2 164
York ≃ E 5 162
York, Cape ≻ A 6 142
York, Kap ≻ B 13 148
Yorke Peninsula ≻1 E 1 144
Yorketown E 1 144
York Factory C 12 158
York Minster ◗1 D 5 72
Yorkshire Dales National Park ♦ C 4 72
York Sound ʏ D 8 140
Yorkton F 7 158
Yorktown E 5 162
Yorkville C 3 164
Yoro, Hond. E 3 186
Yoro, Mali C 4 200
Yoron-jima I K 2 126
Yosemite National Park ♦ C 4 182
Yos Sudarso, Pulau I G 11 134
Yŏsu I 16 128
Yōtei-zan ▲1 C 8 126
You ≃, China G 8 130
You ≃, China D 9 130
Youghal E 4 75
Young, Austl. E 7 144
Young, Az., U.S. E 3 176
Youngstown, Fl., U.S. G 6 170
Youngstown, Oh., U.S. C 3 162
Youngsville A 5 168
Yountville B 1 182
Youxian E 11 130
Youyang D 9 130
Youyi C 18 128
Youyi Feng (Kuytun, Mount) ▲ C 1 124
Yozgat C 6 118
Yozgat □3 C 6 118
Ypsilanti B 2 162
Yreka E 2 178
Yrghyz E 22 110
Yrghyz ≃ E 22 110
Yssingeaux E 2 82
Ystad E 6 66
Ysuk-Köl see Issyk-Kul' A 3 122
Yu ≃ G 9 130
Yuam ≃ F 4 132
Yuan (Hong, Song) (Red River) ≃, Asia C 7 132
Yuan ≃, China E 12 130
Yuan ≃, China D 10 130
Yuanling D 10 130
Yuanmou F 5 130
Yuanyang I 9 128
Yuba □6 A 2 182
Yuba City A 2 182
Yūbari C 8 126
Yubdo F 4 202
Yucaipa E 5 180
Yucatán □3 G 15 184
Yucatan Channel ʏ C 3 186
Yucatan Peninsula ≻1 H 15 184
Yucca Valley F 7 182
Yucheng H 11 128
Yuci H 9 128
Yudu E 12 130
Yuechi C 8 130
Yuendumu H 11 140
Yuendumu Aboriginal Land ✦4 H 11 140
Yueqing D 15 130
Yueyang D 11 130
Yugan D 13 130
Yugoslavia □1 G 12 62
Yukon C 5 172
Yukon ≃ E 12 154
Yukon Territory □3 D 6 150
Yuli, Nig. D 7 200
Yüli, Tai. G 15 130
Yulin, China G 9 130
Yulin, China G 7 128
Yuma, Az., U.S. F 1 176
Yuma, Co., U.S. E 3 174
Yumbi C 2 204
Yumen B 7 122
Yun ≃ C 11 130
Yuna ≃ D 7 186
Yunan G 10 130
Yuncheng, China I 10 128
Yuncheng, China I 8 128
Yunkanjini Aboriginal Land ✦4 H 11 140
Yunlong F 4 130
Yunnan □3 F 5 130
Yunta D 2 144
Yunxian B 10 130
Yunxiao F 13 130
Yunyang C 9 130
Yuqing E 8 130
Yuraygir National Park ♦ B 9 144
Yurimaguas E 3 190
Yurok Indian Reservation ✦4 E 2 178
Yurungkax ≃ B 4 122
Yûsef, Bahr ≡ H 4 118
Yushan D 14 130
Yü Shan ▲ G 15 130
Yushu, China B 3 130
Yushu, China D 16 128
Yushutai E 14 128
Yuste, Monasterio de ◗1 D 5 86
Yutian B 4 122
Yutz A 4 82
Yuxi F 6 130
Yuxian, China G 9 128
Yuxian, China G 10 128
Yuxian, China A 11 130
Yuyao C 15 130
Yuzawa E 8 126
Yvelines □3 D 8 78
Yverdon-les-Bains D 4 82
Yvetot C 7 78
Ywathagyi C 2 132

Z

Za ≃ B 2 130
Zaanstad B 3 69
Zabalac' F 12 66
Zabīd E 5 202
Ząbkowice Śląskie C 9 96
Zabłudów B 12 96
Zābol D 9 116
Zabolotiv E 4 110
Zabrze C 10 96
Zacapa J 15 184
Zacapu H 9 184
Zacatecas F 8 184
Zacatecas □3 F 8 184
Zachodnio-Pomorskie □3 B 9 96
Zaculeu ⊥ J 14 184
Zadar C 5 90
Zafra F 4 86
Żagań C 8 96
Žagare D 11 66
Zagazig G 4 118
Zaghouan G 3 90
Zaghouan □3 G 3 90
Zagora C 3 198
Zagórów B 9 96
Zagreb E 7 102
Zagros Mountains ⋀⋀ F 13 118
Žagubica C 6 104
Za'gya ≃ C 5 122
Zaharovo I 13 108
Zahīrābād F 3 122
Zaḥlah B 5 120
Záhony A 7 104
Zahrebetnoe B 12 108
Zainsk I 20 108
Zaire see Congo, Democratic Republic of the □1 I 10 196
Zaire □3 D 1 204
Zaječar D 7 104
Zakamensk A 4 128
Zakarpattya □6 A 7 104
Zakhidnyy Buh (Bug) (Buh) ≃ C 12 96
Zakho D 10 118
Zaklików C 11 96
Zakopane D 10 96
Zakouma, Parc National de ♦ C 8 200
Zakroczym B 11 96
Zákynthos D 4 106
Zákynthos I D 4 106
Zala □3 B 4 104
Zalaegerszeg D 8 102
Zalalövő D 8 102
Zalamea de la Serena F 5 86
Zalantun C 14 128
Zalaszentgrót D 8 102
Zalău B 7 104
Zalese E 10 66
Zalingei E 1 202
Zalishchyky A 8 104
Zalṭan C 7 198
Zaltbommel C 4 69
Žaludok F 12 66
Zamantı ≃ D 6 118
Zambeze see Zambezi ≃ F 6 204
Zambezi E 3 204
Zambezi (Zambeze) ≃ F 6 204
Zambézia □3 F 6 204
Zambia □1 J 10 196
Zamboanga D 8 134
Zamboanga Peninsula ≻1 D 8 134
Zambrów B 12 96
Žambyl see Zhambyl A 2 122
Zamch C 12 96
Zamfara ≃ C 6 200
Zamora C 5 86
Zamora □6 C 4 86
Zamora de Hidalgo H 8 184
Zamość C 12 96
Zana ⊥ B 6 198
Zanaga C 1 204
Zandvoort B 3 69
Zanesville D 3 162
Zangasso C 3 200
Zanjān D 13 118
Zanjān □3 D 13 118
Zantiébougou C 3 200
Zanzibar D 6 204
Zanzibar I D 6 204
Zanzibar Channel ʏ D 6 204
Zaostrove F 9 108
Zaozërnyj D 12 114
Zaozhuang I 11 128
Zapadnaja Dvina H 10 108
Zapadna Morava ≃ D 6 104
Zapadnyj Sajan ⋀⋀ B 2 124
Západoslovenský □3 B 9 102
Zapala F 2 195
Zapata G 4 172
Zapole C 14 66
Zapoljarnyj B 9 108
Zapopan G 8 184
Zaporizhzhya F 9 110
Zaporizhzhya □6 F 9 110
Zapovednoe E 10 66
Zaqatala I 15 110
Zara C 7 118
Zarāf, Baḥr az- ≃ F 3 202
Zaragoza, Mex. F 3 172
Zaragoza (Saragossa), Spain C 4 88
Zaragoza □6 C 4 88
Zarajsk I 13 108
Zarand G 17 118
Zaranj D 9 116
Zarasai E 13 66
Zárate D 8 195
Zarautz A 2 88
Zard Kūh ▲ F 13 118
Zargān H 15 118
Zarghūn Shahr C 1 122
Zaria C 6 200
Zarichne K 13 64
Žarkovskij I 10 108
Zărnești C 8 104
Zarqā', Raqabat az- ≃ F 2 202
Zarrīneh ≃ D 11 118
Zarrīn Shahr F 14 118
Żary C 8 96
Zarzis C 7 198
Zasa D 12 66
Zašeek C 9 108
Zāskār Mountains ⋀⋀ C 3 122
Zaslauе E 13 66
Zasulle F 13 66
Žatec B 10 100
Zatobyl C 23 110
Zauel G 5 202
Zavallya A 11 104
Zave F 4 204
Zavidovići C 5 104
Zavitinsk A 17 128
Zavodoukovsk H 27 108
Zavodovski Island I J 12 188
Zavolžsk H 14 108
Zawiercie C 10 96
Zâwyet Shammâs A 2 202
Zāyandeh ≃ F 14 118
Zaysan A 13 116
Zaysan, ozero see Zhaysang köli ⊜ A 13 116
Zayü ≃ D 3 130
Zazafotsy I 9 205a
Zbiroh C 10 100
Zbraslav C 11 100
Žd'ár nad Sazavou A 7 102
Zdolbuniv D 4 110
Zduńska Wola C 10 96
Zealandia F 18 156
Zeballos G 8 156
Zebulon B 5 168
Zeebrugge C 2 69
Zeehan i 11 145a
Zeeland □3 C 2 69
Zeerust C 7 206
Zefat D 4 120
Zehdenick D 10 98
Zeil, Mount ▲ H 12 140
Zeist B 4 69
Zeitz E 9 98
Zeja B 9 124
Zeja ≃ D 15 114
Zejskoe vodohranilišče ⊜1 B 9 124
Zela ≃ B 9 124
Zele A 10 78
Żelechów C 11 96
Zelenec E 21 108
Zelenoborskij C 10 108
Zelenodol'sk I 18 108
Zelenogorsk B 14 66
Zelenogradsk B 2 110
Zelenokumsk G 13 110
Železnodorožnyj, Russia E 19 108
Železnodorožnyj, Uzb. H 21 110
Železnogorsk J 11 108
Zelina E 8 102
Zella-Mehlis B 7 100
Zell am See C 4 102
Zelów C 10 96
Zelzate C 2 69
Zemaitijos nacionalnis parkas ♦ D 10 66
Zémio A 3 204
Zemmour ✦1 E 2 198
Zemun C 6 104
Zenica C 4 104
Zephyrhills E 3 168
Zerayshan ≃ C 10 116
Zerbst E 9 98
Žerdevka D 12 110
Zergenta F 14 110
Żerków B 9 96
Zernograd F 12 110
Zerqan B 4 106
Žešart E 18 108
Zetel C 4 98
Žetykol', ozero ⊜ D 22 110
Zeulenroda B 8 100
Zeuthen D 10 98
Zeven C 6 98
Zevenaar C 5 69
Zevenbergen C 3 69
Zevenwouden ✦1 B 5 69
Zeytinbağı B 8 106
Zêzere ≃ E 2 86
Zgierz C 10 96
Zgorzelec C 8 96
Zhag'yab C 4 130
Zhalpaqtal E 16 110
Zhaltyr köli ⊜ F 17 110
Zhambyl A 2 122
Zhambyl □3 A 2 122
Zhangaözen H 18 110
Zhangaqazaly A 9 116
Zhangjiakou F 10 128
Zhangping F 13 130
Zhangpu F 13 130
Zhangqiu H 11 128
Zhangwu E 14 128
Zhangye G 3 128
Zhangzhou F 13 130
Zhanjiang H 10 130
Zhanyu D 14 128
Zhao'an G 13 130
Zhaodong C 15 128
Zhaojue D 6 130
Zhaoping G 10 130
Zhaoqing G 11 130
Zhaoxing C 18 128
Zhaoyuan D 15 128
Zharma A 13 116
Zhashkiv E 6 110
Zhaysang köli ⊜ A 13 116
Zhecheng A 12 130
Zhejiang □3 D 15 130
Zhelin C 15 130
Zhem ≃ F 19 110
Zheng'an D 8 130
Zhengding G 10 128
Zhengfeng F 7 130
Zhenghe E 14 130
Zhenglan Qi E 10 128
Zhengxiangbai Qi E 10 128
Zhengyang B 12 130
Zhengzhou A 11 130
Zhenjiang B 14 130
Zhenlai D 14 128
Zhenning E 7 130
Zhenping B 11 130
Zhenxiong E 7 130
Zhenyuan E 8 130
Zherong E 14 130
Zhetiqara C 22 110
Zhezqazghan A 10 116
Zhijiang E 9 130
Zhijin A 7 132
Zhmerynka E 5 110
Zhob C 1 122
Zhob ≃ D 10 116
Zhongcun B 10 130
Zhonghe E 6 130
Zhongjiang C 7 130
Zhongning H 5 128
Zhongshan, China F 10 130
Zhongshan, China G 11 130
Zhongshan ◗3 C 16 208
Zhongwei H 5 128
Zhongxian C 8 130
Zhongxiang C 11 130
Zhongyaozhan A 15 128
Zhoucun H 11 128
Zhouning E 14 130
Zhouqu B 6 130
Zhoushan Dao I C 16 130
Zhoushan Qundao II C 16 130
Zhouzhi A 8 130
Zhovti Vody E 8 110
Zhovtneve, Ukr. F 8 110
Zhovtneve, Ukr. E 9 110
Zhuanghe G 14 128
Zhuanglang I 5 128
Zhucheng H 12 128
Zhuhe D 11 130
Zhuji D 15 130
Zhujiang Kou c1 G 11 130
Zhujiesi B 3 130
Zhumadian B 11 130
Zhuolu F 10 128
Zhuozhou G 10 128
Zhuozi F 9 128
Zhushan B 10 130
Zhuzhou E 11 130
Zhylgha A 1 122
Zhympīty D 18 110
Zhytomyr D 6 110
Zhytomyr □6 D 6 110
Zi ≃, China H 12 128
Zi ≃, China E 10 130
Zi ≃, China B 2 130
Zia Indian Reservation ✦4 E 5 176
Ziārat C 1 122
Žiar nad Hronom B 10 102
Zibo H 12 128
Zichang H 7 128
Zielona Góra C 8 96
Zierikzee C 2 69
Zifta G 4 118
Žigansk C 15 114
Zigong D 7 130
Ziguéy C 8 200
Ziguinchor C 1 200
Žigulevsk J 18 108
Zihuatanejo I 9 184
Zijin G 12 130
Zilair C 20 110
Zile B 6 118
Žilina A 10 102
Žilino E 10 66
Zillah D 8 198
Zilwaukee B 2 162
Zima B 4 124
Zimba F 4 204
Zimbabwe □1 J 10 196
Zimbabwe Ruins ⊥ G 5 204
Zimi D 2 200
Zimnicea D 8 104
Zimovniki F 13 110
Zinave, Parque National de ♦ A 10 206
Zinder C 6 200
Zinder □3 C 7 200
Zinga Mulike D 6 204
Ziniaré C 4 200
Zin'kiv D 9 110
Zinnowitz B 10 98
Zion D 5 166
Zion National Park ♦ D 2 176
Zionz Lake ⊜ F 13 158
Zirgan C 19 110
Zirndorf C 7 100
Žirovnice C 12 100
Zisterzienserabtei ◗1 C 5 100
Zitong C 7 130
Zittau F 11 98
Zitundo D 10 206
Ziwa Magharibi □3 C 5 204
Ziway Hāyk' ⊜ F 4 202
Ziya ≃ G 11 128
Ziyang C 7 130
Zizhong D 7 130
Zizhou H 7 128
Žižica H 9 108
Zlarin D 3 104
Zlatá Koruna ◗1 D 11 100
Zlaté Moravce B 10 102
Zlatoust I 23 108
Zlín A 9 102
Zlínský □3 D 9 96
Zlīṭan C 7 198
Złoczew C 10 96
Złotoryja C 8 96
Złotów B 9 96
Żmigród C 9 96
Zmiïnyi, ostriv see Serpilor, Insula I C 11 104
Znamensk E 10 66
Znam'yanka E 8 110
Znob-Novhorods'ke C 8 110
Znojmo B 8 102
Žodzina E 14 66
Zoétélé E 7 200
Zoetermeer B 3 69
Zofingen C 5 82
Zogno D 5 92
Zohreh ≃ G 13 118
Zolfo Springs F 4 168
Zollikofen C 5 82
Zollikon C 6 82
Zolochiv, Ukr. D 10 110
Zolochiv, Ukr. E 4 110
Zolotarëvka C 14 110
Zolote E 11 110
Zolotkovo I 14 108
Zolotuhino C 9 110
Zomba F 6 204
Zongo B 2 204
Zonguldak B 9 106
Zonguldak □3 B 5 118
Zonhoven D 4 69
Zörbig E 9 98
Zorita E 5 86
Zorra, Arroyo de la ≃ F 3 172
Zossen D 10 98
Zottegem D 2 69
Zouérat E 2 198
Zourma C 4 200
Zouxian I 11 128
Zrenjanin C 6 104
Zruč nad Sázavou C 12 100
Zschopau F 9 98
Zubova Poljana I 15 108
Zudáñez G 6 190
Zuénoula D 3 200
Zuera C 4 88
Zuevka G 19 108
Zug C 6 82
Zug □3 C 6 82
Zugdidi H 12 110
Zugspitze ▲ E 8 100
Zuid-Beveland ✦1 C 2 69
Zuid-Holland □3 C 3 69
Zújar ≃ F 5 86
Žukovka C 8 110
Zula D 4 202
Zulia □3 F 6 186
Zulia ≃ F 6 186
Zülpich F 3 98
Zumaia A 2 88
Zumbrota C 2 166
Zundert C 3 69
Zune F 6 204
Zungwini D 9 206
Zunhua F 11 128
Zuni Indian Reservation ✦4 E 4 176
Zunyi E 8 130
Zuoxiunulemiao B 10 128
Zuoyun F 9 128
Zupar ✦1 G 7 116
Zurich, On., Can. G 3 160
Zürich, Switz. C 6 82
Zürich □3 C 6 82
Zurich, Lake ⊜ C 6 82
Zürichsee see Zurich, Lake ⊜ C 6 82
Zutphen B 5 69
Žužemberk E 6 102
Zvenyhorodka E 7 110
Zverinogolovskoe I 26 108
Zvishavane G 5 204
Zvolen B 11 102
Zwedru D 3 200
Zweibrücken C 4 100
Zwenkau E 9 98
Zwettl B 7 102
Zwevegem D 2 69
Zwevezele C 2 69
Zwickau F 9 98
Zwiesel C 10 100
Zwijndrecht C 3 69
Zwolle, Neth. B 5 69
Zwolle, La., U.S. G 2 170
Żyrardów B 11 96
Zyrjanovskij H 24 108
Zyryanovsk E 11 114
Żywiec D 10 96

L Waterfall ʏ Strait c Bay, Gulf ⊜ Lake ≡ Swamp ⌂ Ice Feature ⊤ Other Hydrographic Feature ✦ Submarine Feature □ Political Unit ◗ Cultural Institution ⊥ Historical Site ♦ Recreational Site ⊠ Airport ■ Military Installation ✦ Miscellaneous

ACKNOWLEDGMENTS

THE STORY OF THE WORLD

The publishers would like to thank the following artists for their contribution to this book:

Eugene Fleury: pp 10–11 *top left*, 12–13 *top left*, 14–15 *left*, 20–21 *top left*, 26–27 *top right*, 32–33 *top right*, 38–39 *bottom right*, 44–45 *right*, 47–48 *left*, all cartography in Nations of the World pp 209–41

Pavel Kostal: pp 6–7, 8–9 *left & right*, 10–11 *bottom left & right*, 12–13 *centre right*, 16–17 *centre left & right* 18 *bottom left*, 42–43 *bottom left*

Sharon McCausland: 22–23 *left & right*, 24–25 *bottom left*, 26–27 *left & right*, 30–31 *centre left & right*, 34–35 *centre left & right*, 36–37 *bottom left & centre right*, 38–39 *left & bottom right*, 40–41 *left & right*, 42–43 *centre left & right*

Malcolm McGregor: 28–29 *all*, 32–33

Lee Peters: 14–15 *bottom right*, 36–37 *bottom right*, 38–39 *left & bottom right*

James G. Robins: 12–13 *right*, 46–47 *bottom left*

Leslie Smith: 16–17 *top & bottom right*, 46–47 *right*, 50–51 *left & right*

Ed Stuart: pp 8–9 *top right*, 12–13 *right*, 19, 20–21 *bottom left & right*, 24–25 *centre left*, 30–31 *top right*, 34–35 *bottom right*, 42–43 *bottom right*, 48–49 *right*

Andrew Thompson: 34–35 *top right*, 36–37 *bottom right*, 44–45 *left*, 46–47 *left*

Hali Verrider: 24–25 *bottom right*

The projection used for the illustrated maps on pages 19, 37, 39, 46 and 48 is © Bartholomew. Reproduced by permission of Harper Collins Cartographic, Glasgow.

The publishers would like to thank the following photographic libraries for permission to reproduce their material:

Abbreviations:

EPL Environmental Picture Library   **OSF** Oxford Scientific Films
FLPA Frank Lane Picture Agency   **RHPL** Robert Harding Picture Library
GSF Geoscience Features   **SPL** Science Photo Library
NHPA Natural History Photographic Agency

1 SPL/NASA; 2–3 (*L–R*) SPL/NASA; SPL/NASA; SPL/NASA; 4–5 (*L–R*) SPL/NASA; FLPA/David Hosking (aerial view of Grand Canyon, Arizona, USA); Images (rock formations in Colorado valley, Utah, USA); Zefa/Bauer (red bromeliad growing in rock cleft); 6–7 SPL/Hallas; 6 SPL/Baum; 7 *top* SPL/HST; 7 *bottom left* SPL/NRAO; 7 *bottom right* SPL/NRAO; 8 SPL/JISAS-Lockheed; 9 *top left* SPL/NASA; 9 *top centre* SPL/NASA; 9 *top right* SPL/NASA; 9 *bottom left* Image Select; 9 *bottom right* (sequence) Weaver & Smith/Space Telescope Institute/NASA; 10–11 Image Select/Ann Ronan; 11 SPL/ESA/PLI; 12–13 Zefa; 12 *left* RHPL; 12 *centre* RHPL/Tony Waltham; 12 *right* Zefa/T. Stewart; 12 *bottom left* Images; 12 *bottom right* OSF/Ake Lindau/Okapia; 13 *top* Zefa; 13 *left* Spectrum/D. & J. Heaton; 13 *right* Zefa/Kurt Goebel; 14 *top* Rex Features/Butler/Bauer; 14 *centre* SPL/Parker; 14 *bottom* GSF; 15 montage sequence: (*top row L–R*) GSF; Zefa; (*middle row L–R*) Images; Images; Images; (*bottom row L–R*) FLPA/F. Polking; Images; FLPA/Mark Newman; 15 *bottom right* FLPA/USDA; 16 *centre left* SPL/Alfred Pasieka; 16 *centre right* FLPA/Roger Tidman; Box: (*top row*) *left* SPL/Alfred Pasieka; *centre* SPL/Vaughan Fleming; *right* SPL/George Bernard; (*middle row*) *left* SPL/J.C. Revy; *centre* SPL/Roberto de Gugliemo; *right* Natural History Museum; (*bottom row*) *left* SPL/Alfred Pasieka; *centre* SPL/Vaughan Fleming; *right* Natural History Museum; 17 *top left* Zefa; 17 *top right* FLPA/C. Mullen; 17 *centre left* SPL/James Stevenson; 17 *centre right* SPL/George Bernard; 18 SPL/NASA; 18 *right* (inset) RHPL/Liaison; 20–21 Images; 21 SPL/Los Alamos National Laboratory; 22–23 sequence: (*clockwise from top left*) OSF/Kathie Atkinson; OSF/David Fleetham; FLPA/Earthviews; FLPA/David Fleetham/Silvestris; Zefa; NHPA/Norbert Wu; OSF/Norbert Wu; NHPA/Agence Nature; NHPA/Agence Nature; FLPA/D.P. Wilson; 23 cluster (*top*): SPL/Biophoto Associates; SPL/Jan Hinsch; 24–25 Images; 25 *top* FLPA/Wilmshurst; 25 *bottom* OSF/Kay; 26 *top left* Images; 26 *top centre* Images; 26 *top right* Images; 26 *bottom* Telegraph/Sims; 26–27 Impact/Black; 27 *top right* Zefa; 27 *bottom left* Zefa/APL; 27 *bottom right* RHPL/Cavanaugh; 28 *top* RHPL/Craven; 28 *bottom* OSF/Brando; 29 *top* The Hutchison Library/Hughes; 29 *centre* OSF/Jim Holmes; 29 *centre left* Rex Features/Wallace; 30–31 Tony Stone/Bushue; 30 *top* FLPA/Wisniewski; 30 *bottom* Alaska Stock; 31 *top* OSF/Allan; 31 *bottom* OSF/Allan; 32–33 *bottom* Images; 32 *centre* GSF; 32 *right* GSF; 33 *top right* RHPL/Fred Klus; 33 *centre left* RHPL/Paolo Koch; 33 *centre* FLPA/ W. Wisniewski; 33 *centre right* OSF/Tom Ulrich; 34 Images; 35 Zefa/Mehlig; 36–37 Zefa/Floris; 36 *top* FLPA/Newman; 36 *centre* FLPA/Delport; 36 *bottom* Zefa; 37 *top* OSF/Turner; 37 *bottom* FLPA/Hosking; 38–39 SPL/Dr Morley Read; 38 *bottom left* OSF/Richard Packwood; 38 *centre* Images; 38 *top right* Still Pictures; 39 Still Pictures; 40 *top* Images; 40 *left centre* FLPA/Hosking; 40 *centre* FLPA/Hosking; 40 *right centre* OSF/Henry; 40 *bottom* GSF; 41 *top* FLPA/Mullen; 41 *centre* FLPA/Silvestris; 41 *bottom* RHPL/Photri; 42 *bottom left* RHPL; 42 *centre* Images; 42–43 Images; 43 *top* Rex Features/Beghin; 43 *centre* OSF/Reinhard/Okapia; 43 *centre right* OSF/Packwood; 43 *bottom* Images; 44 SPL; 45 (*clockwise from left*): RHPL/Wheeler; Rex Features; Images; Rex Features/Cavali/SIPA; 46–47 Zefa; 46 *top* Zefa; 46 *bottom* RHPL; 47 *top* EPL; 47 *centre* Zefa/Fleumer; 47 *right* RHPL/Woolfitt; 48 Tony Stone/Cunningham; 50–51 SPL/John Mead; 50 *top left* Telegraph/Roger Antrobus; 50 *centre left* RHPL/Dave Jacobs; 50 *centre right* The Hutchison Library/Robert Francis; 50 *bottom right* SPL/Roger Ressmeyer; 51 *centre top* RHPL/Dave Jacobs; 51 *centre left* Panos Pictures/Alain Le Garsmeur; 51 *bottom left* Panos Pictures/Martin Flitman; 51 *bottom centre* The Hutchison Library; 51 *bottom right* Panos Pictures/Sean Sprague; 52–53 RHPL/Bildagentur Schuster/Layda; 52 *left* RHPL; 52 *centre* SPL/World View; 52 *right* Images; 53 *top left* The Hutchison Library/Bernard Régent; 53 *top right* Tony Stone/Robin Smith; 53 *left* The Hutchison Library; 53 *right* Collections/Brian Shuel.

Nations of the World

Flag images supplied courtesy of The Flag Institute, Chester, England.

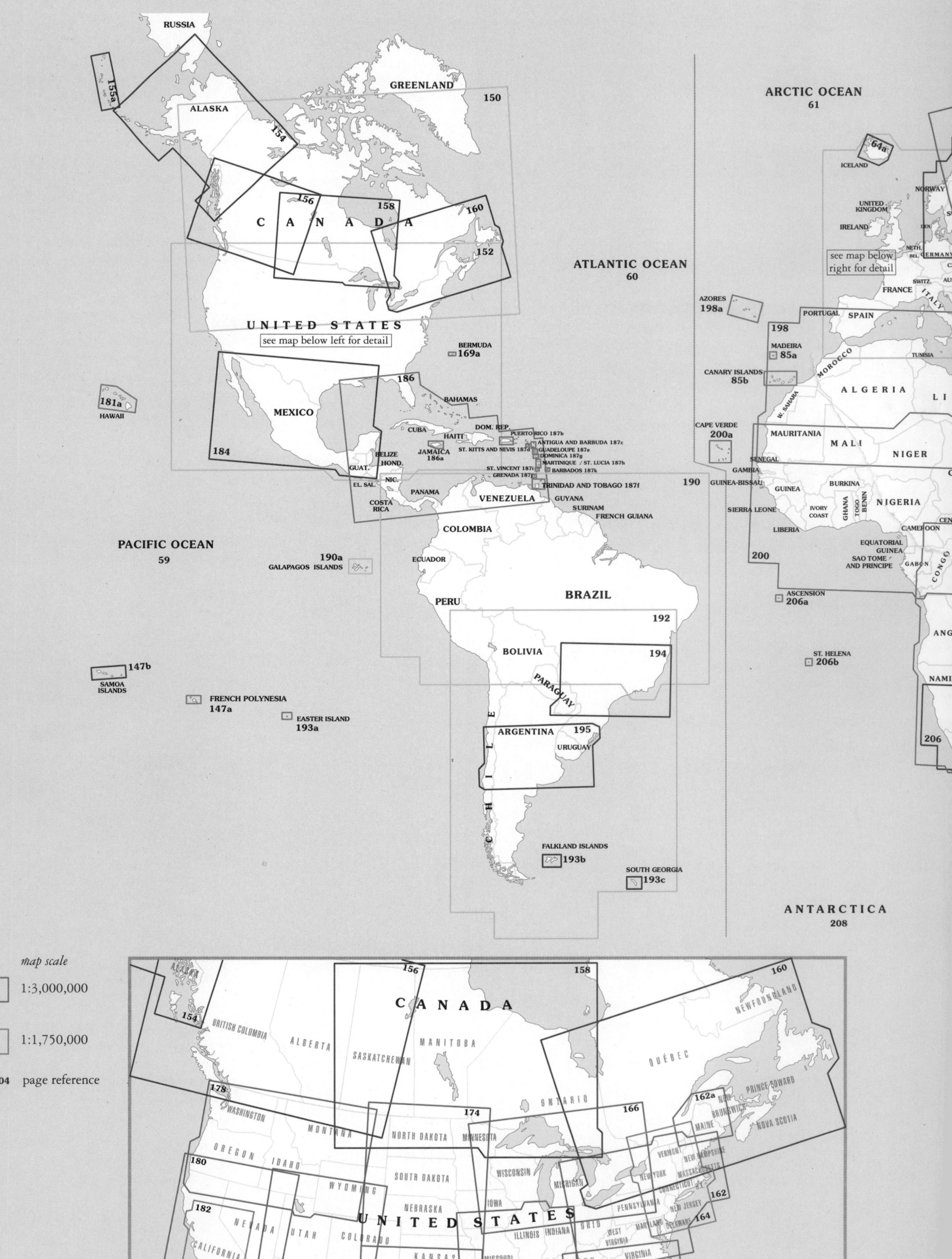

RUSSIA

GREENLAND

ALASKA

150

155a

154

ARCTIC OCEAN
61

C A N A D A

ICELAND

64a

NORWAY

156 **158** **160**

UNITED
KINGDOM

152

IRELAND

see map below
right for detail

FRANCE ITALY

NETH.
BEL. GERMANY
CZ.
SWITZ. AUS.

UNITED STATES
see map below left for detail

ATLANTIC OCEAN
60

PORTUGAL SPAIN

BERMUDA
169a

AZORES
198a

198

MADEIRA
85a

MOROCCO

TUNISIA

186

BAHAMAS

CANARY ISLANDS
85b

A L G E R I A LIB

181a

HAWAII

MEXICO

CUBA
HAITI
DOM. REP.

JAMAICA
186a

PUERTO RICO 187b
ANTIGUA AND BARBUDA 187c
DOMINICA 187g
ST. KITTS AND NEVIS 187d GUADELOUPE 187e
MARTINIQUE / ST. LUCIA 187h
ST. VINCENT 187i BARBADOS 187k
GRENADA 187j
TRINIDAD AND TOBAGO 187f

CAPE VERDE
200a

W. SAHARA

MAURITANIA

MALI

NIGER

184

BELIZE
HOND.

GUATEMALA
EL SAL. NIC.

PANAMA
COSTA
RICA

190

GAMBIA
GUINEA-BISSAU

SENEGAL

BURKINA

GUINEA

NIGERIA

VENEZUELA
GUYANA
SURINAM
FRENCH GUIANA

200

SIERRA LEONE
LIBERIA

IVORY
COAST
GHANA
TOGO
BENIN

CAMEROON

COLOMBIA

EQUATORIAL
GUINEA
SAO TOME
AND PRINCIPE

GABON

CONGO

PACIFIC OCEAN
59

ECUADOR

190a
GALAPAGOS ISLANDS

ASCENSION
206a

ANGO

PERU

BRAZIL

192

147b
SAMOA
ISLANDS

BOLIVIA

194

ST. HELENA
206b

PARAGUAY

NAMIB

FRENCH POLYNESIA
147a

EASTER ISLAND
193a

C
H
I
L
E

ARGENTINA **195**

URUGUAY

206

FALKLAND ISLANDS
193b

SOUTH GEORGIA
193c

ANTARCTICA
208

map scale

1:3,000,000

1:1,750,000

104 page reference

ALASKA

156 **158** **160**

154
BRITISH COLUMBIA

C A N A D A

NEWFOUNDLAND

ALBERTA
SASKATCHEWAN
MANITOBA

QUÉBEC

178

ONTARIO

166

162a
NEW
BRUNSWICK
PRINCE EDWARD

WASHINGTON

MONTANA

174

NORTH DAKOTA
MINNESOTA

MAINE

NOVA SCOTIA

180
OREGON
IDAHO

WYOMING

SOUTH DAKOTA

WISCONSIN

MICHIGAN

VERMONT
NEW HAMPSHIRE

NEW YORK
MASSACHUSETTS

162

182
NEVADA UTAH

NEBRASKA

IOWA

COLORADO

ILLINOIS INDIANA OHIO

PENNSYLVANIA
CONNECTICUT
NEW JERSEY

164

CALIFORNIA

ARIZONA NEW MEXICO

KANSAS

MISSOURI

KENTUCKY

WEST
VIRGINIA
MARYLAND
DELAWARE

VIRGINIA

U N I T E D S T A T E S

TENNESSEE

NORTH CAROLINA

OKLAHOMA
ARKANSAS

SOUTH
CAROLINA

176

TEXAS

MISSISSIPPI

ALABAMA

GEORGIA

LOUISIANA

186

FLORIDA

170

M E X I C O

172

168

184